JANE'S

AMERICAN FIGHTING AIRCRAFT
OF THE 20TH CENTURY

JANE'S

AMERICAN FIGHTING AIRCRAFT

OF THE 20TH CENTURY

COMPILED AND EDITED BY MICHAEL J.H. TAYLOR

PREFACE BY JOHN W.R. TAYLOR

MALLARD PRESS

PUBLISHER'S NOTE

In *Jane's American Fighting Aircraft of the 20th Century* every attempt has been made to include the very large number of combat aircraft that have served, or are serving in the U.S. fighting forces. With few exceptions this has been possible through the licensed extraction of information from editions of *Jane's All The World's Aircraft 1909–1980*. To offer a much greater overview of the military scene, past and present, the majority of support aircraft types have also been included, making this book a valuable source of reference and of much wider scope than the title may at first indicate.

Over the years the shape and format of Jane's has changed, sometimes a minor matter, and at others – like the post-First World War shift from the landscape to the portrait book format – a major but necessary change. The style of writing has also altered over the years, and accuracy of data has improved as information became more readily available to successive editors. These variations have given rise to a mix of styles throughout the book and considerable reorganization of entries, while old age has caused the loss of clarity in some of the photographs. However, in studying the text, the reader has access to aircraft entries written in the period in which the aircraft themselves flew as operational models.

MALLARD PRESS
An Imprint of BDD Promotional Company
666 Fifth Avenue
New York, N.Y. 10103

Mallard Press and its accompanying design and logo
are trademarks of BDD Promotional Book Company, Inc.

Jane's American Fighting Aircraft of the 20th Century.
Originally published by Jane's Publishing Company in
Jane's All The World's Aircraft 1909–1980.

This edition first published by Studio Editions, London.
First published in the United States of America
in 1991 by The Mallard Press.

By arrangement with the proprietor.

ISBN 0-7924-5627-0

Printed and bound in Hong Kong

CONTENTS

WRIGHT BIPLANE AT FORT MYER IN 1908 DURING THE ARMY'S
FIRST MILITARY AEROPLANE TRIALS.

FOREWORD

Military aviation began at Fort Myer, Virginia, just outside Washington, in 1909, the same year in which the first edition of what became *Jane's All the World's Aircraft* was published. Few people at that time were convinced that heavier-than-air aeroplanes had a more assured future than lighter-than-air dirigibles of the kind that Graf (Count) Ferdinand von Zeppelin was building, with considerable success, in Germany. Fred T. Jane hedged his bets by naming his new yearbook *All the World's Air-Ships (Aeroplanes and Dirigibles)*, as a companion to his already established *Jane's Fighting Ships*.

The US Army had informed Wilbur and Orville Wright four years earlier that "the Board (of Ordnance and Fortification) does not care to formulate any requirements for the performance of a flying-machine or take any further action on the subject until a machine is produced which by actual operation is shown to be able to produce horizontal flight and to carry an operator". The Wrights had, in fact, just made a flight of 24 ⅕ miles in 38 minutes 3 seconds in the biplane they called the *Flyer*. It was an improved version of the tail-first aircraft in which they had recorded the world's first controlled, powered and sustained aeroplane flights at Kill Devil Hill, Kitty Hawk, on 17 December 1903.

On 2 August 1909, after demonstration flights at Fort Myer, the Aeronautical Division of the US Army Signal Corps took delivery of a Wright Model A. The first aeroplane ever sold for military use, it cost $30,000, and the Army was given no more money for aircraft until 1912. It then evaluated everything from open-fuselage Curtiss "pushers" to flying-boats and a Burgess-Dunne tailless sweptwing biplane.

Standardization on particular types began after Glenn Curtiss hired B. Douglas Thomas, an engineer with A.V. Roe in England, to use his experience with the outstanding Avro 504 to design what became known as the Curtiss JN Jenny. Eight Jennies formed the equipment of the 1st Aero Squadron, based at San Diego, California, with a complement of 16 officers, who had to be unmarried lieutenants, and 77 enlisted men. It was sent to support a US expedition against Vera Cruz, Mexico, in 1914, but arrived too late and had to return to San Diego without unpacking its aircraft.

When 1st Aero Squadron was dispatched to Texas two years later, to accompany General John Pershing's punitive campaign against the Mexican revolutionary leader, Pancho Villa, its Jennies had been replaced with larger, more powerful Curtiss Rs. Only two of them survived the weather, high mountains, darkness and other hazards; they were condemned and destroyed on return to the US.

Creation of an air force was not easy. Of the dozen US companies considered competent to undertake government contracts, nine contributed to the delivery of a total of 64 aeroplanes out of 366 ordered in 1916. America's industrial expertise finally started to show after it entered the First World War, on 6 April 1917. During the remaining months of the war, US manufacturers built some 11,300 aeroplanes and 41,000 zero-engines, almost from scratch. Many were British-designed de Havilland 4 bombers and, apart from Curtiss twin-engined flying-boats, no combat aircraft of US design were used operationally.

In contrast, America did design, develop and put into mass production with remarkable speed a 400 hp twelve-cylinder V aero-engine known as the Liberty, which was used first in its D.H.4s and was adopted for the British-built D.H.9A, backbone of the postwar Royal Air Force. Fred Jane had recognised, in the very first *All the World's Air-Ships*, that "It is, perhaps, not too much to say that the whole future of aviation rests with the engine and its general reliability". Behind the immense success of the American aeroplanes that fill the major part of this book lie the achievements of companies like Curtiss, Wright, Pratt & Whitney and General Electric that provided their Power plants.

The Air Force, in its successive forms, and the US Navy, also played major roles in the shape of US air power, over more than eighty years. The first man to drop a live bomb from an aeroplane was Lieutenant Myron S. Crissy, from the passenger seat of the Wright biplane, on 7 January 1911. First to fire a rifle from an aeroplane was Lieutenant J.E. Fickel, on a Curtiss pusher on 20 August 1910. Captain Charles de F. Chandler followed by firing a machine-gun from a Wright Model B on 2 June 1912.

Eugene Ely pioneered flying from aircraft carriers when he took off in a Curtiss biplane from a temporary wooden flight deck on the USS *Birmingham* on 14 November 1910, and then landed on a similar platform on the USS *Pennsylvania* on 18 January 1911. A US Navy flying-boat, the Curtiss NC-4, made the first crossing of the North Atlantic by air, with a mid-course stop, in May 1919. In the 1930s, as part of its airship programme, the US Navy designed its USS *Akron* and *Macon* with internal hangars for the four Curtiss Sparrowhawk biplanes, which could be lowered by trapeze, flown to increase enormously the airship's own scouting radius in support of the fleet, and then retrieved by trapeze.

Meanwhile, the Army Air Service, which had grown out of the briefly independent Air Service AEF (American

ELY LANDS ON BOARD USS *PENNSYLVANIA* ON
18 JANUARY 1911.

Expeditionary Force) in wartime France, was equally venture-
some. In 1923, it kept a D.H.4 airborne for 37¼ hours in
the first convincing demonstration of the possibilities of flight
refuelling from another D.H.4. One year later Air Service
crews made the first round-the-world flight, in Douglas

World Cruisers. They showed the vulnerability of large battleships to air attack by sinking former German warships with
Martin MB-2/NBS-1 bombers in 1921; but even a change of
name under the Air Corps Act of 1926 left it still as merely
a combatant branch of the Army, with less prestige than the
Infantry.

It required the immense air battles of the Second World
War to raise the status of US military flying. On 20 June
1941, before America entered the war, the Army Air Forces
came into being, with the Air Corps and Air Force Combat
Command as its major components until they were discontinued in the following March. During the war years the
USAAF grew to a peak of 78,757 aircraft in 243 active groups,
of which 224 were serving overseas. To create and maintain
that vast total, US industry built 303,713 aeroplanes in the
decade to the war's end.

No longer could anyone doubt that the air forces had earned
independence, and the National Security Act of 18 September
1947 created the US Air Force as one of three military
departments. Aircraft for short tactical operations and supply
duties were absorbed into the Army's separate US Army Air
Forces in March 1948, becoming primarily a helicopter
combat service.

SPARROWHAWK BIPLANE FIGHTERS APPROACH USS MACON
IN 1933, THE AIRSHIP'S TRAPEZE LOWERED FOR 'HOOK ON'.

The Naval air arm has undergone similar changes, not only in name but in size and capability. The original Naval Flying Corps had been authorized in August 1916, and trained pilots from the US Marine Corps and US Coast Guard, although these remained under separate command. At peak strength, in July 1945, Naval Aviation had 40,912 aircraft.

Since the Second World War, US Air Force and Naval pilots have continued to play leading roles in research and development flying. For example, on 14 October 1947, Captain Charles 'Chuck' Yeager, USAF, became the first person to fly faster than the speed of sound in the Bell X-1. On 3 October 1967, Major Pete Knight, USAF, flew at 4,534 mph (Mach 6.72) in the North American X-15A-2, the highest speed yet recorded for a piloted aeroplane if we except the Space Shuttle aerospacecraft.

The US military services have helped to fund the aircraft, and provided aircrew for these and many other programmes that have become milestones in the conquest of the air and space. Not all the aircraft are described in this book. Some

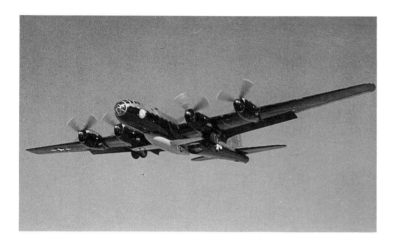

BELL X-1 UNDER ITS B-29 SUPERFORTRESS MOTHERPLANE. ON 14 OCTOBER 1947, PILOT CAPTAIN CHARLES 'CHUCK' YAEGER FLEW THE X-1 THROUGH THE SOUND BARRIER.

NORTH AMERICAN X-15 ROCKETPLANE, AIR-LAUNCHED FROM ITS B-52 STRATOFORTRESS MOTHERPLANE. THE X-15 BECAME THE FASTEST AEROPLANE OF ALL TIME, REACHING MACH 6.72 IN 1967.

ROCKWELL INTERNATIONAL B-1B LANCER SUPERSONIC STRATEGIC BOMBER, 100 OF WHICH WERE BUILT FOR DELIVERY BETWEEN 1985 AND 1988. WING SPAN (VARIABLE) 78 FT 2½ IN TO 136 FT 8½ IN. HIGH SPEED MACH 1.25.

ALREADY USED IN ACTION IN PANAMA IN 1989 AND THE GULF IN 1991, THE SINGLE-SEAT LOCKHEAD F-117A IS THE WORLD'S FIRST OPERATIONAL STEALTH FIGHTER, DESIGNED TO BE VIRTUALLY 'INVISIBLE' TO ENEMY DEFENCES BY DISPERSION OF RADAR ENERGY, USE OF PASSIVE SENSORS AND OFFERING EXTREMELY LOW INFRA-RED EMISSIONS. IT FIRST BECAME OPERATIONAL IN 1983, AND IN EARLY 1991 THE TWO CURRENT TACTICAL FIGHTER SQUADRONS HAD A TOTAL OF 46 AIRCRAFT. WING SPAN 43 FT 4 IN. HIGH SPEED OVER MACH 1.

were pure research vehicles, with no military significance. Others were built too late to appear in the editions of *Jane's* from 1909 to 1980 on which this book is based. But the most effective combat aircraft of the present time, like the B-1B bomber, owe much to the designers and pilots of the research aircraft.

The very latest combat types, such as the F-117A attack aircraft and B-2 bomber, employ low-observables or "stealth" technology that makes them invisible to radar. We can only wait and see if "stealth" represents as much of a breakthrough as the earlier, revolutionary, switches from biplane to monoplane, pistons to jet propulsion, and the ceaseless embodiment of new technologies such as variable-geometry, radar navigation, automatic control, and laser guidance of weapons for pinpoint accuracy.

THE NORTHROP B-2A IS THE PLANNED NEXT-GENERATION STRATEGIC BOMBER FOR THE USAF, TO ENTER SERVICE FROM ABOUT 1993. THE PROTOTYPE FIRST FLEW ON 17 JULY 1989. THE MOST EXPENSIVE AIRCRAFT EVER BUILT, IT IS A FLYING WING USING THE LATEST STEALTH TECHNOLOGIES. WING SPAN IS 172 FT (SEE NORTHROP YB-35/49 IN MAIN SECTION).

MCDONNELL DOUGLAS AND BRITISH AEROPACE COLLABORATED IN THE DEVELOPMENT OF THE SECOND-GENERATION HARRIER FOR THE USMC, THE AV-8B HARRIER II. DELIVERIES BEGAN IN 1984 TO REPLACE AV-8AS AND CS AND SKYHAWKS, WITH EXAMPLES OF THE NIGHT ATTACK VERSION FOLLOWING FROM 1990. WING SPAN 30 FT 4 IN. HIGH SPEED 661 MPH AT SEA LEVEL.

LOCKHEED YF-22A REPRESENTS ONE OF TWO NEW AIRCRAFT CURRENTLY BEING DEVELOPED AS A POSSIBLE FUTURE USAF ADVANCED TACTICAL FIGHTER (THE OTHER IS THE NORTHROP YF-23A). DESIGN GOALS INCLUDE STEALTH CHARACTERISTICS, THE VERY LATEST SENSORS, ADVANCED ENGINES ALLOWING MACH 1.5 CRUISING SPEED WITHOUT AFTERBURNING, AND CONSIDERABLE USE OF COMPOSITE MATERIALS IN ITS CONSTRUCTION.

BELL/BOEING V-22 OSPREY, A TILT-ROTOR AIRCRAFT COMBINING THE VERTICAL TAKE-OFF AND LANDING CHARACTERISTICS OF A HELICOPTER WITH THE SPEED AND CARRYING CAPACITY OF AN AEROPLANE. FIRST FLOWN ON 19 MARCH 1989, IT MAY EVENTUALLY ENTER SERVICE WITH THE US NAVY AS A REPLACEMENT FOR HH-3 HELICOPTERS IN HV-22A FORM (AND POSSIBLY SUPERSEDE THE VIKING FOR ASW IN SV-22A FORM), THE USMC AS A REPLACEMENT FOR SEA KNIGHT AND SEA STALLION HELICOPTERS UNDER THE DESIGNATION MV-22A, AND AS THE USAF'S CV-22A SPECIAL OPERATIONS AIRCRAFT. HIGH SPEED 345 MPH.

SIKORSKY MH-53E SEA DRAGON IS THE US NAVY'S LATEST AIRBORNE MINE COUNTERMEASURES HELICOPTER, BASED ON THE H-53E SUPER STALLION AND DELIVERED TO THE NAVY FROM 1986. ROTOR DIAMETER 79 FT. HIGH SPEED 196 MPH.

MCDONNELL DOUGLAS F-15E EAGLE, THE DUAL-ROLE ATTACK AND FIGHTER VARIANT OF THE F-15 THAT ENTERED USAF SERVICE FROM 1988. THE MARTIN MARIETTA LANTIRN SYSTEM ALLOWS IT TO MAKE PRECISE INTERDICTION ATTACKS AT NIGHT AND IN POOR WEATHER CONDITIONS.

US COAST GUARD AEROSPATIALE HH-65A DOLPHIN SHORT RANGE RECOVERY HELICOPTER (SEE MAIN SECTION).

About this book:

The arrangement is alphabetical, by manufacturers. What must be borne in mind is that the many hundreds of entries are taken from books published over a period of seventy years. In that period, aviation language has changed in style. Much more detail, and higher standards of specification accuracy have been demanded in later years than when *All the World's Aircraft* first appeared.

A phrase such as "It is hoped to fly the . . . this year" means the year in which that particular entry first appeared. Similarly, when the US military simply bought "off the shelf" a basically civil aircraft like the Ford Tri-Motor for military use, the older *Jane's* did not always bother to illustrate or describe any but the basic commercial versions. Finally, many readers will already realise that designation systems have changed through the years. What began life as a P-80 or F8U-1 appeared in later editions as an F-80 or F-8A respec-tively.

It would have been impractical to eliminate, or explain, all such designation changes without resetting the entire book. The time and cost involved in such resetting would put the book beyond the reach of even wealthy readers. At a time when a set of original editions of *Jane's All the World's Aircraft* for the period 1909 to 1980, in less than "as new" condition, would cost tens of thousands of dollars to anyone fortunate enough to be offered them, this book represents quite a treasure.

ONE OF SEVERAL UK AIRCRAFT NOW OPERATING WITH THE US SERVICES IS THE SHORTS SHERPA, USED BY THE USAF AS THE C-23A TRANSPORT FOR EUROPEAN DISTRIBUTION OF SPARES AND OTHER LOADS. C-23S ALSO REPLACED CARIBOUS WITH THE ARMY NATIONAL GUARD. WING SPAN 74 FT 8 IN. CRUISING SPEED 218 MPH.

US NAVY F/A-18A HORNETS, BECOMING OPERATIONAL IN 1873
AS MULTI-MISSION CARRIER FIGHTERS.

U.S.A. MILITARY AERONAUTICS.

By THE BARON LADISLAS DORCY.

THE EARLY BEGINNINGS.

The early development of the American Flying Service rested entirely with the Signal Corps, which had, on December 23rd, 1907, issued specifications for a man-carrying aeroplane that would be capable of remaining in the air for one hour without landing. These conditions were fulfilled the following summer by a *Wright* biplane fitted with a 35 h.p. engine, and the machine was duly purchased; but in spite of this early start the development of American military aeronautics lagged far behind the other Great Powers until the entry of the States into the war. During the eight years that elapsed in the meanwhile less than one million dollars was appropriated by Congress for military aeronautics, and the Flying Service remained a subsidiary branch of the Signal Corps, known as the Aviation Section, which had been established by Act of Congress on July 18th, 1914.

On April 6th, 1917, when the United States declared war on Germany, the establishment of the Aviation Section comprised 65 officers, 1,120 enlisted men, two small flying fields (Mineola and San Diego), and less than 300 very second-rate training aeroplanes.

Manufacturing facilities were comparatively insignificant and experienced aeroplane designers were lacking, and the latter explains why up to that date no modern service machine had been produced in the States, and why most of the American service aeroplanes produced during the war were of British or French design, with the minor alterations the fitting of the Liberty engine necessitated, if such was fitted.

WAR PROGRAMME OF THE AIRCRAFT PRODUCTION BOARD.

The original American War Programme, based on an army of a million men, made of the air service but a relatively insignificant portion of the military forces, and this was to be met by two appropriations—$10,800,000 on May 21st, 1917, and $43,450,000 on June 5th, 1917. However, after the arrival in the States of a British and a French aviation mission, the General Staff revised their views, and concurred with the recommendations made by the Aircraft Production Board, calling for the construction of 22,500 aeroplanes and as many aero engines. For this purpose Congress was asked to appropriate a sum of $640,000,000—the largest ever asked for one specific item—and this was granted in record time, taking only one week till it became law. From this date—July 24th, 1917—the big American aircraft programme was really launched, largely in response to Allied appeals.

As speed was justly deemed the essential of success, it was decided to concentrate at first upon the production of a few types for which specifications and engines were available; thus it came that during 1917, the American aircraft industry produced almost exclusively training aeroplanes. Among these were the *Curtiss* J.N 4 (B., C. and D.) and the *Standard* J. 1 for primary training, and the *Curtiss* J.N. H. (Hispano-Suiza) two-seater, and the *Thomas-Morse* S. 4 (B. and C.) and the *Standard* E. 1 single-seaters for advanced training. Some thirty flying fields were created for the training of aviators, and large numbers of Allied (specially French) specialists in military aeronautics were drawn upon for establishing the Flying Service on a thoroughly up-to-date foundation.

After a lengthy controversy as to whether or not the States should entirely concentrate on training, and have their service machines built to the best available Allied designs in France and Great Britain, a decision was arrived at whereby the United States were to standardize three types of service machines (D.H. 4, *Bristol* F. 2 B. and *Spad de chasse*), and modify them so as to allow the fitting of a standardized aero engine, which was to be built in 4, 6, 8, and 12-cyl. models.

This engine, which was to embody the best features of all existing engines, was designed and constructed with a mixed display of secrecy and advertising within a month, in the summer of 1917, and the initial tests having proven, on the surface, successful, orders were placed in August, 1917, for the construction of this so-called Liberty engine with the following firms, for the quantities stated:—Packard Motor Car Co. and Lincoln Motors Co., 6,000 each; Ford Motor Co., 5,000; Nordyke and Marmon, 3,000; General Motors Corporation, 2,000; Trego Motors Corporation, 500—A total of 22,500 engines. All these were to be of the 12-cyl., 400 h.p. model, for use in the D.H. 4 and the *Bristol* F. 2B.; an 8-cyl. model, rated 225 h.p., was to be developed for use in the modified *Spad*.

A Characteristic Group of U.S. Army Aviators in France.

After some modifications, the Liberty 12 emerged from the experimental stage, and production increased with great rapidity, so that by the time Armistice was signed 13,396 of these engines had been delivered, the output for October, 1918, alone having reached 4,200. The adaptation of the Liberty 12 to the D.H. 4 proved a success, and orders were placed for 9,500 of these machines, of which one-half was delivered during the war; the modification of the *Bristol* F. 2B. and the *Spad* for the fitting of the Liberty 12 and the Liberty 8 respectively was, however, a failure, and the orders had therefore to be cancelled. As a consequence the D.H. 4A. was the only American-built aeroplane that saw service with the American Expeditionary Force, for the war came to an end before the second American aircraft programme could be carried out.

THE ERA OF REORGANISATIONS.

The Aircraft Production Board, which was responsible for the first aircraft programme, was a purely advisory body, which had been appointed after the declaration of war by Howard Coffin, Advisory Commissioner of the Council of National Defence, at the request of the National Advisory Committee for Aeronautics. It consisted of Mr. Coffin, chairman; Brig.-Gen. George O. Squier, Chief Signal Officer, U.S.A.; Rear-Admiral David W. Taylor, Chief Constructor, U.S.N., and Messrs. S. D. Waldon, E. A. Deeds, and R. L. Montgomery.

As the A.P.B. could only make recommendations and had no executive power, there was no assurance that the construction programme it had suggested would be carried out in the most effectual manner. To overcome this drawback, Congress passed, on Sept. 27th, 1917, a bill authorising the creation of an Aircraft Board, consisting of a civilian chairman, the Chief Signal Officer of the Army, the Chief Constructor of the Navy, and two members each taken from the Army, the Navy, and civilian life. This board was empowered, under the direction of the Secretaries of War and the Navy, to supervise and direct the purchase and manufacture of military and naval aircraft. The members, appointed on December 7th, 1917, were:—Howard E. Coffin, chairman; Maj.-Gen. George O. Squier, Rear-Admiral David W. Taylor; Col. E. A. Deeds and Col. R. L. Montgomery, for the Army; Captain H. E. Irwin and Lieut-Comdr. A. Atkins, for the Navy; and Richard F. Howe.

While the Aircraft Production Board had thus been given, with a new name, a legal status, its usefulness was greatly hampered by the fact that the Flying Service of the Army had remained, in spite of its extraordinary expansion, still a branch of the Signal Corps, which it greatly exceeded in numbers and importance—the tail was actually wagging the dog. This anomaly was responsible for many of the errors and delays which hampered the progress of America's aircraft programme, and eventually the Committee on Military Affairs of the Senate started an investigation with a view to determining responsibilities. This investigation, as well as one conducted independently by Mr. Gutzon Borglum, a sculptor, on behalf of President Wilson, resulted in a total re-organisation of the aeronautical establishment. On April 24th, 1918, the Aviation Section was separated from the Signal Corps and re-named Air Service, which was divided into a Division of Military Aeronautics and a Bureau of Aircraft Production. Brig.-Gen. William L. Kenly was appointed Director of Military Aeronautics, in charge of training operations, and Mr. John D. Ryan became Chief of the Bureau of Aircraft Production, and at the same time, Chairman of the Aircraft Board, Mr. Coffin having resigned in the meanwhile. From then on, the Aircraft Board faded into oblivion, and its existence has become purely nominal; but the Act of Congress which created it fortunately made provision for its automatic deletion six months after the ending of war.

THE SECOND AIRCRAFT PROGRAMME.

Under the energetic leadership of Mr. Ryan the aircraft construction programme was pushed to the limit and a new programme was elaborated, calling for the production, beginning early in 1919, of the following standardised types of Air Service machines:—The *Lepère*, or L.U.A.S.C 11, the U.S.D. 9A., the *Martin* bomber, the *Loening* monoplane, the S.E. 5A. the *Handley-Page* and the *Caproni*. When Armistice was signed production was not under way yet, and so the orders were deleted; all of the above machines were to be fitted with Liberty 12 engines, except the *Loening* and the S.E. 5A., for which Hispano-Suiza's were provided.

In August, 1918, a new reorganisation was effected in the Air Service with the view to bringing it under one head, whereas previously dual control had existed in the matter of production and operations. Consequently the Division of Military Aeronautics and the Bureau of Aircraft Production were placed under the Director of Air Service, to which new post Mr. John D. Ryan was appointed, while Mr. William C. Potter became Chief of the Bureau of Aircraft Production.

AEROPLANE PRODUCTION JANUARY 1st, 1919.

The aeroplane production of the Air Service on January 1st, 1919, was, according to figures made public by the Production Division of the Bureau of Aircraft Production, the following:—

Type.	Manufacturer.	Total quantity ordered to Nov. 11th, 1918	Quantity left on order after Armistice cancellations.	Total shipped to Dec. 27th, 1918.
J.1	—Dayton Wright Aeroplane Co... ..	400	400	400
	Fischer Body Corp...	400	400	400
	Standard Aircraft Corp.	750	750	750
	Wright-Martin Aircraft Corp.	50	50	50
	Total	1600	1600	1600
J.N. 4D.	—Liberty Iron Works	300	200	200
	Canadian Aeroplane Co.	680	680	680
	U.S. Aircraft Corp.	50	50	50
	Curtiss Aeroplane & Motor Corp.	2401	2002	2002
	Fowler, Howell & Lesser Co. ..	225	125	125
	Springfield Aircraft Corp. ..	975	625	536
	St. Louis Aircraft Corp... ..	650	450	450
	Total..	5281	4132	4043
J.N. H. :—				
Training	—Curtiss Aerop. & Motor Corp.	402	402	402
Gunnery	—Curtiss Aerop. & Motor Corp.	427	427	427
Bombing	—Curtiss Aerop. & Motor Corp.	100	100	100
	Total	929	929	929
G. 1	—Curtiss Aerop. & Motor Corp.	560	560	471
G. 2	—Curtiss Aerop. & Motor Corp.	90	90	90
J.N, 6H. :—				
Observat'n	—Curtiss Aerop. & Motor Corp.	106	106	100
Pursuit	—Curtiss Aerop. & Motor Corp.	125	125	125
Bombing	—Curtiss Aerop. & Motor Corp.	154	154	154
	Total	1035	1035	940
B.	—Thomas-Morse Aircraft Corp.	100	100	100
S. 4	—Thomas-Morse Aircraft Corp.	50	50	50
C. Le Rhone	—Thomas-Morse Aircraft Corp.	1000	447	447
	Total	1150	597	597
" Penguin "	—Breese Aircraft Co.	300	300	300
E. 1 (M. Defense)	—Standard Aircraft Corp.	30	30	30
	Standard Aircraft Corp.	430	98	96
	Total	460	128	126
D.H. 4	—Dayton-Wright Airplane Co. ..	5000	3104	2899
	Fischer Body Corp.	4000	1600	1599
	Standard Aircraft Corp.	500	140	89
	Total	9500	4844	4587

Type. Manufacturer.	Total quantity ordered to Nov. 11th, 1918	Quantity left on order after Armistice cancellations.	Total shipped to Dec. 27th, 1918.
Handley-Page--Standard Aircraft Corp...	500	107	102
S.E. 5A.—Curtiss Aerop. & Motor Corp. ..	54	54	9
Curtiss Aerop. & Motor Corp. ..	1000	1	1
Total .. '	1054	55	10
L.U.A.S. CII.—Packard Motor Car Co. ..	1025	25	7
(Le Père)—Brewster & Co...	500	0	0
Fischer Body Corp...	2000	0	0
Total	3525	25	7
Martin Bomber—Glenn L. Martin Co. ..	50	4	0
U.S.D. 9A.—Curtiss Aerop. & Motor Corp.	4000	0	0
Caproni—Fischer Body Corp.	500	0	0
Curtiss Aeroplane & Motor Corp.	500	0	0
Total	1000	0	0
U.S.B. 1—Curtiss Aeroplane & Motor Corp.	2000	0	0
V.E. 7.—Sturtevant Co.	500	0	0
Springfield Aircraft Corp.	500	0	0
Total	1000	0	0

A Characteristic Group of U.S. Naval Aviators on Service in France.

THE AIR SERVICE IN FRANCE.

At the date Armistice was signed, the Air Service forces at the front included 2,161 officers and 22,351 soldiers, and those in the supply service in France, 4,643 officers and 28,353 soldiers. With the French armies there were detailed 8 officers, and with the British Expeditionary Force, 49 officers and 525 soldiers. The total personnel in France consisted of 6,861 officers and 51,229 soldiers.

There were in operation on the front 39 aero squadrons, distributed as follows: 20 pursuit, 1 night bombardment, 6 day bombardment, 5 army observation, twelve corps observation, and one night observation squadrons.

Enemy aeroplanes brought down by American aviators included 491 confirmed and 354 unconfirmed, a total of 845, while 82 enemy observation balloons were reported as destroyed, of which 57 were confirmed. The Air Service lost, on the other hand, only 271 aeroplanes and 45 observation balloons, thus showing its marked superiority over the enemy.

The number of aeroplanes, by type, received from all sources by the American Expeditionary Force between September 12th, 1917, and November 16th, 1918, was as follows:

Pursuit for service, 3,337; pursuit for schools, 90.

Observation for service, 3,421; observation for schools, 664.

Day bombing for service, 421; day bombing for schools, 85.

Night reconnaissance, 31.

Other planes received included 2,285 training planes, 30 experimental planes and 108 miscellaneous, making a total of 10,472.

Eight different schools under American control were established in France and designed for training 3,800 officers and 11,700 men, as follows:—

Tours—Observers: 916 officers and 2,121 soldiers.

Issoudun—General flying: 2,175 officers and 6,100 soldiers.

Clermont-Ferrand—Bombardment: 120 officers and 660 soldiers.

St. Jean de Monte—Aerial gunners: 92 officers and 1,500 soldiers.

Souse—Artillery firing point: 256 officers and 750 soldiers.

Coetquidan—Artillery firing point: 25 officers and 120 soldiers.

Meucon—Artillery firing point: 29 officers and 110 soldiers.

Chatillon sur Seine—Observers: 204 officers and 373 soldiers.

A total of 159 officers and soldiers were killed in training.

Casualties at the front included 109 killed, 103 wounded, 200 missing, 27 prisoners and 3 interned, making a total of 442.

The total strength of the Division of Military Aeronautics, Air Service, on November 11th, 1918, was 18,688 officers, 5,775 cadets, and 133,644 soldiers. At that date the Air Service had trained 8,933 reserve military aviators at home, and about 2,300 had been trained in France, Great Britain and Italy.

The personnel of the Bureau of Aircraft Production, Air Service, comprised 32,520 officers and soldiers.

The ground establishments of the Air Service in the United States comprised 40 flying fields, 8 balloon fields, 3 radio schools, 3 photography schools, 5 schools of military aeronautics, and 14 aircraft depots.

THE NEW ORGANISATION SCHEME.

With the return to peace time conditions the Air Service has been greatly reduced and is being wholly reorganised. Mr. Ryan having resigned from the post of Director of Air Service after the signing of Armistice, Major-Gen. Charles T. Menoher was appointed in his place, while Brig.-Gen. William Mitchell was appointed Director of Military Aeronautics in lieu of Gen. Kenly. Since the latter appointment, however, the Division of Military Aeronautics as well as the Bureau of Aircraft Production have disappeared as independent organisations, and have been merged in the general arrangement of the new organisation plan, so that their directors become assistants to the Director of Air Service.

The Executive Officer is the direct representative of the Director of Air Service in the co-ordination, control and direction of the activities of the Air Service, and in the temporary absence of the Director of Air Service issues orders in the latter's name.

The Second Assistant Executive is specifically charged with matters of information, statistics and publicity.

The Fourth Assistant Executive, in addition to the duties outlined above, is specifically charged with all routine executive Air Service functions, such as mail, cable and telegraph service, correspondence, central records and files, office administration and confidential records.

AIR SERVICE STRENGTH ON PEACE FOOTING.

The 1919 organisation plan of the Air Service provides for a personnel strength of 1,923 officers and 21,853 soldiers and for a *materiel* strength of 5,100 aeroplanes of all types, 1,700 of which will be in active commission and 3,400 in reserve.

The Air Service will comprise 87 service aeroplane squadrons, distributed as follows:—42 coast defence (continental and insular), 20 pursuit, and 25 mixed observation and bombing squadrons. The normal squadron comprises 18 aeroplanes and their personnel. Provision is also made for the maintenance of 42 balloon squadrons (some equipped with small airships), which will be divided among three wings of 18 companies each.

In the general plan of the Army reorganisation each army corps will have attached to it five observation and bombing squadrons and four pursuit squadrons, representing a wing formation for each type of machine.

The greater part of the Air Service flying and balloon fields organised during the war will be retained on peace footing; in addition to six fields already owned by the U.S. Government fourteen have been purchased in March, 1919, and leases were extended on eleven others. The status of the remainder has not yet been definitely decided upon at the date of writing.

Air Service Flying Fields.

Barron Field	..	Fort Worth, Texas.
*Bolling Field	..	Anacostia, District of Columbia.
*Brindley Field	..	Commack, Long Island, N.Y.
Brooks Field	..	San Antonio, Texas.
Call Field ..	..	Wichita Falls, Texas.

U.S.A. NAVAL AERONAUTICS.

By THE BARON LADISLAS DORCY.

HISTORICAL.

The U.S. Naval Flying Corps was established in 1911, when Congress appropriated the sum of $25,000 for this purpose. With this sum three naval officers (Lieuts. T. G. Ellyson, John Rodgers and J. T. Towers) were trained as aviators, three shore-going machines (two Curtiss and one Wright biplane) were purchased, and an air station was constructed at Greenbury Point, Md. The latter was removed during the same year to Annapolis, Md., where it remained in operation as a flying school till 1913, when the Pensacola air station and flying school was established, except during the winter months, when the training was conducted at the Curtiss School at San Diego, Cal.

During 1912, a considerable volume of research work was done, under the direction of Capt. W I. Chambers, U.S.N., with regard to seaplane floats, flying boat hulls, and general flotation problems, and a catapult launching apparatus, operated by compressed air was developed. Toward the end of this year a temporary air station was established at Guantanamo, Cuba, but this was broken up the following spring. The development of the N.F.C. was greatly hampered by the inadequate funds available.

In 1913, the Office of Naval Aeronautics was created in the Bureau of Operations, with Captain Mark L. Bristol, U.S.N., as Director of Naval Aeronautics, and naval flying school was established at Pensacola, Fla., whither the U.S.S. *Mississippi* was assigned as an "aeronautic station ship." At the end of this year the N.F.C. had 7 flying boats and 2 float seaplanes in commission, and 3 flying boats on order.

In the spring of 1914, the Atlantic Fleet having been mobilised in Mexican waters, an "aeroplane division" (4 machines) was embarked on the U.S.S. *Mississippi* and *Birmingham*, and sent to Vera Cruz and Tampico, respectively. A number of reconnaissance flights were made in this connection over Vera Cruz. In the summer the U.S.S. *Mississippi* was sold to Greece, and her place was taken by the U.S.S. *North Carolina*.

In February, 1915, specifications were issued and bids asked for one small training airship of the non-rigid type and 6 seaplanes, and in August for 3, 6, 9, and 12 seaplanes, respectively. The specifications asked for a high speed of 60-70 m.p.h., a low speed of 40 m.p.h., a climb of 2,500 ft. in 10 minutes, an endurance of 4 hours at full power, and ability to fly in a wind of 35 m.p.h., and to take off, alight, and drift (afloat) in a wind of 25 m.p.h.

During the summer of this year, Naval Constructor H. C. Richardson, U.S.N., who had previously been identified with extensive research work on flying boat hulls, built an experimental twin-engine seaplane of the float type. Experiments were also continued with the Chambers catapult, and apparently gave satisfactory results, for it was suggested at about this time to equip all the capital ships of the Atlantic Fleet with one or two flying boats and launching devices. As a matter of fact, the first U.S. warship to be so equipped was the *North Carolina*, and this took place in 1916.

The real expansion of the N.F.C. dates from the passage of Naval Act, 1916, the provisions of which are referred to elsewhere. On December 1st, 1916, the N.F.C. had in commission 29 seaplanes and 4 kite balloons—the latter having been developed for the U.S. Navy by the Goodyear Tyre and Rubber Co.—and the flying personnel consisted of 9 officer-aviators, 16 student-aviators, while 24 officers and 120 enlisted men of the Navy, Marine Corps and Naval Militia were about to be sent for a course of training to Pensacola, Fla.

At the time the United States entered the great war (April, 1917), 21 seaplanes of float and boat types were in commission (out of total of 93 delivered to the N.F.C. since its formation), and 135 seaplanes, mostly of the N-9 and R-6 types, were on order. Air stations were in operation at Pensacola, Fla., Bay Shore, N.Y., and Squantum, Mass; the two latter were later removed to Chatham, Mass., and Rockaway, N.Y., respectively. The training airship ordered in 1915 had also been commissioned. The personnel of the N.F.C. consisted of 30 officers and 300 men.

With the granting of a large appropriation for the fiscal year 1917-18, a comprehensive construction programme was begun, and the Naval Aircraft Factory was established at the Navy Yard of Philadelphia at a cost of $3,750,000 for the manufacture of seaplanes as well as the assembly of parts produced by trade firms and concerns not engaged in other war work. This system gave most excellent results, and the Navy aircraft programme was as a rule well ahead of schedule—an achievement much at variance with the progress of the Army aircraft programme, and for which much praise is due to Naval Constructor F. G. Coburn, U.S.N., under whose direction the factory was built and is operated. In October, 1918, the Naval Aircraft Factory employed 3,700 workers, one-fourth of whom were women, and over 7,000 people were employed by various contractors.

During the war the Naval Flying Corps extensively co-operated with the air forces of the Allies. For this purpose air stations were established in Ireland; in France (Le Havre, Brest, La Pallice, Bordeaux), and in Canada (Halifax), from which stations incoming and outgoing merchant vessels were convoyed for considerable distances in addition to patrol flights and bombing raids made for the purpose of combating the submarine menace. With the ending of the war these stations will be turned over to the respective countries in which they were established—if this has not already been done.

On October 2, 1918, the total strength of the Naval Flying Corps was 40,383 officers and men.

ORGANISATION.

The present organisation of the Naval Flying Corps was laid down in Naval Act, 1916, which fixed the personnel strength at 150 officer-aviators and 350 enlisted airmen, and provided for the creation of the Naval Reserve Flying Corps for qualified civilians, and the yearly appointment, from civil life, of fifteen probationary ensigns, for air duty only, and for a duration of three years.

The Naval Appropriation Bill, of March, 1918, increased the strength of the enlisted personnel of the N.F.C. to 10,000 men.

The Naval Flying Corps sub-divides, as to organisation, into four branches, which are attached to four Bureaux of the Navy Department, respectively. The Director of Naval Aviation, in the Bureau of Operations, is in charge of administration, inspection, training, materiel, personnel, and operations. The Aircraft Division of the Bureau of Construction and Repair is responsible for design, specifications, construction and supply of aircraft, minus their motive apparatus, and research work. The Aviation Division of the Bureau of Steam Engineering is in charge of the production of engines and their parts, airscrews, radiators, and station and school equipment, instruments, and balloon gas. The Aviation Section of the Bureau of Ordnance supplies aircraft armament.

NAVAL AIR EXPENDITURES.

1912-13 : $24,532·79.
1913-14 : $56,032·90.
1914-15 : $194,492·46.
1915-16 : $219,429·20.
1916-17 : $684,679·28.
1917-18 : $61,133,000 (appropriation).
1918-19 : $220,383,119 (appropriation).
1919-20 : $35,000,000 (appropriation).

The Curtiss-built N.C.1 Flying Boat, designed by the U.S. Naval Aviation Department.

THE 1919-20 PROGRAMME.

The amount originally asked for aeronautics in the Naval Appropriation Bill, 1919, was $225,000,000, but after Armistice Day this was reduced to $85,000,000, and later to $35,000,000.

The reduced programme provides for the construction of 108 fighting escorts, 54 twin-engine patrol machines, 54 single-engine patrol machines, 108 three-engine fleet seaplanes, and 300 school machines, a total of $88,162,000; and 31 airships, 57 kite-balloons, and 10 free balloons, a total of $19,615,000 for lighter-than-air craft.

It is proposed to have two squadrons of fighting escorts of 18 each, one replacement squadron, and one training squadron : two squadrons and a replacement squadron of large and small patrol machines each ; two squadrons of fleet machines, one replacement squadron, one training squadron. Full replacement is provided for the fleet machines and the fighting escorts.

The fighting escorts are to be of the Dunkirk type ; experiments are now under way with a Curtiss float triplane, which has developed a speed of 140 m.p.h. The large patrol machines are of the F-5-L and F-6 types ; the small patrol machines of the HS-2-L type ; the fleet machines of the NC-1 type ; the school machines of the Curtiss N-9 (100 h.p.) and R-6 (200 h.p.) float-types, the Curtiss F boat type, beside Curtiss JN-4 and Thomas M.I. types for operating from the land and the decks of ships, respectively.

In the airship programme, provision is made for 4 rigid airships, 12 large non-rigid airships, and 64 twin-engine coastal airships : it is not, however, expected to build all these craft during the fiscal year 1919-20.

NAVAL AIRCRAFT STRENGTH.

On Dec. 31, 1918, the following numbers of aircraft were in commission in the United States Navy :

34 twin-engine service seaplanes ;
337 single-engine service seaplanes ;
100 land aeroplanes (Marines, training) ;
401 training seaplanes ;
12 experimental seaplanes ;

a total of 884, in addition to which there were shipped abroad, for the war emergency, the following :

159 twin-engine seaplanes ;
229 single-engine seaplanes ;
140 land aeroplanes ;

that is, a total of 528 machines. The grand total of naval seaplanes and aeroplanes commissioned was therefore 1,412, to which must be added 17 airships and 116 kite-balloons, of which latter 42 were shipped to Europe.

THE U.S. NAVY'S TRANS-ATLANTIC FLIGHT.

THE honour of being the first machine to cross the Atlantic Ocean by air was won by the American Naval Flying Boat N.C.4, commanded by Lieut.-Commander Read, U.S.N.

On May 8th, 1919, three N.C. (Navy-Curtiss) Flying Boats, N.C.1, N.C.3, and N.C.4, left Rockaway Beach, U.S., and flew to Trepassey, Newfoundland, a distance of 950 miles. Owing to slight defects at the start, N.C.4 did not arrive till May 10th.

On May 16th, after adjustments and repairs, the three boats left Trepassey and flew towards the Azores. N.C.4 reached Horta, the first port of the Azores, 1,381 miles from Trepassey, in 15 hours 18 minutes.

N.C.1 (Lieut.-Commander Bellinger) was obliged to descend, owing to fog, and sank before she could be got on board one of the salvage ships which were stationed along the course.

N.C.3 (Commander Towers) was also brought down by fog, but, although badly damaged by the sea, she was brought into Horta under her own power, after navigating for 200 miles on the surface. She was then too badly damaged to fly any further.

The Senior Naval Officer, U.S.N., at the Azores, suggested that Commander Towers, as the organiser of the flight, and as Senior Naval Aviator, should take command of N.C.4. Commander Towers very properly objected to being called upon to supplant one of his own officers in the honour of being the first to cross the Atlantic by air. The Senior Naval Officer telegraphed to the Navy Department at Washington for permission to appoint Commander Towers to N.C.4. This permission was promptly refused, so Lieut.-Commander Read remained in command, as Commander Towers wished.

Unfortunately the telegram of the S.N.O. was widely published, and still more unfortunately the position adopted by Commander Towers was not made equally well-known.

On May 20th, N.C.4 flew from Horta to Porta Delgada—the port in the Azores nearest to Europe—169 miles in 1 hour 45 minutes.

On May 27th, N.C.4 flew from Porta Delgada to Lisbon, 925 miles in 9 hours 44 minutes, and thus achieved the crossing of the Atlantic by air for the first time.

At a later date—May 30th—N.C.4 started for England, but, owing to adverse winds, came down near Ferrol. And on May 31st she flew over Brest and alighted at Plymouth.

The flight was carried out officially by the U.S. Navy, which stationed salvage ships at intervals of 50 miles along the course over which the N.C. boats were to fly. The flying arrangements were made and the organisation was carried out by Commander Towers.—C.G.G.

The Start of the Three N.C. Boats from Rockaway Beach, U.S.A., on May 8th.

FROM 1945–46 *JANE'S ALL THE WORLD'S AIRCRAFT*

Service Aviation in the United States is organized in two separate arms—the Army Air Forces and the Naval Air Service, the latter including Marine Corps Aviation and, for the duration of the War, the Coast Guard Air Service.

The Commander-in-Chief of the Fighting Forces is the President of the United States.

THE ARMY AIR FORCES

On March 2, 1942, a drastic reorganization was approved whereby all branches of the Army were abolished in favour of three main autonomous commands,—Air Forces, Ground Forces and Service of Supply,—all of which are responsible directly to the General Staff.

The placing of the Air Forces under a single command resulted in the abolition of the Air Corps and Combat Command. General of the Army H. H. Arnold was Commander-in-Chief of the Air Forces from March, 1942, until the victory over Japan. On retirement he will be succeeded by General Carl Spaatz.

Further reorganization, which became effective on March 29, 1943, established six Assistant Chiefs of Staff, to direct and control the activities of the Air Forces. This reorganization results in (*a*) H.Q. Army Air Forces being relieved of details of execution and being left free to determine overall policy ; (*b*) the creation of a more cohesive organization within H.Q. ; and (*c*) the delegation of greater responsibility to field commanders.

In 1944 a Continental Air Forces Headquarters was established at Camp Springs, Va. The new organization is responsible for the air defence of the United States. It takes over the operational functions of the A.A.F. H.Q. in the War Department, the latter continuing to handle high-level policies and planning.

THE AIR FORCES

At the end of the war with Japan there were sixteen Air Forces, each theoretically composed of Fighter, Bomber, Air Support and Air Service Commands. The Fighter and Bomber Commands, as their names imply, were made up of fighters and medium and heavy bomber units respectively. The Fighter Commands were responsible for the co-ordination of all types of fighter aircraft, anti-aircraft batteries, balloon-barrages and other air defence elements ranging from searchlights to air-raid warning systems.

The Air Support Commands provided air support for the ground forces of the Army, and operated Fighters, Light and Medium Bombers and Communication aircraft.

Each Air Force had its separate command and staff. The combatant Commands of each Air Force were divided into Divisions, comprising from three to five Wings, the Wing, which generally corresponds to an Army Brigade, being the basic tactical unit. Each Wing was further sub-divided into three Groups, a Group consisting of three to four squadrons of the same category, all based on one airfield. The Group, which generally corresponds to a Regiment, is the basic operational unit. A Squadron may consist of from twelve to twenty-four aircraft according to type. Squadrons are further divided for purposes of flight control into Flights (six aircraft) and Elements (three aircraft).

HOME COMMANDS

There are four Air Forces in the United States. These Air Forces were originally intended for metropolitan defence but after 1942 they became responsible mainly for the operational training of combat groups and units and replacement crews for service in overseas Air Forces.

1st Air Force. H.Q.: Mitchel Field, Long Island, N.Y.
2nd Air Force. H.Q.: Fort George Wright, Spokane, Wash.
3rd Air Force. H.Q.: National Guard Armoury, Tampa, Fla.
4th Air Force. H.Q.: Presidio, San Francisco, Cal.

OVERSEAS COMMANDS

Overseas Air Forces operated in the United Kingdom, Iceland, North and West Africa, Sicily and Italy, the Middle East, India, China, Australia, New Zealand, the Southern Pacific Islands, Hawaii, Alaska, the Caribbean Area, Panama, and at bases outside the Canal Zone and along the Atlantic coast outside the territorial limits of the United States from Newfoundland to the West Indies.

The location of the overseas Air Forces at the end of the war were as follow :—

5th Air Force, Far East Air Force, Okinawa.
First based in Australia. Later incorporated in the U.S. Far East Air Force.
6th Air Force, Caribbean.
Responsible for the defence of the Panama Canal and the Caribbean area.
7th Air Force, Far East Air Force, Okinawa.
Originally based in the Philippines.
8th Air Force, Strategic Air Force, Okinawa.
Originally formed in the British Isles for service in the European Theatre. On the conclusion of the European war, was transferred to the Pacific and re-equipped with B-29 Superfortresses to form part of the Strategic Air Force to bomb Japan.
9th Air Force.
Originally served in the Mediterranean and later in the British Isles and Europe. Was in process of transference to the Pacific on the conclusion of the war. Certain units remained in Germany as part of the forces of occupation.
10th Air Force, China.
Originally formed part of the Allied South-East Asia Command.
11th Air Force, Alaska.
A component of the U.S. Navy North Pacific Command.
12th Air Force.
Formed part of the Mediterranean Allied Air Command in Italy.
13th Air Force, Far East Air Force, Philippines.
Originally served in the Southern Pacific area. Later incorporated in the Far East Air Force.
14th Air Force, China.
Constituted from the former China Air Task Force. Later formed part of the China Theatre Command.
15th Air Force.
Formed in 1943 as part of the U.S. Strategic Bombing Force in Europe to bomb Germany from Italian bases in collaboration with the 8th Air Force (also forming part of the Strategic Bombing Force), which did likewise from British bases.
20th Air Force, Strategic Air Force, Marianas.
Formed to bomb Japan from Indian and, later, Pacific island bases. The first Air Force to be equipped with the B-29 Superfortress.

The U.S.S. Lexington, a Fleet Carrier of the "Essex" Class of 27,000 tons displacement and with accommodation for 80 aircraft.

NAVAL AVIATION

United States Naval Aviation is part of the Naval Organization and is under the direction of the Secretary of the Navy.

ORGANIZATION

The Aircraft Squadron is the standard administrative and tactical unit in all naval operations. Carrier-based squadrons comprise eighteen aircraft, sub-divided into two divisions of nine aircraft each. Patrol squadrons comprise six or twelve aircraft but squadrons operating from battleships and cruisers vary in their complement. Three sections of three aircraft form an Observation Squadron attached to each Battleship Division of three ships. Four cruisers usually form a Division and each cruiser carries a section of four aircraft, the four sections forming a Cruiser Scouting Squadron.

NAVAL AIR STATIONS

On the entry of the United States in the War there were thirty-four naval operational, training, overhaul, test and airship bases in commission in continental United States, the West Indies, the Pacific and Alaska. There were also sixteen Naval Reserve Aviation Bases.

During the fiscal year 1942-43 twenty-three new shore establishments were commissioned, twenty-one naval air stations—eighteen for heavier-than-air and three for lighter-than-aircraft—and two Naval Reserve Aviation Bases. There were to be 134 naval air stations in operation in 1945.

The Naval Reserve Aviation Bases are used as centres for elimination training of candidates seeking enrolment as aviation cadets and to give successful candidates the necessary preparatory flight training to qualify them for further instruction at the Naval Air Training Centres at Pensacola, Jacksonville, Miami, and Corpus Christi.

NAVAL AIR TRANSPORT

A Naval Air Transport Service was authorised on December 12, 1941, as a section of the Naval Transportation Service, a division of the Office of the Chief of Naval Operations. Early in 1942 it was transferred, together with all other aviation activities, to a newly-formed Aviation Division of the Office of the Chief of Naval Operations.

The Naval Transport Service began operations in February, 1942, and one year after authorisation the Service was operating over 40,000 route-miles to Australia, Alaska, the Aleutians, Newfoundland, Brazil, throughout the Caribbean area and all over continental United States.

The Service operates in three main divisions ; Atlantic, West Coast and Pacific.

The Atlantic Command (H.Q.: Patuxent River, Md.) consists of squadrons serving the Atlantic coasts of North, Central and South America, and extending across the Atlantic to Europe and Africa.

The West Coast Command (H.Q.: Alameda, Cal.) operates schedules for the trans-continental service and also serves Western Canada and Alaska.

The Pacific Command (H.Q.: Pearl Harbour, T.H.) operates throughout the Pacific Ocean area.

Pan-American Airways and American Export Airlines supplement the work of the Naval Air Transport Service by operating under contract to the U.S. Navy, air-transport services to naval establishments and fleet units in the War area.

The types of naval transport aircraft used include the Martin PBM-3R Mariner, Consolidated PB2Y-3R Coronado, Douglas R4D and R5D, Lockheed R5O, etc.

U.S. MARINE CORPS AVIATION

Headquarters, U.S. Marine Corps, Washington, D.C.

Director of Marine Corps Aviation : Brigadier-General Field Harris.

Marine Corps Aviation is an integral part of Naval Aviation and its mission is to furnish the Air Forces necessary to the Fleet Marine Force, Carrier Operations with the Fleet and for expeditionary duty, marine advanced base operations and the defence of naval bases outside the continental United States which are defended on shore by the Marines. Its officers are either detailed to aviation duty from permanent line officers of the Corps or are recruited as aviation cadets and appointed to the Marine Corps Reserve. Its enlisted men are marines specially trained for aviation duty. A number of enlisted men are selected each year for flight training.

The Marine Corps also includes Parachute battalions and Airborne troops and all parachute training and air training in both powered aircraft and gliders is undertaken by Marine Corps Aviation. All troop-carrying gliders used by the Marines are amphibians, capable of operating either on land or water.

The Marine Corps is also responsible for the organization and training of barrage balloon units for the protection of Navy and Marine shore establishments.

The administration, training and operations of Marine Corps Aviation are directed by the Director of Aviation Headquarters, U.S. Marine Corps, who is also attached to the Bureau of Aeronautics and whose office also constitutes a division of Headquarters, U.S. Marine Corps.

The following are the principal Marine Air Commands :—

1st Marine Aircraft Wing. Philippine Islands.
2nd Marine Aircraft Wing. Central Pacific.
4th Marine Aircraft Wing. Central Pacific.
Marine Fleet Air. West Coast.
9th Marine Aircraft Wing. East Coast.

The air training of Marine Corps aviation personnel has been co-ordinated with Naval air training since July 1, 1941. Qualified personnel recruited by the Marine Corps now pass through the prescribed course for naval aviation cadets at Pensacola and on completion of the course may apply for appointment as Second Lieutenants, U.S. Marine Corps Reserve.

All aviation material used in Marine aviation is procured by the Navy. In general the same types of aircraft are used. Tactical squadrons have a similar organization. Radio, ordnance equipment and motor transport are identical to those of the Navy.

Marine aviation is responsible for the operation, maintenance and overhaul of its aircraft, aero-engines and equipment and there are two large Marine overhaul bases, one on the East coast and one on the West coast.

LIGHTER-THAN-AIR BRANCH

The Airship Branch of the U.S. Navy has shared in the general expansion of Naval Aviation. A widespread network of major and auxiliary bases has been established, including six new major bases for the East Coast and Gulf of Mexico area, three for the Pacific Coast and others for undisclosed points outside the continental limits of the United States. A greatly augmented training programme was initiated at the Lakehurst base and a second school was established at Moffet Field, Sunnyvale, Cal.

Purchase of 48 non-rigid airships was authorised in June, 1940. Following on the successful demonstration of the value of the airship in anti-submarine patrol in areas where there is no likelihood of attack by enemy aircraft, a Bill was passed on June 8, 1942, which authorised the Navy to build or acquire 200 lighter-than-aircraft of the G, K and M non-rigid types for training, patrol and anti-submarine duties

The U.S.S. Ranger, the first American ship to be built from the keel up as an aircraft-carrier. She was commissioned in June, 1934.

THE AERO COMMANDER 520 and 560
U.S.A.F. designation: U-4
U.S. Army designation: U-9

In addition to civilian sales of the various versions of the Aero Commander, the U.S.A.F. and U.S. Army have purchased a number of these aircraft, under the following designations:—

YL-26. Three Aero Commander 520's for service trials with U.S. Army. Three more for South Korean Air Force.

YL-26A. One Aero Commander 560 for U.S.A.F.

U-4A. Fifteen standard 560A's for U.S.A.F. Used as V.I.P. transports.

U-4B. Aero Commander 680 Super. Two for U.S.A.F. for V.I.P. transport duties.

U-9B (formerly L-26B). Similar to U-4A. One for U.S. Army.

U-9C (formerly L-26C). Similar to U-4B. Four for U.S. Army.

RU-9D (formerly RL-26D). Carries "side-looking" radar. First was modified by University of Illinois for evaluation by U.S. Army Signal Corps. Subsequently two more bought by Army as RU-9D's.

The original Aero Commander 560 received its Type Certificate on May 28, 1954; the 560F was approved on February 8, 1961, and the following details apply to this version.

TYPE.—Twin-engined light transport.

WINGS.—Cantilever high-wing monoplane. Wing section NACA 23012 modified. Aspect ratio 9.45. Chord (root) 8 ft. 4 in. (2.54 m.), (tip) 2 ft. 1½ in. (0.65 m.). Dihedral 4°. Incidence 3° at root, −3.5° at tip. All-metal two-spar structure. Frise-type all-metal ailerons. Hydraulically-operated slotted all-metal flaps. Ground-adjustable tab in starboard aileron. Total area of ailerons 20.52 sq. ft. (1.90 m.²). Total area of flaps 20.82 sq. ft. (1.93 m.²). Gross wing area 255 sq. ft. (23.69 m.²).

FUSELAGE.—All-metal semi-monocoque structure with flush-riveted covering.

TAIL UNIT.—Cantilever all-metal structure with metal covering on all surfaces and 10° dihedral on tailplane. Trim-tabs in elevators and rudder. Areas: fin 24.00 sq ft (2.23 m²), rudder 15.4 sq ft (1.43 m²), tailplane 33.06 sq ft (3.07 m²), elevators 20.54 sq ft (1.91 m²). Span of tailplane 16 ft 9 in. (5.10 m.)

LANDING GEAR.—Retractable tricycle type, with single wheel on each unit. Electrol oleo-pneumatic shock-absorbers. Hydraulic retraction. Hydraulically-steerable nose-wheel. Goodyear wheels and tyres, size 8.50 × 10 on main units, 6.00 × 10 on nose unit. Tyre pressures: main 50 lb/sq in. (3.52 kg/cm²), nose 30 lb/sq in. (2.11 kg/cm²). Goodyear hydraulic single-disc brakes. Track 12 ft 11 in (3.95 m.). Wheelbase 13 ft 11.8 in. (4.26 m.)

The Aero Commander L-26B Light Military Transport.

POWER PLANT.—Two 350 h.p. Lycoming IGO-540-B1A fuel-injection six-cylinder horizontally-opposed air-cooled engines. Hartzell three-blade constant-speed fully-feathering metal airscrews, diameter 7 ft. 9 in. (2.36 m.). Fuel capacity 223 U.S. gallons (843 litres) in bag-type tanks in wings. Oil capacity 10 U.S. gallons (37.8 litres).

ACCOMMODATION.—Enclosed cabin of 177 cub. ft. (5 m.³), with height of 4 ft. 5 in., width of 4 ft. 4 in. and length of 10 ft. 9½ in. (1.35 m. × 1.32 m. × 3.29 m.). Standard seating for two in front on individual adjustable seats with dual controls and full-width seat for three at rear of cabin. One or two additional seats may be added at extra cost. Main entry door, under wing on port side, is 3 ft. 7 in. high and 2 ft. 4 in. wide (1.09 m. × 0.71 m.). Door 20 in. (50.8 cm.) from ground. Cabin heater. All equipment can be removed to permit cabin to be used for freight-carrying, and floor may be reinforced. Optional arrangement provides for both passengers and freight. Baggage compartment aft of cabin with capacity of 32 cub. ft. (0.91 m.³). Baggage compartment door is 1 ft. 11½ in. high and 1 ft. 7½ in. wide (0.60 m. × 0.50 m.). Standard equipment includes blind-flying instruments, rotating beacon, landing lights in nose, passenger reading lights. Radio and radar are to customer's choice.

DIMENSIONS.—
Span	49 ft 6 in. (15.09 m)
Length	35 ft 1¼ in. (10.7 m)
Height	14 ft 6 in. (4.42 m)

WEIGHTS AND LOADINGS.—
Weight empty	4,650 lb (2,110 kg)
Max. T.O. and landing weight	7,500 lb (3,402 kg)
Wing loading	29.4 lb/sq ft (143.5 kg/m²)
Power loading	10.2 lb/hp (4.63 kg/hp)

PERFORMANCE.—
Max. speed at S/L	250 mph (402 kmh)
Max. permissible speed in dive	288 mph (463 kmh)
Cruising speed (70% rated power) at 10,000 ft (3,050 m)	232 mph (373 kmh)
Econ. cruising speed (55% power) at 10,000 ft (3,050 m)	205 mph (330 kmh)
Stalling speed, flaps and landing gear down	73.5 mph (119 kmh)
Rate of climb at S/L	1,587 ft (484 m) min.
Rate of climb at S/L	490 ft (150 m) min.
Service ceiling	21,900 ft (6,675 m)
Service ceiling on one engine	9,800 ft (2,990 m)
T.O. distance to clear 50 ft (15.25 m) no wind	1,350 ft (412 m)
Landing distance from 50 ft (15.25 m)	1,375 ft (419 m)
Range (at 55% S/L rated power, 30 min. fuel reserve) at 10,000 ft (3,050 m)	1,705 miles (2,745 km)

(1963–64)

The Aeromarine modified D.H.4, with high lift wings.

The Aeromarine Plane and Motor Co., Key Port, New Jersey.

The Aeromarine Company has been busy, during the past year, on the construction of twenty-five Martin Bombers for the Army Air Service as well as on general refit and maintenance work of the fleet of the Aeromarine Airways.

The Engineering Department has developed a high-lift wing which has been fitted to an experimental mail aeroplane, greatly improving its performance. The normal Mail DH-4 carries on the average a mail load of 400 lbs. and has a high speed of 120 m.p.h. and a low speed of about 60 m.p.h. Fitted with the Aeromarine Model A-2 wing, the DH-4 carries 800 lbs. of mail, at a high speed of 115 m.p.h., with a landing speed of 50 m.p.h. and a minimum flying speed of 68 m.p.h. The climb with full load is 5,150 ft. in 10 mins., as against 6,500 ft. in 10 mins. for the regular Mail DH-4, and the take-off 11 secs. as against 9 secs.

The Engineering Department has also developed a light weight shutter for aero-engine radiators.

Early in 1923 the Army Air Service placed with the company an order for remodelling twenty-five DH-4 aeroplanes.

AEROMARINE 40

Type of machine	Flying Boat.
Span, upper wing..	48 ft. 6 in.
Span, lower wing..	37 ft. 4 in.
Stagger	8 in.
Chord	75 in.
Gap	78 in.
Dihedral	2 degrees.
Area, upper panel (with ailerons)	304 sq. ft.
Area, lower panel	200 sq. ft.
Ailerons, each	29 sq. ft.
Elevators, each	12.8 sq. ft.
Stabilizer	39.5 sq. ft.
Vertical stabilizer fin	15 sq. ft.
Rudder	17.5 sq. ft.
Skid fin	5.5 sq. ft.
Length overall	28 ft. 11 in.
Weight, light	1,925 lbs.
Weight, loaded	2,485 lbs.
Gasoline	35 gallons.

The Aeromarine 40 (Curtiss 100 h.p. OXX-6 engine).

Seating Arrangement. Model 40-T is arranged for one operator and one passenger, and is an ideal machine for instruction or sporting purposes.

Performance.

Aeromarine 125-130 h.p. motor:

High speed	80 m.p.h.
Landing speed.. ..	38 m.p.h.
Climb	2,500 feet in 10 minutes.

100 h.p. motor:

High speed	70 m.p.h.
Landing speed.. ..	38 m.p.h.
Climb	2,100 feet in 10 minutes.

Hull.—The hulls of these boats are constructed in the most modern and durable fashion.

The bottoms are constructed of two-ply, placed diagonally with cloth between and fastened with brass fastenings.

The sides and decks are of three-ply waterproof veneer.

The decks forward of the cockpit and after the rear beam may be removed, as well as the floors in the passenger compartment, and as it is possible to enter the hull between the wing beams through the hatch, the entire bottom and inside of the boat may be inspected and repaired more easily.

50 of these machines have been delivered to the U.S. Navy. Price : $9,000. (1919)

THE AERONCA GRASSHOPPER.
U.S. Army Air Forces designation: L-3.

The description below applies to the L-3, L-3A, L-3B and L-3C, all of which are generally similar, differing mainly in details of equipment.

TYPE.—Two-seat Light Liaison and Observation monoplane.

WINGS.—High-wing rigidly braced monoplane. NACA 4412 wing section. Wings in two sections attached to top longerons of fuselage and braced to lower longerons by Vee struts. Structure consists of two solid spruce spars, aluminium-alloy ribs, steel-tube compression struts and single-wire drag bracing, the whole being covered with fabric. Ailerons have metal frames with fabric covering.

FUSELAGE.—Welded steel-tube structure covered with fabric over spruce fairing stringers.

TAIL UNIT.—Braced monoplane type. Welded steel-tube framework covered with fabric. Fin built integral with fuselage. Trimming tab in starboard elevator adjustable from cockpit.

LANDING GEAR.—Divided type. Faired-in side Vees hinged to lower fuselage longerons and half-axles hinged to Vee cabane beneath fuselage. Oleo-spring shock-absorber struts incorporated in side Vees. Full swivelling tail-wheel. Mechanical wheel-brakes.

POWER PLANT.—One 65 h.p. Continental O-170-3 four-cylinder horizontally-opposed air-cooled engine on detachable welded steel-tube mounting. Fuel tanks (12 U.S. gallons) in roof of cabin and conforming to curvature of wings.

ACCOMMODATION.—Enclosed cabin seating two in tandem. Dual controls provided but L-3 usually flown from front seat. Observer's seat may face forward or aft and when in latter position a folding table may be brought into use for maps etc. Radio equipment.

DIMENSIONS.—Span 35 ft. (10.67 m.), Length 21 ft. 10 in. (6.67 m.), Height 9 ft. 1 in. (2.74 m.), Wing area (including ailerons) 169 sq. ft. (15.6 sq. m.).

WEIGHTS AND LOADINGS.—Weight empty 835 lbs. (379 kg.), Weight loaded 1,260 lbs. (572 kg.), Wing loading 7.45 lbs./sq. ft. (36.1 kg./sq. m.), Power loading 19.39 lbs./h.p. (8.8 kg./h.p.).

PERFORMANCE.—Maximum speed 87 m.p.h. (139 km.h.), Cruising speed 79 m.p.h. (126.4 km.h.), Stalling speed 46 m.p.h. (73.6 km.h.), Initial rate of climb 404 ft/min. (123 m./min.), Service ceiling 10,000 ft. (3,050 m.), Normal range 218 miles (350 km.).

The U.S. Army also acquired secondhand a number of Aeronca two-seat cabin monoplanes of various models for pre-glider training purposes. These were given designations in the L-3 Series as follow :—

L-3D Model 65TAF Defender. Franklin 4AC-176-B2 engine.
L-3E Model 65TAC Defender. Continental A65-8 engine.
L-3F Model 65CA Super-Chief. Continental A65-8 engine.
L-3G Model 65LB Super-Chief. Lycoming O-145-B1 engine.
L-3H Model 65TL Defender. Lycoming O-145-B1 engine.
L-3J Model 65TC Defender, Continental A65-7 engine.

These are all standard dual control civil models without service modifications. (1945–46)

The Aeronca L-3H Light Liaison and Observation Monoplane (65 h.p. Lycoming O-145-B1 engine).

THE AERONCA 7BC CHAMPION.

U.S. Army designation : L-16A.

This version of the Aeronca Champion has been supplied to the U.S. Army for use by the Ground Forces and the National Guard for liaison and general Communications duties. It differs from the 7AC Champion described below by being fitted with an 85 h.p. Continental engine with fuel injection, the cabin is also provided with a transparent roof and jettisonable doors. Otherwise the two aircraft are structurally similar.

TYPE.—Two-seat Cabin monoplane.
WINGS.—Strut-braced high-wing monoplane. Aerofoil section NACA 4412. Two-spar structure of constant chord built in two sections which are attached directly to top fuselage longerons and braced to lower longerons by V-struts. Solid spruce spars, aluminium-alloy ribs, steel compression ribs and single wire drag-bracing, the whole being fabric-covered. Duralumin ailerons with fabric covering. Wing area 170 sq. ft. (15.79 sq. m.).
FUSELAGE.—Welded steel-tube structure with four longerons, spruce longitudinal stringers and fabric covering.
TAIL UNIT.—Wire-braced monoplane type. Welded steel-tube frame-work with fabric covering attached by metal screws and washers. Fin integral with fuselage. Horn-balanced rudder. Controllable trim-tab in port elevator.
LANDING GEAR.—Fixed divided type consisting of two interchangeable side vees incorporating oleo shock-absorber struts and two half axles hinged to fuselage centre-line. Dual brakes. Steerable tail-wheel. Wheels replaceable by twin float undercarriage.
POWER PLANT.—One 65 h.p. Lycoming four-cylinder horizontally-opposed air-cooled engine driving a Sensenich two-blade fixed-pitch wooden airscrew. Fuel capacity 14 U.S. gallons (53 litres).
ACCOMMODATION.—Enclosed cabin seating two in tandem with dual controls. Moulded one-piece windscreen.
DIMENSIONS.—Span 35 ft. 0 in. (10.66 m.), Length 21 ft. 6 in. (6.56 m.), Height (tail down) 7 ft. 0 in. (2.13 m.).

WEIGHTS AND LOADINGS (Seaplane).—Weight empty 810 lbs. (367 **kg.**), Useful load 510 lbs. (231 **kg.**), weight loaded 1,320 lbs. (598 **kg.**), Wing loading (fully loaded) 7.76 lbs./sq. ft. (37.89 **kg./m.²**), Power loading (fully loaded) 20.3 lbs./h.p. (9.7 kg./h.p.).
PERFORMANCE (Landplane).—Maximum speed 100 m.p.h. (161 **km.h.**), Cruising speed 90 m.p.h. (145 km.h.), Landing speed 38 **m.p.h.** (61 km.h.), Rate of climb 500 ft./min. (152 m./min.), range at **cruising** speed 270 miles (434 km.). (1948)

The Aeronca L-16A Two-seat Military Liason Monoplane (85 h.p. Continental C85 engine). (Peter M. Bowers).

AÉROSPATIALE AS 366 DAUPHIN 2
US Coast Guard designation: HH-65A Dolphin

At the 1979 Paris Air Show, Aérospatiale announced that it had won with this aircraft the competition for a helicopter to perform SRR (Short Range Recovery) duties with the US Coast Guard. The initial requirement is for 90 **AS 366Gs**, basically similar to the AS 365N but with engines and equipment of US manufacture accounting for about 60 per cent of the total cost of each aircraft. The first order, for 23, was received in 1979.

The AS 366G will be powered by two Avco Lycoming LTS 101-750 turboshafts, each rated at 507 kW (680 shp). Rockwell Collins is prime contractor for the advanced communications, navigation and all-weather search equipment. Flight testing was expected to begin in August 1980, to permit civil certification in October 1981 and

deliveries to the Coast Guard between the early months of 1982 and 1986.

A civil counterpart, the **AS 366N**, is planned for the North American market. To meet French military requirements, notably for Aéronavale, a version is projected with two Turboméca Arriel turboshaft engines, strengthened landing gear, deck-landing harpoon, radar, hoist and other special equipment.

DIMENSIONS, EXTERNAL (AS 366G):

Diameter of main rotor	11·68 m (38 ft 4 in)
Length overall	13·35 m (43 ft 9½ in)
Length overall, rotor blades folded	11·40 m (37 ft 4¾ in)
Width, rotor blades folded	3·20 m (10 ft 6 in)
Height overall	3·81 m (12 ft 6 in)

WEIGHTS (AS 366G):

Weight empty, incl mission equipment	2,530 kg (5,577 lb)
Max T-O weight	3,810 kg (8,400 lb)

PERFORMANCE (AS 366G, estimated at max T-O weight):

Max level speed	133 knots (246 km/h; 153 mph)
SRR range	166 nm (307 km; 191 miles)
Range with max passenger load	216 nm (400 km; 248 miles)
Max range, one engine out	327 nm (605 km; 376 miles)
Range with max fuel	420 nm (778 km; 483 miles)
Endurance with max fuel	4 h 11 min
	(1980–81)

THE AMERICAN D.H. 4 BIPLANE

Army Corps Observation Two-seaters. (CO.) Service equipment represented by "Liberty"-engined DH-4B (1920–21), DH-4B2 (1921–22) and DH-4M (1922–23), the latter with a welded steel tube fuselage built by the Boeing Co.

(Built by Dayton Wright Aeroplane Co.)
Specification.

Type of machine	.. ..	Two-seater Biplane.
Name or type No. of machine	..	American D.H. 4.
Purpose for which intended.	..	Reconnaissance.
Span	..	42 ft. 5¾ in.
Overall length	..	30 ft. 5⁶¹⁄₆₄ in.
Maximum height	..	10 ft. 3³⁹⁄₃₂ in.
Chord..	..	5 ft. 6 in.
Span of tail ..	..	13 ft. 7 in.
Engine type and h.p.	..	Liberty 12; 400 h.p.
Weight of machine empty	..	2,391 lbs.
Tank capacity in gallons	..	88 gallons.

Performance.

Speed low down	..	..	124.7 m.p.h.
Speed at 6,500 feet	..	..	120 m.p.h.
Speed at 10,000 feet	..	..	117 m.p.h.
Speed at 15,000 feet	..	..	113 m.p.h.
Landing speed	..	..	58 m.p.h.

Climb

To 10,000 feet in minutes	..	14 minutes.
Ceiling	.. .. ..	19,500 feet.
Endurance at 6,500 feet (full throttle)..	..	2 hrs. 13 mins.
Endurance at 6,500 feet (half throttle)	..	3 hrs. 3 mins.
Track	.. .. ..	6 feet.
Total weight of machine loaded	.. ..	3,582 lbs.
		(1924)

BAe HARRIER
USMC designations: AV-8A (Mk 50) and TAV-8A (Mk 54)

The Harrier was the world's first operational fixed-wing V/STOL strike fighter. Developed from six years of operating experience with the P.1127/Kestrel series of aircraft (see 1968-69 *Jane's*), it is an integrated V/STOL weapon system, incorporating a Ferranti FE 541 inertial navigation and attack system and Smiths head-up display. The first of six single-seat prototypes (XV276) flew for the first time on 31 August 1966.

Harrier Mk 50 (USMC designation AV-8A). Single-seat close-support and tactical reconnaissance version for the US Marine Corps, delivery of which began on 26 January 1971. Dimensionally as GR. Mk 3, but without laser ranger and marked target seeker, and with modifications to customer's specification, including provision for the carriage of Sidewinder missiles. Total of 102 ordered for US Marine Corps, plus eight Harrier **Mk 54s** (a two-seat version designated **TAV-8A**); all of those still in service now have Pegasus 103 engines.

The AV-8As equip three US Marine Corps combat squadrons: VMA 513, VMA 542 and VMA 231 training squadron VMA(T) 203, at Cherry Point, North Carolina.

Beginning in 1979, and continuing until FY 1984, a total of 61 AV-8As are being upgraded to **AV-8C** standard. This involves a service life extension programme (SLEP) of structural improvements aimed at extending the airframe fatigue life to up to 4,000 h; and a CILOP (conversion in lieu of procurement) programme under which the AV-8As are fitted with forward-looking passive radar warning equipment at the wingtips, tail warning radar in the tail 'bullet' fairing, improved UHF com radio, a flare/chaff dispenser in the rear-fuselage equipment bay, the LIDS (lift improvement devices: underfuselage strakes and forward flap) developed for the AV-8B, an onboard oxygen generating system, and KY 58 secure voice system. Conversion of the first few AV-8As to AV-8C standard was undertaken by McDonnell Douglas, from kits supplied by BAe. The remaining conversions will be carried out by the US Marine Corps at NAS Cherry Point, North Carolina.

The following details apply generally to the RAF's Harrier GR, Mk 3 and T. Mk 4, except where a specific version is indicated:

TYPE: V/STOL close support and reconnaissance aircraft.

WINGS: Cantilever shoulder-wing monoplane. Wing section of BAe (HS) design. Thickness/chord ratio 10% at root, 5% at tip. Anhedral 12°. Incidence 1° 45'. Sweepback at quarter-chord 34°. One-piece aluminium alloy three-spar safe-life structure with integrally-machined skins, manufactured by Brough factory of BAe, with six-point attachment to fuselage. Plain ailerons and flaps, of bonded aluminium alloy honeycomb construction. Ailerons irreversibly operated by Fairey tandem hydraulic jacks. Jet reaction control valve built into front of each outrigger wheel fairing. Entire wing unit removable to provide access to engine. For ferry missions, the normal 'combat' wingtips can be replaced by bolt-on extended tips to increase ferry range.

FUSELAGE: Conventional semi-monocoque safe-life structure of frames and stringers, mainly of aluminium alloy, but with titanium skins at rear and some titanium adjacent to engine and in other special areas. Access to power plant through top of fuselage, ahead of wing. Jet reaction control valves in nose and in extended tailcone. Large forward-hinged airbrake under fuselage, aft of main-wheel well.

TAIL UNIT: One-piece variable-incidence tailplane, with 15° of anhedral, irreversibly operated by Fairey tandem hydraulic jack. Rudder and trailing-edge of tailplane are of bonded aluminium honeycomb construction. Rudder is operated manually. Trim tab in rudder. Ventral fin under rear fuselage. Fin tip carries suppressed VHF aerial.

LANDING GEAR: Retractable bicycle type of Dowty Rotol manufacture, permitting operation from rough un-prepared surfaces of CBR as low as 3% to 5%. Hydraulic actuation, with nitrogen bottle for emergency extension of landing gear. Single steerable nosewheel retracts forward, twin coupled mainwheels rearward, into fuselage. Small outrigger units retract inward into fairings slightly inboard of wingtips. Nosewheel leg is of levered-suspension Liquid Spring type. Dowty Rotol telescopic oleo-pneumatic main and outrigger gear. Dunlop wheels and tyres, size 26·00 × 8·75-11 (nose unit), 27·00 × 7·74-13 (main units) and 13·50 × 6·4 (outriggers). GR. Mk 3 tyre pressures 6·21 bars (90 lb/sq in) on nose and main units, 6·55 bars (95 lb/sq in) on outriggers. T. Mk 4 tyre pressures 6·90 bars (100 lb/sq in) on nose unit, 6·55 bars (95 lb/sq in) on main and

Hawker Siddeley AV-8A Harriers in service with US Marine Corps Squadron VMA 231

outrigger units. Dunlop multi-disc brakes and Dunlop-Hytrol adaptive anti-skid system.

POWER PLANT: One Rolls-Royce Pegasus Mk 103 vectored-thrust turbofan engine (95·6 kN; 21,500 lb st), with four exhaust nozzles of the two-vane cascade type, rotatable through 98° from fully-aft position. Engine bleed air from HP compressor used for jet reaction control system and to power duplicated air motor for nozzle actuation. The low-drag intake cowls, with outward-cambered lips, each have 8 automatic suction relief doors aft of the leading-edge to improve intake efficiency by providing extra air for the engine at low forward or zero speeds. Fuel in five integral tanks in fuselage and two in wings, with total capacity of approx 2,865 litres (630 Imp gallons). This can be supplemented by two 455 litre (100 Imp gallon) jettison-able combat tanks or two 1,500 litre (330 Imp gallon) ferry tanks on the inboard wing pylons. Ground refuelling point in port rear nozzle fairing. Provision for in-flight refuelling probe above the port intake cowl.

ACCOMMODATION: Crew of one (Mk 3) or two (Mk 4) on Martin-Baker Type 9D zero-zero rocket ejection seats which operate through the miniature detonating cord equipped canopy of the pressurised, heated and air-conditioned cockpit. AV-8As of the US Marine Corps retrofitted with Stencel SIIIS-3 ejection seats. Manually-operated canopy, rearward-sliding on single-seat, sideways-opening (to starboard) on two-seat versions. Birdproof windscreen, with hydraulically-actuated wiper. Windscreen de-icing.

SYSTEMS: Three-axis limited-authority autostabiliser for V/STOL flight. Pressurisation system of BAe design, with Normalair-Garrett and Marston major components; max pressure differential 0·24 bars (3·5 lb/sq in). Duplicated hydraulic systems, each of 207 bars (3,000 lb/sq in), actuate Fairey flying control and general services and include a retractable ram-air turbine inside top of rear fuselage, driving a small hydraulic pump for emergency power. AC electrical system with transformer-rectifiers to provide required DC supply. One 12kVA Lucas alternator. Two 28V 25Ah batteries, one of which energises a 24V motor to start Lucas gas-turbine starter/APU. This unit drives a 6kVA auxiliary alternator for ground readiness servicing and standby. Normalair-Garrett liquid oxygen system of 5 litres (1 Imp gallon) capacity. Bootstrap-type cooling unit for equipment bay, with intake at base of dorsal fin.

AVIONICS AND EQUIPMENT: Plessey U/VHF, Ultra standby UHF, Hoffman Tacan and Cossor IFF, Ferranti FE 541 inertial navigation and attack system (INAS), with Sperry C2G compass, Smiths electronic head-up display of flight information and Smiths air data computer. INAS can be aligned equally well at sea or on land. The weapon aiming computer provides a general solution for manual or automatic release of free-fall and retarded bombs, and for the aiming of rockets and guns, in dive and straight-pass attacks over a wide range of flight conditions and very considerable freedom of manoeuvre in elevation. Communication equipment ranges through VHF in the 100-156MHz band to UHF in the 220-400MHz band. Ferranti Type 106 laser ranger and marked target seeker (LRMTS) retrofitted to all RAF Harriers.

ARMAMENT AND OPERATIONAL EQUIPMENT: Optically-flat panel in nose, on port side, for F.95 oblique camera, which is carried as standard. A cockpit voice recorder with in-flight playback facility supplements the recon-naissance cameras, and facilitates rapid debriefing and mission evaluation. No built-in armament. Combat load is carried on four underwing and one underfuselage

pylons, all with ML ejector release units. The inboard wing points and the fuselage point are stressed for loads of up to 910 kg (2,000 lb) each, and the outboard underwing pair for loads of up to 295 kg (650 lb) each; the two strake fairings under the fuselage can each be replaced by a 30 mm Aden gun pod and ammunition. At present, the Harrier is cleared for operations with a maximum external load exceeding 2,270 kg (5,000 lb), but has flown with a weapon load of 3,630 kg (8,000 lb). The Harrier is able to carry 30 mm guns, bombs, rockets and flares of UK and US designs, and in addition to its fixed reconnaissance camera can also carry a five-camera reconnaissance pod on the underfuselage pylon. A typical combat load comprises a pair of 30 mm Aden gun pods, a 1,000 lb bomb on the underfuselage pylon, a 1,000 lb bomb on each of the inboard underwing pylons, and a Matra 155 launcher with 19 × 68 mm SNEB rockets on each outboard underwing pylon. A Side-winder installation is provided in the AV-8A version, to give the aircraft an effective air-to-air capability in conjunction with the two 30 mm Aden guns.

DIMENSIONS, EXTERNAL:

Wing span: combat	7·70 m (25 ft 3 in)
ferry	9·04 m (29 ft 8 in)
Wing chord at root	3·56 m (11 ft 8 in)
Wing chord at tip	1·26 m (4 ft 1½ in)
Wing aspect ratio: combat	3·175
ferry	4·08
Length overall: single-seat	13·87 m (45 ft 6 in)
single-seat (laser nose)	13·91 m (45 ft 7·8 in)
two-seat	17·00 m (55 ft 9½ in)
Height overall:	
single-seat	3·45 m (11 ft 4 in)
two-seat	4·17 m (13 ft 8 in)
Tailplane span	4·24 m (13 ft 11 in)
Outrigger wheel track	6·76 m (22 ft 2 in)
Wheelbase, nosewheel to main wheels	approx 3·45 m (11 ft 4 in)

AREAS:

Wings, gross: combat	18·68 m² (201·1 sq ft)
ferry	20·1 m² (216 sq ft)
Ailerons (total)	0·98 m² (10·5 sq ft)
Trailing-edge flaps (total)	1·29 m² (13·9 sq ft)
Fin (excl ventral fin):	
single-seat	2·40 m² (25·8 sq ft)
two-seat	3·57 m² (38·4 sq ft)
Rudder, incl tab	0·49 m² (5·3 sq ft)
Tailplane	4·41 m² (47·5 sq ft)

WEIGHTS AND LOADING:

Basic operating weight, empty, with crew:	
GR.Mk 3 and Mk 50	5,580 kg (12,300 lb)
T.Mk 4 (solo for combat)	5,896 kg (13,000 lb)
T.Mk 4 (dual)	6,237 kg (13,750 lb)
Internal fuel	2,295 kg (5,060 lb)
Max T-O weight (single-seat)	over 11,340 kg (25,000 lb)
Max wing loading (single-seat)	610 kg/m² (125 lb/sq ft)

PERFORMANCE:

Max speed at low altitude	over 640 knots (1,186 km/h; 737 mph) EAS
Max Mach number (in a dive)	1·3
Time to 12,200 m (40,000 ft) from vertical T-O	2 min 22·7 s
Ceiling	more than 15,240 m (50,000 ft)
Range with one in-flight refuelling	more than 3,000 nm (5,560 km; 3,455 miles)
Endurance with one in-flight refuelling	more than 7 h

BEECHCRAFT BARON MODEL 95-B55
US Army designation: T-42A Cochise

The original Baron Model 95-55 was a four/five-seat cabin monoplane developed from the earlier Travel Air but with more power, better all-weather capability and airframe refinements that included a swept tail-fin. It first flew in prototype form on 29 February 1960 and was licensed in the FAA Normal category in November 1960. The Baron Model 95-B55 was similarly licensed in September 1963.

The current Barons are optional four-, five- or six-seaters, with interior features as described for the Bonanza.

In February 1965 the US Army selected the Model 95-B55 as winner of its competition for a twin-engined fixed-wing instrument trainer. Beech identified the military trainer as the Model 95-B55B, and this received FAA Type Approval in the Normal and Utility categories in August 1964. The US Army ordered 65, which were delivered under the designation T-42A. During 1971 Beech delivered five more T-42As to the US Army, for service with the army of Turkey, under the Military Assistance Programme. Export deliveries of the standard Model 95-B55 have also been made, including 19 for the Spanish Air Ministry and six for the Civil Air Bureau of Japan. These aircraft are used as instrument trainers.

TYPE: Four/six weat transport and instrument trainer.

WINGS: Cantilever low-wing monoplane. Wing section NACA 23016·5 at root, NACA 23010·5 at tip. Dihedral 6°. Incidence 4° at root, 0° at tip. No sweepback. Each wing is a two-spar semi-monocoque box beam of conventional aluminium alloy construction. Symmetrical-section ailerons of light alloy construction, with beaded skins. Electrically-operated single-slotted light alloy trailing-edge flaps, with beaded skins. Manually-operated trim tab in port aileron. Pneumatic rubber de-icing boots optional.

FUSELAGE: Semi-monocoque aluminium alloy structure. Hat-section longerons and channel-type keels extend forward from the cabin section, making the support structure for the forward nose section and nosewheel gear an integral part of the fuselage.

TAIL UNIT: Cantilever all-metal structure. Elevators have smooth magnesium alloy skins. Manually-operated trim tab in each elevator and in rudder. Pneumatic rubber de-icing boots optional.

LANDING GEAR: Electrically-retractable tricycle type. Main units retract inward into wings, nosewheel aft. Beech oleo-pneumatic shock-absorbers on all units. Steerable nosewheel with shimmy damper. Cleveland wheels, with 6·50-8 main-wheel tyres, pressure 3·45-3·72 bars (50-54 lb/sq in). Nosewheel tyre size 5·00-5, pressure 3·31-3·59 bars (48-52 lb/sq in). Cleveland ring-disc hydraulic brakes. Parking brake.

POWER PLANT: Two 194 kW (260 hp) Continental IO-470-L flat-six engines, each driving a Hartzell two-blade constant-speed fully-feathering propeller. Optional Hartzell three-blade propellers. Manually-operated cowl flaps. Standard fuel system comprises two interconnected tanks in each wing leading-edge, with total usable capacity of 378 litres (100 US gallons). Optional interconnected fuel tanks may be added in each wing to provide a total usable capacity of 515 litres (136 US gallons). Single refuelling point in each wing for the standard or optional fuel systems. Optional fuel system includes a mechanical sight gauge in each wing leading-edge to give partial fuelling information. Oil capacity 23 litres (6 US gallons). Propeller de-icing optional.

ACCOMMODATION: Standard model has four individual seats in pairs in enclosed cabin, with door on starboard side. Single diagonal strap shoulder harness with inertia reel standard on all seats. Optional wider door for cargo. Folding airline-style fifth and sixth seats optional, complete with shoulder harness and inertia reel. Baggage compartments aft of cabin and in nose, both with external doors on starboard side and with capacity of 181 kg (400 lb) and 136 kg (300 lb) respectively. An extended rear compartment providing for an additional 54 kg (120 lb) of baggage is optional. Pilot's storm window, port side. Openable windows adjacent to the third and fourth seats are used for ground ventilation and as emergency exits. Cabin heated and ventilated. Windscreen defrosting standard. Alcohol de-icing for port side of windscreen optional.

SYSTEMS: Cabin heated by Janitrol 50,000 BTU heater, which serves also for windscreen defrosting. Oxygen system of 1·41 m³ (49·8 cu ft) or 1·87 m³ (66 cu ft) capacity optional. Electrical system includes two 24V 25A generators. One 24V 13·5Ah battery. Two 24V 50A engine-driven alternators and/or two 12V 25Ah batteries optional. Hydraulic system for brakes only. Pneumatic pressure system for air-driven instruments, and optional wing and tail unit de-icing system. Oxygen system optional.

AVIONICS AND EQUIPMENT: Standard avionics comprise King KX 170B 720-channel com transceiver and 200-channel nav receiver with KI 208 VOR/LOC converter indicator, microphone, headset, cabin speaker and com, and nav/GS antennae. A wide range of optional avionics by Bendix, Collins, King, Edo-Aire Mitchell and Narco is available to customer's requirements. Standard equipment includes blind-flying instrumentation, clock, outside air temperature gauge, sensitive altimeter, turn co-ordinator, pilot's storm window, sun visors, ultraviolet-proof windscreen and windows, armrests, adjustable and retractable starboard side rudder pedals, emergency locator transmitter, heated pitot, carpeted floor, glove compartment, hatshelf, headrests for passenger seats, cabin dome light, instrument panel floodlights, map light, trim tab position indicator lights, passenger reading lights, navigation lights, position lights, dual landing lights, soundproofing, heated fuel vents, towbar, and engine winterisation kit. Optional equipment includes control wheel clock or chronograph, engine and flight hour recorders, vertical speed indicator, exhaust gas temperature gauge, dual tachometers with synchroscope, dual controls, alternate static source, cabin fire extinguisher, super soundproofing, entrance door courtesy light, instrument post lights, internally illuminated instruments, rotating beacon, strobe lights, taxi light, wing ice lights, propeller synchroniser, propeller unfeathering accumulator, external power socket, and static wicks.

DIMENSIONS, EXTERNAL:

Wing span	11·53 m (37 ft 10 in)
Wing chord at root	2·13 m (7 ft 0 in)
Wing chord at tip	0·90 m (2 ft 11·6 in)
Wing aspect ratio	7·16
Length overall	8·53 m (28 ft 0 in)
Height overall	2·92 m (9 ft 7 in)
Tailplane span	4·19 m (13 ft 9 in)
Wheel track	2·92 m (9 ft 7 in)
Wheelbase	2·13 m (7 ft 0 in)
Propeller diameter: two-blade	1·98 m (6 ft 6 in)
three-blade	1·93 m (6 ft 4 in)
Passenger door: Height	0·91 m (3 ft 0 in)
Width	0·94 m (3 ft 1 in)
Height to step	0·41 m (1 ft 4 in)

Baggage door (fwd): Height	0·56 m (1 ft 10 in)
Width	0·64 m (2 ft 1 in)
Baggage door (rear):	
Standard: Height	0·57 m (1 ft 10½ in)
Width	0·47 m (1 ft 6½ in)
Height to sill	0·71 m (2 ft 4 in)
Optional: Height	0·57 m (1 ft 10½ in)
Width	0·97 m (3 ft 2 in)

DIMENSIONS, INTERNAL:

Cabin: Length	3·07 m (10 ft 1 in)
Max width	1·07 m (3 ft 6 in)
Max height	1·27 m (4 ft 2 in)
Baggage compartment (fwd)	0·34 m³ (12 cu ft)
Baggage compartment (rear)	0·99 m³ (35 cu ft)

AREAS:

Wings, gross	18·5 m² (199·2 sq ft)
Ailerons (total)	1·06 m² (11·40 sq ft)
Trailing-edge flaps (total)	2·39 m² (25·70 sq ft)
Fin	1·02 m² (11·00 sq ft)
Rudder, incl tab	1·08 m² (11·60 sq ft)
Tailplane	4·46 m² (48·06 sq ft)
Elevators, incl tabs	1·51 m² (16·20 sq ft)

WEIGHTS AND LOADINGS:

Weight empty	1,466 kg (3,233 lb)
Max T-O and landing weight	2,313 kg (5,100 lb)
Max ramp weight	2,322 kg (5,121 lb)
Max wing loading	120·5 kg/m² (25·6 lb/sq ft)
Max power loading	5·96 kg/kW (9·8 lb/hp)

PERFORMANCE (at max T-O weight, except cruising speeds at average cruise weight):

Max level speed at S/L	201 knots (372 km/h; 231 mph)
Max cruising speed, 77% power at 1,830 m (6,000 ft)	188 knots (348 km/h; 216 mph)
Cruising speed, 66% power at 3,050 m (10,000 ft)	184 knots (341 km/h; 212 mph)
Econ cruising speed, 56% power at 3,660 m (12,000 ft)	173 knots (320 km/h; 199 mph)
Stalling speed, flaps up, power off	79 knots (146 km/h; 91 mph) IAS
Stalling speed, flaps down, power off	73 knots (135 km/h; 84 mph) IAS
Max rate of climb at S/L	516 m (1,693 ft)/min
Rate of climb at S/L, one engine out	121 m (397 ft)/min
Service ceiling	5,880 m (19,300 ft)
Service ceiling, one engine out	1,950 m (6,400 ft)
Min ground turning radius	9·00 m (29 ft 6 in)
Runway LCN	2
T-O run	427 m (1,400 ft)
T-O to 15 m (50 ft)	657 m (2,154 ft)
Landing from 15 m (50 ft)	655 m (2,148 ft)
Landing run	447 m (1,467 ft)

Range with 515 litres (136 US gallons) usable fuel, with allowances for engine start, taxi, T-O, climb and 45 min reserves at econ cruise power:

max cruising speed at 1,830 m (6,000 ft)	798 nm (1,479 km; 918 miles)
cruising speed at 3,050 m (10,000 ft)	907 nm (1,680 km; 1,044 miles)
econ cruising speed at 3,660 m (12,000 ft)	991 nm (1,836 km; 1,141 miles)

(1980–81)

THE BEECHCRAFT EXPEDITOR.
U.S. Army Air Forces designation : C-45.
U.S. Navy designation : JRB.

The C-45 is a military utility transport version of the earlier civil Model 18S. The variants of the C-45, all of which are fitted with two Pratt & Whitney R-985 engines, are the C-45 (JRB-1), C-45A (JRB-2), C-45B (JRB-3 and Expediter I), C-45C (Commercial model 18-S) C-45D, C-45E and C-45F (JRB-4 and Expediter II).

TYPE.—Twin-engined Light Personnel or Utility Transport.

WINGS.—Low-wing cantilever monoplane. Centre-section integral with the fuselage. Tapering outer wing sections. Structure consists primarily of a single beam, in the form of a welded tube monospar, which at approximately half-way to the tip is spliced to a duralumin girder. Continuous duralumin ribs are anchored at their ends by a light beam, which carries the aileron and flap hinges. Extruded duralumin stringers extend spanwise, and the whole is covered with a smooth skin riveted to all parts. Duralumin-framed ailerons and flaps, with fabric covering. Trimming-tab in left aileron. Electrical flap operation.

The Beechcraft C-45A Expediter Light Personnel Transport (two Pratt & Whitney R-985 engines).

FUSELAGE.—Oval metal structure, comprising built-up bulkheads and extruded section stringers, the whole covered with a smooth skin riveted to bulkheads and stringers. Single steel-tube spar built into the fuselage to carry engine, landing-gear and wing loads. Remainder of centre-section built up as wings.

TAIL UNIT.—Monoplane, with twin fins and rudders. Stressed-skin tail-plane and fins. Rudder and elevators have welded steel-tube frames with fabric covering. Trimming-tab on port rudder and others on each half of elevator.

LANDING GEAR.—Retractable type. Wheels carried in forks and are electrically retracted backwards into engine nacelles. Air-oil shock-absorbers. Low-pressure wheels and hydraulic brakes.

POWER PLANT.—Two 450 h.p. Pratt & Whitney R-8985-AN-1 or 3 radial air-cooled engines. Hamilton-Standard constant-speed airscrews.

ACCOMMODATION.—Pilot's compartment in nose, seating two side-by-side, with dual controls. Passenger cabin seats six passengers. Baggage compartments in extreme nose and behind cabin. Sound-proofing, controlled ventilation and heating.

DIMENSIONS.—Span 47 ft. 8 in. (14.5 m.), Length 34 ft. 3 in. (10.4 m.), Height 9 ft. 9 in. (2.8 m.), Wing area 349 sq. ft. (32.4 sq. m.).

WEIGHTS.—Weight empty 5,420 lbs. (2,460 kg.), Weight loaded 7,500 lbs. (3,405 kg.).

PERFORMANCE.—Maximum speed 225 m.p.h. (360 km.h.), Landing speed 61 m.p.h. (98 km.h.), Initial rate of climb 1,850 ft./min. (564 m./min.), Service ceiling 26,000 ft. (7,930 m.), Single-engine ceiling (at 50 ft./min. climb) 12,300 ft. (3,752 m.), Range 1,200 miles at 5,000 ft. (1,525 m.) at 160 m.p.h. (256 km.h.).

(1945—46)

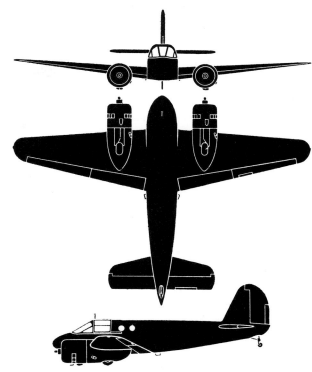

The Beechcraft AT-10 Wichita Advanced Trainer.

THE BEECHCRAFT NAVIGATOR.
U.S. Army Air Forces designation: AT-7.
U.S. Navy designation: SNB-2.

The AT-7 was the first type of aircraft supplied to the Army Air Forces purely for navigational training. It carries a crew of five and is equipped with individual chart tables, aperiodic compasses and stabilised drift signals for each of three navigational students. It is also provided with a rotatable celestial dome for sextant readings.

DIMENSIONS.—Span 47 ft. 8 in. (14.5 m.), Length 34 ft. 3 in. (10.4 m.), Height 9 ft. 9 in. (2.8 m.), Wing area 349 sq. ft. (32.4 sq. m.).

WEIGHTS.—Weight empty 5,800 lbs. (2,633 kg.), Weight loaded 7,850 lbs. (3,564 kg.).

PERFORMANCE.—Maximum speed 224 m.p.h. (358.4 km.h.) at 5,000 ft. (1,525 m.), Landing speed 67 m.p.h. (107 km.h.), Climb to 10,000 ft. (3,050 m.) 6.8 min., Service ceiling 24,000 ft. (7,320 m.), Range 730 miles (1,170 km.) at 5,000 ft. (1,525 m.) at 190 m.p.h. (304 km.h.). (1945—46)

The Beechcraft SNB-2 Navigator Navigational Training Monoplane (two Pratt & Whitney R-985 engines).

A Beechcraft AT-10 Wichita fitted with an experimental Vee tail-unit.

THE BEECHCRAFT WICHITA.
U.S. Army Air Forces designation: AT-10.

The AT-10 is a twin-engined advanced training monoplane intended for the first step in training pilots to operate twin-engined aircraft. Accommodation is provided for two pilots seated side-by-side with dual controls and full instrument equipment is provided, including automatic pilot. The AT-10 is fitted with two 280 h.p. Lycoming R-680-9 radial air-cooled engines driving two-bladed constant-speed airscrews.

The AT-10 was the first all-wood aeroplane designed by the Company and was the first all-wood type to be accepted as an advanced trainer by the U.S. Army.

Although when the AT-10 was designed there was no shortage of light metals, the Beech Company foresaw the difficulties that such a shortage might present and from the outset planned in wood with a view to making as much use of sub-contracting as possible.

One of the most interesting innovations was the use of wooden petrol tanks lined with special synthetic rubber which is unaffected by the fuel. No double-curvature sections were used and no hot-moulding processes were necessary in the forming of the various wooden parts. For this reason it was possible for furniture manufacturers and similar wood-working organizations to undertake the building of major sub-assemblies and 85 per cent. of these parts were built by sub-contractors.

The principal production and assembly of the AT-10 was undertaken by the Beech Aircraft Corpn. and the Globe Aircraft Corpn., but all contracts ceased in 1944.

One AT-10 has been experimentally fitted with a Vee, or "Butterfly", tail-unit. This aircraft is illustrated on this page.

DIMENSIONS.—Span 44 ft. (13.4 m.), Length 34 ft. 4 in. (10.4 m.), Wing area 298 sq. ft. (27.68 sq. m.).
WEIGHTS.—Weight empty 4,750 lbs. (2,156 kg.), Weight loaded 6,130 lbs. (2,783 kg.).
PERFORMANCE.—Maximum speed 198 m.p.h. (317 km.h.), Landing speed 80 m.p.h. (128 km.h.), Climb to 10,000 ft. (3,050 m.) 12.7 min., Service ceiling 16,900 ft. (5,155 m.), Range 770 miles (1,232 km.) at 177 m.p.h. (283 km.h.). (1945–46)

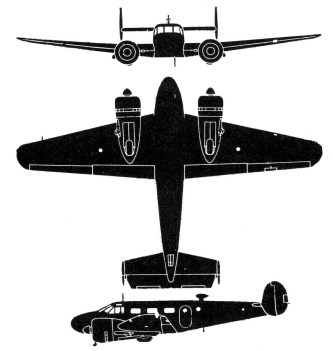

The Beechcraft C-45 Expeditor Light Transport.

THE BEECHCRAFT KANSAN.
U.S. Army Air Forces designation: AT-11.
U.S. Navy designation: SNB-1.

The AT-11 is intended for the specialised training of bombardiers and air-gunners. It is equipped with flexible guns and bomb-racks for the instruction of a crew of three or four, depending upon the instructional mission.

In general design it is similar to the C-45 but has a modified fuselage with transparent nose. Wings, tail-unit and landing gear are the same as for the C-45. The AT-11 is fitted with two 450 h.p. Pratt & Whitney R-985-AN-1 engines.

DIMENSIONS.—Same as AT-7.
WEIGHTS.—Weight empty 6,160 lbs. (2,796 kg.), Weight loaded 8,730 lbs. (3,963 kg.).
PERFORMANCE.—Maximum speed 215 m.p.h. (344 km.h.) at 5,000 ft. (1,525 m.), Landing speed 86 m.p.h. (137.6 km.h.), Climb to 10,000 ft. (3,050 m.) 10 min., Service ceiling 20,000 ft. (6,100 m.), Range 870 miles (1,390 km.) at 5,000 ft. (1,525 m.) at 142 m.p.h. (227 km.h.). (1945–46)

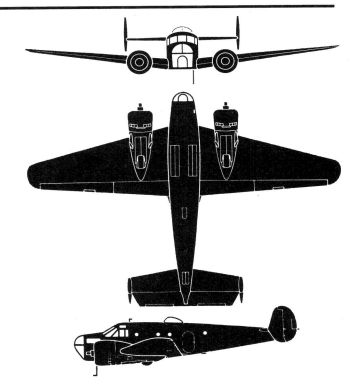

The Beechcraft AT-11 Kansan Advanced Trainer.

THE BEECHCRAFT QUEEN AIR 65
U.S. Army designation: U-8F Seminole

First flown in prototype form on August 28, 1958, the Queen Air 65 is a business aeroplane incorporating the features of a modern airliner. It is instrumented for all-weather operation and is designed to accommodate the latest electronic equipment, including weather-avoidance radar. Junior JATO standby rockets may be fitted as optional equipment.

In addition to commercial deliveries, Beech are producing 68 Queen Airs for the U.S. Army under the designation U-8F.

TYPE.—Seven/nine-seat communications/transport aircraft.
WINGS.—Cantilever low-wing monoplane. Wing section NACA 23,000 series. Aspect ratio 7.51. Chord 7 ft. 0½ in. (2.15 m.) at root, 3 ft. 6 in. (1.07 m.) at tip. Dihedral 7°. Incidence 4.8°. Two-spar all-metal structure of aluminium-alloy. All-metal ailerons of magnesium, each with a trim-tab. Single-slotted aluminium-alloy flaps. Total area of ailerons 13.9 sq. ft. (1.29 m.²). Total area of flaps 29.3 sq. ft. (2.72 m.²). Gross wing area 277.06 sq. ft. (25.73 m.²)
FUSELAGE.—Aluminium-alloy semi-mono-coque structure.
TAIL UNIT.—Cantilever monoplane type. All-metal structure of aluminium alloy. Trim-tabs in rudder and elevators. Areas: fin 14.25 sq. ft. (1.32 m.²), rudder 12.77 sq. ft. (1.19 m.²), tailplane 47.25 sq. ft. (4.39 m.²), elevators 17.87 sq. ft. (1.66 m.²). Tailplane span 17 ft. 1½ in. (5.22 m.).
LANDING GEAR.—Retractable tricycle type. Electric retraction. Air-oil shock-absorbers. Goodyear main wheels, size 8.50 × 10. Goodyear nose-wheel, size 6.50 × 10. Tyre pressures : main wheels 47 lb./sq. in. (3.30 kg./cm².), nose-wheel 35 lb./sq. in. (2.46 kg./cm².). Goodyear single disc hydraulic brakes. Wheel track 12 ft. 9 in. (3.89 m.). Wheelbase 12 ft. 3½ in. (3.75 m.)

POWER PLANT.—Two 340 h.p. Lycoming IGSO-480-A1B6 six-cylinder horizontally-opposed air-cooled geared and supercharged engines, with fuel injection. Hartzell three-blade fully-feathering constant-speed airscrews, diameter 7 ft. 9 in. (2.36 m.). Fuel in two 44 U.S. gallon (166 litre) main tanks and two 71 U.S. gallon (269 litre) auxiliary tanks in wings. Total fuel capacity 230 U.S. gallons (870 litres). Oil capacity 8 U.S. gallons (30 litres).

ACCOMMODATION.—Crew of one or two on flight deck. Six or seven passengers in cabin, which is 9 ft. 4 in. long, 4 ft. 6 in. wide and 4 ft. 9 in. high (2.84 m. × 1.37 m. × 1.45 m.). Cabin volume 199.5 cub. ft. (5.65 m.³). Volume of baggage compartment 42 cub. ft. (1.19 m.³), or 29 cub. ft. (0.82 m.³) with aft toilet. All equipment required by FAA for instrument flying is standard. Optional equipment includes

ARC, Bendix or Collins radar and radio packages, Bendix or RCA weather-avoidance radar, oxygen equipment, standby rocket motors, auto-pilot, and additional sound-proofing.

DIMENSIONS.—
Span	45 ft 10½ in. (13·98 m)
Length	33 ft 4 in. (10·16 m)
Height	14 ft 2 in. (4.32 m)

WEIGHTS.—
Weight empty	4,640 lb (2,105 kg)
Max. T.O. weight	7,700 lb (3,493 kg)
Max. landing weight	7,350 lb (3,334 kg)
Wing loading	27·8 lb/sq ft (135·7 kg/m²)
Power loading	12·03 lb/hp (5·45 kg/hp)

PERFORMANCE.—
Max. speed at 12,000 ft (3,600 m) 239 mph (385 kmh)

Max. cruising speed (70% power) at 15,200 ft (4,630 m) 214 mph (344 kmh)
Econ. cruising speed (45% power) at 15,000 ft (4,575 m) 171 mph (275 kmh)
Stalling speed (wheels and flaps down) 80 mph (129 kmh)
Rate of climb at S/L 1,300 ft (396 m) min.
Service ceiling at 6,500 lb (2,950 kg) A.U.W. 31,300 ft (9,540 m)
Service ceiling, one engine out at 6,500 lb (2,950 kg) A.U.W. 15,500 ft (4,725 m)
T.O. run 1,180 ft (360 m)
T.O. distance to 50 ft (15·25 m) 1,560 ft (475 m)
Landing distance from 50 ft (15·25 m) 1,685 ft (513 m)
Landing run 1,280 ft (390 m)
Range with max. fuel at econ. cruising speed 45 min. reserves 1,200 miles (1,930 km)

BEECHCRAFT MODEL 65-A90-1
US Army designation: U-21A

This twin-turboprop unpressurised utility aircraft is a development of the NU-8F, a turboprop conversion of a Queen Air 80 which Beech produced for the US Army in 1963 (see 1964-65 *Jane's*). The NU-8F was a six-passenger transport powered by two 500 shp Pratt & Whitney (UAC) PT6A-6 engines. By comparison, the U-21A has 550 shp PT6A-20 engines, as fitted in the King Air, and is capable of accommodating up to 10 combat troops or six command personnel in varied interior arrangements, plus a crew of two. It can be adapted quickly for air evacuation ambulance or cargo carrying duties, and is also used for special missions on behalf of the Army Security Agency.

Design of the U-21 began in October 1966, and in the following month construction of the prototype started. Only four months later, in March 1967, the prototype made its first flight, and FAA certification was granted on 27 April 1967.

An initial contract for the U-21A was placed by the US Army in October 1966, covering the manufacture of 48 aircraft and the training of 20 instructor pilots and 20 instructor mechanics by Beech. Subsequent contracts raised the number of U-21A's ordered to 129. The first of these was delivered on May 16, 1967, and deliveries continued until the Spring of 1969.

TYPE: Military utility transport.

WINGS: Cantilever low-wing monoplane. Wing section NACA 23014.10 (modified) at root, NACA 23016.22 (modified) at junction of centre-section and outer panel, NACA 23012.00 (modified) at tip. Aspect ratio 7.51. Dihedral 7°. Incidence 4°48′ at root, 0° at tip. Two-spar structure of aluminium alloy. All-metal ailerons of magnesium, each with anti-servo trim-tab; port tab is also manually adjustable. Single-slotted aluminium alloy flaps. Pneumatic de-icing boots are installed on the wing leading-edges.

FUSELAGE: All-metal semi-monocoque structure, mainly of 2024 aluminium alloy.

TAIL UNIT: Cantilever all-metal structure, mainly of 2024 aluminium alloy, but with magnesium alloy skin on control surfaces. Sweptback vertical surfaces. Controllable trim-tabs in rudder and elevators. Pneumatic de-icing boots on fin and tailplane leading-edges.

LANDING GEAR: Electrically-retractable tricycle type. Main units retract forward, nose-wheel aft. Beechcraft air-oil shock-absorbers. Goodyear main wheels size 7·50 × 10 and tyres size 8·50 × 10, pressure 55 lb/sq in (3·87 kg/cm²). Goodyear steerable nose-wheel and tyre size 6·50 × 10, pressure 50-55 lb/sq in (3·52-3·87 kg/cm²). Goodyear multiple-disc hydraulic brakes.

POWER PLANT: Two 550 shp Pratt & Whitney (UACL) PT6A-20 turboprop engines, driving Hartzell three-blade fully-feathering and reversible constant-speed propellers. Main fuel cell of 58 US gallons (219·5 litres) in each aft nacelle section, plus four interconnected auxiliary cells containing 131 US gallons (496 litres), in each wing. Total capacity 378 US gallons (1,427 litres). The nacelle and inboard wing tanks are self-sealing, the remaining three cells in each wing are conventional bladders. Refuelling points above each nacelle and at the outboard point of each wing. Oil capacity 4·6 US gallons (17 litres) of which 3 US gallons (11 litres) are usable.

ACCOMMODATION: Crew of two, seated side-by-side and separated from the main cabin by a removable half-curtain. The cabin accommodates ten combat-equipped troops on centre-facing bench seats. An alternative ambulance arrangement will accommodate three litter patients, plus three ambulatory patients or medical attendants. A staff transport version accommodates six passengers in forward-facing chairs. With all seats removed, the cabin can hold up to 3,000 lb (1,360 kg) of cargo. Cargo tie-down fittings are installed in the floor. A double door on the port side of the fuselage, aft of the wing, facilitates loading of bulky

items. Both doors are removable. Cabin heated by 100,000 BTU combustion heater. A 22 cu ft (0·62 m³) compartment, forward of the flight deck, houses electronic equipment.

SYSTEMS: Hydraulic system for brakes only. Pneumatic system uses engine bleed-air at 16 lb/sq in (1·12 kg/cm²) to operate air-driven instruments and pneumatic de-icer boots. Bleed-air pressure and vacuum are cycled to the single de-icer inflation system through a valve. A selector switch allows automatic single-cycle operation or manual operation. Electrical system utilises two Beech 250A starter-generators. A BB-433A battery is used with an inverter installed in each wing.

ELECTRONICS: Standard avionics comprise complete all-weather nav/com system, utilising Collins, Bendix, RCA, Sperry and Beechcraft equipment, including weather radar and transponder.

EQUIPMENT: Dual controls and wing icing lights are standard.

DIMENSIONS, EXTERNAL:
Wing span	45 ft 10½ in (13·98 m)
Length overall	35 ft 6 in (10·82 m)
Height overall	14 ft 2½ in (4·33 m)
Tailplane span	17 ft 2⅔ in (5·25 m)
Wheel track	12 ft 9 in (3·89 m)
Wheelbase	12 ft 3½ in (3·75 m)

Passenger and/or cargo doors:
Height	4 ft 3¾ in (1·31 m)
Width	4 ft 6 in (1·37 m)
Height to sill	3 ft 10 in (1·17 m)

DIMENSIONS, INTERNAL:
Cabin:
Length	17 ft 10 in (5·44 m)
Max width	4 ft 7 in (1·40 m)
Max height	4 ft 9 in (1·45 m)
Floor area	70 sq ft (6·50 m²)
Volume	371·5 cu ft (10·52 m³)

AREAS:
Wings, gross	279·7 sq ft (25·98 m²)
Ailerons (total)	13·90 sq ft (1·29 m²)
Trailing-edge flaps (total)	29·30 sq ft (2·72 m²)
Fin	23·67 sq ft (2·20 m²)
Rudder, including tab	14·00 sq ft (1·30 m²)
Tailplane	46·21 sq ft (4·30 m²)
Elevators, including tab	17·87 sq ft (1·66 m²)

WEIGHTS AND LOADINGS:
Weight empty, equipped	5,434 lb (2,464 kg)
Max payload	3,936 lb (1,785 kg)
Max T-O weight	9,650 lb (4,377 kg)
Max landing weight	9,168 lb (4,158 kg)
Max wing loading	34·48 lb/sq ft (168·35 kg/m²)
Max power loading	8·77 lb/shp (3·97 kg/shp)

PERFORMANCE (at max T-O weight):
Max level speed at 10,000 ft (3,050 m) 265 mph (426 kmh) TAS
Max permissible diving speed 299 mph (481 kmh) CAS
Max cruising speed at 10,000 ft (3,050 m) 245 mph (395 kmh) TAS
Econ cruising speed at 10,000 ft (3,050 m) 205 mph (328 kmh) TAS
Stalling speed (flaps and wheels down) 92 mph (148·5 kmh) CAS
Stalling speed (flaps and wheels up) 110 mph (178 kmh) CAS
Rate of climb at S/L 2,160 ft (658 m) min
Service ceiling 26,150 ft (7,970 m)
Service ceiling, one engine out 12,000 ft (3,660 m)
T-O run 1,618 ft (493 m)
T-O to 50 ft (15 m) 1,923 ft (586 m)
Landing from 50 ft (15 m) 2,453 ft (748 m)
Landing run 1,280 ft (390 m)
Range with max fuel (allowances for climb to and cruise at 25,000 ft = 7,620 m, 30 min reserve at altitude, 2,457 lb = 1,114 kg fuel before engine start, one crew member at 200 lb = 90 kg): 1,676 miles (2,697 km)
Range with max payload (allowances for climb to and cruise at 25,000 ft = 7,620 m, 30 min reserve at altitude, 2,120 lb = 961 kg fuel before engine start, one crew member at 200 lb = 90 kg plus 2,000 lb = 907 kg cargo): 1,216 miles (1,956 km)

(1969–70)

BEECHCRAFT KING AIR A100
US Army designation: U-21F

Beech Aircraft announced on 26 May 1969 the addition of a new version of the King Air to its fleet of corporate transport aircraft. Designated King Air 100, this is a pressurised transport with increased internal capacity and more powerful engines, enabling it to carry a useful load of more than two short tons. By comparison with the King Air 90 series, it has a fuselage 1.27 m (4 ft 2 in) longer, reduced wing span, larger rudder and elevator and twin-wheel main landing gear. It is available in a variety of interior configurations, seating six to eight in executive versions, or up to 13 in high-density arrangement, plus crew of two.

The King Air 100 has been approved for Category 2 landing minima by the FAA. Initial deliveries were made in August 1969, following FAA certification. A total of 327 commercial and military King Air 100s had been delivered by 1 January 1980.

First deliveries of the advanced Model A100, comprising five U-21Fs for the Department of the Army, began in October 1971. Supplied under a $2.5 million contract, they represented the first pressurised aircraft in the Army's inventory. Two A100s were supplied to the Spanish Air Force.

Type: Twin-turboprop light passenger, freight or executive transport.

Wings: Cantilever low-wing monoplane. Wing section NACA 23018 at root, NACA 23016.5 at centre-section joint with outer panel, NACA 23012 at tip. Dihedral 7°. Incidence 4° 48′ at root, 0° at tip. Two-spar all-metal light alloy structure. All-metal ailerons of magnesium. Trim tab in port aileron. Single-slotted light alloy trailing-edge flaps. Pneumatic de-icing boots standard.

Fuselage: All-metal light alloy semi-monocoque structure.

Tail Unit: Cantilever all-metal structure with swept vertical surfaces and a ventral stabilising fin. Trim tab in rudder. Electrically-operated adjustment of tailplane incidence. Pneumatic de-icing boots standard.

Power Plant: Two 507 kW (680 ehp) Pratt & Whitney Aircraft of Canada PT6A-28 turboprop engines, each driving a Hartzell four-blade fully-feathering and reversible-pitch constant-speed propeller. Rubber fuel cells in wings, with total capacity of 1,779 litres (470 US gallons). Automatic fuel heating systems; inertial engine inlet de-icing system; engine inlet lips de-iced by electro-thermally heated boots; auto ignition system; environmental fuel drain collector system; magnetic chip detector. Goodrich electrical propeller anti-icing system.

Systems: Cabin pressurisation by engine bleed air with a differential of 0.32 bars (4.6 lb/sq in). Cabin heated by 27,000 BTU electrical heating system. Oxygen system for flight deck and 0.62 m³ (22 cu ft) oxygen system for cabin standard. Cabin oxygen system of 1.39 m³ (49 cu ft), or 1.81 m³ (64 cu ft) optional. Dual vacuum system for instruments. Hydraulic system for brakes only. Pneumatic system for wing and tail unit de-icing only. Two 250A starter/generators. Aircooled nickel-cadmium 28V 45Ah battery with failure detector. Engine fire detection system.

Avionics and Equipment: Standard avionics comprise dual King KTR 905 VHF transceivers, with Gables controls and B3 antennae; King KNR 630 Omni No. 1, with Collins 331A-3G indicator, Gables control and B17 antenna; King KNR 630 Omni No. 2, with Collins 331H-3G indicator and Gables control; dual Omni range filters; dual Collins 356F-3 audio amplifiers, each with 356C-4 isolation amplifiers and audio switches; King KDF 805 ADF less indicator, with KFS 580B control, voice range filter, and Beech flush sense antenna; King KMR 675 marker beacon receiver, with dual marker lights and B16 antenna; dual glideslope receivers integral with No. 1 and No. 2 Omni, with B35 antenna; Bendix RDR-130 weather radar, with phased array antenna and digital scope; Sperry C-14-43 compass system with servo amplifier (pilot); King KNI 581 RMI with VOR-1/ADF on single needle, VOR-2/ADF on double needle; King KXP 755 transponder, with Gables control and B18 antenna; King KDM 706 DME with KDI 572 indicator, Nav-1/Nav-2 switching, DME hold and B18 antenna; dual Flite-Tronics PC-250 250VA inverters with failure light; avionics transient protection; sectional instrument panel; Standard Electric gyro horizon (pilot); CF gyro horizon and directional gyro (co-pilot); Beech edge-lighted radio panel, radio accessories, microphone button in pilot and co-pilot control wheels, static wicks and white lighting; dual microphones, headsets and cockpit speakers; and avionics master switch. A wide range of optional avionics equipment is available, by Bendix, Collins, King, RCA, Sperry and SunAir. Heated main landing gear brake de-icing and tail floodlight offered as optional equipment. Other standard and optional equipment generally as listed for King Air C90.

Dimensions, external:

Wing span	14.00 m (45 ft 11 in)
Wing chord at root	2.15 m (7 ft 0½ in)
Wing chord at tip	1.07 m (3 ft 6 in)
Wing aspect ratio	7.51
Length overall	12.17 m (39 ft 11 in)
Height overall	4.70 m (15 ft 5 in)
Tailplane span	6.83 m (22 ft 5 in)
Wheel track	3.96 m (13 ft 0 in)
Wheelbase	4.55 m (14 ft 11 in)
Propeller diameter	2.29 m (7 ft 6 in)
Propeller ground clearance	0.34 m (1 ft 1½ in)

Dimensions, internal:

Cabin: Length (excl flight deck)	5.08 m (16 ft 8 in)
Max width	1.37 m (4 ft 6 in)
Max height	1.45 m (4 ft 9 in)
Volume, avionics compartment in nose	0.45 m³ (16 cu ft)
Volume, aft baggage compartment	1.51 m³ (53.5 cu ft)

Weights and Loadings:

Weight empty	3,083 kg (6,797 lb)
Max T-O weight	5,216 kg (11,500 lb)
Max ramp weight	5,247 kg (11,568 lb)
Max zero-fuel weight	4,354 kg (9,600 lb)
Max landing weight	5,084 kg (11,210 lb)
Max wing loading	201 kg/m² (41.2 lb/sq ft)
Max power loading	5.14 kg/kW (8.46 lb/ehp)

Performance (at max T-O weight, unless otherwise quoted):

Max cruising speed at 4,762 kg (10,500 lb) AUW:
- at 6,400 m (21,000 ft): 235 knots (436 km/h; 270 mph)
- at 4,875 m (16,000 ft): 243 knots (450 km/h; 280 mph)
- at 3,050 m (10,000 ft): 248 knots (459 km/h; 285 mph)

Stalling speed, power off, wheels and flaps up: 89 knots (164 km/h; 102 mph)

Stalling speed, power off, wheels and flaps down: 75 knots (139 km/h; 86 mph)

Max rate of climb at S/L: 598 m (1,963 ft)/min

Rate of climb at S/L, one engine out: 138 m (452 ft)/min

Service ceiling: 7,575 m (24,850 ft)

Service ceiling, one engine out: 2,835 m (9,300 ft)

Min ground turning radius: 12.2 m (40 ft 0 in)

Runway LCN: 4.5

T-O run: flaps up: 628 m (2,060 ft)
30% flap: 565 m (1,855 ft)

T-O to 15 m (50 ft): flaps up: 989 m (3,245 ft)
30% flap: 817 m (2,681 ft)

Landing from 15 m (50 ft) at max landing weight, without propeller reversal: 897 m (2,944 ft)

Landing run at max landing weight, without propeller reversal: 545 m (1,787 ft)

*Accelerate/stop distance, flaps up: 1,303 m (4,275 ft)

*Accelerate/stop distance, 30% flap: 1,182 m (3,877 ft)

Range at high cruise power, with 1,779 litres (470 US gallons) fuel, incl allowances for starting, taxi, take-off, climb, descent and 45 min reserves:
- at 6,400 m (21,000 ft): 1,212 nm (2,247 km; 1,395 miles)
- at 4,875 m (16,000 ft): 1,064 nm (1,971 km; 1,225 miles)
- at 3,050 m (10,000 ft): 900 nm (1,667 km; 1,036 miles)

Range at long range cruise power, fuel and allowances as above:
- at 6,400 m (21,000 ft): 1,340 nm (2,483 km; 1,542 miles)
- at 4,875 m (16,000 ft): 1,272 nm (2,358 km; 1,464 miles)
- at 3,050 m (10,000 ft): 1,152 nm (2,136 km; 1,326 miles)

*Includes allowance for failure recognition (1980–81)

BEECHCRAFT SUPER KING AIR 200
US military designations: C-12 and RU-21J

Design of the Super King Air 200 began in October 1970, construction of the first prototype and first pre-production aircraft starting simultaneously a year later. The first prototype, serial BB-1, flew for the first time on 27 October 1972, followed by the second aircraft, BB-2, on 15 December 1972. While the flight tests and testing of a static fuselage were under way, construction of the first production aircraft began in June 1973. FAA certification under FAR Part 23 was awarded on 14 December 1973, the aircraft satisfying also the icing requirements of FAR Part 25.

By comparison with the King Air 100, the Super King Air 200 has increased wing span, basically the same fuselage, a T tail, more powerful engines, additional fuel capacity, increased cabin pressurisation and a higher gross weight. The cargo door fitted to some military versions became available as an option on civil Super King Airs in 1979; first deliveries were for air ambulance use in Libya and commuter operations in Australia.

In August 1974, Beech received a military contract to build and support 34 modified versions of the Super King Air, designated **C-12A.** Subsequently, many more C-12s have been ordered, in four versions, as follows:

C-12A. Initial version for US Army (81) and US Air Force (30), with two 559 kW (750 shp) Pratt & Whitney Aircraft of Canada PT6A-38 turboprop engines, each driving a Hartzell three-blade constant-speed fully-feathering reversible-pitch propeller. Total of 111 ordered by 1 January 1980.

C-12A version of the Beechcraft Super King Air 200 for the USAF

UC-12B. US Navy/Marine Corps version, with 634 kW (850 shp) PT6A-41 turboprop engines, cargo door and high-flotation landing gear. Total of 66 ordered by 4 February 1980, which will extend deliveries into 1982.

C-12C. As C-12A, for US Army (14), but with PT6A-41 engines.

C-12D. As C-12C, for US Army, but with cargo door. Total of 21 ordered by 17 July 1980.

Contract value of all 212 C-12s (116 for the Army, 30 for the Air Force, and 66 for the Navy) totals $193 million.

Worldwide deployment of the C-12s began in July 1975. They are described as 'standard off-the-shelf Super King Air types, modified slightly to meet military flight requirements and to orient the control systems for two-pilot operation which is standard military practice'. Accommodation is provided for eight passengers, plus two pilots, with easy conversion to cargo missions. The large baggage area has provisions for storing survival gear.

In addition, during 1974 the US Army added three Super King Airs to its fleet of special mission aircraft, with the designation **RU-21J**. Under an R and D contract, Beech had modified these antenna-laden aircraft for the US Army's Cefly Lancer programme. They are approved for take-off at a special AUW of 6,804 kg (15,000 lb).

In February 1977 Beech delivered to the French Institut Géographique National two specially-modified Super King Airs. These have twin Wild RC-10 Superaviogon camera installations and Doppler navigation systems, and were the first Super King Airs to be equipped with optional wingtip fuel tanks, which increase the total usable fuel capacity from 2,059 litres (544 US gallons) to 2,457 litres (649 US gallons) to provide a max endurance of 10·3 h. Designated **Model 200Ts**, they are fitted with high-flotation main landing gear, and are being operated under a special French airworthiness certificate which allows max T-O and landing weights of 6,350 kg (14,000 lb) and 6,123 kg (13,500 lb) respectively. The aircraft can be operated with or without the wingtip tanks, for high-altitude photographic and weather observation missions.

Beech announced on 25 April 1977 the company's intention to introduce a specially-equipped maritime patrol version of the Super King Air, the **Maritime Patrol 200T**, which is described separately.

During 1978 Beech announced supply to the Egyptian government of a Super King Air which is being used to continue water, uranium and other natural resources exploration in the Sinai and Egyptian deserts which was originated by US ERTS-1 and Landsat satellites. This aircraft is equipped with remote sensing equipment, specialised avionics, and sophisticated cameras. In June 1978, the Japan Maritime Safety Agency announced selection of the Super King Air for maritime patrol in connection with Japan's 174 nm (322 km; 200 mile) fishing limit. A total of 13 aircraft is required at a cost of more than $26 million, and delivery of the first aircraft was made in September 1979. Also in June 1978, Beech delivered to the government of Taiwan a Super King Air equipped to check ground-based navigation systems. A second special-mission aircraft was scheduled for delivery to Taiwan's Ministry of the Interior in May 1979. In late 1978 Beech won an industry-wide competition for the lease of four Super King Airs to the border patrol fleet of the US Customs Service, and these were delivered in Spring 1979.

By 1 January 1980 Beech had delivered 600 Super King Airs to commercial and private operators and 117 military C-12s to the US Air Force, US Navy and US Army.

TYPE: Twin-turboprop passenger or executive light transport.

WINGS: Cantilever low-wing monoplane. Wing section NACA 23018·5 (modified) at root, NACA 23011·3 at tip. Dihedral 6°. Incidence 3°48′ at root, −1° 7′ at tip. No sweepback at quarter-chord. Two-spar light alloy structure. Conventional ailerons of light alloy construction, with trim tab in port aileron. Single-slotted trailing-edge flaps of light alloy construction. Pneumatic de-icing boots standard.

FUSELAGE: Light alloy semi-monocoque structure of safe-life design.

TAIL UNIT: Conventional cantilever T-tail structure of light alloy with swept vertical and horizontal surfaces. Fixed-incidence tailplane. Trim tab in each elevator. Anti-servo tab in rudder. Pneumatic de-icing boots standard, on leading-edge of tailplane only.

LANDING GEAR: Electrically-retractable tricycle type, with twin wheels on each main unit. Single wheel on steerable nose unit, with shimmy damper. Main units retract forward, nosewheel aft. Beech oleo-pneumatic shock-absorbers. Goodrich main wheels and tyres size 18 × 5·5, pressure 7·25 bars (105 lb/sq in). Goodrich nose-wheel size 6·00 × 10, with tyre size 22 × 6·75-10, pressure 3·93 bars (57 lb/sq in). Goodrich hydraulic multiple-disc brakes. Parking brake.

POWER PLANT: Two 634 kW (850 shp) Pratt & Whitney Aircraft of Canada PT6A-41 turboprop engines, each driving a three-blade constant-speed fully-feathering reversible-pitch metal propeller; PT6A-38 engines in C-12A, as noted in introductory copy. Bladder type fuel cells in each wing, with main system capacity of 1,461 litres (386 US gallons) and auxiliary system capacity of 598 litres (158 US gallons). Total fuel capacity 2,059 litres (544 US gallons). Two refuelling points in upper surface of each wing. Oil capacity 29·5 litres (7·8 US gallons). Anti-icing of engine air intakes by hot air from engine exhaust is standard. Electrothermal anti-icing for propellers. Wingtip tanks optional.

ACCOMMODATION: Pilot only, or crew of two side by side, on flight deck, with full dual controls and instruments as standard. Six cabin seats standard, each equipped with seat belts and inertia-reel shoulder harness; alternative

RU-21J version of the Beechcraft Super King Air procured for the US Army's Cefly Lancer programme

layouts for a maximum of 13 passengers in cabin and 14th beside pilot. Partition with sliding door between cabin and flight deck, and partition at rear of cabin. Door at rear of cabin on port side, with integral airstair. Large cargo door optional. Inward-opening emergency exit on starboard side over wing. Lavatory and stowage for up to 186 kg (410 lb) baggage in aft fuselage. Maintenance access door in rear fuselage; radio compartment access doors in nose. Standard equipment includes reading lights and fresh air outlets for all passengers, triple cabin windows with polarised glare control, fully-carpeted floor, 'No smoking—Fasten seat belt' sign, cabin coat rack, fluorescent cabin lighting, aisle and door courtesy lights. Electrically-heated windscreens, hot air windscreen defroster, dual storm windows, sun visors, map pockets and windscreen wipers. Cabin is air-conditioned and pressurised, and can be provided with optional radiant heat panels.

SYSTEMS: Cabin pressurisation by engine bleed air, with a maximum differential of 0·41 bars (6·0 lb/sq in). Cabin air-conditioner of 34,000 BTU capacity. Auxiliary cabin heating by radiant panels optional. Oxygen system for flight deck, and 0·62 m³ (22 cu ft) oxygen system for cabin, with automatic drop-down face masks; standard system of 1·39 m³ (49 cu ft), 1·81 m³ (64 cu ft), or 2·15 m³ (76 cu ft) optional. Dual vacuum system for instruments. Hydraulic system for brakes only. Pneumatic system for wing and tailplane de-icing. Electrical system has two 250A 28V starter/generators and 24V 45Ah aircooled nickel-cadmium battery with failure detector. AC power provided by dual 250VA inverters.

AVIONICS AND EQUIPMENT: Standard avionics include dual Collins VHF-20A VHF transceivers, with Gables controls and B3 antennae; Collins VIR-30AGM automatic Omni No. 1, with 331A-3G indicator, Gables control and B17 antenna; Collins VIR-30AG automatic Omni No. 2, with 331H-3G indicator and Gables control; dual Omni range filters; Collins dual 356-F3 audio amplifiers, each with 356C-4 isolation amplifiers and audio switches; Collins ADF-60A ADF less indicator, with Gables control, voice range filter and ANT-60 antenna; Collins marker beacon, integral with VIR-30 No. 1, with dual marker lights and B16 antenna; dual Collins glideslopes, integral with VIR-30 No. 1 and No. 2, with B35 glideslope antenna; Bendix RDR-130 weather radar, with phased array antenna and digital scope; Sperry C-14-43 compass system, with servo amplifier (pilot); Collins 332C-10 RMI, with Nav 1/ADF on single needle, Nav 2/ADF on double needle; Collins TDR-90 transponder, with Gables control and 237Z-1 antenna; Collins DME-40 with 339F-12 indicator, Nav 1/Nav 2 switching, DME hold and 237Z-1 antenna; dual Flite-Tronics PC-250 250VA inverters with failure light; sectional instrument panel; dual flight instrumentation; Standard Electric gyro horizon (pilot); CF gyro horizon and directional gyro (co-pilot); Beech edge-lighted radio panel, radio accessories, microphone key button in pilot's and co-pilot's control wheels, static wicks, white lighting; dual microphones, headsets and cockpit speakers; and avionics master switch. A wide range of optional avionics by Bendix, Collins, King, RCA, Sperry and SunAir is available to customer's requirements. Standard equipment is generally as listed for King Air C90, plus dual max allowable airspeed indicators, control wheel mounted chrono-

graphs, toilet, fluorescent cabin lighting instead of indirect lighting, aisle courtesy light, transistor controlled blue/white cockpit lighting, entrance door light, engine fire detection light, cabin boost system, and yaw damper system. Optional equipment includes a flight hour recorder, instantaneous vertical speed indicator, cockpit and cabin fire extinguishers, a range of cabin chairs, cabinets and table, flushing toilet, aft cabin air-conditioning installation, radiant heating system, entrance door step lights, wingtip recognition lights, strobe lights, fin illumination lights, engine fire extinguishing system, automatic propeller feathering, propeller synchrophaser, electric pitch trim, oversize and/or 10-ply main-wheel tyres.

DIMENSIONS, EXTERNAL:

Wing span	16·61 m (54 ft 6 in)
Wing chord at root	2·18 m (7 ft 1¾ in)
Wing chord at tip	0·90 m (2 ft 11⅝ in)
Wing aspect ratio	9·8
Length overall	13·34 m (43 ft 9 in)
Height overall	4·57 m (15 ft 0 in)
Tailplane span	5·61 m (18 ft 5 in)
Wheel track	5·23 m (17 ft 2 in)
Wheelbase	4·56 m (14 ft 11½ in)
Propeller diameter	2·50 m (8 ft 2½ in)
Propeller ground clearance	0·37 m (1 ft 2½ in)
Distance between propeller centres	
	5·23 m (17 ft 2 in)
Passenger door: Height	1·31 m (4 ft 3½ in)
Width	0·68 m (2 ft 2¾ in)
Height to sill	1·17 m (3 ft 10 in)
Cargo door (optional):	
Height	1·32 m (4 ft 4 in)
Width	1·32 m (4 ft 4 in)
Nose avionics service doors (port and stbd):	
Max height	0·57 m (1 ft 10½ in)
Width	0·63 m (2 ft 1 in)
Height to sill	1·37 m (4 ft 6 in)
Emergency exit door (stbd):	
Height	0·66 m (2 ft 2 in)
Width	0·50 m (1 ft 7¾ in)

DIMENSIONS, INTERNAL:

Cabin (from forward to aft pressure bulkhead:	
Length	6·71 m (22 ft 0 in)
Max width	1·37 m (4 ft 6 in)
Max height	1·45 m (4 ft 9 in)
Floor area	7·80 m² (84 sq ft)
Volume	11·10 m³ (392 cu ft)
Baggage hold, rear of cabin:	
Volume	1·51 m³ (53·5 cu ft)

AREAS:

Wings, gross	28·15 m² (303 sq ft)
Ailerons (total)	1·67 m² (18·0 sq ft)
Trailing-edge flaps (total)	4·17 m² (44·9 sq ft)
Fin	3·46 m² (37·2 sq ft)
Rudder, incl tab	1·40 m² (15·1 sq ft)
Tailplane	4·52 m² (48·7 sq ft)
Elevators, incl tabs	1·79 m² (19·3 sq ft)

WEIGHTS AND LOADINGS:

Weight empty	3,421 kg (7,543 lb)
Max T-O and landing weight	5,670 kg (12,500 lb)
Max ramp weight	5,710 kg (12,590 lb)
Max zero-fuel weight	4,717 kg (10,400 lb)
Max wing loading	201·6 kg/m² (41·3 lb/sq ft)
Max power loading	4·47 kg/kW (7·35 lb/shp)

WEIGHTS AND LOADINGS (C-12A): As Super King Air, except:
Basic empty weight   3,538 kg (7,800 lb)
Max ramp weight   5,708 kg (12,585 lb)
Max power loading   5·07 kg/kW (8·33 lb/shp)
PERFORMANCE (at max T-O weight, ISA, unless specified):
Never-exceed speed
    Mach 0·52 (260 knots; 482 km/h; 299 mph) CAS
Max level speed, average cruise weight at 4,570 m
    (15,000 ft)   289 knots (536 km/h; 333 mph)
Max cruising speed, average cruise weight at 7,620 m
    (25,000 ft)   278 knots (515 km/h; 320 mph)
Econ cruising speed, average cruise weight at 7,620 m
    (25,000 ft)   272 knots (503 km/h; 313 mph)
Stalling, speed, flaps up
    99 knots (183 km/h; 114 mph) IAS
Stalling speed, flaps down
    75·5 knots (138·5 km/h; 86 mph) IAS
Max rate of climb at S/L   747 m (2,450 ft)/min
Rate of climb at S/L, one engine out
    226 m (740 ft)/min

Service ceiling   10,670 m (35,000 ft)
Service ceiling, one engine out   5,835 m (19,150 ft)
T-O run   592 m (1,942 ft)
T-O run, 40% flap   566 m (1,856 ft)
T-O to 15 m (50 ft), flaps up   1,020 m (3,345 ft)
T-O to 15 m (50 ft), 40% flap   786 m (2,579 ft)
Landing from 15 m (50 ft), full flap, without propeller
    reversal   867 m (2,845 ft)
Landing from 15 m (50 ft) with propeller reversal
    632 m (2,074 ft)
Landing run, full flap, without propeller reversal
    536 m (1,760 ft)
Landing run with propeller reversal 341 m (1,120 ft)
Range with 2,059 litres (544 US gallons) usable fuel,
    with allowances for start, taxi, climb, descent and 45
    min reserves at max range power, ISA:
max cruising power at:
    5,485 m (18,000 ft)
        1,190 nm (2,204 km; 1,370 miles)
    7,620 m (25,000 ft)
        1,485 nm (2,750 km; 1,709 miles)

    9,450 m (31,000 ft)
        1,757 nm (3,254 km; 2,022 miles)
econ cruising power at:
    5,485 m (18,000 ft)
        1,487 nm (2,755 km; 1,712 miles)
    7,620 m (25,000 ft)
        1,737 nm (3,217 km; 1,999 miles)
    9,450 m (31,000 ft)
        1,887 nm (3,495 km; 2,172 miles)
PERFORMANCE (C-12A at max T-O weight, except as noted
    otherwise):
Max level speed at 4,265 m (14,000 ft) and AUW of
    4,536 kg (10,000 lb) 260 knots (482 km/h; 299 mph)
Max cruising speed at 9,145 m (30,000 ft) and AUW of
    4,536 kg (10,000 lb) 236 knots (437 km/h; 272 mph)
Service ceiling   9,450 m (31,000 ft)
Service ceiling, one engine out   5,365 m (17,600 ft)
T-O to 15 m (50 ft)   860 m (2,820 ft)
Landing from 15 m (50 ft)   766 m (2,514 ft)
Range at max cruising speed
    1,584 nm (2,935 km; 1,824 miles)
    (1980–81)

THE BEECHCRAFT MODEL 45 MENTOR

U.S.A.F. designation : T-34A
U.S. Navy designation : T-34B

The Beechcraft Mentor is basically a military trainer adaptation of the Bonanza. Standard equipment in the U.S. Air Force and U.S. Navy, it is also operated in Chile, El Salvador, Colombia, Mexico, Venezuela, Spain, Turkey and the Philippines, and is being manufactured under licence by Fuji Heavy Industries of Tokyo, Japan, and by the Argentine Government.

Two versions have been built, as follows :—

T-34A. For U.S.A.F. More than 350 built. Prototype flew on December 2, 1948.

T-34B. For U.S. Navy, with additional equipment. Production completed in October 1957, after 423 built.

TYPE.—Two-seat primary trainer.

WINGS.—Low-wing cantilever monoplane. Same type structure as for the Bonanza, but with incidence of 4°. Wing area 177.6 sq. ft. (16.49 m.²).

FUSELAGE.—Metal structure with flush-riveted metal skin.

TAIL UNIT.—Conventional cantilever monoplane type. All-metal structure of magnesium. Adjustable trim-tabs in elevators and rudder. Areas: fin 10.39 sq. ft. (.97 m.²), rudder 6.54 sq. ft. (.61 m.²), elevators 15 sq. ft. (1.39 m.²), tailplane 37.25 sq. ft. (3.46 m.²). Tailplane span 12 ft. 2¼ in. (3.71 m.)

LANDING GEAR.—Retractable tricycle type. Same as for Bonanza. Electric retraction with emergency hand control. Beech air-oil struts on all wheels. Split-type wheels with single disc hydraulic brakes. Wheel track 9 ft. 8¾ in. (2.94 m.). Wheelbase 7 ft. 5¼ in. (2.28 m.).

POWER PLANT.—One 225 h.p. Continental O-470-13 six-cylinder horizontally-opposed air-cooled engine. Beech Model 278-101 all-metal constant-speed airscrew 7 ft. (2.13 m.) in diameter. Two wing fuel tanks, Capacity 50 U.S. gallons (225 litres). Oil capacity 3 U.S. gallons (11.35 litres). Entire power-plant assembly including engine, airscrew, accessories and oil system, may be changed as a unit.

ACCOMMODATION.—Tandem cockpits under continuous transparent canopy with sections over each seat which may be independently opened or latched in intermediate positions. Conventional three-control system duplicated in each cockpit. Adjustable seats in both cockpits. Heating and ventilation. Windshield de-froster. VHF radio receiver and transmitter. Baggage compartment aft of rear cockpit.

ARMAMENT (optional).—One machine-gun or camera gun in each wing. Bomb racks or rocket rails under wings.

DIMENSIONS.—
Span 32 ft. 10 in. (10 m.)
Length 25 ft. 11 in. (7.9 m.)
Height 9 ft. 7 in. (2.92 m.)

WEIGHTS AND LOADINGS (T-34A).—
Weight empty 2,156 lb. (978 kg.)
Weight loaded 2,950 lb. (1,338 kg.)
Wing loading 16.6 lb./sq. ft. (81.1 kg./m.²)
Power loading 13.1 lb./h.p. (5.95 kg./h.p.)

WEIGHTS AND LOADINGS (T-34B).—
Weight empty 2,254 lb. (1,022 kg.)
Weight loaded 2,985 lb. (1,354 kg.)
Wing loading 16.8 lb./sq. ft. (82.1 kg./m.²)
Power loading 13.3 lb./h.p. (6.04 kg./h.p.)

PERFORMANCE (T-34A).—
Max. speed at S/L 189 m.p.h. (304 km.h.)
Max. cruising speed 173 m.p.h. (277 km.h.) at 10,000 ft. (3,050 m.)
Stalling speed (flaps down) 56 m.p.h. (90 km.h.)
Rate of climb at S/L 1,120 ft./min. (340 m./min.)
Service ceiling 18,200 ft. (5,550 m.)
Max. cruising range 737 miles (1,186 km.)
Take-off to 50 ft. (15.25 m.) no wind (10° flaps) 1,200 ft. (366 m.)
Landing run from 50 ft. (15.25 m.) no wind (full flaps) 960 ft. (293 m.)

PERFORMANCE (T-34B).—
Max. speed 188 m.p.h. (302 km.h.)
Cruising speed 170 m.p.h. (274 km.h.)
Stalling speed (flaps down) 58 m.p.h. (93 km.h.)
Rate of climb at S/L 1,100 ft./min. (335 m./min.)
Service ceiling 18,100 ft. (5,520 m.)
Range with max. payload 728 miles (1,171 km.)
    (1960–61)

BEECHCRAFT MODEL T-34C

US Navy designation: T-34C

In March 1953 the US Air Force selected the Beechcraft Model 45 as its new primary trainer and, under the designation T-34A Mentor, a total of 450 were eventually acquired. Power plant consisted of a 168 kW (225 hp) Continental O-470-13 flat-six engine. Just over a year later the US Navy reached a similar decision, and a total of 423 T-34B Mentors were built for that service.

In 1973 Beech received a US Navy R & D contract to modify two T-34Bs to see whether the type could be upgraded for a continuing training role. This involved the installation of a turboprop engine and the latest avionics equipment, the primary object being to let student pilots have experience of operating turbine-powered aircraft from the beginning of their flight training. The power plant selected was the PT6A-25, which has a torque limiter in this application to restrict engine output to 298 kW (400 shp), ensure long engine life, and provide constant per-

formance over a wide range of temperature and altitude.

Design of the modifications to update the aircraft began in March 1973, and conversion of two T-34Bs (140784 and 140861) started in May 1973. Designated YT-34C, the first of these aircraft (described in previous editions of *Jane's*) flew for the first time on 21 September 1973.

Beech has received US Navy contracts totalling approx $90 million for 184 new-production T-34Cs, and the provision of engineering services and support. The first of the aircraft were delivered to Naval Air Training Command at Whiting Field, Milton, Florida, in November 1977. Student training in the T-34C began in January 1978. An export civil version, known as the **Turbine Mentor 34C**, is in service at the Algerian National Pilot Training School, which received six in 1979.

Production T-34Cs incorporate improvements developed during the flight test programme; structural strength was increased to permit high limit speeds and a fatigue life of 16,000 h in a primary flight training role.

A **T-34C-1** armament systems trainer version is also available and, in addition to its basic role, is capable of carrying out forward air control (FAC) and tactical strike training missions. Contracts were received for the supply of 12 T-34C-1s to the Air Force of Morocco, 20 for the Air Force of Ecuador, 3 for the Ecuadorean Navy, 16 for the Air Force of Indonesia, 6 for the Peruvian Navy, and 15 for the Navy of Argentina. Delivery of all of these has been completed.

TYPE: Two-seat turbine-powered primary training aircraft.

WINGS: Cantilever low-wing monoplane. Wing section NACA 23016·5 (modified) at root, NACA 23012 at tip. Dihedral 7°. Incidence 4° at root, 1° at tip. No sweepback. Conventional box beam structure of light alloy. Ailerons of light alloy construction. Single-slotted trailing-edge flaps of light alloy. Manually operated trim tab in port aileron. Servo tabs in both ailerons.

FUSELAGE: Semi-monocoque light alloy structure.

TAIL UNIT: Cantilever structure of light alloy. Fixed-incidence tailplane. Manually-operated trim tabs in elevators and rudder. Twin ventral fins under rear fuselage.

LANDING GEAR: Electrically-retractable tricycle type. Main units retract inward, nosewheel aft. Beech oleo-pneumatic shock-absorbers. Single wheel on each unit. Main wheels size 7·00-8. Nosewheel and tyre size 5·00-5. Goodyear multiple-disc hydraulic brakes.

POWER PLANT: One 533 kW (715 shp) Pratt & Whitney Aircraft of Canada PT6A-25 turboprop engine, torque limited to 298 kW (400 shp), driving a Hartzell three-blade constant-speed fully-feathering metal propeller. Version of same engine derated to 410 kW (550 shp) is available optionally. Two bladder-type fuel cells in each wing, with a total usable capacity of 492 litres (130 US gallons). Oil capacity 15·1 litres (4 US gallons).

ACCOMMODATION: Instructor and pupil in tandem beneath rearward-sliding cockpit canopy. Cockpit ventilated, heated by engine bleed air and air-conditioned. Dual controls standard. All armament controls in forward cockpit of T-34C-1.

SYSTEMS: Hydraulic system for brakes only. Pneumatic system for emergency opening of cockpit canopy. Diluter demand gaseous oxygen system, pressure 103·5 bars (1,500 lb/sq in). Electrical power supplied by 250A starter/generator. Freon-type air-conditioner for cockpit cooling.

AVIONICS AND EQUIPMENT: Standard avionics can include UHF or VHF com, VOR or Tacan nav, DME, transponder, angle of attack indicator, ADF, marker beacon, compass and intercom system. Area-NAV, Loran, HF and specialised tactical systems available to customer's requirements. Blind-flying instrumentation standard. Electrically-heated pitot.

ARMAMENT (T-34C-1): CA-513 fixed-reticle reflector gunsight. Four underwing hardpoints are provided for the carriage of stores. The inboard stations are rated at 272 kg (600 lb) each, the outboard stations at 136 kg (300 lb) each, with a maximum load of 272 kg (600 lb) each side and 544 kg (1,200 lb) total. Weapons which can be carried on MA-4 racks include AF/B37K-1 bomb containers with practice bombs or flares, LAU-32 or LAU-59 rocket pods, MK 81 bombs, SUU-11 Minigun pods, BLU-10/B incendiary bombs, AGM-22A wire-guided anti-tank missiles and TA8X towed target equipment.

DIMENSIONS, EXTERNAL:

Wing span	10·16 m (33 ft 3⅞ in)
Wing chord at root	2·55 m (8 ft 4½ in)
Wing chord at tip	1·05 m (3 ft 5¼ in)
Wing aspect ratio	6·22
Length overall	8·75 m (28 ft 8½ in)
Height overall	2·92 m (9 ft 7 in)
Tailplane span	3·71 m (12 ft 2⅛ in)
Wheel track	2·95 m (9 ft 8 in)
Wheelbase	2·41 m (7 ft 11 in)
Propeller diameter	2·29 m (7 ft 6 in)
Propeller ground clearance	0·29 m (11¼ in)

DIMENSIONS, INTERNAL:

Cabin: Length	2·74 m (9 ft 0 in)
Max width	0·86 m (2 ft 10 in)
Max height	1·22 m (4 ft 0 in)

AREAS:

Wings, gross	16·69 m² (179·6 sq ft)
Ailerons (total)	1·06 m² (11·4 sq ft)
Trailing-edge flaps (total)	1·98 m² (21·3 sq ft)
Fin	1·20 m² (12·9 sq ft)
Rudder, incl tab	0·64 m² (6·9 sq ft)
Tailplane	3·46 m² (37·2 sq ft)
Elevators, incl tabs	1·26 m² (13·6 sq ft)

WEIGHTS AND LOADING:

Weight empty: T-34C·	1,342 kg (2,960 lb)

Beechcraft YT-34C Turbo Mentor primary trainer (PT6A-25 turboprop engine)

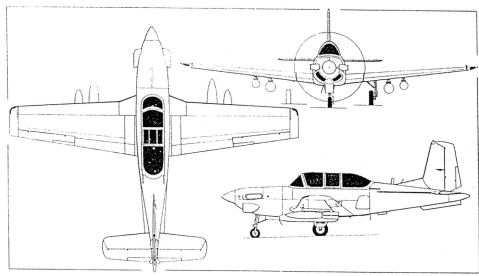

Beechcraft Model T-34C-1 turboprop-powered training/attack aircraft *(Pilot Press)*

T-34C-1	1,356 kg (2,990 lb)

Max T-O and landing weight:

T-34C	1,950 kg (4,300 lb)
T-34C-1, strike role	2,494 kg (5,500 lb)
Max wing loading: T-34C	108·3 kg/m² (22·2 lb/sq ft)

PERFORMANCE (T-34C, preliminary results at max T-O weight):

Never-exceed speed 280 knots (518 km/h; 322 mph)
Max cruising speed at 5,335 m (17,500 ft)
227 knots (420 km/h; 261 mph)
Stalling speed, flaps up
55 knots (102 km/h; 63·3 mph) CAS
Max rate of climb at 3,050 m (10,000 ft)
411 m (1,350 ft)/min
Service ceiling over 9,145 m (30,000 ft)
Range at 6,100 m (20,000 ft)
591 nm (1,094 km; 680 miles)

PERFORMANCE (T-34C-1 with 410 kW; 550 shp engine, estimated. A with two stores at AUW of 2,222 kg; 4,900 lb. B with four stores at AUW of 2,495 kg; 5,500 lb, except where indicated):

Max level speed at 5,500 m (18,000 ft):
A   209 knots (387 km/h; 241 mph)
B   206 knots (382 km/h; 237 mph)
Stalling speed, flaps down, idle power:
A   65 knots (120 km/h; 75 mph) CAS
B   69 knots (128 km/h; 80 mph) CAS
Max rate of climb at S/L: A   540 m (1,771 ft)/min
B   436 m (1,431 ft)/min
Typical combat radius:
FAC mission at AUW of 2,429 kg (5,355 lb), with four stores and optional max fuel, incl 2·6 h loiter over target and 20 min +5% reserves
100 nm (185 km; 115 miles)
Strike mission at AUW of 2,473 kg (5,452 lb), with four stores and optional max fuel, incl 20 min +5% reserves   300 nm (555 km; 345 miles)
(1980-81)

THE BEECHCRAFT TRAVELLER.
U.S. Army Air Forces designation: UC-43.
U.S. Navy designation : GB.
British name : Traveller.

The UC-43 has been supplied to the U.S. Army Air Forces as a light personnel transport.

The GB-1 and GB-2 perform similar functions in the U.S. Naval Air Service as the UC-43 does in the Army Air Forces.

TYPE.—Five-seat Light Personnel Transport.

WINGS.—Equal-span single-bay biplane with back stagger. Upper wing attached direct to the top of the fuselage with one "I"-type heat-treated steel interplane strut on either side of the fuselage. Duplicated flying-wires attached to front spar in upper wing and to fuselage at rear spar attachment of lower wing. Landing wires are attached to fuselage at front spar fitting of upper wing and to rear spar in lower wing. Wing structure consists of two wooden spars, wooden ribs and fabric covering. Statically and aerodynamically-balanced ailerons on upper wings and electrically-operated lift-flaps on lower wings.

FUSELAGE.—Oval structure of metal with two heat-treated steel trusses below lower longerons to carry all main loads. These trusses eliminate cross tubes in cabin and luggage compartments.

TAIL UNIT.—Cantilever monoplane type. Welded steel-tube framework for elevators and rudder, wood framework for tail-plane and fin, all fabric-covered.

LANDING GEAR.—Retractable type. Hydraulic shock-absorbers, semi-balloon wheels and brakes. Electrical retraction. Retractable tail-wheel.

POWER PLANT.—One 450 h.p. Pratt & Whitney R-985-AN-1 or 3 nine-cylinder radial air-cooled engine, driving a two-blade Hamilton Standard constant-speed airscrew. Engine-driven fuel pump with auxiliary hand-pump operated by remote control.

ACCOMMODATION.—Enclosed cabin to accommodate pilot and three passengers, 125 lbs. of baggage and full load of fuel, or pilot and four passengers with reduced fuel load. Adjustable front seats and wide seat across back of cabin. Full vision windows, ventilators and heaters. Large door on left side of cabin to give easy access to both front and back seats.

The Beechcraft GB-2 Traveller Light Transport Biplane (Pratt & Whitney R-985 engine). (*Photograph by Peter Bowers*)

DIMENSIONS.—Span 32 ft. (9.76 m.), Length 26 ft. 2 in. (7.98 m.), Height 10 ft. 3 in. (3.12 m.), Wing area 296 sq. ft. (27.5 sq. m.).

WEIGHTS.—Weight empty 3,085 lbs. (1,400 kg.), Weight loaded 4,250 lbs. (1,928 kg.).

PERFORMANCE.—Cruising speed 195 m.p.h. (312 km.h.) at 5,000 ft. (1,525 m.), Landing-speed 60 m.p.h. (96 km.h.), Initial rate of climb 1,500 ft./min. (455 m./min.), Service ceiling 20,000 ft. (6,100 m.), Range 500 miles (800 km.) at 5,000 ft. (1,525 m.) at 170 m.p.h. (272 km.h.).

The Army Air Forces also acquired a number of second-hand Beechcraft Model 17 biplanes and these were given designations in the UC-43 Series as follow :—

UC-43A	Model D-17R	Wright R-975.
UC-43B	Model D-17S	Pratt & Whitney R-985.
UC-43C	Model D-17D	Jacobs R-915.
UC-43D	Model E-17B	Jacobs L-5.
UC-43E	Model C-17R	Wright R-975.
UC-43F	Model D-17A	Wright R-760E-2.
UC-43G	Model C-17B	Jacobs L-5.
UC-43H	Model B-17R	Wright R-975.
UC-43J	Model C-17L	Jacobs L-4.

(1945–46)

THE BEECHCRAFT MODEL 50 TWIN-BONANZA.
U.S.A.F. designation: L-23A.

A number of Twin-Bonanzas have been acquired by the U.S. Army Field Forces, under the designation L-23A, for staff transport duties.

TYPE.— Twin-engined six-seat Cabin monoplane.

WINGS.— Low-wing cantilever monoplane. All-metal structure. NACA slotted flaps.

FUSELAGE.—Metal structure with flush-riveted metal skin.

TAIL UNIT.—Cantilever monoplane type. Slight dihedral to tailplane. All-metal structure.

LANDING GEAR.—Retractable tricycle type. Main shock-strut assemblies interchangeable on either side. Nose wheel is steerable. Main wheel track 12 ft. 9 in. (3.88 m.). Wheelbase 10 ft. 9 in. (3.28 m.).

The Beechcraft L-23A Twin-Bonanza (two 260 h.p. Lycoming engines).

POWER PLANT.—Two 260 h.p. Lycoming GO-435-C2 six-cylinder horizontally-opposed air-cooled engines each driving a Beech Model B200-116 constant-speed, or Model 214-101 fully-feathering airscrew. Fuel capacity 134 U.S. gallons, 88 gallons in inboard wing tanks and 46 gallons in auxiliary outboard wing tanks.

ACCOMMODATION.—Enclosed cabin seating a maximum of six; pilot, co-pilot and passenger on front seat 54 in. (1.37 m.) wide and three passengers on rear seat 52 in. (1.32 m.) wide. Two baggage compartments one forward and one aft. A stretcher patient can be loaded through rear baggage door without need to climb on wing. Capacity of front baggage compartment 14 cub. ft. (0.4 m.³), rear compartment 41 cub. ft. (1.16 m.³). Equipment includes cabin sound-proofing, heating and ventilation, and choice of radio installations.

DIMENSIONS.—
Span 45 ft. 3¾ in. (13.81 m.).
Length 31 ft. 6½ in. (9.61 m.).
Height 11 ft. 4 in. (3.45 m.).

WEIGHTS AND LOADINGS.—
Weight empty 3,800 lb. (1,700 kg.).
Weight loaded 5,500 lb. (2,500 kg.).
Wing loading 19.87 lb./sq. ft. (96.96 kg./m.²).
Power loading 11.46 lb./h.p. (5.21 kg./h.p.).

PERFORMANCE.—
Max. speed at 2,500 ft. (760 m.) 202.5 m.p.h. (324 km.h.).
Cruising speed (65% power) at 10,000 ft. (3,050 m.) 190 m.p.h. (304 km.h.).
Max. permissible speed 227 m.p.h. (365 km.h.).
Landing speed (full flaps) 64 m.p.h. (103 km.h.).
Rate of climb at S/L 1,500 ft./min. (456 m./min.).
Single-engine climb at S/L 310 ft./min (94 m./min.).
Service ceiling 19,000 ft. (5,780 m.).
Single-engine ceiling 9,000 ft. (2,745 m.).
Max. range (65% power) at 10,000 ft. (3,050 m.) 985 miles (1,580 km.).
Max. range (60% power) at 10,000 ft. (3,050 m.) 1,080 miles (1,728 km.).
Take-off to 50 ft. (15.25 m.) S/L. and no wind 448 yds. (409 m.).
Landing over 50 ft. (15.25 m.) no wind 405 yds. (370 m.).

(1953–54)

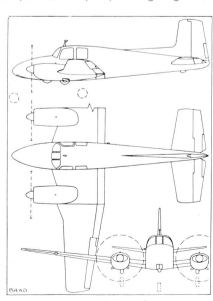

The Beechcraft Twin-Bonanza.

**THE BEECHCRAFT MODEL D50
TWIN-BONANZA
U.S.A.F. designation: L-23B**

The L-23B is a military version of the earlier Model B50 Twin-Bonanza and is used by the U.S. Army as a staff transport and for general liaison duties.

The L-23B is powered by two 260 h.p. Lycoming GO-435-C2 engines with Beech 2-blade variable-pitch propellers, and has

Otherwise the general structural description of the civil Model D50 Twin-Bonanza previously described applies to this aircraft.

DIMENSIONS.—
As for Model D50.

WEIGHTS AND LOADINGS.—
Weight empty 4,015 lb. (1,821 kg.).
Weight loaded 6,000 lb. (2,724 kg.).
Wing loading 21.65 lb./sq. ft. (105.6 kg./m.²).
Power loading 12.25 lb./h.p. (5.57 kg./h.p.).

PERFORMANCE.—
Max. speed at 2,500 ft. (760 m.) 205 m.p.h. (328 km.h.).

Cruising speed (65% power) at 10,000 ft. (3,050 m.) 192 m.p.h. (307 km.h.).
Landing speed (full flaps) 69 m.p.h. (110 km.h.).
Rate of climb at S/L. 1,450 ft./min. (442 m./min.).
Single-engine climb at S/L. 300 ft./min. (91 m./min.).
Service ceiling 20,000 ft. (6,100 m.).
Single-engine ceiling 8,400 ft. (2,560 m.).
Max. range (65% power) at 10,000 ft. (3,050 m.) 961 miles (1,538 km.).
Take-off to 50 ft. (15.25 m.) at S/L. no wind 410 yds. (374 m.).
Landing from 50 ft. (15.25 m.), no wind 458 yds. (418 m.). (1956–57)

**THE BEECHCRAFT MODEL H50
TWIN-BONANZA
U.S. Army designation: L-23D Seminole**

The Model H50 Twin-Bonanza and the equivalent U.S. Army version, the L-23D, have two Lycoming GSO-480-B1B6 super-charged engines for improved performance.

Otherwise the general structural description of the civil Model D50C Twin-Bonanza previously described applies to this aircraft.

Earlier Model L-23A and L-23B versions of the Twin-Bonanza in service with the U.S. Army have been re-manufactured by Beech to L-23D standard.

One L-23D has been fitted with RCA Type AVQ-50 weather-avoidance radar and is being evaluated at Fort Rucker, Alabama. It is the first U.S. Army aircraft equipped in this way and can be recognised by its small nose radome.

Two other L-23D's have been modified into all-weather battlefield surveillance aircraft under the designation RL-23D. They carry Motorola APS-85 radar equipment in a large hemispherical nose fairing and in a long torpedo-like container beneath the fuselage.

Alternative surveillance radars under evaluation on other L-23D's include Texas Instruments' AN/UPD-1, in a large ventral blister, and APQ-86.

Another new development tested on the L-23 is the Beech range extension system. This consists of large wingtip fuel tanks, each complete with stub wings, tail unit and landing gear. Attached as extensions to the aircraft's wings, they provide sufficient lift to offset their weight and the L-23D handles satisfactorily with only one tank fitted.

POWER PLANT.—Two Lycoming GSO-480-B1B6 geared supercharged six-cylinder horizontally-opposed air-cooled engines with 340 h.p. at 3,400 r.p.m. available at take-off and normal rating of 320 h.p. at 3,200 r.p.m. at S/L. Fuel capacity 230 U.S. gallons (872 litres) in two 44 gallon (166 litre) inboard wing tanks, two 46 gallon (174 litre) outboard wing tanks and two optional 25 gallon (96 litre) auxiliary wing tanks. Oil capacity 8 U.S. gallons (30.25 litres).

DIMENSIONS.—
As for Model D50

Beechcraft L-23 fitted with AN/UPD-1 airborne radar

Beechcraft L-23 fitted with two range extension system units (*Howard Levy*)

WEIGHTS AND LOADINGS.—
Weight empty 4,460 lb. (2,023 kg.)
Weight loaded 7,000 lb. (3,175 kg.)
Wing loading 25.2 lb./sq. ft. (123.03 kg./m.²)
Power loading 10.9 lb./h.p. (4.94 kg./h.p.)

PERFORMANCE.—
Max. speed at 9,000 ft. (2,750 m.) 230 m.p.h. (370 km.h.)
Cruising speed (70% power) at 13,300 ft. (4,050 m.) 228 m.p.h. (367 km.h.)
Landing speed (full flaps) 84 m.p.h. (135 km.h.)
Rate of climb at S/L. 1,620 ft./min. (495 m./min.)

Single-engine climb at S/L. (at 6,000 lb.= 2,722 kg. A.U.W.) 445 ft./min. (136 m./min.)
Service ceiling 25,500 ft. (7,770 m.)
Single-engine ceiling (at 6,000 lb.= 2,722 kg. A.U.W.) 15,500 ft. (4,730 m.)
Take-off to 50 ft. (15.25 m.) at S/L. no wind 417 yds. (381 m.)
Landing from 50 ft. (15.25 m.), no wind 613 yds. (560 m.)
Max. range 169 m.p.h. (272 km.h.) no reserve at 10,000 ft. (3,050 m.) 1,650 miles (2,655 km.) (1960–61)

The RL-23D version of the Beechcraft Seminole with Motorola APS-85 radar for all-weather battlefield surveillance

THE BEECHCRAFT MODEL D50 TWIN-BONANZA.
U.S. Army designation: L-23E Seminole.

A number of Model D50 Twin-Bonanzas have been acquired by the U.S. Army Field Forces, under the designation L-23E.

THE BELL MODEL 47 HELICOPTER.
U.S.A.F. designations: H-13B (47D), H-13D, H-13E (47-D-1)
U.S. Navy designations: HTL-1 (47B), HTL-2, HTL-3 (47D), HTL-4 and HTL-5 (47-D-1).

Since it delivered its first Model 47 in January, 1947, Bell has produced five commercial models. They are the 47B, which had an enclosed, automobile-type cabin; the 47B-3, which had an open cockpit; the 47D, which had an all-Plexiglas cabin for greater visibility, plus weather protection, the 47D-1, and the 47G, the company's newest model. There have been corresponding military and naval versions to most of these models.

Since the delivery of the first commercial Model 47 in December, 1946, more than 1,000 Bell helicopters have been bought by the U.S. armed forces and by commercial operators in the United States and abroad.

The versatile usefulness of the helicopter was emphasised by the performance of rotary-wing aircraft in Korea. They were used for liaison, cable-laying, transport and a wide variety of purposes. But its most dramatic rôle was that of aerial ambulance, evacuating wounded U.N. troops from the front lines to mobile hospitals several miles to the rear.

During hostilities in Korea in 1951-53, Bell helicopters, flown by Army and Marine pilots, evacuated over 20,000 casualties.

THE BELL MODEL 47G, 47G-2 and 47G-3
U.S.A.F. designation: H-13.
U.S. Army name: Sioux.
U.S. Navy designation: HTL.

The 2,000th model 47, a 47J, was completed on December 11, 1957.

XH-13F. (Bell Model 201). This is an experimental craft powered by a Continental-Turbomeca T51-T-3 Artouste shaft turbine engine.

H-13G. Military version of standard 47G. Can carry two external litters.

H-13H. Military version of 47G-2, with stretcher evacuation kits, two radios, dual controls, new-type skid landing gear and bonded all-metal rotor blades.

Original U.S. Army contract for 189 increased to over 300, extending production into 1960. An H-13H set up an international helicopter endurance record of 57 hr. 50 min. in 1956, by refuelling whilst hovering just clear of the ground at regular intervals. Others are being evaluated for close support duties, carrying machine-guns, rockets and other armament in packs mounted on the landing gear.

OH-13S. US Army observation version of 47G-3B, of which production continues during 1971. Powered by 260 hp Lycoming TVO-435-25 engine.

TH-13T. Two-seat instrument training version of standard 47G-3B-1 with additional avionics equipment, including VOR, ADF, marker beacon receiver, ILS glideslope, gyro-magnetic compass and attitude gyro system, and blind-flying hood for pupil pilot. Order for 103 for US Army announced in June 1964, followed by further orders for 26 on 17 August 1965, 91 on 15 October 1965, 54 on 16 June 1966 and 141 on 22 June 1967, making a total of 415 ordered. First delivery made in December 1964; deliveries completed in 1968. Powered by 270 hp Lycoming TVO-435-D1B engine.

H-13J. See under Bell Model 47J.

HTL-6. Naval training version of 47G. All supplied with skid landing-gear but float kits provided for proportion.

HTL-7. See under Bell Model 47J.

The description which follows refers specifically to the three-seat utility model 47G.

TYPE.—Three-seat General Utility Helicopter.

ROTORS.—Two-blade main rotor and controllable-pitch anti-torque rotor. Main rotor hub mounted on transmission mast by universal joint and provided with a stabilizing bar below and at right angles to the blades. A swash-plate revolving with the mast but free to move up and down provides cyclic pitch-control.

The Bell H-13H Utility Helicopter (200 h.p. Lycoming VO-435 engine).

The Bell HTL-7, the U.S. Naval training version of the Bell Model 47J.

Lower half of swash-plate which does not revolve alters pitch of the blades differentially for directional control. Main rotor drive through a centrifugal clutch and a two-stage planetary transmisson with a 9 : 1 reduction ratio. Free-wheeling mechanism incorporated in transmission. Transmission furnishes power take-offs for tail rotor drive, cooling fan and accessories and pulleys. Main rotor blades of symmetrical aerofoil section, are of laminated wood with a steel insert in leading-edge for strength and mass-balance. (H-13H has bonded metal blades). Blade area (each) 17.67 sq. ft. (1.64 m.²). Disc area 965 sq. ft. (89.65 m.²). Pre-coning angle 2.5 degrees. Metal anti-torque rotor blades. Blade area (each) 1.2 sq. ft. (0.11 m.²). Disc area 25.31 sq. ft. (2.35 m.²).

FUSELAGE.—In three sections; centre, tail and cabin. Centre section has a welded tubular steel framework which provides for mounting the engine and supports the cabin. Rear section is also a tubular structure, is triangular in cross-section and serves as a support for the anti-torque rotor drive-shaft. Small synchronised elevator surface at rear end of fuselage responds to the fore and aft motion of the cyclic-pitch control, provides better stability and allows a greatly increased C.G. travel.

LANDING GEAR.—Tubular skid type. Skid tread 7 ft. 6 in. (2.28 m.). Small ground handling wheels and tie-down and towing attachments provided. Four-wheel landing-gear may be supplied for training and other missions requiring considerable handling. The two forward self-castoring wheels capable of swivelling through 360°, the two rear wheels fixed. Wheel track 5 ft. 10¼ in. (1.78 m.). For amphibious use two air-inflated nylon floats are easily attached.

POWER PLANT.—One vertically-mounted 200 h.p. Franklin 6V4-200-C32AB (0-355-5) six-cylinder horizontally-opposed fan-cooled engine with clutch, drive shaft and rotor assembly in an integral unit in a steel-tube framework with the engine supported in rubber mounts at the top and bottom and attached to the welded framework of the forward fuselage. The engine-mounting structure has three attachment points for the rear fuselage. Engine controls include throttle, carburettor, hot air and carburettor mixture. The throttle is located on the main rotor pitch control lever and drives through a cam which automatically compensates for varying power requirements as the main rotor pitch control lever is actuated. Two interconnected saddle-mounted fuel tanks (43 U.S. gallons =172.5 litres total capacity) on C.G. and with gravity feed.

ACCOMMODATION.—Side-by-side seating for three in enclosed compartment. The compartment is covered by a full-blown Plexiglas canopy with doors attached. For fair weather or specialised operations the doors are quickly removable. The Model 47G-2 can carry 440 lb. (200 kg.) cargo instead of passengers.

CONTROLS.—Conventional control stick for tilting main rotor by cyclic rotor blade angle change. Adjustable friction device on stick used to regulate control sensitivity. Main rotor pitch control lever located at left side of each seat. Rudder pedals connected to pitch-changing mechanism on tail rotor for torque compensation and directional control.

EQUIPMENT.—Standard equipment includes complete VFR flight and engine instruments, hydraulic boost control, 28-volt/50 amp. generator, electric starter, ground handling wheels, heavy-duty battery, etc. Additional accessories available in CAA-approved kits include floats, night flying equipment, dusting and spraying equipment, cargo carriers, dual controls, etc.

DIMENSIONS.—
Diameter of main rotor 35 ft. 1½ in. (10.72 m.).
Overall length (main rotor fore-and-aft) 41 ft. 5 in. (12.62 m.).
Length of fuselage (tail rotor vertical) 27 ft. 4 in. (8.33 m.).
Width (over landing gear) 8 ft. 6 in. (2.59 m.).
Height 9 ft. 5 in. (2.87 m.).
Diameter of tail rotor 5 ft. 8 in. (1.72 m.).

WEIGHTS (Model 47G).—
Weight empty (standard 2 or 3 seater) 1,435 lb. (651 kg.).
Max. certificated weight 2,350 lb. (1,067 kg.).

WEIGHTS (Model 47G-2).—
Weight empty 1,564 lb. (709 kg.).
Weight loaded 2,450 lb. (1,111 kg.).

PERFORMANCE (Model 47G at 2,350 lb.=1,066 kg. A.U.W.).—
Max. speed 86 m.p.h. (138 km.h.).
Cruising speed 70 m.p.h. (113 km.h.).
Max. rate of climb at S/L 780 ft./min. (238 m./min.).
Time to 5,000 ft. (1,525 m.) 8.2 min.
Service ceiling 10,900 ft. (2,718 m.).
Absolute ceiling 12,500 ft. (3,815 m.).
Hovering ceiling in ground effect 3,600 ft. (1,098 m.).
Range 212 miles (341 km.).
Endurance 3.5 hours.

PERFORMANCE (Model 47G-2).—
Max. speed 100 m.p.h. (161 km.h.).
Hovering ceiling in ground effect 10,850 ft. (3,310 m.).
Range 238 miles (383 km.). (1958–59)

THE BELL MODEL 47J RANGER.
U.S.A.F. designation: H-13J.
U.S. Navy designations: HUL-1 and HTL-7.

The Model 47J is a four-seat utility version of the 47G. The enclosed cabin seats the pilot centrally in front, with three passengers on a cross bench aft. The passenger seat can be removed to allow for the installation of two stretchers on a parallelogram rack such as is used in typical Army field ambulances, plus a jump seat for a medical attendant; with the port door removed a trap can be raised to permit use of an internal electrically-powered hoist for rescue work; or the passenger seat can be folded back to leave clear space for cargo. Conversion to any of the cabin configurations can be made in the field in a matter of minutes without the use of tools. Alternative skid or pontoon landing gear can be fitted.

The 47J is powered by a 260 h.p. Lycoming VO-435 engine de-rated to develop 240 h.p. for two minutes, with a continuous output of 220 h.p.

Three military versions have been announced, as follows :—

H-13J. Two for use by President Eisenhower. Equipped to carry three persons. Specially furnished.

HUL-1. Standard Model 47J in production for general utility and ice breaker patrol duties with U.S. Navy. Alternative pontoon landing gear. Two HUL-1's were fitted with HTL-7 flight instruments for operational tests in the Antarctic with the U.S. Navy's IGY Operation Deepfreeze III expedition in 1957-58.

The Bell H-13J, one of two supplied for Presidential use.

HTL-7. Training version for U.S. Navy, ordered into production in 1957. Has HUL-1 airframe from the firewall back, with completely re-styled cabin containing all-weather flight instruments, dual controls and side-by-side seating for pilot and co-pilot. The Navy will use this helicopter for both basic flying and instrument training, eliminating present need for two different types. Eighteen ordered, of which the first was delivered in December, 1957. Two will be used by Bell for Army-Navy Instrument Programme to develop ideal helicopter instrumentation and for Navy helicopter development programmes.

DIMENSIONS.—
Diameter of main rotor 37 ft. 2 in. (11.33 m.).
Overall length (main rotor fore and aft) 43 ft. 4 in. (13.2 m.).
Height 9 ft. 4 in. (2.84 m.).

WEIGHTS.—
Weight empty 1,618 lb. (734 kg.).
Max. loaded weight 2,800 lb. (1,270 kg.).

PERFORMANCE (at normal A.U.W. of 2,565 lb. =1,164 kg.).—
Max. speed 105 m.p.h (169 km.h.).
Cruising speed 100 m.p.h. (160 km.h.).
Service ceiling 17,000 ft. (5,180 m.).

Hovering ceiling in ground effect 7,400 ft. (2,257 m.).
Normal range 200 miles (322 km.). (1958–59)

THE BELL MODEL 61.
U.S. Navy designation: HSL-1.

The HSL-1 is a large tandem-rotored helicopter which was designed specifically for anti-submarine warfare. The prototype flew on March 4, 1953, followed within a year by the first production type HSL-1's for the U.S. Navy.

The tandem-rotored HSL-1 marks the Bell company's first departure from its familiar single-rotor configuration which has been used in all Bell helicopters since 1942. Each of the two rotors incorporates the basic Bell rotor principles, characterised by the rigid two-blade rotor and automatic stabilising bar. The fore and aft rotors are interconnected and power is supplied by a 1,900 h.p. Pratt & Whitney R-2800-50 engine in a buried installation. The rotors can be folded to enable the helicopter to negotiate the elevators in aircraft-carriers or other types of ship. Total fuel capacity is 425 U.S. gallons (1,610 litres).

The HSL-1 is equipped with dipping sonar for submarine detection and is armed with lightweight homing weapons for the destruction of undersea craft. A Bell-developed helicopter auto-pilot permits the HSL-1 to hover motionless for long periods during a search operation.

The HSL-1 carries a crew of four, a pilot, co-pilot and two sonar operators. It has a flight endurance of nearly four hours and maximum speed of 115 m.p.h. (185 km.h.) at sea level.

DIMENSIONS.—
Rotor diameter (both) 51 ft. 6 in. (15.7 m.).
Length of fuselage 39 ft. 2¾ in. (11.9 m.).
Overall height (over rear rotor pylon) 14 ft. 6 in. (4.4 m.).
Width (rotors folded) 11 ft. 8½ in. (3.5 m.).
Rotor disc area 4,170 sq. ft. (387.4 m.²).

WEIGHT.—
Loaded weight 26,500 lb. (12,020 kg.).

(1958–59)

The Bell HSL-I Anti-Submarine Helicopter (1,900 h.p. Pratt & Whitney R-2800 engine). (1958–59)

BELL MODEL 204
US Military designations: UH-1A/B/C/E/F/L, HH-1K and TH-1F/L Iroquois.

In 1955 the Bell Model 204 won a US Army design competition for a utility helicopter suitable for front-line casualty evacuation, general utility and instrument training duties. The production version was originally designated HU-1, giving rise to the nickname "Huey-copter" or "Huey", which survived the change of designation to UH-1. Official US Army name for the UH-1 series is Iroquois.

The following versions of the Model 204 have appeared:

XH-40. Three prototypes, of which the first flew on 20 October 1956.

YH-40. Six service test models.

UH-1. Nine pre-production models.

UH-1A. Initial production version, incorporating changes requested as a result of service testing. Six-seater, powered by an 860 shp Lycoming T53-L-1A turboshaft engine, derated to 770 shp. Deliveries to US Army began on 30 June 1959 and were completed in March 1961. Thirteen operated by Utility Tactical Transport Helicopter Company in Vietnam were modified to carry 16 × 2·75-in air-to-surface rockets and two 0·30-in machine-guns. Fourteen were delivered for use as helicopter instrument trainers with dual controls and a device for simulated instrument instruction.

UH-1B. Development of UH-1A, initially with 960 shp T53-L-5 turboshaft. Subsequent deliveries with 1,100 shp T53-L-11. Crew of two and seven troops, or three litters, two sitting casualties and medical attendant, or 3,000 lb (1,360 kg) of freight. Rotor diameter 44 ft (13·41 m). Normal fuel capacity 165 US gallons (625 litres); overload capacity 330 US gallons (1,250 litres). For armed support duties, a rocket pack and electrically-controlled machine-gun can be mounted on each side of cabin. Other armament installations tested on UH-1B included General Electric M-5 nose-mounted 40-mm grenade launcher and XM-30 armament system, consisting of two side-mounted XM-140 30-mm cannon with central ammunition reservoir and fire-control system. Deliveries began in March 1961. This version was super-seded by the UH-1C on the Bell assembly line, but continues in production by Fuji in Japan, where delivery of 89 to the JGSDF will be completed in 1973.

Model 204B. Commercial and military export version of UH-1B, with ten seats, 1,100 shp T5311A turboshaft and 48 ft (14·63 m) rotor. Tail boom incorporates a 35 cu ft (0·99 m³) baggage compartment. Cabin doors with jettisonable emergency exits, passenger steps on each side of cabin, improved outside lights, commercial radio equipment, fire detection and extinguishing systems. Received FAA certification on 4 April 1963. More than 60 delivered for commercial service up to end 1967. Military deliveries included 24 for RAAF and 8 for RAN. Deliveries from licence manufacture by Fuji in Japan have included 2 for Asahi Helicopter Company, 2 for All-Nippon Airways, 1 for Tokyo Metropolitan Police and 7 for Bell to meet US civil orders. Licence-built versions (AB 204B) by Agusta SpA in Italy can have Rolls-Royce Bristol Gnome H.1200 or General Electric T58-GE-3 turboshaft as alternative to T5311A and have standard 242 US gallon (916 litre) fuel tanks. Military versions have been supplied to the armed services of Italy, Spain Sweden, the Netherlands, Austria, Turkey and Saudi-Arabia; commercial AB 204Bs are flying in Italy, Norway, Sweden, Switzerland and Lebanon. A special ASW version supplied to the Italian and Spanish Navies is designed for individual or dual-role search and attack missions, with armament of two Mk 44 torpedoes. Equipment includes dipping sonar, automatic stabilisation and automatic approach to hover and all-weather instrumentation.

UH-1C. In September 1965, Bell introduced its Model 540 "door-hinge" rotor, with blades of increased (27 in = 69 cm) chord, on this developed version of the UH-1B, offering some increase in speed and a substantial increase in manoeuvrability through resistance to blade stall. Through reduced vibration and stress levels, the 540 rotor eliminates previous limitations on max level flight speed. T53-L-11 turboshaft, accommodation and armament as for UH-1B. Normal fuel capacity 242 US gallons (916 litres); overload capacity 592 US gallons (2,241 litres). Superseded UH-1B in production for US Army, but is itself superseded by AH-1G HueyCobra.

UH-1E. In March 1962, Bell won a design competition for an assault support helicopter for the US Marine Corps, to replace Cessna O-1B/C fixed-wing aircraft and Kaman OH-43D helicopters. Designated UH-1E, this version is generally similar to the UH-1B/C, but has a personnel hoist, rotor brake and Marine electronics. The 540 rotor and increased fuel capacity (as UH-1C) were introduced in 1965. Payload consists of a pilot and eight passengers or 4,000 lb (1,815 kg) of freight. Initial small purchase was made in 1962 for evaluation, and first UH-1E flew in February 1963. Larger contracts have followed; the latest for 48 in November 1966 and 18 in early 1967 extended production until the Summer of 1968. First delivery to an operational unit, Marine Air Group 26 at New River, NC, was made on 21 February 1964. UH-1Es operational on

Bell TH-1L, training version of the Model 204 for the US Navy

Bell UH-1L, a utility version of the TH-1L for the US Navy

troop-carrying and escort duties in Vietnam have two fixed 7·62-mm M-60 machine-guns, on pylons on each side of the cabin, and two pods, each containing seven or eighteen 2·75-in rockets, also one on each side.

UH-1F. Following a design competition, it was announced in June 1963 that an initial batch of 25 UH-1F helicopters, based on the UH-1B, were to be built for the USAF in 1963-64, and many more later, for missile site support duties. Each has a 1,272 shp General Electric T58-GE-3 turboshaft (derated to 1,100 shp), a 48 ft (14·63 m) rotor, normal fuel capacity of 250 US gallons (945 litres) and overload capacity of 410 US gallons (1,552 litres). This version can handle up to 4,000 lb (1,815 kg) of cargo at missile site silos, or carry a pilot and 10 passengers. The first UH-1F flew on 20 February 1964. Subsequent contracts for a further 121 aircraft were completed in 1967. First delivery to an operational unit was made to the 4486th Test Squadron at Eglin AFB in September 1964. This model has been used for classified psychological warfare missions in Vietnam.

TH-1F. Training version of UH-1F for USAF. Production completed.

HH-1K. Sea-air rescue version for US Navy, which placed letter contract for 27 late in 1968, with deliveries to be made in 1970. Has UH-1E airframe, T53-L-13 turboshaft engine (derated to 1,100 shp) and revised avionics.

TH-1L. Training version for US Navy. Similar to UH-1E but with 1,400 shp Lycoming T53-L-13 turboshaft (derated to 1,100 shp) and improved electronics. Contract for 45 received on 16 May 1968; the first of these was delivered to the USN at Pensacola, Florida, on 26 November 1969.

UH-1L. Utility version of TH-1L for US Navy. Eight ordered, and delivered during 1969.

UH-1M. US Army version fitted with Hughes Aircraft Iroquois night fighter and night tracker (Infant) system to detect and acquire ground targets under low ambient lighting conditions. Two sensors mounted on nose of cabin serve a low-light-level TV system with three cockpit displays and a direct-view system using an image intensifier at cockpit/gunner's station. Three UH-1Ms deployed with hunter-killer helicopter groups in Vietnam in early 1970 to evaluate system.

RH-2 (Research Helicopter 2). One UH-1A was used as a flying laboratory for new instrument and control systems. Installations included an electronic control system and high-resolution radar in a large fairing above the flight deck, enabling the pilot to detect obstacles ahead of the aircraft in bad visibility.

HueyTug. It was announced on 3 September 1968 that a UH-1C had been retrofitted with a 2,850 shp Lycoming T55-L-7C turboshaft and 50 ft (15·24 m) "door-hinge" rotor as the prototype of a new flying crane version able to lift a three-ton external payload. Associated modifications, all of which can be applied retrospectively to existing UH-1s, include substitution of a 2,000 hp transmission and larger tail rotor, reinforcement of the airframe and fitment of a larger tail boom, and use of a stability control and augmentation system instead of the normal stabiliser bar. The HueyTug is designed to hover out of ground effect at 4,000 ft (1,220 m), 95°F, at 14,000 lb (6,350 kg) max T-O weight. Max level speed, clean, is 140 knots (161 mph; 259 kmh).

DIMENSIONS, EXTERNAL (HH-1K, TH-1L, UH-1C, E and L):
Diameter of main rotor   44 ft 0 in (13·41 m)
Diameter of tail rotor   8 ft 6 in (2·59 m)
Length overall (main rotor fore and aft)
   53 ft 0 in (16·15 m)
Length of fuselage   38 ft 5 in (11·70 m)
Overall height   12 ft 7¼ in (3·84 m)
DIMENSIONS, INTERNAL (204B):
Cabin:
Length   8 ft 6 in (2·59 m)

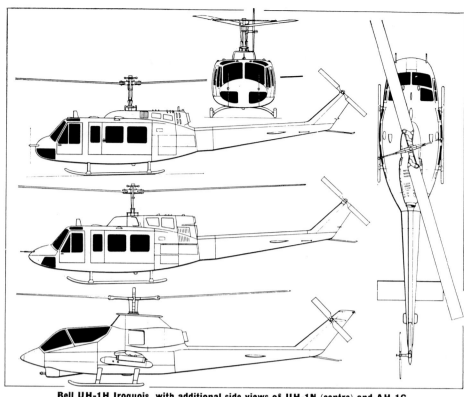

Bell UH-1H Iroquois, with additional side views of UH-1N (centre) and AH-1G HueyCobra (bottom)

Max width	7 ft 10 in (2·39 m)	
Max height	4 ft 10 in (1·47 m)	
Baggage compartment	30 cu ft (0·85 m³)	

AREAS (HH-1K, TH-1L, UH-1C, E and L):
Main rotor disc   1,520 sq ft (141·2 m²)
Tail rotor disc   56·8 sq ft (5·27 m²)

WEIGHTS AND LOADINGS:
Weight empty:
UH-1C (incl 2 armoured crew seats)
   5,071 lb (2,300 kg)
UH-1E   5,055 lb (2,293 kg)
Operating weight, including two crew:
HH-1K   5,811 lb (2,635 kg)
TH-1L   5,686 lb (2,579 kg)
UH-1F   4,902 lb (2,223 kg)
UH-1L   6,045 lb (2,742 kg)
Mission weight:
HH-1K, TH-1L, UH-1L   6,600 lb (2,993 kg)
UH-1F   8,474 lb (3,843 kg)
Max gross weight (military qualified):
HH-1K, TH-1L, UH-1L   8,500 lb (3,855 kg)
UH-1F   9,000 lb (4,082 kg)
Max overload weight:
HH-1K, TH-1L, UH-1C, E, L
   9,500 lb (4,309 kg)
Max zero-fuel weight:
UH-1C   7,927 lb (3,596 kg)
Max disc loading:
UH-1C   6·25 lb/sq ft (30·5 kg/m²)
Max power loading:
UH-1C   8·63 lb/hp (3·91 kg/hp)
PERFORMANCE (at max overload weight, except where stated otherwise):
Max level speed:
HH-1K, TH-1L, UH-1L
   125 knots (144 mph; 231 km/h)
UH-1C   128 knots (148 mph; 238 km/h)
UH-1E   140 knots (161 mph; 259 km/h)
UH-1F   100 knots (115 mph; 185 km/h)
Max permissable speed at mission gross weight:
HH-1K, TH-1L, UH-1L
   140 knots (161 mph; 259 km/h)
UH-1F   105 knots (121 mph; 194·5 km/h)

Max cruising speed at S/L:
UH-1C   128 knots (148 mph; 238 km/h)
UH-1E   120 knots (138 mph; 222 km/h)
Econ cruising speed at 5,000 ft (1,525 m):
UH-1C   124 knots (143 mph; 230 km/h)
Max rate of climb at S/L:
HH-1K, TH-1L, UH-1L   1,160 ft (353 m)/min
UH-1C   1,400 ft (425 m)/min
UH-1E   1,849 ft (563 m)/min
UH-1F (at mission gross weight)
   1,230 ft (375 m)/min

Hovering ceiling, out of ground effect:
HH-1K, TH-1L, UH-1L at 8,500 lb (3,855 kg)
AUW   7,400 ft (2,255 m)
UH-1C at 8,500 lb (3,855 kg) AUW
   10,000 ft (3,050 m)
UH-1E   11,800 ft (3,595 m)
UH-1F at 9,000 lb (4,082 kg) AUW
   4,000 ft (1,219 m)

Vertical rate of climb at S/L:
UH-1C at 8,500 lb (3,855 kg) AUW
   540 ft (165 m)/min
Service ceiling:
HH-1K, TH-1L, UH-1L   10,000 ft (3,050 m)
UH-1C   11,500 ft (3,500 m)
UH-1E   21,000 ft (6,400 m)
UH-1F (at mission gross weight)
   13,450 ft (4,100 m)
Hovering ceiling in ground effect:
HH-1K, TH-1L, UH-1L   10,400 ft (3,170 m)
UH-1C   10,600 ft (3,230 m)
UH-1E   15,800 ft (4,815 m)
UH-1F (at mission gross weight)
   10,300 ft (3,139 m)

Range with max fuel, no allowances:
HH-1K, TH-1L, UH-1L
   270·5 nm (312 miles; 502 km)
UH-1C   331 nm (382 miles; 615 km)
UH-1E   248 nm (286 miles; 460 km)
UH-1F (at mission gross weight)
   301 nm (347 miles; 558 km)

(1971–72)

BELL MODEL 205
US military designations: UH-1D/H and HH-1H Iroquois
Canadian military designation: CH-118 Iroquois

Although basically similar to the earlier Model 204 (see 1971-72 *Jane's*), the Model 205 introduced a longer fuselage, increased cabin space to accommodate a much larger number of passengers, and other changes. The following military versions have been built:

UH-1D. This US Army version of the Model 205 Iroquois has a 1,100 shp Lycoming T53-L-11 turboshaft, 48 ft (14·63 m) rotor, normal fuel capacity of 220 US gallons (832 litres) and overload capacity of 520 US gallons (1,968 litres). Relocation of the fuel cells increases cabin space to 220 cu ft (6·23 m³), providing sufficient room for a pilot and twelve troops, or six litters and a medical attendant, or 4,000 lb (1,815 kg) of freight. A contract for a service test batch of seven YUH-1Ds was announced in July 1960 and was followed by further very large production orders from the US Army and from many other nations of the non-Communist world. First YUH-1D flew on 16 August 1961 and delivery to US Army field units began on 9 August 1963,

when the second and third production UH-1Ds went to the 11th Air Assault Division at Fort Benning, Georgia. The UH-1D was superseded in production for the US Army by the UH-1H, but 352 UH-1Ds were built subsequently under licence in Germany for the German Army and Air Force. Prime contractor was Dornier.

UH-1H. Following replacement of the original T53-L-11 turboshaft by the 1,400 shp T53-L-13, the version of the Model 205 currently in production by Bell for the US Army is designated UH-1H. Deliveries of an initial series of 319 aircraft for the US Army began in September

Bell HH-1H Iroquois local base rescue helicopter in USAF service

Additional orders for a total of 560 UH-IHs were placed in 1971-73. An add-on contract for 54 more UH-1Hs, valued at $11·9 million, was awarded in September 1974, with delivery extending into 1976.

Under a licensing agreement concluded in 1969, the Republic of China is producing UH-1Hs for the Nationalist Chinese Army, with much of the manufacturing and assembly process being carried out at Taichung, Taiwan. The initial production programme was for 50 helicopters, already delivered. Subsequent orders have increased the total procurement to 118.

CH-118. Similar to UH-1H, for Mobile Command, Canadian Armed Forces. First of ten delivered on 6 March 1968. Originally designated CUH-1H.

HH-1H. It was announced on 4 November 1970 that a fixed price contract worth more than $9·5 million had been received from the USAF for 30 HH-1H aircraft (generally similar to the UH-1H) for use as local base rescue helicopters. Deliveries were completed during 1973.

The commercial Model 205A-1 is described separately.

The 7,000th Model 205/205A helicopter was completed in 1973.

The following details refer specifically to the military UH-1H:

TYPE: Single-rotor general-purpose helicopter.

ROTOR SYSTEM: Two-blade all-metal semi-rigid main rotor with interchangeable blades, built up of extruded aluminium spars and laminates. Stabilising bar above and at right angles to main rotor blades. Underslung feathering axis hub. Two-blade all-metal tail rotor of honeycomb construction. Blades do not fold.

ROTOR DRIVE: Shaft-drive to both main and tail rotors. Transmission rating 1,100 shp. Main rotor rpm 294-324.

FUSELAGE: Conventional all-metal semi-monocoque structure.

TAIL SURFACE: Small synchronised elevator on rear fuselage is connected to the cyclic control to increase allowable CG travel.

LANDING GEAR: Tubular skid type. Lock-on ground handling wheels and inflated nylon float-bags available.

POWER PLANT: One 1,400 shp Lycoming T53-L-13 turboshaft mounted aft of the transmission on top of the fuselage and enclosed in cowlings. Five interconnected rubber fuel cells, total capacity 220 US gallons (832 litres). Overload fuel capacity of 520 US gallons obtained by installation of kit comprising two 150 US gallon (568 litre) internal auxiliary fuel tanks interconnected with the basic fuel system.

ACCOMMODATION: Cabin space of 220 cu ft (6·23 m³) provides sufficient room for pilot and 11-14 troops, or six litters and a medical attendant, or 3,880 lb (1,759 kg) of freight. Crew doors open forward and are jettisonable. Two doors on each side of cargo compartment; front door is hinged to open forward and is removable, rear door slides aft. Forced air ventilation system.

EQUIPMENT: Bleed air heater and defroster, comprehensive range of engine and flight instruments, power plant fire detection system, 30V 300A DC starter/generator, navigation, landing and anti-collision lights, controllable searchlight, hydraulically-boosted controls. Optional equipment includes external cargo hook, auxiliary fuel tanks, rescue hoist, 150,000 BTU muff heater.

ELECTRONICS: FM, UHF, VHF radio sets, IFF transponder, Gyromatic compass system, direction finder set, VOR receiver and intercommunications set standard. Optional nav/com systems.

DIMENSIONS, EXTERNAL:
Diameter of main rotor	48 ft 0 in (14·63 m)
Main rotor blade chord	1 ft 9 in (0·53 m)
Diameter of tail rotor	8 ft 6 in (2·59 m)
Tail rotor blade chord	8·4 in (0·213 m)
Length overall (main rotor fore and aft)	57 ft 1 in (17·40 m)
Length of fuselage	41 ft 10¾ in (12·77 m)
Height overall	14 ft 6 in (4·42 m)

AREAS:
Main rotor disc	1,809 sq ft (168·06 m²)
Tail rotor disc	56·7 sq ft (5·27 m²)

WEIGHTS AND LOADINGS:
Weight empty	4,667 lb (2,116 kg)
Basic operating weight (troop carrier mission)	5,557 lb (2,520 kg)
Mission weight	9,039 lb (4,100 kg)
Max T-O and landing weight	9,500 lb (4,309 kg)
Max zero-fuel weight	8,070 lb (3,660 kg)
Max disc loading	5·25 lb/sq ft (25·6 kg/m²)
Max power loading	8·63 lb/hp (3·91 kg/hp)

PERFORMANCE (at max T-O weight):
Max never-exceed speed	110 knots (127 mph; 204 km/h)
Max level and cruising speed	110 knots (127 mph; 204 km/h)
Econ cruising speed at 5,700 ft (1,735 m)	110 knots (127 mph; 204 km/h)
Max rate of climb at S/L	1,600 ft (488 m)/min
Service ceiling	12,600 ft (3,840 m)
Hovering ceiling in ground effect	13,600 ft (4,145 m)
Hovering ceiling out of ground effect	1,100 ft (335 m)
Range with max fuel, no allowances, no reserves, at S/L at 9,500 lb (4,309 kg) AUW	276 nm (318 miles; 511 km)

(1975–76)

BELL MODEL 206A JETRANGER
US Navy designation: TH-57A SeaRanger

Design of this five-seat turbine-powered general-purpose helicopter was started in April 1965. Construction of a prototype began in July 1965 and this aircraft was first flown on 10 January 1966. It received a provisional Type Certificate within four months, at which time two further examples had joined the flight test programme. Full certification was received on 20 October 1966, and deliveries began early in 1967. By December 1970, a total of 600 commercial models had been built, excluding JetRangers produced under licence by Agusta in Italy.

In addition to the standard commercial version, there are two military versions of the JetRanger, as follows:

TH-57A SeaRanger. Primary light turbine training helicopter, of which 40 were ordered by the US Navy on 31 January 1968, to replace Bell TH-13Ms used by Naval Air Training Command at Pensacola, Florida. Basically similar to Model 206A, with naval electronics and control equipment. Intended initially for VFR operation. Dual controls standard. All 40 were delivered during 1968.

Under a five-year programme, covered by contracts valued at more than $75 million, Beech Aircraft is producing airframes for both the commercial and the military versions of the Model 206A. The work involves manufacture of the fuselage, skid gear, tail-boom, spar, stabiliser and two rear fairing assemblies. The first Beech-produced airframe was delivered to Bell on 1 March 1968.

TYPE: Turbine-powered general-purpose light helicopter.

ROTOR SYSTEM: Two-blade semi-rigid see-saw type main rotor, employing pre-coning and underslinging to ensure smooth operation. Blades are of standard Bell "droop-snoot" section. They have a D-shape aluminium spar, bonded aluminium alloy skin, honeycomb core and a trailing-edge extension. Each blade is connected to the hub by means of a grip, pitch-change bearings and a tension-torsion strap assembly. Two tail rotor blades have bonded aluminium skin but no core. Main rotor blades do not fold, but modification to permit manual folding is possible. Rotor brake available as optional kit.

ROTOR DRIVE: Rotors driven through tubular steel alloy shafts with spliced couplings. Initial drive from engine through 90° spiral bevel gear to single-stage planetary main gearbox. Shaft to tail rotor single-stage bevel gearbox. Free-wheeling unit ensures that main rotor continues to drive tail rotor when engine is disengaged. Main rotor/engine rpm ratio 1:15; main rotor rpm 374-394. Tail rotor/engine rpm ratio 1:2·3.

FUSELAGE: Forward cabin section is made up of two aluminium alloy beams and 1 in (2·5 cm) thick aluminium honeycomb sandwich. Rotor, transmission and engine are supported by upper longitudinal beams. Upper and lower structure are interconnected by three fuselage bulkheads and a centre-post to form an integrated structure. Intermediate section is of aluminium alloy semi-monocoque construction. Aluminium monocoque tail-boom.

TAIL UNIT: Fixed stabiliser of aluminium monocoque construction, with inverted aerofoil section. Fixed vertical tail-fin in sweptback upper and ventral sections, made of aluminium honeycomb with aluminium skin.

LANDING GEAR: Aluminium alloy tubular skids bolted to extruded cross-tubes. Tubular steel skid on ventral fin to protect tail rotor in tail-down landing. Special high-skid gear (10 in = 25 cm greater ground clearance) available for use in areas with high brush. Inflated bag-type pontoons or stowed floats capable of in-flight inflation available as optional kits.

POWER PLANT: One 317 shp Allison 250-C18A turboshaft engine. Fuel tank below and behind passenger seat, capacity 76 US gallons (288 litres). Refuelling point on starboard side of fuselage, aft of cabin. Oil capacity 5·5 US quarts (5·2 litres).

ACCOMMODATION: Two seats side-by-side in front and rear bench seat for three persons. Two forward-hinged doors on each side, made of formed aluminium alloy with transparent panels. Baggage compartment aft of rear seats, capacity 250 lb (113 kg), with external door on port side.

SYSTEMS: Hydraulic system, pressure 600 lb/sq in (42 kg/cm²), for cyclic, collective and directional controls. Electrical supply from 150A starter-generator. One 24V 13Ah nickel-cadmium battery.

ELECTRONICS: Full range of electronics available in form of optional kits, including VHF communications and omni navigation kit, glideslope kit, ADF, DME, marker beacon, transponder and intercom and speaker system.

EQUIPMENT: Standard equipment includes night lighting equipment, dynamic flapping restraints, door locks, fire extinguishers and first aid kit. Optional items include dual controls, custom seating, external cargo sling with 1,200 lb (545 kg) capacity, heater, high-intensity night lights, turn and slip indicator, clock, engine oil vent, fire detection system, engine fire extinguisher, fairing kit, camera access door, engine hour meter, internal litter kit and stability and control augmentation system.

DIMENSIONS, EXTERNAL:
Diameter of main rotor	33 ft 4 in (10·16 m)
Main rotor blade chord	13 in (33 cm)
Diameter of tail rotor	5 ft 2 in (1·57 m)
Distance between rotor centres	19 ft 6½ in (5·96 m)
Length overall, blades turning	39 ft 1 in (11·91 m)
Length of fuselage	31 ft 2 in (9·50 m)
Height overall	9 ft 6½ in (2·91 m)
Stabiliser span	6 ft 5¼ in (1·96 m)
Width over skids	6 ft 3½ in (1·92 m)

DIMENSIONS, INTERNAL:
Cabin: Length	7 ft 0 in (2·13 m)
Max width	4 ft 2 in (1·27 m)
Max height	4 ft 3 in (1·28 m)
Baggage compartment	16 cu ft (0·45 m³)

AREAS:
Main rotor blades (total)	36·1 sq ft (3·35 m²)
Tail rotor blades (total)	2·26 sq ft (0·21 m²)
Main rotor disc	873 sq ft (81·1 m²)
Tail rotor disc	20·97 sq ft (1·95 m²)
Stabiliser	9·65 sq ft (0·90 m²)

WEIGHTS AND LOADING:
Weight empty, including oil	1,480 lb (671 kg)
Max T-O and landing weight	3,000 lb (1,360 kg)
Max zero-fuel weight	2,510 lb (1,138 kg)
Max disc loading	3·44 lb/sq ft (16·79 kg/m²)

PERFORMANCE:
Max level speed at S/L:
  at 2,100 lb (953 kg) AUW
    130 knots (150 mph; 241 km/h)
  at 3,000 lb (1,360 kg) AUW
    130 knots (150 mph; 241 km/h)
Max permissible diving speed
    130 knots (150 mph; 241 km/h)
Max cruising speed:
  at 2,100 lb (953 kg) AUW
    122 knots (140 mph; 225 km/h)
  at 3,000 lb (1,360 kg) AUW
    114 knots (131 mph; 211 km/h)
Max rate of climb at S/L:
  at 2,100 lb (953 kg) AUW
    2,740 ft (835 m)/min
  at 3,000 lb (1,360 kg) AUW
    1,430 ft (436 m)/min
Service ceiling:
  at 2,100 lb (953 kg) AUW

at 3,000 lb (1,360 kg) AUW
    over 17,000 ft (5,182 m)
Hovering ceiling in ground effect (standard day):
  at 2,100 lb (953 kg) AUW 19,300 ft (5,880 m)
  at 3,000 lb (1,360 kg) AUW 7,900 ft (2,410 m)
Hovering ceiling out of ground effect (standard day):
  at 2,100 lb (953 kg) AUW 15,600 ft (4,755 m)
  at 3,000 lb (1,360 kg) AUW 3,500 ft (1,067 m)
Maximum range at S/L:
  at 2,100 lb (953 kg) AUW
    313 nm (361 miles; 581 km)
  at 3,000 lb (1,360 kg) AUW
    304 nm (351 miles; 564 km)
Maximum range at 8,000 ft (2,440 m):
  at 2,100 lb (953 kg) AUW
    399 nm (460 miles; 740 km)
  at 3,000 lb (1,360 kg) AUW
    340 nm (392 miles; 630 km)
Max endurance at S/L:
  at 2,100 lb (953 kg) AUW 4 hr 42 min
  at 3,000 lb (1,360 kg) AUW 4 hr 0 min
Max endurance at 8,000 ft (2,440 m):
  at 2,100 lb (953 kg) AUW 5 hr 24 min
  at 3,000 lb (1,360 kg) AUW 4 hr 36 min
    (1971–72)

BELL KIOWA
US Army designation: OH-58
Canadian military designation: CH-136

On 8 March 1968 the US Army named Bell as winner of its reopened light observation helicopter competition, and awarded the company the first increment of a total order for 2,200 **OH-58A** Kiowa aircraft, generally similar to the Model 206A and each powered by a 236·5 kW (317 shp) Allison T63-A-700 turboshaft engine. Major difference concerns the main rotor, that of the Kiowa having an increased diameter. There are also differences in the internal layout and avionics.

The first OH-58A was delivered to the US Army on 23 May 1969 and deployment in Viet-Nam began in the early Autumn of 1969.

Seventy-four similar COH-58As were delivered to the Canadian Armed Forces, and are now designated **CH-136**.

Under a co-production agreement with the Australian government 56 Model 206B-1 Kiowa military light observation helicopters (similar to the OH-58A) were delivered over an eight-year period. The initial 12 206B-1s were built by Bell. Commonwealth Aircraft Corporation was prime Australian licensee, with responsibility for final assembly of the remainder. Only the engines and avionics were supplied from US sources. Delivery of 12 **OH-58Bs** to the Austrian Air Force was completed in 1976.

Under a US Army development qualification contract placed on 30 June 1976, Bell converted an OH-58A to an improved standard, under the designation **OH-58C**. This involved installation of a flat glass canopy to reduce glint, an uprated Allison T63-A-720 turboshaft engine, and an IR reduction package. Two additional OH-58As were modified to OH-58C configuration, for pre-production flight testing by Bell and the US Army, and production modification of 435 OH-58As to OH-58C standard began in March 1978 at Bell Helicopter, Amarillo. The final configuration includes a new instrument panel, modifications to reduce vulnerability in combat, CONUS (Continental US) navigation equipment, day optics, improved avionics and improved maintenance features. The additional power significantly improves high-altitude, hot-weather performance. OH-58D and **Kiowa Warrior** conversion followed.

A prototype mast-mounted sight, manufactured by Rockwell, was installed and flight tested on an OH-58C in 1979-80. The sight consists of a TV camera with automatic tracking, and a laser designator/rangefinder.

The following details apply specifically to the OH-58C:
TYPE: Turbine-powered light observation helicopter.
ROTOR SYSTEM: Two-blade semi-rigid see-saw type main rotor, employing pre-coning and underslinging to ensure smooth operation. Blades of standard Bell 'droop-snoot' section, with D-shape aluminium spar, bonded light alloy skin, honeycomb core and trailing-edge extension. Each blade is connected to the hub by means of a grip, pitch-change bearings and a tension-torsion strap assembly. The two tail rotor blades have bonded aluminium skin but no core. Main rotor blades do not fold, but modification to permit manual folding is possible. Rotor brake available as optional kit.
ROTOR DRIVE: Rotors driven through tubular steel alloy shafts with spliced couplings. Initial drive from engine through 90° spiral bevel gear to single-stage planetary

Bell OH-58A Kiowa turbine-powered light observation helicopter in US Army service

main gearbox. On OH-58C, transmission improvements include a four-pinion upper planetary, with new thrust bearing and 'fly dry' capability. Shaft to tail rotor single-stage bevel gearbox protected by cover. Free-wheeling unit ensures that main rotor continues to drive tail rotor when engine is disengaged. Redundant tail rotor control for improved safety if primary system is disabled. Main rotor/engine rpm ratio 1 : 17·44; main rotor rpm 354. Tail rotor/engine rpm ratio 1 : 2·353.
FUSELAGE: Forward cabin section is made up of two aluminium alloy beams and 25 mm (1 in) thick aluminium honeycomb sandwich. Rotor, transmission and engine are supported by upper longitudinal beams. Upper and lower structures are interconnected by three fuselage bulkheads and a centrepost to form an integrated structure. Intermediate section is a light alloy semi-monocoque. Aluminium monocoque tailboom. A low-glare canopy design reduces the solar glint signature of the OH-58C. The windscreens are slightly convex to assist rain removal and increase their strength.
TAIL UNIT: Fixed stabiliser of aluminium monocoque construction, with inverted aerofoil section. Fixed vertical fin in sweptback upper and ventral sections, constructed of aluminium honeycomb with light alloy skins.
LANDING GEAR: Light alloy tubular skids bolted to extruded cross-tubes. Tubular steel skid on ventral fin to protect tail rotor in tail-down landing. Special high skid gear available, with 0·25 m (10 in) greater ground clearance, for use in areas with high brush. Inflated bag-type pontoons, or stowed floats capable of in-flight inflation, available as optional kits.
POWER PLANT: One 313 kW (420 shp) Allison T63-A-720 turboshaft engine. 'Black Hole' exhaust stacks and hot metal shroud for infra-red suppression. Fuel tank below

and behind aft passenger seat, total usable capacity 276 litres (73 US gallons). Refuelling point on starboard side of fuselage, aft of cabin. Oil capacity 5·6 litres (1·5 US gallons).
ACCOMMODATION: Forward crew compartment seats pilot and co-pilot/observer side by side. Entrance to this compartment is provided by single door on each side of fuselage. The cargo/passenger compartment, which has its own doors on each side, provides approximately 1·13 m³ (40 cu ft) of cargo space, or provision for two passengers by installation of two seat cushions, seat belts and shoulder harnesses. A redesigned instrument panel on the OH-58C houses new avionics, and all flight instruments have been modified for night operations using night vision goggles. An improved defrost/defog air circulation system increases the aircraft's mission readiness.
SYSTEMS: Hydraulic system, pressure 41·5 bars (600 lb/sq in) for cyclic and collective controls. Electrical supply from 150A starter/generator. One 24V 13Ah nickel-cadmium battery.
AVIONICS: C-6533/ARC intercommunication subsystem, AN/ARC-114 VHF/FM, AN/ARC-115 VHF/AM, AN/ARC-116 UHF/AM, AN/ARN-89 ADF, AN/ASN-43 gyro magnetic compass, AN/APX-100 IFF transponder, TSEC/KY-28 communications security set, C-8157/ARC control indication, MT-3802/ARC mounting. TS-1843/APX transponder test set and mounting, KIT-1A/TSEC computer and mounting, duplicate AN/ARC-114, AN/APR-39 radar warning, ID-1351 C/A HBI, ID-1347 C/ARN CDI; and provisions for AN/ARN-123(V)1 CONUS nav, AN/APN-209 radar altimeter and YG-1054 proximity warning.

ARMAMENT: Standard equipment is the M-27 armament kit, utilising the 7·62 mm Minigun.

DIMENSIONS, EXTERNAL: As JetRanger III, except:
Diameter of main rotor — 10·77 m (35 ft 4 in)
Length overall, blades turning — 12·49 m (40 ft 11¾ in)
Length of fuselage · — 9·93 m (32 ft 7 in)

AREAS: As JetRanger III, except:
Main rotor blades (total) — 3·55 m² (38·26 sq ft)
Main rotor disc · — 90·93 m² (978·8 sq ft)

WEIGHTS AND LOADINGS (A: OH-58A; C: OH-58C):
Weight empty: A — 664 kg (1,464 lb)
C — 719 kg (1,585 lb)
Operating weight: A — 1,049 kg (2,313 lb)

C — 1,104 kg (2,434 lb)
Max T-O and landing weight: A — 1,360 kg (3,000 lb)
C — 1,451 kg (3,200 lb)
Max zero-fuel weight: A — 1,145 kg (2,525 lb)
C — 1,200 kg (2,646 lb)
Max disc loading: A — 14·9 kg/m² (3·07 lb/sq ft)
C — 15·9 kg/m² (3·27 lb/sq ft)

PERFORMANCE (OH-58A at observation mission gross weight of 1,255 kg; 2,768 lb, ISA, except where indicated):
Never-exceed speed at S/L — 120 knots (222 km/h; 138 mph)
Cruising speed for max range — 102 knots (188 km/h; 117 mph)

Loiter speed for max endurance — 49 knots (90·5 km/h; 56 mph)
Max rate of climb at S/L — 543 m (1,780 ft)/min
Service ceiling — 5,760 m (18,900 ft)
Hovering ceiling IGE — 4,145 m (13,600 ft)
Hovering ceiling OGE — 2,682 m (8,800 ft)
Hovering ceiling OGE (armed scout mission at 1,360 kg; 3,000 lb) — 1,828 m (6,000 ft)
Max range at S/L, 10% reserves — 259 nm (481 km; 299 miles)
Max range at S/L, armed scout mission at 1,360 kg (3,000 lb), no reserves — 264 nm (490 km; 305 miles)
Endurance at S/L, no reserves — 3 h 30 min
(1980–81)

BELL MODEL 209 HUEYCOBRA and SEACOBRA

US Army designations: AH-1G, AH-1Q and AH-1R
US Navy/Marine Corps designations: AH-1J and AH-1T

Bell Helicopter Textron initiated the Model 209 in March 1965 as a company-funded development of the UH-1B/C Iroquois intended specifically for armed helicopter missions. The original design combined the basic transmission and rotor system and (in its standard form) the power plant of the UH-1C with a new, streamlined fuselage designed for maximum speed, armament load and crew efficiency. Relatively small, its low silhouette and narrow profile make it easy to conceal with small camouflage nets or to move under cover of trees. Tandem seating provides the best possible field of view for the crew of two.

The Model 209 prototype made its first flight on 7 September 1965, and was sent to Edwards AFB in December 1965 for US Army evaluation. The Army's intention to order the aircraft was announced on 11 March 1966, the initial model being known as the AH-1G HueyCobra. Total orders to date exceed 1,800.

Versions announced so far are as follows:

AH-1G HueyCobra. Original version for US Army, powered by a single 1,044 kW (1,400 shp) Avco Lycoming T53-L-13 turboshaft engine, derated to 820 kW (1,100 shp) for T-O and max continuous rating. Development contract for two pre-production aircraft placed on 4 April 1966, followed on 13 April by an initial order for 110 aircraft plus long-lead-time spares. Subsequent contracts raised the total US Army order to 1,078 by mid-1971. Deliveries began in June 1967, and two months later the AH-1G was deployed operationally in Viet-Nam; it played a particularly important part in the Tet offensive in 1968, and in Laos in the Spring of 1971. The US Marine Corps acquired 38 AH-1Gs during 1969, for transition training and initial deployment pending deliveries of the AH-1J; these are included in the above total. The Spanish Navy received 20, for anti-shipping strike duties, and six were supplied to Israel in 1974. A number of AH-1Gs have been converted to TH-1G dual-control trainers. Following the decision to equip the HueyCobra with TOW missiles, 93 AH-1Gs were converted to interim AH-1Q standard; all of these have been updated further to Mod AH-1S standard. One AH-1G was converted to **JAH-1G** as a testbed aircraft, initially for the Hellfire laser-guided air-launched missile. More recent tests with this aircraft have included demonstrations of a General Electric M-197 three-barrel 20 mm gun with an improved rate of fire of 1,500 rds/min. An increase to 3,000 rds/min is possible with this gun, and GE is also developing fast-firing 25 mm and 30 mm weapons for helicopter applications, with the emphasis on air-to-air anti-helicopter combat.

AH-1J SeaCobra. Initial twin-turboshaft version for US Marine Corps, powered by a 1,342 kW (1,800 shp) Pratt & Whitney Aircraft of Canada T400-CP-400 coupled free-turbine turboshaft engine, a military version of the PT6T-3 Turbo Twin Pac. Engine and transmission flat rated at 820 kW (1,100 shp) continuous output, with increase to 932 kW (1,250 shp) available for 2½ or 5 min emergency power. Following an initial US Marine Corps order for 49, placed in May 1968, a pre-production example was displayed to representatives of the US armed forces at Enless, Texas, on 14 October 1969. Deliveries of these 49 began in mid-1970 and were completed in 1971; a further 20, ordered in early 1973, were delivered between April 1974 and February 1975. The last two of this batch were converted later as prototypes for the AH-1T. Under a $38.5 million contract announced on 22 December 1972, 202 TOW-capable AH-1Js were supplied to the Imperial Iranian Army Aviation from 1974, the US Army acting as purchasing agent.

AH-1Q HueyCobra. Interim anti-armour version for US Army, converted from AH-1G to fire Hughes TOW

Bell AH-1S HueyCobra with flat plate canopy and missile launchers

anti-tank missiles. First of eight 'pre-production' examples delivered in early 1973; first 'production' deliveries on 10 June 1975. Total of 93 converted; subsequently upgraded to Mod AH-1S standard.

AH-1R HueyCobra. As AH-1G, but with 1,342 kW (1,800 shp) T53-L-703 turboshaft engine. No TOW missile installation.

AH-1S HueyCobra. Advanced and modernised TOW-capable version for US Army; described separately.

AH-1T Improved SeaCobra. Improved version of twin-engined AH-1J for US Marine Corps. Last two of 69 AH-1Js modified as prototypes under a US Army Aviation Systems Command contract, with uprated components for significantly increased payload and performance. Incorporates features of AH-1J airframe, but embodies dynamic system of Bell Model 214, some technology developed for Bell Model 309 Kingcobra, and upgraded power plant (1,529 kW; 2,050 shp T400-WV-402) and transmission. Lengthened fuselage. Initial contract for 10 announced in June 1975; total of 57 ordered by 1979, of which 23 are scheduled to be modified to TOW configuration. First AH-1T (USN serial number 59228) delivered to US Marine Corps on 15 October 1977.

Under US Navy contract, Hughes is adapting its Black Hole infra-red suppression system (developed for the YAH-64) for interchangeable use on the AH-1J and **AH-1W SuperCobra.** Latest USMC version.

The following description applies primarily to the AH-1G and AH-1Q, except where indicated otherwise:

TYPE: Single-engined (AH-1G/Q/R/S) and twin-engined (AH-1J/T) close support and attack helicopters.

ROTOR SYSTEM AND DRIVE (AH-1G/J/Q/R): Model 540 two-blade wide-chord 'door-hinge' main rotor, similar to that of UH-1C. Interchangeable blades, built up of extruded aluminium spars and laminates. Rotor brake fitted. Blades do not fold. Two-blade all-metal flexbeam tractor tail rotor on starboard side, of honeycomb construction; blade chord increased on AH-1J, which also has push/pull tail rotor controls. Shaft drive to both main and tail rotors. Main rotor rpm 294-324.

ROTOR SYSTEM AND DRIVE (AH-1T): Similar to that of Bell Model 214, with strengthened main rotor hub incorporating Lord Kinematics Lastoflex elastomeric and Teflon-faced bearings. Main rotor blades have increased chord, and swept tips which reduce noise and improve high-speed performance. Tail rotor also similar to that of Model 214, with increased diameter and blade chord.

WINGS: Small mid-mounted stub-wings, to carry armament and offload rotor in flight.

FUSELAGE: Conventional all-metal semi-monocoque structure, with low silhouette and narrow profile. AH-1T has forward fuselage lengthened by insertion of a 0·305 m (1 ft 0 in) plug, to accommodate tankage for additional 181·5 kg (400 lb) of fuel, and tailboom lengthened by 0·79 m (2 ft 7 in).

TAIL UNIT: Sweptback vertical fin/tail rotor pylon, strengthened on twin-engined models to cater for increased power. Elevator, of inverted aerofoil section, mid-mounted on tailboom forward of fin.

LANDING GEAR: Non-retractable tubular skid type. Ground handling wheels optional.

POWER PLANT: Single or twin turboshaft engines, as detailed under model listings. Fuel capacity (G and J) 1,014 litres (268 US gallons). (Fuel loads, where known, are given under 'Weights' heading.) Refuelling point in port side of fuselage, aft of cockpits.

ACCOMMODATION: Crew of two in tandem, with co-pilot/gunner in front seat and pilot at rear. Crew are protected by seats and side panels of Norton Co 'Noroc' armour; other panels protect vital areas of aircraft.

SYSTEMS: Hydraulic system, with Abex pumps, for flight controls and other services. Battery-powered 28V DC electrical system. Environmental control and fire detection systems.

AVIONICS: Communications equipment in AH-1G includes AN/ARC-54/131 FM radio; AN/ARC-51 and AN/ARC-134 voice com; KY-28 secure voice system.

ARMAMENT AND OPERATIONAL EQUIPMENT (AH-1G): Initial production AH-1Gs were fitted with GAU-2B/A 7·62 mm Minigun in Emerson Electric TAT-102A undernose turret (see 1978-79 Jane's). This was superseded by an M-28 turret, able to mount either two Miniguns (each with 4,000 rds), or two M-129 40 mm grenade launchers (each with 300 rds), or one Minigun and one M-129. The Miniguns in these turrets have two rates of fire, controlled by the gunner's trigger: 1,600 rds/min for searching or registry fire, or 4,000 rds/min for attack. The M-129 fires at a single rate of 400 rds/min. Four external stores attachments under stub-wings can accommodate seventy-six 2·75 in rockets in four M-159 launchers, 28 similar rockets in four M-157 launchers, or two M-18E1 Minigun pods. An initial batch of six AH-1Gs were delivered to the US Army in December 1969 equipped with a Bell/General Electric M-35 armament subsystem. This unit consists of an M-61 six-barrel 20 mm automatic cannon on the port inboard wing station, having a firing rate of 750 rds/min. Two ammunition boxes faired flush to the fuselage below the stub-wings each accommodate 500 rds, and total installed weight of the system is 531 kg (1,172 lb). A total of 350 M-35 kits was ordered subsequently by the US Army. All wing stores are symmetrically or totally jettisonable. In normal operation, the co-pilot/gunner controls and fires the turret armament, and the pilot (aided by an M-73 adjustable reflex rocket sight) normally fires the wing stores. The pilot can fire the turreted weapons only in the stowed (ie, dead ahead) position; the turret returns to the stowed position automatically when the gunner releases his grip on the slewing switch. The gunner also has the capability to fire the wing stores if required. Other operational equipment on the AH-1G includes an M-130 chaff dispenser.

ARMAMENT (AH-1J): Electrically operated General Electric undernose turret, housing an M-197 three-barrel 20 mm weapon (a lightweight version of the M-61 cannon). A 750-rd ammunition container is located in the fuselage directly aft of the turret; firing rate is 750 rds/min, but a 16-round burst limiter is incorporated in the firing switch. Barrel length of 1·52 m (5 ft) makes it imperative that the M-197 is centralised before wing stores are fired. Gun can be tracked 110° to each side, 18° upward, and 50° downward. Four attachments under stub-wings for various loads, including LAU-68A/A (seven-tube) or LAU-61A/A (19-tube) 2·75 in rocket launchers, or M-18E1 Minigun pods. Total possible armament load 245 kg (542 lb) internal, 998 kg (2,200 lb) external.

ARMAMENT (AH-1Q): M-28 turreted weapons as for AH-1G. Anti-armour configuration involves installation of eight Hughes TOW missile containers, disposed as two two-round pods on each of the outboard underwing stations. The inboard wing stations remain available for other stores, as listed for AH-1G. In the TOW configuration, a Sperry Univac helmet sight is used by both crew members to cue the turreted weapon or the TOW stabilised sight. In addition, the co-pilot/gunner may use the 2x or 13x magnification offered by the M-65 TOW system's telescopic sight unit for turret weapon engagements.

DIMENSIONS, EXTERNAL:
Diameter of main rotor: G, J, Q, R 13·41 m (44 ft 0 in)
  T   14·63 m (48 ft 0 in)
Main rotor blade chord: G, J, Q, R 0·69 m (2 ft 3 in)
  T   0·84 m (2 ft 9 in)
Diameter of tail rotor: G, J, Q, R 2·59 m (8 ft 6 in)
  T   2·96 m (9 ft 8½ in)
Tail rotor blade chord: G, Q, R 0·21 m (8·4 in)
  J   0·29 m (11½ in)
  T   0·305 m (1 ft 0 in)
Wing span (all)   3·15 m (10 ft 4 in)
Length overall, main rotor fore and aft:
  G, Q, R   16·14 m (52 ft 11½ in)
  J   16·26 m (53 ft 4 in)
  T   17·68 m (58 ft 0 in)

Bell AH-1T improved version of the Model 209 SeaCobra for the US Marine Corps

Length of fuselage: G, J, Q, R 13·59 m (44 ft 7 in)
  T   14·68 m (48 ft 2 in)
Width of fuselage: G, Q, R   0·965 m (3 ft 2 in)
  J, T   0·98 m (3 ft 2½ in)
Height overall: G, Q, R   4·12 m (13 ft 6¼ in)
  J   4·15 m (13 ft 8 in)
Elevator span (all)   2·11 m (6 ft 11 in)
Width over skids (all)   2·13 m (7 ft 0 in)
Width over TOW missile pods:
  G, Q   3·26 m (10 ft 8¾ in)
AREAS:
Main rotor disc: G, J, Q, R 141·26 m² (1,520·53 sq ft)
  T   168·11 m² (1,809·56 sq ft)
Tail rotor disc: G, J, Q, R   5·27 m² (56·75 sq ft)
  T   6·88 m² (74·03 sq ft)
WEIGHTS:
Operating weight empty, incl amounts shown for crew, fluids, avionics and armour:
  G (404 kg; 891 lb)   2,754 kg (6,073 lb)
  J (398 kg; 877 lb)   3,294 kg (7,261 lb)
Weight empty: T   3,635 kg (8,014 lb)
Operating weight empty: T   3,904 kg (8,608 lb)
Mission fuel load:
  G (871 litres; 230 US gallons)   680 kg (1,500 lb)
  J   725 kg (1,600 lb)
Max useful load (fuel and disposable ordnance):
  J   1,144 kg (2,523 lb)
  T   2,445 kg (5,392 lb)

Mission weight: G   4,266 kg (9,407 lb)
  J   4,523 kg (9,972 lb)
Max T-O and landing weight:
  G, Q, R   4,309 kg (9,500 lb)
  J   4,535 kg (10,000 lb)
  T   6,350 kg (14,000 lb)
PERFORMANCE (at max T-O weight, ISA):
Never-exceed speed:
  G, Q, R   190 knots (352 km/h; 219 mph)
  J   180 knots (333 km/h; 207 mph)
Max level speed: G, Q 149 knots (277 km/h; 172 mph)
  J   180 knots (333 km/h; 207 mph)
Max crosswind speed for hovering:
  J   40 knots (74 km/h; 46 mph)
Max rate of climb at S/L, normal rated power:
  G, Q   375 m (1,230 ft)/min
  J   332 m (1,090 ft)/min
Service ceiling, normal rated power:
  G, Q   3,475 m (11,400 ft)
  J   3,215 m (10,550 ft)
Hovering ceiling IGE: G, Q   3,015 m (9,900 ft)
  J   3,794 m (12,450 ft)
Range with max fuel:
  G, Q, both at S/L, 8% reserves
     310 nm (574 km; 357 miles)
  J, no reserves   311 nm (577 km; 359 miles)
     (1980–81)

BELL MODEL 209 HUEYCOBRA (MODERNISED VERSION)

US Army designation: AH-1S

The AH-1S is an advanced version of the single-engined TOW-capable HueyCobra for the US Army, with upgraded power plant, gearbox, transmission and many other improvements. Current Army planning calls for the acquisition of 690 of this model by mid-1981, and the supply of an undisclosed number to Israel has been authorised. Two are being delivered to Japan in 1979-80, and will be evaluated by the JGSDF for potential large-scale procurement.

The first of a succession of US Army contracts was placed in 1975, and orders to the beginning of 1979 were as follows:

Mod AH-1S. This designation (the 'Mod' in this case indicating 'Modified') applies to 290 AH-1Gs already brought up to 'Production AH-1S' standard and redelivered to the US Army. These include the 93 AH-1Gs previously converted to AH-1Qs, which were further modified by Bell and Dornier to Mod AH-1S.

Production AH-1S. Under Step 1 of a three-step new-production programme, 100 Production AH-1S HueyCobras were built and delivered to the US Army between March 1977 and September 1978. These aircraft have a new flat-plate canopy, improved nap-of-the-earth (NOE) instrument panel layout, continental United States (CONUS) navigation equipment, radar altimeter, improved communication radios, uprated engine and

Bell Modernised AH-1S HueyCobra, fitted with the advanced rotor system designed for the Model 412

transmission, push/pull anti-torque controls, and (from the 67th aircraft onwards) new Kaman-developed composite rotor blades. First unit to receive this version, in August 1977, was the 82nd Airborne Division at Fort Bragg, North Carolina. New designation AH-1P.

Up-gun AH-1S. The next 98 new-production aircraft (Step 2) have all the improvements detailed for the Production AH-1S, plus a new universal 20/30 mm gun turret, an improved wing stores management system for the 2·75 in rockets, automatic compensation for off-axis gun firing, and a 10kVA alternator to provide the necessary additional electric power. Deliveries of this version began in September 1978 and were completed in October 1979. New designation AH-1E.

Modernised AH-1S. This version, not to be confused with the 'Mod AH-1S' referred to earlier, represents the fully-upgraded AH-1S, and became standard from the 199th new-production aircraft. To the improvements already mentioned for the two preceding stages are being added, as Step 3, a new fire control subsystem (comprising a laser rangefinder and tracker, ballistics computer, low-airspeed sensor, and pilot's head-up display), air data system, Doppler navigation system, IFF transponder, infra-red jammer, hot-metal and plume infra-red suppressor, closed-circuit refuelling, and new secure voice communications. Deliveries of the 99 Modernised AH-1S so far ordered are taking place between November 1979 and June 1981. Now designated AH-1F.

Under a $13 million contract awarded by the US Army Missile Command, Hughes Aircraft Company began the manufacture in early 1980 of 44 Laser Augmented Airborne TOW (LAAT) stabilised sights for installation in Modernised AH-1S aircraft. The very small (13 × 13 × 4 cm; 5 × 5 × 1·5 in) laser transmitter has been developed to fit within the existing sight turret of the AH-1S; initial delivery of production sights was scheduled for July 1980.

Three engineering development models of the LAAT were used for flight testing by Bell at Yuma Proving Grounds, Arizona. They demonstrated that the LAAT can significantly improve first-burst accuracy of gun and rocket fire. In use, the gunner sights a target and fires the laser. Reflected from the target, the returning beam provides accurate and almost instantaneous range information, enabling the aircraft's fire control computer to integrate range, wind and ammunition ballistics data to direct weapon firing with great accuracy.

The US Army hopes eventually to bring all of its AH-1S HueyCobras up to the full Modernised AH-1S standard over a period of about five years. Current plans envisage, first, the conversion of a further 372 AH-1Gs to Modernised AH-1S in 1979-82; the 290 'Mod AH-1S' aircraft would then be upgraded to Modernised AH-1S in 1982-83; and finally, the 100 Step 1 aircraft (in 1983-84) and 98 Step 2 aircraft (in 1984) would be brought up to the full Step 3 standard. The US National Guard is to receive 12 Modernised AH-1S from April 1981, under a US Army contract announced in July 1980.

One Modernised AH-1S was tested in 1979-80 with the standard two-blade rotor replaced by a four-blade advanced rotor of the kind used on the Bell Model 412 transport helicopter. It had achieved speeds of up to 170 knots (315 km/h; 195 mph) by February 1980.

The major differences between the standard AH-1S and earlier single-engined HueyCobras may be summarised as follows:

TYPE: Anti-armour attack helicopter.

ROTOR SYSTEM AND DRIVE: Upgraded gearbox and transmission, the latter rated at 962 kW (1,290 shp). From 67th new-production AH-1S onward, new main rotor blades of composite construction are fitted, developed by Kaman Aerospace Corporation and equipped with tungsten carbide bearing sleeves. The outer 15% of these blades, which are tolerant of damage by weapons of up to 23 mm calibre, is tapered in both chord and thickness.

FUSELAGE: Tailboom strengthened to increase survivability against weapons of up to 23 mm calibre. Entire airframe has an anti-infra-red paint finish.

POWER PLANT: One 1,342 kW (1,800 shp) Avco Lycoming T53-L-703 turboshaft engine. Closed-circuit refuelling on Modernised AH-1S.

ACCOMMODATION: New flat-plate canopy has seven planes of viewing surfaces, designed to minimise glint and reduce possibility of visual detection during nap-of-the-earth (NOE) flying; it also provides increased headroom for pilot. Improved instrument layout and lighting, compatible with use of night vision goggles. Improved, independently-operating window/door ballistic jettison system to facilitate crew escape in emergency.

SYSTEMS: 10kVA AC alternator added to electrical system. Battery-driven Abex standby pump, for use in event of main hydraulic system failure, can be used for collective pitch control and for boresighting turret and TOW missile system. Improved environmental control and fire detection systems.

AVIONICS AND EQUIPMENT: Standard lightweight avionics equipment (SLAE) includes AN/ARC-114 FM, AN/ARC-164 UHF/AM voice com, and E-Systems (Memcor Division) AN/ARC-115 VHF/AM voice com (compatible with KY-58 single-channel secure voice system). Other avionics include AN/ARN-123 CONUS navigation system with VOR/ILS receivers, glideslope, marker beacon and indicator lights (Doppler navigation system in Modernised AH-1S); HSI; VSI; radar altimeter; push/pull anti-torque controls for tail rotor; co-pilot's standby magnetic compass.

ARMAMENT AND OPERATIONAL EQUIPMENT: M-65 system with eight TOW missiles on outboard underwing stations, as in AH-1Q. Beginning with the 101st new-production AH-1S (the first 'Up-gun' example), the M-28 (7·62/40 mm) turret in earlier HueyCobras is replaced by a new electrically-powered General Electric universal turret, designed to accommodate either a

20 mm or a 30 mm weapon and to improve stand-off capability. Initially, the 20 mm M-197 three-barrel Vulcan (with 750 rds) is mounted in this turret, with the 30 mm Hughes XM-230E1 single-barrel Chain Gun (with 500 rds) scheduled for installation in mid-1981. Rate of fire of both guns is 730 rds/min. Turret position is controlled by the pilot or co-pilot/gunner through helmet sights, or by the co-pilot using the M-65 TOW missile system's telescopic sight unit. Field of fire is up to 110° to each side of aircraft, 20·5° upward and 50° downward. Also from the first 'Up-gun' AH-1S, the helicopter is equipped with a new Baldwin Electronics XM-138 wing stores management subsystem, providing the means to select and fire, singly or in groups, any one of five types of external 2·75 in rocket store. These are mounted in launchers each containing from 7 to 19 tubes, and are additional to the TOW missile capability. In addition to these installations the 199th new-built AH-1S (the first to full 'Modernised' standard) introduces a fire control subsystem which includes a Kaiser head-up display for the pilot, Teledyne Systems digital fire control computer for the turreted weapon and underwing rockets, omnidirectional airspeed system to improve cannon and rocket accuracy, Hughes laser rangefinder (accurate to 10,000 m; 32,800 ft), and AN/AAS-32 airborne laser tracker. Other operational equipment includes a Marconi Avionics air data subsystem, AN/APX-100 solid-state IFF transponder, Sanders AN/ALQ-144 infra-red jammer, suppressor for infra-red signature from engine hot metal and exhaust plume, AN/APR-39 radar warning receiver, AN/ALQ-136 radar jammer (with M-130 chaff system as backup), Perkin-Elmer laser warning receiver.

DIMENSIONS, EXTERNAL: As AH-1G except:

Main rotor blade chord (from 67th new-production AH-1S)	0·76 m (2 ft 6 in)
Tail rotor blade chord	0·29 m (11½ in)

WEIGHTS:

Operating weight empty	2,939 kg (6,479 lb)
Mission weight	4,524 kg (9,975 lb)
Max T-O and landing weight	4,535 kg (10,000 lb)

PERFORMANCE (at max T-O weight, ISA):

Never-exceed speed (TOW configuration)	170 knots (315 km/h; 195 mph)
Max level speed (TOW configuration)	123 knots (227 km/h; 141 mph)
Max rate of climb at S/L, normal rated power	494 m (1,620 ft)/min
Service ceiling, normal rated power	3,720 m (12,200 ft)
Hovering ceiling IGE	3,720 m (12,200 ft)
Range at S/L with max fuel, 8% reserves	274 nm (507 km; 315 miles)

(1980–81)

BELL MODEL 212 TWIN TWO-TWELVE
US military designation: UH-1N
Canadian military designation: CH-135

Bell announced on 1 May 1968 that the Canadian government had approved development of a twin-engined UH-1 helicopter to be powered by a Pratt & Whitney Aircraft of Canada PT6T power plant. Subsequently, the Canadian government ordered 50 of these aircraft (designated CUH-1N) for the Canadian Armed Forces, with options on 20 more. Simultaneously, orders totalling 141 aircraft for the US services were announced, comprising 79 for the US Air Force, 40 for the US Navy and 22 for the US Marine Corps, all having the designation **UH-1N**. Subsequent orders covered the delivery of 159 more UH-1Ns to the US Navy and Marine Corps in 1973-78.

Initial deliveries for the US Air Force began in 1970, and the first CUH-1N for the Canadian Armed Forces was handed over officially at Uplands Airport, Ottawa, on 3 May 1971; the Canadian order was completed one year later. Deliveries to the US Navy and US Marine Corps began during 1971. Canadian aircraft are now designated **CH-135**. Six were delivered to the air force of Bangladesh in early 1977, and the Argentinian Air Force ordered eight in 1978.

A commercial version, known as the Twin Two-Twelve, is also in full-scale production. This received FAA type certification in October 1970, and on 30 June 1971 the Two-Twelve was granted FAA Transport Type Category A certification. The Model 212 has the capability of carrying an external load of 2,268 kg (5,000 lb), and the military UH-1N a load of 1,814 kg (4,000 lb).

Bell announced in January 1973 that two Twin Two-Twelves had been modified and flown in a programme to gain IFR certification from the UK's CAA and America's FAA. Conversion of the Model 212 from VFR to IFR configuration requires a new avionics package, new instrument panel and aircraft stabilisation controls. The Model 212 has also qualified for IFR certification by the Norwegian DCA and the Canadian DoT. In June 1977, it

Bell UH-1N of Antarctic Development Squadron Six (VXE-6), US Navy

became the first helicopter FAA-certificated for single-pilot IFR operations with fixed floats.

An order for eight Model 212s, to support energy and natural resources development in China, was received in early 1979, and all were delivered by the end of the year. Operated by the Civil Air Authority of China (CAAC), they represent the first order received from the People's Republic of China by a US helicopter manufacturer.

ROTOR SYSTEM: Two-blade all-metal semi-rigid main rotor with interchangeable blades, built up of extruded aluminium spars and laminates. Stabilising bar above and at right angles to main rotor blades. Underslung feathering axis hub. Two-blade all-metal tail rotor. Main rotor blades do not fold. Rotor brake standard.

ROTOR DRIVE: Shaft drive to both main and tail rotors.

FUSELAGE: Conventional all-metal semi-monocoque structure.

TAIL SURFACE: Small fixed stabiliser on rear fuselage.

LANDING GEAR: Tubular skid type. Lock-on ground handling wheels, fixed floats and inflatable nylon float-bags optional.

POWER PLANT: Pratt & Whitney Aircraft of Canada PT6T-3 Turbo Twin Pac, comprising two PT6 turboshaft engines coupled to a combining gearbox with a single output shaft. Producing 1,342 kW (1,800 shp), the Twin Pac is flat rated to 962 kW (1,290 shp) for T-O and 842 kW (1,130 shp) for continuous operation. In the event of an engine failure, the remaining engine can deliver 671 kW (900 shp) for 30 minutes or 596 kW (800 shp) continuously. Five interconnected rubber fuel cells, total capacity 814 litres (215 US gallons). Auxiliary fuel tanks optional, to provide a max total capacity of 1,495 litres (395 US gallons). Single-point refuelling on starboard side of cabin.

ACCOMMODATION: Pilot and up to 14 passengers. In cargo configuration there is a total internal volume of 7·02 m³ (248 cu ft), including baggage space in tailboom. Forward door on each side of fuselage, opening forward. Two doors on each side of cabin; forward door hinged to open forward, rear door sliding aft. Accommodation heated and ventilated. Garrett-AiResearch air-cycle environmental control unit available optionally.

SYSTEMS: Dual hydraulic systems. 28V DC electrical system supplied by two completely independent 30V 200A starter/generators. Secondary AC power supplied by two completely independent 250VA single-phase solid-state inverters. A third inverter can acquire automatically the load of a failed inverter.

AVIONICS AND EQUIPMENT: Optional IFR avionics include dual King KTR 900A com transceivers; dual King KNR 660A VOR/LOC/RMI receivers; King KDF 800 ADF; King KMD 700A DME; King KXP 750A transponder; King KGM 690 marker beacon/glideslope receiver; dual Sperry Tarsyn-444 three-axis gyro units; stability control augmentation system; and an automatic flight control system. Optional equipment includes a cargo sling, rescue hoist, emergency pop-out flotation gear and high skid gear.

DIMENSIONS, EXTERNAL:
Diameter of main rotor (with tracking tips)
    14·69 m (48 ft 2¼ in)
Diameter of tail rotor   2·59 m (8 ft 6 in)
Main rotor blade chord   0·59 m (1 ft 11¼ in)
Tail rotor blade chord   0·292 m (11½ in)
Length overall (main rotor fore and aft)
    17·46 m (57 ft 3¼ in)
Length of fuselage   12·92 m (42 ft 4¾ in)
Height overall   4·53 m (14 ft 10¼ in)
Width overall (main rotor fore and aft)
    2·86 m (9 ft 4½ in)

AREAS:
Main rotor disc   168·06 m² (1,809 sq ft)
Tail rotor disc   5·27 m² (56·74 sq ft)
WEIGHTS:
VFR empty weight plus usable oil
    2,787 kg (6,143 lb)
Max T-O weight and mission weight
    5,080 kg (11,200 lb)
PERFORMANCE (at max T-O weight):
Never-exceed speed at S/L
    140 knots (259 km/h; 161 mph)
Max cruising speed at S/L
    124 knots (230 km/h; 142 mph)
Max rate of climb at S/L   402 m (1,320 ft)/min
Service ceiling   4,330 m (14,200 ft)
Hovering ceiling IGE   3,350 m (11,000 ft)
Max range with standard fuel at S/L, no reserves
    227 nm (420 km; 261 miles)
    (1980–81)

THE BELL AIRACOBRA.
U.S. Army Air Forces designation: P-39.
British name : Aircobra.

The first contract for the P-39 was awarded by the U.S. Army on September 13, 1939. The original XP-39 was fitted with the Allison V-1710-17 engine and a turbo-supercharger but this aeroplane was modified at Wright Field and Langley Field to become the XP-39B. In this model the turbo-super-charger was removed, the cabin was lowered and a turn-over beam and numerous minor changes were added. Thirteen YB-39B's were ordered for service trials.

P-39C. One Allison V-1710-35 (E4) engine rated at 1,150 h.p. at 12,000 ft. (3,660 m.) and with the same power available for take-off. The first combat model and essentially the same as the YP-39B. First flew in 1941. Armament consisted of one 37 m/m. cannon (15 rounds) and two 50 cal. (200 rounds each) and two 30 cal. machine-guns (500 rounds each), all in the fuselage and synchronised to fire through the airscrew. Leakproof fuel tanks and pilot armour added.

Aircobra I and IA. The P-400 export version contracted for by the French Government and taken over by the British Government on the fall of France. Substantially the same as the P-39C except that a 20 m/m. cannon (60 rounds) was substituted for the 37 m/m. weapon and the two 30 cal. fuselage guns were replaced by two unsynchronised 30 cal. guns (1,000 rounds each) in the wings. The Aircobra I first went in action with the R.A.F. in October, 1941, but was withdrawn from service after a few missions. When the United States entered the war the undelivered balance of the British contracts was taken over by the U.S. Army and these aircraft were given the U.S. Army designation P-400 and used for training. A total of 336 of this model was delivered.

P-39D. One Allison V-1710-35 engine. The first of the P-39 Series to go into quantity production for the U.S. Army Air Forces. Except that the P-39D had a 37 m/m. cannon (30 rounds) instead of the 20 m/m. weapon, it was substantially the same as the R.A.F. Airacobra. The first model to carry an auxiliary fuel tank (75 U.S. gallons) under the fuselage. 429 were built. A later contract for 158 of the same type but with an Allison V-1710-63 (E6) with a 2 : 1 airscrew reduction gear ratio was designated the P-39D-2.

XP-39E. One Allison V-1710-47 (E9) engine. An experimental model with re-designed square-cut wings and tail surfaces. Span 35 ft. 10 in. (10.91 m.).

P-39F. Similar to the P-39D but fitted with an Aeroproducts hydraulically-operated constant-speed airscrew instead of a Curtiss Electric airscrew. 229 were built.

P-39K. One Allison V-1710-63 (E6) single-stage low-altitude engine rated at 1,150 h.p. at 12,000 ft. (3,660 m.) and with 1,325 h.p. available for take-off. Aeroproducts airscrew. An additional 15 rounds of 50 cal. ammunition for each of the sychronised fuselage guns. 210 were built.

P-39L. Similar to the P-39K except that a Curtiss Electric airscrew was used and a new low-profile nose wheel was introduced. 250 were delivered.

P-39M. One Allison V-1710-83 (E18) single-stage high-altitude engine rated at 1,125 h.p. at 15,500 ft. (4,730 m.) and with 1,200 h.p. available for take-off. Curtiss Electric airscrew 10 ft. 4½ in. (3.14 m.) diameter. 240 were built.

P-39N. One Allison V-1710-85 (E19) engine with different airscrew reduction gear ratio. Same rating as E18. Aeroproducts airscrew 11 ft. 7 in. (3.52 m.) diameter. At the request of the A.A.F. certain fuel cells were removed to lighten the aeroplane, leaving a fuel capacity of 86 U.S. gallons instead of the former standard 120 U.S. gallons. 500 P-39N-0, 900 P-39N-1, which incorporated several minor changes, and 695 P-39N-5, which had a curved armour head plate in place of the bullet-proof glass behind the pilot, were built.

A Bell P-63A Kingcobra and a P-39Q Airacobra. The differences between these two fighters is well shown in this photograph.

The Bell **P-39Q** Airacobra Single-seat Fighter (Allison V-1710-85 engine).

P-39Q. One Allison V-1710-85 engine and Aeroproducts airscrew. This model carried the first armament change since the P-39D. The 30 cal. wing guns were replaced by two 50 cal. guns mounted in external blisters, one under each wing. Later minor revisions of equipment carried the P-39Q through the Q-5, Q-10, Q-20, Q-21, Q-25 and Q-30 sub-series. A four-bladed Aeroproducts airscrew replaced the three-blader in the Q-21 and Q-25. The internal fuel capacity was increased from 86 to 110 U.S. gallons in the P-39Q-5 and further increased to 120 U.S. gallons in the Q-10. Various other models were provided with different auxiliary fuel tanks for ferrying purposes, the largest having a capacity of 250 U.S. gallons. The description that follows refers to the P-39Q, of which over 4,900 were built.

Production of the Airacobra ceased in July, 1944. Of a total of 9,584 built, approximately 5,000 were supplied to Russia under Lend/Lease.

TYPE.—Single-seat Fighter.

WINGS.—Low-wing cantilever monoplane. Wing section NACA 0015 at root and modified NACA 23009 at tip. Centre-section integral with forward fuselage. Tapering outer-sections have three spars, front, rear and auxiliary, the front and rear spars having extended aluminium booms and sheet webs and the auxiliary spar formed cap strips and solid web. Pressed and beaded aluminium ribs and bulkheads, Z-section spanwise stringers and a flush-riveted smooth aluminium skin. Ailerons, which have metal frames with fabric covering, are differentially-controlled and have modified Frise type nose balance and Venturi-shaped slot. Controllable trimming-tabs in ailerons. These tabs also act as a servo control through a mechanical linkage which automatically rotates them to an angle opposite to the movement of the ailerons. Additional servo tabs not controlled by the pilot are located just outboard of the controllable tabs. Electrically-operated trailing-edge flaps between ailerons and fuselage.

FUSELAGE.—Oval all-metal structure in two sections. Forward section consists primarily of two main longitudinal beams with a horizontal upper deck between and extends from the nose to the bulkhead aft of the engine which is installed inside the fuselage aft of the pilot's cockpit. The fuselage covering above the main beams is in the form of detachable cowling to give easy access to engine, cockpit, armament and radio equipment. The aft section is a metal monocoque.

TAIL UNIT.—Cantilever monoplane type. Fixed surfaces are all-metal and movable surfaces have metal frames and fabric covering. Trimming-tabs in all movable surfaces controllable from cockpit.

LANDING GEAR.—Retractable tricycle type. Electrical retraction with emergency hand gear. Main wheels are raised inwardly into wells in underside of wings aft of the main spar structure. Castoring nose wheel is raised aft into fuselage. Hydraulic suspension to all wheels. Hydraulic multiple disc brakes to main wheels.

POWER PLANT.—One 1,200 h.p. Allison V-1710-85 twelve-cylinder Vee Prestone-cooled engine mounted within the fuselage aft of the pilot's cockpit and driving a tractor airscrew through an extension shaft and remote 2.23 : 1 reduction gear box. Aeroproducts three or four-blade hydraulically controlled constant-speed airscrew 11 ft. 7 in. (3.54 m.) diameter. Coolant radiator in centre-section beneath engine, with two separate air ducts in leading-edge of centre-section and single controllable exit beneath fuselage. Two oil coolers in after portion of centre-section, one on each side of fuselage, with air ducts in leading-edge outboard of coolant air ducts. Two fuel tanks (60 U.S. gallons each), each comprising six leak-proof bags, integrally built in outer wing sections. Droppable auxiliary fuel tank of either 75 or 175 U.S. gallons capacity may be carried beneath centre-section. Engine oil tank (13.8 U.S. gallons) in fuselage aft of engine. Separate reduction-gear oil system in nose of fuselage.

ACCOMMODATION.—Enclosed cockpit over leading-edge of wing. Two outward-swinging doors, one on each side of cabin, the one on the starboard side for normal entrance and exit. Both doors have quickly-releasable hinge-pins operated either inside or out for emergency use. Both doors have roll-down windows. Fume-

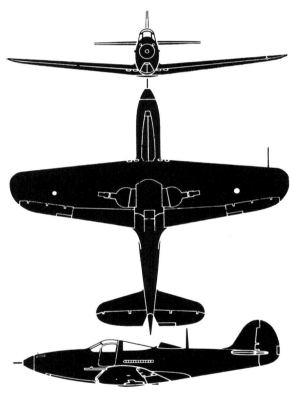

The Bell **P-39** Airacobra Single-seat Fighter.

proof bulkheads between armament compartment and pilot's cabin and between cabin and engine compartment. Cabin heating and ventilation. Armour in nose ahead of airscrew gear-box, on bulkhead ahead of pilot, at pilot's back, ahead of engine accessory compartment and aft of oil tank. Bullet-proof windshield.

ARMAMENT AND EQUIPMENT.—One 37 m/m. cannon on fuselage centreline and firing through gear box and airscrew hub, two 50 cal. machine-guns in forward fuselage and synchronised to fire through airscrew and two 50 cal. guns in fairings under the outer wings and firing outside the airscrew disc. All guns electrically fired. One 500 lb. bomb may be carried under the fuselage on the same shackles as the auxiliary fuel tank. Remotely-controlled two-way radio and storage battery in aft section of fuselage. Radio antenna enclosed in transparent plastic leading-edge of the vertical fin. Full electrical and oxygen equipment.

DIMENSIONS.—Span 34 ft. (10.37 m.), Length 30 ft. 2 in. (9.2 m.), Height to top of airscrew (one blade vertical) 11 ft. 10 in. (3.63 m.), Wing area 213 sq. ft. (19.8 sq. m.).

WEIGHTS AND LOADINGS.—Weight empty 5,968 lbs. (2,709 kg.), Weight loaded 8,052 lbs. (3,656 kg.), Wing loading 37.76 lbs./sq. ft. (184.26 kg./sq. m.).

PERFORMANCE (P-39Q).—Maximum speed 385 m.p.h. (606 km.h.) at 11,000 ft. (3,355 m.), Climb to 15,000 ft. (4,575 m.) 4.5 min., Service ceiling 35,000 ft. (10,670 m.), Range (with external auxiliary tank) 675 miles (1,080 km.) at 240 m.p.h. (384 km.h.). or 1,475 miles (2,360 km.) at 160 m.p.h. (256 km.h.). (1945–46)

The B/J OJ-2 Two-seat Observation Biplane (400 h.p. Pratt & Whitney "Wasp-Junior" engine).

THE B/J OJ-2.

TYPE.—Two-seat naval observation biplane.

WINGS.—Single-bay staggered biplane. Top centre-section carried above fuselage by widely-splayed "N" struts, with one "N"-type interplane strut on either side of the fuselage. Wing structure follows conventional wood box-spar and rib construction, with fabric covering and leading-edge covered with sheet duralumin. "Frise" ailerons on all four wings. This machine is also available with Zap flap and Zap aileron installation, which reduces the landing speed by approximately 25 per cent.

FUSELAGE.—Rectangular welded steel-tube structure, faired to an oval section and covered with fabric on rear and metal on front portion.

TAIL UNIT.—Normal monoplane type. Duralumin framework, with fabric covering. Adjustable tail-plane. Balanced rudder.

UNDERCARRIAGE.—Split type landing gear. Consists of two side Vees, with rigid bracing between the rear legs of the Vees. Oleo springing. Wheel-brakes. Swivelling tail-wheel. The land undercarriage may be replaced by a long single central float of duralumin construction and two duralumin wing-tip stabilising floats. The central float is specially strengthened for catapulting.

POWER PLANT.—One 400 h.p. Pratt & Whitney "Wasp-Junior" radial air-cooled engine. Fuel tanks in fuselage. Townend low-drag engine cowling.

ACCOMMODATION.—Tandem open or closed cockpits, with full equipment for Naval observation work. Arresting gear for deck landing. Armament consisting of one gun firing forward through the airscrew and another gun on a low-drag swivelling mounting over the back cockpit. The rear gun is stowed in the fuselage cowling when not in use. Bomb-racks for 250 or 500 lbs. of bombs can be fitted.

DIMENSIONS.—Span (upper) 33 ft. 8 in. (10.28 m.), Span (lower) 30 ft. 8 in. (9.35 m.), Length 25 ft. 8 in. (7.84 m.), Height 10 ft. 10 in. (3.30 m.), Wing area 284.2 sq. ft. (30.55 sq. m.).

WEIGHTS AND LOADINGS.—Weight empty 2,323 lbs. (1,058 kg.), Useful load 1,390 lbs. (631 kg.), Weight loaded 3,713 lbs. (1,688 kg.), Wing loading 13.1 lbs./sq. ft. (63.9 kg./sq. m.), Power loading 8 9 lbs /h.p. (4.05 kg./h.p.).

PERFORMANCE.—Maximum speed 154 m.p.h. (248 km.h.), Speed at 5,000 ft. (1,525 m.) 150 m.p.h. (242 km.h.), Speed at 10,000 ft. (3,050 m.) 142 m.p.h. (228 km.h.), Speed at 15,000 ft. (4,575 m.) 121 m.p.h. (195 km.h.), Stalling speed 57 m.p.h. (92 km.h.), Initial rate of climb 1,350 ft./min. (411 m./min.), Climb to 10,000 ft. (3,050 m.) 12.1 mins., Service ceiling 15,300 ft. (4,660 m.), Absolute ceiling 16,700 ft. (5,090 m.), Range at cruising speed 530 miles (854 km.).

(1934)

The B/J P-16 Fighter Biplane (600 h.p. Curtiss "Conqueror" engine).

THE B/J P-16 (PB-1)

TYPE.—Two-seat fighter

WINGS.—Unequal-span single-bay staggered biplane. Top and bottom wings attached to small roots which spring from the top and bottom edges of the rectangular fuselage. Wing structure is metal, with fabric covering. Duralumin "wandering-web" type spars, girder type ribs of duralumin tubing, duralumin tube drag-bracing, and sheet duralumin leading-edge. Skew type ailerons, with "Frise" balance on top wings only. Ailerons of metal construction.

FUSELAGE.—Rectangular structure, of welded steel-tube, with fabric covering over light fairing.

TAIL UNIT.—Normal monoplane type. Metal framework, with fabric covering. Adjustable tail-plane.

UNDERCARRIAGE.—Split type. Consists of two side Vees, the front legs of which incorporate oleo springing, and two crossed axles. Bendix wheels and brakes.

POWER PLANT.—One 600 h.p. Curtiss "Conqueror" twelve-cylinder Prestone-cooled engine, with small tunnel-type radiator beneath. Main fuel tank, of 85 U.S. gallons capacity, in the fuselage, with an auxiliary droppable tank, of 75 U.S. gallons capacity, carried below the fuselage. Wright "Cyclone" or Pratt & Whitney

"Hornet" radial air-cooled engines may be installed in place of the liquid-cooled Curtiss "Conqueror" engine.

ACCOMMODATION.—Tandem open cockpits behind the wings. Standard equipment for U.S. Army two-seat pursuit, including oxygen, is carried. Armament consists of two fixed guns firing forward through the airscrew, and one gun on a flexible mounting over the rear cockpit. Bomb-racks below the bottom wings.

DIMENSIONS.—Span 34 ft. (10.37 m.), Length 28 ft. 10 in. (8.8 m.), Chord (top) 6 ft. (1.83 m.), Chord (bottom) 4 ft. (1.22 m.), Stagger 2 ft. 9 in. (0.838 m.), Wing area 250 sq. ft. (23.2 sq. m.).

WEIGHTS.—Weight empty 3,190 lbs. (1,448 kg.), Weight loaded 4,209 lbs. (1,911 kg.), Wing loading 16.35 lbs./sq. ft. (79.8 kg./sq. m.), Power loading 6.82 lbs./h.p. (3.09 kg./h.p.).

PERFORMANCE.—Speed at sea level 170 m.p.h. (272 km.h.), Speed at 5,000 ft. (1,525 m.) 183 m.p.h. (292.8 km.h.), Speed at 12,000 ft. (3,660 m.) 200 m.p.h. (320 km.h.), Speed at 15,000 ft. (4,575 m.) 192 m.p.h. (307 km.h.), Speed at 20,000 ft. (6,100 m.) 178 m.p.h. (285 km.h.), Initial rate of climb 1,600 ft./min. (488 m./min.), Climb to 5,000 ft. (1,525 m.) 2.9 mins., Climb to 12,000 ft. (3,660 m.) 6.9 mins., Climb to 15,000 ft. (4,575 m.) 8.8 mins., Climb to 20,000 ft. (6,100 m.) 12.4 mins., Service ceiling 29,000 ft. (8,845 m.), Absolute ceiling 30,000 ft. (9,150 m.). (1933)

BOEING C AND C-1F

Follow testing of the Model C-5 and C-6, the US Navy ordered 50 two-seat trainers as Model Cs (C-650–699) plus one C-1F single-seat seaplane. Model Cs used the 100 hp Hall-Scott A-7A engine. All were delivered in 1918.

Span, upper	43 ft 10 in	Weight loaded	2,395 lb
Wing area	49 sq ft	High speed	72 mph
Length	27 ft	Range	200 miles
Height	12 ft 7 in	Endurance	3 hours

BOEING FB-1

Almost identical to USAAS PW-9s, the USMC received ten FB-1s by December 1925 as land-based fighters. Nine flew with the Expeditionary Force in China during 1927–28.

A modified version became the FB-3 (only three built), in official trials attaining the remarkable speed of 187 mph. A later production development was the FB-5, of which 27 were delivered from 1926, operating with the Navy (finally with the USMC) from USS *Langley* and *Lexington*.

THE BOEING FB-3.

The Boeing FB-3 is a further modification of the PW-9A, and was produced for the U.S. Navy as a deck-landing fighter easily convertible to a twin-float seaplane fighter. It is fitted with the Packard 2A-1500 engine. Overall dimensions are the same as for the PW-9A. (1927)

The Boeing FB-3 Single-seat Shipboard Fighter (500 h.p. Packard engine).

THE BOEING FB-5.

The Boeing FB-5 is the production model of the FB-3. The principal modifications include increased stagger, a balanced rudder, a cross-axle undercarriage for the attachment of deck-landing hooks, in place of the split-type undercarriage.

TYPE.—Single-seat convertible land or seaplane shipboard fighter.

WINGS.—Single-bay staggered biplane of unequal span and chord. Top plane in one piece. Wings taper in plan and thickness from centre to tips. Top plane is carried above fuselage by struts running from both top and bottom fuselage longerons, with one set of "N" type interplane struts on either side of fuselage. Wing construction of wood, covered with fabric. Narrow chord ailerons on top plane only.

FUSELAGE.—Metal structure, covered with fabric.

TAIL UNIT.—Normal type. Metal framed, covered with fabric. Balanced rudder. Adjustable tail-plane.

UNDERCARRIAGE.—Cross-axle Vee type. Consists of two Vees, incorporating Boeing oleo suspension in the apices and divided cross-axle, which is braced in centre by transverse Vee. Axle fitted with deck-landing hooks. Land undercarriage interchangeable with twin metal floats of the long, single-step type.

POWER PLANT.—One 510 h.p. Packard 2A-1500 water-cooled engine. Radiator under engine, in tunnel equipped with shutters. Main fuel tank in fuselage. Auxiliary tank, of streamline shape, may be slung under fuselage, behind tunnel radiator. This tank is droppable in emergency. Standard steel metal airscrew.

ACCOMMODATION.—Pilot's cockpit aft of trailing-edge of top plane. Armament consists of two .30 calibre Browning guns, mounted on cowling and firing through airscrew.

DIMENSIONS.—Span (top) 32 ft. (9.75 m.), Span (bottom) 22 ft. 5¾ in. (6.85 m.), Chord (max. top) 6 ft. (1.83 m.), chord (max. bottom) 5 ft. (1.52 m.), Length 23 ft. 2¾ in. (7.08 m.), Height 9 ft. 4¾ in. (2.86 m.). (1928)

The Boeing FB-3 single-seat Fighter Seaplane (425 h.p. Pratt & Whitney "Wasp" engine).

THE BOEING F2B-1.

TYPE.—Single-seat convertible landplane or seaplane fighter, for Naval duties.

WINGS.—Unequal winged single-bay biplane, with wings tapering in plan form only. Top plane in one piece, with bottom wing in three sections, the centre-section being a permanent part of the fuselage. One set of "N" type duralumin interplane struts on either side of fuselage. Wings built up of two box spars of spruce flanges and three-ply birch webs, with the grain of the plywood webs running at 45° with the axis of the spars. Ribs are of the Warren truss type, of spruce and plywood. Interplane bracing in the plane of the front spars only.

FUSELAGE.—Welded steel-tube structure, braced with duralumin struts and swaged wire. All fuselage struts forward of pilot's cockpit of steel and those aft of duralumin. The bottom wing struts are built integral with the fuselage, and form the support for the undercarriage.

TAIL UNIT.—Normal type. Of duralumin and steel construction, covered with fabric. Fin and rudder built round steel tubes, with duralumin ribs. Tail plane and elevators entirely of duralumin. Adjustable tail plane and fin, the latter on the ground only.

UNDERCARRIAGE.—Split type. Consists of two Vees, the front legs of which are telescopic and incorporate the Boeing oleo shock-absorbing units, and two axles, which are hinged to the centre-line of the underside of the fuselage, in line with the back legs of the side Vees. Tail-skid equipped with a shoe, which is easily converted for either deck or field landing. Single central metal float of the long single-step type and two wing-tip floats can be fitted in place of land undercarriage.

POWER PLANT.—One 425 h.p. Pratt & Whitney "Wasp" air-cooled radial engine. Main fuel tank, of 50 U.S. gallons (42 Imp. galls. = 189 litres) capacity, in fuselage, with an additional tank of the same capacity, which can be slung under the fuselage. This tank is of streamline shape and can be dropped in emergency. Oil tank of 8 U.S. gallons (6.6 Imp. galls. = 30 litres) capacity, in fuselage. Eclipse inertia hand-starter and Standard Steel adjustable pitch metal airscrew.

ACCOMMODATION.—One cockpit behind cut-out in trailing-edge of top wing. Armament consists of either two .30 calibre or one .30 calibre and one .50 calibre Browning guns, firing through the airscrew. Seat is designed for either back or seat-type parachute.

DIMENSIONS.—Span (top) 30 ft. 1 in. (9.17 m.), Span (bottom) 24 ft. 3 in. (7.39 m.), Length (landplane) 23 ft. (7.01 m.), Height (landplane) 8 ft. 9½ in. (2.68 m.), Wing area 242 sq. ft. (22.7 sq. m.).

WEIGHTS AND LOADINGS (LANDPLANE).—Weight empty 1,900 lbs. (864 kg.), Weight loaded 2,690 lbs. (1,223 kg.), Wing loading 11.15 lbs./sq. ft. (54 kg./sq. m.), Power loading 6.33 lbs./h.p. (2.88 kg./h.p.).

PERFORMANCE (LANDPLANE).—Maximum speed 160 m.p.h. (258 km.h.), Stalling speed 55 m.p.h. (88 km.h.), Climb in 10 mins. 13,000 ft. (3,961 m.), Service ceiling 21,000 ft. (6,398 m.), Range at full speed 215 miles (345 km.), Range at cruising speed 358 miles (577 km.). (1929)

The Boeing F3B-1 Fighter Seaplane (425 h.p. Pratt & Whitney "Wasp" engine).

The United States Aircraft-carrier "Saratoga" leading the Battle Fleet South for a cruise with F3B-1 and other aircraft on board.

THE BOEING F3B-1.

TYPE.—Single-seat convertible land or seaplane shipboard fighter.

WINGS.—Unequal biplane, with backswept top plane. Top plane in one piece, carried above fuselage on splayed-out centre-section struts. One set of splayed-out "N" type interplane struts on either side of fuselage. Ailerons fitted to top plane only. Wings of wooden construction.

FUSELAGE.—Welded steel-tube structure, with swaged-rod internal bracing. Fuselage specially strengthened to withstand catapult loads.

TAIL UNIT.—Normal type. Duralumin construction covered with corrugated duralumin sheet. Adjustable tail-plane.

UNDERCARRIAGE.—Cross-axle type. Consists of two Vees attached to bottom longerons of fuselage, with Boeing type oleo units incorporated in the apices of the Vees. The divided cross-axle is braced laterally by a steel-tube Vee, thus eliminating all wire bracing. Land undercarriage interchangeable with single central duralumin float and two wing-tip floats. Emergency flotation bags provided. Float gear specially designed for catapulting from standard U.S. Navy catapults. Details of land undercarriage deck-arresting gear are not available, but are believed to consist of dog-leash catches on cross-axle and shepherd's crook at aft end of fuselage, to pick up cross-wires on carrier's deck.

POWER PLANT.—One 425 h.p. Pratt & Whitney "Wasp" radial air-cooled engine. Engine cowling provided with adjustable shutters. Main fuel tank in fuselage and an auxiliary fuel tank provided in top plane for use on special operations. Standard Steel metal airscrew.

ACCOMMODATION.—Pilot's cockpit aft of wings. Details of armament not disclosed, but believed to consist of two synchronised machine guns, firing through the airscrew. Pilot's seat is adjustable for height, to facilitate deck-landing, and adjustable rudder pedals are provided.

DIMENSIONS.—Span (top) 33 ft. (9.76 m.), Span (bottom) 26 ft. 7¼ in. (8.1 m.), Length 29 ft. (8.84 m.), Chord (max. top) 5 ft. 9 in. (1.75 m.), Chord (max. bottom) 4 ft. 6 in. (1.37 m.), Height 10 ft. 3¼ in. (3.13 m.). (1929)

THE BOEING F4B-1.

TYPE.—Single-seat shipboard fighter.

WINGS.—Single-bay staggered biplane. Top plane, in one piece, carried above fuselage by two sets of "N" type struts. One set of "N" type interplane struts on either side of the fuselage. Skew ailerons fitted to top plane only. Wings of all-wood construction.

FUSELAGE.—Constructed of duralumin tubes covered with fabric.

TAIL UNIT.—Normal type. Constructed of duralumin and covered with corrugated duralumin sheet.

UNDERCARRIAGE.—Normal Vee cross-axle type, for deck-landing purposes. Wheel undercarriage interchangeable with single central float and two wing-tip floats, suitable for catapult work.

POWER PLANT.—One Pratt & Whitney geared radial air-cooled engine, developing 500 (rated) h.p. at 2,100 r.p.m. When fitted with supercharger, this will increase at high altitudes to about 625 h.p. Nose cowling provided with adjustable shutters for temperature control at altitudes. All cylinders fitted with streamline nose and tail-pieces. High-pitch airscrew, providing maximum engine efficiency at altitude.

ACCOMMODATION.—Pilot's cockpit behind wings. Fuselage narrow and sloping forward from cockpit to nose, providing excellent view for deck-landing and fighting.

DIMENSIONS.—Span 30 ft. (9.15 m.), Length 20 ft. 3 in. (6.17 m.).

WEIGHTS.—Weight empty 1,634 lbs. (746.8 kg.).

PERFORMANCE (approximate).—Maximum speed (low down) 184 m.p.h. (294.4 km.h.), Speed at 5,000 ft. (1,525 m.) 200 m.p.h. (320 km.h.), Climb to 18,000 ft. (5,490 m.) 10 mins., Ceiling 30,000 ft. (9,150 m.). (1929)

THE BOEING F4B-2

Following 27 F4B-1s (delivered in 1929), 46 F4B-2s were received by the Navy in 1931. Although similar to the Army's P-12C, they were restressed and could carry four 116 lb bombs as fighter-bombers. Used on board USS *Lexington* and *Saratoga*. 450 hp Pratt & Whitney R-1340-8 Wasp. Normal take-off weight 2,793 lb and high speed 186 mph. Twenty-one F4B-3s and 92 F4B-4s followed, 21 of the latter for the USMC.

THE BOEING F4B-3.

TYPE.—Single-seat high-performance fighter.

WINGS.—Wings consist of one upper panel and two lower panels. One "N"-type interplane strut on either side of fuselage. Both the interplane and centre-section struts are of streamlined duralumin tubing, with riveted terminal fittings. The wing structure consists of two built-up box spars of spruce and plywood, with Warren girder type ribs of the same materials. Ailerons, of the "Frise" type, are on the top wing only. These are of duralumin construction and covered with corrugated duralumin sheet. The external interplane bracing is of streamlined wire. There are double flying wires from the upper spars to the body and double landing wires from the upper fuselage longeron to the lower front spar. Emergency flotation gear is located in the upper wing.

FUSELAGE.—The main fuselage structure forward of the front lower wing spar is of welded chrome-molybdenum steel tubing, metal cowled. Fuselage aft of this is of duralumin semi-monocoque construction. The engine-mounting is of welded chrome-molybdenum tubing and is not detachable.

TAIL UNIT.—Monoplane type, of metal construction, covered with corrugated duralumin sheet. The tail-plane is adjustable in flight, and the fin is adjustable on the ground. Balanced elevators.

UNDERCARRIAGE.—Cross-axle Vee type, equipped with Boeing oleo type shock-absorbers and brakes. The side loads are taken by a transverse steel-tube Vee from the centre of the axle to the fuselage. Steerable tail-wheel equipped with oleo shock-absorbers.

The Boeing F4B-3 Single-seat Fighter Biplane (500 h.p. Pratt & Whitney "Wasp" engine).

POWER PLANT.—One 500 h.p. Pratt & Whitney supercharged "Wasp" radial air-cooled engine. One main 55 U.S. gallon fuel tank in fuselage and one 55 U.S. gallon auxiliary fuel tank under fuselage. The auxiliary tank is droppable in flight. There is a 7-gallon oil tank of welded aluminium sheet.

ACCOMMODATION.—Single-seat cockpit aft of the trailing-edge of the wings. The pilot's seat has 4 inches vertical adjustment. Armament consists of two .30 calibre Browning synchronised machine-guns, or one .30 calibre and one .50 calibre Browning gun. Special bomb rack with bomb-displacing gear for two 116-lb. bombs is provided under the fuselage. Provision is made for 1,200 rounds of .30 calibre ammunition or 600 rounds of .30 calibre and 200 of .50 calibre ammunition. Equipment includes a wireless receiver, transmitter and generator, with a radio mast mounted abaft the pilot's cockpit.

DIMENSIONS.—Span (upper) 30 ft. (9.13 m.), Span (lower) 26 ft. in. (8.02 m.), Length 20 ft. 41/16 in. (6.2 m.), Height 9 ft. 9 3/32 in. (2.9 m.), Wing area 227.5 sq. ft. (21.1 sq. m.).

WEIGHTS AND LOADINGS.—Weight empty 2,123 lbs. (964 kg.), Disposable load (for bomber) 1,068 lbs. (485 kg.), Disposable load (for fighter) 716.1 lbs. (325 kg.), Weight loaded (for fighter) 2,839 lbs. (1,289 kg.), Weight loaded (for bomber with two 116-lb. bombs) 3,191.6 lbs. (1,449 kg.), Wing loading 12.48 lbs./sq. ft. (60.9 kg./sq. m.), Power loading (450 h.p.) 6.31 lbs./h.p. (2.86 kg./h.p.).

PERFORMANCE (normal carrier fighter).—Speed at sea level 167 m.p.h. (267.2 km.h.), Speed at 6,000 ft. (19,680 m.) 187 m.p.h. (299.2 km.h.), Landing speed 61 m.p.h. (97.6 km.h.), Initial rate of climb 1,980 ft./min. (604 m./min.), Climb to 15,000 ft. (4,575 m.) 9.5 mins., Service ceiling 27,500 ft. (8,387.5 m.). (1932)

THE BOEING F4B-4.

TYPE.—Single-seat high-performance fighter.

WINGS.—Wings consist of one upper panel and two lower panels. One "N"-type interplane strut on either side of fuselage. Both the interplane and centre-section struts are of streamlined duralumin tubing, with riveted terminal fittings. The wing structure consists of two built-up box spars of spruce and plywood, with Warren girder type ribs of the same materials. Ailerons, of the "Frise" type, are on the top wing only. These are of duralumin construction and covered with corrugated duralumin sheet. The external interplane bracing is of streamlined wire. There are double flying wires from the upper spars to the body and double landing wires from the upper fuselage longeron to the lower front spar. Emergency flotation gear is located in the upper wing.

FUSELAGE.—The main fuselage structure forward of the front lower wing spar is of welded chrome-molybdenum steel tubing, metal cowled. Fuselage aft of this is of duralumin semi-monocoque construction. The engine-mounting is of welded chrome-molybdenum tubing and is not detachable.

TAIL UNIT.—Monoplane type, of metal construction, covered with corrugated duralumin sheet. The tail-plane is adjustable in flight, and the fin is adjustable on the ground. Balanced elevators.

The Boeing F4B-4 Single-seat Fighter Biplane (500 h.p. Pratt & Whitney "Wasp" engine).

UNDERCARRIAGE.—Cross-axle Vee type, equipped with Boeing oleo type shock-absorbers and brakes. The side loads are taken by a transverse steel-tube Vee from the centre of the axle to the fuselage. Steerable tail-wheel equipped with oleo shock-absorbers.

POWER PLANT.—One 500 h.p. Pratt & Whitney supercharged "Wasp" radial air-cooled engine. One main 55 U.S. gallon fuel tank in fuselage and one 55 U.S. gallon auxiliary fuel tank under fuselage. The auxiliary tank is droppable in flight. There is a 7-gallon oil tank of welded aluminium sheet.

ACCOMMODATION.—Single-seat cockpit aft of the trailing-edge of the wings. The pilot's seat has 4 inches vertical adjustment. Armament consists of two .30 calibre Browning synchronised machine-guns, or one .30 calibre and one .50 calibre Browning gun. Special bomb rack with bomb-displacing gear for two 116-lb. bombs is provided under the fuselage. Provision is made for 1,200 rounds of .30 calibre ammunition or 600 rounds of .30 calibre and 200 of .50 calibre ammunition. Equipment includes a wireless receiver, transmitter and generator, with a radio mast mounted abaft the pilot's cockpit.

DIMENSIONS.—Span (upper) 30 ft. (9.13 m.), Span (lower) 26 ft. 4in. (8.02 m.), Length 20 ft. $4\frac{11}{16}$ in. (6.2 m.), Height 9 ft. $9\frac{3}{32}$ in. (2.9 m.), Wing area 227.5 sq. ft. (21.1 sq. m.).

WEIGHTS AND LOADINGS.—Weight empty 2,301 lbs. (1045 kg.), Disposable load (for bomber) 1,045 lbs. (474 kg.), Disposable load (for fighter) 714 lbs. (324 kg.), Weight loaded (for fighter) 3,015 lbs. (1,369 kg.), Weight loaded (for bomber with two 116-lb. bombs) 3,356 lbs (1,524 kg.), Wing loading 13.25 lbs./sq. ft. (64.6 kg./sq. m.), Power loading (450 h.p.) 6.03 lbs./h.p. (2.7 kg./h.p.).

PERFORMANCE (normal carrier fighter).—Speed at sea level 167 m.p.h. (267.2 km.h.), Speed at 6,000 ft. (1,830 m.) 187 m.p.h. (299.2 km.h.), Landing speed 61 m.p.h. (97.6 km.h.), Initial rate of climb 1,980 ft./min. (604 m./min.), Climb to 15,000 ft. (4,575 m.) 9.5 mins., Service ceiling 27,500 ft. (8,387.5 m.). (1934)

A Lockheed-built Boeing B-17G Fortress Medium Bomber (four Wright R-1820-97 engines).

THE BOEING MODEL 299 FORTRESS.

U.S. Army Air Forces designations : B-17, XB-38, XB-40, F-9, XC-108, BQ-7, CB-17 and TB-17.

U.S. Navy designation : PB-1.

The Fortress was originally designed to meet a bomber specification issued by the U.S. Army Air Corps in 1934. The prototype first flew on July 28, 1935, and the first Y1B-17 of a production order of thirteen was delivered to the Air Corps in March, 1937. In January, 1939, an experimental Y1B-17A fitted with turbo-supercharged engines was delivered to the Army Air Corps. Following successful trials with this aircraft an order for 39 was placed for this model under the designation B-17B.

B-17B. Four 1,000 h.p. Wright R-1820-51 engines with exhaust driven superchargers. First B-17B delivered to the Army in June, 1939.

B-17C. Four 1,200 h.p. Wright R-1820-65 engines. Similar to B-17B except armament increased from five to seven 0.30 in. (7.7 m/m.) guns. Side gun blisters abandoned in favour of plain openings. Twelve B-17s ferried across the Atlantic in the Spring of 1944 for service with the R.A.F. These were the first Fortresses to go into combat operations in a daylight raid on Brest on July 24, 1941.

B-17D. Similar to B-17C but incorporating self-sealing tanks and armour protection for the crew. Later all B-17Cs were converted to B-17Ds.

B-17E. Major re-design and put into large-scale production by Boeing, Douglas and Vega. First Fortress to incorporate power-driven turrets and a tail-gun position. The total armament consisted of eleven 0.5 in. (12.7 m/m.) machine-guns. Enlarged horizontal and vertical tail-surfaces. First B-17E flew in September, 1941.

B-17F. Similar to the B-17E. Fitted with additional wing fuel tanks and with external racks under inner wings for a maximum of two 4,000 lb. (1,816 kg.) bombs. Later models fitted with four R-1820-97 engines.

B-17G. Four 1,200 h.p. R-1820-97 engines. Similar to B-17F. Various armament changes. Fitted with a remotely-controlled two-gun Bendix chin turret in place of hand-operated nose guns. In later versions the two 0.5 in. (12.7 m/m.) side nose guns were reinstated, the open waist guns were replaced by staggered enclosed waist guns, and a new tail gun mounting with increased angles of fire and a reflector sight instead of ring and bead was installed.

B-17H. Conversion of the B-17G for Air/Sea Rescue duties. Carries airborne lifeboat under fuselage and is fitted with special search radar equipment.

XB-38. One B-17E fitted with four Allison V-1710-89 liquid-cooled engines in place of the standard air-cooled units, and stressed to load factors of the B-17F.

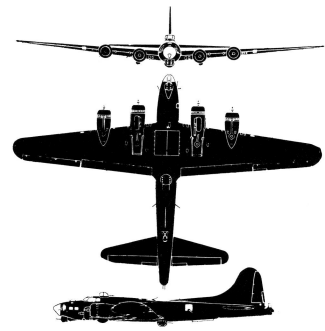

The Boeing B-17G Fortress Bomber.

YB-40. One XB-40 and thirteen YB-40s were modified B-17Fs equipped to serve as escorts for bomber formations in European theatre. Armed with fourteen .5 in. (12.7 m/m.) guns in twin mountings. No bombs carried and bomb-bays fitted to carry extra ammunition which was chute-fed to gun positions. Were not successful and were soon withdrawn from operations.

CB-17. B-17s withdrawn from operations were stripped of armament and used for general utility transport duties under the designation CB-17.

TB-17. Stripped B-17s used for miscellaneous training duties.

The Boeing B-17H Flying Fortress, a conversion from the B-17G for Air/Sea Rescue duties.—(*William T. Larkins*).

XC-108. One B-17E converted to serve as staff aircraft for General Douglas McArthur. Turrets, armour and bomb-racks removed and interior re-arranged to contain three passenger compartments, office facilities and galley. Single .5 in. (12.7 m/m.) nose gun and twin .5 in. (12.7 m/m.) guns in tail retained. XC-108A was a B-17E converted to cargo transport. XC-108B was a fuel tanker conversion.

F-9. A photographic reconnaissance version of the B-17F. Three cameras were installed in the nose and extra fuel tanks carried in the bomb-bay.

BQ-7. Stripped B-17 equipped as a pilotless radio-controlled explosive missile.

PB-1. U.S. Navy modification of the B-17G for over-sea observation duties. Stripped of armament and fitted with special radar equipment for weather observation experiments. PB-1W in service in U.S. Coast Guard for long-range Air/Sea Rescue duties.

Apart from the many variants of the Fortress detailed above, the B-17 is used for many experimental duties, including serving as a launching platform in the U.S.A.A.F. guided-missile programme and in radar and radio-control experiments. Radio-controlled B-17s took part in the Bikini atomic-bomb tests and on the conclusion of these operations two crewless B-17s were flown from Hawaii to Muroc Field, California, a distance of 2,400 miles (3,862 km.) under the control of another aircraft of the same type.

In all, 12,731 B-17s of all models were built, from the XB-17 prototype to the last B-17G which was delivered to the U.S.A.A.F. in April, 1945.

The description below applies to the B-17G, the last operational bomber version of the Fortress. This version is still in service in U.S.A.A.F. bomber squadrons both at home and with the occupation forces overseas.

TYPE.—Four-engined Bomber.

WINGS.—All-metal midwing cantilever monoplane. Aerofoil section varies from NACA 0018 at root to NACA 0010 at tip. Aspect ratio 7.58/1. Taper ratio 2.4 : 1. Incidence 3½°. Dihedral 4½°. Sweepback on leading-edge 8¼°. Structure, consisting of two inner sections carrying the engine nacelles, two outer sections and two detachable tips, chiefly of aluminium-alloy, with two spars, ribs and stressed-skin covering. Electrically-operated split trailing-edge flaps on inner wing sections, ailerons on outer sections. Flaps and ailerons covered with fabric. Ailerons fitted with control trimming-tabs. Gross wing area 1,420 sq. ft. (132 sq. m.).

FUSELAGE.—Semi-monocoque structure, consisting of bulkheads and circumferential stiffeners, tied together with longerons and longitudinal stiffeners, the whole covered with a smooth metal stressed skin.

TAIL UNIT.—Cantilever monoplane type. Aluminium-alloy framework, with fixed surfaces covered with smooth metal sheet and movable surfaces covered with fabric. Elevators and rudder fitted with controllable trimming-tabs.

LANDING GEAR.—Retractable two-wheel type. Air-oil shock-absorber units. Hydraulic wheel-brakes. Electrical retraction. Retractable tail-wheel.

POWER PLANT.—Four 1,200 h.p. Wright R-1820-97 nine-cylinder radial air-cooled engines with General Electric Type B-22 exhaust-driven turbo-superchargers installed in the undersides of the engine nacelles. Hamilton-Standard three-bladed constant-speed full-feathering airscrews 11 ft. 7 in. (3.54 m.) diameter. Self-sealing fuel tanks in wings. Normal fuel capacity carried in six tanks in the inner wing sections 1,700 U.S. gallons (6,435 litres). Nine self-sealing auxiliary feeder tanks in outer wings. Two self-sealing droppable ferry tanks may be carried in bomb-bay. Maximum capacity of all wing tanks 2,789 U.S. gallons (10,523 litres). Self-sealing hopper oil tank in each nacelle. Oil capacity 148 U.S. gallons (561 litres).

ACCOMMODATION.—Normal crew of six to ten. Bomb-aimer's compartment in extreme nose. Pilot's compartment seating two side-by-side with dual controls in front of leading-edge of wing. Aft of pilot's position is an upper electrically-operated two-gun turret. Radio-operator's position amidships. Two gun positions aft of the wings, one two-gun electrically-operated turret beneath the fuselage and one position in the extreme tail. Equipment includes automatic pilot, two-way radio and radio "homing" equipment. Oxygen equipment with points of supply for each member of the crew, de-icers on leading-edges of wings, tail-plane and fin, two collapsible dinghies, etc.

ARMAMENT.—Thirteen .5 in. (12.7 m/m.) machine-guns. From nose to tail these are : two, remotely-controlled, in a chin turret beneath the plastic bomb-aimer's nose ; two in cheek mountings, one on either side of the plastic nose ; two in an electrically-operated turret on top of the fuselage just aft of the pilot's cockpit ; one manually-operated firing through the top of the fuselage above the radio-operator's compartment ; two in a Sperry electrically-operated ball turret below the fuselage ; two on hand-operated mountings and firing through side ports, one on each side of the fuselage midway between wings and tail ; and two in the extreme tail. Internal bomb stowage in fuselage between the main spar frames, the bomb-bay occupying the full cross-section of the fuselage. Normal capacity of bomb-bay is 6,000 lbs. (2,724 kg.). Largest bomb which can be carried internally is the 2,000 lb. (907 kg.). External racks no longer fitted.

DIMENSIONS.—Span 103 ft. 9 in. (31.6 m.), Length 74 ft. 9 in. (22.8 m.), Height 19 ft. 1 in. (5.8 m.).

WEIGHTS AND LOADINGS.—Weight empty 32,720 lbs. (14,855 kg.), Normal weight loaded 49,500 lbs. (22,475 kg.), Maximum overloaded weight 60,000 lbs. (27,216 kg.).

PERFORMANCE.—Maximum speed 295 m.p.h. (472 km.h.) at 25,000 ft. (7,625 m.), Climb to 25,000 ft. (7,625 m.) 41 min., Service ceiling 35,000 ft. (10,670 m.), Normal range (maximum bomb load and normal fuel) 1,100 miles (1,760 km.) at 220 m.p.h. (352 km.h.) at 25,000 ft. (7 625 m.).

(1945–46)

THE BOEING NB NAVAL TRAINING MACHINE

In the spring of 1924 the Boeing Company produced a convertible land-and-water training aeroplane which won the Navy's Training Plane Competition at Pensacola. This machine, which is equipped with the 200 h.p. Wright Radial engine, but may also be fitted with the 220 h.p. Wright E-4 engine, is remarkable for its simple and interchangeable construction. The top and bottom wings, as well as the right and left ailerons and elevators, are interchangeable, which makes the question of maintenance very simple. The landing speed of this machine is 35 m.p.h., a very desirable feature for training. The fuselage is of welded steel tubing. Single or twin float water gears and a land type undercarriage are all equally adaptable to this machine, and can be changed with a minimum of effort.

Span	..	..	..	36 ft. 10 in. (11.2 m.).
Weight empty	..	..	..	1,960 lbs. (890 kgs.).
Weight loaded	..	..	..	2,640 lbs. (1,200 kgs.).
Max. speed	..	..	..	104 m.p.h. (167 km.h.).

The Boeing Training Seaplane (200 h.p. Wright " Whirlwind " engine).

The Boeing P-12B Single-seat Fighter Biplane (400 h.p. Pratt & Whitney "Wasp" engine).

THE BOEING P-12

The P12 was derived from the Navy's F4B. Nine P-12s were delivered to the Army in 1929, followed by 90 P-12Bs, 69 P-12Cs (with R-1340-9 engines instead of previously used R-1340-7), 35 P-12Ds with 500 hp R-1340-17 engines (delivered 1931), 110 P-12Es and 25 P-12Fs (ordered as P-12Es but with SR-1340F engines for high altitude flying).

Details below are for the P-12B and E:—

THE BOEING P-12B.

TYPE.—Single-seat high-performance fighter.

WINGS.—Single-bay biplane of unequal span and chord. Both upper and lower wings are one-piece continuous wings, the upper wing being mounted above the fuselage on splayed-out centre-section struts and the lower wing is bolted directly to fittings suspended from the lower fuselage longerons. There is one set of "N"-type interplane struts on either side of the fuselage. Both the inter-plane and centre-section struts are of streamline duralumin tubing, with the terminal fittings riveted in. The wing structure consists of two built-up box spars of spruce and plywood, with Warren girder type ribs of the same materials. Frise type ailerons on top plane only. These are of duralumin construction and are covered with corrugated duralumin sheet.

FUSELAGE.—A rectangular structure of square duralumin tubing assembled with steel and duralumin fittings, the whole being faired out to an oval section and covered with fabric. The front or engine-section is a welded-up structure of steel-tubing and sheet. This is bolted to the front end of the duralumin longerons, but is not easily detachable.

TAIL UNIT.—Normal monoplane type. Duralumin framework, with corrugated duralumin sheet covering. Balanced rudder. Fin adjustable on ground and the tail-plane is adjustable in the air.

UNDERCARRIAGE.—Split-axle type. Consists of two side Vees, the front legs of which incorporate the Boeing oleo shock-absorbing unit, and two bent axles hinged under the centre-line of the under-side of the fuselage. Bendix wheel brakes, operating from the rudder pedals, are fitted. The tail-skid is of the Boeing oleo type.

POWER PLANT.—One 450 h.p. Pratt & Whitney "Wasp" super-charged radial air-cooled engine. Main fuel tank, of 57 U.S. gallons capacity, is mounted in the fuselage, with an auxiliary tank of 49 U.S. gallons, which can be slung under the fuselage. This auxiliary tank is of streamline shape and is droppable in flight. A 7 U.S. gallons oil tank is mounted forward of the main fuel tank. "Eclipse" inertia starter, which may be released either inside or outside the cockpit. A "Flash" type fire-extinguisher mounted forward of the fireproof bulkhead, with control located in the cockpit.

ACCOMMODATION.—Single-seat cockpit aft of the trailing-edge of the wings. Pilot's seat has 4-inch vertical adjustment, but is only adjustable on the ground. Armament consists of either two 30-calibre or one 30-calibre and one 50-calibre Browning guns firing forward through the airscrew. Provision is made for 600 rounds of 30-calibre ammunition per gun or 200 rounds of ammunition for the 50-calibre gun when this gun is used. Provision is also made for the mounting of a rack for five 30-lb. or two 100-lb. bombs under the fuselage. No wireless or photographic equipment is carried.

DIMENSIONS.—Span (upper) 30 ft. (9.13 m.). Span (bottom) 26 ft. 4 in. (8.02 m.). Length 20 ft. 8 in. (6.29 m.). Height 9 ft. 7 in. (2.92 m.). Wing area 227.5 sq. ft. (21.1 sq. m.).

WEIGHTS AND LOADINGS.—Weight empty 1,894 lbs. (860 kg.). Dis-posable load 701 lbs. (318 kg.). Weight loaded 2,595 lbs. (1,178 kg.). Wing loading 11.4 lbs./sq. ft. (55.6 kg./sq. m.), Power loading 5.76 lbs./h.p. (2.6 kg./h.p.).

PERFORMANCE.—Maximum speed 171 m.p.h. (273.6 km.h.), Landing speed 56 m.p.h. (89.6 km.h.), Initial rate of climb 2,900 ft./min. (885 m./min.), Climb to 16,500 ft. (5,032 m.) 10 mins., Service ceiling 26,900 ft. (8,200 m.). (1931)

The Boeing P-12C Single-seat Fighter (450 h.p. Pratt & Whitney "Wasp" supercharged engine).

Twelve Boeing P-12E Pursuit Biplanes (Pratt & Whitney "Wasp" engine) of the 27th Pursuit Squadron U.S. Army Air Corps.

THE BOEING P-12E.

TYPE.—Single-seat high-performance fighter.

WINGS.—Single-bay biplane of unequal span and chord. Both upper and lower wings are in one piece, the upper wing being mounted above the fuselage on centre-section struts and the lower wing bolted directly to fittings on the lower fuselage longerons. There is one set of "N"-type interplane struts on either side of the fuselage. Both the interplane and centre-section struts are of streamline duralumin tubing, with riveted terminal fittings. The wing structure consists of two built-up box spars of spruce and plywood, with Warren girder type ribs of the same materials. Ailerons on top plane only. These are of duralumin construction and are covered with corrugated duralumin sheet.

FUSELAGE.—The main structure forward of the lower front wing spar is of chrome-molybdenum steel tubing with metal cowling. Aft of this the fuselage is of semi-monocoque duralumin construction. The engine-mounting, of welded steel tubing, is not detachable.

TAIL UNIT.—Normal monoplane type. Duralumin framework, with corrugated duralumin sheet covering. Fin adjustable on ground and the tail-plane is adjustable in the air.

UNDERCARRIAGE.—Cross-axle type. Consists of two side Vees, the front legs of which incorporate the Boeing oleo shock-absorbing units. Side loads are taken by a transverse steel-tube Vee from the centre of the axle to the fuselage. Bendix wheel-brakes, operating from the rudder pedals, are fitted. The tail-skid is of the Boeing oleo type.

POWER PLANT.—One 500 h.p. Pratt & Whitney "Wasp," Series E, supercharged radial air-cooled engine. Main fuel tank, of 55 U.S. gallons capacity, is mounted in the fuselage, with an auxiliary tank of 55 U.S. gallons, slung under the fuselage. This auxiliary tank is of streamline shape and is droppable in flight. A 7 U.S. gallons oil tank is mounted forward of the main fuel tank.

ACCOMMODATION.—Single-seat cockpit aft of the trailing-edge of the wings. Pilot's seat has 7-inch vertical adjustment, but is only adjustable on the ground. Armament consists of either two .30-calibre or one .30-calibre and one .50-calibre Browning guns firing forward through the airscrew. Provision is made for 600 rounds of .30-calibre ammunition per gun or 200 rounds of ammunition for the .50-calibre gun when this gun is used. Provision is also made for the mounting of a rack for five 30-lb. fragmentation or two 122-lb. demolition bombs under the fuselage. No wireless or photographic equipment is carried.

DIMENSIONS.—Span (upper) 30 ft. (9.13 m.), Span (bottom) 26 ft. 4 in. (8.02 m.), Length 20 ft. 8 in. (6.29 m.), Height 9 ft. 7 in. (2.92 m.), Wing area 227.5 sq. ft. (21.1 sq. m.).

WEIGHTS AND LOADINGS.—Weight empty 1,981.3 lbs. (899.5 kg.), Disposable load 693 lbs. (315.6 kg.), Weight loaded 2,674.3 lbs. (1,214.1 kg.), Wing loading 11.75 lbs./sq. ft. (57.3 kg./sq. m.), Power loading 5.35 lbs./h.p. (2.4 kg./h.p.).

PERFORMANCE.—Speed at sea level 171 m.p.h. (275.5 km.h.), Speed at 6,000 ft. (1,830 m.) 189 m.p.h. (304.16 km.h.), Landing speed 60 m.p.h. (96.56 km.h.), Initial rate of climb 2,050 ft./min. (625 m./min.), Climb to 6,000 ft. (1,830 m.) 3.5 mins., Service ceiling 28,000 ft. (8,534 m.). (1935)

THE BOEING P-26A.

First flown as the XP-936 prototype on 20 March 1932, two production versions were produced for the USAAC as the P-26A (111 delivered by 1934) and P-26C (35 delivered from 1936).

TYPE.—Single-seater, high-performance fighter.

WINGS.—Low-wing braced monoplane. All-metal structure consisting of centre-section and outboard panels externally braced with front and rear flying and landing wires. Centre-section spars are of steel with spars, ribs and skin covering of aluminium alloy. Split-type trailing-edge wing-flaps manually-operated from cockpit.

FUSELAGE.—Semi-monocoque structure of aluminium alloy longerons, skin stiffeners, bulkheads and skin. The detachable engine-mounting is of welded steel-tubing.

TAIL UNIT.—Cantilever monoplane type of aluminium alloy spars, ribs and skin covering. The tail-plane is fixed, with longitudinal balance corrected by flaps which are built into the trailing-edge of the elevators and adjustable from the cockpit.

UNDERCARRIAGE.—Treadle type with Boeing oleo shock-absorbers and self-energizing brakes. The tail-wheel is steerable and full swivelling.

POWER PLANT.—One 550 h.p. supercharged Pratt & Whitney "Wasp" engine, with Hamilton Standard airscrew and Boeing ring cowling.

ACCOMMODATION.—Single-seat open cockpit. Pilot's seat and rudder-pedals adjustable in flight.

DIMENSIONS.—Span 27 ft. 11⅝ in. (8.5 m.), Length 23 ft. 7¼ in. (7.2 m.), Height (tail down) 7 ft. 10 in. (2.4 m.), Chord 6 ft. (1.83 m.), Wing area (including ailerons) 149.5 sq. ft. (13.88 sq. m.), Ailerons, 9.38 sq. ft. (0.87 sq. m.), Tail plane 11.6 sq. ft. (1.07 sq. m.), Elevators 12.02 sq. ft. (1.11 sq. m.), Fin 5.52 sq. ft. (0.512 sq. m.), Rudder 6.6 sq. ft. (0.613 sq. m.).

Weight loaded	2,995 lb
High speed	234 mph
Service ceiling	27,400 ft
Range	635 miles
Armament	One 0.30 in and one 0.50 in or two 0.30 in guns, plus 200 lb of bombs.

(1935)

Boeing P-26 Monoplanes of the U.S. Army Air Corps. (1936)

The Boeing P-26 Single-seat Fighter Monoplane (Pratt & Whitney "Wasp" engine).

THE BOEING PW-9A.

The Boeing Airplane Company, one of the largest producers of military aircraft in the United States, produced during 1926 a number of interesting experimental and production types.

The Boeing PW-9 Army and Marine Corps pursuit biplane was continued in production in a modified form, known as the PW-9A. A still later refinement of this type, the PW-9C was produced during the year. One PW-9A was fitted with a 180 h.p. Hispano-Suiza engine and submitted to the Air Corps as a pursuit training biplane. This type is designated the AT-3.

The PW-9A, a modification of the PW-9, is a single-seat pursuit biplane, fitted with a 400 h.p. Curtiss D-12 engine. The fuselage is a welded steel-tube structure. Both wings are tapered in plan form and the bottom plane is much smaller in span and chord than the top wing. The interplane struts, of "N" form, are of steel-tube. The radiator is mounted under the engine, in a tunnel.

Specification.

Span	..	..	.. 32 ft. (9.9 m.).
Length	..	..	.. 23 ft. 7 in.
Wing area	..	..	.. 242 sq. ft.
Weight loaded	..	..	3,043 lbs.
Speed, max.	..	..	163 m.p.h.
Speed, min.	..	..	65 m.p.h.
Climb	..	..	10,000 ft. in $7\frac{3}{4}$ mins.
Service ceiling	..	..	20,175 ft.

THE BOEING AT-3.

The Boeing AT-3 is a modification of the PW-9A, and is fitted with the 180 h.p. Wright E-4 water-cooled engine in place of the Curtiss D-12. It is produced as a pursuit training biplane, and except for the change in engines, the substitution of a nose radiator for the tunnel radiator and the elimination of a certain amount of the armament, it differs little from its prototype.

Specification.

Span, top plane	..	..	32 ft.
Span, bottom plane	..	..	22 ft. $5\frac{3}{4}$ in.
Length	..	..	23 ft. $3\frac{1}{4}$ in.
Height ..	..	..	8 ft. $9\frac{3}{4}$ in.
Chord, max. (top plane)	..	6 ft.
Chord, max. (bottom plane)	..	5 ft.

(1927)

Prototype Boeing Pursuit Machine with untypical cross-axle landing gear (Curtiss D.12 engine).

THE BOEING PW-9D.

Following 40 PW-9Cs with Curtiss D-12D engines and heavier structures (delivered from 1927), the PW-9D was the final development of the PW-9 single-seat fighter. This machine has been delivered to the Air Corps in quantity.

TYPE.—Single-seat fighter biplane.

WINGS.—Single-bay staggered biplane, with wings of unequal span and chord. Top wing is in one piece. Wings taper in plan and thickness from centre to tips. Top wing carried above fuselage on steel tubes running from top and bottom fuselage longerons, with one set of "N" type interplane struts on either side. Wing construction of wood, covered with fabric. Narrow chord ailerons fitted to top plane only.

FUSELAGE.—Welded steel-tube structure, covered with fabric.

TAIL UNIT.—Normal type. Metal-framed, covered with fabric. Balanced rudder. Adjustable tail plane.

UNDERCARRIAGE.—Split type. Wheel brakes fitted as standard.

POWER PLANT.—One 440 h.p. Curtiss D-12D water-cooled engine. Radiator mounted in tunnel, under engine.

ACCOMMODATION.—Pilot's cockpit aft of trailing edge of top plane. Armament consists of two .30 calibre Browning guns, in cowling and firing through airscrew.

DIMENSIONS.—Span (top) 32 ft. (9.75 m.), Span (bottom) 22 ft. 5¼ in. (6.85 m.), Length 23 ft. 11 in. (7.26 m.), Height 8 ft. 9¾ in. (2.99 m.), Wing area 242 sq. ft. (22.3 sq. m.).

WEIGHTS.—Weight loaded 3,043 lbs. (1,383 kg.).

PERFORMANCE.—Maximum speed 163 m.p.h. (273 km.h.), Minimum speed 65 m.p.h. (104 km.h.), Climb to 10,000 ft. (3,047 m.) 7¼ mins., Service ceiling 20,175 ft. (6,146 m.). (1928)

The Boeing PT-17 Kaydet Two-seat Primary Training Biplane (220 h.p. Continental engine).
(Photograph by W. T. Larkins)

THE BOEING (STEARMAN 75) KAYDET.
U.S. Army Air Forces designations : PT-13, PT-17, PT-18 and PT-27.
U.S Navy designation : N2S.

The first service training version of the Stearman Model 75 was the PT-13 (Lycoming R-680-5 engine) which was ordered by the Army in 1935. Then followed the PT-17 (Continental R-670-5 engine) in 1940, the PT-18 (Jacobs R-755-7 engine) and the PT-27. All were similar, except for the engines fitted and certain minor equipment charges, with the exception of the PT-27 which was built for use in Canada. The PT-27 had the same airframe and power-plant as the PT-17 but was fitted with cockpit enclosures and heating, night-flying equipment, blind-flying hood and instruments, etc.

Of the U.S. Navy versions, the N2S-1 and N2S-4 (Continental R-670-4 engine) are similar to the PT-17, the N2S-2 (Lycoming R-680-8 engine) is similar to the PT-13A, the N2S-3 (Continental R-670-4 engine) is similar to the PT-17A, and the N-2S-5 (Lycoming R-680 engine) is identical to the PT-13D, these last two aircraft eventually being standardised for unified production for both services.

Production of the Kaydet was completed in February, 1945, after 10,346 had been built.

TYPE.—Two-seat Primary Training biplane.

WINGS.—Single-bay unequal-span staggered biplane. NACA 2213 wing-section. Centre-section carried above the fuselage by splayed-out wire-braced streamline steel-tube struts. One "N"-type streamline steel-tube interplane strut on each side of the fuselage. Wing structure consists of spruce laminated spars and ribs, duralumin channel compression struts and steel tie-rod bracing, the whole covered with fabric. Ailerons, of duralumin construction, on lower wings only.

FUSELAGE.—Rectangular welded chrome-molybdenum steel-tube, covered forward with metal panels and aft with fabric.

TAIL UNIT.—Monoplane type. Wire-braced tail-plane and fin. Welded chrome-molybdenum steel-tube framework and fabric covering. Trimming-tab in elevator.

LANDING GEAR.—Divided cantilever type. Each leg incorporates a torque-resisting oleo-spring shock-absorber, enclosed in a metal fairing. Hydraulic wheel-brakes. Steerable tail-wheel.

POWER PLANT.—One 220 h.p. Lycoming R-680 (PT-13 or N2S-2) or 220 h.p. Continental R-670 (PT-17, PT-27, N2S-1, N2S-3 or N2S-4) or 225 h.p. Jacobs R-755 (PT-18) radial air-cooled engine, on steel-tube mounting. Two-bladed adjustable-pitch metal airscrew. Petrol tank (43 U.S. gallons = 162.75 litres) in centre-section. Oil tank (4 U.S. gallons = 15.14 litres) in engine compartment.

ACCOMMODATION.—Tandem open cockpits, with complete dual controls. Baggage compartment aft of rear cockpit.

DIMENSIONS.—Span 32 ft. 2 in. (9.8 m.), Length 25 ft. ¼ in. (7.63 m.), Height 9 ft. 2 in. (2.79 m.), Wing area 297.4 sq. ft. (27.6 sq. m.).

WEIGHTS AND LOADINGS.—Weight empty 1,936 lbs. (878 kg.), Weight loaded 2,717 lbs. (1,232 kg.), Wing loading 10.94 lbs./sq. ft. (44.6 kg./sq. m.), Power loading 12 lbs./h.p. (3.85 kg./h.p.).

PERFORMANCE.—Maximum speed 124 m.p.h. (199.5 km.h.), Cruising speed at sea level at 65 per cent. power 106 m.p.h. (171 km.h.), Landing speed 52 m.p.h. (83.6 km.h.), Initial rate of climb 840 ft./min. (256 m./min.), Service ceiling 11,200 ft. (3,413 m.), Range 505 miles (812 km.), Endurance at cruising speed (65 per cent. output) 4.75 hours. (1945-46)

The Boeing B-52A Stratofortress Heavy Bomber (eight Pratt & Whitney J57 turbojet engines).

BOEING B-52 STRATOFORTRESS

Designed originally as an intercontinental, high-altitude nuclear bomber, the B-52, which first entered US Air Force service in 1955, has undergone numerous improvement programmes over the years to ensure that its operational capabilities meet changing defence needs.

The first Seattle-produced B-52A was completed in March, 1954, while the first Wichita-produced Stratofortress, the first B-52D, was completed in December, 1955.

Two prototypes, the XB-52 and YB-52, were built, the YB-52 flying for the first time on April 15, 1952, while the XB-52 made its maiden flight on October 2, 1952.

Although the B-52 is a completely different aircraft from the B-47 insofar as both design and mission are concerned, outwardly the two aeroplanes are somewhat similar in appearance. Both feature a 35-degree angle of wing sweepback, distinctive Boeing-type external jet engine pods and a tandem landing-gear. The B-52 landing-gear is, however, a double side-by-side tandem, with small single outrigged wing-tip "protection" wheels which do not normally come into contact with the ground. In production aircraft the main gear is of the "cross-wind" landing type.

The B-52 is powered by eight Pratt & Whitney J57 turbojet engines (over 10,000 lb.=4,540 kg. s.t. each) which are mounted in pairs in four nacelles on forwardly-inclined cantilever struts under the wings.

All production B-52's are equipped for flight refueling by "Flying Boom" system. The refueling receptacle is located on top of the fuselage aft of the cockpit canopy.

A crew of six is carried. All crew members are provided with means of emergency escape, three being ejected upwards, two downwards, while the tail-gunner is ejected complete with tail turret.

The following production versions of the B-52 have been announced:—

B-52A. Eight Pratt & Whitney J57-P-1W engines. First production model, with "cross-wind" landing gear and equipped to receive "flying boom" flight refuelling. First B-52A flew for first time on August 5, 1954. Fitted with two 1,000 U.S. gallon (3,780 litre) drop tanks under outer wings. Gross weight 350,000 lb. (158,900 kg.).

B-52B. Similar to B-52A but capable of undertaking more than one strategic rôle. In addition to bombing (conventional and nuclear) it can also be provided with "capsule" equipment for photographic reconnaissance and other, secret, duties. The "capsule" which may be winched in and out of the bomb-bay, is fully pressurised, air-conditioned and is equipped with stations for a two-man crew. 30 built.

B-52C. Eight Pratt & Whitney J57-P-19W engines. Developed version of B-52B with same versatility. Larger underwing drop tanks. All-up weight increased to more than 400,000 lb. (181,600 kg.).

B-52D. Similar to B-52C but is a long-range heavy bomber exclusively.

B-52E. Developed version of the B-52D with improved bombing, navigation and electronics systems.

B-52F. Developed version of the B-52E with J57-P-43W engines with increased thrust.

B-52G. Developed version of B-52F with redesigned "wet" wing with integral skinning and integral fuel tanks. Vertical tail surfaces reduced in height. 25% greater range, increased climb performance and greater target altitude. Equipped to carry two GAM-77 Hound Dog air-to-surface missiles. Weight loaded approx. 450,000 lb. (204,000 kg.).

B-52H. Development of the B-52G with Pratt & Whitney TF33 turbofan engines. Intended originally to carry four Skybolt ballistic missiles. Armed with a multi-barrel tail cannon and with forward-firing penetration rocket launchers. First of 102 built flew on 6 March 1961. On 10–11 January 1962, a B-52H flew non-stop from Okinawa to Madrid, a record distance of 12,532.3 miles.

Several programmes involving the **B-52G** and **H** have been undertaken or are now in progress to improve the avionics, equipment and operational capability. Under a 1971 contract, 281 of these two models were modified to carry the Boeing SRAM (short range attack missile), which completely replaced the underwing Hound Dog missiles formerly carried. The first of these became operational on 4 August 1972.

The US Air Force's Rivet Ace programme, initiated in 1974, has progressively updated about 270 B-52Gs and B-52Hs which are currently receiving Phase VI ECM (electronic countermeasures). These aircraft have already an AN/ASQ-151 Electro-optical Viewing System (EVS) to improve low level penetration capability, the EVS sensors being housed in two steerable, side-by-side chin turrets. The starboard turret houses a Hughes Aircraft AAQ-6 forward-looking infra-red (FLIR) scanner, while the port turret contains a Westinghouse AVQ-22 low light level TV camera.

By 1981 the B-52G and H should be ready for flight test with Motorola ALQ-122 SNOE (Smart Noise Operation Equipment) countermeasures, and Northrop AN/ALQ-155(V) power management system; by 1982 with an AFSATCOM kit permitting worldwide communication via satellite; and by 1984 with Northrop ALT-28 and ALT-32 jammers. Sedco Systems has an Air Force contract to design and develop the prototype of an electronically steerable antenna system (ESAS) for the onboard ALT-28s, to improve their defensive electronics (jamming) capability. Other Phase VI avionics include a Dalmo Victor ALR-46 digital radar warning receiver, Westinghouse ALQ-153 pulse-Doppler tail warning radar, and two tail-mounted ITT Avionics ALQ-117 noise/deception jammers.

Boeing has a US Air Force contract to define and design an Offensive Avionics System (OAS) to upgrade the navigation and weapons delivery of the B-52G and H. At a significantly reduced life-cycle cost, this will be a digital (instead of analogue) based, solid-state system, and will include Tercom (terrain comparison) guidance.

Phase I of this programme, to be completed by 1981, involves the equipment of a B-52G test aircraft with the new avionics, followed by 12 months of flight testing. The new equipment includes a Teledyne Ryan Doppler radar, Honeywell AN/ASN-131 gimballed electrostatic airborne inertial navigation system (GEANS), IBM/Raytheon ASQ-38 analogue bombing/navigation system with IBM digital processing, Lear Siegler attitude heading and reference system, Honeywell radar altimeter, Sperry controls and displays, and Norden Systems modernised radar. The programme will be completed in the late 1980s by a Phase II under which a percentage of the B-52 fleet will be equipped for better performance of low-level penetration missions. A major feature of Phase II is an electronically agile radar (EAR), modified from an existing Westinghouse radar, which has been under test since 1978. The EAR will be able to fulfil both mapping and terrain-following functions, and to update the GEANS by measuring ground speed. Automatic terrain-following guidance and a new flight control system also form a part of the Phase II programme, flight testing of which is scheduled for FY 1982-84. A production decision is due to be taken in FY 1983 or 1984.

Following the choice of Boeing's AGM-86B air-launched cruise missile, as a result of its fly-off against the General Dynamics AGM-109 Tomahawk, the B-52G will be adapted as carrier aircraft for the AGM-86B, and development for this role is continuing. Full-scale development of B-52 carrier aircraft equipment, as an integral part of the cruise missile programme, began in early 1978, and three B-52Gs were modified for use in the fly-off programme at Edwards AFB, California.

The following description refers to the B-52A, unless stated otherwise:—

TYPE.—Eight-jet Heavy Bomber.

WINGS.—High-wing cantilever monoplane with anhedral and 35 degree sweepback. All-metal stressed-skin structure. Lateral control by inset ailerons between inner and outer flaps, supplemented by serrated spoilers on upper surface of wings. Spoilers can be used symmetrically as air brakes. Area-increasing flaps. Wing area approximately 4,000 sq. ft. (371.6 m².).

FUSELAGE. — All-metal semi-monocoque structure.

TAIL UNIT.—Cantilever monoplane type, with hydraulically-actuated variable-incidence tailplane. All control surfaces operated manually through servo tabs.

LANDING GEAR.—Retractable tandem type. Four individually-retracted twin-wheel main units in tandem pairs, retracting into fuselage fore and aft of bomb-bay. Two forward units with hydraulic steering. All four units can be set at a selected degree of castor in flight or on ground for "crosswind" landings. Small outrigger units retract inward into wings outboard of outer engine positions. Ribbon braking parachute, 48 ft. (14.6 m.) diameter, in container which extends under rear fuselage.

ACCOMMODATION.—Crew of six. Forward pressurised cabin accommodates pilot, co-pilot and radio operator in upward-ejection seats on flight deck, with navigator and radar observer on downward-ejection seats on lower level. Rest bunk, kitchen and toilet on lower deck. Tail gunner has pressurised compartment linked by a crawlway with forward cabin. Crawlway can be used only when cabins de-pressurised. Tail-gunner's compartment is complete with own toilet and electric stove : entire gun and radar installation can be jettisoned for unobstructed exit in emergency. Cabins pressurised to differential of 8.77 lb./sq. in. (0.617 kg./cm.²). (1958–59)

POWER PLANT (B-52D): Eight 44·5 kN (10,000 lb st) Pratt & Whitney J57-P-19W or -29W turbojet engines. Fuel capacity 135,140 litres (35,700 US gallons) internally, plus two 11,355 litre (3,000 US gallon) underwing drop-tanks.

POWER PLANT (B-52G): Eight 61·2 kN (13,750 lb st) J57-P-43WB turbojet engines. Fuel capacity 174,130 litres (46,000 US gallons) internally, plus two 2,650 litre (700 US gallon) underwing drop-tanks.

POWER PLANT (B-52H): Eight 75·6 kN (17,000 lb st) Pratt & Whitney TF33-P-3 turbofan engines. Fuel capacity as for B-52G.

ACCOMMODATION (B-52D/G/H): Crew of six (pilot and co-pilot, side by side on flight deck, navigator, radar navigator, ECM operator and gunner).

ARMAMENT (B-52D): Four 0·50 in machine-guns in occupied tail turret. Up to eighty-four 500 lb bombs in fuselage weapons bay, and a further twenty-four 750 lb bombs on underwing pylons: total bomb load 27,215 kg (60,000 lb).

ARMAMENT (B-52G): Four 0·50 in machine-guns in tail turret, remotely operated by AGS-15 fire control system, remote radar control, or closed circuit TV. Up to 20 Boeing AGM-69 SRAM short-range attack missiles: eight on rotary launcher in internal weapons bay, and six SRAM or AGM-86 ALCMs under each wing, plus nuclear free-fall bombs.

Boeing B-52G fitted with AN/ASQ-151 Electro-optical Viewing System and with other recent modifications

ARMAMENT (B-52H): As B-52G, except for single 20 mm Vulcan multi-barrel cannon in tail turret instead of four machine-guns.

DIMENSIONS, EXTERNAL:

Wing span	56·39 m (185 ft 0 in)
Wing area, gross	371·6 m² (4,000 sq ft)
Length overall: G, H	49·05 m (160 ft 10·9 in)
Height overall: D	14·74 m (48 ft 4½ in)
G, H	12·40 m (40 ft 8 in)
Width of fuselage	3·00 m (9 ft 10 in)
Tailplane span: G, H	15·85 m (52 ft 0 in)
Wheel track (c/l of shock-struts)	2·51 m (8 ft 3 in)
Wheelbase	15·48 m (50 ft 3 in)

DIMENSION, INTERNAL:

Weapons bay volume	29·53 m³ (1,043 cu ft)

WEIGHTS:

Max T-O weight:

D	more than 204,115 kg (450,000 lb)
G, H	more than 221,350 kg (488,000 lb)

PERFORMANCE (B-52G/H):

Max level speed at high altitude
    Mach 0·90 (516 knots; 957 km/h; 595 mph)

Cruising speed at high altitude
    Mach 0·77 (442 knots; 819 km/h; 509 mph)

Penetration speed at low altitude
    Mach 0·53 to 0·55
    (352-365 knots; 652-676 km/h; 405-420 mph)

Service ceiling	16,765 m (55,000 ft)
T-O run: G	3,050 m (10,000 ft)
H	2,900 m (9,500 ft)

Range with max fuel, without in-flight refuelling:
  G more than 6,513 nm (12,070 km; 7,500 miles)
  H more than 8,685 nm (16,093 km; 10,000 miles)

(1980–81)

THE BOEING STRATOFREIGHTER.
U.S. Air Force designation: C-97.

The C-97 Stratofreighter is the military transport counterpart of the Stratocruiser, from which it differs principally in the arrangement and equipment of the large two-deck fuselage. The XC-97 was, in fact, the forerunner of the civil Stratocruiser and all initial prototype trials of the civil airliner were conducted with the XC-97.

The principal structural modification to the C-97 fuselage involves the provision of large loading doors and an internally operated ramp under the rear fuselage to permit the loading of wheeled and tracked vehicles and other bulky cargo. An electrically-operated cargo hoist runs along the entire length of the fuselage. Three fully-loaded 1½-ton trucks or two light tanks can be driven into the fuselage, the drive-up ramp being raised and lowered by the cargo hoist. Adequate cargo handling and tie-down equipment is provided. The cabins can also be arranged to accommodate 134 fully-equipped troops, or be fitted out as a hospital transport for 83 stretcher cases and four attendants.

Three XC-97's were built and these were followed by ten YC-97's in three different versions of the basic design. These prototype and service test aircraft incorporated the wings, tail-unit, landing-gear and power-plant of the B-29. The C-97A and subsequent production versions use the main components of the B-50.

The 500th Stratofreighter—a KC-97G—was completed on February 8, 1954. The 888th and last KC-97 was wheeled out of the Renton plant on July 18, 1956, the same day on which the first jet-powered KC-135 emerged from the factory. The completion of the last KC-97 marked the end of Boeing's production of piston-engined aircraft.

The principal features of the many versions of the C-97 are given below.

C-97A. Four Pratt & Whitney R-4360-27 engines. First production aircraft delivered to U.S.A.F. on October 15, 1949. C-97A has a normal payload of 41,400 lb. (18,800 kg.) and under special conditions can carry up to 53,000 lb. (24,060 kg.). It can accommodate 134 fully-equipped troops or mixed loads of cargo or troops. As an ambulance it can transport 83 stretcher patients with medical supplies and attendants.

C-97C. Four 3,250 h.p. Pratt & Whitney R-4360-35A engines. Similar to C-97A in general details and performance. New flush-mounted radio antennae, heavier floor, higher payload. First production C-97C delivered to U.S.A.F. in February, 1951.

VC-97D. Three specially-modified C-97A's supplied to U.S.A.F. Strategic Air Command as mobile "command posts." Used as Staff Transports and living quarters for key personnel in overseas training missions.

KC-97E. Four 3,250 h.p. Pratt & Whitney R-4360-35A engines. Multi-purpose transport and tanker. Has permanent fixtures for tanker but can be rapidly converted to cargo or troop carrier, or ambulance. Pod carrying flying boom, operator and controls is detachable and tanks, pumps, etc. on upper deck are removable. First production KC-97E delivered to U.S.A.F. in July, 1951.

KC-97F. Four 3,250 h.p. Pratt & Whitney R-4360-59 engines. Convertible tanker-transport. Other details and performance similar to KC-97E.

KC-97G. Four 3,250 h.p. Pratt & Whitney R-4360-59B engines. Development of KC-97F. Change in location of refuelling tanks and related equipment, so that they need not be removed when aircraft is used as a transport. As a personnel carrier without refuelling equipment can carry 96 fully equipped combat troops, or as an ambulance, 69 stretcher patients, medical attendants and supplies. With refuelling equipment installed can carry 65 fully-equipped troops or 49 stretcher cases, attendants and supplies.

The Boeing KC-97G Tanker-Transport (four Pratt & Whitney R-4360 engines).

Fitted with two external fuel tanks with total capacity for 1,400 U.S. gallons (5,290 litres). Pressurisation system maintains ground atmospheric pressure to 15,500 ft. (4,730 m.). Last KC-97G completed on July 18, 1956.

The particulars below refer specifically to the KC-97G.

DIMENSIONS.—
Span 141 ft. 3 in. (43.1 m.).
Length 110 ft. 4 in. (33.64 m.).
Height 38 ft. 3 in. (11.6 m.).

WEIGHTS.—
Weight empty 82,500 lb. (37,450 kg.).
Weight loaded 153,000 lb. (69,460 kg.).
Max. permissible loaded weight 175,000 lb. (79,450 kg.).

Landing weight 121,000 lb. (54,930 kg.).
PERFORMANCE.—
Max. speed 375 m.p.h. (600 km.h.).
Cruising speed 300 m.p.h. (480 km.h.).
Operating range 4,300 miles (6.880 km.).
Service ceiling over 35,000 ft. (10,675 m.).
(1958–59)

The Boeing ERB-47H Stratojet special reconnaissance aircraft (six General Electric J47 turbojet engines) (Howard Levy)

THE BOEING STRATOJET
U.S. Air Force designation : B-47

The following are the main production versions of the B-47 three-seat medium bomber :—

B-47A. Six General Electric J47-GE-11 engines (5,200 lb. = 2,360 kg. s.t.). 18 individual Jato solid-fuel rockets fitted to give emergency take-off thrust of 20,000 lb. (9,080 kg.). First production B-47A flew for the first time on June 25, 1950. Ten built.

B-47B. Six General Electric J47-GE-23 engines (5,800 lb. = 2,630 kg. s.t.). Gross weight 185,000 lb. (84,000 kg.). Fitted with wing drop tanks. First B-47B flew on April 26, 1951. B-47B's have been modified and modernised up to B-47E standard by Boeing-Wichita. Modifications include installation of J47-GE-25 engines and water-injection system to give 17% increased T.O. power; substitution of droppable 33-rocket T.O.

assist for original internal 18-rocket equipment; installation of 16-foot approach parachutes; installation of ejection seats (pilot and co-pilot up, navigator down); re-arrangement of equipment in flight compartment and substitution of G.E. radar-directed tail

gun-turret armed with two 20 mm. cannon for former .50-cal. guns. Modified B-47B's are known as B-47B II. Total of 398 built.

RB-47B. Conversion of B-47B for high-altitude photographic reconnaissance. Eight cameras and equipment in heated "package" can be installed in and removed from bomb-bay.

B-47E. Six General Electric J47-GE-25 engines (6,000 lb. = 2,724 kg. s.t.). Developed version of B-47B. Remotely-controlled tail armament of two 20 mm. cannon. First B-47E flew on January 30, 1953. Some converted to ETB-47E crew trainers. About 1,500 in service.

RB-47E. Day or night long-range photographic reconnaissance version of B-47E. Longer nose. Heated and air-conditioned camera compartment. Crew of three, pilot, co-pilot and photographer-navigator. First RB-47E flew on July 3, 1953. Length 109 ft. 10 in. (33.5 m.), other dimensions as for B-47E.

RB-47H. Special reconnaissance version. No details available.

RB-47K. Similar to RB-47E but equipped for both photographic and weather reconnaissance.

QB-47. Fourteen B-47E Stratojets modified by Lockheed into pilotless drones for U.S.A.F. Air Research and Development Command. Used to test vulnerability and effectiveness of North American air defences. Controllable from air or ground stations. First flew in September, 1959.

All operational B-47 bombers have been structurally modified to extend their useful life by approximately 3,000 hours, or between 6 and 10 years in normal service with Strategic Air Command.

Structural details of the B-47 have been given in earlier editions of this work.
ARMAMENT.—Remotely-controlled tail armament of two 20 mm. cannon. Designed internal bomb load 20,000 lb. (9,080 kg.).
DIMENSIONS.—
Span 116 ft. (35.4 m.)
Length 109 ft. 10 in. (33.48 m.)
Height 27 ft. 11 in. (8.50 m.)
WEIGHTS (B-47E).—
Normal loaded weight 175,000 lb. (79,380 kg.)
Max. loaded weight 202,000 lb. (91,625 kg.)
PERFORMANCE (B-47E).—
Max. speed 630 m.p.h. (1,014 km.h.)
Cruising speed at 40,000 ft. (12,200 m.) 495 m.p.h. (796 km.h.)
Service ceiling 42,000 ft. (12,800 m.)
Range 3,200 miles (5,150 km.)   (1960–61)

Boeing NKC-135A operated by the US Air Force Systems Command *(Gordon S. Williams)*

BOEING MODEL 717 STRATOTANKER
USAF designation: KC-135

The USAF announced its intention of buying an undisclosed number of tanker-transports, developed from the prototype Model 367-80 jet transport, in August, 1954. The first of these aircraft, designated KC-135A, left the assembly line at Renton on July 18, 1956, and flew for the first time on August 31, 1956.

Initial deliveries to Castle AFB, California, began on June 28, 1957 and a total of 820 were eventually produced under USAF contracts, including the developed versions listed below and the separately-described C-135, RC-135 and WC-135 series operated by MAC. The last four, all RC-135A's for the Air Photographic and Charting Service, were delayed on the production line pending delivery of government-furnished equipment. The production line was closed in January 1965 and the RC-135A's have been finished on an individual basis, for delivery to APCS from mid-1965.

The total of 820 aircraft were produced in the following versions:

KC-135A (Models 717-100A (first 29 aircraft), 717-146 and 717-148). Standard turbojet tanker-transport. Structurally, the KC-135A is similar to the Boeing 707 commercial airliner, but it has a smaller-diameter fuselage. In addition to its high-speed and high-altitude refuelling capabilities, it serves as a long-range transport, carrying 80 passengers or 25 short tons of cargo or a combination of both, on its upper deck. All refuelling equipment is located in the lower fuselage. Originally, it made use entirely of the rigid "flying boom" type of equipment, but drogues are now trailed from the boom when required to permit the refuelling of probe-equipped fighters of USAF Tactical Air Command. The power plant comprises four 13,750 lb (6,237 kg) st Pratt & Whitney J57-P-59W turbojet engines. Maximum fuel capacity is 31,200 US gallons (118,100 litres). 732 built.

Two modified KC-135A's are used by the Federal Aviation Agency to assist in the programme of flight checking air navigational aids throughout the United States. Other modifications of the KC-135A, some without booms and with turbofan engines, are utilised as follows:

KC-135B (Model 717-166). Basically similar to KC-135A, but with turbofan engines. Seventeen built as SAC Airborne Command Posts. Most KC-135B's were redesignated EC-135C (see below) in October 1964.

EC-135A. J57 turbojets. Equipped as flying command post. Used primarily by USAF Strategic Air Command as back-up aircraft for command post duties and as communications relay stations.

EC-135C. Four 18,000 lb (8,165 kg) st Pratt & Whitney TF33 turbofan engines. Equipped as flying command post ("Looking Glass"), in support of SAC's airborne alert role. Replaced EC-135A. Has flight refuelling receptacle in nose as well as boom under tail. Can refuel other aircraft in flight and can itself be refuelled by SAC tankers. Can also receive fuel in flight from bomber aircraft through reverse fuelling process. Each EC-135C contains a miniaturised version of the SAC control centre at Offutt AFB, and could direct the bomber and missile force if ground control were put out of action. At least one is airborne at all times, manned by a flight crew of five, a general officer and staff of ten. Aircraft is fitted with many additional antennae, above wingtips, under fuselage and elsewhere for communications equipment. Seventeen built.

EC-135G. Turbojet. Same as EC-135A, but with different arrangement of interior equipment.

EC-135H (turbojet) and **EC-135J** (turbofan). Equipped as flying command posts; used by Headquarters Command of USAF (Night Watch).

EC-135K. Turbojet. Equipped as flying command post; used by USAF Tactical Air Command. One only.

EC-135L. Turbojet. KC-135A's modified as dual-rôle communications relay stations and flying command posts.

JKC-135A, NKC-135A, KC-135A and C-135A. Turbojet. Four versions operated by USAF Systems Command in test programmes. Some fitted with sophisticated electronic gear.

RC-135D (turbojet), **RC-135C** and **RC-135E** (turbofans). Equipped for electronic reconnaissance. No refuelling boom.

C-135F (Model 717-165). Turbojet. Twelve aircraft supplied to the French Air Force to serve as dual-purpose transports and tankers to

flight refuel the Mirage IV-A bomber force. As a transport, performance is similar to that of the C-135A Stratolifter, with accommodation for 126 passengers, 75 fully-equipped troops, 44 stretchers and 54 sitting casualties or 34 tons of freight.

C-135A, RC-135A and B, C-135B, VC-135B, WC-135B. Non-tanker versions, described separately.

In addition to the above versions, in military service, the following aircraft are operated on research work.

NC-135A. Turbojet. Similar to NKC-135A in general appearance. Three aircraft modified by General Dynamics/Fort Worth for nuclear weapons blast-detection duties and operated by Sandia Corp, the USAF's Cambridge Research Laboratory and Atomic Energy Commission's Los Alamos Scientific Laboratory. After further minor modification and installation of special equipment, these aircraft were used for complex observations and experiments in the South Pacific during the total solar eclipse of May 30, 1965.

Boeing EC-135C flying command post operated by USAF Strategic Air Command

Boeing RC-135D fitted with extensive radar and reconnaissance equipment *(Toyokazu Matsuzaki)*

On September 17, 1958, a KC-135A commanded by Capt C. E. Gibbs, USAF, set up a speed record of 587·13 mph (944·907 kmh) around a 5,000 km (3,107 mile) closed circuit, carrying a 10,000 kg (22,046 lb) payload. This qualified for official records in the 1,000, 2,000, 5,000 and 10,000 kg speed-with-payload categories, and had not been beaten by mid-1964.

Since 1975 Boeing at Wichita has been engaged in a programme to extend the flying life of each KC-135A by 27,000 hours, by replacing the lower wing skins. This will enable the aircraft to remain fully operational well past the year 2000, and has justified a programme to retrofit modern technology engines, to improve fuel economy and reduce noise. Selection of the 97·86 kN (22,000 lb st)

General Electric/SNECMA CFM56 turbofan for evaluation on a KC-135A testbed aircraft was announced in early 1980, and retrofit of an unspecified number of KC-135As will be undertaken by Boeing Military Airplane Company. Subsequent versions have included the **EC-135J, N** and **P**.

The following details refer to the standard KC-135A:

DIMENSIONS, EXTERNAL:
Wing span	130 ft 10 in (39·88 m)
Length overall	136 ft 3 in (41·53 m)
Height overall	38 ft 4 in (11·68 m)
Wheel track	22 ft 1 in (6·73 m)
Wheelbase	45 ft 8 in (13·92 m)

WEIGHTS (basic tanker version):
Operating weight empty	98,466 lb (44,663 kg)
Design T-O weight	245,000 lb (111,130 kg)
Max T-O weight	297,000 lb (134,715 kg)
Design landing weight	185,000 lb (83,915 kg)

PERFORMANCE (refuelling mission at max T-O weight):
Average cruising speed at 30,500-45,000 ft (9,300-13,700 m)	532 mph (856 kmh)
T-O speed	192 mph (310 kmh)
Rate of climb at S/L	1,290 ft (393 m) min
Rate of climb at S/L, one engine out	580 ft (177 m) min
Time to 30,500 ft (9,300 m)	27 min
T-O run	9,050 ft (2,760 m)
T-O field length	10,690 ft (3,260 m)
Landing run at 105,200 lb (47,720 kg)AUW	1,900 ft (580 m)
Transfer radius with 6,734 lb (3,055 kg) fuel reserve	1,150 miles (1,850 km)
Total mission time	5·5 hours
	(1966–67)

BOEING MODEL 717 STRATOLIFTER AND MODEL 739
USAF designations: C-135, RC-135

The C-135 Stratolifter is a long-range jet transport developed from the KC-135A Stratotanker. External and internal dimensions of the two types are similar, the most noticeable change being the deletion of the refuelling "flying boom" fitted to the tanker. Minor internal changes provide improved standard accommodation for 126 troops or 44 stretchers and 54 sitting casualties. These include additional sound-proofing, improved lighting and two air-conditioning packs. Galley and toilet facilities are located aft. Luggage can be stowed in the forward cabin and in a lower deck compartment under the galley.

In a freight-carrying rôle, typical loads for the C-135 are 376 boxes of 30-cal. ammunition (a 2½-day supply for one airborne division), or 1,090 cases of "C" rations (a daily supply for three battle groups). To facilitate cargo handling, the aircraft has a metal floor, with a special transfer plate opposite the loading door to permit easy manoeuvring of cargo pallets.

The USAF signed an initial contract for 30 C-135's for operation by the Military Airlift Command (formerly Military Air Transport Service) in February, 1961. A further order for 15 aircraft was placed later.

Six versions of the C-135 have been developed, as follows:

C-135A (Model 717-157). First 15 aircraft, with 13,750 lb (6,240 kg) st Pratt & Whitney J57-P-59W engines. The first one flew on May 19, 1961, and was delivered on June 8, becoming the first strategic jet transport in the MATS force.

C-135B (Model 717-158). Sixteenth and subsequent C-135's, with 18,000 lb (8,165 kg) st Pratt & Whitney TF33-P-5 turbofan engines. Tailplane span increased. First one delivered in March, 1962. All 30 had been delivered by the end of August 1962.

Both "A" and "B" models are now being phased out of the airlift force and will be converted to other USAF missions.

RC-135A. Four built. Scheduled to be equipped and delivered in late 1965 and early 1966. Same as C-135, but specially equipped with multiple cameras and electronic equipment for photo-mapping and electronic surveying of terrain, utilising SHIRAN. Has three camera ports in belly behind nose-wheel, covered by remotely-controlled aerodynamic fairing when not in use. Special navigation equipment for improved mapping accuracy. For 1,370th Photo Mapping Wing of MAC. Boeing **Model 739-700.**

RC-135B. Ten built. Electronic reconnaissance aircraft, similar to RC-135A but with turbofan engines. Equipment installed at military establishments. Boeing **Model 739-445B.**

Subsequent versions have included the RC-135S, T, U, V and W.

VC-135B. Version of C-135B with revised interior for VIP transportation.

VC-137A. Three Model 707-120's delivered to USAF for use by VIP personnel. Same as 707-120, except for interior furnishing and electronic equipment installed. Forward area of cabin contains communications centre, galley, toilet and 8-seat compartment. Centre portion is designed as an airborne HQ, with conference table, swivel chairs, projection screen for films and two convertible sofa/bunks. Aft cabin contains 14 double reclining passenger seats, two tables, three galleys, two toilets and closets. First VC-137A flew for the first time on 7 April 1959. All three have since been re-engined with JT3D turbofans and are now designated VC-137B.

VC-137B. This is the current designation of the three USAF VC-137A's following their conversion to turbofan power. They continue in service with the 89th Military Airlift Wing of Military Airlift Command, carrying a crew of seven or eight and 40 passengers. Max T-O weight 258,000 lb (117,025 kg).

VC-137C. One 707-320B, with JT3D-3 turbofan engines and internal furnishing similar to VC-137B. Crew of seven or eight and 49 passengers. Delivered to Special Air Missions Squadron of the USAF Military Airlift Command, but now

with 89th Military Airlift Wing. Used to carry government officials, including the President, and visiting dignitaries of foreign countries. Max T-O weight 322,000 lb (146,055 kg).

WC-135B. Same as C-135B. Ten aircraft modified for long-range weather reconnaissance missions for MAC Air Weather Service.

On April 17, 1962, a C-135B commanded by Major D. W. Craw, USAF, set up an official payload-to-height record by lifting 66,139 lb (30,000 kg) to a height of 47,171 ft (14,377·74 m), qualifying also for records in the 15,000, 20,000 and 25,000 kg categories. Also on April 17-18, 1962, a C-135B commanded by Major V. W. Hamann, USAF, set up records for carrying payloads of 5,000, 10,000 15,000, 20,000, 25,000 and 30,000 kg around a 2,000 km (1,243 mile) closed circuit at 615·79 mph (991·01 kmh).

DIMENSIONS, EXTERNAL:
Same as for KC-135A, except:
Length overall	134 ft 6 in (41·0 m)

WEIGHTS (C-135B):
Operating weight empty	102,300 lb (46,400 kg)
Max payload	87,100 lb (39,500 kg)
Max T-O weight (dry)	275,500 lb (124,960 kg)
Max landing weight	200,000 lb (90,720 kg)

PERFORMANCE (C-135B at max T-O weight, except where indicated):
Max level speed	600 mph (965 kmh)
Average cruising speed at 35,000 ft (10,670 m)	530 mph (850 kmh)
T-O speed	193 mph (310 kmh)
T-O run	7,150 ft (2,180 m)
Rate of climb at S/L, one engine out at AUW of 200,000 lb (90,720 kg)	1,500 ft (457 m) min
Range with 54,000 lb (24,500 kg) payload	4,625 miles (7,445 km)
Max ferry range	9,000 miles (14,485 km)
	(1966–67)

The Boeing B-29 Superfortress Heavy Bomber (four Wright R-3350-23 engines).

THE BOEING MODEL 345 SUPERFORTRESS.
U.S. Air Force designations: B-29 and F-13.
U.S. Navy designation: P2B.

The original specification for a large four-engined bomber to succeed the B-17 Fortress was issued by the U.S. War Department in January, 1940, but it was considerably modified some months later to incorporate increased armament and load requirements. To meet the original specification the Boeing

company designed the Model 341, and this was modified into the Model 345 to incorporate the later requirements.

The contract for three XB-29 prototypes was placed with the Boeing company on August 24, 1940, and a service development order for 13 YB-29's was placed in the following May. With America's entry into the war a vast production programme for the B-29 was initiated, involving five main production plants and hundreds of sub-contractors.

The Boeing B-29 "Pacusan Dreamboat" which flew non-stop from Pearl Harbour to Cairo, Egypt, a distance of 9,500 miles in 39 hours 36 minutes in 1946.

The Boeing SB-29 with Edo A-3 airborne lifeboat for Sea Rescue duties.

The first XB-29 prototype built at Seattle flew on September 21, 1942, and the first YB-29 built at Wichita flew on April 15, 1943. Production of the B-29 ceased in May, 1946, after a total of 4,221 had been built.

A number of B-29s which were put into storage after the war are being modernised before being returned to service. Modifications include the addition of fuel-injection systems to those aircraft not already so equipped; provision of improved electronic equipment; addition of pneumatic bomb-bay doors and modifications for re-fuelling in the air. Some aircraft will be fitted as tankers for flight re-fuelling.

The modernised B-29s will equip new groups required for the recently-authorised 70-Group Air Force.

The successor to the B-29 as the standard heavy bomber in the U.S.A.F. Strategic Air Command will be the B-50, deliveries of which began in 1947.

The power-plant consists of four 3,500 h.p. Pratt & Whitney R-4360 engines, resulting in a 59 per cent. increase in horsepower over the B-29. All four power-plant nacelles are completely interchangeable.

The tail-unit has vertical surfaces some 5 ft. (1.525 m.) higher than those of the B-29. These surfaces are hinged to fold horizontally over the starboard tailplane to allow the B-50 to be housed in existing hangar facilities.

The wings, tail-unit, landing-gear and many accessory items of the B-50 are interchangeable with the C-97A transport.

The following are the principal models and modifications of the Superfortress:—

B-29. Four Wright R-3350-23 engines. In later B-29s 20 mm. gun in tail-turret removed and a four-gun turret replaced the forward upper fuselage two-gun turret.

B-29A. Four Wright R-3350-57 engines. Built by Boeing (Renton).

B-29B. Four Wright R-3350-51 engines. Fuselage turrets and sighting blisters removed. A new three-gun tail turret and two .5 in. (12.7 mm.) hand-held waist guns on special mountings in gunner's pressurised compartments. Reduction of drag gave 10 m.p.h. (16 km.h.) increase in speed and reduction in weight permitted an additional 3,000 lbs. (1,360 kg.) of bombs to be carried.

B-29C and D. Cancelled after VJ-Day. B-29D became B-50 (which see).

XB-29E. One B-29 used to study and test fire-control projects.

B-29F. Six modified B-29s. No armament. Special engines fitted with reversible-pitch airscrews.

XB-29G. One B-29 modified for special engine testing.

XB-29H. One B-29 assigned to special armament tests.

YB-29J. Fitted with new 2,700 h.p. Wright R-3350-CA2 engines and Curtiss airscrews. No further details.

B-29K. Rebuilt and modernised version. No details.

B-29L. Modernised version. No details.

KB-29M. Fitted as tanker with British Flight Refuelling equipment.

KB-29P. Fitted as tanker with Boeing "Flying Boom" refuelling equipment.

SB-29. Sixteen B-29's modified for Air/Sea-Rescue duties. Lower forward turret removed to permit carrying an Edo A-3 airborne lifeboat.

(1951–52)

F-13A. B-29A equipped as a long-range high-altitude photographic-reconnaissance aircraft. Full B-29 armament and long-range fuel tanks retained.

P2B. US Navy test-beds. Four ex-USAF B-29s.

The description which follows refers to the standard B-29A, which is still in service in U.S.A.F. bomber squadrons at home and with the occupation forces overseas.

TYPE.—Four-engined Heavy Bomber.

WINGS.—Mid-wing cantilever monoplane. Boeing 117 aerofoil section. Aspect ratio 11.5/1. Dihedral 4½ degrees. 7 degrees sweep-back on leading-edge, straight trailing-edge. Centre-section and two outer sections with detachable wing-tips. All-metal web-type structure covered with a flush-riveted butt-jointed metal skin. Detachable leading-edge to give access to controls, etc. Electrically-operated flaps of the extensible type which when fully extended increase the wing area by 19 per cent. The trailing-edge of the flaps between the inboard nacelles and fuselage extend aft of the normal wing trailing-edge line and hook downward to decrease aerodynamic interference between wings and body and over tail when flaps extended. Statically and aerodynamically-balanced ailerons fitted with combination trim and servo tabs. Gross wing area 1,739 sq. ft. (1,615 m.²).

FUSELAGE.—Circular section semi-monocoque structure in five sections. Built up of a series of circumferential bulkheads and frames, extruded longerons and stringers and a flush-riveted butt-jointed stressed metal skin. The stringers are riveted to the skin and the circumferentials are attached to the stringers by means of clips. Three pressurised compartments, one forward and one aft of the bomb-bay and one in the extreme tail. Crawl tunnel over the bomb-bays interconnects the two forward compartments but the tail compartment is isolated.

TAIL UNIT.—Cantilever monoplane type with single fin and rudder. All-metal fixed surfaces, and metal-framed fabric-covered aerodynamically and statically-balanced control surfaces. Controllable trim-tabs.

LANDING GEAR.—Retractable tricycle type. Main gear has two oleo-pneumatic shock-struts and twin wheels. Double nose wheel has single strut. Electrical retraction, the main wheels being raised backwards into the inboard engine nacelles and the nose wheel into a well in the fuselage below the flight deck. Hydraulic wheel-brakes. Retractable tail bumper skid.

POWER PLANT.—Four 2,200 h.p. Wright R-3350-57 eighteen-cylinder radial air-cooled engines, each engine with two General Electric exhaust-driven turbo-superchargers mounted vertically, one on each side of the nacelle. Hamilton-Standard Hydromatic four-blade constant-speed full-feathering airscrews 16 ft. 7 in. (5 m.) diameter. Self-sealing fuel cells integral with wing structure. Normal capacity 5,608 U.S. gallons (21,227 litres). Self-sealing oil tank in each nacelle.

ACCOMMODATION.—Crew of ten to fourteen. Normal crew consists of pilot, co-pilot, navigator, bombardier, engineer, radio-operator and four gun-control operators. Forward pressurised compartment accommodates bombardier, pilot and co-pilot side-by-side with aisle in between, navigator facing forward behind pilot, engineer facing aft behind co-pilot and radio-operator behind engineer. Engineer's station has all power-plant controls and instruments but pilot's master throttle controls may override engineer's throttles. Crawl-tunnel over bomb-bays connects with second pressurised compartment which contains three gun-sighting stations in transparent blisters, one on top and one on each side of the fuselage. Tail-gunner's pressurised compartment in extreme tail of fuselage. All crew positions armoured or protected with armoured *flak* curtains. The three pressurised compartments are served by two superchargers driven off two inboard engines.

ARMAMENT.—Four General Electric remotely-controlled and electrically-operated turrets, two above and two below the fuselage. Forward upper turret with four 0.5 in. (12.7 mm.) guns, remainder with two 0.5 in. (12.7 mm.) guns each. Bell electrically-operated tail turret with two 0.5 in. (12.7 mm.) guns. Five sighting stations, one in the nose, three in the middle pressurised compartment and one in tail compartment. Mid-upper station controls either or both upper turrets, side sighting stations control lower rear turret, nose sighting station controls lower front turret and tail station control over turret. Some stations have secondary control over certain other turrets but only one sight may be in control of a given turret at one time. Two bomb-bays, one forward and one aft of the wing centre-portion which passes through the fuselage, and in order that the balance of the aircraft is preserved during bomb-dropping a system is used whereby bombs are dropped alternately from the two bays. Total maximum bomb load 20,000 lbs. (9,072 kg.). Electrically-operated bomb-bay doors.

DIMENSIONS.—Span 141 ft. 3 in. (43.1 m.), Length 99 ft. (30.2 m.), Height (over tail) 27 ft. 9 in. (8.46 m.).

WEIGHTS AND LOADINGS.—Weight empty 74,500 lbs. (33,823 kg.), Normal loaded (combat) weight 120,000 lbs. (54,480 kg.), Maximum permissible loaded weight 140,000 lbs. (63,560 kg.), Wing loading 80 lbs./sq. ft. (391 kg./m.²), Power loading 15.8 lbs./h.p. (7.15 kg./h.p.)

PERFORMANCE (at normal loaded weight).—Maximum speed 351 m.p.h. (562 km.h.) at 25,000 ft. (7,625 m.), Climb to 25,000 ft. (7,625 m.) 43 min., Range (maximum continuous cruising power) 2,850 miles (4,560 km.) or 12.8 hours at 10,000 ft. (3,050 m.). (1948)

The Boeing Superfortress B-50D Medium Bomber (four Pratt & Whitney R-4360 engines).

THE BOEING SUPERFORTRESS.
U.S. Air Force designation: B-50.

The B-50, while retaining the general characteristics of its predecessor, the B-29, is, in fact, 75 per cent. a new aeroplane, with new wings, tail-unit, landing-gear and power-plant; all of which, incidentally, are interchangeable with the C-97 transport.

Until the B-47 reaches service units in any number, the B-50, and its forerunner, the B-29, continue to be the standard U.S.A.F. medium bombers. B-29's which were put into storage after the war have been modernised before being returned to service. Modifications include the addition of fuel-injection systems to those aircraft not already so equipped; provision of improved electronic equipment; addition of pneumatic bomb-bay doors and modifications for re-fuelling in the air. Some aircraft have been fitted as tankers for flight re-fuelling.

The modernised B-29's have equipped new groups formed under the U.S.A.F. expansion programme. Seventy have been supplied to the Royal Air Force under the terms of the North Atlantic Treaty.

Full details of the B-29 and its many versions and sub-types have appeared in previous editions of "All the World's Aircraft." The following are the principal models of the B-50 Superfortress:—

B-50A. Four Pratt & Whitney R-4360 Wasp-Major engines with turbo-superchargers and driving four-blade constant-

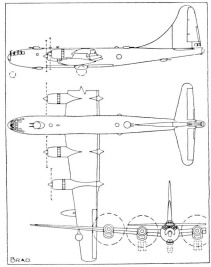

The Boeing B-50D Superfortress.

speed full-feathering and reversible airscrews. First production version. First B-50A flew for the first time on June 25, 1947.

B-50B. Certain structural changes increasing gross weight to 164,500 lb. (74,910 kg.), to permit greater load and range. Subsequently modified to RB-50B.

RB-50B. Photographic reconnaissance conversion of B-50B. Retains bombing equipment but is fitted with four camera stations with a total of nine cameras, improved radar, flight refuelling equipment and weather recording instruments. May also carry two 700 U.S. gallon dropable wing-tip tanks. Photo-flash bombs for night photography carried in bomb-bay.

B-50D. Development of B-50B with increased bomb load or fuel capacity. Carries either two 700 U.S. gallon external fuel tanks or two 4,000 lb. (1,816 kg.) bombs under outer wings. Optically-flat bomb-aimer's panel in nose, changes in radar installation, etc. Provision for in-flight refuelling by Boeing "Flying-Boom" system.

TB-50D. Modified B-50D to train triple-duty crew members who will serve as combined bombardier-navigator-radar operators in high speed jet bombers. All armament removed. Normal flight crew stations in forward fuselage, plus provisions for two student navigators and one instructor. Rear bomb-bay sealed and used for installation of a large part of the electronic equipment used in training. Rear crew compartment contains installations for one instructor and two student radar operators.

RB-50E. Photographic reconnaissance version of B-50D. No details.

RB-50F. Conversion of B-50D with Shoran gear. No details.

RB-50G. Photographic reconnaissance version of B-50D. No details.

TB-50H. Production version of TB-50D.

The description which follows refers to the standard B-50 bomber.

TYPE.—Four-engined Medium Bomber.

WINGS.—Mid-wing cantilever monoplane. Boeing 117 aerofoil section. Aspect ratio 11.5/1. Dihedral 4½ degrees. 7 degrees sweep-back on leading-edge, straight trailing-edge. All-metal stressed-skin structure. Electrically-operated Fowler type flaps which when fully extended increase the wing area by 19 per cent. Statically and aero-dynamically-balanced ailerons fitted with combination trim and servo tabs. Thermal anti-icing. Gross wing area 1,769 sq. ft. (164.2 m.²).

FUSELAGE.—Circular section semi-mono-coque structure with flush-riveted and butt-jointed stressed metal skin.

TAIL UNIT.—Cantilever monoplane type with single fin and rudder. All-metal fixed surfaces, and metal-framed fabric-covered control surfaces. Upper portion of fin and rudder fold down onto starboard tailplane. Thermal anti-icing.

LANDING GEAR.—Retractable tricycle type. Electrical retraction. Hydraulic wheel-brakes. Track of main wheels (centre-line of shock struts) 28 ft. 6 in. (8.69 m.). Wheel base 34 ft. 4 in. (10.47 m.).

POWER PLANT.—Pratt & Whitney R-4360-35 twenty-eight-cylinder radial air-cooled engines each rated at 2,650 h.p. and with 3,500 h.p. available for take-off with water injection. Four-blade Curtiss Electric constant-speed full-feathering and reversing airscrews 17 ft. 2 in. (5.23 m.) in diameter. Each engine fitted with one General Electric CH-7A exhaust-driven turbo-supercharger. All engine nacelles interchangeable. Self-sealing fuel cells integral with wing structure. Self-sealing oil tank in each nacelle.

ACCOMMODATION.—Crew of eleven. Normal crew consists of pilot, co-pilot, navigator, bombardier, engineer, radio-operator and four gun-control operators. Forward pressurised compartment accommodates bombardier, pilot and co-pilot side-by-side navigator facing forward behind pilot, engineer facing aft behind co-pilot and radio-operator behind engineer. Crawl-tunnel over bomb-bays connect with second pressurised compartment which contains three gun-sighting stations in transparent blisters, one on top and one on each side of the fuselage. Tail-gunner's pressurised compartment in extreme tail of fuselage.

ARMAMENT.—Four General Electric remotely-controlled and electrically-operated turrets, two above and two below the fuselage. Forward upper turret with four 0.5 in. (12.7 mm.) guns, remainder with two 0.5 in. (12.7 mm.) guns each. Three 0.5 in. (12.7 mm.) guns in tail position. Five sighting stations, one in the nose, three in the middle pressurised compartment and one in tail compartment. Two bomb-bays, one forward and one aft of the wing centre-portion which passes through the fuselage. Total maximum bomb load 28,000 lb. (12,710 kg.). Pneumatically-operated bomb-bay doors.

DIMENSIONS.—
Span 141 ft. 3 in. (43.1 m.).
Length 99 ft. (30.2 m.).
Height (over tail) 32 ft. 8 in. (10.0 m.).

WEIGHTS.—
Normal loaded (combat) weight 140,000 lb. (63,560 kg.).
Max. permissible loaded weight 164,500 lb. (74,780 kg.).

PERFORMANCE.—
Max. speed over 400 m.p.h. (640 km.h.).
Cruising speed over 300 m.p.h. (480 km.h.).
Ceiling over 40,000 ft. (22,000 m.).
Operating range over 6,000 miles (9,600 km.) with 10,000 lb. (4,540 kg.) of bombs.
(1952–53)

BOEING E-3 SENTRY
USAF designations: EC-137D and E-3

The E-3A Sentry AWACS (Airborne Warning And Control System) aircraft offers the potential of long-range high- or low-level surveillance of all air vehicles, manned or unmanned, in all weathers and above all kinds of terrain. Its data storage and processing capability can provide real-time assessment of enemy action, and of the status and position of friendly resources. By centralising the co-ordination of complex, diverse and simultaneous air operations in wartime, such an aircraft can command and control the total air effort: strike, air superiority, support, airlift, reconnaissance and interdiction.

In US Air Force service, the system has a dual use: as a command and control centre to support quick-reaction deployment and tactical operations by Tactical Air Command units; and as a survivable early-warning airborne command and control centre for identification, surveillance and tracking of airborne enemy forces, and for the command and control of NORAD (North American Air Defense) forces over the continental USA. The E-3A provides comprehensive surveillance out to a range of more than 200 nm (370 km; 230 miles) for low-flying targets, and still further for targets flying at higher altitudes.

Boeing's Aerospace Group was awarded an initial contract as prime contractor and systems integrator for the AWAC system on 23 July 1970. Its design submission was based on the airframe of the Model 707-320B commercial jet transport. Two of these aircraft, with the prototype designation EC-137D, were modified initially for comparative trials with prototype downward-looking radars designed by Hughes Aircraft Company and Westinghouse Electric Corporation.

After several months of airborne tests the Westinghouse radar was selected, on 5 October 1972. On 26 January 1973 the US Air Force announced that, following satisfactory completion of Phase 1, approval had been given for full-scale development of AWACS, and production was authorised in the Spring of 1975. The full-scale development test programme involved a fleet of three aircraft completely equipped with mission avionics, and a fourth aircraft equipped for airworthiness testing, and was completed at the end of 1976.

In December 1976 Boeing awarded Westinghouse a contract to develop a maritime surveillance capability that could be incorporated in the E-3A radar. An aircraft began flight testing this system in June 1979. All E-3A aircraft, beginning with production system 22 scheduled for delivery in early 1981, will be equipped for maritime surveillance.

The first production E-3A Sentry was delivered on 24 March 1977 to Tactical Air Command's 552nd Airborne Warning and Control Wing, based at Tinker AFB, Oklahoma. A total of five were delivered by the end of 1977, followed by ten more during 1978, and five during 1979. E-3As achieved initial operational status in April 1978, and have since completed deployments to Alaska, Iceland, Saudi Arabia, the Mediterranean area, and the Pacific. They began assuming a role in US continental air defence on 1 January 1979, when 30 NORAD personnel started to augment TAC E-3A flight crews on all operational NORAD missions from Tinker AFB. This unit was expected to be fully operational by Summer 1979.

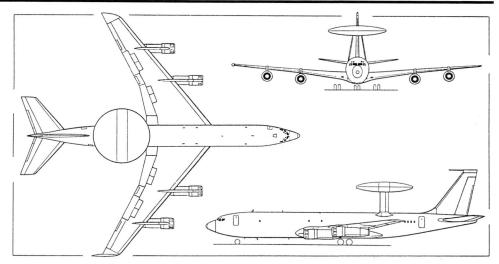

Three-view drawing (Pilot Press) and photograph of a Boeing E-3A Sentry airborne warning and control system (AWACS) aircraft for the USAF

Funding for a total of 28 E-3As had been approved by the end of 1980, and two more will be requested under each Fiscal Year budget until the planned force of 34 USAF AWACS is complete. In addition, NATO has approved the acquisition of 18, under a cost-sharing agreement, to be based in the Federal Republic of Germany. For these, much of the avionics will be produced in West Germany, with Dornier as systems integrator; deliveries to NATO will begin in early 1982. These, too, will have a maritime surveillance capability. Avionics and equipment in the NATO aircraft are generally similar to those in US Air Force E-3As, though in some cases the supplier is different.

From aircraft No. 24, US Air Force and NATO E-3As were to an upgraded standard of which the main ingredients include a joint tactical information distribution system (JTIDS), funded by the US Air Force, and improved data processing capability, funded by NATO.

E-3As now upgraded to latest E-3B and E-3C standards.

TYPE: Airborne early-warning and command post aircraft.

WINGS, FUSELAGE, TAIL UNIT AND LANDING GEAR: Basically as Boeing 707-320B, with strengthened fuselage structure and installation of rotodome.

POWER PLANT: Four Pratt & Whitney TF33-PW-100/100A turbofan engines, each rated at 93.4 kN (21,000 lb st), mounted in pods beneath the wings.

ACCOMMODATION: Basic operational crew of 17 includes a flight crew complement of four plus thirteen AWACS specialists, though this latter number can vary for tactical and defence missions. Aft of flight deck, from front to rear of fuselage, are communications, data processing and other equipment bays; multi-purpose consoles; communications, navigation and identification equipment; and crew rest area.

SYSTEMS: A liquid cooling system provides protection for the radar transmitter. An air-cycle pack system and a closed-loop ram-cooled environmental control system ensure a suitable environment for crew and avionics equipment. Electrical power generation has a 600kVA capability. The distribution centre for mission equipment power and remote avionics is located in the lower forward cargo compartment. The aft cargo compartment houses the radar transmitter and an APU. External sockets allow intake of power when the aircraft is on the ground. Two separate and independent hydraulic systems power flight-essential and mission-essential equipment, but either system has the capability of satisfying the requirements of both equipment groups in an emergency.

AVIONICS AND EQUIPMENT: Prominent above the fuselage is the elliptical cross-section rotodome which is 9·14 m (30 ft) in diameter and 1·83 m (6 ft) in depth. It comprises four essential elements: a strut-mounted turntable, supporting the rotary joint assembly to which are attached sliprings for electrical and waveguide continuity between rotodome and fuselage; a structural centre section of aluminium skin and stiffener construction, which supports the AN/APY-1 surveillance radar and IFF/TADIL C antennae, radomes, auxiliary equipment for radar operation and environmental control of the rotodome interior; liquid cooling of the radar antenna; and two radomes constructed of multi-layer glassfibre sandwich material, one for the surveillance radar and one for the IFF/TADIL C array. For surveillance operations the rotodome is hydraulically driven at 6 rpm, but during non-operational flights it is rotated at only ¼ rpm, to keep the bearings lubricated. The

Westinghouse radar operates in the S band; by use of pulse Doppler technology, with a high pulse repetition frequency, this radar features long range and accuracy in addition to a normal downlook capability. Its antenna, spanning about 7·32 m (24 ft), and 1·52 m (5 ft) deep, scans mechanically in azimuth, and electronically from ground level up into the stratosphere. Heart of the data processing in the first 23 aircraft is an IBM 4 Pi CC-1 high-speed computer, the entire group consisting of arithmetic control units, input/output units, main storage units, peripheral control units, mass memory drums, magnetic tape transports, punched tape reader, line printer, and an operator's control panel. Processing speed is in the order of 740,000 operations/s; input/output data rate has a maximum of 710,000 words/s; main memory size is 131,072 words (expandable to 180,224), and mass memory size 802,816 words (expandable to 1,204,224). An interface adapter unit developed by Boeing is the key integrating element interconnecting functional data between AWACS avionics subsystems, data processing group, radar, communications, navigation/guidance, display, azimuth and identification. From the 24th production aircraft, an improved IBM computer will be installed, with a main storage capacity of 665,360 words. Data display and control is provided by Hazeltine Corporation multi-purpose consoles (MPC) and auxiliary display units (ADU); in present configuration each AWACS aircraft carries nine MPCs and two ADUs. Navigation/guidance relies upon three principal sources of information: two Delco AN/ASN-119

(Carousel IV) inertial platforms; a Northrop AN/ARN-120 Omega navigation set; and a Ryan AN/APN-213 Doppler velocity sensor. Communications equipment, supplied by Collins Radio, Electronic Communications Inc, E-Systems, and Hughes Aircraft, provides HF, VHF and UHF communication channels by means of which information can be transmitted or received in clear or secure mode, in voice or digital form. Identification is based on an AN/APX-103 interrogator set developed by Cutler-Hammer's AIL Division. It is the first airborne IFF interrogator set to offer complete AIMS Mk X SIF air traffic control and Mk XII military identification friend or foe (IFF) in a single integrated system. Simultaneous Mk X and Mk XII multi-target and multi-mode operations allow the operator to obtain instantaneously the range, azimuth and elevation, code identification and IFF status of all targets within radar range.

DIMENSIONS, EXTERNAL:

Wing span	44·42 m (145 ft 9 in)
Length overall	46·61 m (152 ft 11 in)
Height overall	12·60 m (41 ft 4 in)

WEIGHT:

Max T-O weight	147,400 kg (325,000 lb)

PERFORMANCE:

Max level speed	460 knots (853 km/h; 530 mph)
Service ceiling	over 8,850 m (29,000 ft)
Endurance on station, 870 nm (1,610 km; 1,000 miles)	
from base	6 h
	(1980–81)

Boeing E-4B advanced airborne command post operated by the USAF Strategic Air Command

BOEING ADVANCED AIRBORNE COMMAND POST

USAF designation: E-4

On 28 February 1973 the US Air Force's Electronic Systems Division announced from its headquarters at Hanscom Field, Bedford, Massachusetts, that it had awarded The Boeing Company a $59 million fixed-price contract for the supply of two Model 747-200Bs to be adapted as **E-4A** airborne command posts under the 481B Advanced Airborne Command Post (AABNCP) programme. A contract valued at more than $27·2 million was awarded, in July 1973, for a third aircraft; in December 1973 the fourth aircraft was contracted at $39 million.

The third and fourth aircraft differed initially from the first two in having General Electric F103-GE-100 turbofan engines, each rated at 233·5 kN (52,500 lb st), instead of the JT9Ds that were then fitted normally to aircraft of the 747 series; F103-GE-100s were fitted retrospectively to the first two aircraft during 1976. The fourth aircraft is fitted with more advanced equipment (see below) and is designated **E-4B.**

On 15 January 1976 it was stated that the total planned force was six E-4Bs, comprising the fourth aircraft, two more similar aircraft, and the three E-4As brought up to the same standard retrospectively. Contracts covering modification of one E-4A to E-4B configuration, with options to modify the other two, were announced on 26 June 1980. E-Systems Inc of Greenville, Texas, is teamed with Boeing Aerospace in the E-4A/B modification programme.

The E-4s are intended to replace EC-135 Airborne Command Posts of the National Military Command System and Strategic Air Command, which are military variants of the Model 707. E-Systems won the contract to install interim equipment in the three E-4As. This involved transfer and integration of equipment removed from EC-135s, providing aircraft with increased endurance and the ability to carry an expanded battle staff. The E-4A's 429·2 m² (4,620 sq ft) of floor space accommodates almost three times the payload of the EC-135. The main deck is divided into six areas: the National Command Authorities' (NCA) work area, conference room, briefing room, battle staff work area, communications control centre and rest area. The flight deck accommodates the flight crew, navigation station and flight crew rest area. Lobe areas, beneath the main deck, house a technical control facility and a limited onboard maintenance storage area.

The first E-4A flew for the first time on 13 June 1973, and was delivered to Andrews AFB, Maryland, in December 1974. The second and third, also consigned to Andrews AFB, were received in May and September 1975. In their present form, they are able to operate as National Emergency Airborne Command Posts (NEACPs), and provided operational experience that proved invaluable in finalising the design of equipment installed in the E-4B. The E-4 is capable of remaining airborne for up to 72 hours.

Boeing, E-Systems and a team comprising Electrospace Systems Inc of Richardson, Texas; Collins Radio Division of Rockwell International Corporation, Dallas, Texas; RCA Corporation of Morristown, NJ; and Burroughs

Corporation, Federal and Special Systems Group, of Paoli, Pennsylvania, are responsible for designing and installing the advanced command post equipment in the E-4B. The first E-4B was delivered to the US Air Force in August 1975 in testbed configuration, with flight refuelling equipment installed but without the planned command, control and communications equipment. Next stage involved installation of the 1,200kVA electrical system (two 150kVA generators on each engine) that had been designed to support the advanced avionics. Finally the operational systems were added, and the first flight of the fully equipped E-4B took place in June 1978. US Air Force tests of operational capability began later that year.

The first E-4B (75-0125) was redelivered to the US Air Force on 21 December 1979, and entered service in January 1980. It has accommodation for a larger battle staff than that carried by the E-4A; an air-conditioning system of 226·5 m³ (8,000 cu ft)/min capacity to cool avionics components; nuclear thermal shielding; acoustic controls; an improved technical control facility; and new super high frequency (SHF) and Collins LF/VLF communications systems, the latter employing a trailing-wire antenna that is trailed several miles behind the aircraft in flight. The SHF antennae are housed in a dorsal fairing which is a recognition characteristic of the E-4B.

Strategic Air Command (SAC) is now sole operational manager of the AABNCP force. Transfer of operational responsibility from Headquarters Command USAF to SAC began in October 1975 and became effective as from 1 November 1975. The main operating base for the E-4 fleet is at Offutt AFB, Nebraska. (1980–81)

BOEING T-43A

Experience gained during the war in Vietnam alerted the USAF to the need to increase its supply of trained navigators. To meet this requirement and to improve the standard of training, it was decided to replace the existing fleet of Convair T-29 piston-engined trainers by more modern aircraft of greater capacity.

Boeing's Model 737-200 was selected as the most suitable off-the-shelf basic aircraft for this role, and 19 of these, modified to meet the military requirement, were ordered with the designation T-43A under an $81·7 million contract.

Generally similar to the commercial model, they differ primarily in having only two doors, one on each side of the fuselage; nine windows only on each side; strengthened floor to carry avionics consoles; provision of overhead sextant viewing ports; and installation of an 800 US gallon (3,027 litre) auxiliary fuel tank in the aft cargo compartment.

The first of these navigational trainers was rolled out at Boeing's Renton, Washington, factory on 2 March 1973, and made its first flight on 10 April 1973, prior to obtaining FAA certification in the new configuration. Following certification, this first T-43A was delivered to Mather AFB, California, for operational test and evaluation by the USAF, and all 19 had been delivered by July 1974.

At Mather the T-43As replaced 77 T-29s which had been in use for navigation training. Only 19 T-43As were needed to replace this fleet as they each accommodate up to twelve trainee

navigators, four navigator proficiency students and three instructors, and were expected to have double the utilisation factor of the T-29s.

They are being used in conjunction with Honeywell T-45 electronic simulators to form a new Undergraduate Navigator Training System. The new ground-based equipment provides simulation of a wide range of missions, including low-level flights over land and water, night flights, airways navigation, high-altitude operations up to 70,000 ft (21,340 m) and at speeds of up to Mach 2. On-board avionics equipment of the T-43As is the same as that used in the most

advanced USAF operational aircraft, including celestial, radar and inertial navigation systems, LORAN and other radio systems.

The specification and performance figures quoted for the Boeing Model 737-200 equipped with Pratt & Whitney JT8D-9 turbofan engines apply in general to the T-43A, except as follows:

PERFORMANCE:
Econ cruising speed at 35,000 ft (10,670 m)
Mach 0·7
Operational range, MIL-C-5011A reserves
2,600 nm (2,995 miles; 4,820 km)
Endurance 6 hr

Boeing T-43A navigational trainer, evolved from the Model 737-200 (1975–76)

THE BOEING TB-1.

The Boeing TB-1 is a three-purpose bomber, torpedo or scout biplane, fitted with one 850 h.p. Packard 2A-2500 engine. It is of all-metal construction, can be equipped with either wheel landing gear or twin floats, and is provided with folding wings. The pilot and navigator are accommodated in a side-by-side cockpit, situated under the leading edge of the top wing, and the cowling slopes away forward, giving them an excellent view.

The back gunner's cockpit is situated midway between the trailing edge of the main planes and the tail unit.

Specification.

Span	..	..	..	55 ft.
Length	..	..	..	40 ft. 6 in.
Height	..	..	..	15 ft.
Chord	..	..	..	8 ft. 6 in.

(1927)

BOEING VERTOL MODELS 114 and 414
US Army designation: CH-47 Chinook
Canadian Armed Forces designation: CH-147
Royal Air Force designation: Chinook HC. Mk 1

Development of the CH-47 Chinook series of helicopters began in 1956, and the first of five YCH-47As (formerly YHC-1B) made its initial hovering flight on 21 September 1961. Since then, effectiveness of the CH-47 has been increased by successive improvement programmes.

The CH-47 was designed to meet the US Army's requirement for an all-weather medium transport helicopter and, depending upon the series model, is capable of transporting specified payloads under severe combinations of altitude and temperature conditions. The primary mission radius criterion established by the US Army is 100 nm (185 km; 115 miles). The primary mission take-off gross weight is based on the capability of hovering out of ground effect at 1,830 m/35°C (6,000 ft/95°F). The CH-47C has demonstrated its ability to hover out of ground effect with a useful load of 11,453 kg (25,250 lb) at sea level under standard atmospheric conditions.

The following versions of the Chinook have been produced:

CH-47A. Initial production version, powered by two 1,640 kW (2,200 shp) Avco Lycoming T55-L-5 or 1,976 kW (2,650 shp) T55-L-7 turboshaft engines. Operation of the CH-47A by the Viet-Nam Air Force (VNAF) began in 1971. Four delivered to Royal Thai Air Force. Production completed. Transmissions uprated to CH-47C standard under 1978 Army contract.

CH-47B. Developed version with 2,125 kW (2,850 shp) T55-L-7C turboshaft engines, redesigned rotor blades with cambered leading-edge, blunted rear rotor pylon, and strakes along rear ramp and fuselage for improved flying qualities. First of two prototypes flew for the first time in early October 1966. Deliveries began on 10 May 1967. Production completed. Transmissions uprated to CH-47C standard under 1978 Army contract.

CH-47C. Increased performance from a combination of strengthened transmissions, two 2,796 kW (3,750 shp) T55-L-11A engines and increased integral fuel capacity. First flight of original CH-47C made 14 October 1967; production deliveries began in Spring 1968. First deployed in Viet-Nam in September 1968. Total of 210 US Army CH-47Cs currently undergoing retrofit with glassfibre rotor blades.

A Crash-worthy Fuel System (CWFS) and an Integral Spar Inspection System (ISIS) were made available during

The three Boeing Vertol CH-47D prototypes, converted from CH-47A/47B/47C Chinooks

1973. Incorporation of the CWFS on US Army CH-47Cs was accomplished by retrofit kits, deliveries of which began in March 1973. Chinooks delivered to Australia have this system, which provides a total fuel capacity of 3,944 litres (1,042 US gallons).

CH-147. Designation of nine CH-47Cs delivered to Canada from September 1974. These aircraft have T55-L-11C engines, ISIS, CWFS, forward door rescue hoist, ferry range tank kit, up to 44 troop seats, advanced

flight control system, rear ramp with water dam, 12,700 kg (28,000 lb) cargo hook, T-O weight of 22,680 kg (50,000 lb), and weight for water operations of 16,330 kg (36,000 lb) normal or 20,865 kg (46,000 lb) emergency.

CH-47D. Three Chinooks (one each of the CH-47A, CH-47B, and CH-47C models) have been modernised to CH-47D configuration under a $75 million contract received from the US Army in June 1976. The three aircraft were stripped down to their basic airframes, and were then rebuilt with improved components and systems to provide three CH-47D prototypes.

Conversion included the installation of Avco Lycoming T55-L-712 engines, which have an emergency power rating; the introduction of improved rotor transmissions with a rating of 5,593 kW (7,500 shp); the introduction of integral lubrication and cooling for the transmission systems, and of glassfibre rotor blades. Other improvements include a redesigned cockpit to reduce the pilot's workload; the introduction of redundant and improved electrical systems, modularised hydraulic systems, an advanced flight control system, and improved avionics equipment. In addition, a T62T-2B APU and a triple cargo hook suspension system have been installed.

The first CH-47D, converted from a CH-47A airframe, was rolled out four months ahead of schedule on 6 March 1979. After flight testing had been completed by Boeing Vertol, this aircraft was accepted by the US Army, at Fort Rucker, Alabama, on 13 December 1979, and by mid-1980 the three prototypes had completed a 920-hour programme of flight testing, as well as an extensive series of ground tests, by Boeing Vertol and the US Army. Two of the CH-47D prototypes were allocated to an operational test programme, conducted by the 101st Airborne Division (Air Assault) at Fort Campbell, Kentucky, which took place in April and May 1980. The third aircraft was then being used for climatic tests. A decision was due in August/September 1980 on US Army plans calling for 436 earlier-model Chinooks to be remanufactured to CH-47D standard. Meanwhile, what Boeing Vertol describes as "an orderly transition to the start of CH-47D production" has been under way since January 1979.

Chinook HC.Mk 1. Version for Royal Air Force, which ordered 33 for delivery by the end of 1981. First example (ZA670) made its initial flight on 23 March 1980. Deliveries were due to begin in September 1980. Generally similar to Canadian CH-147, with Avco Lycoming T55-L-11E turboshaft engines, but with provision for glassfibre/carbonfibre rotor blades and three external cargo hooks (capacity 12,700 kg; 28,000 lb on centre hook, or 9,072 kg; 20,000 lb total on forward and rear hooks); accommodation for up to 44 troops or 24 standard NATO stretchers; engine and windscreen de-icing; provision for two self-ferry fuel tanks in cabin; and amphibious capability in sea states of up to 3. Intended for use on logistic support, tactical troop lift, casualty evacuation, air-mobility, and external load-carrying duties. Will equip one squadron based in the UK, a small training unit (also in the UK), and No. 18 Squadron at RAF Gutersloh in West Germany. Extensive range of British avionics and equipment, including Decca tactical navigation system, Doppler Mk 71 radar and Mk 19 area navigation; Marconi Avionics ARC340 VHF/FM com and homing system, AD120 VHF/AM com, AD380 ADF, AD2770 Tacan and AD27733 interface unit; Lucas 40kVA generators; and UHF/AM, VOR/ILS, HF/SSB, radar altimeter, UHF/VHF homing, and IFF transceiver.

Model 234. Commercial version, described separately.

CH-47 helicopters are in service in many places, including Alaska, Australia, West Germany, Hawaii, Iran, Italy, Korea, Spain and Thailand, as well as at numerous US National Guard and US Army installations within the continental United States. Total US Army procurement of CH-47A/B/C models had reached 727 by 1 January 1980.

Of these, 358 then equipped active Army units, with 94 more in Reserve/ANG service. Other customers for US-built CH-47Cs include Argentina (3), Australia (12), Canada (9), Spain (10), Thailand (4), and the UK (33). Deliveries of Agusta/EM-built CH-47Cs have been made to the air forces of Italy (26), Iran (95, of which 60 delivered by the end of 1979), Libya (20, of which 16 delivered) and Morocco (6).

Details apply specifically to the CH-47C.

TYPE: Twin-engined medium transport helicopter.

ROTOR SYSTEM: Two three-blade rotors, rotating in opposite directions and driven through interconnecting shafts which enable both rotors to be driven by either engine. Rotor blades, of a modified NACA 0012 section, have cambered leading-edge, a strengthened steel spar structure and honeycomb-filled trailing-edge boxes. Two blades of each rotor can be folded manually. Rotor heads are fully articulated, with pitch, flapping and drag hinges. All bearings are submerged completely in oil.

ROTOR DRIVE: Power is transmitted from each engine through individual overrunning clutches, into the combiner transmission, thereby providing a single power output to the interconnecting shafts. Rotor/engine rpm ratio 64 : 1.

FUSELAGE: Square-section all-metal semi-monocoque structure. Loading ramp forms undersurface of upswept rear fuselage. Fairing pods along bottom of each side are made of metal honeycomb sandwich and are sealed and compartmented, as is the underfloor section of the fuselage, for buoyancy during operation from water.

LANDING GEAR: Menasco non-retractable quadricycle type, with twin wheels on each forward unit and single wheels on each rear unit. Oleo-pneumatic shock-absorbers on all units. Rear units fully castoring and steerable; power steering installed on starboard rear unit. All wheels are government-furnished size 24 × 7·7-VII, with tyres size 8·50-10-III, pressure 4·62 bars (67 lb/sq in). Two single-disc hydraulic brakes. Provision for fitting detachable wheel-skis.

POWER PLANT: Two 2,796 kW (3,750 shp) Avco Lycoming T55-L-11A turboshaft engines, mounted one each side of rear rotor pylon. Combined transmission rating 5,369 kW (7,200 shp); max single-engine transmission limit 3,430 kW (4,600 shp). Self-sealing fuel tanks in external pods on sides of fuselage. Total fuel capacity is 4,137 litres (1,093 US gallons), or 3,944 litres (1,042 US gallons) when equipped with Crashworthy Fuel System. Refuelling points above tanks. Total oil capacity 14 litres (3·7 US gallons).

ACCOMMODATION: Two pilots on flight deck, with dual controls. Jump seat is provided for crew chief or combat commander. Jettisonable door on each side of flight deck. Depending on seating arrangement, 33 to 44 troops can be accommodated in main cabin, or 24 litters plus two attendants, or vehicles and freight. Typical loads include a complete artillery section with crew and ammunition. All components of the Pershing missile system are transportable by Chinooks. Extruded mag-

nesium floor designed for distributed load of 1,465 kg/m² (300 lb/sq ft) and concentrated load of 1,136 kg/m² (2,500 lb) per wheel in tread portion. Floor contains eighty-three 2,270 kg (5,000 lb) tiedown fittings and eight 4,540 kg (10,000 lb) fittings. Rear loading ramp can be left completely or partially open, or can be removed to permit transport of extra-long cargo and in-flight parachute or free-drop delivery of cargo and equipment. Main cabin door, at front on starboard side, comprises upper hinged section which can be opened in flight and lower section with integral steps. Lower section is jettisonable. Up to 12,700 kg (28,000 lb) can be carried on external cargo hook.

SYSTEMS: Cabin heated by 200,000 BTU heater-blower. Hydraulic system provides pressures of 207 bars (3,000 lb/sq in) for flying controls, and 276 bars (4,000 lb/sq in) for engine starting. Electrical system includes two 20kVA alternators driven by transmission drive system. Solar T62 APU runs accessory gear drive, thereby operating all hydraulic and electrical systems.

AVIONICS AND EQUIPMENT: All government furnished, including UHF communications and FM liaison sets, transponder, intercom, omni-receiver, ADF and marker beacon receiver. Blind-flying instrumentation standard. Special equipment includes dual electro-hydraulic stability augmentation system, automatic/manual speed trim system, hydraulically-powered winch for rescue and cargo handling purposes, cargo and rescue hatch in floor, integral work stands and steps for maintenance, rearview mirror, provisions for paratroops' static lines and for maintenance davits for removal of major components.

DIMENSIONS, EXTERNAL:
Diameter of rotors (each)	18·29 m (60 ft 0 in)
Main rotor blade chord	0·64 m (2 ft 1¼ in)
Distance between rotor centres	11·94 m (39 ft 2 in)
Length overall, rotors turning	30·18 m (99 ft 0 in)
Length of fuselage	15·54 m (51 ft 0 in)
Width, rotors folded	3·78 m (12 ft 5 in)
Height to top of rear rotor hub	5·68 m (18 ft 7·8 in)
Wheel track (c/l of shock-absorbers)	3·20 m (10 ft 6 in)
Wheelbase	6·86 m (22 ft 6 in)
Passenger door (fwd, stbd):	
Height	1·68 m (5 ft 6 in)
Width	0·91 m (3 ft 0 in)
Height to sill	1·09 m (3 ft 7 in)
Rear loading ramp entrance:	
Height	1·98 m (6 ft 6 in)
Width	2·31 m (7 ft 7 in)
Height to sill	0·79 m (2 ft 7 in)

DIMENSIONS, INTERNAL:
Cabin, excl flight deck: Length	9·20 m (30 ft 2 in)
Width (mean)	2·29 m (7 ft 6 in)
Width at floor	2·51 m (8 ft 3 in)
Height	1·98 m (6 ft 6 in)
Floor area	21·0 m² (226 sq ft)
Usable volume	41·7 m³ (1,474 cu ft)

CH-47C CHINOOK WEIGHTS AND PERFORMANCE

	Condition 1	Condition 2	Condition 3	Condition 4
Weight empty	9,736 kg (21,464 lb)	9,736 kg (21,464 lb)	9,812 kg (21,633 lb)	9,599 kg (21,162 lb)
Payload	5,284 kg (11,650 lb)	2,903 kg (6,400 lb)	9,843 kg (21,700 lb)	—
T-O weight	17,463 kg (38,500 lb)	14,968 kg (33,000 lb)	20,593 kg (45,400 lb)	20,865 kg (46,000 lb)
Max speed, S/L, ISA at normal rated power	155 knots (286 km/h; 178 mph)	164 knots (304 km/h; 189 mph)	127 knots (235 km/h; 146 mph)	—
Average cruising speed	139 knots (257 km/h; 160 mph)	137 knots (254 km/h; 158 mph)	114 knots (211 km/h; 131 mph)	133 knots (246 km/h; 153 mph)
Max rate of climb, S/L, ISA at normal rated power	649 m (2,130 ft)/min	878 m (2,880 ft)/min	421 m (1,380 ft)/min	402 m (1,320 ft)/min
Service ceiling, ISA, normal rated power	3,290 m (10,800 ft)	4,570 m (15,000 ft)	2,560 m (8,400 ft)	2,440 m (8,000 ft)
Hovering ceiling OGE, ISA, max power	2,805 m (9,200 ft)	4,145 m (13,600 ft)	Sea level	—
Mission radius	100 nm (185 km; 115 miles)	100 nm (185 km; 115 miles)	20 nm (37 km; 23 miles)	—
Ferry range	—	—	—	1,156 nm (2,142 km; 1,331 miles)

Condition 1 Criteria: Take-off gross weight equals gross weight to hover OGE at 1,830 m/35°C (6,000 ft/95°F). Radius of action 100 nm (185 km; 115 miles). Fuel reserve 10%. Payload carried internally.

Condition 2 Criteria: Take-off gross weight equals design gross weight. Radius of action 100 nm (185 km; 115 miles). Fuel reserve 10%. Payload carried internally.

Condition 3 Criteria: Take-off gross weight equals gross weight to hover OGE at S/L ISA. Radius of action 20 nm (37 km; 23 miles). Fuel reserve 10%. Payload carried externally. Except for the mission average cruising speed, all other performance is predicated on internal loading of cargo.

Condition 4 Criteria: Take-off gross weight represents alternative design gross weight. Max ferry range (integral and internal auxiliary fuel only), cruise at optimum altitude and standard temperature, no payload, 10% fuel reserves.

(1980–81)

AREAS:
Rotor blades (each)   5·86 m² (63·1 sq ft)
Main rotor discs (total)   525·3 m² (5,655 sq ft)
WEIGHTS (CH-47C: see accompanying table. CH-47D as follows, A: guaranteed; B: estimated, based on whirl test results):
Internal payload over 100 nm (185 km; 115 miles) at 1,220 m (4,000 ft), hovering OGE at T-O:
A   5,896 kg (13,000 lb)
B   6,496 kg (14,322 lb)

External payload over 30 nm (55·5 km; 34·5 miles) at 1,220 m (4,000 ft), 61 m (200 ft)/min vertical climb at T-O, 35°C: A   6,803 kg (15,000 lb)
B   7,155 kg (15,775 lb)
Gross weight, hovering OGE at S/L, ISA:
A   22,680 kg (50,000 lb)
B   24,267 kg (53,000 lb)

PERFORMANCE (CH-47C: see accompanying table. CH-47D: as follows):
Max level speed at S/L, ISA, at AUW of 14,968 kg (33,000 lb): A   155 knots (287 km/h; 178 mph)
B   161 knots (298 km/h; 185 mph)
Single-engine service ceiling at 14,968 kg (33,000 lb) AUW, ISA: A   3,050 m (10,000 ft)
B   4,270 m (14,000 ft)
(1980–81)

Brewster F2A-2 "Buffalo" Single-seat Fighter Monoplane (850 h.p. Wright "Cyclone" engine).
(*Photograph by Peter Bowers*).

THE BREWSTER F2A BUFFALO

The Brewster Aeronautical Corpn., formed in 1932, took over the equipment, plant, designs and goodwill of the Aircraft Division of Brewster & Co., Inc., a company which had been manufacturing carriages and, later, automobile bodies since 1810.

At the outset the Company concentrated on the manufacture of seaplane floats, wings and tail surfaces, but later it undertook the design and construction of complete aircraft.

It has specialised in the design of Naval shipboard aircraft. Its first design was the SBA-1 two-seat Scout-Bomber, a quantity of which was built for the U.S. Navy by the Naval Aircraft Factory under the designation SBN-1.

This was followed by the F2A-1 single-seat fighter, a production order for which was placed by the U.S. Navy in the Summer of 1938, and the F2A-2 which was ordered by the U.S. Navy, the British Government and the Netherlands East Indies Government in 1940. The third production model was the F2A-3, delivered in 1941. The US Navy/Marines received 11 F2A-1s, 43 F2A-2s and 108 F2A-3s.

THE BREWSTER F2A-1.

TYPE.—Single-seat Naval shipboard fighter.
WINGS.—Mid-wing cantilever monoplane. All-metal structure with smooth stressed metal skin. Metal-framed ailerons covered with fabric. Hydraulically-operated split flaps between ailerons and fuselage.
FUSELAGE.—Oval metal monocoque with smooth stressed-skin covering.
TAIL UNIT.—Cantilever monoplane type. Metal framework with metal-covered tail-plane and fin and fabric-covered rudder and elevators. Trimming-tabs in elevators and rudder.
UNDERCARRIAGE.—Retractable type. Wheels are retracted inwardly, the struts fairing into the underside of the wings and the wheels into the sides of the fuselage below the wings. Hydraulic retraction with emergency hand-turning gear. Retractable tail-wheel.
POWER PLANT.—One 850 h.p. Wright "Cyclone" nine-cylinder radial air-cooled engine driving a Hamilton-Standard three-bladed hydromatic airscrew. Quickly-detachable N.A.C.A. cowling. Fuel tank in fuselage.
ACCOMMODATION.—Enclosed cockpit over trailing-edge of wing. Sliding canopy over pilot's seat and transparent panels in fairing aft for visibility to the rear. Downward visibility through transparent panel in fuselage bottom.
ARMAMENT AND EQUIPMENT.—Two machine-guns in top cowling and firing through airscrew and two machine-guns or shell-firing guns in wings, one on either side of the fuselage and outside area swept by the airscrew. Equipment includes radio, full oversea navigation equipment, deck-arrester hook in tail of fuselage, etc.   (1939)

BREWSTER F2A-2 (EXPORT MODEL 339)

Details apply to the Model 339:—
TYPE.—Single-seat fighter monoplane.
WINGS.—Mid-wing cantilever monoplane. The central box beam is a single unit passing through the fuselage. To it are attached the leading and trailing-edge sub-assemblies, the portion of the fuselage beneath the beam and the two detachable wing-tips. The main wing beam structure is built up of front and rear webs, extruded corner angles and top and bottom flange plates of aluminium-alloy. Fore-and-aft bulkheads are located throughout the length of the beam, those nearest the fuselage forming the integral fuel tanks. The leading-edge is built up of nose ribs, lateral stringers and aluminium-alloy skin. The trailing-edge has former ribs, auxiliary beams and aluminium-alloy skin. The entire skin of the wing is flush-riveted. "Frise"-type ailerons. Split trailing-edge flaps.
FUSELAGE.—Section forward of the fireproof bulkhead is of welded steel tubing. Aft of the bulkhead the fuselage is an aluminium-alloy monocoque built up of bulkheads, formers and stringers, the whole covered with flush-riveted aluminium-alloy skin. Removable tail-cone to give access to controls. Steel-tube structure provided aft of the pilot for protection in case of a nose-over.
TAIL UNIT.—Cantilever monoplane type. Fin and tail-plane of aluminium-alloy construction with stressed-skin covering. Rudder and elevators have metal frames and fabric covering. Fin mounted 14 in. ahead of tail-plane. Control surfaces are statically and aerodynamically balanced and have controllable trimming-tabs.
UNDERCARRIAGE.—Retractable type. Comprises two aluminium-alloy box struts carrying at their lower ends the oleo shock-absorber struts which have integral wheel axles and two retracting struts which are connected to the hydraulic retracting mechanism in the fuselage. When raised the box-struts are housed in the lower leading-edge of the wings in wells and the wheels and shock-absorber struts in the sides of the fuselage. Fixed tail-wheel with streamline tyre.
POWER PLANT.—One Wright "Cyclone" GR-1820-G205A nine-cylinder radial air-cooled geared and supercharged engine rated at 1,200 h.p. to 1,800 ft. (550 m.) and 1,000 h.p. at 13,500 ft. (4,120 m.). Curtiss electric constant-speed airscrew. Carburetter air and oil-cooling air taken in through faired scoops in leading-edge of engine cowling. Self-sealing fuel tanks (160 U.S. gallons total capacity) integral with wing structure. Oil tank (11 U.S. gallons) in upper forward section of fuselage.
ACCOMMODATION.—Pilot's enclosed cockpit over trailing-edge of wing. Bullet-proof windshield and sliding "Plexiglas" canopy over pilot. Window in bottom of fuselage provides direct downward vision. Cockpit provided with armour protection.
ARMAMENT.—Four .50-cal. machine-guns, two in the upper portion of the cowling and synchronised to fire through the airscrew, and two in the wings, one on either side of the fuselage and firing outside the airscrew disc. All guns are fired electrically. Provision for carrying two 100-lb. bombs under the wings.
DIMENSIONS.—Span 35 ft. (10.67 m.), Length 25 ft. 8 in. (7.83 m.), Height 12 ft. 1 in. (3.66 m.), Wing area 209 sq. ft. (19.4 sq. m.).
WEIGHTS AND LOADINGS.—Weight loaded 6,840 lbs. (3,105 kg.), Wing loading 32.8 lbs./sq. ft. (160 kg./sq. m.), Power loading 5.7 lbs./h.p. (2.58 kg./h.p.).
PERFORMANCE.—Maximum speed 337 m.p.h. (542.4 km.h.) at 15,000 ft. (4,575 m.), Initial rate of climb 2,070 ft./min. (936 m./min.), Service ceiling 30,650 ft. (9,350 m.), Maximum range 1,428 miles (2,385 km.).   (1941)

The Brewster SBA-1 Two-seat Scout-bomber Monoplane (750 h.p. Wright "Cyclone" engine). (1940)

THE BREWSTER SBA-1 (EXPORT MODEL 138).

TYPE.—Two-seat Scout-Bomber monoplane. May also be supplied as a two-seat Fighter, Attack and Reconnaissance type with appropriate variations of equipment.

WINGS.—Mid-wing cantilever monoplane. Centre-section, which carries the main undercarriage fittings, integral with the fuselage. Structure, of riveted aluminium-alloy, consists of a central box made up of extruded corner flanges, stressed sheet webs and cover plates and built-up bulkheads. Former ribs attached to front and back of box. Leading-edge metal-covered, trailing-edge fabric-covered. Leading-edge and main box are watertight. Split all-metal flaps between ailerons and fuselage. Ailerons have steel-tube frames and fabric covering.

FUSELAGE.—Riveted aluminium-alloy monocoque.

TAIL UNIT.—Cantilever monoplane type. Fixed surfaces are of riveted aluminium-alloy construction with stressed-skin covering. Movable surfaces have welded steel-tube frames and fabric covering. Trimming-tabs in elevators and rudder.

UNDERCARRIAGE.—Retractable type. Main legs hinged to extremities of centre-section beam and swing inwards to fair into the under-surface of the centre-section with the wheels fairing into the sides of the fuselage below the centre-section. Hydraulic retraction. Oleo-pneumatic shock-absorber struts on the sides of the streamline wheels. Full swivelling tail-wheel.

POWER PLANT.—One Wright "Cyclone" Series G nine-cylinder radial air-cooled engine rated at 750 h.p. at 15,200 ft. (4,636 m.) and giving 950 h.p. for take-off. Three-bladed Hamilton-Standard constant-speed airscrew. Fuel (136 U.S. gallons) carried in centre-section beam.

ACCOMMODATION.—Tandem closed cockpits. Pilot situated in front of wing beam and observer aft of trailing-edge. Continuous canopy over cockpits, with sliding section over pilot and sliding and hinged section over observer.

ARMAMENT AND EQUIPMENT.—Armament consists of both fixed and flexible machine-guns. Bombs stowed internally with sliding panels in bottom of fuselage for release. Equipment includes radio, oxygen equipment, fixed landing light in the port wing, and full instrument equipment.

DIMENSIONS.—Span 39 ft. (11.89 m.), Length 27 ft. 10 in. (8.5 m.), Height 7 ft. 7 in. (2.28 m.), Wing area 259 sq. ft. (24 sq. m.).

WEIGHTS AND LOADINGS.—Weight empty 4,017 lbs. (1,825 kg.), Weight loaded 5,381 lbs. (2,445 kg.), Wing loading 20.8 lbs./sq. ft. (101.5 kg./sq. m.), Power loading 6.35 lbs./h.p. (2.89 kg./h.p.).

PERFORMANCE.—Speed at sea level 262 m.p.h. (422 km.h.), Maximum speed 302 m.p.h. (486 km.h.) at 17,000 ft. (5,185 m.), Cruising speed 226.5 m.p.h. (364 km.h.) at 17,000 ft. (5,185 m.), Landing speed 65 m.p.h. (104.4 km.h.), Initial rate of climb 2,220 ft. min. (678 m./min.), Service ceiling 30,000 ft. (9,150 m.), Cruising range at 17,000 ft. (5,185 m.) at 75% power 776 miles (1,250 km.).

The Brewster "Bermuda" Two-seat Scout-Bomber monoplane (1,650 h.p. Wright "Cyclone 14" engine). (1943–44)

THE BREWSTER "BERMUDA."

U.S. Navy designation: SB2A (formerly named "Buccaneer").

R.A.F. name: "Bermuda."

The "Bermuda" is a mid-wing all-metal monoplane fitted with a 1,650 h.p. Wright Double-Row "Cyclone 14" GR2600 engine which drives a Curtiss electric full-feathering airscrew. Equipment includes armour plating, bullet-proof fuel tanks, etc.

Several important changes have been made since the prototype was produced as a two-seat Scout-Dive-Bomber for operation from aircraft-carriers. In this form it had folding wings, catapult spools, arrester-gear and its rear armament mounted in a turret midway between wings and tail (SB2A-1). Later versions have been fitted with fixed wings and hand-operated rear armament (SB2A-2), with folding wings and hand-operated rear armament (SB2A-3) and with fixed wings and hand-operated rear armament but without catapult spools and arrester-gear (SB2A-4).

A version of the Model 340 was ordered by the British Government and given the type name "Bermuda." This version was intended for use as a land based dive-bomber and has fixed wings and manually-operated rear armament. The "Bermuda" has not come up to expectations and the examples delivered are being used for training purposes only.

The U.S. naval version was originally known as the "Buccaneer" but this name was later abandoned in favour of "Bermuda" by which both the American and British versions are now known. It was intended to serve as a carrier-based Scout-Dive-Bomber but the elimination of catapult and arrester equipment and the use of fixed wings in the later models suggests that the "Bermuda" has been modified for use on shore-going training duties.

DIMENSIONS.—Span 47 ft. (14.3 m.), Length 39 ft. 2¼ in. (11.9 m.), Height 10 ft. 10 in. (3.3 m.).

WEIGHTS (SB2A-4).—Weight empty 9,780 lbs. (4,440 kg.), Weight loaded 12,674 lbs. (5,754 kg.).

WEIGHTS ("Bermuda").—Weight empty 9,518 lbs. (4,321 kg.), Weight loaded 12,782 lbs. (5,803 kg.).

PERFORMANCE.—Maximum speed at optimum height 296 m.p.h. (474 km.h.), Stalling speed 77.7 m.p.h. (124.3 km.h.), Service ceiling 28,000 ft. (8,540 m.), Normal range 1,680 miles (2,690 km.).

THE BRISTOL 156 BEAUFIGHTER

The Beaufighter was a Private Venture design which in its original form incorporated about 75 per cent. of the airframe of the Beaufort, the only entirely new components being the main fuselage and engine mountings. The wide use of Beaufort components and parts made it possible for the prototype Beaufighter with two Hercules III engines to fly on July 17, 1939, only eight months after the design began.

The Mk. I went into operation as a Home Defence Night Fighter in August, 1940, but by the Spring of 1941 the Beaufighter was serving at home and in the Middle East on long-range escort fighter and ground attack duties. It has since gone into action in the India-Burma and South-west Pacific theatres and has been adapted to many other duties, including those of bomber, torpedo-carrier and rocket fighter.

The first American night fighter squadrons in Europe were trained on and went into action with Beaufighters in the Mediterranean theatre in March, 1944. (1945-46)

Beaufighter VI. Two Bristol Hercules VI or XVI engines. First type to be fitted with one .303 in. Vickers "K" gas-operated machine-gun at the observer's station. First type to be fitted with dihedral tailplane to improve fore and aft stability. This modification was also made retrospective. First type to be fitted with long-range fuel tanks in place of wing guns, a 50 gallon tank in the starboard gun-bay and a 24 gallon tank in the port bay. Two 29 gallon tanks also installed outboard of the engine nacelles. First type to be fitted with rocket projectiles. Various combinations of armament available to suit operational tactics, e.g. (1) four cannon and six wing guns, (2) cannon only with long-range tanks in lieu of wing guns for long-range armed reconnaissance, (3) two 500 lb. bombs with cannon and wing guns, and (4) four cannon and eight rockets, the latter in lieu of wing guns. The Mk.VI was the first to be used by the R.A.F. in India and Burma and the South-west Pacific. Mk.VIF was also the first mark to be used by the United States Army Air Forces, received from June 1943 by four night fighter squadrons of the 12th Air Force. (1966-67)

THE CESSNA BOBCAT.

U.S. Army Air Forces designations: AT-17 and UC-78.
U.S. Navy designation: JRC-1.
R.C.A.F. name: Crane.

The Bobcat is a military adaptation of the T-50 five-seat commercial monoplane which appeared in 1940. It was first built in military form in 1941 as an advanced trainer for the R.C.A.F. as the Crane (two Jacobs engines) and for the U.S. Army Air Forces as the AT-8 (two Lycoming R-680-9 engines). Later the Jacobs power-plant was standardised for both models, the U.S.A.A.F. version being re-designated AT-17. In 1942-3

the aircraft was adopted for light personnel transport use as the C-78 (later UC-78) and JRC-1.

Both the AT-17 and UC-78 were fitted with Hamilton Standard constant-speed airscrews, but subsequent series of both models have had two-blade fixed-pitch wooden airscrews. Otherwise only minor variations in equipment distinguish the various series models.

With the reduction in U.S.A.A.F. training requirements, all AT-17B and AT-17D trainers delivered after January 1, 1943, were re-designated UC-78B and UC-78C respectively.

CESSNA MODEL 172G
USAF designation: T-41A

The Model 172 is available in two versions:
Model 172G. Standard version, described below.
Skyhawk. de luxe version of 172G, described separately.

In addition, a version designated F-172 is being produced in France by Reims Aviation.

On July 31, 1964, the USAF ordered 170 Model 172's, under the designation T-41A, for delivery between September 1964 and July 1965. USAF student pilots complete about 30 hours of basic training on the T-41A before passing on to the T-37B jet primary trainer. Eight T-41A's have been bought by the Ecuadorian Air Force, and 26 by the Peruvian government. In August 1966, the US Army ordered 255 similar aircraft for training and installation support duties.

A total of 11,149 aircraft in the Model 172/Skyhawk series had been built by January 1966.

TYPE: Four-seat cabin monoplane.

WINGS: Braced high-wing monoplane. NACA 2412 wing section. Aspect ratio 7.52. Chord 5 ft 4 in (1.63 m) at root, 3 ft 8½ in (1.12 m) at tip. Dihedral 1° 44'. Incidence 1° 30' at root, —1° 30' at tip. All-metal structure. Single bracing strut on each side. Modified Frise all-metal ailerons Electrically-controlled NACA all-metal single-slotted flaps inboard of ailerons

FUSELAGE: All-metal semi-monocoque structure.

TAIL UNIT: Cantilever all-metal structure. Sweepback on fin 35° at quarter-chord. Trimtab in starboard elevator.

LANDING GEAR: Non-retractable tricycle type. Cessna "Land-o-Matic" cantilever spring steel main legs. Nose-wheel is carried on an oleopneumatic shock-strut and is steerable with rudder up to 10° and controllable up to 30° on either side. Cessna main wheels size 6.00 × 6 and nose-wheel size 5.00 × 5 (optionally 6.00 × 6), with nylon cord tube-type tyres. Tyre pressure: main wheels 23 lb/sq in (1.62 kg/cm²), nose-wheel 26 lb/sq in (1.83 kg/cm²) Hydraulic disc brakes. Alternative float gear.

POWER PLANT: One 145 hp Continental O-300-C six-cylinder horizontally-opposed air-cooled engine. McCauley type 1C172/EM7653 two-blade fixed-pitch metal propeller, diameter 6 ft 4 in (1.93 m). One fuel tank in each wing, total capacity 42 US gallons (159 litres). Usable fuel 39 US gallons (147.5 litres). Oil capacity 2 US gallons (7.5 litres).

Cessna T-41A of 3560 Training Wing, USAF *(S. P. Peltz)*

ACCOMMODATION: Cabin seats four in two pairs. Baggage space aft of rear seats, capacity 120 lb (54 kg). Alternatively, a "family seat" can be fitted in baggage space, for one or two children not exceeding 120 lb (54 kg) total weight. Door on each side of cabin giving access to all seats and to simplify loading if rear seats are removed and cabin used for freight. Baggage door on port side. Combined heating and ventilation system. Glass-fibre sound-proofing.

ELECTRONICS AND EQUIPMENT: Optional extras include Cessna 300 90-channel nav/com, 300 nav/omni with full VOR/LOC/glideslope receiver and optional marker beacon, 300R nav/com, ADF 300, Cessna Nav-o-Matic 200 and 300 single-axis autopilots or Nav-o-Matic 400 two-axis autopilot, dual controls, rotating beacon and blind flying instrumentation.

DIMENSIONS, EXTERNAL:

Wing span	36 ft 2 in (11.02 m)
Length overall	26 ft 6 in (8.07 m)
Height overall	8 ft 11 in (2.72 m)
Tailplane span	11 ft 4 in (3.45 m)
Wheel track	7 ft 2 in (2.18 m)
Wheelbase	5 ft 7 in (1.70 m)
Passenger doors (each):	
Height	3 ft 3¾ in (1.01 m)
Width	2 ft 11 in (0.89 m)

AREAS:

Wings, gross	174 sq ft (16.16 m²)
Ailerons (total)	18.3 sq ft (1.70 m²)
Trailing-edge flaps (total)	21.23 sq ft (1.97 m²)
Fin	11.24 sq ft (1.04 m²)
Rudder	7.30 sq ft (0.68 m²)
Tailplane	20.16 sq ft (1.87 m²)
Elevators, including tab	16.15 sq ft (1.50 m²)

WEIGHTS AND LOADINGS:

Weight empty, equipped	1,260 lb (572 kg)
Max T-O weight	2,300 lb (1,043 kg)
Max wing loading	13.2 lb/sq ft (64.45 kg/m²)
Max power loading	15.9 lb/hp (7.21 kg/hp)

PERFORMANCE (at max T-O weight):

Max level speed at S/L	138 mph (222 kmh)
Max permissible diving speed	174 mph (280 kmh)
Max cruising speed (75% power) at 7,000 ft (2,135 m)	130 mph (209 kmh)
Econ cruising speed at 10,000 ft (3,050 m)	102 mph (164 kmh)
Stalling speed	49 mph (79 kmh)
Rate of climb at S/L	645 ft (197 m) min
Service ceiling	13,100 ft (3,995 m)
T-O run	865 ft (264 m)
T-O to 50 ft (15 m)	1,525 ft (465 m)
Landing from 50 ft (15 m)	1,250 ft (381 m)
Landing run	520 ft (158 m)
Range with max fuel at max cruising speed, no reserve	595 miles (958 km)
Range with max fuel at econ cruising speed, no reserve	720 miles (1,158 km)

CESSNA MODEL R172E

US Army designation: T-41B Mescalero
US Air Force designations: T-41C/D Mescalero

The Cessna Model R172E is a more powerful version of the original Model 172. Its design was started in late 1963, and a prototype was then built, with a 134 kW (180 hp) Continental O-360 engine. Type Approval was received in 1964, but the original power plant was replaced in the production Model R172E by a fuel-injection IO-360 engine.

In August 1966, the US Army ordered 255 aircraft of this type, under the designation **T-41B**, for training and installation support duties. Delivery of these was completed in March 1967.

In October 1967, the US Air Force ordered 45 similar aircraft, with fixed-pitch propellers, under the designation **T-41C**, for cadet flight training at the USAF Academy in Colorado. A total of 52 had been produced by 1 February 1976. Thirty **T-41Ds**, with constant-speed propellers and 28V electrical systems, were ordered initially for the Colombian Air Force, and deliveries of this version to all operators totalled 311 by 1 January 1979.   (1979–80)

A version known as the Reims Rocket was produced by Reims Aviation in France (which see) until the end of the 1976 model year, by which time a total of 572 had been built. (1979–80)

The description of the Skyhawk applies also to the R172E, except for the following details:

POWER PLANT: One 156·5 kW (210 hp) Continental IO-360-D flat-six engine, driving a McCauley 2A34-C209/78CCA-2 constant-speed propeller. Two fuel tanks in wings with total capacity of 197 litres (52 US gallons), of which 174 litres (46 US gallons) are usable. Provision for long-range tanks, giving total usable capacity of 238 litres (63 US gallons). Refuelling points above wing. Oil capacity 9·5 litres (2·5 US gallons).

ACCOMMODATION: Basically as for Skyhawk. The T-41B has special crew seatbacks and shoulder harnesses, with forward-hinged door on each side of cabin by crew seats. Baggage capacity 90·5 kg (200 lb).

AVIONICS AND EQUIPMENT: The T-41B, C and D have variations in their avionics and other equipment consistent with their military roles.

DIMENSIONS, EXTERNAL:
Propeller diameter	1·93 m (6 ft 4 in)

WEIGHTS AND LOADINGS:
Weight empty, equipped	637 kg (1,405 lb)
Max T-O and landing weight	1,156 kg (2,550 lb)
Max wing loading	71·3 kg/m² (14·6 lb/sq ft)
Max power loading	7·39 kg/kW (12·1 lb/hp)

PERFORMANCE (at max T-O weight):
Never-exceed speed	158 knots (293 km/h; 182 mph)
Max level speed at S/L	133 knots (246 km/h; 153 mph)
Max cruising speed at 1,675 m (5,500 ft)	126 knots (233 km/h; 145 mph)
Econ cruising speed at 3,050 m (10,000 ft)	91 knots (169 km/h; 105 mph)
Stalling speed, flaps up	55·6 knots (103 km/h; 64 mph)
Stalling speed, flaps down	46 knots (85 km/h; 53 mph)
Max rate of climb at S/L	268 m (880 ft)/min
Service ceiling	5,180 m (17,000 ft)
T-O run	226 m (740 ft)
T-O to 15 m (50 ft)	375 m (1,230 ft)
Landing from 15 m (50 ft)	387 m (1,270 ft)
Landing run	189 m (620 ft)
Range with max fuel at econ cruising speed at 3,050 m (10,000 ft)	877 nm (1,625 km; 1,010 miles)

CESSNA MODEL 185 SKYWAGON

US military designation: U-17

The prototype of the Model 185 Skywagon flew for the first time in July 1960 and the first production model was completed in March 1961. It is generally similar to the Model 180 Skywagon, except for installation of a 224 kW (300 hp) Continental IO-520 engine.

Cessna has received important contracts to supply U-17A/B/C Skywagons to the US Air Force for delivery to overseas countries, under the US Military Assistance Programme.

A total of 3,869 Model 185 Skywagons, including U-17A/B/Cs, had been built by 1 January 1980. The 4,000th aircraft was delivered on 22 February 1980.

TYPE: One/six-seat cabin monoplane.

WINGS AND FUSELAGE: Similar to Model 180.

TAIL UNIT: Same as for Model 180, except for fin of increased area and manually-operated rudder trim as standard equipment.

LANDING GEAR: Similar to Model 180, except for tyre pressures: main wheels (6·00-6) 2·41 bars (35 lb/sq in), main wheels (8·00-6) 1·72 bars (25 lb/sq in), tailwheel 3·79-4·83 bars (55-70 lb/sq in) depending on load. Manual tailwheel lock standard. Wheel and brake fairings optional. Optional amphibian, float or ski gear.

POWER PLANT: One 224 kW (300 hp) Continental IO-520-D flat-six engine, driving a McCauley three-blade constant-speed metal propeller. Fuel in two tanks in wings, total capacity 333 litres (88 US gallons), of which 318 litres (84 US gallons) are usable. Oil capacity 11·5 litres (3 US gallons).

ACCOMMODATION, AVIONICS AND EQUIPMENT: Generally as for Model 180, except omni-flash beacon and manual tailwheel lock standard, plus availability of optional agricultural kit comprising 571 litre (151 US gallon) capacity Sorensen fan-driven spraygear with electric spray valve, deflector cable, windscreen and landing gear wire cutters, and external finish of Jet-flo polyurethane paint to provide extra corrosion protection.

DIMENSIONS, EXTERNAL:
Wing span	10·92 m (35 ft 10 in)
Wing chord at root	1·63 m (5 ft 4 in)
Wing chord at tip	1·11 m (3 ft 7¾ in)
Wing aspect ratio	7·52
Length overall: Landplane	7·81 m (25 ft 7½ in)
Skiplane	8·47 m (27 ft 9½ in)
Floatplane	8·23 m (27 ft 0 in)
Amphibian	8·38 m (27 ft 6 in)
Height overall:	
Landplane, skiplane	2·36 m (7 ft 9 in)
Floatplane	3·71 m (12 ft 2 in)
Amphibian	3·86 m (12 ft 8 in)
Tailplane span	3·35 m (11 ft 0 in)
Wheel track, landplane	2·33 m (7 ft 8 in)
Passenger doors (each): Height	1·01 m (3 ft 3¾ in)
Width	0·89 m (2 ft 11 in)

AREAS:
Wings, gross	16·16 m² (174 sq ft)
Ailerons (total)	1·70 m² (18·3 sq ft)
Trailing-edge flaps (total)	1·97 m² (21·23 sq ft)
Fin	0·84 m² (9·01 sq ft)
Dorsal fin	0·19 m² (2·04 sq ft)
Rudder	0·68 m² (7·29 sq ft)
Tailplane	1·94 m² (20·94 sq ft)
Elevators	1·40 m² (15·13 sq ft)

WEIGHTS AND LOADINGS:
Weight empty, equipped:	
Skywagon landplane	765 kg (1,688 lb)
Floatplane	902 kg (1,990 lb)
Amphibian	1,018 kg (2,245 lb)
Skiplane	830 kg (1,830 lb)
Skywagon II landplane	789 kg (1,739 lb)
Max T-O and landing weight:	
Landplane, skiplane	1,519 kg (3,350 lb)
Floatplane	1,506 kg (3,320 lb)
Amphibian, land take-off	1,481 kg (3,265 lb)
Amphibian, water take-off	1,406 kg (3,100 lb)
Max ramp weight:	
Landplane	1,525 kg (3,362 lb)
Max wing loading:	
Landplane, skiplane	94·2 kg/m² (19·3 lb/sq ft)
Floatplane	93·3 kg/m² (19·1 lb/sq ft)
Amphibian	91·8 kg/m² (18·8 lb/sq ft)
Max power loading:	
Landplane, skiplane	6·78 kg/kW (11·2 lb/hp)
Floatplane	6·72 kg/kW (11·1 lb/hp)
Amphibian	6·61 kg/kW (10·9 lb/hp)

PERFORMANCE (at max T-O weight):
Never-exceed speed:	
Landplane	182 knots (338 km/h; 210 mph)
Max level speed at S/L:	
*Landplane	154 knots (285 km/h; 177 mph)
Floatplane	140 knots (259 km/h; 161 mph)
Amphibian	135 knots (249 km/h; 155 mph)
Skiplane	136 knots (252 km/h; 157 mph)
Max cruising speed (75% power) at 2,135 m (7,000 ft):	
*Landplane	147 knots (272 km/h; 169 mph)
Floatplane	133 knots (246 km/h; 153 mph)
Amphibian	129 knots (240 km/h; 149 mph)
Skiplane	131 knots (243 km/h; 151 mph)

Stalling speed, flaps up, power off:	
Landplane, skiplane, floatplane	56 knots (104 km/h; 64·5 mph) CAS
Amphibian	55 knots (102 km/h; 63 mph) CAS
Stalling speed, flaps down, power off:	
Landplane, skiplane	49 knots (90·5 km/h; 56 mph) CAS
Amphibian	51 knots (94 km/h; 58 mph) CAS
Floatplane	52 knots (96 km/h; 60 mph) CAS
Max rate of climb at S/L:	
Landplane	328 m (1,075 ft)/min
Floatplane	293 m (960 ft)/min
Amphibian	290 m (950 ft)/min
Skiplane	262 m (860 ft)/min
Service ceiling: Landplane	5,455 m (17,900 ft)
Floatplane	5,000 m (16,400 ft)
Amphibian	4,907 m (16,100 ft)
Skiplane	4,725 m (15,500 ft)
T-O run: Landplane	251 m (825 ft)
Floatplane	436 m (1,430 ft)
Amphibian, on land	238 m (780 ft)
Amphibian, on water	343 m (1,125 ft)
T-O to 15 m (50 ft): Landplane	436 m (1,430 ft)
Floatplane	648 m (2,125 ft)
Amphibian, on land	404 m (1,325 ft)
Amphibian, on water	521 m (1,710 ft)
Landing from 15 m (50 ft):	
Landplane	427 m (1,400 ft)
Floatplane	477 m (1,565 ft)
Amphibian, on land	378 m (1,240 ft)
Amphibian, on water	450 m (1,480 ft)
Landing run: Landplane	186 m (610 ft)
Floatplane	253 m (830 ft)
Amphibian, on land	174 m (570 ft)
Amphibian, on water	236 m (775 ft)

Range with max fuel (recommended lean mixture, with allowances for engine start, taxi, T-O, climb and 45 min reserves at 45% power):
75% power at 2,135 m (7,000 ft):	
Landplane	645 nm (1,196 km; 743 miles)
Floatplane	585 nm (1,085 km; 674 miles)
Amphibian	570 nm (1,056 km; 656 miles)
Skiplane	575 nm (1,065 km; 662 miles)
econ cruising power at 3,050 m (10,000 ft):	
Landplane	850 nm (1,575 km; 979 miles)
Floatplane	745 nm (1,381 km; 858 miles)
Amphibian	715 nm (1,324 km; 823 miles)
Skiplane	665 nm (1,233 km; 766 miles)

* *These speeds are 1 knot (1·9 km/h; 1·2 mph) higher with optional speed fairings installed*

THE CESSNA MODEL 195.

U.S.A.F. designation: LC-126.

The U.S.A.F. has acquired a number of Model 195's under the designation LC-126. These aircraft have been specially equipped with interchangeable wheel, float and ski landing-gear.

TYPE.—Four/five-seat Cabin monoplane.

WINGS.—High-wing cantilever monoplane. NACA 2412 wing section. Aspect ratio 5.94. Two-spar all-metal structure tapering in chord and thickness from root to tip. All-metal ailerons. Electrically-operated split flaps inboard of ailerons. Total area of ailerons 12.32 sq. ft. (1.14 m².). Total flap area 8.68 sq. ft. (0.79 m².). Gross wing area 218.125 sq. ft. (20.2 m².).

FUSELAGE.—Oval section all-metal monocoque structure.

TAIL UNIT.—Cantilever monoplane type. All-metal structure including covering. Areas: fin 8.78 sq. ft. (0.81 m².), rudder 7.77 sq. ft. (0.72 m².), elevators (total) 15.41 sq. ft. (1.43 m².), tailplane 19.80 sq. ft. (1.84 m².). Tailplane span 10 ft. 6½ in. (3.20 m.).

LANDING GEAR.—Cessna patented gear of chrome-vanadium spring steel, the flexing of the two aerodynamically-clean legs providing the only means of shock-absorption. Wheel brakes. Steerable tail-wheel. Track 8 ft. 6 in. (2.59 m.). Edo 3420 all-metal floats may be substituted for wheel landing-gear.

POWER PLANT.—One 275 h.p. Jacobs R-755B-2 seven-cylinder radial air-cooled engine driving a Hamilton Standard Hydromatic constant-speed airscrew. Fuel tanks in wings. Total fuel capacity 80 U.S. gallons (302 litres). The 300 h.p. Jacobs R-755A engine may be supplied in place of the R-755B.   (1980–81)

The Cessna LC-126A (300 h.p. Jacobs engine).

ACCOMMODATION.—Enclosed cabin seating four or five, two forward with throw-over control column, and two or three on seat across the back of the cabin. Luggage compartment aft of rear seat accessible from cabin or from outside through door on starboard side. Sound-proofing and cabin heating and ventilation. Two-way radio with loud speaker. Retractable steps to entrance doors on each side of cabin. Rear seat may be removed by undoing four bolts to provide 85 cub. ft. of cargo space.

DIMENSIONS.—
Span 36 ft. 2 in. (11 m.).
Length 27 ft. 4 in. (8.33 m.).
Height 7 ft. 2 in. (2.16 m.). (1954–55)

CESSNA MODEL 305 BIRD DOG
US Army and Marine Corps designation: O-1

The Bird Dog was developed for the US Army Field Forces as a light reconnaissance and observation aircraft, which could also be used for liaison and training duties. The prototype flew in January 1950, and the first contract for 418 aircraft was placed in June 1950. The type remained in continuous production until late 1958, by which time a total of 3,332 had been built. The Bird Dog re-entered production under a new US Army contract in the early Spring of 1962 and total production had increased to 3,431 by March 1964.

The following versions have been delivered to the US and foreign services.

O-1A (formerly L-19A). Observation and liaison version for US Army Field Forces. First delivered in December 1950.

O-1B (formerly OE-1). Similar to O-1A for US Marine Corps. 60 built.

O-1C (formerly OE-2) (**Model 321**). Redesigned development of O-1B for US Marine Corps, with Continental O-470-2 engine. 25 built. Described in previous editions of *Jane's*.

TO-1D (formerly TL-19D). Trainer with dual controls, comprehensive instruments and radio communications and navigation equipment. Received FAA Type Approval, as Cessna Model 305B, on April 11, 1956.

O-1E (formerly L-19E). Current version of standard observation and liaison aircraft. Further US Army contracts for 18 received in 1963, of which four were allocated to the US Navy's Military Assistance Programme and 14 to the US Army's Programme.

O-1D and **O-1F**. Modified TO-1Ds transferred to USAF for FAC duties in Vietnam.

O-1G. Modified O-1As transferred to USAF for FAC duties in Vietnam.

A licence to build the O-1 in Japan is held by Fuji Heavy Industries of Tokyo.

The O-1 seats a pilot and observer in tandem. Cabin features include a wide door, a swing-up window, large rear cabin and baggage compartment.

The power plant consists of a 213 hp Continental O-470-11 (O-470-15 in TO-1D) six-cylinder horizontally-opposed air-cooled engine. Fuel

Cessna O-1E Bird Dog (213 hp Continental O-470-11 engine)

is carried in tanks built into the wings, with a capacity of 41 US gallons (155 litres).

Four of the standard US Army O-1's were delivered with amphibious float landing gear and all late production models have provision for floats.

A winterisation kit has been developed by Cessna, which permits the O-1 to operate in temperatures as low as 60° below zero. The equipment includes a 25,000 BTU heater, a collapsible 4-inch pre-heater hose, nose shutters, electric oil dilution unit, electric primer, internal de-frosters and a carburettor heater unit.

DIMENSIONS, EXTERNAL:
Wing span   36 ft 0 in (10·9 m)
Length overall   25 ft 10 in (7·89 m)
Height overall   7 ft 4 in (2·23 m)
WEIGHTS AND LOADINGS (O-1E):
Weight empty   1,614 lb (680 kg)

Max T-O weight (primary mission)
                     2,400 lb (1,090 kg)
Max T-O weight (alternative missions)
                     2,430 lb (1,103 kg)
Max wing loading   13·79 lb/sq ft (67·3 kg/m²)
Max power loading   11·26 lb/hp (5·11 kg/hp)
PERFORMANCE (O-1E at max T-O weight):
Max level speed   115 mph (184 kmh)
Econ cruising speed (29% power) at 5,000 ft
(1,525 m)   104 mph (166·4 kmh)
Stalling speed   54 mph (86·4 kmh)
Rate of climb at S/L 1,150 ft (350 m) min
Service ceiling   18,500 ft (5,640 m)
Absolute ceiling   24,800 ft (7,565 m)
T-O to 50 ft (15 m) from grass 560 ft (171 m)
Landing from 50 ft (15 m) on grass
                     600 ft (183 m)
Cruising range   530 miles (848 km)
                     (1964–65)

THE CESSNA MODEL 310.
U.S.A.F. designation: L-27A. Later U-3.

The Model 310 is a twin-engined five-seat cabin monoplane, the prototype of which first flew on January 3, 1953. More than 700 have been built since the Model 310 went into production late in 1954.

The Cessna 310 has been in service with the USAF since 1957, when it won a competition for a light twin-engined administrative liaison and cargo aircraft. Initial orders for a total of 160 "off-the-shelf," under the designation U-3A (formerly L-27A), were followed by a contract for 35 later models, designated U-3B, which were delivered between December 1960 and June 1961.

The Cessna L-27A, the military version of the Model 310.

TYPE.—Twin-engined Five-seat Cabin monoplane.

WINGS.—Low-wing cantilever monoplane. All-metal flush-riveted structure. Electrically-operated split flaps between ailerons and fuselage. Maximum flap depression 45°. Wing area 175 sq. ft. (16.2 m.²).

FUSELAGE.—All-metal flush-riveted structure.

TAIL UNIT.—Cantilever monoplane type. All-metal flush-riveted structure. Trim-tabs in rudder and elevators.

LANDING GEAR.—Retractable nose-wheel type. Electro-mechanical retraction. Cessna type oleo shock-absorber struts. Nose-wheel steerable to 15° and castoring from 15° to 55° in both directions.

POWER PLANT.—Two 240 h.p. Continental O-470-M six-cylinder horizontally-opposed air-cooled engines. Each engine exhausts into two stainless steel augmenter tubes terminating above wing ahead of trailing-edge. Two-blade metal constant-speed full-feathering airscrews. Fuel in two permanently-attached wing-tip tanks, each of which contains a bladder-type fuel cell holding 50 U.S. gallons (189 litres). Cross-feed fuel system. Each wing tank is also fitted with an electrical fuel boost pump. An optional 30 U.S. gallon (113 litres) auxiliary fuel system became available during 1956. It consists of two 15 U.S. gallon (56.5 litres) rubber fuel cells which are installed between the wing spars outboard of each engine nacelle and connected to the main fuel system. Total extra weight of the auxiliary fuel system is only 16 lb. (7.25 kg.). Oil capacity 6 U.S. gallons (22.7 litres).

ACCOMMODATION.—Cabin seats five, two in front and three on cross bench behind. Controlled heating provided by Stewart-Warner thermostatically-controlled blower-type heater. Large door on starboard

side giving access to all seats. Baggage compartment aft of cabin with internal and external access. Baggage capacity 200 lb. (91 kg.).

DIMENSIONS.—
Span 36 ft. (11.0 m.).
Length 27 ft. 1 in. (8.26 m.).
Height 10 ft. 5 in. (3.17 m.).

WEIGHTS AND LOADINGS (Model 310).—
Weight empty 2,900 lb. (1,315 kg.).
Weight loaded (5 people, max. fuel and oil 225 lb.=102 kg. baggage and optional equipment) 4,600 lb. (2,088 kg.).
Wing loading 26.2 lb./sq. ft. (127.7 kg./m.²).
Power loading 9.6 lb./h.p. (4.35 kg./h.p.).

WEIGHT (Model 310B).—
Max. loaded weight 4,700 lb. (2,132 kg.).

PERFORMANCE (Model 310B at 4,700 lb.= 2,132 kg. A.U.W.).—
Max. speed at S/L 232 m.p.h. (373 km.h.).
Cruising speed (70% power) at 8,000 ft. (2,440 m.) 213 m.p.h. (343 km.h.).
Rate of climb at S/L 1,660 ft./min. (505 m./min.).
Rate of climb on one engine at S/L 415 ft./min. (126 m. min.).
Service ceiling 20,500 ft. (6,250 m.).
Service ceiling on one engine 7,750 ft. (2,360 m.).
Cruising range (70% power) at 8,000 ft. (2,440 m.) 850 miles (1,368 km.).
Cruising range at 169 m.p.h. (272 km.h.) at 10,000 ft. (3,050 m.) 975 miles (1,570 km.).
Cruising range with auxiliary tanks (70% power) 1,107 miles (1,782 km.). **(1958–59)**

CESSNA MODEL 318
USAF designation: T-37

The T-37 was the first jet trainer designed as such from the start to be used by the USAF. The first of two prototype XT-37s made its first flight on 12 October 1954, and the first of an evaluation batch of 11 T-37As flew on 27 September 1955.

A total of 1,247 T-37s had been delivered by 1 March 1974, with production continuing. In addition to aircraft supplied to the USAF, there have been substantial deliveries to foreign governments by direct purchase, or through the Military Assistance Programme.

Three versions have been built in quantity:

T-37A. Initial production version with Continental J69-T-9 turbojets (each 920 lb; 417 kg st). 534 built. Converted to T-37B standard by retrospective modification.

T-37B. Two Continental J69-T-25 turbojets (each 1,025 lb; 465 kg st). New Omni navigational equipment, UHF radio and instrument panel. First T-37B was accepted into service with the USAF in November 1959. The T-37B has also been supplied to the Royal Thai Air Force and the Cambodian, Chilean and Pakistan Air Forces. Forty-seven ordered by the Federal German government are being used to train Luftwaffe pilots at Sheppard AFB in Texas.

Equipment can be added to the T-37B to enable it to perform military surveillance and low-level attack duties, in addition to training. Range can be extended by two 65 US gallon (245 litre) wingtip fuel tanks. Two armed T-37Bs were evaluated at the USAF Special Air Warfare Center, and were followed by two prototypes of the more powerful and more heavily armed YAT-37D (see entry on A-37). Thirty-nine T-37Bs were later converted to A-37A standard. To replace these and to meet further requirements, the USAF placed further contracts for the T-37B in 1967 and again in 1968, bringing the total on order to 447.

T-37C. Basically similar to T-37B, but with provision for both armament and wingtip fuel tanks. Initial order for 34 placed by USAF for supply to foreign countries under Military Assistance Programme. Portugal received 30, of which 18 were supplied under this Programme. Peru had 15 and others were supplied to Chile, Greece, Pakistan, Thailand, Turkey, Brazil and Colombia. In production. Total orders exceed 250.

Following 133 bird strikes encountered in 1965-70, the USAF ordered new windscreens for more than 800 T-37s to be replaced with a birdproof type. Developed by Cessna, using General Electric-developed Lexan polycarbonate plastics, the material is formed by Texstar of Dallas, Texas, and Cessna fabricates the complete windscreen assembly. These screens are 0·5 in (1·27 cm) thick, weigh about 35 lb (16 kg) and can resist the impact of a 4 lb (1·8 kg) bird at a speed of 250 knots (288 mph; 463 km/h).

The following details refer to the T-37B:

TYPE: Two-seat primary trainer.
WINGS: Cantilever low-wing monoplane. Wing section NACA 2418 at root, NACA 2412 at tip. Dihedral 3°. Incidence at root 3° 30'. Two-spar aluminium alloy structure. Hydraulically-operated all-metal high-lift slotted flaps inboard of ailerons.
FUSELAGE: All-metal semi-monocoque structure. Hydraulically-actuated speed brake below forward part of fuselage in region of cockpit.
TAIL UNIT: Cantilever all-metal structure. Fin integral with fuselage. Tailplane mounted one-third of way up fin. Movable surfaces all have electrically-operated trim tabs.
LANDING GEAR: Hydraulically-retractable tri-

Cessna T-37C two-seat primary jet trainer with armament provisions (1975–76)

cycle type. Bendix oleo-pneumatic shock-absorbers. Steerable nosewheel. Tyres by General Tire and Rubber Co. Main-wheel tyres size 20 × 4·4. Nosewheel tyre size 16 × 4·4. General Tire and Rubber Co multiple-disc hydraulic brakes.
POWER PLANT: Two Continental J69-T-25 turbojet engines (each 1,025 lb; 465 kg st). Six rubber-cell interconnected fuel tanks in each wing, feeding main tank in fuselage aft of cockpit. Total usable fuel capacity 309 US gallons (1,170 litres). Automatic fuel transfer by engine-driven pumps and a submerged booster pump. Provision for two 65 US gallon (245 litre) wingtip fuel tanks on T-37C only. Oil capacity 3·12 US gallons (11·8 litres).
ACCOMMODATION: Enclosed cockpit seating two side by side with dual controls. Ejection seats and jettisonable clamshell type canopy. Standardised cockpit layout, with flaps, speed brakes, trim tabs, radio controls, etc, positioned and operated as in standard USAF combat aircraft.
ELECTRONICS: Standard USAF UHF radio; Collins VHF navigation equipment and IFF.
ARMAMENT AND EQUIPMENT (T-37C only): Provision for two 250 lb bombs or four Sidewinder missiles. Associated equipment includes K14C computing gunsight and AN-N6 16 mm gun camera. For reconnaissance duties, KA-20 or KB-10A cameras, or HC217 cartographic camera, can be mounted in fuselage.

DIMENSIONS, EXTERNAL:

Wing span	33 ft 9·3 in (10·30 m)
Wing chord (mean)	5 ft 7 in (1·70 m)
Wing chord at tip	4 ft 6 in (1·37 m)
Wing aspect ratio	6·2
Length overall	29 ft 3 in (8·92 m)
Height overall	9 ft 2·3 in (2·80 m)
Tailplane span	13 ft 11¼ in (4·25 m)
Wheel track	14 ft 0½ in (4·28 m)
Wheelbase	7 ft 9 in (2·36 m)

AREAS:

Wings, gross	183·9 sq ft (17·09 m²)
Ailerons (total)	11·30 sq ft (1·05 m²)
Trailing-edge flaps (total)	15·10 sq ft (1·40 m²)
Fin	11·54 sq ft (1·07 m²)
Rudder, incl tab	6·24 sq ft (0·58 m²)
Tailplane	34·93 sq ft (3·25 m²)
Elevators, incl tabs	11·76 sq ft (1·09 m²)

WEIGHTS AND LOADINGS (A: T-37B; B: T-37C):

Max T-O weight:	
A	6,600 lb (2,993 kg)
B	7,500 lb (3,402 kg)
Max wing loading:	
A	35·9 lb/sq ft (175·3 kg/m²)
B	40·8 lb/sq ft (199·2 kg/m²)
Max power loading:	
A	3·21 lb/lb st (3·21 kg/kg st)
B	3·65 lb/lb st (3·65 kg/kg st)

PERFORMANCE (at max T-O weight except as noted. A: T-37B; B: T-37C):

Max level speed:	
A, at 25,000 ft (7,620 m)	370 knots (426 mph; 685 km/h)
B, at 25,000 ft (7,620 m)	349 knots (402 mph; 647 km/h)
Normal cruising speed:	
A, at 25,000 ft (7,620 m)	330 knots (380 mph; 612 km/h)
B, at 25,000 ft (7,620 m)	310 knots (357 mph; 574 km/h)
Stalling speed:	
A	72 knots (83 mph; 134 km/h)
B	77 knots (89 mph; 143 km/h)
Max rate of climb at S/L:	
A	3,020 ft (920 m)/min
B	2,390 ft (728 m)/min
Service ceiling:	
A	35,100 ft (10,700 m)
B	29,900 ft (9,115 m)
Service ceiling, one engine out:	
A	20,100 ft (6,125 m)
B	13,500 ft (4,115 m)
T-O to 50 ft (15 m):	
A	2,050 ft (625 m)
B	2,750 ft (838 m)
Landing from 50 ft (15 m):	
A	2,700 ft (823 m)
B	3,400 ft (1,036 m)
Range with MIL-C-5011A reserve at 25,000 ft (7,620 m):	
A	472 nm (543 miles; 874 km)
B	703 nm (809 miles; 1,302 km)
Range at normal rated power, 5% reserve at 25,000 ft (7,620 m):	
A	525 nm (604 miles; 972 km)
B	738 nm (850 miles; 1,367 km)
Maximum range, 5% reserve at 25,000 ft (7,620 m):	
A	576 nm (663 miles; 1,067 km)
B	819 nm (943 miles; 1,517 km)

(1975–76)

CESSNA MODEL 318E DRAGONFLY
USAF designation: A-37

The A-37 is a development of the T-37 trainer, intended for armed counter-insurgency (COIN) operations from short unimproved airstrips. Two YAT-37D prototypes were produced initially, for evaluation by the USAF, by modifying existing T-37 airframes. The first of these flew for the first time on 22 October 1963, powered by two 2,400 lb (1,090 kg) st General Electric J85-GE-5 turbojets. There are two production versions, as follows:

A-37A (Model 318D). First 39 aircraft, converted from T-37B trainers. Withdrawn from service in 1974. Details in 1974-75 *Jane's*.

A-37B (Model 318E). Production version, of which design began in January 1967. Construction of prototype started in following month and it flew for the first time in September 1967. A-37B has two General Electric J85-GE-17A turbojets, giving more than double the take-off power available for the T-37, permitting an almost-doubled take-off weight. A total of 434 had been delivered by 31 January 1975. In addition to USAF, operators include the air forces of Chile (16) and Guatemala (8).

The following details apply to the A-37B:

TYPE: Two-seat light strike aircraft.

WINGS: Cantilever low-wing monoplane. Wing section NACA 2418 (modified) at root, NACA 2412 (modified) at tip. Dihedral 3°. Incidence 3°38′ at root, 1° at tip. No sweep at 22½% chord. Two-spar aluminium alloy structure. Conventional all-metal ailerons, with forward skin of aluminium alloy and aft skin of magnesium alloy. Electrically-operated trim tab on port aileron with force-sensitive boost tabs on both ailerons, plus hydraulically-operated slot-lip ailerons forward of the flap on the outboard two-thirds of flap span. Hydraulically-operated all-metal slotted flaps of NACA 2h type. No de-icing equipment.

FUSELAGE: All-metal semi-monocoque structure. Hydraulically-operated speed brake, measuring 3 ft 9 in (1·14 m) by 1 ft 0 in (0·30 m), below forward fuselage immediately aft of nosewheel well. Mountings for removable probe for in-flight refuelling on upper fuselage in front of cockpit.

TAIL UNIT: Cantilever all-metal structure. Fin integral with fuselage. Fixed-incidence tailplane mounted one-third of way up fin. Electrically-operated trim tabs in port elevator and rudder. No de-icing equipment.

LANDING GEAR: Retractable tricycle type. Cessna oleo-pneumatic shock-absorber struts on all three units. Hydraulic actuation, main wheels retracting inward, nosewheel forward. Steerable nosewheel. Goodyear tyres and single-disc brakes. Main-wheel tyres size 7·00-8 (14PR). Nosewheel tyre size 6·00-6 (6PR). Tyre pressure: main wheels 110 lb/sq in (7·73 kg/cm²), nosewheel 37 lb/sq in (2·60 kg/cm²).

POWER PLANT: Two General Electric J85-GE-17A turbojet engines, each rated at 2,850 lb (1,293 kg) st. Fuel tank in each wing, each with capacity of 113 US gallons (428 litres); two non-jettisonable tip-tanks, each of 95 US gallons (360 litres) capacity; sump tank in fuselage, aft of cockpit, capacity 91 US gallons (344 litres). Total standard usable fuel capacity 507 US gallons (1,920 litres). Single-point refuelling through in-flight refuelling probe, with adaptor. Alternative refuelling through flush gravity filler cap in each wing and each tip-tank. Four 100 US gallon (378 litre) auxiliary tanks can be carried on underwing pylons. Provision for in-flight refuelling through nose-probe. Total oil capacity 2·25 US gallons (9 litres).

ACCOMMODATION: Enclosed cockpit seating two side by side, with dual controls, dual throttles, full flight instrument panel on port side, partial panel on starboard side, engine instruments in between. Full blind-flying instrumentation. Jettisonable canopy hinged to open upward and rearward. Standardised cockpit layout as in standard USAF combat aircraft. Cockpit air-conditioned but not pressurised. Flak-curtains of layered nylon are installed around the cockpit. Windscreen defrosted by engine bleed air. A polycarbonate bird-resistant windscreen is available optionally.

SYSTEMS: AiResearch air-conditioning system of expansion turbine type, driven by engine bleed air. Hydraulic system, pressure 1,500 lb/sq in (105 kg/cm²), operates landing gear, main landing gear doors, flaps, thrust attenuator, nosewheel steering system, speedbrake, stall spoiler, inlet screen. Pneumatic system, pressure 2,000 lb/sq in (140 kg/cm²), utilises nitrogen-filled 50 cu in (819 cm³) air bottle for emergency landing gear extension. Electrical system includes two 28V DC 300A starter/generators, two 24V nickel-cadmium

Cessna A-37B Dragonfly light strike aircraft (two General Electric J85-GE-17A turbojets)

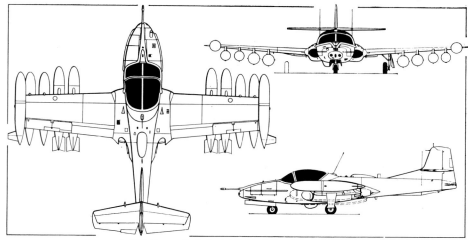

Cessna A-37B Dragonfly twin-jet light strike aircraft (*Pilot Press*)

batteries, and provision for external power source. One main inverter (2,500VA 3-phase 115V 400Hz), and one standby inverter (750VA 3-phase 115V 400Hz), to provide AC power.

ELECTRONICS: Radio and radar installations include UHF communications (AN/ARC-109A, ARC-151 and ARC-164), FM communications (FM-622A), TACAN (AN/ARN-65), ADF (AN/ARN-83), IFF (AN/APX-72), direction finder (AN/ARA-50) VHF communications (VHF-20B), VOR/LOC, glideslope, marker beacon (VIR-31A) and interphone (AIC-18).

ARMAMENT AND OPERATIONAL EQUIPMENT: GAU-2B/A 7·62 mm Minigun installed in forward fuselage. Each wing has four pylon stations, the two inner ones carrying 870 lb (394 kg) each, the intermediate one 600 lb (272 kg) and the outer one 500 lb (227 kg). The following weapons, in various combinations, can be carried on these underwing pylons: SUU-20 bomb and rocket pod, MK-81 or MK-82 bomb, BLU/32/B fire bomb, SUU-11/A gun pod, CBU-24/B or CBU-25/A dispenser and bomb, M-117 demolition bomb, LAU-3/A rocket pod, CBU-12/A, CBU-14/A or CBU-22/A dispenser and bomb, BLU-1C/B fire bomb, LAU-32/A or LAU-59/A rocket pod, CBU-19/A canister cluster and SUU-25/A flare launcher. Associated equipment includes an armament control panel, Chicago Aerial Industries CA-503 non-computing gunsight, KS-27C gun camera and KB-18A strike camera.

DIMENSIONS, EXTERNAL:
Wing span over tip-tanks 35 ft 10½ in (10·93 m)
Wing chord at root 6 ft 7·15 in (2·01 m)
Wing chord at tip 4 ft 6 in (1·37 m)
Wing aspect ratio 6·2
Length overall, excl refuelling probe
  28 ft 3¼ in (8·62 m)
Height overall 8 ft 10½ in (2·70 m)
Tailplane span 13 ft 11½ in (4·25 m)
Wheel track 14 ft 0½ in (4·28 m)
Wheelbase 7 ft 10 in (2·39 m)

AREAS:
Wings, gross 183·9 sq ft (17·09 m²)
Ailerons (total) 11·30 sq ft (1·05 m²)
Trailing-edge flaps (total) 15·10 sq ft (1·40 m²)
Fin 11·54 sq ft (1·07 m²)
Rudder, incl tab 6·24 sq ft (0·58 m²)
Tailplane 34·93 sq ft (3·25 m²)
Elevators, incl tab 11·76 sq ft (1·09 m²)

WEIGHTS AND LOADINGS:
Weight empty, equipped 6,211 lb (2,817 kg)
Max T-O and landing weight
  14,000 lb (6,350 kg)
Normal landing weight 7,000 lb (3,175 kg)
Max zero-fuel weight 10,710 lb (4,858 kg)
Max wing loading 65·4 lb/sq ft (319·3 kg/m²)
Max power loading 2·1 lb/lb st (2·1 kg/kg st)

PERFORMANCE (at max T-O weight, except as detailed otherwise):
Max never-exceed speed (Mach limitation)
  455 knots (524 mph; 843 km/h)
Max level speed at 16,000 ft (4,875 m)
  440 knots (507 mph; 816 km/h)
Max cruising speed at 25,000 ft (7,620 m)
  425 knots (489 mph; 787 km/h)
Stalling speed at max landing weight, wheels and flaps down
  98·5 knots (113 mph; 182 km/h)
Stalling speed at normal landing weight, wheels and flaps down
  75 knots (86·5 mph; 139 km/h)
Max rate of climb at S/L 6,990 ft (2,130 m)/min
Service ceiling 41,765 ft (12,730 m)
Service ceiling, one engine out
  25,000 ft (7,620 m)
T-O run 1,740 ft (531 m)
T-O to 50 ft (15 m) 2,596 ft (792 m)
Landing from 50 ft (15 m) at max landing weight
  6,600 ft (2,012 m)
Landing run at max landing weight
  4,150 ft (1,265 m)
Landing run at normal landing weight
  1,710 ft (521 m)
Range with max fuel, including four 100 US gallon (378 litre) drop-tanks, at 25,000 ft (7,620 m) with reserves
  878 nm (1,012 miles; 1,628 km)
Range with max payload, including 4,100 lb (1,860 kg) ordnance
  399 nm (460 miles; 740 km)
  (1975–76)

CESSNA MODEL 337 SKYMASTER and SKYMASTER II
USAF designation: O-2

This unique all-metal 4/6-seat business aircraft resulted from several years of study by Cessna aimed at producing a twin-engined aeroplane that would be simple to fly, low in cost, safe and comfortable, while offering all the traditional advantages of two engines. Construction of a full-scale mockup was started in February 1960 and completed two months later. The prototype flew for the first time on 28 February 1961, followed by the first production model in August 1962. FAA Type Approval was received on 22 May 1962 and deliveries of the original Model 336 Skymaster, with non-retractable landing gear, began in May 1963.

544 examples of two military versions (O-2A and O-2B) were delivered to the US Air Force and Imperial Iranian Air Force.

O-2A. Equipped for forward air controller missions, including visual reconnaissance, target identification, target marking, ground-to-air co-ordination and damage assessment. Dual controls standard. Four underwing pylons for external stores, including rockets, flares or other light ordnance, such as a 7·62 mm Minigun pack. Modified 60A electrical system to support special electronics systems, including UHF, VHF, FM, ADF, TACAN and APX transponder.

Initial contract, dated 29 December 1966, called for 145 O-2As; a follow-on contract awarded in June 1967 brought the total on order to 192, all of which had been delivered by early 1968. A further contract was announced on 26 June 1968, for 45 O-2As, together with modification services and spares, and this was amended in September 1968 to increase the quantity to 154 aircraft. The additional 109 O-2As have lightweight electronics. In early 1970 Cessna delivered 12 O-2As to the Imperial Iranian Air Force for training, liaison and observation duties.

O-2B. Generally similar to the commercial version, but equipped for psychological warfare missions. Advanced communications system and high-power air-to-ground broadcasting system, supplied by University Sound division of LTV Ling Altec and utilising three 600W amplifiers with highly directional speakers. Manual dispenser fitted, for leaflet dropping. Initial contract for 31 placed on 29 December 1966, and the programme was initiated by the repurchase of 31 commercial aircraft, six of which were used for pilot training at Eglin AFB, Florida. First O-2B accepted by USAF on 31 March 1967 and was assigned to Vietnam. A combined total of 510 O-2As and O-2Bs were delivered by December 1970.

The following details apply to the standard commercial Skymasters:

TYPE: Tandem-engined cabin monoplane.

WINGS: Braced high-wing monoplane, with single streamlined bracing strut each side. Wing section NACA 2412 at root, NACA 2409 at tip. Dihedral 3°. Incidence 4° 30′ at root, 2° 30′ at tip. Conventional all-metal two-spar structure. Conical-camber glassfibre wing-tips. All-metal Frise ailerons. Electrically-operated all-metal single-slotted flaps. Ground-adjustable tab in port aileron. Pneumatic de-icing optional.

FUSELAGE: Conventional all-metal semi-monocoque structure.

TAIL UNIT: Cantilever all-metal structure with twin fins and rudders, carried on two slim metal booms. Trim tab in elevator, with optional electric actuation. Optional pneumatic de-icing system.

LANDING GEAR: Hydraulically-retractable tricycle type. Cantilever spring steel main legs. Steerable nosewheel with oleo-pneumatic shock-absorber. Main wheels and tyres size 6·00-6. Nosewheel and tyre size 5·00-5. Main-wheel tyre pressure 45 lb/sq in (3·16 kg/cm²). Hydraulic disc brakes. Parking brake. Oversize wheels and heavy-duty brakes optional.

POWER PLANT: Two 210 hp Continental IO-360-C six-cylinder horizontally-opposed aircooled engines, each driving a McCauley two-blade fully-feathering constant-speed metal propeller. Electrically-operated cowl flaps. Propeller de-icing optional for forward propeller. Fuel in two main tanks in each outer wing, with total usable capacity of 92 US gallons (348 litres), and two additional tanks in inner wings with total usable capacity of 56 US gallons (212 litres) provide for optional long-range system. Total usable capacity with optional tanks 148 US gallons (560 litres). Refuelling points above wings. Oil capacity 4 US gallons (15 litres).

Cessna O-2A forward air control aircraft, with underwing rocket pods (1975–76)

ACCOMMODATION: Standard accommodation for pilot and co-pilot on fully-articulating individual seats, with rear bench seat for two passengers. Alternative arrangements include individual seats for fifth and sixth passengers. Optional cabin equipment includes fully-articulating individual seats for passengers and matching headrests. Space for 365 lb (165 kg) of baggage in four-seat version. Airstair door on starboard side. Cabin is heated, ventilated and soundproofed. Adjustable air vents and reading lights available to each passenger. Provision for carrying glassfibre cargo pack, with capacity of 300 lb (136 kg), under fuselage; this reduces cruising speed by only 2·6 knots (3 mph; 5 km/h).

SYSTEMS: Electrical system supplied by two 38A 28V engine-driven alternators. 24V battery. Hydraulic system for landing gear retraction and brakes.

ELECTRONICS AND EQUIPMENT: Standard equipment includes sensitive altimeter, airspeed indicator, rate of climb indicator, electric clock, outside air temperature gauge, audible stall warning device, engine synchronisation indicator, turn co-ordinator indicator, elevator and aileron control locks, windscreen defroster, dome light, map light, reading lights, baggage net, sun visors, hinged window starboard side, all-weather window, tinted windscreen and windows, omni-flash beacon, taxi light, navigation light detectors, retractable tie-down rings, towbar and quick drain fuel tank valves. Optional avionics include Cessna Series 300 nav/com with 720-channel com and 200-channel nav with remote VOR/LOC or VOR/ILS indicator, ADF with digital tuning, marker beacon with three lights and aural signal, DME, 10-channel HF transceiver, and Nav-O-Matic single-axis autopilot and integrated flight control system; or Series 400 nav/com with 720-channel com and 200-channel nav with VOR/LOC or VOR/ILS indicator, 40-channel glideslope receiver, ADF with digital tuning and BFO, transponder with 4096 code capability, Nav-O-Matic 400 or 400A two-axis autopilot and integrated flight control system. Optional equipment includes all-purpose control wheel with provision for map light, boom microphone switch, pitch trim switch, autopilot/electric trim disengage switch, dual controls, blind-flying instrumentation, economy mixture indicator, true airspeed indicator, instrument post lights, approach plate holder, flight hour recorder, alternate static source, cabin fire extinguisher, baggage net, wall-mounted table, safety belts for 3rd, 4th, 5th and 6th seats, oxygen system, portable stretcher, cargo tie-down installation, full-flow oil filters, oil dilution system, external power socket, propeller synchrophaser, winterisation kit, internal corrosion proofing, ice detection system, white strobe lights, photographic provisions, static wicks, windscreen anti-icing panel, pitot heating system, flush glideslope antenna, cargo pack, and emergency exit window for port side.

DIMENSIONS, EXTERNAL:

Wing span	38 ft 2 in (11·63 m)
Wing chord at root	6 ft 0 in (1·83 m)
Wing chord at tip	4 ft 0 in (1·22 m)
Wing aspect ratio	7·18
Length overall	29 ft 9 in (9·07 m)
Height overall	9 ft 2 in (2·79 m)
Tailplane span	10 ft 0½ in (3·06 m)
Wheel track	8 ft 2 in (2·49 m)
Wheelbase	7 ft 10 in (2·39 m)

Propeller diameter:

Front	6 ft 6 in (1·98 m)
Rear	6 ft 4 in (1·93 m)

Passenger door:

Height	3 ft 10 in (1·17 m)
Width	3 ft 0 in (0·91 m)

DIMENSIONS, INTERNAL:

Cabin: Length	9 ft 11 in (3·02 m)
Max width	3 ft 8¼ in (1·12 m)
Max height	4 ft 3¼ in (1·30 m)
Volume	128 cu ft (3·62 m³)
Baggage space	17 cu ft (0·50 m³)

AREAS:

Wings, gross	202·5 sq ft (18·81 m²)
Ailerons (total)	15·44 sq ft (1·43 m²)
Trailing-edge flaps (total)	36·88 sq ft (3·43 m²)
Fins (total)	30·68 sq ft (2·85 m²)
Rudders (total)	10·70 sq ft (0·99 m²)
Tailplane	32·82 sq ft (3·05 m²)

WEIGHTS AND LOADINGS:

Weight empty:	
Skymaster	2,710 lb (1,229 kg)
Skymaster II	2,840 lb (1,288 kg)
Max T-O weight	4,630 lb (2,100 kg)
Max landing weight	4,400 lb (1,995 kg)
Max wing loading	22·9 lb/sq ft (112 kg/m²)
Max power loading	11·0 lb/hp (5·0 kg/hp)

PERFORMANCE (at max T-O weight):

Max level speed at S/L	179 knots (206 mph; 332 km/h)
Max cruising speed, 75% power at 5,500 ft (1,675 m)	170 knots (196 mph; 315 km/h)
Econ cruising speed at 10,000 ft (3,050 m)	128 knots (147 mph; 237 km/h)
Stalling speed, flaps up, power off	70 knots (80 mph; 129 km/h)
Stalling speed, flaps down, power off	61 knots (70 mph; 113 km/h)
Max rate of climb at S/L	1,100 ft (335 m)/min
Rate of climb at S/L, front engine only	270 ft (82 m)/min
Rate of climb at S/L, rear engine only	320 ft (98 m)/min
Service ceiling	18,000 ft (5,490 m)
Service ceiling, front engine only	6,100 ft (1,860 m)
Service ceiling, rear engine only	7,100 ft (2,160 m)
T-O run	1,000 ft (305 m)
T-O to 50 ft (15 m)	1,675 ft (510 m)
Landing from 50 ft (15 m)	1,650 ft (503 m)
Landing run	700 ft (213 m)
Range at max cruising speed, standard fuel, no reserve	677 nm (780 miles; 1,255 km)
Range at max cruising speed, long-range fuel, no reserve	1,098 nm (1,265 miles; 2,035 km)
Range at econ cruising speed, standard fuel, no reserve	872 nm (1,005 miles; 1,617 km)
Range at econ cruising speed, long-range fuel, no reserve	1,402 nm (1,615 miles; 2,600 km)

(1975–76)

The Chance Vought AU-1 Close-Support Fighter (Pratt & Whitney R-2800 engine).

THE CHANCE VOUGHT CORSAIR.
U.S. Navy designations: F4U and AU.

The prototype XF4U-1 was delivered to the U.S. Navy in 1940 and after protracted tests the Corsair was ordered in quantity in the Autumn of 1941. The first production F4U-1 flew in June, 1942.

The following versions of the Corsair have been or are being built in quantity :

F4U-1. Pratt & Whitney R-2800 8 (B) engine. First production version of the Corsair. Underwent considerable development in successive production batches.

F4U-4. Pratt & Whitney R-2800-18W engine. Similar to F4U-1 except for engine installation and new cockpit arrangement. Withdrawn from production late in 1947 after 2,356 had been built.

F4U-5. Pratt & Whitney R-2800-32W (-E) two-stage supercharged engine. Considerable internal redesign, particularly in cockpit arrangement and equipment. Various sub-types such as F4U-5N night fighter, F4U-5P photo-reconnaissance aircraft and F4U-5NL winterised night fighter, the last specially developed for carrier operations off Korea in winter of 1950-51. See below.

F4U-5NL. F4U-5 with wing and tail Goodrich boot de-icers, windshield de-icers, Hamilton Standard airscrew de-icers, larger heater, extra oxygen, exhaust glare dampeners, completely duplicated radio equipment, with antenna for emergency set on rear fuselage aft of rudder. A.I. radar in nacelle on starboard wing and auxiliary fuel tank under fuselage. First F4U-5NL flew on November 4, 1950.

F4U-7. Pratt & Whitney R-2800-18W engine and heavier armament. Ordered through M.D.A.P. for French Navy. In production in 1952.

AU-1. Adaptation of F4U-5 for close support of ground forces in Korea. Pratt & Whitney R-2800-83WA engine with single-stage blower. First AU-1 flew on December 29, 1951. In production in 1952.

In addition, Goodyear Aircraft Corporation built over 4,000 F4U-1 types as FG-1s and developed the F2G-1/2 which entered very limited production, and Brewster Aeronautical Corporation built F4U-1 types as F3A-1s.

The specification below refers to the AU-1 attack version of the Corsair :—

TYPE.—Single-seat Fighter.

WINGS.—Cantilever inverted gull-wing monoplane. Wing section NACA 23018/23009. Aspect ratio 5.35. Outer wing dihedral 8.5°. All-metal single-spar structure with spot-welded metal skin. Outer wings fold upwards hydraulically for stowage. Wood ailerons with wood covering. All-metal slotted trailing-edge flaps. Total area of ailerons 18.1 sq. ft. (1.68 m.²). Total flap area 36.4 sq. ft. (3.38 m.²). Gross wing area 314 sq. ft. (29.2 m.²).

FUSELAGE.—All-metal monocoque structure with spot-welded metal skin.

TAIL UNIT.—Cantilever monoplane type. Structurally similar to wings. Spot-welded metal skin on fin. Metalite skin on tailplane and fabric-covering on movable surfaces. Balanced rudder with controllable trim-tab. Balance and trim-tabs in elevators.

LANDING GEAR.—Retractable tail-wheel type. Wheels turn through 90 degrees as they retract backwards to lie flat within wings. Tail-wheel with deck arrester hook attached retracts into fuselage. Hydraulic operation. Goodyear main wheels with brakes. Solid tail-wheel.

POWER PLANT.—One 2,400 h.p. Pratt & Whitney R-2800-83WA Double Wasp eighteen-cylinder two-row radial air-cooled engine employing water injection and driving a Hamilton Standard Hydromatic four-blade constant-speed airscrew, 13 ft. 2 in. (4 m.) in diameter. Fuel tank in fuselage with capacity for 234 U.S. gallons (850 litres). Two auxiliary drop tanks (150 U.S. gallons=567 litres each) may be carried either one under each wing or under right wing and fuselage centre-line.

ACCOMMODATION.—Pilot's cockpit has bulged enclosure which slides backwards for access. Bullet-resisting windscreen and armour-plate protection.

ARMAMENT.—Four 20 mm. cannon two in each outer wing, outboard of airscrew disc. Racks below wings for ten 5-in. (12.7 cm.) rocket projectiles and two 1,000 lb. (454 kg.) or 1,600 lb. (726 kg.) bombs under wings.

DIMENSIONS.—
Span 40 ft. 11¾ in. (12.48 m.).
Span (folded) 17 ft. 0 in. (5.18 m.).
Length 34 ft. 6½ in. (10.5 m.).
Height (tail down) 14 ft. 9¼ in. (4.49 m.).
Height (folded) 16 ft. 4¼ in. (4.98 m.).
WEIGHT LOADED.—
12,845 lb. (5,830 kg.).
PERFORMANCE.—
Max. speed over 450 m.p.h. (720 km.h.).
(1952–53)

The Chance Vought F4U-5NL Single-seat Night Fighter.

The Chance Vought F7U-3M Cutlass armed with four Sparrow I missiles. (*Gordon Williams*).

THE CHANCE VOUGHT CUTLASS.
U.S. Navy designation: F7U.

The Cutlass is a swept-wing tail-less single-seat twin-jet aircraft which is in service with the U.S. Navy in several forms. Production of the F7U-3 ceased in December, 1955.

The Cutlass wing, which is of symmetrical section and has a sweepback of 35° at quarter chord, is fitted with full-span leading-edge slats, air brakes, power-operated irreversible "ailavators," or combined ailerons and elevators, and vertical fin and rudder surfaces. The "ailavators" are operated by two completely independent hydraulic power control systems connected in tandem. There is no direct mechanical linkage between control stick in the cockpit and the "ailavator" surfaces.

The Cutlass was the first production naval aircraft to achieve supersonic flight, the first to release bombs at a speed greater than that of sound and the first to be catapulted from a carrier while carrying nearly 5,000 lb. of external stores and weapons. The Cutlass was the first fighter to have incorporated in its design the use of afterburners, full power controls with an "artificial feel" system and an automatic stabilisation system.

The four following versions of the Cutlass have been announced :—

F7U-1. Two Westinghouse J34-WE-32 turbojets with afterburners. First prototype XF7U-1 flew on September 29, 1948. First production F7U-1 flew on March 1, 1950. Fourteen built. Used for training and operational evaluation for aircraft-carrier use.

The Chance Vought F7U-3P, the Photographic Reconnaissance version of the Cutlass.

F7U-3. Two Westinghouse J46-WE-8 turbojet engines (6,000 lb. = 2,725 kg. s.t. each) with afterburners. It is larger, has more power, carries a heavier armament load and has better maintenance characteristics than the F7U-1. Fitted with folding wings and arrester-gear for carrier operations. Standard armament consists of four 20 mm. cannon and a new type of rocket launcher carrying "Mighty Mouse" missiles. Normally one pack is mounted under the fuselage but two further packs can be carried under the wings for "strike" missions.

The first production F7U-3 flew for the first time on December 20, 1951, and the aircraft went into production in 1953. First deliveries to the U.S. Navy were made in February, 1954.

F7U-3P. Photographic reconnaissance version of F7U-3. Elongated nose to house camera equipment. This version is illustrated on page 271. First flew July, 1955.

F7U-3M. Missile-carrying version of the F7U-3. Armed with four Sparrow I supersonic beam-riding missiles.

DIMENSIONS (F7U-3).—
Span 39 ft. 8¼ in. (12.10 m.).
Length 44 ft. 3¼ in. (13.50 m.).
Height 14 ft. 7.4 in. (4.45 m.).
WEIGHTS.—
Weight empty 18,210 lb. (8,267 kg.).
Normal loaded weight 27,340 lb. (12,412 kg.).
Max. loaded weight 31,642 lb. (14,365 kg.).

PERFORMANCE.—
Max. speed more than 650 m.p.h. (1,040 km.h.).
Rate of climb (with afterburner) approx. 13,000 ft./min. (3,965 m./min.).
Service ceiling approx. 40,000 ft. (12,200 m.).
(1957—58)

THE CHANCE VOUGHT KINGFISHER.
U.S. Navy designation : OS2U (also OS2N when built by Naval Aircraft Factory).
Fleet Air Arm name : Kingfisher.

The XOS2U-1 protype was delivered to the U.S. Navy in 1938 and the first production OS2U-1's went into service in 1940. Two further and generally similar series, the OS2-U2 and OS2U-3 followed, the latter model also going into production at the Naval Aircraft Factory as the OS2N-1. The British Kingfisher I was a counterpart of the OS2U-3.

The Kingfisher is no longer in production, but it was still in service at the end of 1944.

TYPE.—Two-seat Observation-Scout seaplane or landplane.
WINGS.—Mid-wing cantilever monoplane. Centre-section integral with fuselage. Two tapering outer panels. Structure comprises a single-spar with a D-shaped torque-resisting metal leading-edge. Aft of spar wing is covered with fabric. The trailing-edge includes deflector-plate type flaps and drooping ailerons. Spoilers are built into the upper wing surfaces to provide lateral control when the ailerons are drooped.

FUSELAGE.—All-metal monocoque of riveted and spot-welded construction. The skin panels, reinforced by spot-welded stiffeners or channels, are riveted to two upper longerons and one keel member.
TAIL UNIT.—Cantilever monoplane type. Fixed surfaces are all-metal. Movable surfaces have fabric-covered metal frames. The movable surfaces are equipped with trimming-tabs controllable in flight by the pilot.
LANDING GEAR.—Split type. Each oleo shock-absorbing strut forms one leg of a tripod bolted to fuselage fittings. Duo-servo hydraulic brakes and high pressure tyres. Free swivelling lockable tail-wheel equipped with smooth-contour pneumatic tyre. The tail-wheel shock-strut is of the oleo-air cushion type. As a seaplane, a single main float is attached to the fuselage by two centre-line struts and bracing wires. Wing-tip floats are connected to the wing by five aluminium-alloy streamline struts.
POWER PLANT.—One Pratt & Whitney Wasp-Junior R-985-AN-2 radial air-cooled engine rated at 400 h.p. at 5,000 ft. (1,525 m.) and at 450 h.p. for take-off. NACA cowling, adjustable trailing-edge gills, Hamilton-Standard constant-speed airscrew. Cartridge starter. The fuel tank is built integral with the centre-section of the wing and has a capacity of 144 U.S. gallons. The oil tank is of welded aluminium-alloy construction mounted in

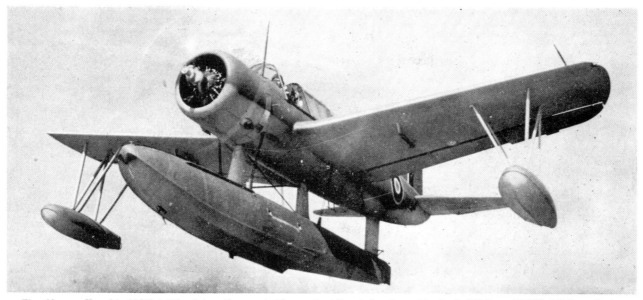

The Chance Vought OS2U-3 Kingfisher Two-seat Observation Scout Seaplane (Pratt & Whitney R-985-AN-2 engine).

the engine compartment and has an oil capacity of 10 U.S. gallons. An oil-cooler, and automatic oil-temperature control-unit are included in the lubricating system.

ACCOMMODATION.—Pilot and gunner in enclosed cockpits. Complete flying, engine, and navigation instruments.

ARMAMENT.—One fixed 30-cal. synchronized machine-gun firing through the airscrew, 500 rounds of ammunition ; and one flexible machine-gun in rear cockpit mounted on a rotating and tilting seat, 600 rounds of ammunition. Bomb-racks in the outer panels, for carrying two 100-lb. bombs or eight 30-lb. bombs. Provision for camera-gun, radio, smoke-tank and other equipment for special missions.

DIMENSIONS (Seaplane).—Span 35 ft. 10 11/16 in. (10.96 m.), Length 33 ft. 7 3/16 in. (10.25 m.), Height 14 ft. 8 in. (4.47 m.), Wing area 261.9 sq. ft. (24.4 sq. m.).

WEIGHTS AND LOADINGS (Observation Seaplane).—Weight empty 3,335 lbs. (1,514 kg.), Weight loaded 4,980 lbs. (2,260.8 kg.), Wing loading 19.0 lbs./sq. ft. (92.6 kg./sq. m.), Power loading 12.45 lbs./h.p. (5.63 kg./h.p.).

PERFORMANCE (Observation Seaplane).—Maximum speed at 5,000 ft. (1,525 m.) 171 m.p.h. (275 km.h.), Cruising speed at 75% power at 6,000 ft. (1,830 m.) 152 m.p.h. (244.7 km.h.), Landing speed 55 m.p.h. (88.5 km.h.), Rate of climb at 4,000 ft. (1,220 m.) 960 ft./min. (292.8 m./min.), Service ceiling 18,200 ft. (5,550 m.), Cruising range at 6,000 ft. (1,830 m.) at 75% power 908 miles (1,460 km.).

(1945–46)

The Chance Vought XF6U-1 Pirate (one Westinghouse 24C gas-turbine engine).

THE CHANCE VOUGHT PIRATE.
U.S. Navy designation : F6U-1.

The F6U-1 is a single-seat jet-propelled fighter which has been developed for the U.S. Navy. The experimental prototype underwent its preliminary flying trials at the U.S.A.F. test base at Muroc, California, where it made its first flight on October 2, 1946.

The first production F6U-1 flew in July, 1949, and the last aircraft of an order for thirty was delivered to the U.S. Navy in February, 1950.

TYPE.—Single-seat jet-propelled Naval Fighter.

WINGS.—Low-wing cantilever monoplane. Metal structure with Metalite skin with high-gloss finish. Metalite consists of two sheets of high-strength aluminium-alloy bonded to a balsa-wood core. It eliminates skin wrinkling and saves weight as fewer ribs and stiffeners are necessary. Large sections can be molded as single units thereby reducing number of external joints.

FUSELAGE.—Oval-section structure of metal with Metalite skin.

TAIL UNIT.—Cantilever monoplane type. Tailplane mounted on fin above fuselage. Metal and Metalite structure.

LANDING GEAR.—Retractable tricycle type. Main wheels raised inward into wings and nose-wheel backward into fuselage.

POWER PLANT.—One Westinghouse J-34-WE-30A axial-flow gas-turbine mounted in fuselage aft of wings, with air intakes in leading-edge of wing on either side of fuselage. Solar after-burner in tail-pipe. Main fuel tanks in fuselage. Jettisonable wing-tip fuel tanks.

ACCOMMODATION.—Pilot's cockpit in nose of fuselage well forward of wings. Jettisonable bubble-type canopy.

DIMENSIONS.—
Span 32 ft. 10 in. (9.20 m.).
Length 37 ft. 8 in. (11.48 m.).
Height 12 ft. 11 in. (3.95 m.).

WEIGHTS.—
Normal loaded weight 11,300 lb. (5,130 kg.).

PERFORMANCE:—Maximum speed 546 mph (902 km/h).

(1950–51)

The Consolidated "Trainer" Light Training Biplane (170 h.p. Kinner C-5 engine).

THE CONSOLIDATED SERIES 21 TRAINING BIPLANES.

The Consolidated Model 21 convertible primary and advanced training biplane was produced under a design competition inaugurated by the U.S. Army Air Corps for the purpose of finding a successor to the Consolidated PT-1 and PT-3 biplanes, of which the Corporation has produced more than a thousand.

The Corporation's dominance in the training aeroplane field has been maintained by the new Series 21 military trainers, the 21-A, 21-B and 21-C, which are known in the U.S. Army Air Corps as the PT-11B, PT-11D and BT-7 respectively, and the "Fleet" 2, 7 and 7-A commercial sport and training designs.

TYPE.—Two-seat light training biplane.

WINGS.—Equal-span staggered biplane. N-22 wing section. Top centre-section carried above fuselage on splayed-out "N" type struts, with one set of "N" type interplane struts on either side of the fuselage. Wing structure consists of two laminated wood spars and the usual number of duralumin ribs, the whole being covered with fabric. The ailerons, on bottom planes only, are built up of duralumin tube spars and duralumin ribs, with fabric covering. For conversion from primary to advanced training, involving change of engine, to preserve longitudinal balance the whole wing cellule is moved forward 9 ins. to additional fittings provided

FUSELAGE.—Rectangular welded steel-tube structure, covered with fabric.

TAIL UNIT.—Normal monoplane type. Welded steel-tube framework covered with fabric. Adjustable tail-plane. Fin is adjustable on the ground.

UNDERCARRIAGE.—Split-axle type. Consists of two steel-tube Vees, which incorporate a built-in oleo shock-absorber leg, hinged to the bottom fuselage longerons, with two half-axles hinged at their inner ends to a transverse steel-tube Vee. The side Vees are faired with streamline covers. Semi-balloon wheels and brakes are standard. Interchangeable tail-skid and tail-wheel.

POWER PLANT.—One 170 h.p. Kinner C-5 five-cylinder radial air-cooled engine on detachable mounting. For advanced training or light observation duties, the 300 h.p. Pratt & Whitney "Wasp-Junior" or 400 h.p. Pratt & Whitney "Wasp-Junior" engines are fitted. Fuel tank, of 43 U.S. gallons capacity, in centre-section. An additional 30 U.S. gallons fuel tank may be mounted in the fuselage, forward of the front cockpit, and still further additional fuel may be carried in a "belly" tank under the fuselage.

ACCOMMODATION.—Tandem open cockpits, with complete dual control. Standard control column and rudder pedals. Elevators and ailerons operated by push-pull rods. All engine-controls are by push-pull rods. Tail-plane adjustable from both cockpits. All cockpit installation mounted inside fuselage fairing, to leave cockpits free of obstructions. Fire-extinguisher is carried in a streamline container, partially outside fuselage, where it can be reached from both cockpits or from ground. Instrument boards covered with mousse rubber crash-pads and instruments are indirectly lighted. A metal-lined baggage compartment of 4.5 cub. ft. capacity behind rear cockpit.

DIMENSIONS.—Span 31 ft. 6 in. (9.6 m.), Wing area 266 sq. ft. (24.7 sq. m.).

WEIGHTS AND LOADINGS (Primary Trainer).—Weight empty 1,700 lbs. (772 kg.), Weight loaded 2,400 lbs. (1,090 kg.), Wing loading 9.02 lbs./sq. ft. (44 kg./sq. m.), Power loading (Kinner C-5 at 175 h.p.) 13.7 lbs./h.p. (6.2 kg./h.p.).

WEIGHTS AND LOADINGS (Basic or Advanced Trainer).—Weight empty 2,090 lbs. (949 kg.), Weight loaded 3,000 lbs. (1,362 kg.), Wing loading 11.28 lbs./sq. ft. (55 kg./sq. m.), Power loading (Pratt & Whitney "Wasp-Junior" at 300 h.p.) 10 lbs./h.p. (4.5 kg./h.p.), Power loading (Pratt & Whitney "Wasp-Junior" at 400 h.p.) 7.5 lbs./h.p. (3.4 kg./h.p.).

PERFORMANCE (175 h.p. Kinner C-5).—Maximum speed 119 m.p.h. (190.4 km.h.), Initial rate of climb 750 ft./min. (228.75 m./min.), Service ceiling 12,550 ft. (3,828 m.).

PERFORMANCE (300 h.p. Pratt & Whitney "Wasp-Junior").—Maximum speed 150 m.p.h. (240 km.h.), Initial rate of climb 1,130 ft./min. (345 m./min.), Service ceiling 18,500 ft. (5,642.5 m.).

PERFORMANCE (400 h.p. Pratt & Whitney "Wasp-Junior").—Maximum speed 160 m.p.h. (256 km.h.), Initial rate of climb 1,650 ft./min (503 m./min.), Service ceiling 22,700 ft. (6,923.5 m.). (1932)

The Consolidated 21 Two-seat Training Biplane (Pratt & Whitney "Wasp-Junior" engine).

A Consolidated "Fleet" Type 5 Two-seat Training Biplane (100 h.p. Kinner engine) with apparatus for hooking onto airship trapezes.

CONSOLIDATED "FLEET" TYPES 5, 10 AND 11.

TYPE.—Two-seat open-cockpit biplane.

WINGS.—Single-bay biplane, with dihedral angle on lower planes only. "N" type interplane struts. Centre-section struts also of "N" type, splayed outwards. Spruce spars. Aluminium-alloy ribs built up from stampings. Chrome-molybdenum steel-tube drag struts with tie-rod drag-bracing. Leading-edge, trailing-edge and wing-tips are duralumin. Balanced ailerons, with inset hinges on lower wings only. Wood structure. One long hinge-pin inserted at extremity. All aileron control mechanism within wing.

FUSELAGE.—Welded chrome-molybdenum steel-tube structure. Wood fairing clipped to structure. Fabric covering.

TAIL UNIT.—Chrome-molybdenum steel-tube spars, sheet steel channel ribs, sheet steel trailing-edges. Tubular leading-edges. Fabric covering. Fin adjustable on the ground. Screw-type tail-plane adjustment.

UNDERCARRIAGE.—Divided type. Two Vees hinged to lower longerons contain oleo-cum-spring shock-absorber gear. Axles hinged to cabane beneath fuselage. Leaf-spring tail-skid, with renewable manganese steel shoe. Land undercarriage may be replaced by twin floats.

POWER PLANT.—One 100 h.p. Kinner K-5 (Model 5), 125 h.p. Kinner B-5 (Model 10), or 160 h.p. Kinner R-5 (Model 11) five-cylinder radial air-cooled engine. Gravity fuel tank (24 U.S. gallons) in centre-section. "Belly" tank (25 U.S. gallons) may be installed under fuselage, and extra tank (35 U.S. gallons) may be installed in front cockpit. Oil tank (3 U.S. gallons) in fuselage.

ACCOMMODATION.—Two open cockpits in tandem behind centre-section. Dual control of normal stick type and rudder pedals.

EQUIPMENT.—In Model 11 provision is made for installing one fixed machine-gun synchronised to fire through airscrew, one or two bomb-racks under fuselage or wings, and gun on movable mounting may be installed over rear cockpit.

DIMENSIONS.—Span 28 ft. (8.53 m.), Length 21 ft. 6 in. (6.5 m.), Height 7 ft. 11½ in. (2.4 m.), Wing area 194 sq. ft. (18 sq. m.).

PERFORMANCE (Model 5 as dual-control trainer).—Maximum speed 106 m.p.h. (171 km.h.), Initial rate of climb 640 ft./min. (195 m./min.), Service ceiling 11,600 ft. (3,536 m.), Cruising range 360 miles (580 km.).

PERFORMANCE (Model 10 as dual-control trainer).—Maximum speed 115 m.p.h. (185 km.h.), Initial rate of climb 990 ft./min. (302 m./min.), Service ceiling 15,900 ft. (4,846 m.), Cruising range 313 miles (504 km.).

PERFORMANCE (Model 10 as dual-control training seaplane).—Maximum speed 109 m.p.h. (175 km.h.), Initial rate of climb 670 ft./min. (204 m./min.), Service ceiling 11,400 ft. (3,475 m.), Cruising range 605 miles (974 km.).

PERFORMANCE (Model 11 as dual-control trainer).—Maximum speed 124 m.p.h. (200 km.h.), Initial rate of climb 1,100 ft./min. (335 m./min.), Service ceiling 17,800 ft. (5,425 m.), Cruising range 296 miles (477 km.).

PERFORMANCE (Model 11 as single-seat long-range bomber).—Maximum speed 120 m.p.h. (193 km.h.), Initial rate of climb 950 ft./min. (290 m./min.), Service ceiling 14,600 ft. (4,450 m.), Cruising range 659 miles (1,061 km.). (1933)

THE CONSOLIDATED VULTEE MODEL 28 CATALINA.
U.S. Navy designation : PBY.
R.A.F. name: Catalina.

The prototype XPBY-1 made its first flight in the Spring of 1935 and the type has been in continuous service in the U.S. Navy since 1936. The PBY-5 went into service in 1939-40 and this was the model which was adopted by the R.A.F. and named the Catalina. This name was recognised by the U.S. Navy in 1941.

Apart from its primary rôle as a patrol bomber, the Catalina has been used as a torpedo-carrier, as a night bomber, as a convoy protection and anti-submarine weapon, for long-range reconnaissance and air/sea rescue duties, and as a glider-tug. The U.S. Navy has also used the Catalina as a mail and freight transport. On an empty weight of 17,500 lbs. (7,945 kg.) the modified Catalina has a cargo capacity of up to 15,000 lbs. (6,810 kg.).

The Catalina has also been built by the Naval Aircraft Factory (PBN-1), Boeing Aircraft of Canada, Ltd. (PB2B-1) and by Canadian Vickers, Ltd. (PBV-1).

The last version built by Consolidated Vultee—the PBY-6A—embodied the modifications incorporated in the PBN-1 (see under "Naval Aircraft Factory").

TYPE.—Twin-engined Long-range Patrol-Bomber flying-boat.

WINGS.—Semi-cantilever high-wing monoplane. Wing in three sections, the centre-section supported above the hull by a streamline superstructure and braced by two pairs of parallel streamline struts to the sides of the hull. Wing structure is of the beam bulkhead and stressed-skin type, the skin being reinforced with "Z" section extruded stiffeners. The trailing-edge section consists of aluminium alloy ribs cantilevered from the main beam and covered with fabric. Aluminium-alloy-framed balanced ailerons covered with fabric.

HULL.—Two-step semi-circular topped hull, of all-metal construction. Aluminium-alloy bulkheads, framing stringers and skin. All-metal retractable wing-tip floats. When the floats are retracted they form tips to the wings and the float struts and bracing structure are recessed flush with the lower surface of the wings. Electrical and mechanically-operated retracting mechanism. Automatic locks and warning lights.

TAIL UNIT.—Monoplane cantilever type. Lower fin built integral with the hull. Tail-plane and upper section of fin covered with smooth metal sheet reinforced with extruded sections. Elevators and rudder are aluminium-alloy structures with fabric covering. Trimming-tabs in elevators and rudder.

POWER PLANT.—Two 1,200 h.p. Pratt & Whitney Twin-Wasp R-1830-92 radial air-cooled engines on welded steel-tube mountings in the leading-edge of the centre-section. NACA cowling. Hamilton-Standard Hydromatic constant-speed airscrews. Protected fuel tanks (1,750 U.S. gallons) in centre-section.

The Consolidated Vultee PBY-5 Catalina Patrol Bomber Flying-boat (two Pratt & Whitney R-1830-92 engines).

ACCOMMODATION.—Bow compartment for mooring gear, etc. Enclosed pilot's compartment seating two side-by-side with dual controls. Engineer's station in hull below centre-section. Two large transparent gun-blisters each with one Browning gun on the sides of the hull aft of the wings. Details of military equipment not available.

DIMENSIONS.—Span 104 ft. (31.72 m.), Length 63 ft. 10 in. (19.52 m.), Height 18 ft. 10 in. (5.65 m.), Wing area 1,400 sq. ft. (130 sq. m.).

WEIGHTS AND LOADINGS.—Weight empty 17,564 lbs. (7,974 kg.), Weight loaded 34,000 lbs. (15,436 kg.), Wing loading 24.3 lbs./ sq. ft. (118.5 kg./sq. m.), Power loading 14.1 lbs./h.p. (6.4 kg./h.p.).

PERFORMANCE.—Maximum speed at 7,500 ft. (2,290 m.) 196 m.p.h. (314 km.h.), Cruising speed 130 m.p.h. (208 km.h.) at 10,000 ft. (3,050 m.), Stalling speed at sea level 76 m.p.h. (112 km.h.), Climb to 5,000 ft. (1,525 m.) 4.5 mins., Climb to 15,000 ft. (4,755 m.) 16 mins., Service ceiling 18,200 ft. (5,550 m.), Maximum range (1,570 U.S. gallons of fuel) at critical altitude 3,100 miles (4,960 km.).

(1945–46)

The Consolidated Vultee PBY-5A Catalina Amphibian (two Pratt & Whitney R-1830-92 engines).

THE CONSOLIDATED VULTEE MODEL 28-5A CATALINA AMPHIBIAN.

U.S. Navy designation: PBY-5A.
U.S. Army Air Forces designation: OA-10.
R.A.F. name: Catalina III.
R.C.A.F. name: Canso.

The Model 28-5A is an amphibian version of the previously-described flying-boat.

It is fitted with a tricycle landing gear, with single wheel under the nose and two aft. The side wheels and supporting mechanism, complete with oleo shock-absorbers, retract into wells in the sides of the hull. The nose wheel in the bow is completely enclosed in the retracted position by automatically-operated hatches.

All three wheels are operated by a central hydraulic power drive and the operations are carried out in sequence automatically. A single lever controls both the extension and retraction of the landing gear. Hydraulic power is derived from the main power plant or from an auxiliary engine, but the landing-gear may be manually-operated if necessary.

PERFORMANCE.—Same as for Catalina flying boat except, Cruising speed 125 m.p.h. (200 km.h.) at 10,000 ft. (3,050 m.), Service ceiling 15,800 ft. (4,820 m.), Range 2,520 miles (4,030 km.).

(1945–46)

THE NAVAL AIRCRAFT FACTORY CATALINA.

U.S. Naval designation : PBN-1.

The Naval Aircraft Factory has produced a modified version of the Catalina to incorporate changes which, if undertaken by plants already in full production, would have seriously interfered with deliveries to the U.S. Navy. These changes, which resulted in improved take-off with heavy load and increased range, were later introduced into the design of the Consolidated Vultee PBY-6A Catalina.

The modifications made in the PBN may be summarised as follows :—

HULL.—Bow extended 2ft and sharpened ; 20° taper step amidships ; after step extended aft some 5 ft ; and shallow breaker step added just forward of the tail.

WINGS.—Strengthened to meet a 28,000 lb. (12,710 kg.) gross load (2,000 lbs. = 908 kg. more than PBY). Shape and size of wing-tip floats changed to provide improved lift and planing characteristics.

TAIL UNIT.—Re-designed with new upper fin and horn-balanced rudder of greater aspect ratio.

FUEL TANKS.—Two additional integral fuel tanks in centre-section to raise total capacity from 1,495 to 2,095 U.S. gallons. Tanks equipped with vapour-dilution system and dump valves. Range increased by ¼ over PBY.

ARMAMENT.—Increased fire-power at all stations and guns equipped with continuous-feed mechanisms.

EQUIPMENT.—Modernised electrical system with greater load capacity. Auxiliary power-plant installed. Storage batteries re-located in hull instead of leading-edge of centre-section. (1945–46)

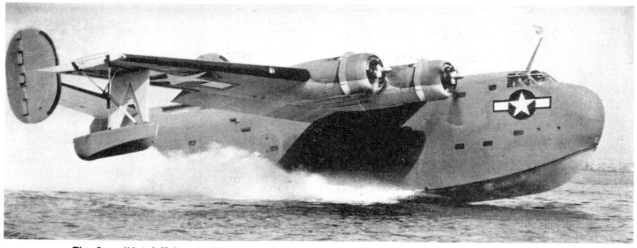

The Consolidated Vultee PB2Y-3R Naval Transport (four Pratt & Whitney R-1830-92 engines).

THE CONSOLIDATED VULTEE MODEL 29 CORONADO.
U.S. Navy designation : PB2Y-3 and 5 and PB2Y-3R.

The XPB2Y-1 prototype of the Coronado, ordered in 1936, was delivered to the U.S. Navy in August, 1938. After service trials it served for some time as Flagship of Aircraft, Scouting Force, U.S. Navy. The first PB2Y-2, the production development of the XPB2Y-1, went into service in January, 1941. The PB2Y-3 was ordered in quantity in 1941 and remained in production until 1944.

Following on the successful power-plant modification in the PB2Y-3R (see below), the PB2Y-3 was submitted to the same change, the Patrol-Bomber conversion with R-1830-92 engines being designated the PB2Y-5.

The PB2Y-5H is fitted as a naval ambulance with accommodation for 25 stretcher cases.

Many Coronado flying-boats were converted into transports under the designation PB2Y-3R. Conversion was undertaken by the Rohr Aircraft Corpn. of Chula Vista, Cal.

In the process of conversion all military equipment has been removed and the nose and tail turret positions faired over. All control cables within the hull have been re-routed and the interior accommodation completely redesigned.

On C deck over the crew's quarters, formerly used as stowage for life-rafts, etc., have been installed a galley, auxiliary power-plant, main cabin heater and emergency water-still. Below the flight deck is the forward sound-proofed sleeping compartment equipped with bunks which let down to form seats for day use.

The main cabin and rear portion of the hull has been provided with a smooth wood and duralumin floor (stepped-up towards the tail) and cargo tie-down rings have been fitted in the floor and sides of the hull. A large cargo loading hatch replaces the former small entrance door beneath the wing and hoisting eyes have been fitted both inside and outside the hull. All seats in the main cabin and tail space are easily removable.

The PB2Y-3R can be used for either passenger or cargo transport. Without cargo there is accommodation for a crew of five and 44 passengers. With 8,600 lbs. (3,905 kg.) of cargo, 24 passengers may be carried. With no passengers 16,000 lbs. (7,264 kg.) of cargo can be transported on a range of 1,000 miles (1,600 km.).

The former standard Coronado power-plant units (Pratt & Whitney R-1830-88 engines with two-speed superchargers) have been replaced by modified Catalina units (Pratt & Whitney R-1830-92 single-stage low-altitude engines) complete with accessories and oil tanks. Airscrews on the inboard engines

are four-bladed, and those on the outer engines three-bladed. The outer wings have been strengthened to carry larger wing-tip floats.

The modified PB2Y-3R in its unladen state weighs 8,000 lbs. (3,624 kg.) less than the former PB2Y-3 Patrol-Bomber flying-boat.

TYPE.—Four-engined Patrol (PB2Y-3) or Transport (PB2Y-3R) flying-boat.

WINGS.—High-wing cantilever monoplane. Wings mounted direct to top of hull and taper in chord and thickness, with a swept-back leading-edge and a straight trailing-edge. All-metal structure with stressed aluminium-alloy skin. Entire trailing-edge hinged, the outer portions acting as ailerons and inner portions between ailerons and hull as flaps. Ailerons and flaps have metal frames with fabric covering.

HULL.—Two-step semi-circular-topped hull of all-metal construction. The after step terminates in a vertical knife-edge. Hull treated inside and out with anti-corrosion finishes. Stabilising floats retract to form wing-tips, the supporting struts being recessed flush with the underside of the wings.

TAIL UNIT.—Cantilever monoplane type with twin fins and rudders. All-metal structure with fabric-covered elevators and rudders. Statically and aerodynamically-balanced movable surfaces, which are also fitted with trimming-tabs.

POWER PLANT.—Four 1,200 h.p. Pratt & Whitney R-1830-88 (PB2Y-3) or R-1830-92 (PB2Y-5 and PB2Y-3R) radial air-cooled engines in line along the leading-edge of the wings. NACA cowlings. Hamilton-Standard Hydromatic full-feathering airscrews.

ACCOMMODATION.—Patrol-Bomber version (PB2Y-3 and 5) accommodates crew of ten. Internal arrangements include sleeping quarters, galley with electric range and refrigerator, workshop, independent electric generating system, intercommunication telephone system, etc. Equipment includes breaching gear, lifting slings for engines etc. The Transport version (PB2Y-3R) has a maximum capacity for 16,000 lbs. (7,264 kg.) with strengthened flooring, large loading door and facilities for handling cargo (see above).

ARMAMENT.—Three power-operated turrets armed with 50 cal. machine guns. Stowage for bombs or depth-charges in wings.

DIMENSIONS.—Span 115 ft. (35 m.), Length 79 ft. 3 in. (24.2 m.), Height 27 ft. 6 in. (8.4 m.), Wing area 1,780 sq. ft. (175.4 sq. m.).

WEIGHTS.—Maximum cargo capacity 16,000 lbs. (7,264 kg.), Weight loaded 66,000 lbs. (29,964 kg.).

PERFORMANCE.—Maximum speed 194 m.p.h. (310.4 km.h.), Cruising speed 170 m.p.h. (272 km.h.), Maximum range 1,070 miles (1,710 km.) at 131 m.p.h. (210 km.h.) (1945-46)

THE CONSOLIDATED VULTEE MODEL 33 DOMINATOR.
U.S. Army Air Forces designation : B-32.

The B-32 was the last U.S. heavy bomber to go into action in the war, aircraft of this type flying a score or so of sorties before Japan surrendered.

Although the B-32 was designed to the same specification as the B-29 Super-fortress and the prototypes of both aircraft were flying at the same time, considerably more development was necessary with the B-32. Pressurisation and remote control of gun turrets were abandoned and the twin-ruddered B-24 type tail used in the three XB-24 prototypes was replaced by the gigantic single fin and rudder shown in the accompanying illustrations.

With the end of the war production of the B-32, which was undertaken as possible insurance against tactical or production failure of the B-29, was cancelled.

The power-plant consisted of four Wright R-3350-23 engines driving four-blade Curtiss Electric reversible-pitch airscrews.

The B-32 carried a normal crew of eight and was provided with an armament of ten 50 cal. guns in five turrets. The tandem bomb-bays had a maximum capacity for 20,000 lb. (9,080 kg.) of bombs.

DIMENSIONS.—Span 135 ft. (41.2 m.), Length 83 ft. 1 in. (25.3 m.), Height 32 ft. 2 in. (9.8 m.), Wing area 1,422 sq. ft. (132 sq. m.).

WEIGHTS.—Weight empty 60,272 lbs. (27,365 kg.), Weight loaded 100,000 lbs. (45,400 kg.), Maximum overloaded weight 120,000 lbs. (54,480 kg.).

PERFORMANCE.—Maximum speed over 360 m.p.h. (576 km.h.) at 25,000 ft. (7,625 m.), Ceiling over 35,000 ft. (10,680 m.), Range with maximum bomb load 800 miles (1,280 km.), Maximum range 3,800 miles (6,080 km.). (1945-46)

The Consolidated Vultee B-32 Dominator Heavy Bomber (four Wright R-3350-23 engines).

THE CONSOLIDATED VULTEE MODEL 32 LIBERATOR.
U.S. Army Air Forces designations : B-24, TB-24, C-109, F-7.
U.S. Navy designation : PB4Y.

The contract for the construction of the first Model 32 was signed with the U.S. Army on March 30, 1939. The prototype XB-24 flew nine months later, on December 29, 1939. It was put into production in the Autumn of 1940, for the U.S., French and British Governments, and when France fell the French contracts were taken over by the British authorities. Development of the B-24 progressed through several stages before it went into large scale use in the U.S. Army Air Forces, the early production Liberators being mainly delivered under British contracts.

The Liberator was finally withdrawn from production on May 31, 1945, after a total of over 19,000 had been built, over 10,000 by Consolidated Vultee at San Diego and Fort Worth, and a further 9,000 by Ford, Douglas and North American.

B-24 (LB-30A). The first twenty-six Liberators off the production lines at San Diego were released to the British Government and delivered by air to Great Britain. They were found to be unsuitable for European combat conditions and were converted into unarmed transports for use on the trans-Atlantic Return Ferry service.

B-24A (Liberator I). As with the B-24, fitted with four Pratt & Whitney R-1830-33 engines with two-speed superchargers and driving Hamilton Standard Hydromatic full-feathering airscrews. The B-24A had an armament of six 50 cal. and two 30 cal. flexible guns, the latter in the tail position. The Liberator I was put into service with R.A.F. Coastal Command and was armed with four 20 m/m. cannon in a fairing beneath the forward fuselage, two .303 in. waist guns, one .303 in. tunnel gun and two .303 in. tail guns.

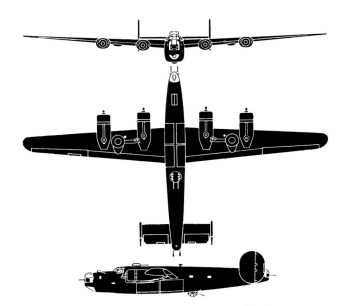

The Consolidated Vultee B-24J Liberator.

The Consolidated Vultee B-24J Liberator Long-range Bomber (four Pratt & Whitney R-1830-43 engines).

The Consolidated Vultee B-24J Liberator Long-range Bomber (four Pratt & Whitney R-1830-65 engines).

Liberator II (LB-30). Had no B-24 counterpart (LB-30 designation signifies Liberator built to British specifications). Four Pratt & Whitney R-1830-S3C4G engines with two-speed superchargers and driving Curtiss Electric full-feathering air-screws. Armed with eleven .303 in. guns, eight in two Boulton Paul power turrets, one dorsal and one tail, one in the nose and two in waist positions.

XB-24B. The first B-24 to be fitted with turbo-supercharged engines, self-sealing tanks, armour, and other modern refinements.

B-24C. Four Pratt & Whitney R-1830-41 engines with exhaust-driven turbo-superchargers. Armament augmented to include two power-driven turrets, one dorsal and one tail, each fitted with two 50 cal. guns. In addition, there was one 50 cal. nose gun and two similar guns in waist positions.

B-24D (PB4Y-1 and Liberator B.III and G.R.V.). Four Pratt & Whitney R-1830-43 engines. Armament further increased by the addition of two further nose guns and one tunnel gun, making a total of ten 50 cal. guns. Fuel capacity increased by the addition of auxiliary self-sealing fuel cells in the outer wings and there was provision for long-range tanks in the bomb-bay. The first model to be equipped to carry two 4,000 lb. bombs on external racks, one under each inner wing. The Liberator G.R.V. was used as a long-range general reconnaissance type by R.A.F. Coastal Command. Fuel capacity was increased at the expense of armour and tank protection. Armament consisted of one .303 in. or 50 cal. gun in the nose, two 50 cal. guns in the upper turret, four .303 in. or two 50 cal. guns in waist positions and four .303 in. guns in a Boulton Paul tail turret. Bombs or depth charges 5,400 lbs.

B-24E (Liberator IV). Similar to B-24D except for minor equipment details. Built by Consolidated (Forth Worth), Ford (Willow Run) and Douglas (Tulsa).

B-24F. An experimental version of the B-24E fitted with exhaust-heated surface anti-icing equipment on wings and tail surfaces.

B-24G, B-24H and B-24J (PB4Y-1 and Liberator B.VI and G.R.VI). Similar except for details of equipment and minor differences associated with different manufacturing methods. B-24G built by North American (Dallas). B-24H built by Consolidated (Forth Worth), Ford (Willow Run) and Douglas (Tulsa). B-24J built by Consolidated (San Diego and Fort Worth), Ford, Douglas and North American (Dallas). Four Pratt & Whitney R-1830-43 or 65 engines. Armament further improved to include four two-gun turrets, in nose and tail and above and below the fuselage (details below). Later models of the B-24J were fitted with exhaust-heated anti-icing equipment. The Liberator G.R.VI was used as a long-range general reconnaissance type by R.A.F. Coastal Command. Armament consisted of six 50 cal. guns, two each in nose and dorsal turrets and in waist positions, and four .303 in. guns in a Boulton Paul tail turret. Bombs or depth charges 4,500 lbs. (2,045 kg.).

XB-24K. The first Liberator to be fitted with a single fin and rudder. An experimental model only.

B-24L. Similar to the B-24J but fitted with a new tail turret with two manually-operated 50 cal. guns. The two guns had a wider field of fire and the new turret, which was designed by the Consolidated Vultee Modification Center at Tucson, permitted a saving of 200 lbs. (91 kg.) in weight.

B-24M. Same as the B-24L except fitted with a new Motor Products two-gun power-operated tail turret. A B-24M was the 6,725th and last Liberator built by Consolidated Vultee at San Diego.

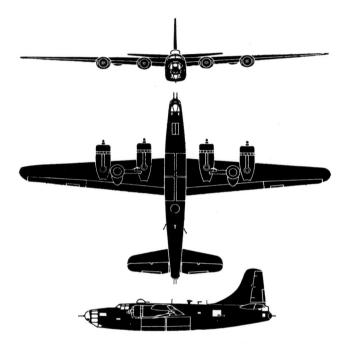

The Consolidated Vultee B-24N Liberator.

B-24N. The first production single-tail Liberator. Fitted with new nose and tail gun mountings. Only a few were built before the Liberator was withdrawn from production on May 31, 1945.

CB-24. Numbers of B-24 bombers withdrawn from operational flying in the European Theatre of Operations were stripped of all armament and adapted to various duties, including utility transport, etc. Painted in distinctive colours and patterns, they were also used as Group Identity Aircraft to facilitate the assembly of large numbers of bombers into their battle formations through and above overcast weather. All these carried the designation CB-24.

TB-24 (formerly AT-22). A conversion of the B-24D for specialised advanced training duties. All bombing equipment and armament removed and six stations provided in the fuselage for the instruction of air engineers in power-plant operation, essentially for such aircraft as the Boeing B-29 and the Consolidated Vultee B-32, which are the first large combat aircraft in the U.S.A.A.F. to have separate completely-equipped engineer's stations.

C-109. A conversion of the B-24 into a fuel-carrying aircraft. The first version, modified by the U.S.A.A.F., had metal tanks in the nose, above the bomb-bay and in the bomb-bay holding a total of 2,900 U.S. gallons. Standard fuel transfer system for loading and unloading through single hose union in side of fuselage. Inert gas injected into tanks as fuel pumped out to eliminate danger of explosion. Developed for transporting fuel from India to China to supply the needs of the B-29's operating therefrom. Later version, modified by the Glenn L. Martin Company, fitted with collapsible Mareng fuel cells.

The Consolidated Vultee B-24N Liberator Long-range Bomber (four Pratt & Whitney R-1830-75 engines).

F-7. A long-range photographic reconnaissance version of the Liberator bomber. The first conversion was made at the Northwest Airlines Modification Center at St. Paul, Minn., in the Autumn of 1943. Bomb racks and other structural obstructions in the fuselage were removed and extra fuel tanks installed in the front section of the bomb-bay to give increased range. The crawl deck over the former bomb compartment was raised to permit head clearance and an upholstered cabin built in aft of the fuel tanks and provided with five windows for the cameras. Photographic equipment of eleven cameras includes a tri-metrogon camera which takes three photographs simultaneously, one vertically downward and two at angles of 30 degrees from the horizontal, to cover an area of 40 square miles from a height of 20,000 ft. The standard Liberator armour and armament of ten 50 cal. machine-guns are retained.

The description below applies specifically to the B-24J Liberator bomber.

TYPE.—Four-engined Long-range Bomber.

WINGS.—High-wing cantilever monoplane. Davis wing of high aspect ratio and constant taper from roots to tips. Wing in three sections comprising centre-section and two outer sections with detachable tips. All-metal two-spar structure. Spars have angle-section booms and reinforced sheet webs. Pressed or built-up former ribs. Spanwise stringers support the flush-riveted smooth metal skin. Statically-balanced ailerons have metal frames and fabric covering. Hydraulically-operated Fowler flaps between ailerons and fuselage.

FUSELAGE.—Aluminium-alloy monocoque structure. Five main bulkheads and intermediate secondary frames, longitudinal Z-section stringers, and a smooth stressed Alclad skin.

TAIL UNIT.—Cantilever monoplane type with twin fins and rudders. Light-alloy framework, the fixed surfaces being metal-covered. The rudders have metal-leading-edges, the remainder being covered with fabric. The elevators are fabric-covered.

LANDING GEAR.—Retractable tricycle type. Main wheels retract outwards into wells in the underside of the wings just inboard of the outer engine nacelles. Nose wheel retracts backwards into the fuselage. Hydraulic retracting mechanism and wheel-brakes.

POWER PLANT.—Four 1,200 h.p. Pratt & Whitney Twin-Wasp R-1830-65 fourteen-cylinder two-row radial air-cooled engines with single-stage engine-driven superchargers and exhaust-driven turbo-superchargers. Hamilton-Standard Hydromatic constant-speed full-feathering airscrews 11 ft. 7 in. (3.54 m.) diameter. Twelve self-sealing fuel cells in centre-section between spars, and speed full-feathering airscrews 11 ft. 7 in. (3.54 m.) diameter. Twelve self-sealing fuel cells in centre-section between spars, and three auxiliary self-sealing fuel cells in each outer wing outboard of the wheel wells. Two further long-range ferrying tanks may be installed in the bomb-bay. Normal fuel capacity : 2,344 U.S. gallons. Each engine has independent oil system. Hopper type self-sealing oil tank (32.9 U.S. gallons) in each engine nacelle.

ACCOMMODATION.—Crew of ten. Power-driven turret in nose with bombardier's prone position below. Aft of the navigator's compartment, with astro-dome in roof, is the pilot's compartment, seating two side-by-side with dual controls. Then follows the radio operator's compartment with turret in roof. A cat-walk through the bomb-bay leads to the after fuselage, which contains the lower retractable "ball" turret, two side gun positions and the tail turret. All crew positions are armoured.

ARMAMENT AND EQUIPMENT.—Ten 0.5 in. machine-guns. One Consolidated or Emerson electrically-operated two-gun turret in nose. One Martin two-gun electrically-operated dorsal turret in the roof of the radio operator's compartment. One retractable Briggs-Sperry two-gun electrically-operated "ball" turret aft of the bomb-bay. Two "waist" guns on manually-operated mountings firing through side ports, one on each side of the fuselage midway between wings and tail. One Consolidated or Motor Products two-gun electrically-operated turret in extreme tail. Tail turret has ammunition feed tracks from magazines amidships. Tandem bomb-bays in fuselage beneath wings, each containing two vertical racks accommodating bombs of from 100 to 1,600 lbs. Special carriers may be installed for four 2,000 lb. bombs. Maximum internal bomb load : 8,000 lbs. Bomb doors of "roll-top desk" type are hydraulically operated, the doors sliding outwards and upwards from the centre-line. Emergency hand operation is provided. Two 4,000 lb. bombs may be carried on external racks, one under each inner wing. Equipment includes two inflatable dinghies, high-pressure oxygen system, full radio and intercommunication equipment, automatic pilot, cameras in rear fuselage, sound-proofing and heating of bombardier's position and flight deck forward of wings, etc. Heating system provides warm-air sprays for pilot's windscreen and bombardier's sighting panel.

DIMENSIONS.—Span 110 ft. (33.5 m.), Length 67 ft. 2 in. (20.5 m.), Height 17 ft. 7½ in. (5.4 m.), Wing area 1,048 sq. ft. (97.4 sq. m.).

WEIGHT LOADED.—Over 60,000 lbs. (27,240 kg.).

PERFORMANCE.—Maximum speed 297 m.p.h. (475.2 km.h.) at 25,000 ft. (7,625 m.), Normal range 1,540 miles (2,465 km.) at 237 m.p.h. (379 km.h.) at 25,000 ft. (7,625 m.) with normal fuel and maximum internal bomb load, Service ceiling 28,000 ft. (8,540 m.).

(1945–46)

THE CONSOLIDATED VULTEE MODEL 32 LIBERATOR TRANSPORT.

U.S. Army Air Forces designation : C-87.
U.S. Navy designation : RY.
British Name : Liberator.

The C-87 Liberator is a military transport version of the B-24 and is in service in both the U.S. Army Air Forces and the U.S. Navy, as well as in the R.A.F.

During the Battle of Java the B-24, because of its capacious fuselage, was used to carry personnel and cargo in the evacuation to Australia. The adaptability of the B-24 to this work and the growing need for air transport to the spreading theatres of war led the U.S. Army to order Consolidated to produce a special transport version of the bomber.

The bomb-bay and rear fuselage were replaced by a passenger or freight compartment, the nose and tail gun positions were closed in and a 6 ft. square door was cut in the rear fuselage for loading purposes. Production of the C-87 Liberator Express was begun at Fort Worth in April, 1942, and moved to San Diego in 1944.

There are also certain freight and passenger-carrying versions of the Liberator bomber which have been converted in Great Britain and Canada for use by R.A.F. Transport Command and the British Overseas Airways Corporation. These have no equivalents in the C-87 Series.

The following are the principal versions of the standard U.S. Liberator Express :—

C-87 (RY-2 and Liberator C.VII). General transport to carry cargo, personnel and their equipment, or both. Tie-down fittings in the floor and sides of the main compartment and 20 easily-removable seats. Originally fitted with one 50 cal. tail gun, but later replaced by a faired tail-cone.

C-87A (RY-1). De luxe passenger transport with seats for 16 passengers by day or five folding berths and four single seats by night. There is a galley aft. Only a few were so equipped.

C-87B. This was an armed version of the C-87. It was fitted with two fixed nose guns fired by the pilot, a top turret and a ventral rear-firing tunnel gun. All crew positions were armoured. Only a few were so equipped.

C-87C (RY-3 and Liberator C.IX). A modified version of the Liberator Express with single fin and rudder, dihedral tailplane and a lengthened forward fuselage.

The Consolidated Vultee RY-3 Liberator' Naval Transport (four Pratt & Whitney R-1830-94 engines).

TYPE.—Four-engined military transport.
WINGS, FUSELAGE, TAIL UNIT AND LANDING GEAR.—Same as B-24.
POWER PLANT.—Four 1,200 h.p. Pratt & Whitney R-1830-43 fourteen-cylinder radial air-cooled engines with General Electric exhaust-driven turbo superchargers. Hamilton-Standard Hydromatic airscrews 11 ft. 7 in. (3.54 m.) diameter. Fuel tanks in wings, either self-sealing or non-self-sealing cells or integral with structure. Total fuel capacity: 2,910 U.S. (2,425 Imp.) gallons.

ACCOMMODATION.—Crew of four—pilot, co-pilot, navigator and radio-operator, with provision for fifth crew member—on flight deck above nose-wheel well. Nose compartment used for baggage and equipment stowage, and can also accommodate two extra passengers. Main compartment with large loading door, 70 × 70 inches (1.8 × 1.8 m.) on port side aft and smaller hatch opposite. Dimensions of main compartment: length 33 ft. (10 m.), width 4 ft. (1.22 m.) and maximum height 8 ft. (2.44 m.). Alternative fittings and furnishings as detailed above. Rear compartment includes lavatory and is used for further equipment stowage. Heating and ventilation. Oxygen for crew and occupants of main compartment. Life-rafts stowed in top and fuselage, with two additional rafts in main compartment. For range of 1,000 miles (1,600 km.) average cargo capacity of 10,000 lbs. (4,540 kg.) or on trans-ocean routes 6,000 lbs. (2,725 kg.).

DIMENSIONS.—Span 110 ft. (33.55 m.), Length 66 ft. 4 in. (20.23 m.), Height 17 ft. 11 in. (5.47 m.).
WEIGHTS.—Weight empty 30,645 lbs. (13,913 kg.). Normal loaded weight 56,000 lbs. (25,424 kg.).
PERFORMANCE.—Maximum speed 300 m.p.h. (480 km.h.) at 25,000 ft. (7,625 m.), Climb to 20,000 ft. (6,100 m.) 60 min., Service ceiling 30,000 ft. (9,150 m.). Normal range (60% power) 1,400 miles (2,240 km.) at 215 m.p.h. (344 km.h.) at 10,000 ft. (3,050 m.), Maximum range 3,300 miles (5,280 km.) at 188 m.p.h. (300 km.h.) at 10,000 ft. (3,050 m.).

(1945–46)

The Consolidated Vultee RY-3 Transport.

THE CONSOLIDATED VULTEE L-13.

The L-13 is a two/three-seat monoplane designed as a general liaison, observation, photographic and ambulance aircraft.

L-13A. Franklin O-425-9 six-cylinder horizontally-opposed air-cooled engine. Production version of the XL-13, three of which were built. U.S.A.F. contract for 300.

L-13B. Modified L-13A for operation in sub-zero temperatures. Principal modifications include installation of 40,000 BTU combustion heater and ducting; sealing of all floor and door cracks; provision of form-fitting covers to protect wings and tail surfaces when moored in the open; provision of exterior heat openings in cabin and engine cowling and modified engine covers to fit; provision of heat-retaining blankets on side walls, aft wall, aft side window and aft upper window, etc.

TYPE.—Two/three-seat Liaison and Ambulance monoplane.

POWER PLANT.—One 245 h.p. Franklin O-425-9 six-cylinder horizontally-opposed air-cooled engine driving two-blade variable-pitch wooden airscrew 9 ft. 0 in. (2.74 m.) diameter. Airscrew clearance (tail up) 9 in. (22.86 cm.). Fuel capacity 60 U.S. gallons (226 litres). Provision for 52½ U.S. gallon (198 litre) auxiliary tank.

The Consolidated Vultee L-13 Military Liaison Monoplane (245 h.p. Franklin O-425 engine).

DIMENSIONS.—
Span 40 ft. 5½ in. (12.33 m.).
Length 31 ft. 9 in. (9.67 m.).
Height (tail down, over cabin) 8 ft. 5 in. (2.97 m.).
Height (tail up, over rudder) 13 ft. 10 in. (4.22 m.).
WEIGHTS AND LOADINGS.—
Weight empty 2,070 lb. (940 kg.).
Disposable load 830 lb. (376 kg.).
Weight loaded 2,900 lb. (1,316 kg.).
Wing loading 10.74 lb./sq. ft. (52.43 kg./m.²).
Power loading 11.8 lb./h.p. (5.34 kg./h.p.).
Max. overloaded weight 3,738 lb. (1,697 kg.).

PERFORMANCE.—
Max. speed 115 m.p.h. (185 km.h.).
Cruising speed 92 m.p.h. (148 km.h.).
Landing speed 43.5 m.p.h. (70 km.h.).
Service ceiling 15,000 ft. (4,570 m.).
Range 368 miles (592 km.).
Range (with extra tank) 750 miles (1,207 km.).
Take-off run 97 yds. (89 m.).
Take-off distance to 50 ft. (15 m.) 187 yds. (171 m.).
Landing run 76 yds. (69 m.).
Landing distance from 50 ft. (15 m.) 161 yds. (147 m.).

(1950–51)

The Consolidated P2Y-1 Patrol Flying-boat (two 575 h.p. Pratt & Whitney "Hornet" engines).

THE CONSOLIDATED P2Y-1.

The Consolidated P2Y-1, twenty-five of which were produced in 1932-33, is a development of the PY-1, which was first described in this Annual in 1929.

The original PY-1 won a design competition for a Naval patrol-type flying-boat. A commercial modification of the PY-1, known as the "Commodore," is in service on Pan-American Airways.

The P2Y-1 differs from the PY-1 mainly in the power plant, which now consists of two 575 h.p. Pratt & Whitney "Hornet" geared engines enclosed in low-drag cowlings and the addition of two short lower wings to make the machine a sesquiplane instead of a high-wing braced monoplane. The pilot's cockpit has also been enclosed.

The Consolidated P2Y-3 Patrol Flying-boat (two Wright "Cyclone" engines). (1937)

THE CONSOLIDATED P2Y-3.

The Consolidated P2Y-3 is a progressive development of the PY-1, which was first described in this Annual in 1929. Although this type was, in 1937, out of production for the U.S. Navy, after a contract for the supply of twenty-three had been fulfilled, the Company was completing a contract for six of these boats for the Argentine Government.

TYPE.—Twin-engined patrol flying-boat.

WINGS.—Sesquiplane arrangement with Warren type interplane bracing. Upper centre-section supported above hull by splayed-out struts, outer sections by inclined struts, the lower apices of which coincide with the attachment of the stabilising floats to the lower wings. Wing structure of metal with fabric covering. Ailerons on outer sections.

HULL.—Two-step type with rear step terminating in a vertical knife-edge. Semi-circular top with shallow Vee bottom. Structure consists of four main watertight bulkheads with intermediate belt-frames and keel. The aluminium-alloy sheet skin is reinforced with "Z"-section extruded aluminium-alloy stringers.

TAIL UNIT.—Monoplane type. Tail-plane mounted on top of fin built integral with the hull. Twin fins and rudders strut-braced to tail-plane which, in turn, is strut-braced to hull. All-metal construction except fins which are fabric-covered.

POWER PLANT.—Two Wright "Cyclone" R-1820-90 nine-cylinder radial air-cooled engines each developing 700 h.p. at 1,950 r.p.m. at 4,000 ft. (1,220 m.). Engines mounted at extremities of leading-edge of centre-section. N.A.C.A. cowlings. Curtiss three-bladed electrically-controllable-pitch airscrews. Fuel tanks 1,620 U.S. gallons (6,120 litres) total capacity in hull. Oil tanks (90 U.S. gallons (341 litres) total capacity, in engine nacelles.

ACCOMMODATION.—Gunner-observer's cockpit in nose, with bomb-sights, mooring equipment, etc. Enclosed pilot's compartment seating two side-by-side with dual controls in front of engines. Details of interior accommodation unknown. Two open cockpits aft of wings with gun mountings. Equipment includes radio receiving and transmitting apparatus, full electrical equipment, flares, life-raft, leading-edge landing lights, navigation lights, etc.

DIMENSIONS.—Span 100 ft. (30.5 m.), Length 61 ft. 9 in. (18.8 m.), Height 17 ft. 3 in. (5.3 m.), Wing area 1,514 sq. ft. (143 sq. m.).

WEIGHTS AND LOADINGS.—Weight empty 11,700 lbs. (5,300 kg.), Weight loaded 20,000 lbs. (9,080 kg.), Maximum permissible loaded weight 24,000 lbs. (10,880 kg.), Wing loading 13.65 lbs./sq. ft. (66.6 kg./sq. m.), Power loading 14.75 lbs./h.p. (6.7 kg./h.p.).

PERFORMANCE.—Maximum speed 140 m.p.h. (225 km.h.), Cruising speed 117.5 m.p.h. (189 km.h.), Alighting speed 61 m.p.h. (98 km.h.), Initial rate of climb 790 ft./min. (213 m./min.), Service ceiling 16,500 ft. (5,040 m.), Cruising range 2,650 miles (4,270 km.).

The Consolidated PB-2A Two-seat Fighter Monoplane (Curtiss "Conqueror" engine).

THE CONSOLIDATED PB-2A

The PB-2A is a high-performance two-seat fighter monoplane with the Curtiss "Conqueror" liquid-cooled engine and retractable undercarriage.

Fifty production P-30As were ordered in December 1934, being redesignated PB-2A two-seat fighters soon after.

Engine:	700 hp Curtiss V-1570-61
Span:	43 ft 11 in (13.39 m)
Length:	30 ft (9.14 m)
Weight loaded:	5,643 lb (2,560 kg)
High Speed:	274 mph (441 km/h)
Range:	508 miles (817 km)
Arrangement:	Three 0.30-in guns, one in rear cockpit.

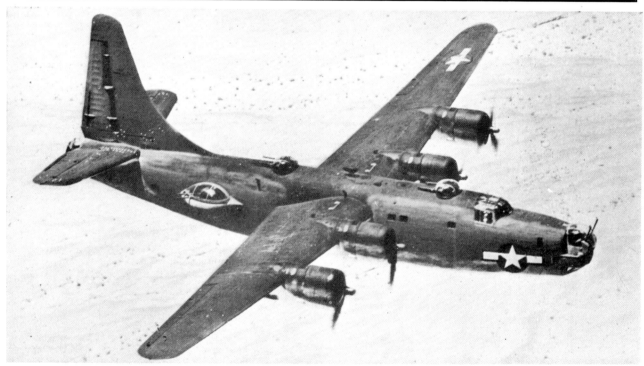

The Consolidated Vultee PB4Y-2 Privateer (four Pratt & Whitney R-1830-94 engines).

THE CONSOLIDATED VULTEE PRIVATEER.
U.S. Navy designation : PB4Y-2.

The PB4Y-2 is a long-range oversea Bomber-Reconnaissance development of the PB4Y-1 Liberator. The original contract for the PB4Y-2 was placed with the Consolidated Vultee Corpn. by the U.S. Navy in May, 1943, and work on three prototypes was begun almost immediately. Four months later, on September 20, the first prototype flew, followed on October 30 and December 15 by the second and third respectively.

The PB4Y-2 uses the same Davis wing and landing-gear as the Liberator. Otherwise it is a new design embodying most of the structural features of its predecessor.

The fuselage forward of the wings has been lengthened by 7 ft. (2.135 m.) and the armament has been rearranged to include a Consolidated nose-turret, two Martin dorsal turrets, one forward and one aft of the wings, a Consolidated tail-turret and two Erco "blister" type waist turrets, one on each side of the fuselage midway between the wings and tail. Each turret is armed with two 50 cal. Browning machine-guns. The fuselage bomb-bay is similar to that of the Liberator and can accommodate on normal missions 6,000 lbs. (2,725 kg.) of bombs or depth charges.

(1945–46)

The Consolidated Vultee SNV-2 Valiant Two-seat Basic Trainer (Pratt & Whitney R-985 engine).

THE CONSOLIDATED VULTEE (VULTEE 74D) VALIANT.
U.S. Army Air Forces designations : BT-13 and BT-15.
U.S. Navy designation : SNV.

The original contract for the BT-13 was awarded in September 1939. Production ceased in the Summer of 1944 after 11,537 Valiants had been delivered to the U.S. Army Air Forces and the U.S. Navy.

There have been several variants of the Valiant. These include the BT-13, BT-13A (SNV-1) and BT-13B (SNV-2), all with the Pratt & Whitney R-985 Wasp Junior engine, and the BT-15 with the Wright R-975-11 engine. The differences between the various models have been mainly in matters of equipment.

TYPE.—Two-seat Basic Trainer.

WINGS.—Low-wing cantilever monoplane. Wing section NACA Symmetrical 18% at root tapering to NACA Symmetrical 9% at tips. Wide centre-section, two outer sections and detachable and interchangeable semi-circular wing-tips. All-metal structure with flush-riveted stressed-skin covering. Ailerons on three-quarters of span of outer wing sections. Slotted flaps with hydraulic operation between ailerons and fuselage. Ailerons and flaps have metal frames and fabric covering.

FUSELAGE.—Oval all-metal structure of composite construction. Forward section including cockpits of welded steel tubing covered with detachable metal panels. Rear section is a semi-monocoque with flush-riveted stressed-skin covering. (1945–46)

TAIL UNIT.—Cantilever monoplane type. All-metal structure with metal-covered fixed surfaces and fabric-covered movable surfaces. Trimming-tabs in elevators and rudder.

LANDING GEAR.—Fixed type. Cantilever units provided with air-oil shock-absorbers. Wheels carried at extremities in cranked extensions on stub-axles to permit easy removal of wheels. Hydraulic brakes and parking brake. Steerable tail-wheel.

POWER PLANT.—One 450 h.p. Pratt & Whitney Wasp-Junior R-985-AN-1 or AN-3 nine-cylinder radial air-cooled engine. NACA cowling. Hamilton-Standard two-position variable-pitch air-screw. Fuel tanks in wings. Total capacity 120 U.S. gallons.

ACCOMMODATION.—Tandem cockpits beneath continuous transparent hooding. Dual controls. Full navigation and night-flying equipment.

DIMENSIONS.—Span 42 ft. 2 in. (12.86 m.), Length 28 ft. 8½ in. (8.76 m.), Height 12 ft. 4⅜ in. (3.75 m.), Wing area 238 sq. ft. (22.2 sq. m.).

WEIGHTS AND LOADINGS.—Weight empty 3,345 lbs. (1,520 kg.), Disposable load 1,015 lbs. (460 kg.), Weight loaded 4,360 lbs. (1,980 kg.), Wing loading 18.3 lbs./sq. ft. (89.3 kg./sq. m.), Power loading 9.7 lbs./h.p. (4.4. kg./h.p.).

PERFORMANCE.—Maximum speed at sea level 164 m.p.h. (293 km.h.), Maximum speed at 1,400 ft. (425 m.) 166 m.p.h. (265.6 km.h.), Cruising speed at 5,500 ft. (1,675 m.) 140 m.p.h. (224 km.h.), Stalling speed 75 m.p.h. (120 km.h.), Climb to 10,000 ft. (3,050 m.) 13 mins., Service ceiling 16,500 ft. (5,030 m.), Maximum range 516 miles (826 km.).

The Consolidated Vultee Vengeance IV Dive Bomber (Wright R-2600-13 engine).

THE CONSOLIDATED VULTEE (VULTEE 72) VENGEANCE.
U.S. Army Air Forces designations : A-31 and A-35.

The Vultee Model 72 was designed to a British specification by Vultee Aircraft, Inc. and was put into production by both the Vultee company and Northrop Aircraft, Inc. When the United States entered the War, the Vengeance was given the U.S. Army designation A-31.

Vengeance I, II and III (A-31). Fitted with the 1,600 h.p. Wright R-2600-A5B5 (R-2600-19) engine. British armament and equipment, the armament consisting of four .303 in. machine-guns

in the wings and two .303 in. guns on a flexible mounting in the rear cockpit. The Vengeance I was built by Northrop, the others by Consolidated Vultee.

Vengeance IV (A-35). One 1,700 h.p. Wright R-2600-13 engine. Fitted with American armament and equipment and built to American contracts for the U.S.A.A.F. and for delivery to the British under Lend/Lease. Early models fitted with four 50 cal. guns in the wings, but on later versions six wing guns were installed. One 50 cal. gun in the rear cockpit. The Vengeance was only used operationally by the R.A.F. and the Royal Indian Air Force in the India-Burma theatre.

The U.S.A.A.F. A-35 was mainly used as a high-speed target-tug. Production of the Vengeance ceased at the Nashville plant of Consolidated Vultee in the Autumn of 1944, after 1,528 had been built. The last batch off the production lines was delivered to the Brazilian Government.

Type.—Two-seat Dive-Bomber.

Wings.—Mid-wing cantilever monoplane. Flat centre-section with swept-back leading-edge and straight trailing-edge. Outer sections have straight leading-edges and swept forward trailing-edges. All-metal single-spar structure with stressed skin covering. Hydraulically-operated dive-brakes on both upper and lower surfaces of outer sections hinge upwards and backwards and forward and downward respectively. Differentially-operated and statically, and aerodynamically-balanced ailerons have metal frames and smooth sheet covering. Electrically-operated trim-tabs in both ailerons. Hydraulically-operated slotted trailing-edge flaps between ailerons and fuselage.

Fuselage.—Oval all-metal structure in two sections, the forward section a semi-monocoque and the rear section a monocoque. Entire skin is flush-riveted and lap-jointed.

Tail Unit.—Cantilever monoplane type. Fin forward of the tail-plane. Fin and tailplane are all-metal structures. Elevators have metal frames and metal and fabric covering. Statically and aerodynamically-balanced control surfaces. Rudder has a metal frame and fabric covering. Controllable trim-tabs in rudder and port elevator.

Landing Gear.—Retractable type. Cantilever oleo legs retract backward and rotate through 90 degrees for wheels to lie flat in undersurface of centre section. Legs are enclosed by hinged fairings. Partially retractable non-steerable tail-wheel. Hydraulic retraction.

Power Plant.—One Wright Cyclone R-2600-13 fourteen-cylinder radial air-cooled engine on welded steel-tube mounting. Hamilton-Standard Hydromatic constant-speed airscrew. Ten self-sealing fuel cells in the wings and fuselage interconnected to form three separate tanks, with a total capacity of 275 U.S. gallons. Electrically-driven booster pumps for use in power dives.

Accommodation.—Crew of two. Tandem cockpits under continuous transparent canopy with sliding sections over each seat. Armour protection for pilot and rear gunner.

Armament.—Four or six 50 cal. machine-guns in wings, two or three in each extremity of the centre-section. One 50 cal. machine-gun on flexible mounting in rear cockpit. Internal bomb-bay in fuselage can accommodate two 500 lb. bombs. As overload two further 250 lb. bombs may be carried on external wing racks.

Dimensions.—Span 48 ft. (14.64 m.), Length 39 ft. 9 in. (12.12 m.), Height 14 ft. 6 in. (4.4 m.), Wing area 332 sq. ft. (30.8 sq. m.).

Weight Loaded.—13,500 lbs. (6,130 kg.).

Performance.—Maximum speed 279 m.p.h. (446.4 km.h.), Service ceiling 27,000 ft. (8,235 m.). (1945-46)

The Convair B-36J Long-Range Strategic Bomber (six 3,800 h.p. Pratt & Whitney R-4360 piston and four G.E. J47 turbojet engines).

THE CONVAIR B-36.

Production of the B-36 ceased in August, 1954, and, after a life of eleven years, it was declared obsolete in 1957. 382 were built. Ninety-five have already been scrapped and a further 105 were due to be reduced to produce by the Spring of 1958.

The B-36 has been built in the following versions :—

XB-36. First prototype. Originally fitted with two 110-in. (2.79 m.) single main landing gear wheels, but later equipped with the multi-wheel main gears introduced on the B-36A. First flew on August 8, 1946.

YB-36. Production prototype. Roof of crew compartment raised above fuselage top line for improved vision, re-location of crew stations and installation of nose turret. First flew on December 4, 1947.

B-36A. Six 3,000 h.p. Pratt & Whitney R-4360-25 engines. First production model. Single main wheels of prototypes replaced by four-wheel bogies to reduce structure weight and improve weight distribution on runways. Twenty-two built. Originally without armament and used for training and type familiarisation. Modified into RB-36E (which see).

B-36B. Second production model. Six 3,500 h.p. Pratt & Whitney R-4360-41 engines with water-injection. Fully-equipped for combat with full armament. First flew on August 8, 1948. Last of 130 B-36B's modified by Convair to RB-36D standard, with additional jet power and installation of latest radar and electronic equipment, delivered to U.S.A.F. in December, 1951.

B-36D. Third production model. B-36B with additional power primarily to increase speed over target area. Has four General Electric J47-GE-19 turbojet engines in podded pairs under outer wings to supplement the six 3,500 h.p. R-4360-41 engines. Prototype, a converted B-36B with four Allison J35 engines, first flew on March 26, 1949. Over-target speed of B-36D with J47 turbojets increased to over 435 m.p.h. (696 km.h.). Has new snap-action bomb-bay doors instead of sliding type used in earlier models. Maximum gross weight 358,000 lb. (162,390 kg.).

RB-36D. Long-range strategic reconnaissance version of B-36D. Same defensive armament. Fourteen cameras in forward bomb-bay. First flight on December 18, 1949.

RB-36E. B-36A modified for strategic reconnaissance. Re-engined with six 3,500 h.p. R-4360-41 engines and fitted with additional jet-power as for B-36D.

B-36F. Six 3,800 h.p. Pratt & Whitney R-4360-53 engines, plus four J47-GE-19 jet engines. Fourth production model.

RB-36F. Long-range reconnaissance version of B-36F.

B-36H. Six 3,800 h.p. Pratt & Whitney R-4360-53 engines plus four J47-GE-19 turbojets. Fifth production model, incorporating new two-station flight-engineer's panel and improved radar and electronic equipment.

NB-36H. In January, 1956 the U.S.A.F. announced that a B-36 had been flying for several months with an atomic reactor installed in the fuselage. The reactor, which does not power the aircraft, has been fitted "to investigate the problem of shielding against radiation on aircraft materials and systems, and to develop airbourne nuclear instruments." The cooling air scoops on the fuselage mid-way between the wings and tail give a clue to the location of the reactor. The nose has been extensively modified for crew shielding.

RE-36H. Long-range reconnaissance version of B-36H.

B-36J. Six 3,800 h.p. Pratt & Whitney R-4360-53 engines, plus four General Electric J47-GE-19 turbojets. Sixth production model. Same power-plant as B-36H. Strengthened landing-gear. Maximum gross weight increased to over 400,000 lb. (181,600 kg.). Last production aircraft completed on August 14, 1954.

GRB-36. "Aircraft carrier." Formerly known as FICON (Fighter Conveyor) project. An undisclosed number of RB-36's are being converted into carriers for Republic RF-84K reconnaissance fighters, which can carry cameras or atomic weapons. GRB-36's are fitted with special gear to launch and retrieve the RF-84K's in the air including bomb-bay lights to facilitate retrieving at night. This combination has an operational radius of action of up to 5,000 miles (8,000 km.).

The first unit of the U.S.A.F. to be equipped with GRB-36 aircraft in 1955 was the 99th Strategic Reconnaissance Wing, which operates the RF-84K fighters of the 91st Strategic Reconnaissance Squadron.

One GRB-36 capable of carrying three RF-84F's, one above the fuselage and one at each wing-tip, has been flown experimentally.

The following detailed information applies to the B-36J.

The Convair GRB-36 "Carrier" with a Republic RF-84K reconnaissance fighter in its stowed position.

TYPE.—Ten-engined Heavy Bomber.

WINGS. — Shoulder-wing cantilever monoplane. NACA laminar-flow wing section. Aspect ratio 11. Wing mounted slightly forward of mid point of fuselage. All-metal structure with stressed skin. Leading-edge sweepback 15° 5' 39", trailing-edge sweepback 3°. Gross wing area 4,772 sq. ft. (443.3 m.²). Statically-balanced ailerons with controllable trim-tabs. Electrically-operated trailing-edge flaps in three sections on each side of fuselage. Total flap area 519 sq. ft. (48.2 m.²). Heated surface anti-icing.

FUSELAGE.— Circular section all-metal structure.

TAIL UNIT.—Cantilever monoplane type. All-metal structure. Tailplane span 73 ft. 5 in. (22.38 m.). Total horizontal area 978 sq. ft. (90.85 m.²). Total vertical area 542 sq. ft. (50.34 m.²). Thermal anti-icing in leading-edges of tailplane and fin.

LANDING GEAR.—Retractable tricycle type. Main gear consists of two four-wheel bogies on single shock-absorber struts, each unit retracting inwards into wing. Twin nose wheel gear raised forward into fuselage. Hydraulic retraction. Wheel track 46 ft. (14 m.), wheel base 59 ft. (18.0 m.).

POWER PLANT.—Six 3,800 h.p. Pratt & Whitney R-4360 twenty-eight cylinder radial air-cooled piston engines and four General Electric J47 turbojet engines (5,200 lb.= 2,360 kg. s.t. each). Piston engines mounted as pushers aft of rear spars and drive Curtiss Electric three-blade constant-speed full-feathering and reversing propellers with hollow steel blades and thermal anti-icing. Propeller diameter 19 ft. (5.79 m.). Each engine fitted with two turbo superchargers. Inlets for induction and cooling air in and below leading-edge of wings. Turbojet engines are paired in pods under the outer wings. Wing fuel tanks with total capacity of over 30,000 U.S. gallons (113,400 litres). Oil capacity over 1,200 U.S. gallons (4,542 litres).

ACCOMMODATION.—Crew of sixteen, including 5-man relief crew. Pressurised crew compartments forward and aft of bomb-bay with pressurised intercommunication tunnel 85 ft. (25.9 m.) long and 25 in. (0.63 m.) in diameter on left side of fuselage and below wings. Four-wheel truck for passage through tunnel. Thermal anti-icing and de-frosting for pilot's and bombardier's compartments and for gun-sighting blisters in forward and rear crew compartments. Total pressurised fuselage volume 3,924 cub. ft. (111 m.³).

ARMAMENT AND EQUIPMENT.—Six retractable remotely-controlled turrets, each mounting twin 20 mm. cannon, plus two 20 mm. cannon on flexible mounting in nose and two in radar-controlled tail turret. General Electric central fire-control system. Four-section bomb-bay with total volume of 12,300 cub. ft. (348 m.³). Designed bomb load for 10,000 mile range, 10,000 lb. (4,540 kg.). Maximum bomb load 84,000 lb. (38,140 kg.).

DIMENSIONS.—
Span 230 ft. (70.14 m.).
Length 162 ft. (49.4 m.).
Height 46 ft. 9 in. (14.26 m.).

WEIGHTS AND LOADINGS.—
Max. gross weight over 400,000 lb. (181,600 kg.).
Wing loading 83.8 lb./sq. ft. (408.9 kg./m.²).

PERFORMANCE. –
Max. speed over 435 m.p.h. (696 km.h.).
Stalling speed 95 m.p.h. (152 km.h.).
Service ceiling over 45,000 ft. (13,725 m.).
Max. designed range 10,000 miles (16,000 km.).
Take-off to 50 ft. (15.25 m.) 1,666 yards (1,523 m.).   (1956–57)

THE CONVAIR DELTA DAGGER
U.S.A.F. designation: F-102

The F-102 is a supersonic single-seat all-weather delta-wing interceptor which is now operational with more than 25 U.S.A.F. air defence squadrons.

Design of the F-102 began in 1951, after Convair had won a U.S.A.F. competition for an interceptor to carry the Falcon and its associated fire control system. As far as possible, it was a direct scale-up of the earlier Convair XF-92A research aircraft, which was the first true delta-wing aeroplane to fly; but in detail the F-102 was largely re-designed, making extensive use of large pressed forgings.

The following versions have appeared:—

YF-102. Two prototypes, powered by Pratt & Whitney J57-P-11 turbojet with afterburner. First YF-102 flew on October 24, 1953; second on January 11, 1954. Initial production aircraft of this type were subsequently modified to virtual F-102A standard.

YF-102A. Developed version incorporating major design changes found essential for flight to transonic and supersonic speeds. Longer fuselage incorporating the NACA "area-rule" that gives the fuselage a pinched-in waisted effect just forward of streamlined fairings at the aft end of the fuselage. Delta wing given cambered leading-edges and swept-up wing-tips. Canopy re-designed to give the pilot greater visibility. More powerful J57 turbojet. Design generally improved for easier production and servicing. Re-design took 117 working days and first YF-102A flew on December 20, 1954. It exceeded the speed of sound in level flight on the following day.

F-102A. Production version, described below. One F-102A was converted for

Convair F-102A Delta Dagger (Pratt & Whitney J57 turbojet engine)

evaluation in tactical rôle in the Spring of 1957. Many F-102A's have been modernised, including improvements to their fire-control system. A further modernisation programme, under way in 1961, is designed to increase overall effectiveness at low altitude and against enemy countermeasures. Five major modifications include the installation of an infra-red search and tracking device.

TF-102A. Two-seat combat proficiency trainer and tactical interceptor version of F-102A. Length reduced to 63 ft. 4½ in. (19.32 m.)

F-102B. Developed and extensively re-designed all-weather interceptor version. Redesignated F-106A and described separately.

The last F-102 was completed in April, 1958, after about 1,000 of the two production

versions—F-102A and TF-102A—had been built.

CONVAIR DELTA DAGGER
USAF designation: F-102

Modification and updating of F-102 fighter aircraft has been a continuing process. Latest modifications include the installation of standby vertical gyro indicators. Radar homing and warning (RHAW) will be incorporated in a limited number of aircraft and equipment complying with the DOD's aircraft identification monitoring systems (AIMS) programme will be installed in the near future under the direction of the San Antonio Air Materiel Area, USAF.

Convair has proposed a Close Air Support Mission re-configuration for this aircraft to provide improved air-to-ground weapon accuracy, maximum use being made of off-the-shelf USAF inventory equipment to effect the modification. The aim is to achieve simplified systems requiring a minimum of maintenance. Improvements would include installation of an internal "Gatling" gun; two additional external pylon stations; increased internal fuel capacity with provision for in-flight refuelling; expanded nav/com equipment and better flight instrumentation. The modifications would allow a large variety of optional weapons to be carried externally.

TYPE.—Single-seat all-weather interceptor.

WINGS.—Cantilever mid-wing monoplane of delta shape. Leading-edge sweepback 60° 6′ 13″. Root chord 29 ft. $9\frac{1}{4}$ in. (9.07 m.). All-metal structure with five forged one-piece spars in each wing. Machined aluminium alloy (Alcoa 2024-T86) skins. Conical camber leading edge. Integral fuel tank bays fore and aft of landing gear bay. Elevons of bonded honeycomb construction, each divided into inner and outer sections operated by irreversible hydraulic jacks. Wing area 661.5 sq. ft. (61.45 m.^{2})

FUSELAGE.—All-metal semi-monocoque structure, with titanium alloy frames in vicinity of power plant.

TAIL UNIT.—Vertical fin and rudder only, of all-metal construction. Height of fin increased from 104 in. (264 cm.) to 137 in. (348 cm.) on later production aircraft by reducing leading-edge sweepback to 52° 30′. Areas: fin 83.75 sq. ft. (7.78 m.^{2}), rudder 11.25 sq. ft. (1.04 m.^{2}). Braking parachute housed inside forward-opening speed brakes aft of fin.

LANDING GEAR.—Retractable tricycle type. Hydraulic actuation. Menasco shock-absorber units. Wheel track 14 ft. $2\frac{1}{4}$ in. (4.32 m.). Wheelbase 22 ft. $4\frac{1}{2}$ in. (6.86 m.)

POWER PLANT.—One Pratt & Whitney J57-P-35 turbojet engine, rated at 10,900 lb. (4,945 kg.) dry and 17,000 lb. (7,710 kg.) with afterburner in operation. Fuel in two integral tanks in each wing and in fuselage aft of missile bay. A jettisonable external fuel tank can be carried under each wing.

ACCOMMODATION.—Pilot seated on Weber ejection seat in air-conditioned and pressurised cockpit. Normal pressurisation 7.2 lb./sq. in. (0.506 kg./cm.^{2}) requires use of MC-1 partial-pressure suit above 50,000 ft. (15,240 m.). Vee-shaped windscreen with de-misting. Rearward-hinged stretched plastic canopy.

ARMAMENT.—Six Hughes GAR-1D or -2A Falcon air-to-air guided missiles mounted on short rails which extend from three missile bays when rapid-acting doors are opened. Secondary armament of 24 × 2.75 in. folding fin rockets in firing channels built into missile bay doors. Primary armament fired automatically by Hughes MG-10 fire control system mounted in fuselage nose. This can also take over complete task of controlling aircraft and effecting interception, with aid of new "Digitair" computer, leaving pilot free to monitor mission.

DIMENSIONS.—
- Span 38 ft. $1\frac{1}{2}$ in. (11.62 m.)
- Length 68 ft 3 in. (20.81 m.)
- Height 21 ft. $2\frac{1}{2}$ in. (4.46 m.)

WEIGHT.—
- Weight loaded approx. 27,000 lb. (12,250 kg.)

PERFORMANCE (estimated).—
- Max. speed at 36,000 ft. (11,000 m.) Mach 1.25
- Service ceiling 54,000 ft. (16,460 m.)

(1961–62)

CONVAIR DELTA DART

USAF designation: F-106

The F-106 is a developed version of the F-102 which was described in earlier editions of this work. It was originally designated F-102B; but, because of structural changes and use of the more powerful Pratt & Whitney J75 turbojet with afterburner, was redesignated.

Design of the F-106 was started in 1954 and construction of the prototype began in 1955. Two versions were subsequently produced for the USAF, as follows:—

F-106A. Single-seat all-weather interceptor. Prototype first flew at Edwards Air Force Base, Calif, on December 26, 1956. Deliveries to North American Air Defense Command began in July, 1959. Total of 257 built.

F-106B. Tandem two-seat dual-purpose all-weather combat/trainer version, ordered into parallel production with F-106A in April, 1957. Prototype flew for first time on April 9, 1958. Total of 63 built.

Production of the F-106 was completed on December 29, 1960.

Both versions are supersonic all-weather interceptors and carry a highly-sophisticated electronic guidance and fire control system. Produced by Hughes Aircraft Company and designated MA-1, this system is designed to operate with the Semi-Automatic Ground Environment (SAGE) defence system.

The MA-1 can fly the F-106 from soon after take-off, through climb and cruise, to attack position. Once the aircraft's radar detects the target, it locks onto it and, at the proper time for the greatest kill probability, fires the selected armament. Immediately afterwards, the electronic system breaks the F-106 from its intercept course and searches for other targets, since the aircraft has multiple attack capability, before flying it back to its home base or to a nearer base. There the pilot resumes control of the aircraft for landing.

During the intercept mission, the pilot acts principally as a monitor of the electronic guidance and fire control system, but he can override it in case of emergency. Basis of the system is a device called Digitair, an exceedingly compact and rapid-acting airborne computer that translates data received from ground control intercept (GCI) stations into commands to the aircraft flying control systems.

If the SAGE system were inoperative or completely knocked out, the F-106 could utilise the airborne computer with only meagre voice vectoring information.

An up-rated version of the MA-1, with horizontal situation indicator and other refinements, has been fitted retrospectively in many F-106's by Convair division of General Dynamics under a USAF modernisation programme. This work involved fitting a completely new nose and cockpit section and introduced also supersonic ejection seats and vertical display instrument panels.

A subsequent modernisation programme has increased the overall effectiveness of the aircraft at low altitude and against enemy countermeasures. It introduced five major modifications, including the installation of an infra-red search and tracking device.

On December 15, 1959, an F-106A piloted by Major Joseph W. Rogers set up an official world absolute speed record of 1,525·95 mph (2,455·736 kmh) at Edwards AFB, California. This has since been beaten.

Convair F-106A Delta Dart (Pratt & Whitney J75 turbojet engine)

In 1960, Major Frank Forsythe flew a production F-106A on a completely automatic flight 2,400 miles (3,860 km) non-stop from Edwards AFB, California, to Jacksonville, Florida, and back to Tyndall AFB, Florida, without refuelling.

Under contracts awarded by the San Antonio Air Materiel Area of the USAF, F-106 fighter aircraft continue to be updated and modified.

Included in this work are programmes for improved reliability of operating systems (IROS), improved maintainability and reliability (IMRS), and improved mission probability success (IMPS).

Among these improvements are MEISR, which enhances the reliability of the radar system, and RIPS, which deals with reliability of the electrical power distribution/generation system. A feasibility demonstration of an internally mounted "Gatling" gun and a clear-top canopy was conducted successfully in 1969. The USAF is planning modification programmes to incorporate these features to enhance the weapon system's capability to operate in global rôles as well as in continental US defence in conjunction with the USAF advanced airborne warning and control systems (AWACS).

TYPE: Single-seat all-weather interceptor (F-106A) or two-seat all-weather interceptor/trainer (F-106B).

WINGS: Cantilever mid-wing monoplane of delta planform. Wing section NACA 0004-65 (modified). Aspect ratio 2·198. Chord at root 29 ft $9\frac{1}{4}$ in (9·07 m). Thickness/chord ratio 4%. No dihedral or incidence. Sweepback on leading-edge 60° 6′ 13″. All-metal fail-safe structure with five forged one-piece spars in each wing. Machined aluminium alloy (Alcoa 2024-T86) skins. Conical camber leading-edge. Integral fuel tank bays fore and aft of main landing gear bays. Elevons of bonded honeycomb construction, each divided into inner and outer sections operated by Clemco irreversible hydraulic jacks. No trim-tabs. No flaps. Hot-air de-icing ducts in leading-edges.

FUSELAGE: All-metal (Alcoa 2024-T6) semi-monocoque fail-safe structure, with titanium alloy frames in vicinity of power plant. Glycol de-icing system for nose radome.

TAIL UNIT: Vertical fin and rudder only, of all-metal construction and using same aerofoil section as wings. Rudder operated by Clemco irreversible hydraulic jacks. No trim-tabs. No de-icing system. Braking parachute housed inside paired 60° forward-opening speed-brakes at base of fin.

LANDING GEAR: Hydraulically-retractable tricycle type, with steerable twin-wheel nose unit. Main units retract inward, nose unit forward. Menasco shock-absorbers. Bendix Type 7 wheels and Goodrich tyres, size 30 × 8·8 on main wheels, 18 × 4·4 on nose-wheels. Tyre pressure: main wheels over 225 lb/sq in (15·8 kg/cm^2), nose-wheels over 100 lb/sq in (7·05 kg/cm^2). Bendix $12\frac{3}{4}$ × 6·4 rotor brakes.

POWER PLANT: One Pratt & Whitney J75-P-17 turbojet engine, rated at 24,500 lb (11,123 kg) st with afterburner in operation. Fuel in two integral tanks in each wing and one tank in fuselage aft of missile bay. A jettisonable external fuel tank can be carried under each wing.

ACCOMMODATION (F-106A): Pilot seated on Weber ejection seat in air-conditioned and pressurised cockpit. Rearward-hinged combination Vee-shaped windscreen and stretched plastic canopy. Nesa type windscreen de-icing.

SYSTEMS: Fairchild-Stratos air-cycle air-conditioning system, pressure differential 5 lb/sq in (0·35 kg/cm^2). Two 3,000 lb/sq in (210 kg/cm^2) hydraulic systems, utilising Vickers pumps. Two pneumatic systems, one operating at 3,000 lb/sq in (210 kg/cm^2), the other at 250 lb/sq in (17·5 kg/cm^2) variable. AC electrical supply for aircraft services, DC for MA-1 fire-control system. Emergency hydraulic generator and air-turbine generator.

ARMAMENT: One AIR-2A Genie nuclear-warhead air-to-air rocket, plus several AIM-4E and AIM-4F Super Falcon guided missiles, in internal weapon bay.

DIMENSIONS, EXTERNAL (F-106A):

Wing span	38 ft $3\frac{1}{2}$ in (11·67 m)
Length overall	70 ft $8\frac{3}{4}$ in (21·56 m)
Height overall	20 ft $3\frac{1}{3}$ in (6·18 m)
Wheel track	15 ft $5\frac{1}{2}$ in (4·71 m)
Wheelbase	24 ft $1\frac{1}{2}$ in (7·35 m)

AREAS:

Wings, gross	697·83 sq ft (64·83 m^2)
Vertical tail surfaces (total)	105·0 sq ft (9·76 m^2)

WEIGHTS:

Weight empty, equipped	23,646 lb (10,726 kg)
Max T-O weight	over 35,000 lb (15,875 kg)

PERFORMANCE (at max T-O weight):

Max level speed	Mach 2
Service ceiling	over 50,000 ft (15,250 m)
Range with max fuel	approx 1,500 miles (2,400 km)

(1964–65)

THE CONVAIR T-29.

Military versions of the Convair 240 carry the designation T-29, of which the following versions have been built:—

T-29A. Original Convair-Liner 240 crew trainer conversion. Non-pressurised but fitted with oxygen equipment for high-altitude training, permitting 6 hour's duration at 20,000 ft. (6,100 m.) at 250 m.p.h. (400 km.h.). Cabin has fourteen fully-equipped stations for students and one radio operator's station. Each student has access to a map table, Loran scope, altimeter indicator and radio compass panel. In roof of fuselage are four astrodomes. Five drift-meters also included. First T-29A flew on September 22, 1949. All T-29A's later modified with additional outer wing fuel tanks for increased range at operational height. 48 built.

T-29B. Development of T-29A with pressurised cabin, increased fuel capacity and greater A.U.W. of 43,575 lb. (19,780 kg.) compared with 40,500 lb. (18,390 kg.) of T-29A. Major external difference is the fitting of three astrodomes and one periscopic sextant on top of fuselage instead of the four astrodomes of the A Series. First T-29B flew on July 30, 1952. 105 built.

T-29C. Similar to T-29B but fitted with two advanced model 2,500 h.p. Pratt & Whitney R-2800 engines. Accommodation for 14 students and instructors. First T-29C flew on July 28, 1953. About 20 of these aircraft, assigned to the Air Force Academy at Colorado Springs, are being fitted with two wingtip-mounted Fairchild J44 turbojets to provide improved take-off and climb performance at the high-altitude airfields used by the Academy. 119 built.

T-29D. Similar to T-29C but equipped for advanced navigation/bombardment

The Convair T-29D Aircrew Trainer (two Pratt & Whitney R-2800 engines).

training. Accommodation for six students and two instructors. Training equipment for all phases of radar and optical bombing and navigation, including use of the "K" system bombsight. Only external difference compared with T-29B is the absence of astrodomes. First T-29D flew on August 11, 1953. 93 built.

VT-29E. This designation covers four Convair-Liner 240 personnel transports for MATS use. Two are furnished for V.I.P. use and two have standard high-density seating.

The following data refers specifically to the T-29B which is powered with two 2,500 h.p. Pratt & Whitney R-2800-99W engines.

DIMENSIONS.—
Span 91 ft. 9 in. (27.98 m.).
Length 74 ft. 8 in. (22.77 m.).

Height over tail 27 ft. 3 in. (8.31 m.).
Wing area 817 sq. ft. (75.9 m.²).
WEIGHT.—
T.O. weight 43,575 lb. (19,780 kg.).
PERFORMANCE.—
Max. speed 300 m.p.h. (480 km.h.).
Average cruising speed 230 m.p.h. (368 km.h.).
Stalling speed (with flaps) 92 m.p.h. (147 m./min.).
Initial rate of climb 1,370 ft./min. (418 m./min.).
Service ceiling 24,000 ft. (6,320 m.).
Service ceiling on one engine 7,500 ft. (2,290 m.).
T.O. distance to 50 ft. (15.25 m.) 1,030 yds. (945 m.).
Landing distance from 50 ft. (15.25 m). 780 yds. (714 m.).
Cruising range 1,500 miles (2,400 km.).
(1958–59)

The Convair C-131A Samaritan Transport (two 2,500 h.p. Pratt & Whitney R-2800-99W engines). (*Gordon Williams*).

THE CONVAIR C-131.

The C-131A Samaritan is a military transport version of the Convair-Liner 240. It was the first pressurised twin engined air-evacuation transport to be ordered by the Military Air Transport Service. 26 were built.

The cabin can be arranged to carry 37 passengers in backward-facing seats or 27 stretcher cases, or several combinations of both. For loading stretchers a large hydraulically-operated door, opening upwards, is provided on the port side of the cabin aft of the wings. A standard Convair-Liner integral stairway which folds into the aircraft is located on the starboard side forward of the wings.

The C-131A is powered by two 2,500 h.p. Pratt & Whitney R-2800-99W engines.

DIMENSIONS.—
As for Convair-Liner 240.
WEIGHTS.—
Weight empty 29,000 lb. (13,166 kg.).
Weight loaded 43,575 lb. (19,783 kg.).
PERFORMANCE.—
Max. speed 313 m.p.h. (500 km.h.).
Stalling speed 95.4 m.p.h. (153 km.h.).
Initial rate of climb 1,410 ft./min. (430 m./min.).
Service ceiling 24,500 ft. (7,470 m.).
Service ceiling on one engine 7,100 ft. (2,165 m.).
Range with max. fuel (1,530 U.S. gallons = 5,780 litres) 1,600 miles (2,560 km.).
Take-off distance to 50 ft. (15.25 m.) 1,100 yds. (1,006 m.).
Whereas the C-131A previously described is based on the Convair-Liner 240, there are several other aircraft in the C-131 series which are developments of the slightly larger Convair-Liner 340. These are :—

C-131B. This designation is applied to several aircraft which are used as flying laboratories to test electronic equipment, either by the Air Force itself for research projects or by firms engaged in the development of special electronic devices under Air Force contract. The C-131B is pressurised, has the Convair-Liner's integral passenger stairway forward of the wings, and is equipped with fittings to accommodate 48 passenger seats so that the aircraft can be quickly converted for transport duties. Large cargo door on port side of fuselage aft of wings for loading test equipment, etc. Provision for installation of radome beneath fuselage. 36 built.

The Convair YC-131C (two 3,750 s.h.p. Allison YT56 turboprop engines).

One C-131B has been fitted with two Solar T41 gas-turbine units, mounted in special plastic and metal pods on pylons, one under each wing. It is the first aircraft to carry these units, which drive generators to supply electrical power to the aircraft, externally.

First C-131B flew for the first time on December 1, 1954.

DIMENSIONS.—
Same as for Convair-Liner 340.
WEIGHTS.—
Weight empty 29,000 lb. (13,166 kg.).
Weight loaded 47,000 lb. (21,340 kg.).
PERFORMANCE.—
Max. speed 305 m.p.h. (488 km.h.).
Cruising speed 276 m.p.h. (442 km.h.).
Service ceiling over 20,000 ft. (6,100 m.).
Range with max. fuel 1,900 miles (3,040 km.). (1958–59)

YC-131C. This designation covers two Convair-Liner 340's which are powered by two 3,750 h.p. Allison YT56-A-3 turboprop engines. They have been flown intensively by No. 1700 Test Squadron, as part of the U.S.A.F.'s turbo-prop test and evaluation programme. The gross weight of the YC-131C is 53,200 lb. (24,153 kg.), and it has an average true air speed of approximately 320 m.p.h. (515 km.h.), cruising at 21,000 ft. (6,400 m.).

The first YC-131C made its maiden flight on June 29, 1954.

VC-131D. Military transport version of the Convair-Liner 340 for use in the Air Force's domestic transport service. 33 built. Last six incorporate modifications for speed improvement and sound reduction introduced in Model 440 (which see.)

TC-131E. Ten built as electronic countermeasure trainers for Strategic Air Command. Nine now being converted into air evacuation transports for M.A.T.S. Incorporates sound-proofing and speed improvements introduced in Model 440 (which see). Extruded magnesium floor stressed to 300 lb./sq. ft. 10-foot cargo door on port side aft of wing. Integral passenger stairway.

Five basically-similar C-131E aircraft with special equipment employed by the C.A.A. for testing facilities along the Federal Airways above 10,000 ft. (3,050 m.).

RC-131F. Similar to TC-131E. Six for Military Air Transport Service (MATS).

RC-131G. Similar to RC-131F. One for Military Air Transport Service.

The Convair R4Y-1 Naval Transport (two 2,500 h.p. Pratt & Whitney R-2800-52W engines).

THE CONVAIR R4Y.

U.S. Navy versions of the Convair 340 and 440 carry the designation R4Y, of which the following versions have been built :—

R4Y-1. Cargo / personnel / ambulance version of 340, with two 2,500 h.p. Pratt & Whitney R-2800-52W (Mod.) engines. Thirty-six for U.S. Navy. Reinforced plastic-covered extruded magnesium floor stressed to 300 lb./sq. ft. Tie-down rings in floor to withstand 6,000 lb. strain. 10-foot cargo door on starboard side. Integral passenger stairway. As personnel transport can carry 44 passengers in removable upholstered seats which can face either forward or backward. Seats are interchangeable with those used in

R3Y flying-boat transport. Military bucket seats may also be installed. No galley or baggage compartment. Toilet at rear of cabin. As ambulance can carry 27 stretcher patients and as freighter its payload is 12,000 lb. Flight deck similar to 340. First production R4Y-1 flew on June 29, 1955.

R4Y-1Z. This is an executive transport version of the Convair-Liner 340 in service with the U.S. Navy. Seats 24 passengers and sleeps 6, plus crew. Based at the U.S. Naval Air Station, Anacostia.

Structurally, the R4Y-1 and R4Y-1Z are generally similar to the Model 440 (which see). Altogether, 36 were built.

R4Y-2. Two 440's used by the U.S. Navy Bureau of Aeronautics as combined transport and research aircraft.

DIMENSIONS.—
Same as for Convair Metropolitan 440.
WEIGHTS.—
Weight empty 30,464 lb. (13,918 kg.).
Weight loaded 47,000 lb. (21,319 kg.).
Landing weight 46,500 lb. (21,092 kg.).
PERFORMANCE.—
Max. speed at 16,000 ft. (4,875 m.) 294 m.p.h. (473 km.h.).
Cruising speed (1,200 h.p. per engine) at 20,000 ft. (6,100 m.) 289 m.p.h. (465 km.h.).
Landing speed 85 m.p.h. (137 km.h.).
(1958–59)

CURTISS. Military Biplane. The military machine supplied to the U.S. army is in all respects similar to the standard, except in supporting surface. The passenger sits behind the pilot. The spread of this machine is 28 feet 6 inches, not including ailerons. It has a 60 h.p. 8-cyl. Curtiss engine, as have all the present Curtiss machines.

The U.S. navy has one of this size equipped with pontoons and with double controls, so that either passenger or pilot, sitting side by side, can take the control wheel and pillar. This is the machine used by Lieuts. Ellyson and Towers in their flight of 138 miles and back. The army has one Curtiss, and the navy two Curtiss machines.

U.S. Navy's Machine

CURTISS. Hydroplane. On January 26, 1911, the first successful flights were made. The first water machine had 2 floats or pontoons, one under the engine section and one where the front wheel usually comes. Wheels were also attached at one time, these were capable of being drawn up out of the way when starting from water. (For details of this flight see *Aeronautics*, March, 1911, pages 86 and 87).

Later, but one pontoon was used, running the entire distance formerly occupied by the two, measuring approximately 12 feet by 13 inches deep by 2 feet wide.

This machine has been flown with a third upper plane added as an extension.

Flights of Curtiss Hydroplanes.

Glenn H. Curtiss flew from his winter station on North Island, San Diego (Calif.) Bay, alongside a battleship, the machine and himself was hoisted on board; later, returned to the water and flew home. For this the propeller and engine were put in front and Curtiss sat behind.

Lieuts. Ellyson and Towers flew 138 miles non-stop from Annapolis to Fortress Monroe, Va., and back again later with one stop. Also a previous flight of 75 miles non-stop.

Hugh Robinson flew 314 miles down the Mississippi River carrying mail in three days. Many exhibition flights were made during the year.

(1912)

The Curtiss C-46A Commando Military Transport (two Pratt & Whitney R-2800-51 engines).

THE CURTISS COMMANDO.
U.S. Army Air Forces designation : C-46A.
U.S. Navy designation : R5C.

The Commando is the largest twin-engined transport in production. It was evolved from the Curtiss-Wright CW-20 which was originally laid out as a 36-passenger commercial transport in 1937. The prototype CW-20 was built at the St. Louis plant and it first flew there on March 26, 1940. During its C.A.A. flight tests, the U.S. Army was impressed with the possibilities of the CW-20 and authorisation was obtained for the purchase of a large number as cargo transports. In the meantime the prototype was bought, modified and given the Army designation C-55. It was later re-converted for civil use and sold to the British Government.

The Army production model of the CW-20, designated the C-46, was a re-design not only to fit it to the duties of a military freight or task force aircraft but to suit it to large-scale production. It was produced at the Buffalo, St. Louis and Louisville plants and has been in widespread use by the U.S. Army Air Transport Command, Air Service Command and Troop Carrier Command and by the U.S. Naval Air Transport Service (160 acquired by the USMC as r5Cs).

TYPE.—Twin-engined Military Troop or Cargo Transport.

WINGS.—Low-wing cantilever monoplane of all-metal construction. In three sections, comprising a rectangular centre-section and two tapering outer sections with detachable tips. Centre-section has three built up-spars with extruded flanges, the landing-gear fittings and nacelles attaching to the front spars. Centre-section ribs are of the girder type built up of rolled and extruded sections. The stressed skin of 24ST Alclad has spanwise hat-shaped stiffeners riveted to the skin, the stiffeners being riveted to the ribs through the medium of special clips. Outer sections have two spars, girder type ribs (except at the roots where the first four are web type with cut-outs for the fuel tanks and the fifth is a solid rib) and 24ST Alclad skin with internal spanwise stringers as in the centre-section. Flush-riveting over the leading-edges and back to about one-third of the chord, with modified brazier-head rivets over the remainder of the wing surfaces. Hydraulically-operated flaps on centre-section and on outer sections inboard of the ailerons. Flaps have single-spar, stamped ribs and sheet metal covering. Statically and dynamically balanced ailerons have single spar, metal-covered nose, stamped ribs and fabric covering.

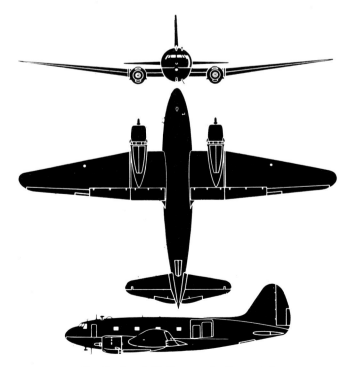

The Curtiss C-46 Commando Transport.

FUSELAGE.—All-metal semi-monocoque structure in four sections. In cross-section the fuselage, except for the extreme rear portion, is formed by two intersecting circles with the common chord of intersection as the cabin floor line. Structure comprises a series of transverse rings and bulkheads and longitudinal stringers, the whole covered with a smooth 24ST Alclad skin. Flush-riveting in the "drag-sensitive" areas.

TAIL UNIT.—Cantilever monoplane type. All-metal structure. Tailplane in two interchangeable sections, each with three beams and a stressed skin reinforced by intermediate bulb-angle stiffeners. Interchangeable elevators have two beams, stamped ribs and a smooth skin. Fin has six beams and a reinforced stressed skin. Rudder has the same structure as the elevators. All tail surfaces, fixed and movable, have detachable tips. Elevators and rudder are dynamically balanced and are fitted with trim-tabs.

LANDING GEAR.—Retractable type. Each unit comprises one Cleveland "Aerol" oleo-pneumatic shock-absorber strut, braced fore and aft by tubular drag struts which are aligned by forged upper and lower drag links. Sideways bracing by similar tubes. Hydraulic jack operates on bell-crank which is part of the outboard side bracing strut. When the lock at the top of the oleo leg is released the upper end of the leg moves backwards while the wheel moves upward and forward, being guided into the nacelle by the rear drag struts and drag links and side struts. When fully retracted the gear is locked by a latch. Hydraulically-operated fairing doors operated by a sequence valve follow the wheel up to enclose it fully when retracted. Emergency lowering of the gear by auxiliary manual extension system. Tail-wheel has a shimmy-dampened shock strut and is fully retractable.

POWER PLANT.—Two 2,000 h.p. Pratt & Whitney R-2800-51 Double Wasp eighteen-cylinder radial air-cooled engines on steel-tube mountings in semi-monocoque nacelles. Curtiss Electric four-bladed constant-speed full-feathering airscrews. Diameter 13 ft. 6 in. (4.12 m.). Entire power-plant, engine-mounting, fireproof bulkhead and all accessories forward of the bulkhead can be removed as a unit with complete interchangeability between right and left units and vice-versa. Three fuel tanks in the root of each outer wing section, 242 U.S. gallons in the front tank, 283 U.S. gallons in the mid tank and 175 U.S. gallons in the rear tank. Total fuel capacity in the wings: 1,400 U.S. gallons. An additional 800 U.S. gallons may be carried in eight fuselage tanks for long-range operations. Separate oil system for each engine, with a 40 U.S. gallon tank aft of the fire-proof bulkhead at the outboard side of each nacelle.

ACCOMMODATION.—Pilot's cabin accommodates pilot, co-pilot, navigator and radio operator. A door connects the pilot's cabin with the main cargo compartment. This compartment is 48 ft. (14.6 m.) long, 9 ft. 10 in. (3 m.) wide and 6 ft. 8 in. (2 m.) high, and has a capacity of 2,300 cu. ft. (69 cu. m.). Main loading door on port side, 8 ft. (2.4 m.) wide and 6 ft. (1.8 m.) high and divided vertically so that each section opens upward and outward, and opposite a loading floor which is level when the aircraft is in a normal three-point ground position. Three extra openings, 20 × 26 in. (46 × 66 cm.), one on each side of main compartment just above the wing and one on starboard side opposite the main door. Tie-down rings in floor and on walls. Tracks set in floor for engine-loading, with loading winch at forward end of compartment. Main compartment can accommodate, in addition to general cargo, 40 fully-armed troops on seats which fold down from the walls, a maximum of 33 stretcher cases, five Wright R-3350 engines or their weight equivalent. Fittings are provided beneath the fuselage for the carriage of complete airscrews. There is also additional cargo space beneath the main cabin floor in two compartments fore and aft of the wing centre-section, the forward compartment with a capacity of 197.2 cu. ft. (5.9 cu. m.) and the rear compartment with a capacity of 258.4 cu. ft. (7.7 cu. m.). Both these compartments are accessible from the ground through doors on the starboard side, while the forward compartment has additional access through a trap-door in the main floor just behind the pilot's seat. Adequate electric and natural lighting. Heating and ventilation systems.

DIMENSIONS.—Span 108 ft. 1 in. (32.9 m.), Length 76 ft. 4 in. (23.3 m.), Height (tail down) 21 ft. 9 in. (6.6 m.), Wing area 1,360 sq. ft. (126.3 sq. m.).

WEIGHTS AND LOADINGS.—Standard weight empty (with fixed equipment) 29,483 lbs. (13,385 kg.), Normal loaded weight 45,000 lbs. (20,430 kg.), Maximum overloaded weight 50,000 lbs. (22,700 kg.), Wing loading 33.09 lbs./sq. ft. (161.5 kg./sq. m.), Power loading 14.06 lbs./h.p. (6.38 kg./h.p.).

PERFORMANCE (at 45,000 lbs. (20,430 kg.) loaded weight).—Maximum speed 265 m.p.h. (424 km.h.) at 13,000 ft. (3,965 m.), Cruising speed (67% power) 227 m.p.h. (363.2 km.h.) at 10,000 ft. (3,050 m.), Climb to 10,000 ft. (3,050 m.) 13.5 mins., Service ceiling 24,500 ft. (7,470 m.), Service ceiling (one engine) 12,000 ft. (3,660 m.).
(1945–46)

THE CURTISS C-46D and F COMMANDO

Follow on military versions, with R-2800-51 and R-2800-75 engines respectively. Production totalled 1,410 C-46Ds and 234 C-46Fs.

A Curtiss C-46E Commando with the stepped windscreen and revised side windows to be introduced in the

THE CURTISS CW-20E COMMANDO AIRLINER.

Profiting from the experience gained with the large-scale production of the C-46 Commando military transport, the Curtiss company in 1944 prepared designs and mock-up of a commercial version of the Commando for immediate post-war production. At least two American air-line companies placed orders for the CW-20E before the end of 1944.

The CW-20E will accommodate 36 passengers. Among the major changes in the new model are the re-designed nose with a stepped windscreen and deeper side-windows to the pilot's compartment already incorporated in the later models in the C-46A Series, all-metal control surfaces, the introduction of welded easily-removable fuel tanks, and the fitting of two 2,100 h.p. Wright R-3350 (C18B2) eighteen-cylinder engines in place of the Pratt & Whitney R-2800 eighteen-cylinder radials fitted to the C-46.

Seventeen military C-46Es entered service, with R-2800-34 engines. C-46G and H derivatives were cancelled with the end of the war.

The following is a provisional specification of the new commercial version of the Commando :—

DIMENSIONS.—Same as for C-46.

WEIGHTS.—Weight empty 32,100 lbs. (14,573 kg.), Maximum Payload 12,430 lbs. (5,643 kg.), Design disposable load 15,900 lbs. (7,219 kg.), Normal take-off loaded weight 48,000 lbs. (21,792 kg.), Maximum gross landing weight 46,400 lbs. (21,066 kg.).

PERFORMANCE.—Maximum cruising speed 242 m.p.h. (387 km.h.) at 10,000 ft. (3,050 m.). (1945–46)

The Curtiss "Condor" (B-2) Night-bomber (two 600 h.p. Curtiss "Conqueror" (V-1550) geared engines).

THE CURTISS B-2 "CONDOR."

The Curtiss "Condor" is used by the U.S. Air Corps as a standard twin-engined night-bomber.

TYPE.—Twin-engined, all-metal, military night-bomber

WINGS.—Equal span, unstaggered biplane. Wings in three sections, consisting of centre-section and two outer sections. Top centre-section is carried above the fuselage by two pyramids of steel tubes, bottom wing-roots attached direct to bottom of fuselage, the top and bottom units being united by one set of vertical interplane struts on either side of fuselage. Outer wing-sections are of two-bay type, with vertical steel-tube interplane struts. Top planes flat, bottom planes have slight dihedral. Balanced "Frise" ailerons fitted to all four planes. Wing structure of metal, fabric-covered. Spars and drag-truss members are of welded steel-tubing and ribs are of duralumin.

FUSELAGE.—Constructed of duralumin tubing, except bomb-bay, which is of steel-tubing, using a Warren-truss with steel fittings.

TAIL UNIT.—Biplane tail, with twin fins and rudders. Duralumin tube framed, covered with fabric. Tail-plane adjustable in flight, and rudders fitted with automatic compensating device, to allow for adjustment when flying on one engine.

UNDERCARRIAGE.—In two separate units. Each consists of a vertical Vee mounted under the wing engine, the front leg of which incorporates an oleo and spring shock-absorbing unit with 14 in. travel. The axle runs to the front spar attachment at the fuselage. Wheels are of duralumin disc construction with internal brakes, mechanically operated, which may be used together or independently.

POWER PLANT.—Two 600 h.p. Curtiss geared V-1550 "Conqueror" water-cooled engines. Engines carried on detachable mountings on bottom planes. Engines completely cowled, and engine nacelles, extending aft of planes, accommodate one gunner each Long narrow radiators mounted above nacelles on interplane struts. One 192 U.S. gallon (160 Imp. galls. = 727 litres) petrol tank in each engine nacelle and one 60 U.S. gallons (50 Imp. galls. = 227 litres) on top plane. Either engine can take fuel from any one of the three tanks and in case of failure of fuel pump of either engine, the other will supply fuel to both engines. Two two-blade Curtiss adjustable-pitch duralumin airscrews.

ACCOMMODATION.—Gunner and bomber's cockpit, provided with Scarff ring and twin Lewis guns, in nose of fuselage. Unsplinterable glass windows in nose and floor of compartment for bomb-sighting. Pilot's cockpit in advance of planes, with accommodation for two side-by-side. Single central wheel-type control, the top end of which may be swung in front of either seat. Two sets of rudder pedals. Seats and rudder pedals adjustable. Sliding floors provide access from pilot's cockpit to bomber's compartment. Under wings, standard Army type G-5 bomb-rack is carried within fuselage. Rear gunner's positions are located in tails of engine nacelles, each being provided with Scarff ring and twin Lewis guns. Crew of five carried, comprising one pilot, one bomber and three gunners.

DIMENSIONS.—Span 90 ft. (27.45 m.), Length 47 ft. 4½ in. (14.4 m.), Height 16 ft. 6 in. (5.93 m.), Wing area 1,496 sq. ft. (138.9 sq. m.).

WEIGHTS AND LOADINGS.—Weight empty 9,300 lbs. (4,222.2 kg.), Disposable load 7,291 lbs. (3,310.1 kg.), Weight loaded 16,591 lbs. (7,532.3 kg.), Wing loading 11.08 lbs./sq. ft. (54 kg./sq. m.), Power loading 13.1 lbs./h.p. (5.94 kg./h.p.).

PERFORMANCE.—Maximum speed 132 m.p.h. (211.2 km.h.), Cruising speed 105.5 m.p.h. (168.8 km.h.), Stalling speed 55.9 m.p.h. (89.4 km.h.), Initial rate of climb 850 ft./min. (260 m./min.), Service ceiling 17,100 ft. (5,215.5 m.), Range at cruising speed 805 miles (1,288 km.). (1931)

The Curtiss Central Float Seaplane (Curtiss K. 12 400 h.p. engine).

CURTISS F

Developed from earlier Curtiss pusher seaplanes of the Navy's A types, the F was a true flying-boat of historical importance. The Army bought three but the Navy received 154, starting with five that were originally military designated C types but became ABs in 1914. On 25 April 1914 Navy AB-3 conducted the very first US operational sortie by aeroplane, searching for sea mines during the Vera Cruz incident in Mexico, having been catapult-launched from USS *Mississippi*. AB-3 was hit by rifle fire on 6 May, the first US aeroplane to sustain such damage. Fs remained operational until 1918 or thereabouts.

Span:	45 ft 1½ in
Wing area:	387.0 sq ft
Length:	27 ft 9¾ in
Weight loaded:	2,460 lb
High speed:	69 mph
Endurance:	over 5 hours
Engine:	One 100 hp Curtiss OXX

Curtiss "Falcon" (O.1) (400 h.p. Curtiss D.12 engine).

THE CURTISS "FALCON" (O.1).

The Curtiss "Falcon" was originally designed in 1924 and was arranged to be fitted with either the Liberty or Packard engine, in accordance with the regulations of the Army Air Service competition.

Structurally, the machine differs from usual Curtiss practice. The wings are of wood construction, with duralumin fittings and fabric covering. In addition to a pronounced stagger, the top plane has a sweepback of 9 degrees, allowing for excellent vision and at the same time provides stability necessary for accurate gunnery.

The fuselage is of duralumin tubing, using a Warren truss with riveted joints. This type of construction has given entire satisfaction and works out much lighter than steel or wood.

The undercarriage is of the usual Curtiss split type, using rubber compression disc suspension housed inside the fuselage.

The tail unit and ailerons are of duralumin construction, fabric-covered. Ailerons and elevators are differentially controlled, providing excellent control at all speeds, with minimum control stick loads. The rudder is balanced and the tail plane is adjustable in flight.

Fuel is carried in a droppable tank within the fuselage and an auxiliary tank, also droppable, can be installed under the fuselage for long-distance flying.

The 1925 "Falcon" is fitted solely with the Curtiss D.12 engine and the following performance concerns the D.12 "Falcon" :—

Weight empty (with water)	..		**2,388 lbs.**
Useful load	..	..	**1,748 lbs.**
Crew (2)	..	..	**360 lbs.**
Fuel and oil	..	..	**756 lbs.**
Equipment	..	..	**632 lbs.**
Weight loaded	..	..	**4,136 lbs.**

Performance.

High speed	..	..	153 m.p.h.
Speed at 15,000 ft...	..		136 m.p.h.
Landing speed	..	..	63 m.p.h.
Rate of climb	..	..	1,235 ft. per min.

Service ceiling	..	..	18,700 ft.
Absolute ceiling	..	..	20,300 ft.

Climb.

In 10 mins.	..	..	9,400 ft.

The following data concerns the Curtiss "Falcon" fitted with the 500 h.p. Packard engine, and has been taken from the Lampert Report :—

Official Performance Tests on Curtiss X.O.1.

Engine	.. .. ..	**Packard 1-A-1500.**
Rated power	.. ..	**510 h.p. at 2,080 r.p.m.**
Weights :—		
Empty, with water	..	2,277 lbs.
Armament (one 30 cal. fixed gun, two flexible Lewis guns, bombing racks, etc.)		218 lbs.
Equipment (K.3 map camera, complete W/T., etc.)	.. ..	377 lbs.
Crew	.. .. ..	360 lbs.
Fuel and oil	.. ..	625 lbs.
Weight loaded	..	3,875 lbs.
Wing area (including ailerons)		350 sq. ft.
Wing loading	.. ..	11.01 lbs./sq. ft.
Power loading	.. ..	7.56 lbs./h.p.

Performance Converted to Standard Atmosphere.

Density.	Temp.	Stand. Altitude.	Climbing Speed.		Climb.		Level Speed.	
			m.p.h.	r.p.m.	Min.	Rate.	m.p.h.	r.p.m.
1.036	5C	0	93.6	1,900	0	1,725	154.1	2,080
.887	−3	5,000	96.3	1,800	3.2	1,380	151.4	2,060
.842	−4	6,000	97.1	1,800	4.3	1,275	150.4	2,055
.744	−6	10,000	98.8	1,795	7.4	1,032	147.4	2,035
.634	−15	15,000	100.9	1,785	13.2	685	141.4	1,990
.536	−24	20,000	101.8	1,770	23.4	337	131.6	1,910
.475	−29	23,000	102.0	1,750	38.8	100	118.5	1,810
—	—	24,800	absolute ceiling.		—	—	102.1	1,735

Landing Speed .. Approximately 62–63 m.p.h.
Endurance .. Full throttle : ½-hour at sea level and 3 hours at 15,000 ft.
(1926)

A Curtiss "Falcon" (XO-18) with the 600 h.p. Curtiss "Chieftain" air-cooled engine.

A Curtiss "Falcon" (O-1B) Biplane with a 600 h.p. Curtiss V-1550 "Conqueror" engine and Ethylene-Glycol cooling.

THE CURTISS O-1B "FALCON."

The Curtiss O-1, or "Falcon," was designed in 1924 as a' two-seat observation biplane, to be fitted with either a Liberty or Packard engine, in accordance with the regulations of the then existing Army Air Service competition.

This requirement called for the design of a quickly-detachable engine-mounting, and since then this feature has been made full use of in equipping the "Falcon" with various types of engines, to fulfil a number of different Army, Navy, Marine Corps and National Guard requirements.

The O-1B has been adopted as a standard two-seat observation biplane of the U.S. Air Corps.

TYPE.—Two-seat military observation biplane.

WINGS.—Staggered single-bay biplane. The top wings are swept back outside the centre-section, while the bottom wings are straight. Centre-section is mounted above fuselage on widely-splayed streamlined steel-tube struts. One pair of splayed-out "N" struts on either side of fuselage. Differential ailerons fitted to all four planes. Wings of wooden construction, with duralumin fittings and fabric covering.

FUSELAGE.—Duralumin tube, Warren-truss structure, with riveted joints.

TAIL UNIT.—Normal type. Duralumin-tube-framed, covered with fabric. Elevators are differentially controlled, giving excellent control at all speeds. Rudder is balanced and the tail-plane adjustable in flight.

UNDERCARRIAGE.—Split type. Consists of two Vees, hinged on the bottom fuselage longerons and two bent axles crossing at the centre, which are provided with rubber compression disc suspension, housed within the fuselage.

POWER PLANT.—One 435 h.p. Curtiss D-12 water-cooled engine. Radiator mounted under engine, in tunnel, and fitted with shutters. Main fuel tank slung under the fuselage and is droppable in case of emergency. Curtiss-Reed duralumin airscrew.

ACCOMMODATION.—Crew of two, in tandem cockpits, aft of the top wing. Pilot in front provided with two fixed Browning guns, firing through the airscrew, and Scarff ring with mounting for twin Lewis guns over the rear cockpit.

DIMENSIONS.—Span 38 ft. (11.58 m.), Length 27 ft. 10 in. (8.28 m.), Height 10 ft. 3 in. (3.12 m.), Wing area 353 sq. ft. (32.7 sq. m.).

WEIGHTS AND LOADINGS.—Weight empty (with water) 2,388 lbs. (1,085 kg.), Weight of fuel 756 lbs. (343 kg.), Weight of crew 360 lbs. (164 kg.), Weight of equipment 632 lbs. (287 kg.), Total disposable load 1,748 lbs. (795 kg.), Weight loaded 4,136 lbs. (1,880 kg.), Wing loading 11.7 lbs./sq. ft. (57.5 kg./sq. m.), Power loading 9.5 lbs./h.p. (4.3 kg./h.p.).

PERFORMANCE.—Maximum speed 153 m.p.h. (246 km.h.), Speed at 15,000 ft. (4,570 m.) 136 m.p.h. (219 km.h.), Landing speed 59 m.p.h. (95 km.h.), Initial rate of climb 1,235 ft./min. (376 m./min.), Climb in 10 mins. 9,400 ft. (2,864 m.), Service ceiling 18,700 ft. (5,697 m.), Absolute ceiling 20,300 ft. (6,515 m.).

During 1927, the O-1B was experimentally produced as a seaplane. The conversion consists of the substitution of a single central float and two small wing-tip floats for the standard wheel undercarriage.

The main float is built of wood, using a shell of two-ply mahogany planking over a wooden skeleton. This float is of the concave vee-bottom type, with a single step.

For the use of the U.S. Navy and Marine Corps, the "Falcon" has also been produced fitted with the 425 h.p. Pratt & Whitney "Wasp" air-cooled engine, and experimental versions of this type have also been delivered to the Air Corps.

THE CURTISS O-11 "FALCON."

The Curtiss O-11 differs from the standard O-1B in that it is fitted with the 400 h.p. Liberty engine instead of the Curtiss D-12. This type has been produced for the use of the National Guard air units.

THE CURTISS O-1C "FALCON."

The Curtiss O-1C is a special version of the "Falcon," four of which are in use in the Air Corps for the personal use of high officials.

A Curtiss "Falcon" (O-1C) (435 h.p. Curtiss D-12 engine) fitted for the personal use of Army Air Corps officials.

The Curtiss O-39 "Falcon" Two-seat Observation Biplane (Curtiss "Conqueror" engine).

The back cockpit of each machine has been upholstered, in leather, fitted with a folding table and a special instrument board and a roomy baggage compartment for suitcases and personal effects is provided. Each machine is also fitted with dual control.

THE CURTISS A-3 "FALCON."

The A-3 has been designed for Ground Attack purposes, and differs from the O-1B only with regard to the comprehensive armament fitted.

This armament consists of two Browning 30 calibre guns in the cowling firing through the airscrew, two similar guns, one mounted in each bottom plane, firing outside the airscrew disc, and twin Lewis guns on a Scarff ring mounted over the observer's cockpit. The two wing guns are arranged so that only the muzzle protrudes through the leading edge and several hundred rounds of ammunition are carried within the wings. These guns are operated by electric triggers and are so arranged that they can be fired independently or simultaneously.

In addition to the above, two bomb racks are fitted into the under surface of the bottom wings and these can carry twenty five-pound fragmentation bombs, which can be released individually or in salvo by the pilot.

Another version of the A-3 is being produced for the Air Corps and Marine Corps, fitted with the Pratt & Whitney "Wasp" engine, and is exactly similar except for the change in engines.

In preliminary tests, the A-3 has made a top speed of 147 m.p.h.

THE CURTISS XO-18 "FALCON."

The XO-18 is a standard "Falcon" fitted with the 600 h.p. Curtiss "Chieftain" twelve-cylinder air-cooled engine.

DIMENSIONS.—Same as O-1B, except length, 27 ft. 11 in. (8.51 m.).

WEIGHTS.—Weight empty 2,771 lbs. (1,255 kg.), Weight loaded 4,284 lbs. (1,940 kg.).

PERFORMANCE.—Maximum speed 158 m.p.h. (254 km.h.), Cruising speed 126 m.p.h. (203 km.h.), Stalling speed 60 m.p.h. (96.5 km.h.), Initial rate of climb 1,600 ft./min. (488 m./min.), Service ceiling 21,600 ft. (6,590 m.). (1929)

THE CURTISS O-1E "FALCON."

The Curtiss O-1E "Falcon" resembles the "Conqueror Falcon" in all respects, except for its power plant, which consists of a 435 h.p. Curtiss D-12 water-cooled, twelve-cylinder engine, which gives the craft different performance characteristics.

DIMENSIONS.—Span 38 ft. (11.58 m.), Length 27 ft. 7 in. (8.4 m.), Height 10 ft. 3 in. (3.12 m.), Wing area 351 sq. ft. (32.97 sq. m.).

WEIGHTS AND LOADINGS.—Weight empty 2,897 lbs. (1,315.2 kg.), Disposable load 1,435 lbs. (651.5 kg.), Weight loaded 4,332 lbs. (1,966.7 kg.), Wing loading 12.35 lbs./sq. ft. (60.26 kg./sq. m.), Power loading 9.97 lbs./h.p. (4.51 kg./h.p.).

PERFORMANCE.—Maximum speed 140.8 m.p.h. (225.3 km.h.), Speed at 5,000 ft. (1,525 m.) 135.1 m.p.h. (216.2 km.h.), Speed at 10,000 ft. (3,050 m.) 128.3 m.p.h. (205.3 km.h.), Speed at 15,000 ft. (4,575 m.) 118.2 m.p.h. (189.1 km.h.), Cruising speed 114 m.p.h. (182.4 km.h.), Stalling speed 60.9 m.p.h. (97.4 km.h.), Climb to 5,000 ft. 6.05 mins., Climb to 10,000 ft. 14.1 mins., Climb to 15,000 ft. 36 mins., Service ceiling 15,300 ft. (4,666 m.), Absolute ceiling 17,000 ft. (5,185 m.). (1930)

THE CURTISS A-3B "FALCON."

The A-3B has been designed for Ground Attack purposes, and differs from the O-1E only with regard to the comprehensive armament fitted.

This armament consists of two Browning 30 calibre guns in the cowling firing through the airscrew, two similar guns, one mounted in each bottom plane, firing outside the airscrew disc, and twin Lewis guns on a Scarff ring mounted over the observer's cockpit. The two wing guns are arranged so that only the muzzle protrudes through the leading edge and several hundred rounds of ammunition are carried within the wings. These guns are operated by electric triggers and are so arranged that they can be fired independently or simultaneously.

In addition to the above, two bomb racks are fitted into the under surface of the bottom wings and these can carry twenty five-pound fragmentation bombs, which can be released individually or in salvo by the pilot. (1930)

THE CURTISS XO-1G "FALCON."

The Curtiss XO-1G is a development of the "Falcon" and is very similar in outward appearance to that type, as can be seen from the photograph. This observation type is fitted with the 425 h.p. Curtiss D.12 engine, and in preliminary tests showed a speed of 147 m.p.h. (223.2 km.h.).

THE CURTISS O-39 "FALCON."

The O-39 is the latest development of the Curtiss "Falcon" series, for years a standard observation and attack type of the U.S. Army Air Corps.

TYPE.—Two-seat military observation biplane.

WINGS.—Single-bay, staggered, unequal-span biplane. The upper wing is swept back outboard of the centre-section, which is mounted above the fuselage on widely-splayed-out streamline steel-tube struts. The lower wing is straight. There is one set of streamline steel-tube "N" struts on each side of the fuselage. There are four ailerons of duralumin construction, fabric-covered, with "Frise" type balance. Wings are of wood construction and are covered with fabric.

FUSELAGE.—Steel and duralumin tube Warren-truss structure, with riveted joints and covered with fabric.

TAIL UNIT.—Normal monoplane type. Duralumin framework, covered with fabric. Horizontal tail-plane is externally braced by two streamline steel struts. Rudder and elevators are balanced. Tail-plane is adjustable.

UNDERCARRIAGE.—Split type. Consists of two Vees hinged to the lower longerons and two bent axle struts hinged to the apex of a Vee below the fuselage. Oleo and spring shock-absorbers. Wheels are enclosed in fairings. Bendix brakes. The tail-wheel is steerable.

POWER PLANT.—One Curtiss "Conqueror" model V-1570-C Prestone-cooled engine, on a detachable welded steel-tube mount. There is a 106 U.S. gallon main fuel tank in the fuselage and a 36 U.S. gallon droppable auxiliary tank beneath the fuselage, giving a cruising range of 730 miles. The oil tank is forward of the fireproof bulkhead and has a capacity of 14 U.S. gallons. Hamilton-Standard metal airscrew. "Eclipse" electric inertia-starter.

ACCOMMODATION.—Tandem cockpits for pilot and observer. Armament consists of one fixed synchronised gun forward, with 300 rounds of ammunition. Rear gun over rear cockpit on new Curtiss type flexible mount, with 600 rounds of ammunition. One bomb rack beneath fuselage capable of carrying 244 lbs. of bombs. Either radio or camera equipment is carried. Two parachute flares and two signal pistols are carried. Controls comprise standard column and rudder-pedals in duplicate. Ailerons operated by positive push-pull rods; rudder and elevators operated by cables. Navigation lights and provision for landing lights. Cockpit lights and indirect lighting on pilot's instrument board.

DIMENSIONS.—Span 38 ft. (11.58 m.), Length overall 27 ft. 7 in. (8.38 m.), Height 10 ft. 3 in. (3.09 m.), Wing area 348 sq. ft. (32.3 sq. m.).

WEIGHTS AND LOADINGS.—Weight empty 3,366 lbs. (1,528 kg.), Special military equipment 130 lbs. (59 kg.), Crew 400 lbs. (182 kg.), Fuel and oil (for 530 miles) 676 lbs. (307 kg.), Armament (military useful load) 128 lbs. (58 kg.), Total disposable load 1,334 lbs. (606 kg.), Weight loaded 4,700 lbs. (2,134 kg.), Wing loading 13.5 lbs./sq. ft. (65.8 kg./sq. m.), Power loading 7.8 lbs./h.p. (3.5 kg./h.p.).

PERFORMANCE.—Maximum speed at sea level 172 m.p.h. (275.2 km.h.), Maximum speed at 5,000 ft. (1,525 m.) 168 m.p.h. (268.8 km.h.), Maximum speed at 10,000 ft. (3,050 m.) 164 m.p.h. (262.4 km.h.), Maximum speed at 15,000 ft. (4,575 m.) 156 m.p.h. (249.6 km.h.), Initial rate of climb 1,200 ft./min. (366 m./min.), Climb to 5,000 ft. (1,525 m.) 4.7 mins., Climb to 10,000 ft. (3,050 m.) 11 mins., Climb to 15,000 ft. (4,575 m.) 20.4 mins., Service Ceiling 20,900 ft. (6,374 m.), Absolute ceiling 22,800 ft. (6,954 m.), Range at cruising speed 530 miles (848 km.) with normal fuel load, 730 miles (1,168 km.) with full tanks. (1931)

The Curtiss SNC-1 "Falcon" Two-seat Advanced Training Monoplane 420 h.p. Wright "Whirlwind" engine).

THE CURTISS "FALCON."

U.S. Navy designation: SNC-1.

TYPE.—Two-seat Naval Advanced Combat Training monoplane.

WINGS.—Cantilever low-wing monoplane of all-metal multi-cellular construction, built up with five longitudinal webs, and an "Alclad" skin stiffened by extruded angles. Ailerons have metal frames and fabric covering and are dynamically and statically-balanced. The wing is equipped with hydraulically-operated split flaps extending over 55% of the wing.

FUSELAGE.—All-metal monocoque structure with pressed rings and longitudinal stiffeners formed of extruded angles, the whole covered with flush-riveted smooth "Alclad" skin.

TAIL UNIT.—Monoplane type. Tail-plane and fin are both of canti-lever, all-metal, multi-cellular construction similar to wing. Both elevators and rudder have metal frames and "Alclad" covering and are statically and dynamically-balanced. Trimming-tabs on the elevators are operated by an irreversible mechanism, and are dynamically-balanced.

LANDING GEAR.—Retractable type. Single-strut cantilever legs with Cleveland "Aerol" shock-absorbers. Wheels retract back-wards and are completely enclosed by split fairings beneath wings. Non-retractable tail-wheel.

POWER PLANT.—One 420 h.p. Wright "Whirlwind" R-975-E3 nine-cylinder air-cooled radial engine with pressure-cooling baffles and a special engine cowling which exhausts air only at the bottom. Engine is mounted with rubber bushings to a chrome-molybdenum steel structure which is quickly demountable from the main fuselage. Two fuel tanks in the wings provide a total capacity of 68 U.S. gallons. Hamilton-Standard two-position controllable-pitch airscrew.

ACCOMMODATION.—Tandem enclosed cockpits. Provision for all types of naval training, including gunnery, bombing and instrument flying. It can be fitted with machine-guns and light bombs and has provision for radio transmitting and receiving equipment and oxygen apparatus for high altitude training. The front cockpit is reserved for the pilot and contains complete flight instruments, power plant and armament controls. The rear cockpit is equipped for use by an instructor, gunner or observer, and all flight and power plant controls of the front cockpit are duplicated.

DIMENSIONS.—Span 35 ft. (10.7 m.), Length 26 ft. 6 in. (8.1 m.), Height 7 ft. 6 in. (2.3 m.), Wing area 174.3 sq. ft. (16.2 sq. m.).

WEIGHTS AND LOADINGS.—Weight empty 2,610 lbs. (1,185 kg.), Disposable load 1,016 lbs. (461 kg.), Weight loaded 3,626 lbs. (1,646 kg.), Wing loading 20.8 lbs./sq. ft. (101.5 kg./sq. m.), Power loading 6.6 lbs./h.p. (3 kg./h.p.).

PERFORMANCE.—Maximum speed 201 m.p.h. (322 km.h.) at sea level, Cruising speed 195 m.p.h. (312 km.h.) at 2,500 ft. (762 m.), Landing speed 65 m.p.h. (104 km.h.), Service ceiling 21,900 ft. (6,680 m.) Cruising range 515 miles (824 km.).

THE CURTISS N2C-1 "FLEDGLING."

The Curtiss "Fledgling" was designed by the Curtiss Company to participate in a competition held by the United States Navy to select a machine to serve for both primary and advanced training as either a land or seaplane. Fourteen other designs were submitted in the competition, over which the "Fledgling" was adjudged the winner.

In addition to producing the "Fledgling" as a military training plane, the Curtiss Company also built a commercial version for civilian aircraft schools, from which the military equipment has been omitted and the 170 h.p. Curtiss "Challenger" engine substituted for the 230 h.p. Wright 'Whirlwind' engine.

TYPE.—A two-seat convertible land or sea training biplane.

WINGS.—Staggered equal-winged, two-bay biplane. Spars of routed spruce and plywood ribs with fabric covering. Leading-edge of top plane reinforced with sheet duralumin, and of bottom plane with plywood. The front spar of the bottom plane is almost directly under the back spar of the bottom plane. Two sets of "N" interplane struts on either side of the fuselage, with only one set of flying and landing wires in the plane of the centre cross strut of the "N" struts. Wing section, Curtiss C-72.

FUSELAGE.—Welded steel-tube Warren truss, covered with fabric.

TAIL UNIT.—Normal design. Steel-tube-framed, with fabric covering. Tail-plane adjustable in flight. Rudder balanced.

UNDERCARRIAGE.—Land undercarriage consists of two steel-tube Vees, hinged to the bottom longerons, to the apices of which are attached two long telescopic legs, the top ends of which are attached to the top longerons, one on each side. The tail-skid is steerable. For sea use one long central float and two wing-tip floats, all of wood, are fitted.

POWER PLANT.—One 230 h.p. Wright "Whirlwind" J-5 radial air-cooled engine.

ACCOMMODATION.—Crew of two accommodated in tandem cockpits, both behind the wings. The rear cockpit has removable dual control. For fighting training, one fixed Browning gun is mounted in the cowling in front of the pilot and a Lewis gun on a Scarff mounting over the back cockpit. Provision is also made for the installation of bomb-sights, wireless transmitting and receiving apparatus, etc. The lay-out of the military equipment follows closely that used in actual service aircraft.

The Curtiss "Fledgling" (N2C-1) Naval Training Biplane (230 h.p. Wright "Whirlwind" engine).

DIMENSIONS.—Span 39 ft. 1 in. (11.9 m.), Chord 5 ft. (1.52 m.), Length 26 ft. 9 in. (7.85 m.), Height 10 ft. 4 in. (3.14 m.), Wing area 365 sq. ft. (34 sq. m.).

WEIGHTS AND LOADINGS.—Weight empty 1,989 lbs. (904 kg.), Disposable load 711 lbs. (323 kg.), Weight loaded 2,700 lbs. (1,227 kg.), Wing loading 7.4 lbs./sq. ft. (35.2 kgs./sq. m.), Power loading 11.7 lbs./h.p. (5.32 kg./h.p.). (1929)

The Curtiss "Fledgling" Two-seat Training Biplane (240 h.p. Wright "Whirlwind" engine). (1931)

THE CURTISS N2C-2 "FLEDGLING."

TYPE.—A two-seat all-purpose training biplane.

WINGS.—Staggered, equal-winged, two-bay biplane. Curtiss C-72 wing section. Spars of routed spruce and plywood ribs with fabric covering. Leading-edge of top plane reinforced with sheet duralumin, and of bottom plane with plywood. The front spar of the bottom plane is almost directly under the back spar of the bottom plane. Two sets of "N" interplane struts on either side of the fuselage, with only one set of flying and landing wires in the plane of the centre cross strut of the "N" struts. Wing section, Curtiss C-72.

FUSELAGE.—Welded steel-tube Warren truss, covered with fabric.

TAIL UNIT.—Normal design. Steel-tube-framed, with fabric covering. Tail-plane adjustable in flight. Rudder balanced.

UNDERCARRIAGE.—Land undercarriage consists of two steel-tube Vees, hinged to the bottom longerons, to the apices of which are attached two long telescopic legs, the top ends of which are attached to the top longerons, one on each side. Bendix wheel-brakes. The tail-skid is steerable.

POWER PLANT.—One 240 h.p. Wright "Whirlwind" R-760 radial air-cooled engine, attached to ring-type engine-mount. One 40 U.S. gallon fuel tank mounted in fuselage, giving a range of 300 miles at cruising speed. One 5 U.S. gallons oil tank mounted in front of fireproof bulkhead. Curtiss or Hamilton-Standard metal airscrew. "Eclipse" hand intertia-starter.

ACCOMMODATION.—Two seats, in tandem, with dual controls. Push-rod aileron control mechanism. Rudder and elevators actuated by cable mechanism. Small luggage compartment. For training purposes, the following alternative installations are provided :—
(a) Synchronised fixed gun and 250 rounds of ammunition ; (b) Flexible gun on Scarff ring mount and 291 rounds of ammunition ; (c) 10 miniature bombs, bomb-sight and pilot director ; (d) Wireless transmitting and receiving set and wind driven generator.

DIMENSIONS.—Span 39 ft. 5 in. (12.01 m.), Length 28 ft. 2½ in. (8.6 m.), Height 10 ft. 8½ in. (3.26 m.), Wing area 365 sq. ft. (33.9 sq. m.).

WEIGHTS AND LOADINGS.—Weight empty 2,135 lbs. (969 kg.), Special military equipment 36 lbs. (16 kg.), Crew 400 lbs. (182 kg.), Fuel and oil (for 300 miles) 278 lbs. (126 kg.), Armament (military useful load) 8 lbs. (3.6 kg.), Total disposable load (for primary training) 722 lbs. (328 kg.), Weight loaded 2,857 lbs. (1,297 kg.). Wing loading 7.8 lbs./sq. ft. (38 kg./sq. m.), Power loading 11.9 lbs./h.p. (5.4 kg./h.p.).

PERFORMANCE.—Maximum speed at sea level 116 m.p.h. (185.6 km.h.), Speed at 5,000 ft. (1,525 m.) 111 m.p.h. (177.6 km.h.), Speed at 10,000 ft. (3,050 m.) 104 m.p.h. (166.4 km.h.), Speed at 15,000 ft. (4,575 m.) 92 m.p.h. (147.2 km.h.), Initial rate of climb 785 ft./min. (239 m./min.), Climb to 5,000 ft. (1,525 m.) 7.5 mins., Climb to 10,000 ft. (3,050 m.) 17.5 mins., Climb to 15,000 ft. (4,575 m.) 35.5 mins., Service ceiling 17,800 ft. (5,429 m.), Absolute ceiling 20,800 ft. (6,344 m.), Range at cruising speed 300 miles (480 km.).

THE CURTISS F11C-2 "GOSHAWK."

TYPE.—Single-seat shipboard fighter and light bomber biplane.

WINGS.—Single-bay, staggered, unequal-span biplane. The wings are tapered in plan form and are built up of wood spars and ribs, covered with fabric. One set of "N" type splayed-out streamline steel-tube interplane struts on either side of the fuselage. Ailerons are fitted to the upper wing only and are of sheet duralumin construction, fabric-covered.

FUSELAGE.—Welded steel-tube structure, fabric-covered.

TAIL UNIT.—Normal type. Metal framed, fabric-covered. Adjustable tail-plane.

UNDERCARRIAGE.—New Curtiss single-strut type. Oleo shock-absorbers and low-pressure tyres. Wheels are enclosed in fairings. Bendix brakes. The tail-wheel is steerable.

POWER PLANT.—One Wright "Cyclone" model R-1820-F.2 radial air-cooled engine, rated at 600 h.p. at 1,850 r.p.m. 94 U.S. gallons main fuel tank in the fuselage, 52 U.S. gallons droppable auxiliary fuel tank below main tank. Oil tank is located forward of fireproof bulkhead and has 8 U.S. gallons normal and 9 U.S. gallons maximum capacity. Detachable-blade metal airscrew. Hand inertia-starter.

ACCOMMODATION.—Pilot's cockpit aft of upper wing. Control consists of normal column and rudder-pedals. Ailerons operated through positive push-pull rods, rudder and elevators operated through cables. Armament consists of two fixed guns firing through airscrew and 1,200 rounds of ammunition. Bomb-racks under wings and fuselage for carrying 474 lbs. of bombs. The bombs can be released from any angle in a dive up to and including the vertical. Equipment includes arresting gear, life-raft, emergency flotation bags in wings, oxygen apparatus, wiring and mast for installation of wireless.

DIMENSIONS.—Span 31 ft. 6 in. (9.6 m.), Length overall 22 ft. 6½ in. (6.8 m.), Height 8 ft. 11 in. (2.74 m.), Wing area 252 sq. ft. (23.4 sq.m.).

WEIGHTS AND LOADINGS.—Weight empty 2,980 lbs. (1,353 kg.), Special military equipment 114 lbs. (51.7 kg.), Crew 200 lbs. (91 kg.), Fuel and oil (for 285 miles) 330 lbs. (150 kg.), Armament (military normal useful load) 156 lbs. (70.8 kg.), Total normal disposable load 1,094 lbs. (497 kg.), Weight loaded 4,074 lbs. (1,847 kg.), Wing loading 16.1 lbs./sq. ft. (78.5 kg./sq. m.), Wing loading 16.1 lbs./sq. ft. (78.5 kg./sq. m.), Power loading 7 lbs./h.p. (3.2 kg./h.p.).

The Curtiss F11C-2 "Goshawk" Single-seat Shipboard Fighter (700 h.p. Wright "Cyclone" engine).

PERFORMANCE.—Maximum speed at sea level 193 m.p.h. (309 km.h.), Maximum speed at 5,000 ft. (1,525 m.) 190 m.p.h. (304 km.h.), Maximum speed at 10,000 ft. (3,050 m.) 187 m.p.h. (299 km.h.), Maximum speed at 15,000 ft. (4,575 m.) 180 m.p.h (288 km.h.), Initial rate of climb 1,820 ft./min. (555 m./min.), Climb to 5,000 ft. (1,525 m.) 3.1 mins., Climb to 10,000 ft. (3,050 m.) 6.9 mins., Climb to 15,000 ft. (4,575 m.) 12.2 mins., Service ceiling 25,400 ft. (7,750 m.), Absolute ceiling 26,700 ft. (8,145 m.), Range at cruising speed 285 miles (457 km.) with normal fuel load, 570 miles (914 km.) with full tanks. (1933)

THE CURTISS "HAWK" BF2C-1

The BF2C-1 is the latest version of the F11C-2 Goshawk (redesignated BFC-2) single-seat fighter and is the US Naval version of the "Hawk" Type III export fighter. Twenty-eight machines of this type were delivered to the US Navy in 1935. These form the Fighting Group in the new US aircraft carrier *Ranger*.

The Curtiss ''Hawk'' BF2C-1 Single-seat Fighter Biplane (Curtiss ''Cyclone'' engine). (1936)

The Curtiss H. 12 Boat (two 160 h.p Curtiss engines).

In 1914, much attention was paid to flying boats, and a huge two-engined machine was built to the order of mr. Wanamaker and designed by Lieut. John Porte, R.N., the intention being that it should fly the Atlantic.

Just before the war this machine was fitted with three engines. Later on a big triplane with four 250 h.p. Curtiss engines was built, and it was reported in the American papers that it had been taken over by the British Navy.

CURTISS H.12, H.16 and F-5L

Flying boats of similar type to the original Wanamaker *America* were produced by Curtiss as H.4s, used by the British RNAS and nicknamed 'America boats' or 'Small Americas'. In 1916 the US Navy ordered larger flying-boats based on the H.4, becoming H.12s with two 200 hp Curtiss VXX engines (some later becoming H.12Ls when fitted with Liberty engines).

A further scaling up produced the H.16 with Liberty engines, built by Curtiss and the Naval Aircraft Factory. Meanwhile, in Britain the Curtiss H.12 had been redesigned under the instruction of Sqn Cdr John C. Porte of the RNAS as the Felixstowe F.2 (the F.1 having been an H.4 improvement), and later models became the F.2A, F.3 and F.5. Under US Navy instructions, the F.5 was built in USA and Canada as the F-5L, replacing British engines with Liberty 12As.

CURTISS MODEL H. 16A. FLYING BOAT.
Specification.

General Dimensions.

Wing span, upper plane..	96 ft. 6⅝ in.
Wing span, lower plane ..	68 ft. 11¾ in.
Depth of wing chord ..	84¹⁷⁄₆₄ in.
Gap between wings ..	96⁹⁄₁₆ in.
Stagger	None.
Length of machine overall ..	46 ft. 1¹⁵⁄₃₂ in.
Height of machine overall ..	17 ft. 8¾ in.
Angle of incidence ..	4 degrees.
Dihedral angle	1 degree.
Sweepback	None.

Wing curve	R.A.F. No. 6.
Horizontal stabilizer—angle of incidence	2 degrees pos.

Areas.

Wings, upper (without ailerons)	616.2 sq. ft.
Wings, lower	443.1 sq. ft.
Ailerons	131 sq. ft.
Horizontal stabilizer	108 sq. ft.
Vertical stabilizer	31.1 sq. ft.
Elevators	58.4 sq. ft.
Rudder	27.9 sq. ft.
Non-skids	24 sq. ft.
Total supporting surface ..	119.3 sq. ft.
Loading (weight carried per sq. ft. of supporting surface) ..	8.54 lbs.
Loading (per r.h.p.)	15.42 lbs.

Weights.

Net weight, machine empty	6,956 lbs.
Gross weight, machine and load	10,172 lbs.
Useful load	3,216 lbs.
Fuel and oil	1,527 lbs.
Crew	660 lbs.
Useful load	1,029 lbs.
Total	3,216 lbs.

Performance.

Speed, max. (horizontal flight) ..	95 m.p.h.
Speed, min. (horizontal flight) ..	55 m.p.h.
Climbing speed	4,000 ft. in 10 mins. (1919)

The U.S. Navy's H.16 type Flying Boat ashore.

Motor.
    Two Liberty 12-cylinder, Vee,
        four-stroke cycle   ..   ..   Water cooled.
    Horse power (each motor 330) ..   660
    Weight per rated h.p. 2.55
    Bore and stroke ..   ..   ..   5 in. × 7 in.
    Fuel consumption (both motors)   62.8 galls. per hour.
    Fuel tank capacity   ..   ..   300 galls.
    Oil capacity provided   ..   ..   10 galls.
    Fuel consumption per b.h.p.   ..   0.57 lbs. per hour.
    Oil consumption per b.h.p.   ..   0.03 lbs. per hour.
Propeller.
    Material.—Wood.
    Diameter.—According to requirements of performance.
    Pitch.—According to requirements of performance.

Maximum Range.
    At economic speed, about 675 miles.
Shipping Data.
    Hull Box.—Dimensions : 44 ft. 9 in. × 11 ft. × 9 ft. 4 in. ;
        gross weight, 1,300 lbs.
    Panel Box.—Dimensions : 30 ft. 4 in. × 7 ft. 7 in. × 6 ft. 6 in. ;
        gross weight, 4,850 lbs.
    Panel Box.—Dimensions : 21 ft. 2 in. × 7 ft. 5 in. × 3 ft. 6 in. ;
        gross weight, 2,170 lbs.
    Engine Box.—Dimensions : 6 ft. 2 in. × 4 ft. 4 in. × 2 ft. 9 in. ;
        gross weight, 1,645 lbs.   (1922)

The U.S. Navy's F.5.L. Flying Boat afloat.

F.5.L. SEAPLANE.

Specification.

Type of machine   ..   ..   ..   Twin Tractor Flying-boat.
Name or type No. of machine   ..   F.5.L.
Purpose for which intended ..   ..   Coast Patrol.
Armament   ..   ..   1—1½ pdr., 4 M.G., and
                2—500 lbs. (or 4—230
                lbs.) bombs.
Crew   ..   ..   5 men.
Span   ..   ..   103 ft. 9 in. (U).
Overall length   ..   ..   ..   49 ft. 3 in.
Maximum height   ..   ..   ..   18 ft. 9 in.
Total wing area   ..   ..   ..   1,397 sq. ft.
Engine type and h.p. ..   ..   ..   Two 420 h.p. Liberty
                "Twelves" (high com-
                pression type)

Weight empty   ..   ..   ..   8,250 lbs.
Weight loaded   ..   ..   ..   13,000 lbs.
Performance.
    High speed ..   ..   87 m.p.h.
    Low speed ..   ..   57 m.p.h.
Climb.
    To 2,625 feet   ..   ..   ..   10 mins.
    Range, at full speed   ..   ..   850 miles.

Note.—This seaplane is the American version of the Felixtowe boats.   (1922)

THE CURTISS "HAWK" SEAPLANE (F6C-1 AND F6C-2).

The U.S. Navy has recently adopted the Curtiss "Hawk," equipped as an interchangeable seaplane and deck-landing aeroplane. The deck-landing type is identical with the Army P-1 type, with the exception of the landing gear, which has been re-designed for the special service required. In the seaplane, this landing gear has been replaced by twin floats, similar in appearance to the Curtiss racer floats. The performance of this seaplane is exceptionally good.

Specification.

Span	31 ft. 6 in.	
Length	25 ft. 5 in.	
Height	10 ft. 8½ in.	
Wing area	250 sq. ft.	
Weight empty ..	2,519 lbs.	
Useful load	744 lbs.	
Weight loaded	3,263 lbs.	
Wing loading	13.05 lbs./sq. ft.	
Power loading	7.41 lbs./h.p.	

Performance.

Max. speed, sea level	159 m.p.h.	
Max. speed, at 15,000 ft.	138.7 m.p.h.	
Landing speed ..	65.4 m.p.h.	
Cruising speed	128 m.p.h.	
Service ceiling ..	18,100 ft.	
Absolute ceiling ..	19,300 ft.	

Climb.

In 10 mins.	10,850 ft.	

The Curtiss "Hawk" (F6C-1) Pursuit Seaplane (400 h.p. Curtiss D.12 engine). (1926)

The Curtiss "Hawk" (F6C-3) single-seat Fighter Seaplane (440 h.p. Curtiss D-12 engine).

THE CURTISS "HAWK" SEAPLANE (F6C-3).

The U.S. Navy has adopted the "Curtiss "Hawk," equipped as an interchangeable seaplane and deck-landing aeroplane. The deck-landing type is identical with the Army P-1 type, with the exception of the landing gear, which has been re-designed for the special service required. In the seaplane, this landing gear has been replaced by twin floats, similar in appearance to the Curtiss racer floats. The performance of this seaplane is exceptionally good.

Specification.

Span	31 ft. 6 in.	
Length	25 ft. 5 in.	
Height	10 ft. 8½ in.	
Wing area	250 sq. ft.	
Weight empty ..	2,519 lbs.	
Useful load	744 lbs.	
Weight loaded	3,263 lbs.	
Wing loading	13.05 lbs./sq. ft.	
Power loading	7.41 lbs./h.p.	

Speed:—

Max., sea level	159 m.p.h.	
Max., at 15,000 ft. ..	138.7 m.p.h.	
Landing	65.4 m.p.h.	
Cruising	128 m.p.h.	
Service ceiling ..	18,100 ft.	
Absolute ceiling ..	19,300 ft.	
Climb in 10 mins. ..	10,850 ft.	

THE CURTISS "HAWK" (F6C-4).

Another modification of the "Hawk" is the F6C-4, which is fitted with the 425 h.p. Pratt & Whitney "Wasp" engine.

The Curtiss "Hawk" (F6C-4) single-seat Fighter (425 h.p. Pratt & Whitney "Wasp" engine).

The Curtiss " Hawk " (P.1) Pursuit Biplane (400 h.p. Curtiss D.12 engine).

THE CURTISS " HAWK " (P-1 AND P-2).

The Curtiss " Hawk " pursuit plane, in its present form, has been adopted as the standard pursuit machine of the U.S. Army Air Service, and is being purchased in quantities to replace the previous types. This machine is the result of four years of intensive development by the Curtiss organization, in close co-operation with the military services.

The " Hawk " is a single-bay tractor biplane with a pronounced stagger, which affords the pilot exceptionally good vision.

The wings are tapered in plan form, and are of the conventional two-spar type, with fabric covering, the upper wing having a greater span and chord than the lower. Interplane struts are of the " N " type, using streamline steel tubing, and the wires are of streamline section.

All tail surfaces, as well as ailerons, are of metal construction, fabric-covered. The ailerons are operated through a positive push-pull rod linkage, adjustable to permit of various degrees of differential or synchronous aileron motion. The tail controls are cable operated, with a differential action incorporated in the elevator controls. This differential control of elevators and ailerons provides excellent control at all speeds, and avoids excessive stick loads.

The fuselage is of welded-steel tube, Pratt truss type, fabric-covered. The landing gear is of the usual Curtiss split-axle type, using rubber compression discs, housed within the fuselage. The tail-skid is also of the compression disc type, and is steerable, a feature which provides excellent ground control.

The power plant consists of either the 440 h.p. Curtiss D-12 motor (used in the P-1) or the 500 h.p. Curtiss V-1400 motor (used in the P-2). Both motors fit on the same motor-mount, which, in accordance with usual Curtiss practice, is a detachable welded-steel unit. The water and oil systems, incorporating a tunnel radiator and Curtiss oil temperature regulator, have been so refined that the " Hawk," in freezing weather, can be started, warmed up and flown in less than half the time usually required.

The petrol tank is " leak-proof," and an auxiliary droppable petrol tank of 50 gallons capacity can be hung under the fuselage for use in long-distance flights. A Curtiss-Reed duralumin airscrew is used.

The armament consists of two fixed Browning machine guns, firing through the airscrew disc, and provision is made for carrying bombs to be used in ground attack. The equipment includes the regulation Army parachute and oxygen equipment.

Specifications.

The Curtiss " Hawk " (P-1 and P-1a) (D-12 engine).

Span	31 ft. 6 in.
Length	22 ft. 5½ in.
Height	8 ft. 10¾ in.
Wing area	250 sq. ft.
Weight empty	2,041 lbs.
Useful load	800 lbs.
Weight loaded	2,841 lbs.

Performance.

Max. speed, sea level ..	170 m.p.h.
Max. speed, at 15,000 ft. ..	154.5 m.p.h.
Landing speed	61 m.p.h.

Climb.

To 15,000 ft.	14 mins.
Service ceiling	21,000 ft.
Absolute ceiling	22,150 ft.
Climb in 10 mins.	12,350 ft.

The Curtiss " Hawk " (P-2) (V-1400 engine).

Dimensions	Same as P-1.
Weight empty	2,013.5 lbs.
Useful load	794.5 lbs.
Weight loaded	2,808 lbs.
Wing loading	11.24 lbs./sq. ft.
Power loading	5.3 lbs./h.p.

Performance.

Max. speed, sea level ..	180 m.p.h.
Max. speed, at 15,000 ft. ..	172 m.p.h.
Landing speed	60.5 m.p.h.

Climb.

To 15,000 ft.	9 mins.
Service ceiling	24,400 ft.
Absolute ceiling	25,400 ft.
Climb in 10 mins.	16,000 ft.

(1926)

THE CURTISS " HAWK " (AT-4).

A still further modification of the " Hawk " is the AT-4. This type was produced by the Company for the U.S. Air Corps as a pursuit training type. It is essentially a standard " Hawk," fitted with a 180 h.p. Wright E-4 water-cooled engine in place of the Curtiss D-12. This arrangement provides the Air Corps with a standardised approved type, particularly suited for training purposes and possessing excellent performance and maintenance features at low cost. In addition, the 180 h.p. engine can be replaced with a standard D-12 engine, thus converting the AT-4, in time of emergency, into a standard type " Hawk."

Specification.

Span		31 ft. 6 in.
Length		22 ft. 2 in.
Height		8 ft. 6 in.
Wing area		250 sq. ft.
Weight empty, with water ..		1,847 lbs.
Useful load:—		
Crew ..	180 lbs.	
Fuel and oil ..	325 lbs.	
Equipment	31 lbs.	
Armament	101 lbs.	
		637 lbs.
Weight loaded		2,484 lbs.

Speed:—

Max., at 1,820 r.p.m. ..	132.8 m.p.h.
Cruising	108.5 m.p.h.
Landing	54.6 m.p.h.
Rate of climb	920 ft. per min.
Climb to 5,000 ft. ..	6.5 mins.
Climb to 10,000 ft. ..	16.5 mins.
Range, full throttle ..	394 miles.
Range, at 1,500 r.p.m. ..	490 miles.
Service ceiling	15,150 ft.
Absolute ceiling	17,000 ft.

(1927)

THE CURTISS AT-5 "HAWK."

The Curtiss AT-5 is a pursuit training biplane, fitted with the 225 h.p. Wright "Whirlwind" engine. It is identical to the standard "Hawk," except for the engine, and it can, in case of national emergency, be fitted with the standard D-12 or "Wasp" engine to convert it into a standard "Hawk" single-seat fighter.

(1926)

The Curtiss "Hawk" (P-1B) single-seat Fighter (440 h.p. Curtiss D-12 engine). (1928)

THE CURTISS P1-B "HAWK."

The Curtiss P1-B "Hawk" is the standard single-seat pursuit biplane in the U.S. Air Corps.

This machine incorporates a quickly detachable engine-mounting, and like the "Falcon" has been adapted to a number of varying purposes by the installation of different power plant.

TYPE.—Single-seat military pursuit biplane.

WINGS.—Single-bay, staggered, unequal biplane. The wings are tapered in plan form and are built up of wooden spars and ribs, covered with fabric. One set of "N" type splayed-out streamline steel-tube interplane struts on either side of the fuselage. Ailerons fitted to top plane only and are of metal construction, covered with fabric. Ailerons operated through positive push-pull rods, adjustable to permit of various degrees of differential or synchronous aileron motion.

FUSELAGE.—Welded steel-tube structure, covered with fabric.

TAIL UNIT.—Normal type. Metal framed, covered with fabric. Tail controls are cable-operated, with a differential action incorporated in the elevator controls.

UNDERCARRIAGE.—Split type. Consists of two Vees hinged on the bottom fuselage longerons and two bent axles crossing at the centre. Suspension by rubber compression discs, housed within the fuselage. Steerable tail-skid sprung by rubber compression discs. Interchangeable wheels and skis.

POWER PLANT.—One 435 h.p. Curtiss D-12 water-cooled engine on a detachable welded steel-tube mounting. The water and oil systems incorporating a tunnel radiator and Curtiss oil temperature regulator, allow the machine to be warmed up and flown in freezing weather in less than half normal time. Main fuel tank carried under fuselage, behind tunnel radiator, and is droppable in case of emergency. Curtiss-Reed duralumin airscrew.

ACCOMMODATION.—Pilot's cockpit aft of top plane. Armament consists of two fixed Browning guns, firing through airscrew, and provision is made for carrying small fragmentation bombs for ground attack work. Equipment includes regulation Army parachute and oxygen equipment.

DIMENSIONS.—Span 31 ft. 6 in. (9.60 m.), Length 22 ft. 5½ in. (6.83 m.), Height 8 ft. 10¾ in. (2.71 m.), Wing area 250 sq. ft. (23.2 sq. m.).

WEIGHTS AND LOADINGS.—Weight empty (with water) 2,041 lbs. (928 kg.), Weight of crew 180 lbs. (82 kg.), Weight of fuel and oil 325 lbs. (147 kg.), Weight of equipment 295 lbs. (134 kg.), Total disposable load 800 lbs. (363 kg.), Weight loaded 2,841 lbs. (1,291 kg.), Wing loading 11.36 lbs./sq. ft. (55.6 kg./sq. m.), Power loading 6.53 lbs./h.p. (2.97 kg./h.p.).

PERFORMANCE.—Maximum speed 165 m.p.h. (266 km.h.), Speed at 15,000 ft. (4,570 m.) 154.5 m.p.h. (249 km.h.), Landing speed 58.7 m.p.h. (95 km.h.), Initial rate of climb 1,800 ft./min. (548 m./min.), Climb in 10 mins. 12,350 ft. (3,762 m.), Service ceiling 21,000 ft. (6,398 m.), Absolute ceiling 22,150 ft. (6,750 m.).

THE CURTISS P1-C "HAWK."

The Curtiss P1-C "Hawk" is the standard single-seat pursuit biplane in the U.S. Air Corps.

This machine incorporates a quickly detachable engine-mounting, and like the "Falcon" has been adapted to a number of varying purposes by the installation of different power plants.

TYPE.—Single-seat military pursuit biplane.

WINGS.—Single-bay, staggered, unequal-span biplane. The wings are tapered in plan form and are built up of wooden spars and ribs, covered with fabric. One set of "N" type splayed-out streamline steel-tube interplane struts on either side of the fuselage. Ailerons fitted to top plane only and are of metal construction, covered with fabric. Ailerons operated through positive push-pull rods, adjustable to permit of various degrees of differential or synchronous aileron motion.

FUSELAGE.—Welded steel-tube structure, covered with fabric.

TAIL UNIT.—Normal type. Metal framed, covered with fabric. Tail controls are cable-operated, with a differential action incorporated in the elevator controls.

UNDERCARRIAGE.—Split type. Consists of two Vees hinged on the bottom fuselage longerons and two bent axles crossing at the centre. Suspension by rubber compression discs, housed within the fuselage. Steerable tail-skid sprung by rubber compression discs. Interchangeable wheels and skis.

POWER PLANT.—One 435 h.p. Curtiss D-12 water-cooled engine on a detachable welded steel-tube mounting. The water system incorporates a tunnel radiator. Auxiliary fuel tank carried under fuselage, behind tunnel radiator, and is droppable in case of emergency. Curtiss-Reed duralumin airscrew.

ACCOMMODATION.—Pilot's cockpit aft of top plane. Armament consists of two fixed Browning guns, firing through airscrew, and provision is made for carrying small fragmentation bombs for ground attack work. Equipment includes regulation Army parachute and oxygen equipment.

DIMENSIONS.—Span 31 ft. 6 in. (9.6 m.), Length 23 ft. (7.01 m.), Height 8 ft. 9 in. (2.67 m.), Wing area 252 sq. ft. (23.4 sq. m.).

WEIGHTS AND LOADINGS.—Weight empty (with water) 2,195 lbs. (998 kg.), Weight of crew 200 lbs. (90.6 kg.), Weight of fuel and oil 330 lbs. (149.6 kg.), Weight of equipment 27 lbs. (12.2 kg.), Total disposable load 765 lbs. (347 kg.), Weight loaded 2,960 lbs. (1,345 kg.), Wing loading 11.74 lbs./sq. ft. (57.4 kg./sq. m.), Power loading 6.8 lbs./h.p. (3.08 kg./h.p.).

PERFORMANCE.—Maximum speed 165 m.p.h. (266 km.h.), Speed at 15,000 ft. (4,570 m.) 154.5 m.p.h. (249 km.h.), Landing speed 58.7 m.p.h. (95 km.h.), Initial rate of climb 1,800 ft./min. (548 m./min.), Climb in 10 mins. 12,350 ft. (3,762 m.), Service ceiling 21,000 ft. (6,398 m.), Absolute ceiling 22,150 ft. (6,750 m.).

(1929)

The Curtiss P-6E "Hawk" Single-seat Fighter (675 h.p. Curtiss "Conqueror" engine).

THE CURTISS P-6 "HAWK."

The Curtiss P-6 is the latest development of the "Hawk" series, for years the standard single-seat pursuit biplane in the U.S. Air Corps.

TYPE.—Single-seat military pursuit biplane.

WINGS.—Single-bay, staggered, unequal-span biplane. The wings are tapered in plan form and are built up of wooden spars and ribs, covered with fabric. One set of "N" type splayed-out streamline steel-tube interplane struts on either side of the fuselage. Ailerons fitted to top plane only and are of metal construction, covered with fabric. Ailerons operated through positive push-pull rods, adjustable to permit of various degrees of differential or synchronous aileron motion.

FUSELAGE.—Welded steel-tube structure, covered with fabric.

TAIL UNIT.—Normal type. Metal framed, covered with fabric. Tail controls are cable-operated, with a differential action incorporated in the elevator controls.

UNDERCARRIAGE.—Split type. Consists of two Vees hinged on the bottom fuselage longerons and two bent axles crossing at the centre. Oleo and spring shock-absorber units in both undercarriage and tail-skid units. Interchangeable wheels and skis.

POWER PLANT.—One 600 h.p. Curtiss "Conqueror" water-cooled engine on a detachable welded steel-tube mounting. The water system incorporates a tunnel radiator. Auxiliary fuel tank carried under fuselage, behind tunnel radiator, and is droppable in case of emergency. Curtiss-Reed duralumin airscrew.

ACCOMMODATION.—Pilot's cockpit aft of top plane. Armament consists of two fixed Browning guns, firing through airscrew, and provision is made for carrying small fragmentation bombs for ground attack work. Equipment includes regulation Army parachute and oxygen equipment.

DIMENSIONS.—Span 31 ft. 6 in. (9.6 m.), Length 23 ft. (7.01 m.), Height 8 ft. 9 in. (2.67 m.), Wing area 252 sq. ft. (23.4 sq. m.).

WEIGHTS AND LOADINGS.—Weight empty 2,545 lbs. (1,055.4 kg.), Disposable load 724 lbs. (328.6 kg.), Weight loaded 3,269 lbs. (1,484 kg.), Wing loading 13 lbs./sq. ft. (6.34 kg./sq. m.), Power loading 5.45 lbs./h.p. (2.47 kg./h.p.).

PERFORMANCE.—Maximum speed 178 m.p.h. (284.8 km.h.), Speed at 5,000 ft. (1,525 m.) 175 m.p.h. (280 km.h.), Speed at 10,000 ft. (3,050 m.) 170 m.p.h. (272 km.h.), Speed at 15,000 ft. (4,575 m.) 162 m.p.h. (265.2 km.h.), Cruising speed 142 m.p.h. (227.2 km.h.), Stalling speed 62.4 m.p.h. (105.84 km.h.), Climb to 5,000 ft. 2.7 mins., Climb to 10,000 ft. 6.2 mins., Climb to 15,000 ft. 11.2 mins., Service ceiling 22,600 ft. (6,890 m.), Absolute ceiling 23,800 ft. (7,260 m.).

THE CURTISS P-6E "HAWK."

TYPE.—Single-seat military pursuit biplane.

WINGS.—Single-bay, staggered, unequal-span biplane. The wings are tapered in plan form and are built up of wooden spars and ribs, covered with fabric. One set of "N" type splayed-out streamline steel-tube interplane struts on either side of the fuselage. Ailerons fitted to top plane only and are of metal construction, covered with fabric.

FUSELAGE.—Welded steel-tube structure, covered with fabric.

TAIL UNIT.—Normal type. Metal framed, covered with fabric. Adjustable tail-plane.

UNDERCARRIAGE.—New Curtiss single-strut type landing gear. Oleo shock-absorbers and low-pressure tyres. Wheels fitted with Bendix brakes and wheel fairings.

POWER PLANT.—One 675 h.p. Curtiss high-compression "Conqueror" Prestone-cooled engine, on a detachable welded steel-tube mounting. The radiator is beneath the fuselage, just forward of the landing gear. There is a main fuel tank in the fuselage, of 50 U.S. gallons capacity, and a droppable auxiliary tank just below it, with 50 U.S. gallons capacity. Cruising range with both tanks full is 480 miles. Oil tank is located forward of fireproof bulkhead and has 4 U.S. gallons normal and 8 U.S. gallons maximum capacity. Detachable-blade duralumin airscrew. "Eclipse" hand inertia starter.

ACCOMMODATION.—Pilot's cockpit aft of top plane. Armament consists of two fixed Browning guns, firing through airscrew, and 1,200 rounds of ammunition. A bomb rack may be mounted under the fuselage and 240 lbs. of bombs carried. Equipment includes oxygen apparatus.

DIMENSIONS.—Span 31 ft. 6 in. (9.6 m.), Length overall 22 ft. 7 in. (6.87 m.), Height 8 ft. 11 in. (2.74 m.), Wing area 252 sq. ft. (23.4 sq. m.).

WEIGHTS AND LOADINGS.—Weight empty 2,715 lbs. (1,231 kg.), Special military equipment 31 lbs. (9.5 kg.), Crew 200 lbs. (91 kg.), Fuel and oil (for 240 miles) 330 lbs. (150 kg.), Armament (military useful load) 140 lbs. (63 kg.), Total disposable load 691 lbs. (313 kg.), Weight loaded 3,406 lbs. (1,546 kg.), Wing loading 13.5 lbs./sq. ft. (65.8 kg./sq. m.), Power loading 5.0 lbs./h.p. (2.27 kg./h.p.).

PERFORMANCE.—Maximum speed at sea level 198 m.p.h. (317 km.h.), Maximum speed at 5,000 ft. (1,525 m.) 196 m.p.h. (314 km.h.), Maximum speed at 10,000 ft. (3,050 m.) 189 m.p.h. (303 km.h.), Maximum speed at 15,000 ft. (4,575 m.) 182 m.p.h. (291 km.h.), Initial rate of climb 2,400 ft./min. (732 m./min.), Climb to 5,000 ft. (1,252 m.) 2.4 mins., Climb to 10,000 ft. (3,050 m.) 5.3 mins., Climb to 15,000 ft. (4,575 m.) 9.5 mins., Service ceiling 24,700 ft. (7,525 m.), Absolute ceiling 25,800 ft. (7,865 m.), Range at cruising speed 285 miles (455 km.) with normal fuel load, 570 miles (910 km.) with full tanks.

The Curtiss F8C-4 "Helldiver" Two-seat Shipboard Fighter (450 h.p. Pratt & Whitney "Wasp" engine).

CURTISS F8C-4 "HELLDIVER."

The Curtiss F8C-4 is a two-seater shipboard fighter and light bomber equipped with a 450 h.p. Pratt & Whitney "Wasp" engine. It is noteworthy for its ability to dive vertically under full power in bombing operations.

TYPE.—Two-seat shipboard fighter.

WINGS.—Equal-span, staggered biplane. Upper wing has 12° of sweepback. Bottom wings are straight. Centre-section is mounted above fuselage on widely-splayed "N" type duralumin tube struts. Interplane bracing consists of one pair of "N" type struts in either side of fuselage. Wings are of wooden construction, employing C-72 airfoil section, with spruce box-spars, wood ribs, and fabric covering. Wing-bracing consists of double flying wires and single landing wires. Lower ailerons are balanced.

FUSELAGE.—Constructed of steel and duralumin tubing, with Warren-truss bracing.

TAIL UNIT.—Normal type. All-duralumin construction, fabric-covered. Rudder balanced. Tail-plane adjustable in flight, fin adjustable on ground.

UNDERCARRIAGE.—Split type. Consists of two Vees, the front leg of each incorporating an oleo and spring shock-absorber. The rear legs of each Vee hinges to the lower longerons. Two radius-rods hinge to an attachment on the under side of the fuselage in line with the Vee hinges.

POWER PLANT.—One 450 h.p. Pratt & Whitney "Wasp" engine. Fuel is carried in two tanks, one in either side of fuselage, aft of firewall.

ACCOMMODATION.—Two seats for pilot and gunner, arranged in tandem aft of upper wing. Flotation bags, which can be inflated with carbon dioxide in a few seconds, are carried in canvas packs on either side of fuselage, and provide ample buoyancy to keep plane afloat in event of a forced landing in the sea.

DIMENSIONS.—Span 32 ft. (9.76 m.), Length 25 ft. 11⅞ in. (7.92 m.), Height 10 ft. 2 in. (3.09 m.), Wing area 308 sq. ft. (28.6 sq. m.).

WEIGHTS AND LOADINGS.—Weight empty 2,449 lbs. (1,112 kg.), Disposable load (fighter) 1,261 lbs. (572.5 kg.), Disposable load (bomber) 1,523 lbs. (691.4 kg.), Weight loaded (fighter) 3,710 lbs. (1,684.5 kg.), Weight loaded (bomber) 3,972 lbs. (1,803.4 kg.), Wing loading (fighter) 12.04 lbs./sq. ft. (58.75 kg./sq. m.), Wing loading (bomber) 12.9 lbs./sq. ft. (64 kg./sq. m.), Power loading (fighter) 8.25 lbs./h.p. (3.74 kg./h.p.), Power loading (bomber) 8.83 lbs./h.p. (40 kg./h.p.).

PERFORMANCE (fighter).—Maximum speed 141 m.p.h. (225.6 km.h.), Speed at 10,000 ft. (3,050 m.) 134 m.p.h. (214.4 km.h.), Speed at 15,000 ft. (4,575 m.) 125 m.p.h. (200 km.h.), Initial rate of climb 1,250 ft./min. (381 m./min.), Service ceiling 18,800 ft. (5,734 m.), Absolute ceiling 20,500 ft. (6,252.5 m.). (1931)

THE CURTISS F8C-5.

An adaptation of the F8C-4 is the F8C-5 used by the Marine Corps, and equipped only as a landplane, not for carrier operations. (1931)

The Curtiss F8C-7 "Helldiver" (575 h.p. Wright "Cyclone" engine).

CURTISS F8C-7 "HELLDIVER."

TYPE.—Two-seat shipboard fighter.

WINGS.—Equal-span, staggered biplane. Upper wing has 12° of sweepback. Bottom wings are straight. Centre-section is mounted above fuselage on widely-splayed "N" type duralumin tube struts. Interplane bracing consists of one pair of "N" type struts in either side of fuselage. Wings are of wooden construction, employing C-72 airfoil section, with spruce box-spars, wood ribs, and fabric covering. Wing-bracing consists of double flying wires and single landing wires. Lower ailerons are balanced.

FUSELAGE.—Constructed of steel and duralumin tubing, with Warren-truss bracing.

TAIL UNIT.—Normal type. All-duralumin construction, fabric-covered. Rudder balanced. Tail-plane adjustable in flight, fin adjustable on ground.

UNDERCARRIAGE.—Split type. Consists of two Vees, the front leg of each incorporating an oleo and spring shock-absorber. The rear legs of each Vee hinges to the lower longerons. Two radius-rods hinge to an attachment on the under side of the fuselage in line with the Vee hinges. Wheels are enclosed in fairings and equipped with brakes. Steerable tail-wheel. Deck-landing arresting gear.

POWER PLANT.—One 575 h.p. Wright "Cyclone." Fuel is carried in two tanks, one in either side of fuselage, aft of firewall.

ACCOMMODATION.—Two seats for pilot and gunner, arranged in tandem aft of upper wing. The pilot's seat is enclosed and the covering is extended aft to protect the rear gunner. The rear gun is mounted on new Curtiss-type flexible mounting. Flotation bags, which can be inflated with carbon dioxide in a few seconds, are carried in canvas packs on either side of fuselage, and provide ample buoyancy to keep plane afloat in event of a forced landing in the sea.

DIMENSIONS.—Span 32 ft. (9.76 m.), Length 25 ft. 11⅞ in. (7.92 m.), Height 10 ft. 2 in. (3.09 m.), Wing area 308 sq. ft. (28.6 sq. m.).

THE CURTISS SBC-3 AND SBC-4.

The Curtiss SBC-3 and SBC-4 are two-seat Scout-Bomber biplanes, 141 of which have been built for the U.S. Navy. The basic design incorporates single-bay biplane wings with tapered upper wings, "I"-type interplane struts, metal monocoque fuselage and a retractable undercarriage. The crew is accommodated in enclosed tandem cockpits aft of the wings. The engine of the SBC-3 is a Pratt & Whitney "Twin-Wasp" enclosed in a N.A.C.A. cowling with controlled flaps. The SBC-4 is identical to the SBC-3 but is fitted with the Wright "Cyclone" engine. (1938)

The Curtiss SBC-4 Two-seat Scout-Bomber Biplane (850 h.p. Wright "Cyclone" engine).
(*Photograph by Peter Bowers*)

THE CURTISS SBC-4. "HELLDIVER."

TYPE.—Two-seat scout-bomber biplane.

WINGS.—Single-bay biplane with single "I"-struts and wire bracing. Upper wing of one-piece multi-cellular construction. Lower wings are of aluminium-alloy spar and rib construction and attached directly to fittings on either side of the fuselage. All are fabric-covered. Ailerons on upper wings and double-split trailing-edge flaps on lower wings.

FUSELAGE.—All-metal semi-monocoque structure, using aluminium-alloy skin, bulkhead and stringers with forged fittings.

TAIL UNIT.—Monoplane type. Tail-plane and fin of aluminium-alloy sheet construction with metal skin. The rudder and elevators have aluminium-alloy spar and nose box sections, aluminium-alloy ribs and fabric covering. Trimming-tabs in elevators and rudder.

UNDERCARRIAGE.—Retractable type. Wheels are raised with sides of fuselage just aft of engine compartment. Air-oil type shock-absorbers. Hydraulic retraction. The tail-wheel retracts simultaneously with the landing gear.

POWER PLANT.—One Wright "Cyclone" R-1820-34 radial air-cooled engine, rated at 850 h.p. at 2,100 r.p.m. at 9,800 ft. (2,990 m.) and 1,000 h.p. at 2,200 r.p.m. for take-off. The main fuel tank has a capacity of 135 U.S. gallons (511 litres) and a streamlined auxiliary tank carrying 50 U.S. gallons (189 litres) and may be installed under the fuselage. Oil capacity 10 U.S. gallons (37.8 litres). Three-bladed Hamilton Standard Hydromatic constant-speed airscrew.

ACCOMMODATION.—Tandem cockpits are completely enclosed by a canopy consisting of a windshield, three sliding hoods and a fixed section.

ARMAMENT.—Various combinations of fuselage and observer guns of .30 cal. or .50 cal. are available as well as medium and heavy bomb-loads carried beneath the fuselage and wings.

DIMENSIONS.—Span 34 ft. (10.36 m.), Length 27 ft. 5 in. (8.42 m.), Height 10 ft. 3½ in. (3.18 m.), Wheel track 7 ft. 3 in. (2.28 m.).

WEIGHTS AND LOADINGS.—Weight empty 4,548 lbs. (2,065 kg.), Disposable load 1,708 lbs. (775 kg.), Weight loaded 6,256 lbs. (2,840 kg.), Wing loading 19.7 lbs./sq. ft. (96.13 kg./sq. m.), Power loading 6.6 lbs./h.p. (3 kg./h.p.).

PERFORMANCE.—Maximum speed 235 m.p.h. (376 km.h.) at 15,000 ft. (4,575 m.), Cruising speed 176 m.p.h. (282 km.h.) at 15,000 ft. (4,575 m.), Landing speed 68 m.p.h. (109 km.h.), Service ceiling 24,500 ft. (7,470 m.), Absolute ceiling 25,400 ft. (7,750 m.), Cruising range 855 miles (1,368 km.). (1941)

THE CURTISS HELLDIVER.

U.S. Navy designation : SB2C. (Also SBF when built by Fairchild and SBW when built by Canadian Car & Foundry).

U.S. Army Air Forces designation: A-25.

The experimental contract for the Helldiver was awarded by the the U.S. Navy on May 15, 1939, and the prototype XSB 2C-1 first flew in November, 1940. From that date the Helldiver has been the subject of constant development. Armour, self-sealing tanks, protected fuel and oil lines, increased armament, a lengthened fuselage and a completely new tail unit with greatly enlarged fixed and moveable surfaces were incorporated in the production SB2C-1, the first of which flew in June, 1942. From that date until November, 1943, when the Helldiver first went into action in the Pacific, over 880 major design changes were made, some of which were part of the Army-Navy standardisation programme to permit the production of an Army version of the Helldiver under the designation A-25. The A-25 is now in service with the Marine Corps.

SB2C-1 (A-25). Wright R-2600-8 engine driving a three-blade Curtiss Electric constant-speed airscrew. Armament consists of four 50 cal. machine-guns in the wings and one 50 cal. gun on an hydraulic mounting in the rear cockpit. SBW-1 and SBF-1 similar.

XSB2C-2. An experimental long-range reconnaissance-bomber seaplane development of the SB2C-1 and delivered for test in 1943. Fitted with twin Edo floats.

SB2C-3. Wright R-2600-20 engine of greater output driving a four-blade Curtiss Electric airscrew. Wing armament changed to two 20 m/m. cannon, one in each extremity of the centre-section just outboard of the landing-gear. SBW-3 and SBF-3 similar.

SB2C-4 and **SB2C-5.** Developments of the SB2C-3 with perforated wing flaps and wing bomb racks. Also fitted with racks under the outer wings for eight 4.5 in. rockets, four under each wing. SBW-4, SBW-5 and SBF-4 similar.

The Helldiver contracts with the Canadian Car & Foundry Co., Ltd. and Fairchild Aircraft, Ltd. were terminated in 1945.

TYPE.—Two-seat Dive-Bomber.

WINGS.—Low-wing cantilever monoplane. Wing in four sections. Centre panel in two portions bolted to fuselage. Outer wing sections fold upward. Two-spar stressed skin aluminium-alloy structure. Dynamically and statically-balanced ailerons have upper surface and fabric on the lower surface. Split perforated flaps opening both upward and downward as dive-brakes. Hydraulic locks for upper flaps to permit lower flaps to operate as landing flaps. Wing-tip slats extend when landing-gear is lowered.

FUSELAGE.—Aluminum-alloy semi-monocoque structure with a flush-riveted smooth Alclad skin.

TAIL UNIT.—Cantilever monoplane type. Fixed surfaces have aluminium-alloy frames with flush-riveted Alclad skin. Movable surfaces have aluminium-alloy frames and fabric covering.

LANDING GEAR.—Retractable type. Comprises two Curtiss oleo-pneumatic shock-absorber struts which are raised inwardly into the underside of the wings, the apertures being closed by fairings attached to the struts and wheels. Hydraulic retraction. The steerable tail-wheel is partly retractable. Deck arrester gear. Retractable catapult spools.

POWER PLANT.—One Wright R-2600-20 fourteen-cylinder radial air-cooled geared and supercharged engine. Curtiss Electric four-blade constant-speed airscrew. Three self-sealing fuel tanks, two in centre-section and one in fuselage. Provision for auxiliary tank to be carried in bomb-bay. Oil tank in engine compartment. Protected fuel and oil lines.

ACCOMMODATION.—Enclosed pilot's and observer's cockpits. Heating and ventilation. Both crew positions armoured. Auto pilot. Inflatable dinghy stowed in cylindrical container under canopy forward of the gunner.

The Curtiss SB2C-4 Helldiver Two-seat Dive-Bomber with wings folded.

ARMAMENT.—Two 20 m/m. cannon or four .50 cal. machine-guns in wings. One .50 cal. gun on a hydraulic mounting in rear cockpit. Collapsible decking aft of cockpit to increase field of fire aft. Internal bomb stowage. Hydraulically-operated bomb-doors. Two external bomb-racks under wings. Camera in rear cockpit.

(1945–46)

Details for SB2C-4:—

Span	49 ft 9 in (15.15 m)
Length	36 ft 8 in (11.18 m)
Wing area	422 sq ft (39.2 m²)
Weight loaded	16,615 lb (7,536 kg)
High speed	295 mph (475 km/h)
Range	1,165 miles (1,870 km)
Engine	One 1,900 hp Wright

CURTISS MODEL H.S. 2L. FLYING BOAT.
Specification.

General Dimensions.

Wing span, upper plane	74 ft. 0½³ in.
Wing span, lower plane	64 ft. 1³¹⁄₃₂ in.
Depth of wing chord	6 ft. 3⁵⁄₃₂ in.
Gap between wings (front)	7 ft. 7⅛ in.
Gap between wings (rear)	7 ft. 5³⁹⁄₃₂ in.
Stagger	None.
Length of machine overall	38 ft 6 in
Height of machine overall	14 ft. 7¼ in.
Angle of incidence, upper plane	5¼ degrees.
Angle of incidence, lower plane	4 degrees.
Dihedral angle	2 degrees.
Sweepback	0 degrees.
Wing curve	R.A.F. No. 6.
Horizontal stabilizer—angle of incidence	0 degrees.

Areas.

Wings, upper	380.32 sq. ft.
Wings, lower	314.92 sq. ft.
Ailerons (upper 62.88, lower 42.48)	105.36 sq. ft.
Horizontal stabilizer	54.8 sq. ft.
Vertical stabilizer	19.6 sq. ft.
Elevators (each 22.8 sq. ft.)	45.6 sq. ft.
Rudder	26.5 sq. ft.
Total supporting surface	800.6 sq. ft.
Loading (weight carried per sq. ft. of supporting surface)	7.77 lbs.
Loading (per r.h.p.)	18.85 lbs.

Weights.

Net weight, machine empty		4,359 lbs.
Gross weight, machine and load		6,430 lbs
Useful load		1,864 lbs
Fuel		977 lbs.
Crew		360 lbs.
Useful load		527 lbs.
Total		1,864 lbs.

Performance.

Speed, max. (horizontal flight)	91 m.p.h.
Speed, min. (horizontal flight)	55 m.p.h.
Climbing speed	1,800 ft. in 10 mins.

Motor.

Liberty 12-cylinder, Vee, four-stroke cycle	Water cooled.
Horse power (rated)	330.
Weight per rated h.p.	2.55 lbs.
Bore and stroke	5 in. × 7 in.
Fuel consumption	32 galls per hour.
Fuel tank capacity	152·8 galls.
Oil tank capacity	8 galls.
Fuel consumption per b.h.p.	0.57 lbs. per hour.
Oil consumption per b.h.p.	0.03 lbs. per hour.

The Curtiss H-A Dunkirk fighter Central Float Seaplane of 1918 (Curtiss K.12 400 h.p. engine). Three built for the Navy. Max speed 132 mph.

Propeller.
Material.—Wood.
Pitch.—According to requirements of performance.
Diameter.—According to requirements of performance.
Direction of rotation, viewed from pilot's seat.—Clockwise.

Maximum Range.
At economic speed, about 575 miles.

Shipping Data.
Hull Box.—Dimensions: 35 ft. 5 in.×8 ft. 6 in×6 ft. 4 in.; gross weight, 8,525 lbs.
Panel Box.—Dimensions: 23 ft. 6 in.×6 ft. 9 in.×3 ft. 5 in.; gross weight, 2,900 lbs.
Engine Box.—Dimensions: 6 ft. 2 in.×4 ft. 4 in.×2 ft. 9 in.; gross weight, 1,645 lbs.

(1919)

A U.S. Naval Flying Boat of the H.S. 2 L. type, built by the Standard Aircraft Corporation. (1919)

CURTISS MODEL M.F. FLYING BOAT.
Specification.

General Dimensions.

Wing span, upper plane	49 ft. 9⅜ in.
Wing span, lower plane	38 ft. 7 5/32 in.
Depth of wing chord	60 in.
Gap between wings at engine section	6 ft. 4 5/64 in.
Stagger	None.
Length of machine overall ..	28 ft. 10 9/16 in.
Height of machine overall ..	11 ft. 9⅜ in.
Angle of incidence	6 degrees.
Dihedral angle, lower panels only	2 degrees.
Sweepback	None.
Wing curve	U.S.A. No. 1.
Horizontal stabilizer—angle of incidence	0 degrees.

Areas.

Wings, upper	187.54 sq. ft.
Wings, lower	169.10 sq. ft.
Ailerons (each 22.43 sq. ft.) ..	44.86 sq. ft.
Horizontal stabilizer	33.36 sq. ft.
Vertical stabilizer	15.74 sq. ft.
Elevators (each 15.165 sq. ft.) ..	30.33 sq. ft.
Rudder	20.42 sq. ft.
Total supporting surface ..	401.50 sq. ft.
Loading (weight carried per sq. ft. of supporting surface) ..	6·05 lbs.
Loading (per r.h.p.)	24.32 lbs.

Weights.

Net weight, machine empty		1,796 lbs.
Gross weight, machine and load		2,432 lbs.
Useful Load		636 lbs.
Fuel	240 lbs.	
Oil	22.5 lbs.	
Water	36 lbs.	
Pilot	165 lbs.	
Passenger	165 lbs.	
Miscellaneous accessories ..	7·5 lbs.	
Total	636.0 lbs.	

Performance.

Speed, max. (horizontal flight) ..	69 m.p.h.
Speed, min. (horizontal flight) ..	45 m.p.h.
Climbing speed	5,000 ft. in 27 mins.

Motor.

Model O.X.X. 8-cylinder, Vee, four-stroke cycle	Water cooled.
Horse power (rated) at 1400 r.p.m.	100.
Weight per r.h.p...	4.01 lbs.
Bore and stroke	4½ in. × 5 in.
Fuel consumption	10 galls. per hour.
Fuel tank capacity	40 galls.
Oil capacity provided (crankcase)	5 galls.
Fuel consumption per b.h.p. ..	0.60 lbs. per hour.
Oil consumption per b.h.p. ..	0.030 lbs. per hour.

Propeller.

Material.—Wood.
Pitch.—According to requirements of performance.
Diameter.—According to requirements of performance.
Direction of rotation, as viewed from pilot's seat.—Clockwise.

Details.

Dual control.
Standard Equipment.—Tachometer, oil gauge, gasoline gauge, complete set of tools.
Other equipment on special order.

Maximum Range.

At economic speed, about 325 miles.

Shipping Data—Foreign Shipment.

Hull Box.—Dimensions : 26 ft. 6 in. × 6 ft. 3 in. × 4 ft. 11 in. ; gross weight, 2,390 lbs.
Panel Box.—Dimensions : 22 ft. 3 in. × 5 ft. 11 in. × 3 ft. 9 in. ; gross weight, 730 lbs.
Engine Box.—Dimensions : 5 ft. 4 in. × 3 ft. 3 in. × 2 ft. 9 in. ; gross weight, 680 lbs.
For domestic shipment, sidewalks and engine section are crated with hull ; gross weight, 2,680 lbs.

The Curtiss M.F, Sporting type Flying Boat (100 h.p. Curtiss O.X.X. engine). (1919)

The Curtiss AT-9 "Jeep" Advanced Training Monoplane (two 280 h.p. Lycoming engines). (*Photograph by W. T. Larkins*)

THE CURTISS "JEEP."

U.S. Army Air Forces designation: AT-9.

TYPE.—Twin-engined Advanced Training monoplane.

WINGS.—Low-wing cantilever monoplane. Centre-section permanently attached to the fuselage. Tapering outer panels, which carry the engine nacelles and landing gear, bolted to centre-section through extruded match angles. Two-spar all-metal neo-geodetic construction, with top-hat section stringers and a smooth "Alclad" skin. Hydraulically-operated split trailing-edge flaps between ailerons and fuselage.

FUSELAGE.—Oval section structure built up of sheet metal rings and extruded angle skin stiffeners, the whole covered with a smooth aluminium-alloy stressed skin. Entire nose forward of the windshield is removable for servicing.

TAIL UNIT.—Cantilever monoplane type. All-metal structure similar to wings. Elevators and rudder are of all-metal construction with "Alclad" skin.

LANDING GEAR.—Retractable type. Comprises two single-strut cantilever legs with oleo-pneumatic shock-absorbers which are hinged to engine nacelle structure and swing backwards until wheels are almost completely enclosed within tails of nacelles. Fixed tail-wheel.

POWER PLANT.—Two 280 h.p. Lycoming R-680 seven-cylinder radial air-cooled engines completely enclosed in special cowling which exhausts air only at the bottom. Hamilton-Standard two-bladed constant-speed airscrews. Fuel capacity 130 U.S. gallons.

ACCOMMODATION.—Enclosed cabin seating two side-by-side with provision for two additional seats immediately behind. Door on either side of cabin. Details of equipment not available.

DIMENSIONS.—Span 40 ft. 3¼ in. (12.3 m.), Length 31 ft. 8 in. (9.65 m.), Height 9 ft. 10 in. (3 m.).

WEIGHTS AND LOADINGS.—Weight empty 4,494 lbs. (2,040 kg.). Disposable load 1,270 lbs. (576 kg.). Weight loaded 3,764 lbs. (2,616 kg.), Wing loading 24.78 lbs./sq. ft. (120.9 kg./sq. m.), Power loading 10.29 lbs./h.p. (4.67 kg./h.p.).

PERFORMANCE.—Maximum speed 200 m.p.h. (320 km.h.). Cruising speed 175 m.p.h. (280 km.h.), Landing speed 65 m.p.h. (104 km.h.). Cruising range 750 miles (1,200 km.). (1942)

CURTISS J and JN JENNY

Designed as a tandem-seat trainer by Englishman, B. Douglas Thomas, the J was bought by the Army (2) and formed the basis of the subsequent JN. The similar Curtiss N adopted modified wings (described separately). The Navy took into service one JN-1 as a gunnery trainer and two JN-1S seaplanes, while the Army acquired eight JN-2s and two JN-3s.

Massive production started with the JN-4, being ordered in thousands by the US forces from 1916 for training and observation. Early versions were the JN-4, JN-4A (350 for Army; 2 for Navy), JN-4B (73 for Army; 9 for Navy), and JN-4C. The main version was the JN-4D, built by Curtiss plus other companies. The final version was the JN-4H, which led to the development of the JN-6H bombing and gunnery trainer and observation type with the JN-4H's 150 hp Hispano-Suiza engine.

Weights.

Net weight, machine empty	..	..	1,580 lbs.
Gross weight, machine and load	..	..	2,130 lbs.
Useful load ..	..	..	..	550 lbs.
Fuel ..	..	..	..	130 lbs.
Oil ..	..	..	..	38 lbs.
Pilot..	..	..	..	165 lbs.
Passenger and other load..	..	217 lbs.
Total	..	..	550 lbs.

CURTISS MODEL J.N. 4D. 2 TRACTOR.

Specification.

General Dimensions.

Wing span, upper plane..	..	43 ft. 7⅜ in.
Wing span, lower plane ..	..	33 ft. 11¼ in.
Depth of wing chord ..	..	59¼ in.
Gap between wings ..	..	61¼ in.
Stagger	..	16 in.
Length of machine overall ..	..	27 ft. 4 in.
Height of machine overall ..	..	9 ft. 10⅝ in.
Angle of incidence ..	..	2 degrees.
Dihedral angle	..	1 degree.
Sweepback	..	0 degrees.
Wing curve	..	Eiffel No. 6.
Horizontal stabilizer—angle of incidence	..	0 degrees.

Areas.

Wings, upper ..	..	167.94 sq. ft.
Wings, lower ..	..	149.42 sq. ft.
Ailerons, upper ..	..	35.2 sq. ft.
Horizontal stabilizer ..	..	28.7 sq .ft.
Vertical stabilizer ..	..	3.8 sq. ft.
Elevators (each 11 sq. ft.) ..	..	22 sq. ft.
Rudder	..	12 sq. ft.
Total supporting surface ..	..	352.56 sq. ft.
Loading (weight carried per sq. ft. of supporting surface) ..	..	6.04 lbs.
Loading (per r.h.p.) ..	..	23·65 lbs.

The Standard type Curtiss J.N. Training Tractor. The type most used by the U.S. Army. (1919)

CURTISS MODEL J.N. TRACTOR—*continued*

Performance.

Speed, max. (horizontal flight) ..	75 m.p.h.
Speed, min. (horizontal flight) ..	45 m.p.h.
Climbing speed	3,000 ft. in 10 mins.

Motor.

Model O.X. 8-cylinder, Vee, four-stroke cycle	Water cooled.
Horse power (rated) at 1400 r.p.m.	90.
Weight per rated h.p.	4.33 lbs.
Bore and stroke	4 in. × 5 in.
Fuel consumption per hour ..	9 galls.
Fuel tank capacity	21 galls.
Oil capacity provided (crankcase) ..	4 galls.
Fuel consumption per b.h.p. ..	0.60 lbs. per hour.
Oil consumption per b.h.p. ..	0.030 lbs. per hour.

Propeller.

Material.—Wood.

Pitch.—According to requirements of performance.
Diameter.—According to requirements of performance.
Direction of rotation, viewed from pilot's seat.—Clockwise.

Details.

One gasoline tank located in fuselage.
Tail skid independent of tail post.
Landing gear wheel, size 26 in. × 4 in.
Standard Equipment.—Tachometer, oil gauge, gasoline gauge, complete set of tools.
Other equipment on special order.

Maximum Range.

At economic speed, about 250 miles.

Shipping Data.

Fuselage Box.—Dimensions: 24 ft. 6 in. × 5 ft. 3 in. × 3 ft. 1 in.; gross weight, 2,380 lbs.
Panel Box.—Dimensions: 20 ft. 9 in. × 5 ft. 8 in. × 3 ft.; gross weight, 1,450 lbs. (1919)

The "J.N." type CURTISS biplane, with ailerons integral with the upper plane, and 90 h.p. Curtiss motor. (1916)

CURTISS N-9, one of 14 used by the Army as JN-4-type single-float seaplane trainers with extended span from 1917. The Navy received 560 from 1917, remaining operational until 1926. Originally given OXX-6 engines, some later received 150 hp Hispano-Suiza As. (1918)

CURTISS N.9.

Specification.

Type of machine	Tractor Sea Biplane.
Name or type No. of machine ..	N.9.
Purpose for which intended ..	Training.
Accommodation	2 seats.
Span	53 ft. 4 in. (U), 43 ft. (L).
Overall length	29 ft. 10 in.
Total wing area	496 sq. ft.

Engine type and h.p.	100 h.p. Curtiss "OXX."
Weight empty	2,000 lbs.
Weight loaded	2,510 lbs.

Performance.

High speed	70 m.p.h.
Low speed	45 m.p.h.
Range	200 miles.

Note.—This is the standard "primary training" seaplane of the U.S. Naval Air Service. (1920)

The Curtiss O-52 "Owl" Two-seat Army Observation Monoplane (550 h.p. Pratt & Whitney "Wasp" engine).
(Photograph by Peter Bowers)

THE CURTISS "OWL."

U.S. Army Air Forces designation: O-52.

TYPE.—Two-seat Army Observation monoplane.

WINGS.—High-wing braced monoplane. Structure comprises aluminium-alloy spars and transverse members, the whole covered with a stressed flush-riveted smooth metal skin. Slots extend over full span and when slots extend flaps are automatically lowered. Ailerons have aluminium-alloy frames and fabric covering. Flaps are of all-metal construction with an "Alclad" stressed-skin covering.

FUSELAGE.—Oval monocoque structure with longerons, bulkheads and flush-riveted skin.

TAIL UNIT.—Cantilever monoplane type. Fixed surfaces have flush-riveted stressed-skin covering. Movable surfaces have metal frames and fabric covering.

LANDING GEAR.—Retractable type. Wheels are raised hydraulically into pockets in sides of fuselage. Oleo springing. Oleo-sprung non-retractable tail-wheel.

POWER PLANT.—One 550 h.p. Pratt & Whitney "Wasp" nine-cylinder radial air-cooled engine driving a three-bladed Hamilton-Standard constant-speed airscrew.

ACCOMMODATION.—Tandem enclosed cockpits. Access to pilot's cockpit by side door, to observer's cockpit by means of sliding canopy. Folding doors in bottom of fuselage between pilot and observer facilitate use of camera equipment. Dual flight controls in observer's cockpit.

ARMAMENT.—In accordance with U.S. Army Air Forces specification. Consists of one .30-cal. machine-gun in fuselage and synchronised to fire through airscrew and one .30-cal. machine-gun on flexible mounting in observer's cockpit.

DIMENSIONS.—Span 40 ft. 9½ in. (12.4 m.), Length 26 ft. 4 in. (8 m.), Height 9 ft. 3¼ in. (2.82 m.).

WEIGHTS AND LOADINGS.—Weight empty 4,231 lbs. (1,921 kg.), Disposable load 1,133 lbs. (514 kg.), Weight loaded 5,364 lbs. (2,435 kg.), Wing loading 25.5 lbs./sq. ft. (124.4 kg./sq. m.), Power loading 8.94 lbs./h.p. (4 kg./h.p.).

PERFORMANCE.—Maximum speed 220 m.p.h. (352 km.h.), Cruising speed 192 m.p.h. (307 km.h.), Landing speed 65 m.p.h. (104 km.h.), Service ceiling 21,000 ft. (6,400 m.), Cruising range 700 miles (1,120 km.). (1942)

The Curtiss P-36A Single-seat Fighter (1,100 h.p. Pratt & Whitney S3C3G engine), the U.S. Air Forces' version of the "Hawk" 75A.

THE CURTISS "HAWK" 75-A.

U.S. Army Air Forces designation : P-36A.

R.A.F. name: "Mohawk."

TYPE.—Single-seat fighter monoplane.

WINGS.—Low-wing cantilever monoplane. Structure consists of longitudinal stringers, shear beams and bulkheads of aluminium-alloy riveted to smooth "Alclad" skin. Aluminium-alloy-framed ailerons with fabric covering. Metal trailing-edge flaps between ailerons.

FUSELAGE.—Aluminium-alloy monocoque with smooth "Alclad" skin.

TAIL UNIT.—Cantilever monoplane type. Aluminium-alloy framework, fixed surfaces covered with smooth sheet, movable surfaces with fabric.

UNDERCARRIAGE.—The undercarriage, including the tail-wheel, is fully retractable by hydraulic hand-pump in the pilot's cockpit. This pump also operates the split flaps. The front portion of the landing gear hinges at a point under the main wing spar and folds back and up, the wheels rotating approximately 90 degrees to allow them to fit flat into the wings. Doors in the rear of the fuselage close the opening when the tail-wheel is retracted. This retraction operates simultaneously and by the same pump as the main landing-gear.

POWER PLANT.—One 1,200 h.p. Wright "Cyclone" R-1820-G205A radial air-cooled engine with two-speed supercharger. Curtiss three-bladed electrically-controlled constant-speed full-feathering airscrew. Normal fuel capacity 105 U.S. gallons. Overload fuel capacity 163 U.S. gallons. Normal oil capacity 7.5 U.S. gallons.

ACCOMMODATION.—Enclosed cockpit, with sliding top. Heating and ventilation. Baggage compartment.

ARMAMENT AND EQUIPMENT.—Various combinations of fuselage and wing guns of 30 cal. and 50 cal. are available, as well as light and medium bomb loads. Racks for various combinations of bomb loads may be installed flush with underside of wings. Equipment includes radio, oxygen, flare and signal pistol installation.

DIMENSIONS.—Span 37 ft. 3¼ in. (11.37 m.), Length 28 ft. 9½ in. (8.78 m.), Height 9 ft. 3 in. (2.82 m.), Wing area 236 sq. ft. (21.92 sq. m.).

WEIGHTS AND LOADINGS.—Weight empty 4,541 lbs. (2,060 kg.), Pilot 200 lbs. (91 kg.), Fuel (105 U.S. gallons = 397 litres) 630 lbs. (285.8 kg.), Oil (10 U.S. gallons = 13.8 litres) 75 lbs. (34 kg.), Fuselage guns (one .30-cal., one .50-cal. Colt) 174 lbs. (78.9 kg.), Radio receiver and transmitter 112 lbs. (50.8 kg.), Oxygen equipment 15 lbs. (6.8 kg.), Signal pistol 3 lbs. (1.4 kg.), Total disposable load 1,209 lbs. (548.4 kg.), Normal loaded weight 5,750 lbs. (2,610 kg.), Wing loading 24.3 lbs./sq. ft. (118.5 kg./sq. m.), Power loading 4.8 lbs./h.p. (2.6 kg./h.p.).

PERFORMANCE.—Maximum speed (15,100 ft. = 4,600 m. high blower gear) 323 m.p.h. (520 km.h.), Cruising speed at 15,000 ft. (4,575 m.) 262 m.p.h. (422 km.h.), Stalling speed (sea level) 69 m.p.h. (111 km.h.), Service ceiling 32,700 ft. (9,970 m.), Absolute ceiling 33,600 ft. (10,240 m.). (1941)

Curtiss P.W.8 Biplanes of the 1st Pursuit Group, U.S. Army Air Service, operating under winter conditions on skiis.

THE CURTISS PW-8 PURSUIT PLANE.

This machine, which was designed and built in 1923 and put into production early in 1924, is one of the standard service machines of the U.S. Army. It is a development of the original Curtiss 1922 pursuit plane. The outstanding achievement of this machine to date was the Atlantic to Pacific flight of Lt. Maughan, between dawn and dusk of June 20th. This flight covering 2,700 miles in 17 hours and 52 minutes flying time, with but five stops, is probably the most severe service test ever given a pursuit ship.

The PW-8 is a two-bay biplane designed around the Curtiss D-12 motor. The wings are of the multi-spar planked veneer construction developed for the Curtiss racing planes. The fuselage is a welded steel tubes truss braced with wire, and cloth covered. Most of the internal bracing is of duralumin. The tail surfaces and ailerons are of steel, cloth covered, the former being externally braced. The landing gear is of the split-axle type sprung upon rubber compression discs.

The power-plant is characterized by wing radiators, water-cooled oil cooler and hand-starting crank.

Aside from the generally excellent performance attained by this machine, it is well liked on account of its manœuvrability and its freedom from the more common maintenance difficulties. The squadron of PW-8 planes which attended the Dayton Races performed throughout with uniform reliability, and created a very favourable impression.

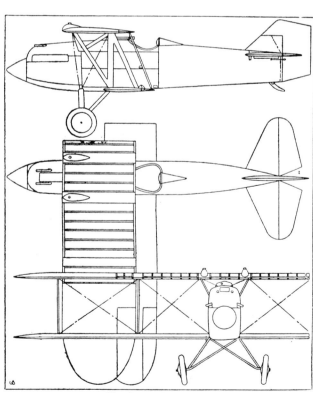

The Curtiss PW-8 (1925)

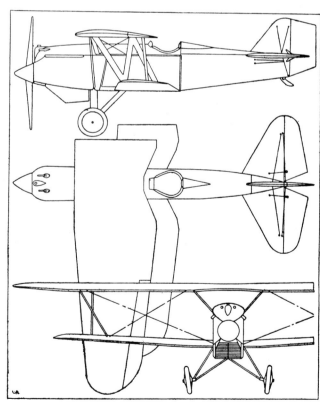

The Curtiss "Hawk" (tapered wings) (1925)

THE CURTISS "HAWK" (PW-8-A).

The most recent Curtiss pursuit plane, the "Hawk," has been built with two different wing arrangements. The first arrangement is a single-bay biplane with straight wings, using a thin, high-speed wing section. The second arrangement is also a single-bay biplane, but with tapered wings of thicker section and slightly higher lift.

The machine is characterized by pronounced stagger, which permits the pilot to have unusual vision. Two fixed Browning machine-guns fire through the propeller, the bore being 30 and 50 calibre, respectively. The military load includes parachute, pyrotechnics, and oxygen apparatus, besides ammunition for the guns. Provision is also made to carry bombs or an auxiliary fuel tank for long cross-country flights.

The straight biplane wings are of the usual Curtiss racer construction, being multi-spar planked with two-ply spruce and covered with a light cloth. The tapered wings, which taper in plan only, maintaining a similar geometrical section throughout, are of the more conventional two-spar, cloth-covered type. The two sets of wings are interchangeable.

Like the earlier Curtiss PW-8, the fuselage is a cloth-covered, welded steel-tube, Pratt truss. The seat, gun supports, etc., are of duralumin. Tail and ailerons are also of duralumin, cloth-covered. The ailerons are operated through a positive push-and-pull rod linkage, adjustable to permit of various degrees of differential or synchronous aileron motion. The tail controls, including the stabilizer adjustment, are cable operated. A split-axle chassis of usual Curtiss design is employed, the compression shock-absorbers being housed within the fuselage.

The motor, a Curtiss D-12, is carried on a semi-detachable unit, which also supports the radiator and radiator tunnel beneath, as well as the water-cooled oil-cooler, hand-starting crank and other motor equipment. Gasoline and oil are carried in the bay immediately aft of the motor, the gasoline tank being droppable in case of emergency landings in rough country, thus doing away with the fire hazzard without the excessive weight required for "crash-proof" fuel tanks. The carburettors are fed by motor-driven fuel pumps. A Curtiss-Reed duralumin propeller is used.

Due to the refinements in design and the general compactness of the machine, the "Hawk" shows a marked improvement in performance and manoeuvrability over its predecessor, the PW-8, and it is expected to show a similar improvement in field maintenance.

The PW-8A was a single modified XPW-8 prototype, and the PW-8B was the further modified PW-8A.

Specification.

PW-8-A—Straight Wings.

Span, top	30 ft. (9.14 m.).
Span, bottom	28 ft. (8.53 m.).
Length	22 ft. 2 in. (6.75 m.).
Height	8 ft. 6 in. (2.59 m.).
Wing area	254 sq. ft. (23.6 sq. m.).
Weight empty	1,986 lbs. (905 kgs.).
Weight loaded	2,800 lbs. (1,270 kgs.).
Engine	Curtiss D12, 420 h.p.
Wing loading	11.05 lbs./sq. ft. (53.8 kgs./sq. m.).
Power loading	6.67 lbs./h.p. (3.0 kgs./h.p.).
Max. speed	178 m.p.h. (287 km.h.).
Landing speed	65 m.p.h. (105 km.h.).
Climb to 12,000 ft. 3,660 m.)	10 mins.
Ceiling	23,400 ft. (7,120 m.).

PW-8-B—Tapered Wings.

Span, top	31 ft. 6 in. (9.6 m.).
Span, bottom	26 ft. (7.92 m.).
Length	22 ft. 2 in. (6.75 m.).
Height	8 ft. 6 in. (2.59 m.).
Wing area	250 sq. ft. (23.2 sq. m.).
Weight empty	1,988 lbs. (906 kgs.).
Weight loaded	2,802 lbs. (1,271 kgs.).
Engine	Curtiss D-12, 420 h.p.
Wing loading	11.2 lbs./sq. ft. (54.8 kgs./sq. m.).
Power loading	6.67 lbs./h.p. (3.0 kgs./h.p.).
Max. speed	170 m.p.h. (275 km.h.).
Landing speed	58 m.p.h. (94 km.h.).
Ceiling	24,000 ft. (7,300 m.).

(1925)

CURTISS R-2, -3, -4, -6 and D -9

R-series biplanes entered US Navy (R-3, R-6 and R-9) and US Army (R-2, R-4 and R-6) service from 1916 to 1918, undertaking a variety of roles including observation, bombing, training, scouting, and utility. Six Army R-4s became R-4LM mailplanes.

Details for R-4:—

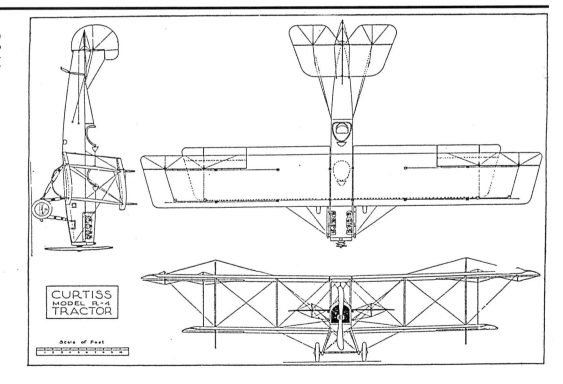

CURTISS MODEL R-4 TRACTOR

Scale of Feet

General Dimensions.

Span { Upper	48' 4"
{ Lower	38' 5"
Chord	6' 3"
Gap	6' 2"
Stagger	10¾"
Length, overall,	28' 11¾"
Height	13' 2¼"
Incidence	2½ degrees
Dehedral	3 degrees
Wing Cvrve	R.A.F. 6
Tail Plane	No incidence

Areas.

Surface (total)	505 sq. ft.
Wings (upper)	257 sq. ft.
„ (lower)	193 sq. ft.
Aileron (upper)	17 sq. ft.
„ (lower)	10¼ sq. ft.

Total Aileron Surface	54½ sq. ft.	
Tail Plane	40½ sq. ft.	
Elevators (two)	27½ sq. ft.	
Fin (vertical)	7 sq. ft.	
Rudder	16½ sq. ft.	
Load per sq. ft.	6·42 lbs.	

Other Figures.

Load per B.H.P.	15·89 lbs.
Net Weight (empty)	2225 lbs.
Gross „ (full)	3245 lbs.
Useful Load	1020 lbs.
Petrol carried	625 lbs. (90 galls.)
Speed (max.)	90 m.p.h.
„ (min.)	48 m.p.h.
Climb	4000 ft. in 10 mins.
Motor (V 2 type)	200 h.p. 8-cyl. Curtiss

(1917)

The Curtiss SOC-1 "Seagull" Two-seat Scout-Observation Biplane (550 h.p. Pratt & Whitney "Wasp" engine).

THE CURTISS SOC-1 "SEAGULL."

TYPE.—Two-seat scout-observation biplane.

WINGS.—Single-bay staggered biplane. Folding wings. "N"-type centre-section and interplane struts. Structure consists of two "I" spars, ribs, etc., all of aluminium-alloy, the whole being covered with fabric. Handley Page slots and trailing-edge flaps.

FUSELAGE.—Welded chrome-molybdenum steel-tube structure, covered forward with aluminium-alloy panels and aft with fabric. A large proportion of the fittings, especially the complicated ones, are steel forgings welded into the main structure.

TAIL UNIT.—Monoplane type. Tail-plane and fin of aluminium-alloy sheet construction, including the covering. Rudder and elevators have aluminium-alloy spars and ribs and are covered with fabric.

UNDERCARRIAGE.—Single-strut cantilever type, with tension-type oleo shock-absorbers inside the fuselage. Steel forgings at the fuselage attachment and knuckle fitting. Legs and wheels faired with aluminium-alloy casings. Mechanical brake controls. Swivelling tail-wheel with centre-lock.

FLOAT.—Single main float and wing-tip floats interchangeable with land undercarriage. Floats of riveted aluminium-alloy construction. Auxiliary fuel tank in the main float.

POWER PLANT.—One Pratt & Whitney "Wasp" radial air-cooled engine rated at 550 h.p. at 2,200 r.p.m. at 5,000 ft. (1,525 m.). Normal fuel capacity 144 U.S. gallons. Oil capacity 10 U.S. gallons. Curtiss one-piece two-bladed metal airscrew.

ACCOMMODATION.—Tandem cockpits for pilot and observer entirely enclosed by a continuous coupé top with sliding sections to provide easy access.

ARMAMENT.—One 30-cal. Browning machine-gun firing forward through the airscrew, with 500 rounds of ammunition. One 30-cal. Browning gun on flexible mounting in observer's cockpit, with 600 rounds of ammunition. Camera-gun. Racks for two 100-lb. bombs beneath lower wings. Equipment includes radio, flares, etc.

DIMENSIONS.—Span 36 ft. (10.96 m.), Width folded 12 ft. 6 in. (3.82 m.), Length 26 ft. 6 in. (80.08 m.) Landplane, 31 ft. 5 in. (9.65 m.) Seaplane, Height 13 ft. (3.99 m.) Landplane, 14 ft. 9 in. (4.49 m.) Seaplane, Wing area 342 sq. ft. (31.8 sq. m.).

WEIGHTS.—Weight empty Landplane 3,543 lbs. (1,607 kg.), Seaplane 3,788 lbs. (1,718 kg.), Pilot and observer 400 lbs. (181.5 kg.), Petrol (144 U.S. gallons) 864 lbs. (392 kg.), Oil (10 U.S. gallons) 75 lbs. (34 kg.), Fixed gun 64 lbs. (29 kg.), Flexible gun 79 lbs. (36 kg.), Pyrotechnics 4 lbs. (1.8 kg.), Radio 155 lbs. (70 kg.), Navigating equipment 8 lbs. (3.6 kg.), Useful load 1,649 lbs. (748 kg.), Weight loaded Landplane 5,192 lbs. (2,355 kg.), Seaplane 5,437 lbs. (2,466 kg.).

PERFORMANCE (Landplane).—Maximum speed at 5,000 ft. (1,525 m.) 168 m.p.h. (270 km.h.), Cruising speed 137 m.p.h. (221 km.h.), Stalling speed at sea level 56 m.p.h. (90 km.h.), Service ceiling 16,070 ft. (4,900 m.), Range at cruising speed at 5,000 ft. (1,525 m.) 697 miles (1,122 km.).

PERFORMANCE (Seaplane).—Maximum speed at 5,000 ft. (1,525 m.) 165 m.p.h. (266 km.h.), Cruising speed 133 m.p.h. (214 km.h.), Stalling speed at sea level 57 m.p.h. (92 km.h.), Service ceiling 14,900 ft. (4,540 m.), Range at cruising speed at 5,000 ft. (1,525 m.) 675 miles (1,086 km.). (1940)

The Curtiss SOC-4 Two-seat Scout-Observation Biplane (550 h.p. Pratt & Whitney "Wasp" engine).
(Photograph by Peter Bowers)

THE CURTISS SOC-4.

TYPE.—Two-seat scout-observation biplane.

WINGS.—Single-bay staggered biplane. Folding wings. "N"-type centre-section and interplane struts. Structure consists of two "I" spars, ribs, etc., all of aluminium-alloy, the whole being covered with fabric. Handley Page slots and trailing-edge flaps.

FUSELAGE.—Welded chrome-molybdenum steel-tube structure covered forward with aluminium-alloy panels and aft with fabric. A large portion of the fittings, especially the complicated ones, are steel forgings welded into the main structure.

TAIL UNIT.—Monoplane type. Tail-plane and fin of aluminium-alloy sheet construction, including the covering. Rudder and elevators have aluminium-alloy spars and ribs and are covered with fabric.

UNDERCARRIAGE.—Single-strut cantilever type, with tension-type oleo shock-absorbers inside the fuselage. Steel forgings at the fuselage attachment and knuckle fitting. Legs and wheels faired with aluminium-alloy casings. Mechanical brake controls. Swivelling tail-wheel with centre-lock.

FLOAT.—Single main float and wing-tip floats interchangeable with land undercarriage. Floats of riveted aluminium-alloy construction. Auxiliary fuel tank in the main float.

POWER PLANT.—One Pratt & Whitney "Wasp" radial air-cooled engine rated at 550 h.p. at 2,200 r.p.m. at 5,000 ft. (1,525 m.), Normal fuel capacity 144 U.S. gallons. Oil capacity 10 U.S. gallons. Curtiss one-piece two-bladed metal airscrew.

ACCOMMODATION.—Tandem cockpits for pilot and observer entirely enclosed by a continuous coupé top with sliding sections to provide easy access.

ARMAMENT.—One 30-cal. Browning machine-gun firing forward through the airscrew, with 500 rounds of ammunition. One 30-cal. Browning gun on flexible mounting in observer's cockpit, with 600 rounds of ammunition. Camera-gun. Racks for two 100-lb. bombs beneath lower wings. Equipment includes radio, flares, etc.

DIMENSIONS.—Span 36 ft. (10.96 m.), Width folded 12 ft. 6 in. (3.82 m.), Length 26 ft. 6 in. (80.08 m.), Landplane, 31 ft. 5 in. (9.65 m.) Seaplane, Height 13 ft. (3.99 m.) Landplane, 14 ft. 9 in. (4.49 m.) Seaplane, Wing area 342 sq. ft. (31.8 sq. m.).

WEIGHTS.—Weight empty Landplane 3,543 lbs. (1,607 kg.), Seaplane 3,788 lbs. (1,718 kg.), Pilot and observer 400 lbs. (181.5 kg.), Petrol (144 U.S. gallons) 864 lbs. (392 kg.), Oil (10 U.S. gallons) 75 lbs. (34 kg.), Fixed gun 64 lbs. (29 kg.), Flexible gun 79 lbs. (36 kg.), Pyrotechnics 4 lbs. (1.8 kg.), Radio 155 lbs. (70 kg.), Navigating equipment 8 lbs. (3.6 kg.), Useful load 1,649 lbs. (748 kg.), Weight loaded Landplane 5,192 lbs. (2,355 kg.), Seaplane 5,437 lbs. (2,466 kg.).

PERFORMANCE (Landplane).—Maximum speed at 5,000 ft. (1,525 m.) 168 m.p.h. (270 km.h.), Cruising speed 137 m.p.h. (221 km.h.), Stalling speed at sea level 56 m.p.h. (90 km.h.), Service ceiling 16,070 ft. (4,900 m.), Range at cruising speed at 5,000 ft. (1,525 m.) 697 miles (1,222 km.).

PERFORMANCE (Seaplane).—Maximum speed at 5,000 ft. (1,525 m.) 165 m.p.h. (266 km.h.), Cruising speed 133 m.p.h. (214 km.h.), Stalling speed at sea level 57 m.p.h. (92 km.h.), Service ceiling 14,900 ft. (4,540 m.), Range at cruising speed at 5,000 ft. (1,525 m.) 675 miles (1,086 km.).

THE CURTISS F7C-1 "SEA HAWK."

The Curtiss F7C-1 is a single-seat shipboard fighter, fitted with the 425 h.p. Pratt & Whitney "Wasp" engine. It differs in many features from the standard "Hawk," particularly with regard to arrangement of wings, undercarriage and general equipment.

The Curtiss "Sea-Hawk" (F7C-1) Single-seat Shipboard Fighter Biplane (425 h.p. Pratt & Whitney "Wasp" engine).

TYPE.—Single-seat naval shipboard fighter.

WINGS.—Unequal span staggered biplane. Top planes have 7 degrees of sweepback outside the centre-section. Bottom planes are straight. Centre-section is mounted above fuselage on widely-splayed "N" type steel-tube struts. One pair of splayed "N" type steel-tube interplane struts on either side of fuselage. Ailerons on inset hinges on top planes only. Wings of Curtiss C-72 section, of wooden construction, with spruce box spars and ribs, covered with fabric.

FUSELAGE.—Constructed of riveted steel and duralumin tubing, with steel fittings, and is designed to take catapult and deck-landing loads.

TAIL UNIT.—Normal type. Metal-framed, covered with fabric. Balanced rudder. Adjustable tail-plane.

UNDERCARRIAGE.—Split type. Consists of two Vees hinged to bottom fuselage longerons and two half-axles hinged to a Vee cabane under fuselage. Oleo shock-absorbers and hydraulic wheel-brakes, housed entirely within the wheels. The shock-absorbing medium is a combination of a two-cylinder oleo gear and rubber discs. Hydraulically operated wheel brake-shoes bear on the inner surface of the wheel rims. Entire undercarriage may be replaced by a single central float and two wing-tip floats, and the machine can be catapulted with either type of landing gear.

POWER PLANT.—One 425 h.p. Pratt & Whitney "Wasp" air-cooled radial engine. Main petrol tank, carried in fuselage, is fitted with dumping valve, to lighten machine and provide extra buoyancy in event of forced landing in the sea.

ACCOMMODATION.—Pilot's cockpit in rear of trailing-edge of top plane. Pilot's seat is provided with 11 ins. up-and-down adjustment, and rudder pedals slide back and forth in conjuncton with seat. In turtle-deck, behind cockpit, is carried a pneumatic life-raft which can be inflated in a few seconds with carbon dioxide, a bottle of which, in liquid form, is carried in same compartment. All petrol pipe lines kept outside pilot's cockpit and pressure fire-extinguisher carried in engine compartment.

THE CURTISS SEAHAWK.

U.S. Navy designation : SC-1.

The development of the Seahawk began in June, 1942, when the U.S. Navy Bureau of Aeronautics invited the Curtiss company to submit proposals for an improved scout seaplane to replace the Kingfisher and Seamew. The Curtiss proposals were submitted on August 1 and on the 25th of that month a contract was placed with the company for seven aircraft, two experimental models for flight testing and five additional aircraft for equipment and service testing.

The first XSC-1 flew on February 16, 1944, and by April 28 all seven experimental aircraft had flown. The Seahawk was developed by and is in production at the Curtiss Columbus plant.

It was first reported in action with the U.S. Fleet in the pre-invasion bombardment of Borneo in June, 1945.

TYPE.—Single-seat Shipborne Scout.

WINGS.—Low-wing cantilever monoplane. Rectangular centre-section with dihedral. Outer sections have taper and dihedral with square detachable wing-tips. Wings fold back for shipboard stowage. All-metal stressed-skin structure. Full-span automatic leading-edge slots. Slotted flaps inboard of ailerons.

FUSELAGE.—All-metal stressed-skin structure of circular section forward and changing to oval section aft.

TAIL UNIT.—Cantilever monoplane type. All-metal structure. Trim-tabs in elevators and rudder.

FLOATS.—Central single-step float on streamline pedestal mounting and two wing-tip stabilising floats on single cantilever struts. Main float accommodates bomb load or auxiliary fuel tanks. Wheel landing-gear for ferrying operations may replace float gear, the same attachments points being used for both gears. Catapult points and hook under nose of main float for net pick-up.

POWER PLANT.—One Wright R-1820-62 nine-cylinder radial air-cooled engine driving a Curtiss electrically-operated airscrew with four hollow steel paddle-type blades. Fuel tanks in centre-section. Auxiliary tanks may be carried in the main float.

ACCOMMODATION.—Pilot's cockpit over wing with sliding blister-type canopy. For sea-rescue work a bunk can be fitted in the fuselage aft of the pilot's seat into which a man can crawl.

ARMAMENT.—Two 50-cal. machine-guns in the centre-section, one on each side of the fuselage. Bombs or depth-charges may be carried in the central float, which has bomb-doors controllable from the pilot's cockpit.

DIMENSIONS.—Span 41 ft. (12.5 m.), Length 36 ft. 5 in. (11.1 m.).

WEIGHTS AND PERFORMANCE.—No data available.

The Curtiss SC-1 Seahawk Single-seat Shipborne Scout (Wright R-1820-62 engine).

The Curtiss SC-1 Seahawk Single-seat Shipborne Scout (Wright R-1820-62 engine).

The Curtiss SO3C-1 "Seamew" Scout-Observation Monoplane (520 h.p. Ranger V-770-6 engine).

THE CURTISS "SEAMEW."

U.S. Navy designation: SO3C-1 (formerly named "Seagull").
Fleet Air Arm name: "Seamew."

TYPE.—Two-seat Scout-Observation shipboard monoplane.

WINGS.—Cantilever mid-wing monoplane. Centre-section and two detachable outer sections. Outer sections taper in chord and thickness and have square upturned wing-tips. Structure of aluminium-alloy with flush-riveted smooth "Alclad" skin. Ailerons have aluminium-alloy frames and fabric covering. Split trailing-edge flaps between ailerons and fuselage.

FUSELAGE.—All-metal monocoque with flush-riveted "Alclad" stressed skin.

TAIL UNIT.—Cantilever monoplane type. Fin mounted forward of tail-plane. Single-piece elevator. Fixed surfaces of all-metal construction with metal covering. Rudder and elevator have metal frames with fabric covering. Trimming-tabs in control surfaces.

LANDING GEAR.—Single-strut cantilever type landing gear with wheels and struts fully encased in aluminium-alloy fairings. Curtiss oleo shock-absorbers. Wheel landing gear may be replaced by large single-step metal float which is attached to the fuselage by a single cantilever strut. Wing-tip floats are also mounted on single cantilever struts.

POWER PLANT.—One 520 h.p. Ranger V-770-6 twelve-cylinder inverted Vee air-cooled engine. Two-bladed Hamilton-Standard Hydromatic constant-speed airscrew.

ACCOMMODATION.—Tandem enclosed cockpits, that for pilot being in line with leading-edge with the observer's cockpit aft of the trailing-edge.

ARMAMENT.—Standard observation armament conforming to U.S. Navy requirements.

DIMENSIONS.—Span 38 ft. (11.6 m.), Length (Landplane) 34 ft. 2 in. (10.4 m.), Length (Seaplane) 36 ft. 10 in. (11.25 m.), Height (Landplane) 11 ft. 5 in. (3.47 m.), Height (Seaplane) 15 ft. (4.57 m.), Wing area 290 sq. ft. (26.9 sq. m.).

WEIGHTS AND PERFORMANCE.—No data available.   (1943–44)

The Curtiss A-8 ''Shrike'' Two-seat Attack Monoplane (600 h.p. Curtiss ''Conqueror'' engine).

THE CURTISS A-8 ''SHRIKE.''

TYPE.—Two-seat military attack monoplane.

WINGS.—Low-wing wire-braced monoplane, with slots and flaps. Entire wing of metal construction. Box-type spars made up of corrugated duralumin sections. Duralumin stressed-skin covering.

FUSELAGE.—Oval-sectioned structure, of all-metal construction. Welded steel tubing structure to station 5 and monocoque construction aft to rudder-post.

TAIL UNIT.—Cantilever monoplane. Overhung type rudder balance and modified ''Frise'' elevator balance. All-metal construction. Tail-plane adjustable in flight. Fin adjustable on ground.

UNDERCARRIAGE.—Divided type. Oleo and spring shock-absorbers. Wheels fitted with Bendix brakes and wheel fairings. Prior to take-off. wheels can be locked in ''up'' position limited by travel of oleo. Steerable tail-wheel.

POWER PLANT.—One 600 h.p. Curtiss ''Conqueror'' Prestone-cooled engine, on detachable welded steel-tube mounting. The radiator is beneath the fuselage, just forward of the landing gear. The main fuel tank, having a capacity of 104 U.S. gallons, is located in the fuselage, and a 52 U.S. gallons capacity, dirigible type, droppable auxiliary fuel tank is located beneath the fuselage. Cruising range

with both tanks full is 715 miles. The oil tank, of 10 U.S. gallons capacity, is located on the right-hand side of the fuselage, just aft of the firewall, and is shaped to fair in with the fuselage cowling. Air circulates around all sides of the tank for cooling purposes, in addition to which core-type oil-coolers are used. Detachable-blade duralumin airscrew. ''Eclipse'' hand electric inertia starter.

ACCOMMODATION.—Tandem cockpits for pilot and gunner. The pilot's cockpit is provided with a cabin and the gunner's cockpit is provided with a sliding semi-cabin. Four Browning fixed guns, two in each side of landing gear, with a total of 2,400 rounds of ammunition, are provided. The flexible gun over the rear cockpit is mounted on a track and is provided with 600 rounds of ammunition. Bomb-racks inside and beneath the fuselage permit carrying 488 lbs. of bombs. Dual controls are provided. Ailerons operated by positive push-pull rods ; elevators operated by push-pull rod and cable controls ; rudder operated by cables. Navigation lights, cockpit lights and indirect lighting on pilot's instrument board. Provision for carrying two parachute flares.

DIMENSIONS.—Span 44 ft. (13.42 m.), Length overall 32 ft. (9.75 m.), Height 9 ft. (2.74 m.), Wing area 256 sq. ft. (23.7 sq m.). (1933)

The Curtiss A-12 ''Shrike'' Two-seat Attack Monoplane (750 h.p. Wright ''Cyclone'' engine).   (1936)

THE CURTISS A-12 ''SHRIKE.''

TYPE.—Two-seat attack monoplane.

WINGS.—Low-wing wire-braced monoplane, with slots and flaps. Entire wing of metal construction. Box-type spars made up of corrugated duralumin sections. Duralumin stressed-skin covering.

FUSELAGE.—Oval-sectioned structure, of all-metal construction. Welded steel tubing structure to bulkhead 5 and monocoque construction aft to rudder-post.

TAIL UNIT.—Cantilever monoplane. Rudder has overhang-type balance. Elevators have Handley Page type balance. All-metal construction. Tail-plane adjustable in flight. Fin adjustable on ground.

UNDERCARRIAGE.—Divided type. Oleo and spring shock-absorbers. Wheels fitted with Bendix brakes and wheel fairings. Prior to take-off, wheels can be locked in ''up'' position, limited by travel of oleo. Steerable tail-wheel.

POWER PLANT.—One Wright ''Cyclone'' SR-1820F-52 nine-cylinder radial air-cooled engine, rated at 775 h.p. at 2,100 r.p.m. at 6,800 ft., mounted in rubber and on a detachable welded steel-tube mounting. The main fuel tank (114 U.S. gallons) located in the fuselage, streamline auxiliary fuel tank (52 U.S. gallons) located beneath the fuselage. The main and auxiliary tanks are droppable. The oil tank (12 U.S. gallons) in engine compartment. Fuel and oil tanks are mounted in rubber. Core-type oil-cooler. Adjustable-pitch duralumin airscrew. Curtiss cowling ring. ''Eclipse'' electric inertia-starter.

ACCOMMODATION.—Tandem cockpits for pilot and gunner. The pilot's cockpit is provided with a cabin and the gunner's cockpit

is provided with a sliding semi-cabin. Four Browning fixed guns, two in each side of landing gear, with a total of 2,400 rounds of ammunition, are provided. The flexible gun over the rear cockpit is mounted on a track and is provided with 600 rounds of ammunition. Bomb-racks inside and beneath the fuselage permit carrying 488 lbs. of bombs. Dual controls are provided. Ailerons operated by positive push-pull rods ; elevators operated by push-pull rod and cable controls ; rudder operated by cables. Navigation lights, cockpit lights and indirect lighting on pilot's instrument board. Provision for carrying two parachute flares.

DIMENSIONS.—Span 44 ft. (13.42 m.), Length overall 31 ft. 6 in. (9.6 m.), Height 9 ft. 4½ in. (2.86 m.), Wing area (including ailerons) 285 sq. ft. (26.41 sq. m.).

WEIGHTS.—Weight empty 4,025 lbs. (1,825.3 kg.), Pilot, observer and parachutes 400 lbs. (181.4 kg.), Petrol (114 U.S. gallons) 684 lbs. (310.3 kg.), Bombs 300 lbs. (136.1 kg.), Oil (8 U.S. gallons) 60 lbs. (27.2 kg.), Fixed gun and ammunition 258 lbs. (117.0 kg.), Flexible gun and ammunition 87 lbs. (39.5 kg.), Pyrotechnics 38 lbs. (17.2 kg.), Camera equipment 74 lbs. (33.6 kg.), Useful load 1,901 lbs. (862.3 kg.), Weight loaded 5,925 lbs. (2,687.6 kg.).

PERFORMANCE.—Maximum speed at 6,800 ft. (2,070 m.) 202 m.p.h. (325 km.h.), Cruising speed at 6,800 ft. (2,070 m.) 171 m.p.h. (275.2 km.h.), Maximum speed at 16,400 ft. (5,000 m.) 183.5 m.p.h. (295.3 km.h.), Maximum speed at sea level 182.3 m.p.h. (293.5 km.h.), Stalling speed at sea level 67.9 m.p.h. (109.2 km.h.), Service ceiling 20,790 ft. (6,310 m.), Absolute ceiling 21,950 ft. (6,690 m.), Range at cruising speed at 6,800 ft. (2,070 m.) 481.5 miles (775 km.).

The Curtiss 76-D (A-18) Two-seat Attack Monoplane (two 850 h.p. Wright "Cyclone" engines).

THE CURTISS 76-D (A-18).

TYPE.—Two-seat twin-engined Attack monoplane.

WINGS.—Mid-wing cantilever monoplane consisting of centre-section and two detachable outer sections. Ailerons are installed on the outer panels and flaps on both outer panels and centre panels. The centre-section of aluminium-alloy construction using three main spars with metal ribs and covering. Outer sections taper in chord and thickness from the root to the tip and are of aluminium-alloy monospar construction. Metal-covering from the leading-edge to single spar aft of the main beam. Fabric-covering over aluminium-alloy ribs to trailing-edge. Split flaps between ailerons and under fuselage.

FUSELAGE.—All-metal semi-monocoque construction with "Alclad" aluminium-alloy stressed skin. In three sections which may be dismantled for shipment or major repair.

TAIL UNIT.—Cantilever monoplane type. Fin and tail-plane of stressed-skin construction with "Alclad" covering. The elevators and rudder are aluminium-alloy structures with fabric-covered trimming-tabs controlled from the pilot's cockpit.

UNDERCARRIAGE.—The undercarriage and tail-wheel retract by means of an electrically-driven pump operating hydraulic struts with automatic integral locks. This same system also actuates the flaps which can be operated simultaneously with the landing-gear.

POWER PLANT.—Two 850 h.p. Wright "Cyclone" BR-1820-G3 nine-cylinder radial air-cooled engines on steel-tube mountings at extremities of centre-section. Curtiss automatic full-feathering airscrews. Fuel carried in five tanks with a total normal capacity of 291 U.S. gallons (1,105 litres). Over-load capacity 639 U.S. gallons (2,419 litres). Normal oil capacity 13 U.S. gallons (49 litres) in each of two tanks. Overload oil capacity 28 U.S. gallons (106 litres).

ACCOMMODATION.—Front and rear cockpits are completely enclosed with sliding canopies. Each cockpit is provided with an emergency release panel. A retractable deck is provided in the rear cockpit to allow free movement of the flexible gun. Flying controls in both cockpits.

ARMAMENT AND EQUIPMENT.—Normal armament includes four fixed .30-cal. machine-guns mounted in the nose of the fuselage and one flexible gun mounted on a track in the rear cockpit. Wing-guns or guns of heavier calibre may also be installed. A rack is provided in the fuselage to carry 20 chemical or fragmentation bombs. Racks in each side of the centre-section outboard of the fuselage carry two 100-lb. bombs. Additional equipment includes flares and signal pistol installation.

DIMENSIONS.—Wings pan 59 ft. 6 in. (18.13 m.), Length over all 41 ft. (12.5 m.), Height 11 ft. 6 in. (3.5 m.), Tread (landing gear) 14 ft. (4.27 m.).

WEIGHTS.—Weight empty 9,388 lbs. (4,258.3 kg.), Crew (2) 400 lbs. (181.4 kg.), Fuel (291 U.S. gallons = 1,101 litres) 1,746 lbs. (792.0 kg.), Oil (26 U.S. gallons = 96.4 litres) 195 lbs. (88.5 kg.), Fixed guns (nose) 263 lbs. (107 kg.), Flexible gun 116 lbs. (52.6 kg.), Bombs 600 lbs. (272.2 kg.), Radio equipment 112 lbs. (50.8 kg.), Total useful load 3,405 lbs. (1,544.5 kg.), Weight loaded 12,793 lbs. (5,302.8 kg.).

PERFORMANCE.—Maximum speed at 10,200 ft. (3,100 m.) 266 m.p.h. (428 km.h.), Cruising speed at 10,200 ft. (3,100 m.) 224 m.p.h. (360 km.h.), Stalling speed at sea level 72 m.p.h. (116 km.h.), Service ceiling 30,900 ft. (9,120 m.), Normal cruising range at critical altitude 744 miles (1,200 km.), Maximum cruising range at critical altitude 1,600 miles (2,575 km.). (1940)

The Curtiss F9C-2 "Sparrowhawk" Single-seat Airship Fighter (420 h.p. Wright "Whirlwind" engine).

THE CURTISS F9C-2 "SPARROWHAWK."

TYPE.—Single-seat light shipboard fighter, built for the U.S. Navy.

WINGS.—Single-bay staggered biplane. Wings are of the "gull" type, attaching directly to the fuselage and faired into it. Upper wings have 3 degrees of dihedral, lower wings are flat. One set of "N" type steel-tube interplane struts on each side of fuselage. Wings are of Clark "YH" airfoil section. The structure is of all-metal construction, fabric covered. There are two spars made from oval duralumin tubes, ribs of stamped duralumin sheet, drag-struts of duralumin tubes with steel end-fittings. Ailerons are on upper wings only and have "Frise" type balance. There are no interplane aileron operating struts. Ailerons have duralumin skeleton and fabric covering.

FUSELAGE.—A duralumin monocoque of excellent streamline form. It is elliptical in cross-section, fairing into a circular section at the nose, to conform to the radial engine-cowling.

TAIL UNIT.—Normal monoplane type. All surfaces are cantilever and are of all-duralumin construction, with smooth duralumin skin. The rudder is balanced. The tail-plane is not adjustable, but the elevator control incorporates an adjustable rubber cord, which holds the elevators in the proper position to trim the aeroplane in any flight attitude.

UNDERCARRIAGE.—Single-strut type. Oleo and spring shock-absorbers. Bendix wheels and brakes.

POWER PLANT.—One Wright "Whirlwind" Model R-975-E nine-cylinder radial air-cooled engine, rated at 420 h.p. at 2,200 r.p.m., attached to ring-type engine-mounting of tubular construction. One 60 U.S. gallons fuel tank mounted in fuselage, giving a cruising range of 420 miles. Oil tank is located forward of firewall and has a capacity of 4.8 U.S. gallons. Detachable-blade duralumin airscrew. Hand-inertia starter.

ACCOMMODATION.—Pilot's cockpit behind wings. Controls consist of control column and rudder-pedals. Ailerons operated by push-rods in fuselage and torque shafts out through upper wings. Rudder and elevators operated by cables. Rudder-pedals are adjustable. Armament consists of two 30-calibre synchronised guns in fuselage. 1,200 rounds ammunition (78 lbs.). Equipment includes arresting gear, special airship hook, emergency flotation bags in wings inflated by carbon dioxide, wiring and provision for aerial and for installation of wireless.

DIMENSIONS.—Span 25 ft. 6 in. (7.7 m.), Length overall 19 ft. 5 in. (5.9 m.), Height 7 ft. 1 in. (2.1 m.), Wing area (without ailerons) 153.9 sq. ft. (14.3 sq. m.), Area of ailerons 18.9 sq. ft. (1.75 sq. m.).

WEIGHTS AND LOADINGS.—Weight empty 2,090 lbs. (950 kg.), Special Military equipment 57 lbs. (25.9 kg.), Crew 180 lbs. (82 kg.), Fuel and oil (for 300 miles' range) 284 lbs. (129 kg.), Armament (military useful load) 141 lbs. (64 kg.), Total disposable load 662 lbs. (300 kg.), Weight loaded 2,752 lbs. (1,250 kg.), Wing loading 15.9 lbs./sq. ft. (77.2 kg./sq. m.), Power loading 6.6 lbs./h.p. (2.9 kg./h.p.).

PERFORMANCE. Maximum speed 176 mph (283 km/h). Service ceiling 19,200 ft (5,850). Range 350 miles (563 km). (1934)

The Curtiss P-40K-1 Warhawk Single-seat Fighter with modified fin introduced before the fuselage was lengthened in later models. (*Photograph by Peter Bowers*).

THE CURTISS WARHAWK.
U.S. Army Air Forces designation : P-40.
British names : Tomahawk and Kittyhawk.

The Curtiss Warhawk went into production in the Summer of 1939 and from then until December, 1944, when the Warhawk was withdrawn from production, it has been the subject of continuous development and has served in the Air Forces of the Allies in practically every theatre of war. In all, the Warhawk has worn the insignia of twenty-eight Allied and friendly nations.

On November 22, 1944, the Curtiss Airplane Division delivered to the Army Air Forces the 15,000th fighter built for service in the present war. This aeroplane was a P-40N Warhawk.

Hereafter follows a brief outline of the development of the Warhawk.

XP-40. The prototype, evolved from the radial-engined P-36A by the installation of the Allison V-1710-19 (C-13) engine, the first altitude-rated Allison with built-in supercharger, and a liquid-cooling system with the radiator mounted under the fuselage aft of the trailing-edge of the wings. Standard P-36 wings, fuselage, tail-unit and landing-gear. Won a U.S. Army Pursuit Competition at Wright Field, Dayton, Ohio, in 1939, as the result of which the largest peacetime order for fighter aircraft, valued at nearly $13,000,000, was placed for the P-40.

P-40 (Tomahawk I, IA and IB). Fitted with the Allison V-1710-33 (C15) engine. Considerably revised in structure of both wings and fuselage and stressed to take the increased horse-power of the new engine. Landing-gear and other structural members strengthened to take care of the increased gross weight. Radiators moved forward under the nose. Armament consisted of two 50 cal. machine-guns in the engine cowling and two 30 cal. guns, one in each wing. The Tomahawk I had British .303 in. machine-guns and equipment.

P-40B (Tomahawk IIA and IIB). Same as P-40 but fitted with pilot armour, bulletproof windscreen and leakproof fuel tanks. Wing armament increased to four 30 cal. guns, two in each wing. The Tomahawk II retained the U.S. armament, the IIA having British radio and the IIB American radio.

P-40C. Same as the P-40B but fitted with improved self-sealing tanks.

P-40D (Kittyhawk I). Fitted with the Allison V-1710-39 (F3R) engine, which differed from the V-1710-33 by having an external spur airscrew reduction gear. This resulted in a shorter reduction gear casing and a higher airscrew thrust-line which, in turn, permitted the fuselage to be shortened by 6 in., the cross-section to be reduced, the cowling to be redesigned and the landing-gear to be reduced in height. The synchronised fuselage guns were abandoned, the entire armament of four 50 cal. guns being mounted in the wings. Shackles under the fuselage for a 52 U.S. gallon drop tank or a 300-500 lb. bomb. Racks under the outer wings for six 20 lb. bombs.

P-40E (Kittyhawk IA). Similar to the P-40D but fitted with six 50 cal. guns, three in each wing. A few P-40E's were converted into two-seat trainers by having the fuselage fuel tank removed and a second seat and dual controls added.

P-40F (Kittyhawk II). The P-40F was the first in the P-40 Series to be fitted with the Packard V-1650-1 (Rolls-Royce Merlin 28 engine) engine rated at 1,240 h.p. at 11,500 ft. (3,510 m.), 1,120 h.p. at 18,500 ft. (5,640 m.) and with 1,300 h.p. available for take-off. With this engine the air intake was removed from the top of the cowling and incorporated in the cooling scoop beneath the engine. Armament consisted of six 50 cal. machine-guns, three in each wing, with 235 rounds per gun. A rack under the fuselage could accommodate an auxiliary fuel tank (75 U.S. gallons) or a single bomb (100 to 600 lbs.). Racks for three light fragmentation or practice bombs mounted under each wing outboard of the guns. Later models of the F had a lengthened fuselage. This moved the rudder hinge aft of the elevator hinges and gave increased manoeuvrability and improved control characteristics.

P-40G. The same as the P-40 except fitted with pilot armour, self-sealing fuel tanks, bullet-proof windscreen and P-40B wings and wing armament.

P-40K (Kittyhawk III). Fitted with the Allison V-1710-73 (F4R) engine, rated at 1,150 h.p. at 12,000 ft. (3,660 m.) and with 1,325 h.p. available for take-off. This model ran through the production lines simultaneously with the P-40F and as with that version the longer fuselage was introduced in the later models. Later P-40K's were winterised and many saw service in Alaska and the Aleutians.

P-40L (Kittyhawk II). Fitted with the Packard V-1650-1 (Merlin 28) engine. A development of the P-40F but much lighter. Saving in weight achieved by the elimination of head armour and the removal of the Prestone tank and the front portions of the multiple wing fuel tanks. All had the long fuselage.

P-40M (Kittyhawk III and IV). Fitted with the Allison V-1710-81 (F20R) engine rated at 1,000 h.p. at 16,400 ft. (5,000 m.) and with 1,200 h.p. available for take-off. A development of the P-40L.

P-40N (Kittyhawk III). Fitted successively with the Allison V-1710-81 (F20R), V-1710-99 (F26R) and V-1710-115 (F31R) engine. A further development of the P-40L. The first production models were further lightened by the removal of two of the six machine-guns, and smaller and lighter landing wheels and aluminium radiators and oil coolers were installed. The head armour, however, was reintroduced, together with improved rear vision panels. After the first few hundred had come off the production lines the two machine-guns and the front portions of the wing multiple fuel tanks were reinstated. In 1943 the P-40N was fitted with two additional bomb racks under the

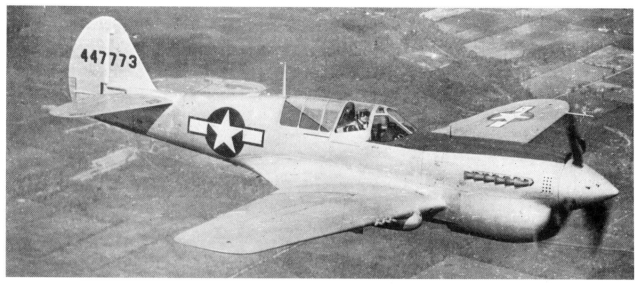

The Curtiss P-40N-40 Warhawk Single-seat Fighter (Allison V-1710-115 engine).

wings, each capable of carrying a bomb of from 100 to 500 lbs. or a droppable "ferry" tank. Other new features included improved non-metallic self-sealing fuel tanks, new radio and oxygen equipment, flame-damping exhaust stacks, etc.

XP-40Q. Fitted with the Allison V-1710-121 engine. A greatly cleaned-up version of the Warhawk. Re-designed fuselage with the coolant radiators removed to the wings, "blister" type sliding cockpit hood and a shallower rear fuselage. Clipped wings with squared tips. The Allison engine fitted with water-injection and driving a four-blade airscrew. Only one built.

P-40R. Several hundred P-40F and P-40L Warhawks were modified by having their Merlin engines replaced by the Allison V-1710-81 (F20R) engine. This conversion was given the designation P-40R. All had the lengthened fuselage.

TYPE.—Single-seat Fighter and Fighter-Bomber.

WINGS.—Low-wing cantilever monoplane. Aerofoil section NACA 2215 at root, 2209 at tip. Wing in two panels joined at the centre-line of the fuselage. Structure consists of longitudinal stringers and shear beams of aluminium-alloy, Alclad bulkheads and flush-riveted Alclad skin. Ailerons have Alclad frames and fabric covering. Hydraulically-operated split trailing-edge flaps extend between ailerons and fuselage.

FUSELAGE.—Semi-monocoque structure made up of Alclad bulkheads, aluminium-alloy stringers and a flush-riveted Alclad skin.

TAIL UNIT.—Cantilever monoplane type. All-metal framework. Fixed surfaces have smooth metal covering, movable surfaces covered with fabric. Adjustable trim-tabs in rudder and elevators.

LANDING GEAR.—Retractable type. Curtiss oleo-pneumatic shock-absorber legs and wheels are retracted hydraulically aft and up, rotating about bevel gears until the wheels in raised position lie flush within the wing. In both lowered and retracted positions landing-gear main wheels are automatically locked by hydraulically-operated mechanical locks. Fully-retractable steerable tail-wheel has positive-action hinged fairing which smoothly cover the aperture after the wheel is retracted.

POWER PLANT.—One Allison V-1710 or Packard V-1650-1 (Merlin 28) twelve-cylinder Vee liquid-cooled engine driving a three-bladed Curtiss electrically-controlled multi-position constant-speed airscrew. Ducted coolant and oil radiators beneath engine with controllable air exit. Fuel carried in two wing tanks, a fuselage tank and an auxiliary "belly" tank. Each wing tank and the fuselage tank consists of a multiple self-sealing fuel cell contained in an aluminium-alloy shell. Auxiliary tank carried on bomb-rack beneath the fuselage. Oil system incorporates provision for oil dilution for cold weather starting.

ACCOMMODATION.—Enclosed pilot's cockpit over trailing-edge of wing. Bullet-proof windscreen with glycol spray and warm air de-frosting. Sliding cockpit cover with rear vision side panels in fuselage aft of cockpit. Armour plate forward of the instrument panel and aft of the pilot's seat and head. Cockpit heating and ventilating system. Heat may also be ducted to gun compartments in wings. 24-volt electrical system. Radio equipment.

ARMAMENT.—Three .50-cal. machine-guns in each wing and firing outside the airscrew disc. 235 rounds of ammunition per gun. Bomb rack beneath fuselage may carry a single bomb ranging from 100 to 600 lbs. Racks under wing to carry two 100-500 lb. bombs or two auxiliary "belly" fuel tanks.

DIMENSIONS.—Span 37 ft. 3½ in. (11.36 m.), Length (short fuselage) 31 ft. 8¾ in. (9.68 m.), Length (long fuselage) 33 ft. 3¾ in. (10.14 m.), Height (thrust-line horizontal) 12 ft. 2 in. (3.7 m.), Wing area 236 sq. ft. (21.9 sq. m.).

WEIGHTS (P-40F).—Weight empty 6,550 lbs. (2,974 kg.), Weight loaded 8,720 lbs. (3,960 kg.).

PERFORMANCE (P-40F—Packard V-1650-1 engine).—Maximum speed 364 m.p.h. (582 km.h.) at 20,000 ft. (6,100 m.), Cruising speed 300 m.p.h. (480 km.h.) at critical height, Economical cruising speed 220-245 m.p.h. (352-392 km.h.) according to mission, Climb to 15,000 ft. (4,575 m.) 7.5 mins., Climb to 20,000 ft. (6,100 m.) 10 mins. Service ceiling 33,000 ft. (10,060 m.), Normal range 610 miles (976 km.) at 310 m.p.h. (496 km.h.), Maximum range (with auxiliary fuel tank) 1,200 miles (1,920 km.) at 210 m.p.h. (336 km.h.).

(1945-46)

THE CURTISS-NAVY CS.

The CS machines were designed by the Curtiss Company and the U.S. Navy, the first machine being completed by the Curtiss Company late in 1923. The CS-1 aeroplane is powered with a Wright T-2 525 h.p. engine, while the CS-2 uses a Wright T-3 600 h.p. engine. Both machines are convertible from a land plane with a wide tread, split-axle type landing gear, to a twin-float seaplane. In addition, each plane is designed to fill the triple purpose of torpedo carrying, bombing and scouting. In its first capacity, the plane carries its torpedo under the fuselage in a specially cowled recess. When bombing, the torpedo is replaced by the bomb load. For long range scouting, the wider cowling is removed and special auxiliary fuel tanks fitted in its place.

The wings are single-bay of conventional wood and cloth construction. They are made to fold back for storage. For this reason, diagonal braces are run out to the lower wings from the top of the fuselage. The juncture of these braces and the wing beams serve as attachment points for landing gear or floats. The elevator and rudder are of metal construction, and

the rudder is balanced by extending the leading edge forward of the hinge-point. The stabilizer and fin, which are of unusually thick section, are externally braced.

The fuselage is made entirely of steel tubing braced with wire. The joints are reinforced by sleeve fittings brazed screwed to the members. The engine mount is detachable. The main fuel and oil tanks are carried between the engine fire-wall and the pilot. Cooling is by a core radiator on either side of the fuselage. However, the arrangement of fuel tanks and cooling system has been varied considerably on different machines. All of the CS-2 planes have four fuel tanks in the centre-section of the upper wing, in addition to the tanks slung beneath the fuselage in place of the torpedo.

The CS planes are remarkable in that they serve so many purposes so well. Their general ruggedness has been proved by extensive flying, while their high performance has been amply attested by the record-breaking duration flights of Lts. Weed and Price. (1925)

The Curtiss Navy CS (Wright T-2 engine), with wing radiators. (1925)

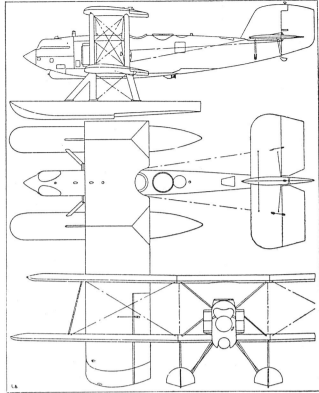

The Curtiss CS as a Seaplane. (1925)

Specification.

		Seaplane.	Land Machine.
Span, top	.. ..	52 ft. 3 in. (15.9 m.).	
Span, bottom	.. .. ..	56 ft. 6 in. (17.24 m.).	
Length (seaplane)	.. .. ..	40 ft. 3 in. (12.25 m.).	
Length (land machine)	.. ..	38 ft. 5 in. (11.7 m.).	
Wing area	.. ..	856 sq. ft. (79.5 sq. m.).	
Engine	.. ..	Wright T-2, 520 h.p.	
Weight empty		5,390 lbs. (2,460 kgs.).	4,690 lbs. (2,135 kgs.).
Weight loaded		8,670 lbs. (3,940 kgs.).	7,908 lbs. (3,590 kgs.).
Wing loading		10.1 lbs./sq. ft. (49.7 kgs./sq. m.).	9.2 lbs./sq. ft. (45.2 kgs./sq. m.).
Power loading		16.6 lbs./h.p. (7.58 kgs./h.p.).	15.2 lbs./h.p. (6.9 kgs./h.p.).
Max. speed		102 m.p.h. (165 km.h.).	105 m.p.h. (170 km.h.).
Ceiling		7,200 ft. (2,200 m.).	9,300 ft. (2,840 m.).

THE CURTISS-WRIGHT "CONDOR" TRANSPORT.

The "Condor" Transport is produced in two versions, as a standard passenger transport for normal day-time flying, and as a convertible day-and-night transport. In the latter version the machine was designed basically as a "sleeper" with six compartments each accommodating two sleeping berths convertible into two seats. The US Navy received 10 in 1934 as R4C transports.

TYPE.—Twin-engined fifteen-passenger commercial biplane.

WINGS.—Unequal-span biplane. Upper centre-section carried above fuselage by single pair of struts at centre-line, with two "N"-struts at extremities running down to outer ends of two lower wing-stubs. One pair of slightly splayed-out interplane struts to each outer wing-section. Metal wing-structure of normal two-spar type, with duralumin ribs at 10-inch intervals. Long narrow-chord ailerons on entire trailing-edges of upper wing outer sections only.

FUSELAGE.—Rectangular structure of welded chrome-molybdenum steel tubing, faired to streamline section and covered with fabric.

TAIL UNIT.—Normal monoplane type. Metal frame, covered with fabric. Adjustable tail-plane.

UNDERCARRIAGE.—Two separate retractable units. Each unit a tripod, one leg of which is an oleo shock-absorber leg. This leg and sloping axle is hinged to the extremity of lower wing-stub and lower fuselage longeron respectively. Unit swings back and up until only lower portion of wheel protrudes through lower surface of engine nacelle. Electrical operation with emergency hand-lever. Swivelling tail-wheel.

POWER PLANT.—Two Wright "Cyclone" R-1820F nine-cylinder geared air-cooled engines, either of F-2 model developing 720 h.p. at 4,000 ft. (1,220 m.), or of F-3 model developing 710 h.p. at 7,000 ft. (2,135 m.), mounted in nacelles at extremities of lower wing-stubs. Townend-type cowling rings. Four fuel tanks (300 U.S. gallons total capacity) in upper centre-section, with gravity feed to engines.

ACCOMMODATION.—Pilot's compartment in nose of fuselage, with dual controls. Control wheels mounted on central column, and engine control-unit between seats. Adjustable seats and rudder-pedals. Wireless apparatus behind pilots' seats. Openable side windows and emergency exit in roof. Aft of bulkhead is main cabin which, in standard model, has seats for fifteen passengers, three abreast, with gangway between second and third seats. In sleeper model cabin is divided by transverse partitions giving three compartments on each side of a central gangway. Each compartment has two seats and for night flying may be converted into sleeping compartment with two bunks. Toilet, wash rooms with running water, etc., at aft end of cabin. Mail and baggage in compartment below cabin floor. Controlled ventilating and heating. Full night-flying and wireless equipment.

DIMENSIONS.—Span 82 ft. (25 m.), Length 48 ft. 7 in. (14.8 m.), Height 16 ft. 4 in. (5 m.), Wing area 1,208 sq. ft. (122.2 sq. m.).

WEIGHTS.—Weight empty 11,465 lbs. (5,192 kg.), Crew 510 lbs. (231 kg.), Fuel and oil 2,325 lbs. (1,054 kg.), Passengers 2,550 lbs. (1,157 kg.), Mail 200 lbs. (91 kg.), Total pay load 3,200 lbs. (1,451 kg.), Weight loaded 17,500 lbs. (7,937 kg.).

WEIGHTS (Sleeper model).—Weight empty 12,235 lbs. (5,540 kg.), Crew 340 lbs. (154 kg.), Fuel and oil 2,325 lbs. (1,054 kg.), Passengers 2,040 lbs. (923 kg.), Baggage 360 lbs. (163 kg.), Mail 200 lbs. (91 kg.), Total pay load 2,600 lbs. (1,178 kg.), Weight loaded 17,500 lbs. (7,937 kg.).

PERFORMANCE.—Maximum speed 190 m.p.h. (306 km.h.), Cruising speed 167 m.p.h. (269 km.h.), Initial rate of climb 1200 ft./min. (366 m./min.), Service ceiling 23,000 ft. (7,010 m.), Absolute ceiling 25,000 ft. (7,620 m.), Range at cruising speed 716 miles (1152 km.).

(1935)

DASSAULT MYSTÈRE-FALCON 20 SERIES G

US Coast Guard designation: HU-25A Guardian

When Dassault-Breguet released preliminary details of the Garrett-engined version of its Mystère-Falcon 20 twin-turbofan business jet in the late Spring of 1976, it stated that the new power plant, complete with nacelles and thrust reversers, would be offered initially as a retrofit for existing aircraft, with full production of the new model, designated Mystère-Falcon 20G, scheduled for a later date.

A further statement, in the Autumn of 1976, announced that a tender by Falcon Jet Corporation, distributor and support centre for Falcons in the USA, had proved the lowest bid to meet a US Coast Guard requirement for a medium-range surveillance aircraft known by the project designation HX-XX. This was confirmed on 5 January 1977, when William T. Coleman Jr, then US Secretary of Transportation, authorised the Coast Guard to award a contract for 41 aircraft to Falcon Jet Corporation.

A prototype (F-WATF) flew for the first time on 28 November 1977, and was the 362nd Mystère-Falcon 20 to be completed. Production aircraft are expected to have 44 per cent French content and 56 per cent US content.

The 41 Falcon 20Gs ordered by the US Coast Guard, as **HU-25As**, are to be delivered at the rate of about one a month, from early 1981. In choosing the type to meet its HX-XX requirement, the Coast Guard had expressed a preference for a turbofan-powered aircraft, with a minimum cabin/cockpit volume of 17 m³ (600 cu ft), able to perform the full range of MRS (medium-range surveillance) missions. These were listed as search and rescue (28.5% of total flight hours), marine environmental protection (30.3%), enforcement of laws and treaties (18.9%), marine science activities (10.6%), logistics support (5.4%), engineering support (3.8%), domestic icebreaking (1.7%) and short-range aids to navigation (0.8%).

The basic airframe of the HU-25A is little changed from that of the Mystère-Falcon 20F. The most significant new features are as follows:

AIRFRAME: Fuselage is modified to embody a drop hatch, and one search window on each side. Four hardpoints under fuselage: two for 500 kg (1,100 lb) loads, two for 200 kg (440 lb) loads. Four underwing hardpoints: two for 660 kg (1,455 lb) loads, two for 230 kg (507 lb) loads.

POWER PLANT: Two Garrett-AiResearch ATF 3-6-2C turbofan engines (each 24.65 kN; 5,538 lb st) meeting current and proposed FAR Pt 36 noise standards. Entire engine open to borescope inspection. Fuel tankage, total capacity 5,770 litres (1,269 Imp gallons; 1,524 US gallons), divided into two identical halves, one for each engine with cross-feed capability. Wing feeder tanks pressurised with bleed air, so that fuel will continue to flow to engines with all pumps turned off. Provision for auxiliary fuel tank in rear of cabin. Single-point refuelling in about nine minutes. Fuel heaters and bacterial protection standard.

ACCOMMODATION: Normal crew of five to seven. Typical complement will comprise two pilots, one surveillance system operator (SSO) at a console on the starboard side at the rear of the cabin, two search crew members at side windows. A three-seat sofa is provided for passengers, on the port side. A drop-hatch for stores, with floor-mounted roller conveyor, is located towards the front of the cabin. Galley and retractable toilet on port side. Provision for carrying four stretchers.

SYSTEMS: Pressurisation and air-conditioning by engine bleed air; max pressure differential 0.585 bars (8·5 lb/sq in). Two independent hydraulic systems, with twin engine-driven pumps; electric standby pump to power primary flight control system in emergency. All primary flight controls utilise dual hydraulic actuators, artificial feel, electric trim and manual backup. Each half of the dual actuator is fed by one of the hydraulic systems; failure of either system will not affect handling, as each actuator has sufficient power for full control deflection. DC electrical system, with two 9kW engine-driven starter/generators, two nickel-cadmium batteries and two 1,000VA static inverters. Ground power receptacle. One 20kVA alternator driven by hydraulic motor, plus one 4kVA alternator driven by APU. Wings and nacelles anti-iced by engine bleed air, permitting flight under maximum icing conditions with one engine out.

AVIONICS: Basic avionics package includes dual HF, VHF-AM, IFF, single VHF-FM and UHF. Nav equipment includes inertial sensor system, Omega, dual VOR/ILS/MBR, DME, ADF, radio altimeters, area navigation system and single Tacan. Sensors include maritime search and weather radar and optional SLAR, infra-red and ultra-violet scanners, FLIR, aerial reconnaissance camera and steerable TV camera with laser illumination invisible to human eyes.

Dassault Mystère-Falcon Guardian, prototype for the US Coast Guard's HU-25A

DIMENSIONS, EXTERNAL:	
Wing span	16·30 m (53 ft 6 in)
Wing aspect ratio	7·02
Length overall	17·15 m (56 ft 3 in)
Height overall	5·32 m (17 ft 5 in)
Tailplane span	6·74 m (22 ft 1 in)
AREA:	
Wings, gross	41·80 m² (450 sq ft)
WEIGHTS:	
Weight empty	8,620 kg (19,000 lb)
Operating weight empty, with 5 crew and complete avionics package	9,475 kg (20,890 lb)
Max fuel	4,636 kg (10,220 lb)
Max zero-fuel weight	10,215 kg (22,520 lb)
Max T-O weight	14,515 kg (32,000 lb)
Max landing weight	12,510 kg (27,580 lb)

PERFORMANCE (at max T-O weight, except where indicated):
Max cruising speed at 12,200 m (40,000 ft) Mach 0·8
(461 knots; 855 km/h; 531 mph)
Econ cruising speed at 12,500 m (41,000 ft) Mach 0·72
Min manoeuvring speed at low altitude
150 knots (278 km/h; 173 mph)
Initial cruising height 12,500 m (41,000 ft)
T-O run 1,235 m (4,050 ft)
FAR 25 landing run at typical landing weight
625 m (2,050 ft)
Range with 5 crew, reserves of 5% total fuel plus 30 min at S/L 2,250 nm (4,170 km; 2,590 miles)
(1980–81)

DAYTON-WRIGHT.

It is reported that the Dayton-Wright Company, which is the aeronautic branch of the General Motors Corporation, will shut down its factory on June 1st, 1923, and cease all aeronautic activities, but this report is not confirmed by the firm.

The Dayton Wright Co. have built two types of training machines for the U.S. Army Service, known as the types T.A.3 and T.W.3. These are respectively for primary and advanced training, and are better known to the Trade generally as the Dayton-Wright "Chummy" aeroplanes. The T.A.3 has been built round the 80 and 110 h.p. Le Rhône engines and the T.W.3 around the 180 h.p. Wright. The general construction and layout of these machines are identical.

The two seats are side-by-side, greatly facilitating the rapid instruction of pupils.

In the design of the machine the number of parts has been reduced to the minimum. The upper and lower planes are interchangeable, and the same tail surface can be used for left or right hand elevator or as the rudder.

The engine-controls and petrol and oil feed lines are short and direct, and ample head of petrol under all conditions, is obtained by placing the petrol tanks on the top plane. The fuselage, interplane struts, landing gear members and tail surface framework are constructed of ordinary commercial grade low-carbon steel tubing, without heat treatment.

The wings only are of wooden construction, fabric covered.

The single bay wings are braced externally by only three wires on each side, the incidence being controlled by a vernier adjustment on the middle member of each N strut. The portion of the fuselage aft of the pilot's cockpit is attached by four pins, and the entire engine installation can be removed by undoing four nuts, thus rendering the entire power plant and fuel system accessible for adjustment, replacement or repair.

The undercarriage is so designed to withstand the worst kind of "pancake" landings. Two steel tube Vees form the principal members, but, instead of a cross axle, two steeply inclined members are hinged at the centre-point between the Vees and cross to the opposite Vee, where they are bent horizontally to take the landing wheels. The axles are sprung in the usual manner by rubber shock-absorber. The rotary-engined machine is adapted to take either the 80 h.p. or 110 h.p. Le Rhône, the 130 h.p. Clerget, or the 100 h.p. Gnôme.

Specification (with 80 h.p. Le Rhone engine).

Length	..	..	..	22 ft. 1 in.
Height ..	..	..	..	9 ft. 7 in.

The Dayton-Wright T.W.3 Training Machine (180 h.p. Wright engine).

Span (upper) ..	..	..	..	31 ft.
Span (lower) ..	..	..	..	25 ft. 11 in.
Chord ..	..	..	..	54 in.
Gap ..	..	..	..	58½ in.
Stagger ..	..	..	..	15 in.
Dihedral ..	..	..	..	2¾°.
Wing curve ..	..	..	..	U.S.A. 27.
Total area ..	..	..	..	231.5 sq. ft.
Fin area ..	..	..	..	5.6 sq. ft.
Elevator area ..	..	..	..	13.2 sq. ft.
Rudder area ..	..	..	..	6.6 sq. ft.
Weight empty ..	..	..	..	1,134 lbs.
Fuel ..	..	..	..	132 lbs.
Oil ..	..	..	..	33 lbs.
Crew ..	..	..	..	360 lbs.
Weight fully loaded ..	..	..	..	1,675 lbs.
Wing loading ..	..	..	..	7.2 lbs. per sq. ft.
Power loading ..	..	..	..	18.8 lbs. per h.p.
Fuel consumption (at cruising speed)			6 galls. per hour (13 miles per gall.)
				(1923)

A Canadian-built Mosquito as supplied to the U.S. Army Air Forces under the designation F-8.

THE D.H.98 MOSQUITO.

The Mosquito was originally conceived in 1938 as a small bomber which was to rely for its safety upon speed rather than armament, and was to be built of wood for industrial economy and quickness of production. Capt. de Havilland then envisaged it as having two Rolls-Royce engines and a crew of two. Directly the war was declared the idea was submitted to the Air Ministry and after considerable discussion the D.H. Company was instructed to proceed with the design, aiming at a 1,500 mile range with a 1,000 lb. bomb load and a performance in the fighter class.

The Mosquito prototype unarmed bomber first flew on November 25, 1940, eleven months from the start of the design work. The makers' basic trials were completed in three months and the aircraft was handed over for R.A.F. trials on February 19, 1941. Meanwhile a fighter version was also being developed and the growing importance of long-range photographic reconnaissance also called for an adapted form of the bomber version. The fighter prototype was first flown on May 15, 1941, and the photographic reconnaissance prototype followed on June 10, 1941.

In July, 1941, the first three Mosquitos were delivered to the R.A.F. and in that month a production scheme which included manufacture by the Canadian de Havilland plant was planned. Plans to manufacture the Mosquito in Australia were negotiated nine months later.

The USAAF received British PR.XVIs for operation by Light Weather Squadrons of the 8th Air Force, plus Canadian-built B.VIIs and B.XXs from 1943. These versions are detailed below.

Mosquito P.R. Mk. XVI. Photographic Reconnaissance version of the B. Mk. XVI. An astro-dome is a distinguishing feature of this model.

CANADIAN PRODUCTION.

Mosquito B. Mk. VII. Packard Merlin 31 engines. Canadian version of the Unarmed Bomber developed from the B. Mk. V. All remained in Canada.

Mosquito B. Mk. XX. Packard Merlin 31 or 33 engines. Designed from B. Mk. V drawings in Canada and similar to B. Mk. VII except fitted with Canadian-American equipment. First Canadian-built Mosquitos delivered to England flew via Greenland in August, 1943, and went into action from an English R.A.F. base on November 29, 1943, in a raid on Berlin.

(1945–46)

DHC-2 Mark I BEAVER
US Military designation: U-6A

The prototype DHC-2 Mark I Beaver flew for the first time in August, 1947, and type certification was received from the Canadian Department of Transport on March 12, 1948. More than 1,600 production aircraft had been delivered by early 1966. Of these, 968 were supplied to the US Armed Forces, under the designation U-6A (originally L-20A). Forty-six have been acquired for service with the British Army as the Beaver AL.Mk 1. In all, Beavers are now in civil and military service in 65 countries and production is continuing.

A single Beaver Mark II was built with a 570 hp Alvis Leonides 502/4 engine and correspondingly improved performance. A description of this aircraft can be found in the 1955-56 edition of *Jane's*.

TYPE: Single-engined STOL utility transport.

WINGS: Braced high-wing monoplane with single streamline-section bracing strut each side. Wing section NACA 64A series type $C_L = 0.4$. Aspect ratio 9·2. Constant chord of 5 ft 2½ in (1·59 m). Dihedral 2°. Incidence 0°. Sweepback at quarter-chord 0°. Aluminium alloy two-cell box structure with built-up front and rear spars and lateral stringers. NACA slotted ailerons, of aluminium alloy construction, droop 15° with flaps. Hydraulically-operated NACA slotted flaps of aluminium alloy construction. Trim-tabs on ailerons adjustable on ground.

FUSELAGE: Front fuselage of welded steel tubes covered with dural skin. Centre portion of aluminium alloy channel members and stressed skin. Rear portion is conventional aluminium alloy stressed-skin semi-monocoque structure.

TAIL UNIT: Cantilever aluminium alloy stressed-skin structure with single-piece fixed-incidence tailplane. Controllable elevator and rudder trim-tabs·

LANDING GEAR: Non-retractable tail-wheel type. Rubber-in-compression shock-absorption on main units. DH shock-absorber strut on steerable tail-wheel. Main units have Goodyear 95-2902 wheels and 8·50 × 10 6-ply tyres and tubes, pressure 25 lb/sq in (1·75 kg/cm²). Tail unit has Goodyear 512129M wheel, Dunlop 5·50 × 4TC tyre and Goodyear 5·00 × 4 tube, pressure 35 lb/sq in (2·46 kg/cm²). Goodyear disc brakes. Alternatively, can be fitted with Edo 58-4580 floats, or Bristol 348-4580 amphibious floats (this version described separately), or fixed skis of DH design, or combination wheel-ski gear of DH design. With wheel-ski gear, the changeover from wheels to skis or *vice versa* is accomplished normally from the cockpit by a manually-operated hydraulic pump, but an electric pump unit is available as optional equipment.

POWER PLANT: One 450 hp Pratt & Whitney R-985 Wasp Junior* nine-cylinder radial air-cooled engine, driving a two-blade Hamilton Standard 2D30-237 controllable-pitch propeller, diameter 8 ft 6 in (2·59 m). Fuel in three metal or rubber cell tanks under cabin floor. Front and centre tanks each have capacity of 29 Imp gallons (132 litres), rear tank capacity is 21 Imp gallons (95 litres). Total standard capacity 79 Imp gallons (359 litres). Provision for two 18 Imp gallon (82 litre) tanks in wingtips to raise total capacity to 115 Imp gallons (523 litres). Refuelling point for standard tanks on port side of fuselage. Oil capacity 4·5 Imp gallons (20·5 litres).

* *Standard engine is Wasp Junior SB-3. Alternative models are the military R-985-AN-2, -4, -6, -6B, -8, -10, -12, -12B, -14B or 14BM1. Engines in the U-6A are R-985-AN-1, -3, -14B, -39 and -39A.*

ACCOMMODATION: Pilot's compartment with pilot on port side and removable seat on starboard side. Dual rudder pedals and Y-type control column with throw-over wheel. Door with automobile-type sliding window on each side. Cabin seats up to seven passengers (six when both seats occupied in pilot's compartment). Cabin heating. Floor stressed for freight carrying. Lightweight collapsible bush seats are interchangeable with cargo attachments. Two cabin doors, one each side, are wide enough to roll a 45-gallon petrol drum into cabin on its side. Hatches in rear wall of cabin to enable long pieces of freight, such as 10 ft drilling rods, to be loaded and stowed. Baggage space at back of cabin, with separate locker aft for emergency rations, etc.

SYSTEMS: Manual low-pressure hydraulic system for brakes and flaps. Engine-driven 24V DC 50-amp or 100-amp generator. Outside receptacle for ground APU.

ELECTRONICS AND EQUIPMENT: Radio to operator's requirements. Blind-flying instrumentation is not standard. Provision for navigation lights, instrument lighting, anchor riding light and cabin lights, agricultural spraying or dusting equipment etc.

The DHC-2 Beaver as supplied to the U.S. Army.

DIMENSIONS, EXTERNAL:

Wing span	48 ft 0 in (14·64 m)
Length overall:	
Landplane	30 ft 4 in (9·24 m)
Seaplane	32 ft 9 in (9·98 m)
Height over tail:	
Landplane	9 ft 0 in (2·75 m)
Seaplane	10 ft 5 in (3·18 m)
Tailplane span	15 ft 10 in (4·83 m)
Wheel track	10 ft 2 in (3·10 m)
Wheelbase	22 ft 9 in (6·94 m)
Float track (C/L of floats)	9 ft 6¾ in (2·92 m)
Cockpit door (each side):	
Height	3 ft 4 in (1·02 m)
Width	1 ft 5 in (0·43 m)
Height to sill	4 ft 8 in (1·42 m)
Cabin door (each side):	
Height	3 ft 4 in (1·02 m)
Width	3 ft 3 in (0·99 m)
Height to sill	4 ft 1 in (1·24 m)

DIMENSIONS, INTERNAL:

Cabin, including cockpit:	
Length	9 ft 0 in (2·74 m)
Max width	4 ft 0 in (1·22 m)
Max height	4 ft 3 in (1·30 m)
Floor area	31·5 sq ft (2·93 m²)
Volume	120 cu ft (3·40 m³)
Baggage hold (in rear fuselage)	14 cu ft (0·40 m²)

AREAS:

Wings, gross	250 sq ft (23·2 m²)
Ailerons (total)	24·6 sq ft (2·29 m²)
Trailing-edge flaps (total)	20·0 sq ft (1·86 m²)
Fin	16·0 sq ft (1·49 m²)
Rudder, including tab	9·4 sq ft (0·87 m²)
Tailplane	25·4 sq ft (2·36 m²)
Elevators, including tab	23·0 sq ft (2·14 m²)

WEIGHTS AND LOADINGS:

Basic operating weight:	
Landplane	3,000 lb (1,361 kg)
Seaplane	3,316 lb (1,506 kg)
Max T-O weight:	
Landplane	5,100 lb (2,313 kg)
Seaplane	5,090 lb (2,309 kg)
Max landing weight (landplane)	5,100 lb (2,313 kg)
Max wing loading (landplane)	20·4 lb/sq ft (99·6 kg/m²)
Max power loading (landplane)	11·3 lb/hp (5·1 kg/hp)

PERFORMANCE (landplane, at max T-O weight):

Max level speed at S/L	140 mph (225 kmh)
Max permissible diving speed	180 mph (290 kmh)
Max cruising speed at S/L	135 mph (217 kmh)
Econ cruising speed at S/L	125 mph (201 kmh)
Stalling speed	60 mph (97 kmh)
Rate of climb at S/L	1,020 ft (311 m) min
Service ceiling	18,000 ft (5,490 m)
T-O run	560 ft (170 m)
T-O to 50 ft (15 m)	1,015 ft (310 m)
Landing from 50 ft (15 m)	1,000 ft (305 m)
Landing run	500 ft (152 m)
Range with max fuel, 45 min reserve	778 miles (1,252 km)
Range with max payload, 45 min reserve	483 miles (777 km)

(1966–67)

DHC-3 Otter (600 h.p. Pratt & Whitney R-1340 engine)

DHC-3 OTTER
US Military designation: U-1A

The Otter, which flew for the first time on December 12, 1951, received its Canadian Certificate of Airworthiness as both a landplane and seaplane in November, 1952, and thereupon became the first single-engined aircraft to qualify for approval in accordance with ICAO Category D airworthiness requirements.

A total of 443 Otters had been built by July 31, 1964, including many supplied to the US Army, under the designation U-1A. Aircraft of this type accompanied the US Navy's "Operation Deep-freeze" expedition to the Antarctic in 1956-58. Nine other nations, including the United Kingdom, have used Otters and Beavers for duty in the Antarctic.

The 66 Otters ordered by the RCAF are engaged on Arctic Search and Rescue operations, paratroop dropping and aerial photographic duties. Other air forces with which Otters are in service include those of Australia, Burma, Chile, Colombia, Ghana, India, Indonesia and Norway.

Commercially, Otters are operating over a wide range of climatic conditions, including territories such as Norway, Colombia, India and the Philippine Islands.

An RCAF Otter was modified extensively for STOL research under Canadian Defence Research Board contracts. Details can be found in the 1965-66 Jane's.

The following data apply to the standard production Otter.

TYPE: Single-engined STOL utility transport.

WINGS: Braced high-wing monoplane, with single streamline-section bracing strut each side. Wing section NACA 64A series type CL₁=0·4. Aspect ratio 8·97. Constant chord of 6 ft 6 in (1·98 m). Dihedral 2°. Incidence 2° 30′. Sweepback at quarter-chord 0°. Aluminium alloy two-cell box structure with built-up front and rear spars and lateral stringers. NACA slotted ailerons of aluminium alloy construction droop 26° with flaps. Slotted flaps of aluminium alloy construction. Trim-tabs on ailerons adjustable on ground.

FUSELAGE: Conventional all-metal semi-monocoque stressed-skin structure.

TAIL UNIT: Cantilever all-metal structure. Adjustable-incidence tailplane mounted half-way up fin, which is integral with fuselage. Controllable trim-tabs in rudder and elevator.

LANDING GEAR: Non-retractable tail-wheel type. Main units have rubber-in-compression shock-absorption. Goodyear 530884M main wheels, tyres and tubes, size 11·00 × 12, pressure 28 lb/sq in (1·97 kg/cm²). Goodyear 511500M-1 tail-wheel, tyre and tube, size 6·00 × 6 pressure 36 lb/sq in (2·53 kg/cm²). Goodyear disc brakes. Alternatively, can be fitted with Edo 55-7170 floats, Bristol 324 amphibious floats (this version is described separately),

fixed skis of DH design, or combination wheel-skis of DH design. In the wheel-ski version, the change from wheels to skis or vice versa is accomplished normally from the cockpit by a manually-operated hydraulic pump, but an electric pump unit is available as optional equipment.

POWER PLANT: One 600 hp Pratt & Whitney R-1340-S1H1-G or S3H1-G nine-cylinder radial air-cooled engine, driving a three-blade Hamilton Standard 3D40 Hydromatic propeller, diameter 10 ft 10 in (3·30 m). Fuel in three rubber cell tanks under cabin floor. Front tank has capacity of 51 Imp gallons (233 litres), centre tank 85 Imp gallons (389 litres) and rear tank 42 Imp gallons (192 litres). Total fuel capacity 178 Imp gallons (814 litres). Three refuelling points on port side of fuselage. Oil capacity 9 Imp gallons (41 litres).

ELECTRONICS AND EQUIPMENT: Navigation lights, controllable-intensity instrument lights, a 250-watt sealed-beam landing-light in the port wing leading-edge and cabin lights are provided. Radio and navigation equipment as specified by the operator.

DIMENSIONS, EXTERNAL:

Wing span	58 ft 0 in (17·69 m)
Length overall	41 ft 10 in (12·80 m)
Height over tail:	
Landplane	12 ft 7 in (3·83 m)
Seaplane	15 ft 0 in (4·57 m)
Tailplane span	21 ft 2 in (6·46 m)
Wheel track	11 ft 2 in (3·42 m)
Wheelbase	27 ft 10 in (8·49 m)
Float base (C/L of floats)	10 ft 6 in (3·20 m)
Landing from 50 ft (15 m):	
Landplane	880 ft (268 m)
Seaplane	1,200 ft (366 m)
Landing run (landplane)	440 ft (134 m)
Max range:	
Landplane	945 miles (1,520 km)
Seaplane	855 miles (1,375 km)
Range with 2,100 lb (953 kg) payload	875 miles (1,410 km)
Max endurance:	
Landplane	8·6 hours
Seaplane	7·9 hours

NOTE: Range and endurance include allowances for 10 min warm-up, take-off, climb to 5,000 ft (1,525 m) and fuel reserves for 45 minutes at cruise power.

Cockpit door (each side):	
Height	3 ft 8 in (1·12 m)
Width	2 ft 2 in (0·66 m)
Height to sill	6 ft 1 in (1·85 m)

Cabin door (port):	
Height	3 ft 9 in (1·14 m)
Width	3 ft 10½ in (1·18 m)
Height to sill	4 ft 1 in (1·24 m)

Cabin door (starboard):	
Height	3 ft 9 in (1·14 m)
Width	2 ft 6 in (0·76 m)
Height to sill	4 ft 1 in (1·24 m)

DIMENSIONS, INTERNAL:

Cabin, excluding flight deck:	
Length	16 ft 5 in (5·0 m)
Max width	5 ft 2 in (1·58 m)
Max height	4 ft 11 in (1·50 m)
Floor area	79 sq ft (7·34 m²)

AREAS:

Wings, gross	375 sq ft (34·84 m²)
Ailerons (total)	26·3 sq ft (2·44 m²)
Trailing-edge flaps (total)	98·0 sq ft (9·10 m²)
Fin	33·2 sq ft (3·08 m²)
Rudder, including tab	27·0 sq ft (2·51 m²)
Tailplane	39·0 sq ft (3·62 m²)
Elevators, including tab	46·0 sq ft (4·27 m²)

WEIGHTS AND LOADINGS:

Basic operating weight:	
Landplane	4,431 lb (2,010 kg)
Seaplane	4,892 lb (2,219 kg)
Skiplane	4,652 lb (2,110 kg)
Wheel-ski version	4,734 lb (2,147 kg)

Max T-O weight:	
Landplane	8,000 lb (3,629 kg)
Seaplane	7,967 lb (3,614 kg)
Max landing weight (landplane)	8,000 lb (3,629 kg)
Max wing loading (landplane)	21·3 lb/sq ft (104 kg/m²)
Max power loading (landplane)	13·3 lb/hp (6·03 kg/hp)

PERFORMANCE (at max T-O weight):

Max speed at S/L (landplane)	153 mph (246 kmh)
Max speed at 5,000 ft (1,525 m):	
Landplane	160 mph (257 kmh)
Seaplane	153 mph (246 kmh)
Skiplane	158 mph (254 kmh)
Max permissible speed in dive	192 mph (309 kmh)
Max cruising speed at S/L (landplane)	132 mph (212 kmh)
Econ cruising speed at S/L (landplane)	121 mph (195 kmh)
True cruising speed (400 hp) at 5,000 ft (1,525m):	
Landplane	138 mph (222 kmh)
Seaplane	129 mph (207 kmh)
Skiplane	133 mph (214 kmh)
Stalling speed (landplane)	58 mph (93 kmh)
Max rate of climb at S/L (landplane)	850 ft (259 m) min
Rate of climb at S/L (550 hp):	
Seaplane	650 ft (198 m) min
Skiplane	690 ft (210 m) min

Service ceiling (S1H1-G engine):	
Landplane	18,800 ft (5,730 m)
Seaplane	17,900 ft (5,455 m)
Skiplane	18,500 ft (5,640 m)
Service ceiling (S3H1-G engine):	
Landplane	17,400 ft (5,300 m)
Seaplane	16,400 ft (5,000 m)
Skiplane	17,100 ft (5,210 m)
T-O run (landplane)	630 ft (192 m)
T-O to 50 ft (15 m):	
Landplane	1,155 ft (352 m)
Seaplane	1,925 ft (586 m)
Landing from 50 ft (15 m):	
Landplane	880 ft (268 m)
Seaplane	1,200 ft (366 m)
Landing run (landplane)	440 ft (134 m)
Max range:	
Landplane	945 miles (1,520 km)
Seaplane	855 miles (1,375 km)
Range with 2,100 lb (953 kg) payload (landplane)	875 miles (1,410 km)
Max endurance:	
Landplane	8·6 hours
Seaplane	7·9 hours

NOTE: Range and endurance include allowances for 10 min warm-up, take-off, climb to 5,000 ft (1,525 m) and fuel reserves for 45 minutes at cruise power. (1966-67)

The DHC-4 Caribou (two 1,450 h.p. Pratt & Whitney R-2000 engines) as supplied to the U.S. Army

DHC-4A CARIBOU
CAF designation: CC-108
USAF designation: C-7

The Caribou was developed with the co-operation of the Canadian Department of Defence Production and an order for one prototype was placed by the Royal Canadian Air Force. Construction began in 1957 and the prototype flew for the first time on 30 July 1958.

The original DHC-4 Caribou obtained US Type Approval on 23 December 1960, at a gross weight of 26,000 lb (11,793 kg). The DHC-4A was approved on 11 July 1961, at the current maximum gross weight of 28,500 lb (12,928 kg).

Five YAC-1 Caribou were delivered to the US Army for evaluation in 1959. The US Army subsequently ordered a total of 159 aircraft under the designation CV-2 (originally AC-1). The 134 aircraft still in service on 1 January 1967 were transferred to the USAF. Versions of the Caribou delivered to the US Army were the CV-2A (equivalent to the DHC-4), and the C-7A (formerly CV-2B), equivalent to the DHC-4A. The change of designation of the latter version followed transfer from the US Army to the USAF.

Versions of the Caribou delivered to the US Army were as follows:

CV-2A. Equivalent to DHC-4.

C-7A (formerly CV-2B). Equivalent to DHC-4A, with higher AUW. Delivery began in 1963. Change of designation followed transfer from US Army to USAF.

One Caribou (see 1972-73 *Jane's*) was converted into a flying command post by Collins Radio for operation with the US 1st (Air) Cavalry Division in Vietnam.

TYPE: Twin-engined all-weather STOL utility transport.

WINGS: Cantilever high-wing monoplane. Wing section NACA 64₂A417·5 throughout one-piece centre-section, varying to NACA 63₂A615 near tips of outer panels. Dihedral on outer panels 5°. Incidence 3° inboard, 0° outboard. Sweepback at quarter-chord 0°. All-metal two-spar fail-safe structure. Full-span double-slotted flaps, outer trailing portions operated independently as ailerons. Trim tabs on ailerons. Goodrich flush-mounted inflatable de-icing boots in four sections.

FUSELAGE: All-metal fail-safe semi-monocoque structure. Rear portion is upswept aft of wings, with upward and inward hinged door forming underside of rear fuselage.

TAIL UNIT: Cantilever all-metal structure. Variable-incidence tailplane. Glassfibre fairings at top and bottom of rudder. Spring tabs on rudder and elevators. Goodrich inflatable de-icing boots.

LANDING GEAR: Retractable tricycle type. Hydraulic retraction, main units forward, nose unit rearward. Main gear, produced by Jarry Hydraulics, shortens as it retracts. Dual wheels on all units. Hydraulically-steerable nosewheels. Goodyear wheels and tyres, size 11·00 × 12 on main units, 7·50 × 10 on nose unit. Tyre pressures (nominal) 40 lb/sq in (2·81 kg/cm²). Goodyear four-cylinder single-disc brakes.

POWER PLANT: Two 1,450 hp Pratt & Whitney R-2000-7M2 fourteen-cylinder two-row radial air-cooled engines, each driving a Hamilton Standard 43D50-7107A three-blade constant-speed fully-feathering propeller. Fuel in two wing tanks, each of 10 cells, with total capacity of 690 Imp gallons (3,137 litres). Refuelling point in upper surface of each wing. Oil capacity 50 Imp gallons (227 litres).

ACCOMMODATION: Flight compartment seats two side by side. Civil version accommodates 30 passengers, with access via two doors, at rear of cabin on each side (an airstair type can be provided), or via the large rear loading ramp, formed by lowering electrically the sloping undersurface of the rear fuselage. The military version carries 32 troops on inward-facing folding seats or 26 fully-equipped paratroops, or, in an ambulance role, up to 22 stretcher patients, 4 sitting casualties and 4 attendants. Typical freight loads are three tons of cargo or two fully-loaded jeeps. The floor is stressed to support distributed loads of 200 lb/sq ft (975 kg/m²) and has tie-down fittings on a 20 in (0·50 m) grid pattern over the entire area. Tie-down rings can be fitted at 36 points on the side walls.

SYSTEMS: Flaps, brakes, landing gear retraction and nosewheel steering actuated by 3,000 lb/sq in (210 kg/cm²) hydraulic system. No pneumatic system. Two engine-driven generators, 24V 300A DC/115V 400Hz AC.

ELECTRONICS AND EQUIPMENT: To customer's requirements. Blind-flying instrumentation standard.

DIMENSIONS, EXTERNAL:

Wing span	95 ft 7½ in (29·15 m)
Wing chord at root	11 ft 10 in (3·60 m)
Wing chord at tip	5 ft 7¾ in (1·72 m)
Wing aspect ratio	10
Length overall	72 ft 7 in (22·13 m)
Height over tail	31 ft 9 in (9·70 m)
Tailplane span	36 ft 0 in (11·00 m)
Wheel track	23 ft 1½ in (7·05 m)
Wheelbase	25 ft 8 in (7·82 m)
Propeller diameter	13 ft 1½ in (3·99 m)
Propeller ground clearance	21·9 in (55·6 cm)
Passenger door (each side):	
Height	4 ft 7 in (1·40 m)
Width	2 ft 6 in (0·76 m)

Main cargo door (rear fuselage):
Height   6 ft 3 in (1·90 m)
Width   6 ft 1½ in (1·86 m)
Height to sill   3 ft 9½ in (1·16 m)
DIMENSIONS, INTERNAL:
Cabin, excluding flight deck:
Length   28 ft 9 in (8·76 m)
Max width   7 ft 3 in (2·21 m)
Max height   6 ft 3 in (1·90 m)
Floor area   176 sq ft (16·35 m²)
Volume   1,150 cu ft (32·57 m²)
AREAS:
Wings, gross   912 sq ft. (84·72 m²)
Ailerons (total)   91 sq ft (8·45 m²)
Trailing-edge flaps (total)   285 sq ft (26·47 m²)
Fin   127 sq ft (11·80 m²)
Rudder, including tab   84 sq ft (7·80 m²)
Tailplane   144 sq ft (13·37 m²)
Elevators, including tab   86 sq ft (7·99 m²)

WEIGHTS AND LOADINGS:
Basic operating weight (including 2 crew)
     18,260 lb (8,283 kg)
Max payload   8,740 lb (3,965 kg)
Normal max T-O weight   28,500 lb (12,928 kg)
Max permissible weight for ferry missions
     31,300 lb (14,197 kg)
Max zero-fuel weight   27,000 lb (12,250 kg)
Max landing weight   28,500 lb (12,928 kg)
Normal max wing loading
     31·2 lb/sq ft (152·3 kg/m²)
Normal max power loading
     9·83 lb/hp (4·45 kg/hp)
PERFORMANCE (at normal max T-O weight):
Max level speed at 6,500 ft (1,980 m)
     188 knots (216 mph; 347 km/h)
Max diving speed
     208 knots (240 mph; 386 km/h)

Max and econ cruising speed at 7,500 ft (2,285 m)
     158 knots (182 mph; 293 km/h)
Stalling speed   59 knots (68 mph; 109 km/h)
Rate of climb at S/L   1,355 ft (413 m)/min
Service ceiling   24,800 ft (7,560 m)
Service ceiling, one engine out 8,800 ft (2,680 m)
T-O run   725 ft (221 m)
T-O to 50 ft (15 m)   1,185 ft (361 m)
Landing from 50 ft (15 m)   1,235 ft (376 m)
Landing run   670 ft (204 m)
Range with max fuel
     1,135 nm (1,307 miles; 2,103 km)
Range with max payload
     210 nm (242 miles; 390 km)
NOTE: Ranges are for long-range cruising speed at 7,500 ft (2,285 m), with allowances for warm-up, taxi, take-off, climb, descent, landing and 45 min reserve   (1973–74)

The Douglas A-33 Two-seat Attack Bomber (1,200 h.p. Wright "Cyclone" engine).

THE DOUGLAS 8A-5.

U.S. Army Air Forces designation: A-33.

TYPE.—Two-seat Attack-Bomber monoplane.

WINGS.—Low-wing cantilever monoplane. In three sections, with detachable wing-tips. All-metal stressed-skin cellular structure. Metal-framed fabric-covered ailerons. Split trailing-edge flaps.

FUSELAGE.—Light alloy monocoque, with smooth stressed skin. Made in two halves divided along horizontal centre-line. Lower half is built integral with the wing centre-section.

TAIL UNIT.—Cantilever monoplane type. All-metal framework, with stressed-skin covering to fixed surfaces and fabric covering for rudder and elevators. Rudder and elevators have inset-hinge balances and trimming-tabs.

LANDING GEAR.—Retractable type. Orientable tail-wheel.

POWER PLANT.—One Wright "Cyclone" GR-1820-G205A nine-cylinder radial air-cooled engine rated at 860 h.p. at 10,000 ft. (3,050 m.) and with 1,200 h.p. available for take-off. NACA cowling, with controllable gills. Curtiss electric constant-speed airscrew.

ACCOMMODATION.—Tandem seats under a transparent canopy, with sliding section over pilot's seat and hinged section over gunner's cockpit.

ARMAMENT.—Six machine-guns, four in the leading-edge of the wing and two on a flexible mounting in the gunner's cockpit. Racks and chutes for twenty internally-stowed 30-lb. bombs. External racks for bombs of 120, 300 or 600-lbs. Maximum bomb load 1,800 lbs. (818 kg.).

DIMENSIONS.—Span 47 ft. 8.75 in. (14.56 m.), Length 32 ft. 5 in. (9.85 m.), Height 9 ft. 9 in. (2.97 m.), Wing area 363 sq. ft. (33.8 sq. m.).

WEIGHTS AND LOADINGS.—Weight empty 5,370 lbs. (2,436 kg.), Normal disposable load (attack) 2,130 lbs. (965 kg.), Normal disposable load (bomber) 3,830 lbs. (1,736 kg.), Weight loaded (attack) 7,848 lbs. (3,560 kg.), Weight loaded (bomber) 8,948 lbs. (4,060 kg.), Wing loading (attack) 21.6 lbs./sq. ft. (105.4 kg./sq. m.), Power loading 7.5 lbs./h.p. (3.4 kg./h.p.).

PERFORMANCE.—Maximum speed at 9,000 ft. (2,745 m.) 265 m.p.h. (424 km.h.), Cruising speed at 10,000 ft. (3,050 m.) 200 m.p.h. (322 km.h.), Landing speed 65 m.p.h. (105 km.h.), Initial rate of climb 1,570 ft./min. (474 m./min.), Service ceiling 32,000 ft. (9,760 m.), Cruising range 910 miles (1,465 km.).   (1942)

Two views of the Douglas B-18 Bomber Monoplane (two 1,000 h.p. Wright "Cyclone" engines).

THE DOUGLAS B-18.

The B-18 is a twin-engined Army bomber and an adaptation of the well-known Douglas DC-3 transport. It is a mid-wing cantilever monoplane, is fitted with two Wright "Cyclone" engines and is said to have a speed of 225 m.p.h. (360 km.h.). It has internal bomb stowage and gun positions in the nose and above and below the fuselage aft of the wings.

This machine won the U.S. Army Air Corps Bomber Competition in 1936. The original contract for 133 machines of this type has been completed. A further contract for 255 B-18A's is in course of fulfilment.

Details for B-18A

Wing span:	89 ft 6 in (27.28 m)
Length:	57 ft 10 in (17.63 m)
Height:	15 ft 2 in (4.62 m)
Weight loaded:	27,673 lb (12,552 kg)
Bomb load:	6,500 lb (2,948 kg)
Maximum speed:	215 mph (346 km/h)

(1938)

The Douglas B-23 Reconnaissance-Bomber (two Wright "Cyclone" GR-2600-A5B engines).

THE DOUGLAS B-23.

The B-23 is a twin-engined reconnaissance bomber which is now in service in the U.S. Army Air Forces. It is a development of the earlier B-18A bomber, which was a service derivation of the DC-3 airliner. The B-23 is fitted with two 1,600 h.p. Wright Double-Row "Cyclone" GR-2600-A5B engines which drive three-bladed Hamilton-Standard Hydromatic full-feathering airscrews. (1941)

THE DOUGLAS C-1.

The Douglas C-1 is the standard cargo and troop carrier of the U.S. Army Air Service. It follows the lines of the "World Cruiser" and the O-2 and M-2 types.

The fuselage is constructed of chrome molybdenum steel tubing and swaged steel tie rods. The joints are welded in the approved manner. The engine-section and pilot's bay, back to the front wing spar, are covered with quickly detachable aluminium cowling, the rest of the fuselage being fabric-covered. The engine is a Liberty. Immediately behind the engine is the pilot's cockpit. The pilot is placed on the left side of the fuselage, with the mechanic or spare pilot on the left. The passenger compartment has a clear cross-sectional size of 46 in. width by 50 in. height. It is about 10 ft. long. The six passenger seats are readily removable, to permit the stowage of freight. An opening in the floor of the cabin allows for the hoisting-in of heavy objects, such as a Liberty engine, and a Tee rail may be fitted to the roof for use in transporting heavy weights, such as a Liberty engine, forward to the centre of the compartment, after being hoisted into the fuselage. Six seats for passengers are normally provided, but a seating capacity of eight people in the present enclosed compartment may be easily

provided. A baggage compartment, 4 × 4 × 4 × 10 ft. is provided to carry any baggage for the passengers. The wings consist of two box spars, built up of spruce capping strips and two-ply spruce veneer sides, together with the necessary spruce and ply-wood gussets, stiffeners and filler blocks. The ribs are of the girder type and are made of spruce throughout, except for the corner truss gussets, which are of three-ply mahogany veneer. The internal wing-bracing is by steel tie-rods attached to duralumin fittings, bolted to the spars. Folding wings may be provided if required, resulting in small increase in weight. The tail unit is normal. The undercarriage is of the divided axle type, as fitted to the O-2 and M-2.

Specification.

Span	..	..	..	60 ft.
Length				36 ft.
Height ..	..	..	..	14 ft.
Wing area	..	..	..	800 sq. ft.
Total dead load	..	..		3,900 lbs.
Petrol ..	..	..	..	900 lbs.
Oil ..	..	..	..	120 lbs.
Crew of 7 passengers and pilot				1,440 lbs.

Total normal pay load of 7 passengers	1,260 lbs.
Total normal pay load of 9 passengers	1,620 lbs.
Max. pay load (cargo)	2,500 lbs.
Gross weight normal load of 7 passengers and pilot ..	6,360 lbs.
Gross weight, 9 passenger load	6,540 lbs.
Gross weight, max. pay load	7,420 lbs.

This method of loading would vary the wing loading from 7.9 to 9.3 lbs. per sq. ft.

Performance.

Max. speed ..	..	..	119.7 m.p.h.
Landing speed	..	..	46 m.p.h.
Service ceiling	..	..	15,950 ft.
Absolute ceiling	..	..	18,700 ft.

The Douglas C.1 Army Transport Biplane (400 h.p. Liberty engine).

(1926)

The Douglas O-2 Biplane (400 h.p. Liberty engine).

THE DOUGLAS M-2.

The Douglas M-2 Air Mail Plane is a development of the Douglas O-2, already described. Its construction is identical with the machine, which, built in accordance with Air Service Specifications, has withstood the required loads on the wing truss, fuselage, undercarriage and tail-surfaces.

The mail compartment is of 58 cubic feet and has a capacity for 1,000 lbs. of mail. It is situated in front of the pilot's cockpit and is isolated from the engine by a fireproof bulkhead and, in addition, is lined with reinforced duralumin.

The length of the mail compartment is six feet, which permits of the stowage of long packages. The mail compartment is further provided with two quickly removable seats, thus permitting the carrying of two passengers or for ferrying reserve pilots from one aerodrome to another. The petrol capacity of 130 gallons is sufficient for a range of 650 miles. The engine is a 400 h.p. Liberty.

Specification.

Span ..	..	..	..	39 ft. 8 in.
Length	..	..	..	28 ft. 11 in.
Height ..	..	..	..	10 ft. 1 in.
Chord ..	..	..	..	5 ft. 8 in.
Wing area	..	..	..	411 sq. ft.
Weight empty	..	..	..	2,910 lbs.
Useful load	..	..	..	2,058 lbs.
Weight loaded	..	..	..	4,968 lbs.
Wing loading ..	..	..	12 lbs./sq. ft.
Power loading	..	..	..	11.8 lbs./sq. ft.
Max. speed	..	..	..	145 m.p.h.
Stalling speed ..	..	..	58 m.p.h.
Landing speed	..	..	..	55 m.p.h.
Cruising speed	..	..	..	110 m.p.h.
Service ceiling	..	..	..	17,000 ft.
Climb, at ground level	..	..	1,100 ft. per min.

THE DOUGLAS CARGOMASTER
U.S.A.F. designation: C-133

The C-133 is a four-engined transport which, although not much bigger in overall dimensions than the earlier C-124 Globemaster II, can carry payloads equivalent to twice the normal cargo capacity of the C-124. Detailed design work on the aircraft began in February, 1953. The first production C-133 was completed in February, 1956, and made its first flight on April 23, 1956. The first operational C-133 was delivered on August 22, 1957. Production was completed in April, 1961.

The C-133's main freight hold is 90 ft. (27.45 m.) long with the floor at truck-bed height. There are two loading doors and

virtually all types of military vehicles can be driven up the integral ramp and through the main doors beneath the rear of the fuselage. Typical loads are two prime-movers weighing more than 40,000 lb. (18,160 kg.) each, 16 loaded Jeeps, 20 jet engines or various combinations of vehicles, heavy ordnance and general cargo. It can also accommodate the American IRBM and ICBM surface-to-surface missiles. Roller conveyors can be installed in existing fittings in the aircraft in approximately five minutes to speed the loading of heavy items of freight.

Although designed primarily for air freight, the basic configuration of the C-133 can easily be modified to permit the transportation of

more than 200 fully-armed troops. It can also be used as an ambulance.

Two versions of the C-133 have been produced, as follows:—

C-133A. Initial production version with four 6,500 e.h.p. Pratt & Whitney T34-P-7WA (initially T34-P-3) turboprop engines and loaded weight of 275,000 lb. (124,735 kg.). Total of 34 delivered.

On December 16, 1958, a C-133A broke the international payload-to-height record by lifting 117,900 lb. (53,478.5 kg.) to 10,000 ft. (3,050 m.). It required a take-off run of only 4,500 ft. (1,370 m.) and climbed at the rate of 2,000 ft./min. (610 m./min.). This record has since been beaten.

Douglas C-133B Cargomaster heavy transport (four Pratt & Whitney T34 turboprop engines) (Peter M. Bowers)

C-133B. Developed version with four Pratt & Whitney T34-P-9W turboprop engines, increased loaded weight and an enlarged main cargo door to permit easier loading of the Atlas ICBM and Thor and Jupiter IRBM's. Fifteen C-133B's have been delivered. The first one flew for the first time on October 31, 1959. Delivery to the 1,501st Air Transport Wing, MATS, at Travis Air Force Base, California, began on March 21, 1960. Details below refer to this version.

TYPE.—Four-turboprop long-range transport.

WINGS.—High-wing cantilever monoplane. Chord at tip 5 ft. 6½ in. (1.69 m.). Dihedral 2°. All-metal two-spar stressed-skin construction, with thick inter-spar skins 58 ft. 6 in. (17.83 m.) long. Hydraulically-actuated double-slotted flaps between ailerons and fuselage. Thermal anti-icing system. Vortex generators on upper and lower wing surfaces forward of ailerons. Total area of ailerons 142.0 sq. ft. (13.19 m.²). Total area of flaps 496.5 sq. ft. (46.13 m.²). Wing area 2,673.1 sq. ft. (248.3 m.²).

FUSELAGE.—All-metal semi-monocoque structure. Crew accommodation and freight hold pressurised to maintain 10,000 ft. (3,050 m.) cabin altitude to 35,000 ft. (10,675 m.).

TAIL UNIT.—Cantilever monoplane type. All-metal stressed-skin structure. Pneumatic boot de-icing system. Areas : fin 354.6 sq. ft. (32.92 m.²), rudder 182.4 sq. ft. (16.95 m.²), tailplane 459.2 sq. ft. (42.66 m.²), elevators 341.5 sq. ft. (31.73 m.²). Tailplane span 60 ft. (18.29 m.).

LANDING GEAR.—Retractable type. Steerable dual nose-wheel unit. Two main units of four wheels each retract into faired pods on sides of fuselage. Hydraulic actuation. Main tyres 20.00 × 20. Nose tyres 15.00 × 16. Twin wheels, with solid rubber tyres, under rear fuselage to cater for nose-high landings. Wheel track 20 ft. 1 in. (6.12 m.). Wheelbase 58 ft. 11 in. (17.95 m.).

POWER PLANT.—Four 7,500 e.s.h.p. Pratt & Whitney T34-P-9W turboprop engines, each driving a Curtiss-Wright Turboelectric three-blade 18 ft. (5.49 m.) constant-speed reversing airscrew. Fuel in four bladder-type cells in centre-section, three integral tanks in each centre wing panel and one integral tank in each outer wing panel. Total fuel capacity 18,112 U.S. gallons (68,557 litres). Single-point pressure re-fuelling system with nozzle adaptor in forward portion of starboard landing-gear pod. Engine starting by compressed air supplied by auxiliary gas-turbine installation located in port landing gear pod.

ACCOMMODATION.—Normal crew of four. Quarters for relief crew of three for extended operation. Usable hold is 90 ft. (27.45 m.) long and constant floor width is 11 ft. 10 in. (3.60 m.). Capacity of hold is 13,000 cub. ft. (368 m.³). Hold floor is 4 ft. 2 in. (1.27 m.) above ground. Loading doors in port side of fuselage forward and at rear of hold beneath fuselage. Main rear loading area has clam-shell doors opening in four directions, the lower door forming loading ramp, which is able to support a load of 25,000 lb. (11,340 kg.) in horizontal position and raise from ground with a 10,000 lb. (4,536 kg.) load. Doors, which are hydraulically-operated, are sealed to support full cabin pressure. Vehicles and other prime-movers up to 12 ft. (3.66 m.) high can drive into fuselage through rear door. Forward side door, 8 ft. 4 in. × 8 ft. 10 in. (2.54 m. × 2.69 m.) for direct loading of freight from truck or trailer. Entire accommodation pressurised and heated, the heating system having a capacity of 900,000 B.Th.U's. All pressurisation and ventilating requirements supplied by AiResearch GTU-85-2 auxiliary dual gas-turbine power installation in port landing gear pod. Four automatically ejected and inflated life-rafts in centre-section, two on each side of fuselage and accessible from emergency exits. Separate life-raft for crew in forward fuselage.

DIMENSIONS.—
Span 179 ft 8 in. (54·75 m)
Length 157 ft 6½ in. (48·0 m)
Height 48 ft 3 in. (14·70 m)

WEIGHTS.—
Weight empty 120,363 lb (54,595 kg)
Normal T.O. weight 286,000 lb (129,730 kg)
Overload gross weight 300,000 lb (136,080 kg)
Wing loading 107 lb/sq ft (522 kg/m²)
Power loading 9·73 lb/eshp (4·41 kg/eshp)

PERFORMANCE.—
Max. speed at 9,000 ft (2,740 m) 347 mph (558 kmh)
Normal cruising speed 310 mph (500 kmh)
Landing speed at 250,500 lb (113,625 kg) A.U.W. 133 mph (214 kmh)
Rate of climb at S/L 1,315 ft (400 m) min.
Service ceiling 20,100 ft (6,125 m)
Range with max. fuel and 43,706 lb (19,825 kg) payload 4,360 miles (7,015 km)
Range with 91,240 lb (41,386 kg) payload 2,250 miles (3,620 km)
(1963–64)

THE DOUGLAS DAUNTLESS.
U.S. Navy designation : SBD.
U.S. Army Air Forces designation : A-24.

The Dauntless went into production in June, 1940, as the SBD-1, the first deliveries being to the U.S. Marine Corps. By December, 1941, the SBD-3 was the standard carrier-borne dive-bomber with the U.S. Fleet and for two years the Dauntless fulfilled the entire Scout Dive-Bomber requirements of the naval forces operating in the Pacific.

In 1941 the U.S. Army took delivery of a military version of the Dauntless designated the A-24. This was a counterpart of the SBD-3 and differed from it in only minor equipment details and by the elimination of deck-landing gear. The A-24A (SBD-4) and A-24B (SBD-5) followed. While all SBD models were built at El Segundo, the A-24 versions emanated from the Douglas Tulsa plant. Production of the A-24 ceased in November, 1943.

With the completion of the 5,936th Dauntless on July 22, 1944, production of the SBD ceased. Although the type was still in operational service at the end of 1944 it was gradually being replaced by aircraft of more recent design.

The following information details briefly the development of the Dauntless :—

SBD-1. Wright R-1820-32 engine with two-speed supercharger, rated at 950 h.p. at 5,000 ft. (1,525 m.), 800 h.p. at 16,000 ft. (4,880 m.) and with 1,000 h.p. available for take-off. Welded fuel tanks, all in centre-section. Total capacity 210 U.S. gallons. Armament consisted of two 50 cal. guns in fuselage and one 30 cal. flexible gun in rear cockpit. Delivered to U.S. Marine Corps.

SBD-2. Similar to SBD-1 except for revision of fuel system to two tanks in centre-section (90 U.S. gallons each) and two in outer wings (65 U.S. gallons each). Total capacity 310 U.S. gallons. Armament consisted of one 50 cal. fuselage gun and one 30 cal. flexible gun. Automatic pilot installed. Delivered to U.S. Navy.

SBD-3 (A-24). Wright R-1820-52 engine with same output as previous power-unit. Aluminium-alloy fuel tanks with self-sealing liners. Two centre-section tanks (75 U.S. gallons each) and two outer wing tanks (55 U.S. gallons each). Total capacity 260 U.S. gallons. Same armament as SBD-1, but flexible armament revised in service to two 30 cal. guns to agree with later models. Armour protection and bullet-proof windscreen.

SBD-4 (A-24A). Similar to SBD-3 except Hydromatic airscrew, installation of 24-volt electrical system in place of former 12-volt, and other minor equipment changes.

SBD-5 (A-24B). Wright R-1820-60 engine rated at 1,000 h.p. at 4,500 ft. (1,370 m.), 900 h.p. at 14,000 ft. (4,270 m.) and with 1,200 h.p. available for take-off. Illuminated Mk. VIII sight for fixed guns and Mk. IX for flexible guns in place of former telescopic and ring sights respectively. Ammunition capacity increased. Radar installed. Otherwise as for SBD-4.

SBD-6. Wright R-1820-66 engine rated at 1,200 h.p. at 5,500 ft. (1,680 m.), 900 h.p. at 18,500 ft. (5,640 m.) and with 1,350 h.p. available for take-off. Non-metallic self-sealing fuel cells of increased capacity. Total fuel, 284 U.S. gallons. Otherwise as for SBD-5.

The Douglas SBD-3 "Dauntless" Two-seat Naval Dive-Bomber (Wright "Cyclone" R-1820 engine).

TYPE.—Two-seat Scout Bomber (SBD) or Dive-Bomber (A-24).

WINGS.—Low-wing cantilever monoplane. Rectangular centre-section with outer sections tapering in chord and thickness and with detachable wing-tips. Duralumin multi-cellular structure with flush-riveted stressed-skin covering. Metal-framed ailerons with fabric-covering. Trim-tab in port aileron. Slots in wings ahead of ailerons. Hydraulically-operated perforated metal dive-brakes above and below trailing-edges of outer wings and below trailing-edge only of centre-section beneath fuselage.

FUSELAGE.—Oval duralumin monocoque structure. For manufacture fuselage split longitudinally, the upper half in one piece and lower in three, plus a tail cone. Forward lower section includes built-in centre-section. Fuselage structure built up of channel-section transverse frames, extruded stringers and 24ST Alclad skin. Aft of rear cockpit solid bulkheads divided the rear fuselage into a series of watertight compartments.

TAIL UNIT.—Cantilever monoplane type. Fin built integral with fuselage. All-metal tailplane with stressed-skin covering. Rudder and elevators have metal frames and fabric covering. Trimming-tabs in movable surfaces.

LANDING GEAR.—Retractable type. The two cantilever oleo shock-absorber legs are hinged at the extremities of the centre-section and are raised inwardly, the wheels being buried in wells in the underside of the centre-section. Hydraulic retraction with emergency hand-operated mechanical gear. Locked or free swivelling solid-tyre tail-wheel. Deck-landing hook under rear fuselage.

POWER PLANT.—One Wright R-1820-66 Cyclone nine-cylinder radial air-cooled engine rated at 1,200 h.p. at 5,500 ft. (1,680 m.) 900 h.p. at 18,500 ft. (5,640 m.) and with 1,350 h.p. available for take-off. NACA cowling. Hamilton-Standard Hydromatic full-feathering airscrew, 10 ft. 10 in. (3.3 m.) diameter. Fuel tanks (4) in centre-section and roots of outer wings. Total capacity :

284 U.S. gallons. Oil tank (15.5 U.S. gallons) in engine compartment with oil cooler below. Controllable air scoop for oil cooler at bottom of cowling with fixed exit louvres on either side of cowling.

ACCOMMODATION.—Tandem cockpits beneath continuous transparent canopy. Bullet-proof windscreen. Sliding hood over pilot's and gunner's cockpits. Armour protection for crew. Duplicate set of controls in rear cockpit. Equipment includes Sperry automatic pilot, full radio equipment, automatically inflatable two-seat dinghy, oxygen, 24 volt electrical system, etc.

ARMAMENT.—Two 0.50 in. Browning machine-guns in fuselage firing through the airscrew. Two 0.30 in. machine-guns on flexible mounting in rear cockpit. Swinging bomb cradle beneath fuselage and bomb-racks mounted under roots of outer wing sections. For dive-bombing one 1,000 lb. is carried beneath fuselage, and two 100 lb. bombs, may be carried beneath wings. On scout-bombing missions, with increased fuel, one 500 lb. and two 100 lb. can be carried. Certain versions of the SBD are equipped for long-range photographic reconnaissance duties.

DIMENSIONS.—Span 41 ft. (12.5 m.), Length 32 ft. (9.76 m.), Height 13 ft. (3.96 m.), Wing area 325 sq. ft. (30.2 sq. m.).

WEIGHTS AND LOADINGS.—Weight empty 6,535 lbs. (2,970 kg.), Weight loaded (Dive-bomber) 9,519 lbs. (4,320 kg.), Wing loading 29.3 lbs./sq. ft. (142.9 kg./sq. m.), Power loading 9.5 lbs./h.p. (4.3 kg./h.p.).

PERFORMANCE.—Maximum speed 255 m.p.h. (408 km.h.) at 14,000 ft. (4,270 m.), Cruising speed 185 m.p.h. (296 km.h.) at 14,000 ft. (4,270 m.), Stalling speed 78 m.p.h. (125 km.h.), Climb to 10,000 ft. (3,050 m.) 7 mins., Service ceiling 25,200 ft. (7,690 m.), Range (Dive-bomber) 456 miles (730 km.), Range (Scout-bomber) 773 miles (1,240 km.). (1945—46)

A Douglas DC-2 Monoplane as used by the U.S. Army Air Corps for transport duties.

THE DOUGLAS DC-2 "TRANSPORT."

The Douglas "Transport" was originally developed for T.W.A., Inc., and was put into production in 1933. The first machines were delivered early in 1934 and they were so successful that by June, 1934, orders for seventy-five had been received from firms both in the United States and abroad. Subsequent orders were received from American Air Lines, Eastern Air Lines, Pan-American Airways, and from numerous foreign concerns throughout the world.

In 1934, Mr. Antony Fokker acquired the exclusive European rights for the manufacture and sale of the Douglas "Transport" in Europe.

TYPE.—Twin-engined commercial monoplane.

WINGS.—Cantilever low-wing monoplane, of Douglas-Northrop cellular multi-web construction. Wings tapered in plan form and thickness. The centre portion of the wing extends underneath the fuselage and serves as a mounting for both engine nacelles. The outer wing-panels are detachable by multi-bolted flange joints. The entire trailing-edge of the wing between the ailerons, including the portion beneath the fuselage, incorporates an adjustable flap, which greatly reduces the landing speeds and gives a consequent increase in the speed range. The material used is a newly-developed high-tension strength aluminium-alloy. The ailerons are metal-framed and covered with fabric. The right aileron is equipped with a trailing-edge trimming-flap.

FUSELAGE.—The fuselage is constructed entirely of the same new alloy as the wing. It is semi-monocoque construction, consisting of transverse frames of formed sheet, longitudinal members of extruded bulb angles, with a covering of smooth sheet.

TAIL UNIT.—Tail-plane and fin are of multi-cellular construction using the same alloy as the wing and fuselage. Rudder and elevators have aluminium-alloy framework covered with fabric. The elevators and rudder carry trimming flaps, which are adjustable in the air. Full swivelling tail-wheel, with oleo shock-absorber unit.

UNDERCARRIAGE.—Retractable type. Consists of two units, each comprising two oleo type shock-absorbers and a wheel fitted with hydraulic brakes. These brakes are operated by either pilot and are differentially controlled through the rudder-pedals. When retracted, the wheels move upward and forward into the nacelles, leaving a small portion protruding, to allow an emergency landing to be made with the wheels retracted. Complete control of the brakes is maintained with the wheels in the retracted position.

POWER PLANT.—Two supercharged, geared Wright "Cyclone" SGR-1820 F-52 air-cooled engines, each rated at 760 h.p. at 2,100 r.p.m. at 5,800 ft. (1,766 m.). Two main fuel tanks, each of 180 U.S. gallons (681.3 litres) capacity, and two auxiliary fuel tanks, each of 75 U.S. gallons (283.9 litres) capacity, carried in the centre-section of the wing. One oil tank, of 19 U.S. gallons (71.9 litres), in each nacelle. Hand and direct electric starters. Controllable pitch, three-bladed metal airscrews. The engine mounting, with all accessories, forward of the fireproof bulkhead in the nacelles, including the oil system and engine cowling, is quickly detachable as well as interchangeable right and left.　(1936)

ACCOMMODATION.—Pilot's cockpit is forward of the wing and is normally reached through a corridor from the passenger cabin. Emergency exit is provided in the roof. Dual controls are of the individual wheel type, with pedal foot-controls. The passenger cabin is 26 ft. 4 in. (7.8 m.) long, 6 ft. 3 in. (1.91 m.) high and 5 ft. 6 in. (1.68 m.) wide, and is normally fitted to accommodate fourteen passengers. The passengers' seats are fully adjustable for reclining or facing backward and are mounted in rubber, to minimise vibration. Passengers are seated high enough above the wing for excellent vision from all seats. Ventilating and steam heating systems are provided. The cargo and mail compartment is located in the plane of the engines and airscrews and is separated from the rest of the machine by a sound-deadening bulkhead 2.5 in. (6.35 cm.) thick. This compartment has a capacity for 1,000 lbs. (454 kgs.) and is provided with a loading door in the side of the fuselage. An additional cargo and baggage compartment, with an outside door for loading, is located aft of the cabin. The passenger cabin is entered by a door on the left side of the fuselage. Aft of this door is the buffet, complete with refrigerator and facilities for serving meals in flight. Lavatory at the rear of the cabin. Opposite the main entrance door is an emergency exit door. Equipment for night-flying and radio telephone communication is provided.

DIMENSIONS.—Span 85 ft. (25.91 m.), Length 61 ft. 11¾ in. (18.9 m.), Height 16 ft. 3¾ in. (4.95 m.), Wing area 939 sq. ft. (87.2 sq. m.).

WEIGHTS AND LOADINGS.—Weight empty 12,408 lbs. (5,620 kg.), Useful load 6,152 lbs. (2,790 kg.), Weight loaded 18,560 lbs. (8,410 kg.), Wing loading 19.76 lbs./sq. ft. (96.4 kg./sq. m.), Power loading 12.21 lbs./h.p. (5.53 kg./h.p.).

PERFORMANCE.—Maximum speed (airscrew-pitch set for cruising) 210 m.p.h. (338 km.h.), Cruising speed (at 8,000 ft. = 2,438 m.) 190 m.p.h. (306 km.h.), Cruising speed (at 13,000 ft. = 3,958 m.) 200 m.p.h. (320 km.h.), Landing speed 62 m.p.h. (100 km.h.), Initial rate of climb 1,000 ft./min. (305 m./min.), Service ceiling 22,450 ft. (6,840 m.), Absolute ceiling 24,300 ft. (7,410 m.), Absolute ceiling on one engine 9,100 ft. (2,770 m.), Absolute ceiling on one engine with one-half normal fuel 10,600 ft. (3,228 m.).

The Douglas SC-54 Search and Rescue version of the C-54 Skymaster.　(1956–57)

THE DOUGLAS DC-5.

U.S. Navy designations: R3D-1 and R3D-2.

Only a small number of DC-5 commercial transports were built but there are two service variants of this type which are still in service.

The R3D-1 is a Navy personnel transport and accommodates a crew of four, comprising pilot, second pilot, engineer and radio operator, and sixteen passengers.

The R3D-2, in service with the Marine Corps, is primarily a cargo transport but can be converted to passenger type by the addition of seats. It has been specially designed to carry aircraft engines, airscrews and other heavy freight. Special handling equipment including winch, hoist, loading platform, and ramp, is provided and a loading door 66 in. × 80 in. permits the handling of complete aero-engines on their shipping stands.

Both models are fitted with two 900 h.p. Wright "Cyclone" engines and have a similar performance to that of the DC-5 described herewith.

TYPE.—Twin-engined Transport.

WINGS.—High-wing cantilever monoplane. All-metal structure, similar to that of DC-3. Wing-tips are detachable. Ailerons have metal frames with fabric covering. Hydraulically-operated trailing-edge flaps.

FUSELAGE.—Semi-monocoque construction, circular at the wing-root. Incorporates a substantial keel along the bottom of the fuselage. Structure consists essentially of transverse frames, longitudinal stiffeners and light-gauge sheet covering.

TAIL UNIT.—Cantilever monoplane type with the tail-plane set at a dihedral angle. Tail-plane and fin of metal-covered two-spar construction. Elevators and rudder are fabric-covered metal structures. Trim-tabs, controllable in flight, are provided for rudder and elevators.

LANDING GEAR.—Fully retractable tricycle type. All three units of the landing gear, consisting of the two main gears and the nose gear, are shock-mounted. Hydraulically-operated wheel-brakes.

POWER PLANT.—Two Wright "Cyclone" GR-1820-G102A nine-cylinder radial air-cooled engines, each rated at 900 h.p. at 2,300 r.p.m. at 6,700 ft. (2,043 m.). Two fuel tanks, each accommodating approx. 275 U.S. gallons (1,041 litres); total fuel capacity approx. 550 U.S. gallons (2,082 litres). Each nacelle carries a stainless steel oil tank of approx. 17 U.S. gallons (64.3 litres) and approx. 3½ gallons (13.2 litres) foaming space. Starters are direct hand-electric type. Three-bladed hydromatic, full-feathering airscrews. Engine mountings of welded steel-tubing are interchangeable with DC-3 mountings when Wright engines are installed. Entire nacelle forward of fireproof bulkhead is detachable.

ACCOMMODATION.—Crew of three, with two pilots side-by-side, in nose. Sixteen passengers are accommodated in the standard version. Alternative arrangements accommodate eighteen or twenty-two passengers. Ventilating, steam heating and sound-proofing systems. A lavatory and buffet are provided. Provisions are made for the installation of radio equipment and baggage is accommodated in three compartments—the left forward compartment with approximately 98 cub. ft. (2.77 cub. m.) space; the right forward compartment with approximately 34 cub. ft. (.96 m.) space; and the rear baggage compartment with approximately 146 cub. ft. (4.06 cub. m.) of space.

DIMENSIONS.—Span 78 ft. (23.8 m.), Length 62 ft. 2 in. (18.96 m.), Height 19 ft. 10 in. (6.05 m.), Wing area 824 sq. ft. (76.6 sq. m.).

WEIGHTS AND LOADINGS.—Weight empty 13,674 lbs. (6,**200** kg.), Useful load 6,326 lbs. (2,870 kg.), Gross weight 20,000 lbs. (9,070 kg.), Wing loading 24.2 lbs./sq. ft. (118.2 kg./sq. m.), Power loading 11.1 lbs./h.p. (5 kg./h.p.).

PERFORMANCE.—Maximum speed at 7,700 ft. (2,350 m.) 230 m.p.h. (370 km.h.), Cruising speed at 10,000 ft. (3,050 m.) (65% power) 202 m.p.h. (325 km.h.), Initial rate of climb (take-off power) 1,585 ft./min. (486 m./min.), Service ceiling 23,700 ft. (7,230 m.), Absolute ceiling on one engine 11,400 ft. (3,480 m.), Maximum range 1,600 miles (2,575 km.).　(1942)

The Douglas R3D-2 Service Transport (two 900 h.p. Wright "Cyclone" engines) developed from the DC-5 Airliner.

THE DOUGLAS DC-6A.
U S. Air Force designation: C-118.
U.S. Navy designation: R6D-1.

The DC-6A is a freight-carrying version of the standard DC-6. It uses the wings, tail-unit and landing-gear of the DC-6 but has an entirely new fuselage incorporating features which experience has shown to be necessary for successful military and commercial cargo operation.

The new fuselage is 5 ft. (1.525 m.) longer than that of the DC-6, giving the DC-6A a total cargo space of 5,000 cub. ft. (141.5 m.³). The main cabin, of constant cross-section throughout, is 68 ft. (20.74 m.) long, 7 ft. 9 in. (2.36 m.) high, and 8 ft. 9 in. (2.67 m.) wide at floor level. Two large doors, one forward and the other aft of the wings, are hinged at their top edges and swing upward to be clear of loading equipment. A self-powered loading elevator, which folds up for storage within the aircraft, can be attached to either front or rear cargo door and will lift 4,000 lb. (1,820 kg.) from truck-bed height to cabin floor level.

The DC-6A has automatically controlled cabin pressurisation and air-conditioning systems to permit high-altitude transportation of perishable cargoes.

Production of the military versions of the DC-6A—the C-118 and C-118A for the U.S.A.F. and the R6D-1 for the U.S. Navy—came to an end on December 29, 1955, after one C-118, 101 C-118A's and 65 R6D-1's had been delivered. These transports, which are in service with MATS and the U.S. Navy Fleet Logistic Air Wings, can carry 74 passengers, or 60 stretcher cases or 27,000 lb. (12,260 kg.) of cargo. The take-off weight is 107,000 lb. (48,530 kg.).

POWER PLANT.—Four Pratt & Whitney Double-Wasp R-2800-CB17 eighteen-cylinder radial air-cooled engines each developing 1,900 h.p. at max. continuous cruise and with 2,500 h.p. available for take-off with alcohol-water injection. Hamilton Standard or Curtiss Electric full-feathering and reversible airscrews. Standard fuel capacity 3,992 U.S. gallons (15,111 litres), with optional capacities of 5,406 U.S. gallons (20,550 litres) and 5,512 U.S. gallons (20,918 litres).

DIMENSIONS.—
As for DC-6 except Length 105 ft. 7 in. (32.20 m.).

WEIGHTS AND LOADINGS.—
Weight empty 49,767 lb. (22,595 kg.).
Gross T.O. weight 106,000 lb. (48,125 kg.).
Wing loading 72.5 lb./sq. ft. (353.8 kg./m.²).
Power loading 10.6 lb./h.p. (4.81 kg./h.p.).

PERFORMANCE.—(At 95,000 lb.= 42,800 kg. gross weight).—
Max. speed 360 m.p.h. (576 km.h.) at 18,100 ft. (5,520 m.).
Cruising speed 307 m.p.h. (494 km.h.) at 22,400 ft. (7,390 m.).
Landing speed 93 m.p.h. (149 km.h.).
Initial rate of climb 1,120 ft./min. (374 m./min.).
Initial rate of climb (one engine out) 620 ft./min. (203 m./min.).
T.O. distance to 50 ft. (15.25 m.) at max. A.U.W. (no wind) 4,500 ft. (1,492 m.).
Landing distance from 50 ft. (15.25 m.) 3,010 ft. (918 m.).
Landing distance from 50 ft. (15.25 m.) with reversible airscrews 2,250 ft. (686 m.).
Normal range 3,860 miles (6,176 km.).
Max. range 4,910 miles (7,856 km.).

(1956–57)

THE DOUGLAS DESTROYER
U.S.A.F. designations: B-66 and RB-66

The B-66, which is in service with the U.S.A.F., is based on the A3D previously described, with design and engineering changes to modify the carrier-based aircraft design into a land-based bomber.

Versions of the basic B-66 so far announced are :—

RB-66A. First five production aircraft, used for service test only. Allison J71-A-9 turbojet engines. First RB-66A flew on June 28, 1954.

One RB-66A has been re-engined with General Electric CJ-805-23 turbofan engines in Convair 600 nacelles. Flown for the first time at the end of February, 1960, it is illustrated under the "General Electric" heading in the "Aero-Engines" section of this work. Earlier, the General Electric CJ-805-3 turbojet had also been flight tested in an RB-66 flying test-bed aircraft.

B-66B. First production bomber version, fitted with in-flight refuelling equipment. First B-66B flew on January 4, 1955. Early machines with Allison J71-A-11 turbojets ; later models with J71-A-13. Crew of three. Deliveries to U.S.A.F. began on March 16, 1956.

RB-66B. Production development of RB-66A for night photographic reconnaissance, incorporating improvements introduced on B-66B. Crew of three. First RB-66B flew on June 28, 1954. Deliveries to U.S.A.F. started on February 1, 1956.

The Douglas B-66B Destroyer light bomber (two Allison J71 turbojet engines)

The Douglas WB-66D, the weather reconnaissance version of the RB-66B   (*Gordon Williams*)

The RB-66 is in the 600-700 m.p.h. (965-1,126 km.h.) class and has a range of 1,500-1,750 miles (2,415-2,815 km.), but no other performance data is available for publication.

RB-66C. Development of RB-66B for all-weather electronics reconnaissance. Crew of four. First RB-66C flew on October 29, 1955. Deliveries to U.S.A.F. started on May 11, 1956.

WB-66D. First production aircraft ever designed specifically for weather reconnaissance. Equipped with instruments to collect meteorological data over combat area or for normal Air Weather Service duties. Data fed into electronic computer to obtain complete weather report. Crew of five. Deliveries to U.S.A.F. started on June 26, 1957.

The structural description given for the A3D can be assumed to apply in general to the B-66. The information given below, however, refers primarily to the latter aircraft.

TYPE.—Twin-jet bomber (B-66), tactical reconnaissance (RB-66) or weather reconnaissance (WB-66) aircraft.

WINGS.—As for A3D but without wing folding. All-metal stressed-skin structure. All-metal single-slotted flaps. All-metal internal-pressure-balanced ailerons. Thermo-cyclic de-icing system. Areas : flaps (total) 108.8 sq. ft. (10.11 m.²), ailerons (total) 32.6 sq. ft. (3.03 m.²). Gross wing area 780 sq. ft. (72.5 m.²)

FUSELAGE.—Aluminium-alloy and magnesium semi-monocoque structure.

TAIL UNIT.—As for A3D but vertical surfaces non-folding. Thermo-cyclic de-icing to fin and tailplane. Areas: fin 129.9 sq. ft. (12.07 m.²), rudder 32.5 sq. ft. (3.02 m.²), tailplane 114.8 sq. ft. (10.66 m.²), elevators (total) 52.2 sq. ft. (4.85 m.²)

LANDING GEAR.—Retractable nose-wheel type. Hydraulic actuation. Air-oil shock struts designed by Douglas and manufactured by Cleveland Pneumatic Tool Co. Bendix disc brakes. Large ribbon braking parachute stowed under rear gun turret Wheelbase 27 ft. 7 in. (8.41 m.). Track 10 ft. 10 in. (3.30 m.)

POWER PLANT.—Two Allison J71-A-13 turbo-jet engines (10,200 lb. = 4,627 kg. s.t. each) in underwing pods. Two wing and two fuselage tanks. Normal internal fuel capacity 4,489 U.S. gallons (16,993 litres.) Auxiliary fuel in pylon-mounted underwing tanks. Equipment for probe and drogue flight refuelling. Provision for attaching six JATO bottles to lower part of rear fuselage.

ACCOMMODATION (B-66B and RB-66B).—Pilot seated in front of navigator and gunner. All three face forward in ejector seats, with explosively-jettisonable roof hatches. Pressurised and air-conditioned. Normal pressure differential of 5 lb./sq. in. (0.35 kg./cm.²) reduced to 2.75 lb./sq. in. (0.19 kg./cm.²) for combat. Automatic electrical control system eliminates at least 10 pilot functions. Western Electric K-5 navigation system.

ARMAMENT AND EQUIPMENT.—Two 20 mm. cannon in tail ball-turret. General Electric electronic fire-control system. Provision for wide selection of bomb combinations, including nuclear weapons, in internal bay (B-66). Photographic equipment, comprising three K46 night cameras and a K38 day camera, photoflash bombs and cartridges, in RB-66. Meteorological instruments and computer in WB-66.

DIMENSIONS.—
Span 72 ft. 6 in. (22.11 m.)
Length 75 ft. 2 in. (22.9 m.)
Height 23 ft. 7 in. (7.18 m.)

WEIGHTS (B-66B).—
Weight empty 42,788 lb. (19,408 kg.)
Normal bomb load 15,000 lb. (6,800 kg.)
Normal loaded weight 78,000 lb. (35,380 kg.)
Max. overloaded weight 83,000 lb. (37,648 kg.)
Wing loading (normal) 100 lb./sq. ft. (488 kg./m.²)

WEIGHTS (RB-66B).—
Weight empty 43,819 lb. (19,875 kg.)
Normal loaded weight 70,000 lb. (31,750 kg.)
Max. overloaded weight 83,000 lb. (37,648 kg.)

PERFORMANCE.—
Max. speed 700 m.p.h. (1,125 km.h.)
Service ceiling over 45,000 ft. (13,700 m.)
Range over 1,500 miles (2,400 km.)

(1960–61)

Douglas RB-66C all-weather electronics reconnaissance aircraft   (*AiReview, Japan*)

The Douglas TBD-1 "Devastator" Three-seat Torpedo-Bomber (825 h.p. Pratt & Whitney "Twin Wasp-Junior" engine).

THE DOUGLAS TBD-1 "DEVASTATOR."

TYPE.—Three-seat Torpedo-Bomber.

WINGS.—Low-wing cantilever monoplane. Wings taper in chord and thickness and arranged to fold upwards at points about midway between roots and tips. All-metal two-spar structure with corrugated covering from points of attachment of landing gear to tips. Balanced ailerons on outer folding portion of wings. Split flaps on inner sections of wings.

FUSELAGE.—Oval metal structure with stressed-skin covering. Compartment for internal stowage of torpedo or bombs in forward portion of fuselage gives pigeon-chested lower lines. Fuselage stressed for deck-arrester gear.

TAIL UNIT.—Cantilever monoplane type. Fin built integral with fuselage. Triangular tail-plane. Balanced elevators and rudder. All metal framework with metal-covered fixed surfaces and fabric-covered elevators and rudder. Trimming-tabs in control surfaces.

LANDING GEAR.—Retractable type. Semi-cantilever shock-absorber legs hinged to front spar and are raised backwards, the wheels being half buried in the undersides of the wings when retracted. Hydraulic retraction. Non-retractable tail-wheel. Deck-arrester hook forward of tail-wheel.

POWER PLANT.—One 825 h.p. Pratt & Whitney "Twin-Wasp Junior" SB4G fourteen-cylinder radial air-cooled engine in NACA cowling. Hamilton-Standard controllable-pitch airscrew.

ACCOMMODATION.—Crew of three in tandem under continuous transparent canopy with sliding sections over each cockpit. Bomb-aimer's position beneath pilot with bomb-sights and releases, intercommunication between bomb-aimer and pilot, etc. Full radio equipment, automatic pilot, night-flying equipment, deck-arrester gear, etc. Internal stowage for one 21-in. Bliss-Leavitt aircraft torpedo or large armour-piercing bomb. Armament consists of one fixed .3-in. machine-gun in top cowling and synchronised to fire through the airscrew and one .5-in. machine-gun on a movable mounting in rear cockpit.

DIMENSIONS.—Span 50 ft. (15.25 m.), Length 35 ft. 6 in. (10.8 m.), Height 18 ft. 1 in. (5.5 m.).

WEIGHT LOADED.—9,300 lbs. (4,220 kg.).

PERFORMANCE.—Maximum speed 225 m.p.h. (360 km.h.) at 9,000 ft. (2,745 m.), Range 985 miles (1,576 km.) at 180 m.p.h. (288 km.h.).

(1942)

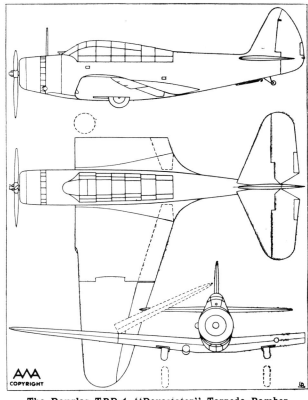

The Douglas TBD-1 "Devastator" Torpedo-Bomber.

THE DOUGLAS "DOLPHIN."

The Douglas "Dolphin" is a six-eight-seat amphibian which was originally produced for commercial use. Its outstanding success, both on air lines and in private operation, attracted the attention of the U.S. Government, with the result that contracts have been awarded by the Army, Navy and the Coast Guard.

TYPE.—Six-eight-seat monoplane amphibian.

WINGS.—A single-piece cantilever monoplane, attached direct to top of the hull by nickel steel bolts. The wing structure consists of two spruce box-spars, girder ribs, chrome-molybdenum steel fittings, and the whole wing is covered with spruce plywood. Ailerons, of the Handley Page slot type, are metal framed and are covered with fabric.

HULL.—A semi-monocoque structure with two steps, the rear one terminating in a vertical knife-edge. Structure is of duralumin, with the outer skin riveted together above the waterline and screwed below. There are five watertight compartments, with three external hatchways.

TAIL UNIT.—Monoplane type, with two small auxiliary fins on either side of the main fin. Framework is of aluminium-alloy. Covering of rudder and elevator is fabric and of tail-plane and fins of aluminium-alloy sheet. Balanced rudder and elevators. Adjustable tail-plane.

UNDERCARRIAGE.—Retractable type. Main chassis and tail-wheel retract in one operation. Main wheels are raised upwards to position above waterline with axles acting as radii about their hull attachment fittings by shortening of the oleo legs. Tail-wheel pivots upward around lower attaching fitting until it is close to the hull aft of the rear step. The retracting and lowering is operated by a hydraulic system, with control valves and hand-pump conveniently arranged in the cockpit, for use by either pilot. Air strut shock-absorbers are installed in both the main chassis and tail-wheel assemblies. The tail-wheel swivels through 360°.

POWER PLANT.—Two 420 h.p. Pratt & Whitney "Wasp" nine-cylinder radial air-cooled engines are mounted in nacelles carried above and in front of the wing. The nacelles are of welded chrome-molybdenum steel, covered with conventional aluminium-alloy cowling. Two 96 U.S. gallons fuel tanks and two 37 U.S. gallons reserve fuel tanks are carried in the wing. Oil tank in each engine nacelle. Electric inertia starters. Two two-bladed metal airscrews.

(1932)

ACCOMMODATION.—Pilot's compartment, seating two side-by-side, with complete dual control, is located in line with the leading-edge of the wing. Watertight doors front and rear, and an exit hatch in the roof are provided. Under the wing is a cabin for six passengers. This also has watertight doors front and rear and also one removable exit window on each side. A lavatory is located aft of the cabin. Space for baggage is provided both in a compartment forward of the pilot's compartment and abaft the rear cabin hatchway.

DIMENSIONS.—Span 60 ft. (18.3 m.), Length 45 ft. (13.7 m.), Height 14 ft. (4.3 m.), Wing area 575 sq. ft. (48 sq. m.).

WEIGHTS AND LOADINGS.—Weight empty 6,100 lbs. (2,769 kg.), Disposable load 2,850 lbs. (1,294 kg.), Weight loaded 8,950 lbs. (4,063 kg.), Wing loading 15.1 lbs./sq. ft. (73.6 kg./sq. m.), Power loading 10.9 lbs./h.p. (4.9 kg./h.p.).

PERFORMANCE.—Maximum speed 151 m.p.h. (241.6 km.h.), Cruising speed 108 m.p.h. (172.8 km.h.), Landing speed 61 m.p.h. (97.6 km.h.), Initial rate of climb 860 ft./min. (262.3 m./min.), Service ceiling 17,200 ft. (5,246 m.). (1932)

The Douglas "Dolphin" Six-seat Cabin Amphibian (two 420 h.p. Pratt & Whitney "Wasp" engines).

A Douglas D.T.2 Torpedo Carrier (Liberty engine).

THE DOUGLAS DT-2 TORPEDO PLANE.

The Douglas DT-2 Torpedo Plane is a machine of extremely sturdy construction, a requirement naturally desired for operations at sea with the fleets. It is a single-bay tractor biplane with the 400 h.p. "Liberty" engine and nose radiator. The first model, DT-1, had side radiators.

The fuselage is of welded steel tubing, braced with tie-rods and provided with stiffening gussets. It is built in three detachable sections—engine section, mid section and tail section—the two first-named being plated with · aluminium, while the tail section is covered with fabric.

The vertical tail surfaces have conventional wood frames, while the horizontal tail surfaces are made of welded steel tubing. The tail skid is a steel tube and is steerable.

The undercarriage is remarkable for its wide tread—10 ft.—and consists of two steel tube Vees, laterally braced to the fuselage by two steel tubes faired with wood, and carrying rubber-sprung wheel for land use. For sea use two long wooden floats may quickly be substituted. There is no tail float.

The wings are of standard box beam and built-up rib construction of wood and fabric covered. The top wings are in three panels, the bottom wings in two panels.

Specification of the Douglas DT-2 Plane.

Seats	..	..	1.
Span, upper and lower	..	..	50 ft. (15.25 m.).
Length	..	..	37 ft. 7½ in. (11.5 m.) (with floats).
Height	..	..	15 ft. (4.57 m.).
Chord	..	..	7 ft. 6 in. (2.43 m.).
Wing area	..	..	707 sq. ft. (66 sq. m.).
Engine	..	..	400 h.p. "Liberty."
Performance.			
High speed	..	..	100 m.p.h. (161 km.h.).
Low speed	..	..	50 m.p.h. (80 km.h.).
Climb.			
To 3,000 ft. (915 m.)	..	..	10 mins.
Service ceiling	..	..	6,500 ft. (2,000 m.).

(1925)

THE DOUGLAS DWC WORLD CRUISER

The Douglas World Cruiser, as far as its structure is concerned, is identical with the Douglas DT-2 Torpedo Plane. The internal equipment, however, which was specially designed for the Round-the-World of the U.S. Army Air Service, is of course quite different, insofar as the weights allowed for the standard military load (torpedo with release gear, firing gear, etc.) were used to increase the range of the machine to approximately 2,200 miles by the fitting of extra petrol and oil tanks.

The Douglas WC carries, as a land plane, six petrol tanks of aluminium with a total capacity of 600 galls., or nearly two tons. One tank, of the gravity type, holds 60 galls. and is located in the centre section of the top wing ; the second tank (150 galls.) in the engine section, just aft of the fire wall ; the third (160 galls.) in the mid section, below the pilot's floor ; the fourth (105 galls.) in the tail section, underneath the rear cockpit ; and the fifth and sixth tanks, of 62½ galls. each, are situated one each in the bottom wing roots. When the machine is fitted with floats, the second (150 galls.) petrol tank is removed.

Two oil tanks are mounted, one on each side of the "Liberty" engine, one holding 20 galls., the other 30 galls. They are interconnected.

The radiator is of square form, to allow for easy repairs, and is mounted on the nose of the fuselage. A 10-gall. copper reserve water tank is installed in the pilot's cockpit and is provided with an air pump, so that the pilot may pump water into the radiator if necessary. There is an electric starter, and the machine is equipped with dual controls. A radio direction finder is also included in the equipment.

The Douglas WC was selected for the Round-the-World Flight both for its ruggedness (well proved by the DT-2) and its remarkable weight-carrying capacity. The "Liberty" engine was selected for its long record of reliability. The engine used is the improved "Liberty," which weighs less than 2 lbs. per h.p. and develops 420 h.p. The air intakes have been rearranged to prevent back firing and fire hazard ; petrol pumps for the carburettor are so fitted as to reduce danger from petrol under pressure ; also, stronger timing gears have been provided to operate the two ignition systems.

The wheels are 36 × 8 in. in size and can quickly be replaced by floats.

Specification of the Douglas World Cruiser.

Seats	..	..	..	..	2.
Span	..	..	..	..	50 ft. (15.25 m.).
Length	..	..	..	..	35 ft. 6 in. (11.12 in.).
Height	..	..	..	..	13 ft. 7 in. (4.15 m.).
Wing area	..	..	..	..	721 sq. ft. (67 sq. m.).
Engine	..	..	..	..	420 h.p. " Liberty."
Weight empty	..	..	..	..	4,380 lbs. (1,980 kgs.) (land plane).
					5,180 lbs. (2,350 kgs.) (seaplane).
Weight loaded	..	..			7,380 lbs. (3,355 kgs.) (land plane).
					8,180 lbs. (3,710 kgs.) (seaplane).

Performance, as Land Plane.

High Speed	..	..	..	103 m.p.h. (166 km.h.).
Low speed	..	..	..	53 m.p.h. (86 km.h.).
Service ceiling	..	..	..	10,000 ft. (3,000 m.).
Cruising range	..	.:.	..	2,200 miles (3,550 km.).

Performance as Seaplane.

High speed	..	..	..	100 m.p.h. (161 km.h.).
Low speed	..	..	..	53 m.p.h. (86 km.h.).
Service ceiling	..	..	..	7,000 ft. (2,130 m.).
Cruising range	..	..	..	1,650 miles (2,660 km.h.)

Two of the Douglas World Cruisers taking off from the Orkneys on the " Round-the-World " Flight.

(1925)

The Douglas C-124A Globemaster II Military Transport (four 3,500 h.p. Pratt & Whitney R-4360-20W engines).

THE DOUGLAS GLOBEMASTER II.
U.S.A.F. designation: C-124.

The Globemaster II transport has the ability to load without disassembly 95 per cent. of all types of Army Field Force's equipment. It has nose-loading doors with vehicle ramps, a rear cargo hatch with elevator loading and auxiliary floor for double deck loading.

The last Globemaster II was delivered to the U.S.A.F. on May 9, 1955. In five years 446 C-124's were built at the Long Beach plant.

The following versions of the Globemaster II were built :—

YC-124. Prototype. Four 3,000 h.p. Pratt & Whitney R-4360-35 engines driving four-blade airscrews. First flew on November 27, 1949.

C-124A. First production model. Four 3,500 h.p. Pratt & Whitney R-4360-20W engines driving Curtiss three-blade feathering and reversible airscrews 16 ft. 7 in. (5.06 m.) in diameter. Later fitted with thermal de-icing and APS-42 search radar as originally installed in C-124C.

YC-124B. One Globemaster fitted with four 5,500 h.p. Pratt & Whitney YT34-P-1 turboprop engines. Developed to provide technical data on the operation of turboprop propulsive systems and also

to test the power-plant installation selected for the C-133. Flew for the first time on February 2, 1954. A.U.W. 200,000 lb. (90,800 kg.).

C-124C. Four 3,800 h.p. Ford-built Pratt & Whitney R-4360-63 engines. Development of C-124A. Fitted with APS-42 search radar in nose radome. Second production model. Production ceased in May, 1955.

One C-124 was modified to flight-test the Pratt & Whitney T57 turboprop engine, which was mounted in the nose of the fuselage.

A full structural description of the C-124 has appeared in previous editions of "All the World's Aircraft."

ACCOMMODATION.—Pilot's compartment seating two side-by-side in nose, with compartment immediately behind for flight-engineer, radio-operator and navigator. Galley, crew lavatory and relief crew compartment, with rest bunks, etc., further aft. Main cargo hold 77 ft. (23.48 m.) long, 12 ft. 10 in. (3.91 m.) high and 13 ft. (3.96 m.) wide, providing more than 10,000 cub. ft. (283 m.³) of usable cargo space. Clamshell

doors in nose ahead of nose-wheel provide an opening 11 ft. 8 in. (3.55 m.) high and 11 ft. 4 in. (3.45 m.) wide through which tracked or wheeled vehicles can be driven or rolled up built-in ramps. Electrically-operated elevator in middle of cargo hold, just aft of wing trailing-edge, provides additional loading and unloading facilities. Floor covered with 20 in. (50.8 cm.) grid pattern of heavy-duty tie down fittings. Two overhead travelling cranes, each lifting 8,000 lb. (3,629 kg.) or 16,000 lb. (7,258 kg.) run length of hold. For personnel transport interior of hold can be converted into a double-deck cabin with capacity for 200 troops and their field equipment. Fitted as an ambulance it can accommodate 127 stretcher cases, plus 52 sitting patients and medical attendants.

DIMENSIONS.—
Span 174 ft. 1½ in. (53.10 m.).
Length 130 ft. 5 in. (39.77 m.).
Height 48 ft. 3½ in. (14.72 m.).
WEIGHTS.—
Payload 50,000 lb. (22,700 kg.).
Weight loaded 175,000 lb. (79,450 kg.).
PERFORMANCE.—
No data available. (1958–59)

The Douglas A-20G Havoc Attack Bomber (two Wright R-2600-23 engines).

THE DOUGLAS HAVOC.
U.S. Army Air Forces designations : A-20, P-70 and F-3.
U.S. Navy designation : BD.

The original DB-7 was a private venture and was first produced to the order of the French Government. The first production DB-7 flew at El Segundo on August 17, 1939. When France fell the undelivered portions of the French contracts was taken over by the British Government and the DB-7 was given the type name Boston. The following briefly traces the development of this aeroplane from the Boston I to the A-20K (Boston V), the production of which ceased on September 20, 1944, after 7,097 had been built for the U.S., British and Russian Air Forces. Russia received twice as many as the R.A.F. and only some 800 less than the U.S. Army.

Boston I. Two Pratt & Whitney Twin-Wasp R-1830-S3C4G engines. The undelivered portion of the French contract. Mainly used for training but some experimentally converted for night fighting and given the British name Havoc I.

A-20 (Boston II). This was the first of the DB-7 series to be built to a U.S. Army Specification. The A-20 was fitted with two 1,500 h.p. Wright Cyclone R-2600-7 engines with exhaust-driven turbo-superchargers, and American armament and equipment. The Boston II had R-2600-A5B engines and British armament. Was later converted into a Night Fighter under the British name Havoc. The nose was lengthened and fitted with twelve forward-firing .303 in. guns. Operated as a night fighter without bomb-load but with special radar equipment, or as an intruder fighter-bomber with full armament and bombs. The British name Havoc has now been abandoned.

A-20A (BD-1). Two 1,600 h.p. Wright R-2600-11 engines with integral two-speed superchargers. Crew of three. American armament and bombing equipment.

A-20B (BD-2). Development of the A-20A. Armament consisted of two 50 cal. guns firing forward, one 50 cal. upper flexible gun, one 30 cal. lower flexible gun and one 30 cal. gun in the tail of each engine nacelle and firing aft. Nacelle guns remotely-controlled by foot trigger in rear compartment. Provision for temporary auxiliary fuel tanks to permit flight delivery to various war theatres.

A-20C (Boston III and IIIA). Two 1,600 h.p. Wright R-2600-23 engines. Armament consists of four fixed guns, two on either side of the transparent nose firing forward, two on a flexible mounting in the rear cockpit and one in the lower rear-firing position, all .30 cal. in A-20C or .303 in. in Boston III. Ejector-type exhaust stacks replaced the collector rings used on the earlier models and increased fuel capacity by use of a self-sealing fuel tank in the forward and rear bomb-bay compartments. Provision for carrying one 2,000 lb. naval torpedo. The Boston III was fitted with R-2600-A5BO engines, the light-bomber version accommodating a crew of four ; pilot, bomb-aimer, upper gunner and lower gunner. Boston IIIA same but built by the Boeing Aircraft Company. Some Boston III's and IIIA's fitted as Intruder fighters with four 20 m/m. cannon under forward fuselage, four .303 in. guns in the nose and two .303 in. guns in the upper flexible position. Overall length 47 ft. (14.33 m.).

XA-20E. An experimental model developed from the A-20A. Fitted with a 37 m/m. nose cannon and upper and lower General Electric turrets, each armed with two 50 cal. machine-guns. Only one built.

A-20G. Similar to A-20C except that the transparent bombardier nose replaced by a closed-in nose fitted, in the case of earlier versions of the A-20G, with four 20 m/m. cannon and two 50 cal. machine-guns, and ultimately with six 50 cal. guns. A few A-20G's had a single 50 cal. upper flexible gun, but this was soon replaced by a power-driven turret armed with two 50 cal. guns. One flexible 50 cal. gun in the rear-firing lower position. Thicker armour for increased crew protection on ground attack missions. Fuel capacity augmented by use of one self-sealing fuel-tank in the forward bomb-bay compartment and two in the rear compartment. Droppable streamline "belly" fuel tank also provided for long-range missions or ferrying. Later versions of the A-20G incorporated improved exhaust ejector stacks and fuel system. Wing racks provided for additional bombs or chemical tanks for smoke-screen laying. Contrary to previous models all auxiliary flight controls removed from rear compartment and provisions for photographic equipment deleted. Overall length increased to 48 ft. (14.64 m.).

A-20H. Two 1,700 h.p. Wright R-2600-29 engines. A later model of the A-20G. Various minor improvements incorporated.

A-20J (Boston IV). Identical to the later version of the A-20G except that the attack nose is replaced by a moulded plastic bombardier's nose incorporating bombing controls and flight navigation instruments. One in ten A-20G's completed as A-20J's to serve as squadron lead planes. Armament consists of two 50 cal. machine-guns, one on each side of the transparent nose, two in the dorsal power-operated turret and one in the lower rear-firing position. Overall length, 48 ft. 4 in. (14.7 m.).

A-20K (Boston V). Identical to the A-20H except that the attack nose is replaced by a bombardier's nose, as with the A-20J.

P-70. The P-70 is the night fighter version of the A-20 Havoc. The first P-70 was a conversion of the A-20A, with two 1,600 h.p. Wright R-2600-11 engines. The crew consisted of a pilot and radio-operator, and the armament four 20 m/m. cannon mounted in a fairing beneath the fuselage bomb-bay. The major portion of the radio equipment was installed in the nose.

P-70A. A conversion of the A-20G, with two 1,600 h.p. R-2600-23 engines. Armament consists of six 50 cal. machine-guns in the solid nose, a flexible 50 cal. gun in the upper rear position and a similar gun in the lower tunnel position.

P-70B. A development of the P-70A with six 50 cal. "package" guns, three on each side of the fuselage, and one 50 cal. gun in the lower tunnel position. The nose accommodates the special radar equipment.

F-3. A photographic reconnaissance version of the A-20A. A crew of two, pilot and photographer/rear-gunner, was carried. Photographic equipment was installed in the after portion of the bomb-bay. Armament consisted of two 30 cal. machine-guns, one on each side of the standard A-20 transparent nose, two flexible 30 cal. guns in the upper gunner's position, one flexible 30 cal. gun in the lower tunnel position, and two remotely-controlled fixed 30 cal. guns, one in the tail of each engine nacelle and firing directly aft.

Another Havoc project, the XO-53, with provision for photographic equipment in the bomb-bay was cancelled.

TYPE.—Twin-engined Attack Bomber.

WINGS.—Mid-wing cantilever monoplane. Each wing comprises an inner section with integral engine nacelle, an outer section and a wing-tip. Inboard section attached to fuselage at five points, one at leading-edge, two at main spar and two at rear shear web. Five similar attachment points between inner and outer sections. Single-spar aluminium-alloy structure with stressed Alclad skin. Trailing-edge flaps on inner wing sections, ailerons on outer sections. Trimming-tabs in both ailerons, interconnected and operated by single control in pilot's compartment.

FUSELAGE.—Aluminium-alloy monocoque structure with smooth flush-riveted Alclad skin. Detachable nose and tail cone.

TAIL UNIT.—Cantilever monoplane type. Tailplane set at 10 degrees dihedral. Fixed surfaces all metal with stressed-skin covering. Movable surfaces have metal frames with fabric covering. Trimming-tabs in both elevators and rudder controllable from pilot's cockpit.

LANDING GEAR.— Retractable tricycle type. Main wheels retract backwards into tails of engine nacelles, nose-wheel into fuselage. Hydraulic retraction with provision for emergency hand operation. Oleo-pneumatic shock-absorber struts. Goodyear wheels and hydraulic brakes.

POWER PLANT.—Two 1,700 h.p. Wright R-2600-29 fourteen-cylinder radial air-cooled engines with two-speed superchargers on welded steel-tube mountings attached to fireproof bulkheads at four points. Hamilton-Standard Hydromatic three-blade constant-speed full-feathering airscrews. Diameter : 11 ft. 3 in. (3.43 m.). Four

main self-sealing fuel tanks in wings, two inboard (136 U.S. gallons each) and two outboard (64 U.S. gallons each) of engine nacelles. Total normal fuel capacity : 400 U.S. gallons. Three auxiliary long-range tanks may be installed in bomb-bay and used in combat. One external long-range tank (374 U.S. gallons) may be carried under fuselage for long-range bombing missions, but must be dropped before bomb-doors can be opened. This tank is boat-shaped with flat top and is of Duramold plywood construction. For long-range ferrying four easily-removable tanks (676 U.S. gallons) may be carried in the bomb-bay.

ACCOMMODATION.—Bomb-aimer's compartment in A-20J and K has moulded transparent plastic nose with optically-flat section for bomb sighting. Replaced by closed-in attack nose in A-20G and H. Pilot's cockpit in front of leading-edge of wings. Entrance through side-hinged hatch in roof, the hinge-pins of which can be withdrawn for emergency exit. Aft of cockpit is the main internal bomb compartment with hydraulically-operated doors. Rear gunner's compartment aft of wings with gun positions above and below fuselage. A door in the floor is used for entry and exit and for the lower flexible gun. Upper emergency hatches are provided for two front and rear view positions for exit in case of descent on water. All crew positions are armoured.

ARMAMENT.—See above.

DIMENSIONS.—Span 61 ft. 3½ in. (17.8 m.), Length 48 ft. 4 in. (14.74 m.), Height 18 ft. 1½ in. (5.5 m.), Wing area 465 sq. ft. (43.2 sq. m.).

WEIGHTS AND LOADINGS.—Weight loaded 20,000 lbs. (9,080 kg.), Wing loading 43.01 lbs./sq. ft. (209.88 kg./sq. m.), Power loading 7.4 lbs./h.p. (3.36 kg./h.p.).

PERFORMANCE.—Maximum speed 325 m.p.h. (520 km.h.) at 14,500 ft. (4,420 m.), Cruising speed 280 m.p.h. (448 km.h.) at 14,000 ft. (4,270 m.), Stalling speed 98 m.p.h. (157 km.h.), Initial rate of climb 2,000 ft./min. (610 m./min.), Service ceiling 25,300 ft. (7,720 m.). (1945—46)

The Douglas A-26B Invader Attack Bomber (two 2,000 h.p. Pratt & Whitney R.2800-71 engines).

THE DOUGLAS INVADER.
U.S. Army Air Forces designation : A-26.
U.S. Navy designation : JD-1.

The contract for the prototype XA-26 was placed in June, 1941. Actually three experimental models were produced to the basic design, the XA-26 light bombardment and attack aeroplane, the XA-26A, a modification for use as a night fighter, and the XA-26B attack-bomber, mounting a large calibre cannon.

The XA-26 was flown for the first time on July 10, 1942, and it is interesting to note that this aeroplane carried approximately twice the bomb load required by the original specification and exceeded every performance guarantee. It was also 700 lbs. (318 kg.) under the designed weight. Tests with these three experimental models culminated in the design of the production A-26B which carried additional armour protection for the pilot and a closed-in nose armed with six .5 in. (12.7 m/m.) machine-guns. The A-26C which served as a lead ship, was fitted with a transparent bombardier nose and two forward-firing .5 in. (12.7 m/m.) guns. The FA-26C was the photographic-reconnaissance version.

The A-26D was to have been similar to the A-26B but with a revised armament consisting of eight 0.5 in. (12.7 m/m.) guns in the solid nose and six 0.5 in. (12.7 m/m.) guns in the wings. All orders for this version were cancelled after VJ-Day.

The XA-26F is an experimental conversion of an A-26B fitted with an auxiliary General Electric I-16 (U.S. Army designation J-31) turbo-jet unit in the fuselage and exhausting aft of the tail-unit. The jet installation, which replaces the rear gunner and the defensive turret armament, was made during the war with the aim of adding 35 m.p.h. (56 km.h.) to the maximum speed of the Invader. The project, however, was not completed until two months after VJ-Day.

The air scoop for the jet unit is above the fuselage amidships and the exhaust is through a tube 17 in. (43 c/m.) in diameter

and 19 ft. (5.8 m.) long from engine to tail. A standard 125 U.S. gallon (473 litre) fuel tank modified to carry kerosene was installed in the upper rear section of the bomb-bay, providing sufficient jet fuel for 25 minutes at full r.p.m.

On June 26, 1946, the XA-26F established a new speed record of 413 m.p.h. (661 km.h.) over 1,000 km. (621 miles) carrying 1,000 kg. (454 lbs.) of useful load. Water injection was not used for the two Pratt & Whitney R-2800-83 engines but the auxiliary jet engine was operated for 45 minutes of the flight, which was made at a height of 22,000 ft. (6,710 m.).

The JD-1 is a stripped version of the Invader used by the U.S. Navy as a target-tug.

The Invader first went into action in the European Theatre of Operations on November 19, 1944.

A total of 2,502 A-26 Invaders were built before production was stopped after VJ-Day. The Invader is still a standard service type in the U.S. Army Air Forces and it is also used to equip light bomber squadrons of the National Guard.

TYPE.—Twin-engined Attack Bomber.

WINGS.—Shoulder-wing cantilever monoplane. NACA low-drag laminar-flow wing section. Incidence (root) 2°, (tip) 1°. Dihedral (on median line) 4.5°. Root chord (on centre-line) 10 ft. 8 in. (3.25 m.), projected tip chord 4 ft. 10 in. (1.47 m.). Complete left and right-hand wing panels attach directly to fuselage without centre-section. Two-spar structure, the spars being built up of unspliced spar caps having integral end fittings. Chordwise stiffeners and flush-riveted Alclad skin. Wing area (less ailerons) 513.3 sq. ft. (47.68 sq. m.). Electrically-operated slotted trailing-edge flaps. Area of flaps 55.9 sq. ft. (5.19 sq. m.).

FUSELAGE.—All-metal semi-monocoque structure. Channel section formers, extruded longitudinal stringers and a flush-riveted Alclad skin.

TAIL UNIT.—Cantilever monoplane type. All-metal structure with stressed-skin covering, except for fabric-covered rudder. Trimming-tabs in elevators and rudder. Tailplane dihedral 10° 35 min. Tailplane span 23 ft. 1 in. (7 m.). Area of fin 48.23 sq. ft. (4.48 sq. m.). Area of rudder 23.1 sq. ft. (2.14 sq. m.).

LANDING GEAR.—Retractable tricycle type. Main wheels on single telescopic legs retract backwards into engine nacelles. Nose wheel on single leg which retracts backwards, turning through 90° to lie flat in the fuselage. Hydraulic actuation. Track 19 ft. 5.6 in. (5.94 m.), Wheel base 13 ft. 4 in. (4 m.).

POWER PLANT.—Two Pratt & Whitney R-2800-71 eighteen-cylinder radial air-cooled engines with two-speed superchargers, each rated at 1,600 h.p. and with 2,000 h.p. available for take-off. Three-blade Hamilton Standard Hydromatic constant-speed quick-feathering airscrews 12 ft. 7 in. (3.84 m.) diameter. Engine mountings, interchangeable right to left or *vice-versa*, built up of a large metal spinning forward and a stainless steel rear part, tied together by six identical forgings. The six engine attachment points pick up the front of the forgings and the bolts for removing the whole power-plant installation tie the aft end of the forgings and the engine mounting to the nacelle. All lines, pipes and wiring grouped together inside skin of mounting and fitted with quick release fittings. Cowling in two halves, upper and lower, and quickly removable. Quick-release access panels and doors in mounting. Access door in fire-wall permits mechanic to enter nacelle to work on engine accessory section. Two main fuel tanks (300 U.S. gallons =1,136 litres each), one in each nacelle. Two wing tanks (100 U.S. gallons=378 litres each) inboard of nacelles. Auxiliary tank (125 U.S. gallons=473 litres) in top forward section for bomb-bay. Total normal fuel capacity 925 U.S. gallons (3,502 litres). Long-range ferrying-tank (675 U.S. gallons=2,555 litres) may be carried in bomb-bay. One 30 U.S. gallon (2,555 litre) oil tank in top of each engine nacelle aft of leading-edge. Oil cooling intakes in leading-edge of wing outboard of nacelles.

ACCOMMODATION.—Normal crew of three. Pilot on port side of cockpit with bomb-aimer/radio-operator/gun-loader on starboard side and slightly to rear. Observer/turret-gunner in rear cockpit facing aft.

ARMAMENT.—Standard armament of A-26B consists of eighteen .5 in. (12.7 m/m.) machine-guns, six in nose (four on starboard side and two on port side) ; four under each wing outboard of airscrew discs in twin "package" mountings ; two in dorsal turret remotely-controlled by the observer with periscopic sighting ; and two in under-turret similarly controlled by the observer. Upper turret can be fixed to fire forward and operated by pilot. Guns in lower turret trained to fire slightly below horizontal and can be depressed downwards 90°. 2,400 maximum rounds for six nose guns, 1,000 rounds for each pair of turret guns. Alternative interchangeable nose armaments may consist of two 37 m./m. guns ; one 37 m/m. with two .5 in. (12.7 m/m.) guns on port side ; one 37 m/m. with four starboard .5 in. (12.7 m/m.) guns ; one 75 m/m. cannon with two port .5 in. (12.7 m/m.) guns ; and one 75 m/m. cannon with one 37 m/m. gun on port side. A-26C has transparent bomb-aimer's nose with only two .5 in. (12.7 m/m.) guns in troughs on starboard side. Later A-26C has three .5 in. (12.7 m/m.) guns in each wing in place of "package" guns. Bomb-bay may accommodate a maximum of four 1,000 lb. (454 kg.) bombs. A maximum of four 500 lb. (454 kg.) bombs may be carried under wings when bomb-bay load reduced to six 500 lb. (227 kg.) bombs. Other alternative bomb-loads up to a maximum of 5,000 lbs. (2,270 kg.). Two 2,000 lb. (907 kg.) torpedoes may be carried in bomb-bay.

ARMOUR.—Heavy dural armour plating along sides of fuselage from nose to rear of observer's cockpit ; under nose and both cockpits ; in front and behind crew positions ; under engine and in tail. Bullet-proof glass in cockpit canopy.

DIMENSIONS.—Span 70 ft. (21.35 m.), Length (A-26B) 50 ft. 9 in. (15.47 m.), Length (A-26C) 51 ft. 3 in. (15.63 m.), Height (over fin and rudder) 18 ft. 6 in. (5.64 m.).

WEIGHTS.—Normal loaded weight 27,000 lbs. (12,260 kg.), Maximum permissible loaded weight 32,000 lbs. (14,530 kg.).

PERFORMANCE.—Maximum speed (normal rated power) 359 m.p.h. (574.4 km.h.) at 16,700 ft. (5,090 m.), Cruising speed (62.5% power) 266 m.p.h. (4,256 km.h.) at 5,000 ft. (1,525 m.), Operational range at cruising speed with designed useful load 700 miles (1,120 km.), Maximum range (without ferry tank) 1,600 miles (2,560 km.) at 5,000 ft. (1,525 m.) at 206 m.p.h. (329.6 km.h.), Maximum range (with ferry tank) 3,000 miles (4,800 km.) at 5,000 ft. (1,525 m.) at 210 m.p.h. (336 km.h.), Service ceiling 28.500 ft. (8,690 m.), Ceiling on one engine 14,400 ft. (4,390 m.). (1947)

THE DOUGLAS O-2.

The Douglas XO-2 was designed by the Douglas Co., of Santa Monica, Cal., in 1924, to participate in the Army competition for observation aircraft. Seventy-five machines of this type were ordered in 1925 to replace the D.H.4B in various squadrons of the U.S. Army Air Service.

In general arrangement the machine follows the lines of the famous "World Cruiser," the principal modifications being in the design of the nose, which now includes the tunnel radiator and very much cleaner cowling lines and a simplified form of undercarriage, consisting of two oleo legs and two Vees hinged at the centre line of the underside of the fuselage and carrying one large diameter wheel at each extremity. Fuselage construction is of welded steel-tube fabric-covered.

The petrol tanks are carried in the bottom plane wing roots and are droppable in emergency.

The machine can be equipped with either the 400 h.p. Liberty or the 500 h.p. Packard engine.

The radiator is mounted under the engine, and shutters are so arranged that when closed they form a streamline section with the nose of the fuselage.

Dimensions.

Span	39 ft. 8 in.
Length	28 ft. 11 in.
Height	10 ft. 6 in.
Chord	5 ft. 8 in.

Performance with Liberty engine.

Max. speed	140 m.p.h.
Stalling speed ..	58 m.p.h.
Landing speed ..	55 m.p.h.
Cruising speed ..	110 m.p.h.
Service ceiling ..	17,000 ft.
Rate of climb at ground ..	1,100 ft. per min.

The following summary of performances of the O-2 type, with the Packard 1-A-1500 engine, is taken from the Lampert Report :—

Date of test	Jan. 12, 1925.
Pilot	Mr. Lockwood.
Engine	Packard 1-A-1500.
Rated power	500 at 2,065 r.p.m.
Airscrew dia. ..	9 ft. 8 in.
Weights :—	
Empty, with water ..	2,580 lbs.
Armament	218 lbs.
Equipment	377 lbs.
Crew	380 lbs.
Fuel	636 lbs.
Oil	82 lbs.
Weight loaded.. ..	4,253 lbs.

The Douglas O-2 biplane (400 h.p. Liberty engine).

Wing area (incl. ailerons) ..	411 sq. ft.
Wing loading	11.5 lbs./sq. ft.
Power loading	8.5 lbs./h.p.
Ground r.p.m.	1,750.

Performance Converted to Standard Atmosphere.

Density.	Temp.	Stand. Altitude.	Climbing Speed.				Level Speed.	
			Speed.	r.p.m.	Time	Rate.	m.p.h.	r.p.m.
1.000	15C	0	87.4	1,800	0	1,270	150.0	2,065
.863	4.5	5,000	90.0	1,800	4.45	992	144.5	2,010
.824	1.5	6,500	91.0	1,800	6 0	910	142.8	2,035
.737	- 4.5	10,000	92.5	1,800	10.33	720	138.0	2,005
.624	- 12.0	15,000	95.2	1,795	19.12	442	129.0	1,945
.502	- 20.0	21,200	98.7	1,770	44.3	100	110.0	1,825
.468	—	23,100	100.0	1,755	—	—	100.0	1,755

In connection with these two performances, it is interesting to note that the load factors required for U.S. Army Air Service Observation Aircraft are as follows :—

Wings at maximum lift, 8.5 ; wings, top load, 3.5 ; horizontal tail, 30 lbs./sq. ft. ; vertical tail, 25 lbs./sq. ft. ; fuselage, 6.

(1926)

THE DOUGLAS O-2C.

Specification.

Span	39 ft. 8 in.
Length	28 ft. 11 in.
Height	10 ft. 6 in.
Chord	5 ft. 8 in.

Speed, max.	140 m.p.h.
Speed, stalling ..	58 m.p.h.
Speed, landing ..	55 m.p.h.
Speed, cruising ..	110 m.p.h.
Service ceiling ..	17,000 ft.
Rate of climb	1,100 ft. per min.

(1927)

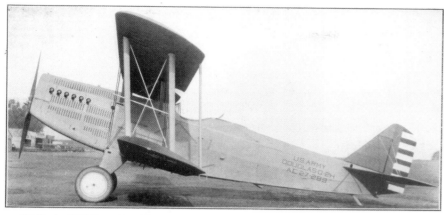

The Douglas O-2H Observation Biplane (400 h.p. Liberty engine).

THE DOUGLAS O-2H.

The Douglas O-2H was developed in 1927 as a replacement for the O-2C and was adopted by the U.S. Air Corps as the standard observation type for the Army. An order for 142 has been placed with the Company for this type.

Type.—Two-seat military observation biplane.

Wings.—Unequal-span, single-bay, staggered biplane. Top wings attached to wide centre-section, which is carried above fuselage on widely-splayed struts. Bottom wings attached direct to bottom rails of fuselage. One pair of splayed struts on either side of fuselage. Wings of wooden construction, covered with fabric. Ailerons fitted to all four planes.

Fuselage.—Welded chrome-molybdenum steel-tube structure, with rolled rod bracing. Covered with fabric aft of fire-wall and easily demountable metal cowling forward to radiator. With exception of fabric covering, entire fuselage structure of metal, including floors, fairing stringers, etc.

Tail Unit.—Normal type. Metal-framed, covered with fabric. Adjustable tail-plane. Balanced rudder.

Undercarriage.—Split type. Consists of two Vees, faired in, hinged to the bottom longerons, and two bent axles, hinged to a small Vee cabane under fuselage. Front legs of side Vees incorporate oleo type suspension.

Power Plant.—One 400 h.p. Liberty water-cooled engine and nose radiator. Main fuel tanks fitted with dump valves for released petrol, in emergency, are now installed in the fuselage. Oil tank carried behind engine, on fireproof bulkhead. Standard Steel airscrew.

Accommodation.—Crew of two, in tandem cockpits, aft of top wing. Pilot in front cockpit and observer-gunner in rear. Armament and other equipment installation have been greatly improved, both for convenience and comfort.

Dimensions.—Span 39 ft. 8 in. (12.09 m.), Length 30 ft. (9.14 m.), Height 10 ft. (3.05 m.), Chord 5 ft. (1.52 m.).

Performance.—Maximum speed 137 m.p.h. (220 km.h.), Cruising speed 110 m.p.h. (177 km.h.), Landing speed 58 m.p.h. (93 km.h.), Stalling speed 55 m.p.h. (89 km.h.), Initial rate of climb 1,250 ft./min. (2,809 m./min.), Service ceiling 18,200 ft. (5,545 m.). (1929)

THE DOUGLAS O-22.

The Douglas O-22 was produced in 1929 as a new and improved observation aeroplane for the U.S. Air Corps.

THE DOUGLAS O-25A.

The Douglas O-25A was produced in 1930 as an observation aeroplane for the U.S. Air Corps.

Type.—Two-seat military observation biplane.

Wings.—Unequal-span, single-bay staggered biplane. Top wings attached to fuselage by means of widely-splayed struts. Bottom wings attached direct to bottom rails of fuselage. One pair of splayed struts on either side of fuselage. Wings of wooden construction, covered with fabric. Ailerons of metal construction, with fabric covering, fitted to top and bottom wings.

Fuselage.—Welded chrome-molybdenum steel-tube structure, with rolled rod-bracing. Covered with fabric aft of fireproof bulkhead and with easily-demountable metal cowling forward to engine. With the exception of fabric covering, entire fuselage structure is of metal, including floors, fairing, stringers, etc.

Tail Unit.—Normal monoplane type, of metal frame construction, covered with fabric. Adjustable tail-plane. Balanced rudder. Steerable tail-wheel, with oleo-type shock-absorber.

Undercarriage.—Split type. Consists of two faired-in Vees, hinged to the bottom longerons, and two bent axles hinged to a small Vee cabane under fuselage. Front legs of side Vees incorporate oleo-type suspension.

Power Plant.—One 600 h.p. Curtiss "Conqueror" twelve-cylinder Vee type water-cooled engine. Main fuel tank, of 110 U.S. gallons capacity, and an auxiliary tank, of 36 U.S. gallons capacity, are located in front of the front cockpit. Oil tank carried in engine-compartment.

Accommodation.—Crew of two, in tandem cockpits, aft of top wing. Armament and other equipment common to observation aircraft. New swinging-arm type machine-gun mounting developed by the Douglas Aircraft Company in the rear cockpit. This permits the use of a front cockpit-type windshield on the rear cockpit and makes for better streamline of the fuselage in general.

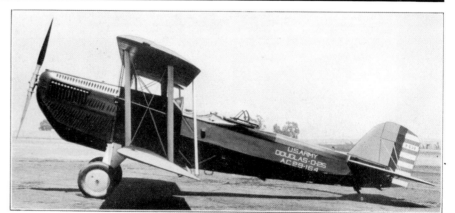

The Douglas O-25A Two-seat Observation Biplane (600 h.p. Curtiss "Conqueror" engine).

Dimensions.—Span 40 ft. (12.2 m.), Length 30 ft. 4 in. (9.2 m.), Height 10 ft. 10 in. (3.3 m.), Chord 5 ft. (1.52 m.), Stagger 1 ft. 10 in. (0.55 m.), Gap 6 ft. ¼ in. (1.8 m.).

Weights and Loadings.—Weight empty 3,400 lbs. (1,544 kg.), Disposable load 1,405 lbs. (637 kg.), Weight loaded 4,805 lbs. (2,181 kg.), Wing loading 13.3 lbs./sq. ft. (64.9 kg./sq. m.), Power loading 8 lbs./h.p. (3.6 kg./h.p.).

Performance.—Maximum speed 156.6 m.p.h. (250.6 km.h.), Cruising speed 125 m.p.h. (200 km.h.), Landing speed 62 m.p.h. (99.2 km.h.), Initial rate of climb 1,515 ft./min. (462 m./min.), Service ceiling 22,180 ft. (6,765 m.). (1931)

THE DOUGLAS O-38B.

The Douglas O-38B is an improved model observation biplane delivered to the U.S. Army Air Corps. It belongs to the same series as the types O-25A and O2MC described in the previous volume.

Type.—Two-seat military observation biplane.

Wings.—Unequal-span, single-bay staggered biplane. Top wings attached to fuselage by means of widely-splayed struts. Bottom wings attached direct to bottom rails of fuselage. One pair of splayed struts on either side of fuselage. Wings of wooden construction, covered with fabric. Ailerons of metal construction, with fabric covering, fitted to top and bottom wings.

Fuselage.—Welded chrome-molybdenum steel-tube structure, with rolled rod-bracing. Covered with fabric aft of fireproof bulkhead and with easily-demountable metal cowling forward to engine. With the exception of fabric covering, entire fuselage structure is of metal, including floors, fairing, stringers, etc.

Tail Unit.—Normal monoplane type, of metal construction and covered with fabric. Adjustable tail-plane. Balanced rudder. Tail-wheel rotatable through 360°.

Undercarriage.—Split type. Consists of two faired-in Vees, hinged to the bottom longerons, and two bent axles hinged to a small Vee cabane under fuselage. Front legs of side Vees incorporate oleo-type suspension.

Power Plant.—One 525 h.p. Pratt & Whitney "Hornet" nine-cylinder radial air-cooled engine. Main fuel tank, of 110 U.S. gallons capacity, is located in front of the front cockpit. Oil tank, of 14 U.S. gallons capacity, carried in engine-compartment. Two-bladed metal airscrew.

Accommodation.—Crew of two, in tandem cockpits, aft of top wing. Armament and other equipment common to observation aircraft. New swinging-arm type machine-gun mounting developed by the Douglas Aircraft Company in the rear cockpit. This permits the use of a front cockpit-type windshield on the rear cockpit and makes for better streamline of the fuselage in general.

Dimensions.—Span 40 ft. (12.2 m.), Length 30 ft. 4 in. (9.2 m.), Height 10 ft. 10 in. (3.3 m.), Chord 5 ft. (1.52 m.), Stagger 2 ft. 2 in. (0.65 m.), Gap 6 ft. ¼ in. (1.8 m.).

Weights and Loadings.—Weight empty 3,032 lbs. (1376.5 kg.), Disposable load 1,372 lbs. (623 kg.), Weight loaded 4,404 lbs. (1,999 kg.), Wing loading 12.16 lbs./sq. ft. (59.3 kg./sq. m.), Power loading 8.38 lbs./h.p. (3.8 kg./h.p.).

Performance.—Maximum speed 149 m.p.h. (238.4 km.h.), Cruising speed 128 m.p.h. (204.8 km.h.), Landing speed 59 m.p.h. (94.4 km.h.), Initial rate of climb 1,240 ft./min. (378 m./min.), Service ceiling 20,700 ft. (6313.5 m.). (1932)

THE DOUGLAS O-43A

The O-43A is a two-seat Army observation monoplane (developed from the earlier O-3I, of which 8 were built), a large number of which have been delivered to the Army Air Corps. It is a wire-braced "gull-wing" monoplane with a 675 h.p. liquid-cooled Curtiss "Conqueror" engine. It is reported to have a top speed of 188 m.p.h. (300 km.h.) and to have climbed to 10,000 ft. (3,050 m.) in a little over 7 minutes.

(1925)

THE DOUGLAS O-46-A.

The O-46-A is a two-seat observation monoplane which has been produced in quantity for the U.S. Army and National Guard. It is an all-metal high-wing braced monoplane with enclosed accommodation for a crew of two, has a single-leg cantilever undercarriage and is fitted with a 725 h.p. Pratt & Whitney "Twin-Wasp Junior" engine and Hamilton-Standard controllable-pitch airscrew.

(1937)

The Douglas PD-1 Coastal Patrol Flying-boat (two 525 h.p. Wright "Cyclone" engines).

THE DOUGLAS PD-1.

The Douglas PD-1 was developed from a U.S. Navy Bureau of Aeronautics' design for a twin-engined coastal-patrol flying-boat. It is a modification of the PN-10 and PN-12 types which were built by the U.S. Naval Aircraft Factory at Philadelphia.

TYPE.—Coastal patrol and bombing flying-boat.

WINGS.—Unequal-span, single-bay, unstaggered biplane. U.S.A.27 airfoil section. Top wings attached to wide centre-section, which is carried above the hull by the engine-mounting struts. Bottom wings are in four sections, two outer and two stub. Bottom stub wings are attached to hull and carry engines. Wings of aluminium alloy construction, fabric-covered. Ailerons fitted to upper wings only. Stabilising floats are fitted to tips of lower wings.

HULL.—Metal F-5 type hull. Framework of sheet duralumin channels riveted together. Covering is of duralumin sheet riveted to framework above waterline and screwed below. Floors of corrugated duralumin sheet. Two watertight transverse bulkheads.

TAIL UNIT.—Normal monoplane type. Metal framework covered with fabric. Adjustable tail-plane. Balanced rudder.

POWER PLANT.—Two 525 h.p. Wright "Cyclone" air-cooled radial engines. 677 U.S. gallons of petrol carried in seven tanks in hull and a further 110 U.S. gallons in two gravity tanks in upper centre wing panel. One oil tank carried in each engine nacelle. Two three-blade Standard Steel airscrews.

ACCOMMODATION.—Crew of four. Pilot and auxiliary pilot (who is also navigator and bomber) side-by-side in nose. Radio operator in midship cabin. Gunner-mechanic in cockpit aft of wings. Clear passage-way inside hull from bow to stern. Armament and other equipment common to machines of the type.

DIMENSIONS.—Span 72 ft. 10 in. (22.2 m.), Length 49 ft. 2 in. (15 m.), Height 16 ft. 4 in. (4.9 m.), Chord 9 ft. (2.7 m.), Gap 9 ft. 4 in. (2.8 m.).

WEIGHTS AND LOADINGS.—Weight empty 7,885 lbs. (3,580 kg.), Disposable load 6,995 lbs. (3,176 kg.), Weight loaded 14,880 lbs. (6,756 kg.), Wing loading 12.75 lbs./sq. ft. (62.1 kg./sq. m.), Power loading 14.15 lbs./h.p. (6.42 kg./h.p.).

PERFORMANCE.—Maximum speed 120.8 m.p.h. (193.3 km.h.), Cruising speed 100 m.p.h. (160 km.h.), Landing speed 51.8 m.p.h. (82.8 km.h.), Initial rate of climb 605 ft./min. (212 m./min.), Service ceiling 11,600 ft. (3,540 m.). (1931)

THE DOUGLAS P2D-1.

The Douglas P2D-1 is a new improved patrol biplane for the U.S. Navy. It bears many resemblances to the T2D-1 of 1928, but embodies complete up-to-date improvements.

TAIL UNIT.—Monoplane type. Consists of tail-plane, elevator, two fins and two rudders. Horizontal tail-plane is adjustable. Rudders balanced. All sections of metal construction. Tail-plane and fins are metal-covered. Elevator and rudders fabric-covered. 360° swivel tail-wheel.

UNDERCARRIAGE.—Divided-axle type. Axles and bracing-struts hinged to bottom longerons of fuselage. Vertical shock-absorber struts attached to front wing-spars below engine nacelles. Wheel-brakes.

FLOATS.—Twin, long, single-step type floats. Each float supported by front and rear "N" struts attached to bottom longerons of fuselage and front and rear stub-wing spars.

POWER PLANT.—Two 575 h.p. Wright "Cyclone" nine-cylinder radial air-cooled engines. 220 U.S. gallons of fuel carried in two tanks in fuselage. Two gravity tanks, of 136 U.S. gallons total capacity, are located in centre-section. An additional supply may be carried by means of two belly tanks, each of 108 U.S. gallons capacity, which may be slung beneath the fuselage. Total capacity of all tanks is 572 U.S. gallons. Oil tanks carried in each engine nacelle. Two three-bladed metal airscrews.

TYPE.—Patrol, torpedo and bombing convertible twin-float seaplane or landplane.

WINGS.—Equal-span, single-bay, unstaggered biplane. Top wings attached to wide centre-section, which is carried above the fuselage by vertical struts from the engine nacelles and inverted Vee struts from the fuselage. Bottom wings are in four sections, two outer and two stub. Bottom stub wings are attached directly to bottom longerons of fuselage and carry engines. Wings of aluminium-alloy construction, covered with fabric. Ailerons, of aluminium-alloy construction, with fabric covering, fitted to upper and lower wings.

FUSELAGE.—Welded chrome-molybdenum steel-tube structure, with rod bracing and fabric covering. Nose section of aluminium-alloy monocoque construction.

ACCOMMODATION.—Crew of three in tandem cockpits. Pilot in centre cockpit. Auxiliary pilot (who is also navigator and bomber) in forward cockpit, which is interconnected with nose section bombing compartment. Gunner-wireless-operator in rear cockpit. Armament and other equipment common to machines of this type.

The Douglas P2D-1 Patrol Biplane (two 575 h.p. Wright "Cyclone" engines) equipped as a landplane.

DIMENSIONS (as seaplane).—Span 57 ft. (17.37 m.), Length 44 ft. (13.42 m.), Height 15 ft. 5 in. (4.6 m.), Chord 8 ft. 6 in. (2.6 m.), Gap 8 ft. (2.4 m.).

WEIGHTS AND LOADINGS (as seaplane).—Weight empty 7,577 lbs. (3,440 kg.), Disposable load 5,323 lbs. (2,417 kg.), Weight loaded 12,900 lbs. (5,857 kg.), Wing loading 11.22 lbs./sq. ft. (54.75 kg./sq. m.), Power loading 14.20 lbs./h.p. (6.4 kg./h.p.).

PERFORMANCE (as seaplane).—Maximum speed 135 m.p.h. (216 km.h.), Cruising speed 108 m.p.h. (172.8 km.h.), Landing speed 61 m.p.h. (97.6 km.h.), Initial rate of climb 885 ft./min. (270 m./min.), Service ceiling 11,950 ft. (3,665 m.). (1932)

The Douglas F3D-2 Skyknight Two-seat All-weather Fighter (*Warren Bodie*).

THE DOUGLAS SKYKNIGHT.
U.S. Navy designation: F3D.

The Skyknight is a two-seat jet-propelled carrier-based all-weather fighter, the prototype of which first flew on March 22, 1948.

F3D-1. First production version. Two Westinghouse J34-WE-38 turbojet engines (3,250 lb. = 1,475 kg. s.t. each). First production aircraft flew on February 13, 1950.

F3D-2. Designed, with larger nacelles, for Westinghouse J46 engines but first production aircraft were fitted with J34 engines. Improved air-conditioning, wing spoilers for improved lateral control thicker bullet-proof windscreen, new type of auto-pilot, etc. First F3D-2 flew on February 14, 1951. Production complete. In service with U.S. Marine Corps.

The description which follows refers to the F3D-1.

TYPE.—Two-seat Naval All-weather Fighter.

WINGS.—Mid-wing cantilever monoplane. Laminar-flow wing section. All-metal stressed-skin structure. Wings fold upward for carrier stowage. Hydraulic folding. Slotted flaps inboard of ailerons.

FUSELAGE.—All-metal stressed-skin structure. Hydraulically-operated speed brakes, one on each side and one below fuselage aft of wings as in the AD Skyraider.

TAIL UNIT.—Cantilever monoplane type. Tailplane mounted on fin. All-metal stressed-skin structure.

LANDING GEAR.—Retractable nose-wheel type. Auxiliary tail-wheel under rear fuselage. Hydraulic retraction. Arrester hook under rear fuselage.

POWER PLANT.—Two Westinghouse J34-WE-38 axial-flow turbojet engines (3,250 lb. = 1,475 kg. s.t.) mounted on lower edges of forward fuselage. After removal of cowlings engines may be lowered on to handling trucks with a standard bomb hoist. Complete engine change in 1 hour. Normal fuel in fuselage above engines and aft of cockpit. Auxiliary fuel may be carried in drop tanks under each wing near folding joints.

ACCOMMODATION.—Crew of two side-by-side in pressurised cockpit with flat armoured windscreen and armoured canopy. Cabin pressurisation and air-conditioning by AiResearch expansion turbine fed by engine compressors. Emergency exit through escape chute from rear wall of cabin to underside of fuselage, the hydraulically-operated lower chute door acting as windbreak. Hatch in canopy roof for escape in event of ditching.

ARMAMENT.—20 mm. cannon armament in lower nose below radome. Provision under wings for bombs, rockets and other armament stores.

DIMENSIONS:—
Span 50 ft (15.25 m)
Length 45 ft 6 in (13.87 m)
Height 16 ft (4.88 m)

WEIGHTS:—
Max T–O weight 26,850 lbs (12,179 kg)

PERFORMANCE:—
Max speed 600 mph (965 km/h)
Rate of climb 4,500 ft (1,370 m)/min
Range 1,200 miles (1,931 km)

(1954–55)

The Douglas C-54D Skymaster Military Transport (four Pratt & Whitney R-2000-11 Twin-Wasp engines).—
(*William T. Larkins*).

THE DOUGLAS DC-4 SKYMASTER.
U.S. Army Air Forces designation: C-54.
U.S. Navy designation : R5D.

The design of the original DC-4 was developed by the Douglas Company in collaboration with the technical departments of five of the biggest airline companies in the United States. The prototype received its Approved Type Certificate in May, 1939, and it was then submitted to prolonged service tests under the supervision of United Air Lines. The first model was fitted with four 1,150 h.p. Pratt & Whitney R-2180 Twin-Hornet engines and had accommodation for 52 passengers. It was eventually sold to Japan and subsequently crashed.

On the basis of service tests a new and slightly scaled-down design was prepared for production with accommodation for 40-42 passengers and fitted with four 1,100 h.p. Pratt & Whitney R-2000 Twin-Wasp engines. In 1941 production of provisional orders for sixty aircraft of this type was slowed down owing to defence needs but later in the year the DC-4 design was converted to meet U.S. Army specifications, redesignated C-54, and ordered in large quantities as a long-range military transport. The first production C-54 flew early in 1942 without experimental prototype.

The Skymaster is still the standard four-engined transport in the U.S. Army and Navy air services, but large numbers, mainly of the C-54B and C-54E models, have been sold out of the service for conversion to civil use. Converted C-54Es were used by Pan American World Airways, American Overseas Airlines and T.W.A. to survey and inaugurate their trans-Atlantic landplane services to Europe after the war.

C-54. Four 1,100 h.p. Pratt & Whitney R-2000-3 radial engines. The original military conversion of the DC-4. Did not have the heavy-duty floor and floor support structure found in the later models in the C-54 Series. No large cargo door or facilities for handling military cargo. Main cabin had seats for 26 passengers. Fuel compartment in fuselage housed four fuel tanks to augment the standard wing tanks. Fuel capacity 3,580 U.S. gallons (13,550 litres).

C-54A (R5D-1). Four 1,100 h.p. Pratt & Whitney R-2000-7 engines. Structurally re-designed to provide for carrying heavy cargo. Large cargo-loading door cut in underside of fuselage aft of wings, floor and floor supporting structure strengthened to support heavy items of freight and twin-boom hoist and winch installed to load and unload cargo and ordnance. Provision for suspension beneath fuselage of items of heavy equipment the size and weight of which would prevent them from being loaded in the cabin. Cabin designed to be rapidly converted for carrying cargo or troops, or for the evacuation or transport of wounded. Fuel capacity 3,620 U.S. gallons (13,703 litres).

C-54B (R5D-2). Four 1,100 h.p. Pratt & Whitney R-2000-7 engines. Development of C-54A. Chief structural change consisted of the removal of two fuselage fuel tanks and installation of integral fuel tanks of comparable capacity in outer wings. Standardisation of cabin interior fittings to permit rapid conversion from cargo transport or troop carrier. Removable stretcher fittings and individual oxygen outlets throughout the cabin. Fuel capacity 3,720 U.S. gallons (14,081 litres).

C-54C. One special Skymaster equipped for the personal use of the late President Roosevelt. Fitted with electrically-operated elevator, Presidential state-room, three other state-rooms, main cabin with conference table, etc. Crew of seven and fifteen passengers with sleeping accommodation for six.

C-54D (R5D-3). Cargo model with cabin interior similar to C-54B. Many improvements introduced in C-54E progressively incorporated in C-54D, including later installation of R-2000-11 engines.

C-54E (R5D-4). Four Pratt & Whitney R-2000-11 engines with better altitude performance. Combines passenger features of original C-54 with cargo facilities of C-54A and B. Remaining two fuselage tanks removed and additional collapsible tanks installed in wings. Twenty double passenger seats, ten on each side of central aisle, fit-on combination seat and cargo tie-down fittings. Detachable full-length baggage racks above windows. Buffet, toilet, lavatory and coat-room at aft end of cabin. Sound-proofing, heating and individual oxygen outlets. For cargo carrying, seats, carpets, baggage racks, etc. removed and floor covered with plywood covering. Fuel capacity 3,540 U.S. gallons (13,400 litres).

XC-54F. A modification of the C-54B incorporating special requirements of Troop Carrier Command. None built.

C-54G (R5D-5). Four Pratt & Whitney R-2000-9 engines. Except for power-plant similar to C-54E.

C-54H. Similar to XC-54F troop-carrier. Cancelled after VJ-Day.

C-54J (**R5D-6**). Same power-plant as C-54G. Personnel transport with full airline furnishings. No cargo facilities. Cancelled after VJ-Day.

XC-54K. One C-54E fitted with four 1,425 h.p. Wright R-1820 Cyclone engines.

C-54M. Ambulance aircraft with USAF.

XC-114. C-54 fitted with four 1,620 h.p. Allison V-1710-131 twelve-cylinder Vee liquid-cooled engines. One only.

XC-115. Project for C-54 fitted with four Packard V-1650-209 Merlin engines. Not built.

XC-116. Same as XC-114 but fitted with thermal de-icing for wings and tail.

In addition, a number of standard aircraft have more recently been modified for special duties under the following new designations :—

R5D-2-2. Flying radar laboratory for the U.S. Navy. Four radar installations in under-wing nacelles, with a 15 ft. (4.57 m.) retractable mast on the fuselage housing meteorological instruments. The cabin contains four radar consoles, accessory control equipment and high-speed cine-cameras to record research data. Eight research personnel are carried in addition to the normal flight crew of three.

SC-54. Thirty-six C-54 aircraft have been converted for search and rescue duties by Convair's Fort Worth Division, under this designation. There is a seat for a flight engineer between the pilot and co-pilot, and the crew have 21 new electronic flying and navigation aids including TACAN search radar. Behind the flight deck are two bunks, above large reserve fuel tanks, then a galley, and a flare-launcher from which fluorescent green dye markers can be fired.

There are B-36 type observation blisters on each side of the rear fuselage and an enlarged door on the port side through which MA-1 rescue kits, including two 20-man life rafts, can be dropped to survivors at sea. The MA-1 kits are stowed in bins on the starboard side of the cabin of the SC-54. (1956–57)

TYPE.—Four-engined medium and long-range Troop or Cargo Transport.

WINGS.—Low-wing cantilever monoplane with constant taper from roots to tips. Aerofoil section NACA 23016/23012. Incidence at root 4 degrees. Dihedral 7 degrees. Centre-section of three-spar construction, spars passing through the fuselage to which they are permanently attached. Self-sealing fuel tanks built integrally with structure. Outer wings have single main spar. Structure of centre-section and outer wings completed by former ribs, spanwise stringers and a smooth Alclad skin. Wing area 1,457 sq. ft. (135.35 sq. m.). NACA slotted flaps from fuselage to ailerons. Flap doors on wing undersurface are automatically retracted to permit smooth flow of air through slot when flaps are down. Both flaps and ailerons are single-spar metal structures. Controllable tab in starboard aileron.

FUSELAGE.—Semi-monocoque all-metal structure made up of a series of transverse frames, longitudinal stringers and a flush-riveted smooth Alclad skin.

TAIL UNIT.—Cantilever monoplane type. Fin and tailplane have two-spar frames and are covered with smooth Alclad sheet. Tailplane units have removable leading-edges and detachable tips, and are interchangeable from right to left or vice-versa. Rudder which is statically, aerodynamically and dynamically balanced by lead weights, has single channel spar and fabric covering. Elevators, with similar balances to rudder, have single-spar frames, metal leading-edges and overall fabric covering. Fin area : 90.5 sq. ft. (8.4 sq. m.), Rudder area (aft of hinge including tab) 47.3 sq. ft. (4.39 sq. m.), Total vertical area (including fin extension) 153.6 sq. ft. (14.26 sq. m.), Elevator area (aft of hinge line, including tabs) 86.1 sq. ft. (7.99 sq. m.), Total horizontal surface area 324.8 sq. ft. (30.17 sq. m.).

LANDING GEAR.—Retractable tricycle type. Each unit of main gear has twin-wheels and single shock-strut. Steerable nose wheel has single wheel. Hydraulic retraction, the main wheels being raised forward into inboard engine nacelles and the nose wheel forward into fuselage. Manual emergency gear. Automatic devices provided to prevent retraction while any load remains on the landing-gear. Dual hydraulic brakes on each main wheel.

POWER PLANT.—Four Pratt & Whitney R-2000-7 or 11 fourteen-cylinder radial air-cooled engines with two-speed superchargers, each rated at 1,100 h.p. to 7,000 ft. (2,135 m.), 1,000 h.p. from 7,000 to 14,000 ft. (4,270 m.) and with 1,350 h.p. available for take-off. Hamilton-Standard Hydromatic four-blade constant-speed full-feathering airscrews 13 ft. 2 in. (4 m.) diameter. Fuel tanks in fuselage and wings. Oil tank in each engine nacelle behind fireproof bulkhead. Auxiliary oil tank in fuselage.

ACCOMMODATION.—Crew of six, comprising pilot, co-pilot, navigator, radio-operator and two relief crew members. Flight compartment accommodates pilot and co-pilot side-by-side with dual controls, and navigator and radio-operator behind. Crew compartment aft of flight compartment provides accommodation for two relief crew members, and is provided with rest bunks, toilet, water tank and stowage for parachutes, life-raft, etc. Both these compartments are sound-proofed. In C-54 fuel compartment housing four fuel tanks follows crew compartment and is separated from main compartment by removable partition. Main compartment equipped with 26 seats, overhead baggage racks and stowage for four life-raft. Coatroom, buffet and food storage unit and lavatory and wash-room aft of main compartment. In C-54A main compartment re-arranged to provide troop benches instead of passenger seats. Flooring and floor beams strengthened to withstand heavy concentrated loads. Tie-down fittings for engines, ordnance and cargo installed throughout length of main cabin. Large loading door on starboard side 94 in. (2.38 m.) wide × 67 in. (1.7 m.) high, with provisions for attaching a platform and ramp for loading wheeled vehicles. Built-in twin-boom hoist capable of supporting 4,000 lbs. (1,814 kg.). Provision for removable stretcher installation and for stowage space for sea rescue equipment. Low-pressure continuous-flow oxygen system for pilot's and crew's compartments. In C-54B two of four tanks removed from fuselage and tanks of comparable capacity installed in outer wings. In C-54E remaining two tanks removed. Additional all-purpose floor fittings for passenger seats or troop benches. A demand-type oxygen supply system with individual outlets installed throughout main cabin. Improved hoist permits greater clearance and outreach for handling cargo or stretchers. Emergency exit doors in sides of fuselage over wings. Front (125 cub. ft. = 3.53 cub. m.) and rear (165 cub. ft. = 4.66 cub. m.) belly compartments beneath cabin floor with access from outside. Provision for carrying external loads under fuselage, such as airscrews, etc. Glider-towing cleat and release in aft end of tail-cone. Heating and ventilating system, full radio equipment, including marker beacon and radio compass, etc.

DIMENSIONS.—Span 117 ft. 6 in. (35.8 m.), Length 93 ft. 11 in. (28.6 m.), Height 27 ft. 6⅝ in. (8.4 m.).

WEIGHTS (C-54).—Weight empty 36,400 lbs. (16,526 kg.), Weight loaded 62,000 lbs. (28,150 kg.).

WEIGHTS (C-54A).—Weight empty 37,300 lbs. (16,934 kg.), Maximum loaded weight 65,000 lbs. (29,510 kg.), Maximum landing weight 62,000 lbs. (28,150 kg.).

WEIGHTS (C-54B).—Weight empty 38,200 lbs. (17,343 kg.), Maximum loaded weight 73,000 lbs. (33,142 kg.), Maximum landing weight 62,000 lbs. (28,150 kg.).

PERFORMANCE.—Maximum speed 274 m.p.h. (438 km.h.) at (1947)

The Douglas AD-6 Skyraider with a Douglas-developed in-flight refuelling store on the centre bomb-rack and 2 × 400 U.S. gallon fuel tanks on under-wing pylons.

THE DOUGLAS SKYRAIDER.
U.S. Navy designation : AD.

The Skyraider was the third design conceived by the Douglas company to replace the SBD dive-bomber. Under the original designation XBT2D-1, the design was submitted to the U.S. Navy in July, 1944, and the prototype first flew on March 18, 1945. It went into production under the simplified Naval Attack designation AD. Since then the aircraft has undergone considerable development, resulting in the AD-2, AD-3, AD-4, AD-5, AD-6 and AD-7, and a total of 49 versions of the seven basic types has been produced.

The Skyraider was in continuous production for twelve years until February, 1957, when the last of a total of 3,180 was delivered to the U.S. Navy.

Originally conceived in 1944 to carry a 1,000-lb. bomb, the Skyraider was operating in the Korean war with loads totalling 10,500 lbs., more than that carried by the four-engined B-17 Flying Fortress in World War II. The AD's

conversion to carry atomic bombs was announced by the U.S. Navy Department in 1953.

In addition, Skyraiders can carry Douglas-developed self-contained flight refuelling packs for operation as flying "tankers."

The following are the principal versions of the Skyraider :—

AD-1. 2,400 h.p. Wright R-3350-24 engine. First production series. Sub-types include (*a*) AD-1Q radar counter-measure aircraft with additional radar operator ; (*b*) XAD-1W special search and early-warning radar aircraft with two additional radar operators : and AD-1N night attack aircraft with two additional radar operators. All additional crews carried in rear fuselage.

AD-2. 2,700 h.p. Wright R-3350-26W engine. Increased performance and many internal refinements to give simplified control, improved vision, etc. AD-2Q (and AD-2Q(U) target tug), AD-2W and AD-2N tactical versions (see functions under AD-1).

AD-3. 2,700 h.p. Wright R-3350-26W engine. Strengthened landing-gear and longer-stroke oleo legs, improved canopy. etc., AD-3Q, AD-3W, AD-3N, AD-3S (anti-submarine) and AD-3E (special electronic equipment) versions.

AD-4. Development of AD-3. Redesigned cockpit, auto-pilot fitted, improved radar, etc. AD-4B modified to carry "special weapons" into production in 1952. Also AD-4Q, AD-4W and AD-4N special multi-seat tactical models AD-4W in service with Royal Navy as Skyraider AEW Mk. 1.

AD-5. 2,700 h.p. Wright R-3350-26WA engine. "Multiplex" version permitting basic single-seat aircraft to be converted with standard kits to any one of twelve or more combat or tactical versions, including day or night attack, photographic reconnaissance, target-tug, -Q, -N, -W, and -S special radar-equipped multi-seaters, passenger-carrying (eight persons) and ambulance (four stretchers) versions. Redesigned fuselage with new

A Douglas Skyraider "Hunter-Killer" team, the AD-5W Three-seat Search and (behind) the AD-6 Single-seat Attack versions.

wider cockpit to permit side-by-side seating, direct communication between crew members and complete interchangeability of stations, larger vertical tail surfaces, etc. Normal loaded weight 18,800 lb. (8,535 kg.). 670 built.

AD-6. 2,700 h.p. Wright R-3350-26WA engine. Improved AD-4 with special equipment for attack bombing.

AD-7. Wright R-3350-26WB engine. Strengthened wings and landing gear to prolong service life under increasing tactical loads. Deliveries began in August, 1956, and the 72nd and last AD-7 was delivered on February 18, 1957.

The following description refers to the AD-6 :—

TYPE.—Single-seat Naval Attack monoplane.

WINGS.—Low-wing cantilever monoplane. All-metal structure in three main sections, comprising a centre-section and two upward-folding outer sections. Hydraulic folding controlled from cockpit. Gross wing area 400.33 sq. ft. (37.19 m.²). All-metal ailerons on outer sections with trim and balance tabs in each. Hydraulically operated Fowler-type trailing-edge landing flaps on centre-section.

FUSELAGE.—All-metal monocoque structure with integral fin. The dive-brakes are components of the fuselage and consist of three rectangular surfaces, one on each lower side of the fuselage and one below, hinged at their forward ends in line with the trailing-edge of the wings. These surfaces are extended hydraulically outwards and downwards into the airstream.

TAIL UNIT.—Cantilever monoplane type. All-metal structure including covering of movable surfaces. Electrically-controlled adjustable tailplane. Aerodynamically and statically balanced rudder and elevators. Trim and balance tabs in rudder.

LANDING GEAR.—Retractable two-wheel type. Main wheels on single compression legs are raised backwards and turn through 90 degrees while retracting to lie flat within wing. Hydraulic actuation. Forwardly-retracting tail-wheel. Deck arrester hook aft of tail wheel.

POWER PLANT.—One 2,700 h.p. Wright R-3350-26W eighteen-cylinder two-row radial air-cooled engine. Engine mounted at 4½° downthrust. Aeroproducts four-blade constant-speed airscrew 13 ft. 6 in. (4.11 m.) diameter. Single leakproof fuel cell occupies the entire fuselage bay aft of the pilot's cockpit. Long-range fuel tanks may be carried on the wing bomb shackles.

ACCOMMODATION. — Pilot's cockpit with blister-type blown canopy over fore part of wing with downward vision angle of 15 degrees. Full naval radio and radar equipment.

ARMAMENT.—Two 20 mm. cannon, one in each extremity of the centre-section inboard of the wing-fold hinges. Launchers for twelve 5 in. (12.7 cm.) zero-length and two 12 in. (30.5 cm.) "Tiny Tim" rocket projectiles under wings. Torpedo carried externally in crutches under the fuselage. Bomb racks under the fuselage and each outer wing.

DIMENSIONS.—
Span 50 ft. 9 in. (15.47 m.).
Width folded 24 ft. (7.32 m.).
Length 39 ft. (11.89 m.).
Height (over airscrew) 15 ft. 7 in. (4.75 m.).

WEIGHTS.—
Weight empty 10,550 lb. (4,790 kg.).
Normal loaded weight 19,000 lb. (8,618 kg.).
Max. overload weight 25,000 lb. (11,350 kg.).

PERFORMANCE.—
Max. speed 365 m.p.h. (584 km.h.) at 15,000 ft. (4,575 m.).
Initial rate of climb 2,850 ft./min. (870 m./min.).
Service ceiling over 25,000 ft. (7,620 m.).
Max. combat radius 1,500 miles (2,412 km.).
(1957-58)

THE DOUGLAS SKYRAY
U.S. Navy Designation: F4D

The F4D Skyray is a single-seat carrier-based jet aircraft, which is operational with the U.S. Navy and U.S. Marine Corps and is being flown by a Navy Squadron assigned to the North American Air Defense Command as an all-weather interceptor. It can also perform the duties of a general-purpose fighter and fighter-bomber.

The prototype XF4D-1 flew for the first time on January 23, 1951. Like the second prototype it was powered initially by a 5,000 lb. (2,270 kg.) s.t. Allison J35-A-17 turbojet. Both were re-engined subsequently with a 7,000 lb. (3,175 kg.) s.t. Westinghouse XJ40-WE-6 and then with an 11,600 lb. (5,270 kg.) s.t. XJ40-WE-8 with afterburner. With this last engine, the second prototype, on October 3, 1953, set up a World Speed Record of 752.9 m.p.h. (1,211.746 km.h.) over a 3-km. course. Subsequent records established by Skyrays included an average of 728.11 m.p.h. (1,171.77 km.h.) over a 100-km. closed circuit and five time-to-height records, ranging from 3,000 m. in 44.39 sec. to 15,000 m. in 2 min., 36.05 sec.

The first production F4D-1 Skyray flew on June 5, 1954, with a Pratt & Whitney J57-P-2 turbojet, rated at 13,500 lb. (6,125 kg.) s.t. with afterburning. After a time this engine was superseded by the now-standard J57-P-8, giving 10,500 lb. (4,763 kg.) s.t. dry or 14,500 lb. (6,577 kg.) s.t. with afterburning.

A Douglas F4D-1 Skyray interceptor in the markings of North American Air Defense Command

Designed with a modified delta wing and without a horizontal tail, the Skyray is controlled about its longitudinal and horizontal axes by power-operated "elevons," located at the trailing-edge of the wing, which perform the combined functions of conventional elevators and ailerons. The cockpit is located well forward of the wing to give the pilot excellent visibility. Radar navigation and fire control systems are employed.

Six external armament stations beneath the wings carry a wide range of guided missiles, rocket packages and bombs. Two of the stations are equipped to take 300 U.S. gallon (1,136 litre) external fuel tanks. In addition, four 20 mm. guns are installed in the wings. An Aero 13F fire control system directs the attack.

Delivery of the 419th and last F4D-1, from the El Segundo Division, took place on December 22, 1958.

DIMENSIONS.—
Span 33 ft. 6 in. (10.21 m.)
Length 45 ft. 8¼ in. (13.92 m.)
Height 13 ft. (3.96 m.)
Wing area 557 sq. ft. (51.75 m.²)

WEIGHT.—
Loaded (approx.) 21,000 lb. (9,525 kg.)

PERFORMANCE.—
Max. speed at S/L Mach 0.95
Max. speed at 36,000 ft. (11,000 m.) Mach 1.05
Rate of climb at S/L 18,000 ft./min. (5,500 m./min.)
Time to 40,000 ft. (12,200 m.) 2 min.
Ceiling 55,000 ft. (16,760 m.)
Normal range 400 miles (640 km.)
Range with max. external tankage 950 miles (1,530 km.)

The Douglas C-47A Skytrain Military Transport (two Pratt & Whitney R-1830-92 engines).

THE DOUGLAS SKYTRAIN.
U.S. Army Air Forces designation: C-47.
U.S. Navy designation : R4D.
British name : Dakota.

The most widely-used transport in the World, the DC-3 has now been withdrawn from production after 10,926 had been built, 10,123 as military transports under the designations C-47 and C-53.

The first DC-3 flew on December 18, 1935, and the first transport company to put the DC-3 into commercial service was American Airlines, in June, 1936. Before the war the DC-3 was standard equipment on the major U.S. airlines and on several foreign lines. During the war the DC-3 in military guise became the standard equipment in the Transport Commands of the Allied air forces, serving as cargo-carrier, paratroop carrier, personnel transport, glider-tug, ambulance, etc.

From the welter of variations created from the basic DC-3 transport there now emerge five identifiable civil types and a great number of non-standard converted military transports.

C-47 (**R4D-1 and Dakota I**). Two Pratt & Whitney R-1830-92 engines. All-purpose transport. Large cargo loading doors, reinforced metal floor and tie-down fittings, wood seats folding against sides of cabin, etc. Glider towing-cleat, formerly exclusive to the C-53, is now a standard fitting in the C-47.

C-47A (**R4D-5 and Dakota III**). Same as C-47 except fitted with a 24-volt instead of a 12-volt electrical system. Description below refers to the C-47A.

C-47B (**R4D-6 and Dakota IV**). Same as C-47A except fitted with two Pratt & Whitney R-1830-90C engines with two-stage blowers and provision for carrying increased fuel in the cabin. Evolved for use in the India-China Theatre.

TC-47B (**R4D-7**). Navigational trainer version of the C-47B.

C-47C. Fitted with an Edo twin-float amphibian installation. The floats are of the all-metal single-step type and each is fitted with two retractable wheels, one under the nose and one aft of the step. The space between the two midship bulkheads in each float is used as an auxiliary fuel tank with a capacity of 300 U.S. gallons.

The following list details the various military versions of the DC-3, some of which are conversions from civil models taken over from the airlines by the military authorities early in 1942.

C-47 (**R4D and Dakota**). Two Pratt & Whitney R-1830-92 engines. A cargo re-design of the DC-3 for large-scale military production. Large loading door, reinforced floor, strengthened landing-gear, etc. For further details see Skytrain description.

C-48. Two Pratt & Whitney R-1830 engines. DC-3's taken over from the airlines for use as personnel transports. Furnishings retained but accommodation provided for extra crew member. Some were DTS sleeper transports and used as such.

C-49. Two Wright R-1820-71 engines. DC-3 commercial design modified for military use. Crew of 3 and 21 passengers. Reinforced floor for light cargo and astro-hatch for navigator. This series also included some Wright-engined DC-3's taken over from the airlines, including some DST sleeper transports.

C-50. Two Wright R-1820-85 engines. Some 21-passenger transports and some troop-carriers.

C-51. Two Wright R-1820-83 engines. Paratroop transport. Only one built.

C-52. Two Pratt & Whitney R-1830-51 engines. DC-3's taken over on the production lines before delivery to commercial customers and fitted as paratroop transports.

C-53 (**R4D and Dakota**). Two Pratt & Whitney R-1830-92 engines. Troop-carrying version of the C-47. No heavy cargo facilities, only small door and no reinforced floor. Supply dropper and glider-tug. For further details see Skytrooper description.

C-68. Two Pratt & Whitney R-1830 engines. DC-3A's taken over from the airlines.

C-84. Two Wright R-1820-G202A engines. DC-3B's taken over from the airlines.

C-117A. Two 1,200 h.p. Pratt & Whitney R-1830-90C engines. Combines the original features of the standard 21-seat commercial DC-3 with the latest improvements developed for the C-47 Series, including C-47 wing flaps and landing gear, hot-air cabin heating system and many internal changes. Produced for the A.A.F. at the Oklahoma City plant but production cancelled after surrender of Japan. Many released for sale to the airlines.

The Douglas C-47B Skytrain Military Transport (two Pratt & Whitney R-1830-90C engines).

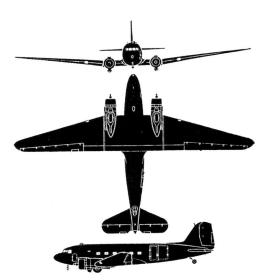

The Douglas C-47 Skytrain Military Transport.

By the end of 1944 all surviving civil DC-3's taken over by the U.S. Army Air Forces in 1942 had been returned to the airlines. In addition numbers of C-47's and C-53's have been released for conversion to civil use.

TYPE.—Twin-engined Military Transport.

WINGS, FUSELAGE, TAIL UNIT AND LANDING GEAR.—Same as DC-3.

POWER PLANT.—Two Pratt & Whitney R-1830-92 Twin-Wasp fourteen-cylinder radial air-cooled geared and supercharged engines each rated at 1,050 h.p. at 7,500 ft. (2,207 m.) and with 1,200 h.p. available for take-off. Three-bladed Hamilton-Standard constant-speed airscrews. Two main fuel tanks (202 U.S. gallons each) located forward of centre-section spar. Two auxiliary tanks (200 U.S. gallons each) aft of spar. Each engine is served by a separate fuel system but cross-feed permits both engines to be supplied by either set of tanks in case of emergency. Oil dilution system. One oil tank (29 U.S. gallons) in each engine nacelle.

ACCOMMODATION.—Crew of three consisting of pilot, co-pilot and radio operator. Fuselage divided into six compartments—pilot's compartment ; port and starboard baggage compartment ; radio operator's compartment ; main cargo hold and lavatory. Pilot's compartment seats two side-by-side with dual controls. Automatic pilot. Full radio equipment includes radio compass, marker beacon receiver and receivers for localised and glide-path reception for the instrument-landing equipment. Steam or hot air heating and ventilation. Main cargo hold equipped with snatch block, idler pulley and tie-down fittings for cargo handling. Large freight door on port side. Cargo load of 6,000 lbs. (2,725 kg.) may include three aero-engines on transport cradles, or two light trucks. Folding seats down sides of cabin for 28 fully-armed airborne or parachute troops. Alternatively fittings for eighteen stretchers together with provision for medical crew of three. Racks and release mechanism for six parachute pack containers under fuselage. Also under the fuselage are fittings for carrying two three-bladed airscrews. Glider-towing cleat in tail. De-icing equipment includes airscrew anti-icing system, rubber de-icer shoes on outer wings, tailplane and fin leading-edges and alcohol-type windscreen de-icer. Oxygen equipment.

DIMENSIONS.—Span 95 ft. (28.9 m.), Length 64 ft. 5½ in. (19.63 m.), Height 16 ft. 11¼ in. (5.2 m.), Wing area 987 sq. ft. (91.7 sq. m.).

WEIGHTS AND LOADINGS.—Weight empty 16,970 lbs. (7,705 kg.), Useful load 8,600 lbs. (3,904 kg.), Weight loaded 26,000 lbs. (11,805 kg.), Wing loading 25.3 lbs./sq. ft. (123.5 kg./sq. m.), Power loading 12 lbs./h.p. (5.45 kg./h.p.).

PERFORMANCE.—Maximum speed 229 m.p.h. (368 km.h.) at 7,500 ft. (2,290 m.), Cruising speed 185 m.p.h. (296 km.h.) at 10,000 ft. (3,050 m.), Stalling speed 67 m.p.h. (107.8 km.h.), Initial rate of climb 1,130 ft./min. (345 m./min.), Service ceiling 23,200 ft. (7,076 m.), Normal range 1,500 miles (2,400 km.).

THE DOUGLAS SKYTRAIN GLIDER.
U.S. Army Air Forces designation : XCG-17.

As an experiment a standard C-47A was converted at Wright Field into a glider suitable for towing behind the C-54. The engines and airscrews were replaced by hemispherical fairings, all excess weight and unnecessary fittings were removed and a towing cleat was fitted under the front spar of the centre-section. The result was a clean and efficient glider with which a towing speed of 290 m.p.h. (464 km.h.) was possible as compared with the previous maximum speed of 200 m.p.h. (320 km.h.). The XCG-17 had a gliding angle of 14/1 and a stalling speed of 35 m.p.h. (56 km.h.).

On a gross weight of 26,000 lbs. (11,805 kg.) the XCG-17 could carry a maximum pay-load of 14,000 lbs. (6,356 kg.) and could accommodate up to 40 fully-armed troops. No ballast was required for flying at minimum weight conditions.

Successful trials were made with the XCG-17 using two tandem-coupled tugs to give assisted take-off, the leading tug casting off on reaching a certain height.

The Douglas C-47C Skytrain Transport fitted with Edo amphibian float gear.

THE DOUGLAS SKYTROOPER.
U.S. Army Air Forces designation: C-53.
U.S. Navy designations: R4D-3 (C-53) and R4D-4 (C-53C).
British name : Dakota II.

The Douglas C-53 Skytrooper is similar to the C-47 but it has not the facilities for carrying heavy cargo. It has a normal wooden floor, fixed metal seats for twenty-eight fully-armed airborne or parachute-troops and a towing cleat for use as a glider-tug. It has no large loading door. Power-plant, dimensions and other general particulars are the same as for the C-47. (1945–46)

The Douglas C-53 Skytrooper Troop-carrier and Glider-tug (two Pratt & Whitney R-1830-92 engines),

THE DOUGLAS SKYWARRIOR
U.S. Navy designation: A3D (later A-3)

Production of this twin-jet carrier-based attack bomber ended in January, 1961, but it remains in front-line service with the U.S. Navy.

The A3D is the most powerful aircraft yet operational on board carriers, and can carry the largest types of bombs, including nuclear weapons. It can be used for high-altitude high-speed attack or for low-level attack or mine-laying. It can also be adapted for photographic reconnaissance duties.

The prototype XA3D-1 flew for the first time on October 28, 1952, powered with two Westinghouse J40 engines. It was followed by the first production aircraft on September 16, 1953.

Five versions have been produced:—

A3D-1. Initial production series with two Pratt & Whitney J57-P-6 turbojet engines. Entered service on March 30, 1956.

A3D-2. Developed version with Pratt & Whitney J57-P-10 turbojet engines (each 10,500 lb. = 4,763 kg. s.t.). Entered service with U.S. Pacific Fleet early in 1957. Claimed to fly at high subsonic speeds above 40,000 ft. (12,200 m.)

A3D-2P. Photographic - reconnaissance version of A3D-2, with crew of three and 12 cameras. Re-designed and reinforced fuselage, pressurised to give equivalent of 8,000 ft. (2,440 m.) at 35,000 ft. (10,670 m.). Tail armament retained. Shorter bomb-bay, housing photoflash bombs. Fuselage length 75 ft. 6 in. (23.0 m.). First flown on July 22, 1958.

A3D-2Q. Radar countermeasures and reconnaissance version of A3D-2, with crew of seven and specialised equipment, including radome under fuselage. First flight December 10, 1958. Deliveries to U.S. Navy began in November, 1959.

A3D-2T. Trainer for bomber or electronic countermeasures crews, with radar bomb sights and navigation gear. Accommodation for pilot, one instructor and six pupils. Tail armament retained. First flight August 29, 1959.

All A3D's have probes for in-flight refuelling and a special bomb-bay pack developed by Flight Refuelling Inc. enables the A3D-2 to be adapted quickly for service as a refuelling tanker, carrying a 1,300 U.S. gallon (4,923 litre) tank and hose reel assembly.

Fitted with a new cambered wing leading-edge, an A3D-2 tanker took off from the U.S.S. *Independence* at a gross weight of 84,000 lb. (38,100 kg.) in the Autumn of 1959.

TYPE.—Twin-jet attack bomber.

WINGS.—Shoulder-wing cantilever monoplane. 36° sweepback at 25% of chord. Aspect ratio 6.75. Taper ratio 6% at root, 8.25% at tip. Dihedral nil. All-metal two-spar torsion-box type structure. Outer wings fold upward hydraulically for carrier stowage. Hydraulically-operated NACA slotted flaps inboard of wing fold. Lateral control by combination of ailerons and spoilers on outer wings. Automatic leading-edge slats outboard of engine pod struts. Gross wing area 730 sq. ft. (67.82 m.²)

FUSELAGE.—All-metal structure in three sections, nose, centre and tail-cone. Air-brakes on sides of rear fuselage. Extendable anti-buffet "rake" forward of weapons bay.

Douglas A3D-2Q Skywarrior, the electronic countermeasures version of the A3D-2 (AiReview, Japan)

TAIL UNIT.—All-metal cantilever mono-plane type with all-moving tailplane. All surfaces swept. Vertical surfaces fold down to starboard for carrier stowage. Hydraulically-powered control system.

LANDING GEAR.—Retractable nose-wheel type. Nose-wheel retracts forward, main wheels sideways and backward, all into fuselage. Hydraulic actuation. Braking parachute stowed under rear gun turret. Retractable tail bumper and arrester hook. Wheel track 11 ft. (3.35 m.)

POWER PLANT.—Two Pratt & Whitney J57 turbojet engines in underwing pods. Fuel in four tanks, two self-sealing in fuselage, one forward and one aft of bomb-bay, and two integral wing tanks, one in each wing

inboard of wing fold. Twelve 4,500 lb. (2,040 kg.) s.t. jettisonable T.O. rockets may be mounted on sides of rear fuselage.

ACCOMMODATION.—Crew of three, pilot and co-pilot/bombardier side-by-side and navi-gator/gunner behind pilot back-to-back, in pressurised cockpit. Emergency exit for all members of crew through floor escape chute. Upper ditching hatch.

ARMAMENT.— Radar-directed Westinghouse Aero 21-B ball-turret in rear end of fuselage armed with two 20 mm. cannon. Bomb-bay 15 ft. (4.57 m.) long adaptable to carriage of variety of offensive stores.

(1961–62)

DIMENSIONS.—
Span 72 ft. 5 in. (22.07 m.)
Length 75 ft. 7 in. (23.04 m.)
Height 22 ft. 8 in. (6.91 m.)

WEIGHTS.—
Weight empty approx. 38,000 lb. (17,240 kg.)

PERFORMANCE (approx.).—
Max. speed 630 m.p.h. (1,014 km.h.)
Landing speed 167 m.p.h. (269 km.h.)
Service ceiling 45,000 ft. (13,720 m.)
Normal range over 2,880 miles (4,630 km.)

The Douglas XB-42 Medium Attack-Bomber (two 1,725 h.p. Allison V-1710-125 engines mounted in the fuselage).

THE DOUGLAS XB-42.

The XB-42 is an experimental mid-wing monoplane developed by the Douglas Company to Air Technical Service Command contract and powered by two Allison liquid-cooled engines mounted in the fuselage and driving contra-rotating pusher propellers behind the rudder through extension shafts. The XB-42 flew for the first time in June, 1944, and on December 8 of that year it made a fast flight from Long Beach, California, to Washington, D.C., a distance of 2,290 miles (3,665 km.), at an average speed of 432 m.p.h. (695 km.h.). Subsequently the prototype XB-42 was crashed at Washington on December 15, 1945, through no fault of either airframe or power-plant installation. A second prototype differs from the original model by having a single cockpit enclosure in place of the twin blister canopies.

TYPE.—Twin-engined Medium Attack bomber.

WINGS.—All-metal cantilever mid-wing monoplane. Laminar flow aerofoil section. All-metal ailerons and slotted trailing-edge flaps.

FUSELAGE.—All-metal monocoque structure.

TAIL UNIT.—All-metal cantilever structure. Twin fins and rudders, one above and one below fuselage.

LANDING GEAR.—Tricycle type. Main and nose wheels retract upward and backward into fuselage. Emergency bumper skid in bottom of lower fin.

POWER PLANT.—Two Allison V-1710-125 twelve-cylinder Vee liquid-cooled engines, each rated at 1,725 h.p. for take-off with water injection, mounted side-by-side in the fuselage aft of the pilot's cockpit and driving two Curtiss Electric three-blade co-axial contra-rotating propellers behind tail-unit by shaft drive. Pro-pellers are independently driven and independently feathering. Engines are connected to propeller reduction gear by steel drive shafts in 5 ft. (1.52 m.) lengths carried at each joint on ball-bearing supports to provide for air load deflections in fuselage.

ACCOMMODATION.—Crew of three. Pilot's compartment ahead of the wing seats two side-by-side with separate blister canopies for pilot and co-pilot/navigator. Glazed nose for bombardier on Bomber version is replaceable by solid nose mounting various arma-ments for Attack version.

ARMAMENT.—Four .5-in. (12.7 m/m.) remotely-controlled and sighted flexibly-mounted guns in trailing-edge of wings inboard of ailerons and firing aft. Attack version has nose-section containing com-bination of guns ranging from eight .5-in. (12.7 m/m.) guns to one 75 m/m. cannon and two .5-in. (12.7 m/m.) guns. Maximum bomb load 8,000 lbs. (3,629 kg.) carried internally.

DIMENSIONS.—Span 70 ft. 0 in. (21.34 m.), Length 53 ft. 0 in. (16.15 m.).

WEIGHTS AND LOADINGS.—Weight empty 19,149 lbs. (8,687 kg.), Weight loaded 35,702 lbs. (16,194 kg.), Power loading (fully loaded) (take-off power) 5.46 lbs./h.p. (2.47 kg./h.p.).

PERFORMANCE.—Maximum level speed 410 m.p.h. (660 km.h.), Range (approximate) 5,000 miles (8,046 km.).

The Fairchild PT-19 "Cornell" Two-seat Primary Training Monoplane (175 h.p. Ranger engine).

THE FAIRCHILD CORNELL.

U.S. Army Air Forces designations: PT-19, PT-23 and PT-26.
R.C.A.F name: Cornell (PT-26).

There were three production versions of the Cornell, the PT-19, the PT-23 and the PT-26.

PT-19A. Fitted with the 175 h.p. Ranger 6-440C-2 six-cylinder in-line inverted engine. Built by the Fairchild Aircraft Division and the Aeronca Aircraft Corpn. Production ceased late in 1943.

PT-23. Built by the Howard Aircraft Corpn., the Aeronca Aircraft Corpn. and the St. Louis Aircraft Corpn. Identical in construction to the PT-19 but fitted with the 220 h.p. Continental R-670-11 seven-cylinder radial air-cooled engine. Production ceased in May, 1944. The PT-23 has been modified to carry two stretcher cases and was the first trainer to be re-designed for overseas duties.

PT-26. Adopted by the Canadian Government as the standard primary trainer for the Commonwealth Joint Air Training Plan and built by Fleet Aircraft, Ltd., Toronto, Canada (which see). Production ceased in May, 1944.

The following general description applies to all three training versions mentioned above.

TYPE.—Two-seat Primary Trainer.

WINGS.—Low-wing cantilever monoplane in three portions, consisting of centre-section and two tapering outer sections. Conventional two-spar construction with spruce spars and girder ribs and formed plywood covering. End ribs, landing gear ribs and those at the fuselage attachment points are of chrome-molybdenum steel. Built-in slots. Manually-controlled split flaps on centre-section. Statically and aerodynamically-balanced ailerons have aluminium-alloy frames and fabric covering.

FUSELAGE.—Welded chrome-molybdenum steel-tube framework. Fabric covering over wooden stringers except on top of fuselage aft of cockpits, which is of Duramold plywood.

TAIL UNIT.—Monoplane type. Fixed surfaces have wooden frames and plywood covering. Movable surfaces have welded steel-tube frames and fabric covering. Cockpit-controlled tabs on elevators.

LANDING GEAR.—Fixed single-leg cantilever type. Streamline wheels and hydraulic brakes. Steerable tail-wheel, which may be disconnected to become full-swivelling for ground manœuvring.

POWER PLANT.—One 175 h.p. Ranger L-440-1 (PT-19A) or 200 h.p. L-440-7 (PT-26) six-cylinder in-line inverted, or 220 h.p. Continental R-670-11 (PT-23) seven-cylinder radial air-cooled engine. Two fuel tanks (22⅜ U.S. gallons each) in each wing.

ACCOMMODATION.—Tandem cockpits, open (PT-19 and PT-23) or under continuous canopy (PT-26). Seats have vertical adjustment and are designed for seat-type parachutes. Dual controls. In PT-26 equipment includes cockpit heating, blind and night-flying instruments, etc.

DIMENSIONS.—Span 36 ft. 11 7/10 in. (11.2 m.), Length (PT-19A and PT-36) 27 ft. 11⅜ in. (8.5 m.), Length (PT-23) 25 ft. 10¾ in. (7.9 m.), Height 7 ft. 6 in. (2.2 m.), Wing area 200 sq. ft. (18.6 sq. m.).

WEIGHTS AND LOADINGS (PT-19A—175 h.p. Ranger engine).—Weight empty 1,851 lbs. (840 kg.), Weight loaded 2,518 lbs. (1,143 kg.), Wing loading 12.6 lbs./sq. ft. (61.5 kg./sq. m.), Power loading 14.4 lbs./h.p. (6.53 kg./h.p.).

WEIGHTS AND LOADINGS (PT-23—220 h.p. Continental engine).—Weight empty 2,046 lbs. (928.8 kg.), Weight loaded 2,747 lbs. (1,247 kg.), Wing loading 13.7 lbs./sq. ft. (66.8 kg./sq. m.), Power loading 12.5 lbs./h.p. (5.67 kg./h.p.).

WEIGHTS AND LOADINGS (PT-26—200 h.p. Ranger engine).—Weight empty 2,022 lbs. (918 kg.), Weight loaded 2,741 lbs. (1,244 kg.), Wing loading 13.7 lbs./sq. ft. (66.8 kg./sq. m.), Power loading 13.7 lbs./h.p. (6.2 kg./h.p.).

PERFORMANCE (PT-19A—175 h.p. Ranger engine).—Maximum speed 125 m.p.h. (200 km.h.), Cruising speed 113 m.p.h. (181 km.h.), Stalling speed (with flaps) 52 m.p.h. (83.2 km.h.), Initial rate of climb 655 ft./min. (200 m./min.), Service ceiling 13,000 ft. (3,965 m.), Normal range 430 miles (690 km.).

PERFORMANCE (PT-23—220 h.p. Continental engine).—Maximum speed 131 m.p.h. (209.6 km.h.), Cruising speed 109 m.p.h. (174.4 km.h.), Stalling speed (with flaps) 54 m.p.h. (86.4 km.h.), Initial rate of climb 965 ft./min. (294 m./min.), Service ceiling 13,250 ft. (4,040 m.), Normal range 370 miles (592 km.).

PERFORMANCE (PT-26—200 h.p. Ranger engine).—Maximum speed 126 m.p.h. (201.6 km.h.), Cruising speed 114 m.p.h. (182 km.h.), Stalling speed (with flaps) 53 m.p.h. (85 km.h.), Initial rate of climb 675 ft./min. (206 m./min.), Service ceiling 17,300 ft. (5,276 m.), Normal range 450 miles (720 km.).

(1945—46)

The Fairchild UC-61K Forwarder Light Utility Transport (200 h.p. Ranger L-440-7 engine).

THE FAIRCHILD FORWARDER.

U.S. Army Air Forces designation: UC-61.
U.S. Navy designation: GK-1.
British name: Argus.

The Forwarder was an adaptation of the Model 24 four-seat commercial monoplane and was originally produced as a light military utility transport in 1942 for the Royal Air Force, under the name Argus I. The Argus I, later adopted by the U.S. Army under the designation C-61, was fitted with the 145 h.p. Warner R-500-1 Super Scarab engine. This was followed by the UC-61A (Argus II) with the more powerful 165 h.p. R-500-7 Super-Scarab engine. Early in 1944 the UC-61K (Argus III), fitted with the 200 h.p. Ranger L-440-7 six-cylinder in-line inverted engine, was developed and was in production from April to November of that year.

The sub-types between UC-61A and K were various commercial models of the Model 24 bought secondhand for various military duties and given designations in the UC-61 Series.

These were :—

  UC-61B Model 24J (Warner Super-Scarab).
  UC-61C Model 24R (Ranger 6-410-B1).
  UC-61D Model 51A (Pratt & Whitney R-985).
  UC-61E Model 24K (Ranger 6-410-B1).
  UC-61F Model 24R (Ranger 6-410-B1).
  UC-61G Model 24W (Warner Super-Scarab).
  UC-61H Model 24G (Warner Super-Scarab).
  UC-61J Model 24C (Ranger 6-390-D3).

A small number of the commercial Model 24R-40 (Ranger engine) was also given the designation UC-86.

Most of these have been illustrated and described in previous issues of this Annual. The description which follows refers to the UC-61K.

TYPE.—Four-seat utility-cargo monoplane.

WINGS.—High-wing braced monoplane. Wing in two sections, each attached to the top fuselage longerons and braced to the bottom longerons by parallel steel-tube struts. No. 22 wing section. Wings taper in plan and section where they join the fuselage. Structure consists of spruce spars and ribs, duralumin and steel-tube compression struts and wire drag bracing, plywood leading-edge, fabric covering. Frise-type statically-balanced ailerons have built-up aluminium-alloy frames and fabric covering. Flaps have aluminium-alloy and wood frames and are covered with aluminium sheet.

FUSELAGE.—Rectangular welded steel-tube structure, covered with fabric.

TAIL UNIT.—Normal monoplane type. Tail-plane and fin have wood spars and plywood covering, rudder and elevators welded steel-tube frames and fabric covering. Adjustable trimming-tabs on elevators.

LANDING GEAR.—Divided type. Each unit consists of a Fairchild oleo leg with 8 in. travel, the top end attached to the front wing-bracing strut, with the bottom end hinged to the bottom fuselage longerons by steel-tube axle and backwardly-inclined radius-rod. Medium-pressure tyres and wheel-brakes. Steerable-automatic swivel oleo-spring tail-wheel.

POWER PLANT.—One 200 h.p. Ranger L-440-7 six-cylinder in-line inverted air-cooled engine on steel-tube mounting. Fuel tanks (two) in wing roots, with a total capacity of 60 U.S. gallons.

ACCOMMODATION.—Enclosed cabin, seating four in two pairs with dual controls for the front pair. Sloping windshield and side windows. Two doors, one on either side, give access to either front seat. Seat cushions may be removed to accommodate seat-type parachutes. Dual controls may be disconnected and removed.

DIMENSIONS.—Span 36 ft. 4 in. (11.7 m.), Length 23 ft. 10¼ in. (7.24 m.), Height 7 ft. 7½ in. (2.3 m.), Wing area 193.3 sq. ft. (18.5 sq. m.).

WEIGHTS AND LOADINGS.— Weight empty 1,813 lbs. (823 kg.), Weight loaded 2,882 lbs. (1,308 kg.), Wing loading 14.9 lbs./sq. ft. (72.7 kg./sq. m.), Power loading 14.4 lbs./h.p. (6.5 kg./h.p.).

PERFORMANCE.—Maximum speed 124 m.p.h. (198.4 km.h.), Cruising speed 112 m.p.h. (179.2 km.h.), Landing speed 57 m.p.h. (91.2 km.h.), Service ceiling 12,700 ft. (3,873 m.), Normal range 465 miles (745 km.). (1945–46)

The Fairchild AT-21 Gunner Gunnery Crew Trainer (two Ranger V-770-15 engines).

THE FAIRCHILD GUNNER.

U.S. Army Air Forces designation : AT-21.

The AT-21 was developed from two previous models, the XAT-13 and XAT-14. It was manufactured by Fairchild and under licence by the Bellanca Aircraft Corpn. and the McDonnell Aircraft Corpn. It was withdrawn from production in October, 1944.

TYPE.—Twin-engined five-seat Advanced Gunnery Crew Trainer.

WINGS.—Mid-wing cantilever monoplane. Centre-section has dihedral, outer sections flat. Wing structure comprises two wooden box spars and girder type former ribs, the whole covered with a Dura-mold skin, in which thin strips of veneer are bonded together and moulded to the requisite form under heat and pressure before assembly. Split flaps on centre-section are of wood and plywood construction. Ailerons on outer-sections have aluminium-alloy frames and fabric covering.

FUSELAGE.—Oval section structure. Forward portion has welded steel-tube framework with Duramold pre-formed skin. After portion from wings to tail is a pure wood monocoque with wood bulkheads and Duramold covering.

TAIL UNIT.—Cantilever monoplane type with twin fins and rudders. Fixed surfaces have wood spars and ribs and Duramold covering. Rudders and elevator have aluminium-alloy frames and fabric covering.

LANDING GEAR.—Retractable tricycle type. Unit under each engine nacelle comprising single air-oleo shock strut braced fore and aft by retracting strut and torque arms to resist torsional motion. Nose-wheel is free swivelling with air-oleo shock absorber unit. Hydraulic brakes on main wheels. Hydraulic wheel retraction with auxiliary hand gear.

POWER PLANT.—Two Ranger V-770-15 twelve-cylinder inverted Vee air-cooled engines, each rated at 450 h.p. at 12,000 ft. (3,660 m.) and with 520 h.p. available for take-off. Welded steel-tube mountings. Two-bladed Hamilton Standard constant-speed air-screws. Four fuel tanks in wings with a total capacity of 225 U.S. gallons.

ACCOMMODATION.—Crew of five comprising pilot, co-pilot (instructor), turret-gunner, nose-gunner and relief gunner.

ARMAMENT AND EQUIPMENT.—One flexible .30-cal. machine-gun in Plexiglas nose and two .30 cal. machine-guns in power-operated turret aft of wings. Equipment includes oxygen supply system, night-flying equipment, radio, radio compass, marker beacon receiver, cabin heaters, interphone system, etc.

DIMENSIONS.—Span 52 ft. 8 in. (16 m.), Length 37 ft. 11⅝ in. (11.6 m.), Height 13 ft. 1⅝ in. (4 m.), Wing area 378 sq. ft. (35.1 sq. m.).

WEIGHTS AND LOADINGS.—Weight empty 8,654 lbs. (3,930 kg.), Weight loaded 11,288 lbs. (5,124 kg.), Wing loading 30.1 lbs./sq. ft. (146.8 kg./sq. m.), Power loading 12.5 lbs./h.p. (5.67 kg./h.p.).

PERFORMANCE.—Maximum speed 225 m.p.h. (360 km.h.) at 12,000 ft. (3,660 m.), Cruising speed 196 m.p.h. (313.6 km.h.) at 67% power at 12,000 ft. (3,660 m.), Initial rate of climb 930 ft./min. (284 m./min.), Service ceiling 22,150 ft. (6,760 m.), Normal range 910 miles (1,460 km.). (1945–46)

THE FAIRCHILD PACKET.

U.S. Air Force designations : C-82 and C-119.
U.S. Navy Designation : R4Q.

The original design of the XC-82 was begun in 1941 and the design and mock-up were approved by the U.S. Army in 1942. The actual detailed development and engineering, including the construction and preliminary testing of the prototype, which first flew on September 10, 1944, took less than 21 months.

The Packet was put into production by both Fairchild and North American, but at the end of the war the North American contract was cancelled after three C-82N's had been built. The Fairchild contract for 200 aircraft was continued and a supplemental order for 20 additional was contracted for in 1948, making a total of 220 aircraft of this type manufactured by Fairchild by Sept-ember, 1948, when production on this model ceased.

C-82A. Two 2,100 h.p. Pratt & Whitney R-2800-85 engines. Production model of the XC-82. By September, 1948, 220 had been delivered to the U.S. A.F., practically all of which were assigned to the Tactical Air Command and the Military Air Transport Service.

TYPE.—Twin-engined Cargo or Troop Transport.

WINGS.—Cantilever high-wing monoplane. Two-spar construction in three main sections consisting of anhedral centre-section let into fuselage and carrying engine nacelles and tail booms and two outer wings. Detachable tips. All-metal structure. Metal ailerons on outer wings in two sections. Aileron span 25 ft. 0⅞ in. (7.65 m.). Controllable trim-tab in starboard aileron which has an area 2.5 sq. ft. (.17 m.²). An automatic mechanical boost tab is installed in both port and starboard ailerons for reduction of aileron loads. Area of each boost tab 2.5 sq. ft. (.17 m.²). Electrically operated NACA slotted trailing-edge flaps between ailerons and fuselage divided by tail booms. Outer flap span 7 ft. 7.6 in. (2.33 m.), inner flap span 5 ft. 9.8 in. (1.78 m.), maximum depression 40 degrees.

FUSELAGE.—All-metal semi-monocoque structure, in six main sections comprising main body, sides, upper front, upper rear, nose compartment, and rear cargo door compartments. Structure consists of Alclad vertical frames, longitudinal stringers and longitudinal and transverse beams, with smooth Alclad skin. Seven longitudinal beams take the floor and tie-down loads beneath a ply covered floor. Rear compartment is split on vertical centre-line, the halves hinging outwards to allow direct loading of freight.

The Fairchild C-82A Packet Military Transport (two 2,100 h.p. Pratt & Whitney R-2800-85 engines).
(*Gordon S. Williams*).

TAIL BOOMS.—All-metal structures of circular cross-section forward tapering to oval-section aft. Each in two main sections. Forward section bolted to engine nacelle structure aft of trailing-edge. Aft section is bolted to forward section at leading-edge of tailplane.

TAIL UNIT.—Cantilever monoplane type with twin fins and rudders extending above and slightly below tail-booms in C-82A and above booms only in C-119. All-metal structures. Tailplane and fins have stressed metal skin covering, one-piece metal framed elevator and rudders, metal noses and fabric covering over all. Controllable elevator trim-tab each side of centre-line and in each top rudder. A spring-loaded torsional rudder-tab is located in the trailing-edge of each bottom rudder for reduction of rudder loads.

LANDING GEAR.—Retractable tricycle type. Gears are electrically retracted and extended. In emergency, the clutch at the electric actuators is released to allow the gears to "free fall" into the down position. Hydraulic brakes on main wheels.

ACCOMMODATION.—Flight deck has two seats side-by-side for pilot (on port) and co-pilot ; navigator's seat and desk are on starboard side of the aircraft ; the radio operator is centrally located behind the pilot and co-pilot. Access to the flight deck is by a ladder on the port side. The aircraft may be equipped as a troop transport, litter carrier or heavy cargo transport. An electrically-operated monorail discharges paracans through a hatch in the bottom of the fuselage. Ramps provided to load wheeled or tracked equipment. Heavy reinforced floors are at truck bed level. Rear cargo doors open on vertical hinge line providing entrance opening as wide as cargo hold.

EQUIPMENT.—Thermal de-iced wings and fixed tail surfaces. Complete facilities for radio and radar for tactical cargo aircraft. 24-volt electrical system. Individual oxygen equipment for crew and troops. Dual doors for simultaneous jumping of two sticks of paratroopers.

POWER PLANT.—Two Pratt & Whitney R-2800-85 eighteen-cylinder radial air-cooled engines, each with a military rating of 2,100 h.p. at 3,000 ft. (915 m.) in low blower and 1,700 h.p. at 16,000 ft. (4,880 m.) in high blower, and a normal rating of 1,700 h.p. at 7,300 ft. (2,230 m.) in low blower and 1,500 h.p. at 17,500 ft. (5,340 m.) in high blower. Three-blade Hamilton Standard Hydromatic airscrews 15 ft. 2 in. (4.62 m.) in diameter. Fluid de-icing. Four fuel tanks in wings. Total capacity 2,614 U.S. gallons (9,881 litres).

ACCOMMODATION. — Interior dimensions of cabin or hold : Length 38 ft. 6 in. (11.74 m.). Width 8 ft. (2.44 m.). Height 7 ft. 8 in. (2.34 m.). Floor area 308 sq. ft. (28.6 m.²). Volume 2,312 cub. ft. (65.4 m.³). Normal seating capacity 41. Max. seating capacity (emergency evacuation) 42. Stretcher patients 34. Monorail capacity 15 bundles each weighing 350 lb. (159 kg.). Glider tow capacity one 30,000 lb. (13,620 kg.) glider.

DIMENSIONS.—
Span 106 ft. 6 in. (32.48 m.).
Length 77 ft. 1 in. (23.51 m.).
Height 26 ft. 5 in. (8.05 m.).

AREAS.—
Wings (including ailerons) 1,400 sq. ft. (130 m.²).

Ailerons 112 sq. ft. (10.4 m.²).
Flaps 100 sq. ft. (9.3 m.²).
Vertical fins 113.2 sq. ft. (10.5 m.²).
Rudders 85.6 sq. ft. (7.95 m.²).
Tailplane 226.7 sq. ft. (21.1 m.²).
Elevators 93.4 sq. ft. (8.6 m.²).

WEIGHTS.—
Weight empty 31,288 lb. (14,205 kg.).
Designed loaded weight 50,000 lb. (22,680 kg.).
Max. permissible overloaded weight 54,000 lb. (24,520 kg.).
Designed landing weight 47,200 lb. (21,430 kg.).
Max. permissible landing weight 50,000 lb. (22,680 kg.).

PERFORMANCE (at 50,000 lb.=22,680 kg. loaded weight).—
Max. speed 238 m.p.h. (381 km.h.) at 17,500 ft. (5,340 m.).
Stalling speed 83 m.p.h. (132.8 km.h.).
Initial rate of climb 920 ft./min. (280 m./min.).
Service ceiling 22,000 ft. (6,710 m.).
Single-engine ceiling 6,000 ft. (1,830 m.).
Max. range at economical cruise 3,900 miles (6,240 km.).
Range with 13,000 lb. (5,900 kg.) cargo load 500 miles (800 km.).
Range with 8,800 lb. (4,000 kg.) load : 750 miles (1,200 km.).
Range with 6,300 lb. (2,860 kg.) load : 1,000 miles (1,600 km.).
Take-off to 50 ft. (15.25 m.) 2,780 ft. (850 m.).
Landing run from 50 ft. (15.25 m.) 1,900 ft. (580 m.).   (1949–50)

The Fairchild C-119G Packet Military Transport (two 3,500 h.p. Wright R-3350 Turbo Compound engines).
(*Gordon Williams*).

THE FAIRCHILD PACKET.
U.S. Air Force designation: C-119.
U.S. Marine Corps designation: R4Q.

The original design of the Packet was begun in 1941 and the design and mock-up were approved by the U.S. Army in 1942. The prototype, under the designation XC-82, first flew on September 10, 1944.

The C-82 was the first production version, but it went out of production in 1948 in favour of a new and improved version known as the C-119. This has been produced in the following versions:—

C-119B. Two Pratt & Whitney R-4360-20 twenty-four cylinder radial engines with two-stage blowers, rated at 2,650 h.p. to 6,000 ft. (1,830 m.), 2,300 h.p. at 18,000 ft. (5.480 m.) and with 3,250 h.p. available for take-off. First production version of C-119.

C-119C. Two Pratt & Whitney R-4360-20W engines developing 3,500 h.p. for take-off. Dorsal fins added to booms.

R4Q-1. U.S. Marine Corps version of C-119C. The two versions are identical.

C-119F. Similar to C-119C but fitted with two 3,500 h.p. Wright R-3350-85 Turbo Compound engines and Hamilton Standard airscrews. Small lower fins added.

R4Q-2. U.S. Marine Corps version of C-119F.

C-119G. As C-119F but with Aero-Products airscrews. First production C-119G flew on October 28, 1952.

The last production C-119, the 1,112th of the type, was built towards the end of 1955.

TYPE.—Twin-engined Cargo and Troop Transport.

ACCOMMODATION.—Flight deck has two seats side-by-side for pilot (on port) and co-pilot ; navigator's seat and table are on starboard side of the aircraft ; the radio operator is centrally located behind the pilot and co-pilot. A crew chief's seat is provided behind the pilot over the entrance hatch. Individual oxygen equipment for all members of crew. Access to the flight deck is by a ladder on the port side. The aircraft is equipped as a troop transport, ambulance or medium cargo transport. An electrically-operated monorail discharges paracans through a hatch in the bottom of the fuselage. Ramps provided to load wheeled or tracked equipment. Heavy reinforced floors are at truck bed level. Rear cargo doors open on vertical hinge line providing entrance opening as wide and high as cargo hold. Small door in each main cargo door for simultaneous jumping of two sticks of paratroopers. Interior dimensions of cabin or hold : Length 36 ft. 11 in. (11.25 m.). Width 9 ft. 10 in. (3.0 m.). Height 8 ft. (2.44 m.). Floor area 353 sq. ft. (32.8 m.²). Volume 3,150 cub. ft. (88.2 m.³). Normal seating capacity 67. Maximum seating capacity (emergency evacuation) 78. Stretcher patients 35. Monorail capacity 20 bundles each weighing 500 lb. (227 kg.). Glider tow capacity one 30,000 lb. (13,620 kg.) glider.

DIMENSIONS.—
Span 109 ft. 3 in. (33.32 m.).
Length 86 ft. 6 in. (26.38 m.).
Height 26 ft. 3 in. (8.0 m.).

WEIGHTS AND LOADINGS (C-119C).—
Weight empty 39,942 lb. (18,134 kg.).
Payload 27,500 lb. (12,485 kg.).
Max. T.O. weight 73,150 lb. (33,210 kg.).
Wing loading 50.5 lb./sq. ft. (246.4 kg./m.²).
Power loading 10.5 lb./h.p. (4.76 kg./h.p.)

The Fairchild R4Q-2 Marine Corps Transport, which is identical to the C-119F.

WEIGHTS AND LOADINGS (C-119F).—
Weight empty 39,809 lb. (18,083 kg.).
Payload 28,000 lb. (12,712 kg.).
Max. T.O. weight 72,800 lb. (33,050 kg.).
Wing loading 50.5 lb./sq. ft. (246.4 kg./m.²).
Power loading 10.5 lb./h.p. (4.76 kg./h.p.).

WEIGHTS AND LOADINGS (C-119G).—
Weight empty 39,982 lb. (18,152 kg.).
Payload 28,000 lb. (12,712 kg.).
Max. T.O. weight 74,400 lb. (33,778 kg.).
Wing loading 51.4 lb./sq. ft. (250.8 kg./m.²).
Power loading 10.6 lb./h.p. (4.81 kg./h.p.).

PERFORMANCE (C-119C—2 × Pratt & Whitney R-4360-20W engines).—
Cruising speed at 70% normal rated power 200 m.p.h. (320 km.h.).
Stalling speed 108 m.p.h. (173 km.h.).
Rate of climb at S/L. 740 ft./min. (226 m./min.).
Rate of climb on one engine at S/L. 100 ft./min. (30.5 m./min.).
Range (max. standard fuel) 1,950 miles (3,120 km.).

PERFORMANCE (C-119F—2 × Wright R-3350-85 engines).—
Cruising speed at 70% normal rated power 205 m.p.h. (328 km.h.).
Stalling speed 108 m.p.h. (173 km.h.).
Rate of climb at S/L. 820 ft./min. (250 m./min.).
Rate of climb on one engine at S/L. 100 ft./min. (30.5 m./min.).
Range (max. standard fuel) 2,300 miles (3,680 km.).

PERFORMANCE (C-119G—2 × Wright R-3350-89W engines).—
Cruising speed at 70% normal rated power 200 m.p.h. (320 km.h.).
Stalling speed 108 m.p.h. (173 km.h.).
Rate of climb at S/L. 750 ft./min. (230 m./min.).
Rate of climb on one engine at S/L. 100 ft./min. (30.5 m./min.).
Range (max. standard fuel) 2,280 miles (3,648 km.). (1957–58)

FAIRCHILD HILLER M484
USAF designation: YC-119K

Fairchild Hiller modified a C-119 military transport to YC-119K standard, by adding two pylon-mounted auxiliary turbojets and installing a more powerful version of the existing piston-engines. Design of the conversion was started in May 1966 and the prototype aircraft flew for the first time in February 1967. A production development is the AC-119K, described separately.

The YC-119K is powered by two 3,700 hp (wet) Wright R-3350-999 TC18EA2 engines and two General Electric J85-GE-17 auxiliary turbojets, each rated at 2,850 lb (1,293 kg) st.

WEIGHTS :
Weight empty	44,747 lb (20,300 kg)
Basic operating weight	45,435 lb (20,610 kg)
Max payload	20,000 lb (9,070 kg)
Max T-O weight	77,000 lb (34,925 kg)
Max landing weight	77,000 lb (34,925 kg)

PERFORMANCE (at max T-O weight) :
Max level speed at 10,000 ft (3,050 m)	243 mph (391 kmh)
Max cruising speed at 10,000 ft (3,050 m)	187 mph (300 kmh)
Stalling speed, wheels and flaps down	112 mph (180 kmh)
Rate of climb at S/L, one engine out	1,050 ft (320 m) min
Service ceiling, one engine out	18,100 ft (5,515 m)
T-O run	1,501 ft (458 m)
T-O to 50 ft (15 m)	2,100 ft (640 m)
Landing from 50 ft (15 m)	3,200 ft (975 m)
Ferry range with four 500 US gal (1,890 litre) Benson tanks	3,460 miles (5,570 km)
Range with max payload	990 miles (1,595 km)

Fairchild Hiller AC-119K Gunship, an armed conversion of the C-119 transport aircraft

FAIRCHILD HILLER AC-119 GUNSHIP
USAF designations: AC-119G and AC-119K

Under a USAF contract, Fairchild Hiller's Aircraft Service Division is modifying 52 C-119 transport aircraft to gunship configuration, under the designations AC-119G and AC-119K. Deliveries began in the Spring of 1968.

The first 26 AC-119G aircraft are each fitted with four 7·62-mm General Electric Miniguns, a sighting system, a flare launcher for night operations and armour protection for the crew of ten. The second series of 26 AC-119K aircraft will have in addition two 20-mm cannon and will be fitted with two General Electric J85 auxiliary turbojets, as described above for the M484/YC-119K. (1969–70)

The Fairchild C-123B Provider Military Transport (two 2,500 h.p. Pratt & Whitney R-2800 engines).

THE FAIRCHILD PROVIDER.
U.S.A.F. designation: C-123B.

The C-123 was designed by the original Chase Aircraft Company, Inc. A production order for 300 C-123B's held by the Kaiser-Frazer Corporation, which had acquired a majority interest in the Chase company in 1953, was cancelled in June of that year. New bids were asked for, as the result of which production of the C-123B was assigned to Fairchild. The first Fairchild-built C-123B flew for the first time on September 1, 1954, and production aircraft entered service with the U.S.A.F.'s 309th Troop Carrier Group in July, 1955.

Orders totalling more than 300 aircraft were completed in mid-1958. Most of these C-123B's are serving with the U.S.A.F.; but six are in service with the Saudi-Arabian Air Force and 18 with the Venezuelan Air Force.

An interesting design feature is that all fuel is carried in jettisonable tanks to reduce fire risk in combat.

In 1955, the prototype C-123B was fitted experimentally with two Fairchild J44 turbojet engines (1,000 lb.=454 kg. s.t. each) mounted at the wing-tips to provide auxiliary power for use in emergency, particularly in the event of failure of one engine on take-off. In tests the C-123B, loaded to its gross all-up weight and with one engine feathered during take-off, showed an increase in rate of climb of from 150 ft./min. to 500 ft./min. with the jet augmenters in operation.

Another C-123B was fitted with a wheel/ski landing gear, on which it took off and landed successfully at a loaded weight of approximately 56,000 lb. (25,400 kg.).

As a result of these private research projects, the U.S.A.F. had ten of its production C-123B's built with wing-tip J44 turbojets and wheel/ski landing gear. These aircraft are used in Arctic areas for logistic support of the DEW-line radar chain and for rescue duties.

TYPE.—Twin-engined Troop and Cargo-carrying Transport for operation from short or unprepared landing fields.

WINGS.—High-wing cantilever monoplane. Aspect ratio 9.89. All metal structure. Flaps inboard of ailerons and divided by tail cones of engine nacelles. Aileron area 83.28 sq. ft. (7.73 m.²), flap area 128.00 sq. ft. (11.89 m.²), gross wing area 1,223.22 sq. ft. (113.64 m.²).

FUSELAGE.—The main fuselage frame is of stressed-skin monocoque construction. The nose is of truss-type welded steel tubing to provide maximum crash protection for flight personnel.

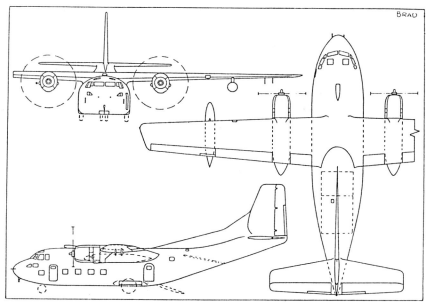

The Fairchild C-123B Provider.

TAIL UNIT.—Cantilever monoplane type. All-metal structure with fabric-covered control surfaces. Trim-tabs in elevators and rudder. Total horizontal tail area 345.5 sq. ft. (32.09 m.²), fin area 127.5 sq. ft. (11.84 m.²) plus dorsal fin 68.3 sq. ft. (6.34 m.²), elevator area 127.8 sq. ft. (11.85 m.²), rudder area 59.19 sq. ft. (5.59 m.²). Tailplane span 39 ft. 2 in. (11.94 m.).

LANDING GEAR.—Retractable tricycle type. Main gear retracts up into fuselage and is completely enclosed when retracted. A high-strength drag link is incorporated to carry drag loads and side loads from the gear to increase the utility of the aircraft for rough field operation. The dual wheel nose wheel unit is also completely retractable. Goodyear wheels of removable-flange type and Goodyear brakes with Westinghouse Decelostat anti-skid equipment. Wheelbase 23 ft. 11 in. (7.3 m.). Track 12 ft. 1 in. (3.69 m.).

POWER PLANT.—Two 2,500 h.p. Pratt & Whitney R-2800-99W radial air-cooled engines driving Hamilton Standard three-blade steel constant-speed feathering and reversing airscrews. Jettisonable self-sealing fuel tanks installed in nacelles. Total internal fuel capacity 1,462 U.S. gallons (5,520 litres). Provision for two auxiliary drop tanks, 450 U.S. gallons (1,700 litres) each. The power-plant installation is such that a complete engine change forward of the fire-wall, may be made in 45 minutes. Quick disconnect fittings are provided in all lines and mechanisms to facilitate the operation.

ACCOMMODATION.—Flight compartment in nose, seats crew of two. Cargo compartment 36 ft. 8 in. (11.18 m.) long, 9 ft. 2 in. (2.79 m.) wide and 8 ft. 2 in. (2.48 m.) high with a usable floor area of 450 sq. ft. (41.8 m.²) and cubic capacity of 3,570 cub. ft. (100 m.³). The compartment floor is stressed to support distributed loads of 250 lb./sq. ft. (1,220 kg./m.²) and two tread-ways accommodate vehicles with loadings up to 6,500 lb. (3,405 kg.) per wheel. Tie-down fittings are spaced over total floor area on a 20 in. (50.8 cm.) grid pattern, each fitting capable of sustaining a 10,000 lb. (4,535 kg.) load in any direction. The large rear loading door is formed by lowering the rear sloping wall of the hold to form a ramp and an upper door which folds inside fuselage to give adequate clearance for vehicles, bulky freight, etc. Ramp is hydraulically operated. Compartment can receive a 155 mm. howitzer and one truck or any comparable combination of wheeled units. As a personnel carrier, plane can accommodate 60 fully-equipped troops, 50 stretcher patients, plus 6 sitting patients and 6 medical attendants. Personnel can enter by side doors which may also be used for parachute jumping.

DIMENSIONS.—
Span 110 ft. (33.55 m.).
Length 76 ft. 3 in. (23.25 m.).
Height 34 ft. 1 in. (10.38 m.).
WEIGHTS AND LOADINGS.—
Weight empty 31,058 lb. (14,100 kg.).
Max. gross weight 60,000 lb. (27,240 kg.).

Wing loading 49.0 lb./sq. ft. (239.12 kg./m.²).
Power loading at max. A.U.W. 12.0 lb./h.p. (5.44 kg./h.p.).
PERFORMANCE.—
Max. speed 245 m.p.h. (392 km.h.).
Cruising speed (at 61% power) 190 m.p.h. (304 km.h.).

Stalling speed 75 m.p.h. (120 km.h.).
Rate of climb 1,150 ft./min. (350 m./min.).
Service ceiling 23,000 ft. (7,015 m.).
Range with max. cargo and optimum cruising speed at 5,000 ft. (1,525 m.) 1,470 miles (2,350 km.).   (1958–59)

FAIRCHILD HILLER M473

USAF designation: C-123K

To meet a USAF requirement, Fairchild Hiller has developed a modification scheme to increase the payload capacity of the C-123B Provider tactical transport aircraft and to improve its take-off performance.

Design of the modification began in February 1966. Basically, it involves the addition of two pylon-mounted General Electric J85-GE-17 auxiliary turbojet engines (each 2,850 lb = 1,293 kg st) in low-drag nacelles with integral intake doors, outboard of the standard piston-engines. New Goodyear high-capacity wheels, brakes and anti-skid units, and a new stall warning system are installed.

Present contracts cover 181 installations of the modification and 187 kits. The first modified aircraft, redesignated C-123K, flew in September 1966, and 27 conversions had been produced by mid-May 1967. By that date, the first C-123K's were already operating in Vietnam.

Details of the standard C-123B last appeared in the 1958-59 Jane's.

WEIGHTS:
Weight empty	35,366 lb (16,042 kg)
Basic operating weight	36,576 lb (16,590 kg)
Max payload	15,000 lb (6,800 kg)
Max T-O weight	60,000 lb (27,215 kg)
Max landing weight	60,000 lb (27,215 kg)

PERFORMANCE (at max T-O weight):
Max level speed at 10,000 ft (3,050 m) 228 mph (367 kmh)

Fairchild Hiller C-123K Provider, a conversion of the C-123B with General Electric J85-GE-17 auxiliary turbojet engines   (Denis Hughes)

Max cruising speed at 10,000 ft (3,050 m) 173 mph (278 kmh)
Stalling speed, wheels and flaps down 95 mph (152 kmh)
Rate of climb at S/L, one engine out 1,220 ft (372 m) min
Service ceiling, one engine out 21,100 ft (6,430 m)

T-O run 1,167 ft (356 m)
T-O to 50 ft (15 m) 1,809 ft (551 m)
Landing from 50 ft (15 m) 1,800 ft (549 m)
Ferry range, with two 500 US gallon (1,890 litre) Benson tanks 3,280 miles (5,280 km)
Range with max payload 1,035 miles (1,665 km)   (1969–70)

FAIRCHILD REPUBLIC THUNDERBOLT II
USAF designation: A-10A

On 18 December 1970, Fairchild Republic and Northrop were selected as the two companies that were each to build two prototypes for evaluation under the US Air Force's A-X programme, initiated in 1967, for a close-support aircraft. The first Fairchild Republic prototype (71-1369), designated YA-10A, flew for the first time on 10 May 1972. On 18 January 1973 it was announced that the Fairchild A-10A had been selected as the winner. The first of six DT and E aircraft flew on 15 February 1975. Details of them can be found in the 1977-78 Jane's.

The first flight by a production A-10A (75-00258) was made on 21 October 1975.

The first combat-ready A-10A wing was the 354th Tactical Fighter Wing, based at Myrtle Beach, South Carolina, to which deliveries began in March 1977. In May 1977 several A-10As were assigned to the 422nd Fighter Weapons Squadron of the 57th Tactical Training Wing at Nellis AFB, Nevada, for operational training and testing purposes. On 15 October 1977 the 356th Tactical Fighter Squadron of 354 TFW became the first combat-ready A-10 squadron.

In August 1977, six A-10As flew to Europe for the first live firing of the aircraft's 30 mm cannon and the anti-armour Maverick air-to-ground missile in the NATO theatre, expending 7·5 tons of conventional 500 lb bombs and 9,000 rounds of 30 mm ammunition during 117 close support sorties.

The first flight by a production A-10A (75-00258) was made on 21 October 1975. Production totalled 713.

25 January 1979, with the arrival of 14 Thunderbolt IIs at RAF stations Bentwaters and Woodbridge in the UK, to equip the US Air Force's 81st Tactical Fighter Wing. Six squadrons will eventually be based at the two UK stations.

Deliveries of new production A-10As to four Tactical Fighter Groups of the Air National Guard are under way, the A-10 being the first first-line aircraft to be assigned to ANG units. Air Force Reserve units also are scheduled to receive A-10As in 1980-81.

A two-seat night/adverse weather attack version of the A-10A is described separately.

TYPE: Single-seat close-support aircraft.
WINGS: Cantilever low-wing monoplane, with wide-chord, deep aerofoil section (NACA 6716 on centre-section and at start of outer panel, NACA 6713 at tip) to provide low wing loading. Incidence −1°. Dihedral 7° on outer panels. Aluminium alloy three-spar structure, consisting of one-piece constant-chord centre-section and tapered outer panels with integrally stiffened skins

Fairchild Republic A-10A Thunderbolt II single-seat close-support aircraft

and drooped (cambered) wingtips. Outer panel leading-edges and cores of trailing-edges are of honeycomb sandwich. Four-point attachment of wings to fuselage, at front and rear spars. Two-segment, three-position trailing-edge slotted flaps, interchangeable right with left. Wide-span ailerons, made up of dual upper and lower surfaces that separate to serve as air-brakes. Flaps, airbrakes and ailerons actuated hydraulically. Ailerons pilot-controlled by servo tab during manual reversion. Small leading-edge slat inboard of each main-wheel fairing. Redundant and armour-protected flight control system.
FUSELAGE: Semi-monocoque structure of aluminium alloy (chiefly 2024 and 7075), with four main longerons, multiple frames, and lap-jointed and riveted skins. Built in front, centre and aft portions. Single-curvature components aft of nose portion, interchangeable right with left. Centre portion incorporates wing box carry-through structure.
TAIL UNIT: Cantilever aluminium alloy structure, with twin fins and interchangeable rudders mounted at the tips of constant-chord tailplane. Interchangeable

elevators, each with an electrically-operated trim tab. Rudders and elevators actuated hydraulically. Redundant and armour-protected flight control system.
LANDING GEAR: Menasco retractable tricycle type with single wheel on each unit. All units retract forward, and have provision for emergency gravity extension. Interchangeable main-wheel units retract into non-structural pod fairings attached to the lower surface of the wings. When fully retracted approximately half of each wheel protrudes from the fairing. Steerable nosewheel is offset to starboard to clear firing barrel of gun. Main wheels size 36 × 11, Type VII; nosewheel size 24 × 7·7-10, Type VII.
POWER PLANT: Two General Electric TF34-GE-100 high bypass ratio turbofan engines, each rated at 40·3 kN (9,065 lb st), enclosed in separate pods, each pylon-mounted to the upper rear fuselage at a point approximately midway between the wing trailing-edges and the tailplane leading-edges. Fuel is contained in two tear-resistant and self-sealing cells in the fuselage, and two smaller, adjacent integral cells in the wing centre-

section. Maximum internal fuel capacity 4,853 kg (10,700 lb). All fuel cells are internally filled with reticulated foam, and all fuel systems pipework is contained within the cells except for the feeds to the engines, which have self-sealing covers. Three 2,271 litre (600 US gallon) jettisonable auxiliary tanks can be carried on underwing and fuselage centreline pylons. Provision for in-flight refuelling using universal aerial refuelling receptacle slipway installation (UARRSI).

ACCOMMODATION: Single-seat enclosed cockpit, well forward of wings, with large transparent bubble canopy to provide all-round view. Bulletproof windscreen. Canopy is hinged at rear and opens upward. Douglas ejection seat operable at speeds from 450 knots (834 km/h; 518 mph) down to zero speed at zero height. Entire cockpit area is protected by an armoured 'bathtub' structure of titanium, capable of withstanding projectiles of up to 23 mm calibre.

SYSTEMS: Redundant control system incorporates two 207 bar (3,000 lb/sq in) primary hydraulic flight control systems, each powered by an engine-driven pump, and a manual backup. Hydraulic systems actuate flaps, flying control surfaces, landing gear, brakes and nosewheel steering. Two independent hydraulic motors, either of which is sufficient to sustain half-rate firing, supply drive for 30 mm gun barrel rotation. Electrical system includes two 30/40kVA 115/200V AC engine-driven generators and a standby battery and inverter. Auxiliary power unit. Environmental control system, using engine bleed air for cockpit pressurisation and air-conditioning, pressurisation of pilot's *g* suit, windscreen anti-icing and rain clearance, fuel transfer, gun compartment purging, and other services.

AVIONICS AND EQUIPMENT: Head-up display giving airspeed, altitude and dive angle; weapons delivery package with dual reticle optical sight for use in conjunction with underfuselage Pave Penny laser target seeker pod; target penetration aids; associated equipment for Maverick and other missile systems; IFF/SIF (AIMS); UHF/AM; VHF/AM; VHF/FM; Tacan; UHF/ADF; ILS/FDC; X-band transponder; INS; heading and attitude reference system (HARS); radar homing and warning (RHAW); secure voice communications; active or passive electronic countermeasures (ECM); armament control panel; and gun camera. Space provisions for HF/SSB, and other 'growth' avionics and equipment.

ARMAMENT: General Electric GAU-8/A Avenger 30 mm seven-barrel cannon, mounted in nose with 2° depression and offset slightly to port so that as the barrels rotate the firing barrel is always on the aircraft centre-line. Gun and handling system for the linkless ammunition are mechanically synchronised and driven by two motors fed from the aircraft's hydraulic system. The single-drum magazine has a capacity of 1,174 rounds, and has a dual firing rate of either 2,100 or 4,200 rds/min. Four stores pylons under each wing (one inboard and three outboard of each main-wheel fairing), and three under fuselage, for max external load of 7,250 kg (16,000 lb). External load with full internal fuel is 6,640 kg (14,638 lb). The centreline pylon and the two flanking fuselage pylons cannot be occupied simultaneously. The centreline pylon has a capacity of 2,268 kg (5,000 lb); the two fuselage outer pylons and two centre-section underwing pylons 1,587 kg (3,500 lb) each; the two innermost outer-wing pylons 1,134 kg (2,500 lb) each; and the four outermost wing pylons 453 kg (1,000 lb) each. These allow carriage of a wide range

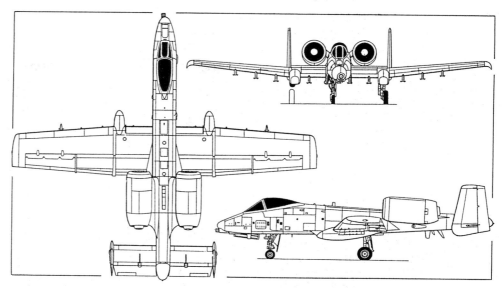

Fairchild Republic A-10A Thunderbolt II single-seat twin-engined close-support aircraft *(Pilot Press)*

of stores, including twenty-eight 500 lb Mk-82 LDGP or Mk-82 retarded bombs; six 2,000 lb Mk-84 general-purpose bombs; eight BLU-1 or BLU-27/B incendiary bombs; four SUU-25 flare launchers; twenty Rockeye II cluster bombs, sixteen CBU-52/71 dispenser weapons; six AGM-65A Maverick missiles; Mk-82 and Mk-84 laser-guided bombs; Mk-84 electro-optically-guided bombs; two SUU-23 gun pods; ALE-40 chaff/flare system; ALQ-119 ECM pods, or other jammer pods; or up to three drop-tanks.

DIMENSIONS, EXTERNAL:

Wing span	17·53 m (57 ft 6 in)
Wing chord at root	3·04 m (9 ft 11½ in)
Wing chord (mean)	2·73 m (8 ft 11·32 in)
Wing chord at tip	1·99 m (6 ft 6·4 in)
Wing aspect ratio	6·54
Length overall	16·26 m (53 ft 4 in)
Height overall	4·47 m (14 ft 8 in)
Tailplane span	5·74 m (18 ft 10 in)
Wheel track	5·25 m (17 ft 2½ in)
Wheelbase	5·40 m (17 ft 8¾ in)

AREAS:

Wings, gross	47·01 m² (506·0 sq ft)
Ailerons (total, incl tabs)	4·42 m² (47·54 sq ft)
Trailing-edge flaps (total)	7·99 m² (85·99 sq ft)
Leading-edge slats (total)	0·98 m² (10·56 sq ft)
Airbrakes (total)	8·06 m² (86·78 sq ft)
Fins (total)	7·80 m² (83·96 sq ft)
Rudders (total)	2·18 m² (23·50 sq ft)
Tailplane	8·31 m² (89·40 sq ft)
Elevators (total, incl tabs)	2·69 m² (29·00 sq ft)

WEIGHTS AND LOADINGS:

Manufacturer's empty weight	9,761 kg (21,519 lb)
Operating weight empty	11,302 kg (24,918 lb)
*Basic design weight, equipped	14,420 kg (31,790 lb)
**Forward airstrip weight	14,846 kg (32,730 lb)
Internal fuel load	4,853 kg (10,700 lb)
Max external ordnance	7,250 kg (16,000 lb)

Max external ordnance with full internal fuel	
	6,640 kg (14,638 lb)
Max T-O weight	22,680 kg (50,000 lb)
Max wing loading	457·4 kg/m² (93·68 lb/sq ft)
Max power loading	266·7 kg/kN (2·61 lb/lb st)
Thrust/weight ratio	0·4

*incl six 500 lb bombs, 750 rds of ammunition, and fuel for 300 nm (555 km; 345 miles) with 20 min reserves
**with four Mk-82 bombs and 750 rds

PERFORMANCE: (at max T-O weight except where indicated):

Never-exceed speed	450 knots (834 km/h; 518 mph)
Max level speed	368 knots (681 km/h; 423 mph)
Combat speed at 1,525 m (5,000 ft), with six Mk-82 bombs	387 knots (717 km/h; 446 mph)
Cruising speed at S/L	
	300 knots (555 km/h; 345 mph)
Cruising speed at 1,525 m (5,000 ft)	
	336 knots (623 km/h; 387 mph)
Stabilised 45° dive speed below 2,440 m (8,000 ft), AUW of 15,932 kg (35,125 lb)	
	260 knots (481 km/h; 299 mph)
Max rate of climb at S/L at basic design weight	
	1,828 m (6,000 ft)/min
T-O distance:	
at max T-O weight	1,220 m (4,000 ft)
at forward airstrip weight	433 m (1,420 ft)
Landing distance:	
at max T-O weight	610 m (2,000 ft)
at forward airstrip weight	457 m (1,500 ft)
Operational radius, 20 min reserve:	
close air support, 1·8 h loiter	
	250 nm (463 km; 288 miles)
deep strike	540 nm (1,000 km; 620 miles)
Ferry range, headwind of 50 knots (93 km/h; 58 mph)	
	2,208 nm (4,091 km; 2,542 miles)
	(1980–81)

FEDERAL AT-20

The Canadian "Anson" II is basically the English Avro "Anson" but has been modified to provide for the installation of two 330 h.p. Jacobs L-6BM engines in place of the Armstrong Siddeley "Cheetah" engines, which calls for new cowling and nacelles ; and the fitting of Dowty hydraulic landing-gear retraction instead of the manually-operated type ; and the use of Canadian-made auxiliaries—controls, instruments, piping, flexible tubing, conduits and all other materials and parts. An interesting feature of the Canadian "Anson" II is the use of a moulded plastic-plywood nose section made by the Vidal process. Otherwise, similarity in design permits parts being approximately 75 per cent. interchangeable with the British "Anson."

The first "Anson" II flew in August, 1941, and by the end of August, 1943, Federal Aircraft Ltd. had supervised the construction of over 2,000 aircraft, with a spares replacement varying from 10 to 50 per cent. Federal-built "Anson II" advanced trainers are now being supplied to the U.S. Army Air Forces under the designation AT-20. (1943)

THE FOKKER C-2A MONOPLANE.

The Fokker C-2A has been developed for the U.S. Army and Navy as a cargo transport type and differs only from the F-7 in regard to certain minor details. It was on a machine of this type that Lieuts. Maitland and Hegenberger flew from Oakland, Cal., to Wheeler Field, near Honolulu, on June 28-29, 1927. This was the first flight across the Pacific, and the distance of 2,400 miles over open sea was covered in 25 hrs. 50 mins.

THE FOKKER TA-1 MONOPLANE.

The Fokker TA-1 is similar to the C-2A, and three have been supplied to the U.S. Marine Corps for use in Nicaragua in the quadruple capacity of bombing, cargo, ambulance and attack. (1928)

The USAAC received 13 Tri-Motor monoplane transports from 1928, carrying the military designations C-3, C-4 and C-9. These were based on the commercial 4-AT-B, 5-AT-B and 5-AT-D. Nine 4-ATs and 5-ATs were also acquired by the Navy/Marine Corps as JR-2 and -3s (later redesignated RR-2 and -3) plus RR-4/5s.

POWER PLANT.—Three 300 h.p. Wright J-6, three 300 h.p. Pratt & Whitney "Wasp-Junior," three 420 h.p. Pratt & Whitney "Wasp" or one 420 h.p. Pratt & Whitney "Wasp" and two 300 h.p. Wright J-6 radial air-cooled engines, one fitted in the nose of the fuselage and two suspended under the wing, one on either side. Fuel tanks carried in the wing. Standard Steel metal airscrews.

ACCOMMODATION.—Pilot's cockpit, with accommodation for two side-by-side, in advance of leading-edge. Cockpit is covered with transparent cupola, providing excellent vision. Side windows openable. Dual control fitted. Entrance to cockpit through passenger's cabin. Passengers' cabin under the wing has accommodation for either eleven or fourteen passengers, in wicker chairs with ample leg room. Dimensions of cabin 16 ft. 3 in. (4-AT-E), 18 ft. 9 in. (5-D and 7-AT) long × 4 ft. 6 in. wide × 6 ft. high (4.95 m. × 1.37 m. × 1.83 m.). Openable windows of unsplinterable glass, fitted throughout length of cabin. Electric dome lights, ventilating systems and cabin exhaust heater fitted. Machine fitted with navigation lights for night-flying.

DIMENSIONS (4-AT-E).—Span 74 ft. (22.55 m.), Length 49 ft. 10 in. (15.20 m.), Height 11 ft. 9 in. (3.85 m.), Wing area 765 sq. ft. (73 sq. m.).
DIMENSIONS (5-D).—Span 77 ft. 10 in. (23.72 m.), Length 50 ft. 3 in. (16.5 m.), Height 12 ft. 8 in. (4.1 m.), Wing area 835 sq. ft. (77.5 sq. m.).
WEIGHTS AND LOADINGS (4-AT-E).—Weight empty 6,500 lbs. (2,951 kg.), Weight loaded 10,130 lbs. (4,590 kg.), Wing loading 12.9 lbs./sq. ft. (63 kg./sq. m.), Power loading 11.3 lbs./h.p. (5.2 kg./h.p.).
WEIGHTS AND LOADINGS (5-D).—Weight empty 7,840 lbs. (3,560 kg.), Weight loaded 13,500 lbs. (6,129 kg.), Wing loading 16.1 lbs./sq. ft. (78.5 kg./sq. m.), Power loading 10.7 lbs./h.p. (4.8 kg./h.p.).
PERFORMANCE (4-AT-E).—Maximum speed 132 m.p.h. (211.2 km.h.), Cruising speed 107 m.p.h. (171.2 km.h.), Landing speed 57 m.p.h. (91.2 km.h.), Ceiling 16,500 ft. (5,412 m.), Normal radius 570 miles (912 km.).
PERFORMANCE (5-D).—Maximum speed 150 m.p.h. (240 km.h.), Cruising speed 122 m.p.h. (195.2 km.h.), Landing speed 64 m.p.h. (102.4 km.h.), Ceiling 20,500 ft. (6,724 m.), Normal cruising range 560 miles (896 km.). (1931)

THE G.A. F-14

The Army received 20 as YIC-14 transports, one becoming the YIC-15.

TYPE.—Single-engined passenger and mail carrier.
WINGS.—Cantilever monoplane wing, in one piece, carried above the fuselage on four short struts. Wing structure follows standard Fokker practice and is plywood covered.
FUSELAGE.—Welded steel-tube structure, covered with fabric aft and with corrugated aluminium on sides of cabin.
TAIL UNIT.—Normal monoplane type. Welded steel-tube framework, covered with fabric. Adjustable tail-plane. All surfaces balanced.
UNDERCARRIAGE.—Divided type. Each side consists of a vertical compression strut, incorporating oleo-pneumatic suspension, the top end of which is attached to the front wing-spar and the bottom end hinged to the bottom fuselage longerons by steel-tube axle and radius-rod. Internal expanding wheel-brakes. Swivelling tail-wheel.
POWER PLANT.—One 525 h.p. Pratt & Whitney "Hornet" or Wright "Cyclone" radial air-cooled engine. Electric hand-inertia starter and "booster" coil. Adjustable metal airscrew. Nose cowling with adjustable shutters operated from cockpit.
ACCOMMODATION.—The pilot's cockpit is an open one and is located aft of the wing. The cabin is under the wing and has accommodation for six passengers. Normally, the cabin is intended for transport of freight, and no seats are supplied unless specified. Side windows throughout length of cabin. Door on left side. Forward of cabin is a separate mail compartment. Full night-flying equipment, including navigation cabin, instrument and retractable landing lights, is installed.

The G.A. Y1C-15 Military Ambulance Monoplane (525 h.p. Wright "Cyclone" engine).

DIMENSIONS.—Span 59 ft. (17.9 m.), Length 43 ft. 4 in. (13.2 m.), Height 12 ft. 11 in. (3.9 m.), Wing area 550 sq. ft. (51 sq. m.).
WEIGHTS.—Pay load 1,625 lbs. (737.75 kg.), Disposable load 2,955 lbs. (1,341.5 kg.).
PERFORMANCE.—Maximum speed 140 m.p.h. (224 km.h.), Cruising speed 115 m.p.h. (184 km.h.), Landing speed 55 m.p.h. (88 km.h.), Initial rate of climb 1,000 ft./min. (305 m./min.), Service ceiling 18,000 ft. (5,490 m.). Range at cruising speed 7 hrs. or 800 miles (1,280 km.). (1932)

GENERAL DYNAMICS F-16

USAF designations: F-16A and F-16B

The F-16 had its origin in the USAF's Lightweight Fighter (LWF) prototype programme, in 1972. The history of this programme and a description of the YF-16 prototypes can be found in the 1978-79 and 1977-78 editions of *Jane's* respectively.

The first of two YF-16 prototypes (72-01567) made its official first flight on 2 February 1974. A level speed of Mach 2 at 12,200 m (40,000 ft) was attained on 11 March 1974. The second YF-16 (72-01568) flew for the first time on 9 May 1974. During subsequent weapon trials, this aircraft extended the planned operational capability of the design by completing successfully the initial launch of Sparrow missiles on 6 October 1977 and of a Sky Flash missile in November 1977.

On 13 January 1975 the Secretary of the USAF announced that the F-16 had been selected for full-scale engineering development. The original YF-16 requirement for an air superiority day fighter was expanded, to give equal emphasis to the air-to-surface role, including provision of radar and all-weather navigation capabilities. Finalised contracts covered the manufacture of eight pre-production aircraft, comprising six single-seat **F-16As** and two two-seat **F-16Bs**, construction of which began in July 1975.

The first development F-16A made its first flight on 8 December 1976, and the first F-16B on 8 August 1977. The last of the eight development aircraft was the second two-seater, which made its first flight in June 1978. Meanwhile, the USAF had indicated its intention to procure a total of 1,388 F-16s, including 204 two-seaters.

On 7 June 1975 a joint announcement by the four NATO countries of Belgium, Denmark, the Netherlands and Norway confirmed their selection of the F-16 to replace F-104s in current service. The initial order was for 348 aircraft (Belgium 116, Denmark 58, the Netherlands 102 and Norway 72), of which 58 will be two-seaters.

Under co-production agreements, final assembly lines for these aircraft have been established in Belgium and the Netherlands. About 30 European companies are producing F-16 components, avionics and equipment.

In August 1977 Israel announced plans to acquire a minimum of 75 F-16s, of which deliveries are scheduled to begin in January 1980.

A $1·9 billion programme announced in the Spring of 1978 authorised the start of production by General Dynamics of 105 aircraft for the USAF, 192 of the 348 for Europe, and 55 of the 160 that had been ordered by Iran, but which were cancelled in January 1979. The first production F-16A (78-0001) flew for the first time on 7 August 1978 and was delivered formally to the USAF ten days later; five had been delivered by the end of 1978, with deliveries planned of a further 55 in 1979. First F-16 to enter operational service was delivered to the USAF's 388th Tactical Fighter Wing on 6 January 1979. The first F-16 for Europe was delivered to the Belgian Air Force on 26 January 1979.

General Dynamics announced on 7 April 1978 that company-funded preliminary design work had begun to evolve a sophisticated two-seat 'Wild Weasel' version of the F-16. This would be able to operate in an autonomous hunter-killer mode, or in direct support of strike aircraft. The USAF has no current requirement for such a version of the F-16, but allied nations have expressed an interest. Weapons under consideration for this version include AGM-45 Shrike anti-radiation missiles on wing stations 2 and 8, and either AGM-78 'F' Standard ARM, AGM-65 Maverick or AGM-88 HARM missiles on wing stations 3 and 7. The Wild Weasel F-16 can also carry 1,400 litre (370 US gallon) external fuel tanks on wing stations 4 and 6, and an electronic countermeasures pod on the fuselage centreline.

In late 1978 an F-16 prototype, fitted with a Martin Marietta ATLIS II (Automatic Tracking Laser Illumination System) pod, became the first single-seat fighter to hit ground targets with GBU-10 and GBU-16 laser-guided bombs, without assistance from air/ground locators. In December 1978 the USAF selected the F-16 as a testbed to explore promising new fighter aircraft technologies, under the Advanced Fighter Technology Integration (AFTI-16) programme.

Later versions include the **F-16 (ADF)**, **F-16C/D** and naval **F-16N**.

The following description applies to the F-16A and F-16B, as indicated:

TYPE: Single-seat lightweight air combat fighter (F-16A) and two-seat fighter/trainer (F-16B).

WINGS: Cantilever mid-wing monoplane, of blended wing/body design and cropped-delta planform. The blended wing/body concept is achieved by flaring the wing/body intersection, thus not only providing lift from the body at high angles of attack but also giving less wetted area and increased internal fuel volume. In addition, thickening of the wing root gives a more rigid structure, with a weight saving of some 113 kg (250 lb). Basic wing is of NACA 64A-204 section, with 40° sweepback on leading-edges. Structure is mainly of aluminium alloy, with 11 ribs, 5 spars and single upper and lower skins, and is attached to fuselage by machined aluminium fittings. Vortex lift and control is provided by sharp, highly-swept strakes extending along the fuselage forebody. This permits significant reduction in wing area. Variable wing camber is achieved by the use of leading-edge manoeuvring flaps that are programmed automatically as a function of Mach number and angle of attack. The increased wing camber maintains effective lift coefficients at high angles of attack. These flaps are one-piece bonded aluminium honeycomb sandwich structures, actuated by an AiResearch drive system using rotary actuators. The trailing-edges carry large flaperons (flaps/ailerons), which are interchangeable left with right and are actuated by National Water Lift integrated servo-actuators. The maximum rate of flaperon movement is 80°/s.

FUSELAGE: Semi-monocoque all-metal structure of frames and longerons, built in three main modules: forward (to just aft of cockpit), centre and aft. Nose radome built by Brunswick Corporation. Highly-swept vortex control strakes along the fuselage forebody.

TAIL UNIT: Cantilever structure with sweptback surfaces. Fin is multi-spar multi-rib aluminium structure with graphite-epoxy skins, aluminium tip, and glassfibre dorsal fin and root fairing. Interchangeable all-moving tailplane halves, constructed of graphite-epoxy composite laminate skins with full-depth bonded aluminium honeycomb sandwich core, titanium spar, steel leading-edge caps and aluminium tips. Ventral fins are bonded aluminium honeycomb core with aluminium skins. Split speed-brake inboard of rear portion of each horizontal tail surface to each side of nozzle, each deflecting 60° from the closed position. National Water Lift servo-actuators for rudder and tailplane.

LANDING GEAR: Menasco hydraulically-retractable type, nose unit retracting aft and main units forward into fuselage. Nosewheel is located aft of intake, to reduce the risk of foreign objects being drawn into the engine during ground operation, and rotates 90° during retraction to lie horizontally under engine air intake duct. Oleo-pneumatic struts on all units. Goodyear main wheels and brakes; B. F. Goodrich main-wheel tyres, size 25·5 × 8-14. Steerable nosewheel with B. F. Goodrich tyre, size 18 × 5·5-8. All but two main unit components interchangeable. Brake-by-wire system on main gear, with Goodyear anti-skid units. Runway arrester hook under rear fuselage.

POWER PLANT: One Pratt & Whitney F100-PW-100(3) turbofan engine, rated at approx 111·2 kN (25,000 lb st) with afterburning, mounted within the rear fuselage. Fixed-geometry intake, with boundary layer splitter plate, beneath fuselage. A variable-geometry intake can be fitted later, without difficulty, if desirable to improve high-speed performance. The underfuselage intake position was chosen because here the airflow suffers least disturbance throughout the entire range of aircraft manoeuvres, and because it eliminates the problem of gun gas ingestion. Foreign object damage is avoided by placing the nose gear aft of the inlet lip. Standard fuel contained in wing and five fuselage cells which function as two tanks; internal fuel weight is 3,162 kg (6,972 lb) in F-16A, and approx 17% less in F-16B. In-flight refuelling receptacle in top of centre-fuselage, aft of cockpit. Auxiliary fuel can be carried in drop-tanks on underwing and underfuselage hardpoints.

ACCOMMODATION: Pilot only in F-16A, in air-conditioned cockpit. McDonnell Douglas Aces II zero-zero ejection seat. Texstar transparent bubble canopy, made of polycarbonate, an advanced plastics material. The windscreen and forward canopy are an integral unit without a forward bow-frame, and are separated from the aft canopy by a simple support structure which serves also as the break-point where the forward section pivots upward and aft to give access to the cockpit. A redundant safety-lock feature prevents canopy loss. Windscreen/canopy design provides 360° all-round view, 195° fore and aft, 40° down over the side, and 15° down over the nose. Supersonic drag penalty is considered to be more than offset by the improved rearward view afforded to the pilot. To enable the pilot to sustain high-g forces, and for pilot comfort, the seat is inclined 30° aft and the heel-line is raised. In normal operation the canopy is pivoted upward and aft by electrical power; the pilot is also able to unlatch the canopy manually and open it with a backup handcrank. Emergency jettison is provided by explosive unlatching devices and two forward-mounted rockets. A limited-displacement, force-sensing control stick is provided on the right hand console, with a suitable armrest, to provide precise control inputs during combat manoeuvres. The F-16B has two cockpits arranged in tandem and equipped with all controls, displays, instruments, electronics and life-support systems required to perform both training and combat missions. The layout of the F-16B second station is essentially the same as that of the F-16A, and is fully systems-operational. A single-enclosure polycarbonate transparency, made in two pieces and spliced aft of the forward seat with a metal bow-frame and lateral support member, provides outstanding view from both cockpits.

SYSTEMS: Regenerative bootstrap air-cycle environmental control system by United Technologies' Hamilton Standard Division, using engine bleed air, for pressurisation and cooling. Two separate and independent hydraulic systems supply power for operation of the primary flight control surfaces and the utility functions. Electrical system powered by engine-driven Westinghouse 40kVA and Lear Siegler 5kVA generators and ground control units, with Sundstrand constant-speed drive. Four dedicated, sealed-cell batteries provide transient

The first production example of the General Dynamics F-16A multi-role fighter

First production example of the General Dynamics F-16B two-seat fighter/trainer

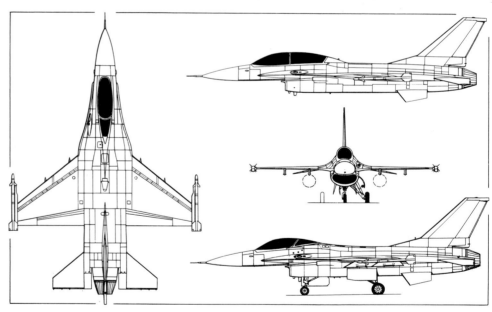

General Dynamics F-16A, with additional side view (top) of F-16B *(Pilot Press)*

electrical power protection for the fly-by-wire flight control system. Application of the control configured vehicle (CCV) principle of relaxed static stability produces a significant reduction in trim drag, especially at high load factors and supersonic speeds. The aircraft centre of gravity is allowed to move aft, reducing both the tail drag and the change in drag on the wing due to changes in lift required to balance the down-load on the tail. Relaxed static stability imposes a requirement for a highly-reliable, full-time-operating, stability augmentation system, including reliable electronic, electrical and hydraulic provisions. The signal paths in this quad-redundant system are used to control the aircraft, replacing the usual mechanical linkages. Direct electrical control is employed from pilot controls to surface

actuators. An onboard Sundstrand/Solar jet fuel starter is provided for engine self-start capability. Hamilton Standard turbine compressor, and Sundstrand accessory drive gearbox. Simmonds fuel measuring system. AiResearch emergency power unit automatically drives a standby generator and pump to provide uninterrupted electrical and hydraulic power for control in the event of the engine or primary power systems becoming inoperative.

AVIONICS AND EQUIPMENT: Westinghouse pulse-Doppler range and angle track radar, with planar array in nose. The radar has a lookdown range, in ground clutter, of 20-30 nm (37-56 km; 23-35 miles), and a lookup range of 25-40 nm (46-74 km; 29-46 miles). Forward avionics bay, immediately forward of cockpit, contains radar, air data equipment, inertial navigation system and flight control computer; rear avionics bay contains ILS, Tacan and IFF. A Dalmo Victor ALR-69 radar warning system, with AEL antennae, is installed. Communications equipment includes Magnavox AN/ARC-164 UHF transceiver; provisions for a Magnavox KY-58 secure voice system; Memcor AN/ARC-115 VHF transceiver; government furnished AN/AIC-18/25 intercom; and Novatronics interference blanker. Sperry Flight Systems central air data computer. Singer-Kearfott modified SKN-2400 inertial navigation system; Collins AN/ARN-108 ILS; Collins AN/ARN-118 Tacan; Teledyne Electronics AN/APX-101 air-to-ground IFF transponder with a government furnished IFF control; government furnished National Security Agency KIT-2A/TSEC cryptographic equipment; Lear Siegler stick force sensors; Marconi Avionics electronic head-up display set; a government-furnished horizontal situation indicator; Teledyne Avionics angle of attack transmitter; Gull Airborne angle of attack indicator; Clifton Precision attitude director indicator; Delco fire control computer; Photo-Sonics gun camera; Kaiser radar electro-optical display. Landing/taxying light on each main landing gear strut.

ARMAMENT: General Electric M61A-1 20 mm multi-barrel cannon in the port-side wing/body fairing, equipped with a General Electric ammunition handling system and a 'snapshoot' gunsight (part of the head-up display system) and 500 rounds of ammunition. There is a mounting for an infra-red air-to-air missile at each wingtip, one underfuselage hardpoint and six underwing hardpoints for the carriage of additional stores. The underfuselage station is stressed for a load of up to 1,000 kg (2,200 lb), the two inboard underwing stations for 1,587 kg (3,500 lb) each, the two centre underwing stations for 1,134 kg (2,500 lb) each, all at 5·5g; the two outboard underwing stations and the two wingtip sta-

tions 113 kg (250 lb) each, all at 9·0g. Total possible external weapon load, with reduced internal fuel, is 6,894 kg (15,200 lb), and a total load of approximately 4,763 kg (10,500 lb) can be carried with full internal fuel. Typical stores loads can include two wingtip-mounted AIM-9J/L Sidewinders, with up to four more on the outer underwing stations; Sargent-Fletcher 1,400 litre (370 US gallon; 308 Imp gallon) drop-tanks on the inboard underwing stations; a 1,136 litre (300 US gallon; 250 Imp gallon) drop-tank or a 2,200 lb bomb on the underfuselage station; a Martin Marietta Pave Penny laser tracker pod along the starboard side of the nacelle; and single or cluster bombs, air-to-surface missiles, or flare pods, on the four inner underwing stations. Stores can be launched from Aircraft Hydro-Forming MAU-12C/A bomb ejector racks, Hughes LAU-88 launchers, or Orgen triple or multiple ejector racks. Westinghouse AN/ALQ-119 ECM (jammer) pods and pod control system have been listed among probable equipment, and can be carried on the centreline and two underwing stations. Modified Tracor ALE-40 internal pyrotechnic/chaff dispensers have been specified. Weapon delivery capabilities include air-to-air combat with gun and Sidewinder missiles, and air-to-ground attack with gun, rockets, conventional bombs, special weapons, laser-guided and electro-optical weapons. Weapons already launched successfully from F-16s include radar-guided Sparrow and Sky Flash air-to-air missiles and TV-guided Maverick air-to-surface missiles.

DIMENSIONS, EXTERNAL:

Wing span over missile launchers	9·45 m (31 ft 0 in)
Wing span over missiles	10·01 m (32 ft 10 in)
Wing aspect ratio	3·0
Length overall, excl probe	14·52 m (47 ft 7·7 in)
Height overall	5·01 m (16 ft 5·2 in)
Tailplane span	5·495 m (18 ft 0·34 in)

Wheel track	2·36 m (7 ft 9 in)
Wheelbase	4·00 m (13 ft 1·44 in)
AREA:	
Wings, gross	27·87 m² (300·0 sq ft)
WEIGHTS AND LOADINGS:	
Operational weight empty:	
F-16A	6,607 kg (14,567 lb)
F-16B	6,868 kg (15,141 lb)
Internal fuel load: F-16A	3,162 kg (6,972 lb)
F-16B	2,624 kg (5,785 lb)
Max external load (F-16A)	6,894 kg (15,200 lb)
Structural design gross weight with full internal fuel (F-16A)	10,205 kg (22,500 lb)
Maximum symmetric design load factor with full internal fuel at 10,205 kg (22,500 lb) gross weight (F-16A)	9·0
Max T-O weight:	
F-16A, air-to-air, no external tanks	10,335 kg (22,785 lb)
F-16B, air-to-air, no external tanks	10,051 kg (22,160 lb)
F-16A with external load	16,057 kg (35,400 lb)
Wing loading:	
at 10,070 kg (22,200 lb) AUW	361 kg/m² (74 lb/sq ft)
at 14,968 kg (33,000 lb) AUW	537 kg/m² (110 lb/sq ft)
Thrust/weight ratio ('clean')	1·1 to 1
PERFORMANCE (F-16A):	
Max level speed at 12,200 m (40,000 ft)	above Mach 2·0
Service ceiling	more than 15,240 m (50,000 ft)
Radius of action	more than 500 nm (925 km; 575 miles)
Ferry range, with drop-tanks	more than 2,100 nm (3,890 km; 2,415 miles)
	(1979–80)

GENERAL DYNAMICS F-111

Following a detailed evaluation of design proposals submitted by General Dynamics and Boeing, the US Department of Defense announced on 24 November 1962 that General Dynamics had been selected as prime contractor for development of the F-111 variable-geometry tactical fighter (known originally by the designation TFX), with Grumman Aircraft as an associate. An initial contract was placed for 23 development aircraft (18 F-111As for the USAF, five F-111Bs for the US Navy), of which the first were scheduled for delivery within 2½ years. Subsequently, further orders were placed, covering F-111D, E and F improved tactical fighters for the USAF, 24 F-111Cs for the Royal Australian Air Force, and the FB-111A strategic bomber version for the USAF.

A total of 562 F-111s of all types, including the 23 development models, were covered by these contracts.

The specification to which the F-111 was designed called for a maximum speed of about Mach 2·5, capability of supersonic speed at sea level, short take-off capability from rough airfields in forward areas and short landing capability. The F-111 had to be able to fly between any two airfields in the world in one day and to carry a full range of conventional and nuclear weapons including the latest air-to-surface tactical weapons.

Versions are as follows:

F-111A. USAF two-seat tactical fighter-bomber. Development models built with two P & W TF30-P-1 turbofan engines; production version has TF30-P-3 engines and Mk I electronics. First F-111A flew for the first time (with wings locked at sweepback of 26°) on 21 December 1964. Contracts covered the 18 development aircraft and 141 production models for the USAF Tactical Air Command. Production completed.

EF-111A. ECM jamming version. Under development by Grumman, which has converted two F-111As to this configuration for evaluation. Details under Grumman entry.

RF-111A. Reconnaissance conversion of No. 11 F-111A, tested in prototype form. No further development planned.

YF-111A. Two strike/reconnaissance fighters completed prior to cancellation of the British government's order for 50 aircraft, under the designation F-111K, were subsequently assigned to the USAF for use in its research, development, test and evaluation programme, with the designation YF-111A. Included in F-111A total of 141 production aircraft.

F-111B. US Navy version, designed for carrier-based fleet defence duties. Powered initially by TF30-P-1 turbofan engines; production models were programmed to have more powerful TF30-P-12 engines. First F-111B, assembled by Grumman, flew for the first time on 18 May 1965.

General Dynamics FB-111A of the USAF's Strategic Air Command, armed with four SRAM missiles

Original orders covered five development aircraft and 24 production models for the US Navy. The sixth aircraft, the first to be fitted with TF30-P-12 engines, flew on 29 June 1968. The seventh (and last) has been used as a testbed for the Phoenix missile. Continued development, production and support of the F-111B were halted by Congress in mid-1968.

F-111C. Strike aircraft. Outwardly similar to FB-111A, with Pratt & Whitney TF30-P-3 engines, Mk I electronics, cockpit ejection module and eight underwing attachments for stores. 24 built for RAAF.

F-111D. Similar to F-111A, but with Mk II electronics, offering improvements in navigation and in air-to-air weapon delivery. TF30-P-9 engines. Delivery of 96 completed in February 1973. Equips 27th Tactical Fighter Wing, Cannon AFB, New Mexico.

F-111E. Superseded F-111A from 160th aircraft. Modified air intakes improve engine performance above Mach 2·2. Total of 94 built; followed by F-111D. Most equip the 20th Tactical Fighter Wing, USAFE, at Upper Heyford, Oxon, England, the remainder serving with the 474th Tactical Fighter Wing, Nellis Air Force Base, Nevada.

F-111F. Fighter-bomber. Generally similar to F-111D, but with electronics that combine the best features of the F-111E and FB-111A systems, to provide effective tactical electronics at the lowest possible cost. TF30-P-100 engines, producing 25% more thrust than the basic TF30 and providing a significant improvement in T-O performance, single-engine rate of climb, payload capability, acceleration and max speed at low level without use of afterburning. 106 ordered for Tactical Air Command. The 366th Tactical Fighter Wing at Mountain Home AFB, Idaho, is equipped with F-111Fs.

It was announced in late 1970 that all F-111F aircraft would have a boron-epoxy doubler applied to the wing pivot fitting to increase fatigue life. This was to be retrofitted to all tactical F-111 aircraft already in service during each aircraft's inspect-and-repair-as-needed (IRAN) programme.

F-111K. See YF-111A.

FB-111A. Two-seat strategic bomber version for USAF Strategic Air Command with Mk IIB advanced electronics and TF30-P-7 engines. Requirement for 210 announced by US Secretary of Defense on 10 December 1965; to replace B-52C/F versions of the Stratofortress and B-58A

General Dynamics F-111E fighter-bomber of the USAF

Hustler. Initial contract for 64 signed in Spring of 1967. Subsequently, on 20 March 1969, the US Secretary of Defense stated that FB-111A production would total 76 aircraft. First of two prototypes converted from development F-111As flew on 30 July 1967, followed by first production FB-111A on 13 July 1968 (fitted temporarily with TF30-P-3 engines). Long-span wings. Strengthened landing gear. Increased braking capacity. Max load of six nuclear bombs, or six SRAM missiles (four under wings, two in weapons bay), or combinations of these weapons. Conventional weapon loadings of up to 14,288 kg (31,500 lb) of bombs can also be delivered.

First FB-111A was delivered to the 340th Bomb Group, a training unit of Strategic Air Command, at Carswell AFB, Texas, on 8 October 1969. FB-111A units (each two squadrons) are the 509th Bomb Wing at Pease AFB, New Hampshire, and the 380th Strategic Aerospace Wing at Plattsburgh AFB, New York. Production completed.

The following details apply to the F-111A except where otherwise indicated:

TYPE: Two-seat variable-geometry multi-purpose fighter.

WINGS: Cantilever shoulder wing. Wing section of NACA 63 series, with conventional washout. Sweepback of outer portions variable in flight or on the ground from 16° to 72° 30'. Wing-actuating jacks by Jarry Hydraulics. Five-spar structure, with stressed and sculptured skin panels, each made in one piece between leading- and trailing-edge sections, from root to tip. Leading- and trailing-edge sections of honeycomb sandwich. Airbrake/lift dumpers above wing operate as spoilers for lateral control at low speeds. Full-span variable-camber leading-edge slats and full-span double-slotted trailing-edge flaps. General Electric flight control system.

FUSELAGE: Semi-monocoque structure, mainly of aluminium alloy, with honeycomb sandwich skin. Some steel and titanium. Main structural member is a T-section keel, under the arms of which the engines are hung.

TAIL UNIT: Conventional cantilever sweptback surfaces, utilising honeycomb sandwich skin, except for tailplane tips and central area of fin on each side. All-moving horizontal surfaces operate both differentially and symmetrically to provide aileron and elevator functions. Two long narrow ventral stabilising fins.

LANDING GEAR: Hydraulically-retractable tricycle type. Single wheel on each main leg. Twin-wheel nose unit retracts forward. Main gear is a triangulated structure with hinged legs which are almost horizontal when the gear is extended. During retraction, the legs pivot downward, the wheels tilt to lie almost flat against them, and the whole gear rotates forward so that the wheels are stowed side by side in fuselage between engine air intake ducts. Low-pressure tyres on main wheels, size 47-18 (42-13 in on F-111C and FB-111A). Disc brakes, with anti-skid system. Main landing gear door, in bottom of fuselage, hinges down to act as speed brake in flight.

POWER PLANT: Two Pratt & Whitney TF30-P-3 turbofan engines, each giving 82·3 kN (18,500 lb st) with afterburning. Fuel tanks in wings and fuselage. Pressure fuelling point in port side of fuselage, forward of engine air intake. Gravity fuel filler/in-flight refuelling receptacle in top of fuselage aft of cockpit. Hamilton Standard hydro-mechanical air intake system with movable shock-cone.

ACCOMMODATION: Crew of two side by side in air-conditioned and pressurised cabin. Portion of canopy over each seat is hinged on aircraft centreline and opens upward. Zero-speed, zero-altitude (including underwater) emergency escape module developed by

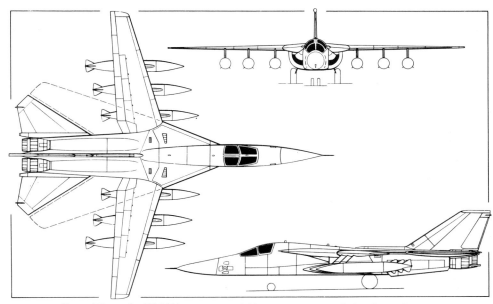

General Dynamics FB-111A two-seat variable-geometry strategic bomber *(Pilot Press)*

McDonnell Douglas Corpn and utilising a 178 kN (40,000 lb st) Rocket Power Inc rocket motor. Emergency procedure calls for both crew members to remain in capsule cabin section, which is propelled away from aircraft by rocket motor and lowered to ground by parachute. Airbags cushion impact and form flotation gear in water. Entire capsule forms survival shelter.

ARMAMENT: Tactical fighter versions carry one M61 multi-barrel 20 mm gun or two 750 lb bombs in internal weapon bay. External stores are carried on four attachments under each wing. The two inboard pylons on each side pivot as the wings sweep back, to keep the stores parallel with the fuselage. The two outboard pylons on each wing are jettisonable and non-swivelling.

DIMENSIONS:
Wing span:
  F-111A, F-111D, F-111E, F-111F:
    spread   19·20 m (63 ft 0 in)
    fully swept   9·74 m (31 ft 11·4 in)
  F-111B, F-111C, FB-111A:
    spread   21·34 m (70 ft 0 in)
    fully swept   10·34 m (33 ft 11 in)
Wing chord at root   2·11 m (6 ft 11 in)
Length overall:
  F-111A, F-111C, F-111D, F-111E, F-111F, FB-
  111A   22·40 m (73 ft 6 in)
Height overall:
  F-111A, F-111C, F-111D, F-111E, F-111F, FB-
  111A   5·22 m (17 ft 1·4 in)
WEIGHTS (F-111A):
Weight empty   20,943 kg (46,172 lb)
Max T-O weight   41,500 kg (91,500 lb)
PERFORMANCE (F-111A):
Max speed at height   Mach 2·2
Max speed at S/L   Mach 1·2
Service ceiling   over 15,500 m (51,000 ft)
T-O and landing run   under 915 m (3,000 ft)
Range with max internal fuel
                      over 2,750 nm (5,093 km; 3,165 miles)

Important avionics update programmes are continuing to maintain the effectiveness of Tactical Air Command F-111s. Details of some of those programmes follow:

F-111A/E. Current effort, scheduled to continue in RDT & E phases through FY 1981, involves replacement of current analogue bombing and navigation systems with digital equipment. This will provide capacity to handle modern guided munitions and advanced sensors, as well as growth potential for future systems such as the Navstar global positioning system and JTIDS (Joint Tactical Information Distribution System).

F-111F. Two F-111Fs fitted with Pave Tack pods were delivered to TAC's 4485th Test Squadron in 1977, and this 585 kg (1,290 lb) pack is expected to be deployed eventually throughout the F-111 force. Pave Tack, for which Ford Aerospace is prime contractor, is carried inside the aircraft's weapon bay on a cradle which rotates 180° in 5 s to expose it for use. Embodying a data link for stand-off delivery, Pave Tack provides a day/night all-weather capability to acquire, track and designate ground targets for laser, infra-red and electro-optically guided weapons, from very low altitudes if necessary.

Six more to be converted to ECM jamming aircraft under USAF contract of April 1979 (see description of EF-111A below and under Grumman entry).

EF-111A. ECM jamming version. Developed by Grumman, which converted two F-111As to this configuration for evaluation. Details under Grumman entry.

RF-111C. Four of the RAAF's 21 remaining F-111C strike aircraft have been allocated to an electronic/photographic reconnaissance role. An accompanying illustration shows the first of them, which was modified at Fort Worth and returned to Australia in the second quarter of 1979. Reconnaissance kits for the other three aircraft are being installed by RAAF personnel. They include a Fairchild KA-56E low-altitude panoramic camera, Fairchild KS-87C split vertical camera, Honeywell AN/AAD-5 infra-red linescan and Cardion Electronics TV.

(1976–77 / 79–80)

GENERAL DYNAMICS HUSTLER
USAF designation: B-58

The B-58 Hustler is a four-jet supersonic delta-wing bomber which grew from a USAF design study competition won by Fort Worth division of General Dynamics in 1949. This "generalised bomber" study contract examined the feasibility of a manned supersonic bombing system.

The B-58 received its numerical designation in March, 1951, with another design contract which continued the generalised bomber study.

A third USAF competition resulted in the MX-1964 contract, awarded in August, 1952, to produce the B-58 as a flyable bomber under the "weapon system" management concept which made the company responsible not only for the airframe, but for managing the development of all B-58 systems (except engines).

The B-58 carries a crew of three in tandem in individual cockpits. It was designed around the "minimum size" concept, packing maximum performance and flexibility into minimum weight and space. An important part of the "minimum size" concept is the two-component disposable armament and fuel pod which is carried beneath the B-58's slender fuselage. The lower component carries only fuel. In combat, this lower component would be dropped as soon as the fuel it contains became exhausted. The upper component contains both fuel and one of the aircraft's weapons; which can be either nuclear or conventional. (Additional weapons are carried externally under the wings). With its weapons dropped the B-58 is completely "clean" aerodynamically for the return flight to its home base. In this way, the two-component pod obviates the necessity of hauling useless empty structure within the aircraft.

The B-58 is the first aircraft in which the crew have individual escape capsules for emergency use at supersonic speeds. The first manned ejection test of one of these capsules was performed on February 28, 1962, at Edwards AFB. Escape capsules have been fitted retrospectively to all operational B-58's that were delivered without them.

The first B-58 prototype flew for the first time on November 11, 1956. The second prototype, first flown in February, 1957, was the first to be tested with the under-fuselage pod, which initially contained both fuel and weapon load in a single component.

The sharp temperature rise from aerodynamic friction associated with the Mach 2 speeds of which the B-58 is capable, made necessary an entirely new approach to the design and manufacture of skin and primary structures. The B-58's heat and fatigue resistant skin is made of a glass-fibre, aluminium and stainless steel honeycomb, sandwiched between two layers of metal. About 90 per cent of the wing surface is made of honeycomb sandwich panels.

The following versions of the B-58 have been produced:—

B-58A. Standard production version. Original USAF contract for 13 service test models followed by further order for 17 in Spring of 1957. The first eight aircraft had General Electric J79-GE-1 turbojet engines. The remainder were fitted with J79-GE-5 turbojets, like the fully-operational B-58A, of which 86 were built before production ended in the Autumn of 1962. In addition to these 86 genuine tactical B-58A's ten of the service test models have been brought up to fully-operational standard. Eight more of the test series have been converted into TB-58A advanced trainers. Delivery of the operational B-58A to SAC's 43rd Bombardment Wing at Carswell AFB, Texas, began in December, 1959 and the first of three squadrons became operational in August, 1960. Equipment of the 305th Wing at Bunker Hill AFB began in 1961.

NB-58A. One of the service test B-58A's has been used as a flying test bed for the General Electric J93-GE-3 turbojet, which was carried in an under-fuselage pod.

TB-58A. Eight service test models have been converted into dual-control trainers. The first of these flew on May 10, 1960, and was delivered to the USAF on August 13, 1960. Identified by extended cockpit windows, which enable the aircraft to be flown visually from either of the two forward cockpits, it is similar to the operational version except for deletion of the bomb-navigation system, electronic countermeasures equipment and defence systems. Flight refuelling equipment is retained.

During flight trials, B-58's attained speeds of up to Mach 2·09 (equivalent to 1,380 mph=2,220 kmh) at 50,000 ft (15,250 m). Low-level capabilities were demonstrated with a 1,400-mile (2,250 km) flight from Fort Worth, Texas, to Edwards AFB, California, at nearly 700 mph (1,125 kmh) while never exceeding 500 ft (150 m) above the ground.

Six international closed-circuit speed records were set up by USAF crews flying B-58A's from Edwards AFB in January, 1961. On January 12, Major Henry J. Deutschendorf and crew

General Dynamics B-58A Hustler (four General Electric J79 turbojet engines)

averaged 1,061·81 mph (1,708·82 kmh) around a 2,000-km circuit, carrying a 2,000 kg (4,409 lb) payload. This raised the records also for 1,000 kg payload and no payload over this distance. Two days later, Major Harold E. Confer and crew set up records for 2,000 kg payload, 1,000 kg payload and no payload over a 1,000-km circuit with an average speed of 1,284·73 mph (2,067·58 kmh).

On May 10, 1961, another B-58A piloted by Major Elmer E. Murphy, flew at a sustained speed of 1,302 mph (2,095 kmh) for 30 minutes, thereby winning the Aero Club de France Blériot Trophy for the first aircraft to average 2,000 kmh for 30 minutes. The same aircraft, piloted by Major W. R. Payne and crew, flew non-stop 3,669 miles (5,905 km) from New York to Paris in 3 hours, 19 min, 41 sec, on May 26, 1961, at an average speed of 1,105 mph (1,778 kmh). This was one leg of a non-stop flight of 5,183 miles (8,341 km) from Carswell AFB, Texas, to Paris, during which the B-58A was three times refuelled in flight by KC-135A Stratotankers.

Three more official records were set on March 5, 1962, during a Los Angeles to New York return flight, covering speed in both directions and for the round trip. The Los Angeles-New York leg was timed at 2 hr, 58·7 sec. On September 14, 1962, a USAF B-58A climbed to 85,360·84 ft (26,018 m) over Edwards AFB, California, establishing records for height with 5,000 kg and 2,000 kg payloads.

On October 16, 1963, the B-58 brought its total of speed and altitude/payload records to 19. Most significant of the new records was the longest supersonic flight yet made, from Tokyo to London, in 8 hr 35 min. The officially-recognised distance for this flight is 8,028 miles (12,920 km), measured as a great circle route between the two cities. In fact, the B-58 covered a significantly greater distance, in order to keep over friendly territory at all times.

TYPE: Three-seat medium bomber.

WINGS: Cantilever mid-wing monoplane of delta-configuration. All-metal structure making extensive use of honeycomb sandwich skin panels. Conical camber leading-edge. Wide-chord elevons from wing-root fairings to outboard engine pods.

FUSELAGE: All-metal semi-monocoque structure, conforming with the Area Rule and making extensive use of honeycomb skin panels. Large ribbon braking parachute housed under tail.

TAIL UNIT: Vertical fin and rudder only. All-metal construction.

LANDING GEAR: Retractable tricycle type. Each main unit has an eight-wheel bogie which retracts vertically upward into wings. Nose-unit has twin wheels and retracts rearward.

POWER PLANT: Four General Electric J79-GE-5B turbojet engines (each 15,600 lb=7,075 kg st with afterburning) in underwing pods with variable air-inlet ducts. Fuel in wings and under-fuselage pod. Normal fuel capacity more than 15,000 US gallons (56,780 litres). Flight refuelling socket for "flying boom" system on port side of fuselage nose.

ACCOMMODATION: Crew of three (pilot, navigator-bombardier and defence systems operator) in separate tandem cockpits with individual hinged canopies and individual self-contained emergency escape capsules capable of being used at Mach 2.

SYSTEMS AND EQUIPMENT: Bendix electronic powered-control and autopilot system which continually senses and computes maximum control surface movement permitted by structural limitations over the entire speed range. Sperry bombing-navigation system, providing automatic internal guidance. Hamilton Standard automatic air conditioning and pressurisation system provides cooling for the cockpits, wheel wells and electronic installations, controls heating, de-humidifies the cabin air and provides demisting and rain removal air for windscreen.

ARMAMENT: One General Electric T-171E3 Vulcan 20-mm multi-barrel cannon in flexible mounting in fuselage tail-cone.

DIMENSIONS, EXTERNAL:

Wing span	56 ft 10 in (17·32 m)
Length overall	96 ft 9 in (29·49 m)
Height overall	29 ft 11 in (9·12 m)

WEIGHT:

Max T-O weight	over 160,000 lb (72,570 kg)

PERFORMANCE (at max T-O weight):

Normal max speed at 44,000 ft (13,400 m)	Mach 2 (1,324 mph=2,118 kmh)
Service ceiling	over 60,000 ft (18,300 m)

(1965–66)

GREAT LAKES BG-1

The Great Lakes Aircraft Corporation is a contractor to the U.S. Army and Navy and a producer of commercial aircraft.

The Company is principally engaged in the development and manufacture of naval and military aircraft for the U.S. Government. The BG-1 or TBG-1 is a two-seat Torpedo-Bomber for aircraft carrier operation. It is a single-bay biplane with folding wings and is equipped with a two-row Pratt & Whitney "Wasp" engine, controllable N.A.C.A. cowling and V.P. airscrew.

(1936)

Sixty production BG-1s were acquired by the Navy and Marine Corps from 1934, remaining on aircraft carriers until 1938 and thereafter serving on land in bomber and utility roles.

Wing span 36 ft (10.7 m). Length 28 ft 9 in (8.76 m). Height 11 ft (3.35 m). Weight loaded 6,347 lbs (2,879 kg). Maximum speed 188 mph (302 km/h). Range 549 miles (883 km). Armament two 0.30-in guns and bombs.

THE GREAT LAKES TG-1.

TYPE.—Single-engined torpedo bomber landplane or seaplane.

WINGS.—Equal-span, single-bay, folding-wing biplane. Upper wing in three sections, consisting of centre-section and two outer sections. Lower wing in four sections, consisting of two stub-sections and two outer-sections. Outer-sections of both upper and lower wings fold round the rear spar joints. Construction is entirely of aluminium-alloy except for the fabric covering. Ailerons on all four outer-sections.

FUSELAGE.—Rectangular structure of riveted aluminium-alloy members, with welded steel-tube fittings, the whole being covered with fabric.

TAIL UNIT.—Normal monoplane type. Aluminium alloy framework with fabric covering. Adjustable tail-plane. Balanced rudder.

UNDERCARRIAGE.—Split type with oleo pneumatic suspension. Full swivel tail-wheel with oleo-pneumatic suspension. Land undercarriage is interchangeable with twin long single-step Vee-bottomed floats.

POWER PLANT.—One 550 h.p. Pratt & Whitney "Hornet" radial air-cooled engine. Main fuel tanks in fuselage, with gravity tank in centre-section.

ACCOMMODATION.—Three open cockpits on centre-line of machine and internal wireless compartment. Cockpit for bomber-pilot in front, pilot's cockpit under cut-out in trailing-edge of wing, with third cockpit for gunner behind.

DIMENSIONS.—Span 53 ft. (16.15 m.), Length 34 ft. 7 $\frac{3}{16}$ in. (10.56 m.), Height (landplane) 12 ft. 7$\frac{3}{4}$ in. (3.8 m.), (seaplane) 14 ft. 4$\frac{1}{2}$ in. (4.38 m.).

The Great Lakes TG-1 Torpedo-bomber Biplane (550 h.p. Pratt & Whitney "Hornet" engine).

WEIGHTS.—Weight empty (landplane) 4,134 lbs. (1,875.18 kg.), (seaplane) 4,607 lbs. (2,089.7 kg.), Disposable load (landplane) 3,460 lbs. (1,569.45 kg.), (seaplane) 3,489 lbs. (1,582.6 kg.).

PERFORMANCE.—No data available.

(1931)

THE GREAT LAKES TG-2.

TYPE.—Single-engined torpedo bomber landplane or seaplane.

WINGS.—Equal-span, single-bay, folding-wing biplane. Upper wing in three sections, consisting of centre-section and two outer sections. Lower wing in four sections, consisting of two stub-sections and two outer-sections. Outer-sections of both upper and lower wings fold round the rear spar joints. Construction is entirely of aluminium-alloy except for the fabric covering. Ailerons on all four outer-sections.

FUSELAGE.—Rectangular structure of riveted aluminium-alloy members, with welded steel-tube fittings, the whole being covered with fabric.

TAIL UNIT.—Normal monoplane type. Aluminium-alloy framework with fabric covering. Adjustable tail-plane. Balanced rudder.

UNDERCARRIAGE.—Split type with oleo pneumatic suspension. Full swivel tail-wheel with oleo-pneumatic suspension. Land undercarriage is interchangeable with twin long single-step Vee-bottomed floats.

POWER PLANT.—One 575 h.p. geared Curtiss "Cyclone" radial air-cooled engine. Main fuel tanks in fuselage, with gravity tank in centre-section.

ACCOMMODATION.—Three open cockpits on centre-line of machine. Cockpit for bomber-gunner in front, pilot's cockpit under cut-out in trailing-edge of wing, with third cockpit for gunner-wireless operator behind.

DIMENSIONS.—Span 53 ft. (16.15 m.), Length 34 ft. 7 $\frac{3}{16}$ in. (10.56 m.), Height (landplane) 13 ft. 5$\frac{1}{4}$ in. (4.09 m.), (seaplane) 14 ft. 7$\frac{7}{16}$ in. (4.46 m.).

WEIGHTS.—Weight empty (landplane) 4,546 lbs. (2,062 kg.), (seaplane) 5,073 lbs. (2,530 kg.), Disposable load (landplane) 3,794 lbs. (1,722 kg.), (seaplane) 3,794 lbs. (1,722 kg.).

PERFORMANCE.—Maximum speed (landplane) 127.8 m.p.h. (204.5 km.h.), Maximum speed (seaplane) 124.8 m.p.h. (199.6 km.h.), Stalling speed (landplane) 58 m.p.h. (92.4 km.h.), Stalling speed

The Great Lakes TG-2 Torpedo Bomber (575 h.p. Wright "Cyclone" engine).

(seaplane) 59.5 m.p.h. (95.2 km.h.), Climb in 10 mins. (landplane) 5,450 ft. (1,662 m.). Climb in 10 mins. (seaplane) 4,850 ft. (1,480 m.), Service ceiling (landplane) 13,150 ft. (4,011 m.), Service ceiling (seaplane) 11,450 ft. (3,492 m.).

(1934)

THE GRUMMAN FF-1 AND SF-1.

TYPE.—Two-seat fighting (FF-1) or scouting (SF-1) biplane.

WINGS.—Single-bay staggered biplane of unequal span. Aluminium-alloy spars and ribs, fabric covering. "N"-type interplane struts. Ailerons on upper wings only.

FUSELAGE.—Metal monocoque structure, details of the construction of which are unknown. The fuselage forward is shaped to accommodate the entire undercarriage when it is retracted.

TAIL UNIT.—Normal monoplane type of all-metal construction.

UNDERCARRIAGE.—Two-wheel retractable type. When retracted the wheels are drawn into recesses in the sides of the fuselage. Retractable tail-wheel.

POWER PLANT.—One Wright "Cyclone" SR-1820-F (775 h.p. at 5,800 ft. = 1,770 m.) nine-cylinder air-cooled radial engine, enclosed in a Townend low-drag cowling ring. Fuel tanks in fuselage.

ACCOMMODATION.—Two open cockpits, in tandem, for pilot and rear gunner. Cockpits fitted with a coupé top. Armament consists of one fixed Browning gun firing forward through the airscrew and two Browning guns on a movable mounting in the observer's cockpit. Equipment includes emergency flotation and deck landing gear.

DIMENSIONS.—Span 34 ft. 6 in. (10.5 m.), Length 24 ft. 6 in. (7.6 m.), Height 9 ft. 5 in. (2.9 m.), Wing area 310 sq. ft. (28.8 sq. m.).

WEIGHTS AND LOADINGS.—Weight empty 3,221 lbs. (1,461 kg.), Disposable load 1,579 lbs. (716 kg.), Weight loaded 4,800 lbs. (2,177 kg.), Wing loading 15.5 lbs./sq. ft. (74.7 kg./sq. m.), Power loading 6.22 lbs./h.p. (2.8 kg./h.p.).

PERFORMANCE.—Maximum speed at 7,000 ft. (2,135 m.) 220 m.p.h. (352 km.h.), Cruising speed at 7,000 ft. (2,135 m.) 200 m.p.h. (320 km.h.), Landing speed 65 m.p.h. (104.6 km.h.), Initial rate of climb 1,800 ft./min. (487.7 m./min.), Service ceiling 25,000 ft. (6,858 m.), Cruising range 647 miles (1,030 km.).

(1936)

Scouting Aeroplanes of the United States Navy in Line-abreast Formation.

THE GRUMMAN F2F-1.

TYPE.—Single-seat fighter biplane.

WINGS.—Unequal-span single-bay staggered biplane. Aluminium-alloy spars and ribs, fabric covering. Arrangement of wings and bracing similar to J2F-1. Ailerons on upper wings only.

FUSELAGE.—Aluminium-alloy monocoque, using .032 in. minimum sheet.

TAIL UNIT.—Monoplane type. Aluminium-alloy structure, fixed surfaces covered with metal sheet, movable surfaces with fabric. Trimming-tabs in elevator and rudder.

UNDERCARRIAGE.—Retractable type. Wheels are retracted into recesses in sides of fuselage by chains and sprockets. Retractable tail-wheel.

POWER PLANT.—One Pratt & Whitney R-1535-72 fourteen-cylinder radial air-cooled engine rated at 650 h.p. at 7,500 ft. (2,290 m.). N.A.C.A. cowling. Alternatively, the Wright "Cyclone" R-1820-F53 engine rated at 745 h.p. at 10,500 ft. (3,160 m.) may be installed. Fuel tank in fuselage.

ACCOMMODATION.—Pilot's cockpit over trailing-edge of lower wing, with sliding cabin enclosure. Large baggage compartment and radio compartment behind cockpit.

ARMAMENT.—Two fixed Browning machine-guns firing forward through the airscrew.

DIMENSIONS.—Span 28 ft. 6 in. (8.69 m.), Length 21 ft. 5 in. (6.65 m.), Height 8 ft. 6 in. (2.59 m.), Wing area 230 sq. ft. (21.36 sq. m.).

WEIGHTS AND LOADINGS.—Weight empty 2,625 lbs. (1,192 kg.), Disposable load 1,156 lbs. (525 kg.), Weight loaded 3,781 lbs. (1,717 kg.), Wing loading 16.5 lbs./sq. ft. (80.5 kg./sq. m.), Power loading 5.85 lbs./h.p. (2.65 kg./h.p.).

PERFORMANCE.—Maximum speed (Pratt & Whitney R-1535-72 engine) 237 m.p.h. (379 km.h.) at 7,500 ft. (2,290 m.), Maximum speed (Wright "Cyclone" R-1820-F53 engine) 257 m.p.h. (411 km.h.) at 10,500 ft. (3,160 m.), Landing speed 65.5 m.p.h. (86.8 km.h.), Initial rate of climb 2,700 ft./min. (823.5 m./min.), Service ceiling 27,500 ft. (8,390 m.), Cruising range 750 miles (1,200 km.). (1939)

The Grumman F3F-2 Single-seat Fighter Biplane (Wright "Cyclone" engine).

THE GRUMMAN F3F-1, F3F-2 AND F3F-3.

These are developments of the F2F-1 single-seat fighter. The F3F-1 is fitted with the 650 h.p. Pratt & Whitney "Twin-Wasp Junior" and the F3F-2 and F3F-3 with the 750 h.p. Wright "Cyclone" engine. In general arrangement and construction they are identical to the F2F-1 previously described.

DIMENSIONS.—Span 32 ft. (9.7 m.), Length 23 ft. 3 in. (7.1 m.), Height 8 ft. 9 in. (2.7 m.), Wing area 260 sq. ft. (24 sq. m.).

WEIGHTS AND LOADINGS (F3F-1).—Weight empty 2,870 lbs. (1,302 kg.), Disposable load 1,230 lbs. (558 kg.), Weight loaded 4,100 lbs. (1,860 kg.), Wing loading 15.8 lbs./sq. ft. (77.1 kg./sq. m.), Power loading 6.3 lbs./h.p. (2.8 kg./h.p.).

WEIGHTS AND LOADINGS (F3F-2).—Weight empty 3,215 lbs. (1,458 kg.), Disposable load 1,338 lbs. (607 kg.), Weight loaded 4,553 lbs. (2,065 kg.).

PERFORMANCE (F3F-1—Pratt & Whitney "Twin-Wasp-Junior").—Maximum speed 240 m.p.h. (386.2 km.h.) at 7,500 ft. (2,290 m.), Cruising speed 215 m.p.h. (346 km.h.) at 7,500 ft. (2,290 m.), Landing speed 65 m.p.h. (104.6 km.h.), Initial rate of climb 2,700 ft./min. (822 m./min.), Service ceiling 29,000 ft. (8,840 m.), Cruising range 720 miles (1,160 km.).

PERFORMANCE (F3F-2—Wright "Cyclone").—Maximum speed 270 m.p.h. (434.4 km.h.), Cruising speed 243 m.p.h. (390.0 km.h.), Landing speed 67 m.p.h. (107.6 km.h.), Initial rate of climb 3,000 ft./min. (914.4 m./min.), Service ceiling 32,000 ft. (9,753.6 m.).

(1939)

Grumman Albatross, equipped for anti-submarine duties, with MAD tail-sting extended

GRUMMAN G-64/G-111 ALBATROSS
US Air Force, Navy and Coast Guard designation: HU-16
RCAF designation: CSR-110

The prototype of this general-utility amphibian flew in October, 1947, and the Albatross entered military service in July, 1949. More than 450 have been built. Production has ended, but conversion of existing airframes for new duties continues.

The following versions of the Albatross are in service:

HU-16A (formerly SA-16A) **(G-64)**. Amphibian used by the USAF for sea rescue duties. 305 built. A few fitted with triphibious sprung skis to make possible operation from ice and snow as well as land and water. USAF machines being converted to HU-16B standard as they come in to Grumman for inspection and repair. HU-16A's also supplied to the Argentine, Brazil (13), Italy, Nationalist China, Pakistan, Peru, the Philippines, Portugal, Spain and Venezuela.

HU-16B (formerly SA-16B) **(G-111)**. Improved version, with higher speed, increased range and improved single-engine performance. Span increased by 16 ft 6 in (5·03 m). Larger tail surfaces. Wing slots replaced by cambered leading-edges. Antenna housings modified to reduce drag. New high-pressure de-icing boots on wings and tail. Prototype first flown January 16, 1956. First HU-16A aircraft modified to HU-16B standard on January 25, 1957. Also supplied to Chile (6).

Sixteen special models have been produced for the Royal Norwegian Air Force, for anti-submarine warfare duties. These aircraft have a large nose radome, retractable MAD tail "sting" wingtip ECM antennae, sonobuoy stowage and launcher in rear fuselage, depth charge and marine marker stowage in centre fuselage, searchlight under starboard wing, and four underwing attachments for Mk 42-1 torpedoes, 5-in HVAR rockets, depth bombs, Zuni rocket packs or fuel tanks.

CSR-110. Ten specially-modified HU-16B's for air-sea rescue duties with the RCAF. Each has two 1,525 hp Canadian-built Wright R-1820-82 engines, and a new retractable tricycle landing gear designed to facilitate beaching.

HU-16C (formerly UF-1). Amphibian for US Navy and Coast Guard, similar to HU-16A. Being modified to HU-16D standard as received for inspection and repair. Also delivered to Republic of Indonesia (12) and the Federal Republic of Germany (5).

HU-16D (formerly UF-2). US Navy utility amphibian similar to HU-16B. Six supplied to Japanese Maritime Self-Defence Force in Spring of 1961.

HU-16E (formerly UF-2G). Similar to HU-16D, for US Coast Guard.

The following details apply specifically to the HU-16B and D versions of the Albatross.

TYPE: Twin-engined general-utility triphibian or amphibian flying-boat.

WINGS: Cantilever high-wing monoplane. Wing section NACA 23017 with extended leading- and trailing-edges. Aspect ratio 9·0. Chord 14 ft 2¾ in (4·33 m) at root, 6 ft 11¾ in (2·13 m) at tip. Dihedral 1° 10'. Incidence 5° at root. Aluminium alloy box-beam structure. Wing in three sections: a centre-section permanently attached to hull and two outer sections. Frise ailerons with aluminium alloy structure and fabric covering. Aluminium alloy split flaps. Trim-tab in each aileron. Pneumatic de-icing boots on leading-edges.

HULL: Two-step aluminium alloy semi-monocoque structure.

TAIL UNIT: Cantilever all-metal structure, with dihedral tailplane. Fin integral with hull. Trim-tabs in rudder and each elevator. Pneumatic de-icing boots on leading-edges.

LANDING GEAR: Retractable tricycle type. Main wheels raised into sides of hull, twin nose wheels into nose of hull. Hydraulic retraction. Bendix oleo-pneumatic shock-absorbers. Main wheels and tyres size 40 × 12, pressure 107 lb/sq in (7·52 kg/cm²). Nose-wheels size 26 × 6, pressure 62 lb/sq in (4·36 kg/cm²). Disc brakes.

POWER PLANT: Two 1,425 hp Wright R-1820-76A or B nine-cylinder radial air-cooled engines, each driving a three-blade Hamilton Standard constant-speed and reversing propeller. Internal fuel in two tanks in centre-section outboard of hull with total capacity of 675 US gallons (2,550 litres). Drop tanks of 100, 150 or 300 US gallons (378, 567 or 1,135 litres) each may be carried on bomb-racks under centre-section, one on each side of hull. Each wing-tip float can carry a further 200 US gallons (756 litres). Oil capacity 58 US gallons (200 litres).

ACCOMMODATION: Crew of five. Cabin may be adapted for various missions. As an ambulance 12 litters can be carried, and for transport work 10-22 passengers in addition to crew. With seats removed cargo or special equipment can be accommodated. A "dutch-type" door is provided on port side for sea rescue operations or for loading stretchers. Door is split horizontally, the lower half being left in place to give higher freeboard in rough weather. A rescue platform may be attached to bottom door sill from which a crewman secured by safety belt may haul persons aboard from water. Smaller emergency door on starboard side. Both doors may be used for oblique photography and for handling sea anchor. Hatch in roof to facilitate loading of freight. Three life-rafts carried, two in cabin, and one of automatically inflatable type in compartment in top of hull aft of wing. Lavatory and tail compartment for stowing equipment and gear.

SYSTEMS AND EQUIPMENT: Stewart-Warner air-conditioning equipment. Auxiliary power-plant in compartment aft of main cabin. Separate oxygen supplied for crew and passengers with 20 outlets for oxygen masks in cabin. Racks under each wing can carry bombs, auxiliary fuel tanks, rescue boat or other packaged equipment. Radome on nose. Provision for Jato units to be attached to cabin doors from inside hull. Stowage for four Jato units below cabin floor between wheel wells. Stowage for two parachute flares in tail compartment.

DIMENSIONS, EXTERNAL (HU-16B):

Wing span	96 ft 8 in (29·46 m)
Length overall	62 ft 10 in (19·18 m)
Height overall	25 ft 10 in (7·87 m)
Draught	3 ft 3½ in (1·0 m)
Tailplane span	31 ft 0 in (9·45 m)
Wheel track	17 ft 8 in (5·38 m)
Wheelbase	18 ft 3¾ in (5·58 m)

DIMENSIONS, INTERNAL (HU-16B):

Cabin: Length	26 ft 1 in (7·95 m)
Max width	7 ft 5 in (2·26 m)
Max height	6 ft 4 in (1·93 m)
Floor area	145 sq ft (13·5 m²)
Volume	568 cu ft (16·08 m³)

AREAS (HU-16B):

Wings, gross	1,035 sq ft (96·2 m²)
Ailerons (total)	90·4 sq ft (8·40 m²)
Flaps (total)	135·4 sq ft (12·58 m²)
Fin	95·0 sq ft (8·83 m²)
Rudder	45·5 sq ft (4·23 m²)
Tailplane	139·8 sq ft (12·98 m²)
Elevators	87·8 sq ft (8·16 m²)

WEIGHTS AND LOADINGS (HU-16B):

Weight empty equipped	22,883 lb (10,380 kg)
Normal T-O weight	30,353 lb (13,768 kg)
Max T-O weight	37,500 lb (17,010 kg)
Max zero-fuel weight	27,486 lb (12,467 kg)
Max wing loading	29·33 lb/sq ft (143·2 kg/m²)
Max power loading	15·56 lb/hp (7·06 kg/hp)

PERFORMANCE (HU-16B at max T-O weight):

Max level speed at S/L	236 mph (379 kmh)
Max cruising speed	224 mph (362 kmh)
Cruising speed for max endurance	124 mph (200 kmh)
Stalling speed	74 mph (119 kmh)
Rate of climb at S/L	1,450 ft (442 m) min
Service ceiling	21,500 ft (6,550 m)
Service ceiling, one engine out	9,300 ft (2,835 m)
T-O run	2,100 ft (640 m)
T-O run with JATO	700 ft (213 m)
T-O to 50 ft (15 m)	4,450 ft (1,356 m)
T-O to 50 ft (15 m) with JATO	1,500 ft (457 m)
Landing from 50 ft (15 m)	2,200 ft (670 m)
Landing run	1,100 ft (335 m)
Range with max fuel 5% reserve, 30 min hold-off	2,850 miles (4,587 km)

(1964–65)

The Grumman TBF-1 Avenger Three-seat Torpedo Bomber (Wright R-2600-8 engine).

THE GRUMMAN AVENGER.
U.S. Navy designation : TBF. (TBM when built by Eastern Aircraft Division, General Motors Corpn.).

The XTBF-1 prototype of the Avenger was ordered by the U.S. Navy in 1940 and was delivered in 1941. The TBF-1 went into production in the same year and it began to go into service as a replacement for the TBD early in 1942. It was first reported in action in the Battle of Midway in June, 1942.

The Avenger was latterly in production solely by the Eastern Aircraft Division, General Motors Corpn., under the designation TBM. The first TBM-1 assembled from parts supplied by Grumman flew on November 11, 1942, and by December, 1943, all production of the Avenger by Grumman had ceased.

The last model of the Avenger was the TBM-4. This version was fitted with a Wright R-2600-20 engine, and had a strengthened airframe.

TYPE.—Three-seat Torpedo-Bomber.

WINGS.—Mid-wing cantilever monoplane. Rectangular centre-section and equally-tapered folding outer wing-sections. All-metal single-spar structure with flush-riveted smooth metal skin. Split trailing-edge flaps between ailerons and centre-section. Outer wings fold. Hydraulic folding and unfolding, the locking-pins being operated in the proper sequence by one motion of the hydraulic control lever.

FUSELAGE.—Oval section semi-monocoque structure built up of a series of angle frames and stamped bulk-heads and covered with a smooth metal skin which is reinforced internally by longitudinal Z and channel type stringers, with suitable stiffening at highly-stressed points.

TAIL UNIT.—Cantilever monoplane type. Integral fin with the cantilever tail-plane mounted above fuselage. All-metal structure with metal-covered fixed surfaces and fabric-covered rudder and elevators. Trimming-tabs in control surfaces.

LANDING GEAR.—Retractable type. Cantilever oleo legs hinged at extremities of centre-section and are raised outwardly into recesses in underside of outer wing-sections. Fully-retractable tail-wheel. Catapult points and electrically-operated retractable arrester hook. Provision for "Jato" rocket boost take-off

POWER PLANT.—One 1,700 h.p. Wright R-2600-8 fourteen cylinder radial air-cooled engine with two-speed supercharger. Three-blade Hamilton-Standard Hydromatic constant-speed airscrew. Three main fuel tanks built integral with centre-section, centre tank (150 U.S. gallons) within fuselage and outer tanks (90 U.S. gallons each) in centre-section stubs. Auxiliary streamline droppable tanks (58 U.S. gallons each) under outer wings. Droppable long-range ferry tank (275 U.S. gallons) in bomb-bay. Oil tank (32 U.S. gallons) in engine compartment.

ACCOMMODATION.—Crew of three—pilot, bomb-aimer and radio-operator. Pilot's cockpit over leading-edge of wing. Pilot fires forward fixed guns and releases torpedo. Bomb-aimer's position in lower fuselage aft of bomb-bay. Bomb-aimer also operates ventral gun. Radio-operator aft of pilot serves as turret-gunner.

ARMAMENT.—One 30 cal. machine-gun in cowling and synchronised to fire through airscrew, one fixed 50 cal. gun in each outer wing, one 50 cal. gun in power operated-turret, and one 30 cal. gun in ventral hatch at aft end of bomb or torpedo bay. Bomb-bay can accommodate one U.S.N. short air torpedo, one 2,000 lb. or one 1,600 lb. armour-piercing bomb, four 500 lb. bombs or equivalent load of bombs of smaller calibre, a smoke-screen tank, droppable fuel tank or tow target and equipment. Hydraulically-operated bomb doors controlled by pilot or bomb-aimer.

DIMENSIONS.—Span 54 ft. 2 in. (16.5 m.), Width folded 19 ft. (5.8 m.), Length 40 ft. 0⅛ in. (12.2 m.), Height 16 ft. 5 in. (5 m.), Wing area 490 sq. ft. (45.5 sq. m.).

NORMAL LOADED WEIGHT.—15,536 lbs. (7,053 kg.).

PERFORMANCE.—Maximum speed 278 m.p.h. (445 km.h.), Rate of climb 1,075 ft./min. (376 m./min.), Service ceiling 22,600 ft. (6,890 m.), Normal range 905 miles (1,450 km.) at 215 m.p.h. (344 km.h.).   (1945–56)

THE GRUMMAN G-58 BEARCAT.
U.S. Navy designation : F8F.

The Bearcat is a single-seat Fighter bearing the characteristic lines of the earlier Grumman fighters from which it was developed. There are three versions in service :—

F8F-1. Pratt & Whitney R-2800-34W engine with 2,800 h.p. take-off output with water injection, driving four-blade Aeroprop constant-speed airscrew. Armament consists of four wing-mounted .5-in. (12.7 mm.) machine-guns.

F8F-1B. Redesigned power-plant section with same basic engine. Armament modified to four 20 mm. cannon, two in each wing. Revised radio and radar equipment.

F8F-2. Latest R-2800-E engine with a maximum rating of 2,500 h.p. Height of fin and rudder increased by 12 in. (30.5 cm.) to increase directional stability where four 20 mm. cannon are firing. The F8F-2 has made a controlled climb from take-off to 10,000 ft. (3,050 m.) in 92 seconds.

TYPE.—Single-seat Carrier Fighter.

WINGS.—Cantilever mid-wing monoplane. All-metal structure in three sections with flush-riveted metal skin. Dihedral from roots. "Safety wing-tips" automatically jettisoned in flight in cases of overload to prevent failure of main wing structure. Sections break away at about 3 ft. (0.91 m.) from the tips, including half the ailerons. Outer wing sections fold upwards for stowage. Gross wing area 244 sq. ft. (22.66 m.²). Fabric-covered metal ailerons and hydraulically-operated slotted flaps. Area of ailerons 20.7 sq. ft. (1.92 m.²).

FUSELAGE.—All-metal monocoque structure with integral fin.

TAIL UNIT.—Cantilever monoplane type. All-metal structure with metal-covered fixed surfaces and fabric-covered rudder and elevators. Fin built integral with fuselage. Trim-tabs in rudder and elevators.

LANDING GEAR.—Retractable two-wheel type. Each main wheel, carried in half-fork on Bendix shock-absorber leg, retracts inwards into wing and fuselage and is fully enclosed by fairing plates attached to leg and by hinged doors under fuselage. Hydraulic operation. Tail-wheel retracts rearwards into fuselage. Deck arrester hook. Track 11 ft. 6 in. (3.5 m.).

POWER PLANT.—One Pratt & Whitney R-2800-34W eighteen-cylinder two-row radial air-cooled engine rated at 1,700 h.p. (normal) or 2,210 h.p. (with water injection) at 10,000 ft. (3,050 m.) and with 2,100 h.p. (normal) or 2,800 h.p. (with water injection) for take-off. Aeroprop four-blade constant-speed airscrew 12 ft. 7 in. (3.82 m.) diameter. Internal bullet-proof fuel tanks with total capacity of 185 U.S. gallons (700 litres). Two long-range drop-tanks each of 150 U.S. gallons (568 litres) capacity may be carried under wings.

ACCOMMODATION.—Pilot's enclosed cockpit with flat bullet-proof windshield and sliding bubble canopy. Armour plating behind pilot.

ARMAMENT.—Four .5 in. (12.7 mm.) machine-guns (F8F-1), or four 20 mm. cannon (F8F-1B) mounted two in each wing outside airscrew disc. Provision for bombs up to total of 2,000 lb. (907 kg.) or four 5 in. (12.7 cm.) rocket projectiles under wings.

DIMENSIONS.
Span 35 ft. 6 in. (10.82 m.).
Width folded 23 ft. 9⅛ in. (7.25 m.).
Length 27 ft. 6 in. (8.38 m.).
Height 13 ft. 10 in. (4.22 m.).
Height (wing folded 13 ft. (3.96 m.).

WEIGHTS AND LOADINGS.
Weight loaded 9,300 lb. (4,222 kg.).
Wing loading 39.3 lb./sq. ft. (191.7 kg./m.²).
Power loading at take-off 4.5 lb./h.p. (2.0 kg./h.p.).

PERFORMANCE.—
Max. speed over 455 m.p.h. (732 km.h.) at rated height.
Speed at sea level 425 m.p.h. (684 km.h.).
Rate of climb (with water injection) 6,500 ft./min. (1,980 m./min.).
Normal rate of climb 5,700 ft. min. (1,525 m./min.).
Service ceiling 42,300 ft. (12,895 m.).
Normal range with drop tank 1,650 miles (2,640 km.).
Max. ferrying range 2,200 miles (3,740 km.).
(1949–50)

The Grumman F8F-2N Bearcat Single-seat Night Fighter (2,500 h.p. Pratt & Whitney R-2800 engine).
(*Harold Martin*).

THE GRUMMAN G-93 COUGAR.
U.S. Navy designation: F9F.

The Cougar is a swept-wing development of the earlier straight-wing G-79 Panther. The fuselage is similar to that of the Panther, but new 35° swept wings and tailplane are incorporated. Spoilers replace the ailerons for lateral control. Production ended on 31 December 1959, when a total of 399 had been built.

Four versions of the Cougar were produced from 1962 receiving new F-9F designations. The F9F-81T continued to serve into the 1980s as the TF-9J.

F9F-6. One Pratt & Whitney J48-P-8 (7,250 lb.=3,290 kg. s.t.). Prototype first flew on September 20, 1951. Armament consists of four 20 mm. cannon. F9F-6P is an unarmed photographic reconnaissance aircraft with longer nose to accommodate K-17 and trimetrogon cameras.

F9F-7. One Allison J33-A-16A (6,350 lb.=2,880 kg. s.t.). Same as F9F-6 except for power-plant.

F9F-8. One Pratt & Whitney J48-P-8 engine. Development of F9F-6 with greater speed and range. Movable leading-edge slats replaced by fixed cambered leading-edge extensions outboard of fences and trailing-edge extended. Elimination of hydraulic system necessary to operate wing slats provides space for 30 additional U.S. gallons of fuel in each wing. Centre fuselage lengthened by 8 inches to make room for additional 80 U.S. gallons in front, or main, fuselage tank. Total internal fuel load increased by 140 U.S. gallons. First production F9F-8 flew for first time on January 18, 1954. F9F-8P (first flown August 21, 1955) is photographic reconnaissance version with extended nose for cameras. Out of production in 1957.

F9F-8T. Two-seat fighter-trainer version of F9F-8, first flown on April 4, 1956. Nose section lengthened 34 in. (86 cm.) to accommodate second cockpit. Both cockpits have Martin-Baker ejector seats and standard F9F-8 controls, instruments, etc. and can be used interchangeably by instructor and pilot. When flown as single-seater forward cockpit is used. Armament consists of two 20 mm. cannon and wide variety of air-to-air or air-to-ground stores can be carried under wings. In addition to training, F9F-8T can be used as an operational fighter. More than 100 ordered for U.S. Navy. First deliveries made in mid-1956.

The Grumman F9F-8 Cougar Naval Carrier Fighter armed with Sidewinder missiles.

TYPE.—Single-seat Naval Carrier Fighter.
WINGS.—Low-wing cantilever swept-wing monoplane. Outboard of air inlets wings have 35° L/E. sweepback. All-metal structure with flush-riveted stressed skin. Trailing-edge flap over ¾ span. Lateral control by hydraulically-operated spanwise spoilers on upper surface of wings at 75% of chord line. Artificial feel system incorporated in lateral control. Electrically operated trim-tab near port wing-tip. Auto-slats on F9F-6 and -7, fixed cambered leading-edge extensions on F9F-8.
FUSELAGE.—All-metal structure with flush-riveted stressed skin. Quickly-detachable nose for servicing equipment and interchangeability of armament, photographic and electronic equipment. Tail section detachable for access to engine compartment.
TAIL UNIT.—Cantilever monoplane type. All-metal structure. Hydraulically adjustable tailplane linked with flap control to provide constant longitudinal trim during flap movement. Electrically-operated trim-tab in rudder.
LANDING GEAR.—Retractable nose-wheel type. Main wheels raised inwardly into thickened wing roots, nose-wheel backwards into fuselage. Hydraulic actuation. Retractable arrester hook in rear end of fuselage below jet pipe.
POWER PLANT.—One Pratt & Whitney J48 or Allison J33 turbojet engine. Two self-sealing fuel tanks in fuselage and two non-sealing bladder tanks in wings. Increased fuel capacity in fuselage and wings in F9F-8. All tanks pressurised and all fuel can be jettisoned from wing-tip outlets by ram pressure. Provision for two 150 U.S. gallon drop tanks to be carried on under-wing bomb shackles.
ACCOMMODATION.—Pressurised cockpit forward of wings with sliding and jettisonable canopy. Ejector seat.
ARMAMENT.—Four nose-mounted 20 mm. cannon. Under-wing racks for either four 1,000 lb. bombs or six HVAR rockets or four Philco/Martin Sidewinder air-to-air missiles.
DIMENSIONS.—
Span 34 ft. 6 in. (10.52 m.).
Length (F9F-6 and -7) 40 ft. 2 in. (12.24 m.).
Length (F9F-6P) 41 ft. 2 in. (12.55 m.).
Length (F9F-8) 41 ft. 7 in. (12.68 m.).
Height 12 ft. 3 in. (3.73 m.).
WEIGHTS.—
Normal loaded weight about 20,000 lb. (9,080 kg.).
PERFORMANCE (F9F-8).—
Max. speed 712 m.p.h. (1,139 km.h.).
Climb to 40,000 ft. (12,200 m.) 7 min.
Service ceiling 42,000 ft. (12,800 m.).
Range 1,100-1,300 miles (1,770-2,090 km.).
(1957–58)

The Grumman J2F-6 Duck General Utility Amphibian built by Columbia Aircraft Corpn.

THE GRUMMAN DUCK.

U.S. Navy designation : J2F-6.

Nine series of this particular aeroplane, which first appeared in 1933, have been built for the U.S. Navy and Coast Guard. The latest J2F-6 series was in production in 1944 by the Columbia Aircraft Corpn. of Valley Stream, Long Island, N.J. under licence from the Grumman Company.

TYPE.—General Utility amphibian for photographic, target-towing, rescue, ambulance and other similar duties.

WINGS.—Equal-span single-bay staggered biplane. Upper wing in two sections joined at the centre-line and carried above the fuselage on splayed-out struts and braced to the lower wings by N-type interplane struts. No transverse bracing in centre-section struts but vertical wires from strut attachments on wings to bottom of fuselage. Lift and anti-lift wires in plane of upper rear and lower front wing spars. Wing structure of metal with fabric covering. Spars have two extruded channel section booms with a wandering web riveted alternately to front and rear faces of channels. Shot-welded steel girder ribs. Frise ailerons on all four wings.

HULL AND FUSELAGE.—Single-step hull is a metal monocoque of aluminium alloy. Internal bracing of cross-floor type with longitudinal stresses taken by skin, with reinforcement from chines and keel and from inverted U-members riveted to deck in forward section. The fuselage is of stressed skin construction. The hull is stressed to catapult launching and deck arresting.

TAIL UNIT.—Braced monoplane type. All-metal fin and tailplane. Rudder and elevators have aluminium-alloy frames and fabric covering. Trim-tabs in rudder and elevators.

LANDING-GEAR.—Retractable type. Consists of two oleo shock-absorber struts with their upper ends hinged to extensions on two fore-and-aft revolving tubes and with their lower ends attached to axle-blocks which are hinged to the chines of the hull by steel-tube Vees. Wheels are raised into recesses in the sides of the hull. Retraction by chains and sprockets. Combined tail-wheel and water-rudder has self-centering lock.

POWER PLANT.—One 900 h.p. Wright R-1820-54 nine-cylinder radial air-cooled engine driving a three-blade Hamilton-Standard constant-speed airscrew. NACA cowling. Fuel tanks in fuselage. Capacities : main tank 150 U.S. gallons, auxiliary tank 65 U.S. gallons.

ACCOMMODATION.—Tandem cockpits under a continuous transparent canopy with opening sections over each cockpit. Folding door in rear cockpit gives access to lower compartment in which two persons may sit side-by-side. External doors on each side of lower compartment, which may also accommodate one stretcher case, target-towing gear, etc.

DIMENSIONS.—Span 39 ft. (11.9 m.), Length 34 ft. (10.37 m.), Height on wheels 13 ft. 11 in. (4.25 m.), Wing area 409 sq. ft. (38 sq. m.).

WEIGHT LOADED 7,700 lbs. (3,496 kg.).

PERFORMANCE.—Maximum speed 190 m.p.h. (304 km.h.), Cruising speed 155 m.p.h. (248 km.h.), Stalling speed 70 m.p.h. (112 km.h.), Service ceiling 20,000 ft. (6,100 m.).

THE GRUMMAN GOOSE.

U.S. Navy designation : JRF.
U.S. Army Air Forces designation : OA-9 and OA-13.

The Goose is a military adaptation of the commercial Model G-21A. It was first put into service in the U.S. Navy as the JRF-1 and the U.S. Coast Guard as the JRF-2 in 1939-40. Further series included the JRF-1A, fitted for target-towing and photography ; the JRF-3 (Coast Guard) fitted with anti-icing equipment and auto-pilot for use in Northern waters ; the JRF-4, a development of the JRF-1 ; the JRF-5, similar to the JRF-4 but fitted for photography ; and the JRF-6B, which was equipped as a navigational trainer.

The JRF-1 and 1A are in service in the U.S. Army Air Forces as the OA-13 and the JRF-6B as the OA-9. The British Goose is similar to the JRF-6B.

TYPE.—Twin-engined General Utility amphibian.

WINGS.—High-wing cantilever monoplane. Centre-section and detachable tapering outer sections. Metal structure consists of a tapering box-spar with its rear face at 36% of the chord from the leading-edge. Elementary rib structure and metal skin plating

complete the leading-edge. The rear 66% of both centre-section and outer sections is fabric-covered over duralumin ribs cantilevered from the rear face of the spar. Vacuum-operated split trailing-edge flaps from hull to ailerons.

HULL.—Two-step all-metal hull. Rectangular section forward, but aft of second step the section is oval and fairs into fin. Six water-tight bulkheads.

TAIL UNIT.—Monoplane type. Cantilever fin built integral with hull. Tail-plane strut-braced to hull. All-metal framework with sheet covering. Movable surfaces have duralumin frames and are covered with fabric. Trimming-tabs in elevators and rudder.

LANDING GEAR.—Grumman type with parallelogram linkage mechanically retracted by worm and gear. Wheels withdrawn into recesses in sides of hull. Retractable tail-wheel, with centering lock.

POWER PLANT.—Two Pratt & Whitney Wasp-Junior R-985-AN6 radial air-cooled engines, each rated at 400 h.p. at 5,000 ft (1,525 m.). Steel-tube mountings bolted to lower flanges of box-spar and to upper edges of duralumin anchors built into upper surface of wing-spar at extremities of centre-section. Fuel tanks integral with box-spars. Total fuel capacity 220 U.S. gallons. Oil tanks in engine-mountings. Total oil capacity 15 U.S. gallons. Hamilton-Standard controllable-pitch airscrews.

ACCOMMODATION.—In the nose is a mooring compartment with stowage for anchor and marine gear, vacuum storage tank, radio units and excess baggage. Pilot's compartment seats two side-by-side, with dual controls and wide aisle between. Thereafter follows cabin, to which access is gained through a wide hatch at the trailing-edge of the wing on the port side. Emergency hatch on starboard side, opposite main hatch. Equipment varies according to function of aircraft. JRF-5 and earlier models still in service are for general utility work, which includes personnel transport, ambulance duties, photographic work, target towing, etc. JRF-6B is a navigational trainer and general utility amphibian.

DIMENSIONS.—Span 49 ft. (14.95 m.), Length 38 ft. 4 in. (11.7 m.), Height (on wheels) 15 ft. (4.57 m.), Wing area 375 sq. ft. (34.8 sq. m.).

WEIGHTS AND LOADINGS.—Weight empty 5,425 lbs. (2,461 kg.), Disposable load (standard equipment) 2,575 lbs. (1,168 kg.), Weight loaded 8,000 lbs. (3,629 kg.), Wing loading 21.3 lbs./sq. ft. (103.9 kg./sq. m.), Power loading 8.9 lbs./h.p. (4 kg./h.p.).

PERFORMANCE.—Maximum speed at 5,000 ft. (1,525 m.) 201 m.p.h. (323 km.h.), Cruising speed at 5,000 ft. (1,525 m.) 191 m.p.h. (307 km.h.), Rate of climb at sea level 1,100 ft./min. (335 m./min.), Service ceiling 21,000 ft. (6,405 m.), Maximum range 640 miles (1,287 km.). (1945—46)

The Grumman JRF-5 Goose General Utility Amphibian (two Pratt & Whitney R-985-AN6 engines).

Grumman C-2A Greyhound Carrier On-Board Delivery Aircraft (1971–72)

GRUMMAN C-2A GREYHOUND

The C-2A Greyhound was developed from the E-2A Hawkeye specifically to deliver cargo to air groups deployed on carriers of the US Navy. It is compatible with elevators and hangar decks on CVS-10 and CVA-19 carriers, can be launched by catapult, using nose-tow gear, and can make arrested landings.

Many components of the C-2A and E-2A are common, including the complete turboprop power plants, and the Greyhound offers similar all-weather capability to the Hawkeye.

The first of three pre-production C-2As (one for static testing) flew for the first time on 18 November 1964, and was accepted formally by the US Navy on 2 December 1964. Deliveries of production C-2As to the US fleet began in 1966, to supplement C-1s of the Navy Carrier On-board Delivery force.

Production of the original series of 17 C-2As ended in 1967, but Grumman announced receipt of an order for 8 more in the FY 1970 budget. The structural description of the E-2A Hawkeye applies equally to the C-2A Greyhound, with the following differences and additions.

TYPE: Twin-turboprop Carrier On-board Delivery (COD) transport.

WINGS: Incidence 4° at root, 1° at tip.

FUSELAGE: Conventional semi-monocoque light alloy structure. Cargo door, with integral ramp, forms undersurface of rear fuselage.

TAIL UNIT: Basically as for E-2A, but without tailplane dihedral.

LANDING GEAR: Basically as for E-2A, but with stronger nose gear (adapted from that of A-6A Intruder) to cater for higher AUW. Each nose-wheel fitted with 20 × 5·5 Type VII 12-ply tyre. Main wheel tyre pressure 200 lb/sq in (14 kg/cm²) on ship, 165 lb/sq in (11·6 kg/cm²) ashore.

POWER PLANT: Two fuel tanks, total capacity 1,824 US gallons (6,905 litres), occupy entire wing centre-section between the beams and the centre-line and wing-fold ribs. Fuelling point on inboard side of starboard nacelle. Provision for carrying 300 US gallon (1,135 litre) or 450 US gallon (1,704 litre) external fuel tanks on sides of fuselage, or Douglas D704 or Beech 385 buddy refuelling packs in similar position. Provision for mounting flight refuelling probe above front fuselage. For long-range ferrying, fuel tanks can be supplemented by two 1,000 US gallon (3,786 litre) tanks in main cabin. Oil capacity (usable) 6·2 US gallons (23·5 litres).

ACCOMMODATION: Pilot and co-pilot side-by-side on flight deck, with dual controls. Lavatory and baggage space aft of flight deck. High-strength cargo compartment floor (300 lb/sq ft = 1,465 kg/m²) incorporates flush tracks for attaching tie-down fittings. Cargo door has integral ramp with detachable treadways. Provision for remotely-controlled cargo handling winch. Compartment can be adapted to accept Military Air Transport Command 463L material handling and support system, with choice of either three 108 × 88-in (2·74 × 2·24 m) master pallets or five 88 × 54-in (2·24 × 1·37 m) modular pallets. Alternative payloads include 39 troops in three longitudinal rows of seats or 20 litters and four attendants. Door at front of cabin on port side.

SYSTEMS: Hydraulic system, pressure 3,000 lb/sq in (210 kg/cm²), consists of two independent systems. Both systems supply control surface actuators. One system is also responsible for actuating wing fold system, cargo door, steering damper, arrester hook, brakes, landing gear, windshield wipers, flaps and auxiliary generator. Air-conditioning system max pressure differential 6·5 lb/sq in (0·46 kg/cm²). Liquid oxygen breathing system, with two 10-litre converters, plus portable unit for cargo or personnel attendant. Primary electrical system supplied by two independent 115/200V 400 Hz three-phase engine-driven generators, each rated at 60kVA. 28V DC secondary sub-system supplied by two independent transformer-rectifiers. Emergency power provided by hydraulically-driven 3kVA AC generator, plus third transformer-rectifier for DC supply. Gas-turbine APU supplies pneumatic power for engine starting.

ELECTRONICS AND EQUIPMENT: Standard equipment includes separate vertical and horizontal attitude control sub-systems, duplicated ID-663 BDHI and ID-387 course indicator, AN/ASW-15 automatic flight control system featuring control wheel steering, heading and altitude hold, and TACAN/VOR radial navigation mode, central air data computer, two VOR receivers, glide-slope receiver, marker beacon receiver, TACAN, UHF and LF ADFs, LORAN, choice of eight receivers and three transmitters in

AN/AIC-14 intercommunication and radio control system, AN/APX-46 IFF transponder and AN/APN-141 radar altimeter, Provision for UHF digital data link, automatic carrier landing system, Doppler radar and weather radar.

DIMENSIONS, EXTERNAL:
Wing span	80 ft 7 in (24·56 m)
Wing chord at root	13 ft 0 in (3·96 m)
Wing chord at tip	4 ft 4 in (1·32 m)
Width, folded	29 ft 4 in (8·94 m)
Length overall	56 ft 8 in (17·27 m)
Height overall	15 ft 11 in (4·85 m)
Cargo door:	
Width	7 ft 6 in (2·29 m)
Height	6 ft 6 in (1·98 m)

DIMENSIONS, INTERNAL
Cargo space: Length	27 ft 6 in (8·38 m)
Width	7 ft 3½ in (2·23 m)
Height	5 ft 6 in (1·68 m)

AREAS:
Wings, gross	700 sq ft (65·03 m²)
Ailerons (total)	62 sq ft (5·76 m²)
Flaps (total)	118·75 sq ft (11·03 m²)
Fins (four, total)	93·02 sq ft (8·64 m²)
Rudders (three, total), including tabs	68·60 sq ft (6·37 m²)
Tailplane	125·07 sq ft (11·62 m²)
Elevators	40·06 sq ft (3·72 m²)

WEIGHTS:
Weight empty	31,154 lb (14,131 kg)
Max payload	10,000 lb (4,535 kg)
Max T-O weight	54,830 lb (24,870 kg)
Max arrested landing weight	44,612 lb (20,236 kg)
Max landing weight ashore	47,372 lb (21,488 kg)

PERFORMANCE (at max T-O weight):
Max level speed at optimum altitude
306 knots (352 mph; 567 km/h)
Stalling speed at max arrested landing weight
78 knots (89 mph; 143 km/h)
Rate of climb at S/L 2,330 ft (710 m)/min
Rate of climb at S/L, one engine out
310 ft (95 m)/min
Service ceiling 28,800 ft (8,780 m)
T-O to 50 ft (15 m) 2,560 ft (780 m)
Landing from 50 ft (15 m) at max arrested landing weight 1,735 ft (530 m)
Combat range at average cruising speed of 258 knots (297 mph; 478 kmh) at 27,300 ft (8,320 m) 1,432 nm (1,650 miles; 2,660 km)

THE GRUMMAN G-82 GUARDIAN.

U.S. Navy designation: AF.

The following versions of the Guardian are in service :—

AF-2W. Search version. Large search and early warning radome beneath forward fuselage.

AF-2S. Attack version. Internal stowage for various offensive stores, which may include one 2,000 lb. (908 kg.) torpedo, or two 1,600 lb. (726 kg.) depth charges, or two 2,000 lb. (908 kg.) bombs. Any of these stores can be duplicated and carried externally beneath wings. Searchlight under port wing and radar scanner under starboard wing, both in identically-shaped casings.

AF-3S. Similar to AF-2S but with additional submarine detection gear.

The Guardian went out of production in March, 1953.

TYPE.—Single-engined multi-seat Anti-submarine Monoplane in two versions, Search (AF-2W) and Attack (AF-2S) and AF-3S.

The Grumman AF-2S Guardian Anti-Submarine (Killer) Monoplane with wings folded. (Harold Martin).

The Grumman AF-2W Guardian Anti-Submarine (Hunter) Monoplane. (*Warren Bodie*).

WINGS.—Mid-wing cantilever monoplane. Wing section NACA 23018 at root, NACA 23012 at tip. Aspect ratio 6.56. Taper ratio 2 : 1. Thickness ratio 1.6 : 1. All-metal structure. Outer wing sections fold back hydraulically about the centre-section rear spar hinges and when stowed lie parallel to fuselage with leading-edges downward. Slotted flaps between ailerons and fuselage. Spoiler flaps. Leading-edge slats ahead of ailerons. Gross wing area 560 sq. ft. (52 m.²).

FUSELAGE.—All-metal structure.

TAIL UNIT.—Cantilever monoplane type. All-metal structure. Auxiliary fin surfaces above and below tailplane.
LANDING GEAR.—Retractable type. Main wheels retract outwardly into outer wings. Dual tail-wheels non-retractable. Catapult points under wings. Sting-type arrester hook.
POWER PLANT.—One 2,400 h.p. Pratt & Whitney R-2800-48W fourteen-cylinder radial air-cooled engine driving a four-blade Hamilton Standard constant-speed airscrew 13 ft. 2 in. (4.01 m.) in diameter. Engine thrust-line at -3 degrees to datum.

ACCOMMODATION.—Crew of three, comprising pilot and two radar operators in AF-2W; or pilot, navigator/bomb-aimer and radar operator in AF-2S and AF-3S.
DIMENSIONS.—
   Span 60 ft. 8 in. (18.5 m.).
   Length 43 ft. 4 in. (13.2 m.).
   Height 16 ft. 2 in. (4.93 m.).
WEIGHTS (Approx.).—
   Weight empty 14,600 lb. (6,630 kg.).
   Weight loaded 25,000 lb. (11,350 kg.).
PERFORMANCE (Approx.).—
   Max. speed 315 m.p.h. (504 km.h.).
   Stalling speed 83 m.p.h. (133 km.h.).
   Range 1,500 miles (2,400 km.).   (1955-56)

Grumman TC-4C, a modified version of the Gulfstream I ordered by the US Navy for avionics training of A-6A Intruder aircrew

GRUMMAN G-159 GULFSTREAM I
US Navy designation: TC-4C
US Coast Guard designation: VC-4A

The Gulfstream I is a 10/24-passenger pressurised light executive transport, powered by two Rolls-Royce Dart turboprop engines. The first Gulfstream I flew for the first time on 14 August 1958, and FAA Type Approval was received on 21 May 1959. The Gulfstream I was the first US twin-engined business aircraft certificated to cruise at 30,000 ft (9,150 m). A total of 188 had been sold by mid-February 1968. Production continues at the rate of about two per month.

There are also two specialised Service versions, as follows:

VC-4A. Two for US Coast Guard for VIP transport duties. Delivered in Summer of 1963.

TC-4C. "Flying classroom" version for US Navy, of which nine were ordered on December 15, 1966. Intended for use in training bombardier/navigators who will serve with A-6A Intruder squadrons. Basic airframe and power plant similar to those of commercial Gulfstream I, with addition of A-6A radome nose, housing search and tracking radar antennae. Aft cabin contains an independent and complete A-6A avionics system, consisting of an A-6A training cockpit which accommodates a student pilot and student bombardier/navigator, an adjacent instructor's seat, and four student radar/computer readout training consoles linked to the displays in the A-6A cockpit. By enabling up to six students to be instructed simultaneously under realistic conditions, the TC-4C is freeing A-6A aircraft for operational duty.

The first TC-4C flew for the first time on 14 June 1967. FAA Type Approval (R-4b) was received on 23 October 1967, by which date a total of 41 flights had been logged by the first three aircraft. In addition, all installed A-6A electronic equipment had been evaluated to ensure that it represented no hazard to the safe operation of the basic Gulfstream I airframe.

The TC-4C is powered by two 2,210 ehp Rolls-Royce Dart Mk 529-8X turboprop engines. Overall length 67 ft 11 in (20.70 m). Max T-O weight 36,000 lb (16,330 kg).

The following details refer to the standard commercial executive transport version.

TYPE: Twin-turboprop executive transport.
WINGS: Cantilever low-wing monoplane. Wing section NACA 63A214 at root, NACA 63A314 at tip. Aspect ratio 10. Chord 11 ft 2 in (3.40 m) at root, 4 ft 5 in (1.35 m) at tip. Dihedral 6° 30'. Incidence 3° at root, 0° at tip. Single box-beam structure with integrally-stiffened machined upper and lower skins. Aluminium alloy ailerons and single-slotted flaps.
FUSELAGE: Aluminium alloy semi-monocoque structure.

TAIL UNIT: Cantilever all-metal structure.

LANDING GEAR: Retractable tricycle type, with twin wheels on all three units. Hydraulic retraction. Main units retract forward of main wing beams to avoid cut-outs in primary wing structure. Nose unit retracts forward into compartment below flight deck. Main landing gear used as speed brake. Bendix oleo-pneumatic shock-absorbers. Goodyear wheels and tyres, size 7.50 × 14. Goodyear single-disc hydraulic brakes.

POWER PLANT: Two 2,210 eshp Rolls-Royce Dart 529-8X or 529-8E (RDa. 7/2) turboprop engines. Four-blade Rotol constant-speed propellers. Integral fuel tanks in wings, with total capacity of 1,550 US gallons (5,865 litres). Oil capacity 7 US gallons (26.5 litres).

ACCOMMODATION: Pressurised accommodation for crew of two and 10-14 passengers in executive version. A 24-passenger high-density interior is also available. Pressurised baggage compartment in addition to luggage space in forward cabin. Toilet compartment with hot and cold water. Hydraulically-operated self-contained stairway forward of cabin. Interior furnishings and equipment of executive versions left to individual choice.

SYSTEMS: Cabin pressurised and air-conditioned by Sir G. Godfrey / AiResearch systems to maintain 5,500 ft (1,680 m) cabin altitude at 25,000 ft (7,625 m). Auxiliary power unit for ground operation of cabin air conditioning equipment, radio, lights, etc, independent of main engines.

ELECTRONICS AND EQUIPMENT: Collins HF radio. Bendix X and C band radar. Full blind-flying instrumentation. Integrated flight system.

DIMENSIONS, EXTERNAL:
Wing span	78 ft 6 in (23.92 m)
Length overall	63 ft 9 in (19.43 m)
Height overall	22 ft 9 in (6.94 m)
Tailplane span	25 ft 6 in (7.77 m)
Wheel track	24 ft 2 in (7.37 m)
Wheelbase	19 ft 9½ in (6.03 m)

DIMENSIONS, INTERNAL:
Cabin, excluding flight deck:
Length	33 ft 0 in (10.06 m)
Max width	7 ft 4 in (2.23 m)
Max height	6 ft 1 in (1.85 m)
Volume	1,040 cu ft (29.45 m³)
Baggage compartment	100 cu ft (2.83 m³)
Luggage space (fwd cabin)	28 cu ft (0.79 m³)

AREAS:

Wings, gross	610·3 sq ft (56·7 m²)
Ailerons (total)	37·0 sq ft (3·44 m²)
Trailing-edge flaps (total)	111·2 sq ft (10·33 m²)
Fin	88·4 sq ft (8·21 m²)
Rudder, including tab	28·7 sq ft (2·66 m²)
Tailplane	98·76 sq ft (9·17 m²)
Elevators, including tab	28·0 sq ft (2·60 m²)

WEIGHTS AND LOADING:

Weight empty equipped	21,900 lb (9,933 kg)
Max payload	4,270 lb (1,937 kg)
Max T-O weight	35,100 lb (15,920 kg)

Max zero-fuel weight	26,170 lb (11,870 kg)
Max landing weight	33,600 lb (15,240 kg)
Max wing loading	57·2 lb/sq ft (279·3 kg/m²)

PERFORMANCE (at max T-O weight):

Max cruising speed at 25,000 ft (7,625 m)	348 mph (560 kmh)
Econ cruising speed at 25,000 ft (7,625 m)	288 mph (463 kmh)
Approach speed	128 mph (206 kmh)
Rate of climb at S/L	1,900 ft (580 m) min

(1968–69)

Service ceiling	33,600 ft (10,240 m)
Service ceiling, one engine out	19,900 ft (6,065 m)
T-O run	2,550 ft (777 m)
T-O to 50 ft (15 m)	2,875 ft (875 m)
FAA T-O field length	4,350 ft (1,325 m)
FAA landing field length	4,000 ft (1,220 m)
Landing from 50 ft (15 m)	2,125 ft (648 m)
Landing run	1,525 ft (465 m)
Range with max fuel and 2,740 lb (1,243 kg) payload, including 45 min holding and 200 mile (320 km) diversion 2,540 miles (4,088 km)	

GRUMMAN HAWKEYE
USN designation: E-2

The E-2 Hawkeye was evolved as a carrier-borne early-warning aircraft, but is suitable also for land-based operations from unimproved fields. The prototype flew for the first time on 21 October 1960, since when the following versions have been built:

E-2A (formerly W2F-1). Initial production version. First flight on 19 April 1961, and first delivery to US Navy on 19 January 1964. Total of 62 built, including three prototypes.

E-2B. Prototype flew for the first time on 20 February 1969. Differs from E-2A by having a Litton Industries L-304 microelectronic general-purpose computer and reliability improvements. A retrofit programme, completed in December 1971, updated all operational E-2As to E-2B standard.

E-2C. First of two E-2C prototypes flew on 20 January 1971. Production began in mid-1971 and the first flight of a production aircraft was made on 23 September 1972. Firm orders from the US Navy cover 79 aircraft, of which 56 had been delivered by the beginning of 1980. Procurement of 22 more is planned by the end of 1986. Israel has four; and in Summer 1979 Japan released funds for four aircraft for delivery in 1982 and 1983. Japan has a requirement for additional E-2C aircraft in the future. The French Air Force conducted an operational evaluation of the 58th production E-2C, from the CEAM, Mont-de-Marsan, in mid-1980.

The E-2C first entered service, with airborne early-warning squadron VAW-123 at NAS Norfolk, Va, in November 1973, and went to sea on board the USS *Saratoga* in late 1974. Nine other squadrons have since received E-2C aircraft, and two **TE-2C** training aircraft are also in service.

The Hawkeye can maintain patrol on naval task force defence perimeters in all weathers, at an operating height of about 9,150 m (30,000 ft), and can detect and assess any threat from approaching high-Mach-number enemy aircraft over ranges approaching 260 nm (480 km; 300 miles). The radar is capable of detecting airborne targets anywhere in a three million cubic mile surveillance envelope. Improvements compared with earlier radars provide increased reliability and easier maintenance. It also monitors movement of enemy ships and land vehicles, enabling each E-2C to track, automatically and simultaneously, more than 250 targets and to control more than 30 airborne intercepts. A Randtron Systems AN/APA-171 antenna system is housed in a 7·32 m (24 ft) diameter saucer-shaped rotodome mounted above the rear fuselage of the aircraft, which revolves in flight at 6 rpm, and can be lowered 0·64 m (1 ft 10¼ in) to facilitate aircraft stowage on board ship. The Yagi type radar arrays within the rotodome are interfaced to the onboard avionic systems, providing radar sum and difference signals plus IFF.

The AN/APS-125 search radar can detect targets as small as a cruise missile at ranges in excess of 100 nm (185 km; 115 miles). The AN/ALR-59 passive detection system (PDS) alerts operators to the presence of electronic emitters at distances up to twice the detection range of the radar system, thus expanding significantly the surveillance capability of the E-2C. Functions of these and other key elements of the E-2C's avionics systems were described more fully in the 1979-80 *Jane's*.

The following details apply to the E-2C Hawkeye:

TYPE: Airborne early-warning aircraft.

WINGS: Cantilever high-wing monoplane of all-metal construction. Centre-section is a structural box consisting of three beams, ribs and machined skins. Hinged leading-edge is non-structural and provides access to flying and engine controls. The outer panels fold rearward about skewed-axis hinge fittings mounted on the rear beams, to stow parallel with the rear fuselage on each side. Folding is done through a double-acting hydraulic cylinder. Trailing-edges of outer panels and part of centre-section consist of long-span ailerons and hydraulically-actuated Fowler flaps. When flaps are lowered, ailerons are drooped automatically. All control surfaces of E-2C are power-operated and incorporate devices to produce artificial feel forces. Automatic flight control system (AFCS) can be assigned sole con-

Grumman E-2C Hawkeye airborne early-warning aircraft from USS *Constellation*

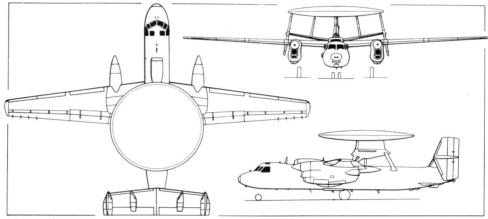

Grumman E-2C Hawkeye twin-turboprop airborne early-warning aircraft (*Pilot Press*)

trol of the system hydraulic actuators, or AFCS signals can be superimposed on the pilot's mechanical inputs for stability augmentation. Pneumatically-inflated rubber de-icing boots on leading-edges.

FUSELAGE: Conventional all-metal semi-monocoque structure.

TAIL UNIT: Cantilever structure, with four fins and three double-hinged rudders. Tailplane dihedral 11°. Portions of tail unit made of glassfibre to reduce radar reflection. Power control and artificial feel systems as for ailerons. Pneumatically-inflated rubber de-icing boots on all leading-edges.

LANDING GEAR: Hydraulically-retractable tricycle type. Pneumatic emergency extension. Steerable nosewheel unit retracts rearward. Main wheels retract forward, and rotate to lie flat in bottom of nacelles. Twin wheels on nose unit only. Oleo-pneumatic shock-absorbers. Main wheel tyres size 36 × 11 Type VII 24-ply, pressure 17·93 bars (260 lb/sq in) on ship, 14·48 bars (210 lb/sq in) ashore. Hydraulic brakes. Hydraulically-operated retractable tailskid. A-frame arrester hook under tail.

POWER PLANT: Two 3,661 kW (4,910 shp) Allison T56-A-425 turboprop engines, driving Hamilton Standard type 54460-1 four-blade fully-feathering reversible-pitch constant-speed propellers. These foam-filled blades which have a steel spar and glassfibre shell that cause minimum interference to the radar equipment. Spinners and blades incorporate electrical anti-icers. Provision for auxiliary fuel tanks in outer wings, and for addition of flight refuelling capability.

ACCOMMODATION: Normal crew of five on flight deck and in ATDS compartment in main cabin, consisting of pilot, co-pilot, combat information centre officer, air control officer and radar operator. Provision for additional operator for long-endurance missions with auxiliary fuel. Downward-hinged doors, with built-in steps, on port side of centre-fuselage.

AVIONICS: AN/APA-171 rotodome (radar and IFF antennae), AN/APS-125 advanced radar processing system (ARPS) with overland/overwater detection capability, RT-988/A IFF interrogator with Hazeltine OL-76/AP IFF detector processor, Litton AN/ALR-59 passive detection system, Hazeltine AN/APA-172 control indicator group, Litton OL-77/ASQ computer programmer (L-304), ARC-158 UHF data link, ARQ-34 HF data link, ASM-440 in-flight performance monitor, ARC-51A UHF com, ARQ-34 HF com, AIC-14A intercom, Litton AN/ASN-92 (LN-15C) CAINS carrier aircraft inertial navigation system, Conrac Corporation CP-1085/AS air data computer, APN-153 (V) Doppler, ASN-50 heading and attitude reference system, ARN-52 (V) Tacan, ARA-50 UHF ADF, ASW-25B ACLS and APN-171 (V) radar altimeter. (1980-81)

DIMENSIONS, EXTERNAL:		Max T-O weight: A	23,541 kg (51,900 lb)	Service ceiling: A	9,390 m (30,800 ft)
Wing span	24·56 m (80 ft 7 in)	B	27,161 kg (59,880 lb)	B	8,840 m (29,000 ft)
Length overall	17·55 m (57 ft 7 in)	PERFORMANCE (at max T-O weight. A: current E-2C; B:		T-O run: A	580 m (1,900 ft)
Height overall	5·59 m (18 ft 4 in)	with auxiliary fuel):		B	884 m (2,900 ft)
Diameter of rotodome	7·32 m (24 ft 0 in)	Max level speed:		T-O to 15 m (50 ft): A	793 m (2,600 ft)
Propeller diameter	4·11 m (13 ft 6 in)	A, B	325 knots (602 km/h; 374 mph)	B	1,128 m (3,700 ft)
AREA:		Cruising speed (ferry):		Ferry range: A	1,394 nm (2,583 km; 1,605 miles)
Wings, gross	65·03 m² (700 sq ft)	A	269 knots (499 km/h; 310 mph)	B	2,170 nm (4,018 km; 2,497 miles)
WEIGHTS (A: current E-2C; B: with auxiliary fuel):		B	270 knots (500 km/h; 310 mph)	Time on station, 175 nm (320 km; 200 miles) from base:	
Weight empty: A	17,241 kg (38,009 lb)	Approach speed:		A	4 h
B	17,504 kg (38,589 lb)	A, B	100 knots (185 km/h; 115 mph)	B	over 6 h
Max fuel (internal): A	5,624 kg (12,400 lb)	Stalling speed (landing configuration):		Endurance with max fuel: A	6 h 6 min
B	8,981 kg (19,800 lb)	A	74 knots (138 km/h; 85·5 mph)	B	9 h 18 min

The Grumman F6F-5 Hellcat Single-seat Fighter (2,000 h.p. Pratt & Whitney R-2800-10W engine).—(*Peter Bowers*). (1947)

THE GRUMMAN HELLCAT.

U.S. Naval designation : F6F.

The Hellcat was designed in the Spring of 1942. The prototype XF6F-1 first flew in August and it was in large-scale production as the F6F-3 by the end of the same year. The Hellcat was first reported in action with a U.S. Carrier Task Force in an attack on Marcus Island on September 1, 1943.

The F6F-5 differed from its predecessor by having a redesigned engine cowling, improved windshield, new ailerons, strengthened tail surfaces, additional armour behind the pilot and a waxed high-gloss skin finish. The F6F-5 could also carry two 1,000 lb. (454 kg.) bombs under the centre-section, drop tanks in place of bombs and was equipped to carry rocket projectile equipment and search radar (F6F-5E). Night Fighter (F6F-5N) and Photographic-Reconnaissance (F6F-5P) versions were also in service.

The F6F-5K is a long-range radio-controlled pilotless drone version of the Hellcat. The modification was undertaken by the Naval Aircraft Modification Unit at Johnsville, Pa. Several F6F-5K drones were used in the Bikini operations.

The F6F-5 was the last operational version of the Hellcat, which was finally withdrawn from production in November, 1945. The 10,000th Hellcat was delivered to the U.S. Navy in the previous March, the Hellcat being the only U.S. aircraft designed and built after Pearl Harbour to be produced in this quantity.

TYPE.—Single-seat Fighter.

WINGS.—Mid-wing cantilever monoplane. Centre-section is flat and of constant thickness but has same constant taper as outer wing sections. Outer sections have dihedral angle and are arranged to fold. All-metal structure with flush-riveted metal skin. Split-flaps between ailerons and fuselage. Gross wing area 344 sq. ft. (31 sq. m.).

FUSELAGE.—All-metal monocoque structure with integral fin.

TAIL UNIT.—Cantilever monoplane type. Fin built integral with the fuselage. All-metal structure.

LANDING GEAR.—Retractable type. Shock-absorber units hinged at extremities of centre-section and are raised backwards, the wheels being turned through 90° to lie flush in wells in underside of centre-section. Hydraulic retraction. Retractable tail-wheel and arrester-hook.

POWER PLANT.—One 2,000 h.p. Pratt & Whitney R-2800-10W eighteen-cylinder double-row radial air-cooled engine driving a Hamilton Standard Hydromatic three-blade constant-speed airscrew 13 ft. 1 in. (4 m.) diameter. Bullet-proof fuel tanks in wings. An auxiliary droppable belly-tank may be fitted.

ACCOMMODATION.—Enclosed cockpit over wing with sliding canopy. Bullet-proof windscreen and armour behind pilot.

ARMAMENT.—Six .5 in. (12.7 m/m.) machine-guns, three in each outer wing.

DIMENSIONS.—Span 42 ft. 10 in. (13.0 m.), Span (folded) 16 ft. 2 in. (4.9 m.), Length 33 ft. 6⅝ in. (10.2 m.), Height 14 ft. 5 in. (4.4 m.).

WEIGHTS.—Weight empty 9,212 lbs. (4,182 kg.), Normal loaded weight 12,730 lbs. (5,780 kg.).

PERFORMANCE.—Maximum level speed 371 m.p.h. (594 km.h.), Stalling speed 85.5 m.p.h. (136.8 km.h.), Initial rate of climb 3,410 ft./min. (1,040 m./min.), Climb to 15,000 ft. (4,575 m.) 4.3 min., Service ceiling 36,700 ft. (11,190 m.), Normal range 1,040 miles (1,665 km.).

GRUMMAN INTRUDER

US Navy designations: A-6, EA-6 and KA-6

The basic A-6A (originally A2F-1) Intruder was conceived as a carrier-borne low-level attack bomber equipped specifically to deliver nuclear or conventional weapons on targets completely obscured by weather or darkness. The Intruder possesses outstanding range and endurance and carries a heavier and more varied load of stores than any previous US naval attack aircraft. It currently equips 17 operational US Navy/Marine Corps squadrons, and three readiness training squadrons.

Competition for the original A-6 contract was conducted from May to December 1957, Grumman's contender being selected on 31 December 1957. Seven variants of the basic design have been built, as follows:

A-6A Intruder. Initial carrier-based attack bomber, described in 1972-73 *Jane's*. The first A-6A flew on 19 April 1960, and this version entered service officially on 1 February 1963, with the US Navy's VA-42 squadron at NAS Oceana. A total of 482 were built, the last delivery taking place in December 1969. A-6As saw considerable service with the Navy and Marine Corps in Vietnam. Most other versions of the Intruder are modifications of A-6As.

Grumman has US Navy contracts covering the modernisation of A-6As by fitting A-6E advanced weapon systems. It is anticipated that the programme will continue until all remaining A-6As in the inventory have been modified to A-6E standard.

EA-6A. First flown in prototype form in 1963, this version retains partial strike capability, but is equipped primarily to support strike aircraft and ground forces by suppressing enemy electronic activity and obtaining tactical electronic intelligence within a combat area. Elements of the A-6A's bombing/navigation system are deleted and the EA-6A carries more than 30 different antennae to detect, locate, classify, record and jam enemy radiation. Externally-evident features include a radome at the top of the tail-fin, and attachment points under the wings and fuselage for ECM pods, fuel tanks and/or weapons. A total of 27 EA-6As were built for the US Marine Corps, including six A-6As modified into EA-6As.

EA-6B Prowler. Advanced electronics development of the EA-6A, described separately.

A-6B Intruder. Conversion of 19 A-6As to provide Standard ARM missile capability. Though primarily an electronics modification, it has three different configurations ranging from limited to full strike capability.

A-6C Intruder. Derived from the A-6A but differing externally by having an underfuselage turret housing forward-looking infra-red (FLIR) sensors and low-light-level television camera, providing additional night attack capability. This equipment is intended to permit detailed identification and acquisition of targets not discernible by the aircraft's radar. A total of 12 A-6As were modified to A-6C configuration.

KA-6D Intruder. An A-6A was modified into a prototype flight refuelling tanker, with hose and reel in the rear fuselage, and flew for the first time on 23 May 1966. The KA-6D production model is fitted with Tacan and can transfer more than 9,500 kg (21,000 lb) of fuel immediately after take-off or 6,800 kg (15,000 lb) at a distance of 250 nm (463 km; 288 miles) from its carrier base. In addition, the KA-6D could act as a control aircraft for air-sea rescue operations or as a day bomber. A total of 62 A-6As were modified to KA-6D configuration.

A-6E Intruder. An advanced conversion of the A-6A with multi-mode radar and an IBM computer similar to that first tested in the EA-6B. First flight of an A-6E was made on 27 February 1970. First squadron deployment was made in September 1972, and the A-6E was approved officially for service use in December 1972. By the end of that month 24 A-6Es had been delivered to the US Navy, and a total procurement of 318 of these aircraft is planned. A total of 119 converted from A-6A, and 58 built as A-6E, delivered by 1 January 1976.

An **A-6E/TRAM** (target recognition attack multisensor) version of the A-6E flew for the first time on 22 March 1974 without sensors, and on 22 October 1974 with sensors. The initial flight test programme was carried out by converting this single aircraft, loaned by the Navy, but three other aircraft were converted and began flight testing in 1975. The conversion adds a turreted electro-optical sensor package, containing both infra-red and laser equipment, to a full-system Intruder, updates the inertial navigation system with CAINS, provides a new CNI system, automatic carrier landing capability and provisions for the Condor missile. The sensor package is integrated with the multi-mode radar, providing the capability of detecting, identifying and attacking a wide range of targets under adverse weather conditions, and with an improved degree of accuracy. It makes possible the viewing of terrain, in addition to conventional radar targets. A high-resolution image is presented on a FLIR (forward-looking infra-red) display by a newly-developed detecting-ranging set (DRS) designed and built by Hughes Aircraft Corporation, allowing the delivery of both conventional and laser-guided weapons. Also of importance is a capability to acquire and attack targets designated by a forward air controller on the ground. The first Intruder squadron to re-equip with the A-6E/TRAM version, VA-165, was deployed aboard the USS *Constellation* in 1977.

Intruder training is carried out using Grumman TC-4C (modified Gulfstream I) aircraft, eight of which are in USN/USMC service. In mid-1978, two of these had been updated to A-6E/TRAM configuration, four others were of A-6A and two of A-6E standard; Grumman plans to update all eight to A-6E/TRAM standard during 1978-79.

The following description applies to the standard A-6E:
Type: Two-seat carrier-based attack bomber.
Wings: Cantilever mid-wing monoplane, with 25° sweepback at quarter-chord. All-metal structure. Hydraulically-operated almost-full-span leading-edge and trailing-edge flaps, with inset spoilers (flaperons) of same span as flaps forward of trailing-edge flaps. Trailing-edge of each wingtip, outboard of flap, splits to form speed-brakes which project above and below wing when extended. Two short fences above each wing. Outer panels fold upward and inward.
Fuselage: Conventional all-metal semi-monocoque structure. Bottom is recessed between engines to carry semi-exposed store.
Tail Unit: Cantilever all-metal structure. All-moving tailplane, without separate elevators. Electronic antenna in rear part of fin, immediately above rudder.
Landing Gear: Hydraulically-retractable tricycle type. Twin-wheel nose unit retracts rearward. Single-wheel main units retract forward and inward into air intake fairings. A-frame arrester hook under rear fuselage.
Power Plant: Two 41·4 kN (9,300 lb st) Pratt & Whitney J52-P-8A turbojet engines. Max internal fuel 7,230 kg (15,940 lb), 9,028 litres (2,385 US gallons). Provision for up to four external fuel tanks under wings, each of 1,136 litres (300 US gallons) capacity. Removable flight refuelling probe projects upward immediately forward of windscreen.
Accommodation: Crew of two on Martin-Baker Mk GRU7 ejection seats. Max internal fuel can be reclined to reduce fatigue during low-level operations. Bombardier/navigator slightly behind and below pilot to starboard. Hydraulically-operated rearward-sliding canopy.
Systems: AiResearch environmental control system for cockpit and electronics bay. Electrical system powered by two AiResearch constant-speed drive starters that combine engine starting and electrical power generation, each delivering 30kVA. An AiResearch ram-air turbine, mounted so that it can be projected into the airstream above the port wing-root, provides in-flight emergency electrical power for essential equipment. Dual hydraulic systems for operation of flight controls, leading-edge and trailing-edge flaps, wingtip speed-brakes, landing gear brakes and cockpit canopy. One electrically-driven hydraulic pump provides restricted flight capability by supplying the tailplane and rudder actuators only.

Grumman A-6E/TRAM (target recognition attack multisensor) version of the A-6E Intruder

Electronics and Equipment: Development of the A-6E began with the substitution of a single simultaneous multi-mode navigation and attack radar, developed by the Norden Division of UAC for the two earlier radar systems in the A-6A. Following the concepts of the EA-6B, the IBM Corporation and Fairchild Camera and Instrument Corporation have supplied a new attack and navigation computer system and an interfacing data converter. Conrac Corporation has designed an armament control unit and RCA has developed a video tape recorder for post-strike assessment of attacks.

The Norden Division's AN/APQ-148 multi-mode radar provides simultaneous ground mapping; identification, tracking, and rangefinding of fixed or moving targets; and terrain-clearance or terrain-following manoeuvres. It can also detect, locate and track radar beacons used by forward air controllers when providing close support for ground forces. The APQ-148 has mechanical scanning in azimuth and utilises a newly-developed electronics system for simultaneous vertical scanning. There are two cockpit displays, one for the pilot and one for the bombardier/navigator, and terrain data is also presented on a vertical display indicator ahead of the pilot.

IBM's AN/ASQ-133 solid-state digital computer is coupled to the A-6E's radar, inertial and Doppler navigational equipment, communications and automatic flight control system. As mission data is measured in flight by onboard aerodynamic and electronic sensors, the computer compares the data with the programmed information, computes any differences, and provides corrective data that can be used to alter the parameters of the mission.

Fairchild Camera and Instrument Corporation's signal data converter for the A-6E accepts analogue input data from up to sixty sensors, and converts that information to a digital output that is fed into the computer of the navigation and attack system.

Conrac Corporation's armament control unit (ACU) for the A-6E provides in a single unit all the inputs and outputs necessary to select and release the Intruder's weapons. The master arming switch has a 'practice' position that allows the ACU to be cycled up to the point of firing command.

The multi-mode AN/AVA-1 display developed by Kaiser Aerospace and Electronics Corporation serves as a primary flight aid for navigation, approach, landing and weapons delivery. The basic vertical display indicator (VDI) is a 0·20 m (8 in) cathode-ray tube which shows a synthetic landscape, sky, and electronically-generated command flight path that move to simulate the motion of these features as they would be seen by the pilot through the windscreen of the aircraft. Symbols are superimposed to augment the basic attitude data, and for attack a second set of superimposed information provides a target symbol, steering symbol, and release and pull-up markers. A solid-state radar data scan converter can provide on the same display an apparent real-world perspective of terrain, ten shades of grey defining terrain elevation at ten different segmented contour intervals up to 8·7 nm (16 km; 10 miles) ahead of the aircraft. This makes it possible for the pilot to fly the Intruder in either a terrain-following or terrain-avoidance mode at low altitude. Flight path and attack symbols can be superimposed over the terrain elevation data on the VDI, enabling the pilot to make his attack while avoiding or following terrain in the target area. Kaiser has also developed a micromesh filter to prevent

'washout' of the data displayed on the VDI in sunlight conditions. Naval pilots use the VDI as a primary flight instrument, for precise steering in navigation, and for weapons cues, progress, and status information during an attack. For carrier landing the unit is used as a flight director and, linked to the APQ-148 radar, it presents steering information, allowing the pilot to select a descent angle for the final approach.

Armament: Five weapon attachment points, each with a 1,633 kg (3,600 lb) capacity (max external stores load 8,165 kg; 18,000 lb). Typical weapon loads are thirty 500 lb bombs in clusters of six, or three 2,000 lb general purpose bombs plus two 1,135 litre (300 US gallon) drop-tanks.

Dimensions, external:

Wing span	16·15 m (53 ft 0 in)
Wing mean aerodynamic chord	3·32 m (10 ft 10¾ in)
Width folded	7·72 m (25 ft 4 in)
Length overall	16·69 m (54 ft 9 in)
Height overall	4·93 m (16 ft 2 in)
Tailplane span	6·21 m (20 ft 4½ in)
Wheel track	3·32 m (10 ft 10½ in)

Areas:

Wings, gross	49·1 m² (528·9 sq ft)
Flaperons (total)	3·81 m² (41·0 sq ft)
Trailing-edge flaps (total)	9·66 m² (104·0 sq ft)
Leading-edge slats (total)	4·63 m² (49·8 sq ft)
Fin	5·85 m² (62·93 sq ft)
Rudder	1·52 m² (16·32 sq ft)

Weights and Loading:

Weight empty	11,675 kg (25,740 lb)
Full load: internal	7,230 kg (15,940 lb)
external (four tanks)	3,638 kg (8,020 lb)
Max payload	7,838 kg (17,280 lb)
Max T-O weight:	
catapult	26,580 kg (58,600 lb)
field	27,397 kg (60,400 lb)
Max zero-fuel weight	20,166 kg (44,460 lb)
Max landing weight:	
carrier	16,329 kg (36,000 lb)
field	20,411 kg (45,000 lb)
Max wing loading	557·6 kg/m² (114·2 lb/sq ft)

Performance (no stores):

Never-exceed speed	689 knots (1,276 km/h; 793 mph)
Max level speed at S/L	563 knots (1,043 km/h; 648 mph)
Cruising speed at optimum altitude	414 knots (767 km/h; 477 mph)
Stalling speed, flaps up	121 knots (225 km/h; 140 mph)
Stalling speed, flaps down	84 knots (156 km/h; 97 mph)
Max rate of climb at S/L	2,804 m (9,200 ft)/min
Rate of climb at S/L, one engine out	945 m (3,100 ft)/min
Service ceiling	14,480 m (47,500 ft)
Service ceiling, one engine out	9,083 m (29,800 ft)
Min T-O run	610 m (2,000 ft)
T-O run to 15 m (50 ft)	795 m (2,610 ft)
Landing from 15 m (50 ft)	689 m (2,260 ft)
Min Landing run	579 m (1,900 ft)
Combat range with max external fuel	2,365 nm (4,382 km; 2,723 miles)
Range with max payload, 5% reserves plus 20 min at S/L	1,671 nm (3,096 km; 1,924 miles)
Ferry range	2,530 nm (4,688 km; 2,913 miles)

(1978–79)

GRUMMAN G-134 MOHAWK
US Army designation: OV-1 (formerly AO-1)

The Mohawk is a high-performance two-seat observation aircraft which Grumman developed for the US Army. The following versions have been built:

YOV-1A. Initial batch of nine service test aircraft, of which the first flew on 14 April 1959. Equipment includes ARC-52 UHF, ARC-44 VHF, AIC-12 ICS, ARN-59 ADF, MA-1 compass, APX-6B IFF, ARN-21 VOR/TACAN, ARN-32 marker beacon, KA-30 high-resolution optical photographic system, ARC-39 HF and APA-89 IFF coder.

OV-1A. First 18 production aircraft similar to YOV-1A, but with addition of FD-105 integrated flight system, ARC-55 UHF instead of ARC-52, ARN-30 VOR/TACAN instead of ARN-21, ARN-68 marker beacon instead of ARN-32 and provision for ARC-73 VHF, APX-44 IFF, radar altimeter, ILS, emergency VHF, autopilot, ground track beacon, Doppler and UAS-4 IR. The 19th and subsequent production aircraft have the radar altimeter, ILS, emergency VHF, auto-pilot and ground track beacon installed and have duplicated VOR/TACAN. All versions can carry 52 flares in each of two removable upward-firing pods mounted above the wing roots for night photography.

OV-1B. Different equipment. Similar to second series of OV-1A, but with APS-94 SLAR (side-looking airborne radar) in under-fuselage container and AKT-16 VHF data link. SLAR provides a permanent radar photographic map of terrain on either side of the flight path, on either 4 × 5 in (10 × 12·7 cm) cut film or 70 mm film strip. An in-flight processer enables the observer to see a developed photograph seconds after the film has been exposed. This version has increased wing span and area.

OV-1C. Different equipment. Similar to second series of OV-1A, but with UAS-4 infra-red surveillance equipment installed.

OV-1D. This final version can be converted from infra-red to SLAR surveillance capability, and vice versa, in an hour, so combining the duties of the OV-1B and OV-1C. Four pre-production prototypes for the US Army were followed by production OV-1Ds, the last of which was completed in December 1970.

More than 375 Mohawks of all versions were delivered. Some are in operational use in Vietnam, with underwing weapons.

The description which follows applies in particular to the OV-1D:

TYPE: Two-seat army observation aircraft.

WINGS: Cantilever mid-wing monoplane. Wing section NACA 2412. Dihedral 6° 30'. Incidence 1° 30'. Aluminium alloy box-beam structure. Aluminium alloy inboard and outboard ailerons. Servo tabs and manually adjustable trim tabs in outboard ailerons. Hydraulically-operated trailing-edge flaps. Pneumatic de-icing boots on wing leading-edges.

FUSELAGE: Aluminium alloy semi-monocoque structure. Forward-opening hydraulically-operated air-brake on each side, aft of wing.

TAIL UNIT: Cantilever aluminium alloy structure. Central and two end-plate fins and rudders. Manually-adjustable trim tabs in elevators and central rudder. Pneumatic de-icing boots on leading-edge of tailplane and fins.

LANDING GEAR: Hydraulically-retractable tricycle type, with a single wheel on each unit. High-pressure pneumatic system for emergency extension. Bendix oleo-pneumatic shock-absorbers. Main units, which retract outward, each have a mechanical shrink-rod to compress the oleo-pneumatic strut so that it can be housed within the engine nacelle. The steerable nosewheel retracts rearward into the fuselage. Main wheels and tyres size 8·50 × 10, pressure 90 lb/sq in (6·33 kg/cm²). Nosewheel tyre size 6·50 × 8, pressure 65 lb/sq in (4·57 kg/cm²). Goodyear hydraulically-operated disc brakes. Provision for wheel/ski gear.

POWER PLANT: Two 1,400 shp Lycoming T53-L-701 turboprop engines, driving Hamilton Standard Type 53C51-27 three-blade constant-speed fully-feathering reversible-pitch metal propellers. Fuel in self-sealing fuselage tank above wing, with capacity of 276 US gallons (1,045 litres). Provision for one 150 US gallon (567 litres) Aero jettisonable tank under each wing, outboard of engine. Oil capacity 5 US gallons (19 litres). Electrical de-icing of propeller blades, spinners and air inlet cowlings.

ACCOMMODATION: Flight compartment seating two side-by-side in nose on Martin-Baker Mk J5 ejection seats. Dual controls, except when electronic surveillance equipment is fitted. Sides of canopy bulged to improve downward visibility. Armouring includes ¼ in (0·64 cm) aluminium alloy cockpit floor, bullet-resistant windshields and removable flak curtains on fore and aft cockpit bulkheads.

Grumman OV-1D Mohawk (two 1,400 shp Lycoming T53-L-701 turboprop engines)

SYSTEMS: Hydraulic system supplied by two engine-driven variable-volume hydraulic pumps, pressure 3,000 lb/sq in (210 kg/cm²), to operate inboard ailerons, flaps, air-brakes, landing gear, wheel-brakes, nosewheel steering and windshield wipers. Electrical power supplied by two engine-driven starter-generators providing up to 400A at 28V DC. Two engine-driven 6·5kVA alternators for de-icing. Three rotary inverters powered from the DC bus-bar generate 115/200V AC three-phase 400 Hz current: 5kVA unit powers inertial navigation and surveillance systems; a 2·5kVA unit powers instruments and navigation aids; and a 750 VA unit provides emergency power. 24V 38Ah nickel-cadmium battery provides power for engine starting and emergency power. An air-cycle system supplies a mixture of heated and cooled engine bleed-air for automatic or manual control of cockpit temperature and window defogging. Ram-air system for cockpit cooling and window defogging. A separate fully-automatic system supplies engine bleed-air to all three camera compartments. Engine inlet struts de-iced by engine bleed-air. Wing and empennage de-icing boots receive pulses of engine bleed-air. Fire extinguishing system for both engines.

EQUIPMENT: Photo surveillance system consists of two KA-60C 180-degree panoramic camera systems and one KA-76 serial frame camera. Infra-red AN/AAS-24 surveillance system. Alternative AN/APS-94D side-looking airborne radar (SLAR) system. ADR-6 radiac system. AN/AYA-10 data annotation system. Nav/com systems include ARN-82 VOR, ARC-102 HF-SSB, ARC-114 VHF-FM primary and auxiliary, ARN-52 TACAN, ARN-89 loop, APX-72 IFF, APN-171(V) radar altimeter, ARC-114 VHF-FM homing, ARC-115 and 116 VHF/UHF, ARN-58 glide-slope and marker beacon, ARN-89 LF-ADF, AN-ASN-33 flight director, PT489/ASQ-104 map readout unit, AN/ASW-12 automatic flight control, C-6533/ARC intercom, ASH-19 aural reproducer and continuous in-flight performance recorder (CIPR). ECM pods and an LS-59A photo-flash unit can be carried on underwing stations.

DIMENSIONS, EXTERNAL:

Wing span:	
OV-1A, C	42 ft 0 in (12·80 m)
OV-1B, OV-1D	48 ft 0 in (14·63 m)
Wing chord at root	10 ft 6 in (3·20 m)
Wing chord at tip	5 ft 3 in (1·60 m)
Wing aspect ratio	5·35
Length overall	41 ft 0 in (12·50 m)
Height overall	12 ft 8 in (3·86 m)
Tailplane span	15 ft 11 in (4·85 m)
Wheel track	9 ft 2 in (2·79 m)
Wheelbase	11 ft 8½ in (3·56 m)
Propeller diameter	10 ft 0 in (3·05 m)

AREAS:

Wings, gross:	
OV-1A, C	330 sq ft (30·65 m²)
OV-1B, OV-1D	360 sq ft (33·45 m²)
Ailerons (total)	22·7 sq ft (2·11 m²)
Flaps (total)	43·6 sq ft (4·05 m²)
Fins (total)	41·3 sq ft (3·84 m²)
Rudders (total)	27·5 sq ft (2·55 m²)
Tailplane	66·0 sq ft (6·13 m²)
Elevators	19·0 sq ft (1·77 m²)

WEIGHTS:

Weight empty, equipped:	
OV-1A	9,937 lb (4,507 kg)
OV-1B	11,067 lb (5,020 kg)
OV-1C	10,400 lb (4,717 kg)
OV-1D	12,054 lb (5,467 kg)
Normal T-O weight:	
OV-1A	12,672 lb (5,748 kg)
OV-1B	13,650 lb (6,197 kg)
OV-1C	13,040 lb (5,915 kg)
OV-1D SLAR	15,741 lb (7,140 kg)
OV-1D IR	15,544 lb (7,051 kg)
Max T-O weight:	
OV-1A	15,031 lb (6,818 kg)
OV-1B, C	19,230 lb (8,722 kg)
OV-1D SLAR	18,109 lb (8,214 kg)
OV-1D IR	17,912 lb (8,124 kg)

PERFORMANCE:

Max level speed at 5,000 ft (1,520 m):	
OV-1A, 1C	267 knots (308 mph; 496 km/h)
OV-1B	258 knots (297 mph; 478 km/h)
OV-1D, maximum rated power at 10,000 ft (3,050 m), 40% fuel:	
SLAR mission	251 knots (289 mph; 465 km/h)
IR mission	265 knots (305 mph; 491 km/h)
Max permissible diving speed	390 knots (450 mph; 724 km/h)
Max cruising speed:	
OV-1A	264 knots (304 mph; 489 km/h)
OV-1B	239 knots (275 mph; 443 km/h)
OV-1C	258 knots (297 mph; 478 km/h)
Econ cruising speed:	
All versions	180 knots (207 mph; 334 km/h)
Stalling speed (landing configuration):	
OV-1A	59 knots (68 mph; 109 km/h)
OV-1B	64 knots (73 mph; 117 km/h)
OV-1C	66 knots (76 mph; 123 km/h)
OV-1D, landing configuration, 10% normal rated power, 60% fuel:	
SLAR mission	73 knots (84 mph; 135 km/h)
IR mission	72 knots (83 mph; 133·5 km/h)
Rate of climb at S/L:	
OV-1A	2,950 ft (900 m)/min
OV-1B	2,350 ft (716 m)/min
OV-1C	2,670 ft (814 m)/min
OV-1D, maximum rated power:	
SLAR mission	3,466 ft (1,056 m)/min
IR mission	3,618 ft (1,102 m)/min
Service ceiling:	
OV-1B	30,300 ft (9,235 m)
OV-1C	29,500 ft (9,000 m)
OV-1D	25,000 ft (7,620 m)
Service ceiling, one engine out:	
OV-1A	13,625 ft (4,152 m)
Min T-O run:	
OV-1A	475 ft (145 m)
OV-1B	580 ft (177 m)
OV-1C	630 ft (192 m)
T-O to 50 ft (15 m):	
OV-1A	922 ft (281 m)
OV-1B	880 ft (268 m)
OV-1C	1,100 ft (335 m)
OV-1D SLAR mission	1,175 ft (358 m)
OV-1D IR mission	1,145 ft (349 m)
Landing from 15 ft (15 m):	
OV-1A, 1C	787 ft (240 m)
OV-1B	866 ft (264 m)
OV-1D SLAR mission	1,060 ft (323 m)
OV-1D IR mission	1,050 ft (320 m)
Landing run:	
OV-1A	454 ft (138 m)
OV-1B	540 ft (165 m)
OV-1C	502 ft (153 m)
Max range with external tanks, 10% reserves:	
OV-1A	1,220 nm (1,410 miles; 2,270 km)
OV-1B	1,065 nm (1,230 miles; 1,980 km)
OV-1C	1,155 nm (1,330 miles; 2,140 km)
Max range with external tanks at 20,000 ft (6,100 m):	
OV-1D SLAR mission	820 nm (944 miles; 1,520 km)
OV-1D IR mission	878 nm (1,011 miles; 1,627 km)
Max endurance at 140 knots (161 mph; 259 km/h) at 15,000 ft (4,560 m):	
OV-1D SLAR mission	4·35 hr
OV-1D IR mission	4·54 hr
	(1972–73)

The Grumman F9F-5 Panther Naval Fighter (Pratt & Whitney J48 turbojet engine). (Harold Martin).

THE GRUMMAN G-79 PANTHER.
U.S. Navy designation : F9F.

The original layout of this aircraft provided for the installation of four wing-mounted Westinghouse 19XB-2B (J30-WE-20) axial-flow jets, but this arrangement was abandoned in favour of one fuselage-mounted high-powered jet engine before the prototype construction began, a change prompted by the successful tests conducted by the U.S. Navy at the Naval Air Materiel Center, Philadelphia, in December, 1946, with two imported Rolls-Royce Nene engines.

The first prototype XF9F-2 was powered with an imported Rolls-Royce Nene engine. The third prototype was similarly fitted, but the second, the XF9F-3, had the Allison J33 engine.

F9F-2. One Pratt & Whitney J42-P-6 (5,000 lb.=2,270 kg. s.t.). Two prototypes (XF9F-2) built, the first flying for first time on November 24, 1947. First production F9F-2 flew on November 24, 1948. 437 delivered to U.S. Navy and Marine Corps.

F9F-3. One Allison J33-A-8 (4,600 lb.=2,090 kg. s.t. dry). Prototype flew on August 15, 1948. 54 ordered but all later converted to F9F-2 standard.

F9F-4. One Allison J33-A-16A (6,350 lb.=2,880 kg. s.t. dry). Original contract for 73, but this and subsequent contracts combined with F9F-5.

F9F-5. One Pratt & Whitney J48-P-4 (6,250 lb.=2,840 kg. s.t. dry) or (later)

J48-P-8 (7,250 lb.=3,290 kg. s.t. dry). Redesigned with larger fuselage and higher tail. The prototype, a modified F9F-2, first flew on December 21, 1949. 640 delivered to U.S. Navy and Marine Corps. F9F-5P is long-range photographic reconnaissance version with longer camera nose and provision for two 150 U.S. gallon underwing drop tanks on bomb shackles.

TYPE.—Single-seat Naval Carrier Fighter.

WINGS.—Low-wing cantilever monoplane. All-metal structure with flush-riveted stressed skin. Trailing-edge flaps inboard of ailerons and beneath fuselage. Variable-camber leading-edge flaps inter-connected with trailing-edge flaps. Hydraulic-operation. Upward-folding wings for carrier stowage.

FUSELAGE.—All-metal structure with flush-riveted stressed skin. Quickly detachable nose for servicing equipment and for interchangeability of armament, photographic and electronic equipment. Tail section quickly removable for access to engine compartment.

TAIL UNIT.—Cantilever monoplane type. Fin integral with fuselage. Tailplane mounted halfway up fin. All-metal structure.

LANDING GEAR.—Retractable tricycle type. Main wheels raised inwardly into thickened wing roots, nose wheel backwards into fuselage. Hydraulic retraction. Retractable arrester hook in rear end of fuselage below jet outlet.

POWER PLANT.—One Pratt & Whitney J42 or J48 or Allison J33 turbojet in plenum chamber amidships with air-inlets in thick-

ened wing-roots and jet exit beneath rear end of fuselage. Four spring-loaded blower doors in sides of plenum chamber may be opened to induce accelerated air-flow through chamber at low flying speeds at take-off and landing to eliminate stalling of air at lower lip of duct intakes at coarse angles of attack. Two additional doors aft release ram pressure in plenum chamber in the event of pressure seal failure. Fuel in internal and wing-tip tanks. Latter are permanent to ensure cleaner fit and to get over difficulty of jettisoning both tanks simultaneously. Fuel can be jettisoned in emergency by ram air valved into front of tanks. Probe-drogue in-flight refuelling equipment.

ACCOMMODATION.—Pilot's pressurised cockpit forward of wings with sliding and jettisonable canopy. Heating and refrigeration. pilot's ejector seat.

ARMAMENT.—Four 20 mm. nose-mounted cannon. May also carry external stores in the form of 5 in. rockets, 500 lb. bombs, Napalm bombs, etc.

DIMENSIONS (F9F-2 and -3).—
Span 38 ft. (11.6 m.).
Length 40 ft. (12.2 m.).
Height (over tail) 15 ft. (4.5 m.).

DIMENSIONS (F9F-4 and -5).—
Span 38 ft. (11.6 m.).
Length 42 ft. (12.8 m.).
Height 16 ft. (4.8 m.).

WEIGHTS.—
Weight empty 8,660 lb. (3,930 kg.).
Weight loaded 17,000 lb. (7,720 kg.).

PERFORMANCE (F9F-5).—
Max. speed about 625 m.p.h. (1,000 km.h.).
Initial rate of climb approx. 9,000 ft./min. (2,745 m./min.).
Service ceiling over 50,000 ft. (15,250 m.).

(1955–56)

GRUMMAN EA-6B PROWLER

The EA-6B is an advanced electronics development of the EA-6A for which Grumman received a prototype design and development contract in the Autumn of 1966. Except for a 1·37 m (4 ft 6 in) longer nose section and large fin pod, the external configuration of this version is the same as that of the basic A-6A.

The longer nose section provides accommodation for a total crew of four, the two additional crewmen being necessary to operate the more advanced ECM equipment. This comprises high-powered electronic jammers and modern computer-directed receivers, which provided the US Navy with its first aircraft designed and built specifically for tactical electronic warfare. The prototype EA-6B flew for the first time on 25 May 1968; deliveries of production aircraft began in January 1971.

The FY 1969 defence budget allocated $139 million for the initial purchase of eight EA-6Bs, and the total programme is expected to cover the supply of 102 aircraft (including the four pre-production and one R and D aircraft), to equip Navy and Marine Corps squadrons.

An ICAP (Increased Capability) version of the EA-6B, which increases substantially the jamming efficiency of the aircraft, has been developed. Current production aircraft are delivered with ICAP as standard, and the first 21 production EA-6Bs have been modified by Grumman to ICAP configuration. Modifications include an expanded

onboard tactical jamming system with eight frequency bands, reduced response time, and a new multi-format display. In addition, an automatic carrier landing system (ACLS) to permit carrier recovery in zero-zero weather, a new defensive electronic countermeasures system (DECM) and new communications-navigation-identification (CNI) equipment are installed. Another advanced version, ICAP-2, is under development; the prototype made its first flight on 24 June 1980.

Ten US Navy squadrons (VAQ-129, 130, 131, 132, 133, 134, 135, 136, 137 and 138) were equipped with the Prowler in mid-1977. The first detachment of US Marine Corps Prowler squadron VMAQ-2 began training on the EA-6B in September 1977 at NAS Whidbey Island, Washington, and the detachment deployed in late 1978. Two additional detachments have since completed training, and at least one is deployed at all times.

Under a $4·8 million contract awarded in 1978, Norden Systems is to supply for the EA-6B an advanced navigation radar system designated AN/APS-130. The contract calls for one prototype and three pre-production systems before the start of full production. This is expected to run to approximately 100 systems.

The description of the standard A-6E Intruder applies also to the EA-6B, except as follows:

TYPE: Four-seat carrier- or land-based advanced ECM aircraft.

WINGS: As for A-6E, but reinforced to cater for increased gross weight, fatigue life and 5·5g load factor.

FUSELAGE: As for A-6E, but reinforcement of underfuselage structure in areas of arrester hook and landing gear attachments, and lengthened by 1·37 m (4 ft 6 in).

TAIL UNIT: As for A-6E, except for provision of a large fin-tip pod to house ECM equipment.

LANDING GEAR: As for A-6E, except for reinforcement of attachments, A-frame arrester hook, and upgrading of structure to cater for increased gross weight.

POWER PLANT: Two 50 kN (11,200 lb st) Pratt & Whitney J52-P-408 turbojet engines, each rated at 49·8 kN (11,200 lb st).

ACCOMMODATION: Crew of four under two separate upward-opening canopies. The two additional crewmen are ECM Officers to operate the ALQ-99 equipment from the rear cockpit. Either ECMO can independently detect, assign, adjust and monitor the jammers. The ECMO in the starboard front seat is responsible for communications, navigation, defensive ECM and chaff dispensing.

SYSTEMS: Generally as for A-6E.

AVIONICS: ALQ-99 advanced electronic countermeasures (ECM) to enable the EA-6B to fulfil a tactical electronic warfare role. Five integrally powered pods, with a total of 10 jamming transmitters, can be carried. Each pod covers one of eight frequency bands. Sensitive surveillance receivers in the fin-tip pod for long-range detection of radars; emitter information is fed to a central digital computer that processes the signals for display and recording. Detection, identification, direction-finding and jammer-set-on sequence can be performed automatically or with manual assistance from crew.

DIMENSIONS, EXTERNAL:
As for A-6E, except:

Width folded	7·87 m (25 ft 10 in)
Length overall	18·24 m (59 ft 10 in)
Height overall	4·95 m (16 ft 3 in)
Wheelbase	5·23 m (17 ft 2 in)

AREAS:
As for A-6E

WEIGHTS AND LOADING:

Weight empty	14,588 kg (32,162 lb)
Internal fuel load	6,995 kg (15,422 lb)
Max external fuel load	4,547 kg (10,025 lb)
T-O weight in stand-off jamming configuration	24,703 kg (54,461 lb)
T-O weight in ferry range configuration	27,492 kg (60,610 lb)
Max T-O weight, catapult or field	29,483 kg (65,000 lb)
Max zero-fuel weight	17,708 kg (39,039 lb)
Max landing weight, carrier or field	20,638 kg (45,500 lb)
Max wing loading	600·5 kg/m² (123 lb/sq ft)

PERFORMANCE (A: no stores; B: 5 ECM pods):

Never-exceed speed	710 knots (1,315 km/h; 817 mph)	
Max level speed at S/L:		
A	566 knots (1,048 km/h; 651 mph)	
B	533 knots (987 km/h; 613 mph)	

Grumman EA-6B Prowler of Squadron VAQ-133 *Wizards* **landing on the USS** *John F. Kennedy (Brian M. Service)*

Cruising speed at optimum altitude:		
A	418 knots (774 km/h; 481 mph)	
B	420 knots (777 km/h; 483 mph)	
Stalling speed, flaps up, max power:		
A	124 knots (230 km/h; 143 mph)	
Stalling speed, flaps down, max power:		
A	84 knots (156 km/h; 97 mph)	

Landing from 15 m (50 ft): A	823 m (2,700 ft)	
Landing run: A	579 m (1,900 ft)	
B	655 m (2,150 ft)	
Combat range with max external fuel:		
A	2,085 nm (3,861 km; 2,399 miles)	
Range with max payload, 5% reserves plus 20 min at		
S/L: A	955 nm (1,769 km; 1,099 miles)	
		(1980–81)

Grumman F11F-1 Tiger carrier-based fighters (Wright J65 turbojet engine with afterburner)

THE GRUMMAN G-98 TIGER
U.S. Navy designation: F11F

The Tiger is a single-seat supersonic fighter which first flew in prototype form on July 30, 1954, less than 15 months after receipt of a letter of intent from the U.S. Navy Bureau of Aeronautics.

The following details apply to the F11F-1 production version, which is in first-line service with the U.S. Navy :—

TYPE.—Single-seat naval carrier fighter.

WINGS.—Cantilever mid-wing monoplane. 30° leading-edge sweepback. 6.5% thickness/chord ratio. All-metal structure. One-piece machined upper and lower skins. Leading-edge slats. Trailing-edge flaps over whole of fixed portion of wings, the wing-tips being manually hinged for carrier stowage. Lateral control by spoilers. Small trim-tab outboard of port flap. Wing area 250 sq. ft. (23.3 m.²)

FUSELAGE.—All-metal structure. Finger-type air brakes on underside of fuselage in line with trailing-edge of wings.

TAIL UNIT.—All surfaces swept. Comprises fixed fin, rudder and low-mounted all-flying tailplane with slight dihedral.

LANDING GEAR.—Retractable tricycle type. All wheels retract into fuselage.

POWER PLANT.—One Wright J65-W-18 turbojet engine (10,500 lb. = 4,770 kg. s.t. with afterburning). Fuel in integral wing and fuselage tanks. Provision for flight refuelling with retractable probe on starboard side of forward fuselage. External fuel tank can be carried under each wing.

ACCOMMODATION. — Pressurised cockpit in nose. Martin-Baker Mk. X5 ejection seat.

ARMAMENT.—Four 20 mm. cannon. Provision for air-to-air (Sidewinder) and air-to-ground missiles.

DIMENSIONS.—

Span 31 ft. 7½ in. (9.65 m.)
Length 44 ft. 11 in. (13.69 m.)
Height 13 ft. 3 in. (4.04 m.)
Width folded 27 ft. 4 in. (8.33 m.)

WEIGHTS.—

Weight empty 13,307 lb. (6,036 kg.)
Normal loaded weight 21,035 lb. (9,541 kg.
Max. loaded weight 24,078 lb. (10,921 kg.

PERFORMANCE.—

Max. speed Mach 1.12 at 35,000 ft. (10,700 m.)
Stalling speed 118 m.p.h. (190 km.h.)
Service ceiling 50,500 ft. (15,400 m.)
(1960–61)

The Grumman F7F-3N Tigercat Two-seat Night Fighter with wings being folded. (*Harold Martin*).

THE GRUMMAN G-51 TIGERCAT.

U.S. Naval designation : F7F.

The Tigercat is a twin-engined single or two-seat Fleet Fighter which has appeared in the following versions :—

XF7F-1. Two Pratt & Whitney R-2800-22 engines. Proto-type aircraft.

F7F-1N. First production version. Single-seat Night Fighter with nose armament.

F7F-2N. Two-seat Night Fighter version with rear seat added for radar-operator. Nose armament.

F7F-2D. F7F-2N equipped for Drone (pilotless radio-controlled target aircraft) control. Crew of two, pilot and radio-operator. Painted yellow all over.

F7F-3. Single-seat Day Fighter. Extra fuel tank carried in place of radar-operator. Nose armament. All converted to F7F-3N.

F7F-3N. Two-seat Night Fighter with radar-operator in place of auxiliary fuel tank. Radar in bulbous nose. Re-designed fin and rudder of greater height and area. Armament in wing roots.

F7F-4N. Development of the F7F-3N with radar enclosed in a streamlined nose. Strengthened landing-gear. Only model of Tigercat approved for use in carriers.

TYPE.—Twin-engined Single or Two-seat Day or Night Fighter.

WINGS.—Cantilever shoulder-wing monoplane. All-metal structure with straight leading-edge and swept-forward trailing-edge. Constant dihedral from roots. Flush-riveted aluminium-alloy stressed skin. All-metal ailerons with trim-tab in each. Slotted trailing-edge flaps in four sections between ailerons and fuselage. Outer wing sections fold upwards for stowage. Gross wing area 455 sq. ft. (42.26 m.²).

FUSELAGE.—Light alloy monocoque structure.

TAIL UNIT.—Cantilever monoplane type of all-metal construction. Trim-tab in rudder and elevators.

LANDING GEAR.—Retractable tricycle type. Each main wheel, on outside of outward-inclined shock-absorber leg, retracts backwards into engine nacelle and is enclosed by twin doors. Nose-wheel, in half-fork on shock-absorber leg, retracts backwards into fuselage and is enclosed by fairing plate attached to front of leg and by twin doors under fuselage. Retractable deck arrester hook under fuselage.

POWER PLANT.—Two Pratt & Whitney R-2800-22W eighteen-cylinder two-row radial air-cooled engines, each with a maximum rating of 2,100 h.p. (2,800 h.p. with water injection). Hamilton-Standard Hydromatic three-blade constant-speed airscrews, 13 ft. 9 in. (4.19 m.) diameter. Main fuel tanks in wings. Provision for 150 U.S. gallon (568 litre) long-range drop-tank under fuselage.

ACCOMMODATION.—Pilot's cockpit in front of leading-edge of wing. Bullet-proof windscreen and body armour. Rear cockpit provided in Night Fighter versions for radar-operator. Radar carried in bulbous nose.

ARMAMENT.—Four 20 mm. cannon mounted in nose on Day Fighter versions and in wing-roots in F7F-3N Night Fighter version. Racks for zero-length R.P. under outer wings. Provision for carriage of up to 4,000 lbs. (1,818 kg.) of bombs or two 22-in. (56 cm.) torpedoes under inner wings.

DIMENSIONS.—Span 51 ft. 6 in. (15.7 m.), Span (folded) 31 ft. 2½ in. (9.5 m.), Length (F7F-1 and -2) 45 ft. 4 in. (13.8 m.), Height 15 ft. 2 in. (4.6 m.).

WEIGHTS AND LOADINGS.—Weight empty 16,200 lbs. (7,355 kg.), Normal loaded weight 21,620 lbs. (9,815 kg.), Wing loading 47.5 lbs./sq. ft. (231.8 kg./m.²), Power loading (take-off) 3.9 lbs./h.p. (1.7 kg./h.p.).

PERFORMANCE.—Maximum level speed 427 m.p.h. (687 km.h.) at 19,200 ft. (5,852 m.), Stalling speed 89.6 m.p.h. (143.3 km.h.), Initial rate of climb 4,260 ft./min. (1,300 m./min.), Climb to 10,000 ft. (3,050 m.) 2.6 min., Climb to 20,000 ft. (6,100 m.) 6.2 min., Service ceiling 36,000 ft. (10,980 m.), Normal range 1,015 miles (1,623 km.). (1948)

GRUMMAN TOMCAT

USN designation: F-14

Grumman announced on 15 January 1969 that it had been selected as winner of the design competition for a carrier-based fighter for the US Navy. Known as the VFX during the competitive phase of the programme, this aircraft was later designated F-14. First flight of the F-14A Tomcat prototype took place on 21 December 1970. It was lost in a non-fatal accident, and flight testing was resumed on 24 May 1971 with the second aircraft.

The F-14 is designed to fulfil three primary missions. The first of these, fighter sweep/escort, involves clearing contested airspace of enemy fighters and protecting the strike force, with support from early-warning aircraft, surface ships and communications networks to co-ordinate penetration and escape. Second mission is to defend carrier task forces via Combat Air Patrol (CAP) and Deck Launched Intercept (DLI) operations. Third role is secondary attack of tactical targets on the ground, supported by electronic countermeasures and fighter escort. It has also been reported that in tests with targets simulating anti-ship missiles, Phoenix-armed F-14s have proved effective against high, fast, relatively small radar cross-

section threats such as the Soviet AS-4/6 air-to-surface missiles.

The configuration of the F-14 is unique, with variable-geometry wings, small foreplanes (glove vanes) which are extended automatically at supersonic speeds to control centre-of-pressure shift, manoeuvring slats and flaps to create a lower effective wing loading, and twin outward-canted fins and rudders. Optimum sweep of the wing is controlled automatically by a Mach sweep programmer, which relates sweep to Mach number and altitude.

Under the initial contracts, Grumman was required to provide the US Navy with a mockup of the F-14A in May 1969, and to build 12 research and development aircraft. Subsequently, the US Navy ordered an initial series of 26 production F-14As, and eventually acquired 557 Tomcats, including the 12 development aircraft. Carrier trials were started in June 1972, and initial deployment with the fleet began in October 1972. Replacement Training Squadron (RTS) VF-124 at Miramar NAS, San Diego, California, was responsible for working up ground and air crews for the new aircraft, and the first two operational squadrons, VF-1 and VF-2, were serving on board the USS *Enterprise* in the Western Pacific in September 1974. Replacement Training Squadron VF-101 was estab-

lished in July 1977 to train ground and flight crews for deployment from NAS Oceana, Virginia.

In mid-1979 the US Navy awarded a $4 million contract to the Northrop Corporation to manufacture pre-production television camera sets (TCSs) for installation on F-14s. Developed by Northrop's Electro-Mechanical Division, the TCS is a closed-circuit TV system, offering both wide-angle (acquisition) and telescopic (identification) fields of view. Mounted beneath the nose of the F-14, the TCS automatically searches for, acquires and locks on to distant targets, displaying them on monitors for the pilot and flight officer. By allowing early identification of targets, the system permits crews of high-speed aircraft to make combat decisions earlier than was possible previously.

The Naval Air Test Center at Patuxent River, Maryland, conducted test and evaluation of a 798 kg (1,760 lb) reconnaissance pod for the F-14 in 1979, and 49 F-14s are being fitted with this pod in 1980-81. Designated **TARPS** (Tactical Air Reconnaissance Pod System), it is mounted 0·38 m (1 ft 3 in) off the centreline of the F-14's under-fuselage, in the tunnel between the two engine nacelles. It has four main compartments: the nose carries a CAI KS-87B frame camera for either forward oblique or verti-

Grumman F-14A Tomcat with tactical air reconnaissance pod system (TARPS)

Northrop TCS under nose of an F-14

cal photographs; the second contains a Fairchild KA-99 low/medium-altitude horizon-to-horizon panoramic camera; the third has a Honeywell AN/AAD-5 infra-red reconnaissance set; and the fourth is an equipment bay containing the ground check maintenance panel and a sensor control data display set.

Without the TARPS pod installed, the F-14 retains its full weapon system capability. The F-14/TARPS aircraft will fulfil an important tactical reconnaissance role pending the evolution of new photo-reconnaissance aircraft.

TYPE: Two-seat carrier-based multi-role fighter.
WINGS: Variable-geometry mid-wing monoplane, with 20° of leading-edge sweep in the fully-forward position and 68° when fully swept. Oversweep position of 75° for carrier stowage. Wing position is programmed automatically for optimum performance throughout the flight regime, but manual override is provided. A short movable wing outer panel, needing only a comparatively light pivot structure, results from the wide fuselage and fixed centre-section 'glove', with pivot points 2·72 m (8 ft 11 in) from the centreline of the airframe. The inboard wing sections, adjacent to the fuselage, arc upward slightly to minimise cross-sectional area and wave-drag, and consist basically of a one-piece electron beam-welded titanium assembly, 6·70 m (22 ft) in span, made from Ti-6A1-4V titanium alloy. Small canard surfaces, known as glove vanes, swing out from the leading-edge of the fixed portion of the wing, to a maximum of 15° in relation to the leading-edge, as sweep of outer panels is increased. Spoilers on upper surfaces of wing. Stabilisation in pitch, provided by the canard surfaces, leaves the differential tailplane free to perform its primary control function. Trailing-edge control surfaces extend over almost entire span. Leading-edge slats.
FUSELAGE: The centre-fuselage section is a simple, fuel-carrying box structure; forward fuselage section comprises cockpit and nose. The aft section has a tapered aerofoil shape to minimise drag, with a fuel dump pipe projecting from the rear. Speed brakes located on the upper and lower surfaces, between the bases of the vertical tail fins.
TAIL UNIT: Twin vertical fins, mounted at the rear of each engine nacelle. Outward-canted ventral fin under each nacelle. The all-flying horizontal surfaces have skins of boron-epoxy composite material.
LANDING GEAR: Retractable tricycle type. Twin-wheel nose unit and single-wheel main units retract forward and upward. Existing beryllium brakes to be replaced with Goodyear lightweight carbon brakes from Spring 1981. Arrester hook under rear fuselage, housed in small ventral fairing. Nose-tow catapult attachment on nose unit.
ENGINE INTAKES: Straight two-dimensional external compression inlets. A double-hinged ramp extends down from the top of each intake, and these are programmed to provide the correct airflow to the engines automatically under all flight conditions. Each intake is canted slightly away from the fuselage, from which it is separated by some 0·25 m (10 in) to allow sufficient clearance for the turbulent fuselage boundary layer to pass between fuselage and intake without causing turbulence within the intake. Engine inlet ducts and aft nacelle structures are manufactured by Rohr Corporation. The

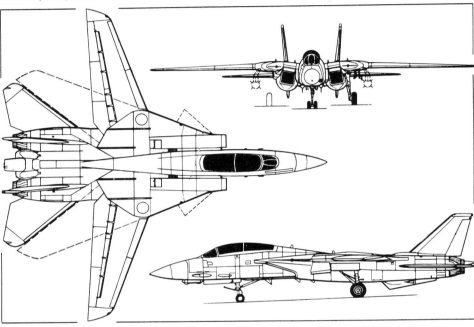

Grumman F-14A Tomcat carrier-based multi-mission fighter *(Pilot Press)*   (1980–81)

inlet duct, constructed largely of aluminium honeycomb, is about 4·27 m (14 ft) long, while the aft nacelle structure, of bonded aluminium honeycomb and conventional aluminium, is about 4·88 m (16 ft) in length.

POWER PLANT: Two Pratt & Whitney TF30-P-412A turbofan engines of 93 kN (20,900 lb st) with afterburning, mounted in ducts which open to provide 180° access for ease of maintenance. Garrett-AiResearch ATS200-50 air-turbine starter. An external auxiliary fuel tank can be carried beneath each intake trunk.

ACCOMMODATION: Pilot and naval flight officer seated in tandem on Martin-Baker GRU-7A rocket-assisted zero-zero ejection seats, under a one-piece bubble canopy, hinged at the rear and offering all-round view.

AVIONICS: Hughes AN/AWG-9 weapons control system, with ability to track 24 enemy targets and attack six of them simultaneously at varied altitudes and distances. Kaiser Aerospace AN/AVG-12 vertical and head-up display system.

ARMAMENT: One General Electric M61A-1 Vulcan 20 mm gun mounted in the port side of forward fuselage. Four Sparrow air-to-air missiles mounted partially submerged in the underfuselage, or four Phoenix missiles carried on special pallets which attach to the bottom of the fuselage. Two wing pylons, one under each fixed wing section, can carry four Sidewinder missiles or two additional Sparrow or Phoenix missiles with two Sidewinders. Various combinations of missiles and bombs to a max external weapon load of 6,577 kg (14,500 lb). ECM equipment includes Goodyear AN/ALE-39 chaff and flare dispensers, with integral jammers.

DIMENSIONS, EXTERNAL:
Wing span: unswept	19·45 m (64 ft 1½ in)
swept	11·65 m (38 ft 2½ in)
overswept	10·15 m (33 ft 3½ in)
Wing aspect ratio	7·28
Length overall	18·89 m (61 ft 11·9 in)
Height overall	4·88 m (16 ft 0 in)
Tailplane span	9·97 m (32 ft 8½ in)
Distance between fin tips	3·25 m (10 ft 8 in)
Wheel track	5·00 m (16 ft 5 in)
Wheelbase	7·02 m (23 ft 0½ in)

AREAS:
Wings, gross	52·49 m² (565·0 sq ft)
Horizontal tail surfaces (total)	13·01 m² (140·0 sq ft)
Vertical tail surfaces (total)	10·96 m² (118·0 sq ft)

WEIGHTS:
Weight empty	17,830 kg (39,310 lb)
Fuel (usable): internal	7,348 kg (16,200 lb)
external	1,724 kg (3,800 lb)
Normal T-O weight	26,553 kg (58,539 lb)
Max useful load (overload)	8,255 kg (18,200 lb)
T-O weight with 4 Sparrow	26,718 kg (58,904 lb)
T-O weight with 6 Phoenix	31,656 kg (69,790 lb)
Max T-O weight	33,724 kg (74,348 lb)
Design landing weight	23,510 kg (51,830 lb)

PERFORMANCE:
Max design speed	Mach 2·4
Max cruising speed	400-550 knots (741-1,019 km/h; 460-633 mph)
Landing speed	120 knots (222 km/h; 138 mph)
Service ceiling	above 15,240 m (50,000 ft)
Min T-O distance	214 m (700 ft)
Min T-O distance at 26,533 kg (58,495 lb) AUW	366 m (1,200 ft)
Min landing distance	488 m (1,600 ft)

Grumman E-1B Tracer early-warning aircraft from Squadron VAW-12 based on the U.S.S. *Forrestal* (S. P. Peltz)

THE GRUMMAN TRACER
U.S. Navy Designation: E-1B (formerly WF-2)

The E-1B Tracer is a modification of the Trader for airborne early warning and fighter direction duties. Suitable for all weather operation, it is equipped with a long-range antenna housed in the largest radome yet in service on a carrier-based aircraft. The aerodynamic prototype flew on March 1, 1957, and the first of 64 production aircraft flew in February, 1958. The type entered service with the U.S. Atlantic Fleet early in 1960.

The E-1B has a completely new tail assembly with twin fins and rudders to reduce possible wake effects from the radome, which is mounted above the fuselage. Production E-1B's also have a re-designed wing folding system, in which the wings fold back to lie alongside the fuselage, instead of upwards as on the C-1A.

A crew of four is carried, with two pilots in the cockpit and two warning system operators in a crew compartment. For airborne early warning operations and training, one pilot moves to the tactical director's position, on a stowable seat located between the operators. This seat is not occupied during take-off and landing.

Production E-1B Tracers are equipped with the APS-82 early warning system produced by Hazeltine Electronics Corporation of Little Neck, New York, who have worked with Grumman in the design and development of the system. The skin of the radar housing, which measures 20 ft × 30 ft (6·10 m × 9·14 m), is of glass-fibre honeycomb sandwich material.

The E-1B is suitable for operation from all Navy attack carriers.

DIMENSIONS.—

Span	72 ft 4 in. (22·05 m)
Length	45 ft 4 in. (13·82 m)
Height	16 ft 10 in. (5·13 m)
Wing area	506 sq ft (47·0 m²)

WEIGHT.—

Weight empty equipped	21,024 lb (9,536 kg)
Normal T.O. weight	27,000 lb (12,250 kg)

(1963–64)

Grumman S-2D Tracker of Air Anti-Submarine Squadron 30, US Navy

GRUMMAN G-89 TRACKER
US Navy designations: S-2, TS-2 and US-2

The Tracker is a twin-engined carrier-based anti-submarine search and attack aircraft which is in production for and in service with the US Navy. Also in service are two developments of the Tracker—the C-1A Trader general-utility transport-trainer and E-1B Tracer airborne early warning and fighter direction aircraft—of which details can be found in the 1963-64 *Jane's*.

The prototype XS-2A made its first flight on December 4, 1952, since when Grumman have delivered more than 1,000 S-2's. Export deliveries have been made to the Royal Netherlands and Italian Navies, which have received 26 and 40 S-2's respectively, and to the Argentine Navy (6) and Brazil (12). Sixty have been delivered to the Japanese Maritime Self-Defence Force. Fourteen of the latest S-2E's have been ordered for the Royal Australian Navy.

The following versions of the S-2 have been produced:

S-2A (formerly S2F-1). Two 1,525 hp Wright R-1820-82 engines. First production model. Supplied to the Argentine, Japan, Italy, Brazil, Taiwan, Thailand, Uruguay and the Netherlands. About 500 built. Production completed.

TS-2A. Training version of S-2A.

S-2B. Redesignation of S-2A's modified to carry Jezebel acoustic search equipment and Julie acoustic echo ranging system.

S-2C (formerly S2F-2). Developed version to carry larger anti-submarine weapons. An enlarged torpedo bay with asymmetrical extension on port side of fuselage accommodates homing torpedoes. To compensate for increased weight the tail surfaces were increased in area. Sixty built. Most converted into **US-2C** utility aircraft.

S-2D (formerly S2F-3). Developed version of S-2A ordered in 1958. Increased span. More roomy crew accommodation. Much improved operational equipment and armament. Twice the endurance of S-2A at 230 miles (370 km) radius. Prototype flew on May 20, 1959. Original contracts for 167, for delivery by end of 1963, were increased by a further order for 48 announced in January 1962. Production completed.

S-2E (formerly S2F-3S). Similar to S-2D, but with more advanced ASW electronic equipment, and provision for new types of armament, including nuclear depth charges, AS.12 air-to-surface missiles and Miniguns. Deliveries to VS-41 began in October 1962. Production continued in 1968.

CS2F-1. Canadian production version of S-2A built under licence for Royal Canadian Navy by de Havilland Aircraft of Canada, Ltd. 100 built. Seventeen supplied to Royal Netherlands Navy.

CS2F-2/3. New designations for CS2F-1 aircraft fitted with improved ASW operational equipment.

A new version of the Tracker, designated **S-2G**, is to enter USN service with ASW units on board CVS-class aircraft carriers, pending introduction of the Lockheed S-3A Viking. Basically similar to the S-2E, it differs in standard of equipment; in particular it has a directional low-frequency analyser and ranging system and an improved avionics system. Trials with YS-2G prototypes were made at Patuxent River during the Summer of 1971, followed by operational evaluation by Squadron VX-1 at NAS Key West, Florida.

The following data apply generally to all versions of the S-2.

TYPE: Twin-engined naval anti-submarine aircraft.

WINGS: Cantilever· high-wing monoplane. All-metal multi-spar structure. Wings fold upward and inward hydraulically from outboard of the engine nacelles. Fixed leading-edge slots on outer wings. Small ailerons, supplemented by wide-span spoilers on upper surfaces. Long-span slotted flaps. Leading-edge de-icer boots.

FUSELAGE: All-metal semi-monocoque structure.

TAIL UNIT: Cantilever all-metal structure. Rudder split vertically into two sections: forward section actuated hydraulically during take-off, landing and single-engined operation to increase rudder area.

LANDING GEAR: Retractable tricycle type, all units retracting rearward. Twin wheels on nose unit only. Small aft wheel-bumper is extendable but not fully retractable.

POWER PLANT: Two 1,525 hp Wright R-1820-82 WA nine-cylinder air-cooled radial engines, driving three-blade constant-speed metal propellers.

ACCOMMODATION: Crew of four consisting of pilot, co-pilot (who serves as navigator, radio-operator and searchlight-operator), radar operator and MAD operator. Dual controls.

ELECTRONICS AND EQUIPMENT: Equipment of S-2D includes UHF direction finder, LF direction finder, TACAN, APN-122 Doppler radar, APN-117 low-altitude radar altimeter, UHF transmitter/receiver, HF transmitter/receiver, APX 6B and APA 89 IFF, ASA-13 ground position indicator, and auto-pilot. S-2D also has ground track plotter on instrument panel, giving aircraft position and ground track, including Doppler correction for drift and ground speed, target position from Julie computer, sonobuoy location, radar position, MAD mark on ground track and exhaust trail mark on ground track.

OPERATIONAL EQUIPMENT (S-2D): AQA-3 Jezebel passive long-range acoustic search equipment, using sonobuoys; ECM instantaneous electronic countermeasures direction finder; Sniffer passive submarine exhaust trail detector; Julie active acoustic echo ranging by means of explosive charges, automatic target computer and automatic target plotting; retractable ASQ-10 MAD (magnetic anomaly detector) tail "sting"; retractable 75kW X-band 42-in × 20-in search radar under fuselage; 85 million candlepower remotely-controlled searchlight under starboard wing.

ARMAMENT (S-2D): Two homing torpedoes or one MK 101 depth bomb or four 385-lb depth charges in bomb bay. Six underwing attachments for torpedoes, 5-in rockets, Zuni rockets or 250-lb bombs. Housing for sonobuoys and marine markers in rear of engine nacelles. Fuselage dispenser for 60 underwater sounding charges for echo ranging.

DIMENSIONS, EXTERNAL (S-2E):

Wing span	72 ft 7 in (22·13 m)
Width folded	27 ft 4 in (8·33 m)
Length overall	43 ft 6 in (13·26 m)

Height overall	16 ft 7 in (5·06 m)
Wheel track	18 ft 6 in (5·64 m)

AREAS:

Wings, gross:	
S-2A, S-2C, CS2F-1 and 2	485 sq ft (45·1 m²)
S-2D, S-2E	496 sq ft (46·08 m²)

WEIGHTS (S-2E):

Weight empty	18,750 lb (8,505 kg)
Max payload	4,810 lb (2,182 kg)
Max internal fuel	4,368 lb (1,981 kg)
Max T-O weight	29,150 lb (13,222 kg)

PERFORMANCE (S-2E at max T-O weight):

Max level speed at S/L over	265 mph (426 kmh)
Patrol speed at 1,500 ft (450 m)	150 mph (241 kmh)
Stalling speed (landing configuration)	74 mph (119 kmh)
Service ceiling	21,000 ft (6,400 m)
Min T-O run	1,300 ft (396 m)
T-O to 50 ft (15 m)	1,875 ft (572 m)
Ferry range	1,300 miles (2,095 km)
Endurance with max fuel, 10% reserves	9 hours

(1969–70)

THE GRUMMAN TRADER
U.S. Navy designations: C-1A and EC-1A
(formerly TF-1)

The C-1A Trader is a general-utility transport-trainer version of the S-2 Tracker. Its larger fuselage can accommodate up to nine passengers in backward-facing easily-removable seats. To secure cargo in arrested carrier landings a "cage" device, comprising two parallel sets of movable vertical bulkheads secured between upper and lower longitudinal rails, is used. Vertical side posts may be fitted at any point along the length of the "cage" depending on size of load. Secured cargo will withstand maximum force of 20G. Life-rafts are stowed in compartments in the rear ends of the engine nacelles.

Except for fuselage assemblies, the main components of the C-1A are interchangeable with those of the S-2, including power-plant assemblies, outer wings, landing-gear, the larger S-2C tail-unit, etc.

Being equipped with the latest navigational devices, the C-1A is suitable for all-weather operational carrier-training, and a version designated EC-1A, with special electronic countermeasures equipment, is also in service.

The first C-1A flew for the first time in January, 1955.   (1963–64)

The Grumman TF-1 Trader general utility transport-trainer

The Grumman J4F-1 Widgeon General Utility Amphibian (two 200 h.p. Ranger L-440-5 engines).

THE GRUMMAN WIDGEON.
U.S. Navy designation: J4F.
U.S. Army Air Forces designation: OA-14.
British name: Gosling.

The Widgeon is a service utility version of the commercial Model G-44. It first went into service in the U.S. Coast Guard as the J4F-1 in 1941 and the U.S. Navy as the J4F-2 in 1942. It has also served in the U.S. Army Air Forces as the OA-14 and in the R.C.A.F. and the Royal Navy as the Gosling.

Its principal functions are coastal patrol, air/sea rescue, light personnel transport and instrument flying training.

TYPE.—Twin-engined light General Utility amphibian.

WINGS.—High-wing cantilever monoplane. All-metal structure with large single box-spar containing integral fuel tanks. Centre-section metal-covered, outer sections metal-covered to rear of spar with fabric aft to trailing-edge. Slotted trailing-edge flaps from hull to ailerons. Flaps pulled down hydraulically but returned to up position by springs within the operating cylinders. Fixed trim-tab in port aileron. Flaps and ailerons fabric-covered.

HULL.—Two-step all-metal structure divided into five watertight compartments. No bulkheads in cabin.

TAIL UNIT.—Cantilever monoplane type. Tail-plane mounted half-way up fin built integral with hull. All-metal construction with metal-covered fixed surfaces and fabric-covered rudder and elevators. Trimming-tabs in movable surfaces.

LANDING GEAR.—Standard Grumman type with wheels fitting nearly flush in sides of hull. Retractable tail-wheel with directional lock. Windows in wheel pockets to check location of gear. Hydraulic retraction with emergency hand-gear.

POWER PLANT.—Two 200 h.p. Ranger L-440-5 six-cylinder in-line inverted air-cooled engines on cantilever mountings from wing spar. Nacelles accessible from upper surface of wing. Fuel capacity 108 U.S. gallons. Each tank normally supplies its own engine but cross-flow valve permits both engines to operate from either tank. Oil tank (3½ U.S. gallons) in each nacelle.

ACCOMMODATION.—Enclosed cabin seating four or five. Anchor compartment and entrance hatch in nose. Main entrance door behind wing on port side. Side-by-side seats with throw-over type control wheel in front of wheel pockets with sliding side windows. One fixed auxiliary seat behind left wheel pocket. Two seats ahead of door. Four fixed windows in cabin.

DIMENSIONS.—Span 40 ft. (12.2 m.), Length 31 ft. 1 in. (9.45 m.), Height 11 ft. 5 in. (3.48 m.), Wing area 245 sq. ft. (22.76 sq. m.).

(1945–46)

The FM-2 Wildcat Single-seat Naval Fighter built by the Eastern Aircraft Division of General Motors.

THE GRUMMAN WILDCAT.

U.S. Naval designation : F4F. (Also FM when built by Eastern Aircraft Division, General Motors Corpn.).
British name : Wildcat.

The Wildcat was first ordered by the U.S. Navy in 1940 and the F4F-3, F4F-4 and F4F-7, the last mentioned a special long-range photographic reconnaissance version of the F4F-4, were all built by the Grumman company. Concurrently, the British Martlet (later renamed Wildcat) Mks. I to IV were Grumman-built.

In 1942 the manufacture of the Wildcat was transferred to the Eastern Aircraft Division, General Motors Corpn. The first FM-1 Wildcat, assembled from parts supplied by Grumman, flew on September 1, 1942. By April 11, 1944, the Eastern Aircraft Division had produced its 2,500th Wildcat.

The FM-1 (Wildcat V) fitted with the Pratt & Whitney R-1830-86 engine, was virtually the same as the F4F-4 (Wildcat IV). The FM-2 (Wildcat VI), which went into production in 1943, is fitted with a Wright R-1820-56 engine of greater output but less weight than the previous power-unit, has a re-designed tail-unit with taller fin and rudder and has the oil-coolers removed from the under-surface of the centre-section to the cowling, which has been revised in shape. The removal of the oil-coolers permits the installation of universal racks under the inner wings for bombs or auxiliary fuel tanks.

The FM-2 and Wildcat VI have served as light escort-carrier fighters.

TYPE.—Single-seat Fighter.

WINGS.—Mid-wing cantilever monoplane. NACA 23015 wing section. Wings attach directly to sides of fuselage. All-metal structure with single aluminium-alloy spar and butt-jointed and flush-riveted smooth metal skin. All-metal vacuum-operated split trailing-edge flaps. Folding wings.

FUSELAGE.—Oval section monocoque structure of aluminium-alloy construction.

TAIL UNIT.—Cantilever monoplane type. Aluminium-alloy construction with metal-covered fin and tail-plane and fabric-covered rudder and elevators.

LANDING GEAR.—Grumman type with wheel retracting into sides of fuselage. Fixed tail-wheel.

POWER PLANT.—One Pratt & Whitney R-1830-86 (FM-1 or Wildcat V) or Wright R-1820-56 (FM-2 or Wildcat VI) radial air-cooled engine. NACA cowling. Curtiss Electric or Hamilton-Standard Hydromatic constant-speed airscrew. Fuel capacity 160 U.S. gallons in self-sealing tanks in wings. Droppable fuel tanks may be carried on wing bomb-racks.

ACCOMMODATION.—Enclosed cockpit with sliding transparent canopy top over centre of wing. Bullet-proof windshield and armour behind pilot.

ARMAMENT AND EQUIPMENT.—Armament consists of six 50 cal. machine guns, three in each wing. Racks for two 250 lb. bombs, one under each wing. Versions of the F4F and FM are equipped for long-range photographic reconnaissance. These have comprehensive camera equipment but no armour or tank protection.

DIMENSIONS.—Span 38 ft. (11.6 m.), Width folded 14 ft. 6 in (4.4 m.), Length 28 ft. 10 in. (8.5 m.), Height 11 ft. 11 in. (3.6 m.), Wing area 260 sq. ft. (24.2 sq. m.).

NORMAL LOADED WEIGHT (FM-1).—7,412 lbs. (3,365 kg.).

PERFORMANCE (FM-1).—Maximum speed 318 m.p.h. (509 km.h.), Rate of climb 1,920 ft./min. (586 m./min.), Service ceiling 34,800 ft. (10,615 m.), Maximum range 925 miles (1,480 km.).

(1945–46)

GRUMMAN (GENERAL DYNAMICS) EF-111A RAVEN

The programme to convert General Dynamics F-111As into EF-111A electronic warfare prototypes, and to evaluate their ability to provide ECM jamming coverage for air attack forces, was initiated in 1972-73. Operational deployment of the F-111A in Southeast Asia, from March 1968, had revealed shortcomings, despite special preparation under the Harvest Reaper programme to provide these aircraft with advanced ECM equipment that would facilitate penetration of enemy airspace. Subsequent enquiry revealed that many factors contributed to the limited success of the F-111A in Southeast Asia; lack of adequate and effective ECM jamming was responsible for many of its problems, as well as those of all other types of combat aircraft in that theatre of operations.

Because of the growing potential of Soviet-built air defence systems, which stretch across Eastern Europe, NATO anti-invasion forces must have the capability of suppressing literally thousands of radar 'eyes', able to locate precisely the route and speed of counter-attacking air strikes. In addition, updated SAM systems and new interceptors with sophisticated ECM equipment are being introduced regularly by the Soviet Union, providing its armed forces with a now-acknowledged lead in electronic warfare, both ground and airborne.

Senior US Air Force officials consider that utilisation of the EF-111 as a tactical jamming system, in combination with the E-3 AWACS, is vital to help offset this Soviet lead. Because of its vast masking power, the EF-111 is essential to provide cover for air-to-ground operations along the forward lines, and for support of penetrating allied strike forces. Should some future circumstances make it necessary to launch a counter-strike against Soviet

One of two Grumman-modified EF-111A prototypes being prepared for anechoic chamber testing of its AN/ALQ-99E tactical jamming system *(Howard Levy)*

penetration of NATO territory, EF-111s operating on the friendly side of the FEBA (forward edge of the battle area) could blind the other side's electronic 'eyes', making it possible for NATO strike forces to attack the armoured spearhead, as well as resupply areas, reserves and SAM installations 17-35 nm (32-64 km; 20-40 miles) behind the opposing lines, with something less than half the anticipated losses that could be expected without use of the EF-111s' jamming systems.

Three basic modes of deployment are foreseen for the EF-111: standoff, penetration, and close air support. In the standoff role, jamming aircraft would operate within their own airspace, at the FEBA. Out of range of the enemy's ground-based weapons, orbiting EF-111s would use their jamming systems to screen the routes of friendly strike aircraft. In the penetration role, the EF-111s would accompany strike aircraft to high-priority targets, their Mach 2 capability making them ideal escort aircraft for such a task. The close air support requirement calls for EF-111 escorts to neutralise anti-air radars while the strike force delivers its attack on enemy armour.

Design study contracts were awarded to General Dynamics and Grumman by the US Air Force in 1974, and in January 1975 it was announced that Grumman had been awarded an $85·9 million contract to convert two existing F-111As to EF-111A prototype configuration. Basic equipment of these prototypes comprises the Raytheon AN/ALQ-99E tactical jamming system, comprising ten transmitters, five exciters and one RF calibrator per aircraft. In addition, each has a modified AN/ALQ-137 Self Protection System, and a modified AN/ALR-62 Terminal Threat Warning System. The ALQ-99E jammers are mounted in the weapons bay, with their antennae covered by a 4·9 m (16 ft) long canoe-shape radome. The fin-tip pod, similar in shape to that of the EA-6B Prowler, houses the receiver system and antennae. Total weight of the new equipment is about three tons.

The two-man crew of an EF-111 comprises a pilot and an electronic warfare officer (EWO). All tactical jamming functions are managed by the EWO who can, through computer management, handle a tactical electronic warfare workload which required previously several operators and more equipment. In addition, the automated system of the EF-111 has exceptional capability for locating, identifying, and assigning jammers to enemy emitters over a wide range of frequencies.

The first flight of an aerodynamic prototype was made on 10 March 1977, and the complete system was flown for the first time on 17 May 1977, on the second prototype. Subsequent Grumman flight testing of the jamming system involved 84 flights totalling 215 flight hours, completed by the two aircraft during a period of 3½ months. US Air Force flight testing involved 78 flights totalling 258 flight hours during a six-month test programme. The US Air Force tests verified various mission operational concepts, flight formations, and the jammer's electromagnetic compatibility with other strike aircraft. These latter tests dispelled an earlier concern that the friendly strike force, as well as enemy threats, might be jammed by the powerful signals emanating from the EF-111. Structural flight tests under all operating conditions demonstrated an 'infinite' life for all modified areas of the aircraft's structure, and flying qualities were considered virtually identical to those of the F-111 strike aircraft.

US Air Force plans envisage the conversion of 42 F-111Fs as ECM jamming aircraft. The production contract for the first six was signed in April 1979; deliveries are due to begin in July 1981 to the 366th Tactical Fighter Wing at Home AFB, Idaho.

The description of the F-111A in the 1976-77 *Jane's* applies also to the EF-111A, except for the following additional or amended details:

TYPE: ECM tactical jamming aircraft.

WINGS: As detailed for F-111A. Wing section NACA 64A210.68 modified at pivot point, NACA 64A209.80 with modified leading-edge at tip. Dihedral, at 16° sweep, 1°. Incidence, at 16° sweep, 1° at root, −3° at tip.

POWER PLANT: As detailed for F-111A. Fuel capacity 19,010 litres (5,022 US gallons). Oil capacity 30·3 litres (8 US gallons).

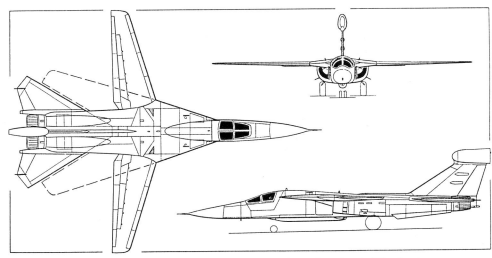

Grumman (General Dynamics) EF-111A electronic warfare aircraft (*Pilot Press*)

AVIONICS: AN/ALQ-99E tactical jamming system; AN/ARC-109 UHF command, AN/AJQ-20A INS, AN/APQ-160 attack radar, AN/APN-167 radar altimeter, AN/APQ-110 terrain-following radar, AN/ARN-58 ILS, AN/ARC-112 HF transceiver, AN/AIC-25 intercom, AN/APX-64 IFF(AIMS), AN/ARN-52 Tacan, AN/ARA-50 UHF/DF, AN/ALQ-137 (modified) SPS, AN/ALR-62 (modified) TTWS, AN/ALR-23 CMRS, and AN/ALE-28 CMDS.

ARMAMENT: None.

DIMENSIONS, EXTERNAL:

Wing span, spread	19·20 m (63 ft 0 in)
Wing span, fully swept	9·74 m (31 ft 11·4 in)
Wing mean aerodynamic chord	2·76 m (9 ft 0 in)
Wing aspect ratio (16° sweep)	7·56
Length overall	23·51 m (77 ft 1·6 in)
Height overall	6·10 m (20 ft 0 in)
Wheel track	3·19 m (10 ft 0·4 in)
Wheelbase	7·44 m (24 ft 4·8 in)

AREA:

Wings, gross (16° sweep)	48·77 m² (525 sq ft)

WEIGHTS:

Weight empty (estimated)	24,230 kg (53,418 lb)
Design T-O weight	33,000 kg (72,750 lb)
Combat T-O weight	28,000 kg (61,729 lb)
Max T-O weight	39,680 kg (87,478 lb)
Max landing weight	36,287 kg (80,000 lb)

PERFORMANCE (estimated for typical mission, A: basic standoff; B: penetration; C: close air support. At max T-O weight unless detailed otherwise):

Max combat speed at combat T-O weight:
A, B, C   1,007 knots (1,865 km/h; 1,160 mph)

Average speed, outbound:
A   450 knots (834 km/h; 518 mph)

B	496 knots (919 km/h; 571 mph)
C	448 knots (830 km/h; 516 mph)

Average speed over combat area:

A	321 knots (595 km/h; 370 mph)
B	336 knots (623 km/h; 387 mph)
C	318 knots (589 km/h; 366 mph)

Average speed, inbound:

A	436 knots (808 km/h; 502 mph)
B	496 knots (919 km/h; 571 mph)
C	438 knots (811 km/h; 504 mph)

Stalling speed, power off:
A, B, C   135·1 knots (250·4 km/h; 155·6 mph)

Rate of climb at S/L, intermediate power:
A, B, C   1,095 m (3,592 ft)/min

Rate of climb at S/L, one engine out, with afterburning:
A, B, C   986 m (3,234 ft)/min

Service ceiling with afterburning, at combat weight:

A	16,670 m (54,700 ft)
B	15,450 m (50,700 ft)
C	16,185 m (53,100 ft)

T-O run: A, B, C   991 m (3,250 ft)

T-O to 15 m (50 ft): A, B, C   1,250 m (4,100 ft)

Landing from 15 m (50 ft):
A, C, at 26,623 kg (58,693 lb)   853 m (2,800 ft)
B, at 32,863 kg (72,451 lb)   1,245 m (4,085 ft)

Landing run:
A, C, at 26,623 kg (58,693 lb)   539 m (1,770 ft)
B, at 32,863 kg (72,451 lb)   759 m (2,490 ft)

Combat radius, with reserves:

A	200 nm (370 km; 230 miles)
B	250 nm (463 km; 287 miles)
C	897 nm (1,661 km; 1,032 miles)
Ferry range	2,157 nm (3,998 km; 2,484 miles)

(1980–81)

GULFSTREAM AMERICAN GULFSTREAM II
US Coast Guard designation: VC-11A

The decision to start production of this twin-turbofan executive transport was announced by Grumman on 17 May 1965. The first production Gulfstream II (no prototype was built) flew for the first time on 2 October 1966. FAA certification was gained on 19 October 1967, and the first production aircraft was delivered to National Distillers & Chemical Corporation on 6 December 1967.

Custom interiors and electronics, with the exception of the Sperry SP-50G automatic flight control system, which is standard, are installed by specialist agencies.

Deliveries totalled more than 200 by 1 January 1977, including a single Gulfstream II operated by the US Coast Guard under the designation **VC-11A**. Two other Gulfstream IIs were converted as flying simulators for the Space Shuttle Orbiter vehicle.

From aircraft No. 166, delivered in July 1975, production aircraft incorporate an engine 'hush-kit', for which Grumman American received FAA certification on 2 May 1975; this modification can be retrofitted to earlier Gulfstream IIs if required.

Flight testing began in 1975 of a Gulfstream II with wingtip tanks, increasing the total fuel capacity to 12,156 kg (26,800 lb). This version has a max ramp weight of 29,937 kg (66,000 lb) and max T-O weight of 29,711 kg (65,500 lb). Increased fuel, amounting to 1,415 kg (3,120 lb), is carried in new wingtip tanks which serve as an extension of the main integral wing tanks. Wind tunnel

tests have shown that the tip-tanks do not affect high-speed handling, that they offer a slight improvement in aircraft stability and lateral control, and that cruise performance penalty is approximately 5 per cent against max fuel range improvements of 12 per cent at long-range cruising speed, 11 per cent at 0·72 constant Mach, and 7 per cent at 0·80 constant Mach. This version is certificated for an NBAA IFR range of 3,180 nm (5,893 km; 3,662 miles) with a 200 nm (370 km; 230 mile) alternate.

The description which follows applies to the standard version:

TYPE: Twin-turbofan executive transport aircraft.

WINGS: Cantilever low-wing monoplane of all-metal construction. Thickness/chord ratio 12% at wing station 50, 9·5% at wing station 145 and 8·5% at wing station 414. Dihedral 3°. Incidence 3° 30' at wing station 50, 1° 30' at wing station 145 and −0° 30' at wing station 414. Sweepback 25° at quarter-chord. One-piece single-slotted Fowler-type trailing-edge flaps. Spoilers forward of flaps assist in lateral control and can be extended for use as airbrakes. All control surfaces actuated hydraulically. Trim tab in port aileron. Anti-icing by engine bleed air.

FUSELAGE: Conventional all-metal semi-monocoque structure. Glassfibre nosecone hinged for access to radar, etc.

TAIL UNIT: Cantilever all-metal T-tail. All surfaces swept-back. Trim tab in rudder and each elevator. Powered controls (see under 'Systems' paragraph).

LANDING GEAR: Retractable tricycle type, with twin wheels on each unit. Inward-retracting main units, with tyres size 34 × 8·25-32, pressure 10·34 bars (150 lb/sq in). Forward-retracting steerable nose unit. Nosewheel tyres size 21 × 7·25-22, pressure 6·55 bars (95 lb/sq in). Goodyear aircooled brakes with Goodyear fully-modulating anti-skid units.

POWER PLANT: Two Rolls-Royce Spey Mk 511-8 turbofan engines, each 50·7 kN (11,400 lb st), mounted in pod on each side of rear fuselage. Rohr target-type thrust reversers form aft portions of nacelles when in stowed position. All fuel in integral tanks in wings, capacity 10,568 kg (23,300 lb). Provision for wingtip tanks, to increase fuel capacity to 12,156 kg (26,800 lb).

ACCOMMODATION: Crew of two or three. Certificated for 19 passengers in pressurised and air-conditioned cabin. Large baggage compartment at rear of cabin, capacity 907 kg (2,000 lb). Integral airstair door at front of cabin on port side. Electrically heated windscreen.

SYSTEMS: Cabin pressurisation system, with max differential of 0·65 bars (9·45 lb/sq in). Two independent hydraulic systems, each 103·5 bars (1,500 lb/sq in). All flying controls hydraulically powered, with manual reversion. APU in tail compartment. Basic 28V DC electrical system, using two 300A generators and a 200A transformer-rectifier. Two 20kVA alternators provide AC power for secondary and auxiliary systems. Third (APU-driven) 20kVA alternator for on-ground power. Three 2·5kVA inverters, powered by the transformer-rectifiers, provide 400Hz fixed-frequency power. Two 24V batteries.

DIMENSIONS, EXTERNAL:
Wing span	20·98 m (68 ft 10 in)
Wing span over tip-tanks	21·87 m (71 ft 9 in)
Length overall	24·36 m (79 ft 11 in)
Length of fuselage	21·74 m (71 ft 4 in)
Height overall	7·47 m (24 ft 6 in)
Tailplane span	8·23 m (27 ft 0 in)
Wheel track	4·16 m (13 ft 8 in)
Wheelbase	10·16 m (33 ft 4 in)
Passenger door: Height	1·57 m (5 ft 2 in)
Width	0·91 m (3 ft 0 in)
Baggage door: Height	0·72 m (2 ft 4½ in)
Width	0·91 m (2 ft 11¾ in)
Ventral door: Width	0·46 m (1 ft 6 in)
Length	0·71 m (2 ft 4 in)

DIMENSIONS, INTERNAL:
Cabin: Length	11·99 m (39 ft 4 in)
Width	2·24 m (7 ft 4 in)
Height	1·85 m (6 ft 1 in)
Volume	40·41 m³ (1,427 cu ft)
Baggage compartment	4·44 m³ (156·85 cu ft)

AREA:
Wings, gross	75·21 m² (809·6 sq ft)

WEIGHTS AND LOADINGS:
Manufacturer's weight empty:
without tip-tanks	13,772 kg (30,363 lb)
with tip-tanks	14,053 kg (30,938 lb)

Typical operating weight empty:
without tip-tanks	16,576 kg (36,544 lb)
with tip-tanks	16,867 kg (37,186 lb)
Max T-O weight	29,711 kg (65,500 lb)
Max ramp weight	29,937 kg (66,000 lb)
Max landing weight	26,535 kg (58,500 lb)
Max zero-fuel weight	19,050 kg (42,000 lb)
Max wing loading	394·8 kg/m² (80·9 lb/sq ft)
Max power loading	293 kg/kN (2·87 lb/lb st)

PERFORMANCE (at max T-O weight except where indicated):
Max cruising speed at 7,620 m (25,000 ft)
Mach 0·85 (505 knots; 936 km/h; 581 mph)
Econ cruising speed at 13,105 m (43,000 ft)
Mach 0·72 (420 knots; 778 km/h; 483 mph)
Approach speed at max landing weight
142 knots (263 km/h; 164 mph)
Max rate of climb at S/L 1,262 m (4,140 ft)/min
Rate of climb at S/L with tip-tanks
1,219 m (4,000 ft)/min

Rate of climb at S/L, one engine out
427 m (1,400 ft)/min
Rate of climb at S/L with tip-tanks, one engine out
366 m (1,200 ft)/min
Service ceiling	13,100 m (43,000 ft)
Service ceiling, one engine out	8,230 m (27,000 ft)

Service ceiling, with tip-tanks, one engine out
7,405 m (24,300 ft)
FAA T-O field length	1,707 m (5,600 ft)

FAA T-O field length, with tip tanks
1,737 m (5,700 ft)
FAA landing field length	1,067 m (3,500 ft)

NBAA IFR range with 200 nm (370 km; 230 mile) alternate, crew of three, plus 907 kg (2,000 lb) 'passenger payload' 2,859 nm (5,298 km; 3,292 miles)
Range, conditions as above, with tip-tanks
3,180 nm (5,893 km; 3,662 miles)
NBAA VFR range with 30 min reserves, crew of three, plus 907 kg (2,000 lb) 'passenger payload'
3,252 nm (6,025 km; 3,744 miles)
Range, conditions as above, with tip-tanks
3,581 nm (6,635 km; 4,123 miles)
(1978–79)

The Hall PH-1 Bombing and patrol Flying-boat (two 575 h.p. Wright "Cyclone" engines).

THE HALL PH-1.

The most recent productions of this company are the Hall PH-1 twin-engined patrol flying-boat, nine of which have been built for the U.S. Navy, and a large four-engined all-metal flying-boat, which is the largest flying-boat yet produced in the United States.

TYPE.—Twin-engined patrol or bomber flying-boat.
WINGS.—Unequal-span single-bay biplane. Clark "Y" wing-section. Upper wing in three sections, consisting of centre-section and two outer sections. Lower wing in four sections, consisting of two strut-wings and two outer sections. Upper centre-section and stub-wings interconnected by engine-struts. One pair of splayed-out interplane struts on each side. Structure entirely of 17ST aluminium-alloy, with exception of steel drag and lift wires. Fabric covering. Ailerons on upper wings only.
HULL.—Two-step hull, with Vee planing bottom and rounded sides and deck. Structure entirely of aluminium-alloy. Lower wings joined to hull through filets of 12-inch radius. Four water-tight bulkheads. Interchangeable wing-tip floats of riveted aluminium-alloy.
TAIL UNIT.—Monoplane type. Central fin and balanced rudder. Rigidly-braced tail-plane and unbalanced elevators. Aluminium-alloy framework, covered with fabric.
POWER PLANT.—Two 575 h.p. Wright "Cyclone" R-1820E geared radial air-cooled engines, mounted between wings in streamline nacelles. Low-drag cowling rings. One half of fuel carried in

tanks in lower wing-stubs, remainder in nacelle tanks behind fireproof bulkheads. Total fuel capacity 900 U.S. gallons. Oil tanks in rear end of each nacelle. Hand-electric inertia starters.
ACCOMMODATION.—Crew of five carried. Bow cockpit used by gunner and bomber-navigator. Aft of this is open cockpit for pilot and assistant, seated side-by-side, with dual controls. Aft of cockpit and inside hull is the wireless compartment and living quarters, complete with bunks, etc. Mechanic's compartment and rear gunner's position aft of wings.
DIMENSIONS.—Span (upper) 72 ft. 10 in. (22.2 m.), Span (lower) 67 ft. 1½ in. (20.4 m.), Length 51 ft. 10⅛ in. (15.8 m.), Height 17 ft. 3 in. (5.26 m.), Wing area 1,170 sq. ft. (108.7 sq. m.).
WEIGHTS AND LOADINGS (Patrol duties).—Weight empty 7,966 lbs. (3,617 kg.), Weight loaded 15,306 lbs. (6,949 kg.), Wing loading 13.2 lbs./sq. ft. (64.4 kg./sq. m.), Power loading 12.4 lbs./h.p. (5.6 kg./h.p.).
WEIGHTS AND LOADINGS (Bombing duties).—Weight empty 8,616 lbs. (3,912 kg.), Weight loaded 16,582 lbs. (7,528 kg.), Wing loading 14.3 lbs./sq. ft. (69.7 kg./sq. m.), Power loading 13.5 lbs./h.p. (6.1 kg./h.p.).
PERFORMANCE (Patrol duties).—Maximum speed 134.5 m.p.h. (215.2 km.h.), Stalling speed 59 m.p.h. (94.4 km.h.), Climb in 10 mins. 5,750 ft. (1,754 m.), Service ceiling 11,400 ft. (3,477 m.), Cruising range (900 U.S. gallons fuel) 1,860 miles (2,976 km.).
PERFORMANCE (Bombing duties).—Maximum speed 129.2 m.p.h. (206.7 km.h.), Stalling speed 61 m.p.h. (97.6 km.h.), Climb in 10 mins. 5,100 ft. (1,555.5 m.), Service ceiling 9,400 ft. (2,867 m.), Cruising range (630 U.S. gallons fuel) 890 miles (1,424 km.).

(1936)

THE HALL PH-2.

The most recent productions of this Company are the Hall PH-2 flying-boat for the U.S. Coast Guard, a development of the PH-1 patrol flying-boat, and the XPTBH-2 experimental patrol-torpedo-bomber seaplane. The PH-2 is intended for patrol and rescue work at the various Coast Guard Air Stations of the United States.

TYPE.—Twin-engined patrol and rescue flying-boat.
WINGS.—Unequal-span single-bay biplane. Clark "Y" wing-section. Upper wing in three sections, consisting of centre-section and two outer sections. Lower wing in four sections, consisting of two stub-wings and two outer sections. Upper centre-section and stub-wings interconnected by engine-struts. One pair of splayed-out interplane struts on each side. Structure entirely of 17ST aluminium-alloy, with exception of steel drag, landing and lift wires. Fabric covering. Ailerons on upper wings only.

HULL.—Two-step hull, with Vee planing bottom and rounded sides and deck. Structure entirely of aluminium-alloy. Lower wings joined to hull through filets of 12-inch radii. Five watertight bulkheads. Interchangeable wing-tip floats of riveted aluminium alloy.
TAIL UNIT.—Monoplane type. Central fin and balanced rudder. Rigidly-braced tail-plane and unbalanced elevators. Aluminium-alloy framework, covered with fabric.
POWER PLANT.—Two Wright "Cyclone" SGR-1820-F51 geared radial air-cooled engines, each rated at 875 h.p. for take-off and 750 h.p. for continuous operation, mounted between wings in streamline nacelles. Three-bladed adjustable-pitch airscrews. Low-drag cowling rings. One half of fuel carried in tanks in lower wing-stubs, remainder in nacelle tanks behind fireproof bulkheads. Total fuel capacity 900 U.S. gallons. Oil tanks in rear end of each nacelle. Ballistic-type engine-starters.

ACCOMMODATION.—Crew of four carried. Mooring and anchoring compartment in nose. Enclosed pilot's cockpit, seating two side-by-side with dual controls. Then follows wireless compartment, aft of which is the mechanic's compartment. Further aft are two compartments with two folding bunks, for use as hospital bays. The forward one is equipped with table for navigator.

DIMENSIONS.—Span (upper) 72 ft. 10 in. (22.2 m.), Span (lower) 67 ft. 1½ in. (20.4 m.), Length 51 ft. (15.5 m.), Height 17 ft. 11 in. (5.46 m.), Wing area 1,170 sq. ft. (108.7 sq. m.).

WEIGHTS AND LOADINGS.—Weight empty 9,277 lbs. (4,208 kg.), Weight loaded 15,547 lbs. (7,052 kg.), Wing loading 13.3 lbs./sq. ft. (64.9 kg./sq. m.), Power loading 10.58 lbs./h.p. (4.80 kg./h.p.).

PERFORMANCE.—Maximum speed at 3,200 ft. (975 m.) 155.2 m.p.h. (249.7 km.h.). Stalling speed 60 m.p.h. (96 km.h.), Climb to 5,000 ft. (1,525 m.) 3.85 mins., Service ceiling 22,200 ft. (6,767 m.), Cruising range at 60 per cent. output (750 U.S. gallons of fuel) 1,928 miles (3,103 km.), Cruising range (892 U.S. gallons of fuel) 2,242 miles (3,608 km.). (1938)

The Hall PH-2 Coastguard Patrol and Rescue Flying-boat (two 750 h.p. Wright "Cyclone" engines).

The Hall PH-3 Patrol Flying-boat (two Wright "Cyclone" engines) as used by the U.S. Coast Guard.

THE HALL PH-3.

The last product of the Hall-Aluminium concern was the PH-3 twin-engined flying-boat, seven of which were delivered to the U.S. Coast Guard for patrol and rescue work in 1940.

TYPE.—Twin-engined patrol and rescue flying-boat.

WINGS.—Unequal-span single-bay biplane. Clark "Y" wing-section. Upper wing in three sections, consisting of centre-section and two outer sections. Lower wing in four sections, consisting of two stub-wings and two outer sections. Upper centre-section and stub-wings interconnected by engine-struts. One pair of splayed-out interplane struts on each side. Structure entirely of 17ST aluminium-alloy, with exception of steel drag, landing and lift wires. Fabric covering. Ailerons on upper wings only.

HULL.—Two-step hull, with Vee planing bottom and rounded sides and deck. Structure entirely of aluminium-alloy. Lower wings joined to hull through filets of 12-inch radii. Five watertight bulkheads. Interchangeable wing-tip floats of riveted aluminium alloy.

TAIL UNIT.—Monoplane type. Central fin and balanced rudder. Rigidly-braced tail-plane and unbalanced elevators. Aluminium-alloy framework, covered with fabric.

POWER PLANT.—Two Wright "Cyclone" GR-1820-F51 geared radial air-cooled engines, each rated at 875 h.p. for take-off and 750 h.p.

for continuous operation at 3,200 ft. (975 m.), mounted between wings in streamline nacelles. Curtiss constant-speed electrically-controllable full-feathering airscrews. Low-drag cowling rings. One half of fuel carried in tanks in lower wing-stubs, remainder in nacelle tanks behind fireproof bulkheads. Total fuel capacity 900 U.S. gallons. Oil tanks in rear end of each nacelle. Breeze cartridge-type engine-starters.

ACCOMMODATION.—Crew of four carried. Mooring and anchoring compartment in nose. Enclosed pilot's cockpit, seating two side-by-side with dual controls. Then follows navigators' compartment, radio compartment, mechanics' compartment, and hospital bay with two folding bunks. Two folding bunks are also provided in the navigators' compartment.

DIMENSIONS.—Span (upper) 72 ft. 10 in. (22.2 m.), Span (lower) 67 ft. 1½ in. (20.4 m.), Length 51 ft. (15.5 m.), Height 17 ft. 11 in. (5.46 m.), Wing area 1,170 sq. ft. (108.7 sq. m.).

WEIGHTS AND LOADINGS.—Weight empty 9,614 lbs. (4,361 kg.), Weight loaded 16,152 lbs. (7,526 kg.), Wing loading 13.8 lbs./sq. ft. (67.4 kg./sq. m.), Power loading 11 lbs./h.p. (5 kg./h.p.).

PERFORMANCE.—Maximum speed at 3,200 ft. (975 m.) 159 m.p.h. (256 km.h.), Cruising speed at 3,200 ft. (975 m.), 136 m.p.h (219 km.h.), Alighting speed 60 m.p.h. (96 km.h.), Climb to 5,000 ft. (1,525 m.) 3.85 mins., Service ceiling 21,350 ft. (6,510 m.), Cruising range at 60 per cent. output (750 U.S. gallons of fuel) 1,937 miles (3,120 km.), Cruising range (892 U.S. gallons of fuel) 2,300 miles (3,800 km.).

HELIO SUPER COURIER MODEL H-295 and TRIGEAR COURIER MODEL HT-295

USAF designation: U-10

The original version of the Super Courier was flown for the first time in 1958 and received FAA Type Approval on 17 November that year. Three were supplied to the USAF for evaluation, under the designation L-28A. Further substantial orders were received subsequently, some aircraft being assigned to Tactical Air Command for counter-insurgency duties.

The current commercial versions of the Courier are the Super Courier Model H-295 with non-retractable tail-wheel landing gear and the Trigear Courier Model HT-295 with non-retractable tricycle-type landing gear.

Design and construction of the prototype H-295 began in late 1964 and it flew for the first time on 24 February 1965, FAA certification being received in the following month. Certification for the Trigear Courier HT-295 was received in March 1974, with the first production deliveries beginning immediately afterwards.

USAF Super Couriers are of three types, as follows:

U-10A. Standard model with fuel capacity of 227 litres (60 US gallons).

U-10B. Long-range version with standard internal fuel capacity of 455 litres (120 US gallons). This version has been operated in South-east Asia, South America, and in other parts of the world, on a wide variety of military missions and has an endurance of more than 10 hours. Paratroop doors standard.

U-10D. Improved long-range version with max AUW increased to 1,633 kg (3,600 lb). Standard internal fuel capacity of 455 litres (120 US gallons). Accommodation for pilot and five passengers.

The following details refer to the standard commercial Super Courier and Trigear Courier, except as noted:

TYPE: Six-seat light STOL personal, corporate and utility monoplane.

WINGS: Cantilever high-wing monoplane. NACA 23012 wing section. Dihedral 1°. Incidence 3°. All-metal single-spar structure. Frise ailerons have duralumin

frames and fabric covering and are supplemented by Arc-type aluminium spoilers, located at 15·5% chord on upper surface of each wing and geared to ailerons for control at low speeds. Ground-adjustable tab on ailerons. Full-span automatic all-metal Handley Page leading-edge slats. Electrically-operated NACA slotted all-metal trailing-edge flaps over 74% of span. No anti-icing equipment.

FUSELAGE: All-metal structure. Cabin section has welded steel tube framework, covered with aluminium; rear section is an aluminium monocoque.

TAIL UNIT: Cantilever all-metal structure. All-moving one-piece horizontal surface is fitted with trim and anti-balance tabs. Electrically-operated elevator trim optional.

LANDING GEAR (H-295): Non-retractable tailwheel type. Cantilever main legs. Oleo-pneumatic shock-absorbers of Helio design and manufacture on all three units. Goodyear crosswind landing gear with main-wheel tyres size 6·50-8, pressure 1·93 bars (28 lb/sq in).

Goodyear 254 mm (10 in) tailwheel tyre, pressure 2·75 bars (40 lb/sq in). Goodyear hydraulic disc brakes. Edo 582-3430 floats, Edo Flying Dolphin amphibious floats or AirGlas Model LW3600 glassfibre wheel-skis optional.

LANDING GEAR (HT-295): Non-retractable tricycle type. Cantilever spring steel main gear, with wheels and tyres size 8·00-6, pressure 2·41 bars (35 lb/sq in). Nosewheel carried on oleo-pneumatic shock-strut, with wheel and tyre size 6·00-6, pressure 2·90 bars (42 lb/sq in).

POWER PLANT: One 220 kW (295 hp) Lycoming GO-480-G1A6 flat-six geared engine, driving a Hartzell three-blade constant-speed propeller. Rajay turbocharger system optional. Two 113·7 litre (30 US gallon) bladder-type fuel tanks in wings. Two further 113·7 litre (30 US gallon) tanks may be fitted to give total fuel capacity of 455 litres (120 US gallons). Oil capacity 11·4 litres (3 US gallons).

ACCOMMODATION: Cabin seats six in three pairs. Front and centre pair of seats individually adjustable. Rear pair comprises double sling seat. FAA standard instrument panel. Special over-strength cabin and seats, stressed to 15g and all fitted with safety harness, are based on Flight Safety Foundation recommendations. Two large doors, by pilot's seat on port side and opposite centre row of seats on starboard side. Baggage compartment aft of rear seats. Second- and third-row seats are removable for carrying over 454 kg (1,000 lb) of freight.

ELECTRONICS AND EQUIPMENT: Radio and blind-flying instrumentation to customer's requirements.

DIMENSIONS, EXTERNAL:

Wing span	11·89 m (39 ft 0 in)
Wing chord (constant)	1·83 m (6 ft 0 in)
Wing aspect ratio	6·58
Length overall	9·45 m (31 ft 0 in)
Height overall:	
H-295	2·69 m (8 ft 10 in)
HT-295	4·52 m (14 ft 10 in)
Tailplane span	4·72 m (15 ft 6 in)
Wheel track	2·74 m (9 ft 0 in)
Wheelbase	7·14 m (23 ft 5 in)
Propeller diameter	2·44 m (8 ft 0 in)
Cabin door (fwd, port):	
Height	1·04 m (3 ft 5 in)
Width	0·85 m (2 ft 9½ in)
Height to sill	0·91 m (3 ft 0 in)

Helio U-10D, military long-range version of the Super Courier

Cabin door (stbd, rear):	
Height	0·98 m (3 ft 2½ in)
Width	0·85 m (2 ft 9½ in)
Height to sill	0·67 m (2 ft 2½ in)
DIMENSIONS, INTERNAL:	
Cabin: Length	3·05 m (10 ft 0 in)
Max width	1·14 m (3 ft 9 in)
Max height	1·22 m (4 ft 0 in)
Floor area	2·79 m² (30 sq ft)
Volume	3·96 m³ (140 cu ft)
Baggage space	0·42 m³ (15 cu ft)
AREAS:	
Wings, gross	21·46 m² (231 sq ft)
Ailerons (total)	1·92 m² (20·7 sq ft)
Flaps (total)	3·54 m² (38·1 sq ft)
Leading-edge slats (total)	2·91 m² (31·3 sq ft)
Spoilers (total)	0·16 m² (1·68 sq ft)
Fin	1·41 m² (15·2 sq ft)
Rudder	0·99 m² (10·6 sq ft)
Tailplane	3·48 m² (37·5 sq ft)
WEIGHTS AND LOADINGS:	
Weight empty:	
H-295	943 kg (2,080 lb)
HT-295	970 kg (2,140 lb)

Max T-O and landing weight	1,542 kg (3,400 lb)
Max wing loading	71·8 kg/m² (14·7 lb/sq ft)
Max power loading	7·01 kg/kW (11·5 lb/hp)
PERFORMANCE (at max T-O weight):	
Never-exceed speed	174 knots (322 km/h; 200 mph)
Max level speed at S/L	
	145 knots (269 km/h; 167 mph)
Max cruising speed (75% power) at 2,600 m (8,500 ft)	143 knots (265 km/h; 165 mph)
Econ cruising speed (60% power)	
	130 knots (241 km/h; 150 mph)
Min flying speed, power on	
	26 knots (48 km/h; 30 mph)
Max rate of climb at S/L	350 m (1,150 ft)/min
Service ceiling	6,250 m (20,500 ft)
T-O run	102 m (335 ft)
T-O to 15 m (50 ft)	186 m (610 ft)
Landing from 15 m (50 ft)	158 m (520 ft)
Landing run	82 m (270 ft)
Range with standard tanks	
	573 nm (1,062 km; 660 miles)
Range with optional tanks	
	1,198 nm (2,220 km; 1,380 miles)
	(1976–77)

The Hiller H-23D Raven Helicopter for the U.S. Army.

HILLER MODEL UH-12
US Army designation: OH-23 Raven
Canadian military designation: CH-112 Nomad

A total of about 2,000 helicopters of this series have been built in various versions, including the military OH-23A, B, C, D, F and G, naval HTE-1 and HTE-2 and civil Models 360, 12B, 12C, 12E and E4. The OH-23D (483 built), now being replaced by the OH-23G, is used in a variety of rôles, including the primary training of all US Army rotorcraft pilots.

H-23A. An air ambulance and field evacuation helicopter for the U.S. Army Ground Forces. Can carry two stretcher patients in completely enclosed externally-carried stretchers, or litters, which are accessible from the cabin.

H-23B. Similar to H-23A but greater power (200 h.p.), greater gross weight, skid landing-gear, simplified stretcher installation and other miscellaneous improvements.

H-23C. Delivered from Autumn 1955.

H-23D. Fitted with 250 h.p. Lycoming engine, new transmission system designed for 1,000 hours' service between overhauls and capable of absorbing up to 300 h.p. and a new tail rotor assembly. First prototype flew on April 3, 1956, and first deliveries were made in December, 1957. Present contracts for a total of 224 aircraft extend production well into 1960.

HTE-1. Two-seat trainer for the U.S. Navy. Special Navy equipment includes a floor control column and other special appointments.

HTE-2. Development of HTE-1 trainer. Greater power (200 h.p.), four-wheel landing-gear, improved vision and other detail changes.

The description which follows refers to the standard commercial Model 360.

OH-23F. Military version of E4 with high-compression pistons as standard equipment, giving the equivalent of 340 hp from the 305 hp

Lycoming VO-540 engine. Twenty-two, ordered in January, 1962, are being used by the US Army's 937th Engineer Company to transport personnel engaged in the Inter-American Geodetic Survey in Central and South America. Delivery of these was completed in mid-1962.

OH-23G. Military counterpart of the 12E. First deliveries made in 1963, when US Army modified its last order for the OH-23D to cover delivery of OH-23G's instead of D's towards the end of the production run. Further US Army contract for 137 G's announced in May 1963, followed by another for 210 aircraft in December 1963, extending production to the Autumn of 1965. Twenty-one used by Royal Navy for pilot training at RNAS Culdrose.

On October 29, 1963, an OH-23G piloted by Capt B. G. Leach, US Army, set up six international helicopter speed records. In class E-1-b, it achieved 121·71 mph (195·872 kmh) over a 100 km closed circuit, 123·59 mph (198·898 kmh) over a 15/25 km course and 123·695 mph (199·067 kmh) over a 3 km course. In class E-1-c, it achieved 119·75 mph (192·718 kmh), 123·76 mph (199·178 kmh) and 123·455 mph (198·682 kmh) respectively over the same distances.

CH-112 Nomad. Canadian designation for OH-23G, which serves as a light reconnaissance helicopter with the Canadian Army in Germany and as a training aircraft at the Canadian Joint Air Training Centre, Rivers, Manitoba.

The following details apply specifically to the Hiller 12E, but are generally applicable to the OH-23G and Model E4, except for differences noted above.

TYPE: Three-seat utility helicopter.

ROTOR SYSTEM: Two-blade main rotor universally mounted on power shaft with small servo rotor, the latter connected directly through universally-mounted transfer bearing and simple linkage with pilot's cyclic control stick. Movement of control stick introduces to the servo rotor paddles positive or negative pitch changes, and aerodynamic forces thus developed tilt the rotor head and produce cyclic pitch changes to the rotor blades. Expanded main rotor and control rotor tilt stops (9°-12° rotor hub). Each main rotor blade has a steel main forward spar and leading-edge skin, extrusion and aluminium trailing-edge skin, extrusion and channels. Blades are individually interchangeable and are bolted to forks which, in turn, are retained at the rotor head by tension-torsion bars. Blades do not fold. Rotor brake available as optional extra. Anti-torque rotor at rear end of fuselage with two aluminium alloy monocoque blades.

ROTOR DRIVE: Mechanical drive through two-stage planetary main transmission. Bevel gear drive to auxiliaries. Also tail rotor gearbox and fan gearbox. Main rotor/engine rpm ratio 1 : 8·64. Tail rotor/engine rpm ratio 1 : 1·45.

FUSELAGE: Aluminium alloy fully-stressed semi-monocoque platform structure supports the non-stressed cabin enclosure, seats and controls, engine mounting and landing gear. Tail-boom of beaded sheet metal with no internal stiffeners.

TAIL UNIT: Single (12E) or twin (E4) horizontal stabiliser, with steel-tube spar, and aluminium alloy ribs and skin. Incidence adjustable on ground.

LANDING GEAR: Wide-track skids carried on spring steel cross-members. Two small wheels can be fitted at rear to facilitate ground handling. Alternative float landing-gear available. Latest "zip-on" pontoons are attached above the normal skids, avoiding the necessity of removing the skids and allowing safe running landings on ground.

POWER PLANT: One 305 hp Lycoming VO-540-C2B six-cylinder horizontally-opposed fan-cooled engine, with dual carburettors. Engine mounted with main shaft vertical on steel-tube quadrapod attached to fuselage engine deck. Single bladder fuel tank, capacity 46 US gallons (174 litres), in fuselage below engine deck. Can be fitted with two 20 US gallon (76 litre) auxiliary tanks, on each side of engine. Oil capacity 3·3 US gallons (12·5 litres).

ACCOMMODATION: Three persons side-by-side. Dual controls optional, comprising floor-type cyclic-pitch control columns, with collective-pitch levers on left side of seats. Electric trim switch on both centre and left-hand cyclic columns, and throttle friction adjustment on collective-pitch levers. Forward-hinged door on each side. Large map storage pocket behind passenger seat. Baggage compartment directly behind engine, capacity 125 lb (57 kg).

ELECTRONICS AND EQUIPMENT: Optional radio installations include King KY 90 transceiver with 90 channels. Civil versions can be adapted easily for agricultural operations, using dust, spray or aerosol equipment. Other optional equipment includes quick-attach litters, hydraulic personnel hoist, cargo racks, air-to-ground broadcast loud-speaker and siren, quick-release external net and load sling for freight transport.

DIMENSIONS, EXTERNAL (12E and E4):

Diameter of main rotor	35 ft 5 in (10·80 m)
Diameter of tail rotor	5 ft 6 in (1·68 m)
Distance between rotor centres	20 ft 3 in (6·17 m)
Length overall, rotors fore and aft	40 ft 8·9 in (12·46 m)
Length of fuselage: 12E	28 ft 6 in (8·69 m)
E4	29 ft 6 in (8·99 m)
Height to top of rotor hub	9 ft 3¼ in (2·83 m)
Skid track	7 ft 6 in (2·29 m)
Cabin doors (each):	
Height: 12E	3 ft 8½ in (1·13 m)
E4	3 ft 7 in (1·09 m)
Max width: 12E	2 ft 6 in (0·76 m)
E4	2 ft 5 in (0·74 m)
Height to sill	1 ft 11 in (0·58 m)

DIMENSIONS, INTERNAL (12E and E4):

Cabin: Length: 12E	5 ft 0 in (1·52 m)
E4	6 ft 11 in (2·11 m)
Max width	4 ft 11 in (1·50 m)
Max height	4 ft 5 in (1·35 m)
Floor area: 12E	12·5 sq ft (1·16 m²)
E4	19·2 sq ft (1·78 m²)

AREAS (12E and E4):

Main rotor blade (each)	16·3 sq ft (1·51 m²)
Tail rotor blade (each)	1 01 sq ft (0·094 m²)
Main rotor disc	990 sq ft (91·97 m²)
Tail rotor disc	27·7 sq ft (2·57 m²)
Horizontal stabiliser: 12E 10·04 sq ft (0·93 m²)	

WEIGHTS AND LOADINGS (12E and E4):

Weight empty: 12E	1,759 lb (798 kg)
E4	1,813 lb (822 kg)
Max normal T-O weight	2,800 lb (1,270 kg)
Max overload T-O weight (FAR 133)	3,100 lb (1,405 kg)
Max normal disc loading	2·83 lb/sq ft (13·81 kg/m²)
Max normal power loading	9·2 lb/hp (4·17 kg/hp)

PERFORMANCE (12E and E4 at max T-O weight):

Max level speed at S/L	96 mph (154 kmh)
Max cruising speed at S/L	90 mph (145 kmh)
Max rate of climb at S/L	1,290 ft (393 m) min
Vertical rate of climb at S/L 740 ft (225 m) min	
Service ceiling	15,200 ft (4,630 m)
Service ceiling, high-compression pistons:	
12E	16,000 ft (4,875m)
E4	21,200 ft (6,460 m)
Hovering ceiling in ground effect	9,500 ft (2,900 m)
Hovering ceiling in ground effect, high-compression pistons	10,800 ft (3,300 m)
Hovering ceiling out of ground effect	5,800 ft (1,770 m)
Hovering ceiling out of ground effect, high-compression pistons	7,200 ft (2,200 m)
Min size of landing area required approx 45 ft × 45 ft (14 m × 14 m)	
Range with auxiliary tanks at AUW of 2,240 lb (1,015 kg)	500 miles (805 km)
Range with auxiliary tanks at AUW of 2,800 lb (1,270 kg)	437 miles (703 km)
	(1966–67)

THE HOWARD NIGHTINGALE.

U.S. Navy designations: GH-1, GH-2, GH-3 and NH-1.

TYPE.—Four-seat Personnel Transport (GH-1) Ambulance (GH-2 and GH-3) or Instrument Trainer (NH-1).

WINGS.—High-wing braced monoplane. Wings attached direct to upper fuselage longerons and braced to lower longerons by Vee struts. Wing structure consists of two rectangular spruce spars, built-up wooden ribs, and a covering of mahogany plywood, and finally fabric. Ailerons on the outer portions of the wings and landing-flaps between the ailerons and the fuselage. The flaps are electrically-operated and may be stopped in any position between neutral and fully deflected.

FUSELAGE.—Rectangular welded chrome-molybdenum steel-tube structure, with the cabin covered with aluminium sheet and the remainder with fabric over a light aluminium and wood fairing structure. The top and sides of the fuselage are flat and underneath is semi-circular.

TAIL UNIT.—Monoplane type. Wire-braced tail-plane and fin. Welded steel-tube framework, covered with fabric. Adjustable tail-plane.

LANDING GEAR.—Divided type. Consists of two fixed tripods of welded chrome-molybdenum round and streamline steel-tube, with the front and drag struts enclosed in streamline fairing. Front struts incorporate oleo shock-absorbers and spring dampers. Hydraulic wheel-brakes. Steerable or swivelling tail-wheel, with spring-damped oleo shock-absorber.

POWER PLANT.—One 450 h.p. Pratt & Whitney R-985-AN-12 Wasp-Junior radial air-cooled engine. Hamilton-Standard Hydromatic constant-speed airscrew. NACA cowling. Fuel tanks below floor of cabin. Normal fuel capacity 152 U.S. gallons.

ACCOMMODATION.—The cabin arrangement in NH-1 is two pairs of two individual seats. Dual controls to front seat with third set of controls and instruments provided for left rear seat for instrument training. Arrangement for GH-2 is two front seats, two standard U.S. Navy litters or stretchers one above the other on left side of cabin and third seat on right side. Stretchers are inserted into and removed from cabin through specially enlarged baggage door on right side. Main cabin door, also on right side, is quickly detachable in flight. Stretchers can be replaced by fourth seat for conversion to personnel transport. Baggage compartment behind cabin.

DIMENSIONS.—Span 38 ft. (11.6 m.), Length 26 ft. (7.9 m.), Height 8 ft. 4 in. (2.5 m.), Wing area 210 sq. ft. (19.5 sq. m.).

WEIGHTS AND LOADINGS.—Weight empty 3,050 lbs. (1,385 kg.), Weight loaded 4,500 lbs. (2,040 kg.), Wing loading 21.4 lbs./sq. ft. (104.4 kg./sq. m.), Power loading 11.3 lbs./h.p. (5.1 kg./h.p.).

The Howard GH-2 Light Personnel Transport (Pratt & Whitney R-985-AN12 engine).

PERFORMANCE.—Speed at sea level 165 m.p.h. (265 km.h.), Maximum speed 175 m.p.h. (282 km.h.) at 6,100 ft. (1,860 m.), Cruising speed 154 m.p.h. (248 km.h.) at 15,000 ft. (4,880 m.), Service ceiling 20,000 ft. (6,100 m.), Cruising range at 6,100 ft. (1,860 m.) 700 miles (1,130 km.) for NH-1 or 875 miles (1,410 km.) for GH-2.

The description above applies to the service adaptations of the DGA-16 which have been supplied to the U.S. Navy.

The U.S. Army also acquired a number of Howard cabin monoplanes of various models from private sources for use as utility or light personnel transports. These were given designations in the UC-70 Series as follow :—

UC-70A Model DGA-12 (Jacobs L-6).
UC-70B Model DGA-15J (Jacobs L-6MB).
UC-70C Model DGA-8 (Wright R-760-E2).
UC-70D Model DGA-9 (Jacobs L-5).

(1945–46)

HUGHES MODEL 77

US Army designation: AH-64

The Model 77 was designed by Hughes to meet the US Army's requirement for an Advanced Attack Helicopter (AAH) capable of undertaking a full day/night/adverse weather anti-armour mission, and of fighting, surviving and 'living with' troops in a front-line environment. Two flight test prototypes were built, for competitive evaluation against Bell's YAH-63, and these made their initial flights on 30 September and 22 November 1975. A ground test vehicle was also completed. The Hughes contract covered, in addition, development of the XM-230 chain gun for installation in the Model 77 prototypes, which have the US Army designation YAH-64.

Selection of the YAH-64 was announced on 10 December 1976. This was followed by Phase 2 of the programme, which involved fitting the prototypes with advanced avionics, electro-optical equipment and weapon fire control systems, for further evaluation; continued development of the airframe; and the manufacture of three more aircraft.

These are identified as AVO.1 to AVO.3. In June 1979 the first was being used by the US Army for continuing evaluation. AVO.3 was transferred to the Army's Yuma Proving Ground, Arizona, on 4 June, equipped with the Northrop TADS/PNVS. AVO.2, with the Martin Marietta TADS/PNVS, followed at the end of the same month. Company R & D with these two aircraft was

expected to continue until the end of the year, with Army testing to follow in 1980 and to be completed in August 1981.

Three additional development aircraft, designated AVO.4 to AVO.6, were flying by the Spring of 1980, described as total systems aircraft.

Teledyne Ryan is responsible for the YAH-64 fuselage, wings, engine nacelles, avionics bays, canopy and tail unit. Martin Marietta and Northrop are developing competitive equipment to fulfil the TADS (Target Acquisition and Designation Sight) and PNVS (Pilot's Night Vision Sensor) tasks in the production AH-64. The former system includes direct-view optics, forward-looking infra-red, TV, laser designator/rangefinder, and a laser tracker. The

PNVS consists of an advanced FLIR installation.

In early 1978 the two Phase 2 helicopters began a new series of tests to evaluate planned design modifications known as Mod 1. These included swept tips on the main rotor blades; a Hughes-developed 'Black Hole' IR suppressor for each engine exhaust; a redesigned T tail; and a 76 mm (3 in) increase in tail rotor diameter. A Mod 2 programme, started later in that year, introduced final airframe improvements, as well as all mission equipment including armament, fire control and nav/com systems. These included cockpit windows of modified shape, with single-curvature side panels; and extending aft, to a point below the wing leading-edges, the fuselage side fairings over the forward avionics bay. The two prototype helicopters then completed a programme to confirm the airworthiness of the Mod 2 airframe changes and initial tests of the weapon system, including the Hellfire missile, 2·75 in rocket, 30 mm chain gun, and the fire control system. By mid-June 1979 five ballistic Hellfire missiles had been fired, without guidance system. The first fully-guided launch of a Hellfire was made successfully on 18 September 1979 at the Yuma, Arizona, proving grounds. Target for the laser-guided system was designated from the ground, and a direct hit was made. Northrop TADS/PNVS was installed and functional in the launch YAH-64, but was not used. Approximately one month later the first test firing was made with the Northrop TADS/PNVS providing illumination of the target. Other systems which were fully integrated and flight tested during 1979 included the Litton LR-80 HARS, and the Singer-Kearfott Doppler navigation system.

Initial Operational Capability was gained in July 1986. Deliveries between 1984 and 1990 had covered 539 aircraft.

The following description applies to the YAH-64 prototypes, except where indicated:

TYPE: Prototype armed helicopter.

ROTOR SYSTEM: Four-blade fully-articulated main rotor and four-blade tail rotor, with blades manufactured by Tool Research and Engineering Corpn (Advanced Structures Division). Main rotor blades are of high-camber aerofoil section and broad chord. Each blade has five stainless steel spars lined with structural glassfibre tubes, a laminated stainless steel skin and a composite aft section, bonded together. Blades are attached to hub by a laminated strap retention system similar to that of the OH-6A, and are fitted with elastomeric lead/lag dampers and offset flapping hinges. Four-blade tail rotor comprises two sets of two blades, mounted on port side of pylon/fin support structure at optimum quiet setting of approx 60°/120° to each other. Rotor mast similar to that of OH-6A, with driveshaft turning within a hollow, fixed outer shaft. Entire system capable of flight in negative g conditions.

ROTOR DRIVE: Transmission to main rotor via Litton (Precision Gear Division) engine nose gearboxes, and to tail rotor via Aircraft Gear Corpn grease-lubricated intermediate and tail rotor gearboxes, with Bendix driveshafts and couplings. Garrett-AiResearch cooling fan for tail rotor gearbox. Redundant flight control system for both rotors. Selected dynamic components constructed of 70/49 aluminium and electro-slag remelt (ESR) steel; critical parts of transmission (gears, bearings) have ESR collars for protection against hits by 12·7 mm or 23 mm ammunition. Rotor/engine rpm ratios approx 66·7 for main rotor, approx 14·3 for tail rotor.

WINGS: Cantilever mid-wing monoplane, of low aspect ratio, aft of cockpit. Trailing-edge flaps deploy automatically as function of control attitude and airspeed (max deflection 20°), and can be deflected 45° upward to offload wings in an emergency autorotative landing. Wings are removable, and attach to sides of cabin for transport and storage. Two hardpoints beneath each wing for the carriage of mixed ordnance.

FUSELAGE: Conventional semi-monocoque aluminium structure, built by Teledyne Ryan Aeronautical. Designed to survive hits by 12·7 mm and 23 mm ammunition.

TAIL UNIT: Hinged and foldable pylon structure with tail rotor mounted on port side. Low-mounted all-flying tailplane (replacing earlier fixed T tail).

LANDING GEAR: Menasco tailwheel type, with single wheel on each unit. Main legs fold rearward to reduce overall height for storage and transportation. Fully-castoring, self-centering tailwheel. Main-wheel tyres size 22 × 8; tailwheel tyre size 13 × 5. Hydraulic brakes.

POWER PLANT: Two 1,145 kW (1,536 shp) General Electric T700-GE-700 turboshaft engines, derated for normal operations to provide reserve power for combat emergencies. Engines mounted one on each side of fuselage, above wings. Two crashproof fuel cells, combined capacity 1,366 litres (361 US gallons).

Hughes YAH-64 armed helicopter prototype equipped with Northrop TADS/PNVS

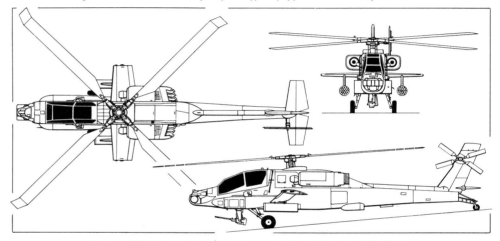

Hughes AH-64 tandem two-seat advanced attack helicopter *(Pilot Press)*

ACCOMMODATION: Crew of two in tandem, co-pilot/gunner in front and pilot aft on 483 mm (19 in) elevated seat. Large, shaped transparent cockpit enclosure for optimum field of view. Lightweight boron armour shields in cockpit floor and sides. Cockpits separated by armour plating and a transparent plastics blast shield offering protection against 23 mm high-explosive and armour-piercing rounds.

SYSTEMS AND EQUIPMENT: Large avionics bay adjacent to gunner's position, in lower fuselage. Parker-Bertea hydraulic control system, with hydraulic actuators ballistic tolerant to direct 12·7 mm hits. In the event of hydraulic control system failure, the system adjusts to secondary fly-by-wire control. Bendix electrical power system, with two fully-redundant engine-driven generators and standby DC battery. Sperry Flight Systems automatic stabilisation equipment. Litton LR-80 strapdown heading and attitude reference system (HARS). Singer-Kearfott lightweight Doppler navigation system. Garrett-AiResearch totally integrated pneumatic system includes a shaft-driven compressor, air turbine starters, pneumatic valves, temperature control unit and environmental control unit. Garrett-AiResearch also supplies the GTP 36-55(C) APU. Sperry Flight Systems all-raster symbol generator is under development to process TV data from IR and other sensors, superimpose symbology and distribute the combination to CRT and helmet-mounted displays in the aircraft. BITE fault detection/location system. Hughes Black Hole IR suppression system, with no moving parts, to protect the aircraft from heat-seeking missiles. This eliminates an engine bay cooling fan, by operating from engine exhaust gas through ejector nozzles to lower the gas plume and metal temperatures.

ARMAMENT AND OPERATIONAL EQUIPMENT: Flexible armament consists of a Hughes-developed XM230E1 30 mm chain gun, mounted in an underfuselage turret between the main-wheel legs, and having a normal rate of fire of 800 rds/min of Honeywell TP, HE and HEDP ammunition. Ammunition max load is 1,200 rds, and is interoperable with NATO Aden/DEFA rounds. Turret designed to collapse into fuselage in the event of a crash-landing. Four underwing hardpoints, on which can be carried up to sixteen Hellfire anti-tank missiles; or up to seventy-six 2·75 in folding-fin rockets in their launchers; or a combination of Hellfire missiles and rockets. CPG stabilised sight in forward fuselage, ahead of cockpit, incorporates day and night (FLIR: forward-looking infra-red) sighting equipment, laser ranger and target designator, and laser tracker equipment. Co-pilot/gunner has primary responsibility for firing guns and missiles, but pilot can override his controls to fire gun or launch missiles. Pilot's night vision sensor (PNVS) in extreme tip of nose. Integrated Helmet And Display Sighting System (IHADSS) by Honeywell Avionics Division, used by both crew members, will enhance speed and flexibility of target acquisition. Forward bay includes avionics for stabilised sight, missiles and fire control computer provided by Teledyne Systems Inc.

DIMENSIONS, EXTERNAL:

Diameter of main rotor	14·63 m (48 ft 0 in)
Diameter of tail rotor	2·54 m (8 ft 4 in)
Main rotor blade chord	0·53 m (1 ft 9 in)
Length of fuselage	15·06 m (49 ft 5 in)
Length overall, rotors turning	17·60 m (57 ft 9 in)
Wing span	4·98 m (16 ft 4 in)
Height to top of rotor hub	3·83 m (12 ft 6⅞ in)
Tailplane span	3·15 m (10 ft 4 in)
Wheel track	2·03 m (6 ft 8 in)

AREA:

Main rotor disc	168·06 m² (1,809 sq ft)

WEIGHTS:
Weight empty	4,657 kg (10,268 lb)
Primary mission gross weight	6,271 kg (13,825 lb)
Structural design gross weight	6,650 kg (14,660 lb)
Max T-O weight	8,006 kg (17,650 lb)

PERFORMANCE (at 6,316 kg; 13,925 lb AUW, ISA except where indicated):
Never-exceed speed	204 knots (378 km/h; 235 mph)
Max level speed	167 knots (309 km/h; 192 mph)
Max cruising speed	158 knots (293 km/h; 182 mph)

Max vertical rate of climb at S/L	878 m (2,880 ft)/min
Max vertical rate of climb at 1,220 m (4,000 ft) at 35°C	259 m (850 ft)/min
Service ceiling	6,250 m (20,500 ft)
Service ceiling, one engine out	3,505 m (11,500 ft)
Hovering ceiling IGE	4,633 m (15,200 ft)
Hovering ceiling OGE	3,780 m (12,400 ft)

Max range, internal fuel 330 nm (611 km; 380 miles)	
Ferry range, max internal and external fuel, still air	974 nm (1,804 km; 1,121 miles)
Endurance at 1,220 m (4,000 ft) at 35°C	1 h 50 min
Max endurance, internal fuel	3 h 23 min
	(1980–81)

Hughes TH-55A (modified) with Allison Model 250-C18 turboshaft engine, similar to the standard engine of the Army OH-6A *(Henry Artof)*

HUGHES MODEL 300
US Army designation: TH-55A Osage

Design and development of the original Hughes Model 269 two-seat light helicopter began in September 1965 and the first of two prototypes was flown 13 months later.

The design was then re-engineered for production with the emphasis on simplicity and ease of maintenance. The resulting Model 269A offered an overall life of over 1,000 hours for all major components.

Five Model 269A pre-production helicopters were purchased by the US Army under the designation YHO-2HU, and completed a highly successful evaluation programme in the command and observation roles.

The Model 269A was then put into production and deliveries began in October 1961.

TH-55A. The Hughes 269A was selected by the US Army as a light helicopter primary trainer in mid-1964, under the designation TH-55A. A total of 792 were eventually delivered, production being completed by the end of March 1969.

It was reported in March 1973 that Hughes had been evaluating a TH-55A powered by a 138 kW (185 hp) Wankel RC 2-60 rotating-piston engine. Another has been fitted experimentally with an Allison 250-C18 turboshaft, similar to the standard engine of the US Army's OH-6As

TYPE: One-, two- or three-seat light helicopter.

ROTOR SYSTEM (all models): Fully-articulated metal three-blade main rotor. Blades are of bonded construction, with constant-section extruded aluminium spar, wraparound skin and a trailing-edge section. Blade section NACA 0015. Two-blade teetering tail rotor, each blade comprising a steel tube spar with glassfibre skin. Blades do not fold. No rotor brake.

ROTOR DRIVE: Vee-belt drive system eliminates need for conventional clutch. Metal-coated and hard-anodised sheaves. Spiral bevel angular drive-shaft. Tail rotor shaft-driven directly from belt-drive. Main rotor/engine rpm ratio 1 : 6.

FUSELAGE: Welded steel tube structure, with aluminium and Plexiglas cabin and one-piece aluminium tube tail-boom.

TAIL UNIT: Horizontal and vertical fixed stabilisers made up of aluminium ribs and skin.

LANDING GEAR: Skids carried on Hughes oleo-pneumatic shock-absorbers. Two cast magnesium ground handling wheels with 0·25 m (10 in) balloon tyres, pressure 4·14-5·17 bars (60-75 lb/sq in). Model 300 is available on floats of polyurethane coated nylon fabric, 4·70 m (15 ft 5 in) long and with total installed weight of 27·2 kg (60 lb).

POWER PLANT: One 134 kW (180 hp) Lycoming HIO-360-A1A (HIO-360-B1A in TH-55A) flat-four engine, mounted horizontally below seats. Aluminium fuel tank, capacity 103·5 litres (30 US gallons), mounted externally aft of cockpit. Provision for aluminium auxiliary fuel tank, capacity 72 litres (19 US gallons), mounted opposite standard tank. Oil capacity 7·5 litres (2 US gallons).

ACCOMMODATION: Two seats (TH-55A) or three seats (Model 300) side by side in Plexiglas-enclosed cabin. Door on each side. Dual controls optional. Baggage capacity 45 kg (100 lb). Exhaust muff or gasoline-heating and ventilation kits available.

ELECTRONICS AND EQUIPMENT (Model 300): Optional equipment includes King KY 90 radio, welded aluminium Stokes litter kit, cargo rack, external load sling of 272 kg (600 lb) capacity.

ELECTRONICS AND EQUIPMENT (TH-55A): Provision for ARC-524M VHF radio.

DIMENSIONS, EXTERNAL:
Diameter of main rotor	7·71 m (25 ft 3½ in)
Main rotor blade chord	0·173 m (6·83 in)
Diameter of tail rotor	1·17 m (3 ft 10 in)
Distance between rotor centres	4·29 m (14 ft 1 in)
Length overall	8·80 m (28 ft 10¾ in)
Length of fuselage	6·80 m (21 ft 11¾ in)
Height overall	2·50 m (8 ft 2¾ in)
Skid track	2·00 m (6 ft 6½ in)
Cabin doors (each):	
Height	1·12 m (3 ft 8 in)
Width	0·81 m (2 ft 8 in)
Height to sill	0·89 m (2 ft 11 in)

DIMENSIONS, INTERNAL:
Cabin: Length	1·40 m (4 ft 7 in)
Max width	1·30 m (4 ft 3 in)
Max height	1·32 m (4 ft 4 in)
Floor area	1·21 m² (13·0 sq ft)

AREAS:
Main rotor blades (each)	0·66 m² (7·1 sq ft)
Tail rotor blades (each)	0·07 m² (0·77 sq ft)
Main rotor disc	46·73 m² (503 sq ft)
Tail rotor disc	0·81 m² (8·70 sq ft)
Fin	0·11 m² (1·22 sq ft)
Horizontal stabiliser	0·32 m² (3·44 sq ft)

WEIGHTS AND LOADINGS:
Weight empty:	
300	434 kg (958 lb)
TH-55A	457 kg (1,008 lb)
Max certificated T-O and landing weight:	
300, TH-55A	757 kg (1,670 lb)
Max recommended weight (restricted operation):	
300, TH-55A	839 kg (1,850 lb)
Max disc loading (at certificated AUW):	
300, TH-55A	16·1 kg/m² (3·3 lb/sq ft)
Max power loading (at certificated AUW):	
300, TH-55A	5·65 kg/kW (9·3 lb/hp)

PERFORMANCE (at max certificated T-O weight):
Never-exceed speed:	
300	75·5 knots (140 km/h; 87 mph)
TH-55A	75 knots (138 km/h; 86 mph)
Max level speed at S/L:	
300	75·5 knots (140 km/h; 87 mph)
TH-55A	75 knots (138 km/h; 86 mph)
Max cruising speed:	
300	69 knots (129 km/h; 80 mph)
TH-55A	65 knots (121 km/h; 75 mph)
Econ cruising speed:	
300, TH-55A	57 knots (106 km/h; 66 mph)
Max water contact speed (on floats)	17 knots (32 km/h; 20 mph)
Max water taxying speed (on floats)	9 knots (16 km/h; 10 mph)
Max rate of climb at S/L:	
300	347 m (1,140 ft)/min
TH-55A (mission weight)	347 m (1,140 ft)/min
Service ceiling:	
300	3,960 m (13,000 ft)
TH-55A (mission weight)	3,625 m (11,900 ft)
Hovering ceiling in ground effect:	
300	2,350 m (7,700 ft)
TH-55A	1,675 m (5,500 ft)
Hovering ceiling out of ground effect:	
300	1,770 m (5,800 ft)
TH-55A	1,145 m (3,750 ft)
Range with max fuel, no reserves:	
300	260 nm (480 km; 300 miles)
TH-55A	177 nm (328 km; 204 miles)
Endurance with max fuel:	
300	3 hr 30 min
TH-55A	2 hr 35 min
	(1976–77)

HUGHES OH-6
US Army designation: OH-6A (formerly HO-6) Cayuse

This aircraft was chosen for development following a US Army design competition for a light observation helicopter in 1961. Five prototypes were ordered for evaluation in competition with the Bell OH-4A and Hiller OH-5A, and the first of these flew on 27 February 1963.

On 26 May 1965 it was announced that the OH-6A had been chosen, as a result of the evaluation, and an initial order for 714 was placed by the US Army; this was increased by subsequent orders to a total of 1,434, all of which were delivered by August 1970.

In March and April 1966, US Army and civilian pilots set up 23 international records in OH-6A helicopters. Among Class E1 (covering all classes of helicopters) records established was one for a distance of 1,922 nm (3,561·55 km; 2,213 miles) in a straight line (California to Florida) nonstop with one pilot.

On 8 April 1971 Hughes announced the existence of a modified OH-6A light observation helicopter known as 'The Quiet One'. Product of a research project funded by the Department of Defense Advanced Research Projects

Agency, Hughes claims that it is the world's quietest helicopter.

Modifications include the installation of a five-blade main rotor, four-blade tail rotor and engine exhaust muffler; sound blanketing of the complete power plant assembly, including engine air intake; and reshaping of the tips of the main rotor blades. The modified aircraft can operate with engine and rotor speeds reduced to 67 per cent of normal in-flight levels and is able to offer a 272 kg (600 lb) increase in payload and 20 knot (37 km/h; 23 mph) increase in airspeed.

A similar aircraft, designated **OH-6C** and powered by a 298 kW (400 shp) Allison 250-C20 turboshaft engine, achieved a speed of 173 knots (322 km/h; 200 mph) during tests at Edwards AFB.

It is reported that an improved version of the OH-6C, with a four-blade tail rotor and max T-O weight of 1,315 kg (2,900 lb), has been offered to the US Army. Designated **OH-6D**, this has been proposed to meet the Army's requirements for an Advanced Scout Helicopter (ASH).

Full-scale production of the Hughes 500 commercial and 500M international military versions of the OH-6A

(which are described separately) began in November 1968.

TYPE: Turbine-powered light observation helicopter.

ROTOR SYSTEM: Four-blade fully-articulated main rotor, with blades attached to laminated strap retention system by means of folding quick-disconnect pins. Each blade consists of an extruded aluminium spar hot-bonded to one-piece wraparound aluminium skin. Trim tab outboard on each blade. Main rotor blades can be folded. Two-blade tail rotor, each blade comprising a swaged steel tube spar and glassfibre skin covering. No rotor brake.

ROTOR DRIVE: Three sets of bevel gears, three drive-shafts and one overrunning clutch. Main rotor/engine rpm ratio 1 : 12·806. Tail rotor/engine rpm ratio 1 : 1·987.

FUSELAGE: Aluminium semi-monocoque structure of pod and boom type. Clamshell doors at rear of pod give access to engine and accessories.

TAIL UNIT: Fixed fin, horizontal stabiliser and ventral fin.

LANDING GEAR: Tubular skids carried on Hughes single-acting shock-absorbers.

POWER PLANT: One 236·5 kW (317 shp) Allison T63-A-5A turboshaft engine, derated to 188·3 kW (252·5 shp) for take-off and 160 kW (214·5 shp) max continuous rating. Two 50% self-sealing bladder fuel tanks under rear cabin floor, capacity 232 litres (61·5 US gallons). Refuelling point aft of cargo door on starboard side. Oil capacity 4·75 litres (1·25 US gallons).

ACCOMMODATION: Crew of two side by side in front of cabin. Two seats in rear cargo compartment can be folded to make room for four fully-equipped soldiers, seated on floor. Crew door and cargo compartment door on each side. Fourteen cargo tie-down points.

ELECTRONICS AND EQUIPMENT: Government-furnished electronics. Sylvania SLAE electronics package installed in 1969/70 production aircraft. ARC-114 VHF-FM and ARC-116 UHF radios, ARN-89 ADF, ASN-43 gyro compass, ID 1351 bearing-heading indicator and ARC-6533 intercoms are standard. ARC-115 may be substituted for ARC-116.

ARMAMENT: Provision for carrying packaged armament on port side of fuselage, comprising XM-27 7·62 mm machine-gun, with 2,000–4,000 rds/min capability, or XM-75 grenade launcher.

DIMENSIONS, EXTERNAL:

Diameter of main rotor	8·03 m (26 ft 4 in)
Main rotor blade chord	0·171 m (6¾ in)
Diameter of tail rotor	1·30 m (4 ft 3 in)
Distance between rotor centres	4·58 m (15 ft 0¼ in)
Length overall, rotors fore and aft	
	9·24 m (30 ft 3¾ in)
Length of fuselage	7·01 m (23 ft 0 in)
Height to top of rotor hub	2·48 m (8 ft 1½ in)
Skid track	2·06 m (6 ft 9 in)
Cabin doors (fwd, each):	
Height	1·19 m (3 ft 11 in)
Width	0·89 m (2 ft 11 in)
Cargo compartment doors (each):	
Height	1·04 m (3 ft 5 in)
Width	0·88 m (2 ft 10½ in)
Height to sill	0·57 m (1 ft 10½ in)

DIMENSIONS, INTERNAL:

Cabin: Length	2·44 m (8 ft 0 in)
Max width	1·37 m (4 ft 6 in)
Max height	1·31 m (4 ft 3½ in)

AREAS:

Main rotor blades (each)	0·69 m² (7·41 sq ft)
Tail rotor blades (each)	0·079 m² (0·85 sq ft)
Main rotor disc	50·60 m² (544·63 sq ft)

Hughes OH-6A Cayuse light observation helicopter, with side-mounted Minigun (*Brian M. Service*)

Tail rotor disc	1·32 m² (14·19 sq ft)
Fin	0·52 m² (5·65 sq ft)
Horizontal stabiliser	0·72 m² (7·70 sq ft)

WEIGHTS AND LOADINGS:

Weight empty, equipped	557 kg (1,229 lb)
Design gross weight	1,090 kg (2,400 lb)
Overload gross weight	1,225 kg (2,700 lb)
Design disc loading	21·48 kg/m² (4·4 lb/sq ft)
Design power loading	5·79 kg/kW (9·5 lb/shp)

PERFORMANCE (at design gross weight):
Never-exceed speed and max cruising speed at S/L
130 knots (241 km/h; 150 mph)
Cruising speed for max range at S/L
116 knots (216 km/h; 134 mph)

Max rate of climb at S/L (military power)	
	560 m (1,840 ft)/min
Max rate of climb at S/L (max continuous power)	
	381 m (1,250 ft)/min
Service ceiling	4,815 m (15,800 ft)
Hovering ceiling in ground effect	3,595 m (11,800 ft)
Hovering ceiling out of ground effect	
	2,225 m (7,300 ft)
Normal range at 1,525 m (5,000 ft)	
	330 nm (611 km; 380 miles)
	(1976–77)

THE INTERSTATE S-1B.
U.S. Army Air Forces designation : XL-6.

TYPE.—Two-seat light cabin monoplane.

WINGS.—High-wing braced monoplane. Wing section NACA 23012. Structure consists of solid spruce spars, girder type ribs, metal leading-edge, steel compression struts and internal bracing, the whole covered with fabric. Steel-tube bracing struts with intermediate jury struts. Mass-balanced ailerons and split flaps.

FUSELAGE.—Welded steel-tube structure, faired with a light super-structure and covered with fabric.

TAIL UNIT.—Braced monoplane type. Metal frames with fabric covering. Fin integral with fuselage. Trimming-tab in port elevator.

LANDING GEAR.—Semi-cantilever type with one oleo-spring shock-absorbing unit mounted within the fuselage serving both legs. Low-pressure wheels and hydraulic brakes. Steerable tail-wheel.

POWER PLANT.—One 115 h.p. Franklin O-200-5 four-cylinder horizontally-opposed geared air-cooled engine.

ACCOMMODATION.—Enclosed cabin seating two in tandem with dual controls. Roof and sides of cabin to a point some way aft of the trailing-edge of the wings provided with Plexiglas panels. The side panels in the region of the seats slope outwards to give down ward vision. Rear seat is reversible to enable observer to use collapsible table for maps, etc. Equipment includes engine-driven generator, electric starter, radio, complete blind-flying equipment, etc.

DIMENSIONS.—Span 35 ft. 6 in. (10.9 m.), Length 23 ft. 5½ in. (7.16 m.), Height 7 ft. 3 in. (2.6 m.), Wing area 173.8 sq. ft. (16.1 sq. m.).

WEIGHTS AND LOADINGS.—Weight empty 1,103 lbs. (500 kg.), Disposable load 547 lbs. (248 kg.), Weight loaded 1,650 lbs. (748 kg.), Wing loading 9.47 lbs./sq. ft. (46.2 kg./sq. m.), Power loading 14.3 lbs./h.p. (6.5 kg./h.p.).

PERFORMANCE.—No data available except Stalling speed (without flaps) 44 m.p.h. (70.4 km.h.), Stalling speed (with flaps) 39 m.p.h. (62.4 km.h.), Range 540 miles (864 km.). (1945–46)

THE KAMAN HTK-1.

The HTK-1 three-seat helicopter has been in service with the U.S. Navy and Marine Corps since early 1952. Used primarily as a trainer, it is adaptable as an ambulance and has been used for anti-submarine activities from the deck of LST's.

It uses the contra-rotating and inter-meshing twin rotor system, with servo-flap control, which has been the feature of all Kaman helicopters.

In this system the solid spruce rotor blades are attached to the hub only by blade lag hinges, the servo flaps eliminating blade-pitch change and associated bearings. The movements of the servo flaps twist the blades, the natural resilience of the blade material being used to obtain torsional deflection.

The HTK-1 also has a horizontal tail surface connected to the collective-pitch control for greater stability to permit "hands-off" flying.

Power is supplied by a 240 h.p. Lycoming O-435 engine.

The Kaman HTK-1 Training Helicopter. (*Gordon Williams*).

For evacuation duties the HTK-1 can carry a pilot and two stretcher cases, one above the other on the left side of the cabin. The left half of the transparent cabin nose opens to facilitate the loading of the stretchers. The change-over from three-seat trainer to ambulance can be made in 2½ minutes.

This helicopter has been awarded a C.A.A. Approved Type Certificate (1H3) and has a commercial designation (K-240) but it will not be produced in civil form until military commitments permit.

DIMENSIONS.—
Rotor diameter (both) 40 ft. (12.20 m.).
Distance between rotor heads 4 ft. 10 in.
  (1.47 m.).
Length of fuselage (over fins) 20 ft. 6½ in.
  (6.25 m.).
Span of tail 8 ft. 0 in. (2.44 m.).
Wheelbase 6 ft. 2 in. (1.88 m.).
Track (rear wheels) 7 ft. 6 in. (2.28 m.).
Track (front wheels) 5 ft. 2 in. (1.57 m.).
WEIGHTS.—
Combat weight (pilot + 1 and 20 U.S.
  gallons of fuel) 2,750 lb. (1,248 kg.).
Normal loaded weight (pilot + 1 and 40
  U.S. gallons of fuel) 2,870 lb. (1,303 kg.).
Max. loaded weight (pilot + 3 stretcher
  cases and 15 U.S. gallons of fuel) 3,100
  lb. (1,407 kg.).

PERFORMANCE (at designed gross weight).—
Max. speed 81 m.p.h. (130 km.h.).
Max. rate of climb 1,050 ft./min. (320 m./
  min.).
Hovering ceiling in ground effect 6,700 ft.
  (2,043 m.).
Service ceiling 14,500 ft. (4,420 m.).
PERFORMANCE (at combat weight).—
Max. speed 81 m.p.h. (130 km.h.).
Max. rate of climb 1,300 ft./min. (396 m./
  min.).   (1956–57)

Under a joint Army-Navy development contract one HTK-1 has been fitted
with two Boeing 502-2 shaft turbine
engines in place of the single standard
Lycoming piston engine. The two turbine engines, which together produce 380
shaft h.p., are placed side-by-side, a simple
gear-box transferring the dual power to
the standard HTK-1 rotor drive system.

Normally both turbines are used for
vertical take-off and hovering with heavy
loads, while one turbine is shut off for
cruising in horizontal flight.

The turbine-powered HTK-1 made its
first flight on March 26, 1954.

The HOK-1 is powered by a 600 h.p.
Pratt & Whitney R-1340-48 radial engine
which is mounted at the rear end of the
fuselage at an angle of 35° from the
horizontal to give direct drive to the dual
rotor gear-box in the roof. The engine is
fan-cooled with the shutter-controlled
main air inlet between the rotor pylons.
Large rear fuselage doors give complete
access to the power-plant. Maximum
fuel capacity is 100 U.S. gallons (378
litres).

The following versions of the Model 600
have been announced :—

HOK-1. Standard production version,
first accepted for service with the U.S.
Navy on April 28, 1953.

HUK-1. Similar to HOK-1. In production for U.S. Navy until 1959.

H-43A. Development of HOK-1 for
local crash rescue duties with the U.S.A.F.,
carrying pilot, rescue crew of three and
a 1,000 lb. (450 kg.) kit of fire-fighting
equipment. 18 ordered. First delivered
in November, 1958. Production completed in mid-1959.

The Kaman H-43A crash-rescue helicopter with fire extinguisher carried externally

THE KAMAN MODEL 600
U.S. Navy and Marine Corps designations: HOK and HUK
U.S.A.F. designation: H-43A

The initial HOK-1 version of the
Kaman 600 was ordered into production
in 1950, after winning a U.S. Navy design
competition for a liaison-type helicopter,
and deliveries of the developed HUK-1
for the Navy and H-43A for the U.S.A.F.
continued until 1959. The turbine-
powered H-43B Huskie is still being
manufactured, but contains so many
design changes that it is described separately.

The standard HOK-1 is a general-
purpose helicopter which normally carries
four or five persons but can be used also
for cargo carrying, medical evacuation,
search and rescue and air-to-ground

photography. As an ambulance it can
accommodate two stretcher patients and
one sitting patient or medical orderly, in
addition to the pilot. Stretcher loading
is through the nose. Optional equipment
includes an externally-mounted hook for
cargo hauling and a power hoist.

The HOK-1 features the Kaman contra-
rotating and intermeshing twin-rotor
system with servo-flap control. The
rotor blades are attached to the hub only
by blade lag hinges, the servo-flaps
eliminating blade-pitch change and associated bearings. The movements of the
servo-flaps twist the blades, the natural
resilience of the blade material being
used to obtain torsional deflection. The
two rotors can be lined up parallel to each
other fore and aft for stowage purposes.

Max. speed at S/L. 104 m.p.h. (167 km.h.)
Cruising speed (max. range) 75 m.p.h.
  (120 km.h.)
Cruising speed (max. endurance) 58 m.p.h.
  (93 km.h.)
Max. rate of climb 1,300 ft./min. (400 m./
  min.)
Vertical rate of climb 800 ft./min. (245 m./
  min.)
Service ceiling 18,000 ft. (5,500 m.)
Hovering ceiling with ground effect 12,000
  ft. (3,660 m.)
Hovering ceiling out of ground effect 9,000
  ft. (2,750 m.)
Range 220 miles (354 km.)
Endurance 3 hr. 20 min.

                                    (1960–61)

KAMAN MODEL 600-3/5
USAF designation: HH-43 Huskie

The Kaman HH-43 Huskie is a turbine-
powered development of the piston-engined
OH-/UH-/HH-43 series of helicopters described
in previous editions of *Jane's*. The prototype
was a modified OH-43D, which was developed
and flown under a USAF contract, through the
Lycoming Division of Avco, as a test-bed for the
first flights of the Lycoming XT53 shaft-turbine.
This aircraft flew for the first time on September
27, 1956.

There are two production versions of the
Huskie, as follows:

HH-43B (Model 600-3). Initial production
version, powered by an 860 shp (derated to 825
shp) Lycoming T53-L-1B shaft-turbine engine.
Normal fuel capacity 200 US gallons (755 litres)
in two flexible interconnected tanks under floor.
Provision for auxiliary tanks with total capacity
of 200 US gallons (755 litres). First production
HH-43B flew in December 1958.

HH-43F (Model 600-5). Development of HH-
43B with a 1,150 eshp (derated to 825 shp)
Lycoming T53-L-11A shaft-turbine engine.
Produced to replace HH-43B in applications where
altitude performance under hot day conditions is
required. Normal fuel capacity increased to 350
US gallons (1,325 litres) by utilising internal
auxiliary tankage. First HH-43F flew in August
1964. Final order for 10, for shipment overseas
under the Military Aid Programme, announced
in November 1964.

The HH-43 incorporates Kaman's contra-
rotating and intermeshing twin-rotor system with
servo-flap control. The rotor blades are attached
to the hub only by blade lag hinges, the servo-
flaps eliminating blade-pitch change and associated bearings. The movements of the servo-flaps
twist the blades, the natural resilience of the blade
material being used to obtain torsional deflection.
The two rotors can be lined up parallel to each
other fore and aft for stowage purposes.

An important feature of the HH-43B/F is that
these versions have twice the cabin space and
payload capacity of the piston-engined HH-43A,
the increased space having been gained by
mounting the lighter and more compact turbine
engine above the cabin and between the rotor
pylons, instead of to the rear of the cabin.
Repositioning of the engine has also made
possible the installation of large clam-shell doors,
forming the rear of the cabin.

The raised tail unit has twin rudders, controlled
by an autostabiliser. Alternative loads include
a pilot, two fully-clothed fire-fighters and 1,000
lb (445 kg) of fire-fighting and rescue gear; pilot,
co-pilot and ten passengers; or pilot, medical
attendant and four stretcher patients.

The four-wheel non-retractable landing gear
is fitted normally with small wheel-skis for
operation from hard or soft surfaces.

Original orders for a total of 116 HH-43B
Huskies were supplemented by further contracts
for both this version and the HH-43F. These

helicopters are used primarily, and with outstanding success, as local crash rescue helicopters at USAF bases throughout the world. They are also operated by the governments of Colombia, Thailand, Morocco, Pakistan and Burma for internal security, VIP transport and communications duties.

At the time of writing, the standard HH-43B held two official international helicopter records, as follows:

Altitude record with 1,000 kg payload of 26,369 ft (8,037·27 m) in Class E.1, set up on May 25, 1961, by Capt W. C. McMeen, USAF; and distance in a straight line of 888·4 miles (1,429·82 km) in Class E.1.d by Capt C. R. Ratcliffe, USAF on July 5, 1962.

DIMENSIONS, EXTERNAL:
Diameter of rotors (each)	47 ft 0 in (14·33 m)
Length of fuselage	25 ft 2 in (7·67 m)
Height to tip of highest blade	15 ft 6½ in (4·73 m)
Height to top of rotor head	12 ft 7 in (3·84 m)
Tailplane span	14 ft 10 in (4·52 m)
Wheel track	8 ft 4 in (2·54 m)

DIMENSIONS, INTERNAL:
Cabin: Max width	5 ft 3 in (1·60 m)
Max height	3 ft 10 in (1·17 m)

WEIGHTS:
Weight empty: HH-43B	4,469 lb (2,027 kg)
HH-43F	4,620 lb (2,095 kg)
Normal T-O weight:	
HH-43B	5,969 lb (2,708 kg)
HH-43F	6,500 lb (2,950 kg)
Max payload: HH-43B	3,880 lb (1,760 kg)
HH-43F	3,970 lb (1,800 kg)
Max T-O weight	9,150 lb (4,150 kg)

PERFORMANCE (HH-43B at 5,969 lb = 2,708 kg AUW; HH-43F at 6,500 lb = 2,950 kg AUW, except where indicated):
Max level speed at S/L	120 mph (193 kmh)
Normal cruising speed	110 mph (177 kmh)
Max rate of climb at S/L	
HH-43B	2,000 ft (610 m) min
HH-43F	1,800 ft (550 m) min
Service ceiling:	
HH-43B	25,000 ft (7,620 m)
HH-43F	23,000 ft (7,010 m)

Kaman HH-43B Huskie crash rescue helicopter with firefighting kit (*S. P. Peltz*)

Hovering ceiling in ground effect:		Range at 5,000 ft (1,525 m), no allowances:	
HH-43B	21,000 ft (6,400 m)	HH-43B	277 miles (445 km)
HH-43F	20,000 ft (6,100 m)	Range at 5,000 ft (1,525 m) at T-O weight of	
Hovering ceiling out of ground effect:		8,270 lb (3,750 kg), no allowances:	
HH-43B	18,000 ft (5,480 m)	HH-43F	504 miles (810 km)
HH-43F	16,000 ft (4,880 m)		(1965–66)

KAMAN SEASPRITE
US Navy designations: UH-2 (formerly HU2K-1), HH-2 and SH-2

The prototype Seasprite flew for the first time on 2 July 1959, and many versions (described in previous editions of *Jane's*) were produced subsequently for the US Navy.

From 1967, all of the original UH-2A/B Seasprites were converted progressively to UH-2C twin-engined configuration, with two 932 kW (1,250 shp) General Electric T58-GE-8B turboshaft engines in place of the former single T58. They have since undergone further modification, under the US Navy's important Mk 1 LAMPS (Light Airborne Multi-Purpose System) programme, to provide helicopters for ASW (anti-submarine warfare) and ASST (anti-ship surveillance and targeting) operations.

The following versions remained available in early 1980:

HH-2D. Two aircraft, without LAMPS modifications, assigned to coast and geodetic survey work.

NHH-2D. Test aircraft assigned to the circulation control rotor (CCR) programme.

SH-2D. LAMPS version, for ASW, ASST and a utility role. The first of 20 SH-2Ds, modified from HH-2D unarmed search and rescue helicopters, made its first flight on 16 March 1971; details of the modifications can be found in the 1979-80 and earlier editions of *Jane's*.

As the LAMPS helicopters became operational, the Navy organised squadrons to provide detachments to fleet units and to train additional personnel to operate and maintain them.

SH-2F. Deliveries of this further-developed Mk I LAMPS version began in May 1973 and the first unit became operational with squadron HSL-33, deployed to the Pacific, on 11 September 1973. A total of 88 SH-2Fs has been delivered. The earlier SH-2Ds and HH-2Ds are being uprated to SH-2F configuration, this programme being scheduled for completion in March 1982.

Other features of the SH-2F include increased-strength landing gear; a shortened wheelbase by relocation of the tailwheel; and T58-GE-8F engines. In early 1980 improvements were being made to the LN-66HP radar, tactical navigation system, ESM, sonobuoys and data link. In January-February 1973 Kaman flight-tested the prototype for flight qualification to a maximum gross weight of 6,033 kg (13,300 lb), which is 227 kg (500 lb) more than the current SH-2F. This could be utilised as increased payload, or in the form of additional fuel in larger auxiliary tanks to provide extended range and endurance in a new production version of the SH-2. US Navy tests have proved the SH-2 suitable for dipping sonar operations,

Kaman SH-2F LAMPS Mk 1 ASW helicopter, showing sensors and stores

air-to-surface missile firing, and equipment with various guns and rockets.

There are currently eight HSL LAMPS squadrons. Operational deployment began on 7 December 1971. By January 1980, 160 LAMPS SH-2D/F detachments had been deployed (not simultaneously) on long cruises, primarily in the Mediterranean and Pacific, on the following ship classes: FFG-7, DD-963, FFG-1, FF-1052, FF-1040, CGN-11, CG-25 and CG-26. The new DD-963 and FFG-7 classes are designed to operate with two LAMPS helicopters per ship.

The following details apply to the SH-2F version of the Seasprite:

TYPE: Naval anti-submarine warfare and anti-ship missile defence helicopter, with secondary capability for search and rescue, observation and utility missions.

ROTOR SYSTEM: Four-blade main and tail rotors. Kaman '101' main rotor utilises titanium hub and retention assemblies, reducing the number of control elements by two-thirds, and offering increased life for the entire rotor system. Blades of aluminium and glassfibre construction, with servo-flap controls. Blades folded manually. Main rotor rpm 287.

FUSELAGE AND TAIL UNIT: All-metal semi-monocoque structure, with flotation hull housing main fuel tanks. Nose split on centreline, to fold rearward on each side to reduce stowage space required. Fixed horizontal stabiliser on tail rotor pylon.

LANDING GEAR: Tailwheel type, with forward-retracting twin main wheels and non-retractable tailwheel. Liquid spring shock-absorbers in main-gear legs; oleo-pneumatic shock-absorber in tailwheel unit, which is fully-castoring for taxying but locked fore and aft for T-O and landing. Main wheels have 8-ply tubeless tyres size 17·5 × 6·25-11, pressure 17·25 bars (250 lb/sq in); tailwheel 10-ply tubeless tyre size 5·00-5, pressure 11·04 bars (160 lb/sq in).

POWER PLANT: Two 1,007 kW (1,350 shp) General Electric T58-GE-8F turboshaft engines, mounted on each side of rotor pylon structure. Normal fuel capacity of 1,499 litres (396 US gallons), including external auxiliary tanks with a capacity of 454·6 litres (120 US gallons).

ACCOMMODATION: Crew of three, consisting of pilot, copilot and sensor operator. One passenger or litter patient with LAMPS equipment installed; four passengers or two litters with sonobuoy launcher removed. Provision for transportation of internal or external cargo.

AVIONICS AND EQUIPMENT: Include Canadian Marconi LN-66HP surveillance radar; ASQ-81 magnetic anomaly detector; ALR-54 passive radiation detection receivers (being replaced by ALR-66); SSQ-41 passive and SSQ-47 active sonobuoys (being replaced by DIFAR and DICASS); smoke markers; one or two torpedoes; PT-429 plotting board system (being replaced by Teledyne Systems ASN-123 tactical navigation system with computer and CRT display); APN-182 Doppler radar; and AYK-2 analogue navigation computer. Cargo hook for external loads, capacity 1,814 kg (4,000 lb). Rescue hoist, capacity 272 kg (600 lb).

DIMENSIONS, EXTERNAL:

Diameter of main rotor	13·41 m (44 ft 0 in)
Main rotor blade chord	0·55 m (21·6 in)

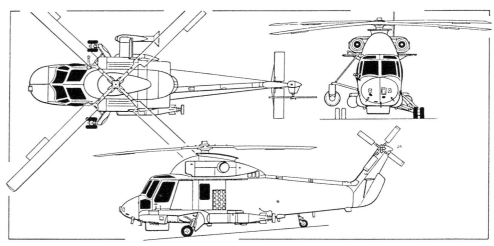

Kaman SH-2F Seasprite Light Airborne Multi-Purpose System (LAMPS) Mk 1 helicopter *(Pilot Press)*

Diameter of tail rotor	2·49 m (8 ft 2 in)
Tail rotor blade chord	0·236 m (9·3 in)
Length overall (rotors turning)	16·03 m (52 ft 7 in)
Length overall, nose and blades folded	11·68 m (38 ft 4 in)
Height overall (rotors turning)	4·72 m (15 ft 6 in)
Height to top of rotor head	4·14 m (13 ft 7 in)
Stabiliser span	2·97 m (9 ft 9 in)
Wheel track (outer wheels)	3·30 m (10 ft 10 in)
Wheelbase	5·11 m (16 ft 9 in)

WEIGHTS:

Weight empty	3,193 kg (7,040 lb)
*Normal T-O weight	5,805 kg (12,800 lb)

*Although not yet certificated for a T-O gross weight of 6,033 kg (13,300 lb), all testing has been accomplished at that weight

PERFORMANCE (at normal T-O weight, except where indicated):

Max level speed at S/L	143 knots (265 km/h; 165 mph)
Normal cruising speed	130 knots (241 km/h; 150 mph)
Max rate of climb at S/L	744 m (2,440 ft)/min
Service ceiling	6,860 m (22,500 ft)
Hovering ceiling IGE	5,670 m (18,600 ft)
Hovering ceiling OGE	4,695 m (15,400 ft)
Normal range with max fuel	367 nm (679 km; 422 miles)

(1980–81)

The Kellett YO-60 Two-seat Observation Autogiro (300 h.p. Jacobs R-915-3 engine).

The Kellett Aircraft Corpn., formerly the Kellett Autogiro Corpn., resumed its former name in June 1943, because of the larger scope of the aviation activities in which it is at present engaged. It is still, however, undertaking the development and manufacture of rotary-wing aircraft, in which it has been engaged since 1929.

In 1943 the Company completed the delivery of a small service development order for the YO-60 Autogiro to the U.S. Army Air Forces.

The YO-60 is a development of the Kellett KD-1A Autogiro, with jump take-off rotor head and a large transparent "bubble" canopy over the tandem cockpits. It is fitted with a 300 h.p. Jacobs R-915-3 radial air-cooled engine.

Kellett has been engaged in helicopter development work for several years and during 1944 the XR-8 helicopter developed for the U.S. Army Air Forces was successfully flown. The Kellet Company is no longer engaged in the production of Autogiros.

During the war the company was also engaged in the production of parts for other aircraft manufacturers.

Earlier, from 1935, nine Kellet KD-1 series autogiros had been taken into service as YG-1/1A/1Bs, two later being modified into YG-1C/XR-2 and XR-3.

THE KELLETT KD-1A AUTOGIRO.

TYPE.—Two-seat direct-control wingless Autogiro.

ROTOR SYSTEM.—Three-bladed rotor turning on a central hub, which is free to be tilted sideways or fore-and-aft, mounted on a large chrome-molybdenum steel-tube pylon strut. The rotor blades are built round a high-tensile steel tubular spar, the inner ends of which contain hydraulic dampers for controlling the position about the vertical hinge-pins. The extension blocks connecting the blades to the hub act as universal blocks, allowing the blades to flap freely and oscillate in the needle bearings. The extension blocks also include the ball-bearing cam-roller used to operate the hydraulic dampers. The central hub is machined from an alloy steel forging and is mounted on a spindle by two thrust and radial ball-bearings. Mechanical starting and braking system. The three blades may be folded back for storage purposes.

CONTROLS.—Control column moves the rotor system and provides for all lateral, longitudinal and directional control. Controls for rotor starter and brake on instrument board, together with engine controls and instruments.

FUSELAGE.—Welded steel-tube rigidly-braced structure, covered with fabric.

TAIL UNIT.—Fixed tail-plane and vertical surfaces to give positive directional stability. Opposite tail surfaces are inverted, the port side to give an upward force and the starboard side a downward force, thereby correcting engine torque reaction. Symmetrical section vertical fins mounted below tail-plane. Small hinged vertical rudder to offset effect of engine torque and not used in normal manoeuvres. Tail-plane has wood frame, fins and rudder welded steel-tube frames, the whole covered with fabric.

UNDERCARRIAGE.—Double fixed tripod type with axles telescoping in the shock-absorber struts to give as near vertical travel as possible. Wheel brakes operated by pedals in cockpit. Tail-wheel may swivel through 360 degrees for ground handling but connects with rudder-bar in cockpit to give positive steering on the ground when taxying.

POWER PLANT.—One 225 h.p. Jacobs L-4-MA radial air-cooled engine on cushioned mounting. Fuel tanks mounted on sides of fuselage outside main structure and held in place by steel straps. Oil tank in engine compartment. "Eclipse" electric engine-starter. Rotor starter driven by bevel gears through clutch off the back of the engine.

ACCOMMODATION.—Tandem open cockpits, with complete dual controls.

DIMENSIONS.—Diameter of rotor 40 ft. (12.2 m.), Length (blades folded) 25 ft. 11 in. (7.9 m.), Width (blades folded) 10 ft 3 in. (3.14 m.), Height (blades folded) 10 ft. 2 in. (3.12 m.).

AREAS.—Horizontal tail area 22 sq. ft. (2.04 sq. m.), Vertical tail area 12 sq. ft. (1.11 sq. m.).

WEIGHTS.—Weight empty 1,580 lbs. (717 kg.), Pilot and passenger 240 lbs. (155 kg.), Parachutes 60 lbs. (27 kg.), Fuel and oil 200 lbs. (91 kg.), Two-way radio 25 lbs. (11 kg.), Weight loaded 2,205 lbs. (1,001 kg.).

PERFORMANCE.—Maximum speed 128 m.p.h. (206 km.h.), Cruising speed 103 m.p.h. (164.8 km.h.), Minimum speed (level flight 17 m.p.h. (27 km.h.), Initial rate of climb 1,250 ft./min. (437 m./min.), Cruising range 200 miles (320 km.), Endurance at cruising speed 2 hours. Take-off run 250 ft. (76 m.), Landing run Nil.

The Keystone B-6A Bomber Biplane (two 575 h.p. Wright "Cyclone" engines).

THE KEYSTONE AIRCRAFT CORPORATION.
(DIVISION OF THE CURTISS-WRIGHT CORPORATION.)

HEAD OFFICE : 30, ROCKEFELLER PLAZA, NEW YORK CITY.
WORKS : BRISTOL, PA.
President : Thomas A. Morgan.
Vice-Presidents : T. P. Wright and W. S. Leaycraft.
Treasurer : W. S. Leaycraft.
Secretary : R. R. Reger.

THE KEYSTONE "PANTHER" B-6A.

TYPE.—Twin-engined military bombardment biplane.
WINGS.—Equal-span biplane, with flat top plane and dihedral angle to the bottom outer wing-sections. All four outer wing-sections and top centre-section of wooden construction. Bottom centre-sections of welded steel-tube. Wing construction consists of plywood box spars and plywood ribs, covered with fabric. Top centre-section carried on an inverted Vee cabane over fuselage and two sets of vertical struts, one on either side of fuselage uniting roots of top and bottom centre-sections. One pair of vertical interplane struts on either side of centre-section. Ailerons, inset from wing-tips, fitted to all four planes.
FUSELAGE.—Welded steel-tube Warren-truss structure, covered with fabric.
TAIL UNIT.—Welded steel-tube monoplane structure. Balanced elevator and rudder. Adjustable tail-plane.
UNDERCARRIAGE.—Divided type. Consists of two Vees, one mounted under each engine, the front legs of which incorporate oleo shock-absorber springing. The apices are hinged to the bottom fuselage longerons by steel-tube axles.
POWER PLANT.—Two 575 h.p. Wright "Cyclone" air-cooled radial engines, mounted one on either side of the fuselage, midway between the planes. Main fuel tanks, with capacity sufficient for

The Keystone Aircraft Corporation, during 1931 and the first part of 1932, delivered over 100 bombardment biplanes to the United States Army Air Corps. Production work has been concentrated during 1932 on building bombers for the United States Army, and amphibians and patrol flying-boats for the United States Navy.　(1934)

6 hours, mounted in top centre-section. Tanks for extra fuel carried in lower centre-sections.
ACCOMMODATION.—Accommodation for crew of five. Gunner's and bomber's cockpit in nose, fitted with flexible gun-mounting above and bomb-sighting and dropping compartment below. Pilot's cockpit, with accommodation for two side-by-side, in front of wings and behind nose cockpit. Under centre-section is carried the standard Air Corps internal bomb-rack for 2,150 lbs. total bomb load. Behind wings and midway between wings and tail is aft gunner's cockpit, armed with twin Lewis guns on flexible gun-ring above and one Lewis gun below, with wireless operator's compartment in fuselage.
DIMENSIONS.—Span 74 ft. 9 in. (22.8 m.), Length 48 ft. 9½ in. (14.8 m.), Height 17 ft. 2 in. (5.2 m.).
WEIGHTS.—Weight empty 8,057 lbs. (3,568 kg.), Weight loaded 13,334 lbs. (6,054 kg.).
PERFORMANCE.—Speed at ground level 120.8 m.p.h. (193.3 km.h.), Speed at 5,000 ft. (1,525 m.) 116.5 m.p.h. (186.4 km.h.), Speed at 10,000 ft. (3,050 m.) 111 m.p.h. (177.6 km.h.), Stalling speed 57 m.p.h. (91.2 km.h.), Initial rate of climb 690 ft./min. (210 m./min.), Ceiling 16,500 ft. (5,032.5 m.), Range (maximum fuel) 825 miles (1,320 km.) or 8 hours.　(1933)

The Keystone OL-9 Two-seat Amphibian Biplane (425 h.p. Pratt & Whitney "Wasp" engine).

THE KEYSTONE OL-9 AMPHIBIAN.

TYPE.—Two-seat flying-boat amphibian, for Navy use.
WINGS.—Equal-winged biplane. Two spruce spars and duralumin or "Alclad" (duralumin coated with pure aluminium) ribs, the whole being covered with fabric. Two sets of "N" type welded steel-tube interplane struts on either side of hull.
FUSELAGE AND HULL.—Framework of fuselage and hull consist of two Warren girders, cross-connected by bulkheads, which, in the case of those in the hull, are solid, thus sub-dividing it up into a series of watertight compartments. Spruce longerons and diagonals joined with flat duralumin gusset-plates bolted throughout with duralumin bolts. Covering is sheet duralumin, bolted to wooden frame with layer of fabric impregnated with marine glue between wood and metal. The hull specially reinforced for deck-landing and to withstand stress of being shot off the U.S. Navy powder-catapult.
TAIL UNIT.—Normal design. Tail-plane and elevator are of usual wood and fabric construction, but fin and rudder are metal-covered.

UNDERCARRIAGE.—The hull is built integral with the fuselage and is Vee-bottomed with two steps. The amphibian undercarriage is in two units, each of triangular form when viewed from the front. Each frame carries a wheel and is revolved round its hinge-point on the chine of the hull by a thrust member, which operates on a slide-tube within the hull. The entire mechanism, with the exception of half a wheel, is withdrawn into the hull. At rear of hull, at the second step, is a tail skid and two floats, each with a skid, are mounted under the wing-tips.
POWER PLANT.—One 425 h.p. Pratt & Whitney "Wasp" air-cooled radial engine. Flanged duralumin engine-plate connected to fuselage by steel tubes and is further braced by two vertical struts running down to the hull. Main fuel tank (140 U.S. gallons = 116 Imp. galls. = 530 litres capacity) is under pilot's seat.
ACCOMMODATION.—Pilot's cockpit forward, under centre-section, with good vision for aircraft-carrier landings. Gunner-observer's cockpit behind and below, in hull, is a cabin for wireless operator. Wheel control in front cockpit and stick control in rear cockpit.

DIMENSIONS.—Span 45 ft. (13.725 m.), Length 35 ft. 2¾ in. (10.74 m.), Height (on wheels) 12 ft. 11 in. (3.93 m.), Height (wheels retracted) 11 ft. 6 in. (3.5 m.), Wing area 502 sq. ft. (46.68 sq. m.).

WEIGHTS AND LOADINGS.—Weight empty 3,253 lbs. (1,476.8 kg.), Disposable load (max.) 2,000 lbs. (908 kg.), Disposable load (Army normal) 1,800 lbs. (817 kg.), Disposable load (Navy catapult) 1,500 lbs. (681 kg.), Weight loaded (max.) 5,253 lbs. (2,384.8 kg.), Wing loading 10.45 lbs./sq. ft. (51 kg./sq. m.), Power loading 12.4 lbs./h.p. (5.62 kg./h.p.).

PERFORMANCE.—Maximum speed 124 m.p.h. (198.4 km.h.), Stalling speed 50 m.p.h. (80 km.h.), Climb in 10 mins. 5,500 ft. (1,650 m.), Range at cruising speed 650 miles (1,040 km.).   (1934)

The Keystone "Pegasus" (800 h.p. Packard 1A-2500 engine).

THE KEYSTONE "PEGASUS."

The Keystone "Pegasus" represents the latest development in light bombing aircraft. It embodies high speed (130 m.p.h.), wide cruising radius, big load-carrying capacity and a high ceiling—essential factors in modern bombing aircraft. It is fitted with one 800 h.p. Packard 1A-2500 engine.

Owing to the fact that there are several new and unusual features in the construction of these planes, many details have been withheld, at the request of the U.S. Air Corps Intelligence Department.

Specification.

Span	..	..	..	66 ft. 6 in.
Length	..	..	..	46 ft. 2 in.
Weight empty	..	..	5,323 lbs.
Weight loaded	..	..	11,224 lbs.
Wing area	..	..	..	1,150 sq. ft.
Wing section	..	..	U.S.A. 45 (modified).

Details of the performance of this machine are also being withheld, at the request of the U.S. Air Corps.   (1927)

The Keystone "Pelican" (200 h.p. Wright "Whirlwind" engine).

THE KEYSTONE "PELICAN."

The Keystone "Pelican" was also produced as a result of the successful experiments made with the various "Petrel" models. It embodies the usual features of strength, low maintenance cost, low minimum flying speed, excellent manœuvrability, and has a good field of vision. This type is known as the Navy Five-Purpose Training Plane. It may be equipped with a single central float, making it an excellent training seaplane. It may be fitted with wheels for landplane training. It may be used as an observation or submarine-spotting plane, or may be equipped for fighting training, with either fixed or movable machine-guns. The fuselage construction is of seamless welded steel tubes, and in general characteristics it is similar to the "Petrel," except that in its seaplane form it is fitted with a single float instead of twin floats, and generally has a somewhat better performance.

Specification.

			Seaplane.	Landplane.
Span	..	33 ft.		
Length	..	28 ft. 6 in.		
Wing area	..	296 sq. ft.		
Wing section	..	Goettingen 387.		
Useful load	..	850 lbs.		
Fuel capacity	..	44 galls.		
Cruising radius	..	250 miles.		
Speed, max.	..		112 m.p.h.	120 m.p.h.
Speed, landing	..		40 m.p.h.	38 m.p.h.
Climb in 10 mins.	..		8,000 ft.	10,000 ft.

(1927)

The Keystone "Pelican" as a Seaplane (200 h.p. Wright "Whirlwind" engine).

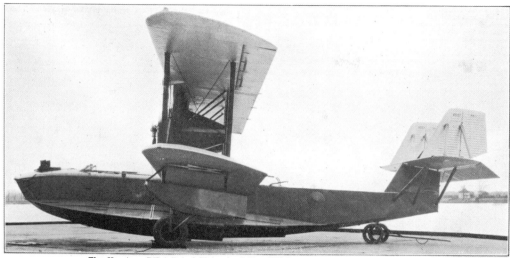

The Keystone PK-1 Patrol Flying-boat (two 575 h.p. Wright "Cyclone" engines).

THE KEYSTONE PK-1.

A development in design of the early type Navy flying-boat known as the PN-12, the PK-1 is built entirely of metal, except for the fabric wing-covering. The hull is all-metal, the rudders, the ailerons, the elevators and the tail-plane and fin are metal and metal-covered.

The PK-1 is fitted with two 575 h.p. Wright "Cyclone" engines. It has a top speed of 120 m.p.h. (192 km.h.) and a ceiling of 12,000 ft.

A crew of five is carried, made up as follows : the pilot, the co-pilot, the navigator-bomber, the radio operator and the gunner mechanic. In action, the crew is disposed in three compartments. Down the centre of the hull, fore and aft, there is a spacious companion-way through which the crew can move about. Hammocks for the crew can be swung in this passage.

The fuel tanks, with a total capacity of 800 gallons, are disposed in the interior of the hull, along the sides of the passage way. When filled, they carry sufficient fuel to permit a cruising range of 1,250 miles (2,000 km.).

The PK-1 is 49 ft. (14.4 m.) long, 16 ft. 9 in. (5.1 m.) high, and has a wing span of 72 ft. 10 in. (22.2 m.). Its regulation equipment includes a 75-lb. anchor and 150 ft. of bronze cable for mooring. Beach landing gear, consisting of wheels which are easily attachable, are also provided for ease in taking the boat up a ramp from the water.

Hand electric-starters for each engine, complete dual control and duplicated instruments, standard navigation lights, two headlights for landing at night, towing tackle for targets, message carriers between the different crew stations, radio transmitting and receiving set, earth inductor compass, drift indicator, bubble sextant, two portable aluminium tanks, each containing 4½ gallons of fresh drinking water, one container for 70 lbs. of food to feed crew for one week, and a life-raft are provided on each PK-1. (1933)

The Lockheed Constellation in military guise. Most C-69 military transports have now been converted for commercial use.

THE LOCKHEED MODELS 49, 649 AND 749 CONSTELLATION.

The original Model 49 Constellation was designed before the war to the requirements of Transcontinental & Western Air, Inc. During its development, and after consultation with T.W.A., Pan American Airways also ordered a number of Constellations but on the entry of the United States into the war both companies waived their rights in favour of the Army Air Forces, to whose requirements the Constellation was completed and put into production as a military transport under the designation C-69.

The following were the designations of the various military versions of the Constellation :—

XC-69. Original Model 49 ordered by airlines and turned over to the U.S.A.A.F.

C-69A. Model 49 fitted to carry up to 100 troops. Cancelled.

C-69B. Fitted to accommodate crew of six and 94 troops on benches. Cancelled.

C-69C. Personnel version to carry crew of six and 43 in chairs. One built, 49 cancelled on VJ-Day and modified by Lockheed for airline use.

C-69D. Three cancelled by U.S.A.A.F. on VJ-Day and modified by Lockheed for delivery to airlines.

XC-69E. One Model 49 fitted with four Pratt & Whitney R-2800 engines in place of standard power plant of four Wright R-3350-35 engines.

When the war ended military contracts were cut and production was converted for civil purposes. The first delivery of a commercial Model 49 was made to T.W.A. on October 1, 1945, and the C.A.B. granted Airworthiness Type Certificate No. 763 for this type of aircraft on December 11, 1945. All the early deliveries of Constellations were conversions of aircraft begun as military C-69 transports.

Owing to several accidents which were at the time attributed to the engine installation the Airworthiness Certificate of the Model 49 was temporarily withdrawn on July 11, 1946, while direct-injection GR-3350 engines were substituted for the original power units, and other minor changes were made to the pressurization system. These modified aircraft are known as the Model 49-46.

The Constellation built throughout as a commercial aeroplane is known as the Model 649. This version is fitted with the slightly more powerful Wright GR-3350-BD1 engines with direct fuel-injection systems, is more luxuriously furnished, and has slightly greater maximum and cruising speeds.

The Model 749 is a long-range version which will be available for delivery in 1947. It will have new wings with additional fuel tankage, thermal de-icing, etc.

Constellations are operated, or have been ordered, by Pan American World Airways, T.W.A., American Overseas Airlines, Eastern Air Lines, Pan American-Grace Airways, British Overseas Airways, Qantas Empire Airways, Air France, K.L.M., K.N.I.L.M., Panair do Brasil and Aer Lingus Tta.

TYPE.—Four-engined Airliner.

WINGS.—Cantilever low-wing monoplane. All-metal structure in five main sections consisting of centre-section carrying engine nacelles, two outer wings and detachable tips. Two-spar structure with flush-riveted stressed metal skin. False spar carrying ailerons and flaps. Fabric-covered metal ailerons each have controllable trim-tab and hydraulic boost control. Lockheed-Fowler trailing-edge flaps extend from ailerons nearly to centre-line of fuselage Flap positions for take-off, landing and manoeuvring. Gross wing area 1,650 sq. ft. (153.5 sq. m.).

FUSELAGE.—All-metal semi-monocoque structure. Circular cross-section throughout length and with centre-line cambered to give longitudinal aerofoil section and maximum length and width of level floor, particularly in nose and tail sections. Structure consists of transversal frames and flush-riveted stressed metal skin.

TAIL UNIT.—Cantilever monoplane type consisting of tailplane and two-piece elevator mounted at top of fuselage, and two inset fins and rudders with third fin and rudder on fuselage centre-line. All-metal structure with stressed metal skin over fixed surfaces and fabric-covered rudders and elevators. Controllable trim-tabs in rudders and elevators. Hydraulically-boosted control surfaces with manual override control for auxiliary use. Tailplane span 50 ft. 0 in. (15.24 m.).

LANDING GEAR.—Retractable tricycle type with dual wheels on all units. Each main unit consists of twin wheels 17.00 × 20 carried on single shock-absorber strut with side and front link members which retract forward into inner engine nacelles and are fully enclosed by twin doors. Low pressure tyres. Track (centre-line of legs) 28 ft. 0 in. (8.50 m.). Nose-unit consists of steerable twin smooth-contour wheels 2 ft. 9 in. (0.84 m.) diameter, carried on single shock-absorber leg which retracts backwards into fuselage and is enclosed by twin doors and fairing plate attached to front of leg. Dual hydraulic brake system on main wheels with manual auxiliary override control. Emergency retractable bumper-skid below rear fuselage.

POWER PLANT.—Four Wright Cyclone GR-3350-BD1 eighteen-cylinder two-row radial air-cooled engines each rated at 2,500 h.p. for take-off and enclosed in long-chord tapered cowlings. Stainless-steel nacelles, with all ducting and controls grouped at fire-proof bulkhead, are completely detachable and can be changed in 30 minutes. Automatic fire-detection and location with positive fire-extinguisher system operated by flight engineer. Hamilton-Standard Hydromatic or Curtiss-Electric three-blade reversible airscrews, 15 ft. 2 in. (4.62 m.) diameter. Four separate fuel systems in wings with total capacity of 4,760 U.S. gallons (15,592 litres). Total oil capacity 186 U.S. gallons (702 litres) in four separate tanks.

ACCOMMODATION.—Pressurized cabin for crew and passengers maintains 8,000 ft. (2,440 m.) cabin atmosphere at 20,000 ft. (6,095 m.). Two fully-automatic cabin superchargers with manual override control. Thermostatically-controlled heating and cooling. Refrigeration unit cools cabin to 75 degrees Fahrenheit with outside temperature at 110 degrees Fahrenheit. Pilot's compartment in forward portion of fuselage with pilot (on port) and co-pilot side-by-side with dual controls. Electric windshield de-icers. Flight engineer behind co-pilot facing outboard. Radio-operator behind pilot facing forward. Steward and stewardess. Entry to crew compartment on starboard side. Aft of crew compartment is fully-insulated forward passenger cabin, followed by compartment which can be arranged as galley, buffet, lounge, etc. Next follows main passenger cabin, insulated against sound, vibration and outside temperature. Many alternative arrangements allow for total accommodation of from 44 to 60 passengers. 48-passenger version convertible to sleeper with 22 berths and 4 seats; 44-passenger version convertible to sleeper with 20 berths and 4 seats. Main entry door at rear on port. Aft of main cabin are lavatories, coatroom and mealtime accommodations. Two freight compartments with total capacity of 440 cub. ft. (12.45 cub. m.) below floor of main cabin with allowance for 5,850 lbs. (2,651 kg.), or 13,400 lbs. (6,077 kg.) with auxiliary flooring. Other freight stowage dependent on passenger accommodation. Additional freight, etc. can be carried in an all-metal pannier, known as a "Speedpak," 33 ft. long × 7 ft. wide × 3 ft. deep (10.05 × 2.13 × 0.9 m.) and weighing 1,700 lbs. (771 kg.). This is carried under and closely fits the contour of fuselage. The "Speedpak" has capacity of 395 cub. ft. (11.17 cub. m.) and a stowage allowance of 10,000 lbs. (4,536 kg.). Built-in electric hoist lowers "Speedpak" to ground for loading or unloading. "Speedpak" reduces speed by about 10 m.p.h. (16 km.h.).

DIMENSIONS.—Span 123 ft. 0 in. (37.49 m.), Length 95 ft. $1\frac{3}{10}$ in. (28.97 m.), Height over fuselage 18 ft. $8\frac{3}{16}$ in. (5.6 m.), Height overall 23 ft. 8 in. (7.2 m.).

WEIGHTS AND LOADINGS (Model 649).—Weight empty (including crew and all passenger equipment) 55,000—60,750 lbs. (24,924—27,556 kg.) depending on interior arrangements. Payload (approximate) 49,280 lbs. (22,353 kg.), Maximum take-off loaded weight 100,000 lbs. (45,359 kg.), Maximum landing weight 78,000 lbs. (35,381 kg.). Wing loading (at maximum take-off weight) 48.3 lbs./sq. ft. (235.8 kg./sq. m.), Power loading (at maximum take-off weight, take-off h.p.) 10 lbs./sq. ft. (4.5 kg./h.p.).

PERFORMANCE (Model 649).—Maximum speed (fully loaded) over 350 m.p.h. (563 km.h.), Maximum cruising speed at 60% power, over 300 m.p.h. (483 km.h.), Landing speed 80 m.p.h. (129 km.h.), Service ceiling 25,000 ft. (7,620 m.), Three-engine ceiling, over 20,000 ft. (6,095 m.), Two-engine ceiling over 8,000 ft. (2,440 m.), Normal range 3,000 miles (4,828 km.), Maximum range 5,000 miles (8,046 km.), Take-off run at sea level with full load, under 667 yds. (610 m.), Take-off distance to 50 ft. (15 m.) with full load, under 933 yds. (853 m.), Landing distance from 50 ft. (15 m.) at maximum landing weight, 833 yds. (762 m.). (1947)

The Lockheed C-121C Military Long-range Transport version of the 1049 Super Constellation.

THE LOCKHEED CONSTELLATION.
U.S. Air Force designation: C-121.
U.S. Navy designation: WV.

C-121A. Military long-range personnel and cargo version of the Model 749.

VC-121B. Military long-range V.V.I.P. transport version of the Model 749.

WV-1. Modified 749 to test advanced electronic systems. Two ordered by U.S. Navy. First flow on June 9, 1949.

THE LOCKHEED 1049 SUPER CONSTELLATION.
U.S. Air Force designation: C-121.
U.S. Navy designations : R7V and WV.

The Super Constellation Model 1049 is basically similar to the Constellation, but with a longer fuselage and other improvements to increase its payload and performance.

There are ten military and naval versions of the 1049 Super Constellation, brief details of which follow :—

C-121C. Military long-range transport version of the Model 1049 with Wright R-3350 Turbo Compound engines. Quickly convertible to carry 75 passengers, 47 litter patients and attendants, or 14 short tons of freight. Take-off weight 135,400 lb. (61,416 kg.).

RC-121C. U.S.A.F. version of WV-2 early-warning radar and reconnaissance aircraft. Total fuel capacity 6,550 U.S. gallons. See WV-2 below.

RC-121D. Developed version of RC-121C. Additional fuel in two wing-tip tanks (600 U.S. gallons each) and one fuselage tank (1,000 U.S. gallons). Total fuel capacity 8,750 U.S. gallons, sufficient for endurance of 24 hours.

VC-121E. Specially-equipped C-121C reserved for the use of the President of the United States.

The Lockheed WV-2E Early-Warning Radar Intelligence aircraft.

The Lockheed R7V-I Naval Transport version of the Model 1049B Super Constellation.

YC-121F. Four 5,700 s.h.p. Pratt & Whitney T34-P-6 turboprop engines with Hamilton Standard three-blade airscrews, 15 ft. (4.57 m.) diameter. Two ordered by U.S.A.F. Similar to Navy R7V-2. Has capacity for 106 passengers, 18 short tons of cargo or 73 stretcher cases. A.U.W. 150,000 lb. (68,100 kg.), landing weight 113,000 lb. (51,300 kg.). Fuel capacity (including tip tanks) 8,770 U.S. gallons (33,150 litres). Cruises at 440 m.p.h. (708 km.h.) and lands at 104 m.p.h. (167 km.h.). Designed range 3,000 miles (4,800 km.), with reserves, carrying 20,000 lb. (9,080 kg.) payload. Absolute range, no reserves, 4,000 miles (6,400 km.). First YC-121F made its first flight on April 5, 1955.

WV-2. After service tests of the WV-1 Constellation, the U.S. Navy ordered into production the WV-2 to serve as a high-altitude reconnaissance and early-warning radar intelligence aircraft, and five orders so far received will extend production into 1958. Developed from Super Constellation and powered by four 3,250 h.p. Wright Turbo Compound engines. Equipped with some five and a half tons of radar and electronics, including G.E. height-finding radar in upper fuselage radome 7 ft. (2.13 m.) high, and G.E. surveillance or distance-measuring radar in the huge under-fuselage radome. Five radar consoles and plotting tables permit observation of various presentations or segments of the same basic radar picture and work on a variety of search and interception problems. Auxiliary radar units provide specialised presentations. CIC (Combat Information Center) co-ordinates all search information for communication to ships, bases or other aircraft. Navigational equipment includes storm-warning radar, Loran, etc. Equipped with bunks, galley, repair shop and all facilities for long missions. Provision for a crew of up to 31, including relief pilots, radar operators, technicians and maintenance specialists.

WV-2E. This new version of the WV-2 carries a very large radar scanner in a 37 ft. (11.28 m.) wide streamlined disc-shaped housing mounted on a pylon above its fuselage.

WV-3. Weather reconnaissance version of the WV-2, with special electronic equipment. In service with the U.S. Navy.

R7V-1. U.S. Navy transport version of the Model 1049B with four Wright R-3350-34W Turbo Compound engines. Carries up to 106 passengers in backward facing 20G removable seats, up to 19 short tons of cargo, or 73 casualties on stretchers. A.U.W. 133,000 lb. (60,380 kg.). Large loading doors fore and aft of wings.

R7V-2 (formerly R7O-2). Two aircraft powered by four 5,700 s.h.p. Pratt & Whitney T34 turboprop engines for evaluation of this type of power-plant for transport aircraft. Fitted with two 600 U.S. gallon wing-tip tanks, with provision for two additional 500 U.S. gallon underwing tanks, to give a total maximum fuel capacity of 8,770 U.S. gallons (33,150 litres). First R7V-2 flew on September 1, 1954.

The R7V-2 programme was cancelled in 1957 and one of the two aircraft, on bailment to Lockheed from the U.S. Navy, has now been fitted with four Allison 501 turboprop engines for a 1,000-hour flight test programme to speed development of these engines for the Electra.

The following description applies mainly to the civil Model 1049C. The structural description applies generally to all versions of the Super Constellation.

TYPE.—Four-engined Airliner.

WINGS.—Cantilever low-wing monoplane. All-metal structure in seven main sections consisting of centre-section, two inner wings carrying engine nacelles, two outer wings and detachable tips. Two-spar structure with flush-riveted stressed metal skin. All-metal ailerons each have controllable trim-tab and hydraulic boost control. Lockheed-Fowler trailing-edge flaps extend from ailerons nearly to centre-line of fuselage. Gross wing area 1,650 sq. ft. (153.5 m.²).

FUSELAGE. — All-metal semi-monocoque structure. Circular cross-section throughout length and with centre-line cambered for aerodynamic cleanliness.

TAIL UNIT.—Cantilever monoplane type, consisting of tailplane and two-piece elevator mounted at top of fuselage, and two inset fins and rudders with third fin and rudder on fuselage centre-line. All-metal structure with stressed metal skin on fins, tailplane and elevators. Metal-framed fabric-covered rudders. Controllable trim-tabs in rudders and elevators. Hydraulically-boosted control surfaces with manual override control for auxiliary use. Tailplane span 50 ft. 0 in. (15.24 m.).

LANDING GEAR.—Retractable tricycle type with dual wheels on all units. Dual hydraulic brake system on main wheels with manual auxiliary override control. Track (centre-line of legs) 28 ft. 0 in. (8.50 m.).

POWER PLANT.—Four Wright R-3350-DA1 Turbo Compound eighteen-cylinder two-row radial air-cooled engines each rated at 3,250 h.p. for take-off. Stainless-steel nacelles, with all ducting and controls grouped at fire-proof bulkhead, are completely detachable and can be changed in 30 minutes. Automatic fire-detection and location with positive fire-extinguisher system operated by flight engineer. Hamilton Standard or Curtiss three-blade reversible airscrews, 15 ft. 2 in. (4.62 m.) diameter. Seven separate fuel systems in wings with total capacity of 6,550 U.S. gallons (24,760 litres). Total oil capacity 227 U.S. gallons (858 litres) in five separate tanks.

ACCOMMODATION.—Pressurized cabin for crew and passengers maintains 8,000 ft. (2,440 m.) cabin atmosphere at 22,800 ft. (6,955 m.). Two fully-automatic cabin superchargers with manual override control. Thermostatically-controlled heating and cooling. Refrigeration unit cools cabin to 80 degrees Fahrenheit with outside temperature at 99 degrees Fahrenheit. Pilot's compartment in forward portion of fuselage with pilot (on port) and co-pilot side-by-side with dual controls. Flight engineer behind co-pilot facing outboard. Radio-operator behind pilot. Two cabin attendants. Entry to crew compartment on starboard side. Aft of crew compartment is a section which may be used as a galley, buffet, etc. Next follows main passenger cabin, insulated against sound, vibration and outside temperature. Many alternative arrangements allow for total accommodation up to 94 passengers. Two passenger doors and one separate crew door. Two freight compartments with total capacity of 728 cub. ft. (20.6 m.³) below floor of main cabin. Other freight stowage dependent on passenger accommodation. On some Models additional freight, etc. can be carried in an all-metal pannier, known as a "Speedpak," 33 ft. long × 7 ft. wide × 3 ft. deep (10.05 × 2.13 × 0.9 m.) and weighing 1,800 lb. (817 kg.). This is carried under and

closely fits the contour of fuselage. The "Speedpak" has capacity of 400 cub. ft. (11.32 m.³) and a stowage allowance of 8,200 lb. (3,723 kg.). Built-in electric hoists lower "Speedpak" to ground for loading or unloading. "Speedpak" reduces speed by about 12 m.p.h. (19.2 km.h.).

DIMENSIONS.—
Span 123 ft. 0 in. (37.49 m.).
Length 113 ft. 7 in. (34.65 m.).
Length with nose radome 116 ft. (35.35 m.).
Height over fuselage 18 ft. 10 in. (5.73 m.).
Height overall 24 ft. 9 in. (7.56 m.).

WEIGHTS (Model 1049E).—
Max. take-off loaded weight 133,000 lb. (60,380 kg.).
Max. landing weight 110,000 lb. (49,940 kg.).

PERFORMANCE (Model 1049E).—
Max. speed (fully loaded) 352 m.p.h. (563 km.h.) at 10,500 ft. (3,200 m.).

Max. speed (at max. landing weight) 376 m.p.h. (602 km.h.) at 20,000 ft. (6,050 m.).
Max. cruising speed at 75% power, 331 m.p.h. (530 km.h.) at 23,000 ft. (7,015 m.).
Landing speed 99.5 m.p.h. (159 km.h.).
Initial rate of climb (at max. A.U.W. at S/L.) 1,140 ft./min. (348 m./min.).
Initial rate of climb (at max. A.U.W. at S/L.) one engine inoperative 640 ft./min. (195 m./min.).
Max. range (full fuel, no reserve) at 10,000 ft. (3,050 m.) 4,820 miles (7,710 km.).
Take-off distance to clear 50 ft. (15 m.) with full load, 4,600 ft. (1,403 m.).
Landing distance from 50 ft. (15 m.) at max. landing weight 3,550 ft. (1,083 m.).
(1958–59)

LAS C-121J SUPER CONSTELLATION VIETNAM AIRBORNE TELEVISION TRANSMITTERS

LAS has remanufactured several C-121J Super Constellation cargo aircraft as airborne television and radio transmitters and studios for service in South Vietnam. Design and modification were performed at the LAS base at J. F. Kennedy International Airport, New York. Technical Materiel Corporation, Mamaroneck, NY, designed and assembled the radio and TV broadcasting and relay equipment for the project.

The aircraft, known as Blue Eagles, are operated under the command of the US Navy Oceanographic Air Survey Unit, Patuxent River Naval Air Station, Maryland. They possess the capability of broadcasting simultaneously on two television channels and on medium, short wave, and FM radio. Programme sources within the aircraft include tape, film and live studio capabilities.

The LAS conversion included the installation of a built-in TV studio, necessary power sources for all equipment, and a complete antenna array for audio and television transmission.

C-121J Super Constellation remanufactured by LAS as an airborne television and radio transmitter and studio for service in Vietnam (1968–69)

Lockheed C-5A Galaxy long-range military heavy transport (four General Electric TF39-GE-1 turbofan engines)

LOCKHEED C-5 GALAXY
USAF designation: C-5A

Design studies for a very large logistics transport for Military Airlift Command (then MATS) began in 1963, when the requirement was for a 600,000 lb (272,200 kg) aircraft known by the designation CX-4. Eventually, this and other requirements evolved into a specification known as CX-HLS (Cargo, Experimental—Heavy Logistics System).

Following an initial design competition in May 1964, contracts were awarded to Boeing, Douglas and Lockheed to develop their designs further. At this time, the requirement was for an aircraft with a gross weight of about 700,000 lb (317,500 kg), to which the definitive designation C-5A and the name Galaxy were allocated. Large contracts also went to Pratt & Whitney and General Electric to finance the development of prototype power plants for the C-5A.

In August 1965, the General Electric GE1/6 turbofan was selected for continued development.

In October, Lockheed was nominated as prime contractor for the airframe. Construction of the first C-5A was started in August 1966, and it flew for the first time on 30 June 1968; the first operational aircraft (the ninth C-5A built) was delivered to Military Airlift Command on 17 December 1969. Lockheed-Georgia and the USAF assigned the first eight aircraft to a flight test programme that extended into mid-1971. Contracts were placed covering the manufacture of 81 C-5As for the USAF. About 50% of the work, in terms of payments, was subcontracted.

In May 1973 the 81st C-5A was delivered, and by the end of 1974 the fleet had accumulated more than 186,000 flight hours. The value of the C-5A for rapid movement of large and/or heavy pieces of equipment has been demonstrated frequently since these aircraft became operational. Loads such as two M-48 tanks, each weighing 99,000 lb (45,000 kg), or three CH-47 Chinook helicopters, have been airlifted over transoceanic ranges.

In early 1978 Lockheed received a $24·3 million USAF contract to manufacture two new sets of wings for the C-5A, of a design intended to reduce stress and increase service life to 30,000 h. Apart from the moving surfaces, these wings are of virtually new design, using 7175-T73511 aluminium alloy for greater strength and increased resistance to corrosion. One set was for ground testing, and one for flight trials, which began in the Summer of 1980. If these tests proved successful it was planned to fit similar new wings to the 77 Galaxies still in operational service with the USAF, between 1982 and 1987. A $68 million contract to begin production of the wings was received by Lockheed in August 1980.

The latest version of the Galaxy is the **C-5B**. Data applies to C-5A.

Type: Heavy logistics transport aircraft.

Wings: Cantilever high-wing monoplane. Wing section NACA 0012 (mod) at 20% span, NACA 0011 (mod) at 43·7% and 70% span. Anhedral 5° 30′ at quarter-chord. Incidence 3° 30′ at root. Sweepback at quarter-chord 25°. Conventional fail-safe box structure of built-up spars and machined aluminium alloy extruded skin panels. Statically-balanced aluminium alloy ailerons. Modified Fowler-type aluminium alloy trailing-edge flaps. Simple hinged aluminium alloy spoilers forward of flaps. No trim tabs. Sealed inboard slats and slotted outboard slats on leading-edges. Ailerons and spoilers operated by hydraulic servo actuators. Trailing-edge flaps and leading-edge slats actuated by ball screwjack and torque tube system.

Fuselage: Conventional semi-monocoque fail-safe structure of 7079-T6 and 7075-T6 aluminium alloy and titanium alloy.

Tail Unit: Cantilever all-metal T-tail. All surfaces swept; anhedral on tailplane. All components are single-cell box structures with integrally-stiffened aluminium alloy skin panels. Variable-incidence tailplane. Elevators in four sections; rudder in two sections. No trim tabs. Rudder and elevators operated through hydraulic servo actuators. Tailplane actuated through hydraulically-powered screwjack. No anti-icing equipment.

Landing Gear: Retractable nosewheel type. Nose unit retracted rearward by hydraulically-driven ballscrews. Main units rotated through 90° and retracted inward via hydraulically-driven gearbox. Single nose shock-strut and four main-gear shock-struts are of Bendix oleo-pneumatic dual-chamber type. Four wheels on nose unit. Four main units (two in tandem on each side) each comprise a "triangular footprint" six-wheel bogie made up of a pair of wheels forward of the shock-strut and two pairs aft. All 28 tyres size 49 × 17-20 type VII 26-ply. Tyre pressures: main 111 lb/sq in (7·80 kg/cm²), nose 137 lb/sq in (9·63 kg/cm²) with in-flight deflation capability. Goodyear aircooled beryllium disc brakes, with fully-modulating anti-skid units. Cross-wind positioning of all units 20° to port or starboard by servo-controlled hydraulically-powered cylinders. Ground manoeuvrability enhanced by castoring forward main units.

Power Plant: Four General Electric TF39-GE-1 turbofan engines, each rated at 41,100 lb (18,642 kg) st. Twelve integral fuel tanks in wings between front and rear spars, comprising four main tanks (each 3,625 US gallons; 13,721 litres), four auxiliary tanks (each 4,625 US gallons: 17,507 litres) and four extended-range tanks (each 4,000 US gallons; 15,142 litres). Total usable capacity 49,000 US gallons (185,480 litres). Two refuelling points each side, in forward part of main landing gear pods. Flight refuelling capability, via inlet in upper forward fuselage, over flight engineer's station (compatible with KC-135 tanker). Oil capacity 36·4 US gallons (138 litres).

Accommodation: Normal crew of five, consisting of pilot, co-pilot, flight engineer, navigator and loadmaster, with rest area for 15 people (relief crew, couriers, etc) at front of upper deck. Basic version has seats for 75 troops on rear part of upper deck, aft of wing box. Provision for carrying 270 troops on lower deck, but aircraft is employed primarily as freighter. Typical freight loads include two M-60 tanks or sixteen ¾ ton lorries; or one M-60 and two Bell Iroquois helicopters, five M-113 personnel carriers, one M-59 2½ ton truck and an M-151 ¼ ton truck; or 10 Pershing missiles with tow and launch vehicles; or 36 standard 463L load pallets. "Visor" type upward-hinged nose, and loading ramp, permit straight-in loading into front of hold, under flight deck. Rear straight-in loading via ramp which forms under-surface of rear fuselage. Side panels of rear fuselage, by ramp, hinge outward to improve access on ground but do not need to open for air-drop operations in view of width of ramp. Provision for Aerial Delivery System (ADS) kits for paratroops or cargo. Two passenger doors on port side, at rear end of upper and lower decks. Two crew doors on port side, at forward end of upper and lower decks. Entire accommodation pressurised and air-conditioned.

Systems: Electronically-controlled air-conditioning and pressurisation systems: pressure differential 8·2 lb/sq in (0·58 kg/cm²). Four separate hydraulic systems, pressure 3,000 lb/sq in (210 kg/cm²) each, supply flying control and utility systems. Electrical system includes four 60/80kVA AC engine-driven generators. Two APUs to provide auxiliary pneumatic, hydraulic and electrical power.

Electronics and Equipment: Communications and navigation radio to military requirements. Norden radar. Nortronics inertial navigation system. Special equipment includes electronic Malfunction Detection, Analysis and Recording subsystem (MADAR) which scans and analyses over 800 test points.

Dimensions, external:

Wing span	222 ft 8½ in (67·88 m)
Wing chord at root	45 ft 5·3 in (13·85 m)
Wing chord at tip	15 ft 4 in (4·67 m)
Wing aspect ratio	7·75
Length overall	247 ft 10 in (75·54 m)
Length of fuselage	230 ft 7½ in (70·29 m)
Height overall	65 ft 1½ in (19·85 m)
Tailplane span	68 ft 8½ in (20·94 m)
Wheel track (between outer wheels)	37 ft 5½ in (11·42 m)
Wheelbase (c/l main gear to c/l nose gear)	72 ft 11 in (22·23 m)
Crew door (lower deck):	
Height	5 ft 11 in (1·80 m)
Width	3 ft 4 in (1·02 m)
Height to sill	12 ft 11 in (3·94 m)
Passenger door (lower deck):	
Height	6 ft 0 in (1·83 m)
Width	3 ft 0 in (0·91 m)
Height to sill	11 ft 8 in (3·56 m)
Aft loading opening (ramp lowered):	
Max height	12 ft 10¾ in (3·93 m)
Max width	19 ft 0 in (5·79 m)
Aft straight-in loading:	
Max height	9 ft 6 in (2·90 m)
Max width	19 ft 0 in (5·79 m)

Dimensions, internal:

Cabins, excl flight deck:	
Length:	
upper deck, forward	39 ft 4 in (11·99 m)
upper deck, aft	59 ft 8½ in (18·20 m)
lower deck, without ramp	121 ft 1 in (36·91 m)
lower deck, with ramp	144 ft 7 in (44·07 m)
Max width:	
upper deck, forward	13 ft 9½ in (4·20 m)
upper deck, aft	13 ft 0 in (3·96 m)
lower deck	19 ft 0 in (5·79 m)
Max height:	
upper deck	7 ft 6 in (2·29 m)
lower deck	13 ft 6 in (4·11 m)
Floor area:	
upper deck, forward	540 sq ft (50·17 m²)
upper deck, aft	776·1 sq ft (72·10 m²)
lower deck, without ramp	2,300·9 sq ft (213·76 m²)
Height to floor (kneeled):	
forward	4 ft 4¾ in (1·34 m)
aft	4 ft 9 in (1·45 m)
Volume:	
upper deck, forward	2,010 cu ft (56·91 m³)
upper deck, aft	6,020 cu ft (170·46 m³)
lower deck	34,795 cu ft (985·29 m³)

Areas:

Wings, gross	6,200 sq ft (576·0 m²)
Ailerons (total)	252·8 sq ft (23·49 m²)
Trailing-edge flaps (total)	991·7 sq ft (92·13 m²)
Leading-edge slats (total)	648·5 sq ft (60·25 m²)
Spoilers (total)	430·7 sq ft (40·01 m²)
Fin	961·1 sq ft (89·29 m²)
Rudder	226·7 sq ft (21·06 m²)
Tailplane	965·8 sq ft (89·73 m²)
Elevators	258·7 sq ft (24·03 m²)

Weights and Loadings (for 2·25*g*):

Basic operating weight	337,937 lb (153,285 kg)
Design payload	220,967 lb (100,228 kg)
Max ramp weight	769,000 lb (348,810 kg)
Max T-O weight	769,000 lb (348,810 kg)
Max landing weight	635,850 lb (288,416 kg)
Max zero-fuel weight	558,904 lb (253,515 kg)
Max wing loading	124·0 lb/sq ft (605·4 kg/m²)
Max power loading	4·69 lb/lb st (4·69 kg/kg st)

Performance (at max T-O weight, except where indicated):

Max never-exceed speed	409·5 knots (472 mph; 760 km/h) CAS or Mach 0·875
Max level speed at 25,000 ft (7,620 m)	496 knots (571 mph; 919 km/h)
High-speed cruise at 25,000 ft (7,620 m) at normal rated thrust	460-480 knots (530-553 mph; 853-890 km/h)
Average cruising speed	450 knots (518 mph; 834 km/h)
Aerial delivery drop speed	130-150 knots (150-173 mph; 241-278 km/h)
Stalling speed, 40° flap at max landing weight	104 knots (120 mph; 194 km/h) EAS
Rate of climb at S/L, ISA, at max rated thrust	1,800 ft (549 m)/min
Service ceiling at AUW of 615,000 lb (278,950 kg)	34,000 ft (10,360 m)
Min ground turning radius	75 ft 0 in (22·86 m)
Runway LCN:	
Concrete	40
Asphalt	64
T-O run	7,000 ft (2,134 m)
T-O to 50 ft (15 m)	8,400 ft (2,560 m)
Landing from 50 ft (15 m)	3,600 ft (1,097 m)
Landing run	2,230 ft (680 m)
Range with 220,967 lb (100,228 kg) payload	3,256 nm (3,749 miles; 6,033 km)
Range with 112,600 lb (51,074 kg) payload	5,670 nm (6,529 miles; 10,505 km)
Ferry range	6,940 nm (7,991 miles; 12,860 km)

(1975–76)

LOCKHEED MODEL 382 HERCULES

USAF designations: C-130, AC-130, DC-130, HC-130, JC-130, RC-130 and WC-130
US Navy designations: C-130, DC-130, EC-130 and LC-130
US Marine Corps designation: KC-130
US Coast Guard designations: EC-130 and HC-130
Canadian Armed Forces designation: CC-130
RAF designations: Hercules C.Mk 1 and W.Mk 2

The C-130 was designed to a specification issued by the USAF Tactical Air Command in 1951. Lockheed was awarded its first production contract for the C-130A in September 1952, and a total of 461 C-130As and C-130Bs was manufactured.

YC-130. The first of two prototypes under this designation flew on August 23, 1954.

C-130A. Initial production version with 3,750 eshp Allison T56-A-1A or -9 turboprops, driving Aeroproducts three-blade constant-speed reversible-pitch propellers, diameter 15 ft 0 in (4·60 m). Fuel capacity originally 5,250 US gallons (19,865 litres). Can now be supplemented by two 450 US gallon (1,705 litre) underwing pylon tanks. First flown on April 7, 1955. Deliveries of this version to USAF began in December 1956, and

Large fairings forward of the fin and under each wing, plus antennae canisters, distinguish the new EC-130E

Lockheed HC-130H Hercules air search, rescue and recovery aircraft with nose-mounted recovery system extended

231 were built before production ended in February 1959, including 12 delivered to the Royal Australian Air Force with T56-A-11 engines.

AC-130A Gunship II. Close support conversion of C-130A Hercules. First aircraft was the 13th production C-130A, with blunt-nose radar, evaluated in Vietnam in 1967-68. Conversion by USAF Aeronautical Systems Division included installation of four 20 mm and four 7·62 mm multi-barrel guns. Next seven were former JC-130As converted by LTV Electrosystems, with standard nose radar, searchlight, forward-looking infra-red target acquisition sensor and direct-view image intensification sights. Deployed to Vietnam in 1968-69. Ninth AC-130A produced by USAF ASD under Surprise Package project, with two 20 mm guns replaced by 40 mm guns, digital fire control computer and other improvements. Nine more aircraft converted to similar standard by LTV Electrosystems under Pave Pronto programme.

C-130A (formerly GC-130A). Drone Launcher/Director. Two C-130A's modified for Air Research and Development Command to test the aircraft's ability to launch realistic targets for support of research, development, operational evaluation and aircrew training of Air Force's air defence weapons systems. C-130 can carry up to four drones under underwing pylons for release at heights of 25,000 to 35,000 ft (7,625 to 10,675 m). Modification systems incorporated permit use of the whole family of drones manufactured by Ryan and Northrop. Fuselage nose lengthened by 30 in (76·2 cm) for installation of ground control antennae and radome equipment. Larger windows provided for camera recording. All electronic equipment for drone launching, control and monitoring in portable consoles for easy removal, permitting aircraft to be used as a cargo carrier, assault transport or ambulance when necessary. Crew of seven or eight.

JC-130A. Eleven early C-130As converted for a missile and spacecraft tracking role, by Temco Aerosystems Division of LTV, in support of operations at Cape Canaveral. Endurance increased to 12-13 hours by standard fitment of normally-optional 450 US gallon (1,703 litre) wing fuel tanks and extra 12 US gallon (45 litre) oil tank. Seven later converted to AC-130A, as noted above.

RC-130A. Photographic version of C-130A. Externally evident features include TV viewfinder blister under nose radome and camera windows in bottom of fuselage. Cabin contains cameras, mapping equipment, dark room and galley. Additional crew stations for photonavigator, photographer, two HIRAN operators and airborne profile recorder operator. Contract for 16 aircraft, including prototype. Deliveries to the 1,370th Photo Mapping Wing, Air Photographic and Charting Service, Military Airlift Command, were completed in 1959.

C-130B. Developed version with additional 1,710 US gallons (6,472 litres) of fuel in wings inboard of inner engine nacelles, strengthened landing gear and four 4,050 hp Allison T56-A-7 turboprops, driving four-blade Hamilton Standard propellers. First C-130B for the USAF Tactical Air Command flew on November 20, 1958, and this version entered service on June 12, 1959. A total of 230 have been delivered, including ten for the Indonesian Air Force, four for the RCAF, six for the Pakistan Air Force, seven for the South African Air Force, four LC-130F's, 12 HC-130B's, 46 KC-130F's and seven C-130F's.

HC-130B (formerly SC-130B). Twelve for US Coast Guard. Deliveries completed in February 1963. Used for search, rescue and other duties. Modifications include addition of radio operator's station in flight compartment, accommodation for two search observer seats and clear-vision panel in rear paratroop doors for low-level search. Able to fly 1,000 miles (1,600 km) off-shore at 25,000 ft (8,200 m) at 370 mph (595 kmh), then cruise for eight hours' search duty at 145-170 mph (233-275 kmh) on two engines, re-start engines and return to base at 300-370 mph (480-595 kmh), with 15 min fuel reserve. Endurance at this range can be increased to 10·2 hours at 150-160 mph (240-257 kmh) if outward flight is made at 335 mph (540 kmh) and return flight at 300 mph (480 kmh). Normal crew of eight. Can carry 24-44 passengers.

JC-130B. Six modified C-130B's equipped for Discoverer satellite recovery. Replaced C-119's of 6593rd Test Squadron, USAF, at Hickam AFB, Hawaii, in mid-1961.

NC-130B. Experimental boundary layer control test-bed for USAF which made its first flight in February 1960. Two Allison YT56-A-6 turbojet engines, pod-mounted under outer wings, are used to blow a constant flow of air over the control surfaces and flaps. Stalling speed, take-off distance and landing distance are greatly reduced. One only. If produced in series, designation would have been C-130C.

RC-130B. Survey and reconnaissance conversions of the basic C-130B.

WC-130B. Seventeen converted from basic C-130B aircraft, with equipment for weather reconnaissance role. Nine issued to 53rd ("Hurricane Hunters") Squadron in Puerto Rico, four to 55th Squadron in California, and three to 54th ("Typhoon Chasers") Squadron on Guam. One updated by Kaman to have advanced Airborne Weather Reconnaissance System (AWRS).

C-130D. Twelve C-130A aircraft modified for service with USAF in Antarctic and elsewhere. Wheel-ski landing gear. Main skis are each approximately 20 ft 0 in (6·10 m) long by 5 ft 6 in wide (5·94 × 1·68 m) and weigh approximately 2,000 lb (907 kg) each. The nose ski is approximately 10 ft 0 in (3·05 m) long and 5 ft 6 in (1·68 m) wide. The total ski installation weighs approximately 5,500 lb (2,495 kg). The main skis and nose ski have 8° and 15° nose-up and nose-down pitch to enable them to follow uneven terrain. They have a bearing surface of Teflon plastic to reduce friction and resist the adhesiveness of ice. JATO fitted. Fuel capacity increased by addition of two 450 US gallon (1,705 litre) underwing pylon tanks. Provision for two 500 US gallon (1,891 litre) tanks in cargo compartment for longer flights such as ferry flights to Antarctic.

C-130E (Lockheed Model 382-44A). Extended-range version of C-130B, with two 1,360 US gallon (5,145 litre) underwing fuel tanks. Normal max T-O weight is 155,000 lb (70,310 kg). Take-off at overload gross weight of 175,000 lb (79,380 kg) increases the range and endurance capabilities, with certain operating restrictions at this higher weight. Total of 383 ordered for USAF Military Airlift Command (130), Tactical Air Command (193), US Navy (4), US Coast Guard (1), Royal Canadian Air Force (20), Iranian Air Force (8), Turkish Air Force (5), Brazilian Air Force (5), Swedish Air Force (1), Saudi-Arabian Air Force (4) and Royal Australian Air Force (12). First C-130E flew on August 25, 1961. Deliveries began in April 1962.

AC-130E. Eight improved close support conversions of C-130E produced by USAF at Warner Robins AFB, Georgia, under Pave Spectre programme. More ammunition, heavier armour and more advanced electronics than in AC-130A. Converted to AC-130H after service in Vietnam.

DC-130E. Version modified by LAS (which see) for drone control duties.

EC-130E. Electronic surveillance version for USAF to replace Lockheed EC-121s. Large blade antennae added above dorsal fin and under each outer wing. Smaller antennae include horizontal blade on each side of rear fuselage. Bullet-shape canisters outboard of each underwing antenna and at extreme tail of aircraft house trailing wire antennae which extend several hundred feet behind the EC-130E in flight.

HC-130E. Sea-air rescue conversion of the basic C-130E Hercules. Three produced for service with the US Coast Guard.

WC-130E. Weather reconnaissance conversions of C-130E for USAF.

C-130F (formerly GV-1U). Seven for transport duties with US Navy. Similar to KC-130F, but without underwing pylons and internal refuelling equipment. AUW 135,000 lb (61,235 kg).

KC-130F (formerly GV-1). Forty-six for US Marine Corps. Deliveries completed in November, 1962. Assault transport, basically similar to C-130B. Equipped for in-flight refuelling to service two jet aircraft simultaneously. Entire refuelling equipment can be quickly and easily installed and removed. Two C-130A's loaned to USMC in the Summer of 1957 for flight refuelling tests. The production tanker version, first flown on January 22, 1960, has a tankage capacity of 3,600 US gallons (13,620 litres) in its cargo compartment. Able to fly 1,000 miles (1,600 km) at cruise ceiling at 340 mph (547 kmh), and transfer 31,000 lb (14,060 kg) of fuel at 25,000 ft (7,620 m) at a refuelling speed of 355 mph (571 kmh) with normal military reserves. Normal crew of five to seven.

LC-130F (formerly C-130BL). Four C-130B's for US Navy with wheel-ski gear (see under C-130D above) for service in Antarctic. Range with skis reduced by 5-10%. First delivered in August 1960.

EC-130G. Redesignation of four C-130Gs acquired by US Navy. Equipped with VLF radio to relay emergency action messages to Fleet Ballistic Missile submarines anywhere in the world.

C-130H. Similar to earlier Hercules models except for more powerful engines: T56-A-15 turboprops rated at 3,661 kW (4,910 ehp) for take-off, but limited to 3,362 kW (4,508 ehp). Deliveries to USAF began in April 1975.

HC-130H. Lockheed was awarded two initial contracts in September 1963 for this extended-range air search, rescue and recovery version to be utilised by the Aerospace Rescue and Recovery Service of the USAF for aerial recovery of personnel or equipment and other duties. The US Coast Guard subsequently ordered seven. A folding nose-mounted recovery system makes possible repeated pickups from ground of persons or objects weighing up to 227 kg (500 lb) including the recoverable gear. Four 3,661 kW (4,910 ehp) (limited to 3,356 kW; 4,500 ehp) Allison T56-A-15 turboprop engines, each driving a Hamilton Standard 54H60-91 four-blade constant-speed propeller. Normal fuel tankage as for C-130H. Provision for installing two 6,184 litre (1,800 US gallon) tanks in cargo compartment. Normal crew of 10, consisting of pilot, co-pilot, navigator, 2 flight mechanics, radio operator, 2 loadmasters and 2 para-rescue technicians, with provision for additional pilot and navigator for long missions. Standard equipment includes four 6-man rafts, two litters, bunks, 16 personnel kits, recovery winches, 10 flare launchers. Total of 66 delivered, of which the first one flew on 8 December 1964. Four modified as **JHC-130H** with added equipment for aerial recovery of re-entering space capsules. One modified by LAS to **DC-130H**.

KC-130H. A tanker version of the C-130H, very similar to the KC-130R. Exported to Argentina (2), Brazil (2), Israel (2), Saudi Arabia (6) and Spain (3).

C-130K. This is basically a C-130H, modified for use by the Royal Air Force. Much of the electronics and instrumentation is of UK manufacture. Sixty-six delivered as **Hercules C. Mk 1**, of which the first one flew on 19 October 1966. One modified by Marshall of Cambridge (Engineering) Ltd in the UK for use by the RAF Meteorological Research Flight, under the designation **Hercules W. Mk 2**. Thirty are each being lengthened by 4·58 m (15 ft 0 in), equivalent to commercial L 100-30 standard, during 1978-82. This will increase payload capacity to seven cargo pallets instead of five, or 128 troops instead of 92, or 92 fully-equipped paratroops instead of 64, or 93 stretcher patients (and six attendants) instead of 70. After modification, these aircraft will be redesignated **Hercules C. Mk 3**.

HC-130N. Search and rescue version for recovery of aircrew and retrieval of space capsules after re-entry, using advanced direction-finding equipment. Fifteen ordered for USAF in 1969.

HC-130P. Twenty HC-130Hs were modified into HC-130Ps with capability of refuelling helicopters in flight, and for mid-air retrieval of parachute-borne payloads. Modification involved the addition of refuelling drogue pods and associated plumbing. Typical helicopter refuelling mission involves taking off at an AUW of 70,310 kg (155,000 lb) with 33,385 kg (73,600 lb) of fuel on board, meeting up with the helicopters at a radius of 500 nm (925 km; 575 miles), transferring 22,000 kg (48,500 lb) of fuel to the helicopters and returning 500 nm to the point of origin.

EC-130Q. Eleven aircraft similar to EC-130G but with improved equipment and crew accommodation, for USN command communications duties.

KC-130R. Tanker version of the C-130H for US Marine Corps. Major changes from the earlier KC-130F include engines of 3,362 kW (4,508 ehp), increased T-O and landing weights, pylon-mounted fuel tanks to provide an additional 10,296 litres (2,720 US gallons) of fuel, plus a removable 13,627 litre (3,600 US gallon) fuel tank located in the cargo compartment. Four ordered in early 1974; ten more subsequently.

LC-130R. Basically a C-130H with wheel-ski gear for US Navy. Main skis each approximately 6·10 m (20 ft 0 in) long by 1·68 m (5 ft 6 in) wide. The nose ski is approximately 3·05 m (10 ft 0 in) long by 1·68 m (5 ft 6 in) wide. The total ski installation weighs approximately 2,540 kg (5,600 lb). The main skis have 8° nose-up and nose-down pitch and the nose skis have 15° nose-up and nose-down pitch, to enable them to follow uneven terrain. The load-bearing surfaces of the skis are coated with Teflon plastics to reduce friction and resist ice adhesion. Provision is made for fitting JATO units. Four converted, for service in the Antarctic. Two more aircraft in this configuration were ordered in late 1975 by the National Science Foundation, for use in the Antarctic.

Advanced versions. The Lockheed-Georgia company has studied several versions of the Hercules which would have improved capabilities. The C-130SS Stretch STOL version features a 2·54 m (8 ft 4 in) cargo compartment stretch, greater payload and better short-field capabilities than the C-130H. The C-130HS offers the above-mentioned fuselage stretch without the improved STOL features. The C-130WBS is a wide-body, stretched STOL version.

The C-130 is able to deliver single loads of up to 11,340 kg (25,000 lb) by the ground proximity extraction method. This involves making a fly-past 1·2-1·5 m (4-5 ft) above the ground with the rear loading ramp open. The aircraft trails a hook which is attached by cable to the palletised cargo. The hook engages a steel cable on the ground and the cargo is extracted from the aircraft and brought to a stop on the ground in about 30 m (100 ft) by an energy absorption system manufactured by All American Engineering of Wilmington, Delaware. An alternative extraction technique involves deploying a 6·70 m (22 ft) ribbon parachute to drag the pallet from the cabin. Loads of up to 22,680 kg (50,000 lb) have been delivered by this method.

By February 1979 firm orders for all versions of the C-130 totalled 1,553 for 44 nations. This total comprised 1,011 C-130s for the US services, 471 for foreign military operators, and 71 commercial Hercules. The 1,500th Hercules, a C-130H for the Sudan Air Force, was delivered on 13 March 1978. Production rate for 1979 was set at three aircraft per month.

The following details refer specifically to the C-130H, except where indicated otherwise:

TYPE: Medium/long-range combat transport.

WINGS: Cantilever high-wing monoplane. Wing section NACA 64A318 at root, NACA 64A412 at tip. Dihedral 2° 30'. Incidence 3° at root, 0° at tip. Sweepback at quarter-chord 0°. All-metal two-spar stressed-skin structure, with integrally-stiffened tapered machined skin panels up to 14·63 m (48 ft 0 in) long. Conventional aluminium alloy ailerons have tandem-piston hydraulic boost, operated by either of two independent hydraulic systems. Lockheed-Fowler aluminium alloy trailing-edge flaps. Trim tabs in ailerons. Leading-edge anti-iced by hot air bled from engines.

FUSELAGE: Semi-monocoque structure of aluminium and magnesium alloys.

TAIL UNIT: Cantilever all-metal stressed-skin structure. Fixed-incidence tailplane. Trim tabs in elevators and rudder. Elevator tabs use AC electrical power as primary source and DC as emergency source. Control surfaces have tandem-piston hydraulic boost. Hot-air anti-icing of tailplane leading-edge, by engine bleed air.

LANDING GEAR: Hydraulically-retractable tricycle type. Each main unit has two wheels in tandem, retracting into fairings built on to the sides of the fuselage. Nose unit has twin wheels and is steerable through 60° each side of centre. Oleo shock-absorbers. Main-wheel tyres size 56 × 20-20, pressure 5·52 bars (80 lb/sq in). Nose-wheel tyres size 39 × 13-16, pressure 4·14 bars (60 lb/sq in). Goodyear aircooled hydraulic brakes with anti-skid units. Retractable combination wheel-skis available.

POWER PLANT: Four 3,362 kW (4,508 ehp) Allison T56-A-15 turboprop engines, each driving a Hamilton Standard type 54H60 four-blade constant-speed fully-feathering reversible-pitch propeller. Eight Aerojet-General 15KS-1000 JATO units (each 4·45 kN; 1,000 lb st for 15 sec) can be carried. Fuel in six integral tanks in wings, with total capacity of 26,344 litres (6,960 US gallons) and two underwing pylon tanks, each with capacity of 5,146 litres (1,360 US gallons). Total fuel capacity 36,636 litres (9,680 US gallons). Single pressure refuelling point in starboard wheel well. Fillers for overwing gravity fuelling. Oil capacity 182 litres (48 US gallons).

ACCOMMODATION: Crew of four on flight deck, comprising pilot, co-pilot, navigator and systems manager. Provision for fifth man to supervise loading. Sleeping quarters for relief crew, and galley. Flight deck and main cabin pressurised and air-conditioned. Standard complements are as follows: troops (max) 92, paratroops (max) 64, litters 74 and 2 attendants. As a cargo carrier, loads can include heavy equipment such as a 12,080 kg (26,640 lb) type F.6 refuelling trailer or a 155 mm howitzer and its high-speed tractor. Up to six preloaded pallets of freight can be carried. Hydraulically-operated main loading door and ramp at rear of cabin. Paratroop door on each side aft of landing gear fairing.

SYSTEMS: Air-conditioning and pressurisation system max pressure differential 0·52 bars (7·5 lb/sq in). Two independent hydraulic systems, pressure 207 bars (3,000 lb/sq in). Electrical system supplied by four 40kVA AC generators, plus one 40kVA auxiliary generator driven by APU. Current production aircraft incorporate many systems and component design changes for increased reliability. There are differences between the installed components for US government and export versions.

DIMENSIONS, EXTERNAL:

Wing span	40·41 m (132 ft 7 in)
Wing chord at root	4·88 m (16 ft 0 in)
Wing chord, mean	4·16 m (13 ft 8½ in)
Wing aspect ratio	10·09
Length overall:	
all except HC-130H	29·79 m (97 ft 9 in)
HC-130H, recovery system folded	
	30·10 m (98 ft 9 in)
HC-130H, recovery system spread	
	32·41 m (106 ft 4 in)
Height overall	11·66 m (38 ft 3 in)
Tailplane span	16·05 m (52 ft 8 in)
Wheel track	4·35 m (14 ft 3 in)
Wheelbase	9·77 m (32 ft 0¾ in)
Propeller diameter	4·11 m (13 ft 6 in)
Main cargo door (rear of cabin):	
Height	2·77 m (9 ft 1 in)
Width	3·05 m (10 ft 0 in)
Height to sill	1·03 m (3 ft 5 in)
Paratroop doors (each): Height	1·83 m (6 ft 0 in)
Width	0·91 m (3 ft 0 in)
Height to sill	1·03 m (3 ft 5 in)

DIMENSIONS, INTERNAL:

Cabin, excl flight deck:	
Length without ramp	12·60 m (41 ft 5 in)
Length with ramp	15·73 m (51 ft 8½ in)
Max width	3·13 m (10 ft 3 in)
Max height	2·81 m (9 ft 2¾ in)
Floor area, excl ramp	39·5 m² (425 sq ft)
Volume, incl ramp	127·4 m³ (4,500 cu ft)

AREAS:

Wings, gross	162·12 m² (1,745 sq ft)
Ailerons (total)	10·22 m² (110 sq ft)
Trailing-edge flaps (total)	31·77 m² (342 sq ft)
Fin	20·90 m² (225 sq ft)
Rudder, incl tab	6·97 m² (75 sq ft)
Tailplane	35·40 m² (381 sq ft)
Elevators, incl tabs	14·40 m² (155 sq ft)

WEIGHTS AND LOADINGS:

Operating weight empty	34,169 kg (75,331 lb)
Max payload	19,872 kg (43,811 lb)
Max normal T-O weight	70,310 kg (155,000 lb)
Max overload T-O weight	79,380 kg (175,000 lb)
Max landing weight	58,970 kg (130,000 lb)
Max zero-fuel weight, 2·5 g	54,040 kg (119,142 lb)
Max wing loading	434·5 kg/m² (89 lb/sq ft)
Max power loading	5·23 kg/kW (8·6 lb/ehp)

PERFORMANCE (at max T-O weight, unless indicated otherwise):

Max cruising speed:		
C-130H	335 knots	(621 km/h; 386 mph)
HC-130H	318 knots	(589 km/h; 366 mph)
Econ cruising speed	300 knots	(556 km/h; 345 mph)
Stalling speed	100 knots	(185 km/h; 115 mph)

Max rate of climb at S/L:

C-130H	579 m (1,900 ft)/min
HC-130H	555 m (1,820 ft)/min
Service ceiling at 58,970 kg (130,000 lb) AUW	10,060 m (33,000 ft)
Service ceiling, one engine out, at 58,970 kg (130,000 lb) AUW	8,075 m (26,500 ft)
Min ground turning radius	19·2 m (63 ft)

Runway LCN at 70,310 kg (155,000 lb) AUW:

asphalt	37
concrete	42
T-O run	1,091 m (3,580 ft)
T-O to 15 m (50 ft)	1,573 m (5,160 ft)
Landing from 15 m (50 ft) at 45,360 kg (100,000 lb) AUW	741 m (2,430 ft)
Landing from 15 m (50 ft) at max landing weight	838 m (2,750 ft)
Landing run at max landing weight	533 m (1,750 ft)

Range with max payload, with 5% reserves and allowance for 30 min at S/L
2,160 nm (4,002 km; 2,487 miles)
Range with max fuel, incl external tanks, 9,070 kg (20,000 lb) payload and reserves of 5% initial fuel plus 30 min at S/L 4,460 nm (8,264 km; 5,135 miles)
(1979-80)

A Lockheed Hudson III carrying the British Mk. I Airborne lifeboat.

THE LOCKHEED MODEL 414 HUDSON.

British name : Hudson.
U.S. Army Air Forces designations : A-28 and A-29.
U.S. Navy designation : PBO-1.

The Hudson was originally built to the order of the British Government as a military conversion of the Type 14 transport. It was in production from 1939 to June, 1943, and thousands were built and delivered to the British, Australian, New Zealand, Canadian, Netherlands, Chinese and American flying services.

Hudson III (A-29 and PBO-1). Two Wright GR-1820-G205A engines driving Hamilton-Standard Hydromatic constant-speed airscrews. Retractable rear firing under-gun position. A-29 fitted with Wright R-1820-87 engines. A-29A similar to A-29 except fitted with benches for troop-carrying. The latter was originally given the designation C-63.

Hudson VI (A-28). Two Pratt & Whitney R-1830-67 engines driving Hamilton-Standard Hydromatic constant-speed airscrews. External D/F loop aerial (no blister). Convertible to troop transport or cargo-carrier when turret removed.

After withdrawal from combatant service with the R.A.F., U.S. Army or Navy, the Hudson continued to be used for miscellaneous duties, including transport, air/sea rescue, training, target-towing, etc.

The Hudson III was the first aeroplane to be fitted to carry the British-developed Mk. I airborne lifeboat. This lifeboat was first used operationally in May, 1943, by an R.A.F. Air/Sea Rescue Squadron equipped with Hudsons to rescue the crew of an R.A.F. bomber forced down in the North Sea, 50 miles from the British coast. (1945–46)

TYPE.—Twin-engined General Purposes monoplane.

WINGS.—Mid-wing cantilever monoplane. Wing in three sections with single spar and stressed-skin covering. Built-in fuel tanks in centre-section. Lockheed-Fowler flaps, between ailerons and fuselage, slide back 42 in. in streamline guides. Ailerons are interconnected to droop with flaps. Low-drag slots in each wing-tip in front of ailerons.

FUSELAGE.—Elliptical cross-section monocoque fuselage of all-metal flush-riveted construction.

TAIL UNIT.—Cantilever monoplane type with twin fins and rudders. All-metal construction.

LANDING GEAR.—Retractable type with wheels retracting backwards into engine nacelles. Hydraulic retraction with emergency hand operation.

POWER PLANT.—Two Wright Cyclone (Hudson I, II and III) or Pratt & Whitney Twin-Wasp (Hudson IV and V) radial air-cooled engines. Hamilton-Standard constant-speed airscrews. NACA cowlings. Built-in fuel tanks in centre-section.

ACCOMMODATION.—Normal crew of five. Bomb-aimer's position in nose. Pilot and navigator over leading-edge of wing. Radio operator and rear gunner in cabin over wing.

ARMAMENT.—Two fixed 0.303 in. Browning machine-guns in top of fuselage in front of pilot. Boulton Paul turret with two 0.303 in. Browning guns at after end of fuselage near tailplane ; two 0.303 in. Browning guns on beam mountings one on each side of fuselage ; and one 0.303 in. Browning gun in retractable prone position beneath fuselage. Internal stowage for bombs or depth-charges (total load : 1,400 lbs.) in fuselage beneath floor of cabin.

DIMENSIONS.—Span 65 ft. 6 in. (19.95 m.), Length 44 ft. 4 in. (13.4 m.), Height 11 ft. 10½ in. (3.63 m.), Wing area 551 sq. ft. (51.2 sq. m.).

WEIGHTS.—Weight empty 12,536 lbs. (5,690 kg.), Weight loaded 18,500 lbs. (8,400 kg.).

PERFORMANCE.—Maximum speed 275 m.p.h. (440 km.h.), Cruising speed 223 m.p.h. (356.8 km.h.) at 8,000 ft. (2,440 m.), Landing speed 72 m.p.h. (115.2 km.h.), Service Ceiling 24,500 ft. (7,470 m.).

Lockheed JetStar light jet transport (four Pratt & Whitney JT12A-6A turbojet engines)

LOCKHEED MODEL 1329 JETSTAR

USAF designation: C-140

First announced in March, 1957, the JetStar is a jet-powered utility transport with normal accommodation for a crew of two and eight or ten passengers. The first prototype, built as a private venture, flew on September 4, 1957, only 241 days after its basic design was finalised.

The two prototype JetStars were each powered originally by two Bristol Siddeley Orpheus turbojets, mounted on each side of the rear fuselage. One of them was re-engined in December, 1959, with four Pratt & Whitney JT12 turbojets mounted in lateral pairs in the same position. This power plant was standardised for the production version, which first flew in the Summer of 1960 and received FAA Type Approval in August 1961.

C-140A. Five for use by the Air Force Communications Service, which is responsible for inspecting world-wide military navigation aids. First delivered in Summer of 1962.

VC-140B. Eleven transport versions for operation by the special air missions wing of MATS. First delivered in late 1961.

All JetStars delivered from the Summer of 1963 have the higher-rated JT12A-6A engine, as described below. This engine has a max continuous rating of 2,570 lb (1,166 kg) st, compared with 2,400 lb (1,090 kg) st for the JT12A-6 engines fitted earlier.

TYPE : Four-jet light utility transport.

WINGS : Cantilever low-wing monoplane. Wing section NACA 63A112 at root, NACA 63A309

(modified) at tip. Aspect ratio 5·27. Chord 13 ft 7⅜ in (4·16 m) at root, 5 ft 1 in (1·55 m) at tip. Dihedral 2°. Incidence 1° at root, —1° at tip. Sweepback at quarter-chord 30°. Conventional fail-safe stressed-skin structure of high-strength aluminium. Bending loads carried by integral skin-stringer extrusion and sheet ribs, shear loads by three beams. Plain aluminium alloy ailerons are mechanically operated with hydraulic boost. Aileron trim-tabs actuated electro-mechanically. Double-slotted all-metal trailing-edge flaps. Hinged leading-edge flaps. No spoilers. Rubber boot de-icers on leading-edge.

FUSELAGE : Semi-monocoque fail-safe structure of aluminium alloy. Hydraulically-operated speed-brake on underside of fuselage aft of pressurised compartment.

TAIL UNIT : Cantilever aluminium alloy structure with tailplane mounted part-way up fin. Fin is pivoted to vary tailplane incidence for trimming. Elevators mechanically operated with hydraulic boost. Rudder mechanically operated with servo assist. Rubber-boot de-icers on leading-edges.

LANDING GEAR : Hydraulically-retractable tricycle type with twin wheels on all units. Manual emergency extension. Main units retract inward, nose-wheels forward. Oleo-pneumatic shock-absorbers. Main wheel tyres size 26 × 6·6 type VII, pressure 205 lb sq in (14·41 kg cm²). Nose-wheel tyres size 18 × 4·4 type VII, pressure 180 lb sq in (12·65 kg cm²). Hydraulic brakes with automatic skid control.

POWER PLANT : Four Pratt & Whitney JT12A-6A turbojet engines (each 3,000 lb = 1,360 kg st) mounted in lateral pairs on sides of rear fuselage. Thrust reversers fitted. Fuel in four integral wing tanks, total capacity 1,530 US gallons (5,792 litres), and two non-removable external tanks on wings. Total fuel capacity 2,660 US gallons (10,070 litres). Refuelling point on each tank. Oil capacity 6·3 US gallons (24 litres).

ACCOMMODATION: Normal accommodation for crew of two and ten passengers, with wardrobe, galley and toilet aft of cabin and baggage compartments fore and aft. Layout and furnishing can be varied to suit customer's requirements. Door on port side between flight deck and cabin.

SYSTEMS: Air-cycle air-conditioning and pressurisation system, using engine-bleed air. Pressure differential 8·9 lb/sq in (0·63 kg/cm²). Two independent hydraulic systems with engine-driven pumps; pressure 3,000 lb/sq in (210 kg/cm²). Four 28V 300A DC engine-driven starter-generators, three 3000VA single-phase 115V inverters and two 24V 36Ah batteries. No APU.

ELECTRONICS AND EQUIPMENT: Provision for full range of radio, radar and all-weather flying equipment, to customer's specification.

DIMENSIONS, EXTERNAL:

Wing span	54 ft 5 in (16·60 m)
Length overall	60 ft 5 in (18·42 m)
Length of fuselage	58 ft 9½ in (17·92 m)
Height overall	20 ft 5 in (6·23 m)
Tailplane span	24 ft 9 in (7·55 m)
Wheel track	12 ft 3½ in (3·75 m)
Wheelbase	20 ft 7 in (6·28 m)

Cabin door:

Height	4 ft 11 in (1·50 m)
Width	2 ft 2½ in (0·67 m)
Height to sill	approx 4 ft 6 in (1·37 m)

DIMENSIONS, INTERNAL:

Cabin, excluding flight deck:

Length	28 ft 2½ in (8·59 m)
Max width	6 ft 2½ in (1·89 m)
Max height	6 ft 1 in (1·85 m)
Volume	700 cu ft (19·82 m³)

AREAS:

Wings, gross	542·5 sq ft (50·40 m²)
Ailerons (total)	24·4 sq ft (2·27 m²)
Trailing-edge flaps (extended, total)	62·6 sq ft (5·82 m²)
Leading edge flaps (total)	34·0 sq ft (3·16 m²)
Fin	94·0 sq ft (8·73 m²)
Rudder, including tab	16·2 sq ft (1·51 m²)
Tailplane	117·8 sq ft (10·94 m²)
Elevators	31·2 sq ft (2·90 m²)

WEIGHTS AND LOADINGS:

Basic operating weight	21,500 lb (9,752 kg)
Max payload	3,000 lb (1,360 kg)
Max T-O weight	40,921 lb (18,550 kg)
Max ramp weight	41,500 lb (18,825 kg)
Max zero-fuel weight	24,500 lb (11,113 kg)
Max landing weight *	30,000 lb (13,600 kg)
Max wing loading	75·5 lb/sq ft (368·5 kg/m²)
Max power loading	3·4 lb/lb st (3·4 kg/kg st)

* Kit available for retrofit to 35,000 lb (15,900 kg)

PERFORMANCE (at max T-O weight):

Max level speed below 22,350 ft (6,810 m) 403 mph (648 kmh) IAS; above 22,350 ft (6,810 m) Mach 0·82

Max permissible diving speed below 17,500 ft (5,330 m) 490 mph (788 kmh) IAS; above 17,500 ft (5,330 m) Mach 0·90

Max cruising speed at 20,000 ft (6,100 m) 550 mph (885 kmh)

Econ cruising speed, reduced AUW, at 40,000 ft (12,200 m) 495 mph (797 kmh)

Stalling speed at max landing weight 122 mph (196 kmh)

Rate of climb at S/L 3,300 ft (1,005 m) min

Service ceiling 33,000 ft (10,050 m)

Service ceiling, one engine out 24,000 ft (7,300 m)

T-O run 3,525 ft (1,075 m)

T-O to 50 ft (15 m) 5,275 ft (1,610 m)

Landing from 50 ft (15 m) 3,950 ft (1,205 m)

Landing run 2,600 ft (792 m)

Range with max fuel at long-range cruising speed at 25,000 ft (7,620 m), 45 min reserve 2,185 miles (3,515 km)

Range with max payload, at long-range cruising speed at 25,000 ft (7,620 m), 45 min reserve 1,980 miles (3,185 km)

(1965–66)

The Lockheed F-5B Photographic-Reconnaissance Monoplane (two Allison V-1710-89/91 engines).

THE LOCKHEED LIGHTNING.

U.S. Army Air Forces designation: P-38 and F-5.

The Lightning was the first military type developed by the Lockheed Aircraft Corpn. It was designed to meet an Air Corps specification issued in 1936 for a twin-engined interceptor fighter a specification which called for, among many other stringent requirements, a minimum speed of 360 m.p.h. (576 km.h.) at 20,000 ft. (6,100 m.). The design was accepted by the Air Corps on June 23, 1937, and the XP-38 prototype was delivered in January 1939. It made its first flight on January 27, 1939, but crashed at the end of a record transcontinental flight from California to New York on February 11. The XP-38 was fitted with two 1,040 h.p. Allison V-1710-33 (C15) engines with exhaust-driven G.E. turbo-superchargers and driving Curtiss electric inwardly-rotating airscrews. The armament consisted of one 23 m/m. Madsen cannon and four 50 cal. machine-guns.

YP-38. A Limited Procurement order for 13 YP-38's followed. Complete structural re-design lightened this model by 1,300 lbs. It was fitted with two 1,150 h.p. Allison V-1710-27/29 (F2R/F2L) engines driving outwardly-rotating airscrews. (*Note:* V-1710-27 (F2R) righthand rotation, V-1710-29 (F2L) lefthand rotation, both from rear end). The turbo and coolant installations were improved. The armament compartment was re-designed to house one 37 m/m. cannon, two 50 cal. and two 30 cal. machine-guns. The YP-38 first flew on September 18, 1940, and first delivery to the Air Corps was made in March, 1941.

P-38. Deliveries were begun in July, 1941. The 30 cal. guns were replaced by two 50 cal. guns and pilot armour was added. Thirty were built.

P-38D. In this model self-sealing tanks were introduced. A change in angle of incidence of the tailplane and redistribution of elevator balance weights improved elevator control, facilitated dive recoveries and eliminated tail-buffeting. Deliveries began in August, 1941.

P-38E. Principal change in this model was in armament. The 37 m/m. cannon was replaced by one of 20 m/m., the standard cannon on all subsequent models. The armament compartment and nose landing gear section were also completely re-designed to accommodate double the quantity of ammunition previously carried. Deliveries began in November, 1941.

P-38F. Power-plant changed to two 1,325 h.p. Allison V-1710-49/53 (F5R/F5L) engines. The P-38F was the first model to be equipped with brackets for 150 gal. auxiliary fuel tanks or 1,000 lb. bombs, one under each inner wing section. The P-38F was also the first model to be converted for training by the removal of all radio equipment and the substitution of a second seat behind the pilot for a trainee to get air experience in the P-38 before taking off alone. Dual control was not fitted. Deliveries began in March, 1942.

P-38G. A further power-plant change to two 1,325 h.p. Allison V-1710-51/55 (F10R/F10L) engines, each giving an additional 100 h.p. for cruising. The first version to use the so-called "manoeuvring" flaps, a feature of all subsequent models. The Fowler-type flaps are given a special combat setting which permits a small extension and droop to provide greatly increased lift for very little drag. The result is a very high degree of manoeuvrability over a wide speed range. The capacity of the auxiliary fuel tanks was doubled and, fitted with two 300 gal. auxiliary fuel tanks, the P-38G was the first American fighter to be ferried across the Atlantic by way of Labrador, Greenland and Iceland. The first trans-ocean flight was made early in 1943 by more than 100 Lightnings, escorted by Boeing Fortresses for navigational purposes. Deliveries began in August, 1942.

P-38H. This model was essentially the same as the P-38G except for the installation of two Allison V-1710-89/91 (F17R/F17L) engines, each developing 1,425 h.p. for take-off and, when needed, 1,600 "war emergency" h.p. Automatic control of coolant radiator shutters was introduced and the electrical system was modified. The P-38H, operating in the Pacific theatre, was the first model to carry two 1,600 lb. bombs. Deliveries began in the Summer of 1943.

P-38J. Fitted with the same engines as the P-38H but with increased take-off and altitude ratings, and driving new airscrews to give improved speed and climb at altitude. The former leading-edge type intercoolers replaced by core-type intercoolers and re-located with the oil radiators in scoops beneath each engine. The engine coolant radiators on the tail booms given greater capacity. Additional fuel tanks installed in the leading-edges of the outer wing sections. An optically-flat bullet-proof windscreen replaced the former curved screen. Late models in the J series were fitted with electrically-operated dive-flaps and an aileron boost system.

To serve as bombing formation leaders a number of P-38J fighters were converted into two-seaters to carry a bombardier and Norden bomb-sight. The first conversion, carried out by Lockheed engineers at Langford Lodge, England, had a typical Boston-type transparent nose and carried instruments for both navigation and bombing. These aircraft, without armament or bombs, led formations of Lightning fighter-bombers, each carrying 3,200 lbs. of bombs, on high-altitude precision bombing missions and were responsible for navigation to the target and for supervising the dropping of all bombs of the formation.

This first version was later superseded by the "Pathfinder" P-38, which had a new elongated cylindrical nacelle with blunt hemispherical nose. This model was developed at the Lockheed Modification Center at Dallas, Texas. The "Pathfinder" was fitted with more advanced instruments than its predecessor, including "Gee" radar equipment for bombing through cloud.

P-38K. This was an experimental model with an improved power-plant but the P-38L was developed so quickly that the K model was never put into production.

P-38L. A development of the P-38J. Fitted with two Allison V-1710-111/113 (F30R/F30L) engines, each with a rated output of 1,475 h.p. and a considerably higher war emergency horsepower than in previous models. A new General Electric turbo regulator replaced the hydraulic regulator used in the P-38J. Some P-38L's were also fitted with bombardier noses introduced in the P-38J (which see).

Two photographs on this page show the rocket projectile installation used on the P-39L Lightning in the closing stages of the war. The upper illustration shows the first installation of the American 5-inch rocket-projectile in two batteries of seven on free flight launchers which released their projectiles after one inch of forward motion. The fitting of seven of these launchers under each wing necessitated changes in the Lightning's wing structure and this arrangement was abandoned in favour of the inverted pyramid mounting

This mounting was installed as standard equipment during the last few months of Lightning production, and it was also issued to squadrons for installation in the field.

F-4. The first unarmed photographic-reconnaissance version of the Lightning. It was a conversion of the P-38E (F-4) and P-38F (F-4A) and was fitted with four cameras. Deliveries began in March, 1942.

F-5. A development of the F-4. From three to five cameras in any one of four different installations may be carried in the nacelle nose. Cameras are remotely controlled by an electrical impulse unit and may be operated either separately or collectively. A shutterless continuous-strip camera is used for low altitude photography. The Sperry A-4 automatic pilot is standard equipment. The photographic Lightning was several hundred pounds lighter than its fighter counterpart and was some 10 m.p.h. faster.

TYPE.—Twin-engined single-seat Fighter or Fighter-Bomber.
WINGS.—Mid-wing cantilever monoplane. Wings taper in chord and thickness and are set at 5°40′ dihedral throughout span. In five sections, comprising centre-section, two outer sections and two tips. All-metal construction, mainly 24ST Alclad. Structure of centre-section consists of a main box spar and front and rear shear members, the whole tied together with corrugated and flat sheet to form a box section in which space is provided for the fuel cells. Outer sections built up of single-web spar, rear shear member, sheet ribs and upper and lower stressed skins. At the rear of shear members and inboard of the ailerons are the trailing-edge ribs which support the rear upper skin and the Lockheed-Fowler flaps. The leading-edge is separate and is built up of upper and lower halves joined at the leading-edge with piano-type

hinges. All-metal hydraulically-operated Fowler-type trailing-edge flaps. Separate electrically-operated dive flaps outboard of engine nacelles and hinged to under surface of wings beneath main spar. All-metal statically and aerodynamically-balanced ailerons on piano-type hinges. Hydraulically-operated aileron "booster" system so that the pilot retains feel but supplies only 17 per cent of the force required to operate ailerons.

NACELLE.—All-metal structure built of bulkheads and covered with flush-riveted smooth metal skin.

TAIL BOOMS.—Booms extend from the fireproof bulkheads to the tail-unit attachments, and are in two portions, front portions accommodating the turbo-superchargers and main landing gear units, and the rear portions the coolant radiators. Semi-monocoque structures built up of bulkheads and rolled sheet covering reinforced internally with extruded bulb angles. Mainly of 24ST Alclad but stainless steel used in region of superchargers in front sections.

TAIL UNIT.—Monoplane type with fins and rudders at extremities of tail booms and single-piece tailplane and elevator between booms. Tailplane built of two spars and smooth flush-riveted skin reinforced internally with extruded bulb angles. Elevator, of similar construction, statically balanced by three weights, one in each boom and one on the centre-line. Elevator attached to tailplane by piano-type hinges. Centrally-placed controllable trim-tab. Fins, including tail-cones of booms, made up of multiple shear webs, ribs and smooth skin covering. Rudders, of similar construction, are statically and aerodynamically-balanced and provided with trim-tabs. Entire tail-unit quickly detachable.

LANDING GEAR.—Retractable tricycle type. All wheels have single oleo struts and retract backwards, the main wheels into the forward portions of the tail booms and the nose wheel into the central nacelle. Hydraulic retraction. Automatically opening and closing wheel-well doors. Brakes on main wheels.

POWER PLANT.—Two 1,520 h.p. Allison V-1710 twelve-cylinder Vee liquid-cooled engines driving oppositely-rotating Curtiss Electric constant-speed full-feathering airscrews. Airscrew diameter: 11 ft. 6 in. (3.5 m.). General Electric turbo-superchargers in upper portions of booms aft of rear shear member of centre-section. Air scoops on outboard sides of booms below trailing-edge of wings feed air to the turbo compressors. Air is then ducted forward to intercoolers beneath engine and thence to engine air induction system. Engine coolant radiators on sides of after sections of tail booms with controllable exit flaps. Separate fuel system for each engine, each consisting of three self-sealing tanks or cells, two (main and auxiliary) in the centre-section and one in outer wing leading-edge. Systems are interconnected so that fuel from any tank, except outer wing tanks, is available for either engine. Droppable fuel tanks may be carried under centre-section midway between central and engine nacelles. Drop tanks are of stream-line form and are made from two steel pressings welded together. They are of two capacities, either 150 or 300 U.S. gallons. Electrically-driven fuel boost pumps assist engine-driven pumps. Oil tank in each engine nacelle with two oil coolers, one on each side of intercooler air duct beneath nose of engine, and with thermostatically-controlled temperature regulator and exit flap.

ACCOMMODATION.—Pilot's cockpit in central nacelle over leading-edge of wing. Centre panel of windshield optically-flat bullet-proof glass. Side windows may be lowered and top centre panel is hinged at aft edge for entrance and exit. Quick release hinges for emergency exit. Pilot armour on front bulkhead, back and bottom of seat and behind seat and head. Armour plate on inboard sides of turbo-superchargers to protect pilot against possible fragmentation of turbo blades. Oxygen equipment. Cockpit heating and canopy de-frosting by hot air.

ARMAMENT.—One 20 m/m. cannon and four 50 cal. machine-guns in compartment in nose of central nacelle. All guns fire straight ahead without converging. Racks under centre-section can carry either bombs ranging from 100 to 1,600 lbs. (45.4 to 726 kg.), drop tanks or chemical tanks for smoke-screen laying. Gun camera installed in fairing of port rack. In photographic-reconnaissance model (F-5) armament removed and compartment redesigned to accommodate varying camera installations.

DIMENSIONS.—Span 52 ft. (15.86 m.), Length 37 ft. 10 in. (11.53 m.), Height 12 ft. 10 in. (3.9 m.), Wing area 327.5 sq. ft. (30.4 sq. m.).

WEIGHTS.—Weight empty (with fixed equipment) 12,700 lbs. (5,766 kg.), Normal loaded weight 15,341 lbs. (6,865 kg.), Designed loaded weight 15,500 lbs. (7,040 kg.), Alternate loaded weight (No. 1) 16,376 lbs. (7,435 kg.), Alternate loaded weight (No. 2) 18,000 lbs. (8,172 kg.).

PERFORMANCE.—Maximum speed over 414 m.p.h. (662 km.h.) at 25,000 ft. (7,625 m.), Service ceiling over 35,000 ft. (10,680 m.), Normal without drop tanks 460 miles (736 km.). (1945–46)

THE LOCKHEED MODEL 18 LODESTAR.

U.S. Army Air Forces designations : C-56, C-57, C-59, C-60 and C-66.
U.S. Navy designation : R50.
British name : Lodestar.

The Lodestar commercial transport, which is still flying for more than a dozen airlines on four continents, normally has accommodation for a crew of three and fourteen passengers. It has also been widely adapted for service transport use by the U.S. Army Air Forces and the U.S. Navy. The following are the various service versions of the Lodestar, of which the C-60 is the most used model.

C-56 (R50-1). Both Army and Navy models equivalent to the civil Model 18-40 and fitted with two Wright GR-1820-G102A Cyclone engines, with the exception of the C-56D which has two Pratt & Whitney R-1830-S1C3G Twin-Wasp engines. Some are fitted with furnishings of the executive type and others for general personnel transportation.

C-57. Similar to the C-56 except for cabin installations and the power-plant. Two Pratt & Whitney R-1830-51 Twin-Wasp engines.

C-59 (R50-2 and Lodestar IA). A military adaptation of the civil Model 18-07 with two Pratt & Whitney R-1690 Hornet engines. Carries a crew of 4 and 14 passengers.

R50-3. A naval executive transport with accommodation for a crew of 4 and four passengers. Similar to the civil Model 18-10 with two Wright R-1820-84 Cyclone engines.

C-60 (R50-4, R50-5, R50-6 and Lodestar II). Developed from the civil Model 18-56 and fitted with two Wright R-1820-87 Cyclone engines. The C-60 (R50-5) has accommodation for 12 passengers ; the R50-4 is an executive version with seats for 7 passengers ; and the C-60A (R50-6 and Lodestar II) is provided with benches for 18 fully-armed troops. The C-60 has also been used to train glider-tug pilots.

C-66. An adaptation of the civil Model 18-10 to carry a crew of 2 and eleven passengers. Fitted with two Wright R-1820 Cyclone engines.

TYPE.—Twin-engined Transport.

WINGS.—Mid-wing cantilever monoplane of single-spar construction. Wing in three sections. Fuel tanks integral with centre-section. Fowler flaps. Ailerons are inter-connected to droop with flaps.

FUSELAGE.—Elliptical cross-section monocoque of all-metal construction.

TAIL UNIT.—Cantilever monoplane type with twin fins and rudders.

LANDING GEAR.—Hydraulically-operated retractable type. May be lowered in six seconds at 250 m.p.h. Low-pressure tyres and hydraulic disc brakes. Pneumatic hydraulic shock-absorbers.

POWER PLANT (C-60A).—Two Wright R-1820-87 nine-cylinder radial air-cooled engines each rated at 1,000 h.p. at 14,200 ft. (4,330 m.) and with 1,200 h.p. available for take-off. Hamilton-Standard constant-speed hydromatic airscrews. Fuel tanks have total maximum capacity of 644 U.S. gallons (536 Imp. gallons = 2,438 litres). Maximum oil capacity 44 U.S. gallons (36.6 Imp. gallons = 166.5 litres).

ACCOMMODATION (C-60A).—Crew of three, pilot, co-pilot and radio operator. Benches in cabin for eighteen troops or other personnel. Dimensions of cabin : 28 ft. (8.54 m.) long × 5 ft. 5½ in. (1.7 m.) wide × 6 ft. 3 in. (1.9 m.) high.

DIMENSIONS.—Span 65 ft. 8 in. (19.96 m.), Length 49 ft. 9⅞ in. (15.19 m.), Height 11 ft. 10½ in. (3.6 m.), Wing area 551 sq. ft. (51.2 sq. m.).

WEIGHTS (C-60A).—Weight empty 12,075 lbs. (5,480 kg.), Normal loaded weight 18,500 lbs. (8,400 kg.), Maximum overloaded weight 21,500 lbs. (9,760 kg.).

PERFORMANCE (C-60A).—Maximum speed 266 m.p.h. (425.6 km.h.) at 17,000 ft. (5,185 m.), Cruising speed 200 m.p.h. (320 km.h.), Climb to 10,000 ft. (3,050 m.) 6.6 min., Service ceiling 30,000 ft. (9,150 m.), Range with full complement and maximum fuel 1,660 miles (2,660 km.).

The Lockheed C-60 Lodestar Military Transport (two Wright R-1820-87 engines).

(1945–46)

Lockheed P-2H Neptune maritime reconnaissance bomber of the U.S. Navy

THE LOCKHEED NEPTUNE
U.S. Navy designation: P-2 (formerly P2V)

The first U.S. Navy contract for the Neptune was placed in April, 1944, for two XP2V-1's. Since then Lockheed has received one contract for the P2V-1, two for the P2V-2, two for the P2V-3, one for the P-2D, three for the P-2E, two for the P-2F and eight for the P-2H. The current P-2H contract, covering aircraft for the U.S. and Royal Netherlands Navies, extended production through to late 1963, bringing the total number of P-2's built to more than 1,000.

In addition a contract was received in October, 1954, for the conversion of P-2E's and P-2F's to P-2H standard with auxiliary jet power. This modification programme required three years to complete.

Four ski-equipped Neptunes were flown by the U.S. Navy in Operation Deepfreeze III at the South Pole.

In addition to world-wide service with the U.S. Navy, the Neptune is also used by the Royal Australian Air Force, the Royal Canadian Air Force, the Royal Netherlands Air Force, the French and Argentine Navies, the Japanese Maritime Self-defence Force, Brazil and Portugal.

Under a contract signed in 1958, Lockheed is providing technical assistance, parts and tooling for the manufacture of the P-2H in Japan by the Kawasaki company. Sixteen aircraft were supplied to Japan by Lockheed. The first of 48 Kawasaki-built Neptunes was delivered on December 11, 1959.

The principal current versions of the Neptune are:—

P-2E (formerly P2V-5). Some have nose turret armed with two 20 mm. cannon in

place of the fixed nose armament of earlier versions. Larger wing-tip tanks carrying radar and searchlight as·well as extra fuel. Considerably more internal radar and electronic equipment. First model to be fitted with elongated tail enclosing anti-submarine magnetic anomaly detection (MAD) gear. All now modified for installation of two Westinghouse J34 turbojet engines in wing-mounted pods as in P-2H.

P-2F (formerly P2V-6). Similar to P-2E but equipped for mine-laying and anti-submarine warfare. Longer nose to give added room for forward crew and improved access to equipment, smaller wing-tip tanks and smaller radome. New features include stainless steel engine nacelles and pressure fuelling. Interchangeability for mine-laying and anti-submarine work permits a wide selection of armament. P-2F's modified for installation of two Westinghouse J34 turbojet engines in wing-mounted pods as in P-2H are now designated **P-2G.**

P-2H (formerly P2V-7). Two 3,500 h.p. Wright R-3350-32W Turbo Compound engines, plus two Westinghouse J34 turbojets (3,400 lb. =1,540 kg. s.t. each) in pods outboard of engine nacelles to augment take-off and combat performance. Enlarged crew space and other interior modifications of a classified nature; bulged cockpit canopy for improved all-round view; modified nose landing-gear unit; redesigned wing-tip tanks; and simplified multi-function control systems. Like all other models, the P-2H can be converted for patrol, mine-laying or torpedo bomber duties.

P2V-7B. Fifteen for Royal Netherlands Navy. Similar to P-2H, but with unglazed

P2V-1. Two Wright R-3350-8 engines each with normal rated power of 2,100 h.p. and with 2,300 h.p. for take-off, driving Hamilton Standard four-blade airscrews with alcohol de-icing. Short nose with armament of two flexible .5-in. (12.7 mm.) machine-guns. Dorsal and tail turrets each armed with two .5-in. (12.7 mm.) guns.

Between September 29 and October 1, 1946, the third production P2V-1, suitably modified, set up a World's Record for Distance in a Straight Line by flying non-stop from Perth, Western Australia, to Columbus, Ohio, U.S.A., a distance of 11,235 miles (17,976 km.). Flight time was 55 hours 17 min.

The aircraft took off at a loaded weight of 85,000 lbs. (38,600 kg.) of which 50,400 lbs. (22,890 kg.) was gasoline, the fuel load alone representing about one and a half times the empty weight of the aircraft. Jato was used for take-off.

P2V-2. Two Wright R-3350-24W engines, each with take-off output of 2,500 h.p. (dry) or 2,800 h.p. (wet) and normal continuous rating of 2,100 h.p. Hamilton Standard three-blade airscrews with paddle blades and electric de-icing. Combustion type heaters for wing and tail de-icing. Longer nose (2½ ft. = 0.76 m. longer than P2V-1) with additional search and tactical radar equipment. Nose armament increased to six 20 mm. cannon, fired by pilot. Dorsal turret armed with two .50-in. machine-guns and tail turret with two 20 mm. cannon. Other war stores as for P2V-1.

Two special ski-equipped versions of the P2V-2, designated P2V-2N, were built in 1949 and flew to the Antarctic as part of Rear Admiral Byrd's Expedition "Deep-freeze" in December, 1955. The skis, made by the Federal Ski Company of Minneapolis, are fitted around the normal wheels, to permit landings on either skis or wheels.

nose containing four 20 mm. guns.

Lockheed has modified 350 P-2E's and P-2H's to accommodate the latest electronic submarine detection system. First deliveries of modified aircraft to operational squadrons began in December, 1958.

Sixty-nine of the modified aircraft and all current production Neptunes are equipped with new electronic systems code-named "Julie" and "Jezebel."

"Julie" is an active system based upon underwater explosions of small depth charges. A pattern of sonobuoys on the ocean surface picks up the resulting sound waves as they bounce off a submerged craft and radios the latter's presence and path to the aircraft. "Jezebel" helps to locate submarines by "listening" for the submerged vessel's own noises. The two complementary systems are linked with electronic equipment in the aircraft which interprets the information quickly and accurately.

The following description applies generally to the P-2 Series:—

TYPE.—Maritime reconnaissance bomber.

WINGS.—All-metal cantilever mid-wing monoplane. Aerofoil section NACA 2419 modified with max. thickness at 38% of chord. Wing designed to give temporary flotation in event of ditching. Centre-section wing box continuous through fuselage and entire bomb-bay load carried directly by wing. All-metal ailerons with controllable trim-tab in each. Lockheed-Fowler flaps on circular arc racks inboard of ailerons. Max. flap depression 32°. Ailerons also droop 10° when flaps lowered. Internal aerodynamic balances on all control surfaces. Thermal leading-edge de-icing. Gross wing area 1,000 sq. ft. (92.9 m.²).

FUSELAGE. — All - metal semi - monocoque structure.

TAIL UNIT.—Cantilever all-metal structure. Tail-unit incorporates "Varicam" (variable camber), a movable trimming surface between fixed tail and elevator which is operated by electrically-driven irreversible screw-jack. Tailplane and fin have detachable thermally-heated leading-edges. Balanced control surfaces, with trim-tab in each elevator. Trim-balance tabs in rudder. Elevator area (each) 39.3 sq. ft. (3.65 m.²). Rudder area 38.4 sq. ft. (3.57 m.²).

LANDING GEAR.—Retractable tricycle type. Hydraulic brakes on main wheels.

POWER PLANT.—Two Wright R-3350 eighteen-cylinder two-row radial air-cooled engines, driving Hamilton Standard Hydromatic constant-speed airscrews. All P-2E, P-2G and P-2H aircraft also have two Westinghouse J34 turbojets (each 3,400 lb.=1,540 kg. s.t.) in underwing pods. Self-sealing fuel tanks with nylon plastic casing. Normal fuel capacity 2,200 U.S. gallons (8,316 litres). Provision for 700 U.S. gallon (2,646 litres) ferrying tank in bomb-bay. Dural armour in nacelles.

ACCOMMODATION.—Crew of up to seven; pilot, co-pilot, navigator/bombardier (who handles radar bombing gear), radar operator, and dorsal and rear gunners. All positions armoured. Galley and sleeping accommodation.

ARMAMENT (P-2H).—Some aircraft have two 0.50 in. guns in dorsal turret. Provision for sixteen 5-in. (12.7 cm.) rocket projectiles under wings. Bomb load of 8,000 lb. (3,629 kg.) carried internally may consist of sixteen 500 lb. (227 kg.), eight 1,000 lb. (454 kg.) or four 2,000 lb. (907 kg.) bombs, two 2,165 lb. (982 kg.) torpedoes, or 2,000 lb. (907 kg.) sea-mines, or twelve 325 lb. (147 kg.) depth-charges. MAD gear. Sonobuoy installation.

DIMENSIONS (P-2H).—
Span (with tip tanks) 103 ft 10 in. (31·65 m)
Length 91 ft 8 in. (27·94 m)
Height 29 ft 4 in. (8·94 m)

WEIGHTS (P-2H).--
Weight empty 49,808 lb (22,592 kg)
Max. T.O. weight 79,788 lb (36,191 kg)

PERFORMANCE (P-2H).—
Max. speed 403 mph (648 kmh)
Max. speed, piston-engines only 356 mph (573 kmh)
Patrol speed at 1,000 ft (300 m) 173-207 mph (278-333 kmh)
Service ceiling 22,000 ft (6,700 m)
Max. range 3,685 miles (5,930 km) (1963–64)

Lockheed P-3C Orion in Update II configuration

LOCKHEED MODEL 185/285 ORION
US Navy designation: P-3
CAF designation: CP-140 Aurora

In 1958 Lockheed won a US Navy competition for an 'off-the-shelf' ASW aircraft with a developed version of its Electra four-turboprop commercial transport. An aerodynamic prototype flew for the first time on 19 August 1958. A second aircraft, designated YP-3A (formerly YP3V-1), with full avionics, flew on 25 November 1959.

Details of the P-3A initial production version (retired from operational use by active-duty USN patrol squadrons on 13 November 1978) and WP-3A can be found in the 1978-79 *Jane's*. Subsequent production versions are as follows:

P-3B. Follow-on production version with 3,661 kW (4,910 ehp) Allison T56-A-14 turboprop engines, which do not need water-alcohol injection. US Navy contracts covered 124 P-3Bs. In addition, five P-3Bs were delivered to the Royal New Zealand Air Force in 1966, ten to the Royal Australian Air Force during 1968 and five to Norway in the Spring of 1969. USN P-3Bs were modified retrospectively to carry Bullpup missiles. Others became **EP-3Bs.** The US Navy and Lear Siegler developed in 1976 a modification kit for retrofitting to P-3B aircraft. This includes a 32K Rom computer, ASN-84 inertial navigation system, Omega, ASA-66 displays and ASN-124 navigation controller, together with the necessary controls and equipment to integrate the new and existing systems. Kits have been made available for the above installation. New Zealand's five P-3Bs are currently undergoing modernisation by Boeing Aerospace, involving upgrading of their data handling and display systems, radar, infra-red detection system, and INS. It is planned to upgrade the ASW equipment in a subsequent programme.

P-3C. Advanced version with the A-NEW system of sensors and control equipment, built around a Univac digital computer that integrates all ASW information and permits retrieval, display and transmission of tactical data

in order to eliminate routine log-keeping functions. This increases crew effectiveness by allowing them sufficient time to consider all tactical data and devise the best action to resolve problems. First flight of this version was made on 18 September 1968 and the P-3C entered service in 1969. A total of 143 of this version had been delivered to the US Navy by early 1978.

All of those delivered from January 1975 have been to **P-3C Update** standard, with new avionics and electronics software developed to enhance the effectiveness of the aircraft. Equipment includes a magnetic drum that gives a sevenfold increase in computer memory capacity, a new versatile computer language, Omega navigation system, improved acoustic processing sensitivity, a tactical display for two of the sensor stations, and an improved magnetic tape transport. A prototype with this equipment was handed over to the US Navy on 29 April 1974.

The US Navy and Lockheed began in 1976 a further P-3C avionics improvement programme known as **Update II.** This added an infra-red detection system (IRDS) and a sonobuoy reference system (SRS). The Harpoon missile and control system are included in Update II, which was incorporated into production aircraft from August 1977. The first Update II P-3C was delivered to the Naval Air Development Center in that same month. The Royal Netherlands Navy has ordered 13 Update II P-3Cs. The first is scheduled for delivery in late 1981.

Update III, of which development began in February 1978, involves mainly ASW avionics, including a new acoustic processor to analyse signals picked up from the sea, a new sonobuoy receiver which replaces DIFAR, an improved APU, and environmental controls to cater for increased heat from the avionics and to further improve crew comfort. A prototype Update III P-3C is scheduled for delivery to the US Navy for test and evaluation in April 1983, with full production to start in April 1984.

Two of the eight international records for turboprop

aircraft set up in a P-3C by Cdr Donald H. Lilienthal, in early 1971, had not been beaten by mid-1980. They were a speed of 434·97 knots (806·10 km/h; 500·89 mph) over a 15/25 km course; and a time-to-height record, to 12,000 m in 19 min 42·24 s.

RP-3D. One P-3C was reconfigured during manufacture for a five-year mission to map the Earth's magnetic field, under Project Magnet, controlled by the US Naval Oceanographic Office. Crew of 17. Range increased to more than 5,000 nm (9,265 km; 5,755 miles) by installation of 4,545 litre (1,200 US gallon) fuel tank in weapons bay. Details of other changes in 1977-78 *Jane's*. Operated by US Navy's Oceanographic Development Squadron 8 (VXN-8) based at the Naval Air Test Center, Patuxent River, Maryland. On 4 November 1972, Cdr Philip R. Hite used it to set up an international closed-circuit distance record for turboprop aircraft, covering 5,451·97 nm (10,103·51 km; 6,278·03 miles).

WP-3D. Two aircraft equipped as airborne research centres, ordered by the US National Oceanic and Atmospheric Administration. Equipped to carry out atmospheric research and weather modification experiments. Pitot static boom on port wingtip; gust probe on fuselage; C-band range heading indicator (RHI) dish antenna in belly radome; and X-band antenna in radome at tail. These aircraft became operational during the Summer of 1976.

EP-3E. Ten P-3As and two EP-3Bs were converted to EP-3E configuration to replace Lockheed EC-121s in service with VQ-1 and VQ-2 squadrons. Identified by large canoe-shaped radars on upper and lower surfaces of fuselage and ventral radome forward of wing.

By mid-1980 Lockheed-California had delivered more than 500 P-3s of all versions. The following data refer to the P-3C, but are generally applicable to other versions, except for the details noted:

TYPE: Four-turboprop ASW aircraft.

WINGS: Cantilever low-wing monoplane. Wing section NACA 0014 (modified) at root, NACA 0012 (modified) at tip. Dihedral 6° at root, 0° 30' at tip. Fail-safe box beam structure of extruded integrally-stiffened aluminium alloy. Lockheed-Fowler trailing-edge flaps. Hydraulically-boosted aluminium ailerons. Anti-icing by engine bleed air ducted into leading-edges.

FUSELAGE: Conventional aluminium alloy semi-monocoque fail-safe structure.

TAIL UNIT: Cantilever aluminium alloy structure with dihedral tailplane and dorsal fin. Fixed-incidence tailplane. Hydraulically-boosted rudder and elevators. Leading-edges of fin and tailplane have electric anti-icing system.

LANDING GEAR: Hydraulically-retractable tricycle type, with twin wheels on each unit. All units retract forward, main wheels into inner engine nacelles. Oleo-pneumatic shock-absorbers. Main wheels have size 40-14 type VII 26-ply tubeless tyres. Nosewheels have size 28-7·7 type VII tubeless tyres. Hydraulic brakes. No anti-skid units.

POWER PLANT: Four 3,661 kW (4,910 ehp) Allison T56-A-14 turboprop engines, each driving a Hamilton Standard 54H60 four-blade constant-speed propeller. Fuel in one tank in fuselage and four wing integral tanks, with total usable capacity of 34,826 litres (9,200 US gallons). Four overwing gravity fuelling points and central pressure refuelling point. Oil capacity (min usable) 111 litres (29·4 US gallons) in four tanks. Electrically de-iced propeller spinners.

ACCOMMODATION: Normal ten-man crew. Flight deck has wide-vision windows, and circular windows for observers are provided fore and aft in the main cabin, each bulged to give 180° view. Main cabin is fitted out as a five-man tactical compartment containing advanced electronic, magnetic and sonic detection equipment, an all-electric galley and large crew rest area.

SYSTEMS: Air-conditioning and pressurisation system supplied by two engine-driven compressors. Pressure differential 0·37 bars (5·4 lb/sq in). Hydraulic system, pressure 207 bars (3,000 lb/sq in), for flaps, control surface boosters, landing gear actuation, brakes and bomb bay doors. Pneumatic system, pressure 207/83 bars (3,000/1,200 lb/sq in), for ASW store launchers (P-3A/B only). Electrical system utilises three 60kVA generators for 120/208V 400Hz AC supply. 24V DC supply. Integral APU with 60kVA generator for ground air-conditioning, electrical supply and engine starting.

AVIONICS AND EQUIPMENT: The ASQ-114 general-purpose digital computer is the heart of the P-3C system. Together with the AYA-8 data processing equipment and computer-controlled display systems, it permits rapid analysis and utilisation of electronic, magnetic and sonic data. Nav/com system comprises two ASN-84 inertial navigation systems, with latitude and longitude indicators; APN-187 Doppler;˙ ARN-81 Loran A and C; ARN-84 Tacan; two ARN-87 VOR receivers; ARN-32 marker beacon receiver; ARN-83 LF-ADF; ARA-50 UHF direction finder; AJN-15 flight director indicator for tactical directions; HSI for long-range flight directions; glideslope indicator; on-top position indicator; two ARC-161 HF transceivers; two ARC-143 UHF transceivers; ARC-101 VHF receiver/transmitter; AGC-6 teletype and high-speed printer; HF and UHF secure communication units; ACQ-5 data link communication set and AIC-22 interphone set; APX-72 IFF transponder and APX-76 SIF interrogator. Electronic computer-controlled display equipment includes ASA-70 tactical display; ASA-66 pilot's display; ASA-70 radar display and two auxiliary readout (computer-stored data) displays. ASW equipment includes two ARR-72 sono receivers; two AQA-7 DIFAR sonobuoy indicator sets; hyperbolic fix unit; acoustic source signal generator; time code generator and AQH-4(V) sonar tape recorder; ASQ-81 magnetic anomaly detector; ASA-64 submarine anomaly detector; ASA-65 magnetic compensator; ALQ-78 electronic countermeasures set; APS-115 radar set (360° coverage); ASA-69 radar scan converter; KA-74 forward computer-assisted camera; KB-18A automatic strike assessment camera with horizon-to-horizon coverage; RO-308 bathythermograph recorder. Additional equipment includes APN-141(V) radar altimeter; two APQ-107 radar altimeter warning systems; A/A24G-9 automatic airspeed computer and ASW-31 automatic flight control system. P-3Cs delivered from 1975 have the avionics/electronics package updated by addition of an extra 393K memory drum and fourth logic unit, Omega navigation, new magnetic tape transport, and an ASA-66 tactical display for the sonar operators. To accommodate the new systems a new operational software computer programme will be written in CMS-2 language. Marconi AQS-901 acoustic signal processing and display system in RAAF P-3Cs.

ARMAMENT: Bomb bay, 2·03 m wide, 0·88 m deep and 3·91 m long (80 in × 34·5 in × 154 in), forward of wing, can accommodate a 2,000 lb MK 25/39/55/56 mine, three 1,000 lb MK 36/52 mines, three MK 57 depth bombs, eight MK 54 depth bombs, eight MK 43/44/46 torpedoes or a combination of two MK 101 nuclear depth bombs and four MK 43/44/46 torpedoes. Ten underwing pylons for stores: two under centre-section each side can carry torpedoes or 2,000 lb mines; three under

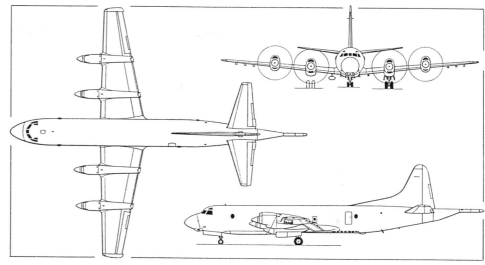

Lockheed P-3C Orion four-turboprop anti-submarine aircraft (*Pilot Press*) (1980–81)

outer wing each side can carry respectively (inboard to outboard) a torpedo or 2,000 lb mine (or searchlight on starboard wing), a torpedo or 1,000 lb mine or rockets singly or in pods; a torpedo or 500 lb mine or rockets singly or in pods. Torpedoes can be carried underwing only for ferrying; mines can be carried and released. Search stores, such as sonobuoys and sound signals, are launched from inside cabin area in the P-3A/B. In the P-3C sonobuoys are loaded and launched externally and internally. Max total weapon load includes six 2,000 lb mines under wings and a 3,290 kg (7,252 lb) internal load made up of two MK 101 depth bombs, four MK 44 torpedoes, pyrotechnic pistol and 12 signals, 87 sonobuoys, 100 MK 50 underwater sound signals (P-3A/B), 18 MK 3A marine markers (P-3A/B), 42 MK 7 marine markers, two B.T. buoys, and two MK 5 parachute flares. Sonobuoys are ejected from P-3C aircraft with explosive cartridge actuating devices (CAD), eliminating the need for a pneumatic system. Australian P-3Cs use BARRA sonobuoys.

DIMENSIONS, EXTERNAL:

Wing span	30·37 m (99 ft 8 in)
Wing chord at root	5·77 m (18 ft 11 in)
Wing chord at tip	2·31 m (7 ft 7 in)
Wing aspect ratio	7·5
Length overall	35·61 m (116 ft 10 in)
Height overall	10·29 m (33 ft 8½ in)
Fuselage diameter	3·45 m (11 ft 4 in)
Tailplane span	13·06 m (42 ft 10 in)
Wheel track (c/l shock-absorbers)	9·50 m (31 ft 2 in)
Wheelbase	9·07 m (29 ft 9 in)
Propeller diameter	4·11 m (13 ft 6 in)
Cabin door: Height	1·83 m (6 ft 0 in)
Width	0·69 m (2 ft 3 in)

DIMENSIONS, INTERNAL:
Cabin, excl flight deck and electrical load centre:

Length	21·06 m (69 ft 1 in)
Max width	3·30 m (10 ft 10 in)
Max height	2·29 m (7 ft 6 in)
Floor area	61·13 m² (658 sq ft)
Volume	120·6 m³ (4,260 cu ft)

AREAS:

Wings, gross	120·77 m² (1,300 sq ft)
Ailerons (total)	8·36 m² (90 sq ft)
Trailing-edge flaps (total)	19·32 m² (208 sq ft)
Fin, incl dorsal fin	10·78 m² (116 sq ft)
Rudder, incl tab	5·57 m² (60 sq ft)
Tailplane	22·39 m² (241 sq ft)
Elevators, incl tabs	7·53 m² (81 sq ft)

WEIGHTS (P-3B/C):

Weight empty	27,890 kg (61,491 lb)
Max expendable load	9,071 kg (20,000 lb)
Max normal T-O weight	61,235 kg (135,000 lb)
Max permissible weight	64,410 kg (142,000 lb)
Design zero-fuel weight	35,017 kg (77,200 lb)
Max landing weight	47,119 kg (103,880 lb)

PERFORMANCE (P-3B/C, at max T-O weight, except where indicated otherwise):

Max level speed at 4,570 m (15,000 ft) at AUW of 47,625 kg (105,000 lb)
411 knots (761 km/h; 473 mph)
Econ cruising speed at 7,620 m (25,000 ft) at AUW of 49,895 kg (110,000 lb)
328 knots (608 km/h; 378 mph)
Patrol speed at 457 m (1,500 ft) at AUW of 49,895 kg (110,000 lb)
206 knots (381 km/h; 237 mph)
Stalling speed, flaps up
133 knots (248 km/h; 154 mph)
Stalling speed, flaps down
112 knots (208 km/h; 129 mph)
Max rate of climb at 457 m (1,500 ft)
594 m (1,950 ft)/min
Service ceiling
8,625 m (28,300 ft)
Service ceiling, one engine out
5,790 m (19,000 ft)
T-O run
1,290 m (4,240 ft)
T-O to 15 m (50 ft)
1,673 m (5,490 ft)
Landing from 15 m (50 ft) at design landing weight
845 m (2,770 ft)
Max mission radius (no time on station) at 61,235 kg (135,000 lb)
2,070 nm (3,835 km; 2,383 miles)
Mission radius (3 h on station at 457 m; 1,500 ft)
1,346 nm (2,494 km; 1,550 miles)

THE LOCKHEED SEASTAR.
U.S. Navy designation: T2V-1.

The SeaStar, developed from the T-33 as a "private venture" two-seat all-purpose jet trainer, has been adopted by the U.S. Navy in modified form as a "sea duty" trainer. The prototype flew for the first time on December 15, 1953, and a production T2V-1 SeaStar completed its carrier suitability trials in the summer of 1957. It is the first U.S. aeroplane to be ordered into production with boundary-layer control as standard equipment, and is the first operational jet trainer designed to perform pilot training operations in sea-going carriers as well as from land bases.

A large additional order announced in November, 1956 extended production into 1958.

TYPE.—Two-seat Naval Jet Trainer.

WINGS.—Low-wing cantilever monoplane. All-metal structure similar to that of T-33 Shooting Star but fitted with movable leading-edge slats and boundary-layer control. Compressed air tapped from engine is ducted in tubes along trailing-edges and blown at high speed through slots in tubes over upper surfaces of flaps to increase lift and delay approach to stall. Powered ailerons. Full-span automatic leading-edge slats.

FUSELAGE.— Light - alloy semi-monocoque structure.

TAIL UNIT.—Cantilever monoplane type. All-metal structure similar to that of T-33 but tailplane raised 20 in. (50.8 cm.) to position on fin, the span increased by 12 in. (30.5 cm.) and dorsal fin extension added.

LANDING GEAR.—Retractable nose-wheel type. Similar in general to that of T-33 but strengthened to absorb four times more energy on landings and take-offs. Nose-wheel strut can be hydraulically lengthened when in extended position to raise nose of aircraft for faster climbs on carrier catapult take-offs. Arrester hook under fuselage is extended hydraulically and maintained in position pneumatically.

POWER PLANT.—One Allison J33-A-22 turbo-jet engine (6,100 lb.=2,770 kg. s.t.) in production T2V-1. Alternatively Pratt & Whitney J48-P-8 (7,250 lb.=3,415 kg. s.t.) may be fitted. Fuel in fuselage tank (300 U.S. gallons=1,134 litres) and two non-jettisonable wing-tip tanks (230 U.S. gallons =870 litres each). Wing-tip fuel can be dumped in flight by ram air. Total fuel capacity 760 U.S. gallons (2,874 litres).

ACCOMMODATION.—Tandem seats with dual controls under jettisonable one-piece clam-shell type canopy. Rear (instructor's) seat 6 in. (15.2 cm.) higher than front seat. Ejector seats. Auxiliary inside windscreen of laminated aluminium in rear cockpit is raised automatically for wind-blast protection when canopy is jettisoned.

The production Lockheed T2V-1 SeaStar Naval Trainer (Allison J33-A-22 turbojet engine).

EQUIPMENT.—Navigational equipment includes radio and ADF installation, glide path receiver and VOR localizer, and BIA attitude gyro, a combination homing device and gyro compass. Two-in-one instruments on control panel which, by use of selector switches, give individual readings from two

devices on one dial.

DIMENSIONS.—
Span (over tip-tanks) 42 ft. (12.8 m.).
Length 38 ft. (11.6 m.).
Height 13 ft. (3.9 m.).

WEIGHTS.—
Weight empty 11,500 lb. (5,217 kg.).
Weight loaded 15,500 lb. (7,030 kg.).

PERFORMANCE.—
Max. speed at 35,000 ft. (10,670 m.) 580 m.p.h. (933 km.h.).
Landing speed 97 m.p.h. (155 km.h.).
Rate of climb at S.L 5,400 ft. min. (1,645 m. min.).
Service ceiling 40,000 ft. (12,200 m.).
Range about 900 miles (1,440 km.).

(1958–59)

The Lockheed F-80B Shooting Star Single-seat Fighter (Allison J-33-23 gas-turbine engine).

THE LOCKHEED MODEL 80 SHOOTING STAR.

U.S. Air Force designation : F-80.
U.S. Navy designation : TO-1.

The Shooting Star was the first jet-propelled combat aircraft to be accepted by the U.S. Army Air Forces. The XP-80 was designed round a British de Havilland H-1 jet-unit which was supplied to the American authorities in July, 1943, and turned over by Wright Field to the Lockheed company to power the prototype. In 143 days Lockheed had designed, built and flown the XP-80, the first flight of the prototype being made on January 9, 1944. Later, a General Electric power-unit was adopted for the YP-80A and the production F-80A.

The first photographic versions of the Shooting Star were designated XF-14 and XF-14A, but only two aircraft were so identified. The P.R. version is now known as the RF-80. The camera nose with three vertical cameras is interchangeable with the gun nose of the F-80.

The following are the principal versions of the Shooting Star :—

F-80A. One Allison J-33-21 engine. First production model. By March, 1948, all F-80As in service were to have been modified to incorporate some features of the F-80B, including water/alcohol injection, provision for Jato take-off, rocket launchers under wings, cockpit cooling and canopy anti-frosting.

TF-80C. Two-seat trainer version of the F-80C with the Allison J-33-23 engine. Fuselage lengthened by 38 in. (0.96 m.) for insertion of second seat, both seats being under continuous canopy. Larger capacity air-conditioning and refrigeration system installed. Instructor in rear seat. Armament : two .50-in. machine-guns. Overall length : 37 ft. 8¾ in. (11.5 m.). Weight empty : 8,000 lbs. (3,632 kg.), Weight loaded : 14,000 lbs. (6,356 kg.).

TO-1. U.S. Navy version of the F-80B for use as a jet trainer. Fifty ordered. A standard F-80A was previously submitted to protracted tests by the U.S. Navy, during which it was successfully launched from and landed on an aircraft-carrier of the *Midway* class. The TO-1 will not have arrester-gear and will not be used in carriers. It will serve as a transitional trainer for the standard U.S. Navy operational jet fighters.

TYPE.—Single-seat jet-propelled Fighter.

WINGS.—Cantilever low-wing monoplane. NACA laminar-flow aero-

F-80B. Improved version of the F-80A. Thinner high-speed wing with thicker skin, stronger bulkheads in the nose section to support greater fire-power, stainless steel armoured engine compartment. Armament : six .50-in. machine-guns (1,200 rounds per gun). Enclosed radio mast and antennae wires. Ordered in quantity in 1947 for the U.S.A.F. and National Guard. The XF-80B was the original modified Shooting Star used for attempts on the World's Speed Record in 1945.

foil section with knife-sharp leading-edge. Centre-line of chord 2 in. (5.08 cm.) behind mid-point of fuselage. Dihedral on chord line 3°50'. Aluminium-alloy structure with I-section spars, T-section longitudinal stringers and stressed metal skin. Wing area 237 sq. ft. (22 m.²). Normal ailerons of all-metal construction with hydraulic boost control. Trim-tab in port aileron. Electrically-operated split trailing-edge flaps inboard of ailerons with separate fuselage flaps interconnected with wing flaps. Fuselage flaps may be operated with or separately from wing flaps.

FUSELAGE.—All-metal semi-monocoque structure in three sections consisting of nose, centre and aft sections. Nose-section detachable. Centre fuselage extending from front of cockpit to wing trailing-edge has main longerons, vertical frames and longitudinal stringers, with flush-riveted smooth metal skin. Detachable inspection panel over jet unit. Aft section consists of tapered longerons, vertical frames and longitudinal stringers and incorporates jet tail pipe and integral tail unit.

TAIL UNIT.—Cantilever monoplane type. All-metal fin and tailplane, integral with rear section of fuselage, have two spars, former ribs and stressed metal covering. Plastic tip to fin houses radio antenna. Balanced rudder and elevators of all-metal construction with metal skin. Controllable inset trim-tab in each elevator; adjustable rudder trim-tab. Tailplane span 15 ft. 7 in. (4.75 m.).

LANDING GEAR.—Retractable tricycle type. Each main wheel, carried on inner side of single shock-absorber leg with side link member, retracts inwards into wing and is completely enclosed by fairing plates attached to outside of leg and under fuselage. Nose-wheel carried on sprung half-fork retracts backwards into fuselage and is enclosed by twin doors. Hydraulic operation.

POWER PLANT.—One Allison J-33 centrifugal-flow jet-propulsion unit in centre-section of fuselage with air-intakes on either side of fuselage forward of wing leading-edge. Water/alcohol injection for increased take-off thrust. Aft section of fuselage, including jet nozzle, removed by detaching three fittings and tail pipe clamp for servicing and maintenance of jet unit. Complete unit may be changed in 20 minutes. Self-sealing kerosene fuel tanks in fuselage and wings. Streamlined long-range fuel-tanks each of 165 U.S.

gallons (623 litres) capacity may be carried on electrically or manually-operated drop shackles under wing-tips.

ACCOMMODATION.—Pressurized cockpit for pilot over wing leading-edge. Moulded cockpit cover slides backwards for access. Pilot's ejection seat. Flat armoured windscreen. Steel armour plate on upper forward side of front bulkhead and behind pilot's seat and head, with duralumin armour plate aft of front bulkhead. Cockpit pressure automatically reduced when combat gun-switch is used to prevent physical injury to pilot from explosive decompression should canopy be pierced. Provision for use of anti-G suit.

ARMAMENT.—Six .5 in. (12.7 mm.) forward-firing machine-guns in lower portion of nose with 1,200 rounds per gun. Electric gyro-lead computing gun sight with reflex optical system. Guns and magazines may be removed and replaced in 15 minutes without use of platforms or ladders. Bombs (100-1,000 lbs. = 45.4-454 kg.) may be carried on wing-tip shackles in place of long-range tanks.

EQUIPMENT.—Complete gun-nose can be replaced by nose-section containing camera equipment for photographic-reconnaissance duties. This includes one K-17 with 6 in. (15.24 cm.) lens and two K-22 with 24 in. (60.9 cm.) lens, and Fairchild automatic RDF sets. Camera gun in slight bulge in starboard intake. Oxygen, radio and adjustable landing-light in nose section; hydraulics in fuselage centre-section below cockpit.

DIMENSIONS.—Span 38 ft. 10½ in. (11.80 m.), Length 34 ft. 6 in. (10.50 m.), Height overall 11 ft. 4 in. (3.45 m.). Total area of control surfaces (ailerons, elevators and rudder) 31.5 sq. ft. (2.92 m.²).

WEIGHTS AND LOADINGS (Approximate).—Weight empty 8,000 lbs. (3,629 kg.), Maximum take-off weight 14,000 lbs. (6,350 kg.), Wing loading (at maximum weight) 59 lbs./sq. ft. (288 kg./m.²).

PERFORMANCE.—Maximum speed 558 m.p.h. (898 km.h.) at sea-level, Maximum speed at 30,000 ft. (9,145 m.) 508 m.p.h. (818 km.h.), Service ceiling, over 45,000 ft. (13,716 m.), Maximum ferry range 1,100 miles 1,760 km.).

Lockheed SR-71A strategic reconnaissance aircraft

LOCKHEED SR-71

Procurement of this aircraft was authorised after consideration of competitive designs from Boeing, General Dynamics, Lockheed and North American, and detail design of the Lockheed submission began in 1959. Known then by the designation A-11, its original purpose was almost certainly to supersede the Lockheed U-2 for long-range high-altitude surveillance missions. Like the U-2, it was designed by a small team led by C. L. Johnson, Lockheed's Vice-President for Advanced Development Projects, in the ADP building at Burbank known as the "Skunk Works". For its construction, a new titanium alloy known as Beta B-120 was evolved specially by Lockheed and the Titanium Metals Corporation, and 93 per cent by weight of the A-11's structure is built of this alloy, which has a tensile strength of up to 200,000 lb/sq in (14,060 kg/cm²).

Existence of the A-11 was not revealed officially until 29 February 1964, when President Lyndon Johnson stated at a news conference that it had already been tested in sustained flight at speeds of more than 1,735 knots (2,000 mph; 3,220 km/h) and at heights in excess of 70,000 ft (21,350 m) at Edwards Air Force Base, California.
The following versions entered service:—

SR-71A. Strategic photographic and electronic reconnaissance aircraft, developed from the YF-12A via the YF-12C prototype. Development began in February 1963, and the first production SR-71A (61-7950) made its first flight at Edwards AFB on 22 December 1964. Existence first revealed officially, by President Johnson, on 24 July 1964.
As in the YF-12C, the SR-71A fuselage is slight-

ly longer than that of the YF-12A, the wing/body chine fairings extend fully forward to meet at the extreme nose, and there are no ventral fins. The SR-71A is substantially heavier than the YF-12A, carries considerably more fuel, and has a longer range. Evaluation by Strategic Air Command began in 1965, and deliveries of production SR-71As, for working up, were made to the 9th (formerly the 4200th) Strategic Reconnaissance Wing at Beale AFB, California, beginning in January 1966. Subsequent operations have reportedly included surveillance of the Suez Canal region in 1970 and, by aircraft detached to Kadena AB, Okinawa, of the Chinese mainland prior to 1971. The SR-71A and the Teledyne Ryan AQM-34L RPV were the only USAF reconnaissance aircraft permitted to overfly North Vietnam after the cessation of bombing on 15 January 1973. One aircraft was operated in the Middle East during and after the Yom Kippur war in late 1973. The SR-71s, although painted dark blue overall, are also referred to unofficially as "Blackbirds".

The initial SR-71A/SR-71B order, placed in FY 1961, is believed to have been for 21 aircraft (61-7950 to 61-7970). An option for six more was taken up in the Spring of 1966, and published photographs have revealed serial numbers up to 61-7980, suggesting that at least 10 more beyond the initial order may have been built. In service, the YF-12/SR-71 series of aircraft have performed several thousand supersonic flights, of which some 40 per cent have been at Mach 3·0 or above. Because of budget constraints, a large percentage of the SR-71 fleet is in storage, but the number of aircraft on active status was increased slightly in late 1973.

SR-71B. Original tandem two-seat operational training version of the SR-71A, with second cockpit elevated aft of front (pilot's) cockpit. Fixed ventral tail-fins under nacelles reintroduced. Two aircraft known (61-7951 and '56), the first of which was delivered to SAC's 9th (formerly 4200th) Strategic Reconnaissance Wing at Beale AFB, California, on 7 January 1966; one aircraft was subsequently lost in a crash.

SR-71C. Revised training version, modified from an SR-71A after the loss of one SR-71B in an accident.

The following description applies primarily to the SR-71A, but is generally applicable to all YF-12 fighter prototype and SR-71 models except where a specific version is indicated:—

TYPE (SR-71A): Two-seat strategic reconnaissance aircraft.

WINGS: Cantilever low/mid-wing monoplane of basically delta planform with rounded tips. Wings have a bi-convex section, a thickness/chord ratio of 3·2%, and a small negative angle of incidence. Leading-edges have 60° sweepback, trailing-edges 10° forward taper. Multi-spar fail-safe structure, predominantly of Lockheed/TMC B-120 series titanium alloy and incorporating engine nacelle ring carry-through structure. Upper and lower skins are bonded to spars, and have preformed chordwise corrugations to aid the airflow in conditions of prolonged thermal soaking. Entire wing structure is designed to withstand sustained skin temperatures of up to about 260°C, and locally up to about 427°C. The leading-edges inboard of the engine nacelles are extended forward along the fuselage sides in blended wing/body chine fairings, which act as a fixed canard surface to reduce trim drag, improve directional stability and provide additional lifting area. On the YF-12C and SR-71 models these chines extend to, and meet at, the extreme nose; on the YF-12A they are cut back to aft of the nose radome, approximately in line with the front cockpit. The leading-edges outboard of the nacelles have marked conical camber, and there is a smaller chine fairing along the outboard side of each nacelle. The outer wings, and the outer half of each nacelle, hinge upward to provide access to the engines. Hydraulically-actuated plain elevons on trailing-edge, inboard and outboard of engine nacelles, each with 12° travel up or down and a triangular cutout adjacent to the nacelle; these are operated in unison or differentially for control and trim in both pitch and roll. No slats, flaps, spoilers, tabs or other movable surfaces.

FUSELAGE: Pressurised fail-safe structure, predominantly of B-120 series titanium alloy, designed to withstand sustained skin temperatures of up to about 260°C, and locally up to about 315°C. Nose, forward of cockpits, is tilted upward 2° to reduce trim drag; the YF-12A has a larger nose than the SR-71A, with a plastics radome. The SR-71 models have an extended tailcone, compared with the YF-12A, to improve boat-tail drag.

POWER PLANT: All versions of the YF-12 and SR-71 are powered by two Pratt & Whitney JT11D-20B (J58) by-pass turbojets (also correctly described as turbo-ramjet engines), each rated at approx 23,000 lb (10,430 kg) st dry and 32,500 lb (14,740 kg) st at sea level with afterburning. Each engine has a very high capacity by-pass duct system which pipes fourth-stage air to the afterburner to cool the jetpipe and increase the compressor stall margin. The engine discharges through an ejector nozzle, which is part of the airframe and is of purely aerodynamic design. The primary nozzle is a ring of blow-in doors which provide tertiary air to fill in the ejector at Mach numbers below 1·1. This tertiary air is provided by suck-in doors around the nacelle, augmented by the cowl (shock trap) bleed and aft by-pass bleed. The main ejector is supported downstream on streamline struts and a ring of Rene 41 alloy, on which are hinged free-floating trailing-edge flaps of Hastelloy X alloy. These open up progressively between Mach 0·9 and Mach 2·4 to provide a divergent shroud around the primary nozzle and the secondary stream. At low Mach numbers the ejector adds nothing to engine thrust; at Mach 2·2 it provides 14 per cent of the total propulsive thrust, and at about Mach 3·2 it provides 28·4 per cent. The power plant also incorporates suck-in doors, to provide tertiary flow, and secondary by-pass doors around the plane of the engine inlet face. The nacelle structure is designed to withstand sustained skin temperatures of up to about 593°C. The fuel used is a special low vapour pressure hydrocarbon known as JP-7. Insulated integral tanks, five occupying the entire upper part of the fuselage and others in the inner portion of each wing, have a total capacity of more than 80,000 lb (36,290 kg) of fuel. This fuel is used as the main heat-sink for the whole aircraft, and is thus heated until at delivery to the engine its temperature is 320°C. Final fuel injection to the engines is made at 130 lb/sq in (9·14 kg/cm²). An automatic fuel feed system maintains CG adjustment as the tanks are depleted; for thermodynamic reasons, due to the high ratio of surface area to volume, the wing tanks are used first, ie in climb. A nitrogen atmosphere is used to pressurise and inert the tanks. All versions of the aircraft have a receptacle on top of the fuselage, aft of the rear cockpit, for in-flight refuelling from KC-135 tanker aircraft.

ACCOMMODATION (SR-71A): Crew of two (pilot and reconnaissance systems officer) on ejection seats in separate tandem cockpits, each under a clamshell canopy which is hinged at the rear and opens upward. Canopies are opaque except for a rectangular window in each side. Front cockpit has a knife-edge windscreen formed by two triangular quarter-lights. Crew members wear Gemini-type *g* suits, and both cockpits are fully pressurised, heated and air-conditioned. Crew escape system is operable from speeds of more than Mach 3·0 at 100,000 ft (30,500 m) down to zero speed at ground level. Duties of the RSO include those of a co-pilot, flight engineer and navigator, and the aircraft can be flown from the rear cockpit if required. This cockpit is elevated in a pronounced "step" in the SR-71B and C, in which versions it is occupied by the instructor.

ELECTRONICS AND EQUIPMENT: Astro-inertial navigation system, providing automatic star tracking even in daylight. Honeywell air data computer and automatic flight control system (AFCS). The latter comprises a three-axis stability augmentation system (SAS), autopilot and Mach trim system, and is designed primarily to provide optimum handling qualities during take-off and landing, in-flight refuelling, subsonic cruise between 25,000 and 50,000 ft (7,625 and 15,250 m), and Mach 3 cruise above 60,000 ft (18,300 m). The SAS incorporates triple-redundant sensors, electronics and gain-scheduling, and is engaged in the yaw and pitch modes at all times to counteract inlet unstarting. A Hamilton Standard control system governs automatically the variable inlets, fuel supply and variable-area nozzles. The pitch axis has two dual-tandem series servos, each driving one inboard elevon; the roll axis has dual redundancy, and a separate channel to drive each inboard elevon; and the yaw axis has four series servos, two for each fin. Triple display indicator (TDI) gives a digital readout of Mach number, altitude, and knots equivalent airspeed (KEAS), and is used for transition to, and cruising at, supersonic speed. Conventional flight director system, modified to present angle of attack information during cruise on the glideslope portion of the attitude display indicator (ADI). Instrumentation duplicated in the rear (RSO's) cockpit includes basic flight instruments, fuel monitoring systems, annunciator warning panels, systems instruments and most communications instruments. Operational equipment in the SR-71A is classified, but includes provision for a wide variety of advanced observation equipment ranging from simple battlefield surveillance systems to multiple-sensor high-performance systems for interdiction reconnaissance and strategic systems capable of specialised surveying of 60,000 sq miles (155,400 km²) in one hour from an altitude of 80,000 ft (24,400 m). Photographic, infra-red and electronic sensors are housed in the forward portions of the wing/body chine fairings.

ARMAMENT: All SR-71 models are unarmed. Details of armament formerly fitted to the YF-12A were given in the 1972-73 *Jane's*.

DIMENSIONS, EXTERNAL (SR-71A):
- Wing span: 55 ft 7 in (16·95 m)
- Length overall: 107 ft 5 in (32·74 m)
- Height overall: 18 ft 6 in (5·64 m)
- Wheel track (c/l of shock-struts): approx 17 ft 0 in (5·18 m)
- Wheelbase: approx 34 ft 0 in (10·36 m)

AREA (SR-71A):
- Wings, nominal: 1,800 sq ft (167·23 m²)

WEIGHTS (SR-71A, approx):
- Weight empty: 60,000 lb (27,215 kg)
- Fuel load: more than 80,000 lb (36,290 kg)
- Max T-O weight: 170,000 lb (77,110 kg)

PERFORMANCE (SR-71A, approx):
- Max level speed at 78,740 ft (24,000 m): more than 1,735 knots (2,000 mph; 3,220 km/h) (more than Mach 3·0)
- Max level speed at 30,000 ft (9,145 m): more than 1,146 knots (1,320 mph; 2,125 km/h) (more than Mach 2·0)
- Typical unstick speed: 200 knots (230 mph; 370 km/h)
- Typical subsonic climb speed: 400 knots (460 mph; 741 km/h)
- Typical approach speed: 180 knots (207 mph; 334 km/h)
- Typical touchdown speed: 150 knots (173 mph; 278 km/h)
- Operational ceiling: above 80,000 ft (24,400 m)
- Air turning radius at 1,735 knots (2,000 mph; 3,220 km/h): 78-104 nm (90-120 miles; 145-193 km)
- Fuel consumption: 8,000 US gallons (6,661 Imp gallons; 30,282 litres)/hr
- Max lift/drag ratio, trimmed:
  - below Mach 1·0: approx 11·5
  - at Mach 3·0 and above: 6·5
- T-O run at 140,000 lb (63,505 kg) AUW: 5,400 ft (1,646 m)
- T-O to 50 ft (15 m) at 140,000 lb (63,505 kg) AUW: 9,000 ft (2,745 m)
- Landing from 50 ft (15 m) at 60,000 lb (27,215 kg): 6,000 ft (1,830 m)
- Landing run at 60,000 lb (27,215 kg): 3,600 ft (1,097 m)
- Typical operational radius: 1,040 nm (1,200 miles; 1,930 km)
- Range at Mach 3·0 at 78,740 ft (24,000 m), without refuelling: 2,589 nm (2,982 miles; 4,800 km)
- Max endurance at Mach 3·0 at 78,740 ft (24,000 m), without refuelling: 1 hr 30 min

(1974–75)

THE LOCKHEED STARFIGHTER

U.S.A.F. designation: F-104

Production of the F-104 for the U.S.A.F. has been completed, but Lockheed's California Division is producing complete aircraft and assemblies for Germany, Japan and Canada, where this fighter is being built under licence. Further licence manufacture is under way in Belgium, the Netherlands and Italy, as detailed below.

Indicative of the aircraft's performance is that an F-104A set up a World Speed Record of 1,404.009 m.p.h. (2,259.54 km.h.) on May 16, 1958; another established a World Aeroplane Height Record of 91,244 ft. (27,811 m.) on May 7, 1958. On December 14, 1959, an F-104C raised the Height Record to 103,389 ft. (31,513 m.) exceeding the height record achieved by a balloon for the first time since 1935.

These records have since been beaten, but at the time of writing the F-104 still held eight climb-to-height records as follows:—

To 3,000 m. (9,840 ft.) 41.85 sec.
To 6,000 m. (19,680 ft.) 58.41 sec.
To 9,000 m. (29,520 ft.) 1 min. 21.14 sec.
To 12,000 m. (39,360 ft.) 1 min. 39.9 sec.
To 15,000 m. (49,200 ft.) 2 min. 11.1 sec.
To 20,000 m. (65,600 ft.) 3 min. 42.99 sec.
To 25,000 m. (82,000 ft.) 4 min. 26.03 sec.
To 30,000 m. (98,400 ft.) 15 min. 4.92 sec.

Development of the design of the F-104 began in 1951 and versions so far announced are:—

XF-104. Two prototypes were built under this designation, with Wright J65-W-6 turbojet engine and afterburner (10,500 lb.=4,760 kg. s.t.), rearward-retracting nose-wheel and downward ejection seat. First flight of first XF-104 February 28, 1954, only 11 months after contract was awarded.

F-104A. Evaluation series of 17 ordered, followed by full production. Basically similar to XF-104, but with air-intake shock-cones, forward-retracting nose-wheel and other refinements. General Electric J79-GE-3A turbojet engine (14,800 lb. = 6,710 kg. s.t. with afterburning). Single-seat interceptor. Ventral fin for improved stability. Flap-blowing system and Lockheed in-flight refuelling equipment with removable probe. The first production F-104A flew for the first time on February 17, 1956 and deliveries to the U.S.A.F. Air Defense Command began on January 26, 1958. No longer in service with the U.S.A.F. Some supplied to American National Guard and Chinese Nationalist Air Force. Others converted into QF-104 target drones.

F-104B. Tandem two-seat development of the F-104A, for use as both combat aircraft and operational trainer. Has considerably greater fin area and fully-powered rudder. Prototype flew on February 7, 1957. Delivered to U.S.A.F. Air Defense Command, but now re-assigned to American National Guard. Total of approximately 195 F-104A's and B's built.

F-104C. General Electric J79-GE-7 turbojet engine (15,800 lb. = 7,165 kg. s.t. with afterburning). Fighter-bomber for U.S.A.F. Tactical Air Command. Deliveries began on October 16, 1958. Total of approximately 100 F-104C's and D's built for U.S.A.F.

F-104D. Two-seat version of F-104C for U.S.A.F. Tactical Air Command. Similar to F-104B but with power-plant in-flight refuelling equipment and other modifications introduced in F-104C.

F-104F. Basically as F-104D, but equipment similar to F-104G. Thirty being built by Lockheed for Federal German Air Force. Deliveries began in mid-1960.

QF-104. Remotely-controlled, recoverable, target drone conversion of F-104A for missile evaluation and firing practice. Initial contracts for 24, with first delivery in 1960.

In January, 1961, it was reported that Lockheed had flown an F-104 with large wing-tip pods designed to carry jet-lift engines, as part of a development programme for a VTOL version of this aircraft. Each pod is large enough to house seven jet-lift engines and additional fuel. Stabilisation in low-speed and hovering flight would be achieved by differential thrust from these engines.

On all standard versions of the Starfighter an automatic pitch control system is fitted to sense and prevent pitch-up, together with a three-axis autostabilizer. A boundary layer control system is used to decrease landing speed. The boundary layer control

Lockheed F-104C Starfighters of the 479th Tactical Fighter Wing, U.S.A.F.

system operates automatically, blowing air bled from the turbojet compressor over the wing flaps whenever the flaps are extended beyond the take-off setting.

Details given below refer specifically to the single-seat F-104G version, but apply generally to all versions of the F-104.

TYPE.—Single-seat supersonic fighter.

WINGS.—Mid-wing cantilever monoplane. Symmetrical supersonic wing section with a thickness/chord ratio of 3.36%. Aspect ratio 2.45. Leading-edge nose radius of 0.016 in. and razor-sharp trailing-edge. All metal structure with two main spars, 12 spanwise intermediate channels between spars and top and bottom one-piece skin panels, tapering from thickness of 0.25 in. (6.3 mm.) at root to 0.125 in. (3.2 mm.) at tip. Each half wing measures 7 ft. 7 in. (2.31 m.) from root to tip and is a separate structure cantilevered from five forged frames in fuselage. Wings have a 10° negative dihedral. Full-span electrically-actuated drooping leading-edge. Entire trailing-edge hinged, with inboard sections serving as landing flaps and outboard sections as ailerons. Ailerons are of steel, operated hydraulically. Flaps are of aluminium, actuated electrically. Above each flap is the air delivery tube of a boundary layer control system, which ejects air bled from the engine compressor over the entire flap span whenever the flaps are lowered more than 15°. Gross wing area 196.1 sq. ft. (18.22 m.²)

FUSELAGE.—All-metal monocoque structure. Hydraulically-operated air-brake on each side of rear fuselage.

TAIL UNIT.—T-type cantilever monoplane unit with "all-flying" one-piece tail hinged at mid-chord point at top of the sweptback vertical fin. Tailplane has similar profile to wing and is all-metal. Rudder is fully-powered. Narrow-chord ventral fin to improve stability. Vertical tail area 43.7 sq. ft. (4.06 m.²). Horizontal tail area 48.2 sq. ft. (4.48 m.²). Tailplane span 11 ft. 11 in. (3.63 m.)

LANDING GEAR.—Retractable tricycle type. Cleveland Pneumatic (Dowty patent) liquid-spring shock-absorbers. Hydraulic actuation. Main wheels raised in and forward. Steerable nose-wheel retracts forward into fuselage. Main wheel legs are hinged on oblique axes so that the wheels lie flush within the fuselage skin when retracted. Goodrich tyres, size 25 × 6.75 on main wheels, 18 × 5.5 on nose-wheel, pressure over 250 lb./sq. in. (17.58 kg./cm.²). Anti-skid multi-disc brakes on main wheels. Drag parachute of 18 ft. (5.50 m.) diameter stowed in lower part of fuselage near end of tailpipe. Wheel track 8 ft. 9 in. (2.67 m.). Wheelbase 15 ft. 1 in. (4.60 m.)

POWER PLANT.—One General Electric J79-GE-7 or GE-11A axial-flow turbojet with afterburner, rated at 15,800 lb. (7,165 kg.) s.t. with afterburning. Electrical de-icing elements fitted to air intakes. Most of the aircraft's hydraulic equipment mounted inside large engine access door under fuselage to facilitate servicing. Internal fuel in five bag-type fuselage tanks with total standard capacity of 896 U.S. gallons (3,392 litres). Optional fuel tanks (capacity 122 U.S. gallons = 462 litres) in ammunition, gun and shell-case compartments of fuselage. Provision for external fuel in 2 × 195 U.S. gallon (740 litre pylon tanks and 2 × 170 U.S. gallon (645 litre) wing-tip tanks. In-flight refuelling can be provided through Lockheed-designed probe-drogue system. Probe, mounted below port sill of cockpit, is removable but when installed is non-retractable.

ACCOMMODATION.—Pressurised and air-conditioned cockpit well forward of wings. Lockheed Model C-2 ejection seat. Equipment includes autopilot with "stick steering," which includes modes for preselecting and holding altitude, speed, heading and constant rate of turn; multi-purpose NASARR radar system; fixed-reticle gunsight; bomb computer; air data computer; dead reckoning navigation device; TACAN radio air navigation system; provision for data link-time division set and UHF radio; lightweight fully-automatic inertial navigation system; and provision for fitting a camera pod under the fuselage for reconnaissance duties.

ARMAMENT.—20 mm. M-61 Vulcan six-barrel cannon developed by General Electric, in port underside of nose (interchangeable with fuel tank on F-104G and CF-104) and one GAR-8 Sidewinder air-to-air missile on each wing-tip. Provision for two more Sidewinders on pylons under fuselage, and for under-wing stores, including podded M-61 cannons, for ground attack or tactical support missions.

EQUIPMENT.—Integrated electronics system in which various communications and navigation components may be installed as a series of interconnecting but self-sustaining units which may be varied to provide for different specific missions.

DIMENSIONS.—
Span (without tip-tanks) 21 ft. 11 in. (6.68 m.)
Length 56 ft. 8 in. (17.34 m.)
Height 13 ft 6 in. (4.11 m.)

WEIGHTS (F-104A).—
Weight empty 11,500 lb. (5,217 kg.)
Normal take-off weight, internal fuel only, 17,000 lb. (7,710 kg.)
Normal take-off weight with tip-tanks 19,200 lb. (8,709 kg.)
Max. take-off weight with tip-tanks and under-wing tanks 22,000 lb. (9,980 kg.)
Landing weight 11,500 lb. (5,215 kg.)

PERFORMANCE (F-104A).—
Max. speed approx. Mach 2.2 to 2.3 at 35,000 ft. (10,670 m.)
Approach speed 200 m.p.h. (322 km.h.)
Landing speed 164 m.p.h. (264 km.h.)
Max. range for ferrying 2,200 miles (3,540 km.)

The Lockheed F-94C Starfire All-weather Fighter (Pratt & Whitney J48 turbojet engine).

THE LOCKHEED STARFIRE.
U.S.A.F. designation: F-94.

The F-94 two-seat All-weather Fighter is a development of the F-80 Shooting Star. It was evolved from the two-seat T-33 trainer and originally used many of the main components and the production facilities of its predecessor. Later versions incorporate much original development.

The structure of the F-94 is generally similar to that of the F-80.

F-94A. Allison J33-A-33 turbojet engine with Solar afterburner. Two-seat all-weather fighter version of T-33 with radar operator replacing pupil pilot in second tandem seat, plus 940 lb. (426 kg.) of radar equipment. Wings, landing-gear and centre fuselage same as for T-33. New nose and rear fuselage sections, former to house radar, latter to accommo-date after-burner installation. All` hydraulic electric and control systems similar to those of the F-80C. The prototype was a converted T-33.

F-94B. Development of F-94A with improved electronic and operational equipment. Square wing-tips with centrally-mounted Fletcher tip tanks of greater capacity (230 U.S. gals.=870 litres each) and improved shape.

F-94C. Pratt & Whitney J48-P-5 engine with afterburner (6,250 lb.= 2,840 kg. s.t. without afterburner). Thinner wings, longer nose, swept horizontal tail surfaces and larger vertical surfaces. All-rocket armament comprising 48×2.75 in. rockets, 24 housed in a ring of firing tubes around the nose, and a further 24 rockets in two cylindrical pods, one on each wing midway between root and tip. Fiberglass noses to pods disintegrate in split second before rockets leave container by gas pressure generated by rockets themselves. The 9 ft. 6 in. (2.89 m.) pods extend about 6 ft. (1.83 m.) from wing leading-edge. 1,200 lb. of electronic equipment, including automatic locating, tracking and firing instruments, Westinghouse auto-pilot, Sperry Zero-Reader, ILS, etc.

DIMENSIONS (F-94C).—
Span 37 ft. 6 in. (11.42 m.).
Length 41 ft. 5 in. (12.64 m.).
Height 13 ft. 7 in. (4.13 m.).
WEIGHT (F-94B).—
Weight loaded over 15,000 lb. (6,810 kg.).
WEIGHT (F-94C).—
Weight loaded over 20,000 lb. (9,080 kg.).
PERFORMANCE.—
Officially stated to be in 600 m.p.h. (965 km.h.) class.   (1956–57)

LOCKHEED MODEL 301 STARLIFTER
USAF designation: C-141A

On March 13, 1961, it was announced that Lockheed-Georgia had won a design contest for a turbofan-powered freighter and troop carrier for operation by the US Military Airlift Command, in competition with Boeing, Douglas and General Dynamics/Convair. The specification to which the entries were designed was SOR-182 (Specific Operational Requirement 182). The initial contract covered five development, test and evaluation aircraft and the USAF has since ordered a total of 284 production aircraft, under the designation C-141A, with all aircraft due for delivery by the end of 1968.

The C-141A, which has been given the name of StarLifter, is the flying element of Logistics Support System 476L. The purpose of this system is to provide global-range airlift for the MAC and strategic deployment capabilities at jet speeds for the US Strike Command, which includes the Strategic Army Corps and the Composite Air Strike Forces of Tactical Air Command. The aircraft received FAA Type Certification in January 1965.

The first flight of the C-141A took place on December 17, 1963, and it began squadron operations with MAC on April 23, 1965. It has made virtually daily flights across the Pacific, to and from Vietnam, since August 1965, carrying troops, cargo and wounded.

A C-141A established a world record for heavy cargo drops of 70,195 lb. (31,840 kg), and is the first jet transport from which US Army paratroops have jumped.

The following details apply to the standard military C-141A:

TYPE: Four-jet long-range transport.
WINGS: Cantilever high-wing monoplane. Chord NACA 0013·00 (modified) at root, NACA 0010·00 (modified) at tip. Aspect ratio 7·90. Chord 33 ft 2 in (10·11 m) at root. Mean aerodynamic chord 22 ft 2½ in (6·77 m). Thickness/chord ratio 13% at root, 10% at tip. Anhedral 1° 26' at quarter-chord. Incidence 4° 53' at root, −42' at tip. Sweepback at quarter-chord 25°. Conventional all-metal two-spar box-beam structure, built on fail-safe principles. Conventional aluminium alloy ailerons with full power actuation by dual hydraulic units and emergency manual control through geared tabs. Lockheed-Fowler aluminium trailing-edge flaps. Hinged spoilers, on upper and lower surfaces of wings, are operated by dual hydraulic systems. No trim-tabs.

Hot-air anti-icing of leading-edges and engine intakes.
FUSELAGE: Conventional aluminium alloy semi-monocoque structure, built on fail-safe principles. Upswept rear fuselage with built-in ramp.
TAIL UNIT: Cantilever all-metal structure with horizontal surfaces mounted at tip of fin. Variable-incidence tailplane provides pitch trim, actuated normally by electric motor or more rapidly by hydraulic motor. Elevators and rudder each controlled by dual hydraulic units. Third hydraulic system takes over elevator control if one of the normal systems fails. Controls can be actuated manually in an emergency. Rudder trim by positioning rudder servo unit control valve with electric trim actuators. Tailplane leading-edge de-iced electrically with metal-clad elements.
LANDING GEAR: Hydraulically-retractable tricycle type, with Cleveland Pneumatic twin-wheel nose unit and Menasco Manuf. Co four-wheel bogie main units. All units retract forward, main bogies into fairings built on to sides of fuselage. Oleo-pneumatic shock-absorbers. Main wheel tyres size 44 × 16 type VII, pressure 150-180 lb/sq in (10·5-12·7 kg/cm²). Nose-wheel tyres size 36 × 11·0 type VII, pressure 200 lb/sq in (14·05 kg/cm²). Hydraulic multiple-disc brakes with independent braking through Bendix Pacific combined brake metering and anti-skid valve.
POWER PLANT: Four Pratt & Whitney TF33-P-7 turbofan engines, each rated at 21,000 lb (9,525 kg) st, mounted in underwing pods and fitted with clamshell-door thrust reversers. Fuel in ten integral tanks in wings, between front and rear spars, with total usable capacity of 23,592 US gallons (89,300 litres). Single-point dual hose adaptor refuelling point in aft section of starboard wheel fairing. Gravity fuelling cap over each tank. Total oil capacity 30·9 US gallons (117 litres).
ACCOMMODATION: Flight crew of four. Main cabin will accommodate 154 troops or 123 fully-equipped paratroops in fore-and-aft seating, or 80 litters with seats for up to 16 ambulatory patients and/or medical attendants. With "comfort pallet" (toilet and galley) at forward end of cabin, accommodation is reduced to 120 passenger-type seats. Galley and coat locker for crew. Two bunks and two seats for relief crew. Crew access door on port side at front. Two paratroop doors near aft end of cabin, on each side. Rear loading ramp for straight-in cargo loading, with opening equivalent to full cabin width and height. Up to 5,283 cu ft (149·6 m³) of freight can be loaded on ten pallets, using the integral USAF Type 463L loading system. The rollers and retaining rails for the pallets can be retracted into recesses to provide a flat floor when not in use. Ramp can be opened in flight for air-drops.
SYSTEMS: Pressurisation and air-conditioning by an air-cycle system utilising engine-bleed air. Pressure differential 8·2 lb/sq in (0·58 kg/cm²). Three independent hydraulic systems, pressure 3,000 lb/sq in (210 kg/cm²). Four 40kVA engine-driven AC generators. Auxiliary 40/50 kVA AC generator on APU for ground use. One 2·5kVA AC/DC hydraulically-driven generator for emergency power. DC power provided normally by two 200A transformer-rectifiers. One 24V 11Ah battery. AiResearch gas-turbine APU in port wheel fairing.
ELECTRONICS AND EQUIPMENT: Standard installations for all-weather operation include dual radio-compass, VOR/localiser, glide-slope and marker beacon equipment, ARN-21 TACAN, APN-147 and ASN-35 Doppler, Loran-C, APN-59B navigation and weather radar, dual HF and VHF communications systems.

DIMENSIONS, EXTERNAL:

Wing span	159 ft 11 in (48·74 m)
Length overall	145 ft 0 in (44·20 m)
Length of fuselage	132 ft 3½ in (40·32 m)
Height overall	39 ft 3½ in (11·98 m)
Tailplane span	50 ft 3½ in (15·32 m)
Wheel track	17 ft 6 in (5·33 m)
Wheelbase	53 ft 0 in (16·16 m)
Crew door:	
Height	approx 4 ft 0 in (1·22 m)
Width	approx 2 ft 6 in (0·76 m)
Height to sill	4 ft 2 in (1·27 m)
Paratroop doors (each):	
Height	6 ft 0 in (1·83 m)
Width	3 ft 0 in (0·91 m)
Height to sill	4 ft 2 in (1·27 m)
Rear loading ramp opening:	
Height	9 ft 1 in (2·77 m)
Width	10 ft 3 in (3·12 m)
Height to sill	4 ft 2 in (1·27 m)

DIMENSIONS, INTERNAL:

Cabin, excluding flight deck:	
Length, without ramp	70 ft 0 in (21·34 m)
Length, with ramp	81 ft 0 in (24·69 m)
Max width	10 ft 3 in (3·12 m)
Max height	9 ft 1 in (2·77 m)
Floor area, excluding ramp	718 sq ft (66·7 m²)
Volume, including ramp	7,340 cu ft (207·8 m³)

Lockheed C-141A StarLifter long-range military transport (four Pratt & Whitney TF33-P-7 turbofan engines)

AREAS:

Wings, gross	3,228 sq ft (299·9 m²)
Ailerons (total)	171·1 sq ft (15·88 m²)
Trailing-edge flaps (total)	528·7 sq ft (49·15 m²)
Spoilers	275 sq ft (25·55 m²)
Fin	416 sq ft (38·65 m²)
Rudder, including tab	86·5 sq ft (8·04 m²)
Tailplane	376·9 sq ft (35·02 m²)
Elevators	106·0 sq ft (9·85 m²)

WEIGHTS AND LOADINGS:

Weight empty, equipped	133,773 lb (60,678 kg)
Max payload	70,847 lb (32,136 kg)
Max T-O weight	316,600 lb (143,600 kg)
Max ramp weight	318,000 lb (144,240 kg)
Design landing weight	257,500 lb (116,800 kg)
Max wing loading	97·9 lb/sq ft (478 kg/m²)
Max power loading	3·8 lb/lb st (3·8 kg/kg st)

PERFORMANCE (at max T-O weight, except where indicated):

Max level speed at 25,000 ft (7,600 m)	571 mph (919 kmh)
Max permissible diving speed	Mach 0·89 or 472 mph (760 kmh) IAS
Max cruising speed at 24,250 ft (7,400 m)	564 mph (908 kmh)
Econ cruising speed	490 mph (788 kmh)
Stalling speed at max landing weight	115 mph (185 kmh)
Rate of climb at S/L	3,000 ft (915 m) min
Service ceiling at 250,000 lb (113,400 kg) AUW	41,600 ft (12,680 m)
Service ceiling, one engine out, at 250,000 lb (113,400 kg) AUW	34,500 ft (10,500 m)
T-O run	4,870 ft (1,485 m)
T-O to 50 ft (15 m)	5,700 ft (1,737 m)
Landing from 50 ft (15 m) at max landing weight	3,990 ft (1,215 m)
Landing run at max landing weight	2,060 ft (628 m)
Range with max fuel and 30,877 lb (14,005 kg) payload, 5% fuel reserve, plus 30 min at S/L	6,040 miles (9,720 km)
Range with design payload, reserves as above	3,965 miles (6,380 km)

(1966–67)

LOCKHEED C-141B STARLIFTER

Operational experience with the Lockheed C-141A StarLifter by the USAF's Military Airlift Command showed that on many occasions the cargo compartment was physically packed to capacity without the aircraft's maximum payload capability being reached. Parametric studies carried out by Lockheed showed that lengthening the fuselage by 7·11 m (23 ft 4 in) would provide an optimum relationship between modification cost and payload improvement, while at the same time allowing the existing wings, landing gear and power plant to be retained.

Under USAF contract, Lockheed-Georgia began work on the conversion of a C-141 in 1976. Designated YC-141B, this prototype was rolled out on 8 January 1977 and made its first flight on 24 March. The fuselage had been lengthened by the insertion of a 4·06 m (13 ft 4 in) plug immediately forward of the wing, and by a similar 3·05 m (10 ft 0 in) plug immediately aft of the wing. These two plug sections are designed so that the lengthened aircraft retains the same operational features and mission versatility as the C-141A. As a result of this modification, the floor area of the cargo compartment is increased by 22·26 m² (239·6 sq ft), and its volume by 61·48 m³ (2,171 cu ft). Thirteen standard 463L cargo pallets can be accommo-

dated in the C-141B StarLifter, instead of the ten carried by an unmodified C-141A. The four 93·4 kN (21,000 lb st) Pratt & Whitney TF33-P-7 turbofan engines are unchanged.

To satisfy another proven requirement, for flight refuelling capability, a Universal Aerial Refuelling Receptacle Slipway Installation (UARRSI) has been incorporated in the upper surface of the forward fuselage, just aft of the flight deck.

The first production C-141B was delivered to the USAF on 4 December 1979, ahead of schedule and below projected cost. Lockheed planned to deliver 80 C-141B conversions during 1980, and is due to complete the modification of all of Military Airlift Command's 271 StarLifters by mid-1982.

DIMENSIONS, EXTERNAL:

Wing span	48·74 m (159 ft 11 in)
Length overall	51·29 m (168 ft 3½ in)
Height overall	11·96 m (39 ft 3 in)

DIMENSIONS, INTERNAL:

Cargo compartment: Length	28·44 m (93 ft 3½ in)
Max height	2·77 m (9 ft 1 in)
Max width	3·11 m (10 ft 2½ in)
Usable cargo volume	322·71 m³ (11,399 cu ft)

WEIGHTS:

Operating weight (MAC)	67,186 kg (148,120 lb)
Max payload (2·5g)	32,025 kg (70,605 lb)
Max payload (2·25g)	41,222 kg (90,880 lb)
Max T-O weight (2·5g)	146,555 kg (323,100 lb)
Max T-O weight (2·25g)	155,580 kg (343,000 lb)
Emergency war planning T-O weight	156,445 kg (344,900 lb)
Max zero-fuel weight (2·5g)	99,210 kg (218,725 lb)
Max zero-fuel weight (2·25g)	108,410 kg (239,000 lb)
Max landing weight	155,580 kg (343,000 lb)

PERFORMANCE (at max 2·5g T-O weight, except where indicated):

Max cruising speed	492 knots (910 km/h; 566 mph)
Long-range cruising speed	430 knots (796 km/h; 495 mph)
Max rate of climb at S/L	890 m (2,920 ft)/min
T-O to 15 m (50 ft)	1,768 m (5,800 ft)
Landing from 15 m (50 ft) at normal landing weight	1,128 m (3,700 ft)
Range with max payload	2,550 nm (4,725 km; 2,935 miles)
Ferry range	5,550 nm (10,280 km; 6,390 miles)

(1980–81)

THE LOCKHEED T-33/TV-2.
U.S. Air Force designations: T-33 and RT-33.
U.S. Navy designation: TV-2.

Developed from the Shooting Star jet-fighter, the T-33A is the standard jet trainer in service in the U.S.A.F., U.S. Navy and U.S. Marine Corps, and has been supplied to the air forces of twelve M.D.A.P. nations. It has also been bought by four Latin-American powers—Cuba, Colombia, Peru and Venezuela.

Current orders for the T-33A will keep it in production until late 1959 and will bring total deliveries of the type to almost 5,700.

The following are the current versions:—

T-33A. Allison J33-A-35 engine (5,200 by = 2,360 kg. s.t.). Fuselage lengthened by 38.6 in. (98.1 cm.), 26.6 in. forward of wings and 12 in. aft, to accommodate extra seat. Both seats under a continuous canopy hinged at rear edge and raised electrically or manually from either inside or outside aircraft. Smaller fuselage fuel tank (95 U.S. gallons = 360 litres) and larger wing tanks, which are nylon cells instead of self-sealing type. Instructor in rear seat. Originally, all T-33A's had a fixed armament of two .50 in. machine-guns in their nose. New production T-33's ordered in 1955 have

all-weather "navigational noses" instead of guns and many of those already in service are being modified. The new equipment includes the first combined radio compass sense antenna and VOR device, and is dual-operated with controls in both cockpits.

The T-33 is built under licence by Canadair, Ltd. Canadian production aircraft are powered by Rolls-Royce Nene engines. It is also being assembled in Japan by Kawasaki from components manufactured by Lockheed.

RT-33A. Single-seat photographic reconnaissance version of the T-33. Carries a battery of four mapping and charting cameras and a wire recorder, to enable the pilot to make a record of the flight over the target, to elaborate on particular features of the terrain and to record height and position. Operational range of the RT-33 is said to be approximately 20 per cent. greater than that of the standard two-seat T-33.

TV-2. U.S. Navy version of the T-33A two-seat trainer.

A full structural description of the T-33 has appeared in previous editions of "All the World's Aircraft."

DIMENSIONS (T-33A).—
Span 38 ft. 10¼ in. (11.85 m.).
Length 37 ft. 8 in. (11.48 m.).
Height 11 ft. 8 in. (3.55 m.).

WEIGHTS (T-33A).—
Weight empty 8,400 lb. (3,810 kg.).
Weight loaded 11,965 lb. (5,432 kg.).

PERFORMANCE (T-33A).—
Max. speed at S/L. 600 m.p.h. (960 km.h.).
Max. speed at 25,000 ft. (7,620 m.) 543 m.p.h. (874 km.h.).
Stalling speed (with flaps) 102 m.p.h. (164 km.h.).
Stalling speed (without flaps) 113 m.p.h. (182 km.h.).

The Lockheed T-33A Shooting Star Two-seat Trainer (Allison J33-A-35 turbojet engine).

Climb to 25,000 ft. (7,620 m.) 6.5 min.
Service ceiling 47,500 ft. (14,480 m.).
T.O. distance to 50 ft. (15.25 m.) (with water injection) 2,560 ft. (780 m.).
Landing distance from 50 ft. (15.25 m.) 3,480 ft. (1,061 m.).
Endurance 3.12 hours.   (1958–59)

Lockheed U-2C electronic intelligence aircraft

U-2CT dual-control conversion trainer

LOCKHEED U-2 and TR-1

Development of the U-2 began in the Spring of 1954 to meet a joint CIA/USAF requirement for a high-altitude strategic reconnaissance and special-purpose research aircraft. It took place in the Lockheed 'Skunk Works' at Burbank, California, where, after acceptance of the design in late 1954, two prototypes were hand-built in great secrecy by a small team of engineers. The aircraft's true purpose was cloaked under the USAF U-for-Utility designation U-2, and the first flight, by Lockheed test pilot Tony LeVier, took place on or about 1 August 1955 at Watertown Strip in the Nevada desert.

The configuration of the U-2 is basically that of a powered sailplane, which explains its unusual 'bicycle' landing gear, combined with underwing balancer units which provide stability during take-off and are then jettisoned. Range can, if necessary, be extended by shutting off the engine and gliding. Because of its configuration the U-2 requires unusually precise handling during take-off and landing—particularly the latter, since there is an extremely small margin between approach speed and stalling speed. After touchdown, the aircraft comes to rest on one of the down-turned wingtips, which serve as landing skids.

Initial quantities of 48 single-seat and five two-seat U-2s were ordered in FY 1956, but after about 30 of these had been completed the increasing weight of special equipment which the aircraft was required to carry had degraded performance to such an extent that a more powerful engine became necessary, and this was installed from 1959 onwards. At the same time a substantial increase in fuel capacity made possible a considerably greater range. In FY 1968 the U-2 was put back into production, to replace some of the two dozen or more aircraft lost over hostile territory or in accidents, and the production line is now to be reopened again to manufacture a new, tactical reconnaissance version, the TR-1.

In service, the U-2 was flown at first by CIA pilots, ostensibly in USAF units known as the 1st, 2nd and 3rd Weather Reconnaissance Squadrons (Provisional). These were based initially at Lakenheath in England, Adana in Turkey, and Edwards AFB, California, with detachments respectively in Germany, Pakistan and Okinawa. From

here, and from bases in Cyprus, the south-west Pacific, Alaska and elsewhere, they were employed for photographic and electronic intelligence (elint) overflights of Eastern Europe, the USSR, the Middle East, China, Cuba and other sensitive areas. These operations, which began in January 1956, were 'blown' when a U-2B flown by Lt Francis Gary Powers was brought down near Sverdlovsk in the Soviet Union on 1 May 1960, during an overflight from Peshawar, Pakistan, to Bodö, Norway.

Deliveries to already-established USAF units began in early 1957, these including the 4028th and 4080th Strategic Reconnaissance Squadrons of Strategic Air Command, and Air Research and Development Command. In addition to their strategic reconnaissance role, they carried out much valuable high-altitude research work, including the monitoring of radioactivity levels in the atmosphere. Two-seat U-2Ds of the 6512th Test Squadron, USAF Systems Command, were also used for atmospheric sampling, for development of equipment for the Midas and Samos satellites, and to track and assist recovery of Discoverer spacecraft. At least six U-2s were transferred from the USAF to the Chinese Nationalist Air Force in the 1960s, most or all of which were subsequently lost.

From 1964, US Air Force U-2s began to operate from Bien Hoa in Viet-Nam, and later from detached bases at Osan, South Korea, and U-Tapao, Thailand. Overflights of mainland China, which had been made from bases in Taiwan, were halted after a Sino-American agreement in 1974, and the U-2s concerned were recalled to the USA. It is often (and wrongly) stated that the Lockheed SR-71 was a 'U-2 replacement', but such is not the case. In 1976 the 349th (formerly the 4080th) Strategic Reconnaissance Squadron was transferred to Beale AFB, California, and redesignated the 99th SRS. It shares this base with the 1st SRS, which flies the SR-71, the two units forming the 9th Strategic Reconnaissance Wing and illustrating that the two types are complementary. In recent years SAC U-2s have, in addition to their usual duties, flown photo-reconnaissance missions on behalf of the US Ministry of Agriculture, Society of Engineers and other agencies, and have been employed to monitor hurricanes, earthquakes and other natural disasters.

The other major operator of the U-2 has been the National Aeronautics and Space Administration and its predecessor, NACA. The first aircraft to appear in NASA markings was NASA 55741, which was shown to the press in June 1960, a month after the Powers incident. It has been suggested that this untypical registration may have been an attempt to disguise a USAF serial number, 55-5741, presumably indicating a prototype aircraft. At least four other U-2s have been operated by NASA (NASA 320,432,708 and 709), the last two of these being of the U-2C version. Work undertaken for NASA has been extensive and varied, and has included flights over ecological test areas, in support of various Earth resources programmes; investigations into clear air turbulence (HI-CAT programme); a NASA/USAF high-altitude atmospheric sampling programme (HASP); and observations in astronomy, atmospheric physics, and geophysics. One NASA U-2, fitted with a microwave radio-meter, was due to undertake a series of flights from Jorge Chavez Airport near Lima, Peru, in Spring 1979, in a programme to measure the speed at which the Earth travels through space.

In view of the continuing classified nature of much of its work, it is not possible to confirm officially many details concerning the U-2; but the list of variants and general description which follow are believed to be substantially correct. It should also be noted that there have been numerous conversions between one model and another during the aircraft's operational career, and that there may be differences between individual aircraft of the same model.

ter; two APQ-107 radar altimeter warning systems; A/A24G-9 true airspeed computer and ASW-31 automatic flight control system. P-3Cs delivered from 1975 have the avionics/electronics package updated by addition of an extra 393K memory drum and fourth logic unit, Omega navigation, new magnetic tape transport, and an ASA-66 tactical display for the sonar operators. To accommodate the new systems a new operational software computer programme will be written in CMS-2 language. Marconi Avionics AQS-901 acoustic signal processing and display system in RAAF P-3Cs.   (1979–80)

ARMAMENT: Bomb bay, 2·03 m wide, 0·88 m deep and 3·91 m long (80 in × 34·5 in × 154 in), forward of wing, can accommodate a 2,000 lb MK 25/39/55/56 mine, three 1,000 lb MK 36/52 mines, three MK 57 depth bombs, eight MK 54 depth bombs, eight MK 43/44/46 torpedoes or a combination of two MK 101 nuclear depth bombs and four MK 43/44/46 torpedoes. Ten underwing pylons for stores: two under centre-section each side can carry torpedoes or 2,000 lb mines; three under outer wing each side can carry respectively (inboard to outboard) a torpedo or 2,000 lb mine (or searchlight on starboard wing), a torpedo or 1,000 lb mine or rockets singly or in pods; a torpedo or 500 lb mine or rockets singly or in pods. Torpedoes can be carried underwing only for ferrying; mines can be carried and released. Search stores, such as sonobuoys and sound signals, are launched from inside cabin area in the P-3A/B. In the P-3C sonobuoys are loaded and launched externally and internally. Max total weapon load includes six 2,000 lb mines under wings and a 3,290 kg (7,252 lb) internal load made up of two MK 101 depth bombs, four MK 44 torpedoes, pyrotechnic pistol and 12 signals, 87 sonobuoys, 100 MK 50 underwater sound signals (P-3A/B), 18 MK 3A marine markers (P-3A/B), 42 MK 7 marine markers, two B.T. buoys, and two MK 5 parachute flares. Sonobuoys are ejected from P-3C aircraft with explosive cartridge actuating devices (CAD), eliminating the need for a pneumatic system. Australian P-3Cs use BARRA sonobuoys.

DIMENSIONS, EXTERNAL:
Wing span 30·37 m (99 ft 8 in)
Wing chord at root 5·77 m (18 ft 11 in)
Wing chord at tip 2·31 m (7 ft 7 in)
Wing aspect ratio 7·5
Length overall 35·61 m (116 ft 10 in)
Height overall 10·29 m (33 ft 8½ in)
Fuselage diameter 3·45 m (11 ft 4 in)

U-2R. Additional batch of 12 single-seat aircraft, ordered for strategic reconnaissance in FY 1968, by which time approx half of original U-2s had been lost through various causes. Serial numbers 68-10329 to 68-10340. Originally designated WU-2C. Bulged intakes, as on U-2C, but longer nose and fuselage, without dorsal spine fairing; increased wing span and internal fuel capacity: rear fuselage slightly bulged on top, just forward of fin; mainwheel unit further aft, tailwheel unit further forward, than on earlier models. Non-US bases have included Mildenhall, England. The U-2R has been selected as the preferred airborne relay vehicle for the Lockheed PLSS (Precision Location Strike System), intended to locate and identify enemy radar emitters, and to direct strike aircraft against them.

TR-1. Tactical reconnaissance version, described officially by the Department of Defense as "to be equipped with a variety of electronic sensors to provide continuously available, day or night, all-weather surveillance of the battle area in direct support of the US and Allied ground and air forces during peace, crises, and war situations". Tooling for the U-2 has been kept in store at the USAF-owned Plant 42 at Palmdale, California, and the FY 1979 defence budget included $10·2 million to reopen the production line in FY 1980. It is understood that the TR-1 will be based on the U-2R, still with the J75-P-13 engine, but with the significant addition of an 'advanced synthetic aperture' radar system (ASARS) in the form of a UPD-X side-looking airborne radar (SLAR) and modern electronic countermeasures (ECM). Seen as a replacement for the now-abandoned Compass Cope RPV (see 1977-78 *Jane's*), the TR-1 is intended primarily for use in Europe, where its SLAR will provide the capability to 'see' approximately 30 nm (55 km; 35 miles) into hostile territory without the need to overfly an actual or potential battle area. An initial $10·2 million was included in the FY 1979 budget for airframe and engine development. A further $43 million was requested by the USAF in FY 1980 for 25 TR-1s. The first two of these will be two-seat **TR-1Bs**, for training.

The new Lockheed TR-1 will resemble closely the U-2R high-altitude strategic reconnaissance aircraft shown here

The following description applies primarily to the single-seat U-2B, C, and R versions, except where indicated otherwise:

TYPE: High-altitude reconnaissance and research aircraft.
WINGS: Cantilever mid-wing monoplane, with wingtips turned down 90° for use as skids during landing. All-metal structure. Trailing-edge flaps occupy approx 60% of each half-span, with ailerons outboard. Small tubular fairing between each flap and aileron: on U-2C/CT/R these are larger and project beyond trailing-edge. Small plate-type spoiler forward of outer portion of each flap. Some aircraft fitted with trim tab on each aileron.
FUSELAGE: All-metal semi-monocoque structure of circular cross-section, with thin-gauge skin. Fineness ratio approx 10:1. Forward-opening door-type airbrake on each side of fuselage aft of wings, used mainly as a landing aid. Large airscoop fairing on fuselage beneath rear of wing root: generally on starboard side, but sometimes on port side and sometimes on both. Since about 1974 some aircraft have had a modified tailpipe, to reduce the infra-red signature from the engine.
TAIL UNIT: Cantilever all-metal structure. Trim tab on rudder and in each elevator. Ventral fin under fuselage of U-2A and WU-2A, immediately aft of wings.
LANDING GEAR: Retractable bicycle type, with twin main wheels and twin small tailwheels in tandem, each unit retracting forward into fuselage. Balancer units under outer wings, each with twin small wheels, are jettisoned on take-off (except on U-2CT). Tailwheels and underwing wheels have solid tyres; castoring tailwheel unit aids manoeuvring on ground. Brakes on main wheels. Braking parachute in container under rudder.
POWER PLANT (except U-2A): One 75·6 kN (17,000 lb st) Pratt & Whitney J75-P-13 turbojet engine. Normal internal fuel capacity 2,970 litres (785 US gallons) in U-2A, approx 4,315 litres (1,140 US gallons) in U-2B, approx 4,448 litres (1,175 US gallons) in U-2C. Provision for two 397·5 litre (105 US gallon) nonjettisonable auxiliary slipper tanks on wing leading-edges; these were designed originally to extend range of U-2A, but may be seen on other models.

ACCOMMODATION: Pilot only in U-2A/B/C/R, on ejection seat (except in early U-2As before 1957). Rearward-sliding transparent canopy, protected internally against ultra-violet radiation. Accommodation is not pressurised. Tandem ejection seats and dual controls in U-2CT and U-2D, the rear cockpit in the U-2CT being 'stepped' above the upper line of the fuselage. Rearview periscope on most aircraft (positions vary).
AVIONICS AND EQUIPMENT: Typical standard avionics in U-2B include Magnavox ARC-34 UHF com, Tacan, ILS, Lear A-10 autopilot, Bendix ARN-6 ADF, MA-1 compass, and (for night flying) astro-compass. Equipment includes one vertical and two lateral cameras for training flights, or up to five 70 mm cameras (U-2) or side-looking airborne radar (TR-1) for operational missions. Panoramic camera(s) originally of Land Polaroid type, but more usually Model 73B or Perkin-Elmer Model 501 in U-2B, with ventral periscopic sight. The U-2B shot down over Sverdlovsk on 1 May 1960 reportedly carried also an electromagnetic receiver for monitoring and recording radio and radar transmissions from the ground, made by Huggins Laboratories, Hewlett-Packard and Raytheon.

DIMENSIONS, EXTERNAL:
Wing span: except U-2R 24·38 m (80 ft 0 in)
U-2R 31·39 m (103 ft 0 in)
Wing area, net: except U-2R 52·49 m² (565 sq ft)
Wing aspect ratio approx 10·2
Length overall: except U-2R 15·11 m (49 ft 7 in)
U-2R 19·20 m (63 ft 0 in)
Height overall: except U-2R 3·96 m (13 ft 0 in)
U-2R 4·88 m (16 ft 0 in)
Wheel track (c/l of wing balancer units):
except U-2R approx 15·24 m (50 ft 0 in)
Wheelbase: except U-2R approx 6·10 m (20 ft 0 in)
WEIGHTS:
Weight empty, without equipment:
U-2C 6,259 kg (13,800 lb)
Fuel and equipment payload:
U-2B approx 1,360 kg (3,000 lb)
U-2R approx 5,443 kg (12,000 lb)
T-O weight without slipper tanks:
U-2A 7,189 kg (15,850 lb)

The Lockheed PV-1 Ventura Naval Patrol Monoplane (two Pratt & Whitney R-2800-31 engines).

THE LOCKHEED (VEGA 37) VENTURA.

U.S. Navy designations : PV-1 and PV-3.
U.S. Army Air Forces designations : B-34 and B-37.
British name : Ventura.

The Ventura, a military development of the Lockheed Lodestar transport, was originally designed and built to the order of the British Government.

Ventura I. Two 1,850 h.p. Pratt & Whitney R-2800-S1A4G engines. First British contracts placed with the Vega Aircraft Corpn. in 1940. Armament consisted of two fixed 50 cal. and two .303 in. machine-guns in the nose, two or four .303 in. guns in a Boulton Paul dorsal turret, and two .303 in. guns in a rear-firing ventral position. First went into service with the R.A.F. as a medium bomber in 1942.

B-34 (Ventura II and IIA). Two 2,000 h.p. Pratt & Whitney R-2800-31 engines. Also built by Vega but under American contracts. Various detail changes, mainly in armament and equipment. B-34 used for coastal patrol, advanced training and as a target tug.

B-37 (Ventura G.R. III). Two 2,000 h.p. Wright R-2600-13 engines. Built by the Lockheed Aircraft Corpn. Originally O-56 but re-designated B-37.

PV-1 (Ventura IV and G.R.V). U.S. Navy Patrol Bomber version of the B-34. Closed-in nose with two fixed forward-firing 50 cal. machine-guns. Remainder of armament same as B-34. Bomb-bay adapted to accommodate bombs, depth-charges or one torpedo. Increased fuel capacity. The description below applies to the PV-1 which was still in production in 1944. The PV-3 was similar to the PV-1 but had British equipment and is obsolete.

TYPE.—Twin-engined Oversea Patrol monoplane.
WINGS.—Mid-wing cantilever monoplane. Centre-section integral with fuselage. Outer sections have detachable wing-tips. Centre-section has one main spar and front and rear shear beams, the main spar passing through fuselage and secondary beams attaching to fuselage sides. Upper smooth Alclad skin reinforced with corrugated sheet, lower skin by stringers. Outer wings have one spar and auxiliary rear beam sheet ribs and Alclad skin. Skin upper surface reinforced by corrugations and stringers, lower surface by stringers only. All-metal ailerons on piano-type hinges, Trim-tabs in ailerons, port tab controllable. Fixed slots in leading-edge ahead of ailerons. Fowler flaps over 34% of trailing-edge between ailerons and fuselage.
FUSELAGE.—All-metal elliptical-section monocoque structure built up of bulkheads and frames, longitudinal members and stringers and a flush-riveted Alclad skin, butt-jointed ahead of pilot's compartment and lapped aft. (1945–46)

TAIL UNIT.—Cantilever monoplane type with twin fins and rudders. All-metal structure. Tailplane comprises centre-section, two outer-sections and two semi-circular tips outboard of fins. Fin and rudder assemblies interchangeable right or left. Trim-tabs in elevators and rudders.
LANDING GEAR.—Retractable type. Aerol shock-absorber units retract backwards into tails of engine nacelles. Units interchangeable right or left with minor adjustments. Hydraulic retraction. Goodyear wheels and hydraulic brakes. Retractable tail-wheel.
POWER PLANT.—Two Pratt & Whitney R-2800-31 eighteen-cylinder radial air-cooled engines with two-speed superchargers, on welded steel-tube mountings. Three-blade Hamilton-Standard Hydromatic broad-blade constant-speed airscrews, 10 ft. 7 in. (3.23 m.) diameter. Main fuel system comprises four tanks in centre-section, two in outer sections, and two cabin tanks, all self-sealing. Two external droppable tanks under outer wings. Provision for long-range ferry tanks in bomb-bay. Main oil tank in each nacelle with reserve tank in fuselage.
ACCOMMODATION.—Crew of four, comprising pilot, navigator/bomb-aimer, radio operator/gunner and turret gunner.
ARMAMENT.—Two fixed 50 cal. machine-guns in nose, two 50 cal. guns in Martin electrically-operated dorsal turret and two 30 cal. tunnel-guns. Internal bomb-bay may accommodate up to 2,500 lbs. of bombs, six 325 lb. depth-charges or one standard 22 in. short aircraft torpedo. Two 500 lb. bombs or two depth-charges may replace external wing tanks.
DIMENSIONS.—Span 65 ft. 6 in. (19.96 m.), Length 51 ft. 7½ in. (15.74 m.), Height 14 ft. 1⅜ in. (4.31 m.), Wing area (with flaps retracted) 551 sq. ft. (51.2 sq. m.), Wing area (with flaps fully lowered) 619 sq. ft. (57.5 sq. m.).
WEIGHTS.—Weight empty 19,373 lbs. (8,795 kg.), Normal loaded weight 26,500 lbs. (12,030 kg.), Maximum permissable overloaded weight 31,000 lbs. (14,075 kg.).
PERFORMANCE.—Maximum speed over 300 m.p.h. (480 km.h.), Service ceiling over 25,000 ft. (7,625 m.), Normal range over 1,000 miles (1,600 km.).

THE LOCKHEED HARPOON.

U.S. Navy designation : PV-2.

The Harpoon is a development of the Ventura PV-1. It has wings of greater span (75 ft. = 22.8 m.) with more taper and with rounded wing-tips, a new rectangular tailplane with new fins and rudders at the outer extremities, a bigger bomb-bay and a heavier armament. The power-plant consists of two Pratt & Whitney R-2800-31 engines, the same as fitted to the PV-1 Ventura.

The armament consists of five fixed 50 cal. machine-guns in the nose, two 50 cal. guns in the dorsal Martin turret, and two 50 cal. guns in a power-operated mounting in the break in the underside of the fuselage. The larger bomb-bay completely encloses the torpedo, which in the PV-1 partly protruded between the bomb-bay doors.

LOCKHEED S-3A VIKING

US Navy designation: S-3A

On 4 August 1969 Lockheed announced the receipt of a $461 million contract from the US Navy to develop a new anti-submarine aircraft under the designation S-3A. Development was carried out by Lockheed in partnership with Vought Systems Division of LTV and Univac Federal Systems Division of Sperry Rand. Vought designed and is building the wing, engine pods, tail unit and landing gear, and Univac is responsible for the digital computer, the heart of the weapon system, which provides high-speed processing of data essential for the S-3A's ASW role. Lockheed is building the fuselage, integrating the electronics, and is responsible for final assembly at Burbank, California.

The selection of Lockheed-California as contractor for this aircraft followed more than a year of intensive competition between North American Rockwell, McDonnell Douglas, Grumman, Convair Division of General Dynamics, and Lockheed-California in conjunction with LTV.

The Lockheed team was responsible for development, test and demonstration of the aircraft and its weapon systems. The first prototype was rolled out on schedule on 8 November 1971 at Burbank, California, and the first flight was made on 21 January 1972. An increased ceiling of $494 million on the contract, funded over a five-year period, provided for production of eight research and development aircraft in two lots.

On 4 May 1972 the US Navy announced an order for the first production lot of 13 S-3As, and orders for 35 and 45 more were received in April and October 1973 respectively. Other orders have followed.

The Viking was introduced into the Fleet officially on 20 February 1974, during ceremonies held at North Island NAS, near San Diego, California. Initial deliveries were made to Squadron VS-41, the S-3A training squadron based at North Island NAS. By 1 January 1976 Lockheed had delivered 101 of the 187 Vikings then on order for the US Navy.

At North Island, USN personnel from Squadron VS-21, VS-22 and VS-29 completed conversion to the S-3A by

mid-1975, and VS-28, 31 and 32 personnel had also qualified by the end of that year. First operational deployment of the Viking, with Squadron VS-21, was made in July 1975, on board the USS *John F. Kennedy*. VS-21's deployment had been completed and the squadron had returned to its home base at North Island NAS by early 1976.

The S-3A has a crew of four, comprising a pilot, co-pilot, tactical co-ordinator (Tacco) and acoustic sensor operator (Senso). The pilot maintains command of the aircraft, while the Tacco formulates strategy and instructs the pilots on the necessary manoeuvres for a successful submarine attack. In addition to flying duties, the co-pilot is responsible for the non-acoustic sensors (such as radar and infra-red) and navigation: the Senso controls the acoustic sensors.

The development of quieter submarines has led to the design of sonobuoys of increased sensitivity, and advanced cathode ray tube displays are provided in the S-3A to maintain flexibility of operation with a limited crew. In

Lockheed S-3A Viking of US Navy Squadron VS-21 landing on board the carrier *John F. Kennedy*

particular, a cathode ray tube is utilised to monitor the acoustic sensors. The information formerly stowed in roll form from paper plotters is now stored in the Univac 1832A computer and is available for instant recall. Other functions of the computer include weapon trajectory calculations and pre-flight navigation. Magnetic anomaly detection (MAD) equipment of increased sensitivity makes it possible to detect submarines at greater depths than has been possible until the present time.

Shipboard maintenance is simplified by the provision of computerised fault-finding equipment, built-in test equipment (BITE), and versatile avionic shop test (VAST) compatibility. Complete deck-level servicing accessibility contributes to the attainment of a quick turnaround time.

Production of 187 S-3As for the US Navy ended in mid-1978. All tooling has been placed in storage at Burbank pending a US Navy decision on further orders, and in early 1980 demonstrator versions of the US-3A (COD) and KS-3 (tanker) were being evaluated by the Navy. No production decision had then been made.

The following description applies to the current production S-3A:

TYPE: Twin-turbofan carrier-borne anti-submarine aircraft.

WINGS: Cantilever shoulder-wing monoplane. Sweepback at quarter-chord 15°. No dihedral. Incidence 3° 15′ at root, −3° 50′ at tip. All-metal fail-safe structure. Wings fold upward and inward hydraulically, outboard of engine pylons, for carrier stowage. Single-slotted Fowler-type trailing-edge flaps, operated by hydraulic power with an integral electric motor for emergency operation. Electrically-operated leading-edge flaps, extending from engine pylons to wingtips, are fully extended after 15° of trailing-edge flap movement. Ailerons augmented by under- and over-wing spoilers for roll control. All primary flight control surfaces are actuated by irreversible servos powered by dual hydraulic systems. Loss of either hydraulic system results in loss of half the available hinge movement, but the remaining system can meet all control requirements. Automatic reversion to manual control in the event of failure of both hydraulic systems. In emergency operation the spoilers are inoperative. Wing anti-icing by engine bleed air, but portions of wing leading-edges are cyclically heated to reduce consumption of bleed air.

FUSELAGE: Semi-monocoque all-metal fail-safe structure, incorporating split weapons bays with clamshell doors. Two parallel beams form a keelson from nose gear to tail-hook, strengthening the fuselage and improving cabin structural integrity by distributing catapult and arrester loads throughout the airframe. Launch tubes for 60 sonobuoys in belly. No provision for in-flight reloading of these launch tubes. Frangible canopies in top of fuselage are so designed that the crew can eject through them in emergency. Electronics bays with external access doors in forward and aft fuselage. An illuminated in-flight refuelling probe, mounted within the fuselage on the top centreline, is operated by an electric drive and protected by a positive-seal door. It can be extended or retracted in emergency by a hand crank. MAD boom, extensible in flight, housed in fuselage tail.

TAIL UNIT: Cantilever all-metal structure with swept vertical and horizontal surfaces. Fin and rudder are folded downward by hydraulic servos for carrier stowage. During fin-folding sequence the pedal input to the rudder servo is disconnected to allow the pilot to steer the nosewheel by the rudder pedals. Variable-incidence tailplane, electrically controlled. Elevator and rudder controlled by hydraulic servos. Trim tabs in elevators and rudder. Anti-icing of tailplane leading-edges by engine bleed air.

LANDING GEAR: Hydraulically-retractable tricycle type. Main units, similar to those of the Vought F-8 Crusader, are fitted with single wheels and retract rearward into wheel wells immediately aft of the split weapons bays. Nose unit similar to that of the Vought A-7 Corsair II, with twin wheels and catapult towbar, retracts rearward into fuselage. Nosewheel steering by hydraulic power. Hydraulic brakes. Arrester hook.

POWER PLANT: Two General Electric TF34-GE-2 high bypass ratio turbofan engines, each rated at 41·25 kN (9,275 lb st), pylon-mounted beneath the wings. Fuel in integral wing tanks, entirely within the wing box beam, one on each side of the fuselage centreline and inboard of the wing fold-line. Usable fuel capacity approximately 7,192 litres (1,900 US gallons). Two 1,136 litre (300 US gallon) jettisonable fuel tanks can be carried on underwing pylons. Single-point pressure refuelling adapter located on starboard side of fuselage aft of main landing gear door. Internal tanks may also be gravity fuelled through overwing connections. Fuel jettison system. Anti-icing of engine inlet nozzles by engine bleed air.

ACCOMMODATION: Crew of four. Pilot and co-pilot side by side on flight deck with transparent canopy. Tacco and Senso accommodated in aft cabin, with individual polarised side windows. All crew on McDonnell Douglas Escapac 1-E zero-zero ejection seats. Each seat has a rigid seat survival kit (RSSK), which can be opened during descent for inflation of life raft. Electric windscreen wipers. Windscreen surfaces electrically heated; side canopy is demisted with conditioned air. Liquid rain-repellent system to augment action of windscreen wipers. Cabin pressurised and air-conditioned, and each crewman's anti-exposure suit is ventilated with conditioned air from this system.

SYSTEMS: Garrett-AiResearch environmental control system, with engine bleed air supply and air-cycle refrigeration unit. Pressurisation system operates on a differential of 0·41-0·55 bars (6-8 lb/sq in), maintaining a cabin altitude of 1,525 m (5,000 ft) to a height of 7,620 m (25,000 ft) and 3,505 m (11,500 ft) cabin altitude to 12,200 m (40,000 ft). Two engine-driven pumps supply hydraulic power for two completely independent 207 bar (3,000 lb/sq in) systems. Port system supplies landing gear, flaps, brakes, wing and tail fold, arrester hook and weapon bay doors. Its secondary function is to power one side of the primary flight control servos. Starboard system powers only the primary flight controls, energising one side of the dual servo actuators; port system energises the other. Electrical system includes two 75kVA generators supplying 115-120V AC at a frequency of 400Hz. Secondary DC power is obtained from two transformer-rectifiers that deliver

28V DC at 200A. Williams Research Corporation gas turbine APU has a 5kVA generator for emergency electrical power, providing 115-120V AC at 400Hz to the essential AC bus and 28V DC at 30A through the transformer-rectifiers. Emergency electrical power is adequate only for essential capabilities such as those required for night flight under instrument conditions.

ELECTRONICS: ASW data processing, control and display includes Univac 1832A general-purpose digital computer, acoustic data processer, sonobuoy receiver, command signal generator and analogue tape recorder. Non-acoustic sensors comprise AN/APS-116 high-resolution radar, OR-89/AA forward-looking infra-red (FLIR) scanner in retractable turret, AN/ASQ-81 MAD and compensation equipment, and ALR-47 passive ECM receiving and instantaneous frequency-measuring system housed in wingtip pods. Primary navigation system composed of ASN-92(V) CAINS inertial navigator, AN/APN-200 Doppler ground velocity system (DGVS), AYN-5 airspeed/altitude computing set (AACS), ASN-107 attitude heading reference system (AHRS), ARS-2 sonobuoy reference system (SRS), APN-201 radar altimeter and altitude warning system (RAAWS), ARN-83 LF/ADF and ARA-50 UHF/DF radio navigation aids, ARN-84(V) Tacan, and the aircraft's flight displays and interface system (FDIS). Communications equipment includes a 1kW ARC-153 HF transceiver for long-range communications, dual ARC-156 UHF transceivers, AN/ARA-63 receiver/decoder set for use with shipboard ILS, data terminal set (DTS), OK-173 integral intercom system (ICS) and APX-72 IFF/APX-76A SIF units with altitude reporting, and AN/ASW-25B automatic carrier landing system (ACLS) communication set. Search stores are designated as LOFAR (SSQ-41), R/O (SSQ-47), DIFAR (SSQ-53), CASS (SSQ-50), DICASS (SSQ-62) and BT (SSQ-36) sonobuoys.

ARMAMENT: Split weapons bays equipped with BRU-14/A bomb rack assemblies can deploy either four MK-36 destructors, four MK-46 torpedoes, four MK-82 bombs, two MK-57 or four MK-54 depth bombs, or four MK-53 mines. BRU-11/A bomb racks installed on the two wing pylons permit carriage of SUU-44/A flare launchers, MK-52, MK-55 or MK-56 mines, MK-20-2 cluster bombs, Aero 1D auxiliary fuel tanks, or two rockets pods of type LAU-68/A (7 FFAR 2·75 in), LAU-61/A (19 FFAR 2·75 in), LAU-69/A (19 FFAR

2·75 in), or LAU-10A/A (4 FFAR 5·0 in). Alternatively, installation of TER-7 triple ejector racks on the BRU-11/A bomb racks makes it possible to carry three rocket pods, flare launchers, MK-20 cluster bombs, MK-82 bombs, MK-36 destructors, or MK-76-5 or MK-106-4 practice bombs under each wing.

DIMENSIONS, EXTERNAL:

Wing span	20·93 m (68 ft 8 in)
Wing span, wings folded	8·99 m (29 ft 6 in)
Length overall	16·26 m (53 ft 4 in)
Length overall, tail folded	15·06 m (49 ft 5 in)
Height overall	6·93 m (22 ft 9 in)
Height overall, tail folded	4·65 m (15 ft 3 in)
Tailplane span	8·23 m (27 ft 0 in)

DIMENSIONS, INTERNAL:

Max height	2·29 m (7 ft 6 in)
Max width	2·18 m (7 ft 2 in)

AREA:

Wings, gross	55·56 m² (598 sq ft)

WEIGHTS AND LOADING:

Weight empty	12,088 kg (26,650 lb)
Max design gross weight	23,831 kg (52,539 lb)
Normal ASW T-O weight	19,277 kg (42,500 lb)
Max landing weight	20,826 kg (45,914 lb)
Max carrier landing weight	17,098 kg (37,695 lb)
Max wing loading	429·2 kg/m² (87·9 lb/sq ft)

PERFORMANCE (at normal ASW T-O weight, unless otherwise indicated):

Max level speed	450 knots (834 km/h; 518 mph)
Max cruising speed	370 knots (686 km/h; 426 mph)
Loiter speed	160 knots (296 km/h; 184 mph)
Approach speed	100 knots (185 km/h; 115 mph)
Stalling speed	84 knots (157 km/h; 97 mph)
Max rate of climb at S/L	over 1,280 m (4,200 ft)/min
Service ceiling	above 10,670 m (35,000 ft)
T-O run	671 m (2,200 ft)
Landing run at landing weight of 16,556 kg (36,500 lb)	488 m (1,600 ft)
Combat range	more than 2,000 nm (3,705 km; 2,303 miles)
Ferry range	more than 3,000 nm (5,558 km; 3,454 miles)

(1976–77)

THE LOENING AMPHIBIAN.

One of the most interesting developments of recent years is the production of the Loening Amphibian.

For the first time, the ordinary tractor type of biplane has been modified, so that the machine is capable of landing on either land or water, with ability to start from or alight on either, at a moment's notice. No extra floats or other devices are used, as the new design obtains its amphibious characteristics by the shape of the main fuselage body itself, the bottom of which is shaped like a flying-boat hull. To this is attached a folding landing gear, an ingenious device, which is operated by an electric motor—the pilot merely throwing a switch in order to raise the wheels for water landing, or to lower them for alighting on the land.

As demonstrated in flight, the new Loening Amphibian, in performance of speed and manœuvrability, compares favourably with other aeroplanes of the same weight equipped with Liberty motors, such as the DH. But the deeper metal body and the unit construction give it a strength and rigidity which should greatly increase the safety of the crew in case of accident. In the sand test, conducted by the Air Service at Dayton, this body stood up without failure to a load of three or four times what is customarily applied.

In addition to the metal covering of the entire hull and body, the interior construction of the wings is largely metal, duralumin being the chief material used.

The Loening Amphibian (400 h.p. inverted Liberty engine).

One of the most interesting features of the machine is the use of the Inverted Liberty Motor. This development places the bulk of the engine cylinders, etc., below the line of thrust of the propeller, so that clearance for the propeller is more readily obtained, and at the same time the centre of gravity of the weight is lowered several feet.

(1926)

During 1925, this Company concentrated on the development of the very successful Loening amphibian.

This machine is the type that was used so successfully on the MacMillan Expedition, last year, where six thousand miles of Arctic flying were covered by Commander Byrd and his men, in less than twelve days flying, and these same planes were subsequently sent down a few months later to Cuba, where they successfully completed the Hydrographic Survey for the United States Navy Department. Planes of this type are in use now in the U.S. Army, U.S. Navy, U.S. Marine Corps, and the U.S. Coast Guard, and have received a wide distribution, and continuously used in the Hawaiian Islands, Philippine Islands, Panama, and Haiti, as well as along both the Atlantic and Pacific Coasts of the United States.

Among the notable Service Missions performed by the Loening Amphibian, was the completion in the Fall of 1925 of the Survey for the United States Army of the Canadian Border around the Rainy Lakes District of Minnesota—a region in the heart of the country where an amphibian was essential, owing to the absence of landing fields and the presence of many lakes.

In March, 1926, a Loening Amphibian was successfully catapulted from a ship of the U.S. Navy by means of high explosive gunpowder charge. In later versions, the new inverted Packard 1-A-1500 engine has been fitted and a number (ten) have been ordered for subsequent use on the new aircraft-carriers "Lexington" and "Saratoga," now completing.

US Army designations: COA-1/OA
US Navy designations: OL-2/4

The Loening Amphibian.
Specification.

Span	45.0 ft. (13.71 m.).
Length	34.08 ft. (10.38 m.).
Height	12.25 ft. (3.73 m.).
Chord	6.0 ft. (1.83 m.).
Wing area	500.0 sq. ft. (46.45 sq. m.).
Area of ailerons	60.0 sq. ft. (5.57 sq. m.).
Weight empty	3,400 lbs. (1,542.64 kgs.).
Load :—	
Petrol and oil	800 lbs. (363.88 kgs.).
Crew	360 lbs. (163.33 kgs.).
Miscellaneous	1,000 lbs. (453.7 kgs.).
Total weight	5,560 lbs. (2,522.55 kgs.).
Max. speed	122 m.p.h.
Ceiling	13,500 ft.

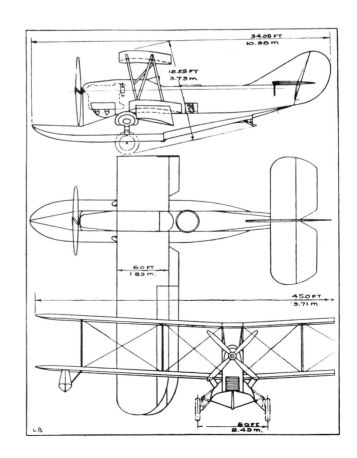

The Loening Amphibian (400 h.p. inverted Liberty engine).

POWER PLANT. One 400 h.p. inverted Liberty water-cooled engine mounted in nose of fuselage. The inverted engine permits a high thrust-line and consequent adequate airscrew clearance above nose of hull, with a low centre of gravity. Main fuel tanks, with capacity of 140 U.S. gallons (116 Imp. galls. = 530 litres) capacity, in fuselage in front of pilot. Radiator mounted in nose of fuselage under airscrew boss.

ACCOMMODATION. Crew of three carried. Pilot's seat under cut-out trailing-edge of top plane, with observer-gunner's cockpit aft. Accommodation provided in fuselage for wireless operator.

DIMENSIONS. Span 45 ft. (13.7 m.). Length 34 ft. 1 in. (10.38 m.). Height 12 ft. 3 in. (3.73 m.). Wing area 500 sq. m. (46.45 sq. m.).

WEIGHTS AND LOADINGS. Weight empty 3,400 lbs. (1,542.64 kg.). Disposable load 2,160 lbs. (980.9 kg.). Weight loaded 5,560 lbs. (2,522.5 kgs.). Wing loading 11.12 lbs./sq. ft. (54.7 kg./sq. m.). Power loading 13.9 lbs./h.p. (6.4 kg./h.p.).

PERFORMANCE. Maximum speed 122 m.p.h. (195.2 km.h.). Ceiling 13,500 ft. (4,200 m.). (1926)

The Loening Amphibian on the water. This machine was one of two used on the MacMillan Arctic Expedition in 1925.

The Loening XO-10 Single-wheel Amphibian (500 h.p. inverted Wright "Typhoon" engine).

The Keystone OL-9 Two-seat Amphibian Biplane (425 h.p. Pratt & Whitney "Wasp" engine).

THE KEYSTONE OL-9 AMPHIBIAN.

TYPE.—Two-seat flying-boat amphibian, for Navy use.

WINGS.—Equal-winged biplane. Two spruce spars and duralumin or "Alclad" (duralumin coated with pure aluminium) ribs, the whole being covered with fabric. Two sets of "N" type welded steel-tube interplane struts on either side of hull.

FUSELAGE AND HULL.—Framework of fuselage and hull consist of two Warren girders, cross-connected by bulkheads, which, in the case of those in the hull, are solid, thus sub-dividing it up into a series of watertight compartments. Spruce longerons and diagonals joined with flat duralumin gusset-plates bolted throughout with duralumin bolts. Covering is sheet duralumin, bolted to wooden frame with layer of fabric impregnated with marine glue between wood and metal. The hull specially reinforced for deck-landing and to withstand stress of being shot off the U.S. Navy powder-catapult.

TAIL UNIT.—Normal design. Tail-plane and elevator are of usual wood and fabric construction, but fin and rudder are metal-covered.

UNDERCARRIAGE.—The hull is built integral with the fuselage and is Vee-bottomed with two steps. The amphibian undercarriage is in two units, each of triangular form when viewed from the front. Each frame carries a wheel and is revolved round its hinge-point on the chine of the hull by a thrust member, which operates on a slide-tube within the hull. The entire mechanism, with the exception of half a wheel, is withdrawn into the hull. At rear of hull, at the second step, is a tail skid and two floats, each with a skid, are mounted under the wing-tips.

POWER PLANT.—One 425 h.p. Pratt & Whitney "Wasp" air-cooled radial engine. Flanged duralumin engine-plate connected to fuselage by steel tubes and is further braced by two vertical struts running down to the hull. Main fuel tank (140 U.S. gallons = 116 Imp. galls. = 530 litres capacity) is under pilot's seat.

ACCOMMODATION.—Pilot's cockpit forward, under centre-section, with good vision for aircraft-carrier landings. Gunner-observer's cockpit behind and below, in hull, is a cabin for wireless operator. Wheel control in front cockpit and stick control in rear cockpit.

DIMENSIONS.—Span 45 ft. (13.725 m.), Length 35 ft. 2¾ in. (10.74 m.), Height (on wheels) 12 ft. 11 in. (3.93 m.), Height (wheels retracted) 11 ft. 6 in. (3.5 m.), Wing area 502 sq. ft. (46.68 sq. m.).

WEIGHTS AND LOADINGS.—Weight empty 3,253 lbs. (1,476.8 kg.), Disposable load (max.) 2,000 lbs. (908 kg.), Disposable load (Army normal) 1,800 lbs. (817 kg.), Disposable load (Navy catapult) 1,500 lbs. (681 kg.), Weight loaded (max.) 5,253 lbs. (2,384.8 kg.), Wing loading 10.45 lbs./sq. ft. (51 kg./sq. m.), Power loading 12.4 lbs./h.p. (5.62 kg./h.p.).

PERFORMANCE.—Maximum speed 124 m.p.h. (198.4 km.h.), Stalling speed 50 m.p.h. (80 km.h.), Climb in 10 mins. 5,500 ft. (1,650 m.), Range at cruising speed 650 miles (1,040 km.). (1931)

LOENING PW2/2A

The Leoning Army Racer (600 h.p. Packard.)

THE PW-2B.

A new version of the PW-2, mentioned in the 1924 volume, has been prepared. This follows the same general arrangement—that is a steel-braced monoplane—but instead of the square tipped wings of the original design, the trailing edge has been rounded off right up to the front spar.

A 300 h.p. Packard engine is to be housed instead of the 300 h.p. Wright. The machine is of 34 ft. (10.36 m.) span, 26 ft. 3 in. (8.0 m.) long, and is expected to have a speed of 145 m.p.h. (234 km.h.).

THE PA-1.

Another new single-seater (pursuit) machine for the new Wright 350 h.p. radial air-cooled engine. This is a heavily-staggered equal-winged biplane, with a single row of "N" interplane struts.

The span is 28 ft. (9.14 m.), length 19 ft. 9¼ in. (6.04 m.), and a speed of 145 m.p.h. (234 km.h.), together with a climb to 10,000 ft. (3,050 m.) in 8 mins., are expected.

THE MAULE BEE DEE M-4

TYPE.—Four-seat light aircraft.

WINGS. — Braced high - wing monoplane. Streamline-section Vee bracing struts each side. All-metal structure, covered with fabric and with a butyrate fire-resistant finish. Ailerons linked with rudder, so that aircraft can be controlled in flight by using only the control wheel in the cockpit. Gross wing area 153 sq ft (14·22 m²).

FUSELAGE.—Steel-tube structure, covered with fabric and with butyrate finish.

TAIL UNIT.—Steel-tube structure, fabric covered and with butyrate finish. Rudder linked to ailerons.

LANDING GEAR.—Non-retractable tailwheel type. Steerable tailwheel. Fairings aft of main wheels.

POWER PLANT.—One 145 hp Continental O-300 six-cylinder horizontally-opposed air-cooled engine, driving a McCauley DM-74/60 airscrew. Fuel capacity 42 U.S. gallons (159 litres). Oil capacity 2 U.S. gallons (7·5 litres).

ACCOMMODATION.—Four seats in pairs in enclosed cabin, 3 ft 8 in. (1·12 m) wide. Three doors. Space for 100 lb (45 kg) baggage.

Max. T.O. weight   2,100 lb (953 kg)

Maule Bee Dee M-4 (145 hp Continental O-300 engine) *(Howard Levy)*

DIMENSIONS.—

Span	29 ft 8 in. (9·04 m)
Length	22 ft 0 in. (6·71 m)
Height	6 ft 2 in. (1·88 m)

WEIGHTS.—

Weight empty	1,100 lb (500 kg)

PERFORMANCE.—

Cruising speed	150 mph (241 kmh)
Stalling speed, flaps down	45 mph (72 kmh)
Rate of climb at S/L	700 ft (213 m) min.
Service ceiling	12,000 ft (3,660 m)
T.O. run	900 ft (274 m)
Range	750 miles (1,205 km)

(1987)

The Martin 139W Bomber Monoplane (two 740 h.p. Wright "Cyclone" engines).

THE MARTIN MODEL 139W. (B-10 and B-12)

The Martin Model 139W is a twin-engined mid-wing monoplane landplane bomber, developed from the Martin experimental Model 123.

During 1934, forty-eight of these machines were delivered to the U.S. Army Air Corps. Fifteen were fitted with Wright "Cyclone" engines (YB-10) and thirty-three with Pratt & Whitney "Hornet" engines (YB-12).

Since 1934, numerous improvements have been made to the type, including the installation of a more powerful "Cyclone" engine, a Sperry automatic pilot, and the addition of wing-flaps, constant-speed airscrews, de-icers, and numerous structural and maintenance refinements.

During 1935 and 1936, 103 of these machines (B-10B) were delivered to the Army Air Corps.

On July 1, 1936, the type was released for export, and since that date orders have been received from six foreign governments, one country contracting a second time for twice the number of machines as called for in the first order.

On the latest export model, the 139W, complete de-icer equipment and automatic pilot have been installed. This model is equipped with special Martin main fuel tanks, providing additional fuel capacity for increased range carrying full load.

A 362 U.S. gallons (1,370 litres) droppable bomb-bay auxiliary fuel tank may also be carried with one 2,000-lb. bomb for extreme range.

TYPE.—Four or five-seat bomber landplane.

WINGS.—Full cantilever tapered mid-wing monoplane. Wing in three sections, a centre-section built into the fuselage and carrying the two engine nacelles in the leading edge, and two detachable outer sections. Wing structure of riveted aluminium-alloy with highly-stressed fittings of heat-treated steel, and aluminium-alloy stressed-skin covering. Balanced ailerons. Split flaps.

FUSELAGE.—Riveted aluminium-alloy monocoque construction. Sheer loads taken by smooth side skin, and top and bottom compression loads by corrugated sections of sheet-metal covering. Fuselage made in three separable units, nose section, centre-section built around centre-section wing, and tail section. Internal bomb bay closed by doors controlled by bomber, or in emergency by pilot.

LANDING GEAR.—Mechanically-retractable landing-gear, with retracting controls in pilot's cockpit. Oleo shock-absorber struts, brakes, Swivelling tail-wheel.

TAIL UNIT.—Full cantilever fin and fixed tail-plane are of riveted aluminium-alloy construction and have aluminium-alloy sheet-metal covering. Rudder and elevator fabric-covered, and fitted with trailing-edge trimming and balance-tabs, adjustable from the pilot's cockpit in flight.

POWER PLANT.—Two Wright "Cyclone" SGR-1820 G3 geared and supercharged radial air-cooled engines, developing 740 h.p. at 11,900 ft. (3,630 m.). Electric inertia-starters are also provided. Riveted aluminium-alloy fuel and oil tanks are in the wings. Several types of American and European engines may be installed as alternatives to the above standard engines.

ACCOMMODATION.—Cockpit in nose of fuselage, equipped with bomb-sights, bomb-release controls, and flexible gun. This cockpit is covered with a transparent cupola. Pilot's cockpit just forward of the leading-edge of wings, with a compartment inside the fuselage aft of the pilot's cockpit for wireless operator. A rear cockpit, behind the wings, has auxiliary flight controls and mounting for flexible top gun and floor-gun.

DIMENSIONS.—Span 70 ft. 10¼ in. (21.6 m.), Length 44 ft. 8⅜ in. (13.63 m.), Height 11 ft. 5 in. (3.48 m.), Wing area 682 sq. ft. (63.4 sq. m.).

WEIGHTS.—Weight empty 9,727 lbs. (4,412 kg.), Crew (four) 800 lbs. (363 kg.), Fuel (main tanks 226 U.S. gallons) 1,356 lbs. (615 kg.), Oil (19 U.S. gallons) 142 lbs. (64 kg.), Armament and equipment 2,970 lbs. (1,347 kg.). Normal loaded weight 14,995 lbs. (6,802 kg.), Overload gross wieght 16,455 lbs. (7,464 kg.), Maximum overload gross weight 18,827 lbs. (8,540 kg.).

PERFORMANCE (Wright "Cyclone" GR-1820-G3 engines developing 760 h.p. at sea level and 840 h.p. at 8,700 ft. = 3,871 m.).—Speed at sea level, 198 m.p.h. (318 km.h.), Speed at 8,700 ft. (2,651.8 m.) 230 m.p.h. (370 km.h.), Climb to 1,000 ft. (3,050 m.) 6.6 mins., Service ceiling 24,300 ft. (7,407 m.), Absolute ceiling on one engine 10,000 ft. (3,050 m.). Range at 160 m.p.h. at 13,000 ft. (257 km.h.) 1,950 miles (3,140 km.).

(NOTE.—*To obtain longer range at altitude, the Wright G-2 engine is recommended. This engine also gives a better sea level high speed.*)

(1937)

The Martin B-57B Tactical Bomber and Night Intruder (two Wright J65 turbojet engines).

THE MARTIN MODEL 272.
U.S.A.F. designation: B-57.

The Martin company has built under licence versions of the English Electric Canberra for the U.S.A.F. The basic American version is powered by two Wright J65 turbojet engines.

In order to convert the Canberra to fulfil its U.S.A.F. missions, as well as to adapt it to American production methods, a considerable amount of re-design was undertaken by the Martin Company.

A Martin-developed feature introduced into the B-57 is a pre-loaded revolving bomb-bay door which rotates through 180 degrees just before the bombs are released, leaving no excrescences to reduce speed on the bombing run.

The following versions of the B-57 have been built :—

B-57A. Two Wright J65-W-1 turbojet engines (7,220 lb.=3,280 kg. s.t. each). Pre-production model externally similar to the British Canberra but incorporating many internal changes. Crew of two—pilot and navigator/radar operator/bombardier. First B-57A flew for the first time on July 20, 1953.

RB-57A. Reconnaissance version of B-57A. First RB-57A delivered to U.S.A.F. in March, 1954.

B-57B. Two Wright J65-W-5 engines (7,220 lb.=3,275 kg. s.t. each). Night intruder or tactical bomber. Crew of two, pilot and radar operator/navigator/bombardier, in tandem beneath continuous jettisonable canopy. Ejector-type seats. Improved bullet-proof windscreen with anti-icing and de-misting. Hydraulically-operated speed brakes added to rear fuselage. These move in co-ordination with "finger" type brakes on each wing. Armament consists of eight wing-mounted .50 in. machine-guns or four 20 mm. cannon. Four Napalm tanks in addition to eight 5-in. HVAR rockets may be carried on pylons under wings. Other stores may be carried on revolving bomb-bay door. Gross weight over 50,000 lb. (22,700 kg.). Maximum speed over 600 m.p.h. (960 km.h.), ceiling over 45,000 ft. (13,725 m.), and range more than 2,000 miles (3,220 km.). First B-57B flew for the first time on June 28, 1954.

B-57C. Basically similar to B-57B, but with dual controls so that it can perform the additional rôle of conversion training. For instrument training, for giving piston-engine pilots experience in jet operation or for giving single-engine fighter pilots multi-jet experience. The first B-57C flew on December 30, 1954.

B-57D. High-altitude version, with two 10,000 lb. (4,536 kg.) s.t. Pratt & Whitney J57 turbojet engines and greatly-increased span. Originally believed to be a flying test-bed, this version is now reported to be in service with the U.S.A.F. in Japan as the RB-57D highly-classified reconnaissance aircraft.

B-57E. Basically similar to B-57B but for dual service as tactical bomber and high-speed target tug. Capable of towing a wide variety of targets, four of which are normally carried in external containers on each flight. Conversion to bomber involves simply removal of the cockpit towing controls, external target containers and the internal cable reels and fittings which are normally carried on the rotary bomb-door. Intended to provide both air-to-air and ground-to-air firing practice at high altitudes.

DIMENSIONS.—
Span 64 ft. (19.5 m.).
Length 65 ft. 6 in. (19.9 m.).
Height 16 ft. (4.88 m.).

(1958–59)

GENERAL DYNAMICS/MARTIN RB-57F

Under USAF contract, the Fort Worth division of General Dynamics has converted an initial series of 12 Martin B-57 (licence-built Canberra) tactical bombers into reconnaissance aircraft with the designation RB-57F. The modifications give the aircraft an increased operating ceiling, greater range, increased payload and improved handling characteristics.

The conversion involves almost complete redesign and rebuilding, and General Dynamics are making use of advanced materials, including honeycomb sandwich panels, for the new components. The original wing is replaced by a new three-spar wing of almost double the span and with a marked anhedral. The ailerons are inset at about mid-span and are supplemented by spoilers. New and larger vertical tail surfaces

are fitted. All control surfaces have tightly-sealed gaps to reduce drag. There are no flaps.

The standard 7,220 lb (3,275 kg) st Wright J65 turbojets are replaced by two 18,000 lb (8,165 kg) st Pratt & Whitney TF33-P-11 turbofan engines, and there are also two 3,300 lb (1,500 kg) st Pratt & Whitney J60-P-9 auxiliary turbojets in underwing pods. The fuselage fuel tank has been deleted to make way for equipment and all fuel is now carried in the wings outboard of the engines.

There are four underwing hard points for external stores, of which two are used normally to carry the auxiliary turbojets. When these turbojets are not required, all four hard points are available for stores or equipment pods.

A great deal of special equipment is carried, including radar in the fuselage nose and unspecified electronics in the streamwise plastic

wingtips. The cockpit layout is unchanged, with ejection seats in tandem for the crew of two. The Lear MC-1 (modified) autopilot is of the type used in the Boeing C-135 transport aircraft.

Delivery of the first RB-57F was made to the USAF's 58th Weather Reconnaissance Squadron at Kirtland AFB, New Mexico, on June 18, 1964, only nine months after design work was started. The aircraft's duties include high-altitude sampling of air for radioactive particles.

DIMENSIONS, EXTERNAL:
Wing span	122 ft 5 in (37·32 m)
Length overall	69 ft 0 in (21·03 m)
Height overall	19 ft 0 in (5·79 m)

AREA:
Wings, gross	2,000 sq ft (185·8 m²)

(1970–71)

The Martin M20-1 Spotter as a land machine (400 h.p. Curtiss D12 engine). (1925)

During 1923 the Glenn Martin Company produced for the U.S. Naval Air Service, thirty MO-1 Observation Planes (see "All the World's Aircraft, 1923"), which type is being issued as the new Service equipment to the Observation Plane Squadrons of the Navy. An experimental biplane version of this type, the M2O-1, was produced during the year.

THE MARTIN M2O-1.

A biplane spotter with the Curtiss D-12 engine, built as a seaplane, but can be fitted with an interchangeable land undercarriage.

Performance.

Max. speed	..	..	..	**110 m.p.h. (177 km.h.).**
Min. speed	..	..	..	**52 m.p.h. (83 km.h.).**
Climb.				
To 5,000 ft. (1,525 m.)	..	..	10 mins.
Ceiling	..	..	14,000 ft. (4,600 m.).
				(1925)

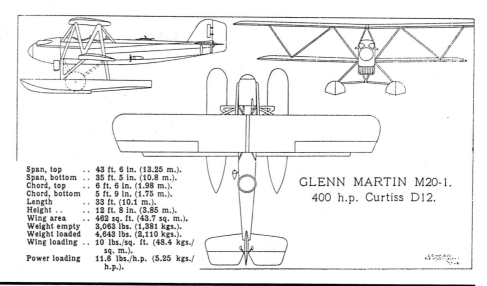

Span, top	43 ft. 6 in. (13.25 m.).
Span, bottom	35 ft. 5 in. (10.8 m.).
Chord, top	6 ft. 6 in. (1.98 m.).
Chord, bottom	5 ft. 9 in. (1.75 m.).
Length	33 ft. (10.1 m.).
Height	12 ft. 8 in. (3.85 m.).
Wing area	462 sq. ft. (43.7 sq. m.).
Weight empty	3,063 lbs. (1,381 kgs.).
Weight loaded	4,643 lbs. (2,110 kgs.).
Wing loading	10 lbs./sq. ft. (48.4 kgs./ sq. m.).
Power loading	11.6 lbs./h.p. (5.25 kgs./ h.p.).

GLENN MARTIN M2O-1.
400 h.p. Curtiss D12.

The Martin 125 Two-seat "Diving Bomber" (575 h.p. Pratt & Whitney "Hornet" engine).

THE MARTIN MODEL 125.

Two squadrons of Martin 125 all-metal "diving bomber," known as Navy Models BM-1 and BM-2, are now operating in the U.S. Navy. This is the first type capable of carrying a 1,000-lb. bomb in a terminal velocity vertical dive and of recovering from the dive without dropping the bomb. A number of successful demonstrations have been conducted in which the diving speeds and accelerations during recovery exceeded those expected in the service use of these machines.

TYPE.—Two-seat "Diving Bomber" landplane. (U.S. Navy BM-1 and BM-2.)

WINGS.—Unequal-span, single-bay biplane. Top centre-section carried above fuselage on splayed-out "N"-type struts, with one "N"-type interplane strut of streamline aluminium-alloy tubing on each side of fuselage. Wing spars and drag struts of riveted aluminium-alloy, ribs of riveted bulb or channel-section aluminium-alloy, drag bracing of standard square steel tie-rods, the whole being covered with fabric. "Frise" type ailerons on all four planes.

FUSELAGE.—All-metal construction and in three sections. The engine-bearer section, of steel tubes, attached to the middle section at four points. The middle section is a girder structure of aluminium-alloy and special Martin riveted sections, covered with aluminium-alloy sheet. The rear section is a monocoque structure with stringers, bulkheads and covering of aluminium-alloy.

TAIL UNIT.—Normal monoplane type. Framework of riveted aluminium-alloy construction, with fin and tail-plane covered with sheet-metal and the rudder and elevators covered with fabric. Tail-plane adjustable through 6 degrees.

UNDERCARRIAGE.—Divided type. Each unit consists of an anti-recoil oleo shock-absorber strut anchored at its top end to the apex of a pyramid of steel tubes on the sides of the fuselage, with the bottom end hinged to the bottom fuselage longerons by axle and radius-rod. Bendix wheels and brakes.

POWER PLANT.—One 575 h.p. Pratt & Whitney "Hornet" direct-drive radial air-cooled engine, equipped with adjustable cowling for temperature control and a carburetter air-heater. A pressure fire-extinguisher, controlled from the pilot's cockpit, is piped to all vital parts of the power plant installation. Complete engine control units in each cockpit. Two main fuel tanks, of riveted aluminium-alloy, each containing 50 U.S. gallons. Auxiliary fuel tank containing 60 U.S. gallons may be carried instead of 1,000-lb. bomb.

ACCOMMODATION.—Pilot's cockpit under cut-out in trailing-edge of centre-section, with observer-gunner's cockpit immediately behind. Armament consists of one fixed gun firing forward through the airscrew and two flexible guns on a rotating mounting over the back cockpit. A bomb-rack for one 1,000-lb. bomb under fuselage. Rear cockpit has auxiliary controls and provision for wireless equipment.

DIMENSIONS.—Span 41 ft. (12.5 m.), Length 28 ft. 4¾ in. (8.6 m.), Height 11 ft. 6½ in. (3.5 m.), Wing area 417 sq. ft. (38.7 sq. m.).

WEIGHTS AND LOADINGS.—Weight empty 3,588 lbs. (1,627 kg.). Weight loaded 6,140 lbs. (2,785 kg.), Wing loading 14.7 lbs./sq. ft. (71.7 kg./sq. m.), Power loading 10.7 lbs./h.p. (4.8 kg./h.p.).

PERFORMANCE (with bomb load—guaranteed by manufacturers).—Maximum speed at 6,000 ft. (1,830 m.) 143 m.p.h. (230 km.h.), Landing speed 61 m.p.h. (98.2 km.h.), Service ceiling 15,100 ft. (4,602 m.), Cruising range (with auxiliary tank) 525 miles (845 km.).

(1936)

THE MARTIN MODEL 179 MARAUDER.
U.S. Army Air Forces designation : B-26.
U.S. Navy designation : JM-1 and JM-2.
British name : Marauder.

The projected design data for the Model 179 Medium Bomber were accepted by the U.S. Army on July 5, 1939 and the first Marauder flew on November 25, 1940. The flow of production Marauders began on February 25, 1941, and by the end of 1944, over 5,000 had been delivered. The Marauder first went into action in the Australian Theatre in April, 1942.

The following briefly outlines the stages of development of the Marauder.

B-26. Two 1,850 h.p. Pratt & Whitney R-2800-5 eighteen-cylinder radial air-cooled engines. Crew of five. Armament consisted of five 50 cal. machine-guns, two in the nose, two in a Martin dorsal turret and one in the extreme tail. Normal bomb load 2,000 lbs., maximum 5,800 lbs. in tandem bomb-bays.

B-26A (Marauder I). Two 2,000 h.p. Pratt & Whitney R-2800-39 engines. Same as B-26 except for minor changes.

B-26B (Marauder IA and II). Two 2,000 h.p. Pratt & Whitney R-2800-43 engines. Span increased from 65 ft. (19.8 m.) to 71 ft. (21.6 m.). Two 50 cal. guns in the tail position. From B-26B-10 (Marauder II) the area of the vertical tail surfaces was increased and armament was raised to include one fixed

The Martin B-26F Marauder Medium Bomber (two Pratt & Whitney R-2800-43 engines).

and one flexible gun in the nose, four "package" guns on the sides of the forward fuselage, two in the Martin dorsal turret, two flexible "waist" guns, one tunnel gun and two tail guns. Crew increased to seven. Maximum bomb load 4,000 lbs. Front bay could carry two 2,000 lb. bombs on special carriers. Use of rear bomb-bay later discontinued.

B-26C (Marauder II). Same as B-26B-10 but built at the Martin Omaha plant.

B-26D. Same as B-26C but fitted experimentally with exhaust-heated surface de-icing equipment. Only one.

B-26E. A special stripped model with the weight reduced by about 2,000 lbs. Upper turret moved forward to the roof of the navigator's compartment. One only.

B-26F and G (Marauder III). Similar to the B-26C except that the incidence of the wing was increased by $3\frac{1}{2}$ degrees. Rear bomb-bay eliminated and no provision for torpedo. Eleven 50 cal. guns, one in the nose, four "package" guns, two in the Martin turret, two waist guns and two tail guns.

TB-26. Certain examples of the earlier versions of the Marauder were stripped of armament and adapted for training and general utility duties, particularly for high-speed target-towing. These were originally given the designation AT-23 but they are now known as TB-26.

JM-1 and JM-2. Stripped versions of the B-26C and B-26G respectively, and used by the U.S. Navy for target-towing and other general utility duties. The JM-1P was equipped for photographic reconnaissance.

TYPE.—Twin-engined Medium Bomber.

WINGS.—Cantilever shoulder-wing monoplane. Wings have equal taper, rounded tips and a flat upper surface. Wings in four sections consisting of two inner sections forming the centre-section and two outer sections with detachable tips. All-metal two-spar corrugated-box-type structure, the whole covered with flush-riveted stressed skin. Ailerons, on outer wing sections, have metal frames and fabric covering. Slotted flaps on inner sections are divided by extensions of engine nacelles.

FUSELAGE.—Circular section all-metal monocoque structure. Built in three sections and bolted together.

TAIL UNIT.—Cantilever monoplane type. Dihedral tailplane. Metal framework with metal-covered fixed surfaces and fabric-covered rudder and elevators. Trimming-tabs in control surfaces.

LANDING GEAR.—Tricycle type. All wheels fully retractable. Main wheels retract into engine nacelles by parallel linkage system. Each main oleo leg hinged about one-third from the top by a "W"

strut and by a pair of drag struts attached near lower end and extending forward and upward at about 60 degrees. Hydraulic retracting jacks operating on "W" strut swing, this strut and drag struts through an arc towards rear end of the nacelle. The shock strut moves aft and upward into the horizontal, bringing the wheel slightly forward and up into the well. Gear held in raised position by lock which hooks onto wheel axle. When lowered the wheel moves aft and down and is held in landing position by down-lock hooking onto a "steeple" extension of shock strut. Gear is balanced so that should hydraulic system fail it will drop by gravity, airstream locking it in landing position. Hinged doors closed when gear fully raised by strut linkage attached to oleo strut. Nose wheel retracts aft into fuselage well. Dual brakes on main wheels.

POWER PLANT.—Two Pratt & Whitney R-2800-43 eighteen-cylinder double-row radial air-cooled engines on welded steel-tube mountings. Four-bladed hollow-steel Curtiss Electric constant-speed full-feathering airscrews. Airscrew diameter: 13 ft. 6 in. (4.12 m.). Fuel tanks in wings. Main tanks, each made up of three Mareng self-sealing cells, inboard of engine nacelles. Two auxiliary tanks, each of two interconnected cells, outboard on nacelles. Long-range ferry tanks may be carried in the bomb-bay.

ACCOMMODATION.—Normal crew of seven. Bombardier in nose; pilot and co-pilot side-by-side; navigator-radio-operator behind pilot, waist-gunner; upper turret gunner or tail gunner. Armour plate protects all crew positions, as well as vital aircraft parts. Life-raft stowed in roof of fuselage aft of pilot's compartment. Main entrance to fuselage in nose wheel well. Pilot's escape hatches in roof of canopy. For rest of crew astro-hatch is used.

ARMAMENT.—Eleven 50 cal. machine-guns, one flexible in nose; four "package" guns in pairs, one pair on each side of the fuselage forward of the wings; two in Martin electrically-operated turret on top of fuselage aft of wings; two in waist positions, one on each side of the fuselage aft of the turret; and two in a Bell tail turret. Tail-gun position has remote-feed ammunition tracks from mid fuselage. Internal bomb-bay with maximum accommodation for two 2,000 lbs. or four 1,000 lb. bombs, latter carried in pairs one above each other on each side of central catwalk. Hydraulically-operated bomb-doors.

DIMENSIONS.—Span 71 ft. (21.65 m.), Length 56 ft. 6 in. (17.23 m.), Height 21 ft. 2 in. (6.45 m.), Wing area 658 sq. ft. (61.1 m.).

WEIGHTS.—Weight empty 25,300 lbs. (11,490 kg.), Maximun loaded weight (with 4,000-lb. bomb load) 38,200 lbs. (17,340 kg.).

PERFORMANCE.—Maximum speed 287 m.p.h. (459.2 km.h.) at 5,000 ft. (1,525 m.), Landing speed 104 m.p.h. (166.4 km.h.), Service ceiling 19,800 ft. (6,040 m.). (1945–46)

THE MARTIN 4-0-4.
U.S. Coast Guard designation: RM-1.

The 4-0-4 is the latest in the Series of Martin commercial transports and is a development of the 2-0-2. It is 39 in. (1.0 m.) longer than the 2-0-2 and is pressurised. C.A.A. type certification of the 4-0-4 was granted on October 5, 1951.

One hundred and three 4-0-4's are being produced, sixty for Eastern Air Lines, forty-one for Trans-World Airlines and two for the U.S. Coast Guard. Deliveries began in the Autumn of 1951.

TYPE.—Twin-engined Airliner.

WINGS.—All-metal cantilever low-wing monoplane. GLM-W 16 laminar-flow aerofoil section. Martin ailerons with total area of 41.8 sq. ft. (3.88 m.²). Double-slotted trailing-edge flaps between ailerons and fuselage, with total area of 150 sq. ft. (13.94 m.²). Hydraulic operation. Gross wing area 864 sq. ft. (79.89 m.²).

FUSELAGE.—All-metal monocoque structure of circular cross-section.

TAIL UNIT.—Cantilever monoplane type of all-metal construction. Dihedral tailplane with variable incidence. Tailplane incidence interconnected with flaps. Statically-balanced rudder and elevators. Elevators interchangeable left and right. Total vertical area 128 sq. ft. (11.89 m.²). Total horizontal area 210 sq. ft. (19.51 m.²). Tailplane span 36 ft. 6 in. (11.13 m.).

LANDING GEAR.—Retractable tricycle type, dual wheels fitted to main legs. Main units each consist of single shock-absorber leg and front link members which retract forward into engine nacelles and are fully enclosed. Steerable nose-wheel, carried in fork on shock-absorber leg, retracts forward into fuselage. Hydraulic operation. Track (centre-line of legs) 25 ft. 0 in. (7.62 m.).

POWER PLANT.—Two Pratt & Whitney R-2800 CB16 Double-Wasp eighteen-cylinder two-row radial air-cooled engines in tapered cowlings and each developing a normal output of 1,800 h.p., and with 2,400 h.p. available for take-off. Hamilton Standard 2H17K3-48R three-blade reversable airscrews, 13 ft. 2 in. (4.01 m.) diameter. Electric anti-icing. Eight Mareng synthetic rubber fuel cells, four in each wing outboard of engine nacelles with under wing refuelling valves and detachable panels underneath wing for removal of cells.

ACCOMMODATION. — Pressurised accommodation for crew of three or four and 40 passengers. Freight and baggage capacity 316 cub. ft. (8.94 m.³). Hydraulically-operated self-contained rear loading ramp. 93 cub. ft. (2.63 m.³) baggage space available under passenger seats. Toilet compartment on starboard at rear, and coat compartment at left forward end of fuselage.

EQUIPMENT.—Hydraulic equipment and other accessory systems carried in space below floor of cabin, with three access panels in fuselage. Thermal anti-icing by four combustion heaters, two in each engine nacelle.

DIMENSIONS.—
Span 93 ft. 3 in. (28.44 m.).
Length 74 ft. 7 in. (22.75 m.).
Height 28 ft. 5 in. (8.61 m.).

WEIGHTS AND LOADINGS.—
Weight empty (equipped) 29,126 lb. (13,223 kg.).
Max. payload 10,205 lb. (4,633 kg.).
Weight loaded 43,650 lb. (19,817 kg.).
Max. landing weight 43,000 lb. (19,522 kg.).
Wing loading 50.5 lb./sq. ft. (246.4 kg./m.²).
Power loading 9.1 lb./h.p. (4.12 kg./h.p.).

PERFORMANCE.—
Max. speed 312 m.p.h. (500 km.h.) at 14,500 ft. (4,420 m.).
Cruising speed (1,200 h.p. per engine) 280 m.p.h. (448 km.h.) at 18,000 ft. (5,490 m.).
Stalling speed at sea level 79 m.p.h. (126.4 km.h.).
Initial rate of climb 1,905 ft./min. (580 m./min.).
Rate of climb at S/L. one engine at T.O. power and max. T.O. weight 460 ft./min. (140 m./min.).

The Martin 4-0-4 Airliner (two 2,400 h.p. Pratt & Whitney R-2800-CB16 engines).

Service ceiling 29,000 ft. (8,845 m.).
Max. *en route* altitude on one engine at 40,000 lb. (18,160 kg.) 10,400 ft. (3,170 m.).
Normal range 1,080 miles (1.730 km.).
Max. range 2,600 miles (4.160 km.).
Take-off distance (max. T.O. weight) to 50 ft. (15.25 m.) 1,980 ft. (604 m.).
C.A.R. take-off field length over 50 ft. (15.25 m.) obstacle max. T.O. weight, one engine out, flaps at 12½° 3,995 ft. (1,218 m.).

Landing distance from 50 ft. (15.25 m.) at max. landing weight and approach speed 10% above stalling speed 1,750 ft. (534 m.).   (1952–53)

THE MARTIN MODEL 237 MARLIN
U.S. Navy designation: P5M

The P5M was the first twin-engined flying-boat to be developed for the U.S. Navy for anti-submarine warfare after the war. Two versions exist. These are identified as follows:—

P5M-1. Two 3,250 h.p. Wright R-3350-36WA or 3,400 h.p. R-3350-32WA Turbo Compound engines. Low tailplane. First production Marlin flew for the first time on June 22, 1951, and the first P5M-1 was delivered to the U.S. Navy in December, 1951. A number of ASR versions of the P5M-1 were delivered to the U.S. Coast Guard in the Autumn of 1953 under the designation P5M-1G.

P5M-2. Two 3,400 h.p. Wright R-3350-32W or -32WA Turbo Compound engines. Development of P5M-1. Chief external difference is the "T" tail with the horizontal surfaces on top of the fin. Also has a lower bow chine line to reduce spray damage to the airscrews, and a rearrangement of much of the interior equipment for greater operational comfort and convenience. The first P5M-2 flew in August, 1953 and the first delivery to the U.S. Navy was made on June 23,

1954. Ten P5M-2's have been supplied to the French Navy under MDAP.

Martin-Baltimore has been engaged on a high-priority modernisation programme of both versions of the Marlin since 1958, with the work scheduled to continue until at least mid-1961.

The initial contract covered the addition of magnetic anomaly detection (MAD) equipment and improvements to the power plant systems, electrical and electronic systems of eighty P5M-1 Marlins. The total number of aircraft involved is reported to be 160.

Improvements currently being built into the P5M-2's include the installation of "Jezebel," a sono-buoy type of anti-submarine detection gear; "Julie," a localisation system to provide range data; and AIDS (aircraft integrated display system) which filters and computes data fed to it from other systems.

The general structure of the P5M-1 and P5M-2 is similar. The description below applies primarily to the P5M-2 except where indicated.

TYPE.—Twin-engined anti-submarine warfare flying-boat.

WINGS.—Gull-wing cantilever monoplane. Wing section NACA 23020 at root, NACA 4412 at tip. Dihedral 16° inner gull section, 3° outboard of nacelles. Gull-wing centre-section integral with hull, outer panels and tips removable. Goodrich de-icing boots on leading-edges. All-metal three-spar box structure. Conventional trailing-edge ailerons have metal D-spar leading-edges, metal ribs and fabric covering. All-metal spoiler ailerons, operating in conjunction with the conventional ailerons to counteract any rolling tendencies that might develop at take-off or alighting in rough water, are located inboard of main ailerons in line of rear spar. All-metal trailing-edge flaps between ailerons and nacelles and nacelles and hull. Total conventional aileron area (including tabs) aft of hinge line 60.8 sq. ft. (5.65 m.²). Total spoiler aileron area 46.49 sq. ft. (4.32 m.²). Total flap area 204.3 sq. ft. (18.97 m.²). Gross wing area (including 103.2 sq. ft. = 9.59 m.² of hull) 1,406.33 sq. ft. (130.65 m.²).

HULL.—All-metal semi-monocoque structure. Single faired V-type step and long planing afterbody. New lower bow chine line, as compared with P5M-1, results in reduction of spray height and permits take-off in heavier seas at greater A.U.W. Martin-developed hydraulically-operated hydro-flaps one on each side of after hull bottom serve as water rudders when operated individually or as water brake or sea anchor when both extended together. All-metal wing-tip stabilising floats.

TAIL UNIT (P5M-2).—Cantilever all-metal T-type structure. Areas : fin, including 33 sq. ft. (3.07 m².) of dorsal fin and 16.7 sq. ft. (1.55 m².) of contained rudder balance 169.31 sq. ft. (15.73 m².), rudder, aft of hinge line 47.65 sq. ft. (4.43 m².), tailplane including 32.02 sq. ft. (2.97 m².) of contained elevator balance 172.08 sq. ft. (15.99 m².), elevators, aft of hinge line 86.4 sq. ft. (803. m².)

POWER PLANT.—Two 3,250 h.p. Wright R-3350-36WA or 3,400 h.p. R-3350-32W or R-3350-32WA Turbo Compound engines. Hamilton Standard airscrews. Fuel tanks in centre wing section are of self-sealing Mareng type. Tanks in hull and two auxiliary tanks outboard of service tanks, one in each wing panel, are non-self-sealing. Provision for jettisoning fuel and for purging interior of auxiliary tanks and spaces surrounding hull tanks with carbon-dioxide for combat protection. Two droppable tanks can be installed, one in each nacelle bomb-bay. Total fuel capacity (P5M-1 and P5M-2) 3,975 U.S. gallons (15,047 litres).

ACCOMMODATION.—Crew of eight. Details of interior accommodation not available.

ARMAMENT.—Bomb-bays in engine nacelles for various types of offensive stores.

EQUIPMENT.—Magnetic airborne detector (AN/ASQ-8 MAD) unit in tubular plastic fairing extending aft from horizontal-vertical tail juncture. APS-80 radar scanner in nose radome. Hoisting points on centre-line of hull at wings for hoisting craft aboard seaplane tender at 60,000 lb. (27,240 kg.) gross weight.

DIMENSIONS (P5M-1).—
Span 118 ft. 2¼ in. (26.03 m.)
Length 94 ft. 11 in. (28.93 m.)
Height 38 ft. 8½ in. (11.80 m.)

DIMENSIONS (P5M-2).—
Span 118 ft. 2¼ in. (36.0 m.)
Length 100 ft. 7¼ in. (30.66 m.)
Height 32 ft. 8½ in. (9.97 m.)

The Martin P5M-2 Marlin anti-submarine flying-boat (two 3,400 h.p. Wright R-3350 engines)

WEIGHTS (P5M-1, A.S.W. mission).—
Weight empty 47,686 lb. (21,630 kg.)
Weight loaded 73,488 lb. (33,333 kg.)

WEIGHTS (P5M-2, A.S.W. mission).—
Weight empty 50,485 lb. (22,900 kg.)
Weight loaded 76,635 lb. (34,761 kg.)

PERFORMANCE.—
Max. speed at S/L. (P5M-1) 246 m.p.h. (396 km.h.)
Max. speed at S/L. (P5M-2) 251 m.p.h. (404 km.h.)

Max. diving speed 303 m.p.h. (487 km.h.)
Alighting speed (at 54,600 lb.=24,766 kg. A.U.W.) 86 m.p.h. (138 km.h.)
Range (A.S.W. mission, with 2,809 U.S. gallons=10,633 litres fuel) 2,050 miles (3,300 km.)
Ferry range (P5M-2 full fuel) 3,100 miles (4,990 km.)   (1960–61)

The Martin JRM-2 Mars Transport Flying-boat (four 3,000 h.p. Pratt & Whitney R-4360 engines).

THE MARTIN 170 MARS.
U.S. Navy designation : JRM-1 and 2.

The Mars was originally built as an experimental Patrol Bomber with the designation XPB2M-1. It was subsequently modified as a cargo transport with reinforced floors, larger hatches and loading equipment and re-designated XPB2M-1R.

The JRM is the production development of the XPB2M-1R. An order for 20 was placed as the result of the successful performance of the prototype with the U.S. Navy Air Transport Services. The first of the new boats was completed in the Summer of 1945. The U.S. Navy contract for the JRM was later reduced to five aircraft. The fourth JRM-1 was delivered to the U.S. Navy in the Summer of 1946, and a fifth aircraft, the JRM-2, with an improved power-plant installation was delivered to the U.S. Naval Air Transport Service in the Autumn of 1947.

TYPE.—Four-engined Military Transport Flying-Boat.

WINGS.—Cantilever high-wing monoplane. Aerofoil section NACA 23020 at root tapering to NACA 23012 at tip. All-metal structure consisting of centre-section, two outer wings and detachable tips. Constant taper in chord and thickness from roots. Metal ailerons with trim and balance-tabs in each. All-metal split trailing-edge flaps in four sections, two each side. Gross wing area 3,686 sq. ft. (342.3 m².)

HULL.—Aluminium-alloy semi-monocoque structure divided into two decks. Total volume 16,655 cub. ft. (471.4 m³.). Gross displacement 995,000 lb. (451,320 kg.). All-metal wing-tip floats carried on cantilever V-struts.

TAIL UNIT.—Cantilever monoplane type. Metal structure with dihedral tailplane. Balanced rudder and elevators with controllable trim-tab in each.

POWER PLANT.—JRM-1: Four Wright R-3350-8 Duplex-Cyclone eighteen-cylinder two-row radial air-cooled engines fitted with single-stage two-speed superchargers, each developing a normal output of 2,100 h.p. at 2,500 ft. (760 m.) ; 1,800 h.p. at 13,600 ft. (4,145 m.), and a max. output of 2,250 h.p. for take-off. JRM-2 : Four Pratt & Whitney R-4360 Wasp-Major twenty-eight-cylinder-four-row radial air-cooled engines fitted with one-stage, variable-speed super-chargers, each developing a normal output of 2,500 h.p. at 5,000 ft. (1,525 m.), 2,200 h.p. at 14,500 ft. (4,420 m.) and a max. output of 3,000 h.p. for take-off. In both engines mounted as power-eggs on welded steel-tube structures and are accessible in flight from wings. Curtiss-Electric four-blade airscrew 16 ft. 8 in. (5.08 m.) diameter. Total fuel capacity 13,220 U.S. gallons (50,040 litres) in six integral fuel tanks under floor of lower deck and two in removable wing-tanks.

ACCOMMODATION.—Hull divided into two decks. Normal crew of eleven. Flight deck forward accommodates duty crew of four, and aft of the pilot's compartment are four bunks for the use of off-duty officers on long flights. Four further bunks provided on the upper rear deck aft of the auxiliary power-plant compartment. Washroom facilities right aft in the tail section which is reached from upper deck. In nose ahead of flight deck is the stowage for anchors and the anchor windlass, and aft of this and ahead of main cargo hold is combined galley and entrance to the flight deck. Main deck provided with cargo tie-down fittings running fore-and-aft and athwartships, metal skid strips for sliding heavy cargo and tracks fore-and-aft and athwartships for handling engine dollies. A 5,000-lb. (2,266-kg.) capacity cargo hoist on overhead track runs out 20 ft. (6.1 m.) under both wings through main loading hatches, each of which is 8 ft. 3 in. wide × 7 ft. 10 in. high (2.52 m. × 3.24 m.) with doors divided vertically and opening outwards. Two further hatches 4 ft. 2 in. wide × 5 ft. 2 in. high (1.27 m. × 1.5 m.) located just forward of the second step with doors which slide up inside the hull. Aft of main cargo hold is a stairway leading to upper deck. Trap doors 4 ft. 2 in. long × 2 ft. wide (1.27 m. × 0.6 m.) in upper deck floor and immediately above the after loading doors for loading low density freight on to the upper deck. Built-in fittings permit rapid conversion into an ambulance to carry 84 stretcher cases and 25 medical attendants ; a passenger transport to carry fifty in chairs all on the main deck ; or a troop-carrier to accommodate 132 troops, all seated.

DIMENSIONS.—
Span 200 ft. 0 in. (60.96 m.).
Length 120 ft. 3 in. (36.65 m.).
Height 44 ft. 7 in. (13.6 m.).

WEIGHTS AND LOADINGS (JRM-1).—
Weight empty 76,805 lb. (34,870 kg.).
Weight loaded 145,000 lb. (65,770 kg.).
Wing loading 39.3 lb./sq. ft. (191.8 kg./m.²).
Power Loading 16.1 lb./h.p. (7.29 kg./h.p.).

WEIGHTS AND LOADINGS (JRM-2).—
Weight empty 80,311 lb. (36,460 kg.).
Weight loaded 165,000 lb. (74,842 kg.).
Wing loading 44.7 lb./sq. ft. (218.2 kg./m.²).
Power loading 13.75 lb./h.p. (6.22 kg./h.p.).

PERFORMANCE (JRM-1).—
Max. speed 222 m.p.h. (355 km.h.) at sea level.
Cruising speed (approximate) 153 m.p.h. (245 km.h.).

PERFORMANCE (JRM-2).—
Max. speed 238 m.p.h. (381 km.h.) at sea level.
Cruising speed 173 m.p.h. (256 km.h.).

(1950–51)

The Martin AM-I Mauler Attack Bomber (3,000 h.p. Pratt & Whitney R-4360 engine).

THE MARTIN 210 MAULER.
U.S. Navy designation : AM-1.

TYPE.—Single-seat Attack Bomber.

WINGS. — Cantilever low - wing monoplane. All-metal box-type structure consisting of centre-section and two outer sections which fold upwards for stowage. All-metal slotted ailerons with trim and balance-tabs in each. Intermeshing finger-type dive-brakes opening on top and bottom surfaces, between ailerons and fuselage, and perforated air-brake under fuselage, limit speed in dive to less than 350 m.p.h. (563 km.h.).

FUSELAGE.—All-metal flush-riveted semi-monocoque structure.

TAIL UNIT.—Cantilever monoplane type. Metal structure with metal covering over all surfaces. Balanced rudder and elevators with trim and balance-tabs in each.

LANDING GEAR.—Retractable two-wheel type. Each main wheel, carried in half-fork on shock-absorber leg, turns through 90 degrees as it retracts backwards so as to lie flat within wing. Tail wheel retracts into fuselage.

POWER PLANT.—One 3,000 h.p. Pratt & Whitney R-4360-4 Wasp-Major 28-cylinder four-row radial air-cooled engine enclosed in long chord cowling with controllable trailing-edge gills, and driving Curtiss-Electric four-blade airscrew, 14 ft. 8 in. (4.47 m.) diameter.

ACCOMMODATION.—Pilot's cockpit has flat bullet-proof forward and side panels and bubble canopy which slides backwards for access.

ARMAMENT.—Four 20 mm. cannon mounted two in each outer wing outside airscrew disc. Max. external load comprises three 2,200 lb. (1,000 kg.) torpedoes and twelve 5-in. (12.7 cm.) rockets, or variety of alternative loads including bombs, mines, search radar equipment, etc. Ejector under fuselage throws bomb clear of airscrew when released.

DIMENSIONS.—
Span 50 ft. 1 in. (15.24 m.).
Length 41 ft. 6 in. (12.6 m.).

WEIGHTS.—
Normal loaded weight (with one 2,000 lb. = 908 kg. bomb) 22,166 lb. (10,633 kg.).

Max. loaded weight over 29,000 lb. (13,166 kg.).

PERFORMANCE.—
Max. speed over 350 m.p.h. (563 km.h.).
Max. diving speed, over 500 m.p.h. (805 km.h.).
Max. range over 1,700 miles (2,736 km.).

THE MARTIN 219 MERCATOR.
U.S. Navy designation : P4M-1.

The Martin Mercator is a long-range naval patrol aircraft with a combined power plant of reciprocating engines and turbo-jets. It is a cantilever shoulder-wing monoplane with a single fin and rudder and a dihedral tailplane. Each engine nacelle contains one Pratt & Whitney R-4360-20 Wasp-Major twenty-eight-cylinder four-row radial air-cooled engine driving a tractor airscrew, and one Allison J-33 jet unit housed in the rear of the nacelle with the air intake below the cowling of the radial engine. The main wheels of the tricycle landing-gear are located outboard of the engine nacelles and retract outwardly into the wings. Armament is carried in nose, mid-upper and tail turrets.

A production order for nineteen P4M-1's was authorised under the 1947 Naval Appropriations Bill and final assembly of the first production aircraft began in April, 1949. This contract was completed in September, 1950.

The Martin P4M-I Mercator Long-range Naval Patrol Monoplane. (1951–52)

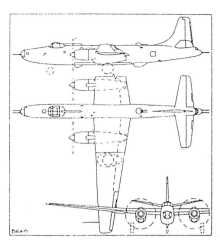

The Martin P4M-I Mercator.

DIMENSIONS.—
Span 114 ft. (34.7 m.).
Length 85 ft. (25.9 m.).
Height 35 ft. 0 in. (10.6 m.).
Wing area 1,311 sq. ft. (12.2 m.²).

WEIGHT LOADED.—
Over 80,000 lb. (36,320 kg.).

PERFORMANCE.—
Max. speed over 350 m.p.h. (560 km.h.)
at 16,400 ft. (5,000 m.).

THE MARTIN TWIN-ENGINED BOMBER.

The *Martin* twin-engined bomber constitutes one of the most important developments in bombing airplanes of original American design. In its official test, at Wilbur Wright Field, the all-round performance of this machine, considering the load carried, has easily excelled any other record from a similar bomber, either here or abroad. The machine shows excellent workmanship and such thoroughness of engineering that the organization is to be complimented upon the talent of their personnel. Mr. Martin is proud of the ability of his assistants, Mr. Lawrence D. Bell, factory manager ; Mr. Eric Springer, pilot ; and Mr. Donald W. Douglas, aeronautical engineer ; and he prophesies important futures in their respective specialties. Lawrence D. Bell, has been with Mr. Martin for seven years, and is noted for his production management. Eric Springer learned to fly at the Martin School five years ago. He is an unusually capable tester and flyer, having made an enviable record in five years of piloting for the Martin Company without an accident. Donald W. Douglas came from the Boston Tech., joining the Martin plant in Los Angeles four years ago, and in that short length of time has grown to be recognised as one of the foremost aeronautical engineers.

The all-round efficiency of the Martin bomber has been proven in its official performance trials. An official high speed at the ground of 118.5 m.p.h. was made on the first trials, with full bombing load on board. This speed has been bettered since, due to the better propeller efficiency arrived at by expensive experiments. With full bomb load, the climbing time to 10,000 feet was 15 minutes, and a service ceiling of between 16,000 and 17,000 feet was attained.

General Description.

As a military machine, the *Martin* "Twin" is built to fulfil the requirements of the four following classes:—(1) Night bomber, (2) day bomber, (3) long-distance photography, (4) gun machine.

(1) As a night bomber it is armed with three flexible Lewis machine guns, one mounted on the front turret, one on the rear, below and to the sides, under the concave lower surface of the body. It carries 1,500 lbs. of bombs and 1,000 rounds of ammunition. A radio-telephone set and the necessary instruments are carried on all four types. The fuel capacity in all four types is sufficient for four and a half hours' full power at the ground and six hours' full power at 15,000 feet. This gives the machine gasoline for the climb to 15,000 feet, and enough more for about six hundred miles.

(2) As a day bomber two more Lewis guns are carried, one more on each turret. The bomb capacity is cut to 1,000 lbs. to give the higher ceiling necessary for day work.

(3) When equipped as a photography machine, the same number of guns as in the case of the day bomber are carried ; but in place of the bombs two cameras are mounted in the rear

Side View of the Glenn L. Martin Bomber (two 400 h.p. Liberty engines).

gunner's cockpit. One camera is a short focal length semi-automatic, and the other is a long focal length hand-operated type.

(4) The gun machine is equipped for the purpose of breaking up enemy formations. In addition to the five machine guns and their ammunition as carried on the photographic machine, a semi-flexible 37 mm. cannon is mounted in the front gun cockpit, firing forward, and with a fairly wide range in elevation and azimuth. This cannon fires either shell or shot, and is a formidable weapon.

The *Martin* "Twin" is easily adaptable to the commercial uses that are now practical. They are :—(1) Mail and express carrying, (2) transportation of passengers, (3) aerial map and survey work.

(1) As a mail or express machine a ton may be carried with comfort, not only because of the ability of the machine to efficiently handle this load, but because generous bulk stowage room is available.

(2) Twelve passengers, in addition to the pilot and mechanic, can be carried for non-stop runs up to six hundred miles.

(3) The photographic machine, as developed for war purposes, is at once adaptable to the aerial mapping of what will become the main flying routes throughout the country. The accuracy that is being obtained in aerial photography should be of vast value in survey and topographical map work. The *Martin* airplane, with its great cruising radius and complete camera installation, presents itself as the logical machine in this field.

General Dimensions and Data.

1,—Power Plant,
Two 12-cyl. Liberty engines.

2.—Wing and Control Surface Areas.

Main planes, total	..	..	..	1,070 sq. ft.
Upper planes, including ailerons	..	550 sq. ft.
Lower planes, including ailerons	..	520 sq. ft.
Ailerons, each	..	..	..	32.5 sq. ft.
No. of ailerons	..	..	..	4
Vertical fins, each	..	..	..	8.8 sq. ft.
No. of fins	..	..	..	2
Stabilizer	..	..	..	62.25 sq. ft.
Elevator	..	..	..	43.20 sq. ft.
Rudders, each	..	..	..	16.50 sq. ft.
No. of rudders	..	..	..	2

3.—Overall Dimensions,

Span, upper and lower	..	..	..	71 ft. 5 in.
Chord, upper and lower	..	..	7 ft. 10 in.
Gap	..	..	..	8 ft. 6 in.
Length overall	..	..	..	46 ft.
Height overall	..	..	..	14 ft. 7 in.
Incidence of wings with propeller axis	.	2 degrees.
Dihedral	..	..	..	None.
Sweep back	..	..	..	None.
Decalage, wings	..	..	..	None.
Stabilizer, setting with wing chord		÷ 1 degree.
adjustable between	..		− 5 degrees.
normal setting	..		− 2 degrees.

(1919)

MARTIN MBT "TORPEDO PLANE".

Specification.

Type of machine	Twin Tractor Biplane.
Name or type No. of machine ..	Martin "Torpedo."
Purpose for which intended ..	Torpedo Carrying.
Armament	1—1,650 lbs. torpedo and 4 M.G. (two forward and two aft).
Crew	4 men.
Span	71 ft. 5 in. (U & L).
Overall length	46 ft. 4 in.
Maximum height	14 ft.
Total wing area	1,070 sq. ft.
Engine type and h.p.	2—400 h.p. Liberty "Twelves."
Weight empty	6,533 lbs.
Weight loaded	11,487 lbs.
Performance.	
High speed	107 m.p.h.
Low speed	60 m.p.h.
Climb.	
To 5,100 feet	10 mins.
Range (economical)	480 miles.

(1920)

The Undercarriage of the Glenn L. Martin Torpedo Carrier, with Torpedo in position.

three-quarter front views of the new Martin bomber M.B.2. (2—420 h.p. Liberty engines.)

THE M.B.2 TYPE BOMBER.

This is a slightly modified edition of the Martin Bomber described in the 1920 volume of "All the World's Aircraft." The modification as to engine mounting, struts and under-carriage, mentioned in connection with the Commercial type, have been embodied therein.

The main dimensions are slightly altered from those of the original type, and are mainly the same as those of the "Commercial" machine.

It is stated to have been a machine of this type which dropped the bombs which sank the ex-German Battleship "Ostfriesland" in the recent bombing trials.

The Martin Bomber M.B.2 is designed for day and night bombardment. The bombs are carried on racks in a compartment in the fuselage, or, in the case of the larger type bombs on special racks or chocks directly under the fuselage.

One of these bombers, equipped with superchargers, recently reached an altitude of 26,500 feet, carrying pilot and three observers. Had it not been for the extreme cold and lack of fuel, a still greater altitude could have been attained.

Following 20 Martin-built M.B.2s, LWF was contracted to build 35, Aeromarine 25 and Curtiss 50, all designated NBS-1s (Night Bombers Short Range).

Specification of the Glenn L. Martin Bomber.

Type of machine	Twin Tractor Biplane.
Name or type No. of machine	Martin Bomber M.B.2.
Purpose for which intended ..	Day and Night Bombing.
Armament	1,800 to 3,000 lbs. bombs, and 5 machine-guns (two forward and three aft).
Crew	4 men.
Span	74 ft. 2 in.
Overall length ..	43 ft. 7⅜ in.
Maximum height ..	15 ft. 6⅜ in.
Total wing area ..	1,121 sq. ft.
Engine type and h.p. ..	2—420 h.p. Liberty "Twelves."
Weight empty	7,000 lbs.
Weight loaded	12,075 lbs.
Performance.	
High speed	107 m.p.h.
Low speed	60 m.p.h.
Climb.	
To 5,000 feet	10 mins.
Range, economical	500 miles. (1922)

THE MARTIN MODEL 125.

Two squadrons of Martin 125 all-metal "diving bomber," known as Navy Models BM-1 and BM-2, are now operating in the U.S. Navy. This is the first type capable of carrying a 1,000-lb. bomb in a terminal velocity vertical dive and of recovering from the dive without dropping the bomb. A number of successful demonstrations have been conducted in which the diving speeds and accelerations during recovery exceeded those expected in the service use of these machines.

TYPE.—Two-seat "Diving Bomber" landplane. (U.S. Navy BM-1 and BM-2.)

PERFORMANCE (with bomb load—guaranteed by manufacturers).—
Maximum speed at 6,000 ft. (1,830 m.) 143 m.p.h. (230 km.h.), Landing speed 61 m.p.h. (98.2 km.h.), Service ceiling 15,100 ft. (4,602 m.), Cruising range (with auxiliary tank) 525 miles (845 km.).

(1934)

THE MARTIN MODEL 120.

TYPE.—Long-range patrol bomber (U.S. Navy P3M-1).

WINGS.—Externally-braced high-wing monoplane. Göttingen 398 wing-section. Wing-bracing structure carries both outboard floats and the two engine nacelles. The wing is in three sections, the centre-section and two outer sections. Wing structure consists of two riveted truss-type spars of aluminium alloy, aluminium-alloy bulb or channel section ribs, a dual system of drag-bracing and fabric covering. "Frise" type ailerons.

HULL.—All-metal hull, with domed top, Vee bottom and two steps. The vertical fin, which carries the tail-unit, is built integral with the hull. Watertight bulkheads fitted with watertight doors between the pilot's cockpit, the wireless compartment, the fuel tank compartment, the rear gunner's compartment and the tail compartment. Removable splash-tight hatches are provided in the hull, over the fuel tanks, to facilitate inspection and removal. Two stabilising floats of riveted aluminium-alloy construction carried by the wing-bracing system, which is so arranged that the strength of the structure is not impaired by the removal of one or both outboard floats.

TAIL UNIT.—Monoplane type, with twin fins and rudders, carried on top of fin, built integral with the hull. Framework of aluminium-alloy construction, with fabric covering. All moving parts have external greasers. Tail-plane adjustable through 6 degrees.

POWER PLANT.—Two 425-h.p. Pratt & Whitney "Wasp" geared radial air-cooled engines, driving tractor airscrews. Main fuel tanks in the hull. Electric inertia starters.

ACCOMMODATION.—The crew, consisting of pilot, assistant pilot, navigator, wireless operator and gunner-mechanic, is comfortably housed in the various appropriate hull compartments.

DIMENSIONS.—Span 100 ft. (30.5 m.), Length 61 ft. 9 in. (18.8 m.), Height 16 ft. 8¼ in. (5 m.), Wing area 1,115 sq. ft. (103.5 sq. m.).

WEIGHTS AND LOADINGS.—Weight empty 9,181.5 lbs. (4,168 kg.), Weight loaded 15,265 lbs. (6,930 kg.), Wing loading 13.69 lbs./sq. ft. (66.8 kg./sq. m.), Power loading 17.96 lbs./h.p. (8.15 kg./h.p.).

PERFORMANCE (with bomb load—guaranteed by manufacturers).—
Maximum speed 113 m.p.h. (180.8 km.h.), Climb in 10 mins. 4,300 ft. (1,311.5 m.), Range at cruising speed (bomber) 450 miles (720 km.), Range at cruising speed (patrol) 1,000 miles (1,600 km.).

(1931)

The Martin 120 (P3M-1) Long-range Patrol Flying-boat (two 425 h.p. Pratt & Whitney "Wasp" engines).

THE MARTIN MODEL 120.

This model has been modified, since the release of the information published last year, by the substitution of two 540 h.p. Pratt & Whitney "Hornet" direct-drive engines for the two 425 h.p. Pratt & Whitney "Wasp" geared engines and by providing an enclosure over the pilot's cockpit.

DIMENSIONS.—Span 100 ft. (30.5 m.), Length 61 ft. 9 in. (18.8 m.), Height 16 ft. 8¼ in. (5 m.), Wing area 1,115 sq. ft. (103.5 sq. m.).

WEIGHTS AND LOADINGS.—Weight empty 9,840 lbs. (4,445 kg.), Weight loaded 15,600 lbs. (7,706 kg.), Wing loading 13.99 lbs./sq. ft. (68.3 kg./sq. m.), Power loading 14.4 lbs./h.p. (6.5 kg./h.p.).

PERFORMANCE (with load—guaranteed by manufacturers).—Maximum speed 115 m.p.h. (185.1 km.h.), Alighting speed 60 m.p.h. (96.5 km.h.), Climb in 10 mins. 4,700 ft. (1,433 m.), Service ceiling 12,050 ft. (3,673 m.).

(1932)

THE MARTIN MODEL 122.

TYPE.—Twin-engined patrol or bomber flying-boat (U.S. Navy PM-2).

WINGS.—Unequal-span single-bay biplane. N-22 wing-section. Top wing in three sections, consisting of centre-section and two outer A removable splash-proof and rainproof hatch provided over the fuel tank compartment to permit inspection and removal of fuel tanks. Wing-tip floats of riveted aluminium-alloy, mounted under interplane struts. These floats are interchangeable.

TAIL UNIT.—Monoplane type, with fins and rudders, carried on central fin which is built integral with the hull. All tail surface frames are of riveted aluminium-alloy, with fabric covering. Tail-plane is in one unit with a continuous torque member and is adjustable through 6 degrees. Balanced elevator and rudders.

POWER PLANT.—Two 550 h.p. Wright "Cyclone" geared air-cooled radial engines, driving tractor airscrews. Fuel tanks, of a total capacity of 750 U.S. gallons, carried in the hull. Oil tanks mounted in engine nacelles. Both engines fitted with electric inertia-starters and may be started from the pilot's cockpit. Engines fitted with Townend type ring cowling and adjustable temperature-control shutters. Adjustable-pitch metal airscrews are standard equipment.

ACCOMMODATION.—Crew of five carried. Bow cockpit for gunner and bomber-navigator, side-by-side cockpit for pilot and assistant-pilot in front of wings. Aft of pilot's cockpit and inside the hull is the wireless compartment, with two folding bunks. Mechanic's compartment and gunner's cockpit aft of wings.

DIMENSIONS.—Span (top) 72 ft. 10 in. (22.2 m.), Span (bottom) 67 ft. 2 in. (20.4 m.), Length 49 ft. (14.9 m.), Height 16 ft. 9 in. (5.1 m.), Wing area 1,189 sq. ft. (110.4 sq. m.).

WEIGHTS AND LOADINGS (Bomber).—Weight empty 9,101 lbs. (4,132 kg.), Weight loaded 16,822 lbs. (7,637 kg.), Wing loading 14.15 lbs./sq. ft. (69 kg./sq. m.), Power loading 14.6 lbs./h.p. (6.6 kg./h.p.).

PERFORMANCE (guaranteed by manufacturers).—Speed 123 m.p.h. (196.8 km.h.), Climb in 10 mins. 3,270 ft. (9,973.5 m.), Service ceiling 7,190 ft. (2,193 m.), Cruising range (bomber) 937 miles (1,500 km.), Cruising range (patrol) 1,450 miles (2,320 km.). (1931)

The Martin 122 (PM-2) Patrol or Bombing Flying-boat (two 550 h.p. Wright "Cyclone" engines).

The Glenn Martin T3M-1, with side-by-side seating (575 h.p. Wright T-3B engine).

THE GLENN MARTIN T3M-2.

The T3M-2 is a further development of the T3M-1. A contract for one hundred of this type was placed with the Company in March, 1927. This machine employs a welded chrome molybdenum steel-tube fuselage, wood wing structure and duralumin tail surfaces. The bombing compartment is retained in the forward part of the fuselage, as in the T3M-1, but the seating arrangement is tandem instead of side-by-side. The split undercarriage incorporates an oleo-pneumatic suspension. The engine fitted is a 730 h.p. Packard 3A-2500.

The Glenn-Martin T3M-1 as a Seaplane (575 h.p. Wright T-3B engine).

Specification.

Span	56 ft. 7 in.
Gap	8 ft. 6 in.
Chord	8 ft. 3 in.
Wing area	883 sq. ft.
Length	42 ft. 6½ in.
Height	15 ft. 10½ in.
Weight empty (seaplane)	6,397 lbs.
Useful load (bomber-torpedo)	3,704 lbs.
Weight loaded (seaplane)	10,101 lbs.
Wing loading (seaplane)	11.44 lbs./sq. ft.
Power loading (seaplane)	12.84 lbs./h.p.
Speed, max.	121 m.p.h.
Speed, stalling	57.5 m.p.h.
Rate of climb	6660 ft. per min.
Climb in 10 mins.	5,050 ft.
Service ceiling	10,000 ft.
Range, full speed (bomber seaplane)	366 miles.
Range, full speed (scout seaplane)	567 miles.
Range, cruising speed (bomber seaplane)	477 miles.
Range, cruising speed (scout seaplane)	755 miles.

(1927)

THE GLENN MARTIN T3M-1.

The Glenn Martin T3M-1 is a development of the SC-1 and SC-2, which were originally designed in conjunction with the Bureau of Aeronautics, U.S. Navy, as a bomber, torpedo-carrier or long-distance scouting plane, being readily convertible by the installation of suitable equipment. They are equipped with twin floats, interchangeable with wheel gear, for use on aircraft-carriers or at land bases.

The fuselage is constructed of mild steel tubing, welded throughout. The wings are of wood and fabric, employing box-type spars of mahogany ply-wood and spruce. The front cockpit is situated just in advance of the wings, and accommodates the pilot and bomber, seated side-by-side. Midway between the wings and the tail unit is a second cockpit, equipped with a rotatable gun-ring above the fuselage and a gun position below. The land undercarriage is of the split type and is sprung by rubber cord. The engine is a 575 h.p. Wright T-3B.

(1927)

Specification.

Span, top plane	52 ft. 4 in.
Span, lower plane	56 ft. 7 in.
Gap	8 ft. 6 in.
Chord	8 ft. 3 in.
Wing area	848 sq. ft.
Length	42 ft. 9 in.
Height	16 ft. ½ in.
Weight empty (seaplane)	6,330 lbs.
Weight loaded (seaplane)	9,750 lbs.
Speed, max.	104 m.p.h.
Speed, stalling	56 m.p.h.
Speed, cruising	68-78 m.p.h.
Service ceiling	6,270 ft.
Endurance (cruising)	13.2 hours or 975 miles.

Martin T3M-2, with tandem seating (730 h.p. Packard 3A-2500 engine).

THE MARTIN-NAVY T4M-1.

The Martin T4M-1, of which 102 are now in active service, is still the main product of the Company, and a further production order from the U.S. Navy is contemplated. The T4M-1 has proved to be very satisfactory in operation from aircraft-carriers as a landplane, as well as for seaplane service.

The Martin T4M-1 is the latest development of the Torpedo-Bombing-Scouting or "Three-Purpose" type of naval aircraft, and is now being produced in quantity for the U.S. Navy.

It can be rapidly converted from landplane to seaplane, or vice-versa, and is particularly suitable for aircraft-carrier use.

TYPE.—Three-seat Naval bombing, torpedo or scouting convertible landplane or seaplane.

WINGS.—Equal-span, unstaggered, single-bay biplane. Top and bottom centre-sections of equal span, braced to the fuselage by parallel struts running from the extremities of the centre-section spars to the top longerons of the fuselage. Outer wing-sections arranged to fold back on rear spar hinges. One pair of parallel struts to each outer section. Wing construction consists of two spars and ribs of aluminium alloy, covered with fabric. Ailerons fitted to all four planes.

FUSELAGE.—Aluminium alloy structure, of rectangular section.

TAIL UNIT.—Normal type. Duralumin framed, covered with fabric. Balanced rudder. Adjustable tail-plane.

UNDERCARRIAGE.—Interchangeable wheel undercarriage and twin floats. In two units, leaving space between for stowage and dropping of torpedo or bombs. Each unit of the land undercarriage consists of an oleo-pneumatic leg, the top of which is attached at the extremity of the bottom centre-section front spar and the bottom to a short horizontal axle. This axle is hinged to the fuselage at two points by four steel-tube struts, two from each end, in the form of an inverted Vee, when viewed from the front and in the form of an ordinary Vee when seen from the side. The twin long single-step floats, of duralumin construction, are attached to the same points on the wings and fuselage by steel-tube struts and one spreader-bar connects the nose of each float.

POWER UNIT.—One 525 h.p. Pratt & Whitney "Hornet" air-cooled radial engine.

ACCOMMODATION.—There are three cockpits, one in advance of the wing immediately behind the engine fireproof bulkhead, one under the centre-section, and one midway between the wings and tail. The front cockpit is occupied by the bomber, the centre cockpit by the pilot, and the rear cockpit by the gunner-observer.

DIMENSIONS.—Span 53 ft. (16.15 m.), Length (landplane) 35 ft. 2 in. (10.7 m.), Length (seaplane) 36 ft. 10 1/16 in. (11.22 m.), Height (landplane) 12 ft. 7 3/4 in. (3.8 m.), Height (seaplane) 15 ft. 10 1/2 in. (4.84 m.), Wing area 656 sq. ft. (61 sq. m.).

WEIGHTS AND LOADINGS (Torpedo-seaplane).—Weight empty 4,231 lbs. (1,923 kg.), Fuel and oil 684 lbs. (311 kg.), Crew 400 lbs. (182 kg.), Equipment 308 lbs. (1,040 kg.), Ordnance 2,099 lbs. (953 kg.), Total disposable load 3,471 lbs. (1,578 kg.), Weight loaded 7,702 lbs. (3,501 kg.), Wing loading 11.74 lbs./sq. ft. (57.5 kg./sq. m.), Power loading 14.81 lbs./h.p. (6.87 kg./h.p.), Weight loaded (scout-seaplane) 7,040 lbs. (3,200 kg.).

PERFORMANCE (Bombing-seaplane).—Maximum speed 116.5 m.p.h. (187 km.h.), Minimum speed 59 m.p.h. (95 km.h.), Climb in 10 mins. 4,790 ft. (1,459 m.), Service ceiling 9,260 ft. (2,830 m.), Range at cruising speed 665 miles (1,070 km.), Duration at cruising speed 8.88 hrs., Range at full speed 502 miles (808 km.), Duration at full speed 4.31 hrs.

The Glenn Martin T4M-1 Three-purpose Landplane (525 h.p. Pratt & Whitney "Hornet" engine).

The McDonnell F2H-3 Banshee Naval Fighter (two Westinghouse J34 turbojet engines).

THE McDONNELL BANSHEE.

U.S. Navy designation : F2H.

The original contract for the design and construction of the XF2H-1 was placed by the U.S. Navy in March, 1945. The first prototype flew on January 11, 1947, and the first production order for the F2H-1 was placed in May, 1947.

The Banshee finally went out of production in October, 1953, after a total of 800 of all versions had been delivered to the U.S. Navy and Marine Corps.

During 1954 the Royal Canadian Navy will be receiving sixty F2H-3 Banshee all-weather fighters, this order being fulfilled by the U.S. Navy.

F2H-1. Two Westinghouse J34-WE-22 (3,000 lb.=1,360 kg. s.t.) engines. First production model, the first example of which flew for the first time on August 10, 1949. Fifty-six built.

F2H-2. Two Westinghouse J34-WE-34 (3,150 lb.=1,430 kg. s.t.) engines. Fuselage lengthened 12 in. forward of wings to accommodate an additional 177 U.S. gallon (670 litre) internal fuel tank and two 200 U.S. gallon (756 litre) wing-tip tanks added. First of an order for 188 was flown in August, 1949. Second contract for 146 placed in September, 1949, completed in April, 1952. All F2H-2's modified for "probe-drogue" flight refuelling.

F2H-2N. Night fighter version of F2H-2. Longer nose to accommodate both armament and A.I. radar. Last of 14 delivered to U.S. Navy in June, 1951.

F2H-2P. Photographic reconnaissance version of F2H-2. New and longer heated nose can accommodate six different types of camera. Combination viewfinder provides pilot with unobstructed

The McDonnell F2H-3 Banshee Naval Fighter.

view of terrain below and ahead. Orientation and operation of all cameras under pilot's control. Last of 58 delivered to U.S. Navy in August, 1952.

F2H-3. Long-range all-weather fighter version. Extra section inserted in mid-fuselage to accommodate two additional fuel tanks. Search radar in nose with cannon armament further aft in fuselage sides. New tailplane with slight dihedral. Fitted with "probe-drogue" flight-refuelling equipment. 173 delivered to U.S. Navy.

F2H-4. Last production model. Production completed on October 30, 1953.

DIMENSIONS.—
Span 41 ft. 7.4 in. (12.68 m.).
Width folded 18 ft. 5½ in. (5.60 m.).

PERFORMANCE.—
Max. speed about 600 m.p.h. (960 km.h.).
Speed at critical height 575 m.p.h. (920 km.h.).
Rate of climb 9,000 ft./min. (2,745 m./min.).
Ceiling 56,000 ft. (17,080 m.).

Tactical radius of action 600 miles (960 km.).
Ferry range with tip tanks 2,250 miles (3,600 km.). (1955–56)

The McDonnell F3H-2M Demon (Allison J71 turbojet engine with afterburner) (Clay Janssen)

THE McDONNELL DEMON
U.S. Navy designation: F3H

The Demon is a single-seat carrier-based fighter which equipped 12 U.S. Navy squadrons on board seven carriers in 1959.

The prototype XF3H-1 flew for the first time on August 7, 1951, and in August, 1952, the U.S. Navy placed an order for 150 F3H-1's, to be powered by the Westinghouse J40-W-22 turbojet.

During development the weight of the F3H-1 was increased from 22,000 lb. to 29,000 lb. (9,980 kg. to 13,150 kg.) to meet an all-purpose fighter requirement and a higher thrust engine, the J40-W-24, was specified in place of the original power-unit. This engine, unfortunately, did not come up to expectations, resulting in the F3H-1 being underpowered.

As a result, the last 90 of the original contract for 150 F3H-1's were re-ordered as F3H-2's with the Allison J71 engine. Of the 56 F3H-1's built, 21 early-production aircraft were retained for use as ground trainers and 29 were modified to take the J71 engine and converted to F3H-2 standard.

The Demon, which is of all-metal construction, has 45° sweptback thin wings and tail surfaces. The primary control system incorporates complete power actuation with separately controlled "feel" forces for the pilot. The wings have power-actuated leading-edge slats and trailing-edge slotted flaps, while speed brakes are fitted on the upper surface of each wing-root trailing-edge and on each side of the fuselage aft of the wings. The entire horizontal tailplane pivots at the fuselage to provide trim and manoeuvring control throughout the entire speed range.

All combat fuel is carried in internal self-sealing tanks. Provision is also made for additional fuel in jettisonable external tanks and a retractable flight refuelling probe is carried in a fairing on the starboard side of the cockpit.

The pressurised cockpit, which is situated well forward for good forward and downward visibility, is provided with an ejection seat and jettisonable canopy.

The following versions of the Demon have been announced :—

F3H-2N. Allison J71-A-2 turbojet engine (9,500 lb. = 4,315 kg. s.t. dry ; 14,250 lb. = 6,463 kg. s.t. with afterburning). Night and all-weather fighter. First F3H-2 production version. Armament consists of four 20 mm. cannon and various types of external stores, including the Sidewinder infra-red homing missile and nuclear weapons.

F3H-2M. Day fighter missile carrier version armed with four 20 mm. cannon and four Sparrow III missiles.

F3H-2P. Photographic reconnaissance version.

The 519th and last F3H was completed in November, 1959.

DIMENSIONS.—
Span 35 ft. 4 in. (10.7 m.)
Length 58 ft. 11 in. (17.9 m.)
Height 14 ft. 7 in. (4.45 m.)
Wing area 519 sq. ft. (48.22 m.)

WEIGHTS (F3H-2N).—
Weight empty 22,130 lb. (10,038 kg.)
Weight loaded 33,900 lb. (15,377 kg.)
Wing loading 65.3 lb./sq. ft. (318.8 kg./m.²)

PERFORMANCE (F3H-2N. estimated).—
Max. speed at S/L. 730 m.p.h. (1,175 km.h.)
Rate of climb at S/L. 12,000 ft./min. (3,660 m./min.)
Normal range 1,500 miles (2,400 km.)

The McDonnell FH-1 Phantom Single-seat Fighter (two Westinghouse 19XB turbojet engines).

THE McDONNELL PHANTOM.
U.S. Navy designation : FH-1.

TYPE.—Single-seat Jet-propelled Fighter.

WINGS.—Cantilever low-wing monoplane. Laminar flow aerofoil section. Aluminium-alloy structure with flush-riveted and high-gloss finish, in three main sections, consisting of centre-section and two outer sections, the latter folding upwards for carrier stowage. Electrical folding gear controlled from cockpit. All-metal ailerons with trim and balance tabs in each. Electrically-operated split trailing-edge flaps in four sections extend under fuselage between ailerons.

FUSELAGE.—Monocoque structure of aluminium-alloy with flush-riveted metal skin.

TAIL UNIT.—Monoplane type. Cantilever fin and dihedral tailplane. All-metal statically-balanced rudder and elevators, with controllable trim-tabs.

LANDING GEAR.—Retractable tricycle type. Main wheels retract inwards into wing, nose-wheel backwards into fuselage below pilot's cockpit. Deck arrester hook below rear fuselage.

POWER PLANT.—Two Westinghouse 19XB-2B (U.S. Navy J-30-WE or J-30-P20) axial-flow turbo-jet units mounted in wing-roots alongside the fuselage and each inclined 1½° outward for jet streams to clear rear fuselage. Air intakes in leading-edge of centre-section have controllable shutters which seal intakes in case of engine failure, or when one engine is shut down for cruising. Self-sealing fuel tanks in fuselage capacity 375 U.S. gallons (1,417 litres). Provision for jettisonable fuselage belly tank, capacity 295 U.S. gallons (1,115 litres). Provision for Jato or catapult launch.

ACCOMMODATION.—Pilot's cockpit has fixed forward portion with bullet-proof panel. Plexiglas bubble canopy slides backwards.

ARMAMENT.—Four .5 in. (12.7 mm.) machine-guns mounted in nose. Eight zero-length rocket launchers may be fitted under wings.

DIMENSIONS.—
Span 40 ft. 9 in. (12.42 m.).
Width folded 16 ft. 3 in. (4.95 m.).
Length 38 ft. 9 in. (11.82 m.).
Height 14 ft. 2 in. (4.32 m.).
Height with wings folded 16 ft. 10 in. (5.13 m.).

WEIGHTS.—
Weight empty 6.683 lb. (3,034 kg.).
Normal loaded weight 10,035 lb. (4,556 kg.).
Max. overloaded weight 12,035 lb. (5,164 kg.).

PERFORMANCE.—
Max. speed 505 m.p.h. (810 km.h.) at 30,000 ft. (9,150 m.).
Service ceiling 43,000 ft. (13,120 m.).
Combat range 690 miles (1,105 km.).
Ferry range 1,400 miles (2,240 km.).

THE McDONNELL MODEL 86.
U.S. Navy designation: XHCH-1.

The XHCH-1 now being developed for the U.S. Navy is a "flying crane" or cargo transporter for short-range work, such as ship-to-shore transfer of heavy equipment, etc. It will have a power winch and retractable cargo sling to lift and carry heavy cargo and will also be able to handle cargo "pods." It is understood that the large folding three-blade rotor will be powered with McDonnell turbojets, one at each rotor-blade tip. No other details are available for publication. (1949–50)

THE McDONNELL VOODOO
U.S. Air Force designation: F-101 and RF-101

The Voodoo is a supersonic twin-jet fighter which is in operational service with the U.S.A.F. It was developed from the XF-88 and XF-88A twin-jet long-range penetration fighters, the latter with afterburners, which underwent successful evaluation by the U.S.A.F. in 1949 and 1950. Owing to a cutback in defense funds and a change in tactical requirements, the experimental contract was terminated in August, 1950. But after a period of over a year the XF-88A was revived and, with modifications, was ordered into production as the F-101A Voodoo. The design has since undergone considerable development, and the following versions of the F-101 are now in service:—

F-101A. Two Pratt & Whitney J57-P-13 turbojet engines (each 11,700 lb. = 5,310 kg. s.t. dry; 14,500 lb. = 6,575 kg. s.t. with afterburning). First F-101A flew on September 29, 1954, and exceeded Mach 1 on its first flight. Intended originally as a long-range escort fighter for Strategic Air Command, but no longer needed in this rôle when the B-36 bomber was superseded by the B-52 Stratofortress. Accordingly, the F-101A was adapted for multi-purpose interceptor/fighter-bomber duties and supplied to Tactical Air Command. Deliveries began in May, 1957.

Armament of the F-101A consists of four 20 mm. M-39E cannon, plus three Hughes GAR-1 Falcon missiles and 12 rockets. It

McDonnell F-101C Voodoo fighter-bomber (Gordon S. Williams)

has a rotary bomb door on which Falcons and other stores of various types can be carried. It can utilise probe-drogue, Flying Boom and "buddy tank" air refuelling systems.

On December 12, 1957, an F-101A flown by Major Adrian Drew, U.S.A.F., set up a World's Speed Record of 1,207.6 m.p.h. (1,943.5 km.h.) over the measured course at Edwards AFB, California. This record has since been beaten.

RF-101A. Two Pratt & Whitney J57-P-13 turbojet engines (each 11,700 lb. = 5,310 kg. s.t. dry; 14,500 lb. = 6,575 kg. s.t. with afterburning). Long range photographic-reconnaissance aircraft. Comprehensive and fully-automatic camera equipment installed in forward fuselage, but otherwise airframe, power-plant, etc. same as F-101A. In service with Tactical Air Command since May, 1957.

F-101B. Two Pratt & Whitney J57-P-55 engines with afterburners. Long-range two-seat interceptor version of F-101A in service with U.S.A.F. Air Defence Command and R.C.A.F., which received the first of 66 on July 24, 1961. First F-101B flew on March 27, 1957. Armed with two Douglas MB-1 Genie unguided air-to-air nuclear missiles carried semi-externally. Three Hughes Falcon air-to-air missiles or bombs carried internally on rotating bomb-door.

F-101C. Similar to F-101A, but strengthened for low-level fighter-bomber operations. Pylon and crutch for atomic weapons under fuselage, between two 450 U.S. gallon (1,705 litre) external tanks. 20 mm. guns retained. In service with U.S.A.F. Tactical Air Command.

RF-101C. Long-range photographic reconnaissance version of F-101C, with cameras in lengthened nose. Delivery completed on April 25, 1959. Some reported in service with Chinese Nationalist Air Force.

Production of the Voodoo ended in March, 1961, with the delivery of the last F-101B. Of the total of 807 Voodoos built, 327 were of the F/RF-101A/C single-seat series. In the Autumn of 1959, nine U.S.A.F. squadrons were equipped with RF-101A's and C's, three with F-101A's and C's and nine with F-101B's.

DIMENSIONS (F-101B).—
   Span 39 ft. 8 in. (12.09 m.)
   Length 67 ft. 5 in. (20.55 m.)
   Height 18 ft. (5.49 m.)
   Wing sweepback 35°.

Cruising speed at 36,000 ft. (11,000 m.) 595 m.p.h. (958 km.h.)
Rate of climb at S/L 14,000 ft./min. (4,270 m./min.)
Service ceiling 52,000 ft. (15,850 m.)
Range with external tanks 2,800 miles (4,500 km.)
WEIGHT (F-101A).—
   Max. loaded weight 49,000 lb. (22,225 kg.)
PERFORMANCE (F-101C).—
   Max. speed at 40,000 ft. (12,200 m.) Mach 1.85.   (1961–62)

McDonnell Douglas C-9B Skytrain II (two Pratt & Whitney JT8D-9 turbofan engines)

MCDONNELL DOUGLAS DC-9
USAF designations: C-9A and VC-9C
US Navy designation: C-9B

Design study data on the DC-9, then known as the Douglas Model 2086, were released in 1962. Preliminary design work began during that year. Fabrication was started on 26 July 1963 and assembly of the first airframe began on 6 March 1964. It flew for the first time on 25 February 1965 and five DC-9s were flying by the end of June 1965. These aircraft were of the basic version now known as the DC-9 Series 10.

There are also three military versions of the DC-9, as follows:

C-9A Nightingale. Aeromedical airlift transport, of which eight were ordered in 1967 for operation by the 375th Aeromedical Wing of the USAF Military Airlift Command. Essentially an 'off-the-shelf' DC-9 Srs 30 commercial transport, but with JT8D-9 engines, the C-9A is able to carry 30 to 40 litter patients, more than 40 ambulatory patients or a combination of the two, together with two nurses and three aeromedical technicians. The interior includes a special-care compartment, with separate atmospheric and ventilation controls. Galleys and toilets are provided fore and aft. There are three entrances, two with hydraulically-operated stairways. The third has a forward door 2·06 m (6 ft 9 in) high and 3·45 m (11 ft 4 in) wide, with a hydraulically-operated ramp, to facilitate loading of litters. First C-9A was rolled out on 17 June 1968 and was delivered to the US Air Force at Scott Air Force Base on 10 August 1968. Orders for the C-9A totalled 21, which were all delivered by February 1973.

C-9B Skytrain II. Fleet logistic support transport, of which five were ordered by the USN under a $25·3 million contract announced on 19 April 1972, increased subsequently to fourteen. Described separately.

VC-9C. DC-9-30 type aircraft with special configuration, ordered in December 1973 by the USAF for service in the Special Air Missions Wing based at Andrews AFB, Maryland, near Washington, DC. Three delivered in 1975.

The following structural details apply to the DC-9 Series 10:

TYPE: Twin-turbofan short/medium-range airliner.
WINGS: Cantilever low-wing monoplane. Mean thickness/chord ratio 11·6%. Sweepback 24° at quarter-chord. All-metal construction, with three spars inboard, two spars outboard and spanwise stringers riveted to skin. Glassfibre trailing-edges on wings, ailerons and flaps. Hydraulically-controlled ailerons, each in two sections, outer sections used at low speed only. Wing-mounted speed brakes. Hydraulically-actuated double-slotted flaps over 67% of semi-span. (Leading-edge slats on Srs 20/30/40/50.) Single boundary-layer fence (vortillon) under each wing. Detachable wingtips. Thermal anti-icing of leading-edges.
FUSELAGE: Conventional all-metal semi-monocoque structure.
TAIL UNIT: Cantilever all-metal structure with hydraulically-actuated variable-incidence T-tailplane. Manually-controlled elevators with servo tabs. Hydraulically-controlled rudder with manual override. Glassfibre trailing-edges on control surfaces.
LANDING GEAR: Retractable tricycle type of Menasco manufacture, with steerable nosewheel. Hydraulic retraction, nose unit forward, main units inward. Twin Goodyear wheels on each unit. Main-wheel tyres size 40 × 14. Nosewheel tyres size 26 × 6·60. Goodyear brakes. Hydro-Aire Hytrol Mk II anti-skid units.
POWER PLANT: Two Pratt & Whitney JT8D turbofan engines

DIMENSIONS, EXTERNAL:
Wing span:
   Srs 10   27·25 m (89 ft 5 in)
   Srs 20, 30, 40, 50   28·47 m (93 ft 5 in)
Wing aspect ratio:
   Srs 10   8·55
   Srs 20, 30, 40, 50   8·71
Length overall:
   Srs 10, 20   31·82 m (104 ft 4¾ in)
   Srs 30   36·37 m (119 ft 3½ in)
   Srs 40   38·28 m (125 ft 7¼ in)
   Srs 50   40·72 m (133 ft 7¼ in)
Height overall:
   Srs 10, 20, 30   8·38 m (27 ft 6 in)
   Srs 40, 50   8·53 m (28 ft 0 in)
Freight and baggage hold doors:
   Height   1·27 m (4 ft 2 in)
   Width:
      fwd   1·35 m (4 ft 5 in)
      rear   0·91 m (3 ft 0 in)
Freight hold (underfloor):
   Srs 10, 20   17·0 m³ (600 cu ft)
   Srs 30   25·3 m³ (895 cu ft)
   Srs 40   28·9 m³ (1,019 cu ft)
   Srs 50   29·3 m³ (1,034 cu ft)

AREAS:
Wings, gross:
   Srs 10   86·77 m² (934·3 sq ft)
   Srs 20, 30, 40, 50 92·97 m² (1,000·7 sq ft)
WEIGHTS AND LOADINGS:
Manufacturer's empty weight:
   Srs 10 Model 11   20,550 kg (45,300 lb)
   Srs 10 Model 15   22,235 kg (49,020 lb)
   Srs 20   23,985 kg (52,880 lb)
   Srs 30   25,940 kg (57,190 lb)
   Srs 40   26,612 kg (58,670 lb)
   Srs 50   28,068 kg (61,880 lb)
Max weight-limited payload:
   Srs 10 Model 15   9,325 kg (20,560 lb)
   Srs 20   10,565 kg (23,295 lb)
   Srs 30   12,743 kg (28,094 lb)
   Srs 40   14,363 kg (31,665 lb)
   Srs 50   15,617 kg (34,430 lb)
Max T-O weight:
   Srs 10 Model 11   35,245 kg (77,700 lb)
   Srs 10 Model 15   41,140 kg (90,700 lb)
   Srs 20   44,450 kg (98,000 lb)
   Srs 30, 40, 50   54,884 kg (121,000 lb)
PERFORMANCE (at max T-O weight, except where indicated):
Never-exceed speed:
   Srs 50   537 knots (994 km/h; 618 mph)
Max level speed:
   Srs 50   500 knots (927 km/h; 576 mph)
Max cruising speed at 7,620 m (25,000 ft):
   Srs 10 Model 11 and 15 and Srs 30:
          490 knots (907 km/h; 564 mph)
   Srs 20   494 knots (915 km/h; 569 mph)
   Srs 40, 50 485 knots (898 km/h; 558 mph)
Average long-range cruising speed at 9,145-10,675 m (30,000-35,000 ft) 443 knots (821 km/h; 510 mph)
Ferry range:
   Srs 10   1,910 nm (3,539 km; 2,199 miles)
   Srs 20   1,865 nm (3,455 km; 2,147 miles)
   Srs 30   1,980 nm (3,669 km; 2,280 miles)
   Srs 40   1,850 nm (3,428 km; 2,130 miles)
   Srs 50   2,185 nm (4,049 km; 2,516 miles)
                             (1976–77)

MCDONNELL DOUGLAS F/A-18 HORNET

In the Spring of 1974 the US Department of Defense accepted a proposal from the US Navy to study a low-cost lightweight multi-mission fighter, then identified as the VFAX. In June 1974 the USN approached the US aircraft industry to submit critiques and comments on such an aircraft. Six companies responded, including McDonnell Aircraft Company; but in August of that year Congress terminated the VFAX concept, directing instead that the Navy should investigate versions of the General Dynamics YF-16 and Northrop YF-17 lightweight fighter prototypes then under evaluation for the USAF.

McDonnell Douglas made a study of the configuration of these two aircraft and concluded that Northrop's contender could be redesigned at minimum cost to meet the Navy's requirements. It then teamed with Northrop to propose a derivative of the YF-17 to meet the Navy's requirement, with McDonnell Douglas as the prime contractor. Identified as the Navy Air Combat Fighter (NACF), this received the designation F-18 Hornet when selected for further development, and the following production versions were originally proposed:

F-18A. Basic single-seat escort fighter/interdictor to replace F-4.

TF-18A. Tandem two-seat version of F-18A for training, with combat capability. Fuel capacity reduced by under 6 per cent.

CF-18A. Version for Canadian Armed Forces, which plan to purchase 137. Selection announced on 10 April 1980.

A-18. Single-seat attack version to replace A-4, A-7 and AV-8A. The A-18 is identical to the F-18 except that FLIR and a laser tracker, which are being developed as part of the Hornet programme, will take the place of fuselage-mounted Sparrows for attack missions.

On 22 January 1976 it was announced that full-scale development had been initiated by the US Navy, with initial funding of $16 million. Total cost of the development programme was expected to be about $1·4 billion, including the production of 11 YF-18s for the flight test programme.

The first Hornet (160775) was rolled out on 13 September 1978, and made its first flight on 18 November 1978; the second flew on 12 March 1979, and all 11 development aircraft were flying by March 1980, including two TF-18A two-seat combat-capable trainers. The first batch of nine production Hornets was authorised in FY 1979, followed by 25 in FY 1980 and 60 in FY 1981. In the fourth quarter of 1979, a Hornet became the first modern jet aircraft to complete initial sea trials within one year of its first flight, and the first production aircraft was delivered to the US Navy for operational evaluation in May 1980. The first development squadron was scheduled to form at NAS Lemoore, California, in the Autumn of 1980. The F-18 is due to become operational with the US Navy in 1982.

The Hornet airframe differs from that of the YF-17 prototype by having increased wing area, a wider and longer fuselage to provide greater internal fuel capacity, an enlarged nose to accommodate the 0·71 m (28 in) radar dish to meet the Navy's search range requirement of over 30 nm (56 km; 35 miles), and strengthening of the airframe structure to cater for the increased loads caused by catapult launches and arrested landings. Approximately 2,000 kg (4,400 lb) of additional fuel is carried to meet Navy mission range requirements.

Ease of maintenance was given careful consideration in formulation of the F-18's design. An engine change can be effected within approx 20 min, and radar equipment is track-mounted so that it can be rolled out for maintenance. Electronics equipment is housed behind quick-release doors at chest height, and the windscreen is hinged to permit easy access behind the instrument panel. A built-in test panel mounted within the nosewheel well pinpoints system failures, and when the indicated access door is opened the assembly which has failed 'flags' confirmation that it needs repair or replacement. Groundcrew have access to a 'go, no go' panel for rapid pre-flight check; this confirms levels of essential liquids, such as engine oil, hydraulic fluid, radar coolant, APU oil and oxygen. Safety features include self-sealing fuel tanks and fuel lines, fire suppressant foam within the fuel tanks, built-in fire extinguishers, filler foam in the fuselage for fire suppression, and a system which detects hydraulic fluid leaks and then isolates the relative section.

Conventional instrumentation has almost disappeared from the cockpit, replaced by three cathode ray tubes and an information control panel directly in front of the pilot. A head-up display is fitted and, so that the pilot will not be distracted by having to move his hands to different controls, every critical switch for air-to-air and air-to-surface engagements is either in the throttle in his left hand, or on the control stick in his right hand. During air-to-air combat the Hughes AN/APG-65 radar can track multiple targets, displaying up to eight target tracks while retaining up to ten in its memory. A raid assessment mode enables

McDonnell Douglas TF-18A, a combat-capable two-seat training version of the Hornet

McDonnell Douglas F-18A Hornet development aircraft in operational finish, using three shades of grey and low-profile markings

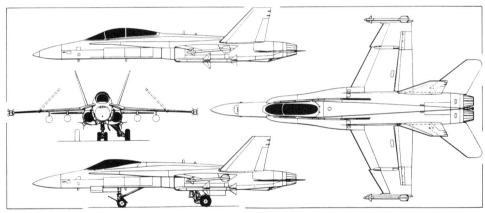

McDonnell Douglas F-18A Hornet, with additional side view (top) of the TF-18A training version *(Pilot Press)*

the pilot to discriminate between closely spaced targets. The radar information is displayed on a clutter-free scope in either lookup or lookdown attitude; it provides also range-while-search capability, long-range search and track, and several modes for close-in combat. Doppler beam sharpening (DBS) achieves greater resolution of radar signal returns during air-to-surface mapping.

McDonnell Douglas is prime contractor for the Hornet, with the centre of activities at St Louis, Missouri. Northrop builds the centre and aft fuselage, which is delivered totally assembled to McDonnell Douglas. Assembly is completed at St Louis and flight testing is carried out at NATC Patuxent River, Maryland.

The decision to combine the A-18 and F-18 into the F/A-18 was taken before production started, and F/A-18As joined USMC and Navy squadrons from 1983. Most recent versions are the **F/A-18C, F/A-18D** and reconnaissance **F/A-18D(CR)**. Data is for the F/A-18:—

TYPE: Single-seat carrier-based naval strike fighter.

WINGS: Cantilever mid-wing monoplane. Moderate-sweep multi-spar structure, primarily of light alloy and graphite/epoxy. Boundary layer control achieved by wing-root slots. Full-span leading-edge manoeuvring flaps have a maximum extension angle of 30°. Single-slotted trailing-edge flaps, actuated by Bertea hydraulic cylinders, deploy to a maximum of 45°. Ailerons, with Hydraulic Research actuators, can be drooped to 45°, providing the advantages of full-span flaps for low approach speeds. Leading- and trailing-edge flaps are computer programmed to deflect for optimum lift and drag in both manoeuvring and cruise conditions. Notched sections on outer wing leading-edge to enhance aileron effectiveness. Wing-root leading-edge extensions (LEX) permit flight at angles of attack exceeding 60°. Wings fold, by means of AiResearch mechanical drive, at the inboard end of each aileron.

FUSELAGE: Semi-monocoque basic structure, primarily of light alloy, with graphite/epoxy used for access doors/panels. Titanium firewall between engines. Airbrake in upper surface of fuselage between tail fins. Pressurised cockpit section of fail-safe construction. Arrester hook for carrier landings under rear fuselage.

TAIL UNIT: Cantilever structure with swept vertical and horizontal surfaces. Twin outward-canted fins and rudders, mounted forward of all-moving horizontal surfaces (stabilators), which are actuated collectively and differentially by National Water Lift servo-cylinder hydraulic units for pitch and roll control.

LANDING GEAR: Retractable tricycle type, manufactured by Cleveland, with twin-wheel nose and single-wheel main units. Nose unit retracts forward, main wheels aft, turning 90° to stow horizontally inside the lower surface of the engine air ducts. Bendix wheels and brakes. Ozone nosewheel steering unit. Nose unit towbar for catapult launch.

POWER PLANT: Two General Electric F404-GE-400 low bypass turbofan engines, each producing approx 71·2 kN (16,000 lb thrust). Self-sealing fuel feed tanks and fuel lines; foam in wing tanks and fuselage voids. Internal fuel load approx 4,990 kg (11,000 lb); provision for up to three 1,192 litre (315 US gallon) external tanks, increasing total fuel capacity to more than 7,257 kg (16,000 lb). Simmonds fuel gauging system. Fixed-ramp air intakes.

ACCOMMODATION: Pilot only, on Martin-Baker US10S ejection seat in pressurised, heated and air-conditioned cockpit. Upward-opening two-part canopy, both sections hinged individually.

SYSTEMS: Two completely separate hydraulic systems. Quadruplex digital fly-by-wire flight control system, with direct electrical backup to all surfaces, and direct mechanical backup to stabilators. Garrett-AiResearch air-conditioning system. GEC electrical power system. Oxygen system. Fire detection and extinguishing systems.

AVIONICS AND EQUIPMENT: Will include an automatic carrier landing system (ACLS) for all-weather carrier operations; a Hughes AN/APG-65 multi-mode digital air-to-air and air-to-ground tracking radar, with air-to-air modes which include Velocity Search (VS), Range While Search (RWS), Track While Scan (TWS), which can track ten targets and display eight to the pilot, and Raid Assessment Mode (RAM). Itek ALR-67 radar warning receiver; General Electric quadruple-redundant flight control system with two AYK-14 digital computers; Litton inertial navigation system; Kaiser multi-purpose cockpit display, including head-up display and three CRTs; Conrac communications system control; Normalair-Garrett digital data recorder for Bendix maintenance recording system; Smiths standby altimeter; and Kearflex standby airspeed indicator, standby vertical speed indicator, and cockpit pressure altimeter. Garrett-AiResearch APU for engine starting and ground pneumatic, electrical and hydraulic power.

ARMAMENT: Nine external weapon stations with a combined capacity of 7,710 kg (17,000 lb) of mixed ordnance at high *g*. These comprise two wingtip stations for AIM-9 Sidewinder air-to-air missiles; two outboard wing stations for an assortment of air-to-ground or air-to-air weapons, including AIM-7 Sparrows; two inboard wing stations for external fuel tanks or air-to-ground weapons; two nacelle fuselage stations for Sparrows or Martin Marietta AN/ASQ-173 laser spot tracker/strike camera (LST/SCAM) and Ford FLIR pods; and a centreline fuselage station for external fuel or weapons. An M61 20 mm six-barrel gun, with 570 rounds, is mounted in the nose and will have a McDonnell Douglas director gunsight, with a conventional sight as backup.

DIMENSIONS, EXTERNAL:

Wing span	11·43 m (37 ft 6 in)
Wing span over missiles	12·31 m (40 ft 4¾ in)
Width, wings folded	8·38 m (27 ft 6 in)
Length overall	17·07 m (56 ft 0 in)
Height overall	4·66 m (15 ft 3½ in)
Tailplane span	6·58 m (21 ft 7¼ in)
Wheel track	3·11 m (10 ft 2½ in)
Wheelbase	5·42 m (17 ft 9½ in)

AREA:

Wings, gross	37·16 m² (400 sq ft)

WEIGHTS:

Fighter mission T-O weight	15,234 kg (33,585 lb)
Attack mission T-O weight	21,319 kg (47,000 lb)

PERFORMANCE (estimated):

Max level speed	more than Mach 1·8
Max speed, intermediate power	more than Mach 1·0
Approach speed	130 knots (240 km/h; 150 mph)
Combat ceiling	approx 15,240 m (50,000 ft)
T-O run	less than 305 m (1,000 ft)
Combat radius, fighter mission	more than 400 nm (740 km; 460 miles)
Combat radius, attack mission	550 nm (1,019 km; 633 miles)
Ferry range, unrefuelled	more than 2,000 nm (3,706 km; 2,303 miles)
	(1980–81)

MCDONNELL DOUGLAS F-15 EAGLE

The USAF requested development funding for a new air superiority fighter in 1965, and in due course design proposals were sought from three airframe manufacturers: Fairchild Hiller Corporation, McDonnell Douglas Corporation, and North American Rockwell Corporation. On 23 December 1969 it was announced that McDonnell Douglas had been selected as prime airframe contractor. The contract called for the design and manufacture of 20 aircraft for development testing, these to comprise 18 single-seat **F-15As** and two **TF-15A** two-seat trainers, with production scheduled at a rate of one aircraft every other month.

First flight of the F-15A was made on 27 July 1972, and the first flight of a two-seat TF-15A trainer, designated subsequently **F-15B**, on 7 July 1973.

A production go-ahead for the first 30 operational aircraft (FY 1973 funds) was announced on 1 March 1973. The FY 1974 Defense Procurement Bill authorised production of 62 aircraft, and the Defense Procurement Bills for FY 1975, 1976/7T, 1977, 1978 and 1979 authorised further production of 72, 135, 108, 97 and 78 aircraft respectively. The FY 1973-74 production contracts included 13 of the two-seat F-15B version; one of these (the 21st Eagle built) was the first Eagle delivered to the USAF, on 14 November 1974. Structural weight of the F-15B is approx 363 kg (800 lb) more than that of the single-seater. Eagles delivered from mid-1979 are to **F-15C** and **F-15D** standard, which provides for an additional 907 kg (2,000 lb) of internal fuel, and the ability to carry FAST Packs (see later paragraphs). Beginning in mid-1980 the APG-63 radar of these aircraft will be equipped with programmable signal processors, providing for future software changes and increased computer capability. F-15C and F-15D aircraft delivered prior to the availability of the programmable signal processor and expanded computer will be retrofitted subsequently to bring them up to standard.

The first F-15C (78-468) flew for the first time on 26 February 1979.

By 1 July 1979 a total of 444 Eagles had been delivered, and were in operational service with the 57th TTW at Nellis AFB, Nevada, the 58th TTW at Luke AFB, Arizona, the 1st TFW at Langley AFB, Virginia, the 36th TFW which was deployed to Bitburg, Germany, with F-15s in April 1977, and the 49th TFW at Holloman AFB, New Mexico, in October 1977. In 1979 the F-15 also equipped the 33rd TFW at Eglin AFB, Florida, and the 32nd Tactical Fighter Squadron based at Soesterburg, The Netherlands. Production was at a rate of ten per month in January 1979. It is planned to procure 749 for the USAF by 1983, including the 20 R & D models. Thirty-five were ordered under an initial contract from the Israeli Air Force, and 60 by Saudi Arabia. The JASDF plans to purchase 100 **F-15Js**, of which all except eight will be licence-built in Japan, with Mitsubishi as the prime contractor.

Designed specifically as an air superiority fighter, the F-15A Eagle has proved equally suitable for air-to-ground missions without degradation of its primary role. It is able to carry a variety of air-to-air and air-to-ground weapons.

A large increase in the normal ferry range of a 'clean' F-15 can be achieved by the use of two low-drag fuel pallets known as FAST Packs (Fuel And Sensor Tactical Packs) developed specially for the F-15 by McDonnell

The first McDonnell Douglas F-15C Eagle overflying St Louis

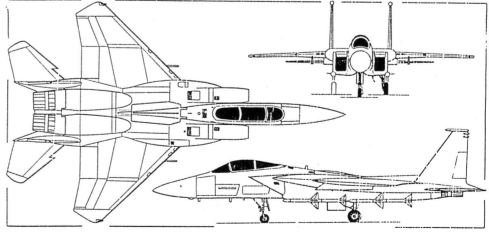

McDonnell Douglas F-15A Eagle twin-turbofan air superiority fighter *(Pilot Press)*

Aircraft Company. Each FAST Pack contains approximately 3,228 litres (114 cu ft) of usable volume, which can accommodate 2,268 kg (5,000 lb) of JP-4 fuel. It attaches to the side of either the port or starboard engine air intake trunk (being made in handed pairs), is designed to the same load factors and airspeed limits as the basic aircraft, and can be removed in 15 minutes. FAST Packs can accommodate avionics such as reconnaissance sensors, radar detection and jamming equipment, a laser designator, low-light-level TV system, and reconnaissance cameras, in addition to fuel. All external stores stations remain available with the pallets in use. AIM-7F missiles and air-to-ground weapons can be attached to the corners of the FAST Packs.

McDonnell Douglas F-15B Eagle two-seat trainer, fitted with FAST Packs

The programmable signal processor for the F-15C/D will enable changes to be incorporated in the radar earlier and more cheaply. An updated radar data processor will be fitted which will increase memory capability from 24K to 96K. These added features will enable the radar to operate in a high-resolution rate assessment mode which can identify clustered targets individually. The PEP-2000 (Production Eagle Package-2,000 lb; 907 kg of additional fuel) expands the fighter's combat endurance considerably, and includes attachment points and fuel plumbing to accommodate FAST Packs.

Minor changes have been made to tyres, wheels and brakes to allow for an increased maximum T-O weight, which could be as high as 30,844 kg (68,000 lb) with full internal fuel, FAST Packs and external tanks. Landing gear and fuel system changes have added about 227 kg (500 lb) to the aircraft's dry weight.

Under a programme dubbed 'Streak Eagle', the F-15 demonstrated its climb capability by capturing eight time-to-height records, between 16 January and 1 February 1975

The dual-task **F-15E** interdiction/attack and air superiority version entered USAF service from 1988.

The following description applies to the F-15A:
TYPE: Single-seat twin-turbofan air superiority fighter, with secondary attack role.
WINGS: Cantilever shoulder-wing monoplane. Leading-edge swept back at 45°.
FUSELAGE: All-metal semi-monocoque structure.
TAIL UNIT: Cantilever structure with twin fins and rudders. All-moving horizontal tail surfaces outboard of fins, with extended chord on outer leading-edges. Rudder servo actuators by Ronson Hydraulic Units Corporation. Actuators for horizontal surfaces by National Water Lift Company. Boost and pitch compensator for control stick by Moog Inc, Controls Division.
LANDING GEAR: Hydraulically-retractable tricycle type, with single wheel on each unit. Nose and main landing gear by Cleveland Pneumatic Tool Company. Wheels and carbon brake assemblies by Goodyear Tire and Rubber Company. Main and nosewheel tyres by B. F. Goodrich Company. Wheel braking skid control system by Hydro-Aire Division of Crane Company. All units retract forward.
POWER PLANT: Two Pratt & Whitney F100-PW-100 turbofan engines of approximately 111·2 kN (25,000 lb st). Internal fuel load 5,260 kg (11,600 lb). Fuel tanks by Goodyear Aviation Products Division. Fuel gauge system by Simmonds Precision Products Inc. FAST Pack conformal fuel pallets attached to side of engine air intakes, beneath wing, can be removed within 15 min. Each has usable volume of 3·23 m³ (114 cu ft) and can contain 2,268 kg (5,000 lb) of JP-4 fuel.
ENGINE INTAKES: Straight two-dimensional external compression inlets, on each side of the fuselage. Air inlet controllers by Hamilton Standard. Air inlet actuators by National Water Lift Company.

ACCOMMODATION: Pilot only, on Aces II ejection seat developed by Douglas. Stretched acrylic canopy and windscreen. Windscreen anti-icing valve by Dynasciences Corporation.
SYSTEMS: Electric power generating system by Lear Siegler Power Equipment Division; transformer-rectifiers by Electro Development Corporation; 40/50kVA generator 'constant-speed drive units by Sundstrand Corporation, Aviation Division. Three independent hydraulic systems (each 207 bars; 3,000 lb/sq in) powered by Abex engine-driven pumps; modular hydraulic packages by Hydraulic Research and Manufacturing Company. The oxygen system includes a liquid oxygen indicator by Simmonds Precision Products Inc. Airconditioning system by AiResearch Manufacturing Company. Automatic flight control system by General Electric, Aircraft Equipment Division. Auxiliary power unit for engine starting, and for the provision of electric or hydraulic power on the ground independently of the main engines, supplied by AiResearch Manufacturing Company.
AVIONICS: Lightweight APG-63 pulse-Doppler radar developed by Hughes Aircraft Company provides long-range detection and tracking of small high-speed targets operating at all altitudes down to treetop level, and feeds accurate tracking information to the airborne central computer to ensure effective launch of the aircraft's missiles or the firing of its internal gun. For close-in dogfights, the radar automatically acquires the target on a head-up display. International Business Machines, Electronic Systems Center, is subcontractor for the central computer, and McDonnell Douglas Electronics Company for the head-up display. This latter unit projects all essential flight information in the form of symbols on to a combining glass positioned above the instrument panel at pilot's eye level. The display presents the pilot with all the information required to intercept and destroy an enemy aircraft without need for him to remove his eyes from the target. The display also provides navigation and other steering control information under all flight conditions. A transponder for the IFF system, developed by Teledyne Electronics Company, informs ground stations and other suitably equipped aircraft that the F-15 is a friendly aircraft. It also supplies data on the F-15's range, azimuth, altitude and identification to air traffic controllers. The F-15 carries an AN/APX-76 interrogator receiver-transmitter, built by Hazeltine Corporation, to inform the pilot if an aircraft seen visually or on radar is friendly. A reply evaluator for the IFF system, which operates with the AN/APX-76, was developed by Litton Systems Inc, Van Nuys. A vertical situation display set, that uses a cathode-ray tube to present radar, electro-optical identification and attitude director indicator formats to the pilot, has been developed by Sperry Rand Corporation, Sperry Flight Systems Division. This permits inputs received from the aircraft's sensors and the central computer to be visible to the pilot under any light conditions. This company has also developed an air data

computer for the F-15, as well as an attitude and heading reference set to provide information on the aircraft's pitch, roll and magnetic heading that is fed to cockpit displays. This latter unit also serves as a backup to the inertial navigation set developed by Litton Guidance and Control Systems Division. This provides the basic navigation data and is the aircraft's primary attitude reference, enabling the F-15 to navigate anywhere in the world. In addition to giving the aircraft's position at all times, the inertial navigation system provides pitch, roll, heading, acceleration and speed information.

Other specialised equipment for flight control, navigation and communications includes a micro-miniaturised Tacan system by Collins Radio Company; a horizontal situation indicator to present aircraft navigation information on a symbolic pictorial display, by Collins Radio Company, which is also responsible for the ADF and ILS receivers. Magnavox provides the UHF transceiver and UHF auxiliary transceiver. The communications sets have cryptographic capability. Dorne and Margolin Aviation Products is responsible for the glideslope localiser antenna, and Teledyne Avionics Company for angle of attack sensors. An internal countermeasures set, designated AN/ALQ-135, which provides automatic jamming of enemy radar signals, is supplied by Northrop's Defense Systems Division; radar warning systems by Loral Electronic Systems; and an electronic warfare warning set by Magnavox.
EQUIPMENT: Tachometer, fuel and oil indicators by Bendix Corporation, Flight and Engine Instrument Division. Feel trim actuators by Plessey Airborne Corporation.
ARMAMENT: Provision for carriage and launch of a variety of air-to-air weapons over short and medium ranges, including four AIM-9L Sidewinders, four AIM-7F Sparrows, and a 20 mm M61A-1 six-barrel gun with 940 rounds of ammunition. A lead-computing gyro has been developed by the General Electric Co. To keep the pilot informed of the status of his weapons and provide for their management, an armament control set has been developed by Dynamic Controls Corporation. Five weapon stations allow for the carriage of up to 7,257 kg (16,000 lb) of bombs, rockets or additional ECM equipment.
DIMENSIONS, EXTERNAL:

Wing span	13·05 m (42 ft 9¾ in)
Length overall	19·43 m (63 ft 9 in)
Height overall	5·63 m (18 ft 5½ in)
Tailplane span	8·61 m (28 ft 3 in)
Wheel track	2·75 m (9 ft 0¼ in)
Wheelbase	5·42 m (17 ft 9½ in)

AREA:

Wings, gross	56·5 m² (608 sq ft)

WEIGHTS (A: F-15A; B: F-15C):

T-O weight (interceptor, full internal fuel and 4 Sparrows): A	18,824 kg (41,500 lb)
B	20,185 kg (44,500 lb)
T-O weight (incl three 2,271 litre; 600 US gallon droptanks): A	24,675 kg (54,400 lb)
B	26,035 kg (57,400 lb)
Max T-O weight: A	25,401 kg (56,000 lb)
B	30,845 kg (68,000 lb)

PERFORMANCE:

Max level speed	more than Mach 2·5
	(800 knots; 1,482 km/h; 921 mph CAS)
Approach speed	125 knots (232 km/h; 144 mph) CAS
T-O run (interceptor)	274 m (900 ft)
Landing run (interceptor), without braking parachute	762 m (2,500 ft)
Absolute ceiling	30,500 m (100,000 ft)
Ferry range: without FAST Pack	
	more than 2,500 nm (4,631 km; 2,878 miles)
with FAST Pack	
	more than 3,000 nm (5,560 km; 3,450 miles)
g limits	+9·0; −3·0
	(1980–81)

MCDONNELL DOUGLAS EXTENDER
US Air Force designation: KC-10A
The USAF announced on 19 December 1977 that, following evaluation of the Boeing 747 and McDonnell Douglas DC-10 to meet its requirement for an Advanced Tanker/Cargo Aircraft (ATCA), the DC-10 ATCA was selected to fulfil this role. Subsequently, the aircraft was designated KC-10A and named Extender.

A force of KC-10As will greatly enhance the ability of the USAF to deploy combat aircraft, men and supplies on a global scale. This point was emphasised in a USAF submission to Congress in which the spokesman commented that 40 Boeing KC-135 tankers and a number of

cargo aircraft would be needed to fuel an F-4 fighter squadron and carry its personnel and equipment from the USA to the Middle East. Just 17 of the proposed KC-10As could fulfil the same task, more economically and efficiently. USAF Military Airlift Command's (MAC) need for support by such aircraft was highlighted during the 1973 Arab-Israeli war, when many countries denied landing rights to MAC aircraft. From these circumstances came the decision to develop an ATCA to support the strategic airlift fleet, under the operational control of the USAF Strategic Air Command.

The initial $28 million contract awarded to McDonnell Douglas covered the funding for initial production planning, engineering and tooling. A second $429,000 contract was for initial planning of a logistics support programme covering the entire KC-10A military tanker fleet.

On 20 November 1978, the USAF authorised McDonnell Douglas to begin production of the KC-10A. This FY 1979 contract called for an expenditure of $148 million by the USAF, for the acquisition of two KC-10As, and in payment of the balance of the non-recurring engineering costs. In addition, under a separate $15·6 million contract, McDonnell Douglas was authorised to purchase the initial spare parts and support equipment for the KC-10A system. Four additional KC-10As were ordered by the USAF in November 1979, under the FY 1980 budget; six were requested in FY 1981. Quantities of KC-10As to be procured over subsequent years will be determined by available funding, but it is anticipated that at least 20 KC-10As may be procured eventually by the USAF. The first KC-10A (USAF serial number 79-0433) made its first flight on 12 July 1980 and was scheduled for delivery to Barksdale AFB, Louisiana, for operation by SAC, in early 1981.

The commercial DC-10 Series 30CF convertible freighter, the basic airframe chosen for conversion to the ATCA role, is currently certificated for operation at a max T-O weight of 267,620 kg (590,000 lb).

The modifications necessary to convert the DC-10-30CF to the ATCA configuration include the installation of fuel cells in the lower fuselage compartment; the provision of a boom operator station, an aerial refuelling boom, a refuelling receptacle, an improved cargo handling system, and some military avionics systems. Various seating layouts are available in the forward area to permit the transport of a fighter squadron's essential support personnel. Seven bladder fuel cells are installed in the lower fuselage compartments, three forward and four aft of the ing, mounted within framework that restrains and sup-;rts the cells. These contain a total of 53,297 kg (117,500) of fuel, equivalent to approx 68,420 litres (18,075 US illons), and are interconnected with the aircraft's basic el system, comprising 108,211 kg (238,565 lb). All can en be used for extended range, or fuel from the lower :ck cells and the aircraft's basic fuel system can be used r in-flight refuelling. The KC-10A is designed to deliver),718 kg (200,000 lb) of fuel to a receiver 1,910 nm .540 km; 2,200 miles) from its home base.

The aerial refuelling operator's station, with access from e upper main deck, is sited in the lower aft fuselage and n accommodate the boom operator, an instructor and an observer, although only the boom operator is needed for a fuelling mission. The station has a rear window and a :riscope observation system to give a wide field of view, d is pressurised and air-conditioned. The advanced aer-l refuelling boom, which is the production version of a om developed and tested in prototype form by McDon-ll Douglas, provides greater capability than the type stalled in the KC-135; in particular, it has a greater insfer flow rate, being rated at 5,678 litres (1,500 US llons)/min. The boom operator 'flies' it by means of a gital fly-by-wire control system supplied by Sperry ight Systems. A hose/reel unit for probe and drogue fuelling is also installed, so that the KC-10A can ser-e USN, USMC, and NATO aircraft, as well as older types fighter still serving with Reserve and ANG units.

The provision of a refuelling receptacle, above the flight ck of the KC-10A, allows greater flexibility on long-nge cargo or refuelling operations, extending the range yond the nominal 6,000 nm (11,112 km; 6,905 miles) th a 45,400 kg (100,000 lb) payload. The improved rgo handling system, by comparison with the basic C-10-30CF, includes an increased floor area covered by ini-directional rollers, power rollers, and a portable nch to move cargo fore and aft.

Changes to the avionics are concerned chiefly with the -letion of equipment intended specifically for commer-l operations, and the addition of UHF and secure com stems, Tacan, IFF, beacon transponder and a radar acon mode.

The description of the DC-10 Series 30CF applies to the C-10A, except as follows:

PE: Military flight refuelling/cargo aircraft.

INGS, FUSELAGE, TAIL UNIT: As for DC-10-30CF, except for omission of most upper-deck cabin windows and lower-deck cargo doors.

LANDING GEAR: As for DC-10-30CF, except Goodyear nosewheels and tyres size 40 × 15·5-16, pressure 13·10 bars (190 lb/sq in). Four-wheel bogie main units and centreline unit have Goodyear wheels and tyres size 52 × 20·5-23. The former have a pressure of 13·79 bars (200 lb/sq in), the latter 10·69 bars (155 lb/sq in). Goodyear disc brakes and anti-skid system, with individual wheel control.

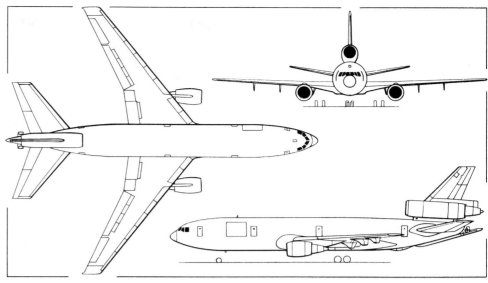

Three-view drawing *(Pilot Press)* **and photograph of the McDonnell Douglas KC-10A Extender advanced tanker/cargo aircraft for the US Air Force**

POWER PLANT: Three 233·53 kN (52,500 lb st) General Electric CF6-50C2 turbofan engines. Basic aircraft fuel system comprises three integral main wing fuel tanks, and an integral auxiliary tank in the wing centre-section with a connected structural compartment fitted with a bladder cell, giving a total capacity of approximately 132,331 litres (34,958 US gallons). Oil capacity 34·1 litres (9 US gallons).

ACCOMMODATION: Three crew on flight deck. Various seating arrangements for a limited number of essential support personnel at forward end of main cabin. Aerial refuelling station, with accommodation for boom operator, instructor and a student observer at aft end of lower fuselage compartment. Five passenger doors on main deck. A 2·59 m × 3·56 m (8 ft 6 in × 11 ft 8 in) cargo door on the port side of the fuselage permits loading of standard USAF 463L pallets, bulk cargo-or wheeled vehicles. Maximum capacity for 25 pallets with access from both sides of the compartment, or 27 pallets with a single aisle on the starboard side.

SYSTEMS: As for DC-10-30CF.

AVIONICS AND EQUIPMENT: Include some additional military avionics, comprising navigation, communication, Tacan, IFF transponder, and modified commercial weather radar. Seven Goodyear Aerospace rubberised fabric fuel cells mounted in the lower fuselage compartments, with combined capacity of 53,446 kg

(117,829 lb) fuel, equivalent to approx 68,610 litres (18,125 US gallons), which are interconnected into the aircraft's basic fuel system. Flight refuelling boom mounted under rear fuselage, plus hose/reel unit for probe and drogue refuelling. Director lights to guide receiver. Flight refuelling receptacle mounted on fuselage upper surface above flight deck.

DIMENSIONS, EXTERNAL: As for DC-10-30CF except:
Length overall	55·35 m (181 ft 7 in)
Height overall	17·70 m (58 ft 1 in)
Wheel track	10·57 m (34 ft 8 in)

AREAS: As for DC-10-30CF

WEIGHTS AND LOADING (estimated):
Operating weight empty:	
tanker	108,973 kg (240,245 lb)
cargo	110,890 kg (244,471 lb)
Max cargo payload	76,897 kg (169,529 lb)
Design max T-O weight	267,620 kg (590,000 lb)
Max wing loading	727·8 kg/m² (149·06 lb/sq ft)

PERFORMANCE (estimated):
Critical field length	3,353 m (11,000 ft)
Max range with max cargo	3,797 nm (7,032 km; 4,370 miles)
Max ferry range, unrefuelled	9.993 nm (18.507 km; 11,500 miles)
	(1980-81)

MCDONNELL DOUGLAS PHANTOM II
US Navy and USAF designations: F-4 and RF-4

The Phantom II was developed initially as a twin-engined two-seat long-range all weather attack fighter for service with the US Navy. A letter of intent to order two prototypes was issued on 18 October 1954, at which time the aircraft was designated AH-1. The designation was changed to F4H-1 on 26 May 1955, with change of mission to missile fighter, and the prototype XF4H-1 flew for the first time on 27 May 1958. The first production Phantom II was delivered to US Navy Squadron VF-101 in December 1960. Trials in a ground attack role led to USAF orders, and the basic USN and USAF versions became the F-4B and F-4C respectively. Many other variants have appeared, as follows:

F-4A (formerly F4H-1F): Basic power plant comprised two General Electric J79-GE-2 turbojet engines, with afterburning. Total of 23 pre-production and 24 production aircraft built. After evaluation of this version, the USAF decided to order land-based versions of the F-4B under the designation F-4C.

F-4B (formerly F4H-1). All-weather fighter for US Navy and Marine Corps, powered by two General Electric J79-GE-8 turbojet engines. Total of 649 built. (See F-4G and F-4N.)

RF-4B (formerly F4H-1P). Multi-sensor reconnaissance version of F-4B for US Marine Corps. No dual controls or armament. Reconnaissance system as for RF-4C. J79-GE-8 engines. High-frequency single sideband radio. First flown on 12 March 1965. Overall length increased to 19·2 m (63 ft). Total of 46 built.

F-4C (formerly F-110A). Variant of F-4B for USAF, with J79-GE-15 turbojets, cartridge starting, wider-tread low-pressure tyres size 30 × 11·5, larger brakes, Litton type LN-12A/B (ASN-48) inertial navigation system, APQ-100 radar, APQ-100 PPI scope, LADD timer, Lear Siegler AJB-7 bombing system, GAM-83 controls, dual controls and boom flight refuelling instead of drogue (receptacle in top of fuselage, aft of cockpit). Folding wings and arrester gear retained. For close support and attack duties with Tactical Air Command, PACAF and USAFE, and with the Air National Guard (ANG) from January 1972. Sufficient F-4Cs were modified to equip two squadrons for a defence suppression role under the USAF's **Wild Weasel** programme. These aircraft carry ECM warning sensors, jamming pods, chaff dispensers

McDonnell Douglas F-4E Phantom II, with leading-edge slats

and anti-radiation missiles. First F-4C flew on 27 May 1963; 36 supplied to Spanish Air Force. The last of 583 was delivered to TAC on 4 May 1966. Replaced in production by F-4D.

RF-4C (formerly RF-110A). Multi-sensor reconnaissance version of F-4C for USAF, with radar and photographic systems in modified nose which increases overall length by 0·84 m (2 ft 9 in). Three basic reconnaissance systems are: side-looking radar to record high-definition radar picture of terrain on each side of flight path on film; infra-red detector to locate enemy forces under cover or at night by detecting exhaust gases and other heat sources; forward and side-looking cameras, including panoramic models with moving-lens elements for horizon-to-horizon pictures. Systems are operated from rear seat. HF single sideband radio. YRF-4C flew on 9 August 1963; first production RF-4C on 18 May 1964. Taken into service with ANG in February 1972. Production ended December 1973. Total of 505 built.

F-4D. Development of F-4C for USAF, with J79-GE-15 turbojets, APQ-109 fire control radar, ASG-22 servoed sight, ASQ-91 weapon release computer, ASG-22 lead computing amplifier, ASG-22 lead computing gyro, 30kVA generators, and ASN-63 inertial navigation system. First F-4D flew on 8 December 1965. Two squadrons of F-4Ds (32 aircraft) delivered to the Imperial Iranian Air Force and 18 to the Republic of Korea. Production completed. Total of 843 built.

F-4E. Multi-role fighter for air superiority, close support and interdiction missions with USAF. Has internally-mounted M-61A1 20 mm multi-barrel gun, improved (AN/APQ-120) fire-control system and J79-GE-17 turbojets (each 79·6 kN; 17,900 lb st). Additional fuselage fuel cell. First production F-4E delivered to USAF on 3 October 1967. Supplied to the Israeli Air Force, Hellenic Air Force, Turkish Air Force, Republic of Korea Air Force and Imperial Iranian Air Force. All F-4Es being fitted retrospectively with leading-edge manoeuvring slats.

In early 1973 F-4Es began to be fitted with Northrop's target identification system electro-optical (TISEO). Essentially a vidicon TV camera with a zoom lens, it aids positive visual identification of airborne or ground targets at long range. The ASX-1 TISEO is mounted in a cylindrical housing on the leading-edge of the port wing of the F-4E.

F-4G (Navy; no longer operational). Development of F-4B for US Navy, with AN/ASW-21 data link communications equipment, first flown on 20 March 1963. In service over Vietnam with Squadron VF-213 from USS *Kitty Hawk* in Spring of 1966. Only 12 were built and these are included in the total quoted for F-4B production.

F-4G (Advanced Wild Weasel). The USAF's Wild Weasel programme is concerned with the suppression of hostile weapon radar guidance systems. The provision of airborne equipment able to fulfil such a role, and modification of the necessary aircraft to create an effective force for deployment against such targets, had first priority in tactical Air Force planning in the Spring of 1975. In the interests of force standardisation and airframe life, the F-4E Phantom (see 1979-80 *Jane's*) was selected for modification to fulfil the Advanced Wild Weasel role, technical studies of the F-4D and F-4E having shown the latter aircraft to be easier to modify. External changes include the addition of a torpedo-shape fairing to the top of the tail fin to carry APR-38 antennae; removal of the M61A-1 gun system and its replacement by a chin pod containing APR-38 subsystems (receiver, homing and warning computer, computer interface system); and the addition of other APR-38 antennae, of which there are 56 in all on the fin-tip and fin sides, along the upper surface of the fuselage, and elsewhere. The new chin pod is of laminated glassfibre construction, and there are new fairing doors in place of the gun muzzle fairings. Internal modifications consist of a number of added and revised systems, chief of which is the McDonnell Douglas AN/APR-38 radar homing and warning system (RHAWS) itself. Changes have been made to the LCOSS (lead-computing optical sight system) amplifier in the upper equipment bay, and the computer interface system (CIS) installations in the front and rear cockpits; suitable cockpit displays have been provided. Additional equipment is installed in the compartment vacated by the ammunition for the M61 gun, and there is provision for further electronics packages if required. The gun purge scoop and entire gun hydraulic system of the F-4E are removed; pitot-static system drains are relocated in the chin pod; and a 7·5 cm (3 in) extension is added to the pitot-static nose boom. The radar cooling duct is modified, to provide open ducting for the APR-38 components on the equipment shelves in the nose. All gun control and APR-36/37 wiring in the F-4E is replaced by new wiring and co-axial cables for the APR-38 system in the radome, nose, inboard wing panels, and forward/centre/aft fuselage locations. New wiring uses F-15 assembly techniques and materials, and additional wiring provides interface with new weapons launchers. The Advanced Wild Weasel F-4G is cleared for operation with AGM-45 Shrike, AGM-78 Standard ARM, and AGM-65 Maverick (including IIR: imaging infra-red version) air-to-surface missiles. Use of the IIR Maverick greatly enhances night and adverse weather capability. Testing with AGM-88 HARM is under way. For self-defence, AIM-7F Sparrow and/or AIM-9L Sidewinder air-to-air missiles can also be carried.

A digital computer receives, processes and displays emitter information to the crew in the form of CRT presentations, digital readouts, advisory/warning lights, and aural tones. Computerised information is also provided to the weapon system for use in munition delivery, and to various instruments used by the crew to perform delivery manoeuvres. This frees both the pilot and the electronics warfare officer (EWO) of many of the analytical and manual duties once required, presents them with an accurate view of the enemy's defence environment, and allows them an unprecedented flexibility in seeking out and destroying those defences. The AN/APR-38 beam receivers (23 cm; 9 in arrays) which obtain range and azimuth information are located on the front and each side of the chin pod, and on the vertical fin looking aft. The range and azimuth information for all ground threats received is displayed on the plan position indicator (PPI), which is one of three scopes in the rear cockpit. There is a repeater PPI in the front cockpit. Priorities are assigned to the top 15 targets by the computer. Threats are indicated by letter and number symbols. A triangle is placed around the highest-priority threat, which is determined by the computer classification table. If desired, the EWO may override and designate a threat for the Weasel to work: this threat is designated by a diamond around the symbol. The homing and warning computer (HAWC) is one of the most important parts of the system. It can be re-programmed to include new or changed threats. The optical sight, which has been modified, indicates the radar emitter position with its red reticle. Ground track of the aircraft in azimuth is indicated by a green cross caged in elevation to the radar boresight of the aircraft. The Weasel pilot can bomb 'blind' by positioning the green cross over the reticle, depressing the bomb button, and starting a recovery. The selected store will release automatically at the correct point. The mission recorder provides the capability to play back the mission on the ground for training and study purposes.

Although the Advanced Wild Weasel F-4G aircraft would be able to operate independently in a hunter/killer role, their main utilisation is likely to be as a component of a strike force, where they would detect, identify, locate

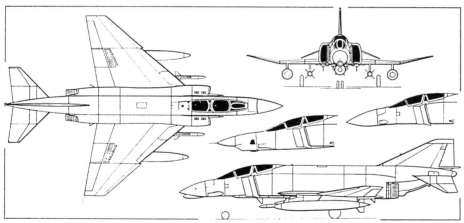

McDonnell F-4C Phantom II tactical fighter with additional scrap views of noses of RF-4C (left) F-4D (right)

McDonnell RF-4C multiple-sensor reconnaissance aircraft, with brake-chute streamed (*S. P. Peltz*)

and warn of hostile electromagnetic emitters, and deploy against them suitable weapons for their suppression or destruction.

The USAF sought funding in FY 1976 for the Advanced Wild Weasel concept, in order to provide an expansion in memory capability of the airborne processor and to extend coverage of low-frequency emissions. The programme provided for the first F-4G operational kit installation in the Spring of 1976 and the second in the Autumn of that year, followed by 15 installations in 1977, 60 in 1978, and 39 in 1979, to provide a force of 116 aircraft (96 for combat units, 20 for training and testing). The first F-4G was delivered on 28 April 1978, and the type entered service with the 35th Tactical Fighter Wing (39th Tactical Fighter Squadron, for training) at George AFB, California, in October 1978. The first two F-4Gs of 24 for the 81st TFS, USAFE, at Spangdahlem, Federal Republic of Germany, were delivered in the Spring of 1979.

F-4J. Development of F-4B for US Navy and Marine Corps, primarily as interceptor but with full ground attack capability. Powered by J79-GE-10 turbojets. Fitted initially with 16½° drooping ailerons and slotted tailplane, to reduce approach speed in spite of increased landing weight; Westinghouse AN/AWG-10 X-band pulse-Doppler fire-control system; Lear Siegler AJB-7 bombing system; and 30 kVA generators. First flight of a production F-4J was made on 27 May 1966; production of 522 examples was completed in January 1972. Before the end of the war in Viet-Nam, production F-4Js underwent a series of retrofit programmes, aimed chiefly at improving the aircraft's electronic warfare equipment. Under a programme named Shoehorn, the F-4J was equipped with an AN/APR-25 warning receiver, AN/APR-27 missile launch warning system, and an AN/ALQ-100 jamming system. Also incorporated at this time was an update of the AN/APX-76 IFF system, known as AIMS (Air traffic control radar beacon IFF Mk XII System). In 1971, the APR-25 and -27 were replaced by improved AN/ALR-45 and AN/ALR-50 warning receivers, which provided better threat response and displayed a letter/number readout instead of coded vectors. During 1973-74, an I-band AN/ALQ-126 jamming system replaced the earlier ALQ-100. In 1979 the Applied Technology Inc AN/APR-43 Compass Sail/Clockwise warning receiver and the AN/ALQ-162 Clockwise jamming system were being considered for installation in the F-4J, the former to replace the ALR-50, the latter as a complement to the ALQ-126. Other avionics in the F-4J included originally an RT-793 UHF com transceiver and AN/APR-69 UHF auxiliary receiver, replaced later by two Collins AN/ARC-159. It is planned to replace the latter, in the early 1980s, with Collins AN/ARC-182 VHF (AM/FM) and UHF (AM/FM) sets. Similarly, the earlier AN/ARN-86 Tacan was scheduled to be replaced from 1980 by the newer Collins AN/ARN-118 system. These new com/nav installations will permit relocation of the AN/APX-76 in a position more accessible for maintenance and overhaul. The original AN/APN-141 radar altimeter has been replaced by a Honeywell AN/APN-194 system.

F-4N. Number updated from F-4B was 227.

F-4S. The US Navy plans to modify up to 265 F-4Js, possibly more, under this designation. Changes include replacement of the original wing leading-edge flaps by highly-cambered, bulbous-nosed leading-edge slats; addition of an inboard leading-edge flap (similar to that on the F/RF-4B); and structural strengthening, including the fitting of steel fatigue straps under the lower skins of the inboard wing panels, at the main spar. Outer wing panels are of entirely new construction. Internally, the aircraft is completely rewired, using lightweight Kapton wiring; and has an improved Westinghouse AN/AWG-10A digital weapon control system. Modifications are undertaken jointly by McDonnell Douglas and the Naval Air Rework

McDonnell Douglas F-4G Advanced Wild Weasel. AN/APR-38 9 in beam receivers are visible in nose and sides of chin pod and on the fin-tip, facing aft

Facility at North Island, California. Deliveries began, with aircraft serial number 155565, to the Naval Air Test Center at Patuxent River, Maryland, on 11 May 1978.

A total of 5,057 completed Phantoms had been delivered from St Louis when production ended on 26 October 1979. This total included 2,597 for the US Air Force, 1,264 for the US Navy/Marine Corps, and 1,196 for foreign customers. In addition, 11 Phantoms were supplied in kit form to Japan for assembly by Mitsubishi, which built a further 127 under licence in that country, bringing total Phantom production to 5,195. McDonnell Douglas also completed, but did not assemble, 16 R F-4Es ordered by Iran before the change of government in that country in 1979. Instructions from the US government for the disposal of these 16 aircraft were still awaited in mid-1980. (1980—81)

A total of 4,742 Phantoms had been delivered by 1 January 1976.

The Phantom II has set up many official records, including a speed of 783·92 knots (1,452·777 km/h; 902·72 mph: Mach 1·2) over a hazardous 3 km low-level course (maximum altitude 100 m; 328 ft), by Lt Hunt Hardisty and Lt E. De Esch in one of the F-4As on 28 August 1961. This exceeded the previous (subsonic) record, set up eight years earlier, by more than 130 knots (240 km/h; 149 mph); and had not been beaten by mid-1976.

The following details apply to the F-4B:

TYPE: Twin-engined two-seat all-weather fighter.

WINGS: Cantilever low-wing monoplane. Average thickness/chord ratio 5·1%. Sweepback 45° on leading-edges. Outer panels have extended chord and dihedral of 12°. Centre-section and centre wings form one-piece structure from wing fold to wing fold. Portion that passes through fuselage comprises a torsion-box between the front and main spars (at 15% and 40% chord) and is sealed to form two integral fuel tanks. Spars are machined from large forgings. Centre wings also have forged rear spar. Centreline rib, wing-fold ribs, two intermediate ribs forward of main spar and two aft of main spar are also made from forgings. Wing skins machined from aluminium panels 0·0635 m (2½ in) thick, with integral stiffening. Trailing-edge is a one-piece aluminium honeycomb structure. Flaps and ailerons of all-metal construction, with aluminium honeycomb trailing-edges. Inset ailerons limited to down movement only, the 'up' function being supplied by hydraulically-operated spoilers on upper surface of each wing. Ailerons and spoilers fully powered by two independent hydraulic systems. Hydraulically-operated trailing-edge flaps and leading-edge flap on outboard half of each inner wing panel are 'blown'. Hydraulically-operated airbrake under each wing aft of wheel well. Outer wing panels fold upward for stowage.

FUSELAGE: All-metal semi-monocoque structure, built in forward, centre and rear sections. Forward fuselage fabricated in port and starboard halves, so that most internal wiring and finishing can be done before assembly. Keel and rear sections make extensive use of steel and titanium. Double-wall construction under fuel tanks and for lower section of rear fuselage, with ram-air cooling.

TAIL UNIT: Cantilever all-metal structure, with 23° of anhedral on one-piece all-moving tailplane. Ribs and stringers of tailplane are of steel, skin of titanium and trailing-edge of steel honeycomb. Rudder interconnected with ailerons at low speeds.

LANDING GEAR: Hydraulically-retractable tricycle type, main wheels retracting inward into wings, nose unit rearward. Single wheel on each main unit, with tyres size 30 × 7·70; twin wheels on nose unit, which is steerable and self-centering and can be lengthened pneumatically to increase the aircraft's angle of attack for take-off. Brake-chute housed in fuselage tailcone.

POWER PLANT: Two General Electric J79-GE-8 turbojet engines (each 75·6 kN; 17,000 lb st with afterburning). Variable-area inlet ducts monitored by air data computer. Integral fuel tankage in wings, between front and main spars, and in six fuselage tanks, with total capacity of 7,569 litres (2,000 US gallons). Provision for one 2,270 litre (600 US gallon) external tank under fuselage and two 1,400 litre (370 US gallon) underwing tanks. Equipment for probe-and-drogue and 'buddy tank' flight refuelling, with retractable probe in starboard side of fuselage.

ACCOMMODATION: Crew of two in tandem on Martin-Baker Mk H7 ejection seats, under individual rearward-hinged canopies. Optional dual controls.

SYSTEMS: Three independent hydraulic systems, each of 207 bars (3,000 lb/sq in). Pneumatic system for canopy operation, nosewheel strut extension and ram-air turbine extension. Primary electrical source is AC generator. No battery.

ELECTRONICS: Eclipse-Pioneer dead-reckoning navigation computer, Collins AN/ASQ-19 communications-navigation-identification package, AiResearch A/A 24G central air data computer, Raytheon radar altimeter, General Electric ASA-32 autopilot, RCA data link, Lear attitude indicator and AJB-3 bombing system. Westinghouse APQ-72 automatic radar fire-control system in nose. ACF Electronics AAA-4 infra-red detector under nose.

ARMAMENT: Six Sparrow III, or four Sparrow III and four Sidewinder, air-to-air missiles on four semi-submerged mountings under fuselage and two underwing mountings. Provision for carrying alternative loads of up to about 7,250 kg (16,000 lb) of nuclear or conventional bombs and missiles on five attachments under wings and fuselage. Typical loads include eighteen 750 lb bombs, fifteen 680 lb mines, eleven 1,000 lb bombs, seven smoke bombs, eleven 150 US gallon napalm bombs, four Bullpup air-to-surface missiles or fifteen packs of air-to-surface rockets.

DIMENSIONS, EXTERNAL:

Wing span	11·70 m (38 ft 5 in)
Width, wings folded	8·39 m (27 ft 6½ in)
Length overall	17·76 m (58 ft 3 in)
Height overall	4·96 m (16 ft 3 in)
Wheel track	5·30 m (17 ft 10½ in)

AREA:

Wings, gross	49·2 m² (530 sq ft)

WEIGHTS:

T-O weight ('clean')	20,865 kg (46,000 lb)
Max T-O weight	24,765 kg (54,600 lb)

PERFORMANCE:

Max level speed with external stores	over Mach 2
Approach speed	130 knots (240 km/h; 150 mph)
T-O run (interceptor)	1,525 m (5,000 ft)
Landing run (interceptor)	915 m (3,000 ft)
Combat radius:	
interceptor	over 781 nm (1,450 km; 900 miles)
ground attack	over 868 nm (1,600 km; 1,000 miles)
Ferry range	1,997 nm (3,700 km; 2,300 miles)

(1976—77)

Prototype of the new F-4J version of the Phantom II for the US Navy

MCDONNELL DOUGLAS SKYHAWK

US Navy designation: A-4

Designed originally to provide the US Navy and Marine Corps with a simple low-cost lightweight attack and ground suppport aircraft, the Skyhawk was based on experience gained during the Korean War. Since the initial requirement called for operation by the US Navy, special design consideration was given to providing low-speed control and stability during take-off and landing, added strength for catapult launch and arrested landings, and dimensions that would permit it to negotiate standard aircraft carrier lifts without the complexity of folding wings.

Construction of the XA-4A (originally XA4D-1) prototype Skyhawk began in September 1953 and the first flight of this aircraft, powered by a Wright J65-W-2 engine (32 kN; 7,200 lb st), took place on 22 June 1954.

Early Skyhawk versions included the A-4A, -4B, -4C and -4E, of which 1,845 examples were built. These were described in the 1973-74 *Jane's*; more recent versions are as follows:

TA-4E. Original designation of prototypes of TA-4F.

A-4F. Attack bomber with J52-P-8A turbojet (41·4 kN; 9,300 lb st), new lift-spoilers on wings to shorten landing run by up to 305 m (1,000 ft), nosewheel steering, low-pressure tyres, zero-zero ejection seat, additional bullet-and flak-resistant materials to protect pilot, updated electronics contained in fairing 'hump' aft of cockpit. Prototype flew for the first time on 31 August 1966. Deliveries to US Navy began on 20 June 1967, and were completed in 1968. 146 built.

TA-4F. Tandem two-seat dual-control trainer version of A-4F for US Navy. Fuselage extended 0·71 m (2 ft 4 in), fuselage fuel tankage reduced to 379 litres (100 US gallons), Pratt & Whitney J52-P-6 or -8A engine optional, Douglas Escapac rocket ejection seats. Provision to carry full range of weapons available for A-4F. Reduced electronics. First prototype flew on 30 June 1965. Deliveries to the US Navy began in May 1966.

A-4G. Similar to A-4F for Royal Australian Navy. Equipped to carry Sidewinder air-to-air missiles. First of eight delivered on 26 July 1967.

TA-4G. Similar to TA-4F for Royal Australian Navy. First of two delivered on 26 July 1967.

A-4H. Designation of version supplied to Israel. Delivery of an initial batch of 48 in 1967-68, followed by 60 more by early 1972.

TA-4H. Tandem two-seat trainer version of the A-4H for Israel. Ten delivered.

TA-4J. Tandem two-seat trainer, basically a simplified version of the TA-4F. Ordered for US Naval Air Advanced Training Command, under $26,834,000 contract, followed by further contract in mid-1971. Deletion of the following equipment, although provisions retained: radar, dead reckoning navigation system, low-altitude bombing system, air-to-ground missile systems, weapons delivery computer and automatic release, intervalometer, gun pod, standard stores pylons, in-flight refuelling system and spray tank provisions. Addition and relocation of certain instruments. J52-P-6 engine standard. Provision for J52-P-8A engine and combat avionics. Prototype flew in May 1969 and the first four were delivered to the US Navy on 6 June 1969. In production.

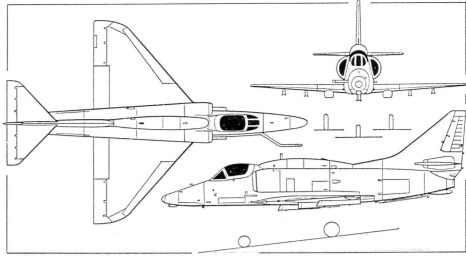

McDonnell Douglas A-4M Skyhawk II single-seat light attack aircraft (*Pilot Press*)

McDonnell Douglas TA-4J tandem two-seat training version of the Skyhawk

A-4K. Similar to A-4F, for Royal New Zealand Air Force. Different radio, and braking parachute. First of ten handed over to the RNZAF on 16 January 1970.

TA-4K. Similar to TA-4F, for Royal New Zealand Air Force. The first of four was handed over to the RNZAF on 16 January 1970.

TA-4KU. Designation of six aircraft, similar to the TA-4F, for Kuwait Air Force.

A-4L. Modification of A-4C with uprated engine, bombing computing system and avionics relocated in fairing "hump" aft of cockpit as on A-4F. Delivery to US Navy Reserve carrier air wing began in December 1969.

A-4M Skyhawk II. Similar to A-4F, but with J52-P-408 turbojet (50 kN; 11,200 lb st) and braking parachute standard, making possible combat operation from 1,220 m (4,000 ft) fields and claimed to increase combat effectiveness by 30%. Larger windscreen and canopy; windscreen bullet-resistant. Increased ammunition capacity for 20 mm cannon. More powerful generator, provision of wind-driven backup generator and self-contained engine starter. First of two prototypes flew for the first time on 10 April 1970. About 50 ordered initially for US Marine Corps, the first of which was delivered on 3 November 1970. Further order was placed subsequently, and the FY 1976 budget includes $70 million for the procurement of a final 24 aircraft. Funds have been allocated also for the installation of improved electronic warfare equipment in service aircraft, and for the continued development of an Angle Rate Bombing System (ARBS) for future installation in A-4Ms (see A-4Y). In production for USMC and Kuwait (36).

A-4N Skyhawk II. Light attack version ordered by US Navy for export. Basically similar to A-4M. First flown on 8 June 1972. In production.

A-4P. Revised A-4B for Argentine Air Force (50).

A-4Q. Revised A-4B for Argentine Navy (16).

A-4S. Designation of 40 Skyhawks for service with Singapore Air Defence Command. Conversion from ex-USN A-4Bs began in 1973, carried out by Lockheed Aircraft Service Company, under which heading all available details are given.

TA-4S. Three two-seat A-4B conversions for Singapore, by Lockheed Aircraft Service Company (which see).

A-4Y. USMC A-4M with updated HUD, redesigned cockpit and Hughes Angle Rate Bombing System (ARBS). All A-4Ms to be modified. Final procurement probably will be new-build A-4Ys.

Current US Navy planning calls for continued production of the Skyhawk into 1977, and logistic support for its continued usage into the 1980s.

The following structural description refers specifically to the A-4M:

TYPE: Single-seat attack bomber.

WINGS: Cantilever low-wing monoplane. Sweepback 33° at quarter-chord. All-metal three-spar structure. Spars machined from solid plate in one piece tip-to-tip. One-

McDonnell Douglas A-4M Skyhawk II attack aircraft of US Marine Corps Squadron VMA-324

FUSELAGE: All-metal semi-monocoque structure in two sections. Rear section removable for engine servicing. Outward-hinged hydraulically-actuated airbrake on each side of rear fuselage. Detachable nose over communications and navigation equipment. Integral flak-resistant armour in cockpit area, with internal armour plate below and forward of cockpit.

TAIL UNIT: Cantilever all-metal structure. Electrically-actuated variable-incidence tailplane. Hydraulically-powered elevators. Powered rudder with unique central skin and external stiffeners.

LANDING GEAR: Hydraulically-retractable tricycle type, with single wheel on each unit. All units retract forward. Free-fall emergency extension. Main legs pre-shorten for retraction and wheels turn through 90° to stow horizontally in wings. Menasco shock-absorbers. Hydraulic nosewheel steering. Ribbon-type braking parachute of 4·88 m (16 ft) diameter contained in canister secured in rear fuselage below engine exhaust. Arrester hook for carrier operation.

POWER PLANT: One 50 kN (11,200 lb st) Pratt & Whitney J52-P-408 turbojet engine. Fuel in integral wing tanks and self-sealing fuselage tank aft of cockpit, total capacity 3,028 litres (800 US gallons). One 568, 1,136 or 1,514 litre (150, 300 or 400 US gallon) auxiliary tank can be carried on the underfuselage bomb-rack, and one 150 or 300 US gallon auxiliary tank on each of the inboard underwing racks. Maximum fuel capacity, internal plus auxiliary tanks, 6,814 litres (1,800 US gallons). Large flight refuelling probe on starboard side of nose. Douglas-developed self-contained flight refuelling unit can be carried on the underfuselage standard bomb shackles. Provisions for JATO.

ACCOMMODATION: Pilot on Douglas Escapac 1-G3 zero-zero lightweight ejection seat. Enlarged cockpit enclosure to improve pilot's view, with rectangular bullet-resistant windscreen.

SYSTEMS: Dual hydraulic system. Oxygen system. Electrical system powered by 20kVA generator, with wind-driven generator to provide emergency power.

ELECTRONICS: Include Bendix Automatic Flight Control, ARC-159 UHF radio transceiver, ARA-50 UHF direction finder, APX-72 IFF, Marconi-Elliott AVQ-24 head-up display system, Douglas angle of attack indicator, electronic countermeasures, ASN-41 nav computer, APN-153(V) radar nav, ARC-114 VHF/FM radio transceiver, ARR-69 auxiliary radio receiver, ARN-84 Tacan and APN-194 radar altimeter.

ARMAMENT: Provision for several hundred variations of military load, carried externally on one underfuselage rack, capacity 1,588 kg (3,500 lb); two inboard underwing racks, capacity of each 1,020 kg (2,250 lb); and two outboard underwing racks, capacity of each 450 kg (1,000 lb). Weapons that can be deployed include nuclear or HE bombs, air-to-surface and air-to-air rockets, Sidewinder infra-red missiles, Bullpup air-to-surface missiles, ground attack gun pods, torpedoes, countermeasures equipment, etc. Two 20 mm Mk 12 cannon in wing roots standard, each with 200 rounds of ammunition. DEFA 30 mm cannon available as optional on international versions, with 150 rounds of ammunition per gun.

McDonnell Douglas A-4M Skyhawk II attack aircraft of the US Marine Corps

DIMENSIONS, EXTERNAL:

Wing span	8·38 m (27 ft 6 in)
Wing chord at root	4·72 m (15 ft 6 in)
Length overall (excl flight refuelling probe):	
A-4M	12·29 m (40 ft 4 in)
TA-4F	12·98 m (42 ft 7¼ in)
Height overall:	
A-4M	4·57 m (15 ft 0 in)
TA-4F	4·66 m (15 ft 3 in)
Tailplane span	3·45 m (11 ft 4 in)
Wheel track	2·37 m (7 ft 9½ in)

AREAS:

Wings, gross	24·16 m² (260 sq ft)
Vertical tail surfaces (total)	4·65 m² (50 sq ft)
Horizontal tail surfaces (total)	4·54 m² (48·85 sq ft)

WEIGHTS:

Weight empty:	
A-4F	4,581 kg (10,100 lb)
TA-4F	4,853 kg (10,700 lb)
A-4M	4,899 kg (10,800 lb)

Normal T-O weight:	
A-4F, M, TA-4F	11,113 kg (24,500 lb)
*A-4F from land base	12,437 kg (27,420 lb)

export version only: overload condition not authorised by US Navy

PERFORMANCE (at combat weight):

Max level speed:	
TA-4F	568 knots (1,052 km/h; 654 mph)
Max level speed (with 1,814 kg; 4,000 lb bomb load):	
A-4F	548 knots (1,015 km/h; 631 mph)
A-4M	561 knots (1,040 km/h; 646 mph)
Max rate of climb (ISA at S/L):	
A-4F	2,440 m (8,000 ft)/min
A-4M	3,140 m (10,300 ft)/min
Rate of climb (ISA at 7,620 m; 25,000 ft):	
A-4F	1,097 m (3,600 ft)/min
A-4M	1,463 m (4,800 ft)/min
T-O run (at 10,433 kg; 23,000 lb T-O weight):	
A-4F	1,030 m (3,380 ft)
A-4M	832 m (2,730 ft)
Max ferry range, A-4M at 11,113 kg (24,500 lb)	
T-O weight with max fuel, standard reserves	
	1,740 nm (3,225 km; 2,000 miles)
	(1975–76)

AV-8B HARRIER II

In late 1973 and early 1974 the British and US governments received for approval various proposals for an advanced version of the BAe (HS) Harrier (see UK section). Subsequent to this came the announcement, on 15 May 1975, of the first British order for Sea Harrier FRS. Mk 1s for the Royal Navy.

Two months before the announcement of this order, the British Secretary of State for Defence, Mr Roy Mason, had stated that there was "not enough common ground on the Advanced Harrier for us to join in the programme with the US", and development studies for a US version have therefore been continued primarily by McDonnell Douglas to meet requirements of the US Navy and Marine Corps.

Essentially, the objective of the Advanced Harrier programme is to evolve a version which, without too much of a departure from the existing Harrier airframe, would virtually double the aircraft's weapons payload/combat radius.

The USMC has stated a requirement for 336 Advanced Harriers, and initially McDonnell Douglas and the USMC modified two AV-8As as prototype YAV-8Bs. The first of these flew for the first time on 9 November 1978, and the second in February 1979. Prototype demonstration was completed in Summer 1979, in 185 test flights totalling 173 flying hours, during which the two aircraft met or exceeded all performance requirements specified by the Marine Corps and Naval Air Systems Command. The second prototype was lost during its 106th flight, on 15 November 1979.

Aim of the AV-8B is to achieve the improved performance capability required of the original AV-16A proposal by aerodynamic means, while retaining the same basic F402-RR-404 (Pegasus 11) engine, thus saving the cost of developing the Pegasus 15 engine that was originally considered necessary for the advanced version.

Aerodynamic changes include use of a supercritical wing; the addition of under-gun-pod strakes and a movable flap panel forward of the pods, to increase lift for vertical take-off; the use of larger wing trailing-edge flaps and drooped ailerons; and redesigned engine air intakes. The landing gear is strengthened to cater for the higher operating weights and greater external stores loads made possible by these changes.

Four full-scale development aircraft are to be built next, contingent on further action by Congress and passage of the 1981 Defense Department budget; the first of these is scheduled to fly in October 1981, with Navy BIS (Bureau of Inspection and Survey) trials following in Spring 1983. The operational date planned for the AV-8B is mid-1985, should production be approved. McDonnell Douglas would be prime contractor for the airframe, with British Aerospace as subcontractor; prime engine contractor would be Rolls-Royce, with Pratt & Whitney as subcontractor.

The following description applies to the proposed production AV-8B:

TYPE: Single-seat V/STOL combat aircraft.

WINGS: Cantilever shoulder-wing monoplane, of broadly similar planform to Harrier/AV-8A but of supercritical section, approx 20% greater in span and 14% greater in area. Thickness/chord ratio 11·5% at root, 7·5% at tip. 10° less sweepback on leading-edges, and non-swept inboard trailing-edges. Composite construction, making extensive use of graphite epoxy in the main multi-spar torsion box, ribs, skins, outrigger fairings and wingtips. Trailing-edge single-slotted flaps, of substantially greater chord than those of AV-8A, with flap slot closure doors. Drooping ailerons, also of graphite epoxy construction.

FUSELAGE: Generally similar to AV-8A, but longer. New forward fuselage, with raised cockpit, constructed from graphite epoxy composite material, and additional lift-augmenting surfaces. These comprise a fixed strake on each of the two underfuselage gun packs, and a retractable forward flap just aft of the nosewheel unit. During VTOL modes the 'box' formed by the ventral strakes and the lowered nose flap augment lift by trapping the cushion of air bounced off the ground by the engine exhaust. This additional lift allows the AV-8B to take off vertically at a gross weight equal to its maximum hovering gross weight.

TAIL UNIT: Taller fin than that of AV-8A, resembling that of UK Sea Harrier. New tailplane planform, with constant sweep on leading-edges and reduced sweep on trailing-edges.

LANDING GEAR: Main landing gear strengthened to cater for higher operating weights. Dowty Rotol/Cleveland outrigger wheels, moved inboard to approx mid-span beneath each wing between flaps and ailerons, and with fairings deleted on production AV-8B.

POWER PLANT: One Rolls-Royce Pegasus (F402-RR-404) vectored-thrust turbofan engine rated at 95·64 kN (21,500 lb st). Engine air intakes redesigned, with elliptical lip shape and double instead of single row of suction relief doors. Increased fuel tankage available in wings, raising total internal fuel capacity (fuselage and wing tanks) from approx 2,268 kg (5,000 lb) in the AV-8A to 3,402 kg (7,500 lb) in the AV-8B. Each of the four inner underwing stations capable of carrying an auxiliary fuel tank. Probe for in-flight refuelling.

ACCOMMODATION: Pilot only, on ejection seat, in pressurised, heated and air-conditioned cockpit. In production configuration the cockpit is raised by comparison with the AV-8B prototype, and has a redesigned windscreen and canopy to provide a better all-round view.

AVIONICS AND EQUIPMENT: Improved attitude and heading reference system, AN/ARN-84 Tacan, AN/ARC-159 UHF, AN/APX-100 IFF, visual landing aids, inertial navigation system, dual combining glass head-up display, and CRT multi-purpose display. Marconi Avionics self-contained pitch and roll autostabilisation computer, with built-in rate gyroscopes and added electronic package to interface with forward reaction control nozzle. Garrett-AiResearch air data computer.

ARMAMENT AND OPERATIONAL EQUIPMENT: Twin underfuselage gun/ammunition packs, each mounting a US 25 mm cannon or a 30 mm Aden gun. Single 454 kg (1,000 lb) stores point on fuselage centreline, between gun packs. Three stores stations under each wing, the inner one capable of carrying a 907 kg (2,000 lb) store, the centre one 454 kg (1,000 lb), and the outer one 286 kg (630 lb). The four inner wing stations are 'wet', permitting the carriage of auxiliary fuel tanks. Including fuel, stores, weapons and ammunition, and water injection for the engine, the maximum useful load for vertical take-off is approximately 3,175 kg (7,000 lb), and for short take-off nearly 7,710 kg (17,000 lb). Typical weapons include Mk 82 Snakeye bombs, and laser or electro-optical guided weapons. Main weapon delivery by Angle Rate Bombing System (ARBS), comprising a dual-mode (TV and laser) target seeker linked to a Marconi head-up display via an IBM digital computer. Passive ECM equipment.

DIMENSIONS, EXTERNAL:
Wing span	approx 9·25 m (30 ft 4 in)
Length overall	14·12 m (46 ft 4 in)
Height overall	3·56 m (11 ft 8 in)

AREA:
Wings, gross	21·37 m² (230 sq ft)

McDonnell Douglas YAV-8B Advanced Harrier, armed with five 500 lb bombs and two Sidewinder missiles, with which it can take off vertically

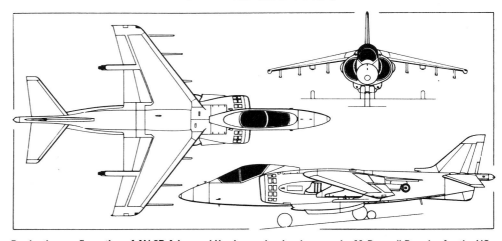

Production configuration of AV-8B Advanced Harrier, under development by McDonnell Douglas for the US Marine Corps (Pilot Press)

WEIGHTS:
Basic operating weight empty	5,783 kg (12,750 lb)
Max fuel, internal and external	7,180 kg (15,829 lb)
Max T-O weight: STO	13,494 kg (29,750 lb)
VTO	8,913 kg (19,650 lb)
Design landing weight	8,799 kg (19,400 lb)

PERFORMANCE (estimated):
Operational radius with external loads shown:
short T-O (305 m; 1,000 ft), twelve Mk 82 Snakeye bombs, internal fuel, 1 h loiter
more than 150 nm (278 km; 172 miles)
short T-O (305 m; 1,000 ft), seven Mk 82 Snakeye bombs, external fuel tanks, no loiter
more than 650 nm (1,204 km; 748 miles)
Unrefuelled ferry range
2,600 nm (4,825 km; 3,000 miles)

BRITISH AEROSPACE/McDONNELL DOUGLAS AV-8C HARRIER

The AV-8C is an updated conversion of the basic AV-8A Harrier that was produced by British Aerospace for the US Marine Corps. All 61 existing AV-8As are to be updated to the improved standard; the first conversions were made by McDonnell Douglas, the remainder will be carried out by the Marine Corps at Cherry Point, North Carolina. Details of the AV-8C can be found in the British Aerospace entry in the UK section. (1980–81)

THE NAVAL AIRCRAFT FACTORY.

The Naval Aircraft Factory is the main supply depôt and test station for U.S. Naval Aviation. It serves as a station for testing materials, structures, engines, catapults, etc., and develops specifications and standards for naval aircraft.

After the War, the factory undertook the design and manufacture of complete aircraft, but after the completion of the PN-9 flying-boat aircraft construction was abandoned.

Under the Vinson-Trammell Treaty Navy Bill of 1935, it was stipulated that at least ten per cent. of the aircraft and aeroengines bought by the Navy should be of Government manufacture, and under the 1936 Naval Appropriations the following construction work was assigned to the Naval Aircraft Factory :— one experimental training aeroplane ; one hundred and eighty-five service type training aircraft ; one twelve-cylinder engine ; one hundred engines for training aircraft ; and a design for a high-speed engine, a two-stroke Vee type engine and a compression-ignition engine. (1941)

The order for 185 training aeroplanes was based on the experimental XN3N-1, which was built at the Factory and tested at Anacostia and Pensacola in 1935. Delivery of the production N3N-1 biplanes began in June, 1936, and was completed in 1938. Twenty of them were fitted with 235 h.p. NAF-R760 engines built under Wright licence. These were followed by the N3N-3, 650 of which have been produced or are being built. An experimental XN5N-1 primary trainer was under test at the time of writing.

The N3N-3 Two-seat Training Biplane produced by the Naval Aircraft Factory.

Naval Aircraft Factory PN-7, -8 and -9

Two new types of Naval Patrol Planes are under construction for the Naval Bureau of Aeronautics. These machines will be seagoing flying-boats with a cruising range of 2,200-2,500 miles.

The other machine, Type PN-9, has been built at the Naval Aircraft Factory in Philadelphia. This machine is a further link in the development of an efficient seagoing patrol plane which started with the PN-7. The next step was the development of the PN-8, which is identical with the PN-7, except for having a metal hull.

PN-9 was produced by replacing the Wright engines of PN-8 by two of the new Packard 1A. 1,500 engines, fitted with reduction gears, which are rated in this form at 480 h.p. for a weight of 850 lbs. each. This new power plant is appreciably lighter than that of PN-8, is practically as powerful, thanks to the geared-down airscrews, and consumes rather less fuel.

At the same time it has been possible appreciably to increase the fuel capacity, which in PN-9 amounts to about 1,200 gallons.

Specification of the PN-9.

Span, top	72 ft. 10 in.
Span, bottom	67 ft. 2 in.
Length	49 ft. 2 in.
Height	16 ft. 6 in.
Wing area (appr.)	1,250 sq. ft.
Weight empty (appr.)	9,000 lbs.
Max. weight loaded (appr.)	18,000 lbs.
Speed level (normal Service load)	128 m.p.h.

The U.S. Navy's P.N.7 Flying Boat (2 Wright T.III engines.).

(1925)

Naval Aircraft Factory PN-12

The Factory has developed numerous types of aircraft since its establishment; the large flying-boats which are used for patrol purposes have been left almost exclusively for development by the Factory. The latest unit of this type is the PN-12. This machine is a further link in the development of an efficient sea-going patrol boat which started with the PN-7. The development of a metal hull was the characteristic feature of the PN-8. Turning attention to long-distance patrol work, geared Packard engines were used in the next model, which embodied all the best features of the PN-7 and PN-8, and was known as the PN-9. The PN-10 was more robustly built and was provided with two 600 h.p. Packard geared engines. The purpose in this instance was to give the service a very sturdy sea-going flying-boat.

The PN-12 development has two improvements, first, the application of the 525 h.p. Wright R-1750 air-cooled engines and the development of a suitable set of metal wings. The reduction in weight obtained by the adoption of air-cooled engines and the development of metal wings has been very marked. The water-cooled installation weighed 9,400 lbs. without personnel, fuel or military load. The air-cooled, metal-winged, machine weighs approximately 7,500 lbs.

THE PN-12.

The PN-12 reached the stage which justified its production in quantity and as it is not the function of the Naval Aircraft Factory to indulge in quantity production in competition with the trade, the general designs of this aircraft were submitted to several aircraft constructors for its ultimate development by them.

The Glenn L. Martin Co., of Baltimore, were entrusted with a production order for a patrol flying-boat of the PN-12 type, and this machine is designated the PM-1.

The Keystone Aircraft Corpn., of Bristol, P.A., and the Douglas Aircraft Co., of Santa Monica, Cal., have constructed a number of patrol flying-boats similar to the PN-12, which is described hereunder. These two types are designated the PK-1 and the PD-1 respectively.

TYPE.—Twin-engined patrol and heavy bomber flying-boat.
WINGS.—Unstaggered single-bay biplane. Top and bottom centre-sections interconnected by a triangulated system of steel-tube struts. Extremities of lower centre-section braced to hull by parallel steel-tube struts. One pair of widely-splayed interplane struts on either side of hull. Spar and rib construction of duralumin with fabric covering. Ailerons on upper planes only and have auxiliary balance surfaces.
HULL.—All-metal, two-step Vee-bottomed type, very similar to the old F-5-L type. Keelson, longitudinals and the transverse frames are of duralumin, with alloy steel fittings at the highly stressed points. Four transverse water-tight bulkheads divide the hull into separate compartments. The outer covering is duralumin sheet, riveted to all constructional members with duralumin rivets.

TAIL UNIT.—Monoplane type. Duralumin framework, with fabric covering. Adjustable tail-plane. Rudder has auxiliary balanced surfaces.
POWER PLANT.—Two 525 h.p. Wright "Cyclone" R-1750D, air-cooled radial engines. Main fuel tanks (six) located amidships in the hull, aft of the pilot's cockpit. Oil tanks are located in the cowling aft of each engine.
ACCOMMODATION.—Crew of five is carried. The navigator-bombers' cockpit is in the nose and has a flexible gun-mounting. This cockpit is also equipped with bomb-sights, navigating instruments and folding chart board, and also serves as the stowage place for anchor and mooring gear. Immediately behind is the open pilot's cockpit, seating two side-by-side, with dual bridge-type control and instruments for each pilot. Aft of the cockpit is the fuel compartment, and this is followed by the gunner-mechanic's station. The wireless compartment is further aft, and this is followed by the after machine-gun station.
DIMENSIONS.—Span (upper) 72 ft. 11 in. (22.23 m.), Span (lower) 67 ft. 2 in. (20.53 m.), Length 49 ft. 2 in. (14.9 m.), Height 16 ft. 4 in. (4.97 m.), Wing area 1,162 sq. ft. (107.9 sq. m.).
WEIGHTS.—Weight empty 7,453 lbs. (3,383.6 kg.), Disposable load 6,669 lbs. (3,027.8 kg.), Weight loaded 14,122 lbs. (6,411.4 kg.).
PERFORMANCE.—Maximum speed 114 m.p.h. (182.4 km.h.), Stalling speed 58 m.p.h. (92.8 km.h.), Service ceiling 10,900 ft. (3,325 m.), Range at cruising speed 1,300 miles (2,080 km.).

(1931)

Naval Aircraft Factory T-Type Seaplanes

During the past year the Naval Aircraft Factory produced several single-seater fighting seaplanes, designated as Types TR and TS. These types were built to the designs of Comdr. J. C. Hunsaker, U.S.N., Chief of the Design Division, Bureau of Aeronautics, Navy Department, for service with Fleet Aviation. For this reason these planes were particularly designed with a view to insuring rapid assembly and dissembly, and minimum encumbrance. Wires and turnbuckles are entirely eliminated in the wing bracing, which is insured by rigid streamlined struts. The fuel tank is carried in the lower wing and is made detachable so that in case of fire, due to incendiary bullets, the pilot can pull a release which will drop the tank and its inflammable contents clear of the machine. Provision is made for an interchangeable landing gear, twin floats or wheels being fitted according to the nature of the service demanded. In landing operations this machine can therefore be used from shore stations too.

The TS and TR types are absolutely identical, save for the wing curve and the power plant. The TS types have the U.S.A.27 wing curve, while the TR types have the R.A.F.15. As to the power plant, the TS1 and the TR1 are both fitted with the 220 h.p. Lawrance J-1 air-cooled radial, the TS2 with the 240 h.p. Aeromarine U-873, and the TR3 with the 220 h.p. Wright E-2 "Alert" engine, the latter two engines being of the water-cooled type.

These four machines were entered by the U.S. Navy, with some older types, in the Curtiss Marine Flying Trophy Race held at Detroit, Mich., on October 7th, 1922, in order to determine which combination of wing curve and power plant would give the best result under the trying conditions of a race involving several obligatory landings on water, taxi-ing and immediate take-offs. As the race was won by Lieut. A. W. Gorton, U.S.N., who was flying the TR1 fitted with the air-cooled Lawrance engine and with the R.A.F.15 aerofoil, the conclusions may be drawn by the reader. This race furnished the American naval authorities with a valuable full-scale experiment for trying out design modifications under competitive conditions, and as such it was of the greatest technical interest.

Specification of the TS and TR Fighting Seaplanes.

Type of machine	Twin-float Tractor Biplane.
Name or type No.	TS or TR.

The American Navy Type T.R.1 (220 h.p. Lawrance engine).

Span, top and bottom..	25 ft. (7.62 m.).	TR3	220 h.p. Wright E-2 "Alert."
Overall length	24 ft. 7 in. (7.5 m.).		
Maximum height	9 ft. 6¾ in. (2.92 m.).	Weight loaded.	
Chord	4 ft. 9 in. (1.45 m.).	TS types	2,025-2,085 lbs. (920-945 kgs.).
Gap	5 ft. 6 in. (1.675 m.).		
Angle of incidence	0°.	TR types	1,790-1,980 lbs. (815-900 kgs.).
Dihedral (bottom only)	3°.		
Total wing area	225 sq. ft. (21 sq. m.).	Performance.	
Engine type and h.p.		High speed	130 m.p.h. (210 km.h.) for all except for TS1, which is 125 m.p.h. (202 km.h.) (1923)
TR1 and TS1	220 h.p. Lawrance J-1.		
TS2	240 h.p. Aeromarine U-873.		

An NC. Boat, (Liberty Engine.)

N.C. (NAVY-CURTISS) SEAPLANE.

The N.C. (Navy-Curtiss) type, which achieved fame through the American Transatlantic Flight Expedition (1919), was not, as is often assumed, specially built for that purpose. The main function of this type, of which a dozen or so have since been built, is to act as "flotilla leaders" to the Atlantic and the Pacific Air Forces of the U.S. Navy, which are chiefly composed of F-5-L flying boats. These forces have, during the past year, made extensive cruises in the Caribbean and along the Pacific Coast, and the matériel has generally given a good account of itself, if one considers the difficult conditions under which it was called to operate.

NC.1, NC.3, NC.4 (1919).

Specification.

Type of machine	Tractor-pusher Flying Boat.
Name or type No. of machine ..	Navy-Curtiss.
Purpose for which intended ..	High Sea Scouting.
Armament	8 M.G.
Crew	5 men.
Span	126 ft. (U), 96 ft. (L).
Overall length	68 ft. 3½ in.
Maximum height	24 ft. 6 in.
Total wing area	2,380 sq. ft.
Engine type and h.p... ..	Four 420 h.p. Liberty "Twelves" (high compression model).
Total horsepower	1,600 h.p.
Airscrews	3 tractors and 1 pusher.
Tank capacity	1,800 U.S. galls.

Weight empty	15,100 lbs.
Weight loaded	28,000 lbs.

Performance.

High speed, with light load ..	90 m.p.h.
High speed, with full load ..	81 m.p.h.

Climb.

To 1,000 feet	5 mins.
Range (economical)	1,470 naut. miles.

Engineering Data.

Weights.—Hull empty, 2,650 lbs. Wing pontoons, 95 lbs. each. Petrol, 11,400 lbs. Oil, 900 lbs. Crew and provisions, 1,000 lbs. Wing loading, 12 lbs. per sq. ft. Power loading, 17.8 lbs. per b.h.p. Carrying efficiency, 47 per cent.

Wings.—Section, Navy Special. Chord, 12 ft. Gap, 14 ft. at centre and 12 ft. at tips. Fittings of chrome vanadium steel, of 150,000 lbs. ultimate strength.

Areas.—Ailerons, 265 sq. ft. Tail plane, 267.6 sq. ft. Elevator. 240.1 sq. ft. Rudders, 69 sq. ft.

Note.—The designs of this type were prepared in the Bureau of Construction and Repair, U.S. Navy Department, by Naval Constructors H. C. Richardson, G. C. Westervelt and J. C. Hunsaker, U.S.N. The construction was carried out by the Curtiss Engineering Corporation at their Works in Garden City, N.Y. The hull of NC.2 and NC.4 was built by the yacht builder Herreshoff, that of the NC.3 by Lawley Bros., Boston.

(1922)

The Noorduyn UC-64A "Norseman" Utility Transport on skis (550 h.p. Pratt & Whitney "Wasp" engine).

THE NOORDUYN "NORSEMAN" Mk V.

The tremendous expansion of this Company's facilities, personnel and output which set in shortly after the outbreak of war, has continued throughout the past year. Aircraft types in production are the "Harvard IIB" (U.S. designation AT-16) advanced trainer for the Joint Air Training Plan, for use in Canada and other British Overseas Dominions, and the Noorduyn "Norseman" (U.S. designation UC-64), as a general utility cargo and passenger transport for the U.S. Army Air Forces. The latter is the only Canadian-designed aircraft now in production and is also used by the R.C.A.F. for the training of wireless operators and for communication duties.

Up to the end of 1942, the number of employees had expanded 600%, factory floor space more than 1,500% and the output of complete aircraft for 1942 exceeded that for 1940 by over 3,000%. For the first 6 months of 1943, the output of complete aircraft was 3.4 times the number delivered during the corresponding period of 1942 and exceeded the output for the whole of 1942. Contract schedules were substantially outpaced.

The firm also operates the main repair department in Canada for "Harvard" and "Norseman" aircraft, and produces ski equipment for these and several other service types.

U.S. Army Air Forces designation: UC-64A.

TYPE.—Single-engined Transport monoplane suitable for various military and civil duties.

WINGS.—High-wing braced monoplane. Wings attached direct to top of fuselage longerons and braced to stubs by steel tube Vee struts. Structure consists of routed solid spruce spars with walnut packing-pieces under fittings, spruce ribs, steel-tube drag struts and swaged wire bracing, duralumin covered leading-edge, fabric covering. Flaps and ailerons have steel tube frame and fabric covering. Slotted mass-balanced ailerons and flaps. Ailerons droop as flaps with first half of flap movement.

FUSELAGE.—Welded chrome-molybdenum steel-tube framework, faired to an oval section by steel-tube frames and "T" section spruce stringers and covered with fabric.

TAIL UNIT.—Braced monoplane type. Tail-plane structure same as for wings. Fin, rudder and elevators have welded steel-tube frames with fabric covering. Trimming-tabs in elevators and rudder.

LANDING GEAR.—Divided type. Consists of two cantilever oleo legs which may be removed from the fuselage stubs by removing two bolts each for substitution of standard Edo type Yd floats or approved skis of Noorduyn or other design. Tail-wheel strut may carry either wheel or tail-ski.

POWER PLANT.—One Pratt & Whitney "Wasp" R-1340-AN1 nine-cylinder radial air-cooled engine rated at 550 h.p. at 5,000 ft. (1,525 m.) and with 600 h.p. available for take-off. NACA cowling. Two-bladed Hamilton-Standard constant-speed airscrew. "Eclipse" direct electric starter with emergency hand-crank. Fuel tanks (two) in wing-roots (100 Imp. gallons = 120 U.S. gallons) with gravity feed to engine-driven pump. One or two additional tanks of 37 Imp. gallons (45 U.S. gallons) and 64 Imp. gallons (75 U.S. gallons) respectively may be installed in baggage space under floor of cabin, thus providing alternative fuel capacities of 100 Imp. gallons (120 U.S. gallons), 137 Imp. gallons (165 U.S. gallons) or 201 Imp. gallons (242 U.S. gallons). Oil capacity 8-16 Imp. gallons (10-20 U.S. gallons). Equipment includes oil dilution system.

ACCOMMODATION.—Pilot's enclosed and heated cockpit seating two side-by-side in front of wings. Full-size doors on each side. Pilot's seat and rudder pedals fully adjustable. Swing-over type dual control. Below wing is main sound-proofed cabin of 150 cub. ft. capacity. Bench-type seats for eight passengers may be instantly removed. Individual upholstered passenger chairs optional. One passenger door hinged on additional removable section to provide 46 in. opening when required. Fixed front and cabin windows, lowering cockpit and cabin door windows. Additional space for baggage or freight below floor of cabin (33 cub. ft.) and behind cabin (10 cub. ft.) with outside doors. Cabin heater with three controllable outlets. Lower part of back wall of cabin may be removed for stowage of long articles of freight into tail of fuselage.

DIMENSIONS.—Span 51 ft. 8 in. (15.8 m.), Length 31 ft. 9 in. (9.68 m.), Height 10 ft. 1 in. (3 m.), Wing area 325 sq. ft. (30.2 sq. m.).

WEIGHTS AND LOADINGS.—Weight empty—Landplane Freighter 4,420 lbs. (2,007 kg.), Seaplane Freighter 4,890 lbs. (2,220 kg.), Skiplane Freighter 4,600 lbs. (2,088 kg.). Additional weight for 6-passenger military cabin equipment 54 lbs. (24.5 kg.), Additional weight for 8-passenger commercial cabin equipment 120 lbs. (54.5 kg.), Weight loaded (Landplane, Seaplane or Skiplane): 7,400 lbs. (3,360 k.g.), Wing loading 22.8 lbs./sq. ft. (111.26 kg./sq. m.), Power loading (take-off) 12.3 lbs./h.p. (5.58 kg./h.p.).

PERFORMANCE.—Cruising speed (75% power)—Landplane: 148 m.p.h. (236.8 km.h.), Seaplane: 130 m.p.h. (208 km.h.), Skiplane: 142 m.p.h. (227.2 km.h.), Landing speed 68 m.p.h. (108.8 km.h.), Climb (Landplane) to 5,000 ft. (1,525 m.) 6.5 min., to 10,000 ft. (3,050 m.) 15.5 min., to 15,000 ft. (4,575 m.) 28.5 min., Service ceiling (Landplane) 17,000 ft. (5,185 m.), Cruising range at 75% power and maximum tankage (Landplane) 1,150 miles (1,840 km.).

(1943–44)

THE NORTH AMERICAN BT-9.

TYPE.—Two-seat advanced training monoplane.

WINGS.—Low-wing cantilever monoplane. Wing in five sections, comprising centre-section, two outer tapering sections and two quickly-removable and interchangeable tip sections. Single-spar construction with spaced ribs and stressed-skin covering. Statically and aerodynamically-balanced ailerons have aluminium-alloy frames and are covered with fabric. Split trailing-edge flaps on centre-section and outer-sections.

FUSELAGE.—Welded chrome-molybdenum steel-tube structure in four sections, comprising the engine mounting, control section, tail section and monocoque bottom aft of wings. All sections are bolted together. Metal decking. Sides covered with detachable fabric-covered aluminium-alloy frames.

TAIL UNIT.—Cantilever monoplane type. Fixed tail-plane. Interchangeable balanced elevators with controllable trimming tabs. Balanced rudder with trimming-tab adjustable on ground only. Aluminium-alloy frames with fabric covering.

UNDERCARRIAGE.—Fixed type. Consists of two single interchangeable shock-absorber legs with half forks, attached by four bolts to built-in castings in centre-section. Air-oil shock absorbers. Duralumin fairings over legs and inner halves of wheels. Streamline wheels accessible without removal of fairings. Hydraulic brakes operated from both cockpits, parking brake in front cockpit only. Steerable tail-wheel with friction damper to prevent oscillation.

POWER PLANT.—One 400 h.p. Wright R-975-E7 radial air-cooled engine in N.A.C.A. cowling. All cowling panels quickly removable and interchangeable. Two fuel tanks (104 U.S. gallons) in centre-section under fuselage. Oil tank (9.5 U.S. gallons) in engine compartment. Controllable-pitch airscrew.

ACCOMMODATION.—Tandem cockpits with individually-operated sliding enclosures of laminated glass in steel frames. Complete dual controls and standard instrument equipment in each cockpit. Blind-flying hood in front cockpit. Complete electrical equipment. Two-way radio and radio compass. Armament consists of one synchronised gun firing forward through the airscrew and (on

The North American BT-9 Two-seat Advanced Training Monoplane (400 h.p. Wright R-975-E7 engine).

Reserve Corps machines) one gun on track mounting to rear cockpit. Rear gun completely housed when not in use. Camera mounting and aperture aft of rear cockpit. Large baggage compartment.

DIMENSIONS.—Span 42 ft. (12.8 m.), Length 27 ft. 3 in. (8.38 m.). Height 8 ft. 8 in. (2.6 m.), Wing area 248 sq. ft. (23 sq. m.).

WEIGHTS.—Weight empty 2,825 lbs. (1,285.37 kg.), Crew 370 lbs.

(168.3 kg.), Fuel and oil 695 lbs. (314 kg.), Weight loaded 3,860 lbs. (1,756.3 kg.).

PERFORMANCE.—Maximum speed 175 m.p.h. (282 km.h.), Cruising speed 155 m.p.h. (250 km.h.), Landing speed 56 m.p.h. (90 km.h.), Maximum rate of climb 1,350 ft./min. (411.75 m./min.), Climb to 10,000 ft. (3,050 m.) 10 mins., Service ceiling 19,000 ft. (5,795 m.), Cruising range 810 miles (1,304 km.). (1936)

The North American BT-14 (NA-16-1) Two-seat Primary Training Monoplane (420 h.p. Wright "Whirlwind" engine).

THE NORTH AMERICAN NA-16-1A.
U.S. Army Air Forces designation: BT-14.
R.A.F. name: "Yale."

TYPE.—Two-seat primary training monoplane.

WINGS.—Low-wing cantilever monoplane. Wing section varies from NACA 2215 to 4412. In five sections, consisting of centre-section, two outer-sections and two wing-tips. Centre-section of parallel chord and thickness, outer-sections have back-swept leading-edge and straight trailing-edge and taper in thickness. Single-spar structure with spaced ribs and covered with a stressed aluminium-alloy skin. Dynamically-balanced ailerons with aluminium-alloy frames and fabric covering. Split trailing-edge flaps between ailerons and under fuselage.

FUSELAGE.—Welded chrome-molybdenum steel-tube framework with fittings integrally welded. Fuselage constructed in four sections, engine-mounting, control section, tail section and monocoque bottom aft of wing. All sections bolt together. Side covering in form of fabric-covered aluminium-alloy frames bolted to fuselage. Cowling all metal and quickly removable.

TAIL UNIT.—Cantilever tail-plane and fin of metal, with sheet covering. Rudder and elevators have light-alloy frames, with fabric covering. Right and left sides of tail-plane and elevators are interchangeable. Metal surfaces are removable by externally-accessible bolts for internal inspection. Non-reversible trimming-tabs on elevators. Fixed tab, adjustable on ground only, on rudder.

UNDERCARRIAGE.—Divided type. Consists of two cantilever oleo struts, with the upper ends built into the ends of the centre-section by sleeves held by four bolts. Right and left units interchangeable. Each unit enclosed in duralumin fairing, which does not enclose the streamline wheel, so that it is accessible for brake adjustment or removal. Hydraulically-operated wheel-brakes. Oleo-sprung steerable tail-wheel.

POWER PLANT.—One Wright "Whirlwind" R-975-E3 radial air-cooled engine, developing 420 h.p. at 1,400 ft. (426 m.), on welded chrome-molybdenum steel-tube mounting. NACA cowling. Fuel tanks (two), of welded aluminium-alloy, in centre-section, one on each side of fuselage. Normal fuel capacity 104 U.S. gallons. Oil tank (9.5 U.S. gallons) in engine compartment and detachable with it.

ACCOMMODATION.—Tandem cockpits, with sliding enclosures. Dual controls, with rear control quickly removable.

DIMENSIONS.—Span 41 ft. (13.1 m.), Length 28 ft. 5 in. (8.7 m.), Height 8 ft. 10½ in. (2.7 m.), Wing area 246 sq. ft. (23 sq. m.).

WEIGHTS AND LOADINGS.—Weight empty 3,247 lbs. (1,473 kg.), Crew 380 lbs. (172.5 kg.), Fuel and oil 695 lbs. (315 kg.), Weight loaded 4,375 lbs. (2,065 kg.), Wing loading 17.7 lbs./sq. ft. (86.7 kg./sq. m.), Power loading 10.4 lbs./h.p. (4.7 kg./h.p.).

PERFORMANCE.—Speed at 1,500 ft. (457.5 m.) 170 m.p.h. (274 km.h.), Cruising speed at 1,500 ft. (457.5 m.) 146 m.p.h. (235 km.h.), Landing speed 65 m.p.h. (105 km.h.), Maximum rate of climb 1,100 ft./min. (336 m./min.), Service ceiling 17,400 ft. (5,310 m.), Cruising range 730 miles (1,180 km.). (1941)

The North American FJ-I Fury Single-seat Naval Fighter (Allison J-35 turbojet engine). (*Hugh J. T. Young*).

THE NORTH AMERICAN FURY.
U.S. Navy designation : FJ-1 (N.A. 141).

The XFJ-1 (N.A. 134) marked the entry of North American into the field of jet-propelled military aircraft. The prototype first flew on November 27, 1946. Early in 1947 it reached a Mach. number of .87, the highest attained by an American fighter up to that time.

Thirty FJ-1's have been delivered to the U.S. Navy and are being used for jet fighter familiarisation. Two squadrons have been equipped with Furies, one with the Pacific and one with the Atlantic Fleet. In March, 1948, Squadron 51 equipped with Furies made the first operational jet landing and take-offs at sea in the U.S.S. *Boxer*.

TYPE.—Single-seat Jet propelled Naval Fighter.

WINGS.—Low-wing cantilever monoplane. Thin laminar-flow wing section. Dihedral 5°. All-metal structure with flush-riveted stressed skin. Perforated "low-swirl" dive brakes above and below wings out-board of landing-gear. Gross wing area 274.8 sq. ft. (26.54 mm.).

FUSELAGE.—Oval all-metal structure with flush-riveted stressed skin.

TAIL UNIT.—Cantilever monoplane type. All-metal structure with stressed skin. Tailplane dihedral 10°. Tailplane span 17 ft. 7 in. (5.36 m.).

LANDING GEAR.—Retractable tricycle type. Hydraulic retraction. Bendix air-oil shock struts. Goodyear wheels and single-disc hydraulic brakes. Nose wheel strut has supplementary independent action to permit aircraft to "kneel" on small two-wheel dolly fitted to nose wheel strut for tail-up carrier stowage. Main landing-gear is set at neutral and kneeling operation conducted externally through radio compartment door by hand-operated hydraulic pump. Wheel track 15 ft. 10½ in. (4.84 m.).

POWER PLANT.—One Allison TG-180 (J-35A-5) axial-flow gas turbine (4,000 lb.=1,820 kg. s.t.) with straight ram air entry in nose of fuselage. Main fuel tanks in fuselage. Wing-tip jettisonable tanks, with built-in wing-tip lights. Total fuel capacity 800 U.S. gallons (3,025 litres), including two 170 U.S. gallon (643 litre) drop tanks.

ACCOMMODATION.—Pilot's cockpit with sliding "bubble" canopy. Cordite ejector seat.

ARMAMENT.—Six 0.50-in. machine-guns in nose of fuselage.

DIMENSIONS.—
Span 38 ft. 1 in. (10.7 m.).
Length 33 ft. 7 in. (10.5 m.).
Height (over tail) 14 ft. 6 in. (4.42 m.).

LOADED WEIGHT.—
12,697 lb. (5,675 kg.).

PERFORMANCE.—
Max. speed over 550 m.p.h. (880 km.h.).
Cruising speed over 350 m.p.h. (560 km.h.).
Stalling speed 102.9 m.p.h. (164.6 km.h.).
Climb at sea level 5,120 ft./min. (1,560 m./min.).

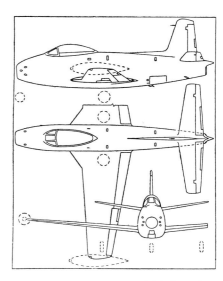

The North American FJ-1 Fury.

Range (with drop tanks) over 1,500 miles (2,400 km.).
Endurance (max.) over 4 hours. (1949–50)

THE NORTH AMERICAN FURY
U.S. Navy designation : FJ

The versions of the Fury currently in service with the U.S. Navy are single-seat swept-wing carrier fighters developed from the F-86 Sabre.

The landing-gear is similar to that of the Sabre but the nose-wheel unit is so designed that the normal nose-up static attitude can be increased for catapulting.

Extension of the nose-wheel shock strut is by hydraulic means and is achieved by a manually-controlled selector valve which is operated by the carrier deck crew. When the landing-gear is retracted after take-off hydraulic fluid returns to the reservoir. The extendable nose-wheel strut increases the angle between the thrust line and deck from 4 to 8 degrees.

Armament consists of four 20 mm. cannon and, on the later versions, six Philco Sidewinder air-to-air missiles. A Navy gun-sight and an improved Navy ejection-seat are fitted.

The following operational versions of the swept-wing Fury were built before production ended in 1958 :—

FJ-2. General Electric J47-GE-2 engine (5,270 lb.=2,390 kg. s.t.). First production version. The prototype

A North American FJ-4B Fury armed with three Bullpup missiles

XFJ-2, which first flew on February 14, 1952, was a semi-navalised F-86E without folding wings or armament. The cannon armament was first installed in the XFJ-2B, which was otherwise a standard F-86E. Produced at Columbus, Ohio, and now in service with U.S. Navy Reserve units.

FJ-3. Wright J65-W-2 engine (7,200 lb.=3,270 kg. s.t.). Larger and slightly heavier version of FJ-2 with enhanced performance. Manufactured at Columbus, Ohio, and in service with U.S. Navy. XFJ-3 prototype flew for first time on July 3, 1953.

FJ-4. Wright J65-W-4 engine (7,800 lb.=3,540 kg. s.t.). Improved version of FJ-3. First aircraft designed, developed and built by Columbus Division of N.A.A. New thin wing with mechanically-drooped leading-edge, slotted flaps and drooping split ailerons, new thinner-section all-moving tail, redesigned long-stroke landing gear, addition of dorsal

spine from fin to cockpit. Can be equipped with "buddy" system of flight refuelling as described under entry for North American Super Sabre. First of two prototype FJ-4's flew on October 28, 1954, and first production model in March, 1955.

FJ-4B. Attack fighter with Wright J65-W-16A engine (approximately 7,800 lb.=3,540 kg. s.t.). Basically similar to FJ-4, with low altitude bombing system and control system improvements for high speeds at very low altitude. Armament comprises four 20 mm. cannon, and six Sidewinder air-to-air missiles, or six bombs, or rockets, or four external tanks with total capacity of 700 U.S. gallons (2,650 litres). First FJ-4B flown on December 3, 1956.

DIMENSIONS (FJ-3).—
Span 37 ft. 1 in. (11.3 m.)
Length 37 ft. 6 in. (11.45 m.)
Height 13 ft. 8 in. (4.16 m.)

DIMENSIONS (FJ-4 and FJ-4B).—
Span 39 ft. 1 in. (11.92 m.)
Length 37 ft. 6 in. (11.45 m.)
Height 12 ft. 8 in. (3.86 m.)
Width folded 27 ft. 6 in. (8.38 m.)

WEIGHTS.—
Max. T.O. weight (FJ-3) over 18,000 lb. (8,170 kg.)
Max. T.O. weight (FJ-4) over 19,000 lb. (8,626 kg.)
Max. T.O. weight (FJ-4B) over 26,000 lb. (11,795 kg.)

PERFORMANCE (FJ-3).—
Max. speed 650 m.p.h. (1,050 km.h.)
Service ceiling 45,000 ft. (13,700 m.)
Combat range over 1,030 miles (1,650 km.)
PERFORMANCE (FJ-4).—
Max. speed over 690 m.p.h. (1,110 km.h.)
Service ceiling over 45,000 ft. (13,700 m.)

(1960–61)

The North American B-25H Mitchell Medium Bomber armed with a 75 m/m. cannon and fourteen 50-cal. machine-guns.

THE NORTH AMERICAN MITCHELL.
U.S. Army Air Forces designations : B-25, F-10.
U.S. Navy designation : PBJ.
British name : Mitchell.

The design of the XB-25 was approved in September, 1939, and the prototype flew on August 19, 1940. The XB-25 and the first few B-25's had wings with constant dihedral from roots to tips but from the 10th aircraft off the production line the outer wings were re-rigged flat to give the characteristic "gull-wing" arrangement which has since been such a distinctive feature of the Mitchell. The armament consisted of four 30 cal. machine-guns, one in the nose and three amidships, and one 50 cal. gun in the tail. The normal bomb load was 2,000 lbs. (910 kg.) with a maximum permissible overload of 3,600 lbs. (1,635 kg.). A crew of five was carried. The power-plant consisted of two 1,700 h.p. Wright R-2600-9 fourteen-cylinder radial engines each driving a Hamilton-Standard airscrew, 12 ft. 7 in. (3.84 m.) diameter.

B-25A. Similar to the B-25 except that self-sealing fuel tanks and armour for the pilot were added.

B-25B (Mitchell I). This model had a completely revised armament. The nose gun remained but the midship and tail guns were replaced by two Bendix electrically-operated turrets each with two 50 cal. machine-guns. The lower turret was retractable and remotely controlled. The former tail gun position became a prone observation post. A separate photographic station was located between the upper turret and the tail. Overall length, 54 ft. 1 in. (16.49 m.). Aircraft of this model were used on the Tokyo raid on April 18, 1942.

B-25C and B-25D (PBJ-1C and D and Mitchell II). These models were virtually the same as the B-25B but were equipped with automatic flight control equipment. Wright R-2600-13 engines with 1,700 h.p. available for take-off were substituted

for the earlier power-units. B-25C built in the Inglewood, Cal., plant, B-25D built in the Kansas City plant. The Mitchell II was first reported in action with the R.A.F. on January 22, 1943.

B-25E and F. One only of each model. Both fitted experimentally with heated-surface anti-icing equipment to wings and tail surfaces, a different system being used for each model.

B-25G (PBJ-1G). The first aircraft to be fitted with a 75 m/m. cannon. This cannon is installed in a new armoured nose which also includes two 50 cal. machine-guns. The 75 m/m. (2.953 in.) M-4 aircraft cannon is 9 ft. 6 in. (2.9 m.) long and weighs about 900 lbs. (410 kg.). It is mounted in a cradle extending aft under the pilot's seat where a hydro-spring mechanism takes care of the 21 in. (53 cm.) recoil. Each shell is 23 in. (58 cm.) long and weighs 15 lbs. (6.8 kg.). Aft of the nose the armament is the same as for the B-25C. The standard bomb-bay is retained but is modified to permit the installation of a standard aircraft torpedo. The crew is reduced to four, comprising the pilot (who fires the nose armament and releases the bombs or torpedo); navigator (who also hand-loads the cannon); gunner (who mans the upper turret and operates the camera); and radio operator (who also mans the lower turret). Overall length, 50 ft. 10 in. (15.50 m.).

B-25H (PBJ-1H). A development of the B-25H but with a greatly enhanced armament. The forward firing-guns are increased to include four 50 cal. machine-guns in the armoured nose and two pairs of 50 cal. "package" guns, one pair on each side of the fuselage in line with the pilot's cockpit.

The top turret is moved forward into the roof of the navigator's compartment. Between the wings and tail are two new waist positions, each armed with one 50 cal. gun. Finally, there is a new tail gun position armed with two 50 cal. guns. The crew is increased to five and their duties rearranged as follows :—pilot (who fires forward-firing armament and releases

The North American B-25J Mitchell Medium Bomber (two Wright R-2600-29 engines).

The North American F-10 Mitchell, an unarmed Photographic-Reconnaissance version of the B-25 Medium Bomber.

bombs or torpedo); navigator-radio operator (who also loads the cannon); flight engineer (who also mans the top turret); midship gunner (responsible for guns in both waist positions and also operates camera); and tail gunner. Overall length, 51 ft. 3¾ in. (15.63 m.).

B-25J (PBJ-IJ and Mitchell III). This is the precision bomber version of the B-25H. A glazed nose of the B-25C type replaces the armoured nose and the nose armament is reduced to one fixed and one flexible 50 cal. machine-guns. Aft of the nose the armament remains the same as for the B-25H. The crew is increased to six to include a bombardier. Internal bomb load increased to from 2,000 to 6,000 lbs. (2,720 m.) for short range operations. Overall length, 53 ft. 5¾ in. (16.3 m.).

TB-25 (formerly AT-24). A number of earlier Mitchells were de-militarised and converted into training aircraft. These were originally given the designation AT-24. This was later cancelled and they are now known by the classification TB-25.

F-10. A specially-equipped photographic reconnaissance version of the B-25. All armament was removed and a variety of cameras installed, including a tri-metrogon camera in the nose.

TYPE.—Twin-engined Medium Bomber.
WINGS.—Mid-wing cantilever monoplane of all-metal construction. Wing in five sections consisting of a two-spar centre-section permanently attached to the fuselage, two outer single-spar sections and two detachable wing-tips. Fuel and oil tanks integral with the centre-section structure. Outer wings have sealed compartments for flotation purposes. Ailerons of sealed type and are fitted with fixed and controllable trimming-tabs. Hydraulically operated slotted trailing-edge flaps inboard of ailerons and divided by tails of engine nacelles. Flaps have fairings which hinge upward into the wings to form a continuous slot opening when the flaps are lowered.
FUSELAGE.—Semi-monocoque four-longeron structure of aluminium-alloy with covering of same material. That portion of the fuselage above the bottom surface of the centre-section and between the front spar and trailing-edge is permanently attached to and removable with the centre-section.
TAIL UNIT.—Cantilever monoplane type with twin fins and rudders. Elevators and rudders have fixed and controllable trimming-tabs.
LANDING GEAR.—Tricycle type with all wheels fully retractable. All wheels retract aft, the main wheels into the engine nacelles and

the nose wheel and tail-skid into the fuselage. Doors cover all openings in both the retracted and extended positions. Hydraulic retraction, with a mechanically-operated emergency system. The swivelling nose-wheel has shimmy damper and centering device and lock. Main wheels have hydraulic brakes.
POWER PLANT.—Two Wright Cyclone R-2600-13 two-row radial air-cooled engines with two-speed superchargers in semi-monocoque nacelles mounted below the extremities of the centre-section. Three-bladed Hamilton-Standard constant-speed full-feathering airscrews with anti-icers. Each engine fitted with independent fuel system consisting of two interconnected fore and aft compartments equipped with bullet-proof self-sealing fuel cells located between fuselage and nacelles. Three auxiliary fuel cells in centre-section outboard of each engine nacelle together with a self-sealing tank in fuselage above bomb-bay. All fuel lines in wings and fuselage are of self-sealing type. Additional droppable long-range ferry tank may be installed in bomb-bay. Each engine has independent oil system.
ACCOMMODATION.—Provision for crew of from four to six. (See above). All crew positions are armoured. Heating and ventilation systems, radio equipment, oxygen etc.
ARMAMENT.—For various models see introduction. Bomb-bay in fuselage beneath wings may accommodate bombs, depth-charges or a torpedo. Maximum internal bomb-load 3,000 lbs. Provision for 2,400 lb. bombs on external wing racks. 2,150 lb. torpedo only partly enclosed in bomb-bay.
DIMENSIONS.—Span 67 ft. 7 in. (20.6 m.), Length 53 ft. 5¾ in. (16.13 m.), Height 16 ft. 4¾ in. (4.6 m.), Wing area 609.8 sq. ft. (56.6 sq. m.).
WEIGHTS—Weight empty 21,100 lbs. (9,580 kg.), Weight loaded 33,500 lbs (15,210 kg.).
PERFORMANCE.—Maximum speed 303 m.p.h. (485 km.h.) at 13,000 ft. (3,965 m.), Landing speed 95 m.p.h. (152 km.h.), Climb to 15,000 ft. (4,575 m.), 11.3 min., Service ceiling 24,200 ft. (7,380 m).
(1945—46)

The North American O-47B (NA-25) Observation Monoplane (1,000 h.p. Wright "Cyclone" GR-1820-G103A engine).
(Photograph by Peter Bowers)

THE NORTH AMERICAN NA-25.

U.S. Army Air Forces designation: O-47B.

TYPE.—Three-seat observation monoplane.

WINGS.—Mid-wing cantilever monoplane. Structure of metal covered aluminium-alloy construction. Centre-section built integral with the fuselage, two removable outer panels and two detachable wing-tips. Front and rear spars of outer structure are of single-web type. Ailerons have metal frames and leading-edges and are fabric-covered. Split trailing-edge flaps between ailerons and fuselage. Flaps are of aluminium-alloy construction and are hydraulically-operated and manually-controlled. Watertight compartments in outer wings for flotation. These compartments are fitted with suitable bilge pump connections, are interconnected and are adequately ventilated and drained to the lowest point.

FUSELAGE.—Semi-monocoque of aluminium-alloy construction. A stainless steel sheet of single thickness forms the fireproof bulkhead and is riveted to the forward end of the fuselage. A chrome-molybdenum steel-tube pylon behind the pilot's compartment forms an emergency nose-over protection of the crew. Provision in this pylon for hoisting.

TAIL UNIT.—Cantilever monoplane type. All-metal fin and tail-plane. Metal-framed and fabric-covered elevators and rudder.

UNDERCARRIAGE.—Retractable type. Wheels raised outwardly into wings by engine-driven hydraulic system. Air-oil shock-absorbers with 8-in. travel. Hydraulically-operated wheel-brakes. Parking brake provided with automatic temperature compensating unit. Fairing is provided to cover units when retracted into wing.

POWER PLANT.—One Wright "Cyclone" GR-1820-G103A nine-cylinder radial air-cooled engine with 1,000 h.p. available for take-off, easily removable as a unit. Fuel tank of 150 U.S. gallons capacity, including reserve. Three-bladed controllable-pitch airscrew.

ACCOMMODATION.—Three seats in tandem. Individual manually-operated sliding sections over pilot's station and auxiliary station. Dual controls except for airscrew control. Ample space provided for radio.

DIMENSIONS.—Span 46 ft. 3⅝ in. (14.1 m.), Length 33 ft. 2⅞ in. (10.1 m.), Height 12 ft. ½ in. (3.6 m.), Wing area 348.63 sq. ft. (32.38 sq. m.).

WEIGHTS AND LOADINGS.—Weight empty 6,035 lbs. (2,737 kg.), Normal disposable load 1,845 lbs. (837 kg.), Weight loaded 7,800 lbs. (3,574 kg.), Maximum overloaded weight 8,312 lbs. (3,770 kg.), Normal wing loading 22.6 lbs. sq./ft. (110.3 kg./sq. m.), Power loading 9.15 lbs./h.p. (4.2 kg./h.p.).

PERFORMANCE (Wright "Cyclone" BR-1820-G103A engine).—Maximum speed 240 m.p.h. (386 km.h.) at 12,000 ft. (3,660 m.), Cruising speed 218 m.p.h. (351 km.h.) at 16,000 ft. (4,875 m.), Landing speed (with flaps) 67 m.p.h. (108 km.h.), Climb to 10,000 ft. (3,050 m.) 5.75 mins., Service ceiling 28,500 ft. (8,690 m.), Cruising range (fuel 100 U.S. gallons) 500 miles (805 km.), Cruising range (fuel 150 U.S. gallons) 750 miles (1,207 km.), Economical cruising range (100 U.S. gallons fuel) 582 miles (937 km.), Economical cruising range (150 U.S. gallons fuel) 853 miles (1,372 km.).

(1941)

THE NORTH AMERICAN MUSTANG.

U.S. Army Air Forces designations : P-51, A-36 and F-6.
British name : Mustang.

The N.A. 73 Mustang was designed and built to a British specification and order. The prototype was actually designed, built and flown in 100 days, its first flight taking place in October, 1940. Passing all tests satisfactorily it was put into production before the end of 1940. The first production Mustang I was delivered to the R.A.F. in Great Britain in November, 1941.

The 5th and 10th aircraft off the production lines were taken over by the American Army for experimental test at Wright Field, Dayton, Ohio, and these two aircraft were given the designation XP-51. The first two batches of Mustangs, amounting to over 600 aircraft, were supplied under British contracts but after the passing of the Lease-Lend Act the aircraft were ordered by the American authorities as the P-51 and allotted to Great Britain. On the entry of America into the war a proportion of the P-51 contracts was diverted to the U.S. Army Air Forces.

Mustang I (P-51). The Mustang I was fitted with the Allison V-1710-F3R engine rated at 1,000 h.p. at 12,000 ft. (3,660 m.) and with 1,150 h.p. available for take-off. Its armament consisted of two 50 cal. and four 30 cal. machine-guns, two of the 50 cal. guns being mounted in the fuselage, one on each side of the engine crankcase and synchronised to fire through the airscrew. All the other guns were in the wings.

Owing to poor performance at height the Mustang I was re-mustered as a low-altitude reconnaissance fighter and posted to the R.A.F. Army Co-operation Command. An oblique camera for tactical photographic reconnaissance was installed in the port backward-vision panel behind the pilot, together with a vertical camera in the rear fuselage. The Mustang I made its first operational sortie with Army Co-operation Command on July 27, 1942.

Mustang IA (P-51). This was the Mustang I with an armament of four 20 m/m. cannon mounted in the wings.

Mustang II (P-51A). Initially the new designation covered solely a change in armament to four 50 cal. machine-guns, all in the wings. Later series were fitted with the Allison V-1710-81 (F20R) engine rated at 1,125 h.p. at 15,500 ft. (4,700 m.) and with 1,200 h.p. available for take-off.

The contracts for this model were equally divided between Great Britain and America. From the American P-51A were developed the A-36A dive-bomber and the F-6A photographic-reconnaissance model (see later).

P-51B and P-51C (Mustang III). These were the first models to be fitted with the Merlin engine and four-bladed airscrew. The original conversion was made in Great Britain by Rolls-Royce, Ltd. by the installation of the Merlin 61 engine in the Mustang II. The success of the conversion was such that steps were immediately taken by N.A.A. to re-design the P-51 to take the 1,520 h.p. Packard V-1650-3 (Packard-built Merlin 68 with two-speed two stage supercharger and aftercooler) which was at that time going into production in the United States. The airframe was strengthened to take the new engine, the radiator installation was re-designed, new ailerons were installed and streamline racks for long-range tanks or two 500 lb. bombs were provided under the wings. The bomb load was later increased to two 1,000 lb. bombs. The new design was originally given the designation XP-78 but this was later changed to P-51B.

The P-51B and P-51C were put into production in 1943, the P-51C at the Dallas plant of North American Aviation, Inc. of Texas. The first Merlin-engined Mustangs were delivered to a U.S. Combat Group of the 8th Air Force in Great Britain, on December 1 of that year. The P-51B first went into action as a fighter on December 17, and on January 15, 1944, P-51B's with drop tanks made their first long-range mission as fighter escort to heavy bombers of the 8th Air Force over Germany.

A modification which had no bearing on the designation was the introduction of the Malcolm backward-sliding bulged cockpit

The North American P-51B Mustang Single-seat Fighter (Packard Merlin V-1650-3 engine).

hood on examples of the P-51B, P-51C and F-6A. This modific-ation was undertaken in the British Isles.

P-51D (Mustang IV). A development of the P-51B with the armament increased to six 50 cal. machine-guns, all in the wings. Fitted with a moulded plastic "blister" type sliding hood and a modified rear fuselage. A later modification was the introduction of a small dorsal extension to the fin. This modification was made retrospective for the P-51B, C and earlier D models.

XP-51F. A complete structural redesign of the Mustang as a pure interceptor, to a combination of the optimum British and American strength requirements. No single structural part interchangeable with earlier P-51 models. New low-drag laminar-flow wing section, new wing plan, improved fuselage and radiator fairing contours, new lightened engine-mounting and landing-gear, substitution of heat exchanger for oil radiator, simplified hydraulic system and cockpit layout, etc. Structural weight reduced by 1,600 lbs. (726 kg.). Armament reduced to four 50-cal. guns. Reduced petrol capacity.

XP-51G. A redesign of the XP-51H into a long-range escort fighter. Higher powered Packard Merlin V-1650-9 engine, which called for a longer fuselage (12 in.) and increase in area and aspect ratio of tail surfaces. Armament reverted to six 50 cal. guns and internal fuel capacity increased with additional fuselage tank behind pilot.

P-51H. Production version of XP-51G with further improve-ments including a new Merlin V-1650-11 engine developing a maximum of over 2,000 h.p. with water injection and 150 grade fuel, changes in control surfaces, etc. 700 lbs. (318 kg.) lighter than P-51D. Armament six 50-cal. guns. Can also carry ten 5-in. rockets or maximum of two 1,000 lb. bombs or two 110 gallon drop tanks.

P-51K. Similar to the P-51D except fitted with the Aero-products instead of the Hamilton Standard Hydromatic four-bladed constant-speed airscrew. All built at the Dallas plant of North American Aviation, Inc.

A-36A. This was an attack or dive-bomber version of the P-51A. Development began in June, 1942 and the first model flew in September of that year.

It was fitted with the 1,325 Allison V-1710-87 (F21R) engine, and had hydraulically-operated dive-brakes and a rack under each wing to carry either a bomb (250, 300 or 500 lb.), or a droppable fuel tank. Armament comprised six 50 cal. machine-guns, two in the fuselage and two in each outer wing.

The A-36 went into service with the U.S.A.A.F. in the Medit-erranean just prior to the invasion of Sicily. Production was completed in March, 1943.

F-6. This is a photographic-reconnaissance version of the P-51. Photographic equipment replaced all armament. The P-51A was fitted with the 1,200 h.p. Allison V-1710-81 (F20R) engine. For improved vision certain aircraft of this model were fitted with the Malcolm bulged sliding hood as shown in the accompanying illustration. The F-6D was similar to the P-51D and the F-6K was similar to the P-51K.

The following specification applies to the P-51H, which was in production until November, 1945.

TYPE.—Single-seat Fighter or Fighter-Bomber.

WINGS.—Cantilever low-wing monoplane. NAA-NACA low-drag laminar-flow aerofoil section. Incidence 1 degree; dihedral 5 degrees; root chord (on fuselage centre-line) 9 ft. 8 in. (2.87 m.), mean aerodynamic chord 6 ft. 10.17 in. (2.1 m.); tip chord 4 ft. 2 in. (1.27 m.). All-metal two-spar structure in two main sections bolted together on the fuselage centre-line. Detachable tips.

A North American P-51D Single-seat Fighter fitted with Bazooka-type rocket projectile equipment.

The North American P-51H Mustang Single-seat Fighter (Packard V-1650-11 Merlin engine).

Inner portion of spars are of I-section composed of two channel-sections, tapering to single channel-section outboard of flaps. Outer portions have flanged lightening holes. Pressed channel-section ribs with lightening holes and stressed-skin covering. Inner sections between spars contain fuel tanks and have top-hat section chordwise stiffeners on top and bottom surfaces. Inter-spar gun-bay outboard of tanks with channel-section chordwise stiffeners on lower surface. Heavy rib between tanks and gun-bay to which landing-gear is attached. Ammunition bay outboard of gun-bay. Gross wing area 235 sq. ft. (21.82 sq. m.). Metal-covered ailerons with trim-tab in port. Aileron area (each) 6.35 sq. ft. (0.57 sq. m.); aileron movement 15 degrees up, 15 degrees down. Tab area 0.71 sq. ft. (0.06 sq. m.), tab movement 10 degrees up, 10 degrees down. Hydraulically-operated slotted trailing-edge flaps between ailerons and fuselage. Flap area (total) 31.74 sq. ft. (2.94 sq. m.), flap depression 45 degrees.

FUSELAGE.—Oval-section all-metal semi-monocoque structure in three main sections consisting of engine section; main fuselage section from engine bulkhead to leading-edge of fin, and rear section. Structure consists of two sides with separate top and bottom. Each side beam consists of two aluminium-alloy longerons (channel-section in front of cockpit tapering to L-section aft) which form the caps, and the aluminium-alloy skin reinforced by vertical channel-section frames forming the webs. L-section longitudinal stringers in main section to aft of cockpit. Radiator tunnel is channel-section structure attaching under and forming lower portion of main fuselage.

TAIL UNIT.—Cantilever monoplane type. One-piece tailplane with detachable tips. Structure of tailplane and fin consists of two channel-section spars, pressed ribs, L-section stringers and stressed metal skin. Fin offset 1 degree to port. Rudder and elevators with sealed dynamic balances and controllable trim-tab in each. Tailplane span 14 ft. 10.16 in. (4.56 m.), tailplane area (including fuselage) 35.50 sq. ft. (3.3 sq. m.). Fin area 14.89 sq. ft. (1.38 sq. m.), Maximum rudder chord 2 ft. 0 in. (0.61 m.), rudder area 10.24 sq. ft. (0.95 sq. m.), rudder movement 30 degrees each way, rudder tab area 0.74 sq. ft. (0.06 sq. m.), tab movement 10 degrees each way. Elevator area (total) 18.25 sq. ft. (1.7 sq. m.), elevator movement 25 degrees up, 25 degrees down, elevator tab area (each) 0.72 sq. ft. (0.06 sq. m.), tab movement 10 degrees up, 25 degrees down.

LANDING GEAR.—Retractable two-wheel type. Each main wheel, on oleo-pneumatic shock-absorber leg hinged on heavy rib outboard of gun-bay, retracts inwards into wing ahead of front spar and is enclosed by light metal plates bolted to legs and by hinged doors under fuselage. Main legs have travel of 8 inches (20.3 c/m.). Hydraulic operation. Track 11 ft. 0 in. (3.35 m.). Goodyear hydraulic brakes. Steerable tail-wheel with multi-tread tyre retracts forward into fuselage and is enclosed by twin resin-bonded plastic fabric doors. Cable-retraction from main gear. Leg travel 7.9 inches (20.06 c/m.).

POWER PLANT.—One Packard-built Rolls-Royce Merlin V-1650-11 twelve-cylinder vee liquid-cooled direct-injection engine rated at 1,380 h.p. at 3,000 r.p.m. at sea-level for take-off and with a normal output of 1,100 h.p. at 2,700 r.p.m. at 17,500 ft. (5,335 m.) and a maximum (war emergency) output of 2,270 h.p. with water injection at 3,000 r.p.m. at 4,000 ft. (1,220 m.). Two-speed two-stage automatic supercharger. Light-weight engine-mounting with outer plate of each side beam flush with outer surface of cowling. Complete power-plant removable forward of firewall. Spot-welded cowling of 20 s.w.g. aluminium-alloy attached by Dzus fasteners. Aeroproducts four-blade constant-speed hollow steel paddle-blade airscrew, 11 ft. 0 in. (3.35 m.) diameter; ground clearance (tail up) 9 in. (23 c/m.). Jet-type exhaust pipes. Collapsible non-metallic self-sealing fuel tanks in wings and fuselage; 105 U.S. gallon (397 litre) tank in port wing; 100 U.S. gallon (378 litre) tank in starboard wing and 50 U.S. gallon (189 litre) tank in fuselage behind cockpit. Wing-tanks removable through rear spar after flaps removed. Two long-range drop-tanks each of 75 U.S. gallons (284 litres) or 110 U.S. gallons (417 litres) capacity can be carried under wings. Maximum fuel capacity 475 U.S. gallons (1,798 litres) Harrison heat-exchanger oil-cooling system.

ACCOMMODATION.—Pilot's enclosed cockpit with 1½ in. (38 m/m.) laminated plate-glass windshield, and long moulded and laminated bubble canopy which slides backwards for access. Hydraulically-adjustable seat. ¼ in. (6.35 m/m.) armour-plating on engine bulkhead; $\frac{5}{16}$ in. (7.9 m/m.) plating forming back of seat, and $\frac{7}{16}$ in. (11 m/m.) armour plating for head and neck protection. Thermo-statically-controlled combustion-type gasoline cockpit heater producing 15,000 B.T.U. per hr. Pressure demand oxygen system positive up to 30,000 ft. (9,145 m.).

ARMAMENT.—Six .5 in. (12.7 m/m.) M-2 machine-guns mounted three in each wing outboard of airscrew disc, with 400 rounds for each inner gun, and 270 rounds for each middle and outer gun. Compensating gun-sight. Access doors to gun and ammunition boxes in upper surface of wing. Provision for ten 5 in. (12.7 c/m.) rocket projectiles; two bombs up to 1,000 lb. (454 kg.) each, or two AN-M-10 chemical smoke tanks under wings.

EQUIPMENT.—Radio equipment consists of AN/ARC/3 Command set; SCR-695-A Identification set and BC-1206 Range Receiver set. AN/APS-13 rear detection radar set. MN-26C radio compass optional. AN-N6 camera gun in port wing leading-edge. For photographic reconnaissance duties the following alternative electrically-operated cameras can be installed in fuselage immediately ahead of tailplane: Type K-17 or K-22 with 6 in., 12 in. or 24 in. (15 c/m., 30.5 c/m. or 61 c/m.) lenses for operating at 5,000 ft., 15,000 ft. or 30,000 ft. (1,525 m., 4,572 m. or 9,145 m.) respectively. Type K-24 with 7-in (17.8 c/m.) lens for vertical or oblique photography for operation up to 10,000 ft. (3,050 m.). Hydraulic system operating at 1,500 lbs./sq. in. (105 kg./sq. c/m.).

DIMENSIONS.—Span 37 ft. 0$\frac{5}{16}$ in. (11.27 m.), Length 33 ft. 4 in. (10.15 m.).

WEIGHTS AND LOADINGS (Interceptor).—Weight empty 6,500 lbs. (2,948 kg.), Disposable load 1,950 lbs. (884 kg.), Weight loaded 8,450 lbs. (3,832 kg.), Wing loading 36 lbs./sq. ft. (185.8 kg./sq. m.), Power loading (normal) 7.7 lbs./h.p. (3.48 kg./h.p.).

WEIGHTS AND LOADINGS (Long-range fighter).—Weight empty 6,500 lbs. (2,948 kg.), Disposable load 3,000 lbs. (1,361 kg.), Weight loaded 9,500 lbs. (4,309 kg.), Wing loading 40.5 lbs./sq. ft. (197.7 kg./sq. m.), Power loading (normal) 8.64 lbs./h.p. (3.9 kg./h.p.).

WEIGHTS AND LOADINGS (Fighter-Bomber).—Weight empty 6,500 lbs. (2,948 kg.), Disposable load 5,000 lbs. (2,266 kg.), Weight loaded 11,500 lbs. (5,214 kg.), Wing loading 49 lbs./sq. ft. (200 kg./sq. m.), Power loading (normal) 10.5 lbs./h.p. (4.75 kg./h.p.).

PERFORMANCE (Interceptor).—Maximum speed (at maximum war emergency power) 488 m.p.h. (785 km.h.) at 25,000 ft. (7,720 m.), Maximum speed (normal output) 410 m.p.h. (660 km.h.) at 22,000 ft. (6,705 km.h.), Maximum rate of climb 6,400 ft./min. (1,950 m./min.) at 5,000 ft. (1,525 m.), Normal rate of climb 2,300 ft./min. (700 m./min.) at 17,500 ft. (5,335 m.), Climb (at normal output) to 20,000 ft. (6,095 m.) 8 minutes.

PERFORMANCE (Long-range Fighter).—Range with maximum fuel (at 307 m.p.h. (494 km.h. at 25,000 ft.=7,720 m., loaded weight 11,054 lbs.=5,014 kg., and with 20 minutes combat allowance) 2,208 miles (3,553 km.).

PERFORMANCE (Fighter-Bomber).—Maximum speed (with two 500 lb.=227 kg. bombs and loaded weight of 10,570 lbs.=4,794 kg., or with ten 5 in.=12.7 c/m. rocket projectiles and loaded weight of 10,980 lbs.=4,980 kg.) 450 m.p.h. (724 km.h.) at 25,000 ft. (7,720 m.), Maximum range (with two 500 h.p.=227 kg. bombs and loaded weight of 10,570 lbs.=4,794 kg.) 960 miles (1,545 km.). (1947)

THE NORTH AMERICAN NA-50 AND NA-68

Fighter development of the NA-16, to be exported to Peru (NA-50) and Siam (NA-68). Six latter aircraft held in US in 1940 and used as P-64 trainers. Details for NA-50, but NA-68 generally similar.

TYPE.—Single-seat fighter monoplane.

WINGS.—Low-wing cantilever monoplane. Wing in five sections, two-spar centre-section, two removable single-spar outer sections and two detachable wing-tips. Spars and ribs of aluminium-alloy with smooth stressed skin. Balanced and differentially-controlled ailerons have aluminium-alloy frames and fabric covering. Split trailing-edge flaps.

FUSELAGE.—Forward section of welded chrome-molybdenum steel-tubing with removable side panels. Rear section of semi-monocoque metal alloy construction. Suitable inspection doors are provided in rear section.

TAIL UNIT.—Cantilever monoplane type. Aluminium-alloy frame-work. Fixed surfaces are metal-covered and non-adjustable. Elevator and rudder are fabric-covered, balanced and fitted with adjustable trimming-tabs.

UNDERCARRIAGE.—Retractable cantilever single-leg half-fork type. Air-oil shock-absorbers. Hydraulically-operated differential brakes and parking brake. Wheel-type skis may be installed. Steerable tail-wheel with full 360° swivel.

POWER PLANT.—One Wright "Cyclone" GR-1820-G203 or G-203A radial air-cooled engine on welded steel-tube mounting. N.A.C.A. cowling. Three-bladed constant-speed airscrew. Two fuel tanks in centre-section (170 U.S. gallons capacity). Oil tank (15.5 U.S. gallons) on top of engine-mounting. Alternatively the Wright "Cyclone" R-1820-F53 or direct-drive or geared R-1820-G3 engines may be used.

ACCOMMODATION.—Pilot's cockpit over wing with sliding enclosure. Windshield of plexiglass, side panels of shatter-proof glass. Baggage space in rear monocoque section. Provision is made for installation of 114 lbs. (52 kg.) of radio equipment. Two synchronized Colt .30-cal. or 7.67 m/m. machine-guns. North American flush-type bomb-racks in outboard wing-sections.

DIMENSIONS.—Span 37 ft. 3 in. (11.36 m.). Length 26 ft. 11¼ in. (8.23 m.). Wing area 236.09 sq. ft. (21.9 sq. m.).

WEIGHTS.—Weight empty 4,470 lbs. (2,029 kg.). Crew 190 lbs. (86 kg.). Weight loaded 5,700 lbs. (2,588 kg.).

PERFORMANCE (with Wright "Cyclone" GR-1820-G203 engine).—Maximum speed at 9,500 ft. (2,900 m.) 295 m.p.h. (475 km.h.), Cruising speed 16,500 ft. (5,030 m.) 255 m.p.h. (410 km.h.), Landing speed (with flaps) 70 m.p.h. (113 km.h.), Climb to 10,000 ft. (3,050 m.) 3 mins. Service ceiling 32,000 ft. (9,755 m.), Range (normal) 645 miles (1,038 km.), Range (overload) 910 miles (1,462 km.).

(1940)

The North American F-86F Sabre Fighter (General Electric J47 turbojet engine).

THE NORTH AMERICAN SABRE.

U.S. Air Force designation: F-86.

The F-86 was the first American swept-wing fighter to go into combat. In two years of fighting in Korea the F-86 maintained its superiority over the Russian MIG-15 and set up an impressive combat record.

Production of the Sabre by North American came to an end in December, 1956, after nine years. Versions have also been built under licence in Canada by Canadair (with a Canadian-designed and built Orenda turbojet), in Italy by Fiat and in Australia by the Commonwealth Aircraft Corporation (with an Australian-built Rolls-Royce Avon turbojet). The Canadian production Sabre has been supplied in quantity to the R.C.A.F., U.S.A.F., R.A.F. and the air forces of several other nations.

Under an agreement signed late in 1955, North American continues to supply parts for the assembly in Japan by the Mitsubishi company of F-86F Sabres for the Japanese Air Self-Defence Force.

The following are the principal versions of the F-86 :—

XF-86. Two prototypes originally fitted with the Allison J35-GE-3 engine. First prototype flew on October 1, 1947. Were later re-engined with the General Electric J47. Re-engined XF-86 first exceeded Mach. 1 on April 25, 1948.

F-86A. First production model. One General Electric J47-GE-1, -3, -9 and -13 engines in successive production series. First production aircraft flew on May 20, 1948. On September 15, 1948, a standard F-86A complete with armament and normal combat equipment and flown by Major Richard L. Johnson, U.S.A.F. established a World's Speed Record of 670.981 m.p.h. (1,073.569 km.h.) over the measured course on Muroc Lake. Out of production in December, 1950.

F-86D. All-weather fighter development of the F-86A. Air intake repositioned under nose, which now encloses radar scanner. General Electric J47-GE-17 engine with G.E. afterburner necessitating a larger rear fuselage. Fully-powered "flying tail," there being no separate elevator surfaces as in F-86E. Equipment includes A.I., armament-laying and tracking, navigation and transponder radar, Sperry Zero-Reader

low approach equipment and Hamilton Standard air-conditioning. Armament consists of 24 × 2.75 in. rockets which are carried in a retractable launching tray located in the underside of the fuselage. Overall length 41 ft. (12.5 m.). Other dimensions as for F-86E. Prototype flew on December 22, 1949. In production at Los Angeles.

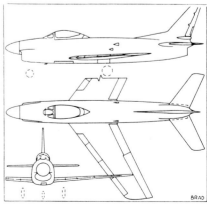

The North American F-86D Sabre.

The North American F-86D Sabre All-weather Fighter (General Electric J47 turbojet engine).

On November 19, 1952, a standard F-86D with full combat load and piloted by Capt. J. Slade Nash, U.S.A.F., set up a World's Speed Record of 698.505 m.p.h. (1,124.137 km.h.). The record was made over a measured 3 km. course at Salton Sea, Cal., which is 240 ft. below sea level (Temp. 76°F.). On July 16, 1953, Lieut.-Col. W. F. Barns, U.S.A.F., also in an F-86D equipped for operational duty, increased the World's Speed Record to 715.697 m.p.h. (1,151.798 km.h.) over the same 3 km. course (Temp. 100.5°F.).

F-86E. One General Electric J47-GE-13 engine. Progressive development of F-86A. New tail with both tailplane and elevators controllable and linked for co-ordinated movement. All controls power-operated and provided with artificial sensing system to give pilot a representative feel in absence of air loads. Irreversible control system also provided with a pressure-sensing unit which increases artificial feel force when longitudinal control is threatened by excessive loads on tail. In other respects similar to F-86A, which it followed on production line at Los Angeles in December, 1950. Production completed in April, 1952.

F-86F. One General Electric J47-GE-27 engine. Slightly larger and more powerful development of F-86E. Wing leading-edge extended forward 6 in. (15.2 cm.) at root and 3 in. (7.6 cm.) at tip, thus slightly increasing the angle of sweepback. Leading-edge slats eliminated and small fences added. First production F-86F flew on March 19, 1952, last delivered on May 26, 1954.

TF-86F. Two-seat trainer version of F-86F. Forward fuselage lengthened by 63 in. (1.6 m.) and wings moved forward 8 in. (20.3 cm.). Wing slats are fitted. Tandem seats under continuous canopy. Complete dual controls and instrumentation. Provision for installation of two .50-cal. machine-guns and fittings provided under wings for the normal two 200 U.S. gallon drop tanks plus an additional pair of 120 U.S. drop tanks or two practice bombs. First TF-86F flew for the first time on December 14, 1953, and was destroyed in an accident soon after. A second TF-86F was completed and flown in the Summer of 1954.

F-86FR. In 1960, North American built and flight tested a "super performance" interceptor version of the F-86F, designed to extend the aircraft's useful life in service with the Japanese Air Self-Defence Force and other air forces. A 6,000 lb. (2,720 kg.) s.t. Rocketdyne AR2-3 liquid-propellent rocket-engine, mounted in a pod under the fuselage, gives the F-86FR supersonic speed in level flight, reduces its turning radius by 50%, gives it a ceiling of over 60,000 ft. (18,300 m.) and a rate of climb above 40,000 ft. (12,200 m.) 15 times faster than that of the standard F-86F. The installation of TACAN ARN-21 navigation equipment enables the F-86FR to operate in adverse weather conditions. Its armament is supplemented with Sidewinder air-to-air missiles.

F-86H. General Electric J73-GE-3 engine (9,300 lb.=4,218 kg. s.t.). Fuselage 6 in. (15.2 cm.) deeper. First armed with six 0.50-in. guns but later with four 20 mm. M-39 cannon. Higher powered fighter-bomber version of F-86F.

Two prototypes built at Los Angeles, the first making its maiden flight on April 30, 1953. First production F-86H flew on September 4, 1953 and the type remained in production at Columbus until August, 1955. Span': 37 ft. 1 in. (11.3 m.). Length: 38 ft. 9 in. (11.8 m.). Height: 15 ft. (4.57 m.).

F-86K. General Electric J47-GE-33 engine (5,600 lb.=2,540 kg. s.t.) with afterburner. Ordered by U.S.A.F. with M.D.A.P. funds for delivery to N.A.T.O. countries. Similar to F-86D but fitted with four 20 mm. cannon instead of rocket armament and Type MG-4 fire control system. Fuselage is 8 in. (20.3 cm.) longer than that of F-86D. Was built under licence by Fiat in Italy. First U.S.-built YF-86K flew on July 5, 1954, and first production F-86K from Los Angeles plant in March, 1955.

F-86L. This designation has been given to F-86D aircraft after modification to new standards at Los Angeles Modification Center and Fresno plant. The F-86L accommodates "Data Link" equipment which receives intercept information and directions from the SAGE (Semi-Automatic Ground Environment) electronic air defence monitoring computer, and links data with pilot's instruments. F-86L's, in service with U.S.A.F. Air Defense Command, are being used to evaluate flying phase of SAGE which, when it becomes fully operational, will form, in conjunction with network of radar "picket" ships, early-warning radar aircraft and land-based radar stations, a solid interlocking radar ring around the United States through and over which it will be impossible to fly undetected. Other changes on the F-86L include a new slotted wing leading edge and new wing-tips that increase span by 2 ft. (0.60 m.). Deliveries began late in 1956. Contracts involve modification of over 800 F-86D interceptors to F-86L standard.

The North American TF-86F Sabre Two-seat Trainer (General Electric J47 turbojet engine).

The description which follows refers to the F-86F.

TYPE.—Single-seat fighter.

WINGS.—Low-wing cantilever monoplane. Modified NACA 0012-64 (root), 0011-64 (tip) wing section. Maximum thickness at 50% of chord. 35° sweepback along 25% chord line. All-metal two-spar structure with upper and lower skins each of which is a sandwich consisting of two sheets milled to tapering thickness separated by "hat" section extrusions, the whole forming a torsion-box structure. Aileron hydraulic boost and artificial feel system. Split flaps inboard of ailerons. Wing area 287.9 sq. ft. (26.75 m.²)

FUSELAGE.—Oval section all-metal structure with flush-riveted stressed skin. Air brakes on fuselage.

TAIL UNIT.—Cantilever monoplane type. All-metal structure. All surfaces have 35° sweep-back. "Flying tail" in which elevators and tailplane are geared together and move differentially with movements of control column to provide in-flight trim.

LANDING GEAR.—Retractable tricycle type with steerable nose-wheel. Hydraulic retraction. Cleveland 8657 air-oil shock struts. Bendix 26 in. (66 cm.) cast magnesium wheels and Bendix rotor-disc hydraulic brakes on main wheels. Track 8 ft. 3 in. (2.5 m.)

POWER PLANT.—One General Electric J47-GE-27 turbojet (5,970 lb.=2,708 kg. s.t.). Nose entry lipped above to maintain adequate air flow in nose-up position. Main fuel tanks in fuselage. External long-range drop-tanks may be carried under wings outboard of landing gear.

ACCOMMODATION.—Pressurised pilot's cockpit with sliding "bubble" canopy. Pilot ejection seat.

ARMAMENT.—Six 0.50-in. (12.7 mm.) machine-guns in nose. Provision for sixteen 5-in. (127 mm.) rockets under wings. May also carry 2 × 1,000-lb. bombs in lieu of auxiliary tanks.

DIMENSIONS.—
Span 37 ft. 1 in. (11.3 m.)
Length 37 ft. 6 in. (11.45 m.)
Height 14 ft. (4.27 m.)

WEIGHTS.—
Weight empty 10,950 lb. (4,967 kg.)
Weight loaded 16,860 kg. (7,647 lb.)

PERFORMANCE.—
Max. speed over 670 m.p.h. (1,072 km.h.)
Service ceiling: 53,000 ft. (16,170 m.)
Normal cruise range: 1,250 miles (2,000 km.)
(1960–61)

The North American AJ-1 Savage (two Pratt & Whitney R-2800 piston engines and one Allison J33 turbojet).
(*Warren Bodie*).

THE NORTH AMERICAN SAVAGE.
U.S. Navy designation : AJ.

The Savage, a large composite-powered carrier-borne Attack Bomber capable of carrying an Atomic bomb, is in production for the U.S. Navy. The unique power-plant of the Savage consists of two Pratt & Whitney R-2800 piston engines under the wings and a single Allison J33 turbojet in the rear fuselage. The turbojet gives added power when required for accelerated take-off or in combat. All the engines use the same type of fuel.

Two XAJ-1 prototypes were built, the first flying for the first time on July 2, 1948.

The following versions of the Savage have been revealed.

AJ-1. Two 2,400 h.p. Pratt & Whitney R-2800-44W piston engines and one

Allison J33-A-10 turbojet (4,600 lb. = 2,090 kg.) s.t. Crew of three. First production AJ-1 flew in May, 1949. First carrier landings in U.S.S. *Coral Sea* on August 31, 1950. Now out of production. AJ-1's being converted into air tankers with Flight Refuelling "probe-drogue" equipment now standard in U.S. Navy. Conversion to tanker by complete pack in bomb-bay comprising hose, drum, fuel pumps, electric power drive, drogue, etc. Additional fuel capacity for tanker duties provided by jettisonable tanks.

AJ-2. Development of AJ-1. Higher vertical fin. Dihedral removed from tailplane. The first AJ-2 flew on February 19, 1953. Production at Columbus, Ohio.

AJ-2P. Photographic-reconnaissance version of AJ-2. 18 cameras for day and night photography at high and low

altitudes. Photo-flash bombs in bomb-bay for night reconnaissance. Automatic control for most of cameras. Additional fuel capacity. Weight (approx.) 50,000 lb. (22,700 kg.). Maximum speed with jet power (approx.) 425 m.p.h. (680 km.h.). First AJ-2P flew on March 6, 1952. In production at Columbus, Ohio.

The general arrangement of the Savage can be gathered from the accompanying photograph. The outer wings fold inboard and the fin and rudder fold down on to the starboard tailplane. There is pressurised accommodation for a crew of three. No other details have been released for publication.

DIMENSIONS.—
Span 71 ft. 5 in. (21.77 m.).
Length 63 ft. 1 in. (19.22 m.).
Height (folded) 15 ft. 2 in. (4.62 m.).
Width (folded) 48 ft. (14.64 m.).
(1955–56)

North American F-100F Super Sabre (Pratt & Whitney J57 turbojet engine and afterburner)

THE NORTH AMERICAN SUPER SABRE
U.S. Air Force designation: F-100

The F-100 was the first supersonic operational fighter to be developed for the U.S.A.F. The prototype YF-100A, powered by a Pratt & Whitney J57-P-7 turbojet engine fitted with an afterburner, flew for the first time on May 25, 1953. It exceeded the speed of sound in level flight on its first 35-minute flight.

Production of the F-100 was completed in October, 1959. Several versions were built as follows:—

F-100A. Initial production version. Day fighter with Pratt & Whitney J57-P-7 or J57-P-39 turbojet, with afterburner. In production at North American's Los Angeles plant from mid-1953 to 1955.

F-100C. Fighter-bomber with Pratt & Whitney J57-P-21 engine. Fitted with in-flight refuelling for internal tanks only and provision for carrying extra drop fuel tanks and bombs under the wings. Improved electronic bombing equipment. Standard armament of four 20 mm. cannon. First F-100C from Los Angeles Division flew on January 17, 1956. Production also undertaken by Columbus Division and first Columbus-built F-100C flown in September, 1955.

F-100D. Fighter-bomber. Similar to F-100C with improvements that include the fitting of flight refuelling probe for replenishing both internal and external tanks, wing flaps on centre-section trailing-edge, tail-warning radar and a Minneapolis Honeywell autopilot. This latter is able to control the aircraft at supersonic speed, leaving the pilot free to concentrate on navigation and tactics. Bomb-load raised to 7,500 lb. (3,400 kg.). First flight of F-100D on January 24, 1956.

Following a series of experimental zero-length launching trials, using a 130,000 lb. (59,000 kg.) s.t. Astrodyne rocket to supplement the J57 turbojet, all late production F-100D's were built with fittings for this type of operation.

F-100F. Two-seat version able to be used as fighter-bomber, air-superiority fighter or trainer. Length increased by 3 ft. (0.91 m.). Fixed armament reduced from four to two M-39 cannon. Ordered into production in 1956. Prototype (designated TF-100C) flew on August 3, 1956 and the first production F-100F on March 8, 1957. Production completed October, 1959.

NF-100F. One F-100F was used, under this designation, in 1960/61 for a low-altitude low-speed control (LALSC) test programme, for which a Rohr thrust reverser replaced the normal afterburner. This aircraft also had variable-area wing flaps with boundary-layer control, a speed brake approximately three times normal size and a special antenna for a radar altimeter. These modifications enabled the NF-100F to simulate the landing approach of advanced boost-glide space vehicles.

RF-100. An illustration shows an F-100 with a modified square-section lower fuselage containing reconnaissance cameras and equipment.

A "buddy" system of flight refuelling has been developed for the F-100 by Flight Refueling Inc. of Baltimore, Maryland. Under this system, one F-100 is able to take fuel from another which trails a hose and drogue from a standard-size streamlined external pod carried under its wing. Upon completion of the operation, the entire equipment retracts automatically into the pod, so that performance is not penalised. In addition to the fuel available within the refuelling pod, the F-100 "tanker" is able to dispense fuel from its external tanks.

Another item of equipment, designed to be fitted to the F-100D but suitable for use on other versions of the Super Sabre, is the North American Center Line Tow Target Boom. With this in place under the fuselage, the pilot can snatch a target off the ground, to provide air-to-air firing practice for other fighters, at supersonic speeds.

The F-100D and F-100F are able to carry either atomic or thermonuclear bombs, in addition to conventional weapons, and 220 are being modified to carry Bullpup air-to-surface missiles.

F-100's have been supplied to NATO air forces, including those of Denmark, France and Turkey, and to the Chinese Nationalist air force, which has received a total of 80.

The following description refers specifically to the F-100C.

TYPE.—Single-seat supersonic fighter-bomber.

WINGS.—Low-wing cantilever monoplane with 7% thickness-chord ratio. 45° sweep-back. Aluminium alloy spars, ribs and tapered skin. Inset ailerons each split into two sections. Automatic leading-edge slats. No flaps.

FUSELAGE.—All-metal structure. Rectangular air brake hinged beneath fuselage approximately in line with front wing spar.

TAIL UNIT.—Monoplane type. All surfaces have 45° sweepback. One-piece "all-flying" horizontal stabiliser. Braking parachute housed in bottom of fuselage. Span of tail 18 ft. (5.5 m.)

LANDING GEAR.—Retractable tricycle type, with steerable twin nose-wheels. Hytrol anti-skid sensing units on segmented-rotor brakes. Track of main wheels 12 ft. (3.6 m.)

POWER PLANT.—One Pratt & Whitney J57-P-21 turbojet engine with afterburner. Automatic fuel system. Total internal fuel capacity 1,185 U.S. gallons (4,487 litres) in wing, fuselage and annular engine-bay tanks, filled from single point on port rear fuselage. Two 250 U.S. gallon (945 litre) and two 225 U.S. gallon (850 litre) tanks may be carried under the wings. Provision for flight-refuelling internal tanks only. Probe on starboard wing inboard of underwing tank shackles. (Some Tactical Air Command F-100's now carry two 450 U.S. gallon (1,700 litre) under-wing tanks which can be replenished in flight).

ACCOMMODATION.—Pilot's cockpit forward of wings with one-piece clamshell-type jettisonable canopy. Automatically-regulated air conditioning and pressurising system. Ejection seat.

ARMAMENT.—Four 20 mm. M-39E cannon with 200 rounds per gun. Six under-wing pylons for up to 6,000 lb. (2,720 kg.) of H.E. or Napalm bombs, 24 × 5 in. rockets, Sidewinder air-to-air missiles, pods of 2.75 in. air-to-air rocket, Bullpup air-to-surface missiles, etc. Type A-4 radar gunsight.

DIMENSIONS.—
Span 38 ft. (11.58 m.)
Length 47 ft. (14.33 m.)
Height 16 ft. (4.88 m.)

RF-100 version of the North American Super Sabre

WEIGHT.—
   Weight loaded approx. 28,000 lb. (12,700 kg.)

PERFORMANCE.—
   Max. speed with afterburner 822 m.p.h. (1,323 km.h.) at 35,000 ft. (10,670 m.)
   Stalling speed approx. 150 m.p.h. (241 km.h.)
   Landing speed approx. 179 m.p.h. (287 km.h.)
   Service ceiling over 50,000 ft. (15.250 m.)
   Combat radius 575 miles (920 km.)
   Take-off run with afterburning approx. 4,500 ft. (1,370 m.)   (1961–62)

North American NF-100F Super Sabre modified for LALSC test programme
(Howard Levy)

The North American T-28C Naval Trainer. *(Gordon Williams)*. (1958–59)

THE NORTH AMERICAN T-28.

The T-28 was originally designed for the U.S.A.F. as a replacement for the T-6 and it went into production for the U.S.A.F. in 1950 as the T-28A.

In 1952, following the policy of standardisation of training aircraft for all the services, the T-28 was adopted by the U.S. Navy and in modified form was put into production under the designation T-28B and, later, as the T-28C.

The three T-28 versions differ in the following respects :—

T-28A. 800 h.p. Wright R-1300-1 seven-cylinder radial engine and Aero Products two-blade constant-speed airscrew. U.S.A.F. advanced trainer. Out of production in 1953.

T-28B. 1,425 h.p. Wright R-1820 engine driving a three-blade Hamilton Standard constant-speed airscrew. U.S. Navy advanced trainer structurally similar to T-28A. New cockpit canopy, which was also introduced in later production T-28A's. Air brake on lower surface of fuselage. All training armament external with gun mounts, rocket and bomb racks under wings. Gunsight and camera in front cockpit. Re-arrangement of radio, electrical and oxygen equipment.

T-28C. Same as T-28B but equipped with arrester hook, etc. for operation from aircraft-carriers. First T-28C flown on September 19, 1955.

Production of the T-28 ended in the Autumn of 1957, when a total of 1,948 of the three different versions had been built.

TYPE.—Two-seat Basic Trainer.

WINGS.—Low-wing cantilever monoplane. Two-spar all-metal structure. Trailing-edge flap between ailerons and fuselage. Total flap area 53.6 sq. ft. (4.98 m.²). Gross wing area 268 sq. ft. (24.89 m.²).

FUSELAGE.—All-metal semi-monocoque structure.

TAIL UNIT.—Cantilever monoplane type. All-metal structure. Area of fin and rudder 30.3 sq. ft. (2.81 m.²), area of tailplane and elevators 59.7 sq. ft. (5.54 m.²).

LANDING GEAR.—Retractable tricycle type. Main wheels with Goodyear single-disc brakes retract inwardly into wings, nose-wheel backwards into fuselage. United Aircraft Products air-oil shock struts. Nose-wheel is steerable from either cockpit by electro-hydraulic boost control. Nose-wheel also carries a movable taxi light. Main wheel track 12 ft. 8 in. (3.86 m.).

POWER PLANT (T-28A).— One Wright R-1300-1 seven-cylinder radial air-cooled engine with a military and take-off rating of 800 h.p. and a normal rating of 700 h.p. Aero Products two-blade constant-speed airscrew 10 ft. (3.05 m.) diameter. Fuel capacity 125 U.S. gallons (473 litres).

POWER PLANT (T-28B).—One 1,425 h.p. Wright R-1820 engine driving a three-blade Hamilton Standard constant-speed airscrew, diameter 9 ft. 4 in. (2.84 m.).

ACCOMMODATION.—Tandem cockpits beneath single bubble canopy. Duplicated flight controls and instruments. Amber screen blind and night flying equipment with ultra-violet and infra-red instrument lighting.

ARMAMENT.—Provision for carrying bombs, 2.25 in. SCA rockets and .50 in. machine-guns.

DIMENSIONS (T-28C).—
   Span 40 ft. 7 in. (12.37 m.).
   Length 34 ft. 4 in. (10.45 m.).
   Height overall 12 ft. 7 in. (3.84 m.).

WEIGHTS AND LOADINGS (T-28A).—
   Weight empty 5,111 lb. (2,320 kg.).
   Normal loaded weight 6,365 lb. (2,890 kg.).
   Max. take-off weight 6,759 lb. (3,068 kg.).
   Wing loading 23.8 lb./sq. ft. (116.14 kg./m.²).
   Power loading 7.96 lb./h.p. (3.61 kg./h.p.).

WEIGHTS AND LOADINGS (T-28B).—
   Weight empty 6,424 lb. (2,916 kg.).
   Normal loaded weight 8,004 lb. (3,634 kg.).
   Max. T.O. weight 8,486 lb. (3,853 kg.).
   Normal wing loading 29 lb./sq. ft. (141.52 kg./m.²).
   Normal power loading 5.6 lb./h.p. (2.54 kg./h.p.).

WEIGHT (T-28C).—
   Max. take-off weight 8,247 lb. (3,741 kg.).

PERFORMANCE (T-28A).—
   Max. speed 285 m.p.h. (456 km.h.) at 5,900 ft. (1,800 m.).
   Cruising speed 190 m.p.h. (304 km.h.).
   Stalling speed 72 m.p.h. (115.2 km.h.).
   Initial rate of climb 2,030 ft./min. (628 m./min.).
   Service ceiling 29,000 ft. (8,845 m.).
   T.O. run to clear 50 ft. (15.25 m.) 570 yds. (521 m.).
   Max. range 1,008 miles (1,612 km.).

PERFORMANCE (T-28B).—
   Max. speed 346 m.p.h. (554 km.h.).
   Cruising speed 310 m.p.h. (496 km.h.) at 30.000 ft. (9,150 m.).

PERFORMANCE (T-28C).—
   Max. speed approx. 346 m.p.h. (554 km.h.).
   Service ceiling 35,000 ft. (10,670 m.).
   Range over 860 miles (1,385 km.).

Initial rate of climb 3,830 ft./min. (1,168 m./min.).
Service ceiling 37,000 ft. (11,285 m.).
T.O. run to clear 50 ft. (15.25 m.) 380 yds. (348 m.).
Max. range 1,060 miles (1,696 km.) at 10,000 ft. (3,050 m.).

THE NORTH AMERICAN T-28D

Under contract to the U.S.A.F. Special Air Warfare Center, North American has converted a total of 147 T-28 two-seat basic training aircraft into light armed reconnaissance and air support aircraft for counter-insurgency operations, under the designation T-28D.

A full description of the basic T-28 can be found in the 1958-59 edition of *All the World's Aircraft*. The T-28D has a 1,425 hp Wright R-1820-56S nine-cylinder air-cooled radial engine (provided by Pacific Airmotive Corporation), driving a three-blade variable-pitch airscrew. It is highly manoeuvrable and can carry a normal underwing combat load of two 0·50-in. machine-gun packs and a variety of napalm, bomb and rocket installations. A typical load, shown in the adjacent illustration, comprises two gun packs, two VLU-11/B 500-lb fire bombs and two MA-3 rocket launchers. Without the gun packs, external fuel tanks can be fitted to give the T-28D a weapon delivery or ferry range of over 1,200 miles (1,930 km).

In combat, the T-28D is flown normally as a single-seater, but a crew of two can be carried, if required.

PERFORMANCE.—
   Max. speed   380 mph (612 kmh)
   Service ceiling   35,000 ft (10,670 m)
   Normal range with full weapon load
                             over 500 miles (800 km)

(1963–64)

North American T-28D, a conversion of the T-28 basic trainer for counter-insurgency operations

The North American AT-6F Texan Two-seat Advanced Trainer (Pratt & Whitney R-1340-AN1 engine).—(*Peter Bowers*).

THE NORTH AMERICAN TEXAN.
U.S. Army Air Forces designation : AT-6.
U.S. Navy designation : SNJ.

The AT-6 was first produced in 1939 and was similar to and eventually replaced the BC-1A basic combat trainer when the Basic Combat classification was abandoned. The BC-1A was a development of the BC-1 (SNJ-1 and Harvard I). Both were fitted with the Pratt & Whitney R-1340-47 engine, the BC-1 having a steel tube fabric-covered fuselage while the BC-1A had a semi-monocoque rear fuselage and a re-designed tail-unit.

Since then several series of AT-6 Advanced Trainers have been built, the various sub-types varying mainly in matters of equipment. These may be summarised as follows :—

AT-6 (Harvard II). Pratt & Whitney R-1340-47 engine. Integral fuel tanks in centre-section.

AT-6A (SNJ-3). Pratt & Whitney R-1340-49 engine. Removable aluminium fuel tanks. The AT-6A built in Canada under licence by Noorduyn Aviation, Ltd. was the Harvard IIB. Canadian-built Harvards were also delivered to the U.S. Army and because of manufacturing and equipment differences these were given the designation AT-16.

AT-6B. Pratt & Whitney R-1340-AN1 engine. Fitted with four internal wing bomb-racks.

AT-6C (SNJ-4 and Harvard IIA). Pratt & Whitney R-1340-AN1 engine. In 1941, owing to possible shortages in strategic materials, the structure of the AT-6C was re-designed partially to eliminate the use of aluminium-alloy and high-alloy steels. The entire rear fuselage, tailplane, floor boards, etc. were made of plywood. A saving of 220 lbs. (100 kg.) of aluminium-alloy per aircraft was achieved. The standard structure was later reverted to.

AT-6D (SNJ-5 and Harvard III). Pratt & Whitney R-1340-AN1 engine. Standard structure as described below. 24-volt electrical system. No photographic equipment.

AT-6F (SNJ-6). Same power-plant as AT-6D. Strengthened outer wings and redesigned rear fuselage. Only external differences are the addition of an airscrew spinner and a moulded plastic rear section of the canopy in place of the earlier built-up unit.

The British Harvard versions of the AT-6 carried no armament and were fitted with British instruments, radio, shoulder harness, etc.

The Texan was in production at Dallas, Texas, right up to VJ-Day and when the Dallas plant closed down a few days after, 15,117 Texans had been built, representing 25.8 per cent. of all trainers built in the United States since July, 1940.

TYPE.—Two-seat Advanced Training (AT-6) or Scout Training (SNJ) monoplane.

WINGS.—Low-wing cantilever monoplane. Two spar rectangular centre-section and two single-spar tapered outer sections with detachable wing-tips. All-metal structure with aluminium-alloy spars and ribs and a smooth Alclad skin. Aerodynamically and statically-balanced ailerons have metal frames and fabric covering. Split trailing-edge flaps between ailerons. Wing area 253.7 sq. ft. (23.6 sq. m.).

FUSELAGE.—Welded chrome-molybdenum steel-tube structure from fireproof bulkhead to rear cockpit, remainder of aluminium-alloy semi-monocoque construction. Side panels of the forward section are of aluminium-alloy and are removable.

TAIL UNIT.—Cantilever monoplane type. Aluminium-alloy framework, fixed surfaces covered with Alclad sheet and movable surfaces with fabric. Elevators and rudder have trim-tabs controllable from both cockpits.

LANDING GEAR.—Retractable cantilever type, with wheels folding inwards. Retraction by engine-driven hydraulic pump. Hydraulic wheel-brakes. Full-swivelling steerable tail-wheel.

POWER PLANT.—One 550 h.p. Pratt & Whitney R-1340-AN1 radial air-cooled engine. Hamilton Standard two-blade constant-speed airscrew. Fuel tanks (111 U.S. gallons capacity) in centre-section. Oil tank (10.2 U.S. gallons=38.6 litres) in engine compartment.

ACCOMMODATION.—Tandem cockpits with individually-operated sliding enclosures. Complete dual flight and engine controls in each cockpit. Adjustable seat in front cockpit, rotating and adjustable gunner's seat in back cockpit.

ARMAMENT.—One 0.30 in. (7.7 m/m.) machine-gun in starboard side of fuselage forward of pilot's cockpit, one 0.30 in. (7.7 m/m.) machine-gun in leading-edge starboard outer wing, and one 0.30 in. (7.7 m/m.) machine-gun on flexible mounting in rear cockpit.

DIMENSIONS.—Span 42 ft. 0¼ in. (12.9 m.). Length 28 ft. 11⅞ in. (8.8 m.), Height 11 ft. 8½ in. (3.5 m.)

WEIGHTS AND LOADINGS.—Weight empty 4,158 lbs. (1,888 kg.), Disposable load 1,142 lbs. (518 kg.), Normal loaded weight 5,250 lbs. (2,383 kg.), Wing loading 20.8 lbs./sq. ft. (101.5 kg./sq. m.), Power loading 9.6 lbs./h.p. (4.35 kg./h.p.).

PERFORMANCE.—Maximum speed at 5,000 ft. (1,525 m.) 205 m.p.h. (331.2 km.h.), Cruising speed at 5,000 ft. (1,525 m.) 170 m.p.h. (272 km.h.), Landing speed 63 m.p.h. (101 km.h.), Service ceiling 21,500 ft. (6,560 m.), Normal range 750 miles (1,200 km.). (1947)

THE NORTH AMERICAN TEXAN.
U.S.A.F. designation: T-6G.

After evaluation of several new post-war designs of primary training aircraft, the U.S.A.F. has, as an economy measure, decided to retain the Texan in modified form as a standard trainer.

In its new form the T-6G retains the basic structural and flying characteristics of the Texan but has modifications in equipment to meet present training requirements. The pilot's cockpit has been simplified to bring it into line with that of the T-28 and the rear cockpit is equipped with complete instrument training equipment. Radio and electronic equipment of the latest design now includes VHF command set, range receiver, marker beacon receiver, interphone system, radio compass and ILS.

Additional fuel tanks are fitted in the roots of the outer wing panels to extend the range to over 1,000 miles (1,600 km.).

Seven hundred wartime-built air frames are to be overhauled, reconditioned and re-equipped to the above standards, 330 of them by North American Aviation, Inc. and the remainder by other manufacturers. (1952–53)

The North American T-6G Two-seat Primary Trainer.

THE NORTH AMERICAN TORNADO.
U.S. Air Force designation: B-45.

The XB-45 was the first American multi-jet heavy aircraft to fly, the prototype making its first flight at Muroc on March 17, 1947.

B-45A. Four General Electric J-47-GE-3 turbojet engines. First production model. 96 built and production complete. Fourteen modified as high-speed target-tugs to tow the Chance Vought 20-ft. span all-metal target glider. Reel assembly in rear bomb-bay and towing cable hydraulically-controlled by target operator in the tail position.

B-45C. Improved version of B-45A. Earmarked as tactical support bomber.

RB-45C. High-altitude photographic reconnaissance aircraft with five camera stations capable of carrying ten different types of cameras for nearly all types of reconnaissance missions. Nose section and rear fuselage section aft of bomb-bay redesigned internally. Crew of three—pilot, co-pilot and photo/navigator. Ejector seats for pilot and co-pilot, escape hatch for navigator. Heating and refrigeration system to maintain 70°F.

temperature in all camera stations. Two 1,200 U.S. gallon wing-tip tanks. 33 for duty with both Tactical and Strategic Commands. Equipped for air-to-air refuelling.

The description and specification below refer to the B-45A bomber.

TYPE.—Four-jet Light Bomber.

WINGS.—Shoulder-wing cantilever monoplane. All-metal structure with flush-riveted stressed skin. Hydraulically-operated trailing-edge flaps betwen ailerons and nacelles and nacelles and fuselage. Hydraulic boost action for aileron control, providing 95° of the energy required to move the surfaces. Electrically-operated trim-tab in port aileron.

FUSELAGE.—Oval section all-metal structure with flush-riveted stressed skin.

TAIL UNIT.—Cantilever monoplane type. All-metal structure with stressed skin. Dihedral tailplane. Hydraulic boost action for elevator and rudder control. Electrically-operated trim-tabs in elevators and rudder. Tailplane span 36 ft. (11 m.).

LANDING GEAR.—Retractable tricycle type. Main wheels raised inwardly into wings, nose wheel into fuselage. Hydraulic retraction. Bendix air-oil shock struts. Bendix rotor-disc hydraulic wheel brakes on

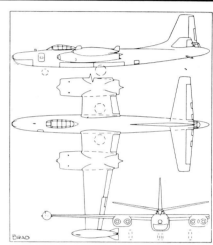

The North American RB-45C Tornado.

The North American B-45C Tornado Light Bomber (four General Electric J-47 turbojet engines).

main wheels. Retractable tail bumper strut. Main wheel track 22 ft. 3 in. (6.78 m.).

POWER PLANT.—Four General Electric J-47-GE-3 axial-flow gas turbines with water injection paired in two nacelles, one on each side of the fuselage. Total static thrust 20,800 lb. (9,443 kg.). Engines entirely ahead of wings for ease of maintenance. Maximum internal fuel capacity 4,500 U.S. gallons (17,010 litres).

ACCOMMODATION.—Crew of four. Pilot and co-pilot in tandem under "bubble" type canopy. Bombardier's compartment in nose. Gunner's position in tail under rudder. Ejector seats for pilot and co-pilot only.

ARMAMENT.—Two .5 in. (12.7 mm.) guns in tail position. Bomb load over 10 tons.

DIMENSIONS.—
Span 89 ft. 6 in. (27.3 m.).
Length 74 ft. (22.6 m.).
Height (over tail) 25 ft. (7.6 m.).
DESIGNED LOADED WEIGHT.—
82,600 lb. (37,500 kg.).
PERFORMANCE.—
Max. speed over 550 m.p.h. (880 km.h.).
Service ceiling 40,000 ft. (12,200 m.).
(1951–52)

The North American F-82F Twin-Mustang Night Fighter landing. (*Gordon S. Williams*).

THE NORTH AMERICAN TWIN MUSTANG.
U.S. Air Force designation : F-82.

The F-82 two-seat long-range escort fighter consists virtually of two Mustang fuselages and port and starboard outer wings, the two fuselages being joined together by a constant-chord centre-section and a rectangular tailplane. The F-82 superseded the F-51H at the North American Los Angeles plant when the latter was withdrawn from production in November, 1945.

The following enumerates the various models of the F-82 which have been built :—

XF-82 (N.A. 120). Two Packard V-1650-23/25 Merlin engines driving oppositely-rotating airscrews. Two built.

F-82B (N.A. 123). Two Packard V-1650-23/25 Merlin engines driving oppositely-rotating airscrews. First production model. Twenty built. One of the batch piloted by Lieut.-Col. R. Thacker and Lieut. J. M. Ard (co-pilot in starboard cockpit) flew from Honolulu to New York non-stop, a distance of 5,051 miles (8,082 km.) in 14 hours 33 minutes, representing an average speed of 334 m.p.h. (550.4 km.h.). 2,215 U.S. gallons (8,375 litres) of fuel were carried internally and in four external drop tanks, two under each outer wing. One external tank was dropped in the sea about 100 miles (160 km.) W. of San Francisco, but failure of the electric release gear made it necessary to carry the remaining three tanks for the whole flight—increasing the air resistance and fuel consumption and reducing the overall speed. The take-off weight of the aircraft, which was standard except for removal of guns and armour, was 50,000 lb. (13,620 kg.) or twice the normal empty weight of a F-82B.

F-82D (N.A. 123). F-82B equipped as night fighter. Radar equipment in large streamline nacelle beneath centre-section. One only. Prototype of F-82F.

F-82E (N.A. 144). Similar to F-82B but fitted with two Allison V-1710-143/145 engines.

F-82F (N.A. 149). Night fighter version of the F-82E. Pilot in port cockpit, radar operator in starboard. Radar

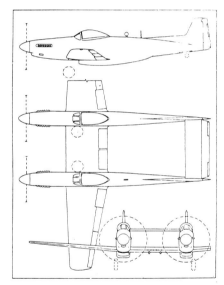

The North American F-82 Twin-Mustang.

equipment carried in large streamline nacelle under centre-section.

F-82G (N.A. 150). Similar to the F-82F the primary difference between the two models being in the type of radar used.

TYPE.—Twin-engined two-seat long-range Escort Fighter.

WINGS.—Cantilever low-wing monoplane. Outer wings on the outboard side of each fuselage. Each aileron constructed in two sections to allow for wing deflection. Controllable trim-tab in inner portion of starboard aileron. Structure of constant-chord centre-section between the fuselages is similar to that of outer wings. Single slotted trailing-edge flap over full span of centre-section. Inter-spar gun-bay and fuel tanks in outboard ends. Heated-surface anti-icing. Gross wing area 408 sq. ft. (37.9 m.²).

FUSELAGES.—All-metal monocoque structures.

TAIL UNIT.—All-metal structure. Single-fin and rudder at extremity of each fuselage. Constant-chord tailplane and elevator between fins. Controllable trim-tab in elevator. Tailplane span (centre-line of each fin) 14 ft. 4 in. (4.37 m.). Rudder height 7 ft. 0½ in. (2.15 m.).

LANDING GEAR.—Retractable type. Each main wheel retracts inwards. Hydraulic operation with emergency mechanical gear. Track 16 ft. 8¾ in. (5.1 m.). Twin retractable tail-wheels, one in each fuselage and cable operated from main gear. Both tail-wheels steered by rudder bar, or are disengaged so as to swivel freely when control column is pushed forward.

POWER PLANT.—Two Allison V-1710-143/145 twelve-cylinder Vee liquid-cooled engines, each normally rated at 1,600 h.p. and with a max. rating of 2,300 h.p. with water-injection. Aeroproducts four-blade oppositely-rotating full-feathering constant-speed airscrews, 11 ft. 0 in. (3.35 m.) diameter, port airscrew rotating L.H. and starboard airscrew R.H. Fuel tanks in outer ends of centre-section and in inner sections of outer wings. Provision for long-range tanks under outer wings and/or centre-section according to stores carried.

ACCOMMODATION.—Two cockpits, one in each fuselage, with dual controls. Pilot in port and co-pilot or, in case of night fighter, radar operator in starboard. Rudder pedals in either fuselage can be disconnected and stowed. Individual cockpit heating, oxygen, etc. Automatic pilot in port cockpit, with manual emergency release in starboard.

ARMAMENT.—Six .5-in. (12.7 mm.) machine-guns in centre-section firing between airscrew discs. Provision for four 1,000 lb. (454 kg.) bombs, one under each outer wing and two under centre-section, or two 2,000 lb. (907 kg.) bombs under centre-section. Alternatively, five racks each carrying a cluster of five rocket projectiles can be carried, two under each outer wing and one under centre-section. Streamline nacelle mounting eight .5-in. (12.7 mm.) machine-guns, with alternative provision for photographic reconnaissance cameras or night-fighting radar, can be installed under centre-section midway between fuselages.

DIMENSIONS.—
Span 51 ft. 2.8 in. (15.61 m.).
Length (tail up) 39 ft. 0⁷⁄₁₆ in. (11.88 m.).
Height 13 ft. 8 in. (4.16 m.).
WEIGHTS AND LOADINGS.—
Weight empty 14,350 lb. (6,509 kg.).
Weight loaded (with max. internal fuel, 2 crew, ammunition and four 1,000 lb. =454 kg. bombs) 20,750 lb. (9,420 kg.).
Wing loading 49 lb./sq. ft. (239 kg./m.²).
PERFORMANCE.—
Max. speed, over 475 m.p.h. (764 km.h.).
Ceiling 45,000 ft. (13,715 m.).
Max. ferrying range 2,500 miles (4,000 km.).
(1946–50)

NORTH AMERICAN ROCKWELL VIGILANTE
US Navy designations: A-5 and RA-5

After a US Navy design competition, the then North American Aviation, Inc, received a contract to build a small number of prototypes of the A-5 (formerly A3J) twin-jet two-seat carrier-based all-weather combat aircraft in September 1956. Design and development of the aircraft was entrusted to the company's Columbus Division, to which the US Navy awarded a large follow-on production contract in January 1959.

Three versions of the A-5 have been built, as follows:

A-5A (formerly A3J-1). Attack bomber designed to carry nuclear or conventional weapons over a range of several hundred miles at high altitudes, with an over-target speed of Mach 2.

The first of two prototype YA-5As flew for the first time on 31 August 1958, and a total of 59 A-5As were delivered to the US Navy. Production was completed in 1963. All remaining A-5As have been converted to RA-5C configuration.

A-5B (formerly A3J-2). Interim long-range version. Extra fuel tank in shape of hump fairing above fuselage aft of cockpit fairing. First flown on 29 April 1962. About 20 built. All converted to RA-5C configuration.

RA-5C (formerly A3J-3). Airborne unit of Integrated Operational Intelligence System (IOIS), which includes also an integrated operational intelligence centre on board a carrier or at a shore base. Primarily a reconnaissance version of the Vigilante, with tactical sensory equipment and cameras in ventral fairing, but retaining an attack capability with externally-carried nuclear or conventional weapons. Cameras include vertical, oblique and horizon-to-horizon scanning types. Non-photographic equipment includes side-looking radar and electro-magnetic sensors for intelligence and counter-measures. Data obtained by these reconnaissance systems are fed to a surface-based tactical data system. Airframe similar to A-5B, with hump-back-fuel tank, enlarged flaps and droop leading-edge BLC. Four underwing attachments, each capable of carrying a 400 US gallon (1,514 litre) fuel tank, bomb or missile.

The RA-5C flew for the first time on 30 June 1962. Production models were assigned to VAH-3, training squadron for Heavy Attack Wing One of the US Navy, at Sanford Naval Air Station, in January 1964. Reconnaissance Attack Squadron 5 became operational on USS *Ranger* in the South China Sea by late 1964. Reconnaissance Attack Squadron 7 also equipped with RA-5Cs in June 1965, so completing the phase-out of the A-5A from carrier-borne operational units. Heavy Attack Wing One was subsequently re-designated Reconnaissance Attack Wing One, and some seven additional RA-5C-equipped Reconnaissance Attack Squadrons have been formed or converted from other heavy bomber types. In 1968 the Wing was transferred to Albany Naval Air Station, Georgia.

Production of 36 new RA-5Cs began early in 1969. The following details refer specifically to the current production version:

TYPE: Carrier-based tactical reconnaissance aircraft.

WINGS: Cantilever high-wing monoplane. Thickness/chord ratio approximately 5%. Sweepback 37° 30′. All-metal structure with integrally-stiffened machined skins of Alcoa 2020-T6 aluminium-lithium alloy. Hydraulically-operated variable-camber leading-edge, in three sections on each wing, with BLC blowing over outboard two sections. Hydraulically-actuated aluminium spoilers in place of ailerons. Hydraulically-operated flaps. Outer wing panels hydraulically-folded upward for carrier stowage.

FUSELAGE: Semi-monocoque structure, widened aft of cockpit to accommodate engines. Built mainly of aluminium, but with several bulkheads and frames of ultra high-strength steel. Titanium alloy skins and frames are used adjacent to turbojets, and gold coating is applied on certain areas of titanium skins to prevent overheating of structural assemblies. Nose radome folds upward for radar maintenance and carrier stowage.

TAIL UNIT: Cantilever all-metal structure. Tail unit has integrally-stiffened machined skins of Alcoa 2020-T6 alloy on horizontal surface, and 7075-T6 alloy on vertical surface. Aluminium honeycomb structures are used for trailing sections. Both vertical and horizontal surfaces are one-piece structures, swept back at 45° and hydraulically-actuated. Lateral trim is by differential operation of horizontal surfaces. Upper section of fin folds to port for carrier stowage.

North American Rockwell RA-5C Vigilante of the US Navy (two General Electric J79 turbojet engines)
(*T. Matsuzaki*)

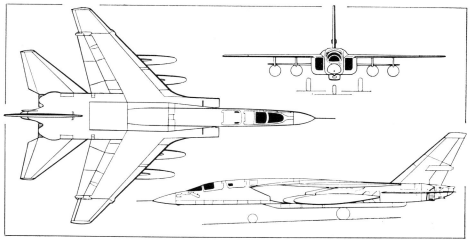

North American Rockwell RA-5C Vigilante naval reconnaissance-attack aircraft

LANDING GEAR: Retractable tricycle type of Bendix manufacture, with single wheel on each unit. All units retract hydraulically into fuselage. Oleo-pneumatic shock-absorbers. Main wheels, size 36 × 11, with hydraulic multiple-disc brakes. Steerable nose-wheel, size 26 × 6·6.

POWER PLANT: Current production RA-5Cs powered by two General Electric J79-GE-10 turbojets (each rated at 11,870 lb = 5,395 kg st dry, and 17,859 lb = 8,118 kg st with after-burning). Aircraft delivered prior to 1969 equipped with two General Electric J79-GE-8 turbojets (each rated at 10,900 lb = 4,944 kg st dry or 17,000 lb = 7,711 kg st with afterburning). Hydraulically-actuated variable-area intakes. Fuel in three bladder-type tanks in fuselage, three integral tanks in the wing, and two or three (varying with reconnaissance configuration) can-type tanks in the former bomb-bay. Retractable flight refuelling probe on port side of nose. Pressure fuelling points under front and rear fuselage. Provision for four 400 US gallon (1,514 litre) jettisonable tanks under wings.

ACCOMMODATION: Crew of two in tandem under separate rearward-hinging canopies. Advanced rocket-powered type HS-1 ejection seats, developed by NAR Columbus Division, using a drogue parachute to stabilise the seats in an upright position after ejection.

ELECTRONICS AND EQUIPMENT: Equipment includes North American Autonetics REINS (radar equipped inertial navigation system) bombing and navigation system, and automatic flight control system. Auto-pilot provides hold for heading, bank, altitude and Mach number; ability to fly selected track through REINS coupling; and ability to perform selected LABS manoeuvres.

SYSTEMS: AiResearch pressurisation and air-conditioning system. Two 3,000 lb/sq in (210 kg/cm²) hydraulic systems, each supplied by two 15 US gallons/min (58·5 litres/min) engine-driven variable-displacement pumps, one on each engine. Each system provides power for independent flight control systems, and one additionally provides utility hydraulic power for flaps, leading-edge droops, landing gear, nose and fin folding, variable-area intakes, etc. Emergency power by AiResearch ram-air turbine, which also supplies emergency AC electrical power. Two 42kVA engine-driven generators supply 115V 400 Hz AC power. Two transformer-rectifiers provide 28V DC supply.

ARMAMENT: Variety of weapons, including thermonuclear bombs, can be accommodated on underwing attachments.

DIMENSIONS, EXTERNAL:
Wing span	53 ft 0 in (16·15 m)
Span, wings folded	42 ft 5 in (12·93 m)
Length overall	75 ft 10 in (23·11 m)
Length, nose and tail folded	68 ft 0 in (20·73 m)
Height overall	19 ft 5 in (5·92 m)
Tailplane span	30 ft 7 in (9·32 m)

AREA:
Wings, gross	769 sq ft (71·44 m²)

WEIGHT (RA-5C):
Max T-O weight (approx)	80,000 lb (36,285 kg)

PERFORMANCE (RA-5C, approx):
Max level speed	Mach 2

(1971–72)

The Northrop A-17 Two-seat Attack Monoplane (750 h.p. Pratt & Whitney "Twin-Wasp Junior" engine).

THE NORTHROP A-17.

TYPE.—Two-seat attack monoplane.

WINGS.—Low-wing cantilever monoplane. In three sections, with detachable wing-tips. All-metal stressed-skin cellular structure. Metal-framed fabric-covered ailerons. Split trailing-edge flaps.

FUSELAGE.—Light alloy monocoque, with smooth stressed skin.

TAIL UNIT.—Cantilever monoplane type. All-metal framework, with stressed-skin covering to fixed surfaces and fabric covering for rudder and elevators. Rudder and elevators have inset-hinge balances and trimming-tabs.

UNDERCARRIAGE.—Fixed cantilever type. Single oleo legs and wheels have fairings, with the wheels only partly enclosed. Orientable tail-wheel.

POWER PLANT.—One 750 h.p. Pratt & Whitney "Twin-Wasp Junior" radial air-cooled engine, enclosed in N.A.C.A. cowling, with controllable gills, and driving a Hamilton-Standard constant-speed airscrew.

ACCOMMODATION.—Tandem seats under a transparent canopy, with sliding section over pilot's seat and hinged section over gunner's cockpit.

ARMAMENT.—Five 30-cal. guns, four in the leading-edge of the wing and one on a flexible mounting in the gunner's cockpit. Provision for 20 small bombs or four large ones of unspecified weight, or an alternative load of chemicals for smoke-screen laying, etc.

DIMENSIONS.—Span 47 ft. 8.5 in. (14.54 m.), Length 31 ft. 8.7 in. (9.67 m.), Height 14 ft. 2.5 in. (4.34 m.), Wing area 363 sq. ft. (33.8 sq. m.).

WEIGHTS AND LOADINGS.—Weight empty 4,875 lbs. (2,213 kg.), Weight loaded 7,440 lbs. (3,380 kg.), Wing loading 20.5 lbs./sq. ft. (100 kg./sq. m.), Power loading 10 lbs./h.p. (4.54 kg./h.p.).

PERFORMANCE.—Maximum speed 206 m.p.h. (330 km.h.), Cruising speed 170 km.h. (272 m.p.h.), Rate of climb at sea level 2,500 ft./min. (762.5 m./min.), Service ceiling 20,700 ft. (6,314 m.), Absolute ceiling 22,150 ft. (6,786 m.).

THE NORTHROP A-17A.

The A-17A is a later modification of the A-17, from which it differs by having a retractable undercarriage. It also has the new Northrop perforated split flaps. The U.S. Army Air Corps has taken delivery of 100 A-17A's during 1936-37.

The A-17A is said to be 15 m.p.h. (24 km.h.) faster than the A-17 described above. (1937)

The Northrop BT-1 Two-seat Dive-Bomber Monoplane (750 h.p. Pratt & Whitney "Twin-Wasp Junior" engine).

THE NORTHROP BT-1.

The Northrop BT-1 is a two-seat Dive Bomber in service in the U.S. Navy. It is generally similar to the Army A-17 but incorporates certain modifications required by the Navy and is fitted with aircraft-carrier equipment. Its power plant is a 750 h.p. Pratt & Witney "Twin Wasp Junior" driving a Hamilton-Standard constant-speed airscrew and, unlike the A-17, it has a retractable undercarriage.

Fifty-four delivered from 1938. Wing span 41 ft 6 in (12.65 m). Length 31 ft 8 in (9.65 m). Height 9 ft 11 in (3.02 m). Weight loaded 7,195 lb (3,263 kg). Maximum speed 222 mph (357 km/h). Range 1,150 miles (1,850 km). Two guns plus 1,000 lb (454 kg) bomb.

NORTHROP F-5
USAF designations: F-5 and RF-5
CAF designations: CF-5A/D

Design of this light tactical fighter started in 1955 and construction of the prototype of the single-seat version (then designated N-156C) began in 1958. It flew for the first time on 30 July 1959, exceeding Mach 1 on its maiden flight. Two more prototypes were built, followed by several production versions, as follows:

F-5A. Basic single-seat fighter. Two General Electric J85-GE-13 afterburning turbojets. First production F-5A flew in October 1963. Norwegian version has ATO and arrester hook for short-field operation.

F-5B. Generally similar to F-5A, but with two seats in tandem for dual fighter/trainer duties. First F-5B flew on 24 February 1964. Production was to be terminated during 1976.

On 4 November 1974, Northrop announced delivery of the 2,500th aircraft in its F-5/T-38 series. The total exceeded 2,800 by early 1976, including more than 300 built under licence in other countries. Eighteen versions of the F-5 are flown by the air forces of 22 countries, including six NATO nations. In addition to those built by Northrop Aircraft Division facilities in California, F-5s have been produced under licensing agreements in Canada and Spain. The F-5 was first ordered into production by the US government, through the USAF, in October 1962, to meet the defence requirements of allied and friendly nations. Initial deliveries, beginning April 1964, were made to Williams AFB, Chandler, Arizona, where the USAF Tactical Air Command has since trained pilots and maintenance personnel of countries receiving F-5s. The first allied air force to receive F-5s was the Imperial Iranian Air Force, which put into service its initial squadron of 13 aircraft on 1 February 1965. The Republic of China, Greece, Republic of Korea, the Philippines and Turkey received F-5s in 1965. Ethiopia, Morocco, Norway and Thailand first received F-5s in 1966, the Republic of Vietnam in 1967 and Libya in 1968.

TYPE: Light tactical fighter and reconnaissance aircraft.

WINGS: Cantilever low-wing monoplane. Wing section NACA 65A004·8 (modified). No dihedral or incidence. Sweepback at quarter-chord 24°. Multi-spar light alloy structure with heavy plate machined skins. Hydraulically-powered sealed-gap ailerons at approximately mid-span with light alloy single-slotted flaps inboard. Continuous-hinge leading-edge flaps of full-depth honeycomb construction. No trim tabs. No de-icing system.

FUSELAGE: Semi-monocoque basic structure of light alloy, with steel, magnesium and titanium used in certain areas. 'Waisted' area rule lines. Two hydraulically-actuated airbrakes on underside of fuselage forward of wheel wells.

TAIL UNIT: Cantilever all-metal structure, with hydraulically-powered rudder and one-piece all-moving tailplane. Single spars with full depth light alloy honeycomb secondary structure. No trim tabs. Longitudinal and directional stability augmentors installed in series with control system.

LANDING GEAR: Hydraulically-retractable tricycle type with steerable nosewheel. Emergency gravity extension. Main units retract inward into fuselage, nosewheel forward. Oleo-pneumatic shock-absorbers. Main wheels fitted with tubeless tyres size 22 × 8·5, pressure 5·86-14·48 bars (85-210 lb/sq in). Nosewheel fitted with tubeless tyre size 18 × 6·5, pressure 4·14-12·41 bars (60-180 lb/sq in). Multiple-disc hydraulic brakes.

POWER PLANT: Two General Electric J85-GE-13 turbojets (each with max rating of 18·15 kN; 4,080 lb st with afterburning). Two internal fuel tanks composed of integral cells with total usable capacity of 2,207 litres (583 US gallons). Provision for one 568 litre (150 US gallon) jettisonable tank on fuselage centreline pylon, two 568 litre (150 US gallon) jettisonable tanks on underwing pylons and two 189 litre (50 US gallon) wingtip tanks. Total fuel, with external tanks, 4,289 litres (1,133 US gallons). Single pressure refuelling point on lower fuselage. Oil capacity 4·5 litres (4·7 US quarts) each engine.

ACCOMMODATION (F-5A): Pilot only, on rocket-powered ejection seat in pressurised and air-conditioned cockpit. (F-5B): Pupil and instructor in tandem on rocket-powered ejection seats in pressurised and air-conditioned cockpits separated by windscreen. Separate manually-operated rearward-hinged jettisonable canopies. Instructor's seat at rear raised 0·25 m (10 in) higher than that of pupil to give improved forward view.

SYSTEMS: Electrical system includes two 8kVA engine-driven generators, providing 115V 400Hz AC power, and 24V battery.

ELECTRONICS AND EQUIPMENT: Standard equipment includes AN/ARC-34C UHF radio, PP-2024 SWIA-Missile AVX, AN/AIC-18 interphone, J-4 compass, Norsight optical sight, AN/APX-46 IFF, and AN/ARN-65 Tacan. Space provision for AN/ARW-77 Bullpup AUX. Blind-flying instrumentation not standard.

ARMAMENT: Basic interception weapons are two Sidewinder missiles on wingtip launchers and two 20 mm guns in the fuselage nose. Five pylons, one under the fuselage and two under each wing, permit the carriage of a wide variety of other operational warloads. A bomb of more than 910 kg (2,000 lb) or high-rate-of-fire gun pack can be suspended from the centre pylon. Underwing loads can include four air-to-air missiles, Bullpup air-to-surface missiles, bombs, up to 20 air-to-surface rockets, gun packs or external fuel tanks. The reconnaissance nose does not eliminate the 20 mm nose gun capability.

DIMENSIONS, EXTERNAL:

Wing span	7·70 m (25 ft 3 in)
Wing span over tip-tanks	7·87 m (25 ft 10 in)
Wing chord at root	3·43 m (11 ft 3 in)
Wing chord at tip	0·69 m (2 ft 3 in)
Length overall:	
F-5A	14·38 m (47 ft 2 in)
F-5B	14·12 m (46 ft 4 in)
Height overall:	
F-5A	4·01 m (13 ft 2 in)
F-5B	3·99 m (13 ft 1 in)
Tailplane span	4·28 m (14 ft 1 in)
Wheel track	3·35 m (11 ft 0 in)
Wheelbase:	
F-5A	4·67 m (15 ft 4 in)
F-5B	5·94 m (19 ft 6 in)

AREAS:

Wings, gross	15·79 m² (170 sq ft)
Ailerons (total)	0·86 m² (9·24 sq ft)
Trailing-edge flaps (total)	1·77 m² (19·0 sq ft)
Leading-edge flaps (total)	1·14 m² (12·3 sq ft)
Fin	3·85 m² (41·42 sq ft)
Rudder	0·57 m² (6·1 sq ft)
Tailplane	5·48 m² (59·0 sq ft)

WEIGHTS AND LOADINGS:

Weight empty, equipped:	
F-5A	3,667 kg (8,085 lb)
F-5B	3,792 kg (8,361 lb)
Max military load	2,812 kg (6,200 lb)
Max T-O weight:	
F-5A	9,379 kg (20,677 lb)
F-5B	9,298 kg (20,500 lb)
Max design landing weight	9,006 kg (19,857 lb)
Max zero-fuel weight:	
F-5A	6,446 kg (14,212 lb)
F-5B	6,237 kg (13,752 lb)
Max wing loading:	
F-5A	590·8 kg/m² (121 lb/sq ft)
F-5B	576 kg/m² (118 lb/sq ft)

PERFORMANCE (F-5A at AUW of 5,193 kg; 11,450 lb: F-5B at AUW of 4,916 kg; 10,840 lb, unless indicated otherwise):

Never-exceed speed	710 knots (1,315 km/h; 818 mph) IAS
Max level speed at 11,000 m (36,000 ft):	
F-5A	Mach 1·4
F-5B	Mach 1·34
Max cruising speed without afterburning, at 11,000 m (36,000 ft)	Mach 0·97
Econ cruising speed	Mach 0·87
Stalling speed, 50% fuel, flaps extended:	
F-5A	128 knots (237 km/h; 147 mph)
F-5B	120 knots (223 km/h; 138 mph)
Max rate of climb at S/L:	
F-5A	8,750 m (28,700 ft)/min
F-5B	9,265 m (30,400 ft)/min
Service ceiling:	
F-5A	15,390 m (50,500 ft)
F-5B	15,850 m (52,000 ft)
Service ceiling, one engine out:	
F-5A, F-5B	over 10,365 m (34,000 ft)
T-O run (with two Sidewinder missiles):	
F-5A at AUW of 6,203 kg (13,677 lb)	808 m (2,650 ft)
F-5B at AUW of 5,924 kg (13,061 lb)	671 m (2,200 ft)
T-O to 15 m (50 ft) (with two Sidewinder missiles):	
F-5A at AUW of 6,203 kg (13,677 lb)	1,113 m (3,650 ft)
F-5B at AUW of 5,924 kg (13,061 lb)	960 m (3,150 ft)
Landing from 15 m (50 ft), with brake-chute:	
F-5A at AUW of 4,504 kg (9,931 lb)	1,189 m (3,900 ft)
F-5B at AUW of 4,363 kg (9,619 lb)	1,158 m (3,800 ft)
Landing run, with brake-chute:	
F-5A at AUW of 4,504 kg (9,931 lb)	701 m (2,300 ft)
F-5B at AUW of 4,363 kg (9,619 lb)	671 m (2,200 ft)
Range with max fuel, with reserve fuel for 20 min max endurance at S/L:	
F-5A, tanks retained	1,205 nm (2,232 km; 1,387 miles)
F-5B, tanks retained	1,210 nm (2,241 km; 1,393 miles)
F-5A, tanks dropped	1,400 nm (2,594 km; 1,612 miles)
F-5B, tanks dropped	1,405 nm (2,602 km; 1,617 miles)
Combat radius with max payload, allowances as above and five minutes combat at S/L:	
F-5A	170 nm (314 km; 195 miles)
F-5B	175 nm (323 km; 201 miles)
Combat radius with max fuel, two 530 bombs, allowances as above and five minutes combat at S/L:	
F-5A	485 nm (898 km; 558 miles)
F-5B	495 nm (917 km; 570 miles)
Operational hi-lo-hi reconnaissance radius with max fuel, 50 nm (93 km; 58 mile) S/L dash to and from target and allowances as for combat radius with max fuel:	
RF-5A	560 nm (1,036 km; 644 miles)

(1976–77)

NORTHROP TIGER II
USAF designations: F-5E and F-5F

The F-5E was selected in November 1970 by the US government as the winner of a competition to determine the single-seat International Fighter Aircraft (IFA) which was to succeed Northrop's F-5A. The two-seat F-5F was developed subsequently.

The F-5E design places particular emphasis on manoeuvrability rather than high speed, notably by the incorporation of manoeuvring flaps, based on the design of a similar system for the Netherlands Air Force's NF-5A/Bs. Full-span leading-edge flaps work in conjunction with conventional trailing-edge flaps, and are operated by a control on the pilot's throttle quadrant.

Wing loading on the F-5E is maintained at approximately the same value as on the F-5A, as the result of an increase in wing area to 17·30 m² (186 sq ft). This is due principally to the widened fuselage, which also increases

Northrop F-5F tandem two-seat fighter-trainer, armed with wingtip-mounted Sidewinder missiles

wing span. The tapered wing leading-edge extension, between the inboard leading-edge and fuselage, was modified to enhance airflow over the wing at high angles of attack.

The F-5E incorporates other features developed for the Canadian, Dutch and Norwegian F-5s. These include two-position nosewheel gear, which increases wing angle of attack on the ground by 3° 22' and which, in conjunction with the more powerful engines, has improved F-5E take-off performance some 30% by comparison with earlier F-5s. Arrester gear permits operation from short runways. It is qualified to carry two 1,040 litre (275 US gallon) underwing fuel tanks, in addition to the centreline 1,040 litre (275 US gallon) tank, and up to seven 500 lb MK-82 bombs, following the addition of a Multiple Ejector Rack (MER) on the centreline stores station.

The first F-5E was rolled out on 23 June 1972, and made its first flight on 11 August 1972. USAF Tactical Air Command, with assistance from Air Training Command, was assigned responsibility for training pilots and technicians of user countries. First deliveries of the F-5E, to the US Air Force's 425th Tactical Fighter Squadron, were made in the Spring of 1973. Twenty aircraft had been supplied for the US Air Force training programme by the end of September 1973, and deliveries to foreign countries began in late 1973. The 1,000th F-5E/F was delivered to the Republic of Korea in August 1979, and production continues at an average rate of about five per month. Customers to date include the US Air Force (112 F-5Es), US Navy (10 F-5Es and 3 F-5Fs), Brazil, Chile, Republic of China, Iran, Jordan, Kenya, South Korea, Malaysia, Saudi Arabia, Singapore, Sudan, Switzerland, Thailand and the Yemen Arab Republic.

In addition to their use as tactical fighters, F-5Es are operated by the US Air Force and US Navy in the 'aggressor' role, to simulate 'enemy' aircraft at major air combat training schools in the USA, England and the Philippines.

Details of the current production versions of the Tiger II are as follows:

F-5E. Standard production version, to which the detailed description applies. In production also, under licence, by AIDC in Taiwan (which see). Can be fitted with an R-843A/ARN-58 localiser receiver and a reconnaissance nose containing four KS-121A 70 mm framing cameras and related equipment. Intended for low/medium-altitude photo-reconnaissance, the nose is similar to that of the RF-5A. New 'shark' profile nose developed for the F-5G (which see) is to be introduced on standard production F-5E and F-5F.

To extend the range of armament options, an F-5E completed a technology flying demonstration with a 30 mm underbelly gun pod developed by General Electric. More than 800 rounds of 30 mm GAU-8 type ammunition were fired on US Air Force test ranges at Edwards AFB, California.

The F-5Es for the Royal Saudi Air Force (RSAF) have a Litton LN-33 inertial navigation system, capable of accuracy exceeding 1·5 nm (2·7 km; 1·7 miles) CEP per flight hour, which provides attitude reference, range and bearing to ten pre-set destinations, as well as true ground track steering. The system is self-aligning in 10 min in the gyro compass mode, and can be aligned in 3 min to a stored heading. In-flight refuelling capability is also provided.

F-5Es of the Brazilian Air Force have a large dorsal fin to accommodate an ADF antenna.

F-5F. Tandem two-seat version of F-5E, with fuselage lengthened by 1·08 m (3 ft 6½ in). Fire control system retained, enabling aircraft to be used for both training and combat duties, but one M-39 gun deleted. Development approved by US Air Force in early 1974. First flight was made on 25 September 1974. Two F-5Fs completed flight test and qualification in early 1976. Total of 118 ordered; deliveries began in the Summer of 1976.

The following details refer to the F-5E, but are generally applicable to the F-5F also, except for details noted under model listings:

TYPE: Single-seat light tactical fighter.

WINGS: Cantilever low-wing monoplane. Wing section NACA 65A004·8 (modified). No dihedral. No incidence. Sweepback at quarter-chord 24°. Multi-spar light alloy structure with heavy plate machined skins. Hydraulically-powered sealed-gap ailerons at approximately mid-span. Electrically-operated light alloy single-slotted trailing-edge flaps inboard of ailerons. Electrically-operated leading-edge manoeuvring flaps. No de-icing system.

FUSELAGE: Light alloy semi-monocoque basic structure, with steel, magnesium and titanium used in certain areas. Two hydraulically-actuated airbrakes of magnesium alloy construction, mounted on underside of fuselage forward of main-wheel wells. Avionics bay and cockpit pressurised; fail-safe structure in pressurised sections.

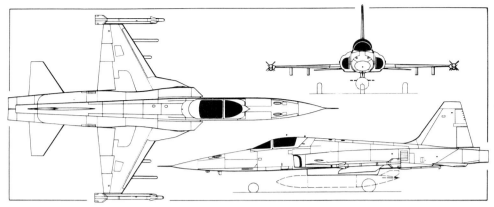

Northrop F-5E Tiger II single-seat twin-jet tactical fighter aircraft *(Pilot Press)*

TAIL UNIT: Cantilever all-metal structure, with hydraulically-powered rudder and one-piece all-moving tailplane. Tailplane incidence varied by hydraulic actuators. No trim tabs. Dual hydraulic actuators of Northrop design for control of rudder and tailplane.

LANDING GEAR: Hydraulically-retractable tricycle type, main units retracting inward into fuselage, nosewheel forward. Oleo-pneumatic struts of Northrop design on all units. Two-position extending nose unit increases static angle of attack by 3° 22' to reduce T-O distance, and is shortened automatically during the retraction cycle. Gravity-operated emergency extension. Main wheels and tyres size 24 × 8·00-13, pressure 14·48 bars (210 lb/sq in). Steerable nose unit with wheel and tyre size 18 × 6·50-8, pressure 8·27 bars (120 lb/sq in). All-metal multiple-disc brakes of Northrop design.

POWER PLANT: Two General Electric J85-GE-21A turbojet engines, each rated at 22·24 kN (5,000 lb st) with afterburning. Two independent fuel systems, one for each engine. Fuel for starboard engine supplied from two rubber-impregnated bladder-type nylon fabric cells, comprising a centre-fuselage cell of 803 litre (212 US gallon) capacity, and an aft-fuselage cell of 640 litre (169 US gallon) capacity. Port engine supplied from a forward fuselage cell of 1,120 litre (296 US gallon) capacity. Total fuel capacity 2,563 litres (677 US gallons). No fuel is carried in the wings. Fuel crossfeed system allows fuel from either or both cell systems to be fed to either or both engines. Auxiliary jettisonable fuel tanks of 568 or 1,040 litres (150 or 275 US gallons) can be carried on the fuselage centreline pylon and the inboard underwing pylons. Single refuelling point on lower fuselage for fuselage fuel cell and external tank installation. Provision for in-flight refuelling by means of a detachable probe. Oil capacity 4·5 litres (1·2 US gallons) per engine.

ENGINE INTAKES: Intakes are supplemented with auxiliary air inlet doors for use during T-O and low-speed flight, to improve compressor face pressure recovery and to decrease distortion. Each door consists of a set of six pivot-mounted louvres in removable panels on each side of the fuselage. The doors are actuated by the pilot at T-O, and controlled automatically in flight by Mach sensor switches, and are maintained in the open position at airspeeds below Mach 0·35-0·4.

ACCOMMODATION: Pilot only in pressurised, heated and air-conditioned cockpit, on rocket-powered ejection seat. Upward-opening canopy, hinged at rear.

SYSTEMS: Cockpit and avionics bay pressurised, heated and air-conditioned by engine bleed air, maximum pressure differential 0·34 bars (5 lb/sq in). Hydraulic power supplied by two independent systems at a pressure of 207 bars (3,000 lb/sq in). Flight control system provides power solely for operation of primary flight control surfaces. Utility system provides hydraulic backup power for the primary flight control surfaces and operating power for the landing gear doors, landing gear doors, airbrakes, wheel brakes, nosewheel steering, gun bay purge doors, gun gas deflectors and stability augmentation system. Electrical power supplied by two 13/15kVA 115/200V three-phase 320-480Hz non-paralleled engine-driven alternators. Each alternator has the capacity to accept full aircraft power load via an automatic transfer function. 250VA 115V 400Hz single-phase solid-state static inverter provides secondary AC source for engine starting. Two 33A 26-32V transformer-rectifiers and a 24V 11Ah nickel-cadmium battery provide DC power. Liquid oxygen system with capacity of 5 litres.

AVIONICS AND EQUIPMENT (F-5E): AN/ARC-164 UHF command radio, 3,500-channel with 50kHz spacing. Emerson Electric AN/APQ-159 lightweight microminiature X-band pulse radar for air-to-air search and range tracking; target information, at a range of up to 20 nm (37 km; 23 miles), is displayed on a 0·13 m (5 in) DVST in cockpit. AN/ARA-50 UHF ADF; AN/AIC-18 intercom system; AN/APX-101 IFF/SIF system; AN/ARN-118 Tacan; attitude and heading reference system; angle of attack system; and central air data computer. Full blind-flying instrumentation. Optional avionics include LN-33 inertial navigation system; AN/ARN-108 instrument landing system; CPU-129/A flight director computer; VHF; VOR/ILS with DME; LF ADF; CRT with scan converter for radar or electro-optical weapon (AGM-65 Maverick); and radar warning receiver.

AVIONICS AND EQUIPMENT (F-5F): AN/ARC-164 UHF/AM command radio, AN/AIC-18 or -25 interphone set, AN/APX-101 IFF/SIF transponder, TS1843/APX transponder test set, AN/ARN-118 Tacan, AN/APQ-159 fire control radar, AN/ASG-29 lead computing optical sight, and AN/ARA-50 UHF/DF. Optional equipment includes photoreconnaissance nose; in-flight refuelling system; pylon jettison conversion kits; anti-skid brakes; and chaff/flare countermeasures package.

ARMAMENT (F-5E): Two AIM-9 Sidewinder missiles on wingtip launchers. Two M-39A2 20 mm cannon mounted in fuselage nose, with 280 rounds per gun. Up to 3,175 kg (7,000 lb) of mixed ordnance can be carried on one underfuselage and four underwing stations, including M129 leaflet bombs; MK-82 GP and Snakeye 500 lb bombs; MK-36 destructors; MK-84 2,000 lb bomb; BLU-1, -27 or -32 U or F napalm; LAU-68 (7) 2·75 in rockets; LAU-3 (19) 2·75 in rockets; CBU-24, 49, -52 or -58 cluster bomb units; SUU-20 bomb and rocket packs; SUU-25 flare dispensers; TDU-10 tow targets (Dart); and RMU-10 reel (Dart). Lead-computing optical gunsight uses inputs from airborne radar for air-to-air missiles and cannon, and provides a roll-stabilised manually-depressible reticle aiming reference for air-to-ground delivery. A 'snapshoot' capability is included for attack on violently manoeuvring and fleeting targets. The gunsight incorporates also a detachable 16 mm reticle camera with 15 m (50 ft) film magazine. Optional ordnance capability includes the AGM-65 Maverick; centreline multiple ejector rack; and laser guided bombs.

ARMAMENT (F-5F): Two AIM-9J Sidewinder missiles on wingtip launchers. One M-39 20 mm cannon in port side of nose with 140 rounds. Underfuselage and underwing stores as detailed for the F-5E. Optional ordnance includes a laser designator in the rear cockpit.

DIMENSIONS, EXTERNAL:

Wing span	8·13 m (26 ft 8 in)
Span over missiles	8·53 m (27 ft 11⅞ in)
Wing chord at root	3·57 m (11 ft 8⅝ in)
Wing chord at tip	0·68 m (2 ft 2⅞ in)
Wing aspect ratio	3·82
Length overall (incl nose-probe):	
F-5E	14·68 m (48 ft 2 in)
F-5F	15·72 m (51 ft 7 in)
Height overall: F-5E	4·06 m (13 ft 4 in)
F-5F	4·01 m (13 ft 1¾ in)
Tailplane span	4·31 m (14 ft 1½ in)
Wheel track	3·80 m (12 ft 5½ in)
Wheelbase	5·17 m (16 ft 11½ in)

AREAS:

Wings, gross	17·3 m² (186 sq ft)
Ailerons (total)	0·86 m² (9·24 sq ft)
Trailing-edge flaps (total)	1·95 m² (21·0 sq ft)
Leading-edge flaps (total)	1·14 m² (12·3 sq ft)
Fin	3·85 m² (41·42 sq ft)
Rudder	0·57 m² (6·10 sq ft)
Tailplane	5·48 m² (59·0 sq ft)

WEIGHTS AND LOADINGS:

Weight empty: F-5E	4,392 kg (9,683 lb)
F-5F	4,793 kg (10,567 lb)
Max T-O weight: F-5E	11,193 kg (24,676 lb)
F-5F	11,442 kg (25,225 lb)
Max landing weight: F-5F	11,406 kg (25,147 lb)
Max zero-fuel weight: F-5E	7,953 kg (17,534 lb)
Max wing loading: F-5E	649·4 kg/m² (133 lb/sq ft)
Max power loading: F-5E	251·6 kg/kN (2·5 lb/lb st)

PERFORMANCE (F-5E at combat weight of 6,055 kg; 13,350 lb, F-5F at combat weight of 6,375 kg; 14,055 lb, unless stated otherwise):

Never-exceed speed
710 knots (1,314 km/h; 817 mph) EAS

Max level speed:

F-5E at 10,975 m (36,000 ft)	Mach 1·63
F-5F at 11,000 m (36,090 ft)	Mach 1·55

Max cruising speed:

F-5E at 10,975 m (36,000 ft)	Mach 0·98
Econ cruising speed	Mach 0·80

Stalling speed, flaps down, power off:

F-5E	124 knots (230 km/h; 143 mph)
F-5F	136 knots (253 km/h; 157 mph)

Max rate of climb at S/L:

F-5E	10,516 m (34,500 ft)/min
F-5F	10,030 m (32,900 ft)/min

Service ceiling: F-5E 15,790 m (51,800 ft)
F-5F 15,484 m (50,800 ft)

Service ceiling, one engine out:

F-5E	over 12,495 m (41,000 ft)
F-5F	12,285 m (40,300 ft)

T-O run:

F-5E at 7,053 kg (15,550 lb)	610 m (2,000 ft)
F-5F at 7,371 kg (16,250 lb)	701 m (2,300 ft)

T-O run at max T-O weight:

F-5E	1,737 m (5,700 ft)
F-5F	1,829 m (6,000 ft)

T-O to 15 m (50 ft):

F-5E at 7,053 kg (15,550 lb)	884 m (2,900 ft)
F-5F at 7,371 kg (16,250 lb)	975 m (3,200 ft)

Landing from 15 m (50 ft):

F-5E at 5,230 kg (11,530 lb), without brake chute
1,417 m (4,650 ft)
F-5F at 5,554 kg (12,245 lb), without brake chute
1,524 m (5,000 ft)

Landing run with brake chute:

F-5E at 5,230 kg (11,530 lb)	762 m (2,500 ft)
F-5F at 5,554 kg (12,245 lb)	792 m (2,600 ft)

Range, F-5E:
with max fuel and reserves for 20 min max endurance at S/L: tanks retained
1,340 nm (2,483 km; 1,543 miles)
tanks dropped
1,545 nm (2,863 km; 1,779 miles)

Combat radius, F-5E:
with max fuel, two Sidewinder missiles, allowances as above and 5 min combat with max afterburning power at 4,570 m (15,000 ft)
570 nm (1,056 km; 656 miles)
with 2,358 kg (5,200 lb) ordnance load, two Sidewinder missiles, max fuel, allowances as above and 5 min combat at military power at S/L, lo-lo-lo mission
120 nm (222 km; 138 miles)
with max fuel, two Sidewinder missiles and two 530 lb bombs, allowances as above and 5 min combat at military power at S/L, hi-lo-hi mission
480 nm (890 km; 553 miles)

Range, F-5F:
ferry range with max fuel, allowances comprising 5 min at normal thrust at S/L, plus 5 min loiter at S/L, plus reserve of 5% of initial fuel: crew of two
1,270 nm (2,353 km; 1,462 miles)

Combat radius, F-5F:
with max internal fuel, and allowances comprising 2 min at normal thrust, 1 min at max thrust, 5 min max thrust for combat at 4,570 m (15,000 ft), 20 min loiter at S/L, plus reserve of 5% of initial fuel
520 nm (964 km; 599 miles)
with max fuel, two Sidewinder missiles and two 530 lb bombs, allowances as above, and 5 min combat at military power at S/L, hi-lo-hi mission
450 nm (834 km; 518 miles)

(1980–81)

The Northrop P-16C Black Widow Night Fighter. Note the supercharger intakes beneath the engine nacelles.

THE NORTHROP BLACK WIDOW

U.S. Army Air Forces designation: P-61.
U.S. Marine Corps designation: F2T

The Black Widow was built to an Army specification issued in 1940. Development began in 1940, an order for two XP-61s was placed in January, 1941, and the first prototype flew on May 26, 1942.

P-61A and P-61B. Generally similar, the earlier P-61A being fitted with two Pratt & Whitney R-2800-10 (B Series) and the later P-61A and P-61B with the R-2800-65 (C Series) engines, both with two-stage superchargers. Only the first 37 P-61As were fitted with the dorsal turret and carried crew of three. Provision for external auxiliary tanks on later P-61Bs. Five P-61As used by USMC from 1946 as trainers.

P-61C. Two Pratt & Whitney R-2800-73 engines with single-stage superchargers and new Curtiss Electric airscrews with paddle-type blades. Aircraft fitted with slatted air-brakes on upper and lower surfaces of outer wings.

XP-61D. Similar to P-61A but fitted with two Pratt & Whitney R-2800-77 engines. One conversion only.

XP-61E. Long-range fighter version of P-61B. Later modified and redesignated XF-15 (which see).

XP-61F. Revised model of P-61C with two Pratt & Whitney R-2800-73 engines. One only. (1947)

TYPE.—Twin-engined Night Fighter.

WINGS.—Shoulder-wing cantilever monoplane. Centre-section panels between central nacelle and points outboard of engine nacelles set a coarser dihedral than outer wings. Two-spar all-metal structure. Landing flaps extend over most of trailing-edge. Aileron system consists of two small conventional ailerons, each with a trim-tab, four retractable aileron panels, all mechanically connected and linked to control system. The retractable panels are perforated metal scoop-shaped strips and when not in use are retracted into slots near trailing-edge. When raised they spoil airflow and reduce lift on one wing.

NACELLE AND TAIL BOOMS.—All-metal structures. The tail booms are metal monocoques extending aft from engine nacelles.

TAIL UNIT.—Monoplane type. Fins built integral with tail booms, the tailplane being located between the fins and above centre-line of booms. Single-piece elevator with centrally-located trim-tabs. Statically and aerodynamically-balanced rudders.

LANDING GEAR.—Retractable tricycle type. Main wheels raise aft into booms and nose wheel into central nacelle.

POWER PLANT.—Two 2,000 h.p. Pratt & Whitney R-2800-10 eighteen-cylinder radial air-cooled engines. Curtiss Electric four-blade constant-speed full-feathering airscrews, 12 ft. 2 in. (3.7 m.) diameter. Self-sealing fuel tanks in wings. Streamline auxiliary drop tanks may be carried under wings outboard of engine nacelles.

ACCOMMODATION.—Crew of three, comprising pilot, gunner and radar operator, in central nacelle. All crew positions armoured.

ARMAMENT.—Four forward firing 20 m/m. cannon in underside of fuselage aft of nose-wheel well and four 50 cal. machine-guns in a 360-degree electrically-operated General Electric dorsal turret. Turret is remotely controlled and fired by the pilot or from either one of two gun-sighting stations, one forward and one aft. Full Radar equipment.

DIMENSIONS.—Span 66 ft. (20.13 m.), Length 48 ft. 11 in. (13.72 m.), Height 14 ft. 2 in. (4.3 m.), Wing area 664 sq. ft. (61.7 sq. m.).

WEIGHT LOADED.—27,000 lbs. (12,260 kg.).

PERFORMANCE.—Maximum speed 375 m.p.h. (600 km.h.) at 17,000 ft. (5,190 m.), Climb to 25,000 ft. (4,575 m.) 13 min., Service ceiling 33,000 ft. (10,070 m.).
(1945–46)

The Northrop R-15A Reporter Long-Range Photographic-Reconnaissance Monoplane.

THE NORTHROP REPORTER.

U.S. Air Force designation : R-15A.

The Reporter is a photographic-reconnaissance aircraft developed from the P-61 (now F-61) Black Widow night-fighter which it closely resembles, the chief difference being in the design of the crew nacelle.

Design work began in the early Summer of 1944, the original specification calling for a long-range fighter aircraft to escort bombing formations in the Pacific Theatre under the designation XP-61E. Two prototypes were completed in January and February, 1945, respectively, but as their development proceeded the military situation rendered the long-range escort-fighter aircraft superfluous, and called for a long-range aircraft carrying comprehensive photographic gear. The XP-61E was duly modified for this purpose and re-designated the F-15 (now R-15) Reporter. 175 were ordered for the U.S.A.F.

TYPE.—Twin-engined Long-range Photographic-Reconnaissance monoplane.

WINGS.—Cantilever shoulder-wing monoplane. All-metal structure in six sections : two inner and two outer sections bolted together, and detachable tips. Two-spar structure, spars continuing through nacelle. Inner wing panels set at dihedral angle to nacelle. Inner wing section span (each) 9 ft. 6.6 in. (2.91 m.), Chord 11 ft. 11.95 in. (3.66 m.), Depth (from bottom at root to top at extremity) 5 ft. 0 in. (1.52 m.). Outer wing section span (each) 19 ft. 9½ in. (6.03 m.), Chord 12 ft. 0 in. (3.66 m.), Depth 1 ft. 10 in. (.56 m.), Tip span 1 ft. 8 in. (.51 m.). Gross wing area 664 sq. ft. (61.68 m.²). Short-span ailerons at wing-tips and four Northrop retractable ailerons acting as spoilers and consisting of perforated scoop-shape strips located near trailing-edge forward of flaps. Full-span trailing-edge flaps in four sections each side of nacelle.

NACELLE AND TAIL BOOMS.—All-metal monocoque nacelle and twin Heliarc-welded magnesium booms extending aft from engine nacelles to carry tail-unit. Nacelle 35 ft. 1.9 in. long × 4 ft. 1.1 in. wide × 6 ft. 5 in. high (10.71 m. × 1.25 m. × 1.96 m.), Tail-booms 9 ft. 0 in. long × 3 ft. 2.1 in. wide × 3 ft. 5.2 in. deep (2.74 m. × .91 m. × .63 m.).

TAIL UNIT.—All-metal twin fins and rudders mounted above ends of tail-booms and connected laterally by constant-chord tailplane and one-piece elevator. Rudders and elevator statically and aero-dynamically-balanced. Trim tabs in rudders ; trim and balance tabs in elevator. Fin height 9 ft. 2.2 in. (2.79 m.), Chord 7 ft. 7.6 in. (2.33 m.), Thickness 9 in. (22.86 cm.), Rudder height 9 ft. 0 in. (2.74 m.), Chord 3 ft. 0 in. (.91 m.), Thickness 7.58 in. (19.25 cm.),

Tailplane span (net) 16 ft. 8 in. (5.08 m.), tailplane chord 4 ft. 8.9 in. (1.44 m.), Thickness 11 in. (27.94 cm.), Elevator span 16 ft. 8 in. (5.08 m.), Chord 2 ft. 10.1 in. (0.86 m.), Thickness 6.3 in. (16 cm.).

LANDING GEAR.—Retractable tricycle type. Each main unit consists of a Bendix wheel and brake assembly carried on inside of a single Bendix shock-absorber leg which retracts backwards into engine nacelle. Nose-wheel carried in half-fork on Bendix shock-absorber leg which retracts backwards into nacelle. Hydraulic operation.

POWER PLANT.—Two Pratt & Whitney R-2800-C Double Wasp eighteen-cylinder two-row radial air-cooled engines each developing a normal output of 2,100 h.p. and with 2,800 h.p. emergency power. Enclosed in long-chord tapered cowlings with trailing-edge controllable gills. Turbo-superchargers, with intake of 11,250 cub. ft. (318 m.³) per minute at 35,000 ft. (10,668 m.). Curtiss Electric four-blade full-feathering airscrews. Diameter 12 ft. 8 in. (3.86 m.). Main fuel tank of 500 U.S. gallons (1,886 litres) capacity in fuselage aft of co-pilot, and secondary tanks in wings. Provision for long-range drop-tanks under both inner and outer wings. Cooling intakes in leading-edge on both sides of engine nacelles.

ACCOMMODATION.—Crew of two, consisting of pilot and co-pilot/navigator seated in tandem in long enclosed cockpit in nacelle. Pilot situated forward with flat bullet-proof panel and deflector plate. Moulded free-blown Plexiglas cover slides backwards for access. Fore and aft armour-plating. Full dual controls, allowing either member to operate cameras.

ARMAMENT.—None carried.

EQUIPMENT.—Provision for six forward shooting, vertical and oblique cameras of eleven different types and twenty-four alternative arrangements. Electrically-operated automatic pilot. Individual oxygen equipment.

DIMENSIONS.—Span 66 ft. 0 in. (20.12 m.), Length overall 50 ft. 3 in. (15.31 m.), Height to wing-tip 9 ft. 2 in. (2.79 m.).

WEIGHTS AND LOADINGS.—Weight loaded 28,000 lbs. (12,700 kg.), Wing loading 45.18 lbs./sq. ft. (220.59 kg./m.²), Power loading (at 2,100 h.p. per engine) 6.66 lbs./h.p. (3.02 kg./h.p.).

PERFORMANCE.—Maximum speed, over 440 m.p.h. (708 km.h.), Landing speed 80 m.p.h. (129 km.h.), Ceiling, over 35,000 ft. (10,668 m.), Maximum range with external tanks, over 4,000 miles (6,437 km.).

(1948)

THE NORTHROP SCORPION.
U.S. Air Force designation: F-89.

The following are the principal versions of the F-89 Scorpion :—

F-89A. Two Allison J35-A-21 engines (4,900 lb.=2,225 kg. s.t. each) with after-burners. First production model. Armament consisted of six nose-mounted 20 mm. cannon.

F-89B. Two Allison J35-A-33 engines (5,000 lb.=2,270 kg. s.t. each). Second production model. Generally similar to the F-89A but with certain internal and equipment changes.

F-89C. Two Allison J35-A-35 engines (5,600 lb.=2,540 kg. s.t. each). Progressive development of F-89B. External mass-balances on elevators suppressed.

F-89D. Two Allison J35-A-35 engines (5,600 lb.=2,540 kg. s.t. each) with Solar afterburners. Rocket-armament replaced

the six 20 mm. nose-mounted cannon of earlier F-89 versions. A total of 104 2.75 in. folding-fin air-to-air rockets carried in permanently mounted wing-tip pods. Electronic aiming and automatic triggering equipment. Two droppable pylon-mounted underwing tanks equipped with Bohanan cartridge-type force ejectors for jettisoning. Additional fuel gives 11 per cent. increase in range as compared with F-89C.

F-89H. Followed F-89D in production. Equipped with new electronic armament and has improved weapons capability. Details below refer to this version.

F-89J. This designation applies to earlier versions of F-89 brought up to F-89H standard.

The following description refers to the F-89H.

TYPE.—Twin-engined two-seat All-weather Interceptor Fighter.

WINGS.—Mid-wing cantilever monoplane. Thin-section high-lift low-drag wing-section. Thickness ratio 8½% at root, 7½% at tip. Taper ratio 2 : 1. Aspect ratio 4.5 : 1. Leading-edge sweep back 5°. All-metal multi-cellular structure. Double slotted flaps inboard of ailerons. The power-operated ailerons, or "decel-erons," are split so as to serve as ailerons or dive-brakes. The upper and lower segments may be opened up and down simultaneously to serve as air brakes ; or with the segments closed the surfaces operate as conventional ailerons. Hot-air anti-icing. Aileron area 45 sq. ft. (4.18 m.²). Flap area 63 sq. ft. (5.85 m.²). Gross wing area 562 sq. ft. (52.20 m.²).

FUSELAGE.—Oval section all-metal structure. Built in halves with joint along vertical centre-line, each half being equipped before assembly to central vertical keel which serves as mounting member for, and inter-vening firewall between, the two engines.

The Northrop F-89H Scorpion here seen with its six Falcon missiles in the extended firing position.

TAIL UNIT.—Cantilever monoplane type. All-metal structure. Power-operated control surfaces operated by aircraft hydraulic system, with emergency electrical actuation should hydraulic power fail. Tailplane span 11 ft. 6 in. (3.50 m.). Tailplane area 110 sq. ft. (10.22 m.²). Elevator area 25 sq. ft. (2.32 m.²). Vertical tail area (fin and rudder) 38 sq. ft. (3.53 m.²).

LANDING GEAR.—Retractable tricycle type. Main wheels are of large diameter and thin enough to permit total enclosure in wings when retracted. 165 lb./sq. in. tyre pressure. Steerable twin nose-wheels. Hydraulic retraction. Wheel track approx. 22 ft. (6.70 m.).

POWER PLANT.—Two Allison J35-A-35 turbo-jet engines, each with a static (dry) thrust rating of 5,450 lb. (2,474 kg.) and thrust

with afterburner in use of 8,000 lb. (3,632 kg.). Engines may be lowered clear of mountings by built-in hydraulic hoist for ground level maintenance. Four light-weight Goodyear bullet-proof tanks in fuselage, twelve Goodyear Pliocel bladder tanks in wings and further fuel tankage in wing-tip pods. Under-wing pylon-mounted auxiliary fuel tanks with Bohanan cartridge type jettison equipment.

ACCOMMODATION.—Crew of two, pilot and radar operator, in tandem in pressurised cockpit. Power-operated jettisonable canopy and ejection seats. Cabin heating and refrigeration.

ARMAMENT.—Six Hughes GAR-1 Falcon air-to-air guided missiles, three in each wing-tip pod, and 42 × 2.75-in. rockets, 21 in each pod in clusters of seven behind

frangible fairings. Can also carry MB-1 Genie air-to-air missile with nuclear warhead. Falcons and rockets can be fired selectively, the Falcons being extended clear of the pod on their launchers prior to firing. Automatic attack system includes sighting radar and fire control computer. Armament is triggered automatically.

DIMENSIONS.—
Span 59 ft. 8 in. (18.19 m.).
Length 53 ft. 4 in. (16.26 m.).
Height 17 ft. 7 in. (5.36 m.).

WEIGHTS.—
Loaded weight over 40,000 lb. (18,160 kg.).

PERFORMANCE.—
Max. speed over 600 m.p.h. (960 km.h.).
Operational ceiling over 50,000 ft. (15,250 m.).
Range over 1,000 miles (1,600 km.).

(1958–59)

Northrop T-38 Talon two-seat supersonic basic trainer

NORTHROP TALON
USAF designation: T-38

Developed for two years as a private venture, the T-38 supersonic lightweight twin-jet trainer has been in continuous production for the USAF under a series of contracts awarded since May 1956. It is powered by two General Electric J85-GE-5 turbojets, and reproduces the flying characteristics of a supersonic operational fighter aircraft.

The first T-38 flew for the first time on 10 April 1959, and production T-38A's became operational on 17 March 1961.

The 1,187th and last T-38 was delivered in January 1972. The **AT-36B** derivative is used for Lead-in Fighter Training, equipped with a gunsight and practice bomb dispensers.

NASA is using T-38's as space flight readiness trainers for astronauts and has acquired a total of 24 aircraft; the US Navy is procuring five T-38's from the Air Force Systems Command.

Another customer is the German government, which took delivery of 46 T-38's through the USAF, in 1967, for the advanced training of German student pilots in the USA. These aircraft retain US military insignia.

TYPE: Two-seat supersonic basic trainer.

WINGS: Cantilever low-wing monoplane. Wing section NACA 65A004·8 (modified). Thickness/chord ratio 4·8%. No dihedral or incidence. Sweepback at quarter-chord 24°. Multi-spar aluminium alloy structure with heavy plate machined skins. Hydraulically-powered sealed-gap ailerons at approximately mid-span with aluminium alloy single-slotted flaps inboard. No trim-tabs. Designed to be flown and landed safely using only one aileron. No de-icing system.

FUSELAGE: Aluminium semi-monocoque basic structure with steel, magnesium and titanium used in certain areas. "Waisted" area-rule lines. Two hydraulically-actuated air-brakes on underside of fuselage forward of wheel wells.

TAIL UNIT: Cantilever all-metal structure, with hydraulically-powered rudder and one-piece "all-moving" tailplane. Single spars with full-depth aluminium honeycomb secondary structure. No trim-tabs. Longitudinal and directional stability augmentors installed in series with control system.

LANDING GEAR: Hydraulically-retractable tricycle type with steerable nose-wheel. Emergency gravity extension. Main units retract inward into fuselage, nose-wheel forward. Oleo-pneumatic shock-absorbers. Main wheel tyres size 20 × 4·4, pressure 236 lb/sq in (16·6 kg/cm²). Nose-wheel tyre size 18 × 4·4, pressure 75 lb/sq in (5·27 kg/cm²). Multiple-disc hydraulic brakes.

POWER PLANT: Two General Electric J65-GE-5 turbojets with afterburners (each 2,680 lb = 1,216 kg st dry, 3,850 lb = 1,748 kg with afterburning). Two independent fuel systems, one for each engine. Fuel for starboard engine provided by forward fuselage tank and dorsal tank just aft of rear cockpit. Fuel for port engine provided by centre and aft fuselage tanks. All tanks of bladder type. Total usable capacity 583 US gallons (2,206 litres). No external tanks. Single refuelling point on lower fuselage. Oil capacity 4·7 US quarts (4·5 litres) each engine. Aircraft supplied to NASA have an engine inlet duct lip anti-ice system.

ACCOMMODATION: Pupil and instructor in tandem on rocket-powered ejection seats in pressurised and air-conditioned cockpits, separated by windshield. Separate manually-operated, rearward-hinged jettisonable canopies. Instructor's seat at rear raised 10 in (0·25 m) higher than that of pupil to give improved forward view.

SYSTEMS: Pressure differential 5 lb/sq in (0·35 kg/cm²). Two separate 3,000 lb/sq in (210 kg/cm²) hydraulic systems, one for flying controls, other for flying controls, air-brakes, landing gear, and nose-wheel steering. No pneumatic system. Two 8·5kVA generators, wide-frequency 320-480 c/s, manufactured by Westinghouse. Two 25A transformer-rectifiers for DC supply. •

ELECTRONICS: Magnavox AN/ARC-34X UHF radio. Hoffmann AN/ARN-65 TACAN, Hazeltine AN/APX-64 IFF, Andrea AN/AIC-18 intercom, Collins AN/ARN-58 ILS, Bendix compass system. Integrated instrument panel.

DIMENSIONS, EXTERNAL:
Wing span 25 ft 3 in (7·70 m)
Wing chord (mean aerodynamic) 7 ft 9 in (2·36 m)
Wing aspect ratio 3·75
Length overall 46 ft 4½ in (14·13 m)
Height overall 12 ft 10½ in (3·92 m)
Tailplane span 14 ft 2 in (4·32 m)
Wheel track 10 ft 9 in (3·28 m)
Wheelbase 19 ft 5½ in (5·93 m)

AREAS:
Wings, gross 170 sq ft (15·80 m^2)
Ailerons (total) 9·24 sq ft (0·86 m^2)
Trailing-edge flaps (total) 19·00 sq ft (1·77 m^2)
Fin 41·42 sq ft (3·85 m^2)
Rudder, including tab 6·37 sq ft (0·59 m^2)
Tailplane 59·00 sq ft (5·48 m^2)

WEIGHTS AND LOADINGS:
Max T-O and landing weight 12,050 lb (5,465 kg)
Max zero-fuel weight 7,663 lb (3,475 kg)
Max wing loading 70·9 lb/sq ft (346·2 kg/m^2)
Max power loading 1·56 lb/lb st (1·56 kg/kg st)

PERFORMANCE (at max T-O weight, except where indicated):
Max level speed (50% fuel) at 36,000 ft (11,000 m) above Mach 1·23
Max permissible diving speed 710 knots (818 mph; 1,316 km/h) IAS
Max cruising speed at 36,000 ft (11,000 m) above Mach 0·95
Econ cruising speed Mach 0·88
Stalling speed flaps extended (50% fuel) 136 knots (156 mph; 252 km/h) IAS
Rate of climb at S/L (50% fuel) 30,000 ft (9,145 m)/min
Service ceiling (50% fuel) 53,600 ft (16,335 m)
Service ceiling, one engine out (50% fuel) 40,000 ft (12,200 m)
T-O run 2,500 ft (762 m)
T-O to 50 ft (15 m) 3,700 ft (1,128 m)
Landing from 50 ft (15 m) at AUW of 8,850 lb (4,014 kg) 4,500 ft (1,372 m)

(1970–71)

ORENCO "D."

Specification.

Type of machine	Tractor Biplane.
Name or type No. of machine	"D."
Purpose for which intended	Single-seater Fighter.
Armament	2 fixed Browning M.G.
Span	30 ft. (U), 28 ft. (L).
Overall length	21 ft. 6 in.
Maximum height	8 ft. 3 in.
Total wing area	261 sq. ft.
Engine type and h.p.	300 h.p. Wright-Hispano "H."
Tank capacity	55 U.S. galls.
Weight empty	1,666 lbs.
Weight loaded	2,432 lbs.
Performance.	
High speed	147 m.p.h.
Low speed	50 m.p.h.
Climb.	
To 5,000 feet	4 mins. 20 secs.
To 15,000 feet	16 mins. 45 secs.
Range	275 miles.

The Orenco Type D Fighter (300 h.p. Wright-Hispano engine).

Side View of the Le Père Fighter (400 h.p. Liberty engine).

THE PACKARD LE PÈRE FIGHTER

Captain G. Lepère, an aeronautical engineer in the French Air service, designed the *Lepère* "Fighter" with a Liberty engine for production in the United States. It was intended for use as a fighter or reconnaissance machine, and carried two fixed guns firing forward, synchronized with the engine, and two Lewis guns attached to a movable Scarff ring surrounding the rear cockpit.

General Dimensions.

Span, upper plane	39 ft. 0¼ in
Span, lower plane	39 ft. 0¼ in.
Chord, both planes	5 ft. 6 in.
Gap between planes	5 ft. 0⅝ in.
Stagger	2 ft. $0\frac{15}{16}$ in.
Length over all	25 ft. 4⅝ in.
Height over all	9 ft. 10⅞ in.

Weights.

Machine empty	2,468 lbs.
Pilot and gunner	360 lbs.
Fuel and oil	475 lbs.
Armament	352 lbs.
Total	3,655 lbs.

Performances.

Height.	Speed.	Time of Climb.
0 ft.	136 m.p.h.	0 mins. 0 secs.
6,000 ft.	132 m.p.h.	5 mins. 35 secs.
10,000 ft.	127 m.p.h.	10 mins. 35 secs.
15,000 ft.	118 m.p.h.	19 mins. 15 secs.
20,000 ft.	102 m.p.h.	41 mins. 0 secs.

Service ceiling, or height beyond which the machine will not climb 100 feet per minute, 20,800 feet.

Centre of gravity occurs at a point 6 ft. 3 ins. from nose of fuselage.

Axle of landing gear 22⅜ ins. forward of centre of gravity. The landing gear wheels have a $65\frac{9}{16}$ ins. track and are 28 ins. in diameter.

Tail Group.

Overall plan of stabilizer, 98¾ ins. ; chord, 35½ ins. It is fixed at a non-lifting angle, and attached to upper fuselage longerons.

Tail flaps or elevators measure 158½ ins. from tip to tip. Their chord is 31⅜ ins., and in addition to this there are small balancing portions extending beyond the tail plane.

Rudder is 30 in. wide and has a balancing portion above the fin, 25 in. wide.

Engine Group.

A Liberty "12" 400 h.p. engine is used. It develops 400 h.p. at 1,750 r.p.m. Bore, 5 ins. ; stroke, 7 ins. ; weight, without propeller and water, 858 pounds. Two Zenith Duplex carburetters are used.

The radiator is located in the upper plane centre section, and its location has necessitated some slight modifications in the engine to increase the water circulation.

Propeller, 9 ft. 4 ins. in diameter. Front propeller plate projects 11¾ ins. forward of fuselage nose.

Propeller axis $15\frac{7}{16}$ ins. below top of upper longerons. In flying position the propeller hub is 5 ft. 2⅞ ins. above the ground line ; when at rest on the ground the propeller hub is 6 ft. 1⅝ ins. above ground.

Main Planes.

Planes are flat in span and have no sweepback. Top plane is in three sections—a centre section over the body and two outer panels. Lower plane in two sections attached at lower sides of fuselage in the usual manner.

Upper and lower planes are similar in shape, and with ailerons 21¾ ins. wide by 94¼ ins. long attached to both. An interconnecting streamlined rod is used between each pair of ailerons, located between the outer wing struts.

Leading edge of outer plane is located $49\frac{9}{16}$ ins. from front of propeller hub. Middle struts located 94⅝ ins. from centre of machine ; outer struts 98½ ins. from middle struts ; overhang, 41 ins. Interplane strut design is unique, inasmuch as it eliminates the usual incidence wires.

Fuselage.

Veneer is used for exterior finish. Overall length of fuselage, 22 ft. 0⅛ in Maximum section at the gunner's cockpit, 32½ ins. wide, 45½ ins. deep.

(1919)

The Piasecki HRP-2 Transport Helicopter (600 h.p. Pratt & Whitney R-1340 engine). (1953–54)

THE PIASECKI RESCUER.
U.S. Navy designation : HRP.

The HRP was the first large tandem-rotored transport helicopter to be put into production by Piasecki. The prototype XHRP-1 was first flown in March, 1945, and an initial service test order for ten HRP-1's was placed by the U.S. Navy in June, 1946, followed later by a further production order for ten. In June, 1948 the U.S. Navy placed a further limited production contract for an improved and modernised development known as the HRP-2. These two versions are distinguished as follows :—

HRP-1. 600 h.p. Pratt & Whitney R-1340 engine. Fabric covering on forward fuselage. Normal accommodation for crew of two (in tandem) and eight passengers, or six stretchers. Maximum load 2,000 lb. (908 kg.). Normal A.U.W. 6,900 lb. (3,133 kg.). Maximum speed 104 m.p.h. (167 km.h.). In service with U.S. Navy, Marine Corps and Coast Guard.

HRP-2. Same power-plant. All-metal fuselage of improved shape and decreased drag. Modified nose section seats crew of two side-by-side with dual controls. Cabin 20 ft. (6.10 m.) long, 5 ft. 6 in.

(1.68 m.) high and 5 ft. 6 in. (1.68 m.) wide. HRP-2's are being used by the U.S. Marine Corps in developing airborne amphibious assault techniques. The data below refers specifically to the HRP-2.

DIMENSIONS.—
Rotor diameter 41 ft. (12.50 m.).
Length 54 ft. (16.47 m.).
Height 14 ft. 10 in. (4.52 m.).
WEIGHTS.—
Empty 5,301 lb. (2,409 kg.).
Loaded 7,225 lb. (3,284 kg.).
PERFORMANCE.—
Max. speed at S.L. 105 m.p.h. (168 km.h.).
Cruising speed 92 m.p.h. (148 km.h.).
Vertical rate of climb 400 ft./min. (121 m./min.).

Pilatus PC-6 Turbo-Porter, one of two operated by the US Army as the UV-20 Chiricahua

PILATUS PC-6 TURBO-PORTER
US Army designation: UV-20 Chiricahua

The Pilatus PC-6 is a single-engined multi-purpose utility aircraft, with STOL characteristics permitting operation from unprepared strips under harsh environmental and terrain conditions. The aircraft can be converted rapidly from a pure freighter to a passenger transport, and can be adapted for a great number of different missions, including supply dropping, ambulance, aerial survey and photography, parachuting, crop spraying, water bombing and target towing as well as operation from soft ground, snow, glacier or water, and long-range operations.

The first of five PC-6 piston-engined prototypes made its first flight on 4 May 1959, and 20 pre-series PC-6s, with 253·5 kW (340 hp) Avco Lycoming engines, had been delivered by the Summer of 1961. Subsequent versions have included the piston-engined PC-6 and PC-6/350 Porters; the PC-6/A, A1, A2, B and C2-H2 Turbo-Porters, with various turboprop power plants.

Swiss-built piston-engined variants have the name Porter, and turboprop-powered variants are known as Turbo-Porters. In the USA, where the PC-6 was manufactured by Fairchild, it is known simply as the Porter, irrespective of the type of power plant fitted.

The current production version is the **PC-6/B2-H2 Turbo-Porter,** certificated on 30 June 1970 and powered by a PT6A-27 turboprop engine. Other versions can be made available on request.

By 1 September 1980, more than 420 PC-6 aircraft, of all models, had been delivered (including US licence manufacture), and were operating in more than 50 countries. Military operators include the air forces of Angola, Argentina, Australia, Austria, Bolivia, Burma, Chad, Ecuador, Oman, Peru, Sudan, Switzerland, Thailand and the US Army. Production by Pilatus was continuing at a rate of two to three per month.

Pilatus markets a Q-STOL (Quiet STOL) conversion kit for the B1 and B2 Turbo-Porters fitted with PT6A-20 or -27 turbine engines. This includes a system whereby propeller speed can be altered independently of the engine power setting, and is claimed to reduce the noise level by more than 10 dB for T-O and 20 dB for landing.

The structural description which follows is applicable to the current B2-H2 version. Details of the agricultural Turbo-Porter are given separately.

TYPE: Single-engined STOL utility transport.
WINGS: Braced high-wing monoplane, with single streamline-section bracing strut each side. Wing section

NACA 64-514 (constant). Dihedral 1°. Incidence 2° Single-spar all-metal structure. Entire trailing-edge hinged, inner sections consisting of electrically-operated all-metal double-slotted flaps and outer sections of all-metal single-slotted ailerons. No airbrakes or de-icing equipment. Trim tabs and/or Flettner tabs on ailerons optional; ground-adjustable tabs are mandatory if these are not fitted.

FUSELAGE: All-metal semi-monocoque structure.

TAIL UNIT: Cantilever all-metal structure. Variable-incidence tailplane. Flettner tabs on elevator.

LANDING GEAR: Non-retractable tailwheel type. Oleo shock-absorbers of Pilatus design on all units. Steerable/lockable tailwheel. Goodyear Type II main wheels and GA 284 tyres size 24 × 7 or 7·50 × 10 (pressure 2·21 bars; 32 lb/sq in); oversize Goodyear Type III wheels and tyres optional, size 11·0 × 12, pressure 0·88 bars (12·8 lb/sq in). Goodyear tailwheel with size 5·00-4 tyre. Goodyear disc brakes. Pilatus wheel/ski gear or Ed⸍ 8-4580 or 679-4930 floats optional.

POWER PLANT (PC-6/B2-H2): One 507 kW (680 shp) Pratt & Whitney Aircraft of Canada PT6A-27 turboprop engine (flat rated to 410 kW; 550 shp at S/L), driving a Hartzell HC-B3TN-3D/T-10178 fully-feathering reversible-pitch propeller with Beta mode control. Standard fuel in integral wing tanks, capacity 480 litres (127 US gallons; 105·5 Imp gallons) normal, 644 litres (170 US gallons; 142 Imp gallons) maximum. Two underwing auxiliary tanks, each of 190 litres (50 US gallons; 42 Imp gallons), available optionally.

ACCOMMODATION: Cabin has pilot's seat forward on port side, with one passenger seat alongside, and is normally fitted with six quickly-removable seats, in pairs, to the rear of these for additional passengers. Up to 11 persons, including the pilot, can be carried in high-density layout. Floor is level, flush with door sill, and is provided with seat rails. Forward-opening door beside each front seat. Large rearward-sliding door on starboard side of main cabin. Double doors, without central pillar, on port side. Hatch in floor 0·58 × 0·90 m (1 ft 10¾ in × 2 ft 11½ in), openable from inside cabin, for aerial camera or for supply dropping. Hatch in cabin rear wall 0·50 × 0·80 m (1 ft 7 in × 2 ft 7 in) permits stowage of six passenger seats or accommodation of freight items up to 5·0 m (16 ft 5 in) in length. Walls lined with lightweight soundproofing and heat-insulation material. Adjustable heating and ventilation systems provided. Dual controls optional.

SYSTEMS: Cabin heated by engine bleed air. Scott 8500 oxygen system optional. 200A 30V starter/generator and 24V 34Ah nickel-cadmium battery.

EQUIPMENT: Generally to customer's requirements, but can include agricultural equipment (see separate description) or a 1,300 litre (286 Imp gallon) water tank in cabin, with quick-release system, for firefighting role.

DIMENSIONS, EXTERNAL:

Wing span	15·13 m (49 ft 8 in)
Wing span over navigation lights	
	15·20 m (49 ft 10½ in)
Wing chord (constant)	1·90 m (6 ft 3 in)
Wing aspect ratio	7·96
Length overall	10·90 m (35 ft 9 in)
Height overall (tail down)	3·20 m (10 ft 6 in)
Elevator span	5·12 m (16 ft 9½ in)
Wheel track	3·00 m (9 ft 10 in)
Wheelbase	7·87 m (25 ft 10 in)
Propeller diameter	2·56 m (8 ft 5 in)
Cabin double door (port) and sliding door (starboard):	
Height	1·04 m (3 ft 5 in)
Width	1·58 m (5 ft 2¼ in)

DIMENSIONS, INTERNAL:

Cabin, from back of pilot's seat to rear wall:	
Length	2·30 m (7 ft 6½ in)
Max width	1·16 m (3 ft 9½ in)
Max height (at front)	1·28 m (4 ft 2½ in)
Height at rear wall	1·18 m (3 ft 10½ in)
Floor area	2·67 m² (28·6 sq ft)
Volume	3·28 m³ (107 cu ft)

AREAS:

Wings, gross	28·80 m² (310 sq ft)
Ailerons (total)	3·83 m² (41·2 sq ft)
Flaps (total)	3·76 m² (40·5 sq ft)
Fin	1·70 m² (18·3 sq ft)
Rudder, incl tab	0·96 m² (10·3 sq ft)
Tailplane	4·03 m² (43·4 sq ft)
Elevator, incl tab	4·22 m² (45·4 sq ft)

WEIGHTS AND LOADINGS:

Weight empty, equipped	1,216 kg (2,680 lb)
Max T-O and landing weight:	
Normal (CAR 3)	2,200 kg (4,850 lb)
Restricted (CAR 8)	2,770 kg (6,100 lb)
Max cabin floor loading	488 kg/m² (100 lb/sq ft)
Max wing loading (Normal)	
	76·4 kg/m² (15·65 lb/sq ft)
Max power loading (Normal)	
	5·37 kg/kW (8·82 lb/shp)

PERFORMANCE (at max T-O weight, Normal category):

Never-exceed speed	
	151 knots (280 km/h; 174 mph) IAS
Max cruising speed at 3,050 m (10,000 ft)	
	140 knots (259 km/h; 161 mph)
Econ cruising speed at 3,050 m (10,000 ft)	
	129 knots (240 km/h; 150 mph)
Max manoeuvring speed	
	106 knots (196 km/h; 122 mph)
Max speed with flaps extended	
	82 knots (152 km/h; 94·5 mph)
Stalling speed, power off, flaps up	
	50 knots (93·5 km/h; 58 mph)
Stalling speed, power off, flaps down	
	44 knots (82 km/h; 51 mph)
Normal rate of climb at S/L	387 m (1,270 ft)/min
Service ceiling	8,535 m (28,000 ft)
T-O run at S/L	110 m (360 ft)
T-O to 15 m (50 ft) at S/L	235 m (771 ft)
Landing from 15 m (50 ft) at S/L	218 m (715 ft)
Landing run at S/L	80 m (262 ft)
Max range, no reserves:	
internal fuel only	560 nm (1,036 km; 644 miles)
with external fuel	875 nm (1,620 km; 1,007 miles)
Endurance, no reserves: internal fuel only	4 h 20 min
with external fuel	6 h 45 min
g limits	+3·72; −1·50
	(1980–81)

THE PIPER AMBULANCE.

U.S. Navy designation: AE-1 (formerly HE-1).

The AE-1 is an ambulance conversion of the J5C Super-Cruiser which has been specially developed for the U.S. Navy. Accommodation is provided for a pilot and one stretcher case. The deck of the fuselage from the trailing-edge of the wing to the fin is arranged to hinge up to permit the loading and unloading of a U.S. Navy standard stretcher.

DIMENSIONS.—Same as for Super-Cruiser.
WEIGHTS.—Weight empty 906 lbs. (411 kg.), Weight loaded 14,26 lbs. (647 kg.).
PERFORMANCE.—Same as for Super-Cruiser except Landing speed 45 m.p.h. (72 km.h.), Initial rate of climb 600 ft./min. (183 m./min.), Range 264 miles (422 km.). (1945–46)

The Piper AE-1 Light Naval Ambulance (100 h.p. Lycoming engine).

The Piper L-4H Grasshopper Light Observation and Liaison Monoplane (65 h.p. Continental O-170-3 engine).

THE PIPER GRASSHOPPER.
U.S. Army Air Forces designation : L-4.
U.S. Navy designation : NE-1.
British name : Piper Cub.

The Piper Grasshopper is a light observation and liaison monoplane which has been developed from the Cub Trainer. It is basically similar to the civil model except that the rear of the cabin has been provided with greater window area. This aircraft was originally given the Army designation O-59 but was subsequently transferred to the liaison category and re-designated the L-4.

The L-4A, L-4B and L-4H were all manufactured under Army contracts and differ from each other only in minor details. Other models in the L-4 Series were civil models which were bought secondhand for pre-glider training and other miscellaneous duties. These civil models are identified as follow :—

L-4C. J3L-65 Cub Trainer. Lycoming O-145-B1 engine.
L-4D. J3F-65 Cub Trainer. Franklin 4AC-176-B2 engine.
L-4E. J4 Coupe. Continental A75-9 engine.
L-4F. (originally UC-83). J5A Cruiser. Continental A75-8 engine.
L-4G. J5B Cruiser. Lycoming GO-145-C2 engine.

The following description applies to the L-4A, L-4B and L-4H models.

TYPE.—Two-seat Light Liaison and Reconnaissance monoplane.
WING, FUSELAGE, TAIL UNIT AND LANDING GEAR.—Same as for Cub J3 Trainer.
POWER PLANT.—One 65 h.p. Continental O-170-3 four-cylinder horizontally-opposed air-cooled engine. Fuel tank (12 U.S. gallons) in fuselage behind fireproof bulkhead.
ACCOMMODATION.—Enclosed cabin seating two in tandem with dual controls. Observer's seat may face forward or aft and when in latter position a small table for maps, etc. is provided. In L-4H two-way radio is standard equipment. No radio in L-4B and L-4A.
DIMENSIONS.—Span 35 ft. 2½ in. (10.7 m.), Length 22 ft. 4½ in. (6.83 m.), Height 6 ft. 8 in. (1.9 m.), Wing area 178.5 sq. ft. (16.5 sq. m.).
WEIGHTS.—Weight empty (L-4A with radio) 740 lbs. (336 kg.), Weight empty (without radio) 695 lbs. (315.5 kg.), Weight loaded 1,220 lbs. (554 kg.).
PERFORMANCE.—Maximum speed 87 m.p.h. (139 km.h.), Cruising speed 75 m.p.h. (120 km.h.), Stalling speed 39 m.p.h. (60.8 km.h.), Initial rate of climb 450 ft./min. (140 m./min.), Service ceiling 11,500 ft. (3,510 m.), Range 260 miles (416 km.). (1945–46)

THE PIPER PA-18 SUPER CUB 95.
U.S.A.F. designation: L-18.

TYPE.—Two-seat Light Cabin monoplane.

WINGS.—High-wing braced monoplane. Wing structure of aluminium spars and aluminium-alloy ribs, the whole being covered with Duroclad. Steel-tube Vee bracing struts. No flaps. Gross wing area 178.5 sq. ft. (16.58 m.²).

FUSELAGE.—Rectangular welded steel-tube structure covered with Duroclad.

TAIL UNIT.—Braced monoplane type. Welded steel-tube framework covered with Duroclad. Tailplane span 9 ft. 6 in. (2.89 m.).

LANDING GEAR.—Fixed divided type. Two side Vees and half axles hinged to cabane below fuselage. Rubber cord shock absorption. Hydraulic wheel-brakes. Leaf-spring steerable tail-wheel.

POWER PLANT.—One 90 h.p. Continental C90 four-cylinder horizontally-opposed air-cooled engine on swinging engine mounting. Two-blade fixed-pitch wood airscrew 6 ft. 2 in. (1.8 m.) diameter. Fuel capacity 18 U.S. gallons (68 litres).

ACCOMMODATION.—Enclosed cabin seating two in tandem with dual controls. Large door on right side and sliding windows on left. Baggage compartment aft of rear seat. Equipment may be installed for spraying, dusting, fertilising, etc.

DIMENSIONS.—
Span 35 ft. 2½ in. (10.72 m.).
Length 22 ft. 4½ in. (6.82 m.).
Height 6 ft. 8 in. (2.03 m.).

WEIGHTS AND LOADINGS.—
Weight empty 800 lb. (363 kg.).
Disposable load 700 lb. (317 kg.).
Weight loaded 1,500 lb. (680 kg.).
Wing loading 8.4 lb./sq. ft. (50 kg./m.²).
Power loading 16.6 lb./h.p. (7.53 kg./h.p.).

PERFORMANCE.—
Max. speed 110 m.p.h. (176 km.h.).
Cruising speed 100 m.p.h. (160 km.h.).
Stalling speed 42 m.p.h. (67.2 km.h.).
Rate of climb 624 ft./min. (190 m./min.).
Service ceiling 13,500 ft. (4,120 m.).
T.O. run 452 ft. (138 m.).
T.O. to 50 ft. (15.25 m.) 952 ft. (290 m.).
Landing run 385 ft. (117 m.).

The Piper L-21, a military version of the Super Cub 125.

THE PIPER PA-18 SUPER CUB 135.
U.S.A.F. designation: L-21.

The Super Cub 125 is identical to the previously-described model except that it is fitted with a 135 h.p. Lycoming O-290-D engine and has wing flaps.

Both versions of the Super Cub may be fitted with tandem wheels for operation on or off rough ground ; and a range of optional equipment is available including electrical system, radio, wood or metal airscrew, extra fuel tank, etc.

DIMENSIONS.—
Same as for Super Cub 95.

WEIGHTS AND LOADINGS.—
Weight empty 845 lb. (384 kg.).
Disposable load 655 lb. (296 kg.).
Weight loaded 1,500 lb. (680 kg.).
Wing loading 8.4 lb./sq. ft. (50 kg./m.²).
Power loading 12 lb./h.p. (5.45 kg./h.p.).

PERFORMANCE (Wood airscrew).—
Max. speed 123 m.p.h. (197 km.h.).
Cruising speed (75% power) 108 m.p.h. (173 km.h.).

Stalling speed (with flaps) 38 m.p.h. (61 km.h.).
Initial rate of climb 870 ft./min. (265 m. min.).
Service ceiling 17.100 ft. (5.215 m.).
Absolute ceiling 19.200 ft. (5.860 m.).
Take-off run 270 ft. (82 m.).
Take-off distance to 50 ft. (15.25 m.) 580 ft. (177 m.).
Landing run 300 ft. (91.5 m.).
Cruising range 250 miles (400 km.).

PERFORMANCE (Sensenich metal airscrew).—
Max. speed 125 m.p.h. (200 km.h.).
Cruising speed (75% power) 110 m.p.h. (176 km.h.).
Stalling speed (with flaps) 38 m.p.h. (61 km.h.).
Initial rate of climb 1.000 ft. min. (305 m. min.).
Service ceiling 19.500 ft. (5.950 m.).
Absolute ceiling 21.700 ft. (6.620 m.).
Cruising range 250 miles (400 km.).
Take-off run 210 ft. (64 m.).
Take-off distance to 50 ft. (15.25 m.) 510 ft. (155.5 m.).
Landing run 300 ft. (91.5 m.).   (1952–53)

Piper UO-1, the U.S. Navy version of the Aztec twin-engined communications monoplane

THE PIPER PA-23-250 AZTEC
U.S. Navy designation: UO-1

The PA-23-250 Aztec is a five-seat twin-engined executive transport, which uses many of the proven systems and components of the PA-23 Apache.

The Aztec is powered by two 250 h.p. Lycoming O-540 direct-drive engines. Hartzell constant speed full-feathering airscrews are standard. Fuel is carried in four 36 U.S. gallon (136 litres) rubber wing cells. The five individual seats are arranged in two pairs and one single seat at the rear of the cabin. The horizontal tail surfaces consist of an all-moving one-piece tailplane with anti-servo tab. There is a servo tab in the rudder.

It was announced in February, 1960, that the U.S. Navy had ordered 20 Aztecs "off the shelf" for service as utility transports, with the designation UO-1.

DIMENSIONS.—
Span 37 ft. (11.28 m.)
Length 27 ft. 7 in. (8.42 m.)
Height 10 ft. 3½ in. (3.14 m.)
Wing area 207 sq. ft. (19.2 m.²)

WEIGHTS AND LOADINGS.—
Weight empty (standard) 2,775 lb. (1,260 kg.)
Weight empty (Super Custom) 2,850 lb. (1,294 kg.)
Weight loaded 4,800 lb. (2,180 kg.)
Wing loading 23.5 lb./sq. ft. (114.73 kg./m.²)
Power loading 9.6 lb./h.p. (4.35 kg./h.p.)

PERFORMANCE.—
Max. speed 215 m.p.h. (344 km.h.)
Cruising speed (75% power) 205 m.p.h. (328 km.h.) at 7,000 ft. (2,135 m.)
Cruising speed (65% power) 200 m.p.h. (320 km.h.) at 9,000 ft. (2,745 m.)
Stalling speed 62 m.p.h. (99 km.h.)
Initial rate of climb 1,650 ft./min. (503 m./min.)
Initial rate of climb on one engine 365 ft./min. (111 m./min.)
Service ceiling 22,500 ft. (6,860 m.)
Single engine service ceiling 7,400 ft. (2,260 m.)
Absolute ceiling 23,750 ft. (7,245 m.)
Single-engine absolute ceiling 8,800 ft. (2,685 m.)
Take-off distance to 50 ft. (15.25 m.) 1,100 ft. (335 m.)
Landing distance from 50 ft. (15.25 m.) 1,360 ft. (415 m.)
Cruising range (max. at 75% power) 1,025 miles (1,640 km.)
Cruising range (max. at 65% power) 1,200 miles (1,920 km.)   (1961–62)

THE REPUBLIC 2-PA "GUARDSMAN."
U.S. Army Air Forces Designation: AT-12.

The 2-PA is a two-seat version of the EP-1. As a light bomber it can carry 1,350 lbs. (615 kg.) of bombs comprising one 750-lb. (340-kg.) fuselage bomb with displacing gear to give airscrew clearance for dive-bombing and six 100-lb. (45.4-kg.) wing bombs. As an attack fighter provision can be made for one 500-lb. (230-kg.) fuselage bomb and ten 35-lb. (16-kg.) wing bombs together with two synchronised fuselage guns of either .30 or .50-cal. and one flexible .30 or .50-cal. gun in the rear cockpit, the after turtle deck of which rotates to allow free movement of the gun. Optional armament includes two fixed .30 or .50-cal. guns in the wings. The pilot has armour protection and a bullet-proof windshield.

A number of aircraft of this type ordered by the Swedish Government before the War was seized by the U.S. Government and taken over by the Army Air Forces. The 2-PA is classified in the U.S. Army Air Forces as an Advanced Trainer and has been given the designation AT-12. Details of the equipment of the AT-12 are not known. The figures for weights and performance given below relate to the 2-PA fighter dive-bomber. Structure and power plant are the same as for the EP-1.

DIMENSIONS.—Span 41 ft. (12.5 m.), Length 27 ft. 8 in. (8.43 m.), Height 9 ft. 9½ in. (2.98 m.), Wing area 250 sq. ft. (23.3 sq. m.).

WEIGHTS AND LOADINGS.—Weight empty 5,146 lbs. (2,334 kg.), Disposable load 2,334 lbs. (1,058 kg.), Weight loaded 7,480 lbs. (3,392 kg.), Wing loading 30 lbs./sq. ft. (145 kg./sq. m.), Power loading 7.12 lbs./h.p. (3.23 kg./sq. ft.).

PERFORMANCE.—Maximum speed 310 m.p.h. (498 km.h.) at 14,300 ft. (4,360 m.), Cruising speed 250 m.p.h. (402 km.h.) at operational height, Initial rate of climb 2,050 ft./min. (624 m./min.), Service ceiling 28,000 ft. (8,534 m.), Cruising range with normal fuel (130 U.S. gallons = 490 litres) 580 miles (932 km.). (1941)

The Republic P-43 "Lancer" Single-seat Fighter Monoplane (1,200 h.p. Pratt & Whitney "Wasp" engine).

THE REPUBLIC "LANCER."
U.S. Army Air Forces designation: P-43.

TYPE.—Single-seat Fighter monoplane.

WINGS.—Low-wing cantilever monoplane. Comprises detachable centre-section, two outer sections and two detachable top sections. Structure consists of five main spars with fore-and-aft ribs and a stressed-skin metal covering. Split trailing-edge flaps.

FUSELAGE.—All-metal semi-monocoque structure of approximately circular cross-section. Structure consists of continuous longitudinal stringers, frames, bulkheads and a stressed-skin covering.

TAIL UNIT.—Cantilever monoplane type. All-metal structure with metal-covered fixed surfaces and fabric-covered rudder and elevators. Trimming-tabs in control surfaces.

LANDING GEAR.—Retractable type. Wheels raised inwardly into wells in the undersurface of the centre-section, the aperture being closed by fairing-plates on the legs and wheels. Hydraulic retraction, with emergency hand-operating gear. Tail-wheel retracted simultaneously with wheels.

POWER PLANT.—One 1,200 h.p. Pratt & Whitney "Wasp" R-1830-B-1 radial air-cooled engine with turbo-supercharger mounted in the fuselage just aft of the baggage compartment. Curtiss electrically-operated constant-speed airscrew. Four fuel tanks (145 U.S. gallons = 550 litres total capacity) integral with the wing structure.

ACCOMMODATION.—Enclosed cockpit over wing. Bullet-proof windshield and armour plating aft of pilot may be provided. Large baggage compartment behind pilot's cockpit.

ARMAMENT.—Two .50-cal. machine-guns in fuselage. Alternatively four .50-cal. guns can be installed in wings, or two in fuselage and two in wings. Provision for carrying six 20-lb. bombs on racks beneath outer wing sections.

DIMENSIONS.—Span 36 ft. (10.97 m.), Length 28 ft. 5¾ in. (8.69 m.), Height 10 ft. 2⁷⁄₁₆ in. (3.11 m.), Wing area 223.7 sq. ft. (20.78 sq. m.).

WEIGHTS AND LOADINGS.—Weight empty 5,627 lbs. (2,552 kg.), Disposable load 1,528 lbs. (693 kg.), Weight loaded 7,155 lbs. (3,245 kg.), Wing loading 32.1 lbs./sq. ft. (156.7 kg./sq. m.), Power loading 5.96 lbs./h.p. (2.68 kg./h.p.).

PERFORMANCE.—Max speed 349 mph (562 km/h), Service ceiling 38,000 ft (11,580 m), Range 800 miles (1,287 km) (1942)

THE REPUBLIC THUNDERBOLT.
U.S. Army Air Forces designation: P-47.
British name : Thunderbolt.

The specification to which the P-47 was designed was drawn up at Wright Field in June, 1940. The original XP-47 design was for a lightweight interceptor fighter fitted with an Allison V-1710 liquid-cooled engine and an armament of one 50 cal. and one 30 cal. guns and provision for two additional 30 cal. wing guns. This was not proceeded with.

The first experimental prototype of the Thunderbolt as it is known to-day was the XP-47B which was flown from Farmingdale to Mitchel Field on May 6, 1941. Production got under way in the following November. The first production P-47B was delivered on March 18, 1942.

P-47's began to arrive in Britain in November, 1942, and the first operational mission with the 8th Air Force was made on April 8, 1943. The first mission with auxiliary fuel tanks took place in July and during the last few weeks of 1943 the first fighter-bomber missions with two 500 lb. bombs were made. The first pairs of 1,000 lb. bombs were carried by P-47's in Italy early in 1944.

The Thunderbolt, in addition to being a standard fighter in the U.S. Army Air Forces, was also supplied, under Lend/Lease, to Great Britain, Russia, France and Brazil. The R.A.F. used the Thunderbolt in India and Burma. The Brazilian fighter squadron which served in Italy was equipped with Thunderbolts.

The 10,000th Thunderbolt came off the assembly lines at Farmingdale on September 20, 1944, just two and a half years after the first P-47B was delivered to the U.S. Army Air Forces.

The following are the principal production and development versions of the Thunderbolt :—

P-47B. 2,000 h.p. Wright R-2800-21 eighteen-cylinder radial air-cooled engine with exhaust-driven turbo-supercharger. Curtiss Electric four-blade constant-speed airscrew 12 ft. 2 in. (3.7 m.) diameter. Self-sealing fuel tanks (307 U.S. gallons capacity). Armour protection for pilot. Eight 50 cal. machine-guns. Length, 34 ft. 10 in. (10.6 m.).

P-47C. Similar to P-47B but fitted with special shackles to carry one 200 U.S. gallon auxiliary fuel tank under the fuselage. Overall, length, 35 ft. 7 in. (10.8 m.).

P-47D (Thunderbolt I and II). First models similar to the P-47C but fitted with universal shackles under fuselage for either droppable fuel tank or 500 lb. bomb, and similar wing racks. Later models fitted with water injection, which added several

The Republic P-47D Thunderbolt Single-seat Fighter (Pratt & Whitney R-2800-21 engine).

hundred horse-power for emergency use; improved turbos; wide-blade airscrews 13 ft. (3.96 m.) diameter, which added 400 ft. per minute to the climb; increased fuel capacity, which increased the radius of action to 637 miles (920 km.); jettisonable standard canopy and, later, a new jettisonable "blister" hood and flat bulletproof windscreen. The bomb load was increased from two 500 lb. to two 1,000 lb. and one 500 lb. bombs, and three auxiliary fuel tanks could be carried externally on the same racks. Various combinations of bombs and tanks could be carried to suit tactical requirements. After the introduction of the "blister hood" in the P-47D-25 a dorsal fin was added. Overall length 36 ft. 1$\frac{3}{16}$ in. (11 m.).

XP-47E. An experimental version of the P-47B fitted with a pressure cabin. Only one aircraft was so fitted.

XP-47F. Another experimental version of the P47B fitted with laminar flow wings.

P-47G. Similar to P-47C and early D but built by Curtiss Airplane Division at Buffalo, N.Y. Progressive developments introduced in P-47D, including water-injection and racks for bombs or auxiliary fuel tanks, also incorporated in P-47G.

XP-47H. A modification of the P-47B to test the experimental Chrysler XIV-2220 inverted Vee liquid-cooled engine.

XP-47J. Similar to the P-47D but with many engineering changes. Weight reduced by 1,000 lbs. (454 kg.). Reduced diameter engine cowling with cooling fan. Redesigned wings. Many features of this experimental model were incorporated in the production P-47M and N.

P-47M. A special model which went into service in Europe early in 1945. Fitted with a P-47D wing. P-47N fuselage and a 2,100 h.p. Pratt & Whitney R-2800-57 engine with larger supercharger and improved water-injection system. Was claimed to be the fastest airscrew-driven aeroplane in service at that time and to be successful in combatting German jet-propelled fighters.

P-47N. A long-range fighter developed for bomber escort duties in the Pacific theatre. Same fuselage and power-unit as the P-47M but fitted with re-designed wings of 18 in. greater span and 22 sq. ft. increased area and with squared wing-tips and larger ailerons; increased petrol capacity with eight additional tanks, one in the leading-edge of each wing and three near each wheel well; and a strengthened landing-gear with wider tread. Armament the same as for previous P-47's but provision for two 500 lb. bombs and ten 5 in. rockets under the wings. Maximum weight over 20,000 lbs. (9.080 kg.).

TYPE.—Single-seat Long-range Fighter or Fighter-Bomber.

WINGS.—Low-wing cantilever monoplane. Republic S-3 wing section. Aspect ratio 5.61 Incidence + 1°. Dihedral (upper surface) 4°. Wings taper in chord and thickness, the leading-edge having a straight taper of 3° and the trailing-edge a curved taper, terminating in rounded detachable wing-tips. Ailerons on skew hinges. Hydraulically-operated NACA slotted trailing-edge flaps between ailerons and fuselage. The flaps are on trapezoidal linkage hinges which permit them, when lowered, to move first aft then down and, when retracted, first up and then forward. Later P-47's have electrically-operated dive-recovery flaps just forward of the main flaps. When in retracted position these lie flush with underside of wing.

FUSELAGE.—Oval-section all-metal monocoque structure.

TAIL UNIT.—Cantilever monoplane type. All-metal structure with metal-covered fixed surfaces, rudder and elevators. Control surfaces statically and aerodynamically balanced and provided with trimming-tabs.

LANDING GEAR.—Retractable type. Cantilever shock-absorber struts retract inwardly, the wheels being raised into wells in the underside of the wings. Fairing plates on legs and wheels and hinged fairings on inner edges of wells close apertures when wheels are raised. Retractable tail-wheel.

The Republic P-47N Thunderbolt Long-range Fighter (Pratt & Whitney R-2800-57 engine).

POWER PLANT (P-47D).—One Pratt & Whitney R-2800-59 Double-Wasp eighteen-cylinder air-cooled supercharged engine rated at 1,625 h.p. at 30,000 ft. (9,150 m.) and with 2,300 h.p. available for take-off. Water-injection equipment provides an emergency increase in power to 2,535 h.p. G.E. turbo supercharger located in rear fuselage. Air fed to impeller through scoop in lower portion of cowling and compressed air led forward to carburetter through intercoolers in side of fuselage. Exhaust gases are ducted aft to supercharger through throttles which control speed of turbine and after passing through turbine are ejected through large diameter pipe near tail-wheel. Four-bladed Curtiss Electric constant-speed full-feathering airscrew. Two self-sealing and armoured fuel tanks in fuselage, the main tank (270 U.S. gallons) aft of the fireproof bulkhead and auxiliary tank (100 U.S. gallons), beneath pilot's seat. Auxiliary droppable fuel tanks of various capacities may be carried beneath fuselage and/or wings. In P-40N greatly increased fuel capacity in eight additional wing tanks, nearly doubling the former total internal capacity. Oil tank in front of firewall and two oil coolers in lower portion of engine cowling, one on each side of main air duct to supercharger.

ACCOMMODATION.—Enclosed cockpit over trailing-edge of wing. Sliding moulded plastic "blister" type canopy. Bullet-proof windscreen and front and rear armour protection for pilot. Cockpit and other vulnerable points armoured.
ARMAMENT.—Eight 50 cal. machine-guns, four in each wing outboard of landing-gear. Guns electrically-fired. Combat cine-camera in port wing root. Bombs may be carried under fuselage or wings. Maximum bomb load : two 1,000 lb. bombs, one under each wing, and one 500 lb. bomb under the fuselage. Ten 5 in. velocity aircraft rockets may be carried, the latest type of rocket needing neither launching-rails or tracks.
DIMENSIONS.—Span 40 ft. 9$\frac{5}{16}$ in. (12.4 m.), Length 36 ft. 1$\frac{1}{16}$ in. (11 m.), Height 14 ft. 2 in. (4.3 m.), Wing area 300 sq. ft. (27.9 sq. m.).
WEIGHT LOADED (P-47D).—12,500 lbs. (5,675 kg.).
PERFORMANCE (P-47D).—Maximum speed 440 m.p.h. (704 km.h.) at 29,000 ft. (8,850 m.), Landing speed 100 m.p.h. (160 km.h.), Climb to 15,000 ft. (4,575 m.) 5.1 min., Service ceiling 40,000 ft. (12,200 m.).

(1945–46)

REPUBLIC AP-63-31 THUNDERCHIEF
USAF designation: F-105

The F-105 was developed to meet USAF requirements for a supersonic single-seat fighter-bomber able to deliver nuclear weapons, as well as heavier loads of conventional bombs and rockets, at very high speeds and over long ranges.

Design work began in 1951 and construction of two YF-105A prototypes began in 1954. The following versions have been built:

YF-105A. The first of two YF-105A's exceeded Mach 1 during its initial test flight on 22 October 1955, powered by a Pratt & Whitney J57 turbojet engine.

F-105B. Single-seat day fighter-bomber with Pratt & Whitney J75-P-3 or -5 turbojet engine (15,000 lb=6,810 kg st dry, approx 25,000 lb= 11,350 kg with afterburner). Introduced swept-forward air intakes. The first example of this developed version flew on 22 May 1956, and was delivered to the USAF Flight Test Center shortly afterwards. The first production aircraft was delivered to USAF Tactical Air Command on 27 May 1958. The 335th Tactical Fighter Squadron, Fourth Tactical Fighter Wing, Eglin AFB, Florida, was first squadron to be equipped with F-105B. Production was completed in 1959 in favour of F-105D after 75 had been built.

JF-105B. Three aircraft of initial test batch of 15 were started as RF-105B's with cameras in nose. When this rôle was dropped, they were redesignated JF-105B for special tests. The first of them flew for the first time on 18 July 1957.

F-105D. Single-seat all-weather fighter-bomber with Pratt & Whitney J75-P-19W turbojet, NASARR monopulse radar system and Doppler for night or bad weather operation. NASARR provides all radar functions for both low and high level missions—air search, automatic tracking, ground mapping and terrain avoidance. First F-105D flew on 9 June 1959, and deliveries to the 4th Tactical Fighter Wing began in May 1960. Over 600 built. Max T-O weight 52,546 lb (23,832 kg). Max level speed Mach 1·11 at sea level, Mach 2·1 above 36,000 ft (11,000 m). Some 30 aircraft of this version are being modified to carry the newly-developed T-Stick II bombing system. The external appearance of these aircraft is changed considerably by the addition of a 'saddle-back' from aft of the cockpit to the base of the fin to house additional avionics.

F-105F. Two-seat dual-purpose trainer/tactical fighter version of F-105D. Only major design changes are an increase in the length of the fuselage and a proportionate increase in the height of the tail fin. Unspecified number ordered for USAF in Autumn of 1962, in lieu of equal number of F-105D's, for service with all F-105D units. First F-105F flew for the first time on 11 June 1963.

Contracts awarded by the USAF in 1968 covered installation in F-105 aircraft of a new bombing system, adaptation of the F-105 to carry the latest missiles, and the design and production of new advanced electronic countermeasures equipment for the F-105.

The following details refer to the F-105F:

TYPE: Two-seat dual-purpose trainer/tactical fighter.

Republic F-105D Thunderchief with 'saddle back' housing avionics for the T-Stick II bombing system

WINGS: Cantilever mid-wing monoplane. Wing section NACA 65A-005·5 at root, NACA 65A-003·7 at t p. Anhedral 3° 30'. No incidence. Sweepback at quarter-chord 45°. Unique swept-forward air intake ducts in wing root leading-edges to provide double shock-wave to slow compressor air and to reduce turbulence in way of tailplane. All-metal stressed-skin structure. Conventional ailerons, of aluminium alloy construction, are used only at low subsonic speeds. Primary roll control is by five sections of hydraulically-actuated aluminium spoiler forward of flaps on each wing. Single-slotted aluminium alloy trailing-edge flaps. Full-span plain aluminium alloy leading-edge flaps, with conical camber. Control surfaces actuated by fully-powered irreversible tandem jacks. No trim-tabs or de-icing system.

FUSELAGE: Semi-monocoque structure of aluminium and magnesium with "wasp-waist" in way of wings in accordance with Area Rule. Radar in nose. Large internal weapons bay under wing position. Hydraulically-operated "clover-leaf" speed brakes, made of titanium and stainless steel, form last 3 ft (0·91 m) of fuselage around tail-pipe.

TAIL UNIT: Cantilever structure of aluminium and magnesium. All surfaces highly swept. Ram air-intake in base of fin to provide cooling air for rear end of aircraft. One-piece "flying tail" and mass-balanced rudder, with flutter-damper, are actuated hydraulically by irreversible tandem jacks. No trim-tabs. Ventral stabilising fin under rear fuselage.

LANDING GEAR: Hydraulically-retractable tricycle type, with single wheel on each unit. Main units retract inward into thickened area of wing-roots created by main air intake ducts. Nose-wheel retracts forward. Bendix oleo-pneumatic shock-absorbers. Main wheel tyres size 36 × 11, pressure 205 lb/sq in (14·4 kg/cm²). Nose-wheel tyre size 24 × 7·7, pressure 140 lb/sq in (9·85 kg/cm²). Multi-pad Goodyear brakes, with anti-skid units.

POWER PLANT: One Pratt & Whitney J75-P-19W turbojet engine (26,500 lb=12,030 kg st with water injection and afterburning). Fuel in three flexible tanks in fuselage (forward, main and aft) with total capacity of 770 US gallons (2,915 litres) and one 390 US gallon (1,477 litre) bomb-bay tank. Provision for one 650 US gallon (2,460 litre) or 750 US gallon (2,840 litre) external tank under fuselage and two underwing tanks on inboard pylons, each of 450 US gallons (1,705 litres). Refuelling point on port side of fuselage, aft of wing. Provision for both flying boom and probe-and-drogue flight refuelling. Retractable refuelling probe on port side of forward fuselage. Oil capacity 6·5 US gallons (24·5 litres).

ACCOMMODATION: Crew of two, in tandem, on ejection seats, in separate pressurised and air-conditioned cockpits. Electrically-operated rearward-hinged canopies.

SYSTEMS: Hamilton Standard air-conditioning and pressurisation system, differential 5 lb/sq in (0·35 kg/cm²). Hydraulic system, pressure 3,000 lb/sq in (210 kg/cm²), operates landing gear, speed brakes, primary flying controls, leading-

Republic F-105F Thunderchief two-seat trainer/tactical fighter

edge flaps, flight refuelling probe and bomb-bay doors. No pneumatic system. Electrical system includes air-turbine motor for AC supply and engine-driven DC generator.

EQUIPMENT: General Electric FC-5 flight-control system connects with AN/APN-131 Doppler for automatic navigation. AN/ARC 70 UHF radio. AN/ASG-19 "Thunderstick" integrated armament control system consisting of NASARR radar, General Electric automatic lead computing sight, toss-bomb computer and associated equipment.

ARMAMENT: Fixed armament consists of one General Electric M-61 20-mm Vulcan auto-matic multi-barrel gun with 1,029 rounds. Typical alternative loads are (1) 650 gal centre-line tank, 450 gal tank on one inner wing pylon, nuclear store on other inner pylon, (2) 650 gal centre-line tank and four GAM-83B Bullpup nuclear missiles, (3) 450 gal tanks on centre-line and inner wing pylons, nuclear weapon in bomb-bay, (4) 650 gal centre-line tank, two 3,000 lb bombs on inner wing pylons, (5) 650 gal centre-line tank and two 450 gal tanks on inner wing pylons, four Sidewinder missiles on outer wing pylons, (6) Three rocket packs on centre-line, two on each inner wing pylon and one on each outer pylon, (7) Nine BLU-1/B fire-bombs or nine MLU-10/B mines in similar arrangement to rocket packs, or sixteen leaflet bombs, 750 lb bombs, or MC-1 toxic bombs.

DIMENSIONS, EXTERNAL (F-105F):

Wing span	34 ft 11·2 in (10·65 m)
Wing chord (mean)	11 ft 6 in (3·50 m)
Wing aspect ratio	3·18
Length overall	69 ft 1·18 in (21·06 m)
Length of fuselage	66 ft 11·85 in (20·42 m)
Height over tail	20 ft 1·96 in (6·15 m)
Tailplane span	17 ft 4·72 in (5·30 m)
Wheel track	17 ft 3·2 in (5·26 m)
Wheelbase	21 ft 1·18 in (6·43 m)

AREAS (F-105F):

Wings, gross	385 sq ft (35·77 m²)
Ailerons (total)	15·37 sq ft (1·43 m²)
Trailing-edge flaps (total)	61·40 sq ft (5·70 m²)
Leading-edge flaps (total)	22·70 sq ft (2·11 m²)
Spoilers (total)	18·70 sq ft (1·74 m²)
Fin	61·52 sq ft (5·72 m²)
Rudder	11·39 sq ft (1·06 m²)
Tailplane	60·37 sq ft (5·61 m²)

WEIGHTS AND LOADINGS (F-105F):

Weight empty	28,393 lb (12,879 kg)
Max T-O weight	54,000 lb (24,495 kg)
Max landing weight	51,038 lb (23,150 kg)
Max wing loading	140 lb/sq ft (683·5 kg/m²)
Max power loading	4·54 lb/lb st (4·54 kg/kg st)

PERFORMANCE (F-105F):

Max level speed at 38 000 ft (11,600 m)	Mach 2·25
Max level speed at S/L	Mach 1·25
Max cruising speed	Mach 0·95
Econ cruising speed, depending on altitude	Mach 0·4-0·88
Stalling speed (minimum)	155 knots (178 mph; 287 km/h)
Rate of climb at S/L	32,000 ft (9,750 m)/min
T-O run (clean)	2,000 ft (610 m)
T-O to 50 ft (15 m) (clean)	2,600 ft (792 m)
Landing from 50 ft (15 m)	4,960 ft (1,510 m)
Landing run, with drag-chute	3,200 ft (975 m)
Range with max fuel	1,797 nm (2,070 miles; 3,330 km)

(1970–71)

The Republic F-84E Thunderjet Single-seat Fighter (Allison J35 turbojet engine).

THE REPUBLIC THUNDERJET.
U.S. Air Force designation: F-84.

The Thunderjet was developed under the joint supervision of the Republic company and the U.S.A.A.F. Air Material command. The first prototype XF-84 flew on February 28, 1946.

F-84A. Differed from XF-84 in brake, armament and other minor details. Thirteen YF-84A's built but converted to F-84B.

F-84B. First production model. Armament increased to six .5 in. (12.7 mm.) guns. Air conditioned cockpit. Provision for R.P. in 86th and subsequent aircraft, with retractable R.P. mounts.

F-84D. Development of F-84B. Thicker metal skins on wings and ailerons, hinged gun deck, winterised fuel system, changes to permit use of gasoline instead of kerosene and substitution of mechanical linkage for hydraulic compression of shock-strut travel to shorten landing-gear for retraction.

F-84E. Fitted with Allison J35-A-17 engine rated at 5,000 lb. (2,270 kg.) s.t. Longer fuselage to give more room in cockpit, wing-tip tanks fitted with fins to permit full manoeuvrability with tanks fitted, structural modifications to increase permissible G loads, and other improvements to simplify maintenance. Addition of two 230 U.S. gallon drop tanks on bomb shackles beneath wings inboard of landing-gear increases combat radius to over 1,000 miles (1,600 km.). In addition to fixed armament, F-84E can carry 32 5-in. rockets ; or two 11.5-in. and 16 5-in. rockets ; or two 1,000-lb. bombs and 18 5-in. rockets or other various combinations of expendable stores. Provision for four 1,000-lb. Jato units for accelerated take-off. First F-84 version to be supplied under M.D.A.P. to nations participating in the North Atlantic Treaty Organization.

F-84G. Progressive development of F-84E. Fitted with in-flight refuelling equipment with wing receptacle in port wing for use with the Boeing "flying-boom" system. Automatic pilot fitted. Allison J35-A-29 engine rated at 5,600 lb. = 2,540 kg. s.t., or 10 per cent. more than F-84E power-plant. Replaced F-84E in production and was delivered to U.S.A.F. and nations participating in the N.A.T.O. Under test an F-84G has remained in the air for 12 hours 5 minutes. receiving four aerial fuelings during the flight. First U.S.A.F. fighter to be equipped with in-flight refuelling equipment. Of the U.S.A.F. F-84G Thunderjets assigned overseas, 631 were flown across the Atlantic and 135 across the Pacific with the aid of flight refuelling. The F-84G was also the first U.S.A.F. fighter-bomber announced as being equipped to carry the atomic bomb. Withdrawn from production in July, 1953.

XF-84H. An experimental aircraft which will be powered with an Allison T54 turboprop engine and an Aero-products six-blade co-axial contra-rotating high-speed small-diameter airscrew, as part of an Air Force supersonic airscrew flight test programme. The XF-84H is not expected to fly until mid-1954.

The description below refers specifically to the F-84E.

TYPE.—Single-seat Jet Fighter.

WINGS.—Low mid-wing cantilever monoplane. Republic high-speed laminar-flow wing-section. Dihedral 5°. All-metal structure with flush-riveted stressed-skin. Flaps between ailerons and fuselage. Root chord 9 ft. 2¼ in. (2.8 m.), tip chord 5 ft. 3 in. (1.6 m.).

FUSELAGE.—Circular section structure. All-metal construction with flush-riveted stressed skin.

TAIL UNIT.—Cantilever monoplane type. Tailplane dihedral 5°. Trim-tabs in elevators and rudder. Tailplane span 14 ft. 11½ in. (4.5 m.).

LANDING GEAR.—Retractable tricycle type. Hydraulic retraction. Track 16 ft. 6 in. (5.03 m.).

POWER PLANT.—One Allison J35-A-17 axial-flow turbojet engine in fuselage aft of wings with nose air inlet and tail exhaust exit. Rear section of fuselage removable for access to engine compartment and to permit complete replacement of engine in 50 minutes. Main fuel tankage in wings. External tanks may be carried on bomb-shackles at wing roots and at wing tips.

ACCOMMODATION.—Pilot's pressurised cockpit ahead of wing leading-edge. Electrically-operated jettisonable bubble canopy. Pilot's ejector seat.

ARMAMENT.—Six .50 in. (12.7 mm.) machine-guns, four in nose of fuselage and two in wings, one on each side of fuselage. Provisions for carrying rocket or bomb loads or various combinations of each up to a maximum weight of 4,500 lb. (2,045 kg.).

DIMENSIONS.—
Span 36 ft. (10.9 m.).
Length 38 ft. (11.6 m.).
Height 12 ft. 10¼ in. (3.9 m.).

WEIGHTS.—
Weight empty over 11,000 lb. (4,995 kg.).
Max. gross weight 18,000 lb. (8,172 kg.).

PERFORMANCE.—
Max. speed over 600 m.p.h. (960 km.h.) at sea level.
Service ceiling, over 45,000 ft. (13,725 m.).
Combat radius 850 miles (1,360 km.).
Combat radius (with four external fuel tanks) 1,000 miles (1,600 km.). (1953–54)

The Republic F-84G Thunderjet, the first operational fighter aircraft to be equipped for air-to-air refuelling.

The Republic F-84F Thunderstreak (Wright J65 turbojet engine).

THE REPUBLIC THUNDERSTREAK.
U.S.A.F. designation: F-84F.

This aircraft was originally intended to be a swept-wing version of the F-84E Thunderjet, with an Allison J35-A-29 engine (5,800 lb.=2,630 kg. s.t.), and a prototype was flown with a lower-powered version of this engine. This prototype was redesignated YF-96A, which was to be the designation of production aircraft; but it later reverted to the designation of XF-84F.

The impending availability of the higher-powered Sapphire engine, for which Curtiss-Wright had acquired a manufacturing licence, resulted in the decision to re-design the airframe to take this engine.

The new power-plant, with its larger dimensions and greater power, called for a considerable number of design and production changes with the result that, compared with the F-84E, the swept-wing F-84F is almost entirely a new aeroplane. The first XF-84F powered by an imported British-built Sapphire engine flew for the first time on February 14, 1951.

The following is the sole production version of the Thunderstreak.

F-84F. Standard production version with Wright J65 engine (7,200 lb.=3,270 kg. s.t.). Production F-84F's went into service with the U.S.A.F. in 1954. The F-84F has also been supplied in quantity to the air forces of several NATO nations.

2,711 were built before production ended in July, 1957.

The description below refers to this version :—

TYPE.—Single-seat Jet Fighter.

WINGS.—Mid-wing cantilever monoplane. Sweepback 40° at quarter-chord. All-metal structure incorporating a high proportion of press forgings in place of built-up components.

FUSELAGE.—All-metal structure with flush-riveted stressed skin. Perforated air-brakes hinged to the fuselage sides aft of the wing trailing-edge. A drag parachute is provided to shorten landing distances.

TAIL UNIT.—Cantilever monoplane type, with one-piece "flying" tailplane high-mounted on fin. Sweepback 40° at quarter-chord. All-metal structure.

LANDING GEAR.—Retractable tricycle type. Hydraulic retraction.

POWER PLANT.—One Wright J65-W-3 turbojet engine (7,200 lb.=3,270 kg. s.t.). External fuel tanks may be carried on wing-root pylons. Normally, two 230 U.S. gallon (870 litre) drop tanks would be carried, but two 450 U.S. gallon (1,700 litre) tanks are permissible for long-range escort missions. Provision for in-flight refuelling, including a new Republic-developed "buddy" system.

ACCOMMODATION.—Pilot's pressurised cockpit ahead of wing leading edge. Upward-hinged jettisonable canopy. Pilot's ejector seat.

ARMAMENT.—Six .50 in. (12.7 mm.) machine-guns, four in the fuselage and one in each wing. Provision for carrying external stores including twenty-four 5 in. rockets, or four 1,000 lb. bombs, or atomic weapons, up to a maximum weight of more than 6,000 lb. (2,720 kg.).

DIMENSIONS.—
Span 33 ft. 6 in. (10.21 m.).
Length 43 ft. 4 in. (13.21 m.).
Height 14 ft. 4 in. (4.37 m.).

WEIGHTS.—
Weight loaded (approx.) 25,000 lb. (11,350 kg.).

PERFORMANCE.—
Max. speed over 650 m.p.h. (1,040 km.h.).
Combat radius over 1,000 miles (1,600 km.).
Service ceiling over 45,000 ft. (13,725 m.).

THE REPUBLIC THUNDERFLASH.
U.S.A.F. designation: RF-84F.

The Thunderflash is the tactical reconnaissance version of the F-84F. Unlike the Thunderstreak which has a nose air-intake, this version has wing-root intakes so as to enable it to carry cameras, radar and electronic equipment in the fuselage nose. An armament of four .50-in. machine-guns, two in each wing, is provided for self protection.

The RF-84F, which went out of production in December, 1956, is in service in several commands of the U.S.A.F., the U.S. Air National Guard and in the air forces of Belgium, France, Italy, Greece, Norway, Turkey and the Netherlands. 715 were built.

The RF-84F is equipped to carry any combination of the 15 standard U.S. aerial cameras, plus the "dicing" camera for close-up photographs of individual targets and several special night cameras. In addition, it can be equipped with the Tri-Metrogon camera which takes horizon-to-horizon photographs. For night operations a large number of magnesium flares in flash ejector cartridges can be carried under the wings.

The Thunderflash has a camera control system with an automatic computer which analyzes factors of light, speed and altitude and automatically sets the cameras. This virtually eliminates camera error. A special viewfinder enables the pilot to see exactly what he is photographing.

Equipment also includes a wire recorder for the pilot to make "notes" during photographic or visual reconnaissance missions.

The standard version of the RF-84F is powered with a Wright J65-W-3 turbojet engine (7,200 lb. = 3,270 kg. s.t.).

The Republic RF-84F Thunderflash, the Tactical Reconnaissance version of the F-84F.

DIMENSIONS.—
Span 33 ft. 6 in. (10.21 m.).
Length 47 ft. 6 in. (14.48 m.).
Height 15 ft. (4.57 m.).
WEIGHTS.—
Restricted.

PERFORMANCE.—
Max. speed over 650 m.p.h. (1,040 km.h.).
Combat radius over 1,000 miles (1,600 km.).
Service ceiling over 45,000 ft. (13,725 m.).

(1957–58)

T-39D with special equipment in modified nose for duty at the Naval Weapons Center, China Lake, California (*Duane A. Kasulka*)

ROCKWELL SABRE SERIES 40 and 60
USAF and US Navy designation: T-39

To meet the USAF's "UTX" requirements for a combat readiness trainer and utility aircraft, Rockwell built as a private venture the prototype of a small sweptwing twin-jet monoplane then named the Sabreliner. Design work began on 30 March 1956 and the prototype, powered by two General Electric J85 turbojet engines, flew for the first time on 16 September 1958.

In January 1959, the USAF ordered the first of 143 **T-39A** pilot proficiency/administrative support aircraft. Subsequently the USAF ordered 6 radar trainer versions which were identified as **T-39Bs**. In 1961 the US Navy ordered 42 radar interception officer trainers, these being designated **T-39D**.

Five commercial versions are now available, as follows:

Series 40. Basic version to carry a crew of two and up to nine passengers. More powerful engines than its predecessors. New brakes with longer life. Three windows instead of two on each side of passenger cabin. Early-model Sabreliners can be modified to Series 40 standard.

Under the designation **CT-39E** the US Navy has acquired seven Series 40 commercial Sabreliners for rapid response airlift of high-priority passengers, ferry pilots and cargo. In early 1972 the USN ordered two **CT-39G** Sabreliners for fleet tactical support squadron use under a $2·9 million contract. Five additional CT-39Gs were delivered during 1973, against a total requirement of 30 aircraft.

TYPE: Twin-engined jet business transport.

WINGS: Cantilever low-wing monoplane. Sweepback 28° 33'. All-metal two-spar milled-skin structure. Electrically-operated trim tab in aileron. Electrically-operated trailing-edge flaps. Aerodynamically-operated leading-edge slats in five sections on each wing. Optional full-span pneumatically-operated de-icing boots.

FUSELAGE: All-metal semi-monocoque structure. Large hydraulically-operated airbrake under centre-fuselage.

TAIL UNIT: Cantilever all-metal structure, with flush antennae forming tip of fin and inset in dorsal fin. Moderate sweepback on all surfaces. Direct mechanical flight controls with electrically-operated horizontal tail surfaces. Electrically-operated trim tab in rudder. Optional full-span pneumatically-operated leading-edge de-icing boots.

LANDING GEAR: Retractable tricycle type. Twin-wheel nose unit retracts forward. Single wheel on each main unit, retracting inward into fuselage. Main-wheel tyres size 26 × 6·60-12, pressure 180 lb/sq in (12·7 kg/cm²). Nosewheel tyres size 18 × 4·40-10, pressure 100 lb/sq in (7·0 kg/cm²). Hydraulic brakes with anti-skid units.

POWER PLANT: Two Pratt & Whitney JT12A-8 turbojet engines (each 3,300 lb; 1,497 kg st) in pods on sides of rear fuselage. Integral fuel tanks in wings, with total capacity of 903 US gallons (3,418 litres). Fuselage tank, capacity 160 US gallons (606 litres). Total fuel capacity 1,063 US gallons (4,024 litres).

ACCOMMODATION: Crew of two and 6-10 passengers in pressurised air-conditioned cabin (see descriptions of individual series). Downward-hinged door, with built-in steps, forward of wing on port side. Emergency exits on starboard side of cabin in the Series 40 and on both sides in the Series 60. Baggage space at front of cabin opposite door in both versions, with adjacent coat rack specified in many interior configurations. Srs 60 has larger lavatory at rear of cabin. With seats removed there is room for 2,500 lb (1,135 kg) of freight.

DIMENSIONS, EXTERNAL:

Wing span	44 ft 5¼ in (13·54 m)
Length overall:	
Srs 40	43 ft 9 in (13·34 m)
Srs 60	48 ft 4 in (14·73 m)
Height overall	16 ft 0 in (4·88 m)
Tailplane span	17 ft 6½ in (5·35 m)
Wheel track	7 ft 2½ in (2·20 m)
Wheelbase:	
Srs 40	14 ft 6 in (4·42 m)
Srs 60	15 ft 10¾ in (4·85 m)
Cabin door:	
Height	3 ft 11 in (1·19 m)
Width	2 ft 4 in (0·71 m)

DIMENSIONS, INTERNAL:

Cabin (excluding flight deck):	
Length:	
Srs 40	16 ft 0 in (4·88 m)
Srs 60	19 ft 0 in (5·79 m)
Max width	5 ft 2½ in (1·59 m)
Max height	5 ft 7½ in (1·71 m)
Volume:	
Srs 40	400 cu ft (11·33 m³)
Srs 60	480 cu ft (13·59 m³)

AREAS:

Wings, gross	342·05 sq ft (31·78 m²)
Ailerons (total)	16·42 sq ft (1·52 m²)
Flaps (total)	40·26 sq ft (3·74 m²)
Slats (total)	36·34 sq ft (3·38 m²)
Fin	41·58 sq ft (3·86 m²)
Rudder	8·95 sq ft (0·83 m²)
Tailplane	77·0 sq ft (7·15 m²)
Elevators	16·52 sq ft (1·53 m²)

WEIGHTS AND LOADINGS:

Basic operating weight, empty:	
Srs 40	9,895 lb (4,488 kg)
Srs 60	11,035 lb (5,005 kg)
Max payload, incl crew:	
Srs 40	2,000 lb (907 kg)
Srs 60	2,215 lb (1,004 kg)
T-O weight with four passengers, baggage and max fuel:	
Srs 40	18,215 lb (8,262 kg)
Srs 60	19,135 lb (8,679 kg)
Max T-O weight:	
Srs 40	18,650 lb (8,498 kg)
Srs 60	20,000 lb (9,060 kg)
Max ramp weight:	
Srs 40	19,035 lb (8,634 kg)
Srs 60	20,372 lb (9,221 kg)
Landing weight with four passengers, baggage and 1 hr reserve fuel:	
Srs 40	12,345 lb (5,600 kg)
Srs 60	13,435 lb (6,094 kg)
Max landing weight	17,500 lb (7,938 kg)
Max zero-fuel weight:	
Srs 40	12,800 lb (5,798 kg)
Srs 60	13,250 lb (6,010 kg)
Max wing loading:	
Srs 40	53·6 lb/sq ft (261·7 kg/m²)
Srs 60	57·6 lb/sq ft (281·2 kg/m²)
Max power loading:	
Srs 40	3·4 lb/lb st (3·4 kg/kg st)
Srs 60	2·97 lb/lb st (2·97 kg/kg st)

PERFORMANCE (Srs 40 and Srs 60 at max T-O weight, unless detailed otherwise):
Max never-exceed speed   Mach 0·85
Max level speed at 21,500 ft (6,550 m)
    489 knots (563 mph; 906 km/h): Mach 0·8
Max cruising speed   Mach 0·8
Econ cruising speed at 39,000-45,000 ft (11,900-13,700 m)   Mach 0·75
Stalling speed, landing configuration, Srs 40 at 12,345 lb (5,600 kg) AUW; Srs 60 at 13,435 lb (6,094 kg) AUW:
    Srs 40   80 knots (92 mph; 148 km/h)
    Srs 60   83·5 knots (96·5 mph; 156 km/h)

Max rate of climb at S/L:
    Srs 40   4,800 ft (1,463 m)/min
    Srs 60   4,700 ft (1,433 m)/min
Max certificated operating altitude
          45,000 ft (13,715 m)

Single-engine ceiling at AUW of 16,000 lb (7,257 kg)   24,000 ft (7,300 m)
Min ground turning radius:
    Srs 40   25 ft 10¾ in (7.89 m)
    Srs 60   28 ft 6 in (8·69 m)

T-O balanced field length:
    Srs 40   4,800 ft (1,463 m)
    Srs 60   5,050 ft (1,539 m)
Landing distance at landing weight with four passengers, baggage and 1 hr reserve fuel:
    Srs 40   2,200 ft (671 m)
    Srs 60   2,275 ft (693 m)
Max range, with four passengers, baggage, max fuel and 45 min reserve:
    Srs 40   1,840 nm (2,118 miles; 3,408 km)
    Srs 60   1,730 nm (1,992 miles; 3,205 km)
          (1974–75)

Fourth Rockwell International B-1 strategic bomber, with its wings in the fully-swept position

ROCKWELL INTERNATIONAL B-1

The B-1 was the outcome of a succession of defence studies, begun in 1962 and leading to the AMSA (Advanced Manned Strategic Aircraft) requirement of 1965, for a low-altitude penetration bomber to replace the Boeing B-52s of USAF Strategic Air Command by 1980. It was to be the third and most flexible component of the US Triad defence system, comprising also land-based and submarine-launched ballistic missiles.

To meet the B-1 requirement, the Department of Defense issued RFPs (Requests For Proposals) to the US aerospace industry on 3 November 1969, and from three airframe and two engine finalists it awarded research, development, test and evaluation contracts on 5 June 1970 to North American Rockwell's Los Angeles Division for the airframe and to the General Electric Company for the F101 turbofan engine. The original cost-plus-incentive contracts were for five flying prototypes, two structural test airframes and 40 engines; in January 1971, in which month the essential design of the B-1 was frozen, these quantities were reduced to three flight test aircraft, one ground test airframe and 27 engines. Procurement of a fourth flight test aircraft, as a pre-production prototype, was approved under the FY 1976 budget. The US Air Force hoped to order 244 B-1s, including prototypes, to replace B-52s now in service.

The B-1 prototypes were assembled in US Air Force facilities known as Plant 42 at Palmdale, California. Assembly of the first aircraft began in late 1972; this aircraft (74-0158) made its first flight, at Palmdale, on 23 December 1974. This occasion was also the first flight of the YF101 engine. The third B-1, used as a testbed for the avionics systems, made its first flight on 1 April 1976, and was followed by the first flight of the second B-1 on 14 June 1976. The second aircraft had been ʾed for proof loads testing; these tests occupied approximately eight months during 1975, after which No. 2 was converted to a flight test aircraft. By 1 January 1979 the three aircraft involved in the test programme had accumulated a total of over 1,200 hours in more than 200 test missions.

The fourth B-1 (76-0174) flew for the first time on 14 February 1979, and represents an operational configuration, with both offensive and defensive avionics systems

installed. The first prototype, devoted to evaluating aircraft stability and control, performance and flutter limits, completed its test programme in 1978 and has been placed in storage. The second prototype, used for air-loads testing and engine/inlet evaluation, completed its testing during 1979 and has been stored in flyable condition.

The third prototype has been modified by the addition of an advanced ECM system, and with a Doppler beam sharpening modification to the forward-looking attack radar. Continued testing of the third and fourth B-1s has been concentrated on defensive system performance and advanced ECM development. Testing is being carried out against simulated enemy threats, defence systems, and against US surrogate threats. Results of the B-1 test programme are expected to contribute greatly to validation and definition of design requirements for any future manned penetration bomber.

In 1978, B-1 derivative designs were included in US Department of Defense studies to evaluate various types of aircraft as cruise missile carriers. In November 1979, as a result of these studies, Rockwell was requested by the US Air Force to submit a proposal for the initial planning and design effort associated with flight demonstration of a prototype B-1 derivative aircraft. Identified as a strategic ALCM launcher (SAL), it will be produced by modification of the third B-1 prototype. This work was authorised in January 1980, and began shortly after, with a planned first flight in late 1981.

DIMENSIONS, EXTERNAL:
Wing span: fully spread   41·67 m (136 ft 8½ in)
    fully swept   23·84 m (78 ft 2½ in)
Wing area, gross   approx 181·2 m² (1,950 sq ft)
Length overall: incl nose probe   45·78 m (150 ft 2½ in)
    excl nose probe   44·70 m (146 ft 8 in)
Height overall   10·24 m (33 ft 7¼ in)
Wheel track (c/l of shock-absorbers)
          4·42 m (14 ft 6 in)
Wheelbase   17·53 m (57 ft 6 in)

WEIGHTS:
Design max T-O weight   179,170 kg (395,000 lb)
Max landing weight   approx 158,755 kg (350,000 lb)

PERFORMANCE (estimated, with VG inlets):
Max level speed at 15,240 m (50,000 ft)
          approx Mach 2·2
    (1,260 knots; 2,335 km/h; 1,451 mph)
Max level speed at 152 m (500 ft)
      approx 650 knots (1,205 km/h; 750 mph)
Cruising speed at 15,240 m (50,000 ft)
    Mach 0·85 (562 knots; 1,042 km/h; 648 mph)
Max range without refuelling   Intercontinental

ROCKWELL INTERNATIONAL B-1B LANCER

Following the cancellation of the B-1, President Reagan authorised development of the B-1B bomber derivative, 100 of which entered USAF service between 1985 and 1988. For details, see *Jane's All The World's Aircraft 1989–90*.

ROCKWELL INTERNATIONAL BRONCO
US military designation: OV-10

This aircraft was North American's entry for the US Navy's design competition for a light armed reconnaissance aeroplane (LARA) specifically suited for counter-insurgency missions. Nine US airframe manufacturers entered for the competition and the NA-300 was declared the winning design in August 1964. Seven prototypes were then built by the company's Columbus Division, under the designation YOV-10A Bronco. The first of these flew on 16 July 1965, followed by the second in December 1965.

A number of modifications were made as a result of flight experience with the prototypes. In particular, the wing span was increased by 3·05 m (10 ft 0 in), the T76 turboprop engines were uprated from 492 kW (660 shp) to 534 kW (716 shp), and the engine nacelles were moved outboard approximately 0·15 m (6 in) to reduce noise in the cockpit.

A prototype with lengthened span flew for the first time on 15 August 1966. The seventh prototype had Pratt & Whitney (Canada) T74 (PT6A) turboprops for comparative testing.

OV-10A. Initial production version ordered in October 1966 and first flown on 6 August 1967. US Marine Corps had 114 in service in September 1969, of which 18 were on loan to the USN; used for light armed reconnaissance, helicopter escort and forward air control duties. At the same date the USAF had 157 OV-10As for use in the forward air control role, as well as for limited quick-response ground support pending the arrival of tactical fighters.

Production of the OV-10A for the US services ended in April 1969; but 15 aircraft were modified by LTV Electrosystems Inc, under the USAF Pave Nail programme, to permit their use in a night forward air control and strike designation role in 1971.

Equipment installed by LTV included a stabilised night periscopic sight, a combination laser rangefinder and target illuminator, a Loran receiver and a Lear Siegler Loran co-ordinate converter. This combination of equipment generates an offset vector to enable an accompanying strike aircraft to attack the target or, alternatively, illuminate the target, enabling a laser-seeking missile to home on to it. These specially configured aircraft reverted to the OV-10A configuration in 1974 by removal of the LTV-installed equipment.

Under the designation **YOV-10A** a single OV-10A was equipped with rotating cylinder flaps for evaluation in a STOL flight test programme by NASA.

OV-10C. Version of OV-10A for Royal Thai Air Force; 32 delivered.

OV-10D. In 1974, Rockwell received a US Navy contract to establish and test a production OV-10D configuration. This led to delivery of 17 US Marine Corps OV-10As to Rockwell's Columbus Aircraft Division, beginning in the Spring of 1978, for conversion to the Night Observation Surveillance (NOS) role. In addition to the NOS systems and the retention of basic OV-10A fuselage stores and external fuel capability, the OV-10D NOS has uprated (775·5 kW; 1,040 shp) engines, wing pylons capable of carrying rocket pods, flare pods, free-fall stores and 378 litre (100 US gallon) external fuel tanks when extended radius/loiter time is required. A Texas Instru-

Rockwell International OV-10A Bronco of US Navy Squadron VAL-4 on a combat sortie

ments FLIR sensor and laser target designator are installed in a rotating ball turret in the nose. The sensor turret can be linked to a turret-mounted General Electric M-97 20 mm cannon, mounted beneath the fuselage, in lieu of normal operation with standard OV-10A armament sponsons and centreline station.

The following details apply to the standard OV-10A, except where stated:

TYPE: Two-seat multi-purpose counter-insurgency aircraft.

WINGS: Cantilever shoulder-wing monoplane. Constant-chord wing without dihedral or sweep. Conventional aluminium alloy two-spar structure. Manually-operated ailerons, supplemented by four small manually-operated spoilers forward of outer flap on each wing, for lateral control at all speeds. Hydraulically operated double-slotted flaps in two sections on each wing, separated by tailbooms.

FUSELAGE: Short pod-type fuselage of conventional aluminium semi-monocoque construction, suspended from wing. Glassfibre nosecone.

TAIL UNIT: Cantilever all-metal structure carried on twin booms of semi-monocoque construction. Tailplane mounted near tips of fins. Manually-operated rudders and elevator.

LANDING GEAR: Retractable tricycle type, with single wheel on each unit, developed by Cleveland Pneumatic Tool Co. Hydraulic actuation, nosewheel retracting forward, main units rearward into tailbooms. Two-stage oleo-pneumatic shock-absorbers. Forged aluminium wheels. Main wheels with tyres size 29 × 11-10, pressure 4·48 bars (65 lb/sq in). Nosewheel tyre size 7·50-10, pressure 5·52 bars (80 lb/sq in). Cleveland hydraulic disc brakes.

POWER PLANT: Two 533 kW (715 ehp) AiResearch T76-G-416/417 turboprops, with Hamilton Standard three-blade propellers. Inter-spar fuel tank in centre portion of wing, capacity 976 litres (258 US gallons). Refuelling points above tank. Provision for carrying 568 or 871 litre (150 or 230 US gallon) jettisonable ferry tank on underfuselage pylon.

ACCOMMODATION: Crew of two in tandem, on ejection seats, under canopy with two large upward-opening transparent door panels on each side. Dual controls standard. Cargo compartment aft of rear seat, with rear-loading door at end of fuselage pod. Rear seat removable to provide increased space for up to 1,452 kg (3,200 lb) of freight, or for carriage of five paratroops, or two stretcher patients and attendant.

ELECTRONICS AND EQUIPMENT: UHF, VHF, HF radios and Tacan are standard, provision of a radar altimeter optional. Gunsight above pilot's instrument panel, the latter having space provisions beneath the gunsight for a TV-type display with applications for night sensor reconnaissance, weapon delivery and navigation, such as in the YOV-10D configuration.

ARMAMENT: Two weapon attachment points, each with capacity of 272 kg (600 lb), under short sponson extending from bottom of fuselage on each side, under wings. Fifth attachment point, capacity 544 kg (1,200 lb) under centre fuselage. Two 7·62 mm M-60C machine-guns carried in each sponson. Provision for carrying one Sidewinder missile under each wing and, by use of a wing pylon kit, various stores including rocket pods, flare pods and free-fall ordnance. Max weapon load 1,633 kg (3,600 lb).

DIMENSIONS, EXTERNAL:
Wing span	12·19 m (40 ft 0 in)
Length overall	12·67 m (41 ft 7 in)
Height overall	4·62 m (15 ft 2 in)
Tailplane span	4·45 m (14 ft 7 in)
Wheel track	4·52 m (14 ft 10 in)
Rear loading door: Height	0·99 m (3 ft 3 in)
Width	0·76 m (2 ft 6 in)

DIMENSIONS, INTERNAL:
Cargo compartment	2·12 m³ (75 cu ft)
Cargo compartment, rear seat removed	3·14 m³ (111 cu ft)

AREA:
Wings, gross	27·03 m² (291 sq ft)

WEIGHTS:
Weight empty	3,161 kg (6,969 lb)
Normal T-O weight	4,494 kg (9,908 lb)
Overload T-O weight	6,563 kg (14,466 lb)

PERFORMANCE (A: OV-10A/C/E/F; B: OV-10B; C: OV-10B(Z); D: OV-10D, with internal 20 mm ammunition only):

Max level speed at S/L, without weapons:
A	244 knots (452 km/h; 281 mph)
D	240 knots (444 km/h; 276 mph)

Max level speed at 3,050 m (10,000 ft) at AUW of 4,536 kg (10,000 lb):
B	241 knots (447 km/h; 278 mph)
C	341 knots (632 km/h; 393 mph)

Max rate of climb at S/L at AUW of 4,494 kg (9,908 lb):
A	808 m (2,650 ft)/min

Max rate of climb at S/L at AUW of 5,443 kg (12,000 lb):
B	701 m (2,300 ft)/min
C	2,073 m (6,800 ft)/min

Max rate of climb at S/L at AUW of 5,644 kg (12,443 lb):
D	812 m (2,665 ft)/min

Rockwell International YOV-10D Night Observation/Gunship System (NOGS)

T-O run:
A, at normal AUW		226 m (740 ft)
B, at 5,443 kg (12,000 lb) AUW	344 m (1,130 ft)	
C, at 5,443 kg (12,000 lb) AUW		168 m (550 ft)
D, at 6,025 kg (13,284 lb) AUW	338 m (1,110 ft)	

T-O to 15 m (50 ft):
A, at normal AUW	341 m (1,120 ft)
A, at overload AUW	853 m (2,800 ft)

Landing from 15 m (50 ft):
A, at normal AUW	372 m (1,220 ft)

Landing run:
A, at normal AUW	226 m (740 ft)
A, at overload AUW	381 m (1,250 ft)
D, at landing AUW	244 m (800 ft)

Combat radius with max weapon load, no loiter:
A	198 nm (367 km; 228 miles)
D	265 nm (491 km; 305 miles)

Ferry range with auxiliary fuel:
A	1,240 nm (2,298 km; 1,428 miles)

(1976–77)

ROCKWELL INTERNATIONAL BUCKEYE
US Navy designation: T-2

After a design competition among several leading US manufacturers, what was then North American's Columbus Division was awarded a contract in 1956 to develop and build a jet training aircraft for the US Navy. The first T2J-1 flew on 31 January 1958. Five versions of the aircraft have since been produced, as follows:

T-2A (formerly T2J-1). Initial version, with single 15·12 kN (3,400 lb st) Westinghouse J34-WE-48 turbojet engine. Initial orders were for 26 production T-2As. Follow-up contracts were awarded in 1958 and 1959, and 217 had been built when production ended in January 1961. The T-2A was used by US Naval Air Training Command, Pensacola, Florida, but was phased out of service in early 1973, having been replaced completely by T-2Bs or -2Cs.

T-2B (formerly T2J-2). To evaluate the potential of the Buckeye airframe, two T-2As were each re-engined with two Pratt & Whitney J60-P-6 turbojets (each 13·34 kN; 3,000 lb st), under US Navy contract, with the designation T-2B. First one flew on 30 August 1962. A US Navy production contract for 10 new T-2Bs was announced in March 1964, and further contracts brought the total ordered to 97. The first production T-2B flew on 21 May 1965; deliveries to Naval Air Training Command were completed in February 1969.

T-2C. Generally similar to T-2B, but powered by two General Electric J85-GE-4 turbojet engines, each rated at 13·12 kN (2,950 lb st). The T-2C entered production in late 1968, following extensive evaluation of J85-GE-4 engines in a T-2B which was redesignated T-2C No. 1. T-2C production began as an amendment of an existing contract. First production T-2C flew on 10 December 1968. Total of 231 T-2Cs ordered by Naval Air Training Command, deliveries of which were completed by the end of 1975.

T-2D. Generally similar to T-2C; differs only in electronics equipment and by deletion of carrier landing capability. A total of 12 were supplied to the Venezuelan Air Force and are used as advanced jet trainers for student pilots; delivery was completed during 1973. An additional 12 T-2D trainers with the attack kit of a T-2E were ordered for delivery during 1976-77.

T-2E. Generally similar to the T-2C, except for new electronics equipment and the provision of an accessory kit which permits utilisation in an attack role. A total of 40 are on order for Greece under a contract managed by US Naval Air Systems Command. The accessory kit provides six wing store stations with a combined capacity of 1,587 kg (3,500 lb), and protection against small arms fire for the fuel tanks. The aircraft will be used by the Hellenic Air Force Training Command as advanced and tactical jet trainers for student pilots in their final stages of training.

Rockwell International T-2D Buckeye in service with the Venezuelan Air Force

Delivery was scheduled to be made during 1976.

The following details apply to the standard T-2C:

TYPE: Two-seat general-purpose jet trainer.

WINGS: Cantilever mid-wing monoplane. Wing section NACA 64A212 (modified). Thickness/chord ratio 12%. All-metal two-spar structure. Interchangeable all-metal ailerons, with hydraulic boost. Large all-metal trailing-edge flaps.

FUSELAGE: All-metal semi-monocoque structure in three main sections: forward fuselage containing equipment bay and cockpit; centre fuselage housing power plant, fuel and wing carry-through structure; and rear fuselage, carrying the arrester hook and a hydraulically-actuated airbrake on each side of the fuselage.

TAIL UNIT: Cantilever all-metal structure. Each half of tailplane and elevators interchangeable. Elevators boosted hydraulically. Rudder manually controlled. Trim tabs in elevators and rudder.

LANDING GEAR: Retractable tricycle type. Oleo-pneumatic shock-absorbers. Hydraulic retraction. Main units retract inward into wings. Nosewheel retracts forward into fuselage. Main wheels size 24 × 5·50. Nosewheel size 20 × 4·40. Main-wheel tyre pressure 10·34 bars (150 lb/sq in), nosewheel tyre pressure 5·17 bars (75 lb/sq in). Goodyear aircooled single-disc hydraulic brakes. Retractable sting-type, universal joint mounted, arrester hook.

POWER PLANT: Two 13·12 kN (2,950 lb st) General Electric J85-GE-4 turbojet engines, with jet outlets under rear fuselage. Fuel in main tanks over engines with capacity of 1,465 litres (387 US gallons), two wingtip tanks each of 386 litres (102 US gallons) capacity, and two tanks in the inboard sections of the wings. Total fuel capacity 2,616 litres (691 US gallons). (1976–77)

ACCOMMODATION: Pupil and instructor in tandem in enclosed cabin, on rocket-powered LS-1 ejection seats, under clamshell canopy. Instructor is raised 0·25 m (10 in) above level of pupil.

ARMAMENT: Optional packaged installations of guns, target-towing gear, 100 lb practice bombs, M-5 or MK76 practice bomb clusters, Aero 4B practice bomb containers, 2·25 in rocket launchers or seven 2·75 in rockets in Aero 6A-1 rocket containers, can be carried on two store stations, one beneath each wing, with a combined capacity of 290 kg (640 lb).

DIMENSIONS, EXTERNAL:
Wing span over tip-tanks	11·62 m (38 ft 1½ in)
Length overall	11·67 m (38 ft 3½ in)
Height overall	4·51 m (14 ft 9½ in)
Tailplane span	5·46 m (17 ft 11 in)
Wheel track	5·61 m (18 ft 4¾ in)

AREAS:
Wings, gross	23·69 m² (255 sq ft)
Trailing-edge flaps (total)	4·23 m² (45·56 sq ft)
Fin	2·54 m² (27·29 sq ft)
Rudder, incl tab	0·84 m² (9·01 sq ft)
Tailplane	3·95 m² (42·55 sq ft)
Elevators, incl tabs	1·95 m² (21·00 sq ft)

WEIGHTS:
Weight empty	3,680 kg (8,115 lb)

THE RYAN MODEL 28 FIREBALL
U.S. Navy designation: FR-1

The Fireball is the first aircraft to be put into production which uses a combined power-plant of a conventional engine driving an airscrew and a jet-propulsion unit. Design work was commenced in 1943 and production was proceeding at the time of the Japanese capitulation. On November 6, 1945, a Fireball, with its nose engine unserviceable, made a successful landing on U.S. aircraft-carrier *Wake Island* off San Diego using only its rear jet unit, and this is claimed to be the first occasion on which a pure jet landing was made on a carrier.

The prototype XFR-1 was powered by a Wright R-1820-56 engine and a General Electric I-16 jet unit. The first and only production version was the FR-1 which was fitted with an R-1820-72W and an I-16.

The Fireball was out of service by 1948. Sixty-five FR-1s were built, together with four experimental models which differed from the production type mainly in power-plant installations.

The last experimental model to be built was the XFR-4, illustrated herewith. This is fitted with a Wright R-1820-74W in the nose and a Westinghouse 24C (J-34) axial-flow jet-unit in the tail. The air intakes for the jet engine are of the flush-entry type, one on each side of the forward fuselage. Electrically-operated duct doors are closed when the aircraft is flying on the nose engine only. The XFR-4 is being used for research and experimental work.

TYPE.—Single-seat Fighter monoplane using both conventional tractor airscrew and a jet propulsion unit.

WINGS.—Low-wing cantilever monoplane of all-metal construction. Laminar flow NACA aerofoil section. Wing of aluminium-alloy built in three sections; centre-section integral with fuselage, and two outer panels which fold upwards hydraulically for stowage. Centre-section built up of two I-section spars, spanwise Z-section stringers, former ribs and flush-riveted metal skin. Outer panels of similar spar construction, semi-monocoque from root to ailerons and full monocoque to tips. Aerodynamically, dynamically and statically-balanced all-metal ailerons. Trim-tab in port aileron. Fowler-type flaps in four sections between ailerons and wing roots.

FUSELAGE.—All-metal structure in two main portions. Forward section of semi-monocoque construction built up on four main longerons with vertical frames and formers stiffened and braced where required. Flush-riveted metal skin. Readily interchangeable rear portion is a monocoque structure and attaches to forward section at points just aft of wing. Firewall of .051 in. (.129 cm.) aluminium-alloy sheet riveted to frame ahead of cockpit. Forward fuselage armoured with face-hardened steel plate and aluminium-alloy plate and sheet. Deck cowling ahead of cockpit of heavy aluminium plate.

TAIL UNIT.—All-metal cantilever structure with stressed metal skin over all surfaces. Elevators and rudder aerodynamically, dynamically and statically-balanced. Trim-tabs in elevators and rudder. Dorsal fin integral with fuselage.

The Ryan FR-1 Fireball Single-seat Fighter (1,350 h.p. Wright R-1820-72W Cyclone engine and General Electric I-16 gas-turbine).

LANDING GEAR.—Tricycle type. Main wheels, of die-cast heat-treated magnesium with Timken roller bearings, are carried on oleo-pneumatic shock-absorber legs attached to front spar at outer ends of centre-section, and retract outwards into outer wing sections and are completely enclosed. Goodyear high-pressure channel-tread tyres and brakes. Self-castering, non-steerable nose-wheel carried in forked shock-absorber leg retracts backwards into fuselage. Hydraulic shimmy-damper and self-aligning device. Firestone low-profile nose-wheel tyre. Hydraulic operation. Wheel base 7 ft. 2 in. (2.2 m.). Retractable self-aligning deck arrester hook. Hydraulic operation.

POWER PLANT.—Combination of conventional engine driving tractor airscrew and gas turbine exhausting aft of the tail unit. Each engine completely independent. Forward unit in FR-1 is a Wright Cyclone R-1820-72W nine-cylinder radial air-cooled engine rated at 1,350 h.p. at 2,700 r.p.m. for take-off. Curtiss-Electric three-blade full-feathering, constant-speed airscrew, 10 ft. (3.05 m.) diameter. Electric starter. Rear engine is a General Electric I-16 or I-20 jet propulsion unit mounted in the forward end of the aft section of the fuselage and ejecting at extreme stern. Air intakes in leading edge of centre-section. Two self-sealing fuel tanks ; one of 125 U.S. gallons (473 litres) in top portion of fuselage behind cockpit, and one of 51 U.S. gallons (191 litres) under cockpit floor immediately aft of firewall. One 100 U.S. gallon (377 litres) drop-tank may be carried under starboard centre-section. Oil capacity 15 U.S. gallons (57 litres).

ACCOMMODATION.—Pilot's cockpit over leading-edge of centre-section. Moulded plastic canopy slides on roller bearings. Emergency jettisonable release. Three-panel windscreen in aluminium alloy channel frame, the front panel of laminated bullet-proof glass 1½ in. (3.8 c/m.) thick. Cockpit back armour of ₅/₁₆ in. (.79 c/m.) and ⅜ in. (.94 c/m.) steel plate welded together.

ARMAMENT.—Four .5 in. (12.7 m/m.) Browning machine-guns, two in each centre-section outboard of air intakes. 1,200 rounds of ammunition carried in wells inboard of guns. Racks for two 1,000 lb. (454 kg.) bombs, one under each centre-section, and racks for two zero-length rocket projectiles under each outer panel. Special Night fighter equipment (FR-1N) may be installed.

DIMENSIONS.—Span 40 ft. 0 in. (12.19 m.), Width folded 17 ft. 6 in. (5.34 m.), Length 32 ft. 4 in. (9.85 m.), Height (on ground, over rudder) 13 ft. 7 in. (4.15 m.), Height folded 16 ft. 9 in. (5.1 m.).

WEIGHTS.—Weight empty 7,635 lbs. (3,470 kg.), Weight loaded 9,862 lbs. (4,480 kg.).

PERFORMANCE (Using both engines).—Maximum speed 425 m.p.h. (860 km.h.) at 18,000 ft. (5,490 m.), Initial rate of climb 4,800 ft./min. (1,465 m./min.), Climb to 10,000 ft. (3,050 m.) 2.4 min., Climb to 20,000 ft. (6,100 m.) 5.6 min., Service ceiling 40,000 ft. (12,200 m.), Normal cruising range 1,030 miles (1,650 km.), Range at cruising speed with drop-tank 1,430 miles (2,290 km.), Maximum speed with front engine only 320 m.p.h. (515 km.h.), Maximum speed with jet unit only 300 m.p.h. (483 km.h.). (1947)

The Ryan L-17B Navion Military Liaison Monoplane. (Warren Bodie).

THE RYAN NAVION.
U.S. Air Force designation : L-17B.

In the Summer of 1947 the Ryan company acquired the design and manufacturing rights of the Navion from North American Aviation, Inc. The Ryan Navion retains all the basic features and flying qualities of the original Navion, but many refinements and additional standard equipment have been introduced in the 1949 model.

These include the addition of landing-gear doors and fairings, greater internal comfort, improved sound-proofing and a new ventilating and heating system, re-location of auxiliary fuel tank under rear seat to give roomier and more accessible baggage compartment, under-wing exhaust outlets, new radio equipment, improved dual fuel system, etc. Both internal and external finish have also been improved.

In 1948, 158 Ryan Navions were ordered by the U.S.A.F. for use as liaison and observation aircraft by the Army Field Forces and the Air National Guard. These aircraft carry the designation L-17B. The L-17A is a North American-built Navion.

TYPE.—Four-seat Cabin monoplane.

WINGS.—Cantilever low-wing monoplane. All-metal two-spar structure in two main sections each attached directly to fuselage. Detachable wing-tips. Channel-section spars, built-up ribs and stressed metal covering. Incidence washed-out 3 degrees at tips. Wing area 184 sq. ft. (17.09 m.²). All-metal mass-balanced ailerons and hydraulically-operated trailing-edge flaps. Flap positions 20 degrees for take-off, 43 degrees for landing.

FUSELAGE.—All-metal semi-monocoque one-piece structure, with four main longerons, transverse bulkheads and frames and aluminium-alloy stressed-skin covering.

TAIL UNIT.—Cantilever monoplane type with detachable tips. Metal structure with metal covering to all surfaces. Two-piece tailplane and elevators interchangeable left and right. Controllable trim-tab in each elevator, rudder tab adjustable on ground.

LANDING GEAR.—Retractable tricycle type. Each main wheel, on single air-oil shock-absorber leg, retracts inwards into wings. Nose-wheel, in fork on air-oil shock-absorber leg, retracts backward into fuselage, leaving small portion projecting. Nose-wheel steerable 20 degrees each way. Hydraulic operation with emergency spring-lowering gear. Track 8 ft. 2½ in. (2.49 m.) wheel base 5 ft. 8½ in. (1.73 m.). Leaf-spring emergency tail-skid.

POWER PLANT.—One Continental E185 six-cylinder horizontally-opposed air-cooled direct-drive engine developing 185 h.p. at 2,300 r.p.m. and with 205 h.p. available for take-off on monocoque mounting integral with fuselage. Hartzell or Aero-matic two-blade variable-pitch airscrew. Normal fuel capacity 40 U.S. gallons (151 litres). Max. fuel capacity (with auxiliary tank) 60 U.S. gallons (227 litres). Oil 2½ U.S. gallons (9.4 litres). Delco-Remy 15-volt generator.

ACCOMMODATION.—Enclosed cabin seating four, two side-by-side with dual controls and two behind on full-width seat. Lucite windshield in aluminium frame. Aluminium-alloy sheet canopy with Plexiglas side panels slides backwards for access. Sound-proofing and controlled ventilation. Cabin interior width 3 ft. 9 in. (1.14 m.). Baggage compartment aft of rear seats.

DIMENSIONS.—
Span 33 ft. 5 in. (10.18 m.).
Length 27 ft. 8 in. (8.43 m.).
Height over tail 8 ft. 8 in. (2.62 m.).

WEIGHTS AND LOADINGS.—
Weight empty 1,680 lb. (763 kg.).
Pilot and three passengers 680 lb. (308 kg.).
Fuel and oil 259 lb. (118 kg.).
Baggage 80 lb. (36 kg.).
Weight loaded 2,750 lb. (1,250 kg.).
Wing loading 14.9 lb./sq. ft. (72.7 kg./m.²).
Power loading 14.8 lb./h.p. (6.72 kg./h.p.).
PERFORMANCE.—
Max. speed 157 m.p.h. (251 km.h.).

Cruising speed at 70% power 155 m.p.h. (241 km.h.) at 5,000 ft. (1,525 m.).
Most economic cruising speed 115 m.p.h. (185 km.h.) at 51% power at 5,000 ft. (1,525 m.).
Landing speed (with flaps) 54 m.p.h. (87 km.h.).

Initial rate of climb 900 ft./min. (253 m./min.).
Service ceiling 15,600 ft. (4,755 m.).
Normal range 500 miles (800 km.).
Take-off run (10 m.p.h. wind, no flaps) 187 yds. (171 m.).
Landing run (10 m.p.h. wind, full flaps) 118 yds. (108 m.).

(1950–51)

THE RYAN S-T (PT-20) MONOPLANE.

TYPE.—Two-seat light monoplane.
WINGS.—Low-wing wire-braced monoplane. High aspect-ratio outer wings attached to stub-wings of steel-tube construction. Outer wing structure consists of two solid spruce spars, stamped aluminium alloy ribs, aluminium alloy leading-edge back to front spar, fabric covering. Wings braced by streamline wires, above to top of fuselage and below to undercarriage. Modified "Frise" ailerons of metal construction. Wing flaps extend over half wing span from stubs to ailerons.
FUSELAGE.—Oval metal monocoque. Internal structure of 24ST aluminium-alloy with 24ST "Alclad" skin.
TAIL UNIT.—Normal monoplane type. Metal framework with fabric covering. Trimming tabs in trailing-edge of elevators.
UNDERCARRIAGE.—Divided type. Consists of two forks, incorporating long-stroke oleo shock-absorbers and two Goodyear Airwheels, the axles of which are hinged to the apices of two steel-tube Vees to which are also anchored the lower wing bracing-wires. Struts and wheels are enclosed in streamline casings. Swivelling or steerable streamline tail-wheel.
POWER PLANT.—One 125 h.p. Menasco C-4 or 150 h.p. Menasco C-4-S (supercharged) four-cylinder in-line air-cooled inverted engine on a steel-tube mounting supported on rubber bushes at the fuselage. N.A.C.A.-type in-line cowling. Fuel tank (24 U.S. gallons) in fuselage.
ACCOMMODATION.—Tandem cockpits which may be either open or closed. A sliding cockpit enclosure may be supplied as optional equipment. Dual controls with controls in front cockpit removable. Luggage compartment between cockpits.
DIMENSIONS.—Span 30 ft. (9.15 m.), Length 20 ft. 4 in. (6.2 m.), Height 6 ft. 3 in. (1.91 m.), Wing area 124 sq. ft. (11.5 sq. m.).
WEIGHTS.—Weight empty 1,027 lbs. (465 kg.), Weight loaded 1,600 lbs. (725 kg.).

The Ryan S-T (PT-20) Two-seat Primary Training Monoplane (125 h.p. Menasco C-4 engine).

PERFORMANCE (Menasco C-4).—Maximum speed 150 m.p.h. (241 km.h.), Cruising speed 127 m.p.h. (203 km.h.), Landing speed 42 m.p.h. (67.2 km.h.), Initial rate of climb 1,200 ft./min. (366 m./min.), Service ceiling 17,500 ft. (5,337 m.), Absolute ceiling 21,200 ft. (6,466 m.). Cruising range 350 miles (560 km.).
PERFORMANCE (Menasco C-4-S).—Maximum speed at sea level 160 m.p.h. (256 km.h.), Maximum speed at 7,500 ft. (2,290 m.) 148 m.p.h. (237 km.h.), Cruising speed at 2,000 ft. (610 m.) 135 m.p.h. (216 km.h.), Landing speed 42 m.p.h. (67.2 km.h.), Initial rate of climb 1,400 ft./min. (427 m./min.), Service ceiling 21,000 ft. (6,405 m.), Range 350 miles (560 km.). (1940)

The Ryan PT-16 Two-seat Military Training Monoplane (125 h.p. Menasco engine).

THE RYAN S-T MONOPLANE.

In 1939 the U.S. Army Air Corps adopted the S-T (PT-16) Trainer for military use, this model being equipped with the Menasco C-4 engine. The only difference between the Army Trainer and the standard commercial model are the larger and differently-shaped cockpits, complete dual Army type instruments, a steerable and full-swivelling tail-wheel and wing tie-down and towing lugs.

TYPE.—Two-seat light monoplane.
WINGS.—Low-wing wire-braced monoplane. High aspect-ratio outer wings attached to stub-wings of steel-tube construction. Outer wing structure consists of two solid spruce spars, stamped aluminium alloy ribs, aluminium alloy leading-edge back to front spar, fabric covering. Wings braced by streamline wires, above to top of fuselage and below to undercarriage. Modified "Frise" ailerons of metal construction. Wing flaps extend over half wing span from stubs to ailerons.
FUSELAGE.—Oval metal monocoque. Internal structure of 24ST aluminium-alloy with 24ST "Alclad" skin.
TAIL UNIT.—Normal monoplane type. Metal framework with fabric covering. Trimming tabs in trailing-edge of elevators.
UNDERCARRIAGE.—Divided type. Consists of two forks, incorporating long-stroke oleo shock-absorbers and two Goodyear Airwheels, the

axles of which are hinged to the apices of two steel-tube Vees to which are also anchored the lower wing bracing-wires. Struts and wheels are enclosed in streamline casings. Swivelling or steerable streamline tail-wheel.
POWER PLANT.—One 125 h.p. Menasco C-4 or 150 h.p. Menasco C-4-S (supercharged) four-cylinder in-line air-cooled inverted engine on a steel-tube mounting supported on rubber bushes at the fuselage. N.A.C.A.-type in-line cowling. Fuel tank (24 U.S. gallons) in fuselage.
ACCOMMODATION.—Tandem cockpits which may be either open or closed. A sliding cockpit enclosure may be supplied as optional equipment. Dual controls with controls in front cockpit removable. Luggage compartment between cockpits.
DIMENSIONS.—Span 30 ft. (9.15 m.), Length 20 ft. 4 in. (6.2 m.), Height 6 ft. 3 in. (1.91 m.), Wing area 124 sq. ft. (11.5 sq. m.).
WEIGHTS.—Weight empty 1,027 lbs. (465 kg.), Weight loaded 1,600 lbs. (725 kg.).
PERFORMANCE (Menasco C-4).—Maximum speed 150 m.p.h. (241 km.h.), Cruising speed 127 m.p.h. (203 km.h.), Landing speed 42 m.p.h. (67.2 km.h.), Initial rate of climb 1,200 ft./min. (366 m./min.), Service ceiling 17,500 ft. (5,337 m.), Absolute ceiling 21,200 ft. (6,466 m.), Cruising range 350 miles (560 km.).
PERFORMANCE (Menasco C-4-S).—Maximum speed at sea level 160 m.p.h. (256 km.h.). Maximum speed at 7,500 ft. (2,290 m.) 148 m.p.h. (237 km.h.), Cruising speed at 2,000 ft. (610 m.) 135 m.p.h. (216 km.h.), Landing speed 42 m.p.h. (67.2 km.h.), Initial rate of climb 1,400 ft./min. (427 m./min.), Service ceiling 21,000 ft. (6,405 m.), Range 350 miles (560 km.). (1939)

THE RYAN ST-3 "RECRUIT."
U.S. Army Air Forces designations: PT-21 and PT-22.
U.S. Navy designation: NR-1.

TYPE.—Two-seat Primary Training monoplane.

WINGS.—Low-wing wire-braced monoplane. Wing section NACA 2412. 4° 10' sweepback, 3° incidence and 4° 30' dihedral. Wing-stubs of riveted aluminium-alloy construction with strut-braced front spar, cantilever rear spar, and metal covering. Outer wings have spruce spars, stamped aluminium-alloy ribs, 24ST "Alclad" covering over leading-edge back to front spar and final fabric covering over all. Streamline tie-rod bracing to fuselage and landing gear. Ailerons and flaps have aluminium-alloy frames and fabric covering.

FUSELAGE.—Oval metal monocoque. Structure consists of nine aluminium-alloy bulkheads and six pieces of pre-formed 24ST "Alclad" skin.

TAIL UNIT.—Braced monoplane type. Aluminium-alloy framework covered with fabric. Rudder trim-tab adjustable on ground. Elevator tabs operated from either cockpit.

LANDING GEAR.—Treadle type with fixed portion acting as anchorage for flying wires. Long-stroke oleo shock-absorber struts. Brakes may be operated hydraulically or mechanically. Oleo-sprung steerable tail-wheel.

POWER PLANT.—One 132 h.p. (PT-21) or 160 h.p. (PT-22 and NR-1) Kinner five-cylinder radial air-cooled engine on quickly-detachable welded steel-tube mounting. Welded aluminium fuel tank (24 U.S. gallons) in fuselage behind stainless-steel fireproof bulkhead. Oil tank (3 U.S. gallons) in engine compartment.

ACCOMMODATION.—Tandem open cockpits with complete dual controls and duplicated instruments. Adjustable seats adapted for the standard U.S. Army-type parachute. Baggage compartment accessible from exterior.

The Ryan PT-22 (ST-3) "Recruit" Two-seat Primary Training Monoplane (160 h.p. Kinner engine).

DIMENSIONS.—Span 30 ft. 1 in. (9.18 m.), Length 22 ft. 5 in. (6.83 m.), Height 6 ft. 10 in. (2 m.), Wing area ·134.25 sq. ft. (12.47 sq. m.).

WEIGHTS AND LOADINGS (PT-21—132 h.p. Kinner engine).—Weight empty 1,278 lbs. (580.2 kg.), Crew (two) 380 lbs. (172.5 kg.), Fuel and oil 167 lbs. (75.8 kg.), Disposable load 547 lbs. (248.3 kg.), Weight loaded 1,825 lbs. (828.5 kg.), Wing loading 13.6 lbs./sq. ft. (66.36 kg./sq. m.), Power loading 13.8 lbs./h.p. (6.26 kg./h.p.).

WEIGHTS AND LOADINGS (PT-22—160 h.p. Kinner engine).—Weight empty 1,313 lbs. (596 kg.), Disposable load 547 lbs. (248.3 kg.). Weight loaded 1,860 lbs. (844.3 kg.), Wing loading 13.8 lbs./sq. ft. (67.3 kg./sq. m.), Power loading 11.6 lbs./h.p. (5.26 kg./h.p.).

PERFORMANCE (PT-21—132 h.p. Kinner engine).—Maximum speed 123 m.p.h. (196.8 km.h.), Cruising speed 112 m.p.h. (179.2 km.h.), Landing speed 54 m.p.h. (864 km.h.), Initial rate of climb 680 ft./min. (208 m./min.), Climb to 3,280 ft. (1,000 m.) 5.9 mins., Climb to 6,560 ft. (2,000 m.) 13.4 mins., Climb to 9,840 ft. (3,000 m.) 27 mins., Climb to 10,000 ft. (3,050 m.) 27.8 mins., Service ceiling 11,900 ft. (3,630 m.), Absolute ceiling 13,900 ft. (4,240 m.), Range 340 miles (544 km.).

PERFORMANCE (PT-22—160 h.p. Kinner engine).—Maximum speed 131 m.p.h. (209.6 km.h.), Cruising speed 123 m.p.h. (196.8 km.h.), Landing speed 54 m.p.h. (86.4 km.h.), Initial rate of climb 1,000 ft./min. (305 m./min.), Climb to 3,280 ft. (1,000 m.) 3.5 mins., Climb to 6,560 ft. (2,000 m.) 8.5 mins., Climb to 9,840 ft. (3,000 m.) 14.9 mins., Climb to 10,000 ft. (3,050 m.) 15.4 mins., Service ceiling 15,500 ft. (4,730 m.), Absolute ceiling 17,500 ft. (5,340 m.), Range 352 miles (560 km.).

The Ryan PT-25 (ST-4) Two-seat Primary Training Monoplane (185 h.p. Lycoming engine).

THE RYAN ST-4.
U.S. Army Air Forces designation: PT-25.

The Ryan Company was one of three firms selected by the Government for the mass-production of military training aircraft under a type standardisation programme and was the first company to manufacture in quantity an all-metal low-wing primary trainer. The S-T (PT-16 and PT-20) was the first low-wing monoplane trainer to satisfy Army requirements, and this model was followed by the ST-3 (PT-21 and PT-22). Both these models were produced in large quantities. Large numbers of Ryan trainers were also supplied to the Air Forces of the Netherlands East Indies, Guatemala, China, Honduras, Mexico, etc.

The ST-3 (PT-22) was in production until 1942 when the Ryan Company, as the result of a request to undertake studies towards the conversion of the PT-22 all-metal trainer to non-strategic materials in order to release essential metals for more urgent purposes, produced the ST-4, an entirely new two-seat trainer built almost entirely of plastic-bonded wood. Aluminium alloys and all strategic materials have been eliminated with the exception of the cowling, firewall and certain simple metal fittings which represent less than 2 per cent. of the total weight of the aircraft. No forgings, castings or extrusions are used, nor any critical steels for any of the fittings or structural parts.

TYPE.—Two-seat Primary Training monoplane.

WINGS.—Low-wing cantilever monoplane. Two-to-one taper ratio. Wing incidence (root) 4 degrees. Dihedral 5 degrees. Sweepback

(leading-edge) 4 degrees 03 mins. All-wood monospar wing structure in five sections comprising centre-section, two outer sections and two removable wing-tips. Structure consists of single wood spar, built-up wooden girder ribs, plywood-covered nose torque box extending from spar over leading-edge, and a final covering of lightweight fabric. Root ends of wing spar reinforced with hardwood blocks. Outer wing attached to centre-section at four points at spar root and one at leading-edge. All ribs, spar flanges and spar assemblies are brought to size from contour plates by routers and shapers to eliminate hand-finishing and to ensure accuracy with speed. Statically-balanced ailerons on outer section have wood spars and ribs and are fabric-covered. Starboard aileron has tab adjustable on ground. Electrically-operated perforated centre-section flap has wood spar and plywood skin.

FUSELAGE.—Ovoid-section monocoque built up of ten laminated bulkheads and a stressed plywood skin. No. 1 bulkhead has black walnut plates at the four engine-mounting points. No. 2 bulkhead which carries torque tube joining leading-edges of outer wings has black walnut inserts at every other lamination. No. 3 bulkhead in three parts and is slotted to receive centre-section spar.

TAIL UNIT.—Cantilever monoplane type. All-wood framework with plywood-covered fixed surfaces and fabric-covered horn-balanced elevators and rudder. Controllable tab operated from either cockpit in starboard elevator. Fixed trailing-edge tab in rudder for directional balance.

LANDING GEAR.—Fixed cantilever type without fairings. Welded truss assembly bolted to centre-section spar. Long-travel oleo shock-absorbers. Hayes wheels and hydraulic brakes. Oleo-sprung tail-wheel steerable from either cockpit, full swivelling beyond steering angles.

POWER PLANT.—One 185 h.p. Lycoming O-435-1 six-cylinder horizontally-opposed air-cooled engine on welded steel-tube mounting. Wickwire Spencer two-blade automatic variable-pitch airscrew. Two plastic fuel tanks in plywood cells in centre-section. Maximum fuel capacity 27 U.S. gallons. Oil carried in engine crankcase. "Eclipse" electric starter and generator.

ACCOMMODATION.—Tandem open cockpits with complete dual controls and instruments. Streamline steel-tube turn-over post between cockpits bolted to centre-section spar. Safety seat-belts and shoulder harness. Blind-flying hood. Full night-flying equipment. Baggage compartment behind rear cockpit with access from within cockpit.

DIMENSIONS.—Span 32 ft. 10½ in. (10 m.), Length 24 ft. 3¼ in. (7.4 m.), Height 6 ft. 7¾ in. (2 m.), Wing area 161.2 sq. ft. (15 sq. m.).

WEIGHTS AND LOADINGS.—Weight loaded 1,800 lbs. (817 kg.), Wing loading 11.1 lbs./sq. ft. (54.2 kg./sq. m.), Power loading 9.7 lbs./h.p. (4.4 kg./h.p.).

PERFORMANCE.—Maximum speed 149 m.p.h. (238.4 km.h.), Cruising speed (75% power) 134 m.p.h. (214.4 km.h.), Initial rate of climb 1,590 ft./min. (485 m./min.), Climb to 6,560 ft. (2,000 m.) 5 mins., Climb to 9,840 ft. (3,000 m.) 8.5 mins., Climb to 10,000 ft. (3,050 m.) 8.7 mins., Service ceiling 20,300 ft. (6,190 m.), Absolute ceiling 21,900 ft. (6,680 m.), Range at operating speed (110 m.p.h. = 176 km.h.) 378 miles (605 km.). (1943-44)

THE SEVERSKY BT-8.

TYPE.—Two-seat basic training monoplane.

WINGS.—Low-wing cantilever monoplane. Single-piece wing tapers in chord and thickness and is attached to the fuselage at five points on each side. Wing structure is of multi-spar construction, with widely-spaced former ribs. The outer skin is reinforced with corrugated sheets on the inside, with the corrugations running along the span. The bottom skin is stiffened internally, with channel stringers at regular intervals. Narrow-chord ailerons inset from wing-tips. Split flaps between ailerons.

FUSELAGE.—Circular section structure, built up of a number of transverse bulkheads interconnected by extruded channel stringers and covered with smooth stressed skin. The front main bulkheads are attached to the corresponding webs of the five wing-spars.

TAIL UNIT.—Cantilever all-metal monoplane type. Tail-plane and fin built integral with the fuselage. Trimming-tabs in elevators and rudder.

UNDERCARRIAGE.—Divided cantilever type. Each unit consists of a stressed-skin casing incorporating oleo shock-absorber and enclosed streamline wheel and tyre. Seversky Training Retractable Gear mechanism installed in cockpit, complete with all necessary handles and warning signals to train pupils in use of retracting gear, although undercarriage of machine is fixed. Landing gear interchangeable with Seversky patent amphibian gear.

POWER PLANT.—One 400 h.p. Pratt & Whitney "Wasp-Junior" nine-cylinder radial air-cooled engine, on welded chrome-molybdenum steel-tube mounting. This mounting is designed to take the 420 h.p. Wright R-975E3 engine. Fuel tank formed by riveting and sealing centre-section of wing to form airtight compartment. Double Venturi engine cowling.

ACCOMMODATION.—Tandem cockpits, with complete dual controls. Crash-proof headrest between cockpits, and over both cockpits are semi-circular transparent hoods, terminating forward in a wind-screen and aft in a streamline tail. Both hoods slide clear of cockpits for entrance and egress. Headrest contains loop antenna for direction-finding radio compass.

DIMENSIONS.—Span 36 ft. (10.9 m.), Length 24 ft. 5 in. (7.5 m.), Height 8 ft. 10 in. (2.68 m.), Wing area 220 sq. ft. (20.4 sq. m.).

The Seversky BT-8 Two-seat Basic Training Monoplane (350 h.p. Wright R-975E engine).

WEIGHTS AND LOADINGS.—Weight empty 2,950 lbs. (1,338 kg.), Weight loaded 4,050 lbs. (1,837 kg.), Wing loading 18.4 lbs./sq. ft. (89.8 kg./sq. m.), Power loading 10.1 lbs./h.p. (4.6 kg./h.p.).

PERFORMANCE.—Maximum speed at sea level 176 m.p.h. (320 km.h.), Cruising speed 154 m.p.h. (248 km.h.), Stalling speed at sea level 60.5 m.p.h. (96.8 km.h.), Initial rate of climb 1,150 ft./min. (348 m./min.), Climb to 10 mins. 12,000 ft. (3,660 m.), Service ceiling 17,000 ft. (5,180 m.), Range at full speed 633 miles (1,012 km.), Range at cruising speed 725 miles (1,170 km.). (1938)

The Seversky P-35 Single-seat Fighter Monoplane (950 h.p. Pratt & Whitney "Twin-Wasp" engine).

THE SEVERSKY P-35.

TYPE.—Single-seat Fighter monoplane.

WINGS.—Low-wing cantilever monoplane. Wing in three sections, a rectangular centre-section and two elliptical outer sections with detachable wing-tips. All-metal aluminium-alloy structure with smooth stressed-skin covering. Split trailing-edge flaps between ailerons.

FUSELAGE.—Light alloy semi-monocoque structure. Built up of continuous longitudinal stringers and transverse frames, covered with smooth stressed skin. Four main longerons pick up the welded steel-tube engine-mounting.

TAIL UNIT.—Cantilever monoplane type. All-metal structure with fixed surfaces covered with smooth metal skin and movable surfaces covered with fabric. Trimming-tabs in elevators and rudder.

UNDERCARRIAGE.—Retractable type. Wheels are raised backwards into fairings under centre-section. Cleveland shock-absorbers. Bendix wheels and brakes.

POWER PLANT.—One 950/1,000 h.p. Pratt & Whitney "Twin-Wasp" fourteen-cylinder radial air-cooled engine on welded steel-tube mounting. N.A.C.A. cowling. Hamilton-Standard constant-speed airscrew. Fuel tanks integral with centre-section.

ACCOMMODATION.—Enclosed cockpit over wing with sliding canopy top.

ARMAMENT AND EQUIPMENT.—One .50 cal. and one .30 cal. machine-guns in top cowling and firing through the airscrew. Provision for light fragmentation bombs. Radio.

DIMENSIONS.—Span 36 ft. (10.9 m.), Length 25 ft. 4 in. (7.7 m.), Height 9 ft. 9½ in. (3 m.), Wing area 220 sq. ft. (20.4 sq. m.).

WEIGHTS AND LOADINGS.—Weight empty 4,318 lbs. (1,958 kg.). Disposable load 1,284 lbs. (582.4 kg.), Weight loaded 5,602 lbs. (2,541 kg.), Wing loading 25.5 lbs./sq. ft. (124.5 kg./sq. m.), Power loading 5.6 lbs./h.p. (2.5 kg./h.p.).

PERFORMANCE.—Maximum speed at 10,000 ft. (3,050 m.), 300 m.p.h. (482.8 km.h.), Rate of climb 3,174.6 ft./min. (666 m./min.), Service ceiling 29,685 ft. (9,048 m.), Cruising range 1,200 miles (1,931 km.) (1938)

SEVERSKY EP-1/P-35A

U.S. Army Air Forces designation: P-35A.

TYPE.—Single-seat fighter monoplane.

WINGS.—Low-wing cantilever monoplane. Wing in five sections, comprising centre-section, two outer sections and two detachable wing-tips. Centre-section is sealed to form fuel tank. Wing structure consists of five main spars, fore-and-aft ribs and stressed-metal skin. "Friso" type aerodynamically and statically-balanced ailerons. Split flaps between ailerons and under fuselage. Trimming-tab on one aileron.

FUSELAGE.—Circular section semi-monocoque. Structure consists of continuous longitudinal stringers, frames and former rings, the whole covered with a smooth stressed skin.

TAIL UNIT.—Cantilever monoplane type. Tail-plane has two converging spars, former ribs and stressed-skin covering. All-metal fin. Elevators and rudder have metal frames and may be covered with either metal or fabric. Aerodynamically-balanced elevators and rudder. Trimming-tabs in elevators.

UNDERCARRIAGE.—Retractable type. Wheels raised backwards into fairings beneath centre-section. Electrical or manual retraction. Steerable and retractable tail-wheel.

POWER PLANT.—One Pratt & Whitney "Twin-Wasp" R-1830-S3C3-G fourteen-cylinder radial air-cooled engine rated at 1,050 h.p. at 2,700 r.p.m. at 12,000 ft. (3,660 m.) and with 1,100 h.p. at 2,700 r.p.m. available for take-off. Hamilton-Standard three-blade constant-speed airscrew. Fuel (200 U.S. gallons = 757 litres) carried in integral tank built into centre-section. NACA cowling with controllable gills.

ACCOMMODATION.—Pilot's cockpit with sliding canopy which may be locked in any one of several intermediate positions. Bullet-proof windshield. Armour protection aft of pilot. Large baggage compartment aft of cockpit with room for an auxiliary passenger seat.

The Republic EP-1 Single-seat Fighter Monoplane (1,050 h.p. Pratt & Whitney "Twin-Wasp" engine).

ARMAMENT.—Normal armament comprises two .30-cal. guns in the fuselage but it can be provided with four .30-cal. or .50-cal. machine-guns, two mounted in the fuselage and synchronised to fire through the airscrew and two in the wings and firing outside the airscrew disc. Internal bomb-racks in outer wings for ten 35-lb. (16-kg.) bombs.

DIMENSIONS.—Span 36 ft. (10.99 m.), Length 26 ft. 10 in. (8.17 m.), Height 9 ft. 9½ in. (2.98 m.), Wing area 225 sq. ft. (20.9 sq. m.).

WEIGHTS AND LOADINGS.—Weight empty 4,708 lbs. (2,135 kg.), Crew 175 lbs. (79 kg.), Fuel and oil 870 lbs. (395 kg.), Armament 172 lbs. (78 kg.), Normal useful load 1,345 lbs. (610 kg.), Weight loaded 6,053 lbs. (2,745 kg.), Wing loading 27 lbs./sq. ft. (131.4 kg./sq. m.), Power loading 5.7 lbs./h.p. (2.61 kg./h.p.).

PERFORMANCE.—Maximum speed at 12,000 ft. (3,660 m.) 320 m.p.h. (515 km.h.), Cruising speed at 15,300 ft. (4,663 m.) 260 m.p.h. (418 km.h.), Rate of climb at sea level 2,800 ft./min. (851 m./min.), Climb to 5,000 ft. (1,525 m.) 1.7 mins., Climb to 10,000 ft. (3,050 m.) 3.6 mins., Climb to 15,000 ft. (4,575 m.) 6.3 mins., Service ceiling 30,000 ft. (9,144 m.), Range at cruising speed at 15,300 ft. (4,663 m.) 600 miles (965 km.). (1941)

The Sikorsky R-4B Two-seat Training Helicopter (185 h.p. Warner R-550-1 engine).

THE SIKORSKY VS-316A.
U.S. Army Air Forces designation : R-4B.
U.S. Navy designation : HNS-1.

The original Sikorsky helicopter—the experimental VS-300—was placed in the Edison Museum in Dearborn, Mich., in 1943.

The first helicopter built for military service—the experimental XR-4—first flew on January 13, 1942, and was delivered by air from Stratford, Conn., to Wright Field, Dayton, Ohio, a distance of 760 miles, by easy stages and under widely-varying weather conditions without any trouble whatsoever.

On the basis of successful tests with the XR-4, a limited production order for a progressive development known as the YR-4 was placed with Sikorsky Aircraft.

These craft were intended for training and service trials. One was sent to Burma and another to Alaska. Others were allocated to the U.S. Navy, Coast Guard and the Royal Navy. Subsequently a production order for 100 R-4B's was placed.

In May, 1943, tests were conducted, through the co-operation of the Army Air Forces, the War Shipping Administration and the Coast Guard, to prove the feasibility of operating the YR-4 from a platform on a ship. These tests were conducted in Long Island Sound from a tanker. The deck used was not specially built but was one which had been used for cargo-carrying purposes and had a clear space only 14 ft. greater than the diameter of the main rotor of the YR-4. Under relatively calm water conditions 24 take-offs and landings were made while the ship was at anchor, while steaming up to 16 knots in a wind of more than 20 m.p.h. and while steaming with the wind and across wind.

Two views of a take-off by the Sikorsky YR-4 Helicopter from the deck of a tanker under way. These show the restricted area from which the tests described alongside were made.

TYPE.—Two-seat Training Helicopter.

ROTORS.—One three-blade main rotor 38 ft. (11.6 m.) dia. and one three-blade vertical controllable-pitch anti-torque and steering rotor 7 ft. 8 in. (2.30 m.) dia. carried on an outrigger extension of the fuselage, both rotors driven through transmission shafts and gear boxes by a single engine. Transmission for the main rotor is through a single plate clutch and double reduction gear. Rotor brake, free-wheel and emergency rotor release to permit auto-rotation in case of transmission seizure provided. Fixed rotor head with cyclic pitch control mounted on a welded steel tube pylon forming integral part of fuselage structure.

FUSELAGE.—Welded steel tube structure covered with detachable metal panels forward and fabric aft.

LANDING GEAR.—Three wheel type. Two main wheels forward have vertical shock-absorber struts supported by steel tube pyramids built into the sides of the fuselage. Tail-wheel mounted under rear fuselage. Wheel gear may be replaced by two low-pressure rubberised floats.

POWER PLANT.—One 185 h.p. Warner R-550-1 seven-cylinder radial fan-cooled engine mounted within fuselage aft of cockpit. Cooling air drawn through louvres in forward face of the rotor pylon casing blown by large-diameter engine-driven fan onto engine and exhausted through openings in underside of fuselage. Cylindrical fuel and oil tanks in fuselage aft of transmission compartment.

ACCOMMODATION.—Enclosed cabin in nose of fuselage seating two side-by-side with dual controls. Two central control columns operate cyclical pitch for forward, sideways and reverse movements. Second lever between seats controls blade pitch in unison for vertical movement. Rudder pedals operate on tail rotor for directional control. Radio equipment originally fitted has been removed. One litter may be carried externally.

DIMENSIONS.—Rotor diameter 38 ft. (11.6 m.), Overall length (including rotor) 48 ft. 1 in. (14.65 m.), Overall height 12 ft. 5 in. (3.78 m.), Wheel track 10 ft. (3.05 m.), Rotor disc area 1,134 sq. ft. (105.3 sq. m.).

WEIGHTS.—Weight empty 2,011 lbs. (913 kg.), Weight loaded 2,540 lbs. (1,153 kg.).

PERFORMANCE.—Maximum speed 75 m.p.h. (120 km.h.), Climb to 8,000 ft. (2,440 m.) 45 min., Service ceiling 8,000 ft. (2,440 m.).

(1945–46)

The Sikorsky R-5A Two-seat Observation Helicopter (450 h.p. Pratt & Whitney R-985-AN1 engine).

THE SIKORSKY R-5A.

U.S. Navy designation: HO2S-1.

TYPE.—Two-seat Observation Helicopter.

ROTORS.—One three-blade main rotor 48 ft. (14.6 m.) dia. and one three-blade vertical controllable-pitch anti-torque rotor 7 ft. (2.1 m.) dia. at rear end of fuselage. Rotor transmission same as for R-4B.

FUSELAGE.—In three sections. Centre-section enclosing power-unit and rotor pylon of welded steel tube and cowled with plastic-impregnated moulded plywood. The nose section enclosing the crew compartment has as a foundation an aluminium monocoque floor on which is built an aluminium-alloy channel superstructure panelled with Plexiglas windows. The tail section is a light wooden monocoque.

LANDING GEAR.—Conventional three-wheel type with the two main wheels sprung at the extremities of two cantilever side members. Tail wheel on steel tube pylon aft of the engine housing at the root of the rear fuselage.

POWER PLANT.—One 450 h.p. Pratt & Whitney R-985-AN-1 radial fan-cooled engine modified for installation within the fuselage with crankshaft vertical. Main rotor drive through conventional reduction gear, with take-off drive in main gear box for auxiliary tail rotor drive. Tail rotor drive shaft runs externally along top of rear fuselage. Cooling air for engine drawn in through aperture in front of face of rotor pylon housing and exhausted through openings in underside of fuselage. Fuel and oil tanks in fuselage aft of transmission compartment.

ACCOMMODATION.—Enclosed compartment in nose seats two in tandem with dual controls. Observer in front. Provision for cameras, radio and other auxiliary equipment. Four litters, two on each side of the fuselage, may be carried.

DIMENSIONS.—Rotor diameter 48 ft. (14.6 m.), Overall length 57 ft. 1 in. (17.4 m.), Wheel track 12 ft. (3.6 m.), Rotor disc area 1,810 sq. ft. (168 sq. m.).

WEIGHT LOADED.—5,000 lbs. (2,270 kg.).

PERFORMANCE.—Maximum speed 90 m.p.h. (144 km.h.). (1945-46)

THE SIKORSKY H-5F (formerly R-5F)

U.S. Air Force designation : H-5F.
U.S. Navy designation : HO3S-1.

The S-51, an enlarged development of the H-5A, was the first Sikorsky helicopter to be licenced by the C.A.A. for commercial operation and went into production in 1946. In addition to its many civil applications the S-51 has also been acquired by the U.S. Air Force and Navy for miscellaneous general utility duties. In January, 1948, forty-six were on order for the U.S. Navy.

TYPE.—Four-seat General Utility Helicopter.

ROTORS.—Three-blade main rotor and three-blade tail anti-torque rotor, the tail rotor being driven by secondary shaft from main gear-box. Rotor blades of composite construction with tapered tubular spar, solid wood leading-edge and fabric covering.

FUSELAGE.—In three main sections, the cabin structure, the centre-section enclosing the engine and rotor transmission, and the rear section. Centre-section of welded chrome-molybdenum steel-tube covered with detachable Alclad panels, cabin and tail sections of light-alloy monocoque construction.

The Sikorsky H-5F General Utility Helicopter (450 h.p. Pratt & Whitney R-985 engine). (Peter Bowers).

A Sikorsky H-5A Search and Rescue Helicopter (450 h.p. Pratt & Whitney R-985 engine). (*William T. Larkins*).

LANDING GEAR.—Fixed three-wheel type. Fully-castoring levered-suspension nose wheel. Oleo-sprung main wheels have hydraulic brakes. Track 12 ft. (3.66 m.).

POWER PLANT.—One 450 h.p. Pratt & Whitney R-985 Wasp Jr. nine-cylinder radial fan-cooled engine mounted horizontally in fuselage centre-section. Two fuel tanks, one forward of engine between two fireproof bulkheads and one aft of engine. Maximum fuel capacity 100 U.S. gallons (379 litres). One tank aft of engine with capacity of 8 U.S. gallons (30 litres).

ACCOMMODATION.—Enclosed cabin seating four, pilot centrally in front and three passengers on cross bench aft. Baggage compartment aft of engine compartment. Maximum width of cabin 4 ft. 8 in. (1.42 m.). Maximum height of cabin 4 ft. 5½ in. (1.36 m.). Sliding door on each side of cabin. Cabin heating and air-conditioning.

DIMENSIONS.—Main rotor diameter 48 ft. 0 in. (14.63 m.), Tail rotor diameter 8 ft. 5 in. (2.56 m.), Length overall 57 ft. 0½ in. (17.39 m.), Length with rotor blades removed 44 ft. 11½ in. (13.69 m.), Main rotor disc area 1,810 sq. ft. (168 sq. m.).

WEIGHTS AND LOADINGS.—Weight empty 3,650 lbs. (1,656 kg.), Disposable load 1,250 lbs. (567 kg.), Weight loaded 4,900 lbs. (2,223 kg.), Rotor disc loading 2.7 lbs./sq. ft. (13.17 kg./m.²), Power loading 10.9 lbs./h.p. (4.9 kg./h.p.).

PERFORMANCE.—Maximum speed at sea level 103 m.p.h. (165 km.h.), Speed at 5,000 ft. (1,525 m.) 100 m.p.h. (160 km.h.), Maximum economical cruising speed 85 m.p.h. (136 km.h.), Rate of climb at sea level 1,200 ft./min. (366 m./min.), Rate of climb at 5,000 ft. (1,525 m.) 950 ft./min. (290 m./min.), Hovering ceiling 5,100 ft. (1,555 m.), Service ceiling 14,000 ft. (4,270 m.), Range 260 miles (420 km.).
(1945–46)

The Sikorsky R-6A Two-seat Observation Helicopter (245 h.p. Franklin O-405-9 engine).

THE SIKORSKY R-6A.
U.S. Navy designation: HOS-1.

TYPE.—Two-seat Observation Helicopter.

ROTORS.—Rotor system and transmission similar to R-4B. Main rotor disc area 1,134 sq. ft. (105.3 sq. m.).

FUSELAGE.—All-metal framework. The cabin section has an aluminium floor and is covered with moulded plastic-impregnated glass fibre cloth and Plexiglas transparent moulded nose and side and roof windows. Paper-based moulded plastic cowling encloses the engine compartment and rotor pylon. The rear fuselage carrying the tail rotor is a light metal monocoque.

LANDING GEAR.—Conventional landing-gear with the main wheels on cantilever oleo struts, a tail-wheel on a steel tube pyramid midway between nose and tail and a small emergency nose wheel. Hydraulic wheel brakes on main wheels. Track 9 ft. (2.7 m.). Landing-gear may be replaced by flotation gear.

POWER PLANT.—One 245 h.p. Franklin O-405-9 six-cylinder horizontally-opposed fan-cooled engine mounted with crankshaft vertical within the fuselage aft of the cabin. Planetary gear transmission to rotor. Fuel and oil tanks in fuselage aft of transmission compartment.

ACCOMMODATION.—Enclosed cabin seating two side-by-side with dual controls. Equipment includes high-frequency radio communication set. An evacuation litter may be installed on each side of fuselage.

DIMENSIONS.—Rotor diameter 38 ft. (11.6 m.), Overall length 47 ft. 11 in. (14.6 m.).

WEIGHT LOADED.—2,600 lbs. (1,180 kg.).

PERFORMANCE.—Maximum speed 100 m.p.h. (161 km.h.), Climb to 5,900 ft. (1,800 m.) 7 min., Service ceiling 10,000 ft. (3,050 m.), Maximum duration 5 hours.
(1947)

THE SIKORSKY S-55
U.S.A.F. and U.S. Army designation: H-19
U.S. Army name: Chickasaw
U.S. Navy and Coast Guard designation: HO4S
U.S. Marine Corps designation: HRS

The S-55 is a twelve-seat utility helicopter suitable for passenger, air mail or cargo transport and for air rescue and military service. The prototype flew on November 9, 1949 and a total of 1,278 were built by Sikorsky before major production ended. The S-55 was put back into production in 1961 to meet a contract for four from the Chilean Air Force.

Apart from being adopted by the U.S.A.F., U.S. Army Field Forces, U.S. Navy, U.S Marine Corps and U.S. Coast Guard, the S-55 is also being built under licence in the United Kingdom by Westland Aircraft Ltd. and in Japan by Mitsubishi. The British-built S-55, known as the Westland Whirlwind, is in service with the Royal Air Force, Royal Navy and other military and civil operators.

The many U.S. naval and military versions are enumerated below:—

H-19A. 600 h.p. Pratt & Whitney R-1340-57 engine. For U.S.A.F. A.U.W. 7,200 lb. (3,263 kg.). Crew of two, plus ten troops or six stretchers.

H-19B. 800 h.p. Wright R-1300-3 engine. For U.S.A.F. A.U.W. 7,500 lb. (3,400 kg.). Crew of two, plus ten troops or six stretchers.

H-19C. Same as H-19A for U.S. Army Field Forces.

H-19D. Same as H-19B for U.S. Army Field Forces.

HO4S-1 and -2. 600 h.p. Pratt & Whitney R-1340 engine. Similar to H-19A. For U.S. Navy for anti-submarine duties.

HO4S-3. 800 h.p. Wright R-1300-3 engine. Similar to H-19B. For U.S. Navy for anti-submarine duties.

HO4S-3G. For U.S. Coast Guard.

The Sikorsky H-19B Utility Helicopter (700 h.p. Wright R-1300 engine).

HRS-1 and -2. 600 h.p. Pratt & Whitney R-1340 engine. Similar to H-19A. For U.S. Marine Corps for assault transport duties. Crew of two and eight fully-armed troops.

HRS-3. 800 h.p. Wright R-1300 engine. Similar to H-19B. U.S. Marine Corps assault transport.

The description and specification which follow refer in general to all current models.

TYPE.—Twelve-seat utility helicopter.

ROTORS.—Three-blade main rotor and two-blade anti-torque tail rotor. All-metal structures.

FUSELAGE.—Structure is primarily aluminium and magnesium semi-monocoque construction. On commercial S-55C's and the versions with R-1300 engine, the tail cone has been sloped down approximately 3½° to increase clearance of main rotor in a rough landing.

LANDING GEAR.—Quadricycle type. Wheel track 11 ft. (3.35 m.). Alternative gear includes all-metal amphibious landing-gear or permanently-inflated rubber bag flotation gear. For use with the normal wheels, "doughnut" pontoons are available which are stowed deflated on each wheel axle and can be inflated in under 5 sec. when needed for landing on water.

POWER PLANT.—One 600 h.p. Pratt & Whitney R-1340 S3H2 or S1H2, or 800 h.p. Wright R-1300-3 radial air-cooled engine, on angular mounting in nose of fuselage with sloping shaft drive to rotor gear box below head. With the R-1300 engine, a hydro-mechanical clutch with freewheel

system is used in the drive to the main transmission, and the drive-shaft from the freewheel unit to the main transmission has flexible rubber couplings on each end. Large clam-shell doors in nose of fuselage allow complete accessibility to engine from ground level. Internal fuel capacity 185 U.S. gallons (700 litres).

ACCOMMODATION.—Pilot's compartment above main cabin seats two side-by-side with dual controls. Cabin located below main lifting rotor may seat from seven (commercial) to ten (military) passengers, the ten passengers being seated three against front and rear walls and two on each side, all facing inwards. Up to six stretchers may be carried, which can be loaded by optional hydraulic power-operated hoist while aircraft is hovering. Pilot's compartment may be entered from the outside or from the cabin so that co-pilot may act as attendant. Cabin dimensions : length 10 ft. (3.05 m.), width 5 ft. 3 in. (1.60 m.), height 6 ft. (1.82 m.). Total capacity 315 cub. ft. (8.9 m.³)

DIMENSIONS.—
Main rotor diameter 53 ft. (16.16 m.)
Tail rotor diameter 8 ft. 9 in. (2.67 m.)
Fuselage length 42 ft. 3 in. (12.88 m.)
Height overall 13 ft. 4 in. (4.07 m.)

WEIGHTS (R-1340 engine).—
Weight empty 4,950 lb. (2,245 kg.)
Max. disposable load 2,250 lb. (1,021 kg.)
Normal weight loaded 7,200 lb. (3,266 kg.)
Overload max. weight (military versions) 7,500 lb. (3,402 kg.)

WEIGHTS (R-1300 engine).—
Weight empty 5,250 lb. (2,381 kg.)
Max. disposable load 2,250 lb. (1,021 kg.)
Weight loaded 7,500 lb. (3,402 kg.)
Overload max. weight (military versions) 7,900 lb. (3,583 kg.)

PERFORMANCE (R-1340 engine at A.U.W. of 7,200 lb.=3,266 kg.).—
Max. speed at S/L. 101 m.p.h. (162 km.h.)
Cruising speed (67% power) at 1,000 ft. (305 m.) 85 m.p.h. (137 km.h.)
Max. rate of climb at S/L. 700 ft./min. (213 m./min.)
Hovering ceiling with ground effect 2,000 ft. (610 m.)
Service ceiling 10,500 ft. (3,218 m.)
Fuel consumption (cruising) 38 U.S. gallons (144 litres) per hour.
Range (with reserve) 400 miles (644 km.).

PERFORMANCE (R-1300 engine).—
Max. speed at S/L. 112 m.p.h. (180 km.h.)
Cruising speed (65% power) 91 m.p.h. (148 km.h.)
Max. rate of climb at S/L. 1,020 ft./min. (311 m./min.)
Vertical rate of climb at S/L. 100 ft./min. (35 m./min.)
Hovering ceiling with ground effect 5,800 ft. (1,770 m.)
Hovering ceiling without ground effect 2,300 ft. (700 m.)
Fuel consumption (cruising) 43 U.S. gallons (163 litres) per hour.
Range (with reserve) 360 miles (578 km.).

(1961–62)

THE SIKORSKY S-56

U.S. Army, Navy and Marine Corps designation: CH-37

U.S. Army name: Mojave

The S-56 is a twin-engined single-rotor transport helicopter which is comparable in size to the Douglas DC-3 transport.

Three versions of the S-56 are in service:—

CH-37A (formerly H-37A). For medium cargo and troop transport duties with U.S. Army. Accommodation for pilot, co-pilot, equipment operator and 23 passengers or 24 litter patients or 1,900 cub. ft. (53.8 m.³) cargo.

CH-37B (formerly H-37B). Designation given to 90 H-37's which Sikorsky are modernising for the U.S. Army. Changes include the installation of Lear autostabilisation equipment, a redesigned cabin door and cargo hatch. Deliveries are being made at the rate of five a month from June, 1961.

CH-37C (formerly HR2S-1). First version of S-56. Basic assault transport for U.S. Marines with accommodation for pilot, co-pilot and 20 passengers or 24 litter patients or 1,900 cub. ft. (53.8 m.³) cargo. Prototype XCH-37C made its first flight on December 18, 1953 and the first production CH-37C flew on October 25, 1955.

The cabin of the S-56 is 30 ft. 4 in. long, 7 ft. 9 in. wide and 6 ft. 8 in. high (9.24 m. × 2.36 m. × 2.03 m.) and is fitted with hydraulically-operated clamshell nose doors. A power-

Sikorsky CH-37A Mojave transport helicopter (two Pratt & Whitney R-2800 engines)

operated 2,000 lb. (907 kg) winch hoist with a monorail facilitates loading and handling cargo. It can be used to draw vehicles up the nose ramp or for making air or ground pick-ups at the rear cargo door for subsequent stowage anywhere in the cabin. Bulky loads can be carried under the aircraft in a sling which is equipped with an automatic release to deposit its load upon touch-down when set by the pilot.

Modifications to the side and clamshell nose doors on the CH-37B model permit loading and unloading while hovering.

The S-56 is powered by two Pratt & Whitney R-2800 engines which are mounted in outboard nacelles on short wing stubs. Each engine is rated at 2,100 h.p. at 2,700 r.p.m. for five minutes, with a normal output of 1,900 h.p. at 2,600 r.p.m.

Power from both engines is transmitted to the five-blade main rotor and the four-blade tail rotor, both of which are of all-metal construction.

This helicopter was one of the first ever built with a retractable landing-gear and is fitted with night flying equipment. It has a hydraulic servo booster control system, and all-weather flying is made possible by installation of automatic stabilisation equipment. Normal fuel capacity is 400 U.S. gallons (1,515 litres) but this can be raised to 1,000 U.S. gallons (3,800 litres) for assault operations by the use of standard external auxil-

iary tanks. The standard tanks of the CH-37B are of the crash-resistant type.

Production of the S-56 series ended in May, 1960, when the 154th and last helicopter of this type (a CH-37A) was completed. Major components of the S-56 will continue to be used on the S-64 Skycrane series and the CH-53A assault helicopter.

DIMENSIONS.—

Main rotor diameter	72 ft (21·95 m)
Tail rotor diameter	15 ft (4·57 m)
Fuselage length	64 ft 10 in. (19·76 m)
Height overall	22 ft (6·71 m)

WEIGHTS.—

Weight empty	20,690 lb (9,385 kg)
Normal T.O. weight	31,000 lb (14,061 kg)

PERFORMANCE.—

Max. speed at S/L	130 mph (209 kmh)
Cruising speed	115 mph (185 kmh)
Max. rate of climb at S/L	910 ft (277 m) min.
Hovering ceiling out of ground effect	1,100 ft (335 m)
Service ceiling	8,700 ft (2,650 m)
Range	145 miles (233 km)
	(1962–63)

The Sikorsky HUS-I equipped experimentally as a Bullpup air-to-ground missile launcher

SIKORSKY S-58

US Navy designations: LH-34 and SH-34 Seabat
US Army designation: CH-34 Choctaw
US Marine Corps designations: UH-34 and VH-34 Seahorse

The first prototype of this helicopter flew on March 8, 1954, and the first production machine on September 20, 1954.

The following military versions of the S-58 remain in service with the US armed forces:

CH-34A (formerly H-34A) **Choctaw.** Transport and general-purpose helicopter, in service with US Army. Has been armed experimentally with rockets, etc.

CH-34C (formerly H-34C) **Choctaw.** Similar to CH-34A, but with airborne search equipment.

LH-34D (formerly HSS-1L). Winterised version of Navy Seabat.

UH-34D (formerly HUS-1) **Seahorse.** Utility version for Marines, first ordered on October 15, 1954 and accepted for service in January, 1957. Bullpup missiles have been fired experimentally from a UH-34D.

VH-34D (formerly HUS-1Z). VIP transport version of Seahorse.

UH-34E (formerly HUS-1A) **Seahorse.** Version with pontoons for emergency operation from water.

SH-34G (formerly HSS-1) **Seabat.** Anti-submarine version, ordered by US Navy on June 30, 1952 and accepted for service in February, 1954.

SH-34J (formerly HSS-1N) **Seabat.** Development of SH-34G for US Navy. This version utilises Sikorsky's automatic stabilisation equipment and is suitable for day and night instrument flying. The changes include (1) incorporation of Ryan-developed AN/APN-97 Doppler and other radar to measure ground speed and altitude accurately; (2) improved flight instrument and cockpit arrangement; (3) addition of automatic engine rpm controls; and (4) introduction of an automatic "hover coupler". With the coupler, which uses the radar to determine ground motion, it is possible for the pilot to place the helicopter on automatic control at 200 ft (60 m) altitude and 92 mph (148 kmh) ground speed and to come automatically to a zero ground speed at a 50 ft (15 m) altitude over a pre-selected spot.

Production of the S-58 series by Sikorsky totalled 1,766 by December 1965, when it term-

inated temporarily. It re-started subsequently to meet new requirements of the US Military Assistance Programme and an overall total of 1,821 aircraft had been delivered by January 1969.

Military S-58's have been supplied to the armed forces of the Argentine, Brazil, Canada, Chile, France, Federal Germany, Italy, Japan, the Netherlands and Thailand. In addition, Sud-Aviation delivered 166 S-58's from their works in France and Westland are producing several turbine-powered versions in the UK, under the name Wessex.

TYPE: General-purpose helicopter.

ROTOR SYSTEM: Four-blade all-metal main and tail rotors, both with servo control. Fully-articulated main rotor blades, each made up of a hollow extruded aluminium spar and trailing-edge pockets of aluminium. Each tail rotor blade has an aluminium spar, sheet aluminium skin and honeycomb trailing-edge. Blades of each rotor interchangeable. Main rotor blades fold. Main and tail rotor brakes.

ROTOR DRIVE: Transmission system has 25% fewer parts than in earlier Sikorsky designs, and provides accessory drives for the generator and its blower, primary servo-control hydraulic pump, rotor tachometer and hydraulic clutch. Steel-tube drive-shafts with rubber couplings. Main gearbox below main rotor, intermediate gearbox at base of tail pylon and tail gearbox behind tail rotor. Main rotor/engine rpm ratio 1 : 11·293. Tail rotor/engine rpm ratio 1 : 1·884.

FUSELAGE: Semi-monocoque structure, primarily of magnesium and aluminium alloys, with some titanium and stainless steel.

TAIL SURFACE: Ground-adjustable stabiliser made of magnesium skin over magnesium and aluminium structure.

LANDING GEAR: Non-retractable three-wheel undercarriage, with tail-wheel towards rear of fuselage. Sikorsky oleo-pneumatic shock-absorber struts. Tail-wheel is fully-castoring and self-centering, with an anti-swivelling lock. Goodyear main wheel tyres size 11·00 × 12, pressure 42 lb/sq in (2·95 kg/cm²). Tail-wheel tyre size 6·00×6 6-ply. Toe-operated Goodyear disc brakes. Provision for amphibious gear, pontoons, "doughnut" or pop-out flotation bags.

POWER PLANT: One 1,525 hp Wright R-1820-84B/D nine-cylinder radial air-cooled engine,

mounted behind large clam-shell doors in nose of fuselage. Fuel in 113 US gallon (427 litre) forward tank, 70 US gallon (265 litre) centre tank, 31·5 US gallon (119 litre) auxiliary tank and 92 US gallon (348 litre) aft tank. Total internal fuel capacity 306·5 US gallons (1,159 litres). Provision for 150 US gallon (568 litre) external metal tank. Refuelling point on starboard side of fuselage. Oil capacity 10·5 US gallons (40 litres).

ACCOMMODATION: Pilot's compartment above main cabin seats two side-by-side with dual controls. Cabin seats 16-18 passengers on inward-facing troop seats or 12 on airline seats in one or two compartments. Two-compartment version has hinged doors, each cabin seating six in rows of three facing each other. Eight stretchers can be carried. Cabin entrance on starboard side. Sliding windows of pilot's compartment removable in an emergency. Cabin and cockpit are heated and sound-proofed.

SYSTEMS: Air-conditioning by 50,000 or 100,000 BTU heater and 1½ hp blower-defroster. Hydraulic system, pressure 1,250 lb/sq in (88 kg/cm²), for hoist, wheel and rotor brakes, clutch, primary and auxiliary servos. 28V DC electrical system. 115V and 26V AC generator, battery and external power supply.

ELECTRONICS AND EQUIPMENT: Optional items include blind-flying instrumentation, ARC-210 VHF, ARC-21A ADF, Collins ILS, HTR-5 HF, cargo sling and military equipment.

DIMENSIONS, EXTERNAL:

Diameter of main rotor	56 ft 0 in (17·07 m)
Diameter of tail rotor	9 ft 6 in (2·90 m)
Distance between rotor centres	33 ft 1 in (10·08 m)
Length overall	56 ft 8½ in (17·27 m)
Length of fuselage	46 ft 9 in (14·25 m)
Width, rotors folded	12 ft 11 in (3·94 m)
Height to top of rotor hub	14 ft 3½ in (4·36 m)
Overall height	15 ft 11 in (4·85 m)
Wheel track	14 ft 0 in (4·27 m)
Wheelbase	28 ft 3 in (8·75 m)
Cabin door:	
Height:	
S-58B	4 ft 0 in (1·22 m)
S-58C	4 ft 8 in (1·42 m)
Width:	
S-58B	4 ft 5½ in (1·36 m)
S-58C	2 ft 5 in (0·74 m)
Height to sill	2 ft 10½ in (0·88 m)

DIMENSIONS, INTERNAL:	
Cabin: Length	13 ft 7 in (4·14 m)
Max width	5 ft 0 in (1·52 m)
Max height	5 ft 10 in (1·78 m)
Floor area	65 sq ft (6·04 m²)
Volume	350 cu ft (9·91 m³)
AREAS:	
Main rotor blade (each)	35·00 sq ft (3·25 m²)
Tail rotor blade (each)	2·67 sq ft (0·25 m²)
Main rotor disc	2,460 sq ft (228·54 m²)
Tail rotor disc	70·88 sq ft (6·59 m²)
Stabiliser	12·38 sq ft (1·15 m²)
WEIGHTS AND LOADINGS:	
Weight empty, equipped:	
CH-34A	7,750 lb (3,515 kg)
UH-34D	7,900 lb (3,583 kg)
SH-34J	8,275 lb (3,754 kg)
S-58	7,630 lb (3,461 kg)

Max normal T-O weight	13,000 lb (5,900 kg)
Max permissible weight	14,000 lb (6,350 kg)
Max disc loading	5·3 lb/sq ft (25·9 kg/m²)
Max power loading	8·53 lb/hp (3·87 kg/hp)
PERFORMANCE (at 13,000 lb = 5,900 kg AUW):	
Max level speed at S/L:	
CH-34A	122 mph (196 kmh)
S-58	123 mph (198 kmh)
Max cruising speed:	
CH-34A	97 mph (156 kmh)
S-58	98 mph (158 kmh)

Max rate of climb at S/L	1,100 ft (335 m) min
Vertical rate of climb at S/L	200 ft (60 m) min
Service ceiling:	
CH-34A	9,500 ft (2,900 m)
S-58	9,000 ft (2,740 m)
Hovering ceiling in ground effect	
	4,900 ft (1,490 m)
Hovering ceiling out of ground effect	
	2,400 ft (730 m)
Range with max fuel, 10% reserve:	
CH-34A	247 miles (400 km)
S-58	280 miles (450 km)
	(1969–70)

Sikorsky SH-3H multi-purpose helicopter for ASW and fleet missile defence

SIKORSKY S-61A and S-61B

US military designations: SH-3 Sea King, HH-3A, VH-3

CAF designation: CH-124

The first version of the S-61 ordered into production was the SH-3A (originally HSS-2) Sea King amphibious anti-submarine helicopter, of which the prototype flew for the first time on 11 March 1959. Deliveries to the US Navy began in September 1961. On 11 March 1979, Sikorsky drew attention to the 20th anniversary of the prototype's first flight, since when more than 900 military S-61s had accumulated over 3 million flight hours, and 130 commercial S-61s had logged a total of more than 815,000 hours.

The S-61 series includes the following military and commercial variants:

SH-3A Sea King. Initial anti-submarine version for the US Navy, powered by 932 kW (1,250 shp) General Electric T58-GE-8B turboshaft engines. A total of 255 were produced by Sikorsky. Also standard equipment in the Japan Maritime Self-Defence Force (see entry for Mitsubishi, which also converted two SH-3As to S-61A standard for use during Antarctic expeditions).

CH-124. Designation of 41 aircraft, similar to SH-3A, for the Canadian Armed Forces. First of these was delivered in May 1963: fifth and subsequent aircraft were assembled by United Aircraft of Canada Ltd. Originally designated CHSS-2.

S-61A. Amphibious transport, generally similar to the US Navy's SH-3A. Accommodates 26 troops, 15 litters, cargo, or 12 passengers in VIP configuration. Rolls-Royce Gnome H.1200 turboshafts available as alternative to standard General Electric T58 engines. Nine delivered to Royal Danish Air Force for long-range air/sea rescue duties, with additional fuel tankage. One delivered to Construction Helicopters.

S-61A-4 Nuri. Thirty-eight delivered to Royal Malaysian Air Force, each with 31 seats, rescue hoists and auxiliary fuel tanks as standard equipment. Used for troop transport, cargo carrying and rescue.

HH-3A. Variant of SH-3A, for search and rescue duties with US Navy. HH-3A conversion kits were supplied to the Navy's overhaul and repair base at Quonset Point, Rhode Island, where 12 conversions were carried out. Changes included installation of two electrically-powered Minigun turrets behind the sponsons, T58-GE-8F turbine engines, a high-speed refuelling and fuel dumping system, a high-speed rescue hoist, modified electronics package, external auxiliary fuel tanks and complete armour installation. The SH-3A's sonar well is covered and a reinforced cabin floor substituted.

SH-3D Sea King. Standard anti-submarine helicopter of the US Navy, with T58-GE-10 engines and more fuel than SH-3A. First SH-3D, delivered in June 1966, was one of 10 for the Spanish Navy, which later ordered 12 more. Four were delivered to the Brazilian Navy and 72 to the US Navy. Versions with Rolls-Royce Gnome turboshaft engines and British anti-submarine equipment are manufactured by Westland Helicopters Ltd (which see). SH-3Ds are also manufactured under licence by Agusta in Italy.

S-61D-4. Four for Argentinian Navy, similar to SH-3D.

VH-3D. Eleven delivered to replace VH-3As of US Executive Flight Detachment.

SH-3G. US Navy conversion of 105 SH-3As into utility helicopters, by removing anti-submarine warfare equipment. Six equipped with Minigun pods for search and rescue missions in combat conditions.

SH-3H. Multi-purpose version of SH-3G with T58-GE-10 engines. US Navy contracts, awarded from 1971, called for conversion of 163 existing aircraft by 1980, to increase fleet helicopter capability against submarines and low-flying enemy missiles. New ASW equipment includes lightweight sonar, active and passive sonobuoys, and magnetic anomaly detection equipment. Electronic surveillance measurement (ESM) equipment enables the SH-3H to make an important contribution to the missile defence of the fleet.

S-61L. Non-amphibious civil transport with longer fuselage than S-61A/B. Described in 1979-80 *Jane's*.

S-61N. Amphibious counterpart of S-61L; described in 1979-80 *Jane's*.

S-61R. Development of S-61B for transport duties with US Air Force, under the designations **CH-3C** and **E**. Described separately.

By mid-1980, more than 750 examples of the S-61 (all models) had been built by Sikorsky, and more than 350 by the company's foreign licensees.

The following details apply to the SH-3D Sea King, but are generally applicable to other versions except for accommodation and equipment:

TYPE: Twin-engined amphibious all-weather anti-submarine helicopter.

ROTOR SYSTEM: Five-blade main and tail rotors. All-metal fully-articulated oil-lubricated main rotor. Flanged cuffs on blades bolted to matching flanges on all-steel rotor head. Main rotor blades are interchangeable and are provided with an automatic powered folding system. Rotor brake standard. All-metal tail rotor.

ROTOR DRIVE: Both engines drive through freewheel units

and rotor brake to main gearbox. Steel drive-shafts. Tail rotor shaft-driven through intermediate and tail gearboxes. Accessories driven by power take-off on tail rotor shaft. Additional freewheel units between accessories and port engine, and between accessories and tail rotor shaft. Main rotor/engine rpm ratio 1 : 93·43. Tail rotor/engine rpm ratio 1 : 16·7.

FUSELAGE: Boat hull of all-metal semi-monocoque construction. Single step. Tail section folds to reduce stowage requirements.

TAIL SURFACE: Fixed stabiliser on starboard side of tail section.

LANDING GEAR: Amphibious. Land gear consists of two twin-wheel main units, which are retracted rearward hydraulically into stabilising floats, and non-retractable tailwheel. Oleo-pneumatic shock-absorbers. Goodyear main wheels and tubeless tyres size 6·50-10 type III, pressure 4·83 bars (70 lb/sq in). Goodyear tailwheel and tyre size 6·00-6. Goodyear hydraulic disc brakes. Boat hull and pop-out flotation bags in stabilising floats permit emergency operation from water.

POWER PLANT: Two 1,044 kW (1,400 shp) General Electric T58-GE-10 turboshaft engines. Three bladder-type fuel tanks in hull; forward tank 1,314 litres (347 US gallons), centre tank 530 litres (140 US gallons), rear tank 1,336 litres (353 US gallons). Total fuel capacity 3,180 litres (840 US gallons). Refuelling point on port side of fuselage. Oil capacity 26·5 litres (7 US gallons).

ACCOMMODATION: Pilot and co-pilot on flight deck, two sonar operators in main cabin. Dual controls. Crew door at rear of flight deck on port side. Large loading door at rear of cabin on starboard side.

SYSTEMS: Primary and auxiliary hydraulic systems, pressure 103·5 bars (1,500 lb/sq in), for flying controls. Utility hydraulic system, pressure 207 bars (3,000 lb/sq in), for landing gear, winches and blade folding. Pneumatic system, pressure 207 bars (3,000 lb/sq in), for blow-down emergency landing gear extension. Electrical system includes one 300A DC generator, two 20kVA 115A AC generators and 24V 22Ah battery. APU optional.

AVIONICS AND EQUIPMENT: Bendix AQS-13 sonar with 180° search beam width. Hamilton Standard auto-stabilisation equipment. Automatic transition into hover. Sonar coupler holds altitude automatically in conjunction with Teledyne APN-130 Doppler radar (Litton AN/APS-503 in CH-124) and radar altimeter. Provision for 272 kg (600 lb) capacity rescue hoist and 3,630 kg (8,000 lb) capacity automatic touchdown-release low-response cargo sling for external loads.

ARMAMENT: Provision for 381 kg (840 lb) of weapons, including homing torpedoes.

DIMENSIONS, EXTERNAL:

Diameter of main rotor	18·90 m (62 ft 0 in)
Main rotor blade chord	0·46 m (1 ft 6¼ in)
Diameter of tail rotor	3·23 m (10 ft 7 in)
Distance between rotor centres	11·10 m (36 ft 5 in)
Length overall	22·15 m (72 ft 8 in)
Length of fuselage	16·69 m (54 ft 9 in)
Length, tail pylon folded	14·40 m (47 ft 3 in)
Width, rotors folded	4·98 m (16 ft 4 in)
Height to top of rotor hub	4·72 m (15 ft 6 in)
Height overall	5·13 m (16 ft 10 in)
Wheel track	3·96 m (13 ft 0 in)
Wheelbase	7·18 m (23 ft 6½ in)
Crew door (fwd, port): Height	1·68 m (5 ft 6 in)
Width	0·91 m (3 ft 0 in)
Height to sill	1·14 m (3 ft 9 in)

Main cabin door (stbd): Height	1·52 m (5 ft 0 in)
Width	1·73 m (5 ft 8 in)
Height to sill	1·14 m (3 ft 9 in)

DIMENSIONS, INTERNAL (S-61A):

Cabin: Length	7·60 m (24 ft 11 in)
Max width	1·98 m (6 ft 6 in)
Max height	1·92 m (6 ft 3½ in)
Floor area	15·1 m² (162 sq ft)
Volume	28·9 m³ (1,020 cu ft)

AREAS:

Main rotor blades (each)	4·14 m² (44·54 sq ft)
Tail rotor blades (each)	0·22 m² (2·38 sq ft)
Main rotor disc	280·5 m² (3,019 sq ft)
Tail rotor disc	8·20 m² (88·30 sq ft)
Stabiliser	1·86 m² (20·00 sq ft)

WEIGHTS:

Weight empty: S-61A	4,428 kg (9,763 lb)
S-61B	5,382 kg (11,865 lb)

Normal T-O weight: S-61A	9,300 kg (20,500 lb)
SH-3A (ASW)	8,185 kg (18,044 lb)
SH-3D (ASW)	8,449 kg (18,626 lb)
Max T-O weight: S-61A	9,750 kg (21,500 lb)
S-61B	9,300 kg (20,500 lb)
SH-3H	9,525 kg (21,000 lb)

PERFORMANCE (at 9,300 kg; 20,500 lb AUW):

Max level speed	144 knots (267 km/h; 166 mph)
Cruising speed for max range	
	118 knots (219 km/h; 136 mph)
Max rate of climb at S/L	670 m (2,200 ft)/min
Service ceiling	4,480 m (14,700 ft)
Hovering ceiling IGE	3,200 m (10,500 ft)
Hovering ceiling OGE	2,500 m (8,200 ft)
Range with max fuel, 10% reserves	
	542 nm (1,005 km; 625 miles)
	(1980–81)

SIKORSKY S-61R

US military designations: CH-3 and HH-3 Jolly Green Giant

Although based on the SH-3A, this amphibious transport helicopter introduced many important design changes. They include provision of a hydraulically-operated rear ramp for straight-in loading of wheeled vehicles, a 907 kg (2,000 lb) capacity winch for internal cargo handling, retractable tricycle-type landing gear, pressurised rotor blades for quick and easy inspection, gas-turbine auxiliary power supply for independent field operations, self-lubricating main and tail rotors, and built-in equipment for the removal and replacement of all major components in remote areas.

The first S-61R flew on 17 June 1963, followed by the first CH-3C a few weeks later. FAA Type Approval was received on 30 December 1963, and the first delivery of an operational CH-3C was made on the same day, for drone recovery duties at Tyndall AFB, Florida. Subsequent deliveries made to USAF Aerospace Defense Command, Air Training Command, Tactical Air Command, Strategic Air Command and Aerospace Rescue and Recovery Service.

There were four Sikorsky-built versions, as follows:

CH-3C. Two 969·5 kW (1,300 shp) T58-GE-1 turboshaft engines. After a total of 41 had been built for the US Air Force, production was switched to the CH-3E. All aircraft delivered as CH-3Cs were modified to CH-3E standard.

CH-3E. Designation applicable since February 1966, following introduction of uprated engines (1,118 kW; 1,500 shp T58-GE-5s). A total of 42 were built as new aircraft to this standard.

HH-3E. For US Air Force Aerospace Rescue and Recovery Service. Additional equipment comprises armour, self-sealing fuel tanks, retractable flight refuelling probe, defensive armament and rescue hoist. Two 1,118 kW (1,500 shp) T58-GE-5 turboshafts. A total of 50 HH-3Es were converted from CH-3Es, and are known as **Jolly Green Giants**.

HH-3F. Similar to HH-3E, for US Coast Guard, which gave them the name **Pelican**. Advanced electronic equipment for search and rescue duties. No armour plate, armament or self-sealing tanks. First order announced in August 1965. Deliveries began in 1968 and 40 were built.

The following details apply to the CH-3E:

TYPE: Twin-engined amphibious transport helicopter.

ROTOR SYSTEM: Five-blade fully-articulated main rotor of all-metal construction. Flanged cuffs on blades bolted to matching flanges on rotor head. Control by rotating and stationary swashplates. Blades do not fold. Rotor brake standard. Conventional tail rotor with five aluminium blades.

ROTOR DRIVE: Twin turbines drive through freewheeling units and rotor brake to main gearbox. Steel driveshafts. Tail rotor shaft-driven through intermediate gearbox and tail gearbox. Main rotor/engine rpm ratio 1 : 93·43. Tail rotor/engine rpm ratio 1 : 16·7.

FUSELAGE: All-metal semi-monocoque structure of pod and boom type. Cabin of basic square section.

TAIL SURFACE: Horizontal stabiliser on starboard side of tail rotor pylon.

LANDING GEAR: Hydraulically-retractable tricycle type, with twin wheels on each unit. Main wheels retract forward into sponsons, each of which provides 2,176 kg (4,797 lb) of buoyancy and, with boat hull, permits amphibious operation. Oleo-pneumatic shock-absorbers. All wheels and tyres tubeless Type III rib, size 22·1 × 6·50-10, manufactured by Goodyear. Tyre pressure 6·55 bars (95 lb/sq in). Goodyear hydraulic disc brakes.

POWER PLANT: Two 1,118 kW (1,500 shp) General Electric T58-GE-5 turboshaft engines, mounted side by side above cabin, immediately forward of main transmission. Fuel in two bladder-type tanks beneath cabin floor; forward tank capacity 1,204 litres (318 US gallons), rear tank capacity 1,226 litres (324 US gallons). Total fuel capacity 2,430 litres (642 US gallons). Refuelling point on port side of fuselage. Total oil capacity 26·5 litres (7 US gallons).

ACCOMMODATION: Crew of two side by side on flight deck, with dual controls. Provision for flight engineer or attendant. Normal accommodation for 25 fully-equipped troops. Alternative arrangements for 30 troops, 15 stretchers or 2,270 kg (5,000 lb) of cargo. Jettisonable sliding door on starboard side at front of cabin. Internal door between cabin and flight deck. Hydraulically-operated rear loading ramp for vehicles, in two hinged sections, giving opening with minimum width of 1·73 m (5 ft 8 in) and headroom of up to 2·21 m (7 ft 3 in).

SYSTEMS: Primary and auxiliary hydraulic systems, pressure 103·5 bars (1,500 lb/sq in), for flying control servos. Utility hydraulic system, pressure 207 bars (3,000 lb/sq in), for landing gear, rear ramp and winches. Pneumatic system, pressure 207 bars (3,000 lb/sq in), for emergency blow-down landing gear extension. Electrical system includes 24V 22Ah battery, two 20kVA 115V AC generators and one 300A DC generator. APU standard.

DIMENSIONS, EXTERNAL:

Diameter of main rotor	18·90 m (62 ft 0 in)
Main rotor blade chord	0·46 m (1 ft 6¼ in)
Diameter of tail rotor	3·15 m (10 ft 4 in)
Distance between rotor centres	11·22 m (36 ft 10 in)
Length overall	22·25 m (73 ft 0 in)
Length of fuselage	17·45 m (57 ft 3 in)
Width over landing gear	4·82 m (15 ft 10 in)
Height to top of rotor hub	4·90 m (16 ft 1 in)
Height overall	5·51 m (18 ft 1 in)
Wheel track	4·06 m (13 ft 4 in)
Wheelbase	5·21 m (17 ft 1 in)
Cabin door (fwd, stbd): Height	1·65 m (5 ft 4¾ in)
Width	1·22 m (4 ft 0 in)
Height to sill	1·27 m (4 ft 2 in)
Rear ramp: Length	4·29 m (14 ft 1 in)
Width	1·85 m (6 ft 1 in)

DIMENSIONS, INTERNAL:

Cabin (excl flight deck):

Length	7·89 m (25 ft 10½ in)
Max width	1·98 m (6 ft 6 in)
Max height	1·91 m (6 ft 3 in)
Floor area	approx 15·61 m² (168 sq ft)
Volume	approx 29·73 m³ (1,050 cu ft)

AREAS:

Main rotor blades (each)	3·71 m² (39·9 sq ft)
Tail rotor blades (each)	0·22 m² (2·35 sq ft)
Main rotor disc	280·5 m² (3,019 sq ft)
Tail rotor disc	7·80 m² (83·9 sq ft)
Stabiliser	2·51 m² (27·0 sq ft)

WEIGHTS:

Weight empty	6,010 kg (13,255 lb)
Normal T-O weight	9,635 kg (21,247 lb)
Max T-O weight	10,000 kg (22,050 lb)

PERFORMANCE (at normal T-O weight):

Max level speed at S/L	
	141 knots (261 km/h; 162 mph)
Cruising speed for max range	
	125 knots (232 km/h; 144 mph)
Max rate of climb at S/L	400 m (1,310 ft)/min
Service ceiling	3,385 m (11,100 ft)
Hovering ceiling IGE	1,250 m (4,100 ft)
Min ground turning radius	11·29 m (37 ft 0½ in)
Runway LCN at max T-O weight	approx 4·75
Range with max fuel, 10% reserves	
	404 nm (748 km; 465 miles)
	(1965–66)

SIKORSKY S-62

US Coast Guard designation: HH-52A

Four versions of the S-62 amphibious helicopter have been announced, as follows:

S-62A. This version incorporates many components of the Sikorsky S-55, including rotor blades, main and tail rotor heads, intermediate and tail gearboxes, shafting, and portions of the flying control and hydraulic systems.

Its empty weight is some 160 lb (72 kg) less than that of the S-55C, largely because it is powered by a 1,250 shp (de-rated to 730 shp) General Electric CT58-110 shaft-turbine, instead of by the latter's heavier piston-engine. Because of this weight saving and the availability of 130 more horsepower for high-altitude or hot weather flight, it can carry a much greater payload than that of the S-55 under all conditions. Full power is available at heights up to 20,000 ft (6,100 m).

First S-62A flew on May 14, 1958, and FAA type approval was received on June 30, 1960. The first delivery was made in the following month to Petroleum Helicopters Inc, to serve off-shore oil-rigs in the Gulf of Mexico.

Sikorsky HH-52A search and rescue helicopter of the US Coast Guard

S-62B. Basically similar to S-62A, but utilising main rotor system of S-58 instead of S-55, with reduced rotor diameter.

S-62C. Commercial and foreign military version of HH-52A.

HH-52A. Ordered for US Coast Guard Service to replace HH-34 for search and rescue duties. First three delivered in January 1963. This version has a 1,250 shp T58-GE-8 engine, automatic stabilisation equipment, towing equipment, and a 4 ft (1·22 m) long rescue platform that folds down from the cabin door and extends over the water, so that a crew member can move out and help survivors aboard after the aircraft has alighted on the water. During evaluation by the Coast Guard, the S-62 operated successfully in 8·10 ft (2·5-3 m) waves.

The S-62 was designed from the start for amphibious operations, so that flotation gear is not required for over-water flights. The bottom of the fuselage is watertight and strengthened to permit landing on either water or snow; and there are two outrigger floats, mounted forward and well away from the fuselage, to resist pitching or rolling during touchdown or while at rest on the water.

Orders for the various versions announced up to March 1965 included the following:

California Oil Company	1
Canadian Department of Transport	1
Fuji Airlines (Japan)	1
Humble Oil and Refining Company	2
Indian Air Force	2
Naka Nihon Airways (Japan)	1
Nishinchon Airways (Japan)	1
Nitto Airlines (Japan)	1
Okanagan Air Services (Canada)	1
Petroleum Helicopters	6
San Francisco & Oakland Helicopter Airlines	4
Thailand Police	2
United Aircraft Corporation	1
US Coast Guard Service	43
World Wide Helicopters	3

A total of 30 S-62's and 29 HH-52A's had been built by mid-March 1964.

The following details refer to the S-62C and HH-52A:

TYPE: Turbine-powered amphibious helicopter.

ROTOR SYSTEM: Three-blade fully-articulated main rotor and two-blade tail rotor. Each blade of the folding main rotor has an extruded aluminium alloy pressurised spar and trailing-edge pockets. Rotor brake standard. Each tail rotor blade is a hollow spar and spacer assembly of aluminium alloy.

ROTOR DRIVE: Steel-tube drive-shafts. Main gearbox below rotor head, intermediate gearbox at base of tail pylon and tail gearbox at top of tail pylon. Main rotor/engine rpm ratio 1:85·757. Tail rotor/engine rpm ratio 1:6·818.

FUSELAGE: Completely amphibious boat hull. Aluminium semi-monocoque structure, with some stainless steel and resin-fabric.

TAIL SURFACE: Horizontal stabiliser on starboard side of tail rotor pylon.

LANDING GEAR: Main units are semi-retractable, being raised hydraulically into the stabilising floats by oleo contraction. Sikorsky oleo-pneumatic shock-absorbers. Goodyear split rim main wheels and tyres, size 6·50 × 10. Non-retractable Goodyear cast aluminium tail-wheel and tyre size 5·00 × 5. Tyre pressure (all) 60-70 lb/sq in (4·22-4·92 kg/cm²). Goodyear hydraulic disc brakes.

POWER PLANT: One 1,250 shp General Electric CT58-110-1 (military T58-GE-8) shaft-turbine engine. Fuel in three under-floor tanks; forward tank capacity 92 US gallons (348 litres), main tank capacity 182 US gallons (689 litres), aft tank capacity 138 US gallons (523 litres). Total usable fuel capacity 412 US gallons (1,560 litres). Refuelling point on port side of fuselage. Oil capacity 2·5 US gallons (9·5 litres).

ACCOMMODATION: Crew of two side-by-side on flight deck. Main cabin accommodates 12 fully-equipped troops or 10 airline passengers and baggage. Airline version has three forward-facing seats at rear of cabin, three on port side at front facing inward, two facing forward and two on starboard side facing inward. Door on starboard side of cabin. Internal door between cabin and flight deck. Cabin heated and ventilated.

SYSTEMS: Primary hydraulic system, pressure 1,000 lb/sq in (70 kg/cm²), and auxiliary system, pressure 1,500 lb/sq in (105 kg/cm²), for flying controls, landing gear, rescue hoist and windscreen wipers. Electrical system includes 28V DC generator, 24V batteries, 26V AC and 115V AC supplies.

ELECTRONICS AND EQUIPMENT: HH-52A has special Coast Guard radio equipment. Optional items on all versions include ARC-210, ARC-21, ICS, Collins 618F radio, blind-flying instrumentation, 600 lb (270 kg) capacity rescue hoist, external cargo sling of 3,000 lb (1,360 kg) capacity, auto-stabilisation equipment, rescue platform, sea anchor and emergency flotation bags.

DIMENSIONS, EXTERNAL:

Diameter of main rotor	53 ft 0 in (16·16 m)
Diameter of tail rotor	8 ft 9 in (2·67 m)
Distance between rotor centres	31 ft 4 in (9·55 m)
Length overall	45 ft 5½ in (13·86 m)
Length of fuselage	44 ft 6½ in (13·58 m)
Width, rotors folded	15 ft 9 in (4·80 m)
Height to top of rotor hub	14 ft 2½ in (4·33 m)
Overall height	16 ft 0 in (4·88 m)
Wheel track	12 ft 2 in (3·70 m)
Wheelbase	17 ft 10 in (5·43 m)
Cabin door:	
Height	5 ft 0 in (1·52 m)
Width	4 ft 0 in (1·22 m)
Height to sill	3 ft 1½ in (0·95 m)

DIMENSIONS, INTERNAL:

Cabin, excluding flight deck:	
Length	14 ft 0 in (4·27 m)
Max width	5 ft 4 in (1·62 m)
Max height	6 ft 0 in (1·83 m)
Floor area	74·6 sq ft (6·93 m²)
Volume	440 cu ft (12·45 m³)
Baggage hold (fwd, stbd side of cabin)	44 cu ft (1·25 m²)

AREAS:

Main rotor blade (each)	32·5 sq ft (3·02 m²)
Tail rotor blade (each)	3·08 sq ft (0·29 m²)
Main rotor disc	2,206 sq ft (205 m²)
Tail rotor disc	60·1 sq ft (5·58 m²)
Stabiliser	8·21 sq ft (0·76 m²)

WEIGHTS AND LOADINGS:

Weight empty, equipped:	
S-62C	4,860 lb (2,204 kg)
HH-52A	4,903 lb (2,224 kg)
Max payload:	
S-62C	2,847 lb (1,291 kg)
HH-52A	3,197 lb (1,450 kg)
Max T-O weight:	
S-62C	7,900 lb (3,583 kg)
HH-52A	8,100 lb (3,674 kg)
Max overload T-O weight (sling load):	
S-62C	8,000 lb (3,629 kg)
HH-52A	8,300 lb (3,765 kg)
Max landing weight:	
S-62C	7,900 lb (3,583 kg)
HH-52A	8,300 lb (3,765 kg)
Max disc loading:	
S-62C	3·58 lb/sq ft (17·48 kg/m²)
HH-52A	3·67 lb/sq ft (17·92 kg/m²)
Max power loading:	
S-62C	10·8 lb/shp (4·90 kg/shp)
HH-52A	11·1 lb/shp (5·04 kg/shp)

PERFORMANCE (at max T-O weight):

Max level speed at S/L:	
S-62C	101 mph (163 kmh)
HH-52A	109 mph (175 kmh)
Max cruising speed:	
S-62C	92 mph (148 kmh)
HH-52A	98 mph (158 kmh)
Max rate of climb at S/L:	
S-62C	1,140 ft (347 m) min
HH-52A	1,070 ft (326 m) min
Vertical rate of climb at S/L:	
S-62C	300 ft (91 m) min
HH-52A	110 ft (33 m) min
Service ceiling:	
S-62C (FAA limit)	6,600 ft (2,010 m)
HH-52A	11,200 ft (3,410 m)
Hovering ceiling in ground effect:	
S-62C	17,800 ft (5,425 m)
HH-52A	12,200 ft (3,720 m)
Hovering ceiling out of ground effect:	
S-62C	4,600 ft (1,400 m)
HH-52A	1,700 ft (520 m)
Range with main and aft tanks, 10% reserve:	
S-62C	462 miles (743 km)
HH-52A	474 miles (763 km)

SIKORSKY S-64 SKYCRANE
US military designation: CH-54 Tarhe

The S-64 flying crane was designed initially for military transport duties. Equipped with interchangeable pods, it is suitable for use as a troop transport, and for minesweeping, cargo and missile transport, anti-submarine or field hospital operations. Equipment includes a removable 9,072 kg (20,000 lb) hoist, a sling attachment and a load stabiliser to prevent undue sway in cargo winch operations. Attachment points are provided on the fuselage and landing gear to facilitate securing of bulky loads.

Versions of the S-64 are as follows:

S-64A. Under this designation the first of three prototypes flew for the first time on 9 May 1962 and was used by the US Army at Fort Benning, Georgia, for testing and demonstration. The second and third prototypes were evaluated by the German armed forces.

CH-54A. Six ordered by US Army in 1963 to investigate the heavy lift concept, with emphasis on increasing mobility in the battlefield. Delivery of five CH-54As (originally YCH-54As) to the US Army took place in late 1964 and early 1965. A sixth CH-54A remained at Stratford, with a company-owned S-64, for a programme leading toward a restricted FAA certification, which was awarded on 30 July 1965. Further US Army orders followed.

The CH-54As were assigned to the US Army's 478th Aviation Company, and performed outstanding service in support of the Army's First Cavalry Division, Airmobile, in Vietnam. On 29 April 1965, a CH-54A of this unit lifted 90 persons, including 87 combat-equipped troops in a detachable van. This is believed to be the largest number of people ever carried by a helicopter at one time. Other Skycranes in Vietnam transported bulldozers and road graders weighing up to 7,937 kg (17,500 lb), 9,072 kg (20,000 lb) armoured vehicles and a large variety of heavy hardware. They retrieved more than 380 damaged aircraft, involving savings estimated at $210 million.

Sikorsky S-64 Skycrane heavy-lift helicopter, operated in Alaska by Rowan Air Cranes *(Norman E. Taylor)*

Sikorsky Aircraft developed an all-purpose van, known as the Universal Military Pod, for carriage by the US Army's CH-54As, and received an order, worth $2·9 million, to supply 22 to the Army. The pods were delivered complete with communications, ventilation and lighting systems, and with wheels to simplify ground handling. They superseded earlier pods which were not approved for the carriage of personnel. The first pod was accepted by the US Army on 28 June 1968, following approval for personnel transport.

Internal dimensions of the pod are length 8·36 m (27 ft 5 in), width 2·69 m (8 ft 10 in) and height 1·98 m (6 ft 6 in).

Doors are provided on each side of the forward area of the pod, and a double-panelled ramp is located aft. With a max loaded weight of 9,072 kg (20,000 lb), each pod accommodates 45 combat-equipped troops, or 24 litters, and in the field may be adapted for a variety of uses, such as surgical unit, field command post and communications post.

CH-54B. On 4 November 1968 Sikorsky announced that it had received a US Army contract to increase the payload capacity of the CH-54 from 10 to 12½ short tons. The contract called for a number of design improvements to the engine, gearbox, rotor head and structure; altitude performance and hot weather operating capability were also to be improved. Two of the improved flying cranes, designated CH-54B, were accepted by the US Army during 1969.

The original JFTD12-4A engines were replaced by two Pratt & Whitney JFTD12-5As, each rated at 3,579 kW (4,800 shp), and a gearbox capable of receiving 5,891 kW (7,900 hp) from the two engines was introduced. Single-engine performance was increased, since the new gearbox receives 3,579 kW (4,800 hp) from one engine, compared with 3,020 kW (4,050 hp) on the CH-54A.

A new rotor system was also introduced, utilising a high-lift rotor blade with a chord some 0·064 m (2·5 in) greater than that of the blades used formerly.

Other changes included the provision of twin wheels on the main landing gear, an improved automatic flight control system and some general structural strengthening throughout the aircraft. Gross weight was increased from 19,050 kg (42,000 lb) to 21,318 kg (47,000 lb).

In October 1970, two US Army CH-54Bs lifted an 18,488 kg (40,760 lb) load during a series of tests being conducted to evaluate the technical feasibility and cost of a twin-lift system for potential application to military requirements for greater helicopter external load capacity. Later in the same month, a single US Army CH-54B lifted an 18,497 kg (40,780 lb) load during tests being conducted to evaluate maximum hover lift capability.

Nine international helicopter records in Class E1 are held by the CH-54B. On 26 October 1971, piloted by B. P. Blackwell, a payload of 1,000 kg was lifted to a height of 9,499 m (31,165 ft). On 29 October CWO E. E. Price flew to 9,595 m (31,480 ft) with 2,000 kg. On 27 October the same pilot had reached 7,778 m (25,518 ft) with a 5,000 kg payload. CWO J. K. Church flew to 5,246 m (17,211 ft) with 10,000 kg on 29 October, and on 12 April 1972 CWO D. L. Spivey reached 3,307 m (10,850 ft) with a 15,000 kg payload. CWO Church set an earlier record on 4 November 1971, by maintaining a height of 11,010 m (36,122 ft) in horizontal flight. Major J. C. Henderson set up two time-to-height climb records in a CH-54B on 12 April 1972, reaching 3,000 m in 1 min 22·7 sec and 6,000 m in 2 min 58·9 sec. Earlier, on 4 November 1971, CWO D. W. Hunt had climbed to 9,000 m in 5 min 57·7 sec.

TYPE: Twin-turbine heavy flying crane helicopter.

ROTOR SYSTEM: Six-blade fully-articulated main rotor with aluminium blades and aluminium and steel head. Four-blade tail rotor with titanium head and aluminium blades. Rotor brake standard.

ROTOR DRIVE: Steel tube drive-shafts. Main gearbox below main rotor, intermediate gearbox at base of tail pylon, tail gearbox at top of pylon. Main gearbox rated at 4,922 kW (6,600 shp) on CH-54A and S-64E, 5,891 kW (7,900 shp) on S-64F.

FUSELAGE: Pod and boom type of aluminium and steel semi-monocoque construction.

LANDING GEAR: Non-retractable tricycle type, with single wheel on each unit of CH-54A/S-64E, twin wheels on main units of S-64F. CH-54A/S-64E main-wheel tyres size 38·45 × 12·50-16, pressure 6·55 bars (95 lb/sq in). S-64F main-wheel tyres size 25·65 × 8·50-10, pressure 6·90 bars (100 lb/sq in). Nosewheels and tyres of all versions size 25·65 × 8·50-10, pressure 6·90 bars (100 lb/sq in).

POWER PLANT (CH-54A/S-64E): Two Pratt & Whitney JFTD12-4A (military T73-P-1) turboshaft engines, each rated at 3,356 kW (4,500 shp) for take-off and with max continous rating of 2,983 kW (4,000 shp). Two fuel tanks in fuselage, forward and aft of transmission, each with capacity of 1,664 litres (440 US gallons). Total standard fuel capacity 3,328 litres (880 US gallons). Provision for auxiliary fuel tank of 1,664 litres (440 US gallons) capacity, raising total fuel capacity to 4,992 litres (1,320 US gallons).

POWER PLANT (CH-54B/S-64F): Two Pratt & Whitney JFTD12-5A turboshaft engines, each rated at 3,579 kW (4,800 shp) for take-off and with max continuous rating of 3,303·5 kW (4,430 shp). Fuel tanks as for CH-54A/S-64E.

ACCOMMODATION: Pilot and co-pilot side by side at front of cabin. Aft-facing seat for third pilot at rear of cabin, with flying controls. The occupant of this third seat is able to take over control of the aircraft during loading and unloading. Two additional jump seats available in cabin. Payload in interchangeable pods.

DIMENSIONS, EXTERNAL:
Diameter of main rotor	21·95 m (72 ft 0 in)
Diameter of tail rotor	4·88 m (16 ft 0 in)
Distance between rotor centres	13·56 m (44 ft 6 in)
Length overall	26·97 m (88 ft 6 in)
Length of fuselage	21·41 m (70 ft 3 in)
Width, rotors folded	6·65 m (21 ft 10 in)
Height to top of rotor hub	5·67 m (18 ft 7 in)
Height overall	7·75 m (25 ft 5 in)
Ground clearance under fuselage boom	
	2·84 m (9 ft 4 in)
Wheel track	6·02 m (19 ft 9 in)
Wheelbase	7·44 m (24 ft 5 in)

AREAS:
Main rotor disc	378·1 m² (4,070 sq ft)
Tail rotor disc	18·67 m² (201 sq ft)

WEIGHTS (CH-54A/S-64E):
Weight empty	8,724 kg (19,234 lb)
Max T-O weight	19,050 kg (42,000 lb)

PERFORMANCE (CH-54A/S-64E at normal T-O weight of 17,237 kg; 38,000 lb):
Max level speed at S/L	
	109 knots (203 km/h; 126 mph)
Max cruising speed	91 knots (169 km/h; 105 mph)
Max rate of climb at S/L	405 m (1,330 ft)/min
Service ceiling	2,475 m (9,000 ft)
Hovering ceiling in ground effect 3,230 m (10,600 ft)	
Hovering ceiling out of ground effect	
	2,100 m (6,900 ft)
Min ground turning radius:	
CH-54A, S-64E, S-64F	16·4 m (54 ft 0 in)
Runway LCN:	
CH-54A, S-64E at max T-O weight of 19,050 kg (42,000 lb)	7·1
S-64F at max T-O weight of 21,318 kg (47,000 lb) 7·7	
Range with max fuel, 10% reserves	
	200 nm (370 km; 230 miles)

(1976–77)

SIKORSKY S-65A
US Navy designation: CH-53A Sea Stallion
USAF designations: HH-53B/C
US Marine Corps designations: CH-53A/D

On 27 August 1962, it was announced that Sikorsky had been selected by the US Navy to produce a heavy assault transport helicopter for use by the Marine Corps. First flight was made on 14 October 1964, and deliveries began in mid-1966. Versions are as follows:

CH-53A. This initial version uses many components based on those of the S-64A Skycrane, but is powered by two General Electric T64 turboshaft engines and has a watertight hull. A full-size rear opening, with built-in ramp, permits easy loading and unloading, with the aid of a special hydraulically-operated internal cargo loading system and floor rollers.

Typical cargo loads include two Jeeps, or two Hawk missiles with cable reels and control console, or a 105 mm howitzer and carriage. An external cargo system permits in-flight pickup and release without ground assistance.

The CH-53A is able to operate under all weather and climatic conditions. Its main rotor blades and tail pylon fold hydraulically for stowage on board ship.

On 17 February 1968, a CH-53A, with General Electric T64-6 (modified) engines, flew at a gross weight of 23,541 kg (51,900 lb) carrying 12,927 kg (28,500 lb) of payload and fuel, establishing new unofficial payload and gross weight records for a production helicopter built outside the Soviet Union.

On 26 April 1968, a Marine Corps CH-53A made the first automatic terrain clearance flight in helicopter history and subsequently concluded flight tests of an Integrated Helicopter Avionics System (IHAS). Prime contractor for the IHAS programme was Teledyne Systems Company. Norden Division of United Aircraft Corporation provided the terrain-clearance radar and vertical structure display.

On 23 October 1968, a Marine Corps CH-53A performed a series of loops and rolls, as part of a joint Naval Air Systems Command and Sikorsky flight test programme, aimed at investigating the CH-53A's rotor system dynamics and manoeuvrability characteristics. Details of these trials have appeared in previous editions of *Jane's*.

Six S-65As were ordered in 1975 by the Imperian Navy.

RH-53A. Fifteen CH-53As borrowed by US Navy for mine countermeasures duties, with T64-GE-413 engines.

HH-53B. Eight ordered by USAF in September 1966 for Aerospace Rescue and Recovery Service. The first of

Sikorsky CH-53D helicopter of the US Marine Corps

these flew on 15 March 1967 and deliveries began in June 1967. Production completed.

The HH-53B is generally similar to the CH-53A, but is powered by 2,297 kW (3,080 shp) T64-GE-3 turboshaft engines. It has the same general equipment as the HH-3E, including a retractable flight refuelling probe, jettisonable auxiliary fuel tanks, rescue hoist, all-weather electronics and armament.

HH-53C. Improved version of the HH-53B, with 2,927 kW (3,925 shp) T64-GE-7 engines, auxiliary jettisonable fuel tanks each of 1,703 litres (450 US gallons) capacity on new cantilever mounts, flight refuelling probe, and rescue hoist with 76 m (250 ft) of cable. External cargo hook of 9,070 kg (20,000 lb) capacity. First HH-53C was delivered to the USAF on 30 August 1968. A total of 72 HH-53B/Cs were built. Production completed.

Eight HH-53Cs are being modified to HH-53H standard for night and adverse weather search and rescue operations under the US Air Force's Pave Low 3 programme, following evaluation of a prototype conversion which flew for the first time in June 1975. The work is being done at the US Naval Air Rework Facility (NARF), Naval Air Station, Pensacola, Florida, on behalf of Military Airlift Command's Aerospace Rescue and Recovery Service.

The **Pave Low 3 HH-53H** has a stabilised Texas Instruments FLIR (forward-looking infra-red) installation mounted below the refuelling boom; a Litton inertial navigation system; a Canadian Marconi Doppler navigation system; an IBM computer; Systems Research symbol generator; and Texas Instruments terrain following/avoidance radar in an offset (to port) 'thimble' fairing on the nose.

The US Air Force accepted the first production Pave Low 3 HH-53H at Pensacola on 13 March 1979.

CH-53D. Improved CH-53A for US Marine Corps, the first of which was delivered on 3 March 1969. Two T64-GE-413 engines, each with a maximum rating of 2,927 kW (3,925 shp). A total of 55 troops can be carried in a high-density arrangement. An integral cargo handling system makes it possible for one man to load or unload one short ton of palletised cargo a minute. Main rotor and tail pylon fold automatically for carrier stowage.

Last CH-53D (the 265th CH-53 built) was delivered on 31 January 1972. All but the first 34 CH-53s were provided with hardpoints for supporting towing equipment and transferring tow loads to the airframe, so that the US Marines could utilise the aircraft as airborne minesweepers, giving an assault commander the capability of clearing enemy mines from harbours and off beaches without having to wait for surface minesweepers. Tow kits installed in the 15 CH-53Ds operated by US Navy Squadron HM-12 included automatic flight control system interconnections to provide automatic cable yaw angle retention and aircraft attitude and heading hold; rearview mirrors for pilot and co-pilot; tow cable tension and yaw angle indicator; automatic emergency cable release; towboom and hook system with 6,803 kg (15,000 lb) load capacity when cable was locked to internal towboom; dam to prevent cabin flooding in emergency water landing with lower ramp open; dual hydraulically-powered cable winches; racks and cradles for stowage of minesweeping gear; auxiliary fuel tanks in cabin to increase endurance.

RH-53D. Specially-equipped minesweeping version for the US Navy, described separately.

YCH-53E. Three-engined development of the CH-53D. Described separately.

VH-53F. Proposed VIP transport version for Presidential Flight, with T64-GE-414 engines. Not built.

CH-53G. Version of the CH-53 for the German armed forces, with T64-GE-7 engines. A total of 112 were produced, the first of two built by Sikorsky being delivered on 31 March 1969. The next 20 were assembled in Germany from American-built components. The remainder embody some 50% components of German manufacture. Prime contractor in Germany was VFW-Fokker, whose first CH-53G flew for the first time on 11 October 1971. Deliveries to the German Army were completed during 1975.

The following details refer to the CH-53A:

TYPE: Twin-turbine heavy assault transport helicopter.

ROTOR SYSTEM AND DRIVE: Generally similar to those of S-64A Skycrane, but main rotor head is of titanium and steel, and has folding blades.

FUSELAGE: Conventional semi-monocoque structure of aluminium, steel and titanium. Folding tail pylon.

TAIL SURFACE: Large horizontal stabiliser on starboard side of tail rotor pylon.

LANDING GEAR: Retractable tricycle type, with twin wheels on each unit. Main units retract into the rear of sponsons on each side of fuselage. Fully-castoring nose unit. Main wheels and nosewheels have tyres size 25·65 × 8·50-10, pressure 6·55 bars (95 lb/sq in).

POWER PLANT: Normally two 2,125 kW (2,850 shp) General Electric T64-GE-6 turboshaft engines, mounted in pod on each side of main rotor pylon. The CH-53A can also utilise, without airframe modification, the T64-GE-1 engine of 2,297 kW (3,080 shp) or the later T64-GE-16 (mod) engine of 2,561·5 kW (3,435 shp). Two self-sealing bladder fuel tanks, each with capacity of 1,192 litres (315 US gallons), housed in forward part of sponsons. Total fuel capacity 2,384 litres (630 US gallons).

ACCOMMODATION: Crew of three. Main cabin accommodates 37 combat-equipped troops on inward-facing

Sikorsky HH-53H modified under the USAF's Pave Low 3 programme

seats. Provision for carrying 24 stretchers and four attendants. Roller-skid track combination in floor for handling heavy freight. Door on starboard side of cabin at front. Rear loading ramp.

DIMENSIONS, EXTERNAL:
Diameter of main rotor	22·02 m (72 ft 3 in)
Diameter of tail rotor	4·88 m (16 ft 0 in)
Length overall, rotors turning	26·90 m (88 ft 3 in)
Length of fuselage, excl refuelling probe	
	20·47 m (67 ft 2 in)
Width overall, rotors folded	4·72 m (15 ft 6 in)
Width of fuselage	2·69 m (8 ft 10 in)
Height to top of rotor hub	5·22 m (17 ft 1½ in)
Height overall	7·60 m (24 ft 11 in)
Wheel track	3·96 m (13 ft 0 in)
Wheelbase	8·23 m (27 ft 0 in)

DIMENSIONS, INTERNAL:
Cabin: Length	9·14 m (30 ft 0 in)
Max width	2·29 m (7 ft 6 in)
Max height	1·98 m (6 ft 6 in)

AREAS:
Main rotor disc	378·1 m² (4,070 sq ft)
Tail rotor disc	18·67 m² (201 sq ft)

WEIGHTS:
Weight empty:	
CH-53A	10,180 kg (22,444 lb)
HH-53B	10,490 kg (23,125 lb)
HH-53C	10,690 kg (23,569 lb)
CH-53D	10,653 kg (23,485 lb)
Normal T-O weight:	
CH-53A	15,875 kg (35,000 lb)
Mission T-O weight:	
HH-53B	16,964 kg (37,400 lb)
HH-53C	17,344 kg (38,238 lb)
CH-53D	16,510 kg (36,400 lb)
Max T-O weight:	
HH-53B/C, CH-53D	19,050 kg (42,000 lb)

PERFORMANCE:
Max level speed at S/L:	
HH-53B	162 knots (299 km/h; 186 mph)
HH-53C, CH-53D	170 knots (315 km/h; 196 mph)
Cruising speed:	
HH-53B/C, CH-53D	
	150 knots (278 km/h; 173 mph)
Max rate of climb at S/L:	
HH-53B	440 m (1,440 ft)/min
HH-53C	631 m (2,070 ft)/min
CH-53D	664 m (2,180 ft)/min
Service ceiling:	
HH-53B	5,610 m (18,400 ft)
HH-53C	6,220 m (20,400 ft)
CH-53D	6,400 m (21,000 ft)
Hovering ceiling in ground effect:	
HH-53B	2,470 m (8,100 ft)
HH-53C	3,565 m (11,700 ft)
CH-53D	4,080 m (13,400 ft)
Hovering ceiling out of ground effect:	
HH-53B	490 m (1,600 ft)
HH-53C	1,310 m (4,300 ft)
CH-53D	1,980 m (6,500 ft)
Min ground turning radius	13·46 m (44 ft 2 in)
Runway LCN at max T-O weight	7·1
Range:	

HH-53B/C, with 4,502 kg (9,926 lb) fuel (two 1,703 litre; 450 US gallon auxiliary tanks), including 10% reserves and 2 min warm-up

468 nm (869 km; 540 miles)

CH-53D, with 1,849 kg (4,076 lb) fuel, 10% reserves at cruising speed and 2 min warm-up

223 nm (413 km; 257 miles)

(1976–77)

SIKORSKY S-65 (MCM)
US Navy designation: RH-53D

On 27 October 1970 the US Navy announced plans to establish helicopter mine countermeasures (MCM) squadrons. The first unit, Helicopter Mine Countermeasures Squadron 12 (HM-12), borrowed 15 CH-53As from the US Marine Corps, pending production of specially equipped helicopters. Details of the tow kits installed in these aircraft are given under the CH-53D entry.

Congress gave approval subsequently for the development of a new and more powerful version of the CH-53 for service with the Navy's mine countermeasures squadrons, and in February 1972 Sikorsky announced that the US Navy had awarded the company an advanced procurement authorisation for 30 helicopters under the designation RH-53D. Production began in October 1972, at a rate of two per month, under a programme extending to December 1973. The first RH-53D flew on 27 October 1972 and first deliveries were made to HM-12 in September 1973. The delivery of six aircraft for the Iranian Navy was to be completed during 1976.

The RH-53D is designed to tow existing and future equipment evolved to sweep mechanical, acoustic and magnetic mines. That for mechanical and acoustic mines can be carried on board the aircraft, and deployed and retrieved in flight. Magnetic sweep equipment, too large to be carried internally by the helicopter, is first streamed behind a surface vessel and then transferred to the aircraft's tow hook. It can also be carried on the external cargo hook, and is lifted from ship to sea or shore to sea by this means. Basic design gross weight is increased to 19,050 kg (42,000 lb), mission gross weight is 18,656 kg (41,130 lb), and the alternate design gross weight is increased to 22,680 kg (50,000 lb). Space, weight and power provisions have been made for installation of a projected advanced navigation system and an approach and hover coupler.

The description of the CH-53A applies also to the RH-53D, except as follows:

ROTOR SYSTEM AND DRIVE: Generally similar to those of the CH-53A, but transmission uprated to 6,458 kW (8,660 shp).

FUSELAGE: As for CH-53A, but heavier-gauge skins are used aft of the transmission area and heavier-gauge stringers around the landing gear.

LANDING GEAR: Stronger landing gear and brakes to cater for the increased gross weights.

POWER PLANT: Two General Electric T64-GE-413A turboshafts with a combined rating of 5,637 kW (7,560 shp) in early models; but it is planned to modify these engines to 3,266 kW (4,380 shp) T64-GE-415 standard by retrofit kits. Standard fuel tankage supplemented by two 1,892 litre (500 US gallon) external tanks. These are standard USAF 2,460 litre (650 US gallon) auxiliary fuel tanks, modified to reduced capacity for better roll control. Flight refuelling capability provided by an HH-53 nose-mounted refuelling probe. In addition, the RH-53D is equipped for ship-to-helicopter refuelling while airborne, with a sensing filter in the helicopter to

Sikorsky RH-53D minesweeping and multi-mission helicopter of the US Navy

EQUIPMENT: Automatic flight control system interconnections to give automatic tow cable yaw angle retention, and aircraft attitude and heading hold. Indicator for tow cable tension and yaw angle, with automatic cable release if limits are exceeded. Nose-mounted adjustable rearview mirrors for pilot and co-pilot. Dual hydraulically-powered winches for streaming tow. Tow system comprising a separate winch and hook, rated at 3,175 kg (7,000 lb) capacity. Towboom rated at 9,072 kg (20,000 lb) capacity with hook locked in retention jaw. External cargo hook capacity rated at 11,340 kg (25,000 lb). Stowage racks and cradles for Mk 103 mechanical and Mk 104 acoustic mine countermeasures gear. Can tow the Marine`105 magnetic and Mk 106 magnetic/acoustic ship-based gear. Anti-exposure suit ventilation system for crew working in cabin. Variable-speed rescue hoist rated at 272 kg (600 lb) capacity.

ARMAMENT: Provision for two 0·50 in machine-guns to detonate surfaced mines.

WEIGHTS:	
Normal T-O weight	19,050 kg (42,000 lb)
Mission T-O weight	18,656 kg (41,130 lb)
Max T-O weight	22,680 kg (50,000 lb)

PERFORMANCE:	
Min ground turning radius	13·46 m (44 ft 2 in)
Runway LCN at max T-O weight	8·0
Endurance	over 4 hr
	(1976–77)

Sikorsky CH-53E heavy-lift helicopter (three General Electric T64-GE-415 turboshaft engines)

SIKORSKY CH-53E
US Navy designation: CH-53E Super Stallion

The Sikorsky S-65 was chosen in 1973 for development with three engines to provide the US Navy and Marine Corps with a heavy-duty multi-purpose helicopter. Other changes to increase performance included installation of a new seven-blade main rotor of increased diameter, with blades of titanium/glassfibre construction, and an uprated transmission of 9,798 kW (13,140 shp) capacity to cater for future development.

Development was initiated by the award of a $1·7 million US Navy cost-plus-fixed-fee contract; in May 1973 Sikorsky announced that construction of two prototypes, designated YCH-53E, was to begin, with the first flight scheduled for April 1974. Bettering this by a month, the first YCH-53E made a successful half-hour flight on 1 March 1974. It was lost subsequently in an accident on the ground, but the programme was resumed on 24 January 1975 with the second YCH-53E. This aircraft flew subsequently at an AUW of 33,793 kg (74,500 lb), the highest gross weight achieved by any helicopter outside the USSR. It was used for preliminary evaluation and testing under Phase I of the development programme. Phase II covered the construction of a static test vehicle and two pre-production prototypes, the first of which flew on 8 December 1975. In February 1978 Sikorsky was awarded a contract to begin full-scale production, with initial approval for six aircraft. The first two of these were in final assembly in mid-1980. A further 14 were ordered in FY 1979 and 15 in FY 1980, with 14 requested in the FY 1981 budget. The eventual production total was 125.

The US Navy plans to use the CH-53E for vertical onboard delivery operations, to support mobile construction battalions, and for the removal of battle-damaged aircraft from carrier decks. In amphibious operations, it would be able to airlift 93 per cent of a US Marine division's combat items, and would be able to retrieve 98 per cent of the Marine Corps' tactical aircraft without disassembly. Features include extended-range fuel tanks, in-flight refuelling capability, an onboard all-weather navigation system, and an advanced dual digital automatic flight control system. It is anticipated that CH-53Es will begin to join the US fleet during the first half of 1981.

The CH-53E is the largest helicopter capable of full operation from the Navy's existing and planned ships, requiring only 10 per cent more deck space than the twin-turbine H-53. It offers double the lift of the latter aircraft with an increase of only 50 per cent in engine power.

TYPE: Triple-turbine heavy-duty multi-purpose helicopter.

ROTOR SYSTEM AND TRANSMISSION: Seven-blade main rotor with blades of titanium/glassfibre construction. Titanium and steel main rotor head. Main rotor blades fold. Four-blade tail rotor mounted on pylon canted 20° to port. Rotor transmission, manufactured by Indiana Gear Works, is rated at 9,798 kW (13,140 shp) for 10 min, 8,628 kW (11,570 shp) for 30 min. Tail rotor pylon folds on starboard side of fuselage.

FUSELAGE: Conventional semi-monocoque structure of light alloy, steel and titanium.

TAIL SURFACE: Initial fixed tailplane on undersurface of fuselage, superseded successively by single high-mounted stabiliser on starboard side and lightweight gull-wing type.

LANDING GEAR: Retractable tricycle type, with twin wheels on each unit. Main units retract into rear of sponsons on each side of fuselage.

POWER PLANT: Three General Electric T64-GE-415 turboshaft engines, each with a max rating of 3,266 kW (4,380 shp) for 10 min, intermediate rating of 3,091 kW (4,145 shp) for 30 min and max continuous power rating of 2,756 kW (3,696 shp).

ACCOMMODATION: Crew of three. Main cabin will accommodate up to 55 troops in a high-density seating arrangement.

DIMENSIONS, EXTERNAL:	
Main rotor diameter	24·08 m (79 ft 0 in)
Tail rotor diameter	6·10 m (20 ft 0 in)
Length overall, rotors turning	30·20 m (99 ft 1 in)
Length, rotor and tail pylon folded	18·44 m (60 ft 6 in)
Length of fuselage	22·35 m (73 ft 4 in)
Width of fuselage	2·69 m (8 ft 10 in)
Width, rotor and tail pylon folded	8·41 m (27 ft 7 in)
Height overall, tail rotor turning	8·66 m (28 ft 5 in)
Height, rotor and tail pylon folded	5·74 m (18 ft 10 in)
Wheel track (c/l of shock-struts)	3·96 m (13 ft 0 in)
Wheelbase	8·31 m (27 ft 3 in)

DIMENSIONS, INTERNAL:	
Cabin: Length	9·14 m (30 ft 0 in)
Max width	2·29 m (7 ft 6 in)
Max height	2·01 m (6 ft 6 in)

WEIGHTS:	
Weight empty	14,913 kg (32,878 lb)
Internal payload (100 nm; 185 km; 115 miles radius)	13,607 kg (30,000 lb)

External payload (50 nm; 92·5 km; 57·5 miles radius)   14,515 kg (32,000 lb)
Max T-O weight   33,339 kg (73,500 lb)
PERFORMANCE (ISA, at T-O weight of 25,400 kg; 56,000 lb):
Max level speed at S/L
170 knots (315 km/h; 196 mph)
Cruising speed at S/L
150 knots (278 km/h; 173 mph)

Max rate of climb at S/L   838 m (2,750 ft)/min
Service ceiling, at max continuous power
5,640 m (18,500 ft)
Hovering ceiling IGE, at max power
3,520 m (11,550 ft)
Hovering ceiling OGE, at max power
2,895 m (9,500 ft)
Range, at optimum cruise condition for best range
1,120 nm (2,075 km; 1,290 miles)

SIKORSKY MH-53E SEA DRAGON

Mine countermeasures variant of the CH-53E. Entered service in 1987.

(1980–81)

SIKORSKY S-70

US Army designations: UH-60 and EH-60 Black Hawk

At the end of August 1972, the US Army selected Sikorsky and Boeing Vertol as competitors to build three prototypes each, plus one ground test vehicle, of their submissions for the Utility Tactical Transport Aircraft System (UTTAS) requirement. Sikorsky's $61 million contract called for flight trials to begin in November 1974, but the first YUH-60A flew on 17 October 1974, six weeks ahead of schedule. The second prototype flew on 21 January 1975, followed by the third on 28 February 1975. Fly-off evaluation against Boeing Vertol's YUH-61A prototypes began in early 1976 and occupied a period of seven months. On 23 December 1976 Sikorsky's design was declared the winner, and it was subsequently named Black Hawk.

Designed to carry 11 fully-equipped troops plus a crew of three, the UH-60A has a large cabin which enables it to be used without modification for medical evacuation, reconnaissance, command and control purposes or troop resupply. For external lift missions its cargo hook has a capacity of up to 3,630 kg (8,000 lb). Design is compact, so that the helicopter itself can be airlifted over long ranges. One can be accommodated in a C-130, two in a C-141 and six in a C-5A.

The UH-60A is intended to serve as the US Army's primary combat assault helicopter, and the Army plans to procure a total of 1,107 by the mid-eighties. The basic production contract awarded to Sikorsky, plus options exercised by mid-1980, covered the construction of 255 aircraft during the first four years of production, which began in the Autumn of 1977. The first flight of a production aircraft was made in October 1978, and Black Hawks were delivered for pilot training to the US Army Aviation Center, Fort Rucker, Alabama, in April 1979. The first delivery of production aircraft to an operational unit was made on 19 June 1979, when four Black Hawks were handed over to the 101st Airborne Division at Fort Campbell, Kentucky. They were used initially by this unit in an extensive Force Development Test and Experimentation (FDTE) programme under field conditions. Later, planned deployment of Black Hawks began to jungle areas of Panama, to desert regions in the southwest USA, and to the Arctic, for testing under a wide variety of temperatures and conditions. A total of 74 Black Hawks had been delivered by 31 August 1980.

In tests carried out during early 1979, the Black Hawk demonstrated its ability to sustain heavy landing impacts without damage. In a series of such tests, the helicopter sustained drop rates of 3·5 m (11·5 ft)/s at a forward speed of 63 knots (117 km/h; 73 mph) and gross weight of 7,632 kg (16,825 lb). Another aircraft, flown under artificial icing conditions, confirmed that safe flight can be made in moderate icing conditions by use of a specially developed de-icing kit.

Two special variants of the Black Hawk have been announced, as follows:

EH-60C. ECM variant, designed to intercept and jam enemy communications. Initial development contract received October 1980. Quick Fix IIB equipment. Subsequent versions have included the trials **JUH-60A, MH-60A** for special operations (Army), **MH-60G Pave Hawk** USAF Aerospace Rescue and Recovery helicopter, special operations **MH-60K, UH-60L** transport, and **VH-60A** USMC executive transport.

The following description applies to the UH-60A:
TYPE: Twin-turbine combat assault squad transport.
ROTOR SYSTEM: Four-blade main rotor. Sikorsky SC-1095 blade section, with thickness/chord ratio of 9·5%. Middle section has leading-edge droop and trailing-edge tab to overcome vortex impingement from preceding blade in cruising flight. Blade twist 18°. Blade tip swept back 20°. Each blade consists of an oval titanium spar, Nomex honeycomb core, graphite trailing-edge and root, covered with glassfibre, and with plastics leading-edge counterweight and titanium leading-edge sheath.

Production example of the Sikorsky UH-60A Black Hawk combat assault helicopter

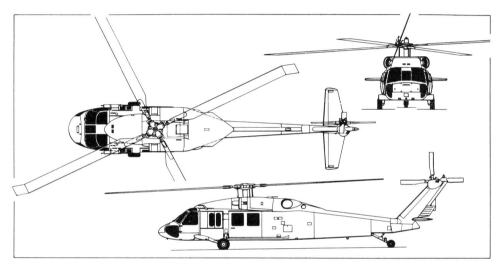

Sikorsky UH-60A Black Hawk combat assault helicopter *(Pilot Press)*

Blades are tolerant to small arms damage, and are pressurised and equipped with gauges providing fail-safe confirmation of blade structural integrity. Electrically-heated de-icing mat in leading-edge of each blade. C/R Industries elastomeric rotor hub bearings require no lubrication, reducing hub maintenance by 60%. Bifilar self-tuning vibration absorbers on rotor head. Manual blade folding. Canting of tail rotor (20° to port) increases vertical lift and allows greater CG travel. 'Cross beam' four-blade tail rotor of composite materials, eliminating all rotor head bearings.

ROTOR DRIVE: Conventional transmission system with both turbines driving through freewheeling units to main gearbox. This is of modular construction to simplify maintenance. Transmission can operate for 30 min following total oil loss. Intermediate and tail rotor gearboxes oil lubricated.

FUSELAGE: Conventional semi-monocoque light alloy crashworthy structure.

TAIL UNIT: Pylon structure with port-canted tail rotor mounted on starboard side. Large variable-incidence tailplane has a control system which senses airspeed, collective-lever position, pitch-attitude rate and lateral acceleration. Tailplane is set at about +34° incidence in the hover, and −6° for autorotation. Tailplane moved by dual electric actuators, with manual backup.

LANDING GEAR: Non-retractable tailwheel type with single wheel on each unit. Energy-absorbing main gear with a tailwheel which gives protection for the tail rotor in taxiing over rough terrain or during a high-flare landing. Axle assembly and main gear shock-absorbers by General Mechatronics.

POWER PLANT: Two 1,151 kW (1,560 shp) General Electric T700-GE-700 advanced technology turboshaft engines; combined transmission rating 2,109 kW (2,828

shp). Two crashworthy, bulletproof fuel tanks, with combined capacity of 1,340 litres (354 US gallons), aft of cabin.

ACCOMMODATION: Pilot and co-pilot on armour protected seats. Main cabin area open to cockpit to provide good communication with flight crew and forward view for squad commander. Accommodation for 11 troops and crew of three. Eight troop seats can be removed and replaced by four litters for medevac missions, or to make room for internal cargo. Cabin heated and ventilated. External cargo hook, having a 3,630 kg (8,000 lb) lift capability. Large aft-sliding door on each side of fuselage for rapid entry and exit. Electrical windscreen de-icing.

SYSTEMS: Solar T-62T-40-1 APU; AiResearch engine start system; Bendix 30/40kVA and 20/30kVA electric power generators; 17Ah nickel-cadmium battery. Engine fire extinguishing system.

AVIONICS: Include VHF/AM, VHF/FM and UHF/AM com, Singer Doppler, LF/ADF, AN/APR-39 radar warning receiver, SIF/IFF, and TSEC/KY-28 secure speech.

ARMAMENT AND OPERATIONAL EQUIPMENT: Provision for one or two M-60 side-firing machine-guns in forward area of cabin, infra-red jamming flares and XM-130 chaff dispenser.

DIMENSIONS, EXTERNAL:
Main rotor diameter   16·36 m (53 ft 8 in)
Main rotor blade chord   0·53 m (1 ft 8¾ in)
Tail rotor diameter   3·35 m (11 ft 0 in)
Length overall (rotors turning) 19·76 m (64 ft 10 in)
Length, rotors and tail pylon folded
12·60 m (41 ft 4 in)

Fuselage length	15·26 m (50 ft 0¾ in)
Fuselage width	2·36 m (7 ft 9 in)
Fuselage depth	1·75 m (5 ft 9 in)
Height overall, tail rotor turning	
	5·13 m (16 ft 10 in)
Height to top of rotor hub	3·76 m (12 ft 4 in)
Height in air-transportable configuration	
	2·67 m (8 ft 9 in)
Tailplane span	4·38 m (14 ft 4½ in)
Wheel track	2·705 m (8 ft 10½ in)
Wheelbase	8·83 m (28 ft 11¾ in)
Cabin doors (each): Height	1·37 m (4 ft 6 in)
Width	1·75 m (5 ft 9 in)

DIMENSION, INTERNAL:

Cabin: Volume	10·90 m³ (385 cu ft)

AREAS:

Main rotor blades (each)	4·34 m² (46·70 sq ft)
Tail rotor blades (each)	0·41 m² (4·45 sq ft)
Main rotor disc	210·05 m² (2,261 sq ft)
Tail rotor disc	8·83 m² (95·0 sq ft)

WEIGHTS:

Weight empty	4,819 kg (10,624 lb)
Mission T-O weight	7,375 kg (16,260 lb)
Max alternative T-O weight	9,185 kg (20,250 lb)

PERFORMANCE (at mission T-O weight, except where indicated):

Never-exceed speed 195 knots (361 km/h; 224 mph)	
Max level speed at S/L	
	160 knots (296 km/h; 184 mph)
Max level speed at max T-O weight	
	158 knots (293 km/h; 182 mph)
Max cruising speed at 1,220 m (4,000 ft)	
	145 knots (269 km/h; 167 mph)
Single-engine cruising speed	
	105 knots (195 km/h; 121 mph)
Vertical rate of climb at S/L	over 137 m (450 ft)/min
Service ceiling	5,790 m (19,000 ft)
Hovering ceiling IGE (35°C)	2,895 m (9,500 ft)
Hovering ceiling OGE: ISA	3,170 m (10,400 ft)
35°C	1,705 m (5,600 ft)
Range at max T-O weight, 30 min reserves	
	324 nm (600 km; 373 miles)
Endurance	2 h 18 min

SIKORSKY S-70L

US Navy designation: SH-60B Seahawk

The S-70L, since designated SH-60B Seahawk, was Sikorsky's submission for the US Navy's LAMPS (Light Airborne Multi-Purpose System) Mk III competition, and was selected as the winner in September 1977 in preference to Boeing Vertol's Model 237.

Detail design of the Seahawk was initiated by a US Navy award to Sikorsky of a $2·7 million sustaining engineering contract. At the same time, General Electric was given a $547,000 contract for further development of the T700 advanced turboshaft engine to provide increased power and improved corrosion resistance, while a $17·9 million contract went to IBM Federal Systems to continue development of the avionics essential for the SH-60B to fulfil the LAMPS Mk III role. On 28 February 1978, it was announced that the US Department of Defense had authorised full-scale development of the SH-60B, and had awarded Sikorsky a $109·3 million contract for the development, manufacture and flight testing of five prototypes, plus a further airframe for ground testing.

First prototype Sikorsky SH-60B Seahawk, developed to meet the US Navy's LAMPS Mk III requirement

Artist's impression of the original abandoned EH-60A communications jamming version of the Black Hawk

Earlier, Sikorsky had updated the original UH-60A Black Hawk mockup to SH-60B configuration, and this was formally reviewed just prior to announcement of the contract award. In July and August 1978, this mockup was used for shipboard compatibility trials on board the frigate USS *Oliver Hazard Perry* (FFG-7) and the Spruance class destroyer USS *Arthur W. Radford* (DD-968).

In February 1979, the main transmission of the SH-60B completed qualification testing, during which it was run at up to 2,685 kW (3,600 shp). This is 447 kW (600 shp) in excess of the Navy's mission performance specification. On 29 March 1979 it was announced that final assembly of the first Seahawk prototype (US Navy serial number 161169) had begun, and the first flight was made on 12 December 1979. The remaining four prototypes were flown on 11 February, 17 March, 26 April and 14 July 1980.

The US Navy has indicated a requirement for 204 of these helicopters for deployment on board Spruance class ASW destroyers, Aegis-equipped guided missile destroyers, and guided missile frigates in the class of the FFG-7 USS *Oliver Hazard Perry*. In addition to the LAMPS Mk III primary missions of anti-submarine warfare (ASW) and anti-ship surveillance and targeting (ASST), the Seahawk is required also to perform secondary missions which include search and rescue (SAR), medical evacuation (Medevac) and vertical replenishment (Vertrep). It is intended for operational deployment in 1984.

Generally similar to the UH-60A Black Hawk, the Seahawk differs in the modifications necessary for shipboard compatibility and in the provision of avionics and equipment suitable for the naval mission. The former includes a rotor brake, automatic blade folding, folding tailplane and tail rotor pylon, a simplified short-wheelbase landing gear, sliding cabin door, and the introduction of recovery assist, secure and traversing (RAST) equipment for rapid hauldown of the helicopter on to a small deck in rough sea

conditions, hovering in-flight refuelling capability, and buoyancy features. Modifications necessary for the mission requirement include the provision of a sensor operator's station, rescue hoist, chin-mounted pods for ESM equipment, pylons for two Mk 46 torpedoes or auxiliary fuel tanks, a pylon on the starboard side to carry MAD equipment, a sonobuoy launcher on the port side, an increased capacity fuel system, and deletion of armour for the pilot's and co-pilot's seats.

Other subsequent versions are the **SH-60F Ocean Hawk** for ASW from aircraft carriers, and **HH-60H/J** rescue/recovery helicopters (USN/USCG).

TYPE: Twin-turbine ASW/ASST helicopter.

ROTOR SYSTEM: As for UH-60A, except that main rotor blades can be folded by electrical power, and a rotor brake is provided.

ROTOR DRIVE: As for UH-60A.

FUSELAGE: As for UH-60A, except for inclusion of flotation bags and sealing of tailboom to provide buoyancy.

TAIL UNIT: As for UH-60A, except that the pylon structure can be folded to port pneumatically, eliminating the necessity to fold the tail rotor, and the tailplane folds upward.

LANDING GEAR: Non-retractable tailwheel type, with single wheels on main units and twin wheels on tail unit. Wheelbase shortened by 46·6%. Landing gear structure is less complex since the SH-60B's vertical impact requirement is 71·5% below that of the UH-60A. Main-wheel tyres size 26 × 10·0-11; tailwheel tyres size 17·5 × 6·00-6. Multiple disc brakes.

POWER PLANT: Two 1,260 kW (1,690 shp) General Electric T700-GE-401 advanced technology turboshaft engines. Crash-resistant twin-cell fuel system in rear fuselage with total capacity of 2,241 litres (592 US gallons). Lower one-third of fuel cells is self-sealing. Single-point refuelling connection on port side. Hovering in-flight refuelling capability. Two auxiliary fuel tanks can be carried on fuselage pylons.

ACCOMMODATION: Pilot and co-pilot/ATO in cockpit, sensor operator in specially-equipped station. Sliding door with jettisonable window on starboard side. Accommodation is heated, ventilated and air-conditioned.

SYSTEMS: Generally as for UH-60A.

AVIONICS AND EQUIPMENT: Avionics include Collins AN/ARC-159 UHF and AN/ARC-174 HF com, Hazeltine AN/APX-76A active IFF, IBM AN/UYS-1 acoustic processor, Raytheon AN/ALQ-142 ESM, Teledyne Ryan AN/APN-217 Doppler, Texas Instruments AN/ASQ-81 MAD and AN/APS-124 search radar. Equipment includes a 25 tube pneumatic launcher for sonobuoys, and a rescue hoist for SAR operations.

ARMAMENT: Includes two Mk 46 torpedoes.

DIMENSIONS, EXTERNAL: As UH-60A except:

Length overall (rotors and tail pylon folded)	
	12·51 m (41 ft 0½ in)
Width (rotors folded)	4·37 m (14 ft 4 in)
Height to top of rotor hub	3·63 m (11 ft 11 in)
Height overall, tail rotor turning	
	5·23 m (17 ft 2 in)
Height overall (pylon folded)	4·01 m (13 ft 2 in)
Tailplane span	4·37 m (14 ft 4 in)
Wheel track	2·79 m (9 ft 2 in)
Wheelbase	4·83 m (15 ft 10 in)

AREAS: As UH-60A
WEIGHTS (estimated. A, ASW mission; B, ASST mission):
Weight empty, equipped: A, B 6,191 kg (13.648 lb)
Desired mission T-O weight: A 8,983 kg (19,804 lb)
B 8,148 kg (17,963 lb)

Max T-O weight: A 9,908 kg (21,844 lb)
B 9,926 kg (21,884 lb)
PERFORMANCE (estimated, at mission T-O weight):
Max cruising speed at 1,525 m (5,000 ft), tropical conditions: A 135 knots (249 km/h; 155 mph)

Vertical rate of climb at S/L:
A 319 m (1,045 ft)/min
Rate of climb at S/L, one engine out:
A, B 198 m (650 ft)/min
(1980–81)

THE SPARTAN MODEL NS-1.
U.S. Navy designation: NP-1.

TYPE.—Two-seat Primary Training biplane.

WINGS.—Unequal-span unstaggered single-bay biplane. Clark Y wing section. Cut-away centre-section carried above fuselage on splayed-out struts. One pair of parallel interplane struts on each side of fuselage. Streamline tie-rod wing-bracing. Wing structure comprises two laminated spruce spars, spruce ribs and drag-struts and fabric covering. Detachable metal wing-tips. Ailerons on all four wings of riveted aluminium-alloy construction with fabric covering.

FUSELAGE.—Rectangular welded chrome-molybdenum steel-tube framework with aluminium-alloy formers and fairing strips and fabric covering aft of cockpits. Removable aluminium-alloy side and bottom panels forward of rear cockpit.

TAIL UNIT.—Wire-braced monoplane type. Fin and tail-plane of stressed-skin aluminium-alloy construction. Elevators and rudder have riveted duralumin framework and fabric covering. Single elevator trimming-tab controllable from cockpit.

LANDING GEAR.—Split type. Consists of two long-stroke Cleveland oleo-spring shock-absorber legs with the upper ends anchored to the upper fuselage longerons and the lower ends hinged to a cabane beneath the fuselage by Vee axles. Oleo-sprung swivelling tail-wheel. Hydraulic wheel-brakes.

POWER PLANT.—One 220 h.p. Lycoming R-680-8 nine-cylinder radial air-cooled engine on welded steel-tube mounting. Hamilton-Standard or Lycoming adjustable-pitch airscrew. Petrol tanks in inner ends of upper outer wings. Fuel capacity 43 U.S. gallons.

ACCOMMODATION.—Tandem open cockpits with complete dual controls.

DIMENSIONS.—Span 33 ft. 8½ in. (10.27 m.), Length 24 ft. 2¾ in. (7.39 m.), Height 8 ft. 4¼ in. (2.85 m.), Wing area 301.3 sq. ft. (28 sq. m.).

The Spartan Model NS-1 (NP-1) Two-seat Primary Training Biplane (220 h.p. Lycoming engine).

WEIGHTS AND LOADINGS.—Weight empty 2,069 lbs. (938.5 kg.), Weight loaded 2,775 lbs. (1,258.7 kg.), Wing loading 9.2 lbs./sq. ft. (44.14 kg./sq. m.), Power loading 12.33 lbs./h.p. (5.59 kg./h.p.).

PERFORMANCE.—Maximum speed 108.5 m.p.h. (174.5 km.h.), Cruising speed 90 m.p.h. (145 km.h.), Landing speed 46.6 m.p.h. (75 km.h.), Initial rate of climb 725 ft./min. (220 m./min.), Service ceiling 13,200 ft. (4,025 m.), Cruising range 315 miles (505 km.).

(1943–44)

SPERRY MESSENGER

(Built to the designs of McCook Field by the Lawrence Sperry Aircraft Corporation, Farmingdale, Long Island, N.Y.)

Type of machine	Tractor Biplane.
Name or type No. of machine	" Messenger."
Purpose for which intended	Communications.
Span	20 ft.
Overall length	17 ft. 9 in.
Maximum height	7 ft.
Total wing area	152 sq. ft.
Engine type and h.p.	60 h.p. Lawrance Radial.
Tank capacity	10 U.S. galls.
Weight empty	581 lbs.
Weight loaded	820 lbs.

Performance.

High speed	95 m.p.h.
Low speed	35 m.p.h.

Climb.

To 10,000 feet	10 mins.
Range	170 miles.

Engineering Data.

Wing section, U.S.A.15. Chord, 4 ft. Gap, 3 ft. 9 in. Dihedral, none. Stagger, 18 in.

Areas : Tail plane, 12.3 sq. ft. ; elevator, 4.7 sq. ft. ; fin, 1.8 sq. ft. ; rudder, 5.3 sq. ft.

Wing loading, 5.4 lbs./sq. ft. Power loading, 13.5 lbs./h.p.

The U.S. Army " Messenger " Biplane (60 h.p. Lawrance engine).

Construction Notes.

This small single-seater, which does not carry any armament, has been developed for communication service between units in the field which for one reason or the other are devoid of other means of communication. It may be considered as an aerial despatch bearer.

The construction is conventional, but much thought has been expended on refining details, particularly in the wing truss.

(1922)

Front View of the Standard Aircraft Corporation's type E.1 Single-seater (80 h.p. Le Rhône engine.)

THE STANDARD E 1 OR M DEFENCE BIPLANE.
Specification.

Type of machine	Single-seater Biplane.
Name or type No. of machine	E. 1. (M. Defence)
Purpose for which intended	Reconnaissance & fighting.
Span	24 ft.
Gap	4 ft.
Overall length	18 ft. 10¹¹⁄₁₆ in.
Maximum height	9 ft. 1in.
Chord	42 ins.
Area of elevators	10.3 sq. ft.
Area of rudder	6.8 sq. ft.
Area of fin	2.5 sq. ft.
Total area of ailerons	23.2 sq. ft.
Engine type and h.p.	80 h.p. Le Rhône,
Airscrew, diameter	8 ft.

Weight of machine empty	..	..	828 lbs.
Load per sq. ft.	..	..	7.5 lbs.
Weight per h.p.	..	..	14.3 lbs.
Tank capacity in hours	..	..	2 hours.

Performance.

Speed low down ..	..	..	99.8 m.p.h.
Speed at 6,400 feet	..	..	94 m.p.h.
Speed at 10,000 feet	..	..	85 m.p.h.
Landing speed ..	..	..	48 m.p.h.

Climb.

To 6,000 feet in minutes	..	10 minutes.	
To 10.000 feet in minutes	..	22 mins. 20 secs.	
Theoretical ceiling	..	14,800 ft.	
Disposable load apart from fuel	..	..	..	201 lbs.
Total weight of machine loaded	..	..	..	1,144 lbs.
Dihedral	..	..	..	3%.
Stagger	..	..	..	13¼ in.
Track	..	..	..	5 ft.	(1919)

THE AMERICAN HANDLEY PAGE TYPE 0-400 BOMBER.

Both in Great Britain and in the United States, the Handley Page has been the principal machine to be put into quantity production for bombing purposes. The American design is similar to the British, except that Liberty "12" 400 h.p. engines are employed in the former, and the Rolls-Royce or Sunbeam in the latter. The Handley Page machines described here were built by the Standard Aero Corporation, Elizabeth, N. J.

Accommodations are made for one pilot and two or three gunners, and an observer who operates the bomb-dropping devices. Their placing is as follows : At the forward end of the fuselage is the gunner who operates a pair of flexible Lewis machine guns. Bowden cables at one side of the cockpit permit the release of bombs. Behind the gunner is the pilot's cockpit from which the gunner's cockpit is reached through an opening in the bulkhead separating the two compartments. The pilot is seated at the right side of the cockpit. Beside him is the observer's seat, hinged so that it may be put raised to permit access. Bomb-releasing controls are placed on the left side of the observer extending to the forward gunner's compartment and running back to the bomb racks located in the fuselage just between the wings.

Forward compartments are reached via a triangular door on the under side of the fuselage.

Aft of the bomb rack compartment, the rear gunners are placed. Two guns are located at the top of the fuselage and a third is arranged to fire through an opening in the under side of the fuselage. One gunner may have charge of all the rear guns, although usually two gunners man them. A platform is situated half way between upper and lower longerons of the fuselage, upon which the gunner stands when operating the upper guns.

THE STINSON 76 SENTINEL.

U.S. Army Air Forces designation : L-5.
U.S. Navy designation: OY-1.
British name : Sentinel.

The Sentinel, which was originally designated the O-56, is a product of the Stinson Division of the Consolidated Vultee Aircraft Corpn. There are three Army versions of the Sentinel, as detailed below.

L-5 and L-5A (OY-1 and Sentinel I). Standard two-seat short-range Liaison and Observation monoplane. The L-5A is identical to the L-5 except that it is fitted with a 24-volt electrical system. The landing gear fairings have been removed from all L-5's.

L-5B (Sentinel II). Adaptation of the L-5 to carry one stretcher case or light cargo up to a maximum of 200 lbs. Fuselage aft of the rear wing spar is deeper and retains its rectangular cross-section to the fin. A large door aft of the observer's door opens downwards to permit the loading of a stretcher. When a stretcher is carried the back of the observer's seat is folded forward and the rear panel of the observer's compartment hinges down to form the front portion of the floor of the stretcher or cargo compartment. Tie-down fittings for light cargo. The L-5B may be fitted with twin-float gear.

The Stinson L-5A Sentinel Two-seat Light Liaison and Observation Monoplane (190 h.p. Lycoming O-435-1 engine).

TYPE.—Two-seat Liaison/Observation or Ambulance monoplane.
WINGS.—High-wing braced monoplane. Structure consists of spruce-spars and ribs, steel tube compression struts and wire bracing, and fabric covering. Vee type steel or duralumin tube bracing struts. Manually-operated trailing-edge flaps between ailerons and fuselage. Flaps have light metal frames and fabric covering.
FUSELAGE.—Welded steel tube structure covered with fabric.
TAIL UNIT.—Cantilever monoplane type. All wood framework with fabric covering. Fin built integral with the fuselage. Fixed tailplane. Horn-balanced control surfaces.
LANDING GEAR.—Single-leg cantilever fixed type. Long-stroke oleo-spring shock absorber units. Hydraulically operated wheel brakes. Steerable tail-wheel with leaf-spring shock-absorber.
POWER PLANT.—One 190 h.p. Lycoming O-435-1 six-cylinder horizontally opposed air-cooled engine. Two fuel tanks, one in root of each wing. Gravity feed. Total maximum fuel capacity: 36 U.S. gallons (30 Imp. gallons). Sesenich fixed-pitch wood airscrew, 7 ft 1 in. (2.16 m.) diameter.
ACCOMMODATION.—Enclosed cockpit seating two in tandem with dual controls. Entire roof of cabin glazed. Side windows inclined slightly outwards to improve downward vision. Doors on starboard side of cabin, pilot's door hinging forward and observers' door downward. In L-5B further stretcher-loading door swings downwards. Normal equipment includes radio, night-flying equipment, fire extinguisher, first-aid kit, etc.
DIMENSIONS.—Span 34 ft. (10.37 m.), Length 24 ft. 1¼ in. (7.33 m.), Height 7 ft. 1 in. (2.13 m.).
WEIGHTS.—Weight empty 1,472 lbs. (668 kg.), Weight loaded 2,158 lbs. (980 kg.).
PERFORMANCE.—Maximum speed 129 m.p.h. (206.4 km.h.), Service ceiling 15,800 ft. (4,820 m.).

THE STINSON RELIANT.

U.S. Army Air Forces designations : AT-19 and UC-81.
British name : Reliant.

The Reliant was originally a four/five-seat commercial monoplane which was in wide use in the United States by sportsmen and business executives.

Although commercial production ceased on America's entry in the War, the Reliant was built in 1942-43 in a modified form as the AT-19, for assignment to the British Government as a navigation trainer for use by the Royal Navy.

TYPE.—Three-seat Navigation Trainer.
WINGS.—High-wing braced monoplane. Wings attached to top longerons and braced to the bottom of the fuselage by single struts.

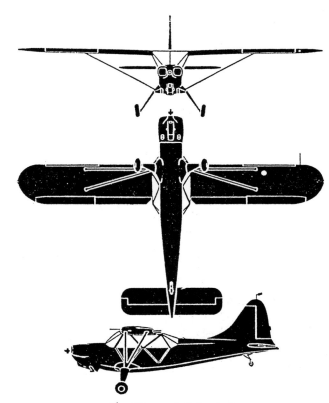

The Stinson L-5 Sentinel.

Clark "Y" wing section. Structure consists of a single steel-tube main spar, steel-tube drag bracing, duralumin auxiliary spar, riveted square duralumin tube ribs, duralumin sheet leading-edge and an overall fabric covering. Vacuum-operated trailing-edge flaps between ailerons and fuselage.

FUSELAGE.—Welded steel-tube structure covered with fabric.

TAIL UNIT.—Braced monoplane type. Welded steel-tube framework covered with fabric.

LANDING GEAR.—Divided type. Cantilever legs incorporating spring shock-absorbers. Hydraulic wheel-brakes. Castoring tail-wheel.

POWER PLANT.—One 290 h.p. Lycoming R-680-13 nine-cylinder radial air-cooled engine on welded steel-tube mounting. Fuel tanks in wing roots.

ACCOMMODATION.—Enclosed cabin seating three, two in front side-by-side with dual controls. Specialised equipment for navigational training.

DIMENSIONS.—Span 41 ft. 10½ in. (12.8 m.), Length 29 ft. 4¼ in. (8.9 m.), Height 8 ft. 7 in. (2.59 m.), Wing area 258.5 sq. ft. (24 sq. m.).

WEIGHTS.—Weight empty 2,810 lbs. (1,276 kg.), Weight loaded 4,000 lbs. (1,816 kg.).

PERFORMANCE.—Maximum speed 141 m.p.h. (226 km.h.), Service ceiling 14,000 ft. (4,270 m.).

The Stinson AT-19 Reliant Navigational Training Monoplane (290 h.p. Lycoming R-680-13 engine).

The U.S. Army also acquired a number of secondhand five-seat commercial Reliants for general utility transport duties and gave them designations in the UC-81 Series. These were as follow :—

UC-81 Model SR-8B (Lycoming R-680-B6 engine).
UC-81A Model SR-10G (Lycoming R-680-E1 engine).
UC-81B Model SR-8D (Wright R-760-E2 engine)
UC-81C Model SR-9C (Lycoming R-680-D5 engine).
UC-81D Model SR-10F (Pratt & Whitney R-985 engine).

UC-81E Model SR-9F (Pratt & Whitney R-985 engine).
UC-81F Model SR-10F (Pratt & Whitney R-985 engine).
UC-81G Model SR-9D (Wright R-760-E1 engine).
UC-81H Model SR-10E (Wright R-760-E2 engine).
UC-81J Model SR-9E (Wright R-760-E2 engine).
UC-81K Model SR-10C (Lycoming R-680-D5 engine).
UC-81L Model SR-8C (Lycoming R-680-B5 engine).
UC-81N Model SR-9B (Lycoming R-680-B6 engine).

(1945—46)

A Supermarine Spitfire VB with clipped wings as supplied to the U.S.A.A.F. in the British Isles for training purposes.

THE SUPERMARINE SPITFIRE.

The first Supermarine aeroplane to bear the name Spitfire was a single-seat fighter designed to meet the Air Ministry F.7/30 specification. It was a low-wing cantilever monoplane with fixed landing-gear and was fitted with a 600 h.p. Rolls-Royce Goshawk engine. From this type, which was not successful, was evolved as a Private Venture a new prototype to which the name Spitfire was transferred and around which the Air Ministry F.37/34 specification was written. Into this prototype Mr. R. J. Mitchell incorporated the fruitful results of the experience gained in the design of his series of high-speed seaplanes which had previously won three successive Schneider Trophy Contests and established three World's Speed Records.

The prototype F.37/34 Spitfire, which was fitted with one of the first Rolls-Royce Merlin engines, flew in March, 1936. With a fixed-pitch wooden airscrew the prototype had a maximum speed of 342 m.p.h. (547.2 km.h.), which classed it at that time as the fastest military aeroplane in the World.

The soundness of the basic design has been proved in six years of war, throughout which the Rolls-Royce-engined Spitfire has, in its many progressive developments, remained a first-line fighter. Apart from its fighter duties the Spitfire has also been used for the past six years for photographic-reconnaissance. The first photographic mission by an unarmed Spitfire was made on November 18, 1939.

Versions of the Spitfire used by the USAAF included the VB, VC (used in North Africa) and XI, mostly for photographic reconnaissance but also for training and fighter roles. Prior to this, US volunteer pilots had flown Spitfires with the RAF from 1940.

Spitfire V. Rolls-Royce Merlin 45, 46, 50, 50A, 55 or 56 engine. Rotol or D.H. three-blade constant-speed airscrew. In other respects Mks. VA and VB similar to Mks. IA and IB respectively. Mk. VC fitted with universal wings with a normal armament of two 20 m/m. cannon and four machine-guns. Mk. V went into service in the Summer of 1941 and was the first mark to be fitted with tropical equipment, to carry drop tanks (on VB and VC), and the first to serve outside the British Isles. In 1942 one Mk. VB was modified into a prototype fighter-seaplane with twin floats, a modified upper fin and an additional lower fin. In 1943 the Mk. V was fitted with clipped wings and the Merlin 45M, 50M or 55M engine for service as a low-altitude fighter, and provision was made for carrying a 250 lb. or 500 lb. bomb on the drop tank fittings. Dimensions : Span (standard wing) 36 ft. 10 in. (11.23 m.), Span (clipped wing) 32 ft. 7 in. (9.93 m.), Length 29 ft. 11 in. (9.12 m.).

Spitfire P.R. XI. Rolls-Royce Merlin 61, 63, 63A or 70 engine. Fuselage as Mk. VC modified for Mk. VII engine installation and wings as for P.R.X. Tropical equipment and universal camera installation.

THE TAYLORCRAFT "GRASSHOPPER."
U.S. Army Air Forces designation: L-2.

The L-2 is a special version of the Tandem Trainer, a large number of which has been supplied to the U.S. Army Air Forces for observation and light liaison duties. It has been supplied in four versions, the L-2, L-2A, L-2B and L-2M, all fitted with the 65 h.p. Continental O-170-3 engine and equipped with two-way radio.

To provide increased vision for the pilot and observer, the fabric formerly covering the cabin roof and the rear deck of the fuselage to a point about midway to the tail has been replaced by transparent "Vinylite" panels. For the same reason, the root ends of the wings have been cut away at the trailing-edge.

The observer has a two-way seat and a table is provided at the rear of the cabin for use by the observer when facing aft.

The latest version in the L-2 Series—the L-2M—has a closed engine cowling and "spoilers" have been fitted to the wings to facilitate landing in small areas. Operation of these "spoilers" has the effect of doubling the rate of descent.

In addition to the versions mentioned above, the U.S. Army also purchased secondhand a number of civil Taylorcraft Model B and Model D monoplanes for pre-glider training. These were given designations in the L-2 Series as follows :—

L-2C	Model DC-65	Continental A-65-8 engine.
L-2D	Model DL-65	Lycoming O-145-B2 engine.
L-2E	Model DF-65	Franklin 4AC-150 engine.
L-2F	Model BF-65	Franklin 4AC-150 engine.
L-2G	Model BFT-65	Franklin 4AC-150 engine.
L-2H	Model BC-12	Continental A-65-7 engine.
L-2J	Model BI-12	Lycoming O-145-B1 engine.
L-2K	Model BF-12	Franklin 4AC-150 engine.
L-2L	Model BF-50	Franklin 4AC-150 engine.

Most of these models have been illustrated and described in previous issues of this Annual. (1945–46)

THOMAS-MORSE.

This Company grew from the original Thomas Brothers Aeroplane Company, which was established in 1912.

They have for some years specialised in metal construction, and during the past year have continued development of the Thomas-Morse O-6B all-metal observation biplane, fitted with a 425 h.p. Pratt & Whitney "Wasp" engine, in conjunction with the Materiel Division of the Air Corps, with satisfactory results. This Company also constructed during the year a quantity of metal wings for pursuit aircraft.

THOMAS-MORSE M.B.3.

During the past year the Thomas-Morse M.B.3, built by this firm (see "All the World's Aircraft, 1920"), was adopted by the U.S. Army Air Service as the standard single-seater pursuit (fighter) aeroplane. An order for 300 machines of this type was placed by the Army Air Service with the Boeing Airplane Company of Seattle, Washington.

Specification.

Type of machine	Tractor Biplane.
Name or type No. of machine	M.B.3.
Purpose for which intended	Fighting.
Armament	2 fixed Browning M.G.
Crew	1 man.
Span	26 ft. (U & L).
Overall length	19 ft. 11 in.
Maximum height	8 ft.
Total wing area	250 sq. ft.
Engine type and h.p.	300 h.p. Wright-Hispano.
Tank capacity	65 galls.

Three-quarter front view of the Thomas-Morse M.B,3 Single-seater Fighter (300 h.p. Wright-Hispano engine).

Weight empty	1,360 lbs.
Weight loaded	2,037 lbs.
Performance.	
High speed	$163\frac{2}{3}$ m.p.h.
Low speed	60 m.p.h.
Climb.	
To 10,000 feet	4 mins. 52 secs. (1920)

The Thomas-Morse O-19E Two-seat Observation Biplane (425 h.p. Pratt & Whitney "Wasp" engine).

Late in 1929, the Company was bought by the Consolidated Aircraft Corpn. and the whole plant was moved to Buffalo, N.Y.

Since its purchase, it has been engaged in the production of approximately 280 all-metal observation aeroplanes of the O-19B, O-19C and O-19E types for the Army Air Corps.

TYPE.—Two-seat observation biplane.

WINGS.—Unequal-span, single-bay, staggered biplane. Clark "Y" wing-section. Top centre-section carried above fuselage by splayed-out struts, with one set of "N" type interplane struts on either side of the fuselage. Wing structure consists of two "I" section spars built up of extruded duralumin sections, the usual number of ribs of duralumin tube, strut and wire drag-bracing, the whole being covered with fabric. Narrow-chord ailerons, inset from the wing-tips, on all four wings. The ailerons are of all-metal construction and covered with corrugated duralumin sheet.

FUSELAGE.—Front portion is a welded steel-tube structure and the rear portion is a monocoque. The whole fuselage is covered with corrugated duralumin sheet.

TAIL UNIT.—Monoplane type. Duralumin framework, covered with corrugated sheet, except the fin, which is fabric-covered. Adjustable tail-plane.

UNDERCARRIAGE.—Divided type. Consists of two side Vees, with the inner ends of the half-axles hinged to the centreline of the underside of the fuselage. Combined oleo and spring shock-absorber units mounted inside the fuselage. Wheel-brakes fitted as standard. Steerable tail-wheel.

POWER PLANT.—One 425 h.p. Pratt & Whitney "Wasp" radial air-cooled engine, on a circular tube engine-mounting and enclosed in a Townend type cowling ring. Main fuel tank, of 80 U.S. gallons capacity, and auxiliary tank, of 45 U.S. gallons capacity, give a cruising range of 450 miles.

ACCOMMODATION.—Tandem open cockpits, behind trailing-edge of top wings. One fixed Browning 30 cal. gun firing forward through the airscrew and one similar type gun on a rotatable mounting over the rear cockpit. Ammunition box for 300 rounds for front gun and racks for 500 rounds for back gun. Single A.3 bomb-rack for 250-lb. load of bombs mounted under fuselage, in vicinity of bottom plane and replaces auxiliary fuel tank. Camera of K3 type in fuselage aft of observer's cockpit. Wireless equipment in front of observer. Seat-type parachutes. Parachute flares in rear section of fuselage.

DIMENSIONS.—Span 39 ft. 9 in. (12.1 m.), Length 28 ft. 9 in. (8.76 m.), Height 11 ft. (3.35 m.), Wing area 348 sq. ft. (32.3 sq. m.).

WEIGHTS AND LOADINGS.—Weight empty 2,786 lbs. (1,265 kg.), Crew 400 lbs. (182 kg.), Fuel and oil for 300 miles range 532.5 lbs. (243 kg.), Military load 233 lbs. (106 kg.), Weight loaded 3,951 lbs. (1,794 kg.), Wing loading 11.4 lbs./sq. ft. (55.6 kg./sq. m.), Power loading 8.8 lbs./h.p. (3.9 lbs./h.p.).

PERFORMANCE.—Maximum speed 157.7 m.p.h. (252.3 km.h.), Service ceiling 21,000 ft. (6,405 m.), Absolute ceiling 25,000 ft. (7,625 m.), Range at cruising speed 300 miles (480 km.). (1931)

THE THOMAS-MORSE SINGLE-SEATER SCOUT BIPLANE.

Type of machine	Single-seater Advanced Trainer, following S-4B
Name or type No. of machine	.. S. 4C.
Purpose for which intended	.. Fighting.
Span	.. 26 ft. 6 in.
Overall length	.. 19 ft. 10 in.
Maximum height	.. 8 ft. 1 in.
Engine type and h.p. ..	.. 80 h.p. Le Rhône.
Weight of machine empty ..	.. 940 lbs.
Petrol tank capacity in gallons	.. 30 gallons.
Performance.	
Speed (maximum) ..	.. 97 m.p.h
Landing speed	.. 45 m.p.h.
Climb.	
To 7,500 feet in minutes	.. 10 minutes.
Total weight of machine loaded	1,330 lbs.

Three-quarter Rear View, of the Thomas-Morse type S.4C. (80 h.p. Le Rhône engine). **(1919)**

The Thomas-Morse S.H. 4 Seaplane.

THE THOMAS-MORSE S.H.4 SEAPLANE

Type of machine	.. Two-seater Seaplane.
Name or type No. of machine	.. S.H. 4.
Purpose for which intended	.. Training and observation; 14 used by Navy from 1917.
Span	.. 44 ft.
Overall length	.. 29 ft. 9 in.
Chord..	.. 5 ft. 9 in.
Engine type and h.p. ..	.. 100 h.p. (type unstated).

THE THOMAS-MORSE S.5 SINGLE SEATER SEAPLANE

Type of machine	.. Single-seater Seaplane.
Name or type No. of machine	.. S. 5.
Purpose for which intended..	.. Scouting; 6 used by Navy from 1917.
Span	.. 26 ft. 6 in.
Overall length	.. 22 ft. 9 in.
Maximum height	.. 9 ft. 7 in.
Total surface of wings (inc. ailerons)	240 sq. ft.
Total area of fixed tail plane ..	16.8 sq. ft.
Area of elevators	.. 22 sq. ft.
Area of rudder	.. 8.5 sq. ft.
Area of fin	.. 3.5 sq. ft.
Total area of ailerons ..	.. 30 sq. ft.
Engine type and h.p. ..	.. 100 h.p. Monosoupape Gnôme.
Airscrew, diameter and revs. ..	8 ft., 1250 r.p.m.
Load per sq. ft.	.. 6.25 lbs.
Weight per h.p.	.. 14·3 lbs.
Tank capacity in hours. ..	.. 3 hours.
Tank capacity in gallons ..	.. 30 galls.
Performance.	
Speed low down	.. 95 m.p.h.
Landing speed	.. 50 m.p.h.
Climb.	
To 5,200 feet in minutes	.. 10 minutes.
Total weight of machine loaded	1,500 lbs.

(1919)

THE TIMM "TUTOR."

On April 2, 1941, the S-160-K was awarded the first Approved Type Certificate ever given to a trainer built entirely of plastic-bonded plywood. The S-160-K was then submitted to tests by the Army and the Navy and as a result the U.S. Navy placed a contract for aircraft of this type fitted with the 220 h.p. Continental W-670 radial engine.

U.S. Navy designation: N2T-1.

TYPE.—Two-seat training monoplane.

WINGS.—Low-wing cantilever monoplane. Wing section NACA 23015 tapered. The entire wing structure is built of "Aeromold" plastic material and comprises laminated plastic-bonded veneer box-spars, plastic-bonded ribs and a laminated plastic-bonded veneer moulded skin. The ailerons and flaps are of the same material with laminated spars and ribs and processed skin. The slotted trailing-edge flaps, between ailerons and fuselage, are hydraulically operated. The outer wing panels are quickly removable at the aileron and flap junction.

FUSELAGE.—Semi-monocoque structure built up of a series of laminated plastic-bonded veneer rings and stringers, the whole covered with a moulded laminated skin.

TAIL UNIT.—Cantilever monoplane type. Structure comprises solid wood spars, resin-bonded ribs and skin.

LANDING GEAR.—Fixed cantilever type. Timm air-oleo shock-absorbers. Low-pressure wheels and hydraulic brakes. Full-swivelling steerable tail-wheel with centre lock.

POWER PLANT.—One 220 h.p. Continental W-670 seven-cylinder radial air-cooled engine. Hamilton-Standard controllable-pitch airscrew. Petrol capacity 42.5 U.S. gallons. Oil capacity 3¾ U.S. gallons.

ACCOMMODATION.—Tandem open cockpits with complete dual controls. Army type adjustable seats. All controls and control surfaces on ball and roller bearings. Baggage compartment.

The Timm N2T-1 "Tutor" Two-seat Training Monoplane (220 h.p. Continental engine).

DIMENSIONS.—Span 36 ft. (11 m.), Length 24 ft. 10 in. (7.6 m.), Height 10 ft. 8 in. (3.24 m.), Wing area 185 sq. ft. (17.2 sq. m.).

WEIGHTS AND LOADINGS.—Weight empty 1,940 lbs. (881 kg.), Crew (two) 380 lbs. (173 kg.), Petrol and oil 283 lbs. (128 kg.), Tools, extras, etc. 122 lbs. (55 kg.), Disposable load 785 lbs. (356 kg.), Weight loaded 2,725 lbs. (1,237 kg.), Wing loading 12.39 lbs./sq. ft. (50.46 kg./sq. m.), Power loading 11.74 lbs./h.p. (5.33 kg./h.p.).

PERFORMANCE.—Maximum speed 144 m.p.h. (232 km.h.), Cruising speed (75% power) 124 m.p.h. (199 km.h.), Landing speed (with flaps) 54 m.p.h. (87 km.h.), Service ceiling 16,000 ft. (4,880 m.), Cruising range 400 miles (640 km.).

(1943–44)

The Vertol (formerly Piasecki) H-21A Work Horse Arctic Rescue Helicopter (1,150 h.p. Wright R-1820 engine).

THE VERTOL WORK HORSE.
U.S.A.F. and Army designation: H-21.

This higher-powered version of the HRP-2 has been supplied to the U.S.A.F., U.S. Army, French Navy and the Royal Canadian Air Force. It exists in the following versions :—

YH-21 and H-21A. One Wright R-1820-103 engine with power limited to 1,150 h.p. Arctic rescue helicopter. Passenger-cargo compartment 20 ft. (6.08 m.) long, 5 ft. 8 in. (1.72 m.) wide and 5 ft. 6 in. (1.67 m.) high. Crew of two, pilot and co-pilot (or medical attendant), and accommodation for twelve stretchers or fourteen troops. 400 lb. (182 kg.) capacity swinging boom-type hydraulic hoist above large sliding door immediately behind pilot on starboard side for transferring loads while hovering, and further door on port side aft for loading and unloading on gound. Each wheel of landing-gear can be surrounded with inflatable ring floats to permit landing on water, marsh and land. Equipment includes cabin insulation and heating, blind-flying instruments, hydraulic control boost, external cargo sling, pilot-controlled searchlight, fixed landing light, tie-down cargo fittings in cabin floor, troop seats and stretcher supports. The Arctic Rescue version of the H-21 has demonstrated its ability to operate at temperatures down to minus 65°F.

H-21B and H-21C. One 1,425 h.p. Wright R-1820-103 engine. Troop and cargo transport capable of performing assault airlift, transport of troops and equipment, and rescue and evacuation missions for U.S. Air Force and Army. Interior and exterior dimensions and crew accommodations same as for H-21A. Cabin accommodates twelve stretchers or twenty troops. Forward door and swinging boom hoist as for H-21A but rear door larger and two extra windows added. Equipment same as for H-21A except for additional items which include autopilot, provision for jettisonable auxiliary fuel tanks, bullet-sealing fuel and oil tanks, readily-removable armour kit for protection of vital components, etc.

H-21D. Two H-21C aircraft have each been fitted with two General Electric T58 gas-turbine engines in place of a single R-1820 piston-engine, under a U.S. Navy/Army contract. Both turbines are mounted aft in such a way that the failure of one will not affect the operation of the other.

The following data apply to the commercial version of the H-21B and C. (Company designation : Vertol 43). This

version will have accommodation for a crew of two and twenty passengers in troop seats or 16-19 passengers in airline seats.

DIMENSIONS.—
Rotor diameter 44 ft. (13.42 m.).
Overall length (rotors turning) 86 ft. 4 in. (26.24 m.).
Width (blades folded) 14 ft. 4 in. (4.31 m.).
Overall height 15 ft. 5 in. (4.68 m.).
Main landing gear tread 13 ft. 4 in. (4.05 m.).
Passenger cabin length 20 ft. 0 in. (6.08 m.).
Passenger cabin width 5 ft. 8 in. (1.72 m.).
Passenger cabin height 5 ft. 6 in. (1.67 m.).

WEIGHTS.—
Weight empty (standard equipment) 8,800 lb. (3.992 kg.).
Normal useful load 4,700 lb. (2,132 kg.).
Normal loaded weight 13,500 lb. (6,124 kg.).

PERFORMANCE (at normal A.U.W.).—
Max. speed at S/L. 130 m.p.h. (209 km.h.).
Cruising speed at S/L. (for best range) 98 m.p.h. (158 km.h.).
Max. rate of climb (normal rated power) 1,080 ft./min. (330 m./min.).
Vertical rate of climb (take-off power) 850 ft./min. (258 m./min.).
Hovering ceiling in ground effect (take-off power) 6,100 ft. (1,859 m.).
Hovering ceiling out-of-ground effect (take-off power) 3,700 ft. (1,128 m.).
Service ceiling 9,450 ft. (2,880 m.).

(1956–57)

THE VERTOL RETRIEVER AND ARMY MULE.
U.S. Navy designation: HUP Retriever.
U.S. Army designation: H-25A Army Mule.

This single-engined tandem-rotored helicopter was designed to meet the requirements of the U.S. Navy for shipboard operation, including carrier plane guard duty, rescue, observation and inter-ship and ship-to-shore utility transport duties. It was required to negotiate the smallest aircraft-carrier lift without blade folding and to go down a standard cruiser aircraft lift with blades folded.

The HUP helicopter has an all-metal soundproofed fuselage with a normal accommodation for a crew of two and four passengers or three stretcher cases. A large loading door and ample cabin dimensions also permit the transport of a wide variety of high or low density cargo. An internally-operated rescue hatch adjacent to the pilot's seat is large enough to allow the passage of a loaded stretcher. A hydraulically-operated hoist above the hatch is used for hoisting survivors while hovering, and if a rescue sling is used the pilot can conduct the entire loading operation without assistance.

The 339th and last HUP was delivered to the U.S. Navy in July, 1954. Others are in service with the Royal Canadian Navy, and French Navy, while the U.S. Army uses the same basic design as the H-25A. The several versions of this helicopter which are in service are identified below.

HUP-1. 525 h.p. Continental R-975-34 engine. First production model. Deliveries started in 1950 and were completed in 1952.

HUP-2. 550 h.p. Continental R-975-46 engine. As the result of successful trials in automatic control in all flight conditions with the prototype XHJP-1, using a modified Sperry automatic pilot, all production HUP-2's have an auto-pilot as primary controller. This permits the

The Vertol HUP-2 Retriever (550 h.p. Continental R-975 engine).
(Gordon Williams).

elimination of the tail stabilising surfaces used in the HUP-1. Fitted with submarine-hunting sonar equipment, the HUP-2S was the first interim anti-submarine warfare helicopter to go into service. HUP-2 also used for plane guard, rescue and utility duties. Deliveries began in 1952 and were completed in 1954.

HUP-3. Medical evacuation and light cargo helicopter. U.S. Navy version of the Army H-25A.

H-25A. U.S. Army version of HUP-type. Incorporates hydraulic boost on all controls, strengthened all-metal cabin floor with cargo tie-down fittings and special modifications to facilitate loading and unloading of stretcher patients. Deliveries began in 1953 and were completed in 1954.

During 1957, the Edo Corporation designed, equipped and tested an amphibious version of the HUP-2. Under a U.S. Navy contract, Edo reinforced and made watertight the bottom of the fuselage, fitted metal outrigger floats on each side of the fuselage and re-ducted the engine cooling system. In initial tests, the

modified aircraft was landed at a forward speed of 35 m.p.h. (55 km.h.) in 18 in. (.45 m.) waves and taxied at 17 m.p.h. (27 km.h.), showing excellent manoeuvrability on water.

The following data specifically concerns the HUP-2 and H-25A.

DIMENSIONS.—
  Length (rotors turning) 56 ft. 11 in. (17.3 m.).
  Length of fuselage (blades folded) 32 ft. (9.75 m.).
  Width (rotors turning) 35 ft. (10.7 m.).
  Width (blades folded) 12 ft. 11 in. (3.91 m.).
  Height (HUP-2) 13 ft. 2 in. (4.0 m.).
  Height (H-25A) 12 ft. 6 in. (3.8 m.).
WEIGHTS.—
  Empty (HUP-2) 4,132 lb. (1,874 kg.).
  Empty (H-25A) 3,928 lb. (1,782 kg.).
  Normal loaded weight 5,750 lb. (2,608 kg.).
  Max. overloaded weight 6,100 lb. (2,767 kg.).
PERFORMANCE.—
  Max. speed at S/L. (normal power) over 105 m.p.h. (170 km.h.).
  Cruising speed over 80 m.p.h. (130 km.h.).
  Best rate of climb (normal power) 1,000 ft./min. (305 m./min.).
  Vertical rate of climb (take-off power) 650 ft./min. (198 m./min.).
  Service ceiling over 10,000 ft. (3,050 m.).
  Max. range approx. 340 miles (630 km.).

(1958–59)

Boeing-Vertol CH-46D Sea Knight (two 1,400 shp General Electric T58-GE-10 shaft-turbine engines)

BOEING-VERTOL MODEL 107
US Navy and Marine Corps designation: CH-46/ UH-46 Sea Knight
RCAF designation: CH-113 Labrador
Canadian Army designation: CH-113A Voyageur

In 1956, Vertol began preliminary design and engineering of a twin-turbine transport helicopter for commercial and military use. The main objective was to take full advantage of the high power, small size and light weight of the shaft-turbine engines then becoming available. To achieve the best possible hovering performance, the traditional Vertol tandem-rotor layout was retained, and the turbines were mounted at the rear of the cabin, on each side of the aft rotor pylon. This results in maximum unobstructed cabin area and permits the use of a large rear ramp for straight-in loading of vehicles and bulky freight.

Construction of a prototype, designated Model 107, was started in May 1957, and this aircraft flew for the first time on 22 April 1958, powered by two 860 shp Lycoming T53 shaft-turbine engines. It was designed for water landing capability, without the addition of special flotation gear or boat hull design, and was intended to carry 23-25 passengers in normal airline standard accommodation.

As a result of experience with this prototype, including extensive demonstration tours in North America, Europe and the Far East, several advanced versions were developed.

CH-46A (formerly HRB-1) **Sea Knight.** This US Marine Corps assault transport version of the 107 Model II has the specified military mission of carrying a crew of 3 and 17-25 fully-equipped troops or 4,000 lb (1,814 kg) of cargo over a combat radius of 115 miles (185 km) at 150 mph (240

kmh). An initial batch of 14 was ordered in February 1961, followed by annual repeat orders which brought the total number ordered to 600 by the end of 1970, including CH-46Ds and CH-46Fs (see below). An integrated loading system permits rapid loading, by one man, under field conditions. A powered blade-folding system enables the rotor blades to be folded quickly by a pilot-operated control, to simplify handling on board aircraft carriers. The CH-46A is powered by two 1,250 shp General Electric T58-GE-8B shaft-turbine engines, and has all-weather capabilities. In a rescue role, it can retrieve 20 persons up to 105 miles (168 km) from its base, and can carry 15 litter patients and two attendants. First CH-46A flew on 16 October 1962. The US Navy Board of Inspection and Survey tests required for fleet release were completed in November 1964, and four Marine Squadrons were operating CH-46As by June 1965. In September 1965, the US Department of Defense ordered Boeing to increase production of the CH-46A/D by 100%. The CH-46 has been in service in Vietnam since March 1966, and had exceeded 280,000 combat flight hours by January 1971.

CH-46D Sea Knight. Generally similar to CH-46A, but with 1,400 shp General Electric T58-GE-10 shaft-turbines and cambered rotor blades. CH-46s delivered from August 1966 to June 1968 are of this version. A CH-46D Sea Knight handed over to the US Marine Corps in August 1968 was the 1,000th twin-turbine tandem-rotor helicopter to be completed by Boeing-Vertol.

CH-46F Sea Knight. Generally similar to CH-46D, with same engines and rotor blades. Contains additional electronic equipment. All CH-46s delivered since July 1968 are of this version.

UH-46A Sea Knight. Similar to CH-46A. Ordered by US Navy for operation from AFS or AOE combat supply ships. UH-46As are utilised to transfer supplies, ammunition, missiles and aviation spares from these ships to combatant vessels under way at sea. Secondary tasks include transfer of personnel, search and rescue. First deliveries to Utility Helicopter Squadron

One, Ream Field, California in July 1964, followed by deliveries to Utility Helicopter Squadron Four at Norfolk in December 1964. Total of 24 delivered. Since mid-1965, UH-46As have been deployed in the Mediterranean and South China Sea.

The war in Vietnam has led to innovations in ship resupply by UH-46A, including bad weather VERTREP (vertical replenishment) and night VERTREP with the aid of small signal lights.

UH-46D Sea Knight. Generally similar to UH-46A, but with 1,400 shp General Electric T58-GE-10 shaft-turbine engines and cambered rotor blades. UH-46s delivered since September 1966 are of this version.

CH-113 Labrador. Six utility models delivered to RCAF in 1963-64 for search and rescue duties. Generally similar to CH-46A. Two 1,250 shp General Electric T58-GE-8B shaft-turbines. Larger-capacity fuel tanks (total of 900 US gallons = 3,408 litres), giving a range of over 650 miles (1,050 km).

CH-113A Voyageur. Twelve aircraft, in a configuration very similar to that of CH-46A, were delivered to the Canadian Army in 1964-65. They are used as troop and cargo carriers in logistical and tactical missions.

A total of 624 basically similar CH/UH-46 aircraft were delivered to the US Marine Corps and US Navy in the 1964-1971 period. With a view to modernising the Marine Corps' fleet of CH-46s, two prototypes were modified by Boeing Vertol in 1975 and have since completed flight testing. The US Marine Corps now plans to update 273 CH-46s to CH-46E configuration, this involving the installation of 1,394 kW (1,870 shp) General Electric T58-GE-16 turboshaft engines, each developing 33·6% more power than the 1,044 kW (1,400 shp) T58-GE-10s installed in production CH-46A/F aircraft. Other modifications include the provision of crash attenuating seats for pilot and co-pilot, a crash and combat resistant fuel system, and improved rescue system. Initial fleet modifications began during 1977, and the first CH-46E modified at the Cherry Point, NC, Naval Air Rework Facility was rolled out on 3 August 1977.

In April 1975 Boeing Vertol received a contract from Naval Air Systems Command to initiate the development of glassfibre main rotor blades for the H-46 fleet. In early 1977 glassfibre rotor blades for testing purposes were manufactured by Boeing Vertol, and these were bench tested, whirl tested and flight tested during the remainder of the year. Due to the satisfactory progress of this programme, the US Marine Corps began in-service testing of the blades in early 1978. The first production order for these glassfibre rotor blades was issued by the US Navy in December 1977, and by early 1980 a total of 811 blades had been ordered. Fifty-six CH-46s had been fitted with the new blades by August 1980. Follow-on orders for an additional 2,100 blades are programmed, to maintain deliveries up to the end of 1984. Boeing Canada (which see) is currently upgrading a number of Canadian Armed Forces CH-113/113As under a programme known as SARCUP.

The following details apply to both the standard commercial 107 Model II and the Sea Knight.

TYPE: Twin-engined transport helicopter.

ROTOR SYSTEM: Two three-blade rotors in tandem, rotating in opposite directions. Each blade on 107 Model II aircraft delivered to New York Airways and Kawasaki is made up of a steel "D" spar to which is bonded a trailing-edge box constructed of aluminium ribs and glass-fibre or aluminium skin. The CH/UH-46 has power-operated blade folding.

ROTOR DRIVE: Power is transmitted from each engine through individually-overrunning clutches into the aft transmission, which combines the engine outputs, thereby providing a single power output to the interconnecting shaft which enables both rotors to be driven by either engine. Engine/rotor rpm ratio: CH-46A 73·722 : 1, CH-113 73·770 : 1.

FUSELAGE: Square-section stressed-skin semi-monocoque structure built primarily of high-strength bare and alclad aluminium alloy. Transverse bulkheads and built-up frames support transmission, power plant and landing gear. Loading ramp forms undersurface of upswept rear fuselage on utility and military models. Baggage container replaces ramp on airliner version. Fuselage is sealed to permit operation from water.

LANDING GEAR: Non-retractable tricycle type, with twin wheels on all three units. Oleo-pneumatic shock-absorbers manufactured by Loud (main gear) and Jarry Ltd (nose gear). Goodyear tubeless tyres, size 8 × 5·5, pressure 150 lb/sq in (10·55 kg/cm²), on all wheels. Goodyear disc brakes.

POWER PLANT (107 Model II-10): Two 1,250 shp General Electric CT58-110-1 shaft-turbine engines, mounted side-by-side at base of rear rotor pylon. Alternatively, two Bristol Siddeley Gnome H.1200 shaft-turbines (in HKP-4).

Boeing Vertol updated CH-46E, for the US Marine Corps, with General Electric T58-GE-16 turboshaft engines

Fuel tanks in sponsons, capacity 350 US gallons (1,323 litres). Newer 1,400 shp CT58-140 engines can be retrofitted and are being incorporated in Kawasaki production aircraft.

POWER PLANT (CH-46/UH-46). Two General Electric T58 shaft-turbine engines (details under model listings above). Two self-sealing fuel tanks in sponsons, with total capacity of 380 US gallons (1,438 litres). Refuelling points above tanks. Total oil capacity 4·2 US gallons (15·9 litres).

ACCOMMODATION (107 Model II): Standard accommodation for two pilots, stewardess and 25 passengers in airliner. Seats in eight rows, in pairs on port side and single seats on starboard side (two pairs at rear of cabin) with central aisle. Airliner fitted with parcel rack and a roll-out baggage container, with capacity of approximately 1,500 lb (680 kg), located in underside of rear fuselage. Ramp of utility model is power-operated on the ground or in flight and can be removed or left open to permit carriage of extra-long cargo.

ACCOMMODATION (CH/UH-46): Crew of three, 25 troops and troop commander. Door at front of troop compartment on starboard side. Door is split type; upper half rolls on tracks to stowed position in fuselage crown, lower half is hinged at the bottom and opens outward, with built-in steps. Loading ramp and hatch at rear of fuselage can be opened in flight or on the water. Floor has centre panel stressed for 300 lb/sq ft (1,464·6 kg/m²). A row of rollers is installed on each side for handling standard military pallets or wire baskets. Outer portion of floor is vehicle treadway stressed for 1,000 lb (454 kg) rubber-tyred wheel loads. Cargo and personnel hoist system includes a variable-speed winch capable of 2,000 lb (907 kg) cable pull at 30 ft (9 m) min for cargo loading or 600 lb (272 kg) cable pull at 100 ft (30 m) min for personnel hoisting, and can be operated by one man. A 10,000 lb (4,535 kg) capacity hook for external loads is installed in a cargo hatch in the floor.

SYSTEMS (CH/UH-46): Cabin heated by Janitrol combustion heater. Hydraulic system provides 1,500 lb/sq in (105 kg/cm²) pressure for flying control boost, 3,000 lb/sq in (210 kg/cm²) for other services. Electrical system includes two 40kVA AC generators and a Leland 200A DC generator. Solar APU provides power for starting and systems check-out.

ELECTRONICS AND EQUIPMENT: Blind-flying instrumentation standard. CH-46 has dual stability augmentation systems and automatic trim system.

DIMENSIONS, EXTERNAL:
Diameter of main rotors (each):
107-II, CH-113, CH/UH-46A   50 ft 0 in (15·24 m)
CH/UH-46D, CH-46F   51 ft 0 in (15·54 m)
Distance between rotor centres   33 ft 4 in (10·16 m)
Length overall, blades turning:
107-II, CH-113, CH/UH-46A   83 ft 4 in (25·40 m)

CH/UH-46D, CH-46F   84 ft 4 in (25·70 m)
Length of fuselage:
107-II, CH-113   44 ft 7 in (13·59 m)
CH/UH-46A, CH-46F   44 ft 10 in (13·66 m)
Width, rotors folded   14 ft 6½ in (4·42 m)
Height to top of rear rotor hub 16 ft 8½ in (5·09 m)
Wheel track   12 ft 10½ in (3·92 m)
Wheelbase   24 ft 10 in (7·57 m)
Passenger door (fwd):
Height   5 ft 3 in (1·60 m)
Width   3 ft 0 in (0·91 m)
DIMENSIONS, INTERNAL:
Cabin, excluding flight deck:
Length   24 ft 2 in (7·37 m)
Normal width   6 ft 0 in (1·83 m)
Max height   6 ft 0 in (1·83 m)
Floor area:
107-II   145 sq ft (13·47 m²)
CH/UH-46A and D, CH-46F and CH-113
(including ramp)   180 sq ft (16·72 m²)
Volume (usable):
107-II, CH-113, CH/UH-46A and D and CH-46F   865 cu ft (24·5 m³)
AREAS:
Main rotor blade (each):
107-II, CH-113, CH/UH-46A
  37·50 sq ft (3·48 m²)
CH/UH-46D, CH-46F   39·85 sq ft (3·70 m²)
Main rotor discs (total):
107-II, CH-113, CH/UH-46A
  3,925 sq ft (364·6 m²)
CH/UH-46D, CH-46F   4,086 sq ft (379·6 m²)
WEIGHTS AND LOADINGS:
Weight empty, equipped:
107-II   10,732 lb (4,868 kg)
CH-113   11,251 lb (5,104 kg)
CH/UH-46A   12,406 lb (5,627 kg)
CH/UH-46D   13,067 lb (5,927 kg)
CH-46F   13,342 lb (6,051 kg)
Mission T-O weight: CH-113 19,394 lb (8,797 kg)
Max T-O and landing weight:
107-II   19,000 lb (8,618 kg)
CH-113, CH/UH-46A   21,400 lb (9,706 kg)
CH/UH-46D, CH-46F   23,000 lb (10,433 kg)
Max disc loading:
107-II   4·84 lb/sq ft (23·60 kg/m²)
CH-113, CH/UH-46A
  5·45 lb/sq ft (26·61 kg/m²)
CH/UH-46D, CH-46F
  5·63 lb/sq ft (27·48 kg/m²)
Max power loading:
107-II   7·8 lb/shp (3·54 kg/shp)
CH-113, CH/UH-46A 8·77 lb/shp (3·98 kg/shp)
CH/UH-46D, CH-46F 8·84 lb/shp (4·00 kg/shp)
PERFORMANCE (107-II and CH/UH-46A at AUW of 19,000 lb = 8,618 kg; CH-113 at AUW of 18,700 lb = 8,482 kg; CH/UH-46D, CH-46F at AUW of 20,800 lb = 9,435 kg):
Max permissable speed:
107-II, CH-113   145 knots (168 mph; 270 km/h)
CH/UH-46A 138 knots (159 mph; 256 km/h)
CH/UH-46D, CH-46F
  144 knots (166 mph; 267 km/h)

Max cruising speed:
107-II, CH-113
    136 knots (157 mph; 253 km/h)
CH/UH-46A 135 knots (155 mph; 249 km/h)
CH/UH-46D, CH-46F
    143 knots (165 mph; 266 km/h)
Econ cruising speed:
107-II, CH-113
    125 knots (144 mph; 232 km/h)
CH/UH-46A 128 knots (147 mph; 237 km/h)
CH/UH-46D, CH-46F
    134 knots (154 mph; 248 km/h)
Max rate of climb at S/L (normal rated power):
107-II   1,440 ft (439 m)/min
CH-113   1,525 ft (465 m)/min
CH/UH-46A   1,439 ft (438·7 m)/min
CH/UH-46D, CH-46F   1,715 ft (523 m)/min
Service ceiling (normal rated power):
107-II   13,000 ft (3,960 m)
CH-113   14,000 ft (4,265 m)
CH/UH-46A   13,000 ft (3,960 m)
CH/UH-46D, CH-46F   14,000 ft (4,265 m)

Service ceiling (military power), one engine out, yaw, 248 rpm:
107-II   350 ft (107 m)
CH-113   1,200 ft (366 m)
CH/UH-46A   S/L
CH/UH-46D, CH-46F   1,050 ft (320 m)
Hovering ceiling in ground effect:
107-II   8,400 ft (2,560 m)
CH-113   9,800 ft (2,985 m)
CH/UH-46A   9,070 ft (2,765 m)
CH/UH-46D, CH-46F   9,500 ft (2,895 m)
Hovering ceiling out of ground effect:
107-II, CH-113   6,600 ft (2,012 m)
CH/UH-46A   5,600 ft (1,707 m)
CH/UH-46D, CH-46F   5,750 ft (1,753 m)
Ranges:
107-II utility with 6,600 lb (3,000 kg) payload, 10% fuel reserve
    94 nm (109 miles; 175 km)
CH-113 with 2,000 lb (907 kg) payload to hover IGE at 10,150 ft (3,090 m), 10% fuel reserve
    577 nm (665 miles; 1,070 km)

CH-113 with 5,000 lb (2,270 kg) payload to hover IGE at 13,350 ft (4,070 m), 10% fuel reserve   405 nm (467 miles; 751 km)
CH/UH-46A at AUW of 19,229 lb (8,722 kg) with 4,000 lb (1,815 kg) payload, 10% fuel reserve   199 nm (230 miles; 370 km)
CH/UH-46A at AUW of 21,400 lb (9,706 kg) with 6,070 lb (2,753 kg) payload, 10% fuel reserve   199 nm (230 miles; 370 km)
CH/UH-46D at AUW of 20,800 lb (9,435 kg) with 4,550 lb (2,064 kg) payload, 10% fuel reserve   206 nm (238 miles; 383 km)
CH/UH-46D at AUW of 23,000 lb (10,433 kg) with 6,750 lb (3,062 kg) payload, 10% fuel reserve   198 nm (228 miles; 366 km)
CH-46F at AUW of 20,800 lb (9,435 kg) with 4,275 lb (1,939 kg) payload, 10% fuel reserve   206 nm (237 miles; 381 km)
CH-46F at AUW of 23,000 lb (10,433 kg) with 6,475 lb (2,937 kg) payload, 10% fuel reserve   198 nm (228 miles; 367 km)

(1971–72)

The Viking Flying Boat Co. has acquired the rights to build the F.B.A-Schreck (French) flying-boat in the U.S.A., and this machine, with the 240 h.p. Wright "Whirlwind" engine, will be known as the Viking flying-boat.

In 1931, the Company moved into new premises on the New Haven Municipal Airport, where they are now actively engaged in the production of the Viking flying-boat, a number of which have been supplied to the U.S. Coast Guard.

THE VIKING V-2 FLYING-BOAT.

Type.—Four-seat single-engined flying-boat.

Wings.—Single-bay biplane. Modified Eiffel 359 wing-section. Centre-section carried above hull by system of struts, which also support the engine-mounting. One pair of parallel hollow spruce interplane struts on either side of hull. Wing structure consists of two routed spruce spars with the usual number of spruce and plywood ribs, the whole being covered with fabric. The leading-edge is reinforced with plywood. Ailerons of two-spar construction, covered with plywood between the spars, on upper wings only.

Hull.—Single-step, flat-bottomed type of wooden construction. Structure consists of four ash chines, an ash keel, and thirty-four poplar frames, the whole covered with plywood. Every fourth frame is a solid bulkhead and two large bulkheads provide the anchorage for the lower wing spars.

Tail Unit.—Monoplane type. Tail-plane carried on fin, which is built integral with hull, and a further fin is mounted above tail. Unbalanced rudder and elevators. The entire structure is of wood, with fabric covering, with the exception of the lower fin, which is plywood-covered as part of the hull.

Power Plant.—One 240 h.p. Wright "Whirlwind" radial air-cooled engine, on welded steel-tube mounting-ring, which is carried above the hull on streamline steel-tube "N" struts. One 48 U.S. gallons fuel tank in hull, behind rear cockpit, and one 12 U.S. gallons tank under rear seat.

Accommodation.—Tandem open cockpits, each seating two side-by-side. Dual controls in front cockpit.

Dimensions.—Span 43 ft. 3¾ in. (13.2 m.), Length 29 ft. 4¼ in. (8.9 m.), Height 10 ft. 4 in. (3.1 m.), Wing area 401.5 sq. ft. (37.3 sq. m.).

Weights and Loadings.—Weight empty 2,300 lbs. (1,044 kg.), Pilot 170 lbs. (77 kg.). Passengers 510 lbs. (231 kg.), Baggage and equipment 72 lbs. (33 kg.), Fuel and oil 398 lbs. (181 kg.), Weight loaded 3,450 lbs. (1,566 kg.), Wing loading 8.6 lbs./sq. ft. (41.7 kg./sq. m.), Power loading 14.4 lbs./h.p. (8.5 kg./h.p.).

Performance.—Maximum speed 105 m.p.h. (168 km.h.), Cruising speed 90 m.p.h. (144 km.h.), Alighting speed 46 m.p.h. (73.6 km.h.), Initial rate of climb 600 ft./min. (183 m./min.), Service ceiling 14,000 ft. (4,270 m.). (1932)

Vought A-7D tactical fighters of the USAF's 23rd Tactical Fighter Wing

VOUGHT CORSAIR II

US military designation: A-7

On 11 February 1964 the US Navy named the former LTV Aerospace Corporation winner of a design competition for a single-seat carrier-based light attack aircraft. The requirement was for a subsonic aircraft able to carry a greater load of non-nuclear weapons than the A-4E Skyhawk. To keep costs to a minimum and speed delivery it had been stipulated by the Navy that the new aircraft should be based on an existing design; the LTV design study was based, therefore, on the F-8 Crusader. An initial contract to develop and build three aircraft, under the designation A-7A, was awarded on 19 March 1964; first flight was made on 27 September 1965.

Since that time several versions of the A-7 have been evolved as Corsair IIs, for the US Navy, the USAF and the Hellenic Air Force, as follows:

A-7A. Initial attack version for the US Navy, powered by a non-afterburning Pratt & Whitney TF30-P-6 turbofan engine, rated at 50·5 kN (11,350 lb st). Delivery of 199 to the Navy was completed in Spring 1968.

A-7B. Developed version for the US Navy with non-afterburning TF30-P-8 engine, rated at 54·3 kN (12,200 lb st). Engine was modified later to TF30-P-408 configuration which provides 59·6 kN (13,400 lb st). Last of 196 was delivered to the Navy on 7 May 1969.

A-7C. Designation applied in late 1971 to the first 67 TF30-engined A-7Es (which see) to eliminate confusion with subsequent Allison-powered A-7Es.

TA-7C. Sixty-five A-7Bs and A-7Cs are being converted into tandem two-seat trainers, with operational capability, under this designation. The first of them (154477) flew for the first time on 17 December 1976. Flight refuelling capability, gun and weapon pylons retained. Configuration similar to YA-7E, but powered by the non-afterburning 54·3 kN (12,200 lb st) Pratt & Whitney TF30-P-8 engine. Entered service with VA-122 and VA-174 in 1978.

A-7D. Tactical fighter for the USAF, with a non-afterburning Allison TF41-A-1 (Spey) turbofan engine of 64·5 kN (14,500 lb st). Production of 459 was completed in December 1976.

From mid-1978, 383 A-7Ds are being modified at the USAF's Oklahoma City Air Logistics Center to carry a Martin Marietta Pave Penny laser target designation pod mounted under the air duct lip.

A-7E. Developed version for the US Navy equipped as a light attack/close air support/interdiction aircraft. First 67 aircraft (since redesignated A-7C, as indicated) powered by TF30-P-408 non-afterburning turbofan engine which provides 59·6 kN (13,400 lb st); 68th and subsequent aircraft by Allison TF41-A-2 (Spey) non-afterburning

turbofan engine, which provides 66·8 kN (15,000 lb st). First flight of an A-7E was made on 25 November 1968 and deliveries began on 14 July 1969. The A-7E entered combat service in Southeast Asia with Attack Squadrons 146 and 147 in May 1970, operating from the aircraft carrier USS *America*. During this conflict USAF and USN A-7 Corsairs of all types flew more than 100,000 combat missions. Production continues at a rate of about one a month.

In early 1977 production began of an A-7E FLIR version, called formerly TRAM (target recognition and attack multi-sensor system). This has a pod under the starboard wing to house equipment which includes a Texas Instruments FLIR sensor, and a Marconi raster-HUD cockpit display, to provide improved night capability. Deliveries of new-production FLIR-equipped A-7Es to the Navy began on 15 September 1978. Several hundred aircraft are to receive the system, mostly by retrofit.

YA-7E. Two-seat version.

A-7K. Two-seat version of the USAF's A-7D. Congress appropriated funds in FY 1979 for the first 12 of a planned procurement of 42 for service with the US Air National Guard from 1981. Basically two-seat trainers, these aircraft will retain combat capability.

Deliveries of all versions totalled 1,477 by 1 January 1979.

The following description, which applies in particular to the A-7E, is generally applicable to other versions of the A-7 except as detailed under the individual model listings:

Type: Subsonic single-seat tactical fighter.

Wings: Cantilever high-wing monoplane. Wing section NACA 65A007. Anhedral 5°. Incidence −1°. Wing sweepback at quarter-chord 35°. Outer wing sections fold upward for carrier parking, and in the A-7D and A-7H to allow best utilisation of revetments at combat airfields. All-metal multi-spar structure with integrally-stiffened aluminium alloy upper and lower skins. Plain sealed inset aluminium ailerons, outboard of wing fold, are actuated by fully-triplicated hydraulic system. Leading-edge flaps. Large single-slotted trailing-edge flaps. Spoiler above each wing forward of flaps.

Fuselage: All-metal semi-monocoque structure. Large door-type ventral speed-brake under centre-fuselage.

A-7D with Pave Penny laser target designation pod under air intake lip

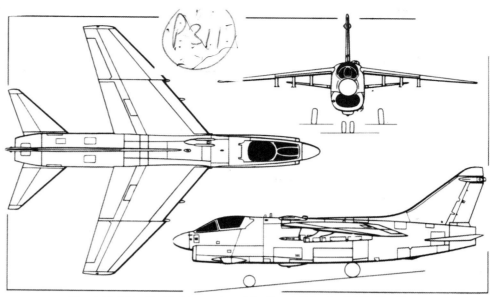

Vought A-7D tactical fighter version of the Corsair II for the USAF *(Pilot Press)*

TAIL UNIT: Large vertical fin and rudder, swept back 44·28° at quarter-chord. One-piece all-moving tailplane, swept back 45° at quarter-chord and set at dihedral angle of 5° 25'. Tailplane is operated by triplicated hydraulic systems, and the rudder powered by two systems.

LANDING GEAR: Hydraulically-retractable tricycle type, with single wheel on each main unit and twin-wheel nose unit. Main wheels retract forward into fuselage, nosewheels aft. Main wheels and tyres size 28 × 9-12; nosewheels and tyres size 22 × 5·50. Nose gear launch bar for carrier catapulting. Sting-type arrester hook under rear fuselage for carrier landings, emergency landings or aborted take-offs. Anti-skid brake system.

POWER PLANT: One Allison TF41-A-2 (Rolls-Royce Spey) non-afterburning turbofan engine, rated at 66·7 kN (15,000 lb st). The A-7E has a pneumatic starter requiring ground air supply; A-7D, A-7H and TA-7H engines have self-start capability through the medium of battery-powered electric motor that spins an air turbine starter, and the A-7K will also have this capability. The engine has self-contained ignition for start/airstart, automatic relight and selective ignition. Integral fuel tanks in wings and additional fuselage tanks. Maximum internal fuel 5,678 litres (1,500 US gallons). Maximum external fuel 4,542 litres (1,200 US gallons). The A-7D has all fuel tanks filled with polyurethane fire-suppressing foam. In the A-7E/H only the fuselage sump tank is filled with foam. Some fuselage tanks and fuel lines self-sealing. The A-7D has an alternate fuel feed system. Flight refuelling capability of first 26 A-7Ds and all A-7Es provided by a probe and drogue system; 27th and subsequent A-7Ds have (and A-7K will have) boom receptacle above fuselage on port side in line with wing leading-edge. The A-7H and TA-7H do not have an air refuelling capability. Boron carbide (HFC) engine armour.

ACCOMMODATION: Pilot on McDonnell Douglas Escapac rocket-powered ejection system, complete with USAF life support system on the A-7D, and a USN life support system on the A-7A/B/C/E/H. Escape system provides a fully-inflated parachute three seconds after sequence initiation; positive seat/man separation and stabilisation of the ejected seat and pilot. Boron carbide (HFC) cockpit armour.

SYSTEMS: Triple-redundant hydraulic system for flight controls; double-redundant system for flaps, brakes and landing gear retraction. Liquid oxygen system. An air-conditioning unit using engine bleed air provides pressurisation and cooling for the cockpit and cooling for certain electronics components. Automatic flight control system provides control-stick steering, altitude hold, heading hold, heading pre-select and attitude hold, which is coupled for automatic carrier landings. Ram-air turbine provides hydraulic pressure and electrical power down to airspeeds below those used in normal landing approaches.

AVIONICS AND EQUIPMENT: The navigation/weapon delivery system is the heart of the A-7D/E/H light attack aircraft. It performs continuously the computations needed for greatly increased delivery accuracy, and for manoeuvring freedom during navigation to a target and the attack, weapon release, pull up, and safe return phases of the mission. The system not only provides the pilot with a number of options during navigation and weapon delivery, but also relieves him of much of his work load. The AN/ASN-91(V) navigation/weapon delivery computer is the primary element of the system, in constant 'conversation' with basic electronic sensors, and computes and displays continuously present position, using computed position and stored data to calculate navigation and weapon delivery solutions, and monitors the reliability of data inputs and outputs. An AN/ASN-90(V) inertial measurement set is the basic three-axis reference system for navigation and weapon delivery. AN/APN-190(V) Doppler measures groundspeed and drift angle. AN/APQ-126(V) forward-looking radar provides the pilot with ten modes of operation: air-to-ground ranging; terrain following; terrain avoidance; ground mapping, shaped beam; ground mapping, pencil beam; beacon; cross-scan terrain avoidance; cross-scan ground mapping, pencil; TV; and SIDS. An AN/AVQ-7(V) HUD receives and displays computed attack, navigation and landing data from the tactical computer; aircraft performance data from flight sensors: and discrete signals from various aircraft systems. CP-953A/AJQ air data computer is a solid-state servomechanical analogue computer which measures and computes continuously required altitude and airspeed information. The Armament Station Control unit integrates and controls the weapon release system; it supplies electrical signals to arm and release or jettison external stores; controls and fires the Vulcan cannon; furnishes store-type information to the tactical computer; supplies weapon status information to the pilot; determines weapon release according to priority of stations; and determines compatibility of selected release mode with the stores on selected stations. Standard aeronautical charts reproduced on 35 mm film in full colour are stored in an AN/ASN-99 Projected Map Display Set which, as a subsystem of the tactical computer, provides a continuous display of the aircraft's geographical position. Other avionics include AN/ASN-54 approach power compensator; AN/ASW-30 AFCS; ARA-63 ACLS; dual AN/ARC-159 UHF com; AN/ARN-84 Tacan; AN/APX-72 IFF transponder; AN/AN-154 radar beacon; AN/ASW-25 data link; AN/ARA-50 ADF; and AN/AIC-25 audio system. ECM equipment includes ALR-45/50 internal homing and warning systems; ALQ-126 active ECM; chaff/flare dispensers; and external pod-mounted systems compatible with the aircraft's internal sytems.

ARMAMENT: A wide range of stores, to a total weight of more than 6,805 kg (15,000 lb), can be carried on six underwing pylons and two fuselage weapon stations, the latter suitable for Sidewinder air-to-air missiles. Two outboard pylons on each wing can each accommodate a load of 1,587 kg (3,500 lb). Inboard pylon on each wing can carry 1,134 kg (2,500 lb). Two fuselage weapon stations, one on each side, can each carry load of 227 kg (500 lb). Weapons carried include air-to-air and air-to-ground (anti-tank and anti-radar missiles); electro-optical (TV) and laser guided weapons; general-purpose bombs; bomblet dispensers; rockets; gun pods; Pave Penny AN/AAS-35 laser target designation pod (A-7D); and auxiliary fuel tanks. In addition, an M61A-1 Vulcan 20 mm cannon is mounted in the port side of the fuselage. This has 1,000-round ammunition storage and selected firing rates of 4,000 or 6,000 rds/min. Strike camera in lower rear fuselage for damage assessment.

DIMENSIONS, EXTERNAL:
Wing span	11·80 m (38 ft 9 in)
Width, wings folded	7·24 m (23 ft 9 in)
Wing chord at root	4·72 m (15 ft 6 in)
Wing chord at tip	1·18 m (3 ft 10¼ in)
Wing aspect ratio	4
Length overall	14·06 m (46 ft 1½ in)
Height overall	4·90 m (16 ft 0¾ in)
Tailplane span	5·52 m (18 ft 1½ in)
Wheel track	2·90 m (9 ft 6 in)

AREAS:
Wings, gross	34·83 m² (375 sq ft)
Ailerons (total)	1·85 m² (19·94 sq ft)
Trailing-edge flaps (total)	4·04 m² (43·48 sq ft)
Leading-edge flaps (total)	4·53 m² (48·74 sq ft)
Spoiler	0·43 m² (4·60 sq ft)
Deflector	0·32 m² (3·44 sq ft)
Fin	10·33 m² (111·20 sq ft)
Rudder	1·40 m² (15·04 sq ft)
Horizontal tail surfaces	5·24 m² (56·39 sq ft)
Speed-brake	2·32 m² (25·00 sq ft)

WEIGHTS:
Weight empty	8,668 kg (19,111 lb)
Max T-O weight	19,050 kg (42,000 lb)

Vought TA-7C tandem two-seat trainer of US Navy Squadron VA-122

Vought A-7E Corsair II close air support/interdiction aircraft of the US Navy

PERFORMANCE:
  Max level speed at S/L
          600 knots (1,112 km/h; 691 mph)
  Max level speed at 1,525 m (5,000 ft):
    with 12 Mk 82 bombs
          562 knots (1,040 km/h; 646 mph)
    after dropping bombs
          595 knots (1,102 km/h; 685 mph)
  Sustained manoeuvring performance at 1,525 m (5,000
    ft), at AUW of 13,047 kg (28,765 lb) with 6 pylons
    and 2 Sidewinder missiles
      1,770 m (5,800 ft) turning radius at 4g and
          500 knots (925 km/h; 575 mph)
  T-O run at max T-O weight   1,830 m (6,000 ft)
  Ferry range:
    max internal fuel
            1,981 nm (3,671 km; 2,281 miles)
    max internal and external fuel
            2,485 nm (4,604 km; 2,861 miles)
                                              (1979–80)

VOUGHT CRUSADER
US Navy designation: F-8

Chance Vought (now Vought Aeronautics Company division of LTV Aerospace Corp) was given a development contract for the F-8 in May 1953 after winning a design competition in which eight airframe manufacturers had participated. The prototype XF-8A Crusader flew for the first time on 25 March 1955, exceeding the speed of sound in level flight. The first production F-8A flew on 20 September 1955, and this version began reaching US Naval operational squadrons in March 1957.

On 21 August 1956 an F-8A set up the first US national speed record of over 1,000 mph (1,600 km/h). Operating under restrictions, it recorded a speed of 1,015·428 mph (1,634·17 km/h) On 16 July 1957 an RF-8A photo-reconnaissance version of the Crusader set up the first supersonic US trans-continental record by flying the 2,445·9 miles (3,936 km) from Los Angeles to New York in 3 hr 22 min 50 sec, at an average speed of 723·52 mph (1,164·39 km/h).

An outstanding feature of the F-8 is its two-position variable-incidence wing. This provides a high angle of attack for take-off and landing, while permitting the fuselage to remain almost parallel to a flight deck or runway for good pilot visibility.

A total of 1,259 production aircraft followed, made up of 318 F-8As, 130 F-8Bs, 187 F-8Cs, 152 F-8Ds, 286 F-8Es, 42 F-8E(FN)s and 144 RF-8As. Production ended in 1965, but subsequent modification programmes involved the remanufacture of a total of 446 aircraft, including 61 F-8Bs redesignated F-8L, 87 F-8Cs into F-8Ks, 89 F-8Ds into F-8Hs, 136 F-8Es into F-8Js and 73 RF-8As into RF-8Gs. Details of all these versions can be found in the 1970-71 Jane's. By July 1970 they had amassed a total of more than two million flying hours.

The following versions of the F-8 have been produced:

XF-8A (formerly XF8U-1). Prototype with Pratt & Whitney J57-P-12 turbojet (approx 16,000 lb=7,257 kg st with afterburning).

F-8A (formerly F8U-1). First production version, initially with J57-P-12 turbojet, later aircraft with J57-P-4A (16,200 lb=7,327 kg st with afterburning). Armed with four 20 mm cannon in nose, belly pack of 32 × 2·75-in folding-fin rockets and two Sidewinders on sides of fuselage. AN/APG-30 gunsight-ranging radar. Phased out of production in 1958. Total of 318 built. Designation now changed to **TF-8A**.

Chance Vought RF-8A Crusader on U.S.S. *Independence* (*Flight International*)

Late production Chance Vought F-8E Crusader with bulged top fuselage

F-8B (formerly F8U-1E). Followed F-8A in production from September 1958, with larger nose radome containing AN/APS-67 radar for limited all-weather capability. J57-P-4A turbojet. First flew on 3 September 1958. Total of 130 built. See also F-8L.

RF-8A (formerly F8U-1P). Reconnaissance version of -8A which flew for first time on 17 December 1956. Fitted with three CAX-12 trimetrogon cameras and two K-17 vertical cameras in place of cannon and fire-control equipment. Capable of special mapping and charting missions, and night reconnaissance, using internally-stowed photoflash bombs. Fuselage undersurface squared around camera bay. J57-P-4A engine. 144 built. Used extensively for surveillance duties over Cuba in 1962-63. A total of 53 were modified to RF-8G standard in 1965-66. Twenty more modified later.

NTF-8A (formerly F8U-1T). The 74th F-8A was converted into a two-seat fighter-trainer under a US Navy contract. It has a J57-P-20 engine, and ventral fins and afterburner airscoops as on the F-8C. An armament of two 20 mm guns and two Sidewinder missiles is retained, enabling this version to serve as an advanced weapons trainer, with full operational capability. Equipment offered on the NTF-8A includes a flying boom flight refuelling receptacle and a brake-chute to reduce landing distance to 2,700 ft (823 m). The NTF-8A flew for the first time on 6 February 1962.

F-8C (formerly F8U-2). Improved version of F-8A with J57-P-16 turbojet (16,900 lb=7,665 kg st with afterburning), giving higher performance, particularly at altitude. F-8C has improved fire control system and additional radar capabilities. Its armament is the same as that of the F-8A, except that it can carry four Sidewinders, in pairs on each side of the fuselage. Externally the two types are similar, except that the F-8C has two fixed ventral fins under the tail section and two afterburner air-scoops mounted on the tail-cone above the tailplane. First prototype, flown in December 1957, had the new engine only. Second prototype, flown in January 1958, was representative of production aircraft, the first of which flew for the first time on 20 August 1958. First production F-8C delivered to the US Navy on 28 January 1959. First operational squadron (VF-84) formed on 4 April 1959. The 187th and last F-8C was delivered on 20 September 1960. See also F-8K.

F-8D (formerly F8U-2N). Limited all-weather interceptor, capable of speeds approaching Mach 2, for service with US Navy and Marine Corps squadrons. Powered by J57-P-20 turbojet (18,000 lb=8,165 kg st with afterburning). Push-button controls, incorporated in a Vought-developed autopilot, perform many of the pilot's routine tasks such as holding an altitude, holding a heading, selecting a new heading or orbiting over a selected point. F-8D also has improved AN/APQ-83 radar, a later type of Martin-Baker ejection seat, revised internal instrumentation and additional internal fuel capacity, extending its endurance to more than three hours without refuelling. It carries four Sidewinder missiles, in pairs on the sides of its fuselage, in addition to the normal fixed armament of four 20 mm guns. Belly rocket pack deleted. First F-8D flew for the first time on 16 February 1960 and the first production model was delivered to the US Navy on 1 June 1960. Deliveries were completed in January 1962. Total of 152 built. See also F-8H.

F-8E (formerly F8U-2NE). Similar to F-8D, but with higher-performance APQ-94 search and fire-control radar. Nose section more rounded back to cockpit, to accommodate larger radar dish. Improved air duct recovery made possible by rounded shape. AN/AAS-15 infra-red scanner for use with the four Sidewinder air-to-air missiles is mounted above the nose forward of the windshield. The prototype F-8E, a conversion of the second F-8D, flew for the first time on 30 June 1961, followed by the first production F-8E in September 1961. More than 250 built by beginning of 1964. Production has been completed.

In 1962 an F-8E was fitted with two underwing pylons to carry a wide variety of bombs and missiles, to test its suitability for attack duties, as well as interception. Loads carried on these pylons included twelve 250 lb bombs, four 500 lb bombs, two 1,000 lb bombs, two 2,000 lb bombs, or 24 Zuni rockets. Eight more Zunis can replace the four standard Sidewinder missiles on fuselage-side pylons. As a result of the success of these trials, which included a week of deck trials on board the USS *Forrestal* in mid-1963, late-model F-8E's (identified by a bulged top fuselage) were equipped with underwing pylons to carry the full range of attack weapons. The trials aircraft was catapult-launched at an AUW of 34,000 lb (15,420 kg), with full fuel, two 2,000 lb bombs and eight Zunis. See also F-8J.

RF-8G. Under a US Navy contract, Vought Aeronautics overhauled and modernised 53 RF-8A photographic-reconnaissance Crusaders to expand their capabilities and extend their service life. Ventral fins and a strengthened wing were fitted, together with fuselage structural reinforcements, a Doppler navigation system and new camera station installations. The modification programme extended through 1965-66, the aircraft being redesignated RF-8G on completion. In 1967 a new contract was negotiated for an additional twenty aircraft, and this programme was scheduled for completion in January 1970.

F-8H. Modernised and remanufactured F-8D, with new extended-service-life wing, addition of attack capabilities identical to those of F-8E/F-8J aircraft, strengthened nose and main landing gear providing an increased carrier landing weight capability, strengthened arresting gear, armament system improvements involving improved fire control computer, expanded missile acquisition envelope and large APQ-94 radar scope. First of 89 F-8H's flew on 17 July 1967.

F-8J. Modified and remanufactured F-8E, incorporating boundary layer control, leading-edge double droops, and larger horizontal tail surfaces for lower landing and catapulting speeds. APQ-124 MAGDARR radar and expanded missile acquisition envelope are added, to provide improvements to the Fire Control System. The F-8J has a new longer-service-life wing identical to that of the F-8H, but also has provision for wing-mounted fuel tanks. The new strengthened landing gear and arresting gear increase carrier landing weight capability. First of 136 F-8J's flew on 31 January 1968.

F-8K. Eighty-seven F-8C's have been modernised and remanufactured with new extended service life wing, wing stores provisions, strengthened fuselage, new nose landing gear, improved lighting and new wiring. This programme was scheduled for completion in the Autumn of 1969.

F-8L. Sixty-three F-8B's have been remanufactured with changes similar to those incorporated in the F-8K's. This programme was scheduled for completion in January 1970.

A total of 375 aircraft have been modernised under the F-8H/J/K/L programme, in the period 1966-70.

The following details apply basically to all versions of the F-8, except for differences detailed above.

Vought F-8J Crusader, a remanufactured F-8E with new wings featuring BLC and double leading-edge droops

TYPE: Supersonic single-seat carrier fighter.

WINGS: Cantilever high-wing monoplane. Thin laminar-flow section. Anhedral 5°. Sweepback 35°. Wing is adjustable to two incidence positions by a hydraulic self-locking actuator. When wing is raised, the ailerons, the flaps and the "dog-tooth" leading-edge are all drooped automatically. Outer wing sections fold upward for carrier stowage. All-metal multi-spar structure with integrally-stiffened aluminium alloy upper and lower skins. Inset aluminium ailerons, inboard of wing fold, are actuated by fully-duplicated hydraulic system and function also as flaps. Small magnesium alloy trailing-edge flaps.

FUSELAGE: All-metal structure in three main assemblies. Both magnesium alloy and titanium are used in the structure, the after section and a portion of the mid-section being of titanium. Ventral speed-brake under centre-fuselage.

TAIL UNIT: Large swept vertical fin and rudder and one-piece horizontal "slab" tail. Tailplane and rudder are actuated by fully-duplicated hydraulic systems.

LANDING GEAR: Hydraulically-retractable tricycle type. Main wheels retract forward into fuselage, nose-wheel aft. Sting-type arrester hook under rear fuselage.

POWER PLANT: One Pratt & Whitney J57 turbojet engine with afterburner. Integral fuel tanks in wings inboard of wing fold. Other tankage in fuselage. Total internal fuel capacity approx 1,165 Imp gallons (5,300 litres). Provision for in-flight refuelling, with retractable probe housed in removable pack on port side of fuselage of F-8A and inside flush panel on RF-8A.

ACCOMMODATION: Pilot on Martin-Baker Mk F7 lightweight ejection seat in pressurised cockpit. Liquid oxygen equipment.

ARMAMENT: Four 20 mm Colt cannon in fuselage nose, with 84 rpg (average) for F-8C/K, F-8H and F-8E/J, and 144 rpg for NTF-8A and F-8F/L. Two Sidewinder missiles (four in F-8C/K, F-8D/H and F-8E/J) mounted externally on sides of fuselage.

DIMENSIONS, EXTERNAL:

Wing span	35 ft 8 in (10·87 m)
Length overall:	
Except F-8E/J	54 ft 3 in (16·54 m)
F-8E/J	54 ft 6 in (16·61 m)
Height overall	15 ft 9 in (4·80 m)
Width folded	22 ft 6 in (6·86 m)
Tailplane span:	
except F-8E(FN), F-8J	18 ft 2 in (5·54 m)
F-8E(FN), F-8J	19 ft 3½ in (5·88 m)
Wheel track	9 ft 8 in (2·94 m)

AREA:

Wings, gross	375 sq ft (34·84 m²)

WEIGHT:

Normal T-O weight:	
F-8C	27,550 lb (12,500 kg)
Max T-O weight: F-8E/J	34,000 lb (15,420 kg)

PERFORMANCE:

Max level speed:		
F-8A and F-8C		
	over 868 knots (1,000 mph; 1,600 km/h)	
F-8D, E		nearly Mach 2
Combat radius:		
F-8A	521 nm (600 miles; 965 km)	

(1970–71)

THE VOUGHT O2U "CORSAIR."

TYPE.—Two-seat Naval land, sea or amphibian shipboard fighter biplane.

WINGS.—Equal-span biplane, with back-swept top plane and straight bottom plane. Top wing in three sections, bottom wing in two sections, attached directly to bottom fuselage longerons. Centre-section carried on splayed-out struts, with one set of "N" type interplane struts on either side. Wing construction consists of deep spruce spars routed out to "I" section and spruce and plywood ribs, the whole being fabric-covered. Narrow chord ailerons fitted to all four planes. Wide sidewalks provided at roots of bottom planes and hand-grips at wing-tips.

FUSELAGE.—Welded chrome-molybdenum steel-tube structure. Metal cowled from nose to rear cockpit and fabric-covered over streamline formers, thence to tail.

TAIL UNIT.—Normal type. Welded steel-tube framed, covered with fabric. Balanced rudder. Adjustable tail-plane.

UNDERCARRIAGE.—Split type. Consists of two Vees, the front legs of which incorporate oleo-spring shock-absorbing units, and two half-axles hinged to a small inverted cabane under fuselage. Bendix wheel-brakes at option. Land type tail-skid, of steerable type. Interchangeable with land undercarriage is one single central float and two wing-tip floats, specially designed for catapult and rough water use. Central float and wing-tip floats of steel and duralumin construction. Built-in nose bumper provided on main float. Amphibian gear can be attached to central float, with two skids on wing-tip floats and tail-skid attached to tail of central float.

POWER PLANT.—One 425 h.p. Pratt & Whitney "Wasp" air-cooled radial engine. Provision made for addition of Root's blower and "hot-spot" heater for high altitude work. Engine nose cowling provided with adjustable shutters to control air-blast on cylinders and crankcase under varying operating conditions. Engine-mounting of welded steel-tubes, quickly removable. Main fuel

The Vought "Corsair" Two-seat Naval Reconnaissance Biplane (425 h.p. Pratt & Whitney "Wasp" engine).

tanks, of 90 U.S. gallons (75 Imp. galls. = 340 litres) capacity, built into side of fuselage fairing. Oil tank, of 6½ U.S. gallons (5½ Imp. galls. = 24 litres) capacity, behind engine. Standard Steel metal airscrew.

ACCOMMODATION.—Tandem cockpits, the front pilot's cockpit being under cut-out in centre-section. Armament consists of two fixed Browning guns mounted in the top centre-section and twin Lewis guns on a flexible mounting over the rear cockpit. Bottom wings provided with internal supports for bomb-racks. Full provision is made in rear cockpit for installation of wireless receiving and sending equipment. Dual control fitted, with rear cockpit stick removable. Adjustable rudder bar in front cockpit adjustable. Grease-gun lubrication to all control connections. Hand fire-extinguisher fitted in each cockpit and large capacity pressure fire-extinguisher in engine compartment operated by remote control from either cockpit.

DIMENSIONS.—Span 34 ft. 6 in. (10.51 m.), Length (landplane) 24 ft. 8 in. (7.52 m.), Length (seaplane) 28 ft. 6 in. (8.68 m.), Height (landplane) 10 ft. ½ in. (3.06 m.), Height (seaplane) 11 ft. 5 in. (3.48 m.).

PERFORMANCE (landplane).—Maximum speed 151 m.p.h. (243 km.h.), Landing speed 48 m.p.h. (77 km.h.), Initial rate of climb 2,100 ft./min. (640 m./min.), Climb in 10 mins. 13,900 ft. (4.234 m.), Service ceiling 22,500 ft. (6,855 m.), Absolute ceiling 24,500 ft. (7,465 m.), Range at cruising speed 580 miles (935 km.), (seaplane) Maximum speed 147 m.p.h. (237 km.h.), Landing speed 50 m.p.h. (80 km.h.), Initial rate of climb 1,900 ft./min. (579 m./min.), Climb in 10 mins. 12,000 ft. (3,656 m.), Service ceiling 21,000 ft. (6,398 m.), Absolute ceiling 22,900 ft. (6,977 m.), Range at cruising speed 520 miles (840 km.).

The Vought "Corsair" Amphibian (425 h.p. Pratt & Whitney "Wasp" engine).

(1929)

The Vought O3U-1 "Corsair" Two-seat Observation Bipane (450 h.p. Pratt & Whitney "Wasp" engine).

THE VOUGHT O3U-1 "CORSAIR."

TYPE.—Two-seat shipboard bomber or observation biplane.

WINGS.—Equal-span biplane, with back-swept top plane and straight bottom plane. Top wing in three sections, bottom wing in two sections, attached directly to bottom fuselage longerons. Centre-section carried on splayed-out struts, with one set of "N" type interplane struts on either side. Wing construction consists of deep spruce spars routed out to "I" section and spruce and plywood ribs, the whole being fabric-covered. The centre-section spars are of the box type. Narrow-chord ailerons fitted to all four wings. Sidewalks provided at roots and along front spars of bottom wings to struts.

FUSELAGE.—Welded chrome-molybdenum steel-tube structure. Metal cowled from nose to rear cockpit and fabric-covered over streamline formers, thence to tail.

TAIL UNIT.—Normal type. Welded steel-tube framed, covered with fabric. Balanced rudder. Adjustable tail-plane.

UNDERCARRIAGE.—Split type. Consists of two Vees, the front legs of which incorporate oleo-spring shock-absorbing units, and two half-axles hinged to a small inverted cabane under fuselage. Mechanically-operated wheel-brakes provided with pedals so arranged as not to be under pilot's fee in normal flying or landing position. Land type tail-skid, of s..erable type. Interchangeable with land undercarriage are one single central float and two wing-tip floats, specially designed for catapult and rough water use. Central float and wing-tip floats of steel and duralumin construction. Built-in nose bumper provided on main float.

Amphibian gear can be attached to central float, with two skids on wing-tip floats and tail-skid attached to tail of central float.

POWER PLANT.—One 450 h.p. Pratt & Whitney "Wasp C" air-cooled radial engine. Engine nose cowling provided with adjustable shutters to control air-blast on cylinders and crankcase under varying operating conditions. Engine-mounting of welded steel tubes, quickly removable. Main fuel tanks, of 110 U.S. gallons capacity built into side of fuselage fairing. Oil tank, of 8 U.S. gallons capacity, behind engine. Standard Steel metal airscrew.

ACCOMMODATION.—Tandem cockpits, the front pilot's cockpit being under cut-out in centre-section. Armament consists of one fixed gun and one gun on a flexible mounting over the rear cockpit. Bottom wings provided with internal supports for bomb-racks. Full provision is made in rear cockpit for installation of wireless receiving and sending equipment. Dual control fitted, with rear cockpit stick removable. Adjustable rudder bar in front cockpit adjustable. Grease-gun lubrication to all control connections. Hand fire-extinguisher fitted in each cockpit and large capacity pressure fire-extinguisher in engine compartment operated by remote control from either cockpit.

DIMENSIONS.—Span 36 ft. (10.9 m.), Length 25 ft. 1 in. (7.64 m.), Height 10 ft. ½ in. (3.06 m.), Wing area 318.5 sq. ft. (29.6 sq. m.).

PERFORMANCE.—Maximum speed 138 m.p.h. (220.8 km.h.), Minimum speed 59.4 m.p.h. (95 km.h.), Initial rate of climb 810 ft./min. (247 m./min.), Service ceiling 16,200 ft. (4,940 m.). (1932)

THE VOUGHT "CORSAIR" SU-1 AND SU-2.

Several modifications of the "Corsair" have been in production during the past twelve months. These include three types of the SU series of Navy scouts, all powered with the 600 h.p. Pratt & Whitney "Hornet" engine.

TYPE.—Two-seat shipboard observation biplane.

WINGS.—Equal-span biplane, with back-swept top plane and straight bottom plane. Top wing in three sections, bottom wing in two sections, attached directly to bottom fuselage longerons. Centre-section carried on splayed-out struts, with one set of "N" type interplane struts on either side. Wing construction consists of deep spruce spars routed out to "I" section and plywood ribs, the whole being fabric-covered. The centre-section spars are of the box type. Balanced ailerons fitted to all four wings.

FUSELAGE.—Welded chrome-molybdenum steel-tube structure. Metal cowled from nose to rear cockpit and fabric-covered over streamline formers, thence to tail.

TAIL UNIT.—Normal type. Welded steel-tube framed, covered with fabric. Balanced rudder. Adjustable tail-plane.

UNDERCARRIAGE.—Cross-axle Vee type, with heavy-duty oleo shock-absorbers designed for severe carrier landings. Bendix wheels and internal brakes, individually operated. Swivelling oleo tail-wheel restrained to trail aft in the air and lockable thus from pilot's cockpit.

POWER PLANT.—One 600 h.p. Pratt & Whitney "Hornet" air-cooled radial engine, with low-drag cowling ring and adjustable nose shutters to control air-blast on cylinders and crankcase under varying operating conditions. Engine-mounting of welded steel tubes, quickly removable. Main fuel tanks, of 130 U.S. gallons capacity, built into side of fuselage fairing. Oil tank, of 8 U.S. gallons capacity, behind engine. Hamilton-Standard metal airscrew.

ACCOMMODATION.—Tandem cockpits, the front pilot's cockpit under cut-out in centre-section. Dual control fitted, with rear cockpit stick removable.

ARMAMENT.—One fixed gun in centre-section, firing outside airscrew, and one gun on a flexible mounting over the rear cockpit. Bottom wings provided with internal supports for bomb-racks. Full provision is made in rear cockpit for installation of wireless receiving and sending equipment.

DIMENSIONS.—Span 36 ft. (10.9 m.), Length 27 ft. 3 in. (8.32 m.), Height 10 ft. 8 in. (3.29 m.), Wing area 325.6 sq. ft. (30.25 sq. m.).

PERFORMANCE.—Maximum speed 170.5 m.p.h. (2.74 km.h.), Minimum speed 60 m.p.h. (96.5 km.h.), Service ceiling 20,500 ft. (6,250 m.).

The Vought "Corsair" Model SU-2 Biplane (600 h.p. Pratt & Whitney "Hornet" engine).

The Vought "Corsair" SU-4 Two-seat Observation Biplane (600 h.p. Pratt & Whitney "Hornet" engine).

THE VOUGHT "CORSAIR" SU-4.

TYPE.—Two-seat shipboard observation biplane.

WINGS.—Equal-span biplane, with back-swept top plane and straight bottom plane. Top wing in three sections, bottom wing in two sections, attached directly to bottom fuselage longerons. Centre-section carried on splayed-out struts, with one set of "N" type interplane struts on either side. Wing construction consists of deep spruce spars routed out to "I" section and spruce and plywood ribs, the whole being fabric-covered. The centre-section spars are of the box type. Balanced ailerons fitted to all four wings.

FUSELAGE.—Welded chrome-molybdenum steel-tube structure. Metal cowled from nose to rear cockpit and fabric-covered over streamline formers, thence to tail.

TAIL UNIT.—Normal type. Welded steel-tube framed, covered with fabric. Balanced rudder. Adjustable tail-plane.

UNDERCARRIAGE.—Cross-axle Vee type, with heavy-duty oleo shock-absorbers designed for severe carrier landings. Bendix wheels and internal brakes, individually operated. Swivelling oleo tail-wheel restrained to trail aft in the air and lockable thus from pilot's cockpit.

POWER PLANT.—One 600 h.p. Pratt & Whitney "Hornet" air-cooled radial engine, with low-drag cowling ring and adjustable nose shutters to control air-blast on cylinders and crankcase under varying operating conditions. Engine-mounting of welded steel tubes, quickly removable. Main fuel tanks, of 130 U.S. gallons capacity, built into side of fuselage fairing. Oil tank, of 8 U.S. gallons capacity, behind engine. Hamilton-Standard metal airscrew.

ACCOMMODATION.—Tandem cockpits, the front pilot's cockpit under cut-out in centre-section. Dual control fitted, with rear cockpit stick removable.

ARMAMENT.—One fixed gun in centre-section, firing outside airscrew, and one gun on a flexible mounting over the rear cockpit. Bottom wings provided with internal supports for bomb-racks. Full provision is made in rear cockpit for installation of wireless receiving and sending equipment.

DIMENSIONS.—Span 36 ft. (10.9 m.), Length 27 ft. 3 in. (8.32 m.), Height 10 ft. 8 in. (3.29 m.), Wing area 325.6 sq. ft. (30.25 sq. m.).

(1934)

THE VOUGHT-SIKORSKY SBU

The Model SBU-1 is a two-seat Scout-Bomber biplane fitted with a 700 h.p. Pratt & Whitney R-1535-80 geared engine, the new N.A.C.A. "flapped" cowling, developed by United Aircraft, and a two-bladed Hamilton-Standard controllable-pitch airscrew. It is of all-metal construction, except for the covering of the wings, fuselage and movable rail surfaces, has tapered wings and is equipped with split landing flaps under the lower wings.

The SBU-1 has been designed to combine the duties of scouting and bombing, hitherto fulfilled by two distinct types of aircraft.

DIMENSIONS. Wing span 33 ft 3 in (10.13 m), Length 27 ft 10 in (8.48 m), Height 11 ft 11 in (3.63 m), Weight loaded 5,520 lb (2,504 kg), Maximum speed 205 mph (330 km/h), Range 545 miles (877 km), Armament two 0.30-in guns, plus bombs.

After 84 SBU-1, 40 SBU-2s followed with R-1535–98 engines.

The Vought-Sikorsky SBU-2 Two-seat Scout-Bomber Biplane (700 h.p. Pratt & Whitney "Twin-Wasp Junior" engine).
(1940)

The Vought-Sikorsky SB2U-1 Two-seat Scout-Bomber Monoplane (700 h.p. Pratt & Whitney "Twin-Wasp Junior" engine).

THE VOUGHT-SIKORSKY "VINDICATOR" SB2U-1.

The Model SB2U-1 is a low-wing Scout-Bomber monoplane, fitted with a 750 h.p. Pratt & Whitney "Twin-Wasp Junior" engine and Hamilton-Standard constant-speed airscrew.

Its structure is of metal, with fabric covering on the movable tail-surfaces and on the after portions of wing and fuselage. The landing gear is retractable, each half of which is arranged to twist during retraction so that the wheels lie flat in recesses in the wing. Night-flying equipment and deck-landing arrester gear are provided.

A considerable number of machines of this type are in use by the U.S. Navy.

THE VOUGHT-SIKORSKY "CORSAIR" SB2U-2.

The Model SB2U-2 is an improved version of the SB2U-1, a number of which are now in service with the U.S. Navy. The power plant, areas and dimensions are the same as for the SB2U-1.
(1939)

The Vought-Sikorsky SB2U-3 "Vindicator" III Scout-Bomber (Pratt & Whitney "Twin-Wasp Junior" engine).

THE VOUGHT-SIKORSKY SB2U-3 "VINDICATOR" III

The Model SB2U-3 is a low-wing Scout-Bomber monoplane, fitted with a 825 h.p. Pratt & Whitney R-1535-02 "Twin-Wasp Junior" engine and Hamilton-Standard constant-speed airscrew.

Its structure is of metal, with fabric covering on the movable tail-surfaces and on the after portions of wing and fuselage. The landing gear is retractable, each half of which is arranged to twist during retraction so that the wheels lie flat in recesses in the wing. Night-flying equipment and deck-landing arrester gear are provided.

Further details and performance data are not yet released for publication.

A considerable number of machines of this type is in use by the U.S. Navy.

Wing span 42 ft 0 in (12.80m). Length 34 ft 0 in (10.36m). Height 10 ft 3 in (3.12m). Weight loaded 9,420 lb (4,273 kg). Maximum speed 243 mph (341 km/h). Range 1,120 miles (1,802 km). Armament two 0.50-in guns plus bombs. (1941)

THE VOUGHT UO-1.

The Vought UO-1 was first produced in 1923, as a Naval Aviation Spotting and Observation Plane, and since then it has been the exclusive equipment for this class of work on the U.S. Navy catapult-equipped battleships and scout cruisers, as well as Navy land bases and on the aircraft-carrier "Langley."

It is fitted with the 200 h.p. Wright "Whirlwind" engine, and is quickly convertible from a landplane to a seaplane.

Specification.

Span	..	..	..	34 ft. 1 in. (10.3 m.).
Length	..	..	..	24 ft. 2 in. (7.4 m.).
Weight empty		..	..	1,419 lbs. (644 kgs.).
Weight loaded		..	..	2,330 lbs. (1,060 kgs.).
Speed, max.	..	..	..	122 m.p.h. (197 km.p.h.).
Speed, min.	..	..	..	53 m.p.h. (65 km.p.h.).
Climb to 8,800 ft. (2,680 m.)..				10 mins.
Ceiling ..	..	..	..	18,200 ft. (5,500 m.).

THE VOUGHT UO-3.

The UO-3 is somewhat similar to the UO-1 in general design and arrangement, but has been adapted for a single-seater observation-fighter.

Specification.

Span	..	..	..	35 ft. 6 in.
Length		..	..	24 ft.
Height ..		..	..	9 ft.
Chord ..		..	..	5 ft. 8 in.
Gap	..	..	..	6 ft.
Speed at 15,000 ft.		..	..	153 m.p.h.
Climb to 21,000 ft.		..	..	20 mins.
Service ceiling		..	..	28,000 ft.
Absolute ceiling		..	..	31,000 ft.
Endurance		..	..	3.75 hours. (1927)

THE VOUGHT UO-4.

The Vought UO-4 was designed and built during 1926 for the newly created U.S. Coast Guard Air Service. These aircraft were the initial aircraft purchased by the Coast Guard under its first appropriation, although several standard UO-1 seaplanes, which had been borrowed from the Navy, had been in use for over two years. These aircraft, equipped with single-float landing gear, will be used on patrol duty against smugglers of liquor, narcotics, etc.

THE VOUGHT FU-1.

The principal production of the Vought plant during 1926 was the new FU-1, a single-seat Naval seaplane-fighter, for catapulting, and designed particularly for high performance at altitudes. The FU-1 is fitted with the Wright "Whirlwind" engine and is the first production type plane in which a supercharger has been used in conjunction with an air-cooled engine. It is similar in general lines to the UO-1, but is equipped with a high-lift wing-section, electric engine-starter, additional armament and other interesting features.

The Vought UO-4 (200 h.p. Wright "Whirlwind" engine) used by the U.S. Coast Guard.

TYPE.—Single-seat Naval high-altitude convertible land or sea fighter biplane.

WINGS.—Equal-span, staggered two-bay biplane. Wing-section is Navy N-9, a medium-thickness, high-lift section. Centre-section carried on slightly splayed-out struts. Ailerons fitted to all four planes.

FUSELAGE.—Welded steel-tube structure, faired to a circular form and covered with fabric. Specially reinforced for launching from Navy type catapults.

TAIL UNIT.—Normal type. Welded steel-tube framed, covered with fabric. Adjustable tail-plane.

UNDERCARRIAGE.—Cross-axle Vee type wheeled undercarriage, interchangeable with single central float and two wing-tip floats. Specially reinforced for launching from Navy type catapults.

POWER PLANT.—One 220 h.p. Wright "Whirlwind" air-cooled radial engine and Root's type supercharger. Electric and standard inertia starter fitted. Petrol tanks faired in side of fuselage, one on either side.

ACCOMMODATION.—Pilot's cockpit aft of planes. Armament consists of two fixed Browning guns, mounted in cowling and firing through airscrew. Provision made for the mounting of bomb-racks to the undersurfaces of bottom wings.

DIMENSIONS.—Span 35 ft. 6 in. (10.82 m.), Length 24 ft. (7.32 m.), Height 10 ft. 6 in. (3.2 m.), Chord 4 ft. 8 in. (1.42 m.), Gap 5 ft. (1.52 m.).

PERFORMANCE.—Speed at sea level 130 m.p.h. (208 km.h.), Speed at 15,000 ft. 151 m.p.h. (242 km.h.), Service ceiling 27,500 ft. (8,378 m.), Absolute ceiling 30,000 ft. (9,150 m.).   (1931)

The Vought UO-1 Naval Observation Biplane (200 h.p. Wright "Whirlwind" engine.

Side View of the Lewis & Vought V.E.7 Training Machine (Hispano-Suiza engine).

THE VOUGHT V.E.Y AND V.E.9 "BLUEBIRD" TRAINING MACHINES

The V.E.7 entered production by Vought and the Naval Aircraft Factory after the end of World War I. One hundred and twenty-eight were built with 180 hp Wright–Hispano E engines (replacing the prototype's 150 hp Hispano–Suiza – details given are for the prototype). V.E.7 variants included armed models, encompassing the V.E.7S developed as a single-seat fighter and the V.E.7H two-seat trainer and observation seaplane (unarmed). The V.E.9 featured a 180 hp Wright–Hispano E-3 and 21 were built as observation aircraft from ships.

Type of machine	Two-seater Biplane.
Name or type No. of machine ..	V.E. 7 "Bluebird."
Purpose for which intended..	Training.
Span	34 ft. 4 in.
Gap	4 ft. 8 in.
Overall length	24 ft. 5⅜ in.
Maximum height	8 ft. 7½ in.
Chord	4 ft. 7½ in.
Span of tail	10 ft.
Engine type and h.p. ..	150 or 180 h.p. Hispano-Suiza.
Airscrew, diameter	8 ft. 8 in.
Weight of machine empty ..	1,392 lbs.

Performance.

Speed low down..	..	..	106 m.p h.
Speed at 6,500 feet	..	..	103 m.p.h.
Speed at 10,000 feet	..	..	97 m.p.h.
Speed at 15,000 feet	..	..	86 m.p.h.
Landing speed	..	..	48 m.p.h.

Climb.

To 6,500 feet in minutes..	..	8 mins. 50 secs.
To 10,000 feet in minutes	..	15 mins. 15 secs.
To 15,000 feet in minutes	..	29 minutes.
Total weight of machine loaded	.. ..	.. 1,937 lbs.

(1919)

THE VULTEE 66 "VANGUARD."

U.S. Air Forces designation: P-66.

TYPE.—Single-seat Fighter monoplane.

WINGS.—Low-wing cantilever monoplane. Wide centre-section, two outer wing-sections and detachable and interchangeable wing-tips. All-metal structure with flush-riveted smooth metal skin. Ailerons on outer wing-sections. Slotted flaps between ailerons and fuselage. Ailerons have fabric covering. Flaps are all-metal and are hydraulically operated.

FUSELAGE.—Oval metal structure of composite construction. Forward section of welded steel-tubing covered with detachable metal panels. Rear section is a semi-monocoque with butt-jointed flush-riveted smooth metal skin.

TAIL UNIT.—Cantilever monoplane type. Metal framework with metal-covered fixed surfaces and fabric-covered movable surfaces. Trimming-tabs in elevators and rudder.

LANDING GEAR.—Retractable type. Wheels are raised hydraulically into underside of fuselage and apertures are closed by fairing plates on legs and wheels and hinged panels on underside of fuselage when wheels are raised. Retractable tail-wheel.

POWER PLANT.—One Pratt & Whitney "Twin-Wasp" R-1830-S3C4-G fourteen-cylinder radial air-cooled engine with two-speed super-charger, rated at 1,200 h.p. at 4,900 ft. (1,495 m.) and 1,050 h.p. at 13,100 ft. (3,995 m.). NACA cowling with controllable gills. Hamilton-Standard Hydromatic constant-speed airscrew. Fuel tanks integral with centre-section structure. Capacity 240 U.S. gallons (908 litres).

ACCOMMODATION.—Enclosed pilot's cockpit over trailing-edge of wing.

ARMAMENT.—Normal armament consists of two fixed synchronised machine-guns in the fuselage. Additional armament may be installed in the wings.

DIMENSIONS.—Span 36 ft. (11 m.), Length 28 ft. (8.5 m.), Height 9 ft. 5 in. (2.9 m.), Wing area 197 sq. ft. (18.3 sq. m.). (1942)

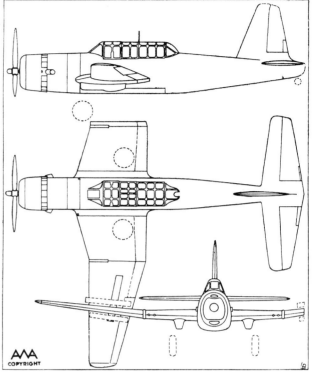

The Vultee "Vengeance" Two-seat Dive-Bomber.

The Vutlee L-1 "Vigilant" Two-seat Observation-Liaison Monoplane (285 h.p. Lycoming R-680 engine).

THE VULTEE 74 "VIGILANT."

U.S. Army Air Forces designation: L-1.

R.A.F. name: "Vigilant."

TYPE.—Two-seat Liaison-Observation or Army Co-operation monoplane.

WINGS.—High-wing rigidly-braced monoplane. Aerofoil section C-72. Wings attached to top of cabin structure and braced to lower fuselage longerons by streamline aluminium-alloy Vee struts. The Vee struts are in turn braced at their mid-points to the wing structure by short vertical jury struts. Two-spar aluminium-alloy wing structure. Leading-edge forward of the front spar and trailing-edge aft of the rear spar covered with aluminium-alloy sheet, remainder with fabric. Entire trailing-edge hinged, the outer sections acting as ailerons and the inner sections as flaps. The slotted flaps are operated manually and when lowered to their maximum position the slotted ailerons droop 20 degrees. Flaps and ailerons have welded steel-tube frames and fabric covering. Automatically-operated leading-edge slats along entire wing span.

FUSELAGE.—Rigidly-braced chrome-molybdenum steel-tube structure covered with fabric.

TAIL UNIT.—Wire-braced monoplane type. Welded stainless steel tube framework covered with fabric. Adjustable tail-plane. Trimming-tab in rudder.

LANDING GEAR.—Fixed type. Each side consists of a chrome-molybdenum heat-treated steel main member hinged at its inner end to a point on the centre-line of the underside of the fuselage and supported at its midpoint by a Cleveland "Aerol" shock-absorber strut and a backwardly-inclined steel drag strut. The upper end of the shock-absorber strut is attached to the lower fuselage longeron and the rear end of the drag strut is hinged to the centre-line of the underside of the fuselage. Hayes wheels and brakes. Full-swivelling tail-wheel which is also steerable through 27 degrees either side of neutral.

POWER PLANT.—One 285 h.p. Lycoming R-680-9 nine-cylinder radial air-cooled engine on a welded chrome-molybdenum steel-tube mounting. Two-blade Hamilton-Standard constant-speed airscrew. Main fuel tank (48 U.S. gallons) in fuselage. Oil tank (5 U.S. gallons) in engine compartment aft of fireproof bulkhead.

ACCOMMODATION.—Enclosed cabin seating two in tandem with dual controls. Cabin enclosure has sloping windshield made up of two curved transparent panels spliced at the centre and extending back to the side panels which slope outwards and upwards to allow downward vision. The domed roof is of transparent plastic material. Two doors on starboard side with sliding window panels and emergency quick-release hinges. Sliding windows on port side. Provision can also be made for carrying one stretcher case with special loading hatch in rear portion of roof (L-1B).

EQUIPMENT.—Includes full radio and electrical equipment, message pick-up hook, cockpit heating and ventilation, anti-glare roller-blinds in domed roof, instrument flying hood (in L-49A only), fire-extinguisher, etc.

DIMENSIONS.—Span 50 ft. $10\frac{7}{8}$ in. (15.5 m.), Length (L-5) 33 ft. $11\frac{1}{2}$ in. (10.37 m.), Length (L-5A) 34 ft. $2\frac{1}{8}$ in. (10.44 m.), Height 10 ft. 6 in. (3.2 m.), Wing area (including flaps and ailerons) 328.9 sq. ft. (30.5 sq. m.).

PERFORMANCE.—Max speed 122 mph (196 km/h).

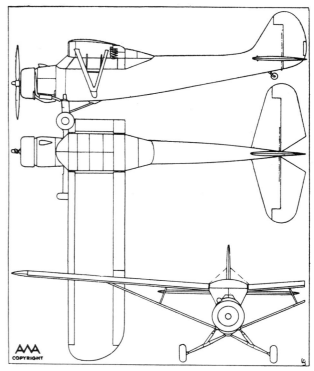

The Vultee 74 "Vigilant" Observation-Liaison Monoplane.

THE WACO CABIN BIPLANES.
U.S. Army Air Forces designation : UC-72 Series.

Since the Model VKS-7F four-seat cabin biplane was specially evolved to meet the requirements for a cross-country navigational trainer for the civilian training programme early in 1942, all production of this type of aircraft has ceased.

A large number of Waco cabin biplanes in the C, E, N and S Series which were in use at the outbreak of war were acquired by the U.S. Army Air Forces from private owners or commercial operators and given designations in the UC-72 Series.

The following is a full list of these aircraft :—
UC-72   Model SRE (Pratt & Whitney R-985).
UC-72A Model ARE (Jacobs L-6).
UC-72B Model EGC-8 (Wright R-760-E2).

UC-72C Model HRE (Lycoming R-680).
UC-72D Model VKS-7 (Continental W-670).
UC-72E Model ZGC-7 (Jacobs L-5).
UC-72F Model CUC-1 (Wright R-760-E).
UC-72G Model AQC-6 (Jacobs L-6).
UC-72H Model ZQC-6 (Jacobs L-5).
UC-72J Model AVN-8 (Jacobs L-6).
UC-72K Model YKS-7 (Jacobs L-4).
UC-72L Model ZVN-8 (Jacobs L-5).
UC-72M Model ZKS-7 (Jacobs L-5).
UC-72N Model YOC-1 (Jacobs L-5 or L-6).
UC-72O Model AGC-1 (Jacobs L-6).   (1945—46)

The Waco F-7 (Army YPT-14) Two-seat Primary Training Biplane.

THE WACO MODEL F-7 (ARMY YPT-14).
TYPE.—Two-seat primary training biplane.
WINGS.—Unequal-span single-bay wire-braced biplane. Centre-section carried above fuselage by splayed-out "N"-struts. One set of "N"-type interplane struts on each side of fuselage. Structure consists of two spruce spars, girder-type spruce ribs with plywood gussets, metal leading-edge back to front spar, the whole covered with fabric. Metal-covered ailerons on all four wings.
FUSELAGE.—Welded steel-tube framework covered with fabric over light wood fairing structure.

TAIL UNIT.—Braced monoplane type. Fixed surfaces have spruce spars and aluminium-alloy flanged web-type ribs, the whole being fabric-covered. Rudder and elevators have welded steel-tube framework covered with fabric.
UNDERCARRIAGE.—Divided type. Consists of two Waco oleo-spring shock-absorber struts braced by backwardly-inclined and transverse streamline steel tubes. Medium-pressure wheels and hydraulic brakes. Fully-castoring tail-wheel.

POWER PLANT.—One 220 h.p. Continental R-670-3 (Model UPF), or 225 h.p. Jacobs R755-5 (Model YPF), or 220 h.p. Lycoming R-680-7 (Model LPF) radial air-cooled engine on welded steel-tube mounting. N.A.C.A. cowling. Curtiss-Reed fixed-pitch metal airscrew. Fuel capacity 50 U.S. gallons (189 litres). Oil capacity 4 U.S. gallons (15.2 litres).

ACCOMMODATION.—Tandem open cockpits with complete dual controls.

DIMENSIONS.—Span 30 ft. (9.14 m.), Length 23 ft. 1 in. (7.06 m.), Height 8 ft. 5 in. (2.56 m.), Wing area 244 sq. ft. (22.67 sq. m.).

WEIGHTS.—Weight empty 1,870 lbs. (848 kg.), Disposable load 746 lbs. (399 kg.), Weight loaded 2,650 lbs. (1,201 kg.).

PERFORMANCE (Model UPF).—Maximum speed at sea level 138.6 m.p.h. (223 km.h.), Cruising speed at 75% power 123 m.p.h. (198 km.h.), Climb to 9,000 ft. (2,745 m.) 15 mins., Service ceiling 15,800 ft. (4,816 m.).

PERFORMANCE (Model YPF).—Maximum speed at sea level 141 m.p.h. (226.8 km.h.), Cruising speed at 75% power 117 m.p.h. (188 km.h.), Climb to 9,000 ft. (2,745 m.) 14 mins., Service ceiling 16,500 ft. (5,030 m.).

PERFORMANCE (Model LPF).—Maximum speed at sea level 136 m.p.h. (219 km.h.), Cruising speed at 75% power 120 m.p.h. (193 km.h.), Climb to 9,000 ft. (2,745 m.) 14.5 mins., Service ceiling 16,000 ft. (4,878 m.). (1940)

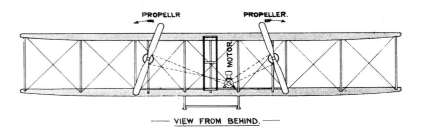

WRIGHT MODEL A

First Army aeroplane, purchased for $25,000 plus a $5,000 bonus for exceeding the required speed of 40 mph. Accepted into service on 2 August 1909.

Dimensions: Span 36 ft 4 in (11.07 m). Length 28 ft 0 in (8.53 m).

Weight: 1,200 lb (544 kg).

Motor.—25–28 h.p. 4-cylinder Barringaud (B.&M.), 1650 r.p.m. Weight, *about* 7.9 lbs. (3.60 kgs.) per h.p.

Speed.—44 m.p.h.

Propellers.—Two 2-bladed, wooden. Diameter, 8¼ feet (2.50 m.) Pitch, 9 feet (2.75 m.) Chain driven in opposite directions, 400 r.p.m. Propellers of 9 ft. (2.75 m) diam., fitted to some.

Steering.—Biplane elevator forward. Area, 70 sq. feet, warpable. *Control,* left hand lever. Double rudder in rear. Area, 23 sq. feet (2 m².) *Control,* right hand lever. Warping wing tips. *Control,* sideways motion of right hand lever.

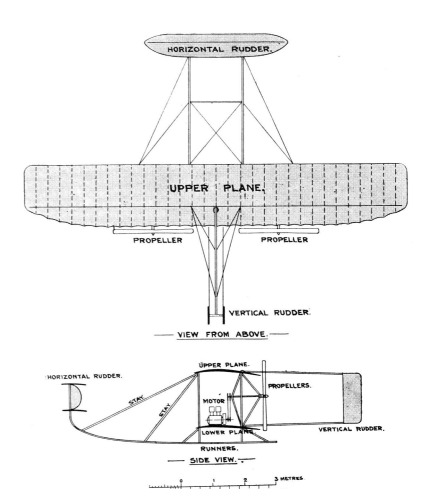

(1910–11)